I0041689

CODE OF FEDERAL REGULATIONS

Title 14
Aeronautics and Space

Parts 110 to 199

Revised as of January 1, 2019

Containing a codification of documents
of general applicability and future effect

As of January 1, 2019

Published by the Office of the Federal Register
National Archives and Records Administration
as a Special Edition of the Federal Register

Table of Contents

Cite this Code: **CFR**

To cite the regulations in this volume use title, part and section number. Thus, 14 CFR 110.1 *refers to title 14, part 110, section 1.*

Explanation

The Code of Federal Regulations is a codification of the general and permanent rules published in the Federal Register by the Executive departments and agencies of the Federal Government. The Code is divided into 50 titles which represent broad areas subject to Federal regulation. Each title is divided into chapters which usually bear the name of the issuing agency. Each chapter is further subdivided into parts covering specific regulatory areas.

Each volume of the Code is revised at least once each calendar year and issued on a quarterly basis approximately as follows:

Title 1 through Title 16...as of January 1
Title 17 through Title 27 ....as of April 1
Title 28 through Title 41 ....as of July 1
Title 42 through Title 50...as of October 1

The appropriate revision date is printed on the cover of each volume.

LEGAL STATUS

The contents of the Federal Register are required to be judicially noticed (44 U.S.C. 1507). The Code of Federal Regulations is prima facie evidence of the text of the original documents (44 U.S.C. 1510).

HOW TO USE THE CODE OF FEDERAL REGULATIONS

The Code of Federal Regulations is kept up to date by the individual issues of the Federal Register. These two publications must be used together to determine the latest version of any given rule.

To determine whether a Code volume has been amended since its revision date (in this case, January 1, 2019), consult the "List of CFR Sections Affected (LSA)," which is issued monthly, and the "Cumulative List of Parts Affected," which appears in the Reader Aids section of the daily Federal Register. These two lists will identify the Federal Register page number of the latest amendment of any given rule.

EFFECTIVE AND EXPIRATION DATES

Each volume of the Code contains amendments published in the Federal Register since the last revision of that volume of the Code. Source citations for the regulations are referred to by volume number and page number of the Federal Register and date of publication. Publication dates and effective dates are usually not the same and care must be exercised by the user in determining the actual effective date. In instances where the effective date is beyond the cutoff date for the Code a note has been inserted to reflect the future effective date. In those instances where a regulation published in the Federal Register states a date certain for expiration, an appropriate note will be inserted following the text.

OMB CONTROL NUMBERS

The Paperwork Reduction Act of 1980 (Pub. L. 96–511) requires Federal agencies to display an OMB control number with their information collection request.

Many agencies have begun publishing numerous OMB control numbers as amendments to existing regulations in the CFR. These OMB numbers are placed as close as possible to the applicable recordkeeping or reporting requirements.

PAST PROVISIONS OF THE CODE

Provisions of the Code that are no longer in force and effect as of the revision date stated on the cover of each volume are not carried. Code users may find the text of provisions in effect on any given date in the past by using the appropriate List of CFR Sections Affected (LSA). For the convenience of the reader, a "List of CFR Sections Affected" is published at the end of each CFR volume. For changes to the Code prior to the LSA listings at the end of the volume, consult previous annual editions of the LSA. For changes to the Code prior to 2001, consult the List of CFR Sections Affected compilations, published for 1949-1963, 1964-1972, 1973-1985, and 1986-2000.

"[RESERVED]" TERMINOLOGY

The term "[Reserved]" is used as a place holder within the Code of Federal Regulations. An agency may add regulatory information at a "[Reserved]" location at any time. Occasionally "[Reserved]" is used editorially to indicate that a portion of the CFR was left vacant and not accidentally dropped due to a printing or computer error.

INCORPORATION BY REFERENCE

What is incorporation by reference? Incorporation by reference was established by statute and allows Federal agencies to meet the requirement to publish regulations in the Federal Register by referring to materials already published elsewhere. For an incorporation to be valid, the Director of the Federal Register must approve it. The legal effect of incorporation by reference is that the material is treated as if it were published in full in the Federal Register (5 U.S.C. 552(a)). This material, like any other properly issued regulation, has the force of law.

What is a proper incorporation by reference? The Director of the Federal Register will approve an incorporation by reference only when the requirements of 1 CFR part 51 are met. Some of the elements on which approval is based are:

(a) The incorporation will substantially reduce the volume of material published in the Federal Register.

(b) The matter incorporated is in fact available to the extent necessary to afford fairness and uniformity in the administrative process.

(c) The incorporating document is drafted and submitted for publication in accordance with 1 CFR part 51.

What if the material incorporated by reference cannot be found? If you have any problem locating or obtaining a copy of material listed as an approved incorporation by reference, please contact the agency that issued the regulation containing that incorporation. If, after contacting the agency, you find the material is not available, please notify the Director of the Federal Register, National Archives and Records Administration, 8601 Adelphi Road, College Park, MD 20740-6001, or call 202-741-6010.

CFR INDEXES AND TABULAR GUIDES

A subject index to the Code of Federal Regulations is contained in a separate volume, revised annually as of January 1, entitled CFR INDEX AND FINDING AIDS. This volume contains the Parallel Table of Authorities and Rules. A list of CFR titles, chapters, subchapters, and parts and an alphabetical list of agencies publishing in the CFR are also included in this volume.

An index to the text of "Title 3—The President" is carried within that volume.

The Federal Register Index is issued monthly in cumulative form. This index is based on a consolidation of the "Contents" entries in the daily Federal Register.

A List of CFR Sections Affected (LSA) is published monthly, keyed to the revision dates of the 50 CFR titles.

REPUBLICATION OF MATERIAL

There are no restrictions on the republication of material appearing in the Code of Federal Regulations.

INQUIRIES

For a legal interpretation or explanation of any regulation in this volume, contact the issuing agency. The issuing agency's name appears at the top of odd-numbered pages.

For inquiries concerning CFR reference assistance, call 202–741–6000 or write to the Director, Office of the Federal Register, National Archives and Records Administration, 8601 Adelphi Road, College Park, MD 20740-6001 or e-mail *fedreg.info@nara.gov*.

SALES

The Government Publishing Office (GPO) processes all sales and distribution of the CFR. For payment by credit card, call toll-free, 866-512-1800, or DC area, 202-512-1800, M-F 8 a.m. to 4 p.m. e.s.t. or fax your order to 202-512-2104, 24 hours a day. For payment by check, write to: US Government Publishing Office – New Orders, P.O. Box 979050, St. Louis, MO 63197-9000.

ELECTRONIC SERVICES

The full text of the Code of Federal Regulations, the LSA (List of CFR Sections Affected), The United States Government Manual, the Federal Register, Public Laws, Public Papers of the Presidents of the United States, Compilation of Presidential Documents and the Privacy Act Compilation are available in electronic format via *www.govinfo.gov*. For more information, contact the GPO Customer Contact Center, U.S. Government Publishing Office. Phone 202-512-1800, or 866-512-1800 (toll-free). E-mail, *ContactCenter@gpo.gov*.

The Office of the Federal Register also offers a free service on the National Archives and Records Administration's (NARA) World Wide Web site for public law numbers, Federal Register finding aids, and related information. Connect to NARA's web site at *www.archives.gov/federal-register*.

The e-CFR is a regularly updated, unofficial editorial compilation of CFR material and Federal Register amendments, produced by the Office of the Federal Register and the Government Publishing Office. It is available at *www.ecfr.gov*.

OLIVER A. POTTS,
Director,
Office of the Federal Register
January 1, 2019

THIS TITLE

Title 14—AERONAUTICS AND SPACE is composed of five volumes. The parts in these volumes are arranged in the following order: Parts 1–59, 60–109, 110–199, 200–1199, and part 1200–End. The first three volumes containing parts 1–199 are comprised of chapter I—Federal Aviation Administration, Department of Transportation (DOT). The fourth volume containing parts 200–1199 is comprised of chapter II—Office of the Secretary, DOT (Aviation Proceedings) and chapter III—Commercial Space Transportation, Federal Aviation Administration, DOT. The fifth volume containing part 1200–End is comprised of chapter V—National Aeronautics and Space Administration and chapter VI—Air Transportation System Stabilization. The contents of these volumes represent all current regulations codified under this title of the CFR as of January 1, 2019.

For this volume, Cheryl E. Sirofchuck was Chief Editor. The Code of Federal Regulations publication program is under the direction of John Hyrum Martinez, assisted by Stephen J. Frattini.

Title 14—Aeronautics and Space

(This book contains parts 110 to 199)

CHAPTER I—FEDERAL AVIATION ADMINISTRATION, DEPARTMENT OF TRANSPORTATION (CONTINUED)

SUBCHAPTER G—AIR CARRIERS AND OPERATORS FOR COMPENSATION OR HIRE: CERTIFICATION AND OPER-ATIONS

PART 110—GENERAL REQUIREMENTS

Sec.
110.1 Applicability.
110.2 Definitions.

AUTHORITY: 49 U.S.C. 106(g), 1153, 40101, 40102, 40103, 40113, 44105, 44106, 44111, 44701–44717, 44722, 44901, 44903, 44904, 44906, 44912, 44914, 44936, 44938, 46103, 46105.

SOURCE: Docket No. FAA–2009–0140, 76 FR 7486, Feb. 10, 2011, unless otherwise noted.

§ 110.1 Applicability.

This part governs all operations conducted under subchapter G of this chapter.

§ 110.2 Definitions.

For the purpose of this subchapter, the term—

All-cargo operation means any operation for compensation or hire that is other than a passenger-carrying operation or, if passengers are carried, they are only those specified in § 121.583(a) or § 135.85 of this chapter.

Commercial air tour means a flight conducted for compensation or hire in an airplane or helicopter where a purpose of the flight is sightseeing. The FAA may consider the following factors in determining whether a flight is a commercial air tour:

(1) Whether there was a holding out to the public of willingness to conduct a sightseeing flight for compensation or hire;

(2) Whether the person offering the flight provided a narrative that referred to areas or points of interest on the surface below the route of the flight;

(3) The area of operation;

(4) How often the person offering the flight conducts such flights;

(5) The route of flight;

(6) The inclusion of sightseeing flights as part of any travel arrangement package;

(7) Whether the flight in question would have been canceled based on poor visibility of the surface below the route of the flight; and

(8) Any other factors that the FAA considers appropriate.

Commuter operation means any scheduled operation conducted by any person operating one of the following types of aircraft with a frequency of operations of at least five round trips per week on at least one route between two or more points according to the published flight schedules:

(1) Airplanes, other than turbojet-powered airplanes, having a maximum passenger-seat configuration of 9 seats or less, excluding each crewmember seat, and a maximum payload capacity of 7,500 pounds or less; or

(2) Rotorcraft.

Direct air carrier means a person who provides or offers to provide air transportation and who has control over the operational functions performed in providing that transportation.

DOD commercial air carrier evaluator means a qualified Air Mobility Command, Survey and Analysis Office cockpit evaluator performing the duties specified in Public Law 99–661 when the evaluator is flying on an air carrier that is contracted or pursuing a contract with the U.S. Department of Defense (DOD).

Domestic operation means any scheduled operation conducted by any person operating any airplane described in paragraph (1) of this definition at locations described in paragraph (2) of this definition:

(1) Airplanes:

(i) Turbojet-powered airplanes;

(ii) Airplanes having a passenger-seat configuration of more than 9 passenger seats, excluding each crewmember seat; or

(iii) Airplanes having a payload capacity of more than 7,500 pounds.

(2) Locations:

(i) Between any points within the 48 contiguous States of the United States or the District of Columbia; or

(ii) Operations solely within the 48 contiguous States of the United States or the District of Columbia; or

(iii) Operations entirely within any State, territory, or possession of the United States; or

(iv) When specifically authorized by the Administrator, operations between any point within the 48 contiguous States of the United States or the District of Columbia and any specifically authorized point located outside the 48 contiguous States of the United States or the District of Columbia.

Empty weight means the weight of the airframe, engines, propellers, rotors, and fixed equipment. Empty weight excludes the weight of the crew and payload, but includes the weight of all fixed ballast, unusable fuel supply, undrainable oil, total quantity of engine coolant, and total quantity of hydraulic fluid.

Flag operation means any scheduled operation conducted by any person operating any airplane described in paragraph (1) of this definition at the locations described in paragraph (2) of this definition:

(1) Airplanes:

(i) Turbojet-powered airplanes;

(ii) Airplanes having a passenger-seat configuration of more than 9 passenger seats, excluding each crewmember seat; or

(iii) Airplanes having a payload capacity of more than 7,500 pounds.

(2) Locations:

(i) Between any point within the State of Alaska or the State of Hawaii or any territory or possession of the United States and any point outside the State of Alaska or the State of Hawaii or any territory or possession of the United States, respectively; or

(ii) Between any point within the 48 contiguous States of the United States or the District of Columbia and any point outside the 48 contiguous States of the United States and the District of Columbia.

(iii) Between any point outside the U.S. and another point outside the U.S.

Justifiable aircraft equipment means any equipment necessary for the operation of the aircraft. It does not include equipment or ballast specifically installed, permanently or otherwise, for the purpose of altering the empty weight of an aircraft to meet the maximum payload capacity.

Kind of operation means one of the various operations a certificate holder is authorized to conduct, as specified in its operations specifications, *i.e.*, domestic, flag, supplemental, commuter, or on-demand operations.

Maximum payload capacity means:

(1) For an aircraft for which a maximum zero fuel weight is prescribed in FAA technical specifications, the maximum zero fuel weight, less empty weight, less all justifiable aircraft equipment, and less the operating load (consisting of minimum flightcrew, foods and beverages, and supplies and equipment related to foods and beverages, but not including disposable fuel or oil).

(2) For all other aircraft, the maximum certificated takeoff weight of an aircraft, less the empty weight, less all justifiable aircraft equipment, and less the operating load (consisting of minimum fuel load, oil, and flightcrew). The allowance for the weight of the crew, oil, and fuel is as follows:

(i) Crew—for each crewmember required by the Federal Aviation Regulations—

(A) For male flightcrew members—180 pounds.

(B) For female flightcrew members—140 pounds.

(C) For male flight attendants—180 pounds.

(D) For female flight attendants—130 pounds.

(E) For flight attendants not identified by gender—140 pounds.

(ii) Oil—350 pounds or the oil capacity as specified on the Type Certificate Data Sheet.

(iii) Fuel—the minimum weight of fuel required by the applicable Federal Aviation Regulations for a flight between domestic points 174 nautical miles apart under VFR weather conditions that does not involve extended overwater operations.

Maximum zero fuel weight means the maximum permissible weight of an aircraft with no disposable fuel or oil. The zero fuel weight figure may be found in either the aircraft type certificate data sheet, the approved Aircraft Flight Manual, or both.

Noncommon carriage means an aircraft operation for compensation or hire that does not involve a holding out to others.

On-demand operation means any operation for compensation or hire that is one of the following:

(1) Passenger-carrying operations conducted as a public charter under part 380 of this chapter or any operations in which the departure time, departure location, and arrival location are specifically negotiated with the customer or the customer's representative that are any of the following types of operations:

(i) Common carriage operations conducted with airplanes, including turbojet-powered airplanes, having a passenger-seat configuration of 30 seats or fewer, excluding each crewmember seat, and a payload capacity of 7,500 pounds or less, except that operations using a specific airplane that is also used in domestic or flag operations and that is so listed in the operations specifications as required by §119.49(a)(4) of this chapter for those operations are considered supplemental operations;

(ii) Noncommon or private carriage operations conducted with airplanes having a passenger-seat configuration of less than 20 seats, excluding each crewmember seat, and a payload capacity of less than 6,000 pounds; or

(iii) Any rotorcraft operation.

(2) Scheduled passenger-carrying operations conducted with one of the following types of aircraft with a frequency of operations of less than five round trips per week on at least one route between two or more points according to the published flight schedules:

(i) Airplanes, other than turbojet powered airplanes, having a maximum passenger-seat configuration of 9 seats or less, excluding each crewmember seat, and a maximum payload capacity of 7,500 pounds or less; or

(ii) Rotorcraft.

(3) All-cargo operations conducted with airplanes having a payload capacity of 7,500 pounds or less, or with rotorcraft.

Passenger-carrying operation means any aircraft operation carrying any person, unless the only persons on the aircraft are those identified in §§121.583(a) or 135.85 of this chapter, as applicable. An aircraft used in a passenger-carrying operation may also carry cargo or mail in addition to passengers.

Principal base of operations means the primary operating location of a certificate holder as established by the certificate holder.

Provisional airport means an airport approved by the Administrator for use by a certificate holder for the purpose of providing service to a community when the regular airport used by the certificate holder is not available.

Regular airport means an airport used by a certificate holder in scheduled operations and listed in its operations specifications.

Scheduled operation means any common carriage passenger-carrying operation for compensation or hire conducted by an air carrier or commercial operator for which the certificate holder or its representative offers in advance the departure location, departure time, and arrival location. It does not include any passenger-carrying operation that is conducted as a public charter operation under part 380 of this chapter.

Supplemental operation means any common carriage operation for compensation or hire conducted with any airplane described in paragraph (1) of this definition that is a type of operation described in paragraph (2) of this definition:

(1) Airplanes:

(i) Airplanes having a passenger-seat configuration of more than 30 seats, excluding each crewmember seat;

(ii) Airplanes having a payload capacity of more than 7,500 pounds; or

(iii) Each propeller-powered airplane having a passenger-seat configuration of more than 9 seats and less than 31 seats, excluding each crewmember seat, that is also used in domestic or flag operations and that is so listed in the operations specifications as required by §119.49(a)(4) of this chapter for those operations; or

(iv) Each turbojet powered airplane having a passenger seat configuration of 1 or more and less than 31 seats, excluding each crewmember seat, that is also used in domestic or flag operations and that is so listed in the operations specifications as required by §119.49(a)(4) of this chapter for those operations.

(2) Types of operation:

(i) Operations for which the departure time, departure location, and arrival location are specifically negotiated with the customer or the customer's representative;

(ii) All-cargo operations; or

(iii) Passenger-carrying public charter operations conducted under part 380 of this chapter.

Wet lease means any leasing arrangement whereby a person agrees to provide an entire aircraft and at least one crewmember. A wet lease does not include a code-sharing arrangement.

When common carriage is not involved or operations not involving common carriage means any of the following:

(1) Noncommon carriage.

(2) Operations in which persons or cargo are transported without compensation or hire.

(3) Operations not involving the transportation of persons or cargo.

(4) Private carriage.

Years in service means the calendar time elapsed since an aircraft was issued its first U.S. or first foreign airworthiness certificate.

[Docket No. FAA–2009–0140, 76 FR 7486, Feb. 10, 2011, as amended by Docket FAA–2018–0119, Amdt. 110–2, 83 FR 9172, Mar. 5, 2018]

PARTS 111–116 [RESERVED]

PART 117—FLIGHT AND DUTY LIMITATIONS AND REST REQUIREMENTS: FLIGHTCREW MEMBERS

AUTHORITY: 49 U.S.C. 106(g), 40113, 40119, 44101, 44701–44702, 44705, 44709–44711, 44713, 44716–44717, 44722, 46901, 44903–44904, 44912, 46105.

SOURCE: Docket No. FAA–2009–1093, 77 FR 398, Jan. 4, 2012, unless otherwise noted.

§117.1 Applicability.

(a) This part prescribes flight and duty limitations and rest requirements for all flightcrew members and certificate holders conducting passenger operations under part 121 of this chapter.

(b) This part applies to all operations directed by part 121 certificate holders under part 91, other than subpart K, of this chapter if any segment is conducted as a domestic passenger, flag passenger, or supplemental passenger operation.

(c) This part applies to all flightcrew members when participating in an operation under part 91, other than subpart K of this chapter, on behalf of the part 121 certificate holder if any flight segment is conducted as a domestic passenger, flag passenger, or supplemental passenger operation

(d) Notwithstanding paragraphs (a), (b) and (c) of this section, a certificate holder may conduct under part 117 its part 121 operations pursuant to 121.470, 121.480, or 121.500.

§117.3 Definitions.

In addition to the definitions in §§1.1 and 110.2 of this chapter, the following definitions apply to this part. In the event there is a conflict in definitions, the definitions in this part control for purposes of the flight and duty limitations and rest requirements of this part.

Acclimated means a condition in which a flightcrew member has been in a theater for 72 hours or has been given at least 36 consecutive hours free from duty.

Airport/standby reserve means a defined duty period during which a

8

flightcrew member is required by a certificate holder to be at an airport for a possible assignment.

Augmented flightcrew means a flightcrew that has more than the minimum number of flightcrew members required by the airplane type certificate to operate the aircraft to allow a flightcrew member to be replaced by another qualified flightcrew member for in-flight rest.

Calendar day means a 24-hour period from 0000 through 2359 using Coordinated Universal Time or local time.

Certificate holder means a person who holds or is required to hold an air carrier certificate or operating certificate issued under part 119 of this chapter.

Deadhead transportation means transportation of a flightcrew member as a passenger or non-operating flightcrew member, by any mode of transportation, as required by a certificate holder, excluding transportation to or from a suitable accommodation. All time spent in deadhead transportation is duty and is not rest. For purposes of determining the maximum flight duty period in Table B of this part, deadhead transportation is not considered a flight segment.

Duty means any task that a flightcrew member performs as required by the certificate holder, including but not limited to flight duty period, flight duty, pre- and post-flight duties, administrative work, training, deadhead transportation, aircraft positioning on the ground, aircraft loading, and aircraft servicing.

Fatigue means a physiological state of reduced mental or physical performance capability resulting from lack of sleep or increased physical activity that can reduce a flightcrew member's alertness and ability to safely operate an aircraft or perform safety-related duties.

Fatigue risk management system (FRMS) means a management system for a certificate holder to use to mitigate the effects of fatigue in its particular operations. It is a data-driven process and a systematic method used to continuously monitor and manage safety risks associated with fatigue-related error.

Fit for duty means physiologically and mentally prepared and capable of performing assigned duties at the highest degree of safety.

Flight duty period (FDP) means a period that begins when a flightcrew member is required to report for duty with the intention of conducting a flight, a series of flights, or positioning or ferrying flights, and ends when the aircraft is parked after the last flight and there is no intention for further aircraft movement by the same flightcrew member. A flight duty period includes the duties performed by the flightcrew member on behalf of the certificate holder that occur before a flight segment or between flight segments without a required intervening rest period. Examples of tasks that are part of the flight duty period include deadhead transportation, training conducted in an aircraft or flight simulator, and airport/standby reserve, if the above tasks occur before a flight segment or between flight segments without an intervening required rest period.

Home base means the location designated by a certificate holder where a flightcrew member normally begins and ends his or her duty periods.

Lineholder means a flightcrew member who has an assigned flight duty period and is not acting as a reserve flightcrew member.

Long-call reserve means that, prior to beginning the rest period required by §117.25, the flightcrew member is notified by the certificate holder to report for a flight duty period following the completion of the rest period.

Physiological night's rest means 10 hours of rest that encompasses the hours of 0100 and 0700 at the flightcrew member's home base, unless the individual has acclimated to a different theater. If the flightcrew member has acclimated to a different theater, rest must encompass the hours of 0100 and 0700 at the acclimated location.

Report time means the time that the certificate holder requires a flightcrew member to report for an assignment.

Reserve availability period means a duty period during which a certificate holder requires a flightcrew member on short call reserve to be available to receive an assignment for a flight duty period.

Reserve flightcrew member means a flightcrew member who a certificate holder requires to be available to receive an assignment for duty.

Rest facility means a bunk or seat accommodation installed in an aircraft that provides a flightcrew member with a sleep opportunity.

(1) *Class 1 rest facility* means a bunk or other surface that allows for a flat sleeping position and is located separate from both the flight deck and passenger cabin in an area that is temperature-controlled, allows the flightcrew member to control light, and provides isolation from noise and disturbance.

(2) *Class 2 rest facility* means a seat in an aircraft cabin that allows for a flat or near flat sleeping position; is separated from passengers by a minimum of a curtain to provide darkness and some sound mitigation; and is reasonably free from disturbance by passengers or flightcrew members.

(3) *Class 3 rest facility* means a seat in an aircraft cabin or flight deck that reclines at least 40 degrees and provides leg and foot support.

Rest period means a continuous period determined prospectively during which the flightcrew member is free from all restraint by the certificate holder, including freedom from present responsibility for work should the occasion arise.

Scheduled means to appoint, assign, or designate for a fixed time.

Short-call reserve means a period of time in which a flightcrew member is assigned to a reserve availability period.

Split duty means a flight duty period that has a scheduled break in duty that is less than a required rest period.

Suitable accommodation means a temperature-controlled facility with sound mitigation and the ability to control light that provides a flightcrew member with the ability to sleep either in a bed, bunk or in a chair that allows for flat or near flat sleeping position. Suitable accommodation only applies to ground facilities and does not apply to aircraft onboard rest facilities.

Theater means a geographical area in which the distance between the flightcrew member's flight duty period departure point and arrival point differs by no more than 60 degrees longitude.

Unforeseen operational circumstance means an unplanned event of insufficient duration to allow for adjustments to schedules, including unforecast weather, equipment malfunction, or air traffic delay that is not reasonably expected.

Window of circadian low means a period of maximum sleepiness that occurs between 0200 and 0559 during a physiological night.

[Doc. No. FAA–2009–1093, 77 FR 398, Jan. 4, 2012; Amdt. 117–1A, 77 FR 28764, May 16, 2012; Amdt. 117–1, 78 FR 69288, Nov. 19, 2013]

§ 117.5   Fitness for duty.

(a) Each flightcrew member must report for any flight duty period rested and prepared to perform his or her assigned duties.

(b) No certificate holder may assign and no flightcrew member may accept assignment to a flight duty period if the flightcrew member has reported for a flight duty period too fatigued to safely perform his or her assigned duties.

(c) No certificate holder may permit a flightcrew member to continue a flight duty period if the flightcrew member has reported him or herself too fatigued to continue the assigned flight duty period.

(d) As part of the dispatch or flight release, as applicable, each flightcrew member must affirmatively state he or she is fit for duty prior to commencing flight.

§ 117.7   Fatigue risk management system.

(a) No certificate holder may exceed any provision of this part unless approved by the FAA under a Fatigue Risk Management System that provides at least an equivalent level of safety against fatigue-related accidents or incidents as the other provisions of this part.

(b) The Fatigue Risk Management System must include:

(1) A fatigue risk management policy.

(2) An education and awareness training program.

(3) A fatigue reporting system.

(4) A system for monitoring flightcrew fatigue.

(5) An incident reporting process.

(6) A performance evaluation.

§117.9 Fatigue education and awareness training program.

(a) Each certificate holder must develop and implement an education and awareness training program, approved by the Administrator. This program must provide annual education and awareness training to all employees of the certificate holder responsible for administering the provisions of this rule including flightcrew members, dispatchers, individuals directly involved in the scheduling of flightcrew members, individuals directly involved in operational control, and any employee providing direct management oversight of those areas.

(b) The fatigue education and awareness training program must be designed to increase awareness of:

(1) Fatigue;

(2) The effects of fatigue on pilots; and

(3) Fatigue countermeasures

(c) (1) Each certificate holder must update its fatigue education and awareness training program every two years and submit the update to the Administrator for review and acceptance.

(2) Not later than 12 months after the date of submission of the fatigue education and awareness training program required by (c)(1) of this section, the Administrator shall review and accept or reject the update. If the Administrator rejects an update, the Administrator shall provide suggested modifications for resubmission of the update.

§117.11 Flight time limitation.

(a) No certificate holder may schedule and no flightcrew member may accept an assignment or continue an assigned flight duty period if the total flight time:

(1) Will exceed the limits specified in Table A of this part if the operation is conducted with the minimum required flightcrew.

(2) Will exceed 13 hours if the operation is conducted with a 3-pilot flightcrew.

(3) Will exceed 17 hours if the operation is conducted with a 4-pilot flightcrew.

(b) If unforeseen operational circumstances arise after takeoff that are beyond the certificate holder's control, a flightcrew member may exceed the maximum flight time specified in paragraph (a) of this section and the cumulative flight time limits in 117.23(b) to the extent necessary to safely land the aircraft at the next destination airport or alternate, as appropriate.

(c) Each certificate holder must report to the Administrator within 10 days any flight time that exceeded the maximum flight time limits permitted by this section or §117.23(b). The report must contain a description of the extended flight time limitation and the circumstances surrounding the need for the extension.

[Doc. No. FAA–2009–1093, 77 FR 398, Jan. 4, 2012; Amdt. 117–1, 78 FR 8362, Feb. 6, 2013; 78 FR 69288, Nov. 19, 2013]

§117.13 Flight duty period: Unaugmented operations.

(a) Except as provided for in §117.15, no certificate holder may assign and no flightcrew member may accept an assignment for an unaugmented flight operation if the scheduled flight duty period will exceed the limits in Table B of this part.

(b) If the flightcrew member is not acclimated:

(1) The maximum flight duty period in Table B of this part is reduced by 30 minutes.

(2) The applicable flight duty period is based on the local time at the theater in which the flightcrew member was last acclimated.

§117.15 Flight duty period: Split duty.

For an unaugmented operation only, if a flightcrew member is provided with a rest opportunity (an opportunity to sleep) in a suitable accommodation during his or her flight duty period, the time that the flightcrew member spends in the suitable accommodation is not part of that flightcrew member's flight duty period if all of the following conditions are met:

(a) The rest opportunity is provided between the hours of 22:00 and 05:00 local time.

(b) The time spent in the suitable accommodation is at least 3 hours, measured from the time that the flightcrew member reaches the suitable accommodation.

(c) The rest opportunity is scheduled before the beginning of the flight duty period in which that rest opportunity is taken.

(d) The rest opportunity that the flightcrew member is actually provided may not be less than the rest opportunity that was scheduled.

(e) The rest opportunity is not provided until the first segment of the flight duty period has been completed.

(f) The combined time of the flight duty period and the rest opportunity provided in this section does not exceed 14 hours.

§ 117.17 Flight duty period: Augmented flightcrew.

(a) For flight operations conducted with an acclimated augmented flightcrew, no certificate holder may assign and no flightcrew member may accept an assignment if the scheduled flight duty period will exceed the limits specified in Table C of this part.

(b) If the flightcrew member is not acclimated:

(1) The maximum flight duty period in Table C of this part is reduced by 30 minutes.

(2) The applicable flight duty period is based on the local time at the theater in which the flightcrew member was last acclimated.

(c) No certificate holder may assign and no flightcrew member may accept an assignment under this section unless during the flight duty period:

(1) Two consecutive hours in the second half of the flight duty period are available for in-flight rest for the pilot flying the aircraft during landing.

(2) Ninety consecutive minutes are available for in-flight rest for the pilot performing monitoring duties during landing.

(d) No certificate holder may assign and no flightcrew member may accept an assignment involving more than three flight segments under this section.

(e) At all times during flight, at least one flightcrew member qualified in accordance with § 121.543(b)(3)(i) of this chapter must be at the flight controls.

§ 117.19 Flight duty period extensions.

(a) For augmented and unaugmented operations, if unforeseen operational circumstances arise prior to takeoff:

(1) The pilot in command and the certificate holder may extend the maximum flight duty period permitted in Tables B or C of this part up to 2 hours. The pilot in command and the certificate holder may also extend the maximum combined flight duty period and reserve availability period limits specified in § 117.21(c)(3) and (4) of this part up to 2 hours.

(2) An extension in the flight duty period under paragraph (a)(1) of this section of more than 30 minutes may occur only once prior to receiving a rest period described in § 117.25(b).

(3) A flight duty period cannot be extended under paragraph (a)(1) of this section if it causes a flightcrew member to exceed the cumulative flight duty period limits specified in 117.23(c).

(4) Each certificate holder must report to the Administrator within 10 days any flight duty period that exceeded the maximum flight duty period permitted in Tables B or C of this part by more than 30 minutes. The report must contain the following:

(i) A description of the extended flight duty period and the circumstances surrounding the need for the extension; and

(ii) If the circumstances giving rise to the extension were within the certificate holder's control, the corrective action(s) that the certificate holder intends to take to minimize the need for future extensions.

(5) Each certificate holder must implement the corrective action(s) reported in paragraph (a)(4) of this section within 30 days from the date of the extended flight duty period.

(b) For augmented and unaugmented operations, if unforeseen operational circumstances arise after takeoff:

(1) The pilot in command and the certificate holder may extend maximum flight duty periods specified in Tables B or C of this part to the extent necessary to safely land the aircraft at the next destination airport or alternate airport, as appropriate.

(2) An extension of the flight duty period under paragraph (b)(1) of this section of more than 30 minutes may occur only once prior to receiving a rest period described in §117.25(b).

(3) An extension taken under paragraph (b) of this section may exceed the cumulative flight duty period limits specified in 117.23(c).

(4) Each certificate holder must report to the Administrator within 10 days any flight duty period that either exceeded the cumulative flight duty periods specified in §117.23(c), or exceeded the maximum flight duty period limits permitted by Tables B or C of this part by more than 30 minutes. The report must contain a description of the circumstances surrounding the affected flight duty period.

[Doc. No. FAA–2009–1093, 77 FR 398, Jan. 4, 2012; Amdt. 117–1A, 77 FR 28764, May 16, 2012; Amdt. 117–1, 78 FR 8362, Feb. 6, 2013; 78 FR 69288, Nov. 19, 2013]

§117.21 Reserve status.

(a) Unless specifically designated as airport/standby or short-call reserve by the certificate holder, all reserve is considered long-call reserve.

(b) Any reserve that meets the definition of airport/standby reserve must be designated as airport/standby reserve. For airport/standby reserve, all time spent in a reserve status is part of the flightcrew member's flight duty period.

(c) For short call reserve,

(1) The reserve availability period may not exceed 14 hours.

(2) For a flightcrew member who has completed a reserve availability period, no certificate holder may schedule and no flightcrew member may accept an assignment of a reserve availability period unless the flightcrew member receives the required rest in §117.25(e).

(3) For an unaugmented operation, the total number of hours a flightcrew member may spend in a flight duty period and a reserve availability period may not exceed the lesser of the maximum applicable flight duty period in Table B of this part plus 4 hours, or 16 hours, as measured from the beginning of the reserve availability period

(4) For an augmented operation, the total number of hours a flightcrew member may spend in a flight duty period and a reserve availability period may not exceed the flight duty period in Table C of this part plus 4 hours, as measured from the beginning of the reserve availability period.

(d) For long call reserve, if a certificate holder contacts a flightcrew member to assign him or her to a flight duty period that will begin before and operate into the flightcrew member's window of circadian low, the flightcrew member must receive a 12 hour notice of report time from the certificate holder.

(e) A certificate holder may shift a reserve flightcrew member's reserve status from long-call to short-call only if the flightcrew member receives a rest period as provided in §117.25(e).

§117.23 Cumulative limitations.

(a) The limitations of this section include all flying by flightcrew members on behalf of any certificate holder or 91K Program Manager during the applicable periods.

(b) No certificate holder may schedule and no flightcrew member may accept an assignment if the flightcrew member's total flight time will exceed the following:

(1) 100 hours in any 672 consecutive hours or

(2) 1,000 hours in any 365 consecutive calendar day period.

(c) No certificate holder may schedule and no flightcrew member may accept an assignment if the flightcrew member's total Flight Duty Period will exceed:

(1) 60 flight duty period hours in any 168 consecutive hours or

(2) 190 flight duty period hours in any 672 consecutive hours.

[Doc. No. FAA–2009–1093, 77 FR 398, Jan. 4, 2012; Amdt. 117–1A, 77 FR 28764, May 16, 2012; Amdt. 117–1, 78 FR 69288, Nov. 19, 2013]

§117.25 Rest period.

(a) No certificate holder may assign and no flightcrew member may accept assignment to any reserve or duty with the certificate holder during any required rest period.

(b) Before beginning any reserve or flight duty period a flightcrew member must be given at least 30 consecutive hours free from all duty within the past 168 consecutive hour period.

(c) If a flightcrew member operating in a new theater has received 36 consecutive hours of rest, that flightcrew member is acclimated and the rest period meets the requirements of paragraph (b) of this section.

(d) A flightcrew member must be given a minimum of 56 consecutive hours rest upon return to home base if the flightcrew member: (1) Travels more than 60° longitude during a flight duty period or a series of flight duty period, and (2) is away from home base for more than 168 consecutive hours during this travel. The 56 hours of rest specified in this section must encompass three physiological nights' rest based on local time.

(e) No certificate holder may schedule and no flightcrew member may accept an assignment for any reserve or flight duty period unless the flightcrew member is given a rest period of at least 10 consecutive hours immediately before beginning the reserve or flight duty period measured from the time the flightcrew member is released from duty. The 10 hour rest period must provide the flightcrew member with a minimum of 8 uninterrupted hours of sleep opportunity.

(f) If a flightcrew member determines that a rest period under paragraph (e) of this section will not provide eight uninterrupted hours of sleep opportunity, the flightcrew member must notify the certificate holder. The flightcrew member cannot report for the assigned flight duty period until he or she receives a rest period specified in paragraph (e) of this section.

(g) If a flightcrew member engaged in deadhead transportation exceeds the applicable flight duty period in Table B of this part, the flightcrew member must be given a rest period equal to the length of the deadhead transportation but not less than the required rest in paragraph (e) of this section before beginning a flight duty period.

[Doc. No. FAA–2009–1093, 77 FR 398, Jan. 4, 2012; Amdt. 117–1A, 77 FR 28764, May 16, 2012; Amdt. 117–1, 78 FR 8362, Feb. 6, 2013]

§ 117.27 Consecutive nighttime operations.

A certificate holder may schedule and a flightcrew member may accept up to five consecutive flight duty peri-

ods that infringe on the window of circadian low if the certificate holder provides the flightcrew member with an opportunity to rest in a suitable accommodation during each of the consecutive nighttime flight duty periods. The rest opportunity must be at least 2 hours, measured from the time that the flightcrew member reaches the suitable accommodation, and must comply with the conditions specified in § 117.15(a), (c), (d), and (e). Otherwise, no certificate holder may schedule and no flightcrew member may accept more than three consecutive flight duty periods that infringe on the window of circadian low. For purposes of this section, any split duty rest that is provided in accordance with § 117.15 counts as part of a flight duty period.

§ 117.29 Emergency and government sponsored operations.

(a) This section applies to operations conducted pursuant to contracts with the U.S. Government and operations conducted pursuant to a deviation under § 119.57 of this chapter that cannot otherwise be conducted under this part because of circumstances that could prevent flightcrew members from being relieved by another crew or safely provided with the rest required under § 117.25 at the end of the applicable flight duty period.

(b) The pilot-in-command may determine that the maximum applicable flight duty period, flight time, and/or combined flight duty period and reserve availability period limits must be exceeded to the extent necessary to allow the flightcrew to fly to the closest destination where they can safely be relieved from duty by another flightcrew or can receive the requisite amount of rest prior to commencing their next flight duty period.

(c) A flight duty period may not be extended for an operation conducted pursuant to a contract with the U.S. Government if it causes a flightcrew member to exceed the cumulative flight time limits in § 117.23(b) and the cumulative flight duty period limits in § 117.23(c).

(d) The flightcrew shall be given a rest period immediately after reaching the destination described in paragraph (b) of this section equal to the length of the actual flight duty period or 24 hours, whichever is less.

(e) Each certificate holder must report within 10 days:

(1) Any flight duty period that exceeded the maximum flight duty period permitted in Tables B or C of this part, as applicable, by more than 30 minutes;

(2) Any flight time that exceeded the maximum flight time limits permitted in Table A of this part and §117.11, as applicable; and

(3) Any flight duty period or flight time that exceeded the cumulative limits specified in §117.23.

(f) The report must contain the following:

(1) A description of the extended flight duty period and flight time limitation, and the circumstances surrounding the need for the extension; and

(2) If the circumstances giving rise to the extension(s) were within the cer-tificate holder's control, the corrective action(s) that the certificate holder intends to take to minimize the need for future extensions.

(g) Each certificate holder must implement the corrective action(s) reported pursuant to paragraph (f)(2) of this section within 30 days from the date of the extended flight duty period and/or the extended flight time.

[Doc. No. FAA–2009–1093, 77 FR 398, Jan. 4, 2012; Amdt. 117–1A, 77 FR 28764, May 16, 2012; Amdt. 117–1, 78 FR 8362, Feb. 6, 2013; 78 FR 69288, Nov. 19, 2013]

TABLE A TO PART 117—MAXIMUM FLIGHT TIME LIMITS FOR UNAUGMENTED OPERATIONS TABLE

Time of report (acclimated)	Maximum flight time (hours)
0000–0459	8
0500–1959	9
2000–2359	8

TABLE B TO PART 117—FLIGHT DUTY PERIOD: UNAUGMENTED OPERATIONS

Scheduled time of start (acclimated time)	Maximum flight duty period (hours) for lineholders based on number of flight segments						
	1	2	3	4	5	6	7 +
0000–0359	9	9	9	9	9	9	9
0400–0459	10	10	10	10	9	9	9
0500–0559	12	12	12	12	11.5	11	10.5
0600–0659	13	13	12	12	11.5	11	10.5
0700–1159	14	14	13	13	12.5	12	11.5
1200–1259	13	13	13	13	12.5	12	11.5
1300–1659	12	12	12	12	11.5	11	10.5
1700–2159	12	12	11	11	10	9	9
2200–2259	11	11	10	10	9	9	9
2300–2359	10	10	10	9	9	9	9

TABLE C TO PART 117—FLIGHT DUTY PERIOD: AUGMENTED OPERATIONS

Scheduled time of start (acclimated time)	Maximum flight duty period (hours) based on rest facility and number of pilots					
	Class 1 rest facility		Class 2 rest facility		Class 3 rest facility	
	3 pilots	4 pilots	3 pilots	4 pilots	3 pilots	4 pilots
0000–0559	15	17	14	15.5	13	13.5
0600–0659	16	18.5	15	16.5	14	14.5
0700–1259	17	19	16.5	18	15	15.5
1300–1659	16	18.5	15	16.5	14	14.5
1700–2359	15	17	14	15.5	13	13.5

PART 118 [RESERVED]

PART 119—CERTIFICATION: AIR CARRIERS AND COMMERCIAL OPERATORS

Subpart A—General

AUTHORITY: Pub. L. 111–216, sec. 215 (August 1, 2010); 49 U.S.C. 106(f), 106(g), 1153, 40101, 40102, 40103, 40113, 44105, 44106, 44111, 44701–44717, 44722, 44901, 44903, 44904, 44906, 44912, 44914, 44936, 44938, 46103, 46105.

SOURCE: Docket No. 28154, 60 FR 65913, Dec. 20, 1995, unless otherwise noted.

Subpart A—General

§ 119.1 Applicability.

(a) This part applies to each person operating or intending to operate civil aircraft—

(1) As an air carrier or commercial operator, or both, in air commerce; or

(2) When common carriage is not involved, in operations of U.S.-registered civil airplanes with a seat configuration of 20 or more passengers, or a maximum payload capacity of 6,000 pounds or more.

(b) This part prescribes—

(1) The types of air operator certificates issued by the Federal Aviation Administration, including air carrier certificates and operating certificates;

(2) The certification requirements an operator must meet in order to obtain and hold a certificate authorizing operations under part 121, 125, or 135 of this chapter and operations specifications for each kind of operation to be conducted and each class and size of aircraft to be operated under part 121 or 135 of this chapter;

(3) The requirements an operator must meet to conduct operations under part 121, 125, or 135 of this chapter and in operating each class and size of aircraft authorized in its operations specifications;

(4) Requirements affecting wet leasing of aircraft and other arrangements for transportation by air;

(5) Requirements for obtaining deviation authority to perform operations under a military contract and obtaining deviation authority to perform an emergency operation; and

(6) Requirements for management personnel for operations conducted under part 121 or part 135 of this chapter.

(c) Persons subject to this part must comply with the other requirements of this chapter, except where those requirements are modified by or where additional requirements are imposed by part 119, 121, 125, or 135 of this chapter.

(d) This part does not govern operations conducted under part 91, subpart K (when common carriage is not involved) nor does it govern operations conducted under part 129, 133, 137, or 139 of this chapter.

(e) Except for operations when common carriage is not involved conducted with airplanes having a passenger-seat configuration of 20 seats or more, excluding any required crewmember seat, or a payload capacity of 6,000 pounds or more, this part does not apply to—

(1) Student instruction;

(2) Nonstop Commercial Air Tours conducted after September 11, 2007, in an airplane or helicopter having a standard airworthiness certificate and passenger-seat configuration of 30 seats or fewer and a maximum payload capacity of 7,500 pounds or less that begin and end at the same airport, and are conducted within a 25-statute mile radius of that airport, in compliance with the Letter of Authorization issued under §91.147 of this chapter. For nonstop Commercial Air Tours conducted in accordance with part 136, subpart B of this chapter, National Parks Air Tour Management, the requirements of part 119 of this chapter apply unless excepted in §136.37(g)(2). For Nonstop Commercial Air Tours conducted in the vicinity of the Grand Canyon National Park, Arizona, the requirements of SFAR 50–2, part 93, subpart U, and part 119 of this chapter, as applicable, apply.

(3) Ferry or training flights;

(4) Aerial work operations, including—

(i) Crop dusting, seeding, spraying, and bird chasing;

(ii) Banner towing;

(iii) Aerial photography or survey;

(iv) Fire fighting;

(v) Helicopter operations in construction or repair work (but it does apply to transportation to and from the site of operations); and

(vi) Powerline or pipeline patrol;

(5) Sightseeing flights conducted in hot air balloons;

(6) Nonstop flights conducted within a 25-statute-mile radius of the airport of takeoff carrying persons or objects for the purpose of conducting intentional parachute operations.

(7) Helicopter flights conducted within a 25 statute mile radius of the airport of takeoff if—

(i) Not more than two passengers are carried in the helicopter in addition to the required flightcrew;

(ii) Each flight is made under day VFR conditions;

(iii) The helicopter used is certificated in the standard category and complies with the 100-hour inspection requirements of part 91 of this chapter;

(iv) The operator notifies the responsible Flight Standards office at least 72 hours before each flight and furnishes any essential information that the office requests;

(v) The number of flights does not exceed a total of six in any calendar year;

(vi) Each flight has been approved by the Administrator; and

(vii) Cargo is not carried in or on the helicopter;

(8) Operations conducted under part 133 of this chapter or 375 of this title;

(9) Emergency mail service conducted under 49 U.S.C. 41906;

(10) Operations conducted under the provisions of §91.321 of this chapter; or

(11) Small UAS operations conducted under part 107 of this chapter.

[Doc. No. 28154, 60 FR 65913, Dec. 20, 1995, as amended by Amdt. 119–4, 66 FR 23557, May 9, 2001; Amdt. 119–5, 67 FR 9554, Mar. 1, 2002; Amdt. 119–7, 68 FR 54584, Sept. 17, 2003; 72 FR 6911, Feb. 13, 2007; Docket FAA–2015–0150, Amdt. 119–18, 81 FR 42214, June 28, 2016; Docket FAA–2018–0119, Amdt. 119–19, 83 FR 9172, Mar. 5, 2018]

§119.3 [Reserved]

§119.5 Certifications, authorizations, and prohibitions.

(a) A person authorized by the Administrator to conduct operations as a direct air carrier will be issued an Air Carrier Certificate.

(b) A person who is not authorized to conduct direct air carrier operations, but who is authorized by the Administrator to conduct operations as a U.S. commercial operator, will be issued an Operating Certificate.

(c) A person who is not authorized to conduct direct air carrier operations, but who is authorized by the Administrator to conduct operations when common carriage is not involved as an operator of U.S.-registered civil airplanes with a seat configuration of 20 or more passengers, or a maximum payload capacity of 6,000 pounds or more, will be issued an Operating Certificate.

(d) A person authorized to engage in common carriage under part 121 or part 135 of this chapter, or both, shall be issued only one certificate authorizing such common carriage, regardless of the kind of operation or the class or size of aircraft to be operated.

(e) A person authorized to engage in noncommon or private carriage under part 125 or part 135 of this chapter, or both, shall be issued only one certificate authorizing such carriage, regardless of the kind of operation or the class or size of aircraft to be operated.

(f) A person conducting operations under more than one paragraph of §§ 119.21, 119.23, or 119.25 shall conduct those operations in compliance with—

(1) The requirements specified in each paragraph of those sections for the kind of operation conducted under that paragraph; and

(2) The appropriate authorizations, limitations, and procedures specified in the operations specifications for each kind of operation.

(g) No person may operate as a direct air carrier or as a commercial operator without, or in violation of, an appropriate certificate and appropriate operations specifications. No person may operate as a direct air carrier or as a commercial operator in violation of any deviation or exemption authority, if issued to that person or that person's representative.

(h) A person holding an Operating Certificate authorizing noncommon or private carriage operations shall not conduct any operations in common carriage. A person holding an Air Carrier Certificate or Operating Certificate authorizing common carriage operations shall not conduct any operations in noncommon carriage.

(i) No person may operate as a direct air carrier without holding appropriate economic authority from the Department of Transportation.

(j) A certificate holder under this part may not operate aircraft under part 121 or part 135 of this chapter in a geographical area unless its operations specifications specifically authorize the certificate holder to operate in that area.

(k) No person may advertise or otherwise offer to perform an operation subject to this part unless that person is authorized by the Federal Aviation Administration to conduct that operation.

(l) No person may operate an aircraft under this part, part 121 of this chapter, or part 135 of this chapter in violation of an air carrier operating certificate, operating certificate, or appropriate operations specifications issued under this part.

[Doc. No. 28154, 60 FR 65913, Dec. 20, 1995, as amended by Amdt. 119–3, 62 FR 13253, Mar. 19, 1997; 62 FR 15570, Apr. 1, 1997]

§ 119.7 Operations specifications.

(a) Each certificate holder's operations specifications must contain—

(1) The authorizations, limitations, and certain procedures under which each kind of operation, if applicable, is to be conducted; and

(2) Certain other procedures under which each class and size of aircraft is to be operated.

(b) Except for operations specifications paragraphs identifying authorized kinds of operations, operations specifications are not a part of a certificate.

§ 119.8 Safety Management Systems.

(a) Certificate holders authorized to conduct operations under part 121 of this chapter must have a safety management system that meets the requirements of part 5 of this chapter and is acceptable to the Administrator by March 9, 2018.

(b) A person applying to the Administrator for an air carrier certificate or operating certificate to conduct operations under part 121 of this chapter after March 9, 2015, must demonstrate, as part of the application process under §119.35, that it has an SMS that meets the standards set forth in part 5 of this chapter and is acceptable to the Administrator.

[Doc. No. FAA–2009–0671, 80 FR 1328 Jan. 8, 2015]

§119.9 Use of business names.

(a) A certificate holder under this part may not operate an aircraft under part 121 or part 135 of this chapter using a business name other than a business name appearing in the certificate holder's operations specifications.

(b) No person may operate an aircraft under part 121 or part 135 of this chapter unless the name of the certificate holder who is operating the aircraft, or the air carrier or operating certificate number of the certificate holder who is operating the aircraft, is legibly displayed on the aircraft and is clearly visible and readable from the outside of the aircraft to a person standing on the ground at any time except during flight time. The means of displaying the name on the aircraft and its readability must be acceptable to the Administrator.

[Doc. No. 28154, 60 FR 65913, Dec. 20, 1995, as amended by Amdt. 119–3, 62 FR 13253, Mar. 19, 1997]

Subpart B—Applicability of Operating Requirements to Different Kinds of Operations Under Parts 121, 125, and 135 of This Chapter

§119.21 Commercial operators engaged in intrastate common carriage and direct air carriers.

(a) Each person who conducts airplane operations as a commercial operator engaged in intrastate common carriage of persons or property for compensation or hire in air commerce, or as a direct air carrier, shall comply with the certification and operations specifications requirements in subpart C of this part, and shall conduct its:

(1) Domestic operations in accordance with the applicable requirements of part 121 of this chapter, and shall be

issued operations specifications for those operations in accordance with those requirements. However, based on a showing of safety in air commerce, the Administrator may permit persons who conduct domestic operations between any point located within any of the following Alaskan islands and any point in the State of Alaska to comply with the requirements applicable to flag operations contained in subpart U of part 121 of this chapter:

(i) The Aleutian Islands.

(ii) The Pribilof Islands.

(iii) The Shumagin Islands.

(2) Flag operations in accordance with the applicable requirements of part 121 of this chapter, and shall be issued operations specifications for those operations in accordance with those requirements.

(3) Supplemental operations in accordance with the applicable requirements of part 121 of this chapter, and shall be issued operations specifications for those operations in accordance with those requirements. However, based on a determination of safety in air commerce, the Administrator may authorize or require those operations to be conducted under paragraph (a)(1) or (a)(2) of this section.

(4) Commuter operations in accordance with the applicable requirements of part 135 of this chapter, and shall be issued operations specifications for those operations in accordance with those requirements.

(5) On-demand operations in accordance with the applicable requirements of part 135 of this chapter, and shall be issued operations specifications for those operations in accordance with those requirements.

(b) Persons who are subject to the requirements of paragraph (a)(4) of this section may conduct those operations in accordance with the requirements of paragraph (a)(1) or (a)(2) of this section, provided they obtain authorization from the Administrator.

(c) Persons who are subject to the requirements of paragraph (a)(5) of this section may conduct those operations in accordance with the requirements of paragraph (a)(3) of this section, provided they obtain authorization from the Administrator.

[Doc. No. 28154, 60 FR 65913, Dec. 20, 1995, as amended by Amdt. 119–2, 61 FR 30433, June 14, 1996; Amdt. 119–3, 62 FR 13254, Mar. 19, 1997]

§ 119.23 Operators engaged in passenger-carrying operations, cargo operations, or both with airplanes when common carriage is not involved.

(a) Each person who conducts operations when common carriage is not involved with airplanes having a passenger-seat configuration of 20 seats or more, excluding each crewmember seat, or a payload capacity of 6,000 pounds or more, shall, unless deviation authority is issued—

(1) Comply with the certification and operations specifications requirements of part 125 of this chapter;

(2) Conduct its operations with those airplanes in accordance with the requirements of part 125 of this chapter; and

(3) Be issued operations specifications in accordance with those requirements.

(b) Each person who conducts non-common carriage (except as provided in §91.501(b) of this chapter) or private carriage operations for compensation or hire with airplanes having a passenger-seat configuration of less than 20 seats, excluding each crewmember seat, and a payload capacity of less than 6,000 pounds shall—

(1) Comply with the certification and operations specifications requirements in subpart C of this part;

(2) Conduct those operations in accordance with the requirements of part 135 of this chapter, except for those requirements applicable only to commuter operations; and

(3) Be issued operations specifications in accordance with those requirements.

[Doc. No. 28154, 60 FR 65913, Dec. 20, 1995, as amended by Amdt. 119–2, 61 FR 30434, June 14, 1996]

§ 119.25 Rotorcraft operations: Direct air carriers and commercial operators.

Each person who conducts rotorcraft operations for compensation or hire must comply with the certification and operations specifications requirements of Subpart C of this part, and shall conduct its:

(a) Commuter operations in accordance with the applicable requirements of part 135 of this chapter, and shall be issued operations specifications for those operations in accordance with those requirements.

(b) On-demand operations in accordance with the applicable requirements of part 135 of this chapter, and shall be issued operations specifications for those operations in accordance with those requirements.

Subpart C—Certification, Operations Specifications, and Certain Other Requirements for Operations Conducted Under Part 121 or Part 135 of This Chapter

§ 119.31 Applicability.

This subpart sets out certification requirements and prescribes the content of operations specifications and certain other requirements for operations conducted under part 121 or part 135 of this chapter.

§ 119.33 General requirements.

(a) A person may not operate as a direct air carrier unless that person—

(1) Is a citizen of the United States;

(2) Obtains an Air Carrier Certificate; and

(3) Obtains operations specifications that prescribe the authorizations, limitations, and procedures under which each kind of operation must be conducted.

(b) A person other than a direct air carrier may not conduct any commercial passenger or cargo aircraft operation for compensation or hire under part 121 or part 135 of this chapter unless that person—

(1) Is a citizen of the United States;

(2) Obtains an Operating Certificate; and

(3) Obtains operations specifications that prescribe the authorizations, limitations, and procedures under which each kind of operation must be conducted.

(c) Each applicant for a certificate under this part and each applicant for operations specifications authorizing a new kind of operation that is subject to §121.163 or §135.145 of this chapter shall conduct proving tests as authorized by the Administrator during the application process for authority to conduct operations under part 121 or part 135 of this chapter. All proving tests must be conducted in a manner acceptable to the Administrator. All proving tests must be conducted under the appropriate operating and maintenance requirements of part 121 or 135 of this chapter that would apply if the applicant were fully certificated. The Administrator will issue a letter of authorization to each person stating the various authorities under which the proving tests shall be conducted.

[Doc. No. 28154, 60 FR 65913, Dec. 20. 1995, as amended by Amdt. 119–2, 31 FR 30454, June 14, 1996]

§119.35 Certificate application requirements for all operators.

(a) A person applying to the Administrator for an Air Carrier Certificate or Operating Certificate under this part (applicant) must submit an application—

(1) In a form and manner prescribed by the Administrator; and

(2) Containing any information the Administrator requires the applicant to submit.

(b) Each applicant must submit the application to the Administrator at least 90 days before the date of intended operation.

[Doc. No. 28154, 62 FR 13254, Mar. 19, 1997; 62 FR 15570, Apr. 1, 1997]

§119.36 Additional certificate application requirements for commercial operators.

(a) Each applicant for the original issue of an operating certificate for the purpose of conducting intrastate common carriage operations under part 121 or part 135 of this chapter must submit an application in a form and manner prescribed by the Administrator to the responsible Flight Standards office.

(b) Each application submitted under paragraph (a) of this section must contain a signed statement showing the following:

(1) For corporate applicants:

(i) The name and address of each stockholder who owns 5 percent or more of the total voting stock of the corporation, and if that stockholder is not the sole beneficial owner of the stock, the name and address of each beneficial owner. An individual is considered to own the stock owned, directly or indirectly, by or for his or her spouse, children, grandchildren, or parents.

(ii) The name and address of each director and each officer and each person employed or who will be employed in a management position described in §§119.65 and 119.69, as applicable.

(iii) The name and address of each person directly or indirectly controlling or controlled by the applicant and each person under direct or indirect control with the applicant.

(2) For non-corporate applicants:

(i) The name and address of each person having a financial interest therein and the nature and extent of that interest.

(ii) The name and address of each person employed or who will be employed in a management position described in §§119.65 and 119.69, as applicable.

(c) In addition, each applicant for the original issue of an operating certificate under paragraph (a) of this section must submit with the application a signed statement showing—

(1) The nature and scope of its intended operation, including the name and address of each person, if any, with whom the applicant has a contract to provide services as a commercial operator and the scope, nature, date, and duration of each of those contracts; and

(2) For applicants intending to conduct operations under part 121 of this chapter, the financial information listed in paragraph (e) of this section.

(d) Each applicant for, or holder of, a certificate issued under paragraph (a) of this section, shall notify the Administrator within 10 days after—

(1) A change in any of the persons, or the names and addresses of any of the persons, submitted to the Administrator under paragraph (b)(1) or (b)(2) of this section; or

(2) For applicants intending to conduct operations under part 121 of this chapter, a change in the financial information submitted to the Administrator under paragraph (e) of this section that occurs while the application for the issue is pending before the FAA and that would make the applicant's financial situation substantially less favorable than originally reported.

(e) Each applicant for the original issue of an operating certificate under paragraph (a) of this section who intends to conduct operations under part 121 of this chapter must submit the following financial information:

(1) A balance sheet that shows assets, liabilities, and net worth, as of a date not more than 60 days before the date of application.

(2) An itemization of liabilities more than 60 days past due on the balance sheet date, if any, showing each creditor's name and address, a description of the liability, and the amount and due date of the liability.

(3) An itemization of claims in litigation, if any, against the applicant as of the date of application showing each claimant's name and address and a description and the amount of the claim.

(4) A detailed projection of the proposed operation covering 6 complete months after the month in which the certificate is expected to be issued including—

(i) Estimated amount and source of both operating and nonoperating revenue, including identification of its existing and anticipated income producing contracts and estimated revenue per mile or hour of operation by aircraft type;

(ii) Estimated amount of operating and nonoperating expenses by expense objective classification; and

(iii) Estimated net profit or loss for the period.

(5) An estimate of the cash that will be needed for the proposed operations during the first 6 months after the month in which the certificate is expected to be issued, including—

(i) Acquisition of property and equipment (explain);

(ii) Retirement of debt (explain);

(iii) Additional working capital (explain);

(iv) Operating losses other than depreciation and amortization (explain); and

(v) Other (explain).

(6) An estimate of the cash that will be available during the first 6 months after the month in which the certificate is expected to be issued, from—

(i) Sale of property or flight equipment (explain);

(ii) New debt (explain);

(iii) New equity (explain);

(iv) Working capital reduction (explain);

(v) Operations (profits) (explain);

(vi) Depreciation and amortization (explain); and

(vii) Other (explain).

(7) A schedule of insurance coverage in effect on the balance sheet date showing insurance companies; policy numbers; types, amounts, and period of coverage; and special conditions, exclusions, and limitations.

(8) Any other financial information that the Administrator requires to enable him or her to determine that the applicant has sufficient financial resources to conduct his or her operations with the degree of safety required in the public interest.

(f) Each financial statement containing financial information required by paragraph (e) of this section must be based on accounts prepared and maintained on an accrual basis in accordance with generally accepted accounting principles applied on a consistent basis, and must contain the name and address of the applicant's public accounting firm, if any. Information submitted must be signed by an officer, owner, or partner of the applicant or certificate holder.

[Doc. No. 28154, 62 FR 13254, Mar. 19, 1997; 62 FR 15570, Apr. 1, 1997, as amended by Docket FAA-2018-0119, Amdt. 119-19, 83 FR 9172, Mar. 5, 2018]

§ 119.37 Contents of an Air Carrier Certificate or Operating Certificate.

The Air Carrier Certificate or Operating Certificate includes—

(a) The certificate holder's name;

(b) The location of the certificate holder's principal base of operations;

(c) The certificate number;

(d) The certificate's effective date; and

(e) The name or the designator of the responsible Flight Standards office.

[Docket No. 28154, 60 FR 65913, Dec. 20, 1995, as amended by Docket FAA–2018–0119, Amdt. 119–19, 83 FR 9172, Mar. 5, 2018]

§ 119.39 Issuing or denying a certificate.

(a) An applicant may be issued an Air Carrier Certificate or Operating Certificate if, after investigation, the Administrator finds that the applicant—

(1) Meets the applicable requirements of this part;

(2) Holds the economic authority applicable to the kinds of operations to be conducted, issued by the Department of Transportation, if required; and

(3) Is properly and adequately equipped in accordance with the requirements of this chapter and is able to conduct a safe operation under appropriate provisions of part 121 or part 135 of this chapter and operations specifications issued under this part.

(b) An application for a certificate may be denied if the Administrator finds that—

(1) The applicant is not properly or adequately equipped or is not able to conduct safe operations under this subchapter;

(2) The applicant previously held an Air Carrier Certificate or Operating Certificate which was revoked;

(3) The applicant intends to or fills a key management position listed in § 119.65(a) or § 119.69(a), as applicable, with an individual who exercised control over or who held the same or a similar position with a certificate holder whose certificate was revoked, or is in the process of being revoked, and that individual materially contributed to the circumstances causing revocation or causing the revocation process; or

(4) An individual who will have control over or have a substantial ownership interest in the applicant had the same or similar control or interest in a certificate holder whose certificate was revoked, or is in the process of being

revoked, and that individual materially contributed to the circumstances causing revocation or causing the revocation process; or

(5) In the case of an applicant for an Operating Certificate for intrastate common carriage, that for financial reasons the applicant is not able to conduct a safe operation.

§ 119.41 Amending a certificate.

(a) The Administrator may amend any certificate issued under this part if—

(1) The Administrator determines, under 49 U.S.C. 44709 and part 13 of this chapter, that safety in air commerce and the public interest requires the amendment; or

(2) The certificate holder applies for the amendment and the responsible Flight Standards office determines that safety in air commerce and the public interest allows the amendment.

(b) When the Administrator proposes to issue an order amending, suspending, or revoking all or part of any certificate, the procedure in § 13.19 of this chapter applies.

(c) When the certificate holder applies for an amendment of its certificate, the following procedure applies:

(1) The certificate holder must file an application to amend its certificate with the responsible Flight Standards office at least 15 days before the date proposed by the applicant for the amendment to become effective, unless the administrator approves filing within in a shorter period; and

(2) The application must be submitted to the responsible Flight Standards office in the form and manner prescribed by the Administrator.

(d) When a certificate holder seeks reconsideration of a decision from the responsible Flight Standards office concerning amendments of a certificate, the following procedure applies:

(1) The petition for reconsideration must be made within 30 days after the certificate holder receives the notice of denial; and

(2) The certificate holder must petition for reconsideration to the Executive Director, Flight Standards Service.

[Docket No. 28154, 60 FR 65913, Dec. 20, 1995, as amended by Docket FAA–2018–0119, Amdt. 119–19, 83 FR 9172, Mar. 5, 2018]

§ 119.43 Certificate holder's duty to maintain operations specifications.

(a) Each certificate holder shall maintain a complete and separate set of its operations specifications at its principal base of operations.

(b) Each certificate holder shall insert pertinent excerpts of its operations specifications, or references thereto, in its manual and shall—

(1) Clearly identify each such excerpt as a part of its operations specifications; and

(2) State that compliance with each operations specifications requirement is mandatory.

(c) Each certificate holder shall keep each of its employees and other persons used in its operations informed of the provisions of its operations specifications that apply to that employee's or person's duties and responsibilities.

§ 119.45 [Reserved]

§ 119.47 Maintaining a principal base of operations, main operations base, and main maintenance base; change of address.

(a) Each certificate holder must maintain a principal base of operations. Each certificate holder may also establish a main operations base and a main maintenance base which may be located at either the same location as the principal base of operations or at separate locations.

(b) At least 30 days before it proposes to establish or change the location of its principal base of operations, its main operations base, or its main maintenance base, a certificate holder must provide written notification to its responsible Flight Standards office.

[Docket No. 28154, 60 FR 65913, Dec. 20, 1995, as amended by Docket FAA–2018–0119, Amdt. 119–19, 83 FR 9172, Mar. 5, 2018]

§ 119.49 Contents of operations specifications.

(a) Each certificate holder conducting domestic, flag, or commuter operations must obtain operations specifications containing all of the following:

(1) The specific location of the certificate holder's principal base of operations and, if different, the address that shall serve as the primary point of contact for correspondence between the FAA and the certificate holder and the name and mailing address of the certificate holder's agent for service.

(2) Other business names under which the certificate holder may operate.

(3) Reference to the economic authority issued by the Department of Transportation, if required.

(4) Type of aircraft, registration markings, and serial numbers of each aircraft authorized for use, each regular and alternate airport to be used in scheduled operations, and, except for commuter operations, each provisional and refueling airport.

(i) Subject to the approval of the Administrator with regard to form and content, the certificate holder may incorporate by reference the items listed in paragraph (a)(4) of this section into the certificate holder's operations specifications by maintaining a current listing of those items and by referring to the specific list in the applicable paragraph of the operations specifications.

(ii) The certificate holder may not conduct any operation using any aircraft or airport not listed.

(5) Kinds of operations authorized.

(6) Authorization and limitations for routes and areas of operations.

(7) Airport limitations.

(8) Time limitations, or standards for determining time limitations, for overhauling, inspecting, and checking airframes, engines, propellers, rotors, appliances, and emergency equipment.

(9) Authorization for the method of controlling weight and balance of aircraft.

(10) Interline equipment interchange requirements, if relevant.

(11) Aircraft wet lease information required by § 119.53(c).

(12) Any authorized deviation and exemption granted from any requirement of this chapter.

(13) An authorization permitting, or a prohibition against, accepting, handling, and transporting materials regulated as hazardous materials in transport under 49 CFR parts 171 through 180.

(14) Any other item the Administrator determines is necessary.

(b) Each certificate holder conducting supplemental operations must obtain operations specifications containing all of the following:

(1) The specific location of the certificate holder's principal base of operations, and, if different, the address that shall serve as the primary point of contact for correspondence between the FAA and the certificate holder and the name and mailing address of the certificate holder's agent for service.

(2) Other business names under which the certificate holder may operate.

(3) Reference to the economic authority issued by the Department of Transportation, if required.

(4) Type of aircraft, registration markings, and serial number of each aircraft authorized for use.

(i) Subject to the approval of the Administrator with regard to form and content, the certificate holder may incorporate by reference the items listed in paragraph (b)(4) of this section into the certificate holder's operations specifications by maintaining a current listing of those items and by referring to the specific list in the applicable paragraph of the operations specifications.

(ii) The certificate holder may not conduct any operation using any aircraft not listed.

(5) Kinds of operations authorized.

(6) Authorization and limitations for routes and areas of operations.

(7) Special airport authorizations and limitations.

(8) Time limitations, or standards for determining time limitations, for overhauling, inspecting, and checking airframes, engines, propellers, appliances, and emergency equipment.

(9) Authorization for the method of controlling weight and balance of aircraft.

(10) Aircraft wet lease information required by §119.53(c).

(11) Any authorization or requirement to conduct supplemental operations as provided by §119.21(a)(3).

(12) Any authorized deviation or exemption from any requirement of this chapter.

(13) An authorization permitting, or a prohibition against, accepting, handling, and transporting materials regulated as hazardous materials in transport under 49 CFR parts 171 through 180.

(14) Any other item the Administrator determines is necessary.

(c) Each certificate holder conducting on-demand operations must obtain operations specifications containing all of the following:

(1) The specific location of the certificate holder's principal base of operations, and if different, the address that shall serve as the primary point of contact for correspondence between the FAA and the name and mailing address of the certificate holder's agent for service.

(2) Other business names under which the certificate holder may operate.

(3) Reference to the economic authority issued by the Department of Transportation, if required.

(4) Kind and area of operations authorized.

(5) Category and class of aircraft that may be used in those operations.

(6) Type of aircraft, registration markings, and serial number of each aircraft that is subject to an airworthiness maintenance program required by §135.411(a)(2) of this chapter.

(i) Subject to the approval of the Administrator with regard to form and content, the certificate holder may incorporate by reference the items listed in paragraph (c)(6) of this section into the certificate holder's operations specifications by maintaining a current listing of those items and by referring to the specific list in the applicable paragraph of the operations specifications.

(ii) The certificate holder may not conduct any operation using any aircraft not listed.

(7) Registration markings of each aircraft that is to be inspected under an

approved aircraft inspection program under § 135.419 of this chapter.

(8) Time limitations or standards for determining time limitations, for overhauls, inspections, and checks for airframes, engines, propellers, rotors, appliances, and emergency equipment of aircraft that are subject to an airworthiness maintenance program required by § 135.411(a)(2) of this chapter.

(9) Additional maintenance items required by the Administrator under § 135.421 of this chapter.

(10) Aircraft wet lease information required by § 119.53(c).

(11) Any authorized deviation or exemption from any requirement of this chapter.

(12) An authorization permitting, or a prohibition against, accepting, handling, and transporting materials regulated as hazardous materials in transport under 49 CFR parts 171 through 180.

(13) Any other item the Administrator determines is necessary.

[Doc. No. 28154, 60 FR 65913, Dec. 20, 1995, as amended by Amdt. 119–10, 70 FR 58823, Oct. 7, 2005; Amdt. 119–13, 75 FR 26645, May 12, 2010]

§ 119.51 Amending operations specifications.

(a) The Administrator may amend any operations specifications issued under this part if—

(1) The Administrator determines that safety in air commerce and the public interest require the amendment; or

(2) The certificate holder applies for the amendment, and the Administrator determines that safety in air commerce and the public interest allows the amendment.

(b) Except as provided in paragraph (e) of this section, when the Administrator initiates an amendment to a certificate holder's operations specifications, the following procedure applies:

(1) The responsible Flight Standards office notifies the certificate holder in writing of the proposed amendment.

(2) The responsible Flight Standards office sets a reasonable period (but not less than 7 days) within which the certificate holder may submit written information, views, and arguments on the amendment.

(3) After considering all material presented, the responsible Flight Standards office notifies the certificate holder of—

(i) The adoption of the proposed amendment;

(ii) The partial adoption of the proposed amendment; or

(iii) The withdrawal of the proposed amendment.

(4) If the responsible Flight Standards office issues an amendment to the operations specifications, it becomes effective not less than 30 days after the certificate holder receives notice of it unless—

(i) The responsible Flight Standards office finds under paragraph (e) of this section that there is an emergency requiring immediate action with respect to safety in air commerce; or

(ii) The certificate holder petitions for reconsideration of the amendment under paragraph (d) of this section.

(c) When the certificate holder applies for an amendment to its operations specifications, the following procedure applies:

(1) The certificate holder must file an application to amend its operations specifications—

(i) At least 90 days before the date proposed by the applicant for the amendment to become effective, unless a shorter time is approved, in cases of mergers; acquisitions of airline operational assets that require an additional showing of safety (e.g., proving tests); changes in the kind of operation as defined in § 110.2; resumption of operations following a suspension of operations as a result of bankruptcy actions; or the initial introduction of aircraft not before proven for use in air carrier or commercial operator operations.

(ii) At least 15 days before the date proposed by the applicant for the amendment to become effective in all other cases.

(2) The application must be submitted to the responsible Flight Standards office in a form and manner prescribed by the Administrator.

(3) After considering all material presented, the responsible Flight Standards office notifies the certificate holder of—

(i) The adoption of the applied for amendment;

(ii) The partial adoption of the applied for amendment; or

(iii) The denial of the applied for amendment. The certificate holder may petition for reconsideration of a denial under paragraph (d) of this section.

(4) If the responsible Flight Standards office approves the amendment, following coordination with the certificate holder regarding its implementation, the amendment is effective on the date the Administrator approves it.

(d) When a certificate holder seeks reconsideration of a decision from the responsible Flight Standards office concerning the amendment of operations specifications, the following procedure applies:

(1) The certificate holder must petition for reconsideration of that decision within 30 days of the date that the certificate holder receives a notice of denial of the amendment to its operations specifications, or of the date it receives notice of an FAA-initiated amendment to its operations specifications, whichever circumstance applies.

(2) The certificate holder must address its petition to the Executive Director, Flight Standards Service.

(3) A petition for reconsideration, if filed within the 30-day period, suspends the effectiveness of any amendment issued by the responsible Flight Standards office unless the responsible Flight Standards office has found, under paragraph (e) of this section, that an emergency exists requiring immediate action with respect to safety in air transportation or air commerce.

(4) If a petition for reconsideration is not filed within 30 days, the procedures of paragraph (c) of this section apply.

(e) If the responsible Flight Standards office finds that an emergency exists requiring immediate action with respect to safety in air commerce or air transportation that makes the procedures set out in this section impracticable or contrary to the public interest:

(1) The responsible Flight Standards office amends the operations specifications and makes the amendment effective on the day the certificate holder receives notice of it.

(2) In the notice to the certificate holder, the responsible Flight Standards office articulates the reasons for its finding that an emergency exists requiring immediate action with respect to safety in air transportation or air commerce or that makes it impracticable or contrary to the public interest to stay the effectiveness of the amendment.

[Doc. No. 28154, 60 FR 65913, Dec. 20, 1995, as amended by Amdt. 119–14, 76 FR 7488, Feb. 10, 2011; Docket FAA–2018–0119, Amdt. 119–19, 83 FR 9172, Mar. 5, 2018]

§119.53 Wet leasing of aircraft and other arrangements for transportation by air.

(a) Unless otherwise authorized by the Administrator, prior to conducting operations involving a wet lease, each certificate holder under this part authorized to conduct common carriage operations under this subchapter shall provide the Administrator with a copy of the wet lease to be executed which would lease the aircraft to any other person engaged in common carriage operations under this subchapter, including foreign air carriers, or to any other foreign person engaged in common carriage wholly outside the United States.

(b) No certificate holder under this part may wet lease from a foreign air carrier or any other foreign person or any person not authorized to engage in common carriage.

(c) Upon receiving a copy of a wet lease, the Administrator determines which party to the agreement has operational control of the aircraft and issues amendments to the operations specifications of each party to the agreement, as needed. The lessor must provide the following information to be incorporated into the operations specifications of both parties, as needed.

(1) The names of the parties to the agreement and the duration thereof.

(2) The nationality and registration markings of each aircraft involved in the agreement.

(3) The kind of operation (e.g., domestic, flag, supplemental, commuter, or on-demand).

(4) The airports or areas of operation.

(5) A statement specifying the party deemed to have operational control and the times, airports, or areas under

27

which such operational control is exercised.

(d) In making the determination of paragraph (c) of this section, the Administrator will consider the following:

(1) Crewmembers and training.

(2) Airworthiness and performance of maintenance.

(3) Dispatch.

(4) Servicing the aircraft.

(5) Scheduling.

(6) Any other factor the Administrator considers relevant.

(e) Other arrangements for transportation by air: Except as provided in paragraph (f) of this section, a certificate holder under this part operating under part 121 or 135 of this chapter may not conduct any operation for another certificate holder under this part or a foreign air carrier under part 129 of this chapter or a foreign person engaged in common carriage wholly outside the United States unless it holds applicable Department of Transportation economic authority, if required, and is authorized under its operations specifications to conduct the same kinds of operations (as defined in §110.2). The certificate holder conducting the substitute operation must conduct that operation in accordance with the same operations authority held by the certificate holder arranging for the substitute operation. These substitute operations must be conducted between airports for which the substitute certificate holder holds authority for scheduled operations or within areas of operations for which the substitute certificate holder has authority for supplemental or on-demand operations.

(f) A certificate holder under this part may, if authorized by the Department of Transportation under §380.3 of this title and the Administrator in the case of interstate commuter, interstate domestic, and flag operations, or the Administrator in the case of scheduled intrastate common carriage operations, conduct one or more flights for passengers who are stranded because of the cancellation of their scheduled flights. These flights must be conducted under the rules of part 121 or

part 135 of this chapter applicable to supplemental or on-demand operations.

[Doc. No. 28154, 60 FR 65913, Dec. 20, 1995, as amended by Amdt. 119–14, 76 FR 7488, Feb. 10, 2011]

§ 119.55 Obtaining deviation authority to perform operations under a U.S. military contract.

(a) The Administrator may authorize a certificate holder that is authorized to conduct supplemental or on-demand operations to deviate from the applicable requirements of this part, part 117, part 121, or part 135 of this chapter in order to perform operations under a U.S. military contract.

(b) A certificate holder that has a contract with the U.S. Department of Defense's Air Mobility Command (AMC) must submit a request for deviation authority to AMC. AMC will review the requests, then forward the carriers' consolidated requests, along with AMC's recommendations, to the FAA for review and action.

(c) The Administrator may authorize a deviation to perform operations under a U.S. military contract under the following conditions—

(1) The Department of Defense certifies to the Administrator that the operation is essential to the national defense;

(2) The Department of Defense further certifies that the certificate holder cannot perform the operation without deviation authority;

(3) The certificate holder will perform the operation under a contract or subcontract for the benefit of a U.S. armed service; and

(4) The Administrator finds that the deviation is based on grounds other than economic advantage either to the certificate holder or to the United States.

(d) In the case where the Administrator authorizes a deviation under this section, the Administrator will issue an appropriate amendment to the certificate holder's operations specifications.

(e) The Administrator may, at any time, terminate any grant of deviation authority issued under this section.

[Doc. No. 28154, 60 FR 65913, Dec. 20, 1995, as amended by Amdt. 119–16, 77 FR 402, Jan. 4, 2012]

§119.57 Obtaining deviation authority to perform an emergency operation.

(a) In emergency conditions, the Administrator may authorize deviations if—

(1) Those conditions necessitate the transportation of persons or supplies for the protection of life or property; and

(2) The Administrator finds that a deviation is necessary for the expeditious conduct of the operations.

(b) When the Administrator authorizes deviations for operations under emergency conditions—

(1) The Administrator will issue an appropriate amendment to the certificate holder's operations specifications; or

(2) If the nature of the emergency does not permit timely amendment of the operations specifications—

(i) The Administrator may authorize the deviation orally; and

(ii) The certificate holder shall provide documentation describing the nature of the emergency to the responsible Flight Standards office within 24 hours after completing the operation.

[Docket No. 28154, 60 FR 65913, Dec. 20, 1995, as amended by Docket FAA–2018–0119, Amdt. 119–19, 83 FR 9172, Mar. 5, 2018]

§119.59 Conducting tests and inspections.

(a) At any time or place, the Administrator may conduct an inspection or test to determine whether a certificate holder under this part is complying with title 49 of the United States Code, applicable regulations, the certificate, or the certificate holder's operations specifications.

(b) The certificate holder must—

(1) Make available to the Administrator at the certificate holder's principal base of operations—

(i) The certificate holder's Air Carrier Certificate or the certificate holder's Operating Certificate and the certificate holder's operations specifications; and

(ii) A current listing that will include the location and persons responsible for each record, document, and report required to be kept by the certificate holder under title 49 of the United States Code applicable to the operation of the certificate holder.

(2) Allow the Administrator to make any test or inspection to determine compliance respecting any matter stated in paragraph (a) of this section.

(c) Each employee of, or person used by, the certificate holder who is responsible for maintaining the certificate holder's records must make those records available to the Administrator.

(d) The Administrator may determine a certificate holder's continued eligibility to hold its certificate and/or operations specifications on any grounds listed in paragraph (a) of this section, or any other appropriate grounds.

(e) Failure by any certificate holder to make available to the Administrator upon request, the certificate, operations specifications, or any required record, document, or report is grounds for suspension of all or any part of the certificate holder's certificate and operations specifications.

(f) In the case of operators conducting intrastate common carriage operations, these inspections and tests include inspections and tests of financial books and records.

§119.61 Duration and surrender of certificate and operations specifications.

(a) An Air Carrier Certificate or Operating Certificate issued under this part is effective until—

(1) The certificate holder surrenders it to the Administrator; or

(2) The Administrator suspends, revokes, or otherwise terminates the certificate.

(b) Operations specifications issued under this part, part 121, or part 135 of this chapter are effective unless—

(1) The Administrator suspends, revokes, or otherwise terminates the certificate;

(2) The operations specifications are amended as provided in §119.51;

(3) The certificate holder does not conduct a kind of operation for more than the time specified in §119.63 and fails to follow the procedures of §119.63 upon resuming that kind of operation; or

(4) The Administrator suspends or revokes the operations specifications for a kind of operation.

(c) Within 30 days after a certificate holder terminates operations under part 135 of this chapter, the operating certificate and operations specifications must be surrendered by the certificate holder to the responsible Flight Standards office.

[Docket No. 28154, 60 FR 65913, Dec. 20, 1995, as amended by Docket FAA–2018–0119, Amdt. 119–19, 83 FR 9172, Mar. 5, 2018]

§ 119.63 Recency of operation.

(a) Except as provided in paragraph (b) of this section, no certificate holder may conduct a kind of operation for which it holds authority in its operations specifications unless the certificate holder has conducted that kind of operation within the preceding number of consecutive calendar days specified in this paragraph:

(1) For domestic, flag, or commuter operations—30 days.

(2) For supplemental or on-demand operations—90 days, except that if the certificate holder has authority to conduct domestic, flag, or commuter operations, and has conducted domestic, flag or commuter operations within the previous 30 days, this paragraph does not apply.

(b) If a certificate holder does not conduct a kind of operation for which it is authorized in its operations specifications within the number of calendar days specified in paragraph (a) of this section, it shall not conduct such kind of operation unless—

(1) It advises the Administrator at least 5 consecutive calendar days before resumption of that kind of operation; and

(2) It makes itself available and accessible during the 5 consecutive calendar day period in the event that the FAA decides to conduct a full inspection reexamination to determine whether the certificate holder remains properly and adequately equipped and able to conduct a safe operation.

[Doc. No. 28154, 60 FR 65913, Dec. 20, 1995, as amended by Amdt. 119–2, 61 FR 30434, June 14, 1996]

§ 119.65 Management personnel required for operations conducted under part 121 of this chapter.

(a) Each certificate holder must have sufficient qualified management and technical personnel to ensure the highest degree of safety in its operations. The certificate holder must have qualified personnel serving full-time in the following or equivalent positions:

(1) Director of Safety.

(2) Director of Operations.

(3) Chief Pilot.

(4) Director of Maintenance.

(5) Chief Inspector.

(b) The Administrator may approve positions or numbers of positions other than those listed in paragraph (a) of this section for a particular operation if the certificate holder shows that it can perform the operation with the highest degree of safety under the direction of fewer or different categories of management personnel due to—

(1) The kind of operation involved;

(2) The number and type of airplanes used; and

(3) The area of operations.

(c) The title of the positions required under paragraph (a) of this section or the title and number of equivalent positions approved under paragraph (b) of this section shall be set forth in the certificate holder's operations specifications.

(d) The individuals who serve in the positions required or approved under paragraph (a) or (b) of this section and anyone in a position to exercise control over operations conducted under the operating certificate must—

(1) Be qualified through training, experience, and expertise;

(2) To the extent of their responsibilities, have a full understanding of the following materials with respect to the certificate holder's operation—

(i) Aviation safety standards and safe operating practices;

(ii) 14 CFR Chapter I (Federal Aviation Regulations);

(iii) The certificate holder's operations specifications;

(iv) All appropriate maintenance and airworthiness requirements of this chapter (e.g., parts 1, 21, 23, 25, 43, 45, 47, 65, 91, and 121 of this chapter); and

(v) The manual required by § 121.133 of this chapter; and

(3) Discharge their duties to meet applicable legal requirements and to maintain safe operations.

(e) Each certificate holder must:

(1) State in the general policy provisions of the manual required by §121.133 of this chapter, the duties, responsibilities, and authority of personnel required under paragraph (a) of this section;

(2) List in the manual the names and business addresses of the individuals assigned to those positions; and

(3) Notify the responsible Flight Standards office within 10 days of any change in personnel or any vacancy in any position listed.

[Docket No. 28154, 60 FR 65913, Dec. 20, 1995, as amended by Docket FAA–2018–0119. Amdt. 119–19, 83 FR 9172, Mar. 5, 2018]

§119.67 Management personnel: Qualifications for operations conducted under part 121 of this chapter.

(a) To serve as Director of Operations under §119.65(a) a person must—

(1) Hold an airline transport pilot certificate;

(2) Have at least 3 years supervisory or managerial experience within the last 6 years in a position that exercised operational control over any operations conducted with large airplanes under part 121 or part 135 of this chapter, or if the certificate holder uses only small airplanes in its operations, the experience may be obtained in large or small airplanes; and

(3) In the case of a person becoming a Director of Operations—

(i) For the first time ever, have at least 3 years experience, within the past 6 years, as pilot in command of a large airplane operated under part 121 or part 135 of this chapter, if the certificate holder operates large airplanes. If the certificate holder uses only small airplanes in its operation, the experience may be obtained in either large or small airplanes.

(ii) In the case of a person with previous experience as a Director of Operations, have at least 3 years experience as pilot in command of a large airplane operated under part 121 or part 135 of this chapter, if the certificate holder operates large airplanes. If the certificate holder uses only small airplanes in its operation, the experience may be obtained in either large or small airplanes.

(b) To serve as Chief Pilot under §119.65(a) a person must hold an airline transport pilot certificate with appropriate ratings for at least one of the airplanes used in the certificate holder's operation and:

(1) In the case of a person becoming a Chief Pilot for the first time ever, have at least 3 years experience, within the past 6 years, as pilot in command of a large airplane operated under part 121 or part 135 of this chapter, if the certificate holder operates large airplanes. If the certificate holder uses only small airplanes in its operation, the experience may be obtained in either large or small airplanes.

(2) In the case of a person with previous experience as a Chief Pilot, have at least 3 years experience, as pilot in command of a large airplane operated under part 121 or part 135 of this chapter, if the certificate holder operates large airplanes. If the certificate holder uses only small airplanes in its operation, the experience may be obtained in either large or small airplanes.

(c) To serve as Director of Maintenance under §119.65(a) a person must—

(1) Hold a mechanic certificate with airframe and powerplant ratings;

(2) Have 1 year of experience in a position responsible for returning airplanes to service;

(3) Have at least 1 year of experience in a supervisory capacity under either paragraph (c)(4)(i) or (c)(4)(ii) of this section maintaining the same category and class of airplane as the certificate holder uses; and

(4) Have 3 years experience within the past 6 years in one or a combination of the following—

(i) Maintaining large airplanes with 10 or more passenger seats, including at the time of appointment as Director of Maintenance, experience in maintaining the same category and class of airplane as the certificate holder uses; or

(ii) Repairing airplanes in a certificated airframe repair station that is rated to maintain airplanes in the same category and class of airplane as the certificate holder uses.

(d) To serve as Chief Inspector under §119.65(a) a person must—

(1) Hold a mechanic certificate with both airframe and powerplant ratings, and have held these ratings for at least 3 years;

(2) Have at least 3 years of maintenance experience on different types of large airplanes with 10 or more passenger seats with an air carrier or certificated repair station, 1 year of which must have been as maintenance inspector; and

(3) Have at least 1 year of experience in a supervisory capacity maintaining the same category and class of aircraft as the certificate holder uses.

(e) A certificate holder may request a deviation to employ a person who does not meet the appropriate airman experience, managerial experience, or supervisory experience requirements of this section if the Manager of the Air Transportation Division, AFS–200, or the Manager of the Aircraft Maintenance Division, AFS–300, as appropriate, finds that the person has comparable experience, and can effectively perform the functions associated with the position in accordance with the requirements of this chapter and the procedures outlined in the certificate holder's manual. Grants of deviation under this paragraph may be granted after consideration of the size and scope of the operation and the qualifications of the intended personnel. The Administrator may, at any time, terminate any grant of deviation authority issued under this paragraph.

[Doc. No. 28154, 60 FR 65913, Dec. 20, 1995, as amended by Amdt. 119–2, 61 FR 30434, June 14, 1996; Amdt. 119–3, 62 FR 13255, Mar. 19, 1997]

§ 119.69 Management personnel required for operations conducted under part 135 of this chapter.

(a) Each certificate holder must have sufficient qualified management and technical personnel to ensure the safety of its operations. Except for a certificate holder using only one pilot in its operations, the certificate holder must have qualified personnel serving in the following or equivalent positions:

(1) Director of Operations.
(2) Chief Pilot.
(3) Director of Maintenance.

(b) The Administrator may approve positions or numbers of positions other than those listed in paragraph (a) of this section for a particular operation if the certificate holder shows that it

can perform the operation with the highest degree of safety under the direction of fewer or different categories of management personnel due to—

(1) The kind of operation involved;
(2) The number and type of aircraft used; and
(3) The area of operations.

(c) The title of the positions required under paragraph (a) of this section or the title and number of equivalent positions approved under paragraph (b) of this section shall be set forth in the certificate holder's operations specifications.

(d) The individuals who serve in the positions required or approved under paragraph (a) or (b) of this section and anyone in a position to exercise control over operations conducted under the operating certificate must—

(1) Be qualified through training, experience, and expertise;
(2) To the extent of their responsibilities, have a full understanding of the following material with respect to the certificate holder's operation—
(i) Aviation safety standards and safe operating practices;
(ii) 14 CFR Chapter I (Federal Aviation Regulations);
(iii) The certificate holder's operations specifications;
(iv) All appropriate maintenance and airworthiness requirements of this chapter (e.g., parts 1, 21, 23, 25, 43, 45, 47, 65, 91, and 135 of this chapter); and
(v) The manual required by § 135.21 of this chapter; and
(3) Discharge their duties to meet applicable legal requirements and to maintain safe operations.

(e) Each certificate holder must—
(1) State in the general policy provisions of the manual required by § 135.21 of this chapter, the duties, responsibilities, and authority of personnel required or approved under paragraph (a) or (b), respectively, of this section;
(2) List in the manual the names and business addresses of the individuals assigned to those positions; and
(3) Notify the responsible Flight Standards office within 10 days of any change in personnel or any vacancy in any position listed.

[Docket No. 28154, 60 FR 65913, Dec. 20, 1995, as amended by Docket FAA–2018–0119, Amdt. 119–19, 83 FR 9172, Mar. 5, 2018]

§ 119.71 Management personnel: Qualifications for operations conducted under part 135 of this chapter.

(a) To serve as Director of Operations under § 119.69(a) for a certificate holder conducting any operations for which the pilot in command is required to hold an airline transport pilot certificate a person must hold an airline transport pilot certificate and either:

(1) Have at least 3 years supervisory or managerial experience within the last 6 years in a position that exercised operational control over any operations conducted under part 121 or part 135 of this chapter; or

(2) In the case of a person becoming Director of Operations—

(i) For the first time ever, have at least 3 years experience, within the past 6 years, as pilot in command of an aircraft operated under part 121 or part 135 of this chapter.

(ii) In the case of a person with previous experience as a Director of Operations, have at least 3 years experience, as pilot in command of an aircraft operated under part 121 or part 135 of this chapter.

(b) To serve as Director of Operations under § 119.69(a) for a certificate holder that only conducts operations for which the pilot in command is required to hold a commercial pilot certificate, a person must hold at least a commercial pilot certificate. If an instrument rating is required for any pilot in command for that certificate holder, the Director of Operations must also hold an instrument rating. In addition, the Director of Operations must either—

(1) Have at least 3 years supervisory or managerial experience within the last 6 years in a position that exercised operational control over any operations conducted under part 121 or part 135 of this chapter; or

(2) In the case of a person becoming Director of Operations—

(i) For the first time ever, have at least 3 years experience, within the past 6 years, as pilot in command of an aircraft operated under part 121 or part 135 of this chapter.

(ii) In the case of a person with previous experience as a Director of Operations, have at least 3 years experience as pilot in command of an aircraft operated under part 121 or part 135 of this chapter.

(c) To serve as Chief Pilot under § 119.69(a) for a certificate holder conducting any operation for which the pilot in command is required to hold an airline transport pilot certificate a person must hold an airline transport pilot certificate with appropriate ratings and be qualified to serve as pilot in command in at least one aircraft used in the certificate holder's operation and:

(1) In the case of a person becoming a Chief Pilot for the first time ever, have at least 3 years experience, within the past 6 years, as pilot in command of an aircraft operated under part 121 or part 135 of this chapter.

(2) In the case of a person with previous experience as a Chief Pilot, have at least 3 years experience as pilot in command of an aircraft operated under part 121 or part 135 of this chapter.

(d) To serve as Chief Pilot under § 119.69(a) for a certificate holder that only conducts operations for which the pilot in command is required to hold a commercial pilot certificate, a person must hold at least a commercial pilot certificate. If an instrument rating is required for any pilot in command for that certificate holder, the Chief Pilot must also hold an instrument rating. The Chief Pilot must be qualified to serve as pilot in command in at least one aircraft used in the certificate holder's operation. In addition, the Chief Pilot must:

(1) In the case of a person becoming a Chief Pilot for the first time ever, have at least 3 years experience, within the past 6 years, as pilot in command of an aircraft operated under part 121 or part 135 of this chapter.

(2) In the case of a person with previous experience as a Chief Pilot, have at least 3 years experience as pilot in command of an aircraft operated under part 121 or part 135 of this chapter.

(e) To serve as Director of Maintenance under § 119.69(a) a person must hold a mechanic certificate with airframe and powerplant ratings and either:

(1) Have 3 years of experience within the past 6 years maintaining aircraft as a certificated mechanic, including, at the time of appointment as Director

33

of Maintenance, experience in maintaining the same category and class of aircraft as the certificate holder uses; or

(2) Have 3 years of experience within the past 6 years repairing aircraft in a certificated airframe repair station, including 1 year in the capacity of approving aircraft for return to service.

(f) A certificate holder may request a deviation to employ a person who does not meet the appropriate airmen experience requirements, managerial experience requirements, or supervisory experience requirements of this section if the Manager of the Air Transportation Division, AFS–200, or the Manager of the Aircraft Maintenance Division, AFS–300, as appropriate, find that the person has comparable experience, and can effectively perform the functions associated with the position in accordance with the requirements of this chapter and the procedures outlined in the certificate holder's manual. The Administrator may, at any time, terminate any grant of deviation authority issued under this paragraph.

[Doc. No. 28154, 60 FR 65913, Dec. 20, 1995, as amended by Amdt. 119–3, 62 FR 13255, Mar. 19, 1997; Amdt. 119–12, 72 FR 54816, Sept. 27, 2007]

§ 119.73 Employment of former FAA employees.

(a) Except as specified in paragraph (c) of this section, no certificate holder conducting operations under part 121 or 135 of this chapter may knowingly employ or make a contractual arrangement which permits an individual to act as an agent or representative of the certificate holder in any matter before the Federal Aviation Administration if the individual, in the preceding 2 years—

(1) Served as, or was directly responsible for the oversight of, a Flight Standards Service aviation safety inspector; and

(2) Had direct responsibility to inspect, or oversee the inspection of, the operations of the certificate holder.

(b) For the purpose of this section, an individual shall be considered to be acting as an agent or representative of a certificate holder in a matter before the agency if the individual makes any written or oral communication on behalf of the certificate holder to the

agency (or any of its officers or employees) in connection with a particular matter, whether or not involving a specific party and without regard to whether the individual has participated in, or had responsibility for, the particular matter while serving as a Flight Standards Service aviation safety inspector.

(c) The provisions of this section do not prohibit a certificate holder from knowingly employing or making a contractual arrangement which permits an individual to act as an agent or representative of the certificate holder in any matter before the Federal Aviation Administration if the individual was employed by the certificate holder before October 21, 2011.

[Doc. No. FAA–2008–1154, 76 FR 52235, Aug. 22, 2011]

PART 120—DRUG AND ALCOHOL TESTING PROGRAM

Subpart A—General

Subpart E—Drug Testing Program Requirements

Subpart F—Alcohol Testing Program Requirements

AUTHORITY: 49 U.S.C. 106(f), 106(g), 40101–40103, 40113, 40120, 41706, 41721, 44106, 44701, 44702, 44703, 44709, 44710, 44711, 45101–45105, 46105, 46306.

SOURCE: Docket No. FAA–2008–0937, 74 FR 22653, May 14, 2009, unless otherwise noted.

Subpart A—General

§120.1   Applicability.

This part applies to the following persons:

(a) All air carriers and operators certificated under part 119 of this chapter authorized to conduct operations under part 121 or part 135 of this chapter, all air traffic control facilities not operated by the FAA or by or under contract to the U.S. military; and all operators as defined in 14 CFR 91.147.

(b) All individuals who perform, either directly or by contract, a safety-sensitive function listed in subpart E or subpart F of this part.

(c) All part 145 certificate holders who perform safety-sensitive functions and elect to implement a drug and alcohol testing program under this part.

(d) All contractors who elect to implement a drug and alcohol testing program under this part.

§120.3   Purpose.

The purpose of this part is to establish a program designed to help prevent accidents and injuries resulting from the use of prohibited drugs or the misuse of alcohol by employees who perform safety-sensitive functions in aviation.

§120.5   Procedures.

Each employer having a drug and alcohol testing program under this part must ensure that all drug and alcohol testing conducted pursuant to this part complies with the procedures set forth in 49 CFR part 40.

§120.7   Definitions.

For the purposes of this part, the following definitions apply:

(a) *Accident* means an occurrence associated with the operation of an aircraft which takes place between the time any individual boards the aircraft with the intention of flight and all such individuals have disembarked, and in which any individual suffers death or serious injury, or in which the aircraft receives substantial damage.

(b) *Alcohol* means the intoxicating agent in beverage alcohol, ethyl alcohol, or other low molecular weight alcohols, including methyl or isopropyl alcohol.

(c) *Alcohol concentration (or content)* means the alcohol in a volume of breath expressed in terms of grams of alcohol per 210 liters of breath as indicated by an evidential breath test under subpart F of this part.

(d) *Alcohol* use means the consumption of any beverage, mixture, or preparation, including any medication, containing alcohol.

(e) *Contractor* is an individual or company that performs a safety-sensitive function by contract for an employer or another contractor.

(f) *Covered employee* means an individual who performs, either directly or by contract, a safety-sensitive function listed in §§ 120.105 and 120.215 for an employer (as defined in paragraph (i) of this section). For purposes of pre-employment testing only, the term "covered employee" includes an individual applying to perform a safety-sensitive function.

(g) *DOT agency* means an agency (or "operating administration") of the United States Department of Transportation administering regulations requiring drug and alcohol testing (14 CFR parts 61, 65, 121, and 135; 46 CFR part 16; 49 CFR parts 199, 219, and 382) in accordance with 49 CFR part 40.

(h) *Employee* is an individual who is hired, either directly or by contract, to perform a safety-sensitive function for an employer, as defined in paragraph (i) of this section. An employee is also an individual who transfers into a position to perform a safety-sensitive function for an employer.

(i) *Employer* is a part 119 certificate holder with authority to operate under parts 121 and/or 135 of this chapter, an operator as defined in § 91.147 of this chapter, or an air traffic control facility not operated by the FAA or by or under contract to the U.S. Military. An employer may use a contract employee who is not included under that employer's FAA-mandated drug and alcohol testing program to perform a safety-sensitive function only if that contract employee is included under the contractor's FAA-mandated drug and alcohol testing program and is performing a safety-sensitive function on behalf of that contractor (i.e., within the scope of employment with the contractor.)

(j) *Hire* means retaining an individual for a safety-sensitive function as a paid employee, as a volunteer, or through barter or other form of compensation.

(k) *Performing* (a safety-sensitive function): an employee is considered to be performing a safety-sensitive function during any period in which he or she is actually performing, ready to perform, or immediately available to perform such function.

(l) *Positive rate for random drug testing* means the number of verified positive results for random drug tests conducted under subpart E of this part, plus the number of refusals of random drug tests required by subpart E of this part, divided by the total number of random drug test results (*i.e.*, positives, negatives, and refusals) under subpart E of this part.

(m) *Prohibited drug* means marijuana, cocaine, opiates, phencyclidine (PCP), and amphetamines, as specified in 49 CFR 40.85.

(n) *Refusal to submit to alcohol test* means that a covered employee has engaged in conduct including but not limited to that described in 49 CFR 40.261, or has failed to remain readily available for post-accident testing as required by subpart F of this part.

(o) *Refusal to submit to drug test* means that an employee engages in conduct including but not limited to that described in 49 CFR 40.191.

(p) *Safety-sensitive function* means a function listed in §§ 120.105 and 120.215.

(q) *Verified negative drug test result* means a drug test result from an HHS-certified laboratory that has undergone review by an MRO and has been determined by the MRO to be a negative result.

(r) *Verified positive drug test result* means a drug test result from an HHS-certified laboratory that has undergone review by an MRO and has been determined by the MRO to be a positive result.

(s) *Violation rate for random alcohol testing* means the number of 0.04, and above, random alcohol confirmation test results conducted under subpart F of this part, plus the number of refusals of random alcohol tests required by subpart F of this part, divided by the total number of random alcohol screening tests (including refusals) conducted under subpart F of this part.

[Doc. No. FAA–2008–0937, 74 FR 22653, May 14, 2009; Amdt. 120–0A, 75 FR 3153, Jan. 20, 2010]

Subpart B—Individuals Certificated Under Parts 61, 63, and 65

§120.11 Refusal to submit to a drug or alcohol test by a Part 61 certificate holder.

(a) This section applies to all individuals who hold a certificate under part 61 of this chapter and who are subject to drug and alcohol testing under this part.

(b) Refusal by the holder of a certificate issued under part 61 of this chapter to take a drug or alcohol test required under the provisions of this part is grounds for:

(1) Denial of an application for any certificate, rating, or authorization issued under part 61 of this chapter for a period of up to 1 year after the date of such refusal; and

(2) Suspension or revocation of any certificate, rating, or authorization issued under part 61 of this chapter.

§120.13 Refusal to submit to a drug or alcohol test by a Part 63 certificate holder.

(a) This section applies to all individuals who hold a certificate under part 63 of this chapter and who are subject to drug and alcohol testing under this part.

(b) Refusal by the holder of a certificate issued under part 63 of this chapter to take a drug or alcohol test required under the provisions of this part is grounds for:

(1) Denial of an application for any certificate or rating issued under part 63 of this chapter for a period of up to 1 year after the date of such refusal; and

(2) Suspension or revocation of any certificate or rating issued under part 63 of this chapter.

[Doc. No. FAA–2008–0937, 74 FR 22653, May 14, 2009; Amdt. 120–0A, 75 FR 3153, Jan. 20, 2010]

§120.15 Refusal to submit to a drug or alcohol test by a Part 65 certificate holder.

(a) This section applies to all individuals who hold a certificate under part 65 of this chapter and who are subject to drug and alcohol testing under this part.

(b) Refusal by the holder of a certificate issued under part 65 of this chapter to take a drug or alcohol test required under the provisions of this part is grounds for:

(1) Denial of an application for any certificate or rating issued under part 65 of this chapter for a period of up to 1 year after the date of such refusal; and

(2) Suspension or revocation of any certificate or rating issued under part 65 of this chapter.

[Doc. No. FAA–2008–0937, 74 FR 22653, May 14, 2009; Amdt. 120–0A, 75 FR 3153, Jan. 20, 2010]

Subpart C—Air Traffic Controllers

§120.17 Use of prohibited drugs.

(a) Each employer shall provide each employee performing a function listed in subpart E of this part, and his or her supervisor, with the training specified in that subpart. No employer may use any contractor to perform an air traffic control function unless that contractor provides each of its employees performing that function for the employer, and his or her supervisor, with the training specified in subpart E of this part.

(b) No employer may knowingly use any individual to perform, nor may any individual perform for an employer, either directly or by contract, any air traffic control function while that individual has a prohibited drug, as defined in this part, in his or her system.

(c) No employer shall knowingly use any individual to perform, nor may any individual perform for an employer, either directly or by contract, any air traffic control function if the individual has a verified positive drug test result on, or has refused to submit to, a drug test required by subpart E of this part and the individual has not met the requirements of subpart E of this part for returning to the performance of safety-sensitive duties.

(d) Each employer shall test each of its employees who perform any air traffic control function in accordance with subpart E of this part. No employer may use any contractor to perform any air traffic control function unless that contractor tests each employee performing such a function for the employer in accordance with subpart E of this part.

[Doc. No. FAA–2008–0937, 74 FR 22653, May 14, 2009; Amdt. 120–0A, 75 FR 3153, Jan. 20, 2010]

§ 120.19   Misuse of alcohol.

(a) This section applies to covered employees who perform air traffic control duties directly or by contract for an employer that is an air traffic control facility not operated by the FAA or the US military.

(b) *Alcohol concentration.* No covered employee shall report for duty or remain on duty requiring the performance of safety-sensitive functions while having an alcohol concentration of 0.04 or greater. No employer having actual knowledge that an employee has an alcohol concentration of 0.04 or greater shall permit the employee to perform or continue to perform safety-sensitive functions.

(c) *On-duty use.* No covered employee shall use alcohol while performing safety-sensitive functions. No employer having actual knowledge that a covered employee is using alcohol while performing safety-sensitive functions shall permit the employee to perform or continue to perform safety-sensitive functions.

(d) *Pre-duty use.* No covered employee shall perform air traffic control duties within 8 hours after using alcohol. No employer having actual knowledge that such an employee has used alcohol within 8 hours shall permit the employee to perform or continue to perform air traffic control duties.

(e) *Use following an accident.* No covered employee who has actual knowledge of an accident involving an aircraft for which he or she performed a safety-sensitive function at or near the time of the accident shall use alcohol for 8 hours following the accident, unless he or she has been given a post-accident test under subpart F of this part or the employer has determined that the employee's performance could not have contributed to the accident.

(f) *Refusal to submit to a required alcohol test.* A covered employee may not refuse to submit to any alcohol test required under subpart F of this part. An employer may not permit an employee who refuses to submit to such a test to perform or continue to perform safety-sensitive functions.

§ 120.21   Testing for alcohol.

(a) Each air traffic control facility not operated by the FAA or the U.S. military must establish an alcohol testing program in accordance with the provisions of subpart F of this part.

(b) No employer shall use any individual who meets the definition of covered employee in subpart A of this part to perform a safety-sensitive function listed in subpart F of this part unless that individual is subject to testing for alcohol misuse in accordance with the provisions of that subpart.

Subpart D—Part 119 Certificate Holders Authorized To Conduct Operations under Part 121 or Part 135 or Operators Under § 91.147 of This Chapter and Safety-Sensitive Employees

§ 120.31   Prohibited drugs.

(a) Each certificate holder or operator shall provide each employee performing a function listed in subpart E of this part, and his or her supervisor, with the training specified in that subpart.

(b) No certificate holder or operator may use any contractor to perform a function listed in subpart E of this part unless that contractor provides each of its employees performing that function for the certificate holder or operator, and his or her supervisor, with the training specified in that subpart.

§ 120.33   Use of prohibited drugs.

(a) This section applies to individuals who perform a function listed in subpart E of this part for a certificate holder or operator. For the purpose of this section, an individual who performs such a function pursuant to a contract with the certificate holder or the operator is considered to be performing that function for the certificate holder or the operator.

(b) No certificate holder or operator may knowingly use any individual to perform, nor may any individual perform for a certificate holder or an operator, either directly or by contract, any function listed in subpart E of this part while that individual has a prohibited drug, as defined in this part, in his or her system.

(c) No certificate holder or operator shall knowingly use any individual to perform, nor shall any individual perform for a certificate holder or operator, either directly or by contract, any safety-sensitive function if that individual has a verified positive drug test result on, or has refused to submit to, a drug test required by subpart E of this part and the individual has not met the requirements of that subpart for returning to the performance of safety-sensitive duties.

[Doc. No. FAA–2008–0937, 74 FR 22653, May 14, 2009; Amdt. 120–0A, 75 FR 3153, Jan. 21, 2010]

§120.35 Testing for prohibited drugs.

(a) Each certificate holder or operator shall test each of its employees who perform a function listed in subpart E of this part in accordance with that subpart.

(b) Except as provided in paragraph (c) of this section, no certificate holder or operator may use any contractor to perform a function listed in subpart E of this part unless that contractor tests each employee performing such a function for the certificate holder or operator in accordance with that subpart.

(c) If a certificate holder conducts an on-demand operation into an airport at which no maintenance providers are available that are subject to the requirements of subpart E of this part and emergency maintenance is required, the certificate holder may use individuals not meeting the requirements of paragraph (b) of this section to provide such emergency maintenance under both of the following conditions:

(1) The certificate holder must give written notification of the emergency maintenance to the Drug Abatement Program Division, AAM–800, 800 Independence Avenue, SW., Washington, DC 20591, within 10 days after being provided same in accordance with this paragraph. A certificate holder must retain copies of all such written notifications for two years.

(2) The aircraft must be reinspected by maintenance personnel who meet the requirements of paragraph (b) of this section when the aircraft is next at an airport where such maintenance personnel are available.

(d) For purposes of this section, emergency maintenance means maintenance that—

(1) Is not scheduled and

(2) Is made necessary by an aircraft condition not discovered prior to the departure for that location.

§120.37 Misuse of alcohol.

(a) *General.* This section applies to covered employees who perform a function listed in subpart F of this part for a certificate holder. For the purpose of this section, an individual who meets the definition of covered employee in subpart F of this part is considered to be performing the function for the certificate holder.

(b) *Alcohol concentration.* No covered employee shall report for duty or remain on duty requiring the performance of safety-sensitive functions while having an alcohol concentration of 0.04 or greater. No certificate holder having actual knowledge that an employee has an alcohol concentration of 0.04 or greater shall permit the employee to perform or continue to perform safety-sensitive functions.

(c) *On-duty use.* No covered employee shall use alcohol while performing safety-sensitive functions. No certificate holder having actual knowledge that a covered employee is using alcohol while performing safety-sensitive functions shall permit the employee to perform or continue to perform safety-sensitive functions.

(d) *Pre-duty use.* (1) No covered employee shall perform flight crewmember or flight attendant duties within 8 hours after using alcohol. No certificate holder having actual knowledge that such an employee has used alcohol within 8 hours shall permit the employee to perform or continue to perform the specified duties.

(2) No covered employee shall perform safety-sensitive duties other than those specified in paragraph (d)(1) of this section within 4 hours after using alcohol. No certificate holder having actual knowledge that such an employee has used alcohol within 4 hours shall permit the employee to perform

or to continue to perform safety-sensitive functions.

(e) *Use following an accident.* No covered employee who has actual knowledge of an accident involving an aircraft for which he or she performed a safety-sensitive function at or near the time of the accident shall use alcohol for 8 hours following the accident, unless he or she has been given a post-accident test under subpart F of this part, or the employer has determined that the employee's performance could not have contributed to the accident.

(f) *Refusal to submit to a required alcohol test.* A covered employee must not refuse to submit to any alcohol test required under subpart F of this part. A certificate holder must not permit an employee who refuses to submit to such a test to perform or continue to perform safety-sensitive functions.

§ 120.39   Testing for alcohol.

(a) Each certificate holder must establish an alcohol testing program in accordance with the provisions of subpart F of this part.

(b) Except as provided in paragraph (c) of this section, no certificate holder or operator may use any individual who meets the definition of covered employee in subpart A of this part to perform a safety-sensitive function listed in that subpart F of this part unless that individual is subject to testing for alcohol misuse in accordance with the provisions of that subpart.

(c) If a certificate holder conducts an on-demand operation into an airport at which no maintenance providers are available that are subject to the requirements of subpart F of this part and emergency maintenance is required, the certificate holder may use individuals not meeting the requirements of paragraph (b) of this section to provide such emergency maintenance under both of the following conditions:

(1) The certificate holder must give written notification of the emergency maintenance to the Drug Abatement Program Division, AAM-800, 800 Independence Avenue, SW., Washington, DC 20591, within 10 days after being provided same in accordance with this paragraph. A certificate holder must

retain copies of all such written notifications for two years.

(2) The aircraft must be reinspected by maintenance personnel who meet the requirements of paragraph (b) of this section when the aircraft is next at an airport where such maintenance personnel are available.

(d) For purposes of this section, emergency maintenance means maintenance that—

(1) Is not scheduled and

(2) Is made necessary by an aircraft condition not discovered prior to the departure for that location.

Subpart E—Drug Testing Program Requirements

§ 120.101   Scope.

This subpart contains the standards and components that must be included in a drug testing program required by this part.

§ 120.103   General.

(a) *Purpose.* The purpose of this subpart is to establish a program designed to help prevent accidents and injuries resulting from the use of prohibited drugs by employees who perform safety-sensitive functions.

(b) *DOT procedures.* (1) Each employer shall ensure that drug testing programs conducted pursuant to 14 CFR parts 65, 91, 121, and 135 comply with the requirements of this subpart and the "Procedures for Transportation Workplace Drug Testing Programs" published by the Department of Transportation (DOT) (49 CFR part 40).

(2) An employer may not use or contract with any drug testing laboratory that is not certified by the Department of Health and Human Services (HHS) under the National Laboratory Certification Program.

(c) *Employer responsibility.* As an employer, you are responsible for all actions of your officials, representatives, and service agents in carrying out the requirements of this subpart and 49 CFR part 40.

(d) *Applicable Federal Regulations.* The following applicable regulations appear in 49 CFR or 14 CFR:

(1) 49 CFR Part 40—Procedures for Transportation Workplace Drug Testing Programs

(2) 14 CFR:

(i) §67.107—First-Class Airman Medical Certificate, Mental.

(ii) §67.207—Second-Class Airman Medical Certificate, Mental.

(iii) §67.307—Third-Class Airman Medical Certificate, Mental.

(iv) §91.147—Passenger carrying flight for compensation or hire.

(v) §135.1—Applicability

(e) *Falsification.* No individual may make, or cause to be made, any of the following:

(1) Any fraudulent or intentionally false statement in any application of a drug testing program.

(2) Any fraudulent or intentionally false entry in any record or report that is made, kept, or used to show compliance with this part.

(3) Any reproduction or alteration, for fraudulent purposes, of any report or record required to be kept by this part.

[Doc. No. FAA–2008–0937, 74 FR 22653, May 14, 2009; Amdt. 120–0A, 75 FR 3153, Jan. 20, 2010]

§120.105 Employees who must be tested.

Each employee, including any assistant, helper, or individual in a training status, who performs a safety-sensitive function listed in this section directly or by contract (including by subcontract at any tier) for an employer as defined in this subpart must be subject to drug testing under a drug testing program implemented in accordance with this subpart. This includes full-time, part-time, temporary, and intermittent employees regardless of the degree of supervision. The safety-sensitive functions are:

(a) Flight crewmember duties.

(b) Flight attendant duties.

(c) Flight instruction duties.

(d) Aircraft dispatcher duties.

(e) Aircraft maintenance and preventive maintenance duties.

(f) Ground security coordinator duties.

(g) Aviation screening duties.

(h) Air traffic control duties.

(i) Operations control specialist duties.

[Doc. No. FAA–2008–0937, 74 FR 22653, May 14, 2009, as amended by Amdt. 120–2, 79 FR 9973, Feb. 21, 2014]

§120.107 Substances for which testing must be conducted.

Each employer shall test each employee who performs a safety-sensitive function for evidence of marijuana, cocaine, opiates, phencyclidine (PCP), and amphetamines during each test required by §120.109.

§120.109 Types of drug testing required.

Each employer shall conduct the types of testing described in this section in accordance with the procedures set forth in this subpart and the DOT "Procedures for Transportation Workplace Drug Testing Programs" (49 CFR part 40).

(a) *Pre-employment drug testing.* (1) No employer may hire any individual for a safety-sensitive function listed in §120.105 unless the employer first conducts a pre-employment test and receives a verified negative drug test result for that individual.

(2) No employer may allow an individual to transfer from a nonsafety-sensitive to a safety-sensitive function unless the employer first conducts a pre-employment test and receives a verified negative drug test result for the individual.

(3) Employers must conduct another pre-employment test and receive a verified negative drug test result before hiring or transferring an individual into a safety-sensitive function if more than 180 days elapse between conducting the pre-employment test required by paragraphs (a)(1) or (2) of this section and hiring or transferring the individual into a safety-sensitive function, resulting in that individual being brought under an FAA drug testing program.

(4) If the following criteria are met, an employer is permitted to conduct a pre-employment test, and if such a test is conducted, the employer must receive a negative test result before putting the individual into a safety-sensitive function:

(i) The individual previously performed a safety-sensitive function for the employer and the employer is not required to pre-employment test the individual under paragraphs (a)(1) or (2) of this section before putting the individual to work in a safety-sensitive function;

(ii) The employer removed the individual from the employer's random testing program conducted under this subpart for reasons other than a verified positive test result on an FAA-mandated drug test or a refusal to submit to such testing; and

(iii) The individual will be returning to the performance of a safety-sensitive function.

(5) Before hiring or transferring an individual to a safety-sensitive function, the employer must advise each individual that the individual will be required to undergo pre-employment testing in accordance with this subpart, to determine the presence of marijuana, cocaine, opiates, phencyclidine (PCP), and amphetamines, or a metabolite of those drugs in the individual's system. The employer shall provide this same notification to each individual required by the employer to undergo pre-employment testing under paragraph (a)(4) of this section.

(b) *Random drug testing.* (1) Except as provided in paragraphs (b)(2) through (b)(4) of this section, the minimum annual percentage rate for random drug testing shall be 50 percent of covered employees.

(2) The Administrator's decision to increase or decrease the minimum annual percentage rate for random drug testing is based on the reported positive rate for the entire industry. All information used for this determination is drawn from the statistical reports required by § 120.119. In order to ensure reliability of the data, the Administrator considers the quality and completeness of the reported data, may obtain additional information or reports from employers, and may make appropriate modifications in calculating the industry positive rate. Each year, the Administrator will publish in the FEDERAL REGISTER the minimum annual percentage rate for random drug testing of covered employees. The new minimum annual percentage rate for random drug testing will be applicable starting January 1 of the calendar year following publication.

(3) When the minimum annual percentage rate for random drug testing is 50 percent, the Administrator may lower this rate to 25 percent of all covered employees if the Administrator determines that the data received under the reporting requirements of this subpart for two consecutive calendar years indicate that the reported positive rate is less than 1.0 percent.

(4) When the minimum annual percentage rate for random drug testing is 25 percent, and the data received under the reporting requirements of this subpart for any calendar year indicate that the reported positive rate is equal to or greater than 1.0 percent, the Administrator will increase the minimum annual percentage rate for random drug testing to 50 percent of all covered employees.

(5) The selection of employees for random drug testing shall be made by a scientifically valid method, such as a random-number table or a computer-based random number generator that is matched with employees' Social Security numbers, payroll identification numbers, or other comparable identifying numbers. Under the selection process used, each covered employee shall have an equal chance of being tested each time selections are made.

(6) As an employer, you must select and test a percentage of employees at least equal to the minimum annual percentage rate each year.

(i) As an employer, to determine whether you have met the minimum annual percentage rate, you must divide the number of random testing results for safety-sensitive employees by the average number of safety-sensitive employees eligible for random testing.

(A) To calculate whether you have met the annual minimum percentage rate, count all random positives, random negatives, and random refusals as your "random testing results."

(B) To calculate the average number of safety-sensitive employees eligible for random testing throughout the year, add the total number of safety-sensitive employees eligible for testing during each random testing period for the year and divide that total by the number of random testing periods. Only safety-sensitive employees are to be in an employer's random testing pool, and all safety-sensitive employees must be in the random pool. If you are an employer conducting random testing more often than once per month (e.g., you select daily, weekly, bi-weekly) you do not need to compute this total number of safety-sensitive employees more than on a once per month basis.

(ii) As an employer, you may use a service agent to perform random selections for you, and your safety-sensitive employees may be part of a larger random testing pool of safety-sensitive employees. However, you must ensure that the service agent you use is testing at the appropriate percentage established for your industry and that only safety-sensitive employees are in the random testing pool. For example:

(A) If the service agent has your employees in a random testing pool for your company alone, you must ensure that the testing is conducted at least at the minimum annual percentage rate under this part.

(B) If the service agent has your employees in a random testing pool combined with other FAA-regulated companies, you must ensure that the testing is conducted at least at the minimum annual percentage rate under this part.

(C) If the service agent has your employees in a random testing pool combined with other DOT-regulated companies, you must ensure that the testing is conducted at least at the highest rate required for any DOT-regulated company in the pool.

(7) Each employer shall ensure that random drug tests conducted under this subpart are unannounced and that the dates for administering random tests are spread reasonably throughout the calendar year.

(8) Each employer shall require that each safety-sensitive employee who is notified of selection for random drug testing proceeds to the collection site immediately; provided, however, that if the employee is performing a safety-sensitive function at the time of the notification, the employer shall instead ensure that the employee ceases to perform the safety-sensitive function and proceeds to the collection site as soon as possible.

(9) If a given covered employee is subject to random drug testing under the drug testing rules of more than one DOT agency, the employee shall be subject to random drug testing at the percentage rate established for the calendar year by the DOT agency regulating more than 50 percent of the employee's function.

(10) If an employer is required to conduct random drug testing under the drug testing rules of more than one DOT agency, the employer may—

(i) Establish separate pools for random selection, with each pool containing the covered employees who are subject to testing at the same required rate; or

(ii) Randomly select covered employees for testing at the highest percentage rate established for the calendar year by any DOT agency to which the employer is subject.

(11) An employer required to conduct random drug testing under the antidrug rules of more than one DOT agency shall provide each such agency access to the employer's records of random drug testing, as determined to be necessary by the agency to ensure the employer's compliance with the rule.

(c) *Post-accident drug testing.* Each employer shall test each employee who performs a safety-sensitive function for the presence of marijuana, cocaine, opiates, phencyclidine (PCP), and amphetamines, or a metabolite of those drugs in the employee's system if that employee's performance either contributed to an accident or can not be completely discounted as a contributing factor to the accident. The employee shall be tested as soon as possible but not later than 32 hours after the accident. The decision not to administer a test under this section must be based on a determination, using the best information available at the time of the determination, that the employee's performance could not have contributed to the accident. The employee shall submit to post-accident testing under this section.

(d) *Drug testing based on reasonable cause.* Each employer must test each employee who performs a safety-sensitive function and who is reasonably suspected of having used a prohibited drug. The decision to test must be based on a reasonable and articulable belief that the employee is using a prohibited drug on the basis of specific contemporaneous physical, behavioral, or performance indicators of probable drug use. At least two of the employee's supervisors, one of whom is trained in detection of the symptoms of possible drug use, must substantiate and concur in the decision to test an employee who is reasonably suspected of drug use; except that in the case of an employer, other than a part 121 certificate holder, who employs 50 or fewer employees who perform safety-sensitive functions, one supervisor who is trained in detection of symptoms of possible drug use must substantiate the decision to test an employee who is reasonably suspected of drug use.

(e) *Return to duty drug testing.* Each employer shall ensure that before an individual is returned to duty to perform a safety-sensitive function after refusing to submit to a drug test required by this subpart or receiving a verified positive drug test result on a test conducted under this subpart the individual shall undergo a return-to-duty drug test. No employer shall allow an individual required to undergo return-to-duty testing to perform a safety-sensitive function unless the employer has received a verified negative drug test result for the individual. The test cannot occur until after the SAP has determined that the employee has successfully complied with the prescribed education and/or treatment.

(f) *Follow-up drug testing.* (1) Each employer shall implement a reasonable program of unannounced testing of each individual who has been hired to perform or who has been returned to the performance of a safety-sensitive function after refusing to submit to a drug test required by this subpart or receiving a verified positive drug test result on a test conducted under this subpart.

(2) The number and frequency of such testing shall be determined by the employer's Substance Abuse Professional conducted in accordance with the provisions of 49 CFR part 40, but shall consist of at least six tests in the first 12 months following the employee's return to duty.

(3) The employer must direct the employee to undergo testing for alcohol in accordance with subpart F of this part, in addition to drugs, if the Substance Abuse Professional determines that alcohol testing is necessary for the particular employee. Any such alcohol testing shall be conducted in accordance with the provisions of 49 CFR part 40.

(4) Follow-up testing shall not exceed 60 months after the date the individual begins to perform or returns to the performance of a safety-sensitive function. The Substance Abuse Professional may terminate the requirement for follow-up testing at any time after the first six tests have been conducted, if the Substance Abuse Professional determines that such testing is no longer necessary.

§ 120.111 **Administrative and other matters.**

(a) *MRO record retention requirements.* (1) Records concerning drug tests confirmed positive by the laboratory shall be maintained by the MRO for 5 years. Such records include the MRO copies of the custody and control form, medical interviews, documentation of the basis for verifying as negative test results confirmed as positive by the laboratory, any other documentation concerning the MRO's verification process.

(2) Should the employer change MRO's for any reason, the employer shall ensure that the former MRO forwards all records maintained pursuant to this rule to the new MRO within ten working days of receiving notice from the employer of the new MRO's name and address.

(3) Any employer obtaining MRO services by contract, including a contract through a C/TPA, shall ensure that the contract includes a recordkeeping provision that is consistent with this paragraph, including requirements for transferring records to a new MRO.

(b) *Access to records.* The employer and the MRO shall permit the Administrator or the Administrator's representative to examine records required to be kept under this subpart and 49 CFR part 40. The Administrator or the Administrator's representative may require that all records maintained by the service agent for the employer must be produced at the employer's place of business.

(c) *Release of drug testing information.* An employer shall release information regarding an employee's drug testing results, evaluation, or rehabilitation to a third party in accordance with 49 CFR part 40. Except as required by law, this subpart, or 49 CFR part 40, no employer shall release employee information.

(d) *Refusal to submit to testing.* Each employer must notify the FAA within 2 working days of any employee who holds a certificate issued under part 61, part 63, or part 65 of this chapter who has refused to submit to a drug test required under this subpart. Notification must be sent to: Federal Aviation Administration, Office of Aerospace Medicine, Drug Abatement Division (AAM-800), 800 Independence Avenue, SW., Washington, DC 20591, or by fax to (202) 267-5200.

(e) *Permanent disqualification from service.* (1) An employee who has verified positive drug test results on two drug tests required by this subpart of this chapter, and conducted after September 19, 1994, is permanently precluded from performing for an employer the safety-sensitive duties the employee performed prior to the second drug test.

(2) An employee who has engaged in prohibited drug use during the performance of a safety-sensitive function after September 19, 1994 is permanently precluded from performing that safety-sensitive function for an employer.

(f) *DOT management information system annual reports.* Copies of any annual reports submitted to the FAA under this subpart must be maintained by the employer for a minimum of 5 years.

§120.113 Medical Review Officer, Substance Abuse Professional, and Employer Responsibilities.

(a) The employer shall designate or appoint a Medical Review Officer (MRO) who shall be qualified in accordance with 49 CFR part 40 and shall perform the functions set forth in 49 CFR part 40 and this subpart. If the employer does not have a qualified individual on staff to serve as MRO, the employer may contract for the provision of MRO services as part of its drug testing program.

(b) *Medical Review Officer (MRO).* The MRO must perform the functions set forth in subpart G of 49 CFR part 40, and subpart E of this part. The MRO shall not delay verification of the primary test result following a request for a split specimen test unless such delay is based on reasons other than the fact that the split specimen test result is pending. If the primary test result is verified as positive, actions required under this rule (e.g., notification to the Federal Air Surgeon, removal from safety-sensitive position) are not stayed during the 72-hour request period or pending receipt of the split specimen test result.

(c) *Substance Abuse Professional (SAP).* The SAP must perform the functions set forth in 49 CFR part 40, subpart O.

(d) *Additional Medical Review Officer, Substance Abuse Professional, and Employer Responsibilities Regarding 14 CFR part 67 Airman Medical Certificate Holders.* (1) As part of verifying a confirmed positive test result or refusal to submit to a test, the MRO must ask and the individual must answer whether he or she holds an airman medical certificate issued under 14 CFR part 67 or would be required to hold an airman medical certificate to perform a safety-sensitive function for the employer. If the individual answers in the affirmative to either question, in addition to notifying the employer in accordance with 49 CFR part 40, the MRO must forward to the Federal Air Surgeon, at the address listed in paragraph (d)(5) of this section, the name of the individual, along with identifying information and supporting documentation, within 2 working days after verifying a positive drug test result or refusal to submit to a test.

(2) During the SAP interview required for a verified positive test result or a refusal to submit to a test, the SAP must ask and the individual must answer whether he or she holds or would be required to hold an airman medical certificate issued under 14 CFR part 67 to perform a safety-sensitive function for the employer. If the individual answers in the affirmative, the

45

individual must obtain an airman medical certificate issued by the Federal Air Surgeon dated after the verified positive drug test result date or refusal to test date. After the individual obtains this airman medical certificate, the SAP may recommend to the employer that the individual may be returned to a safety-sensitive position. The receipt of an airman medical certificate does not alter any obligations otherwise required by 49 CFR part 40 or this subpart.

(3) An employer must forward to the Federal Air Surgeon within 2 working days of receipt, copies of all reports provided to the employer by a SAP regarding the following:

(i) An individual who the MRO has reported to the Federal Air Surgeon under § 120.113 (d)(1); or

(ii) An individual who the employer has reported to the Federal Air Surgeon under § 120.111(d).

(4) The employer must not permit an employee who is required to hold an airman medical certificate under 14 CFR part 67 to perform a safety-sensitive duty to resume that duty until the employee has:

(i) Been issued an airman medical certificate from the Federal Air Surgeon after the date of the verified positive drug test result or refusal to test; and

(ii) Met the return to duty requirements in accordance with 49 CFR part 40.

(5) Reports required under this section shall be forwarded to the Federal Air Surgeon, Federal Aviation Administration, Office of Aerospace Medicine, Attn: Drug Abatement Division (AAM-800), 800 Independence Avenue, SW., Washington, DC 20591.

(6) MROs, SAPs, and employers who send reports to the Federal Air Surgeon must keep a copy of each report for 5 years.

§ 120.115 Employee Assistance Program (EAP).

(a) The employer shall provide an EAP for employees. The employer may establish the EAP as a part of its internal personnel services or the employer may contract with an entity that will provide EAP services to an employee. Each EAP must include education and

training on drug use for employees and training for supervisors making determinations for testing of employees based on reasonable cause.

(b) *EAP education program.* (1) Each EAP education program must include at least the following elements:

(i) Display and distribution of informational material;

(ii) Display and distribution of a community service hot-line telephone number for employee assistance; and

(iii) Display and distribution of the employer's policy regarding drug use in the workplace.

(2) The employer's policy shall include information regarding the consequences under the rule of using drugs while performing safety-sensitive functions, receiving a verified positive drug test result, or refusing to submit to a drug test required under the rule.

(c) *EAP training program.* (1) Each employer shall implement a reasonable program of initial training for employees. The employee training program must include at least the following elements:

(i) The effects and consequences of drug use on individual health, safety, and work environment;

(ii) The manifestations and behavioral cues that may indicate drug use and abuse; and

(2) The employer's supervisory personnel who will determine when an employee is subject to testing based on reasonable cause shall receive specific training on specific, contemporaneous physical, behavioral, and performance indicators of probable drug use in addition to the training specified in § 120.115 (c).

(3) The employer shall ensure that supervisors who will make reasonable cause determinations receive at least 60 minutes of initial training.

(4) The employer shall implement a reasonable recurrent training program for supervisory personnel making reasonable cause determinations during subsequent years.

(5) Documentation of all training given to employees and supervisory personnel must be included in the training program.

(6) The employer shall identify the employee and supervisor EAP training

in the employer's drug testing program.

[Doc. No. FAA–2008–0937, 74 FR 22653, May 14, 2009, as amended by Amdt. 120–1, 78 FR 42003, July 15, 2013]

§120.117 Implementing a drug testing program.

(a) Each company must meet the requirements of this subpart. Use the following chart to determine whether your company must obtain an Antidrug and Alcohol Misuse Prevention Program Operations Specification, Letter of Authorization, or Drug and Alcohol Testing Program Registration from the FAA:

If you are . . .	You must . . .
(1) A part 119 certificate holder with authority to operate under parts 121 or 135.	Obtain an Antidrug and Alcohol Misuse Prevention Program Operations Specification by contacting your FAA Principal Operations Inspector.
(2) An operator as defined in §91.147 of this chapter.	Obtain a Letter of Authorization by contacting the Flight Standards District Office nearest to your principal place of business.
(3) A part 119 certificate holder with authority to operate under parts 121 or 135 and an operator as defined in §91.147 of this chapter.	Complete the requirements in paragraphs 1 and 2 of this chart and advise the Flight Standards District Office and the Drug Abatement Division that the §91.147 operation will be included under the part 119 testing program. Contact the Drug Abatement Division at FAA Office of Aerospace Medicine, Drug Abatement Division (AAM–800) 800 Independence Avenue SW., Washington, DC 20591.
(4) An air traffic control facility not operated by the FAA or by or under contract to the U.S. Military.	Register with the FAA, Office of Aerospace Medicine, Drug Abatement Division (AAM–800), 800 Independence Avenue SW., Washington, DC 20591.
(5) A part 145 certificate holder who has your own drug testing program.	Obtain an Antidrug and Alcohol Misuse Prevention Program Operations Specification by contacting your Principal Maintenance Inspector or register with the FAA, Office of Aerospace Medicine, Drug Abatement Division (AAM–800), 800 Independence Avenue SW., Washington, DC 20591, if you opt to conduct your own drug testing program
(6) A contractor who has your own drug testing program.	Register with the FAA, Office of Aerospace Medicine, Drug Abatement Division (AAM–800), 800 Independence Avenue SW., Washington, DC 20591, if you opt to conduct your own drug testing program.

(b) Use the following chart for implementing a drug testing program if you are applying for a part 119 certificate with authority to operate under parts 121 or 135 of this chapter, if you intend to begin operations as defined in §91.147 of this chapter, or if you intend to begin air traffic control operations (not operated by the FAA or by or under contract to the U.S. Military). Use it to determine whether you need to have an Antidrug and Alcohol Misuse Prevention Program Operations Specification, Letter of Authorization, or Drug and Alcohol Testing Program Registration from the FAA. Your employees who perform safety-sensitive functions must be tested in accordance with this subpart. The chart follows:

If you . . .	You must . . .
(1) Apply for a part 119 certificate with authority to operate under parts 121 or 135.	(i) Have an Antidrug and Alcohol Misuse Prevention Program Operations Specification,
	(ii) Implement an FAA drug testing program no later than the date you start operations, and
	(iii) Meet the requirements of this subpart.
(2) Intend to begin operations as defined in §91.147 of this chapter.	(i) Have a Letter of Authorization,
	(ii) Implement an FAA drug testing program no later than the date you start operations, and
	(iii) Meet the requirements of this subpart.
(3) Apply for a part 119 certificate with authority to operate under parts 121 or 135 and intend to begin operations as defined in §91.147 of this chapter.	(i) Have an Antidrug and Alcohol Misuse Prevention Program Operations Specification and a Letter of Authorization,
	(ii) Implement your combined FAA drug testing program no later than the date you start operations, and
	(iii) Meet the requirements of this subpart.
(4) Intend to begin air traffic control operations (at an air traffic control facility not operated by the FAA or by or under contract to the U.S. military).	(i) Register with the FAA, Office of Aerospace Medicine, Drug Abatement Division (AAM–800), 800 Independence Avenue SW., Washington, DC 20591, prior to starting operations,
	(ii) Implement an FAA drug testing program no later than the date you start operations, and
	(iii) Meet the requirements of this subpart.

(c) If you are an individual or company that intends to provide safety-sensitive services by contract to a part 119 certificate holder with authority to

47

operate under parts 121 and/or 135 of this chapter, an operation as defined in §91.147 of this chapter, or an air traffic control facility not operated by the FAA or by or under contract to the U.S. military, use the following chart to determine what you must do if you opt to have your own drug testing program.

If you . . .	And you opt to conduct your own drug program, you must . . .
(1) Are a part 145 certificate holder.	(i) Have an Antidrug and Alcohol Misuse Prevention Program Operations Specification or register with the FAA, Office of Aerospace Medicine, Drug Abatement Division (AAM–800), 800 Independence Avenue, SW., Washington, DC 20591, (ii) Implement an FAA drug testing program no later than the date you start performing safety-sensitive functions for a part 119 certificate holder with authority to operate under parts 121 or 135, or operator as defined in §91.147 of this chapter, and (iii) Meet the requirements of this subpart as if you were an employer.
(2) Are a contractor	(i) Register with the FAA, Office of Aerospace Medicine, Drug Abatement Division (AAM–800), 800 Independence Avenue, SW., Washington, DC 20591, (ii) Implement an FAA drug testing program no later than the date you start performing safety-sensitive functions for a part 119 certificate holder with authority to operate under parts 121 or 135, or operator as defined in §91.147 of this chapter, or an air traffic control facility not operated by the FAA or by or under contract to the U.S. Military, and (iii) Meet the requirements of this subpart as if you were an employer.

(d) *Obtaining an Antidrug and Alcohol Misuse Prevention Program Operations Specification.* (1) To obtain an Antidrug and Alcohol Misuse Prevention Program Operations Specification, you must contact your FAA Principal Operations Inspector or Principal Maintenance Inspector. Provide him/her with the following information:

(i) Company name.

(ii) Certificate number.

(iii) Telephone number.

(iv) Address where your drug and alcohol testing program records are kept.

(v) Whether you have 50 or more safety-sensitive employees, or 49 or fewer safety-sensitive employees. (Part 119 certificate holders with authority to operate only under part 121 of this

chapter are not required to provide this information.)

(2) You must certify on your Antidrug and Alcohol Misuse Prevention Program Operations Specification issued by your FAA Principal Operations Inspector or Principal Maintenance Inspector that you will comply with this part and 49 CFR part 40.

(3) You are required to obtain only one Antidrug and Alcohol Misuse Prevention Program Operations Specification to satisfy this requirement under this part.

(4) You must update the Antidrug and Alcohol Misuse Prevention Program Operations Specification when any changes to the information contained in the Operation Specification occur.

(e) *Register your Drug and Alcohol Testing Program by obtaining a Letter of Authorization from the FAA in accordance with § 91.147.* (1) A drug and alcohol testing program is considered registered when the following information is submitted to the Flight Standards District Office nearest your principal place of business:

(i) Company name.

(ii) Telephone number.

(iii) Address where your drug and alcohol testing program records are kept.

(iv) Type of safety-sensitive functions you or your employees perform (such as flight instruction duties, aircraft dispatcher duties, maintenance or preventive maintenance duties, ground security coordinator duties, aviation screening duties, air traffic control duties).

(v) Whether you have 50 or more covered employees, or 49 or fewer covered employees.

(vi) A signed statement indicating that your company will comply with this part and 49 CFR part 40.

(2) This Letter of Authorization will satisfy the requirements for both your drug testing program under this subpart and your alcohol testing program under subpart F of this part.

(3) Update the Letter of Authorization information as changes occur. Send the updates to the Flight Standards District Office nearest your principal place of business.

(4) If you are a part 119 certificate holder with authority to operate under

parts 121 or 135 and intend to begin operations as defined in §91.147 of this chapter, you must also advise the Federal Aviation Administration, Office of Aerospace Medicine, Drug Abatement Division (AAM–800), 800 Independence Avenue SW., Washington, DC 20591.

(f) *Obtaining a Drug and Alcohol Testing Program Registration from the FAA.* (1) Except as provided in paragraphs (d) and (e) of this section, to obtain a Drug and Alcohol Testing Program Registration from the FAA, you must submit the following information to the Office of Aerospace Medicine, Drug Abatement Division:

(i) Company name.

(ii) Telephone number.

(iii) Address where your drug and alcohol testing program records are kept.

(iv) Type of safety-sensitive functions you or your employees perform (such as flight instruction duties, aircraft dispatcher duties, maintenance or preventive maintenance duties, ground security coordinator duties, aviation screening duties, air traffic control duties).

(v) Whether you have 50 or more covered employees, or 49 or fewer covered employees.

(vi) A signed statement indicating that: your company will comply with this part and 49 CFR part 40; and you intend to provide safety-sensitive functions by contract (including subcontract at any tier) to a part 119 certificate holder with authority to operate under part 121 or part 135 of this chapter, an operator as defined in §91.147 of this chapter, or an air traffic control facility not operated by the FAA or by or under contract to the U.S. military.

(2) Send this information to the Federal Aviation Administration, Office of Aerospace Medicine, Drug Abatement Division (AAM–800), 800 Independence Avenue SW., Washington, DC 20591.

(3) This Drug and Alcohol Testing Program Registration will satisfy the registration requirements for both your drug testing program under this subpart and your alcohol testing program under subpart F of this part.

(4) Update the registration information as changes occur. Send the up-

dates to the address specified in paragraph (f)(2) of this section.

[Doc. No. FAA–2008–0937, 74 FR 22653, May 14, 2009; Amdt. 120–0A, 75 FR 3154, Jan. 20, 2010, as amended by Amdt. 120–1, 78 FR 42003, July 15, 2013]

§120.119 Annual reports.

(a) Annual reports of testing results must be submitted to the FAA by March 15 of the succeeding calendar year for the prior calendar year (January 1 through December 31) in accordance with the following provisions:

(1) Each part 121 certificate holder shall submit an annual report each year.

(2) Each entity conducting a drug testing program under this part, other than a part 121 certificate holder, that has 50 or more employees performing a safety-sensitive function on January 1 of any calendar year shall submit an annual report to the FAA for that calendar year.

(3) The Administrator reserves the right to require that aviation employers not otherwise required to submit annual reports prepare and submit such reports to the FAA. Employers that will be required to submit annual reports under this provision will be notified in writing by the FAA.

(b) As an employer, you must use the Management Information System (MIS) form and instructions as required by 49 CFR part 40 (at 49 CFR 40.26 and appendix H to 49 CFR part 40). You may also use the electronic version of the MIS form provided by DOT. The Administrator may designate means (e.g., electronic program transmitted via the Internet) other than hard-copy, for MIS form submission. For information on where to submit MIS forms and for the electronic version of the form, *see: http:// www.faa.gov/about/office_org/ headquarters_offices/avs/offices/aam/ drug_alcohol.*

(c) A service agent may prepare the MIS report on behalf of an employer. However, a company official (e.g., Designated Employer Representative as defined in 49 CFR part 40) must certify the accuracy and completeness of the MIS report, no matter who prepares it.

[Doc. No. FAA–2008–0937, 74 FR 22653, May 14, 2009; Amdt. 120–0A, 75 FR 3154, Jan. 20, 2010]

§ 120.121 Preemption.

(a) The issuance of 14 CFR parts 65, 91, 121, and 135 by the FAA preempts any State or local law, rule, regulation, order, or standard covering the subject matter of 14 CFR parts 65, 91, 121, and 135, including but not limited to, drug testing of aviation personnel performing safety-sensitive functions.

(b) The issuance of 14 CFR parts 65, 91, 121, and 135 does not preempt provisions of state criminal law that impose sanctions for reckless conduct of an individual that leads to actual loss of life, injury, or damage to property whether such provisions apply specifically to aviation employees or generally to the public.

§ 120.123 Drug testing outside the territory of the United States.

(a) No part of the testing process (including specimen collection, laboratory processing, and MRO actions) shall be conducted outside the territory of the United States.

(1) Each employee who is assigned to perform safety-sensitive functions solely outside the territory of the United States shall be removed from the random testing pool upon the inception of such assignment.

(2) Each covered employee who is removed from the random testing pool under this section shall be returned to the random testing pool when the employee resumes the performance of safety-sensitive functions wholly or partially within the territory of the United States.

(b) The provisions of this subpart shall not apply to any individual who performs a function listed in § 120.105 by contract for an employer outside the territory of the United States.

§ 120.125 Waivers from 49 CFR 40.21.

An employer subject to this part may petition the Drug Abatement Division, Office of Aerospace Medicine, for a waiver allowing the employer to stand down an employee following a report of a laboratory confirmed positive drug test or refusal, pending the outcome of the verification process.

(a) Each petition for a waiver must be in writing and include substantial facts and justification to support the waiver. Each petition must satisfy the

substantive requirements for obtaining a waiver, as provided in 49 CFR 40.21.

(b) Each petition for a waiver must be submitted to the Federal Aviation Administration, Office of Aerospace Medicine, Drug Abatement Division (AAM-800), 800 Independence Avenue, SW., Washington, DC 20591.

(c) The Administrator may grant a waiver subject to 49 CFR 40.21(d).

Subpart F—Alcohol Testing Program Requirements

§ 120.201 Scope.

This subpart contains the standards and components that must be included in an alcohol testing program required by this part.

§ 120.203 General.

(a) *Purpose.* The purpose of this subpart is to establish programs designed to help prevent accidents and injuries resulting from the misuse of alcohol by employees who perform safety-sensitive functions in aviation.

(b) *Alcohol testing procedures.* Each employer shall ensure that all alcohol testing conducted pursuant to this subpart complies with the procedures set forth in 49 CFR part 40. The provisions of 49 CFR part 40 that address alcohol testing are made applicable to employers by this subpart.

(c) *Employer responsibility.* As an employer, you are responsible for all actions of your officials, representatives, and service agents in carrying out the requirements of the DOT agency regulations.

§ 120.205 Preemption of State and local laws.

(a) Except as provided in paragraph (a)(2) of this section, these regulations preempt any State or local law, rule, regulation, or order to the extent that:

(1) Compliance with both the State and local requirement and this subpart is not possible; or

(2) Compliance with the State or local requirement is an obstacle to the accomplishment and execution of any requirement in this subpart.

(b) The alcohol testing requirements of this title shall not be construed to preempt provisions of State criminal law that impose sanctions for reckless conduct leading to actual loss of life, injury, or damage to property, whether the provisions apply specifically to transportation employees or employers or to the general public.

§ **120.207 Other requirements imposed by employers.**

Except as expressly provided in these alcohol testing requirements, nothing in this subpart shall be construed to affect the authority of employers, or the rights of employees, with respect to the use or possession of alcohol, including any authority and rights with respect to alcohol testing and rehabilitation.

§ **120.209 Requirement for notice.**

Before performing an alcohol test under this subpart, each employer shall notify a covered employee that the alcohol test is required by this subpart. No employer shall falsely represent that a test is administered under this subpart.

§ **120.211 Applicable Federal regulations.**

The following applicable regulations appear in 49 CFR and 14 CFR:

(a) 49 CFR Part 40—Procedures for Transportation Workplace Drug Testing Programs

(b) 14 CFR:

(1) § 67.107—First-Class Airman Medical Certificate, Mental.

(2) § 67.207—Second-Class Airman Medical Certificate, Mental.

(3) § 67.307—Third-Class Airman Medical Certificate, Mental.

(4) § 91.147—Passenger carrying flights for compensation or hire.

(5) § 135.1—Applicability

[Doc. No. FAA–2008–0937, 74 FR 22653 May 14, 2009; Amdt. 120–0A, 75 FR 3154, Jan. 20, 2010]

§ **120.213 Falsification.**

No individual may make, or cause to be made, any of the following:

(a) Any fraudulent or intentionally false statement in any application of an alcohol testing program.

(b) Any fraudulent or intentionally false entry in any record or report that is made, kept, or used to show compliance with this subpart.

(c) Any reproduction or alteration, for fraudulent purposes, of any report or record required to be kept by this subpart.

§ **120.215 Covered employees.**

(a) Each employee, including any assistant, helper, or individual in a training status, who performs a safety-sensitive function listed in this section directly or by contract (including by subcontract at any tier) for an employer as defined in this subpart must be subject to alcohol testing under an alcohol testing program implemented in accordance with this subpart. This includes full-time, part-time, temporary, and intermittent employees regardless of the degree of supervision. The safety-sensitive functions are:

(1) Flight crewmember duties.

(2) Flight attendant duties.

(3) Flight instruction duties.

(4) Aircraft dispatcher duties.

(5) Aircraft maintenance or preventive maintenance duties.

(6) Ground security coordinator duties.

(7) Aviation screening duties.

(8) Air traffic control duties.

(9) Operations control specialist duties.

(b) Each employer must identify any employee who is subject to the alcohol testing regulations of more than one DOT agency. Prior to conducting any alcohol test on a covered employee subject to the alcohol testing regulations of more than one DOT agency, the employer must determine which DOT agency authorizes or requires the test.

[Doc. No. FAA–2008–0937, 74 FR 22653, May 14, 2009, as amended by Amdt. 120–2, 79 FR 9973, Feb. 21, 2014]

§ **120.217 Tests required.**

(a) *Pre-employment alcohol testing.* As an employer, you may, but are not required to, conduct pre-employment alcohol testing under this subpart. If you choose to conduct pre-employment alcohol testing, you must comply with the following requirements:

(1) You must conduct a pre-employment alcohol test before the first performance of safety-sensitive functions by every covered employee (whether a new employee or someone who has transferred to a position involving the

performance of safety-sensitive functions).

(2) You must treat all safety-sensitive employees performing safety-sensitive functions the same for the purpose of pre-employment alcohol testing (*i.e.*, you must not test some covered employees and not others).

(3) You must conduct the pre-employment tests after making a contingent offer of employment or transfer, subject to the employee passing the pre-employment alcohol test.

(4) You must conduct all pre-employment alcohol tests using the alcohol testing procedures of 49 CFR part 40.

(5) You must not allow a covered employee to begin performing safety-sensitive functions unless the result of the employee's test indicates an alcohol concentration of less than 0.04. If a pre-employment test result under this paragraph indicates an alcohol concentration of 0.02 or greater but less than 0.04, the provisions of § 120.221(f) apply.

(b) *Post-accident alcohol testing.* (1) As soon as practicable following an accident, each employer shall test each surviving covered employee for alcohol if that employee's performance of a safety-sensitive function either contributed to the accident or cannot be completely discounted as a contributing factor to the accident. The decision not to administer a test under this section shall be based on the employer's determination, using the best available information at the time of the determination, that the covered employee's performance could not have contributed to the accident.

(2) If a test required by this section is not administered within 2 hours following the accident, the employer shall prepare and maintain on file a record stating the reasons the test was not promptly administered. If a test required by this section is not administered within 8 hours following the accident, the employer shall cease attempts to administer an alcohol test and shall prepare and maintain the same record. Records shall be submitted to the FAA upon request of the Administrator or his or her designee.

(3) A covered employee who is subject to post-accident testing shall remain readily available for such testing or

may be deemed by the employer to have refused to submit to testing. Nothing in this section shall be construed to require the delay of necessary medical attention for injured people following an accident or to prohibit a covered employee from leaving the scene of an accident for the period necessary to obtain assistance in responding to the accident or to obtain necessary emergency medical care.

(c) *Random alcohol testing.* (1) Except as provided in paragraphs (c)(2) through (c)(4) of this section, the minimum annual percentage rate for random alcohol testing will be 25 percent of the covered employees.

(2) The Administrator's decision to increase or decrease the minimum annual percentage rate for random alcohol testing is based on the violation rate for the entire industry. All information used for this determination is drawn from MIS reports required by this subpart. In order to ensure reliability of the data, the Administrator considers the quality and completeness of the reported data, may obtain additional information or reports from employers, and may make appropriate modifications in calculating the industry violation rate. Each year, the Administrator will publish in the FEDERAL REGISTER the minimum annual percentage rate for random alcohol testing of covered employees. The new minimum annual percentage rate for random alcohol testing will be applicable starting January 1 of the calendar year following publication.

(3)(i) When the minimum annual percentage rate for random alcohol testing is 25 percent or more, the Administrator may lower this rate to 10 percent of all covered employees if the Administrator determines that the data received under the reporting requirements of this subpart for two consecutive calendar years indicate that the violation rate is less than 0.5 percent.

(ii) When the minimum annual percentage rate for random alcohol testing is 50 percent, the Administrator may lower this rate to 25 percent of all covered employees if the Administrator determines that the data received under the reporting requirements of this subpart for two consecutive calendar years indicate that the violation rate is less than 1.0 percent but equal to or greater than 0.5 percent.

(4)(i) When the minimum annual percentage rate for random alcohol testing is 10 percent, and the data received under the reporting requirements of this subpart for that calendar year indicate that the violation rate is equal to or greater than 0.5 percent but less than 1.0 percent, the Administrator will increase the minimum annual percentage rate for random alcohol testing to 25 percent of all covered employees.

(ii) When the minimum annual percentage rate for random alcohol testing is 25 percent or less, and the data received under the reporting requirements of this subpart for that calendar year indicate that the violation rate is equal to or greater than 1.0 percent, the Administrator will increase the minimum annual percentage rate for random alcohol testing to 50 percent of all covered employees.

(5) The selection of employees for random alcohol testing shall be made by a scientifically valid method, such as a random-number table or a computer-based random number generator that is matched with employees' Social Security numbers, payroll identification numbers, or other comparable identifying numbers. Under the selection process used, each covered employee shall have an equal chance of being tested each time selections are made.

(6) As an employer, you must select and test a percentage of employees at least equal to the minimum annual percentage rate each year.

(i) As an employer, to determine whether you have met the minimum annual percentage rate, you must divide the number of random alcohol screening test results for safety-sensitive employees by the average number of safety-sensitive employees eligible for random testing.

(A) To calculate whether you have met the annual minimum percentage rate, count all random screening test results below 0.02 breath alcohol concentration, random screening test results of 0.02 or greater breath alcohol concentration, and random refusals as

your "random alcohol screening test results."

(B) To calculate the average number of safety-sensitive employees eligible for random testing throughout the year, add the total number of safety-sensitive employees eligible for testing during each random testing period for the year and divide that total by the number of random testing periods. Only safety-sensitive employees are to be in an employer's random testing pool, and all safety-sensitive employees must be in the random pool. If you are an employer conducting random testing more often than once per month (e.g., you select daily, weekly, bi-weekly) you do not need to compute this total number of safety-sensitive employees more than on a once per month basis.

(ii) As an employer, you may use a service agent to perform random selections for you, and your safety-sensitive employees may be part of a larger random testing pool of safety-sensitive employees. However, you must ensure that the service agent you use is testing at the appropriate percentage established for your industry and that only safety-sensitive employees are in the random testing pool. For example:

(A) If the service agent has your employees in a random testing pool for your company alone, you must ensure that the testing is conducted at least at the minimum annual percentage rate under this part.

(B) If the service agent has your employees in a random testing pool combined with other FAA-regulated companies, you must ensure that the testing is conducted at least at the minimum annual percentage rate under this part.

(C) If the service agent has your employees in a random testing pool combined with other DOT-regulated companies, you must ensure that the testing is conducted at least at the highest rate required for any DOT-regulated company in the pool.

(7) Each employer shall ensure that random alcohol tests conducted under this subpart are unannounced and that the dates for administering random tests are spread reasonably throughout the calendar year.

(8) Each employer shall require that each covered employee who is notified of selection for random testing proceeds to the testing site immediately; provided, however, that if the employee is performing a safety-sensitive function at the time of the notification, the employer shall instead ensure that the employee ceases to perform the safety-sensitive function and proceeds to the testing site as soon as possible.

(9) A covered employee shall only be randomly tested while the employee is performing safety-sensitive functions; just before the employee is to perform safety-sensitive functions; or just after the employee has ceased performing such functions.

(10) If a given covered employee is subject to random alcohol testing under the alcohol testing rules of more than one DOT agency, the employee shall be subject to random alcohol testing at the percentage rate established for the calendar year by the DOT agency regulating more than 50 percent of the employee's functions.

(11) If an employer is required to conduct random alcohol testing under the alcohol testing rules of more than one DOT agency, the employer may—

(i) Establish separate pools for random selection, with each pool containing the covered employees who are subject to testing at the same required rate; or

(ii) Randomly select such employees for testing at the highest percentage rate established for the calendar year by any DOT agency to which the employer is subject.

(d) *Reasonable suspicion alcohol testing.* (1) An employer shall require a covered employee to submit to an alcohol test when the employer has reasonable suspicion to believe that the employee has violated the alcohol misuse prohibitions in §§ 120.19 or 120.37.

(2) The employer's determination that reasonable suspicion exists to require the covered employee to undergo an alcohol test shall be based on specific, contemporaneous, articulable observations concerning the appearance, behavior, speech or body odors of the employee. The required observations shall be made by a supervisor who is trained in detecting the symptoms of alcohol misuse. The supervisor who makes the determination that reasonable suspicion exists shall not conduct the breath alcohol test on that employee.

(3) Alcohol testing is authorized by this section only if the observations required by paragraph (d)(2) of this section are made during, just preceding, or just after the period of the work day that the covered employee is required to be in compliance with this rule. An employee may be directed by the employer to undergo reasonable suspicion testing for alcohol only while the employee is performing safety-sensitive functions; just before the employee is to perform safety-sensitive functions; or just after the employee has ceased performing such functions.

(4)(i) If a test required by this section is not administered within 2 hours following the determination made under paragraph (d)(2) of this section, the employer shall prepare and maintain on file a record stating the reasons the test was not promptly administered. If a test required by this section is not administered within 8 hours following the determination made under paragraph (d)(2) of this section, the employer shall cease attempts to administer an alcohol test and shall state in the record the reasons for not administering the test.

(ii) Notwithstanding the absence of a reasonable suspicion alcohol test under this section, no covered employee shall report for duty or remain on duty requiring the performance of safety-sensitive functions while the employee is under the influence of, or impaired by, alcohol, as shown by the behavioral, speech, or performance indicators of alcohol misuse, nor shall an employer permit the covered employee to perform or continue to perform safety-sensitive functions until:

(A) An alcohol test is administered and the employee's alcohol concentration measures less than 0.02; or

(B) The start of the employee's next regularly scheduled duty period, but not less than 8 hours following the determination made under paragraph (d)(2) of this section that there is reasonable suspicion that the employee has violated the alcohol misuse provisions in §§ 120.19 or 120.37.

(iii) No employer shall take any action under this subpart against a covered employee based solely on the employee's behavior and appearance in the absence of an alcohol test. This does not prohibit an employer with authority independent of this subpart from taking any action otherwise consistent with law.

(e) *Return-to-duty alcohol testing.* Each employer shall ensure that before a covered employee returns to duty requiring the performance of a safety-sensitive function after engaging in conduct prohibited in §§ 120.19 or 120.37 the employee shall undergo a return-to-duty alcohol test with a result indicating an alcohol concentration of less than 0.02. The test cannot occur until after the SAP has determined that the employee has successfully complied with the prescribed education and/or treatment.

(f) *Follow-up alcohol testing.* (1) Each employer shall ensure that the employee who engages in conduct prohibited by §§ 120.19 or 120.37, is subject to unannounced follow-up alcohol testing as directed by a SAP.

(2) The number and frequency of such testing shall be determined by the employer's SAP, but must consist of at least six tests in the first 12 months following the employee's return to duty.

(3) The employer must direct the employee to undergo testing for drugs in accordance with subpart E of this part, in addition to alcohol, if the SAP determines that drug testing is necessary for the particular employee. Any such drug testing shall be conducted in accordance with the provisions of 49 CFR part 40.

(4) Follow-up testing shall not exceed 60 months after the date the individual begins to perform, or returns to the performance of, a safety-sensitive function. The SAP may terminate the requirement for follow-up testing at any time after the first six tests have been conducted, if the SAP determines that such testing is no longer necessary.

(5) A covered employee shall be tested for alcohol under this section only while the employee is performing safety-sensitive functions, just before the employee is to perform safety-sensitive

functions, or just after the employee has ceased performing such functions.

(g) *Retesting of covered employees with an alcohol concentration of 0.02 or greater but less than 0.04.* Each employer shall retest a covered employee to ensure compliance with the provisions of § 120.221(f) if the employer chooses to permit the employee to perform a safety-sensitive function within 8 hours following the administration of an alcohol test indicating an alcohol concentration of 0.02 or greater but less than 0.04.

§ 120.219 Handling of test results, record retention, and confidentiality.

(a) *Retention of records.* (1) *General requirement.* In addition to the records required to be maintained under 49 CFR part 40, employers must maintain records required by this subpart in a secure location with controlled access.

(2) *Period of retention.*

(i) *Five years.*

(A) Copies of any annual reports submitted to the FAA under this subpart for a minimum of 5 years.

(B) Records of notifications to the Federal Air Surgeon of refusals to submit to testing and violations of the alcohol misuse prohibitions in this chapter by covered employees who hold medical certificates issued under part 67 of this chapter.

(C) Documents presented by a covered employee to dispute the result of an alcohol test administered under this subpart.

(D) Records related to other violations of §§ 120.19 or 120.37.

(ii) *Two years.* Records related to the testing process and training required under this subpart.

(A) Documents related to the random selection process.

(B) Documents generated in connection with decisions to administer reasonable suspicion alcohol tests.

(C) Documents generated in connection with decisions on post-accident tests.

(D) Documents verifying existence of a medical explanation of the inability of a covered employee to provide adequate breath for testing.

(E) Materials on alcohol misuse awareness, including a copy of the employer's policy on alcohol misuse.

(F) Documentation of compliance with the requirements of § 120.223(a).

(G) Documentation of training provided to supervisors for the purpose of qualifying the supervisors to make a determination concerning the need for alcohol testing based on reasonable suspicion.

(H) Certification that any training conducted under this subpart complies with the requirements for such training.

(b) *Annual reports.* (1) Annual reports of alcohol testing program results must be submitted to the FAA by March 15 of the succeeding calendar year for the prior calendar year (January 1 through December 31) in accordance with the provisions of paragraphs (b)(1)(i) through (iii) of this section.

(i) Each part 121 certificate holder shall submit an annual report each year.

(ii) Each entity conducting an alcohol testing program under this part, other than a part 121 certificate holder, that has 50 or more employees performing a safety-sensitive function on January 1 of any calendar year shall submit an annual report to the FAA for that calendar year.

(iii) The Administrator reserves the right to require that aviation employers not otherwise required to submit annual reports prepare and submit such reports to the FAA. Employers that will be required to submit annual reports under this provision will be notified in writing by the FAA.

(2) As an employer, you must use the Management Information System (MIS) form and instructions as required by 49 CFR part 40 (at 49 CFR 40.26 and appendix H to 49 CFR part 40). You may also use the electronic version of the MIS form provided by the DOT. The Administrator may designate means (e.g., electronic program transmitted via the Internet) other than hard-copy, for MIS form submission. For information on where to submit MIS forms and for the electronic version of the form, see: *http:// www.faa.gov/about/office_org/ headquarters_offices/avs/offices/aam/ drug_alcohol/.*

(3) A service agent may prepare the MIS report on behalf of an employer. However, a company official (e.g., Designated Employer Representative as defined in 49 CFR part 40) must certify the accuracy and completeness of the MIS report, no matter who prepares it.

(c) *Access to records and facilities.* (1) Except as required by law or expressly authorized or required in this subpart, no employer shall release covered employee information that is contained in records required to be maintained under this subpart.

(2) A covered employee is entitled, upon written request, to obtain copies of any records pertaining to the employee's use of alcohol, including any records pertaining to his or her alcohol tests in accordance with 49 CFR part 40. The employer shall promptly provide the records requested by the employee. Access to an employee's records shall not be contingent upon payment for records other than those specifically requested.

(3) Each employer shall permit access to all facilities utilized in complying with the requirements of this subpart to the Secretary of Transportation or any DOT agency with regulatory authority over the employer or any of its covered employees.

§ 120.221 Consequences for employees engaging in alcohol-related conduct.

(a) *Removal from safety-sensitive function.* (1) Except as provided in 49 CFR part 40, no covered employee shall perform safety-sensitive functions if the employee has engaged in conduct prohibited by §§ 120.19 or 120.37, or an alcohol misuse rule of another DOT agency.

(2) No employer shall permit any covered employee to perform safety-sensitive functions if the employer has determined that the employee has violated this section.

(b) *Permanent disqualification from service.* (1) An employee who violates §§ 120.19(c) or 120.37(c) is permanently precluded from performing for an employer the safety-sensitive duties the employee performed before such violation.

(2) An employee who engages in alcohol use that violates another alcohol misuse provision of §§ 120.19 or 120.37,

and who had previously engaged in alcohol use that violated the provisions of §§ 120.19 or 120.37 after becoming subject to such prohibitions, is permanently precluded from performing for an employer the safety-sensitive duties the employee performed before such violation.

(c) *Notice to the Federal Air Surgeon.* (1) An employer who determines that a covered employee who holds an airman medical certificate issued under part 67 of this chapter has engaged in alcohol use that violated the alcohol misuse provisions of §§ 120.19 or 120.37 shall notify the Federal Air Surgeon within 2 working days.

(2) Each such employer shall forward to the Federal Air Surgeon a copy of the report of any evaluation performed under the provisions of § 120.223(c) within 2 working days of the employer's receipt of the report.

(3) All documents must be sent to the Federal Air Surgeon, Federal Aviation Administration, Office of Aerospace Medicine, Attn: Drug Abatement Division (AAM–800), 800 Independence Avenue, SW., Washington, DC 20591.

(4) No covered employee who is required to hold an airman medical certificate in order to perform a safety-sensitive duty may perform that duty following a violation of this subpart until the covered employee obtains an airman medical certificate issued by the Federal Air Surgeon dated after the alcohol test result or refusal to test date. After the covered employee obtains this airman medical certificate, the SAP may recommend to the employer that the covered employee may be returned to a safety-sensitive position. The receipt of an airman medical certificate does not alter any obligations otherwise required by 49 CFR part 40 or this subpart.

(5) Once the Federal Air Surgeon has recommended under paragraph (c)(4) of this section that the employee be permitted to perform safety-sensitive duties, the employer cannot permit the employee to perform those safety-sensitive duties until the employer has ensured that the employee meets the return to duty requirements in accordance with 49 CFR part 40.

(d) *Notice of refusals* Each covered employer must notify the FAA within 2 working days of any employee who holds a certificate issued under part 61, part 63, or part 65 of this chapter who has refused to submit to an alcohol test required under this subpart. Notification must be sent to: Federal Aviation Administration, Office of Aerospace Medicine, Drug Abatement Division (AAM–800), 800 Independence Avenue, SW., Washington, DC 20591, or by fax to (202) 267–5200.

(e) *Required evaluation and alcohol testing.* No covered employee who has engaged in conduct prohibited by §§ 120.19 or 120.37 shall perform safety-sensitive functions unless the employee has met the requirements of 49 CFR part 40. No employer shall permit a covered employee who has engaged in such conduct to perform safety-sensitive functions unless the employee has met the requirements of 49 CFR part 40.

(f) *Other alcohol-related conduct.* (1) No covered employee tested under this subpart who is found to have an alcohol concentration of 0.02 or greater but less than 0.04 shall perform or continue to perform safety-sensitive functions for an employer, nor shall an employer permit the employee to perform or continue to perform safety-sensitive functions, until:

(i) The employee's alcohol concentration measures less than 0.02; or

(ii) The start of the employee's next regularly scheduled duty period, but not less than 8 hours following administration of the test.

(2) Except as provided in paragraph (f)(1) of this section, no employer shall take any action under this rule against an employee based solely on test results showing an alcohol concentration less than 0.04. This does not prohibit an employer with authority independent of this rule from taking any action otherwise consistent with law.

[Doc. No. FAA–2008–0937, 74 FR 22653, May 14, 2009, as amended by Amdt. 120–1, 78 FR 42004, July 15, 2013]

§ 120.223 Alcohol misuse information, training, and substance abuse professionals.

(a) *Employer obligation to promulgate a policy on the misuse of alcohol.* (1) *General requirements.* Each employer shall provide educational materials that explain these alcohol testing requirements and the employer's policies and procedures with respect to meeting those requirements.

(i) The employer shall ensure that a copy of these materials is distributed to each covered employee prior to the start of alcohol testing under the employer's FAA-mandated alcohol testing program and to each individual subsequently hired for or transferred to a covered position.

(ii) Each employer shall provide written notice to representatives of employee organizations of the availability of this information.

(2) *Required content.* The materials to be made available to employees shall include detailed discussion of at least the following:

(i) The identity of the individual designated by the employer to answer employee questions about the materials.

(ii) The categories of employees who are subject to the provisions of these alcohol testing requirements.

(iii) Sufficient information about the safety-sensitive functions performed by those employees to make clear what period of the work day the covered employee is required to be in compliance with these alcohol testing requirements.

(iv) Specific information concerning employee conduct that is prohibited by this chapter.

(v) The circumstances under which a covered employee will be tested for alcohol under this subpart.

(vi) The procedures that will be used to test for the presence of alcohol, protect the employee and the integrity of the breath testing process, safeguard the validity of the test results, and ensure that those results are attributed to the correct employee.

(vii) The requirement that a covered employee submit to alcohol tests administered in accordance with this subpart.

(viii) An explanation of what constitutes a refusal to submit to an alcohol test and the attendant consequences.

(ix) The consequences for covered employees found to have violated the prohibitions in this chapter, including the requirement that the employee be removed immediately from performing safety-sensitive functions, and the process in 49 CFR part 40, subpart O.

(x) The consequences for covered employees found to have an alcohol concentration of 0.02 or greater but less than 0.04.

(xi) Information concerning the effects of alcohol misuse on an individual's health, work, and personal life; signs and symptoms of an alcohol problem; available methods of evaluating and resolving problems associated with the misuse of alcohol; and intervening when an alcohol problem is suspected, including confrontation, referral to any available employee assistance program, and/or referral to management.

(xii) Optional provisions. The materials supplied to covered employees may also include information on additional employer policies with respect to the use or possession of alcohol, including any consequences for an employee found to have a specified alcohol level, that are based on the employer's authority independent of this subpart. Any such additional policies or consequences must be clearly and obviously described as being based on independent authority.

(b) *Training for supervisors.* Each employer shall ensure that persons designated to determine whether reasonable suspicion exists to require a covered employee to undergo alcohol testing under §120.217(d) of this subpart receive at least 60 minutes of training on the physical, behavioral, speech, and performance indicators of probable alcohol misuse.

(c) *Substance abuse professional (SAP) duties.* The SAP must perform the functions set forth in 49 CFR part 40, subpart O, and this subpart.

§ 120.225 How to implement an alcohol testing program.

(a) Each company must meet the requirements of this subpart. Use the following chart to determine whether your company must obtain an Antidrug and Alcohol Misuse Prevention Program Operations Specification, Letter of Authorization, or Drug and Alcohol Testing Program Registration from the FAA:

If you are . . .	You must . . .
(1) A part 119 certificate holder with authority to operate under part 121 or 135.	Obtain an Antidrug and Alcohol Misuse Prevention Program Operations Specification by contacting your FAA Principal Operations Inspector.
(2) An operator as defined in § 91.147 of this chapter.	Obtain a Letter of Authorization by contacting the Flight Standards District Office nearest to your principal place of business.
(3) A part 119 certificate holder with authority to operate under part 121 or part 135 and an operator as defined in § 91.147 of this chapter.	Complete the requirements in paragraphs 1 and 2 of this chart and advise the Flight Standards District Office and Drug Abatement Division that the § 91.147 operation will be included under the part 119 testing program. Contact Drug Abatement Division at FAA, Office of Aerospace Medicine, Drug Abatement Division (AAM–800), 800 Independence Avenue SW., Washington, DC 20591.
(4) An air traffic control facility not operated by the FAA or by or under contract to the U.S. Military.	Register with the FAA, Office of Aerospace Medicine Drug Abatement Division (AAM–800), 800 Independence Avenue SW., Washington, DC 20591.
(5) A part 145 certificate holder who has your own alcohol testing program.	Obtain an Antidrug and Alcohol Misuse Prevention Program Operations Specification by contacting your Principal Maintenance Inspector or register with the FAA Office of Aerospace Medicine, Drug Abatement Division (AAM–800), 800 Independence Avenue SW., Washington, DC 20591, if you opt to conduct your own alcohol testing program.
(6) A contractor who has your own alcohol testing program.	Register with the FAA, Office of Aerospace Medicine, Drug Abatement Division (AAM–800), 800 Independence Avenue SW., Washington, DC 20591, if you opt to conduct your own alcohol testing program.

(b) Use the following chart for implementing an alcohol testing program if you are applying for a part 119 certificate with authority to operate under part 121 or part 135 of this chapter, if you intend to begin operations as defined in § 91.147 of this chapter, or if you intend to begin air traffic control operations (not operated by the FAA or by or under contract to the U.S. Military). Use it to determine whether you need to have an Antidrug and Alcohol Misuse Prevention Program Operations Specification, Letter of Authorization, or Drug and Alcohol Testing Program Registration from the FAA. Your employees who perform safety-sensitive duties must be tested in accordance with this subpart. The chart follows:

If you . . .	You must . . .
(1) Apply for a part 119 certificate with authority to operate under parts 121 or 135.	(i) Have an Antidrug and Alcohol Misuse Prevention Program Operations Specification,
	(ii) Implement an FAA alcohol testing program no later than the date you start operations, and
	(iii) Meet the requirements of this subpart.
(2) Intend to begin operations as defined in § 91.147 of this chapter.	(i) Have a Letter of Authorization,
	(ii) Implement an FAA alcohol testing program no later than the date you start operations, and
	(iii) Meet the requirements of this subpart.
(3) Apply for a part 119 certificate with authority to operate under parts 121 or 135 and intend to begin operations as defined in § 91.147 of this chapter.	(i) Have an Antidrug and Alcohol Misuse Prevention Program Operations Specification and a Letter of Authorization,
	(ii) Implement your combined FAA alcohol testing program no later than the date you start operations, and
	(iii) Meet the requirements of this subpart.
(4) Intend to begin air traffic control operations (at an air traffic control facility not operated by the FAA or by or under contract to the U.S. military).	(i) Register with the FAA, Office of Aerospace Medicine Drug Abatement Division (AAM–800), 800 Independence Avenue SW., Washington, DC 20591, prior to starting operations,
	(ii) Implement an FAA alcohol testing program no later than the date you start operations, and
	(iii) Meet the requirements of this subpart.

(c) If you are an individual or a company that intends to provide safety-sensitive services by contract to a part 119 certificate holder with authority to operate under parts 121 and/or 135 of this chapter or an operator as defined in § 91.147 of this chapter, use the following chart to determine what you must do if you opt to have your own alcohol testing program.

If you . . .	And you opt to conduct your own Alcohol Testing Program, you must . . .
(1) Are a part 145 certificate holder.	(i) Have an Antidrug and Alcohol Misuse Prevention Program Operations Specifications or register with the FAA, Office of Aerospace Medicine, Drug Abatement Division (AAM–800), 800 Independence Avenue, SW., Washington, DC 20591,

If you . . .	And you opt to conduct your own Alcohol Testing Program, you must . . .
	(ii) Implement an FAA alcohol testing program no later than the date you start performing safety-sensitive functions for a part 119 certificate holder with the authority to operate under parts 121 and/or 135, or operator as defined in §91.147 of this chapter, and (iii) Meet the requirements of this subpart as if you were an employer.
(2) Are a contractor	(i) Register with the FAA, Office of Aerospace Medicine, Drug Abatement Division (AAM–800), 800 Independence Avenue, SW., Washington, DC 20591, (ii) Implement an FAA alcohol testing program no later than the date you start performing safety-sensitive functions for a part 119 certificate holder with authority to operate under parts 121 and/or 135, or operator as defined in §91.147 of this chapter, and (iii) Meet the requirements of this subpart as if you were an employer.

(d)(1) To obtain an Antidrug and Alcohol Misuse Prevention Program Operations Specification, you must contact your FAA Principal Operations Inspector or Principal Maintenance Inspector. Provide him/her with the following information:

(i) Company name.

(ii) Certificate number.

(iii) Telephone number.

(iv) Address where your drug and alcohol testing program records are kept.

(v) Whether you have 50 or more covered employees, or 49 or fewer covered employees. (Part 119 certificate holders with authority to operate only under part 121 of this chapter are not required to provide this information.)

(2) You must certify on your Antidrug and Alcohol Misuse Prevention Program Operations Specification, issued by your FAA Principal Operations Inspector or Principal Maintenance Inspector, that you will comply with this part and 49 CFR part 40.

(3) You are required to obtain only one Antidrug and Alcohol Misuse Prevention Program Operations Specification to satisfy this requirement under this part.

(4) You must update the Antidrug and Alcohol Misuse Prevention Program Operations Specification when any changes to the information contained in the Operation Specification occur.

(e) *Register your Drug and Alcohol Testing Program by obtaining a Letter of Authorization from the FAA in accordance with § 91.147.* (1) A drug and alcohol testing program is considered registered when the following information is submitted to the Flight Standards District Office nearest your principal place of business:

(i) Company name.

(ii) Telephone number.

(iii) Address where your drug and alcohol testing program records are kept.

(iv) Type of safety-sensitive functions you or your employees perform (such as flight instruction duties, aircraft dispatcher duties, maintenance or preventive maintenance duties, ground security coordinator duties, aviation screening duties, air traffic control duties).

(v) Whether you have 50 or more covered employees, or 49 or fewer covered employees.

(vi) A signed statement indicating that your company will comply with this part and 49 CFR part 40.

(2) This Letter of Authorization will satisfy the requirements for both your drug testing program under subpart E of this part and your alcohol testing program under this subpart.

(3) Update the Letter of Authorization information as changes occur. Send the updates to the Flight Standards District Office nearest your principal place of business.

(4) If you are a part 119 certificate holder with authority to operate under part 121 or part 135 and intend to begin operations as defined in §91.147 of this chapter, you must also advise the Federal Aviation Administration, Office of Aerospace Medicine, Drug Abatement Division (AAM–800), 800 Independence Avenue SW., Washington, DC 20591.

(f) *Obtaining a Drug and Alcohol Testing Program Registration from the FAA.* (1) Except as provided in paragraphs (d) and (e) of this section, to obtain a Drug and Alcohol Testing Program Registration from the FAA you must submit the following information to the Office of Aerospace Medicine, Drug Abatement Division:

(i) Company name.

(ii) Telephone number.

(iii) Address where your drug and alcohol testing program records are kept.

(iv) Type of safety-sensitive functions you or your employees perform (such as flight instruction duties, aircraft dispatcher duties, maintenance or preventive maintenance duties, ground security coordinator duties, aviation screening duties, air traffic control duties).

(v) Whether you have 50 or more covered employees, or 49 or fewer covered employees.

(vi) A signed statement indicating that: your company will comply with this part and 49 CFR part 40; and you intend to provide safety-sensitive functions by contract (including subcontract at any tier) to a part 119 certificate holder with authority to operate under part 121 or part 135 of this chapter, an operator as defined in §91.147 of this chapter, or an air traffic control facility not operated by the FAA or by or under contract to the U.S. military.

(2) Send this information to the Federal Aviation Administration, Office of Aerospace Medicine, Drug Abatement Division (AAM–800), 800 Independence Avenue SW., Washington, DC 20591.

(3) This Drug and Alcohol Testing Program Registration will satisfy the registration requirements for both your drug testing program under subpart E of this part and your alcohol testing program under this subpart.

(4) Update the registration information as changes occur. Send the updates to the address specified in paragraph (f)(2) of this section.

[Doc. No. FAA–2008–0937, 74 FR 22653, May 14, 2009; Amdt. 120–0A, 75 FR 3154, Jan. 20, 2010, as amended by Amdt. 120–1, 78 FR 42005, July 15, 2013]

§ 120.227 Employees located outside the U.S.

(a) No covered employee shall be tested for alcohol misuse while located outside the territory of the United States.

(1) Each covered employee who is assigned to perform safety-sensitive functions solely outside the territory of the United States shall be removed from the random testing pool upon the inception of such assignment.

(2) Each covered employee who is removed from the random testing pool under this paragraph shall be returned

to the random testing pool when the employee resumes the performance of safety-sensitive functions wholly or partially within the territory of the United States.

(b) The provisions of this subpart shall not apply to any person who performs a safety-sensitive function by contract for an employer outside the territory of the United States.

PART 121—OPERATING REQUIRE-MENTS: DOMESTIC, FLAG, AND SUPPLEMENTAL OPERATIONS

SPECIAL FEDERAL AVIATION REGULATION NO. 50–2 [NOTE]
SPECIAL FEDERAL AVIATION REGULATION NO. 71 [NOTE]
SPECIAL FEDERAL AVIATION REGULATION NO. 97 [NOTE]

Subpart A—General

Subpart B—Certification Rules for Domestic and Flag Air Carriers [Reserved]

Subpart C—Certification Rules for Supplemental Air Carriers and Commercial Operators [Reserved]

Subpart D—Rules Governing All Certificate Holders Under This Part [Reserved]

Subpart E—Approval of Routes: Domestic and Flag Operations

AUTHORITY: 49 U.S.C. 106(f), 106(g), 40103, 40113, 40119, 41706, 42301 preceding note added by Pub. L. 112–95, sec. 412, 126 Stat. 89, 44101, 44701–44702, 44705, 44709–44711, 44713, 44716–44717, 44722, 44729, 44732; 46105; Pub. L. 111–216, 124 Stat. 2348 (49 U.S.C. 44701 note); Pub. L. 112–95 126 Stat 62 (49 U.S.C. 44732 note).

SPECIAL FEDERAL AVIATION REGULATION
No. 50–2

EDITORIAL NOTE: For the text of SFAR No. 50–2, see part 91 of this chapter.

SPECIAL FEDERAL AVIATION REGULATION
No. 71

EDITORIAL NOTE: For the text of SFAR No. 71, see part 91 of this chapter.

SPECIAL FEDERAL AVIATION REGULATION
No. 97

EDITORIAL NOTE: For the text of SFAR No. 97, see part 91 of this chapter.

Subpart A—General

§121.1 Applicability.

This part prescribes rules governing—

(a) The domestic, flag, and supplemental operations of each person who holds or is required to hold an Air Carrier Certificate or Operating Certificate under part 119 of this chapter.

(b) Each person employed or used by a certificate holder conducting operations under this part including maintenance, preventive maintenance, and alteration of aircraft.

(c) Each person who applies for provisional approval of an Advanced Qualification Program curriculum, curriculum segment, or portion of a curriculum segment under SFAR No. 58 of 14 CFR part 121, and each person employed or used by an air carrier or commercial operator under this part to perform training, qualification, or evaluation functions under an Advanced Qualification Program under SFAR No. 58 of 14 CFR part 121.

(d) Nonstop Commercial Air Tours conducted for compensation or hire in accordance with § 119.1(e)(2) of this chapter must comply with drug and alcohol requirements in §§ 121.455, 121.457, 121.458 and 121.459, and with the provisions of part 136, subpart A of this chapter by September 11, 2007. An operator who does not hold an air carrier certificate or an operating certificate is permitted to use a person who is otherwise authorized to perform aircraft maintenance or preventive maintenance duties and who is not subject to anti-drug and alcohol misuse prevention programs to perform—

(1) Aircraft maintenance or preventive maintenance on the operator's aircraft if the operator would otherwise be required to transport the aircraft more than 50 nautical miles further than the repair point closest to the operator's principal base of operations to obtain these services; or

(2) Emergency repairs on the operator's aircraft if the aircraft cannot be safely operated to a location where an employee subject to FAA-approved programs can perform the repairs.

(e) Each person who is on board an aircraft being operated under this part.

(f) Each person who is an applicant for an Air Carrier Certificate or an Operating Certificate under part 119 of this chapter, when conducting proving tests.

(g) This part also establishes requirements for operators to take actions to support the continued airworthiness of each airplane.

[Doc. No. 28154, 60 FR 65925, Dec. 20, 1995, as amended by Amdt. 121-328, 72 FR 6912, Feb. 13, 2007; Amdt. 121-336, 72 FR 63411, Nov. 8, 2007]

§ 121.2 Compliance schedule for operators that transition to part 121; certain new entrant operators.

(a) *Applicability.* This section applies to the following:

(1) Each certificate holder that was issued an air carrier or operating certificate and operations specifications under the requirements of part 135 of this chapter or under SFAR No. 38–2 of 14 CFR part 121 before January 19, 1996, and that conducts scheduled passenger-carrying operations with:

(i) Nontransport category turbo-propeller powered airplanes type certificated after December 31, 1964, that have a passenger seat configuration of 10–19 seats;

(ii) Transport category turbo-propeller powered airplanes that have a passenger seat configuration of 20–30 seats; or

(iii) Turbojet engine powered airplanes having a passenger seat configuration of 1–30 seats.

(2) Each person who, after January 19, 1996, applies for or obtains an initial air carrier or operating certificate and operations specifications to conduct scheduled passenger-carrying operations in the kinds of airplanes described in paragraphs (a)(1)(i), (a)(1)(ii), or paragraph (a)(1)(iii) of this section.

(b) *Obtaining operations specifications.* A certificate holder described in paragraph (a)(1) of this section may not, after March 20, 1997, operate an airplane described in paragraphs (a)(1)(i), (a)(1)(ii), or (a)(1)(iii) of this section in scheduled passenger-carrying operations, unless it obtains operations specifications to conduct its scheduled operations under this part on or before March 20, 1997.

(c) *Regular or accelerated compliance.* Except as provided in paragraphs (d), (e), and (i) of this section, each certificate holder described in paragraphs (a)(1) of this section shall comply with each applicable requirement of this part on and after March 20, 1997 or on and after the date on which the certificate holder is issued operations specifications under this part, whichever occurs first. Except as provided in paragraphs (d) and (e) of this section, each person described in paragraph (a)(2) of this section shall comply with each applicable requirement of this part on and after the date on which that person is issued a certificate and operations specifications under this part.

(d) *Delayed compliance dates.* Unless paragraph (e) of this section specifies an earlier compliance date, no certificate holder that is covered by paragraph (a) of this section may operate an airplane in 14 CFR part 121 operations on or after a date listed in this paragraph (d) unless that airplane meets the applicable requirement of this paragraph (d):

(1) *Nontransport category turbopropeller powered airplanes type certificated after December 31, 1964, that have a passenger seat configuration of 10–19 seats.* No certificate holder may operate under this part an airplane that is described in paragraph (a)(1)(i) of this section on or after a date listed in paragraph (d)(1) of this section unless that airplane meets the applicable requirement listed in paragraph (d)(1) of this section:

(i) December 20, 1997:

(A) Section 121.289, Landing gear aural warning.

(B) Section 121.308, Lavatory fire protection.

(C) Section 121.310(e), Emergency exit handle illumination.

(D) Section 121.337(b)(8), Protective breathing equipment.

(E) Section 121.340, Emergency flotation means.

(ii) December 20, 1999: Section 121.342, Pitot heat indication system.

(iii) December 20, 2010:

(A) For airplanes described in §121.157(f), the Airplane Performance Operating Limitations in §§121.189 through 121.197.

(B) Section 121.161(b), Ditching approval.

(C) Section 121.305(j), Third attitude indicator.

(D) Section 121.312(c), Passenger seat cushion flammability.

(iv) March 12, 1999: Section 121.310(b)(1), Interior emergency exit locating sign.

(2) *Transport category turbopropeller powered airplanes that have a passenger seat configuration of 20–30 seats.* No certificate holder may operate under this part an airplane that is described in paragraph (a)(1)(ii) of this section on or after a date listed in paragraph (d)(2) of this section unless that airplane meets the applicable requirement listed in paragraph (d)(2) of this section:

(i) December 20, 1997:

(A) Section 121.308, Lavatory fire protection.

(B) Section 121.337(b) (8) and (9), Protective breathing equipment.

(C) Section 121.340, Emergency flotation means.

(ii) December 20, 2010: §121.305(j), third attitude indicator.

(e) *Newly manufactured airplanes.* No certificate holder that is described in paragraph (a) of this section may operate under this part an airplane manufactured on or after a date listed in this paragraph unless that airplane meets the applicable requirement listed in this paragraph (e).

(1) For nontransport category turbopropeller powered airplanes type certificated after December 31, 1964, that have a passenger seat configuration of 10–19 seats:

(i) Manufactured on or after March 20, 1997:

(A) Section 121.305(j), Third attitude indicator.

(B) Section 121.311(f), Safety belts and shoulder harnesses.

(ii) Manufactured on or after December 20, 1997; Section 121.317(a), Fasten seat belt light.

(iii) Manufactured on or after December 20, 1999: Section 121.293, Takeoff warning system.

(iv) Manufactured on or after March 12, 1999: Section 121.310(b)(1), Interior emergency exit locating sign.

(2) For transport category turbopropeller powered airplanes that have a passenger seat configuration of 20–30 seats manufactured on or after March 20, 1997: Section 121.305(j), Third attitude indicator.

(f) *New type certification requirements.* No person may operate an airplane for which the application for a type certificate was filed after March 29, 1995, in 14 CFR part 121 operations unless that airplane is type certificated under part 25 of this chapter.

(g) *Transition plan.* Before March 19, 1996 each certificate holder described in paragraph (a)(1) of this section must submit to the FAA a transition plan (containing a calendar of events) for moving from conducting its scheduled operations under the commuter requirements of part 135 of this chapter to the requirements for domestic or flag operations under this part. Each transition plan must contain details on the following:

(1) Plans for obtaining new operations specifications authorizing domestic or flag operations;

(2) Plans for being in compliance with the applicable requirements of this part on or before March 20, 1997; and

(3) Plans for complying with the compliance date schedules contained in paragraphs (d) and (e) of this section.

(h) *Continuing requirements.* A certificate holder described in paragraph (a) of this section shall comply with the applicable airplane operating and equipment requirements of part 135 of this chapter for the airplanes described in paragraph (a)(1) of this section, until the airplane meets the specific compliance dates in paragraphs (d) and (e) of this section.

(i) Any training or qualification obtained by a crewmember under part 135 of this chapter before March 20, 1997, is entitled to credit under this part for the purpose of meeting the requirements of this part, as determined by the Administrator. Records kept by a certificate holder under part 135 of this chapter before March 20, 1997, can be annotated, with the approval of the Administrator, to reflect crewmember training and qualification credited toward part 121 requirements.

[Doc. No. 28154, 60 FR 65925, Dec. 20, 1995, as amended by Amdt. 121–253, 61 FR 2609, Jan. 26, 1996; Amdt. 121–256, 61 FR 30434, June 14, 1996; Amdt. 121–262, 62 FR 13256, Mar. 19, 1997; Amdt. 121–344, 74 FR 34234, July 15, 2009]

§ 121.4 Applicability of rules to unauthorized operators.

The rules in this part which refer to a person certificated under part 119 of this chapter apply also to any person who engages in an operation governed by this part without the appropriate certificate and operations specifications required by part 119 of this chapter.

[Doc. No. 11675, 37 FR 20937, Oct. 5, 1972, as amended by Amdt. 121–251, 60 FR 65926, Dec. 20, 1995]

§ 121.7 Definitions.

The following definitions apply to those sections of part 121 that apply to ETOPS:

Adequate Airport means an airport that an airplane operator may list with approval from the FAA because that airport meets the landing limitations of § 121.197 and is either—

(1) An airport that meets the requirements of part 139, subpart D of this chapter, excluding those that apply to aircraft rescue and firefighting service, or

(2) A military airport that is active and operational.

ETOPS Alternate Airport means an adequate airport listed in the certificate holder's operations specifications that is designated in a dispatch or flight release for use in the event of a diversion during ETOPS. This definition applies to flight planning and does not in any way limit the authority of the pilot-in-command during flight.

ETOPS Area of Operation means one of the following areas:

(1) For turbine-engine-powered airplanes with two engines, an area beyond 60 minutes from an adequate airport, computed using a one-engine-inoperative cruise speed under standard conditions in still air.

(2) For turbine-engine-powered passenger-carrying airplanes with more than two engines, an area beyond 180 minutes from an adequate airport, computed using a one-engine-inoperative cruise speed under standard conditions in still air.

ETOPS Entry Point means the first point on the route of an ETOPS flight, determined using a one-engine-inoperative cruise speed under standard conditions in still air, that is—

(1) More than 60 minutes from an adequate airport for airplanes with two engines;

(2) More than 180 minutes from an adequate airport for passenger-carrying airplanes with more than two engines.

ETOPS Qualified Person means a person, performing maintenance for the certificate holder, who has satisfactorily completed the certificate holder's ETOPS training program.

Maximum Diversion Time means, for the purposes of ETOPS route planning, the longest diversion time authorized for a flight under the operator's ETOPS authority. It is calculated under standard conditions in still air at a one-engine-inoperative cruise speed.

North Pacific Area of Operation means Pacific Ocean areas north of 40° N latitudes including NOPAC ATS routes, and published PACOTS tracks between Japan and North America.

North Polar Area means the entire area north of 78° N latitude.

One-engine-inoperative-Cruise Speed means a speed within the certified operating limits of the airplane that is specified by the certificate holder and approved by the FAA for —

(1) Calculating required fuel reserves needed to account for an inoperative engine; or

(2) Determining whether an ETOPS alternate is within the maximum diversion time authorized for an ETOPS flight.

South Polar Area means the entire area South of 60° S latitude.

[Doc. No. FAA-2002-6717, 72 FR 1878, Jan. 16, 2007]

§ 121.9 Fraud and falsification.

(a) No person may make, or cause to be made, any of the following:

(1) A fraudulent or intentionally false statement in any application or any amendment thereto, or in any other record or test result required by this part.

(2) A fraudulent or intentionally false statement in, or a known omission from, any record or report that is kept, made, or used to show compliance with this part, or to exercise any privileges under this chapter.

(b) The commission by any person of any act prohibited under paragraph (a) of this section is a basis for any one or any combination of the following:

(1) A civil penalty.

(2) Suspension or revocation of any certificate held by that person that was issued under this chapter.

(3) The denial of an application for any approval under this part.

(4) The removal of any approval under this part.

[Doc. No. FAA-2008-0677, 78 FR 67836, Nov. 12, 2013]

§ 121.11 Rules applicable to operations in a foreign country.

Each certificate holder shall, while operating an airplane within a foreign country, comply with the air traffic rules of the country concerned and the local airport rules, except where any rule of this part is more restrictive and may be followed without violating the rules of that country.

[Doc. No. 16383, 43 FR 22641, May 25, 1978]

§ 121.15 Carriage of narcotic drugs, marihuana, and depressant or stimulant drugs or substances.

If a certificate holder operating under this part permits any aircraft owned or leased by that holder to be engaged in any operation that the certificate holder knows to be in violation of § 91.19(a) of this chapter, that operation is a basis for suspending or revoking the certificate.

[Doc. No. 28154, 60 FR 65926, Dec. 20, 1995]

Subpart B—Certification Rules for Domestic and Flag Air Carriers [Reserved]

Subpart C—Certification Rules for Supplemental Air Carriers and Commercial Operators [Reserved]

Subpart D—Rules Governing All Certificate Holders Under This Part [Reserved]

Subpart E—Approval of Routes: Domestic and Flag Operations

SOURCE: Docket No. 6258, 29 FR 19194, Dec. 31, 1964, unless otherwise noted.

§ 121.91 Applicability.

This subpart prescribes rules for obtaining approval of routes by certificate holders conducting domestic or flag operations.

[Doc. No. 28154, 61 FR 2610, Jan. 26, 1996]

§ 121.93 Route requirements: General.

(a) Each certificate holder conducting domestic or flag operations seeking a route approval must show—

(1) That it is able to conduct satisfactorily scheduled operations between each regular, provisional, and refueling airport over that route or route segment; and

(2) That the facilities and services required by §§ 121.97 through 121.107 are available and adequate for the proposed operation.

The Administrator approves a route outside of controlled airspace if he determines that traffic density is such that an adequate level of safety can be assured.

(b) Paragraph (a) of this section does not require actual flight over a route or route segment if the certificate holder shows that the flight is not essential to safety, considering the availability and adequacy of airports, lighting, maintenance, communication, navigation, fueling, ground, and airplane radio facilities, and the ability of the personnel to be used in the proposed operation.

[Doc. No. 6258, 29 FR 19194, Dec. 31, 1964, as amended by Amdt. 121–3, 30 FR 3638, Mar. 19, 1965; Amdt. 121–253, 61 FR 2610, Jan. 26, 1996]

§ 121.95 Route width.

(a) Approved routes and route segments over U.S. Federal airways or foreign airways (and advisory routes in the case of certificate holders conducting flag operations) have a width equal to the designated width of those airways or routes. Whenever the Administrator finds it necessary to determine the width of other approved routes, he considers the following:

(1) Terrain clearance.

(2) Minimum en route altitudes.

(3) Ground and airborne navigation aids.

(4) Air traffic density.

(5) ATC procedures.

(b) Any route widths of other approved routes determined by the Administrator are specified in the certificate holder's operations specifications.

[Doc. No. 6258, 29 FR 19194, Dec. 31, 1964, as amended by Amdt. 121–253, 61 FR 2610, Jan. 26, 1996]

§ 121.97 Airports: Required data.

(a) Each certificate holder conducting domestic or flag operations must show that each route it submits for approval has enough airports that are properly equipped and adequate for the proposed operation, considering such items as size, surface, obstructions, facilities, public protection, lighting, navigational and communications aids, and ATC.

(b) Each certificate holder conducting domestic or flag operations must show that it has an approved system for obtaining, maintaining, and distributing to appropriate personnel current aeronautical data for each airport it uses to ensure a safe operation at that airport. The aeronautical data must include the following:

(1) Airports.

(i) Facilities.

(ii) Public protection. After February 15, 2008, for ETOPS beyond 180 minutes or operations in the North Polar area and South Polar area, this includes facilities at each airport or in the immediate area sufficient to protect the passengers from the elements and to see to their welfare.

(iii) Navigational and communications aids.

(iv) Construction affecting takeoff, landing, or ground operations.

(v) Air traffic facilities.

(2) Runways, clearways, and stopways.

(i) Dimensions.

(ii) Surface.

(iii) Marking and lighting systems.

(iv) Elevation and gradient.

(3) Displaced thresholds.

(i) Location.

(ii) Dimensions.

(iii) Takeoff or landing or both.

(4) Obstacles.

(i) Those affecting takeoff and landing performance computations in accordance with Subpart I of this part.

(ii) Controlling obstacles.

(5) Instrument flight procedures.

(i) Departure procedure.

(ii) Approach procedure.

(iii) Missed approach procedure.

(6) Special information.

(i) Runway visual range measurement equipment.

(ii) Prevailing winds under low visibility conditions.

(c) If the responsible Flight Standards office charged with the overall inspection of the certificate holder's operations finds that revisions are necessary for the continued adequacy of the certificate holder's system for collection, dissemination, and usage of aeronautical data that has been granted approval, the certificate holder shall, after notification by the responsible Flight Standards office, make those revisions in the system. Within 30 days after the certificate holder receives such notice, the certificate holder may file a petition to reconsider the notice with the Executive Director, Flight Standards Service. This filing of a petition to reconsider stays the notice pending a decision by the Executive Director, Flight Standards Service. However, if the responsible Flight Standards office finds that there is an emergency that requires immediate action in the interest of safety in air transportation, the Executive Director, Flight Standards Service may, upon statement of the reasons, require a change effective without stay.

[Doc. No. 6258, 29 FR 19194, Dec. 31, 1964, as amended by Amdt. 121-162, 45 FR 46738, July 10, 1980; Amdt. 121-207, 54 FR 39293, Sept. 25, 1989; Amdt. 121-253, 61 FR 2610, Jan. 26, 1996; Amdt. 121-329, 72 FR 1878, Jan. 16, 2007; Docket FAA-2018-0119, Amdt. 121-380, 83 FR 9172, 9173, Mar. 5, 2018]

§ 121.99 Communications facilities—domestic and flag operations.

(a) Each certificate holder conducting domestic or flag operations must show that a two-way communication system, or other means of communication approved by the responsible Flight Standards office, is available over the entire route. The communications may be direct links or via an approved communication link that will provide reliable and rapid communications under normal operating conditions between each airplane and the appropriate dispatch office, and between each airplane and the appropriate air traffic control unit.

(b) Except in an emergency, for all flag and domestic kinds of operations, the communications systems between each airplane and the dispatch office must be independent of any system operated by the United States.

(c) Each certificate holder conducting flag operations must provide voice communications for ETOPS where voice communication facilities are available. In determining whether facilities are available, the certificate holder must consider potential routes and altitudes needed for diversion to ETOPS Alternate Airports. Where facilities are not available or are of such poor quality that voice communication is not possible, another communication system must be substituted.

(d) Except as provided in paragraph (e) of this section, after February 15, 2008 for ETOPS beyond 180 minutes, each certificate holder conducting flag operations must have a second communication system in addition to that required by paragraph (c) of this section. That system must be able to provide immediate satellite-based voice communications of landline-telephone fidelity. The system must be able to communicate between the flight crew and air traffic services, and the flight crew and the certificate holder. In determining whether such communications are available, the certificate holder must consider potential routes and altitudes needed for diversion to ETOPS Alternate Airports. Where immediate, satellite-based voice communications are not available, or are of such poor quality that voice communication is not possible, another communication system must be substituted.

(e) Operators of two-engine turbine-powered airplanes with 207 minute ETOPS approval in the North Pacific Area of Operation must comply with the requirements of paragraph (d) of this section as of February 15, 2007.

[Doc. No. 28154, 62 FR 13256, Mar. 19, 1997, as amended by Amdt. 121–329, 72 FR 1878, Jan. 16, 2007; Amdt. 121–333, 72 FR 31680, June 7, 2007; Docket FAA–2018–0119, Amdt. 121–380, 83 FR 9173, Mar. 5, 2018]

§ 121.101   Weather reporting facilities.

(a) Each certificate holder conducting domestic or flag operations must show that enough weather reporting services are available along each route to ensure weather reports and forecasts necessary for the operation.

(b) Except as provided in paragraph (d) of this section, no certificate holder conducting domestic or flag operations may use any weather report to control flight unless—

(1) For operations within the 48 contiguous States and the District of Columbia, it was prepared by the U.S. National Weather Service or a source approved by the U.S. National Weather Service; or

(2) For operations conducted outside the 48 contiguous States and the District of Columbia, it was prepared by a source approved by the Administrator.

(c) Each certificate holder conducting domestic or flag operations that uses forecasts to control flight movements shall use forecasts prepared from weather reports specified in paragraph (b) of this section and from any source approved under its system adopted pursuant to paragraph (d) of this section.

(d) Each certificate holder conducting domestic or flag operations shall adopt and put into use an approved system for obtaining forecasts and reports of adverse weather phenomena, such as clear air turbulence, thunderstorms, and low altitude wind shear, that may affect safety of flight on each route to be flown and at each airport to be used.

[Doc. No. 6258, 29 FR 19194, Dec. 31, 1964, as amended by Amdt. 121–27, 36 FR 13911, July 28, 1971; Amdt. 121–134, 42 FR 27573, May 31, 1977; Amdt. 121–253, 61 FR 2610, Jan. 26, 1996]

§ 121.103   En route navigation facilities.

(a) Except as provided in paragraph (b) of this section, each certificate holder conducting domestic or flag op-

erations must show, for each proposed route (including to any regular, provisional, refueling or alternate airports), that suitable navigation aids are available to navigate the airplane along the route within the degree of accuracy required for ATC. Navigation aids required for approval of routes outside of controlled airspace are listed in the certificate holder's operations specifications except for those aids required for routes to alternate airports.

(b) Navigation aids are not required for any of the following operations—

(1) Day VFR operations that the certificate holder shows can be conducted safely by pilotage because of the characteristics of the terrain;

(2) Night VFR operations on routes that the certificate holder shows have reliably lighted landmarks adequate for safe operation; and

(3) Other operations approved by the responsible Flight Standards office.

[Doc. No. FAA–2002–14002, 72 FR 31681, June 7, 2007, as amended by Docket FAA–2018–0119, Amdt. 121–380, 83 FR 9173, Mar. 5, 2018]

§ 121.105   Servicing and maintenance facilities.

Each certificate holder conducting domestic or flag operations must show that competent personnel and adequate facilities and equipment (including spare parts, supplies, and materials) are available at such points along the certificate holder's route as are necessary for the proper servicing, maintenance, and preventive maintenance of airplanes and auxiliary equipment.

[Doc. No. 28154, 61 FR 2610, Jan. 26, 1996]

§ 121.106   ETOPS Alternate Airport: Rescue and fire fighting service.

(a) Except as provided in paragraph (b) of this section, the following rescue and fire fighting service (RFFS) must be available at each airport listed as an ETOPS Alternate Airport in a dispatch or flight release.

(1) For ETOPS up to 180 minutes, each designated ETOPS Alternate Airport must have RFFS equivalent to that specified by ICAO as Category 4, or higher.

(2) For ETOPS beyond 180 minutes, each designated ETOPS Alternate Airport must have RFFS equivalent to that specified by ICAO Category 4, or

higher. In addition, the aircraft must remain within the ETOPS authorized diversion time from an Adequate Airport that has RFFS equivalent to that specified by ICAO Category 7, or higher.

(b) If the equipment and personnel required in paragraph (a) of this section are not immediately available at an airport, the certificate holder may still list the airport on the dispatch or flight release if the airport's RFFS can be augmented to meet paragraph (a) of this section from local fire fighting assets. A 30-minute response time for augmentation is adequate if the local assets can be notified while the diverting airplane is en route. The augmenting equipment and personnel must be available on arrival of the diverting airplane and must remain as long as the diverting airplane needs RFFS.

[Doc. No. FAA-2002-6717, 72 FR 1879, Jan. 16, 2007]

§121.107 Dispatch centers.

Each certificate holder conducting domestic or flag operations must show that it has enough dispatch centers, adequate for the operations to be conducted, that are located at points necessary to ensure proper operational control of each flight.

[Doc. No. 28154, 61 FR 2610, Jan. 26, 1996]

Subpart F—Approval of Areas and Routes for Supplemental Operations

SOURCE: Docket No. 6258, 29 FR 19195, Dec. 31, 1964, unless otherwise noted.

§121.111 Applicability.

This subpart prescribes rules for obtaining approval of areas and routes by certificate holders conducting supplemental operations.

[Doc. No. 28154, 61 FR 2610, Jan. 26, 1996]

§121.113 Area and route requirements: General.

(a) Each certificate holder conducting supplemental operations seeking route and area approval must show—

(1) That it is able to conduct operations within the United States in accordance with paragraphs (a) (3) and (4) of this section;

(2) That it is able to conduct operations in accordance with the applicable requirements for each area outside the United States for which authorization is requested;

(3) That it is equipped and able to conduct operations over, and use the navigational facilities associated with, the Federal airways, foreign airways, or advisory routes (ADR's) to be used; and

(4) That it will conduct all IFR and night VFR operations over Federal airways, foreign airways, controlled airspace, or advisory routes (ADR's).

(b) Notwithstanding paragraph (a)(4) of this section, the Administrator may approve a route outside of controlled airspace if the certificate holder conducting supplemental operations shows the route is safe for operations and the Administrator finds that traffic density is such that an adequate level of safety can be assured. The certificate holder may not use such a route unless it is approved by the Administrator and is listed in the certificate holder's operations specifications.

[Doc. No. 6258, 29 FR 19195, Dec. 31, 1964, as amended by Amdt. 121-253, 61 FR 2610, Jan. 26, 1996]

§121.115 Route width.

(a) Routes and route segments over Federal airways, foreign airways, or advisory routes have a width equal to the designated width of those airways or advisory routes. Whenever the Administrator finds it necessary to determine the width of other routes, he considers the following:

(1) Terrain clearance.

(2) Minimum en route altitudes.

(3) Ground and airborne navigation aids.

(4) Air traffic density.

(5) ATC procedures.

(b) Any route widths of other routes determined by the Administrator are specified in the certificate holder's operations specifications.

[Doc. No. 6258, 29 FR 19195, Dec. 31, 1964, as amended by Amdt. 121-253, 61 FR 2610, Jan. 26, 1996]

§ 121.117 Airports: Required data.

(a) No certificate holder conducting supplemental operations may use any airport unless it is properly equipped and adequate for the proposed operation, considering such items as size, surface, obstructions, facilities, public protection, lighting, navigational and communications aids, and ATC.

(b) Each certificate holder conducting supplemental operations must show that it has an approved system for obtaining, maintaining, and distributing to appropriate personnel current aeronautical data for each airport it uses to ensure a safe operation at that airport. The aeronautical data must include the following:

(1) Airports.
(i) Facilities.
(ii) Public protection.
(iii) Navigational and communications aids.
(iv) Construction affecting takeoff, landing, or ground operations.
(v) Air traffic facilities.
(2) Runways, clearways, and stopways.
(i) Dimensions.
(ii) Surface.
(iii) Marking and lighting systems.
(iv) Elevation and gradient.
(3) Displaced thresholds.
(i) Location.
(ii) Dimensions.
(iii) Takeoff or landing or both.
(4) Obstacles.
(i) Those affecting takeoff and landing performance computations in accordance with Subpart I of this part.
(ii) Controlling obstacles.
(5) Instrument flight procedures.
(i) Departure procedure.
(ii) Approach procedure.
(iii) Missed approach procedure.
(6) Special information.
(i) Runway visual range measurement equipment.
(ii) Prevailing winds under low visibility conditions.

(c) If the responsible Flight Standards office charged with the overall inspection of the certificate holder's operations finds that revisions are necessary for the continued adequacy of the certificate holder's system for collection, dissemination, and usage of aeronautical data that has been granted approval, the certificate holder shall, after notification by the responsible Flight Standards office, make those revisions in the system. Within 30 days after the certificate holder receives such notice, the certificate holder may file a petition to reconsider the notice with the Executive Director, Flight Standards Service. This filing of a petition to reconsider stays the notice pending a decision by the Director, Flight Standards Service. However, if the responsible Flight Standards office finds that there is an emergency that requires immediate action in the interest of safety in air transportation, the Executive Director, Flight Standards Service may, upon a statement of the reasons, require a change effective without stay.

[Doc. No. 6258, 29 FR 19195, Dec. 31, 1964, as amended by Amdt. 121–162, 45 FR 46738, July 10, 1980; Amdt. 121–207, 54 FR 39293, Sept. 25, 1989; Amdt. 121–253, 61 FR 2610, Jan. 26, 1996; Docket FAA–2018–0119, Amdt. 121–380, 83 FR 9172, 9173, Mar. 5, 2018]

§ 121.119 Weather reporting facilities.

(a) No certificate holder conducting supplemental operations may use any weather report to control flight unless it was prepared and released by the U.S. National Weather Service or a source approved by the Weather Bureau. For operations outside the U.S., or at U.S. Military airports, where those reports are not available, the certificate holder must show that its weather reports are prepared by a source found satisfactory by the Administrator.

(b) Each certificate holder conducting supplemental operations that uses forecasts to control flight movements shall use forecasts prepared from weather reports specified in paragraph (a) of this section.

[Doc. No. 6258, 29 FR 19195, Dec. 31, 1964, as amended by Amdt. 121–76, 36 FR 13911, July 28, 1971; Amdt. 121–253, 61 FR 2611, Jan. 26, 1996]

§ 121.121 En route navigation facilities.

(a) Except as provided in paragraph (b) of this section, no certificate holder conducting supplemental operations may conduct any operation over a route (including to any destination, refueling or alternate airports) unless suitable navigation aids are available to navigate the airplane along the route within the degree of accuracy required for ATC. Navigation aids required for routes outside of controlled airspace are listed in the certificate holder's operations specifications except for those aids required for routes to alternate airports.

(b) Navigation aids are not required for any of the following operations—

(1) Day VFR operations that the certificate holder shows can be conducted safely by pilotage because of the characteristics of the terrain;

(2) Night VFR operations on routes that the certificate holder shows have reliably lighted landmarks adequate for safe operation; and

(3) Other operations approved by the responsible Flight Standards office.

[Doc. No. FAA–2002–14002, 72 FR 31681, June 7, 2007, as amended by Docket FAA–2018–0119, Amdt. 121–380, 83 FR 9173, Mar. 5, 2018]

§121.122 Communications facilities— supplemental operations.

(a) Each certificate holder conducting supplemental operations other than all-cargo operations in an airplane with more than two engines must show that a two-way radio communication system or other means of communication approved by the FAA is available. It must ensure reliable and rapid communications under normal operating conditions over the entire route (either direct or via approved point-to-point circuits) between each airplane and the certificate holder, and between each airplane and the appropriate air traffic services, except as specified in §121.351(c).

(b) Except as provided in paragraph (d) of this section, each certificate holder conducting supplemental operations other than all-cargo operations in an airplane with more than two engines must provide voice communications for ETOPS where voice communication facilities are available. In determining whether facilities are available, the certificate holder must consider potential routes and altitudes needed for diversion to ETOPS Alternate Airports. Where facilities are not available or are of such poor quality that voice communication is not pos-

sible, another communication system must be substituted.

(c) Except as provided in paragraph (d) of this section, for ETOPS beyond 180 minutes each certificate holder conducting supplemental operations other than all-cargo operations in an airplane with more than two engines must have a second communication system in addition to that required by paragraph (b) of this section. That system must be able to provide immediate satellite-based voice communications of landline telephone-fidelity. The system must provide communication capabilities between the flight crew and air traffic services and the flight crew and the certificate holder. In determining whether such communications are available, the certificate holder must consider potential routes and altitudes needed for diversion to ETOPS Alternate Airports. Where immediate satellite-based voice communications are not available, or are of such poor quality that voice communication is not possible, another communication system must be substituted.

(d) Operators of turbine engine powered airplanes do not need to meet the requirements of paragraphs (b) and (c) of this section until February 15, 2008.

[Doc. No. FAA–2002–6717, 72 FR 1879, Jan. 16, 2007]

§121.123 Servicing maintenance facilities.

Each certificate holder conducting supplemental operations must show that competent personnel and adequate facilities and equipment (including spare parts, supplies, and materials) are available for the proper servicing, maintenance, and preventive maintenance of aircraft and auxiliary equipment.

[Doc. No. 28154, 61 FR 2611, Jan. 26, 1996]

§121.125 Flight following system.

(a) Each certificate holder conducting supplemental operations must show that it has—

(1) An approved flight following system established in accordance with subpart U of this part and adequate for the proper monitoring of each flight, considering the operations to be conducted; and

77

(2) Flight following centers located at those points necessary—

(i) To ensure the proper monitoring of the progress of each flight with respect to its departure at the point of origin and arrival at its destination, including intermediate stops and diversions therefrom, and maintenance or mechanical delays encountered at those points or stops; and

(ii) To ensure that the pilot in command is provided with all information necessary for the safety of the flight.

(b) A certificate holder conducting supplemental operations may arrange to have flight following facilities provided by persons other than its employees, but in such a case the certificate holder continues to be primarily responsible for operational control of each flight.

(c) A flight following system need not provide for in-flight monitoring by a flight following center.

(d) The certificate holder's operations specifications specify the flight following system it is authorized to use and the location of the centers.

[Doc. No. 6258, 29 FR 19195, Dec. 31, 1964, as amended by Amdt. 121-253, 61 FR 2611, Jan. 26, 1996]

§ 121.127 Flight following system; requirements.

(a) Each certificate holder conducting supplemental operations using a flight following system must show that—

(1) The system has adequate facilities and personnel to provide the information necessary for the initiation and safe conduct of each flight to—

(i) The flight crew of each aircraft; and

(ii) The persons designated by the certificate holder to perform the function of operational control of the aircraft; and

(2) The system has a means of communication by private or available public facilities (such as telephone, telegraph, or radio) to monitor the progress of each flight with respect to its departure at the point of origin and arrival at its destination, including intermediate stops and diversions therefrom, and maintenance or mechanical delays encountered at those points or stops.

(b) The certificate holder conducting supplemental operations must show that the personnel specified in paragraph (a) of this section, and those in paragraph (a) of this section designates to perform the function of operational control of the aircraft, are able to perform their required duties.

[Doc. No. 6258, 29 FR 19195, Dec. 31, 1964, as amended by Amdt. 121-253, 61 FR 2611, Jan. 26, 1996]

Subpart G—Manual Requirements

§ 121.131 Applicability.

This subpart prescribes requirements for preparing and maintaining manuals by all certificate holders.

[Doc. No. 6258, 29 FR 19196, Dec. 31, 1964]

§ 121.133 Preparation.

(a) Each certificate holder shall prepare and keep current a manual for the use and guidance of flight, ground operations, and management personnel in conducting its operations.

(b) For the purpose of this subpart, the certificate holder may prepare that part of the manual containing maintenance information and instructions, in whole or in part, in printed form or other form acceptable to the Administrator.

[Doc. No. 28154, 60 FR 65926, Dec. 20, 1995]

§ 121.135 Manual contents.

(a) Each manual required by § 121.133 must—

(1) Include instructions and information necessary to allow the personnel concerned to perform their duties and responsibilities with a high degree of safety;

(2) Be in a form that is easy to revise;

(3) Have the date of last revision on each page concerned; and

(4) Not be contrary to any applicable Federal regulation and, in the case of a flag or supplemental operation, any applicable foreign regulation, or the certificate holder's operations specifications or operating certificate.

(b) The manual may be in two or more separate parts, containing together all of the following information, but each part must contain that part of the information that is appropriate for each group of personnel:

(1) General policies.

(2) Duties and responsibilities of each crewmember, appropriate members of the ground organization, and management personnel.

(3) Reference to appropriate Federal Aviation Regulations.

(4) Flight dispatching and operational control, including procedures for coordinated dispatch or flight control or flight following procedures as applicable.

(5) En route flight, navigation, and communication procedures, including procedures for the dispatch or release or continuance of flight if any item of equipment required for the particular type of operation becomes inoperative or unserviceable en route.

(6) For domestic or flag operations, appropriate information from the en route operations specifications, including for each approved route the types of airplanes authorized, the type of operation such as VFR, IFR, day, night, etc., and any other pertinent information.

(7) For supplemental operations, appropriate information from the operations specifications, including the area of operations authorized, the types of airplanes authorized, the type of operation such as VFR, IFR, day, night, etc., and any other pertinent information.

(8) Appropriate information from the airport operations specifications, including for each airport—

(i) Its location (domestic and flag operations only);

(ii) Its designation (regular, alternate, provisional, etc.) (domestic and flag operations only);

(iii) The types of airplanes authorized (domestic and flag operations only);

(iv) Instrument approach procedures;

(v) Landing and takeoff minimums; and

(vi) Any other pertinent information.

(9) Takeoff, en route, and landing weight limitations.

(10) For ETOPS, airplane performance data to support all phases of these operations.

(11) Procedures for familiarizing passengers with the use of emergency equipment, during flight.

(12) Emergency equipment and procedures.

(13) The method of designating succession of command of flight crewmembers.

(14) Procedures for determining the usability of landing and takeoff areas, and for disseminating pertinent information thereon to operations personnel.

(15) Procedures for operating in periods of ice, hail, thunderstorms, turbulence, or any potentially hazardous meteorological condition.

(16) Each training program curriculum required by § 121.403.

(17) Instructions and procedures for maintenance, preventive maintenance, and servicing.

(18) Time limitations, or standards for determining time limitations, for overhauls, inspections, and checks of airframes, engines, propellers, appliances and emergency equipment.

(19) Procedures for refueling aircraft, eliminating fuel contamination, protection from fire (including electrostatic protection), and supervising and protecting passengers during refueling.

(20) Airworthiness inspections, including instructions covering procedures, standards, responsibilities, and authority of inspection personnel.

(21) Methods and procedures for maintaining the aircraft weight and center of gravity within approved limits.

(22) Where applicable, pilot and dispatcher route and airport qualification procedures.

(23) Accident notification procedures.

(24) After February 15, 2008, for passenger flag operations and for those supplemental operations that are not all-cargo operations outside the 48 contiguous States and Alaska,

(i) For ETOPS greater than 180 minutes a specific passenger recovery plan for each ETOPS Alternate Airport used in those operations, and

(ii) For operations in the North Polar Area and South Polar Area a specific passenger recovery plan for each diversion airport used in those operations.

(25)(i) Procedures and information, as described in paragraph (b)(25)(ii) of this section, to assist each crewmember and person performing or directly supervising the following job functions involving items for transport on an aircraft:

(A) Acceptance;

(B) Rejection;

(C) Handling;

(D) Storage incidental to transport;

(E) Packaging of company material; or

(F) Loading.

(ii) Ensure that the procedures and information described in this paragraph are sufficient to assist the person in identifying packages that are marked or labeled as containing hazardous materials or that show signs of containing undeclared hazardous materials. The procedures and information must include:

(A) Procedures for rejecting packages that do not conform to the Hazardous Materials Regulations in 49 CFR parts 171 through 180 or that appear to contain undeclared hazardous materials;

(B) Procedures for complying with the hazardous materials incident reporting requirements of 49 CFR 171.15 and 171.16 and discrepancy reporting requirements of 49 CFR 175.31

(C) The certificate holder's hazmat policies and whether the certificate holder is authorized to carry, or is prohibited from carrying, hazardous materials; and

(D) If the certificate holder's operations specifications permit the transport of hazardous materials, procedures and information to ensure the following:

(1) That packages containing hazardous materials are properly offered and accepted in compliance with 49 CFR parts 171 through 180;

(2) That packages containing hazardous materials are properly handled, stored, packaged, loaded, and carried on board an aircraft in compliance with 49 CFR parts 171 through 180;

(3) That the requirements for Notice to the Pilot in Command (49 CFR 175.33) are complied with; and

(4) That aircraft replacement parts, consumable materials or other items regulated by 49 CFR parts 171 through 180 are properly handled, packaged, and transported.

(26) Other information or instructions relating to safety.

(c) Each certificate holder shall maintain at least one complete copy of

the manual at its principal base of operations.

[Doc. No. 6258, 29 FR 19196, Dec. 31, 1964, as amended by Amdt. 121-104, 38 FR 14915, June 7, 1973; Amdt. 121-106, 38 FR 22377, Aug. 20, 1973; Amdt. 121-143, 43 FR 22641, May 25, 1978; Amdt. 121-162, 45 FR 46739, July 10, 1980; Amdt. 121-251, 60 FR 65926, Dec. 20, 1995; Amdt. 121-250, 60 FR 65948, Dec. 20, 1995; Amdt. 121-316, 70 FR 58823, Oct. 7, 2005; Amdt. 121-329, 72 FR 1879, Jan. 16, 2007]

§ 121.137   Distribution and availability.

(a) Each certificate holder shall furnish copies of the manual required by § 121.133 (and the changes and additions thereto) or appropriate parts of the manual to—

(1) Its appropriate ground operations and maintenance personnel;

(2) Crewmembers; and

(3) Representatives of the Administrator assigned to it.

(b) Each person to whom a manual or appropriate parts of it are furnished under paragraph (a) of this section shall keep it up-to-date with the changes and additions furnished to that person and shall have the manual or appropriate parts of it accessible when performing assigned duties.

(c) For the purpose of complying with paragraph (a) of this section, a certificate holder may furnish the persons listed therein the maintenance part of the manual in printed form or other form, acceptable to the Administrator, that is retrievable in the English language.

[Doc. No. 6258, 29 FR 19196, Dec. 31, 1964, as amended by Amdt. 121-71, 35 FR 17176, Nov. 7, 1970; Amdt. 121-162, 45 FR 46739, July 10, 1980; Amdt. 121-262, 62 FR 13256, Mar. 19, 1997]

§ 121.139   Requirements for manual aboard aircraft: Supplemental operations.

(a) Except is provided in paragraph (b) of this section, each certificate holder conducting supplemental operations shall carry appropriate parts of the manual on each airplane when away from the principal base of operations. The appropriate parts must be available for use by ground or flight personnel. If the certificate holder carries aboard an airplane all or any portion of the maintenance part of its manual in other than printed form, it must carry a compatible reading device that produces a legible image of the maintenance information and instructions or a system that is able to retrieve the maintenance information and instructions in the English language.

(b) If a certificate holder conducting supplemental operations is able to perform all scheduled maintenance at specified stations where it keeps maintenance parts of the manual, it does not have to carry those parts of the manual aboard the aircraft en route to those stations.

[Doc. No. 6258, 29 FR 19196, Dec. 31, 1964, as amended by Amdt. 12–71, 35 FR 17176, Nov. 7, 1970; Amdt. 121–253, 61 FR 2611, Jan. 26, 1996; Amdt. 121–262, 62 FR 13256, Mar. 19, 1997; 62 FR 15570, Apr. 1, 1997]

§121.141 Airplane flight manual.

(a) Each certificate holder shall keep a current approved airplane flight manual for each type of airplane that it operates except for nontransport category airplanes certificated before January 1, 1965.

(b) In each airplane required to have an airplane flight manual in paragraph (a) of this section, the certificate holder shall carry either the manual required by §121.133, if it contains the information required for the applicable flight manual and this information is clearly identified as flight manual requirements, or an approved Airplane Manual. If the certificate holder elects to carry the manual required by §121.133, the certificate holder may revise the operating procedures sections and modify the presentation of performance data from the applicable flight manual if the revised operating procedures and modified performance date presentation are—

(1) Approved by the Administrator; and

(2) Clearly identified as airplane flight manual requirements.

[Doc. No. 28154, 60 FR 65927, Dec. 20, 1995]

Subpart H—Aircraft Requirements

SOURCE: Docket No. 6258, 29 FR 19197, Dec. 31, 1964, unless otherwise noted.

§121.151 Applicability.

This subpart prescribes aircraft requirements for all certificate holders.

§121.153 Aircraft requirements: General.

(a) Except as provided in paragraph (c) of this section, no certificate holder may operate an aircraft unless that aircraft—

(1) Is registered as a civil aircraft of the United States and carries an appropriate current airworthiness certificate issued under this chapter; and

(2) Is in an airworthy condition and meets the applicable airworthiness requirements of this chapter, including those relating to identification and equipment.

(b) A certificate holder may use an approved weight and balance control system based on average, assumed, or estimated weight to comply with applicable airworthiness requirements and operating limitations.

(c) A certificate holder may operate in common carriage, and for the carriage of mail, a civil aircraft which is leased or chartered to it without crew and is registered in a country which is a party to the Convention on International Civil Aviation if—

(1) The aircraft carries an appropriate airworthiness certificate issued by the country of registration and meets the registration and identification requirements of that country;

(2) The aircraft is of a type design which is approved under a U.S. type certificate and complies with all of the requirements of this chapter (14 CFR Chapter 1) that would be applicable to that aircraft were it registered in the United States, including the requirements which must be met for issuance of a U.S. standard airworthiness certificate (including type design conformity, condition for safe operation, and the noise, fuel venting, and engine emission requirements of this chapter), except that a U.S. registration certificate and a U.S. standard airworthiness certificate will not be issued for the aircraft;

(3) The aircraft is operated by U.S.-certificated airmen employed by the certificate holder; and

(4) The certificate holder files a copy of the aircraft lease or charter agreement with the FAA Aircraft Registry, Department of Transportation, 6400 South MacArthur Boulevard, Oklahoma City, OK (Mailing address: P.O. Box 25504, Oklahoma City, OK 73125).

[Doc. No. 6258, 29 FR 19197, Dec. 31, 1964, as amended by Amdt. 121–165, 45 FR 68649, Oct. 16, 1980]

§ 121.155 [Reserved]

§ 121.157 Aircraft certification and equipment requirements.

(a) *Airplanes certificated before July 1, 1942.* No certificate holder may operate an airplane that was type certificated before July 1, 1942, unless—

(1) That airplane meets the requirements of § 121.173(c), or

(2) That airplane and all other airplanes of the same or related type operated by that certificate holder meet the performance requirements of sections 4a.737–T through 4a.750–T of the Civil Air Regulations as in effect on January 31, 1965; or §§ 25.45 through 25.75 and § 121.173(a), (b), (d), and (e) of this title.

(b) *Airplanes certificated after June 30, 1942.* Except as provided in paragraphs (c), (d), (e), and (f) of this section, no certificate holder may operate an airplane that was type certificated after June 30, 1942, unless it is certificated as a transport category airplane and meets the requirements of § 121.173(a), (b), (d), and (e).

(c) *C–46 type airplanes: passenger-carrying operations.* No certificate holder may operate a C–46 airplane in passenger-carrying operations unless that airplane is operated in accordance with the operating limitations for transport category airplanes and meets the requirements of paragraph (b) of this section or meets the requirements of part 4b, as in effect July 20, 1950, and the requirements of § 121.173 (a), (b), (d) and (e), except that—

(1) The requirements of sections 4b.0 through 4b.19 as in effect May 18, 1954, must be complied with;

(2) The birdproof windshield requirements of section 4b.352 need not be complied with;

(3) The provisions of sections 4b.480 through 4b.490 (except sections 4b.484(a)(1) and 4b.487(e)), as in effect May 16, 1953, must be complied with; and

(4) The provisions of paragraph 4b.484(a)(1), as in effect July 20, 1950, must be complied with.

In determining the takeoff path in accordance with section 4b.116 and the one-engine inoperative climb in accordance with section 4b.120 (a) and (b), the propeller of the inoperative engine may be assumed to be feathered if the airplane is equipped with either an approved means for automatically indicating when the particular engine has failed or an approved means for automatically feathering the propeller of the inoperative engine. The Administrator may authorize deviations from compliance with the requirements of sections 4b.130 through 4b.190 and subparts C, D, E, and F of part 4b (as designated in this paragraph) if he finds that (considering the effect of design changes) compliance is extremely difficult to accomplish and that service experience with the C–46 airplane justifies the deviation.

(d) *C–46 type airplanes: cargo operations.* No certificate holder may use a nontransport category C–46 type airplane in cargo operations unless—

(1) It is certificated at a maximum gross weight that is not greater than 48,000 pounds;

(2) It meets the requirements of §§ 121.199 through 121.205 using the performance data in appendix C to this part;

(3) Before each flight, each engine contains at least 25 gallons of oil; and

(4) After December 31, 1964—

(i) It is powered by a type and model engine as set forth in appendix C of this part, when certificated at a maximum gross takeoff weight greater than 45,000 pounds; and

(ii) It complies with the special airworthiness requirement set forth in §§ 121.213 through 121.287 of this part or in appendix C of this part.

(e) *Commuter category airplanes.* Except as provided in paragraph (f) of this section, no certificate holder may operate under this part a nontransport category airplane type certificated after December 31, 1964, and before March 30, 1995, unless it meets the applicable requirements of § 121.173 (a), (b), (d), and (e), and was type certificated in the commuter category.

(f) *Other nontransport category airplanes.* No certificate holder may operate under this part a nontransport category airplane type certificated after December 31, 1964, unless it meets the applicable requirements of §121.173 (a), (b), (d), and (e), was manufactured before March 20, 1997, and meets one of the following:

(1) Until December 20, 2010:

(i) The airplane was type certificated in the normal category before July 1, 1970, and meets special conditions issued by the Administrator for airplanes intended for use in operations under part 135 of this chapter.

(ii) The airplane was type certificated in the normal category before July 19, 1970, and meets the additional airworthiness standards in SFAR No. 23, 14 CFR part 23.

(iii) The airplane was type certificated in the normal category and meets the additional airworthiness standards in appendix A of part 135 of this chapter.

(iv) The airplane was type certificated in the normal category and complies with either section L.(a) or 1.(b) of SFAR No. 41 of 14 CFR part 21.

(2) The airplane was type certificated in the normal category, meets the additional requirements described in paragraphs (f)(1)(i) through (f)(1)(iv) of this section, and meets the performance requirements in appendix K of this part.

(g) *Certain newly manufactured airplanes.* No certificate holder may operate an airplane under this part that was type certificated as described in paragraphs (f)(1)(i) through (f)(1)(iv) of this section and that was manufactured after March 20, 1997, unless it meets the performance requirements in appendix K of this part.

(h) *Newly type certificated airplanes.* No person may operate under this part an airplane for which the application for a type certificate is submitted after March 29, 1995, unless the airplane is type certificated under part 25 of this chapter.

[Doc. No. 6258, 29 FR 19197, Dec. 31, 1964, as amended by Amdt. 121–251, 60 FR 65927. Dec. 20, 1995; Amdt. 121–256, 61 FR 30434, June 14, 1996]

§121.159 Single-engine airplanes prohibited.

No certificate holder may operate a single-engine airplane under this part.

[Doc. No. 28154, 60 FR 65927, Dec. 20, 1995]

§121.161 Airplane limitations: Type of route.

(a) Except as provided in paragraph (e) of this section, unless approved by the Administrator in accordance with Appendix P of this part and authorized in the certificate holder's operations specifications, no certificate holder may operate a turbine-engine-powered airplane over a route that contains a point—

(1) Farther than a flying time from an Adequate Airport (at a one-engine-inoperative cruise speed under standard conditions in still air) of 60 minutes for a two-engine airplane or 180 minutes for a passenger-carrying airplane with more than two engines;

(2) Within the North Polar Area; or

(3) Within the South Polar Area.

(b) Except as provided in paragraph (c) of this section, no certificate holder may operate a land airplane (other than a DC–3, C–46, CV–240, CV–340, CV–440, CV–580, CV–600, CV–640, or Martin 404) in an extended overwater operation unless it is certificated or approved as adequate for ditching under the ditching provisions of part 25 of this chapter.

(c) Until December 20, 2010, a certificate holder may operate, in an extended overwater operation, a nontransport category land airplane type certificated after December 31, 1964, that was not certificated or approved as adequate for ditching under the ditching provisions of part 25 of this chapter.

(d) Unless authorized by the Administrator based on the character of the terrain, the kind of operation, or the performance of the airplane to be used, no certificate holder may operate a reciprocating-engine-powered airplane over a route that contains a point farther than 60 minutes flying time (at a one-engine-inoperative cruise speed under standard conditions in still air) from an Adequate Airport.

(e) Operators of turbine-engine powered airplanes with more than two engines do not need to meet the requirements of paragraph (a)(1) of this section until February 15, 2008.

[Doc. No. 7329, 31 FR 13078, Oct. 8, 1966, as amended by Amdt. 121–162, 45 FR 46739, July 10, 1980; Amdt. 121–251, 60 FR 65927, Dec. 20, 1995; Amdt. 121–329, 72 FR 1879, Jan. 16, 2007]

§ 121.162 ETOPS Type Design Approval Basis.

Except for a passenger-carrying airplane with more than two engines manufactured prior to February 17, 2015 and except for a two-engine airplane that, when used in ETOPS, is only used for ETOPS of 75 minutes or less, no certificate holder may conduct ETOPS unless the airplane has been type design approved for ETOPS and each airplane used in ETOPS complies with its CMP document as follows:

(a) For a two-engine airplane, that is of the same model airplane-engine combination that received FAA approval for ETOPS up to 180 minutes prior to February 15, 2007, the CMP document for that model airplane-engine combination in effect on February 14, 2007.

(b) For a two-engine airplane, that is not of the same model airplane-engine combination that received FAA approval for ETOPS up to 180 minutes before February 15, 2007, the CMP document for that new model airplane-engine combination issued in accordance with § 25.3(b)(1) of this chapter.

(c) For a two-engine airplane approved for ETOPS beyond 180 minutes, the CMP document for that model airplane-engine combination issued in accordance with § 25.3(b)(2) of this chapter.

(d) For an airplane with more than 2 engines manufactured on or after February 17, 2015, the CMP document for that model airplane-engine combination issued in accordance with § 25.3(c) of this chapter.

[Doc. No. FAA–2002–6717, 72 FR 1879, Jan. 16, 2007]

§ 121.163 Aircraft proving tests.

(a) *Initial airplane proving tests.* No person may operate an airplane not before proven for use in a kind of operation under this part or part 135 of this chapter unless an airplane of that type has had, in addition to the airplane certification tests, at least 100 hours of proving tests acceptable to the Administrator, including a representative number of flights into en route airports. The requirement for at least 100 hours of proving tests may be reduced by the Administrator if the Administrator determines that a satisfactory level of proficiency has been demonstrated to justify the reduction. At least 10 hours of proving flights must be flown at night; these tests are irreducible.

(b) *Proving tests for kinds of operations.* Unless otherwise authorized by the Administrator, for each type of airplane, a certificate holder must conduct at least 50 hours of proving tests acceptable to the Administrator for each kind of operation it intends to conduct, including a representative number of flights into en route airports.

(c) *Proving tests for materially altered airplanes.* Unless otherwise authorized by the Administrator, for each type of airplane that is materially altered in design, a certificate holder must conduct at least 50 hours of proving tests acceptable to the Administrator for each kind of operation it intends to conduct with that airplane, including a representative number of flights into en route airports.

(d) *Definition of materially altered.* For the purposes of paragraph (c) of this section, a type of airplane is considered to be materially altered in design if the alteration includes—

(1) The installation of powerplants other than those of a type similar to those with which it is certificated; or

(2) Alterations to the aircraft or its components that materially affect flight characteristics.

(e) No certificate holder may carry passengers in an aircraft during proving tests, except for those needed to make the test and those designated by the Administrator. However, it may carry mail, express, or other cargo, when approved.

[Doc. No. 6258, 29 FR 19197, Dec. 31, 1964, as amended by Amdt. 121–42, 33 FR 10330, July 19, 1968; 34 FR 13468, Aug. 21, 1969; Amdt. 121–162, 45 FR 46739, July 10, 1980; Amdt. 121–251, 60 FR 65927, Dec. 20, 1995]

Subpart I—Airplane Performance Operating Limitations

SOURCE: Docket No. 6258, 29 FR 19198, Dec. 31, 1964; 30 FR 130, Jan. 7, 1965, unless otherwise noted.

EDITORIAL NOTE: Nomenclature changes to subpart I of part 121 appear at 60 FR 65928, Dec. 20, 1995.

§121.171 Applicability.

(a) This subpart prescribes airplane performance operating limitations for all certificate holders.

(b) For purposes of this part, *effective length of the runway* for landing means the distance from the point at which the obstruction clearance plane associated with the approach end of the runway intersects the centerline of the runway to the far end thereof.

(c) For the purposes of this subpart, *obstruction clearance plane* means a plane sloping upward from the runway at a slope of 1:20 to the horizontal, and tangent to or clearing all obstructions within a specified area surrounding the runway as shown in a profile view of that area. In the plan view, the centerline of the specified area coincides with the centerline of the runway, beginning at the point where the obstruction clearance plane intersects the centerline of the runway and proceeding to a point at least 1,500 feet from the beginning point. Thereafter the centerline coincides with the takeoff path over the ground for the runway (in the case of takeoffs) or with the instrument approach counterpart (for landings), or, where the applicable one of these paths has not been established, it proceeds consistent with turns of at least 4,000 foot radius until a point is reached beyond which the obstruction clearance plane clears all obstructions. This area extends laterally 200 feet on each side of the centerline at the point where the obstruction clearance plane intersects the runway and continues at this width to the end of the runway; then it increases uniformly to 500 feet on each side of the centerline at a point 1,500 feet from the intersection of the obstruction clearance plane with the run-

way; thereafter it extends laterally 500 feet on each side of the centerline.

[Doc. No. 6258, 29 FR 19198, Dec. 31, 1964, as amended by Amdt. 121–132, 41 FR 55475, Dec. 20, 1976]

§121.173 General.

(a) Except as provided in paragraph (c) of this section, each certificate holder operating a reciprocating-engine-powered airplane shall comply with §§121.175 through 121.187.

(b) Except as provided in paragraph (c) of this section, each certificate holder operating a turbine-engine-powered airplane shall comply with the applicable provisions of §§121.189 through 121.197, except that when it operates—

(1) A turbo-propeller-powered airplane type certificated after August 29, 1959, but previously type certificated with the same number of reciprocating engines, the certificate holder may comply with §§121.175 through 121.187; or

(2) Until December 20, 2010, a turbo-propeller-powered airplane described in §121.157(f), the certificate holder may comply with the applicable performance requirements of appendix K of this part.

(c) Each certificate holder operating a large nontransport category airplane type certificated before January 1, 1965, shall comply with §§121.199 through 121.205 and any determination of compliance must be based only on approved performance data.

(d) The performance data in the Airplane Flight Manual applies in determining compliance with §§121.175 through 121.197. Where conditions are different from those on which the performance data is based, compliance is determined by interpolation or by computing the effects of changes in the specific variables if the results of the interpolation or computations are substantially as accurate as the results of direct tests.

(e) Except as provided in paragraph (c) of this section, no person may take off a reciprocating-engine-powered airplane at a weight that is more than the allowable weight for the runway being used (determined under the runway takeoff limitations of the operating rules of 14 CFR part 121, subpart I) after taking into account the temperature operating correction factors in the applicable Airplane Flight Manual.

(f) The Administrator may authorize in the operations specifications deviations from the requirements in the subpart if special circumstances make a literal observance of a requirement unnecessary for safety.

(g) The ten-mile width specified in §§ 121.179 through 121.183 may be reduced to five miles, for not more than 20 miles, when operating VFR or where navigation facilities furnish reliable and accurate identification of high ground and obstructions located outside of five miles, but within ten miles, on each side of the intended track.

[Doc. No. 6258, 29 FR 19198, Dec. 31, 1964, as amended by Amdt. 121–251, 60 FR 65928, Dec. 20, 1995]

§ 121.175 Airplanes: Reciprocating engine-powered: Weight limitations.

(a) No person may take off a reciprocating engine powered airplane from an airport located at an elevation outside of the range for which maximum takeoff weights have been determined for that airplane.

(b) No person may take off a reciprocating engine powered airplane for an airport of intended destination that is located at an elevation outside of the range for which maximum landing weights have been determined for that airplane.

(c) No person may specify, or have specified, an alternate airport that is located at an elevation outside of the range for which maximum landing weights have been determined for the reciprocating engine powered airplane concerned.

(d) No person may take off a reciprocating engine powered airplane at a weight more than the maximum authorized takeoff weight for the elevation of the airport.

(e) No person may take off a reciprocating engine powered airplane if its weight on arrival at the airport of destination will be more than the maximum authorized landing weight for the elevation of that airport, allowing for normal consumption of fuel and oil en route.

(f) This section does not apply to large nontransport category airplanes operated under § 121.173(c).

[Doc. No. 6258, 29 FR 19198, Dec. 31, 1964, as amended by Amdt. 121–251, 60 FR 65928, Dec. 20, 1995]

§ 121.177 Airplanes: Reciprocating engine-powered: Takeoff limitations.

(a) No person operating a reciprocating engine powered airplane may takeoff that airplane unless it is possible—

(1) To stop the airplane safely on the runway, as shown by the accelerate stop distance data, at any time during takeoff until reaching critical-engine failure speed;

(2) If the critical engine fails at any time after the airplane reaches critical-engine failure speed V_1, to continue the takeoff and reach a height of 50 feet, as indicated by the takeoff path data, before passing over the end of the runway; and

(3) To clear all obstacles either by at least 50 feet vertically (as shown by the takeoff path data) or 200 feet horizontally within the airport boundaries and 300 feet horizontally beyond the boundaries, without banking before reaching a height of 50 feet (as shown by the takeoff path data) and thereafter without banking more than 15 degrees.

(b) In applying this section, corrections must be made for the effective runway gradient. To allow for wind effect, takeoff data based on still air may be corrected by taking into account not more than 50 percent of any reported headwind component and not less than 150 percent of any reported tailwind component.

(c) This section does not apply to large nontransport category airplanes operated under § 121.173(c).

[Doc. No. 6258, 29 FR 19198, Dec. 31, 1964, as amended by Amdt. 121–159, 45 FR 41593, June 19, 1980; Amdt. 121–251, 60 FR 65928, Dec. 20, 1995]

§ 121.179 Airplanes: Reciprocating engine-powered: En route limitations: All engines operating.

(a) No person operating a reciprocating engine powered airplane may take off that airplane at a weight, allowing for normal consumption of fuel and oil, that does not allow a rate of climb (in feet per minute), with all engines operating, of at least 6.90 V_{So} (that is, the number of feet per minute is obtained by multiplying the number of knots by 6.90) at an altitude of at least 1,000 feet above the highest ground or obstruction within ten miles of each side of the intended track.

(b) This section does not apply to airplanes certificated under part 4a of the Civil Air Regulations.

(c) This section does not apply to large nontransport category airplanes operated under §121.173(c).

[Doc. No. 6258, 29 FR 19198, Dec. 31, 1964, as amended by Amdt. 121–251, 60 FR 65928, Dec. 20, 1995]

§121.181 Airplanes: Reciprocating engine-powered: En route limitations: One engine inoperative.

(a) Except as provided in paragraph (b) of this section, no person operating a reciprocating engine powered airplane may take off that airplane at a weight, allowing for normal consumption of fuel and oil, that does not allow a rate of climb (in feet per minute), with one engine inoperative, of at least

$(0.079–0.106/N)\ V_{so}2$

(where N is the number of engines installed and V_{So} is expressed in knots) at an altitude of at least 1,000 feet above the highest ground or obstruction within 10 miles of each side of the intended track. However, for the purposes of this paragraph the rate of climb for airplanes certificated under part 4a of the Civil Air Regulations is 0.026 $V_{so}2$.

(b) In place of the requirements of paragraph (a) of this section, a person may, under an approved procedure, operate a reciprocating engine powered airplane, at an all-engines-operating altitude that allows the airplane to continue, after an engine failure, to an alternate airport where a landing can be made in accordance with §121.187, allowing for normal consumption of fuel and oil. After the assumed failure, the flight path must clear the ground and any obstruction within five miles on each side of the intended track by at least 2,000 feet.

(c) If an approved procedure under paragraph (b) of this section is used,

the certificate holder shall comply with the following:

(1) The rate of climb (as prescribed in the Airplane Flight Manual for the appropriate weight and altitude) used in calculating the airplane's flight path shall be diminished by an amount, in feet per minute, equal to

$(0.079–0.106/N)\ V_{so}2$

(when N is the number of engines installed and V_{So} is expressed in knots) for airplanes certificated under part 25 of this chapter and by 0.026 $V_{so}2$ for airplanes certificated under part 4a of the Civil Air Regulations.

(2) The all-engines-operating altitude shall be sufficient so that in the event the critical engine becomes inoperative at any point along the route, the flight will be able to proceed to a predetermined alternate airport by use of this procedure. In determining the takeoff weight, the airplane is assumed to pass over the critical obstruction following engine failure at a point no closer to the critical obstruction than the nearest approved radio navigational fix, unless the Administrator approves a procedure established on a different basis upon finding that adequate operational safeguards exist.

(3) The airplane must meet the provisions of paragraph (a) of this section at 1,000 feet above the airport used as an alternate in this procedure.

(4) The procedure must include an approved method of accounting for winds and temperatures that would otherwise adversely affect the flight path.

(5) In complying with this procedure fuel jettisoning is allowed if the certificate holder shows that it has an adequate training program, that proper instructions are given to the flight crew, and all other precautions are taken to insure a safe procedure.

(6) The certificate holder shall specify in the dispatch or flight release an alternate airport that meets the requirements of §121.625.

(d) This section does not apply to large nontransport category airplanes operated under §121.173(c).

[Doc. No. 6258, 29 FR 19198, Dec. 31, 1964; 30 FR 130, Jan. 7, 1965, as amended by Amdt. 121–251, 60 FR 65928, Dec. 20, 1995]

§ 121.183 Part 25 airplanes with four or more engines: Reciprocating engine powered: En route limitations: Two engines inoperative.

(a) No person may operate an airplane certificated under part 25 and having four or more engines unless—

(1) There is no place along the intended track that is more than 90 minutes (with all engines operating at cruising power) from an airport that meets the requirements of § 121.187; or

(2) It is operated at a weight allowing the airplane, with the two critical engines inoperative, to climb at 0.013 $V_{so}2$ feet per minute (that is, the number of feet per minute is obtained by multiplying the number of knots squared by 0.013) at an altitude of 1,000 feet above the highest ground or obstruction within 10 miles on each side of the intended track, or at an altitude of 5,000 feet, whichever is higher.

(b) For the purposes of paragraph (a)(2) of this section, it is assumed that—

(1) The two engines fail at the point that is most critical with respect to the takeoff weight:

(2) Consumption of fuel and oil is normal with all engines operating up to the point where the two engines fail and with two engines operating beyond that point;

(3) Where the engines are assumed to fail at an altitude above the prescribed minimum altitude, compliance with the prescribed rate of climb at the prescribed minimum altitude need not be shown during the descent from the cruising altitude to the prescribed minimum altitude, if those requirements can be met once the prescribed minimum altitude is reached, and assuming descent to be along a net flight path and the rate of descent to be 0.013 $V_{so}2$ greater than the rate in the approved performance data; and

(4) If fuel jettisoning is provided, the airplane's weight at the point where the two engines fail is considered to be not less than that which would include enough fuel to proceed to an airport meeting the requirements of § 121.187 and to arrive at an altitude of at least 1,000 feet directly over that airport.

[Doc. No. 6258, 29 FR 19198, Dec. 31, 1964; 30 FR 130, Jan. 7, 1965, as amended by Amdt. 121–251, 60 FR 65928, Dec. 20, 1995]

§ 121.185 Airplanes: Reciprocating engine-powered: Landing limitations: Destination airport.

(a) Except as provided in paragraph (b) of this section no person operating a reciprocating engine powered airplane may take off that airplane, unless its weight on arrival, allowing for normal consumption of fuel and oil in flight, would allow a full stop landing at the intended destination within 60 percent of the effective length of each runway described below from a point 50 feet directly above the intersection of the obstruction clearance plane and the runway. For the purposes of determining the allowable landing weight at the destination airport the following is assumed:

(1) The airplane is landed on the most favorable runway and in the most favorable direction in still air.

(2) The airplane is landed on the most suitable runway considering the probable wind velocity and direction (forecast for the expected time of arrival), the ground handling characteristics of the type of airplane, and other conditions such as landing aids and terrain, and allowing for the effect of the landing path and roll of not more than 50 percent of the headwind component or not less than 150 percent of the tailwind component.

(b) An airplane that would be prohibited from being taken off because it could not meet the requirements of paragraph (a)(2) of this section may be taken off if an alternate airport is specified that meets all of the requirements of this section except that the airplane can accomplish a full stop landing within 70 percent of the effective length of the runway.

(c) This section does not apply to large nontransport category airplanes operated under § 121.173(c).

[Doc. No. 6258, 29 FR 19198, Dec. 31, 1964; 30 FR 130, Jan. 7, 1965, as amended by Amdt. 121–251, 60 FR 65928, Dec. 20, 1995]

§ 121.187 Airplanes: Reciprocating engine-powered: Landing limitations: Alternate airport.

(a) No person may list an airport as an alternate airport in a dispatch or flight release unless the airplane (at the weight anticipated at the time of arrival at the airport), based on the assumptions in §121.185, can be brought to a full stop landing, within 70 percent of the effective length of the runway.

(b) This section does not apply to large nontransport category airplanes operated under §121.173(c).

[Doc. No. 6258, 29 FR 19198, Dec. 31, 1964; 30 FR 130, Jan. 7, 1965, as amended by Amdt. 121-251, 60 FR 65928, Dec. 20, 1995]

§121.189 Airplanes: Turbine engine powered: Takeoff limitations.

(a) No person operating a turbine engine powered airplane may take off that airplane at a weight greater than that listed in the Airplane Flight Manual for the elevation of the airport and for the ambient temperature existing at takeoff.

(b) No person operating a turbine engine powered airplane certificated after August 26, 1957, but before August 30, 1959 (SR422, 422A), may take off that airplane at a weight greater than that listed in the Airplane Flight Manual for the minimum distances required for takeoff. In the case of an airplane certificated after September 30, 1958 (SR422A, 422B), the takeoff distance may include a clearway distance but the clearway distance included may not be greater than ½ of the takeoff run.

(c) No person operating a turbine engine powered airplane certificated after August 29, 1959 (SR422B), may take off that airplane at a weight greater than that listed in the Airplane Flight Manual at which compliance with the following may be shown:

(1) The accelerate-stop distance must not exceed the length of the runway plus the length of any stopway.

(2) The takeoff distance must not exceed the length of the runway plus the length of any clearway except that the length of any clearway included must not be greater than one-half the length of the runway.

(3) The takeoff run must not be greater than the length of the runway.

(d) No person operating a turbine engine powered airplane may take off that airplane at a weight greater than that listed in the Airplane Flight Manual—

(1) In the case of an airplane certificated after August 26, 1957, but before

October 1, 1958 (SR422), that allows a takeoff path that clears all obstacles either by at least (35 + 0.01D) feet vertically (D is the distance along the intended flight path from the end of the runway in feet), or by at least 200 feet horizontally within the airport boundaries and by at least 300 feet horizontally after passing the boundaries; or

(2) In the case of an airplane certificated after September 30, 1958 (SR 422A, 422B), that allows a net takeoff flight path that clears all obstacles either by a height of at least 35 feet vertically, or by at least 200 feet horizontally within the airport boundaries and by at least 300 feet horizontally after passing the boundaries.

(e) In determining maximum weights, minimum distances, and flight paths under paragraphs (a) through (d) of this section, correction must be made for the runway to be used, the elevation of the airport, the effective runway gradient, the ambient temperature and wind component at the time of takeoff, and, if operating limitations exist for the minimum distances required for takeoff from wet runways, the runway surface condition (dry or wet). Wet runway distances associated with grooved or porous friction course runways, if provided in the Airplane Flight Manual, may be used only for runways that are grooved or treated with a porous friction course (PFC) overlay, and that the operator determines are designed, constructed, and maintained in a manner acceptable to the Administrator.

(f) For the purposes of this section, it is assumed that the airplane is not banked before reaching a height of 50 feet, as shown by the takeoff path or net takeoff flight path data (as appropriate) in the Airplane Flight Manual, and thereafter that the maximum bank is not more than 15 degrees.

(g) For the purposes of this section the terms, *takeoff distance, takeoff run, net takeoff flight path* and *takeoff path* have the same meanings as set forth in the rules under which the airplane was certificated.

[Doc. No. 6258, 29 FR 19198, Dec. 31, 1964, as amended by Amdt. 121-268, 63 FR 8321, Feb. 18, 1998]

§ 121.191 Airplanes: Turbine engine powered: En route limitations: One engine inoperative.

(a) No person operating a turbine engine powered airplane may take off that airplane at a weight, allowing for normal consumption of fuel and oil, that is greater than that which (under the approved, one engine inoperative, en route net flight path data in the Airplane Flight Manual for that airplane) will allow compliance with paragraph (a) (1) or (2) of this section, based on the ambient temperatures expected en route:

(1) There is a positive slope at an altitude of at least 1,000 feet above all terrain and obstructions within five statute miles on each side of the intended track, and, in addition, if that airplane was certificated after August 29, 1959 (SR 422B) there is a positive slope at 1,500 feet above the airport where the airplane is assumed to land after an engine fails.

(2) The net flight path allows the airplane to continue flight from the cruising altitude to an airport where a landing can be made under § 121.197, clearing all terrain and obstructions within five statute miles of the intended track by at least 2,000 feet vertically and with a positive slope at 1,000 feet above the airport where the airplane lands after an engine fails, or, if that airplane was certificated after September 30, 1958 (SR 422A, 422B), with a positive slope at 1,500 feet above the airport where the airplane lands after an engine fails.

(b) For the purposes of paragraph (a)(2) of this section, it is assumed that—

(1) The engine fails at the most critical point en route;

(2) The airplane passes over the critical obstruction, after engine failure at a point that is no closer to the obstruction than the nearest approved radio navigation fix, unless the Administrator authorizes a different procedure based on adequate operational safeguards;

(3) An approved method is used to allow for adverse winds;

(4) Fuel jettisoning will be allowed if the certificate holder shows that the crew is properly instructed, that the training program is adequate, and that

all other precautions are taken to insure a safe procedure;

(5) The alternate airport is specified in the dispatch or flight release and meets the prescribed weather minimums; and

(6) The consumption of fuel and oil after engine failure is the same as the consumption that is allowed for in the approved net flight path data in the Airplane Flight Manual.

[Doc. No. 6258, 29 FR 19198, Dec. 31, 1964; 30 FR 130, Jan. 7, 1965, as amended by Amdt. 121–143, 43 FR 22641, May 25, 1978]

§ 121.193 Airplanes: Turbine engine powered: En route limitations: Two engines inoperative.

(a) *Airplanes certificated after August 26, 1957, but before October 1, 1958* (SR 422). No person may operate a turbine engine powered airplane along an intended route unless he complies with either of the following:

(1) There is no place along the intended track that is more than 90 minutes (with all engines operating at cruising power) from an airport that meets the requirements of § 121.197.

(2) Its weight, according to the two-engine-inoperative, en route, net flight path data in the Airplane Flight Manual, allows the airplane to fly from the point where the two engines are assumed to fail simultaneously to an airport that meets the requirements of § 121.197, with a net flight path (considering the ambient temperature anticipated along the track) having a positive slope at an altitude of at least 1,000 feet above all terrain and obstructions within five miles on each side of the intended track, or at an altitude of 5,000 feet, whichever is higher.

For the purposes of paragraph (a)(2) of this section, it is assumed that the two engines fail at the most critical point en route, that if fuel jettisoning is provided, the airplane's weight at the point where the engines fail includes enough fuel to continue to the airport and to arrive at an altitude of at least 1,000 feet directly over the airport, and that the fuel and oil consumption after engine failure is the same as the consumption allowed for in the net flight path data in the Airplane Flight Manual.

(b) *Aircraft certificated after September 30, 1958, but before August 30, 1959* (SR 422A). No person may operate a turbine engine powered airplane along an intended route unless he complies with either of the following:

(1) There is no place along the intended track that is more than 90 minutes (with all engines operating at cruising power) from an airport that meets the requirements of § 121.197.

(2) Its weight, according to the two-engine-inoperative, en route, net flight path data in the Airplane Flight Manual, allows the airplane to fly from the point where the two engines are assumed to fail simultaneously to an airport that meets the requirements of § 121.197, with a net flight path (considering the ambient temperatures anticipated along the track) having a positive slope at an altitude of at least 1,000 feet above all terrain and obstructions within 5 miles on each side of the intended track, or at an altitude of 2,000 feet, whichever is higher.

For the purposes of paragraph (b)(2) of this section, it is assumed that the two engines fail at the most critical point en route, that the airplane's weight at the point where the engines fail includes enough fuel to continue to the airport, to arrive at an altitude of at least 1,500 feet directly over the airport, and thereafter to fly for 15 minutes at cruise power or thrust, or both, and that the consumption of fuel and oil after engine failure is the same as the consumption allowed for in the net flight path data in the Airplane Flight Manual.

(c) *Aircraft certificated after August 29, 1959* (SR 422B). No person may operate a turbine engine powered airplane along an intended route unless he complies with either of the following:

(1) There is no place along the intended track that is more than 90 minutes (with all engines operating at cruising power) from an airport that meets the requirements of § 121.197.

(2) Its weight, according to the two-engine inoperative, en route, net flight path data in the Airplane Flight Manual, allows the airplane to fly from the point where the two engines are assumed to fail simultaneously to an airport that meets the requirements of § 121.197, with the net flight path (considering the ambient temperatures anticipated along the track) clearing vertically by at least 2,000 feet all terrain and obstructions within five statute miles (4.34 nautical miles) on each side of the intended track. For the purposes of this subparagraph, it is assumed that—

(i) The two engines fail at the most critical point en route;

(ii) The net flight path has a positive slope at 1,500 feet above the airport where the landing is assumed to be made after the engines fail;

(iii) Fuel jettisoning will be approved if the certificate holder shows that the crew is properly instructed, that the training program is adequate, and that all other precautions are taken to ensure a safe procedure;

(iv) The airplane's weight at the point where the two engines are assumed to fail provides enough fuel to continue to the airport, to arrive at an altitude of at least 1,500 feet directly over the airport, and thereafter to fly for 15 minutes at cruise power or thrust, or both; and

(v) The consumption of fuel and oil after the engine failure is the same as the consumption that is allowed for in the net flight path data in the Airplane Flight Manual.

§ 121.195 **Airplanes: Turbine engine powered: Landing limitations: Destination airports.**

(a) No person operating a turbine engine powered airplane may take off that airplane at such a weight that (allowing for normal consumption of fuel and oil in flight to the destination or alternate airport) the weight of the airplane on arrival would exceed the landing weight set forth in the Airplane Flight Manual for the elevation of the destination or alternate airport and the ambient temperature anticipated at the time of landing.

(b) Except as provided in paragraph (c), (d), or (e) of this section, no person operating a turbine engine powered airplane may take off that airplane unless its weight on arrival, allowing for normal consumption of fuel and oil in flight (in accordance with the landing distance set forth in the Airplane Flight Manual for the elevation of the destination airport and the wind conditions anticipated there at the time of landing), would allow a full stop landing at the intended destination airport within 60 percent of the effective length of each runway described below from a point 50 feet above the intersection of the obstruction clearance plane and the runway. For the purpose of determining the allowable landing weight at the destination airport the following is assumed:

(1) The airplane is landed on the most favorable runway and in the most favorable direction, in still air.

(2) The airplane is landed on the most suitable runway considering the probable wind velocity and direction and the ground handling characteristics of the airplane, and considering other conditions such as landing aids and terrain.

(c) A turbopropeller powered airplane that would be prohibited from being taken off because it could not meet the requirements of paragraph (b)(2) of this section, may be taken off if an alternate airport is specified that meets all the requirements of this section except that the airplane can accomplish a full stop landing within 70 percent of the effective length of the runway.

(d) Unless, based on a showing of actual operating landing techniques on wet runways, a shorter landing distance (but never less than that required by paragraph (b) of this section) has been approved for a specific type and model airplane and included in the Airplane Flight Manual, no person may takeoff a turbojet powered airplane when the appropriate weather reports and forecasts, or a combination thereof, indicate that the runways at the destination airport may be wet or slippery at the estimated time of arrival unless the effective runway length at the destination airport is at least 115 percent of the runway length required under paragraph (b) of this section.

(e) A turbojet powered airplane that would be prohibited from being taken off because it could not meet the requirements of paragraph (b)(2) of this section may be taken off if an alternate airport is specified that meets all

the requirements of paragraph (b) of this section.

[Doc. No. 6258, 29 FR 19198, Dec. 31, 1964, as amended by Amdt. 121–9, 30 FR 8572, July 7, 1965]

§ 121.197 Airplanes: Turbine engine powered: Landing limitations: Alternate airports.

No person may list an airport as an alternate airport in a dispatch or flight release for a turbine engine powered airplane unless (based on the assumptions in § 121.195 (b)) that airplane at the weight anticipated at the time of arrival can be brought to a full stop landing within 70 percent of the effective length of the runway for turbopropeller powered airplanes and 60 percent of the effective length of the runway for turbojet powered airplanes, from a point 50 feet above the intersection of the obstruction clearance plane and the runway. In the case of an alternate airport for departure, as provided in § 121.617, allowance may be made for fuel jettisoning in addition to normal consumption of fuel and oil when determining the weight anticipated at the time of arrival.

[Doc. No. 6258, 29 FR 19198, Dec. 31, 1964, as amended by Amdt. 121–9, 30 FR 8572, July 7, 1965; Amdt. 121–179, 47 FR 33390, Aug. 2, 1982]

§ 121.198 Cargo service airplanes: Increased zero fuel and landing weights.

(a) Notwithstanding the applicable structural provisions of the airworthiness regulations but subject to paragraphs (b) through (g) of this section, a certificate holder may operate (for cargo service only) any of the following airplanes (certificated under part 4b of the Civil Air Regulations effective before March 13, 1956) at increased zero fuel and landing weights—

(1) DC–6A, DC–6B, DC–7B, and DC–7C; and

(2) L1049B, C, D, E, F, G, and H, and the L1649A when modified in accordance with supplemental type certificate SA 4–1402.

(b) The zero fuel weight (maximum weight of the airplane with no disposable fuel and oil) and the structural landing weight may be increased beyond the maximum approved in full compliance with applicable regulations only if the Administrator finds that—

(1) The increase is not likely to reduce seriously the structural strength;

(2) The probability of sudden fatigue failure is not noticeably increased;

(3) The flutter, deformation, and vibration characteristics do not fall below those required by applicable regulations; and

(4) All other applicable weight limitations will be met.

(c) No zero fuel weight may be increased by more than five percent, and the increase in the structural landing weight may not exceed the amount, in pounds, of the increase in zero fuel weight.

(d) Each airplane must be inspected in accordance with the approved special inspection procedures, for operations at increased weights, established and issued by the manufacturer of the type of airplane.

(e) Each airplane operated under this section must be operated in accordance with the passenger-carrying performance operating limitations prescribed in this part.

(f) The Airplane Flight Manual for each airplane operated under this section must be appropriately revised to include the operating limitations and information needed for operation at the increased weights.

(g) Except as provided for the carrying of persons under § 121.583 each airplane operated at an increased weight under this section must, before it is used in passenger service, be inspected under the special inspection procedures for return to passenger service established and issued by the manufacturer and approved by the Administrator.

§ 121.199 Nontransport category airplanes: Takeoff limitations.

(a) No person operating a nontransport category airplane may take off that airplane at a weight greater than the weight that would allow the airplane to be brought to a safe stop within the effective length of the runway, from any point during the takeoff before reaching 105 percent of minimum control speed (the minimum speed at which an airplane can be safely controlled in flight after an engine

becomes inoperative) or 115 percent of the power off stalling speed in the takeoff configuration, whichever is greater.

(b) For the purposes of this section—

(1) It may be assumed that takeoff power is used on all engines during the acceleration;

(2) Not more than 50 percent of the reported headwind component, or not less than 150 percent of the reported tailwind component, may be taken into account;

(3) The average runway gradient (the difference between the elevations of the endpoints of the runway divided by the total length) must be considered if it is more than one-half of 1 percent;

(4) It is assumed that the airplane is operating in standard atmosphere; and

(5) The *effective length of the runway* for takeoff means the distance from the end of the runway at which the takeoff is started to a point at which the obstruction clearance plane associated with the other end of the runway intersects the runway centerline.

[Doc. No. 6258, 29 FR 19198, Dec. 31, 1964, as amended by Amdt. 121–132, 41 FR 55475, Dec. 20, 1976]

§ 121.201 Nontransport category airplanes: En route limitations: One engine inoperative.

(a) Except as provided in paragraph (b) of this section, no person operating a nontransport category airplane may take off that airplane at a weight that does not allow a rate of climb of at least 50 feet a minute, with the critical engine inoperative, at an altitude of at least 1,000 feet above the highest obstruction within five miles on each side of the intended track, or 5,000 feet, whichever is higher.

(b) Notwithstanding paragraph (a) of this section, if the Administrator finds that safe operations are not impaired, a person may operate the airplane at an altitude that allows the airplane, in case of engine failure, to clear all obstructions within 5 miles on each side of the intended track by 1,000 feet. If this procedure is used, the rate of descent for the appropriate weight and altitude is assumed to be 50 feet a minute greater than the rate in the approved performance data. Before approving such a procedure, the Administrator considers the following for the route, route segment, or area concerned:

(1) The reliability of wind and weather forecasting.

(2) The location and kinds of navigation aids.

(3) The prevailing weather conditions, particularly the frequency and amount of turbulence normally encountered.

(4) Terrain features.

(5) Air traffic control problems.

(6) Any other operational factors that affect the operation.

(c) For the purposes of this section, it is assumed that—

(1) The critical engine is inoperative;

(2) The propeller of the inoperative engine is in the minimum drag position;

(3) The wing flaps and landing gear are in the most favorable position;

(4) The operating engines are operating at the maximum continuous power available;

(5) The airplane is operating in standard atmosphere; and

(6) The weight of the airplane is progressively reduced by the anticipated consumption of fuel and oil.

§ 121.203 Nontransport category airplanes: Landing limitations: Destination airport.

(a) No person operating a nontransport category airplane may take off that airplane at a weight that—

(1) Allowing for anticipated consumption of fuel and oil, is greater than the weight that would allow a full stop landing within 60 percent of the effective length of the most suitable runway at the destination airport; and

(2) Is greater than the weight allowable if the landing is to be made on the runway—

(i) With the greatest effective length in still air; and

(ii) Required by the probable wind, taking into account not more than 50 percent of the headwind component or not less than 150 percent of the tailwind component.

(b) For the purposes of this section, it is assumed that—

(1) The airplane passes directly over the intersection of the obstruction clearance plane and the runway at a height of 50 feet in a steady gliding approach at a true indicated airspeed of at least 1.3 V_{So};

(2) The landing does not require exceptional pilot skill; and

(3) The airplane is operating in standard atmosphere.

§ 121.205 Nontransport category airplanes: Landing limitations: Alternate airport.

No person may list an airport as an alternate airport in a dispatch or flight release for a nontransport category airplane unless that airplane (at the weight anticipated at the time of arrival) based on the assumptions contained in § 121.203, can be brought to a full stop landing within 70 percent of the effective length of the runway.

§ 121.207 Provisionally certificated airplanes: Operating limitations.

In addition to the limitations in § 91.317 of this chapter, the following limitations apply to the operation of provisionally certificated airplanes by certificate holders:

(a) In addition to crewmembers, each certificate holder may carry on such an airplane only those persons who are listed in § 121.547(c) or who are specifically authorized by both the certificate holder and the Administrator.

(b) Each certificate holder shall keep a log of each flight conducted under this section and shall keep accurate and complete records of each inspection made and all maintenance performed on the airplane. The certificate holder shall make the log and records made under this section available to the manufacturer and the Administrator.

[Doc. No. 28154, 61 FR 2611, Jan. 26, 1996]

Subpart J—Special Airworthiness Requirements

SOURCE: Docket No. 6258, 29 FR 19202, Dec. 31, 1964, unless otherwise noted.

§ 121.211 Applicability.

(a) This subpart prescribes special airworthiness requirements applicable to certificate holders as stated in paragraphs (b) through (e) of this section.

(b) Except as provided in paragraph (d) of this section, each airplane type certificated under Aero Bulletin 7A or part 04 of the Civil Air Regulations in effect before November 1, 1946 must meet the special airworthiness requirements in §§ 121.215 through 121.283.

(c) Each certificate holder must comply with the requirements of §§ 121.285 through 121.291.

(d) If the Administrator determines that, for a particular model of airplane used in cargo service, literal compliance with any requirement under paragraph (b) of this section would be extremely difficult and that compliance would not contribute materially to the objective sought, he may require compliance only with those requirements that are necessary to accomplish the basic objectives of this part.

(e) No person may operate under this part a nontransport category airplane type certificated after December 31, 1964, unless the airplane meets the special airworthiness requirements in § 121.293.

[Doc. No. 28154, 60 FR 65928, Dec. 20, 1995]

§ 121.213 [Reserved]

§ 121.215 Cabin interiors.

(a) Except as provided in § 121.312, each compartment used by the crew or passengers must meet the requirements of this section.

(b) Materials must be at least flash resistant.

(c) The wall and ceiling linings and the covering of upholstering, floors, and furnishings must be flame resistant.

(d) Each compartment where smoking is to be allowed must be equipped with self-contained ash trays that are completely removable and other compartments must be placarded against smoking.

(e) Each receptacle for used towels, papers, and wastes must be of fire-resistant material and must have a cover or other means of containing possible fires started in the receptacles.

[Doc. No. 6258, 29 FR 19202, Dec. 31, 1964, as amended by Amdt. 121–84, 37 FR 3974, Feb. 24, 1972]

§ 121.217 Internal doors.

In any case where internal doors are equipped with louvres or other ventilating means, there must be a means convenient to the crew for closing the flow of air through the door when necessary.

§ 121.219 Ventilation.

Each passenger or crew compartment must be suitably ventilated. Carbon monoxide concentration may not be more than one part in 20,000 parts of air, and fuel fumes may not be present. In any case where partitions between compartments have louvres or other means allowing air to flow between compartments, there must be a means convenient to the crew for closing the flow of air through the partitions, when necessary.

§ 121.221 Fire precautions.

(a) Each compartment must be designed so that, when used for storing cargo or baggage, it meets the following requirements:

(1) No compartment may include controls, wiring, lines, equipment, or accessories that would upon damage or failure, affect the safe operation of the airplane unless the item is adequately shielded, isolated, or otherwise protected so that it cannot be damaged by movement of cargo in the compartment and so that damage to or failure of the item would not create a fire hazard in the compartment.

(2) Cargo or baggage may not interfere with the functioning of the fire-protective features of the compartment.

(3) Materials used in the construction of the compartments, including tie-down equipment, must be at least flame resistant.

(4) Each compartment must include provisions for safeguarding against fires according to the classifications set forth in paragraphs (b) through (f) of this section.

(b) *Class A.* Cargo and baggage compartments are classified in the "A" category if—

(1) A fire therein would be readily discernible to a member of the crew while at his station; and

(2) All parts of the compartment are easily accessible in flight.

There must be a hand fire extinguisher available for each Class A compartment.

(c) *Class B.* Cargo and baggage compartments are classified in the "B" category if enough access is provided while in flight to enable a member of the crew to effectively reach all of the compartment and its contents with a hand fire extinguisher and the compartment is so designed that, when the access provisions are being used, no hazardous amount of smoke, flames, or extinguishing agent enters any compartment occupied by the crew or passengers. Each Class B compartment must comply with the following:

(1) It must have a separate approved smoke or fire detector system to give warning at the pilot or flight engineer station.

(2) There must be a hand fire extinguisher available for the compartment.

(3) It must be lined with fire-resistant material, except that additional service lining of flame-resistant material may be used.

(d) *Class C.* Cargo and baggage compartments are classified in the "C" category if they do not conform with the requirements for the "A", "B", "D", or "E" categories. Each Class C compartment must comply with the following:

(1) It must have a separate approved smoke or fire detector system to give warning at the pilot or flight engineer station.

(2) It must have an approved built-in fire-extinguishing system controlled from the pilot or flight engineer station.

(3) It must be designed to exclude hazardous quantities of smoke, flames, or extinguishing agents from entering into any compartment occupied by the crew or passengers.

(4) It must have ventilation and draft controlled so that the extinguishing agent provided can control any fire that may start in the compartment.

(5) It must be lined with fire-resistant material, except that additional service lining of flame-resistant material may be used.

(e) *Class D.* Cargo and baggage compartments are classified in the "D" category if they are so designed and constructed that a fire occurring therein will be completely confined without endangering the safety of the airplane or the occupants. Each Class D compartment must comply with the following:

(1) It must have a means to exclude hazardous quantities of smoke, flames, or noxious gases from entering any compartment occupied by the crew or passengers.

(2) Ventilation and drafts must be controlled within each compartment so that any fire likely to occur in the compartment will not progress beyond safe limits.

(3) It must be completely lined with fire-resistant material.

(4) Consideration must be given to the effect of heat within the compartment on adjacent critical parts of the airplane.

(f) *Class E.* On airplanes used for the carriage of cargo only, the cabin area may be classified as a Class "E" compartment. Each Class E compartment must comply with the following:

(1) It must be completely lined with fire-resistant material.

(2) It must have a separate system of an approved type smoke or fire detector to give warning at the pilot or flight engineer station.

(3) It must have a means to shut off the ventilating air flow to or within the compartment and the controls for that means must be accessible to the flight crew in the crew compartment.

(4) It must have a means to exclude hazardous quantities of smoke, flames, or noxious gases from entering the flight crew compartment.

(5) Required crew emergency exits must be accessible under all cargo loading conditions.

§ 121.223 Proof of compliance with § 121.221.

Compliance with those provisions of § 121.221 that refer to compartment accessibility, the entry of hazardous quantities of smoke or extinguishing agent into compartments occupied by the crew or passengers, and the dissipation of the extinguishing agent in Class "C" compartments must be shown by tests in flight. During these tests it must be shown that no inadvertent operation of smoke or fire detectors in other compartments within the airplane would occur as a result of fire

96

contained in any one compartment, either during the time it is being extinguished, or thereafter, unless the extinguishing system floods those compartments simultaneously.

§ 121.225 Propeller deicing fluid.

If combustible fluid is used for propeller deicing, the certificate holder must comply with § 121.255.

§ 121.227 Pressure cross-feed arrangements.

(a) Pressure cross-feed lines may not pass through parts of the airplane used for carrying persons or cargo unless—

(1) There is a means to allow crewmembers to shut off the supply of fuel to these lines; or

(2) The lines are enclosed in a fuel and fume-proof enclosure that is ventilated and drained to the exterior of the airplane.

However, such an enclosure need not be used if those lines incorporate no fittings on or within the personnel or cargo areas and are suitably routed or protected to prevent accidental damage.

(b) Lines that can be isolated from the rest of the fuel system by valves at each end must incorporate provisions for relieving excessive pressures that may result from exposure of the isolated line to high temperatures.

§ 121.229 Location of fuel tanks.

(a) Fuel tanks must be located in accordance with § 121.255.

(b) No part of the engine nacelle skin that lies immediately behind a major air outlet from the engine compartment may be used as the wall of an integral tank.

(c) Fuel tanks must be isolated from personnel compartments by means of fume- and fuel-proof enclosures.

§ 121.231 Fuel system lines and fittings.

(a) Fuel lines must be installed and supported so as to prevent excessive vibration and so as to be adequate to withstand loads due to fuel pressure and accelerated flight conditions.

(b) Lines connected to components of the airplanes between which there may be relative motion must incorporate provisions for flexibility.

(c) Flexible connections in lines that may be under pressure and subject to axial loading must use flexible hose assemblies rather than hose clamp connections.

(d) Flexible hose must be of an acceptable type or proven suitable for the particular application.

§ 121.233 Fuel lines and fittings in designated fire zones.

Fuel lines and fittings in each designated fire zone must comply with § 121.259.

§ 121.235 Fuel valves.

Each fuel valve must—

(a) Comply with § 121.257;

(b) Have positive stops or suitable index provisions in the "on" and "off" positions; and

(c) Be supported so that loads resulting from its operation or from accelerated flight conditions are not transmitted to the lines connected to the valve.

§ 121.237 Oil lines and fittings in designated fire zones.

Oil line and fittings in each designated fire zone must comply with § 121.259.

§ 121.239 Oil valves.

(a) Each oil valve must—

(1) Comply with § 121.257;

(2) Have positive stops or suitable index provisions in the "on" and "off" positions; and

(3) Be supported so that loads resulting from its operation or from accelerated flight conditions are not transmitted to the lines attached to the valve.

(b) The closing of an oil shutoff means must not prevent feathering the propeller, unless equivalent safety provisions are incorporated.

§ 121.241 Oil system drains.

Accessible drains incorporating either a manual or automatic means for positive locking in the closed position, must be provided to allow safe drainage of the entire oil system.

§ 121.243 Engine breather lines.

(a) Engine breather lines must be so arranged that condensed water vapor that may freeze and obstruct the line cannot accumulate at any point.

(b) Engine breathers must discharge in a location that does not constitute a fire hazard in case foaming occurs and so that oil emitted from the line does not impinge upon the pilots' windshield.

(c) Engine breathers may not discharge into the engine air induction system.

§ 121.245   Fire walls.

Each engine, auxiliary power unit, fuel-burning heater, or other item of combustion equipment that is intended for operation in flight must be isolated from the rest of the airplane by means of firewalls or shrouds, or by other equivalent means.

§ 121.247   Fire-wall construction.

Each fire wall and shroud must—

(a) Be so made that no hazardous quantity of air, fluids, or flame can pass from the engine compartment to other parts of the airplane;

(b) Have all openings in the fire wall or shroud sealed with close-fitting fireproof grommets, bushings, or firewall fittings;

(c) Be made of fireproof material; and

(d) Be protected against corrosion.

§ 121.249   Cowling.

(a) Cowling must be made and supported so as to resist the vibration inertia, and air loads to which it may be normally subjected.

(b) Provisions must be made to allow rapid and complete drainage of the cowling in normal ground and flight attitudes. Drains must not discharge in locations constituting a fire hazard. Parts of the cowling that are subjected to high temperatures because they are near exhaust system parts or because of exhaust gas impingement must be made of fireproof material. Unless otherwise specified in these regulations all other parts of the cowling must be made of material that is at least fire resistant.

§ 121.251   Engine accessory section diaphragm.

Unless equivalent protection can be shown by other means, a diaphragm that complies with § 121.247 must be provided on air-cooled engines to isolate the engine power section and all parts of the exhaust system from the engine accessory compartment.

§ 121.253   Powerplant fire protection.

(a) Designated fire zones must be protected from fire by compliance with §§ 121.255 through 121.261.

(b) Designated fire zones are—

(1) Engine accessory sections;

(2) Installations where no isolation is provided between the engine and accessory compartment; and

(3) Areas that contain auxiliary power units, fuel-burning heaters, and other combustion equipment.

§ 121.255   Flammable fluids.

(a) No tanks or reservoirs that are a part of a system containing flammable fluids or gases may be located in designated fire zones, except where the fluid contained, the design of the system, the materials used in the tank, the shutoff means, and the connections, lines, and controls provide equivalent safety.

(b) At least one-half inch of clear airspace must be provided between any tank or reservoir and a firewall or shroud isolating a designated fire zone.

§ 121.257   Shutoff means.

(a) Each engine must have a means for shutting off or otherwise preventing hazardous amounts of fuel, oil, deicer, and other flammable fluids from flowing into, within, or through any designated fire zone. However, means need not be provided to shut off flow in lines that are an integral part of an engine.

(b) The shutoff means must allow an emergency operating sequence that is compatible with the emergency operation of other equipment, such as feathering the propeller, to facilitate rapid and effective control of fires.

(c) Shutoff means must be located outside of designated fire zones, unless equivalent safety is provided, and it must be shown that no hazardous amount of flammable fluid will drain into any designated fire zone after a shut off.

(d) Adequate provisions must be made to guard against inadvertent operation of the shutoff means and to make it possible for the crew to reopen the shutoff means after it has been closed.

§121.259 Lines and fittings.

(a) Each line, and its fittings, that is located in a designated fire zone, if it carries flammable fluids or gases under pressure, or is attached directly to the engine, or is subject to relative motion between components (except lines and fittings forming an integral part of the engine), must be flexible and fire-resistant with fire-resistant, factory-fixed, detachable, or other approved fire-resistant ends.

(b) Lines and fittings that are not subject to pressure or to relative motion between components must be of fire-resistant materials.

§121.261 Vent and drain lines.

All vent and drain lines and their fittings, that are located in a designated fire zone must, if they carry flammable fluids or gases, comply with §121.259, if the Administrator finds that the rupture or breakage of any vent or drain line may result in a fire hazard.

§121.263 Fire-extinguishing systems.

(a) Unless the certificate holder shows that equivalent protection against destruction of the airplane in case of fire is provided by the use of fireproof materials in the nacelle and other components that would be subjected to flame, fire-extinguishing systems must be provided to serve all designated fire zones.

(b) Materials in the fire-extinguishing system must not react chemically with the extinguishing agent so as to be a hazard.

§121.265 Fire-extinguishing agents.

Only methyl bromide, carbon dioxide, or another agent that has been shown to provide equivalent extinguishing action may be used as a fire-extinguishing agent. If methyl bromide or any other toxic extinguishing agent is used, provisions must be made to prevent harmful concentrations of fluid or fluid vapors from entering any personnel compartment either because of leakage during normal operation of the airplane or because of discharging the fire extinguisher on the ground or in flight when there is a defect in the extinguishing system. If a methyl bromide system is used, the containers must be charged with dry agent and sealed by the fire-extinguisher manufacturer or some other person using satisfactory recharging equipment. If carbon dioxide is used, it must not be possible to discharge enough gas into the personnel compartments to create a danger of suffocating the occupants.

§121.267 Extinguishing agent container pressure relief.

Extinguishing agent containers must be provided with a pressure relief to prevent bursting of the container because of excessive internal pressures. The discharge line from the relief connection must terminate outside the airplane in a place convenient for inspection on the ground. An indicator must be provided at the discharge end of the line to provide a visual indication when the container has discharged.

§121.269 Extinguishing agent container compartment temperature.

Precautions must be taken to insure that the extinguishing agent containers are installed in places where reasonable temperatures can be maintained for effective use of the extinguishing system.

§121.271 Fire-extinguishing system materials.

(a) Except as provided in paragraph (b) of this section, each component of a fire-extinguishing system that is in a designated fire zone must be made of fireproof materials.

(b) Connections that are subject to relative motion between components of the airplane must be made of flexible materials that are at least fire-resistant and be located so as to minimize the probability of failure.

§121.273 Fire-detector systems.

Enough quick-acting fire detectors must be provided in each designated fire zone to assure the detection of any fire that may occur in that zone.

§121.275 Fire detectors.

Fire detectors must be made and installed in a manner that assures their ability to resist, without failure, all vibration, inertia, and other loads to which they may be normally subjected. Fire detectors must be unaffected by exposure to fumes, oil, water, or other fluids that may be present.

§ 121.277 Protection of other airplane components against fire.

(a) Except as provided in paragraph (b) of this section, all airplane surfaces aft of the nacelles in the area of one nacelle diameter on both sides of the nacelle centerline must be made of material that is at least fire resistant.

(b) Paragraph (a) of this section does not apply to tail surfaces lying behind nacelles unless the dimensional configuration of the airplane is such that the tail surfaces could be affected readily by heat, flames, or sparks emanating from a designated fire zone or from the engine compartment of any nacelle.

§ 121.279 Control of engine rotation.

(a) Except as provided in paragraph (b) of this section, each airplane must have a means of individually stopping and restarting the rotation of any engine in flight.

(b) In the case of turbine engine installations, a means of stopping the rotation need be provided only if the Administrator finds that rotation could jeopardize the safety of the airplane.

§ 121.281 Fuel system independence.

(a) Each airplane fuel system must be arranged so that the failure of any one component does not result in the irrecoverable loss of power of more than one engine.

(b) A separate fuel tank need not be provided for each engine if the certificate holder shows that the fuel system incorporates features that provide equivalent safety.

§ 121.283 Induction system ice prevention.

A means for preventing the malfunctioning of each engine due to ice accumulation in the engine air induction system must be provided for each airplane.

§ 121.285 Carriage of cargo in passenger compartments.

(a) Except as provided in paragraph (b), (c), or (d) or this section, no certificate holder may carry cargo in the passenger compartment of an airplane.

(b) Cargo may be carried anywhere in the passenger compartment if it is carried in an approved cargo bin that meets the following requirements:

(1) The bin must withstand the load factors and emergency landing conditions applicable to the passenger seats of the airplane in which the bin is installed, multiplied by a factor of 1.15, using the combined weight of the bin and the maximum weight of cargo that may be carried in the bin.

(2) The maximum weight of cargo that the bin is approved to carry and any instructions necessary to insure proper weight distribution within the bin must be conspicuously marked on the bin.

(3) The bin may not impose any load on the floor or other structure of the airplane that exceeds the load limitations of that structure.

(4) The bin must be attached to the seat tracks or to the floor structure of the airplane, and its attachment must withstand the load factors and emergency landing conditions applicable to the passenger seats of the airplane in which the bin is installed, multiplied by either the factor 1.15 or the seat attachment factor specified for the airplane, whichever is greater, using the combined weight of the bin and the maximum weight of cargo that may be carried in the bin.

(5) The bin may not be installed in a position that restricts access to or use of any required emergency exit, or of the aisle in the passenger compartment.

(6) The bin must be fully enclosed and made of material that is at least flame resistant.

(7) Suitable safeguards must be provided within the bin to prevent the cargo from shifting under emergency landing conditions.

(8) The bin may not be installed in a position that obscures any passenger's view of the "seat belt" sign "no smoking" sign, or any required exit sign, unless an auxiliary sign or other approved

means for proper notification of the passenger is provided.

(c) Cargo may be carried aft of a bulkhead or divider in any passenger compartment provided the cargo is restrained to the load factors in §25.561(b)(3) and is loaded as follows:

(1) It is properly secured by a safety belt or other tiedown having enough strength to eliminate the possibility of shifting under all normally anticipated flight and ground conditions.

(2) It is packaged or covered in a manner to avoid possible injury to passengers and passenger compartment occupants.

(3) It does not impose any load on seats or the floor structure that exceeds the load limitation for those components.

(4) Its location does not restrict access to or use of any required emergency or regular exit, or of the aisle in the passenger compartment.

(5) Its location does not obscure any passenger's view of the "seat belt" sign, "no smoking" sign, or required exit sign, unless an auxiliary sign or other approved means for proper notification of the passenger is provided.

(d) Cargo, including carry-on baggage, may be carried anywhere in the passenger compartment of a nontransport category airplane type certificated after December 31, 1964, if it is carried in an approved cargo rack, bin, or compartment installed in or on the airplane, if it is secured by an approved means, or if it is carried in accordance with each of the following:

(1) For cargo, it is properly secured by a safety belt or other tie-down having enough strength to eliminate the possibility of shifting under all normally anticipated flight and ground conditions, or for carry-on baggage, it is restrained so as to prevent its movement during air turbulence.

(2) It is packaged or covered to avoid possible injury to occupants.

(3) It does not impose any load on seats or in the floor structure that exceeds the load limitation for those components.

(4) It is not located in a position that obstructs the access to, or use of, any required emergency or regular exit, or the use of the aisle between the crew and the passenger compartment, or is

located in a position that obscures any passenger's view of the "seat belt" sign, "no smoking" sign or placard, or any required exit sign, unless an auxiliary sign or other approved means for proper notification of the passengers is provided.

(5) It is not carried directly above seated occupants.

(6) It is stowed in compliance with this section for takeoff and landing.

(7) For cargo-only operations, paragraph (d)(4) of this section does not apply if the cargo is loaded so that at least one emergency or regular exit is available to provide all occupants of the airplane a means of unobstructed exit from the airplane if an emergency occurs.

[Doc. No. 6258, 29 FR 19202, Dec. 31, 1964, as amended by Amdt. 121–179, 47 FR 33390, Aug. 2, 1982; Amdt. 121–251, 60 FR 65928, Dec. 20, 1995]

§121.287 Carriage of cargo in cargo compartments.

When cargo is carried in cargo compartments that are designed to require the physical entry of a crewmember to extinguish any fire that may occur during flight, the cargo must be loaded so as to allow a crewmember to effectively reach all parts of the compartment with the contents of a hand fire extinguisher.

§121.289 Landing gear: Aural warning device.

(a) Except for airplanes that comply with the requirements of §25.729 of this chapter on or after January 6, 1992, each airplane must have a landing gear aural warning device that functions continuously under the following conditions:

(1) For airplanes with an established approach wing-flap position, whenever the wing flaps are extended beyond the maximum certificated approach climb configuration position in the Airplane Flight Manual and the landing gear is not fully extended and locked.

(2) For airplanes without an established approach climb wing-flap position, whenever the wing flaps are extended beyond the position at which landing gear extension is normally performed and the landing gear is not fully extended and locked.

(b) The warning system required by paragraph (a) of this section—

(1) May not have a manual shutoff;

(2) Must be in addition to the throttle-actuated device installed under the type certification airworthiness requirements; and

(3) May utilize any part of the throttle-actuated system including the aural warning device.

(c) The flap position sensing unit may be installed at any suitable place in the airplane.

[Doc. No. 6258, 29 FR 19202, Dec. 31, 1964, as amended by Amdt. 121–3, 30 FR 3638, Mar. 19, 1965; Amdt. 121–130, 41 FR 47229, Oct. 28, 1976; Amdt. 121–227, 56 FR 63762, Dec. 5, 1991; Amdt. 121–251, 60 FR 65929, Dec. 20, 1995]

§ 121.291 Demonstration of emergency evacuation procedures.

(a) Except as provided in paragraph (a)(1) of this section, each certificate holder must conduct an actual demonstration of emergency evacuation procedures in accordance with paragraph (a) of appendix D to this part to show that each type and model of airplane with a seating capacity of more than 44 passengers to be used in its passenger-carrying operations allows the evacuation of the full capacity, including crewmembers, in 90 seconds or less.

(1) An actual demonstration need not be conducted if that airplane type and model has been shown to be in compliance with this paragraph in effect on or after October 24, 1967, or, if during type certification, with § 25.803 of this chapter in effect on or after December 1, 1978.

(2) Any actual demonstration conducted after September 27, 1993, must be in accordance with paragraph (a) of appendix D to this part in effect on or after that date or with § 25.803 in effect on or after that date.

(b) Each certificate holder conducting operations with airplanes with a seating capacity of more than 44 passengers must conduct a partial demonstration of emergency evacuation procedures in accordance with paragraph (c) of this section upon:

(1) Initial introduction of a type and model of airplane into passenger-carrying operation;

(2) Changing the number, location, or emergency evacuation duties or procedures of flight attendants who are required by § 121.391; or

(3) Changing the number, location, type of emergency exits, or type of opening mechanism on emergency exits available for evacuation.

(c) In conducting the partial demonstration required by paragraph (b) of this section, each certificate holder must:

(1) Demonstrate the effectiveness of its crewmember emergency training and evacuation procedures by conducting a demonstration, not requiring passengers and observed by the Administrator, in which the flight attendants for that type and model of airplane, using that operator's line operating procedures, open 50 percent of the required floor-level emergency exits and 50 percent of the required non-floor-level emergency exits whose opening by a flight attendant is defined as an emergency evacuation duty under § 121.397, and deploy 50 percent of the exit slides. The exits and slides will be selected by the administrator and must be ready for use within 15 seconds;

(2) Apply for and obtain approval from the responsible Flight Standards office before conducting the demonstration;

(3) Use flight attendants in this demonstration who have been selected at random by the Administrator, have completed the certificate holder's FAA-approved training program for the type and model of airplane, and have passed a written or practical examination on the emergency equipment and procedures; and

(4) Apply for and obtain approval from the responsible Flight Standards office before commencing operations with this type and model airplane.

(d) Each certificate holder operating or proposing to operate one or more landplanes in extended overwater operations, or otherwise required to have certain equipment under § 121.339, must show, by simulated ditching conducted in accordance with paragraph (b) of appendix D to this part, that it has the ability to efficiently carry out its ditching procedures. For certificate holders subject to § 121.2(a)(1), this paragraph applies only when a new type or model airplane is introduced into the certificate holder's operations after January 19, 1996.

(e) For a type and model airplane for which the simulated ditching specified in paragraph (d) has been conducted by a part 121 certificate holder, the requirements of paragraphs (b)(2), (b)(4), and (b)(5) of appendix D to this part are complied with if each life raft is removed from stowage, one life raft is launched and inflated (or one slide life raft is inflated) and crewmembers assigned to the inflated life raft display and describe the use of each item of required emergency equipment. The life raft or slide life raft to be inflated will be selected by the Administrator.

[Doc. No. 21269, 46 FR 61453, Dec. 17, 1981, as amended by Amdt. 121–233, 58 FR 45230, Aug. 26, 1993; Amdt. 121–251, 60 FR 65929, Dec. 20, 1995; Amdt. 121–307, 69 FR 67499, Nov. 17, 2004; Docket FAA–2018–0119, Amdt. 121–380, 83 FR 9172, Mar. 5, 2018]

§121.293 Special airworthiness requirements for nontransport category airplanes type certificated after December 31, 1964.

No certificate holder may operate a nontransport category airplane manufactured after December 20, 1999 unless the airplane contains a takeoff warning system that meets the requirements of 14 CFR 25.703. However, the takeoff warning system does not have to cover any device for which it has been demonstrated that takeoff with that device in the most adverse position would not create a hazardous condition.

[Doc. No. 28154, 60 FR 65929, Dec. 20, 1995]

§121.295 Location for a suspect device.

After November 28, 2009, all airplanes with a maximum certificated passenger seating capacity of more than 60 persons must have a location where a suspected explosive or incendiary device found in flight can be placed to minimize the risk to the airplane.

[Doc. No. FAA–2006–26722, 73 FR 63880, Oct. 28, 2008]

Subpart K—Instrument and Equipment Requirements

SOURCE: Docket No. 6258, 29 FR 19205, Dec. 31, 1964, unless otherwise noted.

§121.301 Applicability.

This subpart prescribes instrument and equipment requirements for all certificate holders.

§121.303 Airplane instruments and equipment.

(a) Unless otherwise specified, the instrument and equipment requirements of this subpart apply to all operations under this part.

(b) Instruments and equipment required by §§121.305 through 121.359 and 121.803 must be approved and installed in accordance with the airworthiness requirements applicable to them.

(c) Each airspeed indicator must be calibrated in knots, and each airspeed limitation and item of related information in the Airplane Flight Manual and pertinent placards must be expressed in knots.

(d) Except as provided in §§121.627(b) and 121.628, no person may take off any airplane unless the following instruments and equipment are in operable condition:

(1) Instruments and equipment required to comply with airworthiness requirements under which the airplane is type certificated and as required by §§121.213 through 121.283 and 121.289.

(2) Instruments and equipment specified in §§121.305 through 121.359, 121.321, 121.360, and 121.803 for all operations, and the instruments and equipment specified in §§121.323 through 121.351 for the kind of operation indicated, wherever these items are not already required by paragraph (d)(1) of this section.

[Doc. No. 6258, 29 FR 19202, Dec. 31, 1964, as amended by Amdt. 121–44, 33 FR 14406, Sept. 25, 1968; Amdt. 121–65, 35 FR 12709, Aug. 11, 1970; Amdt. 121–114, 39 FR 44440, Dec. 24, 1974; Amdt. 121–126, 40 FR 55314, Nov. 28, 1975; Amdt. 121–222, 56 FR 12310, Mar. 22, 1991; Amdt. 121–253, 61 FR 2611, Jan. 26, 1996; Amdt. 121–281, 66 FR 19043, Apr. 12, 2001]

§121.305 Flight and navigational equipment.

No person may operate an airplane unless it is equipped with the following flight and navigational instruments and equipment:

(a) An airspeed indicating system with heated pitot tube or equivalent means for preventing malfunctioning due to icing.

(b) A sensitive altimeter.

(c) A sweep-second hand clock (or approved equivalent).

(d) A free-air temperature indicator.

(e) A gyroscopic bank and pitch indicator (artificial horizon).

(f) A gyroscopic rate-of-turn indicator combined with an integral slip-skid indicator (turn-and-bank indicator) except that only a slip-skid indicator is required when a third attitude instrument system usable through flight attitudes of 360° of pitch and roll is installed in accordance with paragraph (k) of this section.

(g) A gyroscopic direction indicator (directional gyro or equivalent).

(h) A magnetic compass.

(i) A vertical speed indicator (rate-of-climb indicator).

(j) On the airplane described in this paragraph, in addition to two gyroscopic bank and pitch indicators (artificial horizons) for use at the pilot stations, a third such instrument is installed in accordance with paragraph (k) of this section:

(1) On each turbojet powered airplane.

(2) On each turbopropeller powered airplane having a passenger-seat configuration of more than 30 seats, excluding each crewmember seat, or a payload capacity of more than 7,500 pounds.

(3) On each turbopropeller powered airplane having a passenger-seat configuration of 30 seats or fewer, excluding each crewmember seat, and a payload capacity of 7,500 pounds or less that is manufactured on or after March 20, 1997.

(4) After December 20, 2010, on each turbopropeller powered airplane having a passenger seat configuration of 10–30 seats and a payload capacity of 7,500 pounds or less that was manufactured before March 20, 1997.

(k) When required by paragraph (j) of this section, a third gyroscopic bank-and-pitch indicator (artificial horizon) that:

(1) Is powered from a source independent of the electrical generating system;

(2) Continues reliable operation for a minimum of 30 minutes after total failure of the electrical generating system;

(3) Operates independently of any other attitude indicating system;

(4) Is operative without selection after total failure of the electrical generating system;

(5) Is located on the instrument panel in a position acceptable to the Administrator that will make it plainly visible to and usable by each pilot at his or her station; and

(6) Is appropriately lighted during all phases of operation.

[Doc. No. 6258, 29 FR 19205, Dec. 31, 1964, as amended by Amdt. 121–57, 35 FR 304, Jan. 8, 1970; Amdt. 121–60, 35 FR 7108, May 6, 1970; Amdt. 121–81, 36 FR 23050, Dec. 3, 1971; Amdt. 121–130, 41 FR 47229, Oct. 28, 1976; Amdt. 121–230, 58 FR 12158, Mar. 3, 1993; Amdt. 121–251, 60 FR 65929, Dec. 20, 1995; Amdt. 121–262, 62 FR 13256, Mar. 19, 1997]

§ 121.306   Portable electronic devices.

(a) Except as provided in paragraph (b) of this section, no person may operate, nor may any operator or pilot in command of an aircraft allow the operation of, any portable electronic device on any U.S.-registered civil aircraft operating under this part.

(b) Paragraph (a) of this section does not apply to—

(1) Portable voice recorders;

(2) Hearing aids;

(3) Heart pacemakers;

(4) Electric shavers;

(5) Portable oxygen concentrators that comply with the requirements in § 121.574; or

(6) Any other portable electronic device that the part 119 certificate holder has determined will not cause interference with the navigation or communication system of the aircraft on which it is to be used.

(c) The determination required by paragraph (b)(6) of this section shall be made by that part 119 certificate holder operating the particular device to be used.

[Doc. No. FAA–1998–4954, 64 FR 1080, Jan. 7, 1999, as amended by Docket FAA–2014–0554, Amdt. 121–374, 81 FR 33118, May 24, 2016]

§ 121.307   Engine instruments.

Unless the Administrator allows or requires different instrumentation for turbine engine powered airplanes to provide equivalent safety, no person may conduct any operation under this part without the following engine instruments:

(a) A carburetor air temperature indicator for each engine.

(b) A cylinder head temperature indicator for each air-cooled engine.

(c) A fuel pressure indicator for each engine.

(d) A fuel flowmeter or fuel mixture indicator for each engine not equipped with an automatic altitude mixture control.

(e) A means for indicating fuel quantity in each fuel tank to be used.

(f) A manifold pressure indicator for each engine.

(g) An oil pressure indicator for each engine.

(h) An oil quantity indicator for each oil tank when a transfer or separate oil reserve supply is used.

(i) An oil-in temperature indicator for each engine.

(j) A tachometer for each engine.

(k) An independent fuel pressure warning device for each engine or a master warning device for all engines with a means for isolating the individual warning circuits from the master warning device.

(l) A device for each reversible propeller, to indicate to the pilot when the propeller is in reverse pitch, that complies with the following:

(1) The device may be actuated at any point in the reversing cycle between the normal low pitch stop position and full reverse pitch, but it may not give an indication at or above the normal low pitch stop position.

(2) The source of indication must be actuated by the propeller blade angle or be directly responsive to it.

§121.308 Lavatory fire protection.

(a) Except as provided in paragraphs (c) and (d) of this section, no person may operate a passenger-carrying airplane unless each lavatory in the airplane is equipped with a smoke detector system or equivalent that provides a warning light in the cockpit or provides a warning light or audio warning in the passenger cabin which would be readily detected by a flight attendant, taking into consideration the posi-

tioning of flight attendants throughout the passenger compartment during various phases of flight.

(b) Except as provided in paragraph (c) of this section, no person may operate a passenger-carrying airplane unless each lavatory in the airplane is equipped with a built-in fire extinguisher for each disposal receptacle for towels, paper, or waste located within the lavatory. The built-in fire extinguisher must be designed to discharge automatically into each disposal receptacle upon occurrence of a fire in the receptacle.

(c) Until December 22, 1997, a certificate holder described in §121.2(a) (1) or (2) may operate an airplane with a passenger seat configuration of 30 or fewer seats that does not comply with the smoke detector system requirements described in paragraph (a) of this section and the fire extinguisher requirements described in paragraph (b) of this section.

(d) After December 22, 1997, no person may operate a nontransport category airplane type certificated after December 31, 1964, with a passenger seat configuration of 10–19 seats unless that airplane complies with the smoke detector system requirements described in paragraph (a) of this section, except that the smoke detector system or equivalent must provide a warning light in the cockpit or an audio warning that would be readily detected by the flightcrew.

[Doc. No. 28154, 60 FR 65929, Dec. 20, 1995]

§121.309 Emergency equipment.

(a) *General:* No person may operate an airplane unless it is equipped with the emergency equipment listed in this section and in §121.310.

(b) Each item of emergency and flotation equipment listed in this section and in §§121.310, 121.339, and 121.340—

(1) Must be inspected regularly in accordance with inspection periods established in the operations specifications to ensure its condition for continued serviceability and immediate readiness to perform its intended emergency purposes;

(2) Must be readily accessible to the crew and, with regard to equipment located in the passenger compartment, to passengers;

(3) Must be clearly identified and clearly marked to indicate its method of operation; and

(4) When carried in a compartment or container, must be carried in a compartment or container marked as to contents and the compartment or container, or the item itself, must be marked as to date of last inspection.

(c) *Hand fire extinguishers for crew, passenger, cargo, and galley compartments.* Hand fire extinguishers of an approved type must be provided for use in crew, passenger, cargo, and galley compartments in accordance with the following:

(1) The type and quantity of extinguishing agent must be suitable for the kinds of fires likely to occur in the compartment where the extinguisher is intended to be used and, for passenger compartments, must be designed to minimize the hazard of toxic gas concentrations.

(2) *Cargo compartments.* At least one hand fire extinguisher must be conveniently located for use in each class E cargo compartment that is accessible to crewmembers during flight.

(3) *Galley compartments.* At least one hand fire extinguisher must be conveniently located for use in each galley located in a compartment other than a passenger, cargo, or crew compartment.

(4) *Flightcrew compartment.* At least one hand fire extinguisher must be conveniently located on the flight deck for use by the flightcrew.

(5) *Passenger compartments.* Hand fire extinguishers for use in passenger compartments must be conveniently located and, when two or more are required, uniformly distributed throughout each compartment. Hand fire extinguishers shall be provided in passenger compartments as follows:

(i) For airplanes having passenger seats accommodating more than 6 but fewer than 31 passengers, at least one.

(ii) For airplanes having passenger seats accommodating more than 30 but fewer than 61 passengers, at least two.

(iii) For airplanes having passenger seats accommodating more than 60 passengers, there must be at least the following number of hand fire extinguishers:

MINIMUM NUMBER OF HAND FIRE EXTINGUISHERS

Passenger seating accommodations:

61 through 200	3
201 through 300	4
301 through 400	5
401 through 500	6
501 through 600	7
601 or more	8

(6) Notwithstanding the requirement for uniform distribution of hand fire extinguishers as prescribed in paragraph (c)(5) of this section, for those cases where a galley is located in a passenger compartment, at least one hand fire extinguisher must be conveniently located and easily accessible for use in the galley.

(7) At least two of the required hand fire extinguisher installed in passenger-carrying airplanes must contain Halon 1211 (bromochlorofluoromethane) or equivalent as the extinguishing agent. At least one hand fire extinguisher in the passenger compartment must contain Halon 1211 or equivalent.

(d) [Reserved]

(e) *Crash ax.* Except for nontransport category airplanes type certificated after December 31, 1964, each airplane must be equipped with a crash ax.

(f) *Megaphones.* Each passenger-carrying airplane must have a portable battery-powered megaphone or megaphones readily accessible to the crewmembers assigned to direct emergency evacuation, installed as follows:

(1) One megaphone on each airplane with a seating capacity of more than 60 and less than 100 passengers, at the most rearward location in the passenger cabin where it would be readily accessible to a normal flight attendant seat. However, the Administrator may grant a deviation from the requirements of this subparagraph if he finds that a different location would be more useful for evacuation of persons during an emergency.

(2) Two megaphones in the passenger cabin on each airplane with a seating capacity of more than 99 passengers, one installed at the forward end and the other at the most rearward location where it would be readily accessible to a normal flight attendant seat.

[Doc. No. 6258, 29 FR 19205, Dec. 31, 1964]

EDITORIAL NOTE: For FEDERAL REGISTER citations affecting § 121.309, see the List of CFR Sections Affected, which appears in the Finding Aids section of the printed volume and at *www.govinfo.gov.*

§ 121.310 Additional emergency equipment.

(a) *Means for emergency evacuation.* Each passenger-carrying landplane emergency exit (other than over-the-wing) that is more than 6 feet from the ground with the airplane on the ground and the landing gear extended, must have an approved means to assist the occupants in descending to the ground. The assisting means for a floor-level emergency exit must meet the requirements of § 25.809(f)(1) of this chapter in effect on April 30, 1972, except that, for any airplane for which the application for the type certificate was filed after that date, it must meet the requirements under which the airplane was type certificated. An assisting means that deploys automatically must be armed during taxiing, takeoffs, and landings. However, if the Administrator finds that the design of the exit makes compliance impractical, he may grant a deviation from the requirement of automatic deployment if the assisting means automatically erects upon deployment and, with respect to required emergency exits, if an emergency evacuation demonstration is conducted in accordance with § 121.291(a). This paragraph does not apply to the rear window emergency exit of DC–3 airplanes operated with less than 36 occupants, including crewmembers and less than five exits authorized for passenger use.

(b) *Interior emergency exit marking.* The following must be complied with for each passenger-carrying airplane:

(1) Each passenger emergency exit, its means of access, and its means of opening must be conspicuously marked. The identity and location of each passenger emergency exit must be recognizable from a distance equal to the width of the cabin. The location of each passenger emergency exit must be indicated by a sign visible to occupants approaching along the main passenger aisle. There must be a locating sign—

(i) Above the aisle near each over-the-wing passenger emergency exit, or

at another ceiling location if it is more practical because of low headroom;

(ii) Next to each floor level passenger emergency exit, except that one sign may serve two such exits if they both can be seen readily from that sign; and

(iii) On each bulkhead or divider that prevents fore and aft vision along the passenger cabin, to indicate emergency exits beyond and obscured by it, except that if this is not possible the sign may be placed at another appropriate location.

(2) Each passenger emergency exit marking and each locating sign must meet the following:

(i) Except as provided in paragraph (b)(2)(iii) of this section, for an airplane for which the application for the type certificate was filed prior to May 1, 1972, each passenger emergency exit marking and each locating sign must be manufactured to meet the requirements of § 25.812(b) of this chapter in effect on April 30, 1972. On these airplanes, no sign may continue to be used if its luminescence (brightness) decreases to below 100 microlamberts. The colors may be reversed if it increases the emergency illumination of the passenger compartment. However, the Administrator may authorize deviation from the 2-inch background requirements if he finds that special circumstances exist that make compliance impractical and that the proposed deviation provides an equivalent level of safety.

(ii) For a transport category airplane for which the application for the type certificate was filed on or after May 1, 1972, each passenger emergency exit marking and each locating sign must be manufactured to meet the interior emergency exit marking requirements under which the airplane was type certificated. On these airplanes, no sign may continue to be used if its luminescence (brightness) decreases to below 250 microlamberts.

(iii) For a nontransport category turbopropeller powered airplane type certificated after December 31, 1964, each passenger emergency exit marking and each locating sign must be manufactured to have white letters 1 inch high on a red background 2 inches high, be self-illuminated or independently, internally electrically illuminated, and have a minimum brightness of at least 160 microlamberts. The color may be reversed if the passenger compartment illumination is essentially the same. On these airplanes, no sign may continue to be used if its luminescence (brightness) decreases to below 100 microlamberts.

(c) *Lighting for interior emergency exit markings.* Except for nontransport category airplanes type certificated after December 31, 1964, each passenger-carrying airplane must have an emergency lighting system, independent of the main lighting system. However, sources of general cabin illumination may be common to both the emergency and the main lighting systems if the power supply to the emergency lighting system is independent of the power supply to the main lighting system. The emergency lighting system must—

(1) Illuminate each passenger exit marking and locating sign;

(2) Provide enough general lighting in the passenger cabin so that the average illumination when measured at 40-inch intervals at seat armrest height, on the centerline of the main passenger aisle, is at least 0.05 foot-candles; and

(3) For airplanes type certificated after January 1, 1958, after November 26, 1986, include floor proximity emergency escape path marking which meets the requirements of § 25.812(e) of this chapter in effect on November 26, 1984.

(d) *Emergency light operation.* Except for lights forming part of emergency lighting subsystems provided in compliance with § 25.812(h) of this chapter (as prescribed in paragraph (h) of this section) that serve no more than one assist means, are independent of the airplane's main emergency lighting systems, and are automatically activated when the assist means is deployed, each light required by paragraphs (c) and (h) of this section must comply with the following:

(1) Each light must—

(i) Be operable manually both from the flightcrew station and, for airplanes on which a flight attendant is required, from a point in the passenger compartment that is readily accessible to a normal flight attendant seat;

(ii) Have a means to prevent inadvertent operation of the manual controls; and

(iii) When armed or turned on at either station, remain lighted or become lighted upon interruption of the airplane's normal electric power.

(2) Each light must be armed or turned on during taxiing, takeoff, and landing. In showing compliance with this paragraph a transverse vertical separation of the fuselage need not be considered.

(3) Each light must provide the required level of illumination for at least 10 minutes at the critical ambient conditions after emergency landing.

(4) Each light must have a cockpit control device that has an "on," "off," and "armed" position.

(e) *Emergency exit operating handles.* (1) For a passenger-carrying airplane for which the application for the type certificate was filed prior to May 1, 1972, the location of each passenger emergency exit operating handle, and instructions for opening the exit, must be shown by a marking on or near the exit that is readable from a distance of 30 inches. In addition, for each Type I and Type II emergency exit with a locking mechanism released by rotary motion of the handle, the instructions for opening must be shown by—

(i) A red arrow with a shaft at least three-fourths inch wide and a head twice the width of the shaft, extending along at least 70° of arc at a radius approximately equal to three-fourths of the handle length; and

(ii) The word "open" in red letters 1 inch high placed horizontally near the head of the arrow.

(2) For a passenger-carrying airplane for which the application for the type certificate was filed on or after May 1, 1972, the location of each passenger emergency exit operating handle and instructions for opening the exit must be shown in accordance with the requirements under which the airplane was type certificated. On these airplanes, no operating handle or operating handle cover may continue to be used if its luminescence (brightness) decreases to below 100 microlamberts.

(f) *Emergency exit access.* Access to emergency exits must be provided as

108

follows for each passenger-carrying transport category airplane:

(1) Each passage way between individual passenger areas, or leading to a Type I or Type II emergency exit, must be unobstructed and at least 20 inches wide.

(2) For each Type I or Type II emergency exit equipped with an assist means, there must be enough space next to the exit to allow a crewmember to assist in the evacuation of passengers without reducing the unobstructed width of the passageway below that required in paragraph (f)(1) of this section. In addition, all airplanes manufactured on or after November 26, 2008 must comply with the provisions of §§25.813(b)(1), (b)(2), (b)(3) and (b)(4) in effect on November 26, 2004. However, a deviation from this requirement may be authorized for an airplane certificated under the provisions of part 4b of the Civil Air Regulations in effect before December 20, 1951, if the Administrator finds that special circumstances exist that provide an equivalent level of safety.

(3) There must be access from the main aisle to each Type III and Type IV exit. The access from the aisle to these exits must not be obstructed by seats, berths, or other protrusions in a manner that would reduce the effectiveness of the exit. In addition—

(i) For an airplane for which the application for the type certificate was filed prior to May 1, 1972, the access must meet the requirements of §25.813(c) of this chapter in effect on April 30, 1972; and

(ii) For an airplane for which the application for the type certificate was filed on or after May 1, 1972, the access must meet the emergency exit access requirements under which the airplane was type certificated; except that,

(iii) After December 3, 1992, the access for an airplane type certificated after January 1, 1958, must meet the requirements of §25.813(c) of this chapter, effective June 3, 1992.

(iv) Contrary provisions of this section notwithstanding, the Director of the division of the Aircraft Certification Service responsible for the airworthiness rules may authorize deviation from the requirements of paragraph (f)(3)(iii) of this section if it is

determined that special circumstances make compliance impractical. Such special circumstances include, but are not limited to, the following conditions when they preclude achieving compliance with §25.813(c)(1)(i) or (ii) without a reduction in the total number of passenger seats: emergency exits located in close proximity to each other; fixed installations such as lavatories, galleys, etc.; permanently mounted bulkheads; an insufficient number of rows ahead of or behind the exit to enable compliance without a reduction in the seat row pitch of more than one inch; or an insufficient number of such rows to enable compliance without a reduction in the seat row pitch to less than 30 inches. A request for such grant of deviation must include credible reasons as to why literal compliance with §25.813(c)(1)(i) or (ii) is impractical and a description of the steps taken to achieve a level of safety as close to that intended by §25.813(c)(1)(i) or (ii) as is practical.

(v) The Director of the division of the Aircraft Certification Service responsible for the airworthiness rules may also authorize a compliance date later than December 3, 1992, if it is determined that special circumstances make compliance by that date impractical. A request for such grant of deviation must outline the airplanes for which compliance will be achieved by December 3, 1992, and include a proposed schedule for incremental compliance of the remaining airplanes in the operator's fleet. In addition, the request must include credible reasons why compliance cannot be achieved earlier.

(4) If it is necessary to pass through a passageway between passenger compartments to reach any required emergency exit from any seat in the passenger cabin, the passageway must not be obstructed. However, curtains may be used if they allow free entry through the passageway.

(5) No door may be installed in any partition between passenger compartments.

(6) No person may operate an airplane manufactured after November 27, 2006, that incorporates a door installed between any passenger seat occupiable

for takeoff and landing and any passenger emergency exit, such that the door crosses any egress path (including aisles, crossaisles and passageways).

(7) If it is necessary to pass through a doorway separating the passenger cabin from other areas to reach required emergency exit from any passenger seat, the door must have a means to latch it in open position, and the door must be latched open during each takeoff and landing. The latching means must be able to withstand the loads imposed upon it when the door is subjected to the ultimate inertia forces, relative to the surrounding structure, listed in § 25.561(b) of this chapter.

(g) *Exterior exit markings.* Each passenger emergency exit and the means of opening that exit from the outside must be marked on the outside of the airplane. There must be a 2-inch colored band outlining each passenger emergency exit on the side of the fuselage. Each outside marking, including the band, must be readily distinguishable from the surrounding fuselage area by contrast in color. The markings must comply with the following:

(1) If the reflectance of the darker color is 15 percent or less, the reflectance of the lighter color must be at least 45 percent.

(2) If the reflectance of the darker color is greater than 15 percent, at least a 30 percent difference between its reflectance and the reflectance of the lighter color must be provided.

(3) Exits that are not in the side of the fuselage must have the external means of opening and applicable instructions marked conspicuously in red or, if red is inconspicuous against the background color, in bright chrome yellow and, when the opening means for such an exit is located on only one side of the fuselage, a conspicuous marking to that effect must be provided on the other side. *Reflectance* is the ratio of the luminous flux reflected by a body to the luminous flux it receives.

(h) *Exterior emergency lighting and escape route.* (1) Except for nontransport category airplanes certificated after December 31, 1964, each passenger-carrying airplane must be equipped with

exterior lighting that meets the following requirements:

(i) For an airplane for which the application for the type certificate was filed prior to May 1, 1972, the requirements of § 25.812 (f) and (g) of this chapter in effect on April 30, 1972.

(ii) For an airplane for which the application for the type certificate was filed on or after May 1, 1972, the exterior emergency lighting requirements under which the airplane was type certificated.

(2) Each passenger-carrying airplane must be equipped with a slip-resistant escape route that meets the following requirements:

(i) For an airplane for which the application for the type certificate was filed prior to May 1, 1972, the requirements of § 25.803(e) of this chapter in effect on April 30, 1972.

(ii) For an airplane for which the application for the type certificate was filed on or after May 1, 1972, the slip-resistant escape route requirements under which the airplane was type certificated.

(i) *Floor level exits.* Each floor level door or exit in the side of the fuselage (other than those leading into a cargo or baggage compartment that is not accessible from the passenger cabin) that is 44 or more inches high and 20 or more inches wide, but not wider than 46 inches, each passenger ventral exit (except the ventral exits on M–404 and CV–240 airplanes), and each tail cone exit, must meet the requirements of this section for floor level emergency exits. However, the Administrator may grant a deviation from this paragraph if he finds that circumstances make full compliance impractical and that an acceptable level of safety has been achieved.

(j) *Additional emergency exits.* Approved emergency exits in the passenger compartments that are in excess of the minimum number of required emergency exits must meet all of the applicable provisions of this section except paragraphs (f)(1), (2), and (3) of this section and must be readily accessible.

(k) On each large passenger-carrying turbojet-powered airplane, each ventral exit and tailcone exit must be—

(1) Designed and constructed so that it cannot be opened during flight; and

(2) Marked with a placard readable from a distance of 30 inches and installed at a conspicuous location near the means of opening the exit, stating that the exit has been designed and constructed so that it cannot be opened during flight.

(l) *Emergency exit features.* (1) Each transport category airplane manufactured after *November 26, 2007* must comply with the provisions of §25.809(i) and

(2) After November 26, 2007 each transport category airplane must comply with the provisions of §25.813(b)(6)(ii) in effect on November 26, 2007.

(m) Except for an airplane used in operations under this part on October 16, 1987, and having an emergency exit configuration installed and authorized for operation prior to October 16, 1987, for an airplane that is required to have more than one passenger emergency exit for each side of the fuselage, no passenger emergency exit shall be more than 60 feet from any adjacent passenger emergency exit on the same side of the same deck of the fuselage, as measured parallel to the airplane's longitudinal axis between the nearest exit edges.

(n) *Portable lights.* No person may operate a passenger-carrying airplane unless it is equipped with flashlight stowage provisions accessible from each flight attendant seat.

[Doc. No. 2033, 30 FR 3205, Mar. 9, 1965]

EDITORIAL NOTE: For FEDERAL REGISTER citations affecting §121.310, see the List of CFR Sections Affected, which appears in the Finding Aids section of the printed volume and at *www.govinfo.gov.*

§121.311 Seats, safety belts, and shoulder harnesses.

(a) No person may operate an airplane unless there are available during the takeoff, en route flight, and landing—

(1) An approved seat or berth for each person on board the airplane who has reached his second birthday; and

(2) An approved safety belt for separate use by each person on board the airplane who has reached his second birthday, except that two persons occupying a berth may share one approved

safety belt and two persons occupying a multiple lounge or divan seat may share one approved safety belt during en route flight only.

(b) Except as provided in this paragraph, each person on board an airplane operated under this part shall occupy an approved seat or berth with a separate safety belt properly secured about him or her during movement on the surface, takeoff, and landing. A safety belt provided for the occupant of a seat may not be used by more than one person who has reached his or her second birthday. Notwithstanding the preceding requirements, a child may:

(1) Be held by an adult who is occupying an approved seat or berth, provided the child has not reached his or her second birthday and the child does not occupy or use any restraining device; or

(2) Notwithstanding any other requirement of this chapter, occupy an approved child restraint system furnished by the certificate holder or one of the persons described in paragraph (b)(2)(i) of this section, provided:

(i) The child is accompanied by a parent, guardian, or attendant designated by the child's parent or guardian to attend to the safety of the child during the flight;

(ii) Except as provided in paragraph (b)(2)(ii)(D) of this section, the approved child restraint system bears one or more labels as follows:

(A) Seats manufactured to U.S. standards between January 1, 1981, and February 25, 1985, must bear the label: "This child restraint system conforms to all applicable Federal motor vehicle safety standards."

(B) Seats manufactured to U.S. standards on or after February 26, 1985, must bear two labels:

(1) "This child restraint system conforms to all applicable Federal motor vehicle safety standards"; and

(2) "THIS RESTRAINT IS CERTIFIED FOR USE IN MOTOR VEHICLES AND AIRCRAFT" in red lettering;

(C) Seats that do not qualify under paragraphs (B)(2)(ii)(A) and (b)(2)(ii)(B) of this section must bear a label or markings showing:

(1) That the seat was approved by a foreign government;

(2) That the seat was manufactured under the standards of the United Nations;

(3) That the seat or child restraint device furnished by the certificate holder was approved by the FAA through Type Certificate or Supplemental Type Certificate; or

(4) That the seat or child restraint device furnished by the certificate holder, or one of the persons described in paragraph (b)(2)(i) of this section, was approved by the FAA in accordance with § 21.8(d) of this chapter or Technical Standard Order C–100b, or a later version. The child restraint device manufactured by AmSafe, Inc. (CARES, Part No. 4082) and approved by the FAA in accordance with § 21.305(d) (2010 ed.) of this chapter may continue to bear a label or markings showing FAA approval in accordance with § 21.305(d) (2010 ed.) of this chapter.

(D) Except as provided in § 121.311(b)(2)(ii)(C)(*3*) and § 121.311(b)(2)(ii)(C)(*4*), booster-type child restraint systems (as defined in Federal Motor Vehicle Safety Standard No. 213 (49 CFR 571.213)), vest- and harness-type child restraint systems, and lap held child restraints are not approved for use in aircraft; and

(iii) The certificate holder complies with the following requirements:

(A) The restraint system must be properly secured to an approved forward-facing seat or berth;

(B) The child must be properly secured in the restraint system and must not exceed the specified weight limit for the restraint system; and

(C) The restraint system must bear the appropriate label(s).

(c) Except as provided in paragraph (c)(3) of this section, the following prohibitions apply to certificate holders:

(1) Except as provided in § 121.311(b)(2)(ii)(C)(*3*) and § 121.311(b)(2)(ii)(C)(*4*), no certificate holder may permit a child, in an aircraft, to occupy a booster-type child restraint system, a vest-type child restraint system, a harness-type child restraint system, or a lap held child restraint system during take off, landing, and movement on the surface.

(2) Except as required in paragraph (c)(1) of this section, no certificate holder may prohibit a child, if requested by the child's parent, guardian, or designated attendant, from occupying a child restraint system furnished by the child's parent, guardian, or designated attendant provided—

(i) The child holds a ticket for an approved seat or berth or such seat or berth is otherwise made available by the certificate holder for the child's use;

(ii) The requirements of paragraph (b)(2)(i) of this section are met;

(iii) The requirements of paragraph (b)(2)(iii) of this section are met; and

(iv) The child restraint system has one or more of the labels described in paragraphs (b)(2)(ii)(A) through (b)(2)(ii)(C) of this section.

(3) This section does not prohibit the certificate holder from providing child restraint systems authorized by this section or, consistent with safe operating practices, determining the most appropriate passenger seat location for the child restraint system.

(d) Each sideward facing seat must comply with the applicable requirements of § 25.785(c) of this chapter.

(e) Except as provided in paragraphs (e)(1) through (e)(3) of this section, no certificate holder may take off or land an airplane unless each passenger seat back is in the upright position. Each passenger shall comply with instructions given by a crewmember in compliance with this paragraph.

(1) This paragraph does not apply to seat backs placed in other than the upright position in compliance with § 121.310(f)(3).

(2) This paragraph does not apply to seats on which cargo or persons who are unable to sit erect for a medical reason are carried in accordance with procedures in the certificate holder's manual if the seat back does not obstruct any passenger's access to the aisle or to any emergency exit.

(3) On airplanes with no flight attendant, the certificate holder may take off or land as long as the flightcrew instructs each passenger to place his or her seat back in the upright position for takeoff and landing.

(f) No person may operate a transport category airplane that was type certificated after January 1, 1958, or a nontransport category airplane manufactured after March 20, 1997, unless it is equipped at each flight deck station with a combined safety belt and shoulder harness that meets the applicable requirements specified in §25.785 of this chapter, effective March 6, 1980, except that—

(1) Shoulder harnesses and combined safety belt and shoulder harnesses that were approved and installed before March 6, 1980, may continue to be used; and

(2) Safety belt and shoulder harness restraint systems may be designed to the inertia load factors established under the certification basis of the airplane.

(g) Each flight attendant must have a seat for takeoff and landing in the passenger compartment that meets the requirements of §25.785 of this chapter, effective March 6, 1980, except that—

(1) Combined safety belt and shoulder harnesses that were approved and installed before March, 6, 1980, may continue to be used; and

(2) Safety belt and shoulder harness restraint systems may be designed to the inertia load factors established under the certification basis of the airplane.

(3) The requirements of §25.785(h) do not apply to passenger seats occupied by flight attendants not required by §121.391.

(h) Each occupant of a seat equipped with a shoulder harness or with a combined safety belt and shoulder harness must have the shoulder harness or combined safety belt and shoulder harness properly secured about that occupant during takeoff and landing, except that a shoulder harness that is not combined with a safety belt may be unfastened if the occupant cannot perform the required duties with the shoulder harness fastened.

(i) At each unoccupied seat, the safety belt and shoulder harness, if installed, must be secured so as not to interfere with crewmembers in the performance of their duties or with the rapid egress of occupants in an emergency.

(j) After October 27, 2009, no person may operate a transport category airplane type certificated after January 1, 1958 and manufactured on or after October 27, 2009 in passenger-carrying operations under this part unless all pas-

senger and flight attendant seats on the airplane meet the requirements of §25.562 in effect on or after June 16, 1988.

(k) *Seat dimension disclosure.* (1) Each air carrier that conducts operations under this part and that has a Web site must make available on its Web site the width of the narrowest and widest passenger seats in each class of service for each airplane make, model and series operated by that air carrier in passenger-carrying operations.

(2) For purposes of paragraph (k)(1) of this section, the width of a passenger seat means the distance between the inside of the armrests for that seat.

[Doc. No. 7522, 32 FR 13267, Sept. 20, 1967]

EDITORIAL NOTE: For FEDERAL REGISTER citations affecting §121.311, see the List of CFR Sections Affected, which appears in the Finding Aids section of the printed volume and at *www.govinfo.gov.*

§121.312 **Materials for compartment interiors.**

(a) *All interior materials; transport category airplanes and nontransport category airplanes type certificated before January 1, 1965.* Except for the materials covered by paragraph (b) of this section, all materials in each compartment of a transport category airplane, or a nontransport category airplane type certificated before January 1, 1965, used by the crewmembers and passengers, must meet the requirements of §25.853 of this chapter in effect as follows, or later amendment thereto:

(1) *Airplane with passenger seating capacity of 20 or more*—(i) *Manufactured after August 19, 1988, but prior to August 20, 1990.* Except as provided in paragraph (a)(3)(ii) of this section, each airplane with a passenger capacity of 20 or more and manufactured after August 19, 1988, but prior to August 20, 1990, must comply with the heat release rate testing provisions of §25.853(d) in effect March 6, 1995 (formerly §25.853(a–1) in effect on August 20, 1986) (see App. L of this part), except that the total heat release over the first 2 minutes of sample exposure must not exceed 100 kilowatt minutes per square meter and the peak heat release rate must not exceed 100 kilowatts per square meter.

113

(ii) *Manufactured after August 19, 1990.* Each airplane with a passenger capacity of 20 or more and manufactured after August 19, 1990, must comply with the heat release rate and smoke testing provisions of § 25.853(d) in effect March 6, 1995 (formerly § 25.853(a–1)(see app. L of this part) in effect on September 26, 1988).

(2) *Substantially complete replacement of the cabin interior on or after May 1, 1972—*(i) *Airplane for which the application for type certificate was filed prior to May 1, 1972.* Except as provided in paragraph (a)(3)(i) or (a)(3)(ii) of this section, each airplane for which the application for type certificate was filed prior to May 1, 1972, must comply with the provisions of § 25.853 in effect on April 30, 1972, regardless of passenger capacity, if there is a substantially complete replacement of the cabin interior after April 30, 1972.

(ii) *Airplane for which the application for type certificate was filed on or after May 1, 1972.* Except as provided in paragraph (a)(3)(i) or (a)(3)(ii) of this section, each airplane for which the application for type certificate was filed on or after May 1, 1972, must comply with the material requirements under which the airplane was type certificated, regardless of passenger capacity, if there is a substantially complete replacement of the cabin interior on or after that date.

(3) *Airplane type certificated after January 1, 1958, with passenger capacity of 20 or more—*(i) *Substantially complete replacement of the cabin interior on or after March 6, 1995.* Except as provided in paragraph (a)(3)(ii) of this section, each airplane that was type certificated after January 1, 1958, and has a passenger capacity of 20 or more, must comply with the heat release rate testing provisions of § 25.853(d) in effect March 6, 1995 (formerly § 25.853(a–1) in effect on August 20, 1986)(see app. L of this part), if there is a substantially complete replacement of the cabin interior components identified in § 25.853(d), on or after that date, except that the total heat release over the first 2 minutes of sample exposure shall not exceed 100 kilowatt-minutes per square meter and the peak heat release rate must not exceed 100 kilowatts per square meter.

(ii) *Substantially complete replacement of the cabin interior on or after August 20, 1990.* Each airplane that was type certificated after January 1, 1958, and has a passenger capacity of 20 or more, must comply with the heat release rate and smoke testing provisions of § 25.853(d) in effect March 6, 1995 (formerly § 25.853(a–1) in effect on September 26, 1988)(see app. L of this part), if there is a substantially complete replacement of the cabin interior components identified in § 25.853(d), on or after August 20, 1990.

(4) Contrary provisions of this section notwithstanding, the Director of the division of the Aircraft Certification Service responsible for the airworthiness rules may authorize deviation from the requirements of paragraph (a)(1)(i), (a)(1)(ii), (a)(3)(i), or (a)(3)(ii) of this section for specific components of the cabin interior that do not meet applicable flammability and smoke emission requirements, if the determination is made that special circumstances exist that make compliance impractical. Such grants of deviation will be limited to those airplanes manufactured within 1 year after the applicable date specified in this section and those airplanes in which the interior is replaced within 1 year of that date. A request for such grant of deviation must include a thorough and accurate analysis of each component subject to § 25.853(a–1), the steps being taken to achieve compliance, and, for the few components for which timely compliance will not be achieved, credible reasons for such noncompliance.

(5) Contrary provisions of this section notwithstanding, galley carts and galley standard containers that do not meet the flammability and smoke emission requirements of § 25.853(d) in effect March 6, 1995 (formerly § 25.853(a–1)) (see app. L of this part) may be used in airplanes that must meet the requirements of paragraphs (a)(1)(i), (a)(1)(ii), (a)(3)(i), or (a)(3)(ii) of this section, provided the galley carts or standard containers were manufactured prior to March 6, 1995.

(b) *Seat cushions.* Seat cushions, except those on flight crewmember seats, in each compartment occupied by crew or passengers, must comply with the requirements pertaining to seat cushions in §25.853(c) effective on November 26, 1984, on each airplane as follows:

(1) Each transport category airplane type certificated after January 1, 1958; and

(2) On or after December 20, 2010, each nontransport category airplane type certificated after December 31, 1964.

(c) *All interior materials; airplanes type certificated in accordance with SFAR No. 41 of 14 CFR part 21.* No person may operate an airplane that conforms to an amended or supplemental type certificate issued in accordance with SFAR No. 41 of 14 CFR part 21 for a maximum certificated takeoff weight in excess of 12,500 pounds unless the airplane meets the compartment interior requirements set forth in §25.853(a) in effect March 6, 1995 (formerly §25.853(a), (b), (b–1), (b–2), and (b–3) of this chapter in effect on September 26, 1978)(see app. L of this part).

(d) *All interior materials; other airplanes.* For each material or seat cushion to which a requirement in paragraphs (a), (b), or (c) of this section does not apply, the material and seat cushion in each compartment used by the crewmembers and passengers must meet the applicable requirement under which the airplane was type certificated.

(e) Thermal/acoustic insulation materials. For transport category airplanes type certificated after January 1, 1958:

(1) For airplanes manufactured before September 2, 2005, when thermal/acoustic insulation is installed in the fuselage as replacements after September 2, 2005, the insulation must meet the flame propagation requirements of §25.856 of this chapter, effective September 2, 2003, if it is:

(i) Of a blanket construction or

(ii) Installed around air ducting.

(2) For airplanes manufactured after September 2, 2005, thermal/acoustic insulation materials installed in the fuselage must meet the flame propagation requirements of §25.856 of this chapter, effective September 2, 2003.

(3) For airplanes with a passenger capacity of 20 or greater, manufactured after September 2, 2009, thermal/acoustic insulation materials installed in

the lower half of the fuselage must meet the flame penetration resistance requirements of §25.856 of this chapter, effective September 2, 2003.

[Doc. No. 28154, 60 FR 65930, Dec. 20, 1995, as amended by Amdt. 121–301, 68 FR 45083, July 31, 2003; Amdt. 121–320, 70 FR 77752, Dec. 30, 2005; Amdt. 121–330, 72 FR 1442, Jan. 12, 2007; Docket FAA–2018–0119, Amdt. 121–380, 83 FR 9173, Mar. 5, 2018]

§121.313 **Miscellaneous equipment.**

No person may conduct any operation unless the following equipment is installed in the airplane:

(a) If protective fuses are installed on an airplane, the number of spare fuses approved for that airplane and appropriately described in the certificate holder's manual.

(b) A windshield wiper or equivalent for each pilot station.

(c) A power supply and distribution system that meets the requirements of §§25.1309, 25.1331, 25.1351(a) and (b)(1) through (4), 25.1353, 25.1355, and 25.1431(b) or that is able to produce and distribute the load for the required instruments and equipment, with use of an external power supply if any one power source or component of the power distribution system fails. The use of common elements in the system may be approved if the Administrator finds that they are designed to be reasonably protected against malfunctioning. Engine-driven sources of energy, when used, must be on separate engines.

(d) A means for indicating the adequacy of the power being supplied to required flight instruments.

(e) Two independent static pressure systems, vented to the outside atmospheric pressure so that they will be least affected by air flow variation or moisture or other foreign matter, and installed so as to be airtight except for the vent. When a means is provided for transferring an instrument from its primary operating system to an alternate system, the means must include a positive positioning control and must be marked to indicate clearly which system is being used.

(f) A door between the passenger and pilot compartments (i.e., flightdeck door), with a locking means to prevent passengers from opening it without the pilot's permission, except that non-transport category airplanes certificated after December 31, 1964, are not required to comply with this paragraph. For airplanes equipped with a crew rest area having separate entries from the flightdeck and the passenger compartment, a door with such a locking means must be provided between the crew rest area and the passenger compartment.

(g) A key for each door that separates a passenger compartment from another compartment that has emergency exit provisions. Except for flightdeck doors, a key must be readily available for each crewmember. Except as provided below, no person other than a person who is assigned to perform duty on the flightdeck may have a key to the flightdeck door. Before April 22, 2003, any crewmember may have a key to the flightdeck door but only if the flightdeck door has an internal flightdeck locking device installed, operative, and in use. Such "internal flightdeck locking device" has to be designed so that it can only be unlocked from inside the flightdeck.

(h) A placard on each door that is the means of access to a required passenger emergency exit, to indicate that it must be open during takeoff and landing.

(i) A means for the crew, in an emergency to unlock each door that leads to a compartment that is normally accessible to passengers and that can be locked by passengers.

(j) After April 9, 2003, for airplanes required by paragraph (f) of this section to have a door between the passenger and pilot or crew rest compartments, and for transport category, all-cargo airplanes that have a door installed between the pilot compartment and any other occupied compartment on January 15, 2002;

(1) After April 9, 2003, for airplanes required by paragraph (f) of this section to have a door between the passenger and pilot or crew rest compartments,

(i) Each such door must meet the requirements of § 25.795(a)(1) and (2) in effect on January 15, 2002; and

(ii) Each operator must establish methods to enable a flight attendant to enter the pilot compartment in the event that a flightcrew member becomes incapacitated. Any associated signal or confirmation system must be operable by each flightcrew member from that flightcrew member's duty station.

(2) After October 1, 2003, for transport category, all-cargo airplanes that had a door installed between the pilot compartment and any other occupied compartment on or after January 15, 2002, each such door must meet the requirements of § 25.795(a)(1) and (2) in effect on January 15, 2002; or the operator must implement a security program approved by the Transportation Security Administration (TSA) for the operation of all airplanes in that operator's fleet.

(k) Except for all-cargo operations as defined in § 110.2 of this chapter, for all passenger-carrying airplanes that require a lockable flightdeck door in accordance with paragraph (f) of this section, a means to monitor from the flightdeck side of the door the area outside the flightdeck door to identify persons requesting entry and to detect suspicious behavior and potential threats.

[Doc. No. 6258, 29 FR 19205, Dec. 31, 1964, as amended by Amdt. 121–5, 30 FR 6113, Apr. 30, 1965; Amdt. 121–251, 60 FR 65931, Dec. 20, 1995; Amdt. 121–288, 67 FR 2127, Jan. 15, 2002; Amdt. 121–299, 68 FR 42881, July 18, 2003; Amdt. 121–334, 72 FR 45635, Aug. 15, 2007; Amdt. 121–353, 76 FR 7488, Feb. 10, 2011]

§ 121.314 Cargo and baggage compartments.

For each transport category airplane type certificated after January 1, 1958:

(a) Each Class C or Class D compartment, as defined in § 25.857 of this Chapter in effect on June 16, 1986 (see Appendix L to this part), that is greater than 200 cubic feet in volume must have ceiling and sidewall liner panels which are constructed of:

(1) Glass fiber reinforced resin;

(2) Materials which meet the test requirements of part 25, appendix F, part III of this chapter; or

(3) In the case of liner installations approved prior to March 20, 1989, aluminum.

(b) For compliance with paragraph (a) of this section, the term "liner" includes any design feature, such as a joint or fastener, which would affect the capability of the liner to safely contain a fire.

(c) After March 19, 2001, each Class D compartment, regardless of volume, must meet the standards of §§25.857(c) and 25.858 of this Chapter for a Class C compartment unless the operation is an all-cargo operation in which case each Class D compartment may meet the standards in §25.857(e) for a Class E compartment.

(d) *Reports of conversions and retrofits.* (1) Until such time as all Class D compartments in aircraft operated under this part by the certificate have been converted or retrofitted with appropriate detection and suppression systems, each certificate holder must submit written progress reports to the FAA that contain the information specified below.

(i) The serial number of each airplane listed in the operations specifications issued to the certificate holder for operation under this part in which all Class D compartments have been converted to Class C or Class E compartments;

(ii) The serial number of each airplane listed in the operations specification issued to the certificate holder for operation under this part, in which all Class D compartments have been retrofitted to meet the fire detection and suppression requirements for Class C or the fire detection requirements for Class E; and

(iii) The serial number of each airplane listed in the operations specifications issued to the certificate holder for operation under this part that has at least one Class D compartment that has not been converted or retrofitted.

(2) The written report must be submitted to the responsible Flight Standards office by July 1, 1998, and at each three-month interval thereafter.

[Doc. No. 28937, 63 FR 8049, Feb. 17, 1998, as amended by Docket FAA–2018–0119, Amdt. 121–380, 83 FR 9173, Mar. 5, 2018]

§121.315 Cockpit check procedure.

(a) Each certificate holder shall provide an approved cockpit check procedure for each type of aircraft.

(b) The approved procedures must include each item necessary for flight crewmembers to check for safety before starting engines, taking off, or landing, and in engine and systems emergencies. The procedures must be designed so that a flight crewmember will not need to rely upon his memory for items to be checked.

(c) The approved procedures must be readily usable in the cockpit of each aircraft and the flight crew shall follow them when operating the aircraft.

§121.316 Fuel tanks.

Each turbine powered transport category airplane operated after October 30, 1991, must meet the requirements of §25.963(e) of this chapter in effect on October 30, 1989.

[Doc. No. 25614, 54 FR 40354, Sept. 29, 1989]

§121.317 Passenger information requirements, smoking prohibitions, and additional seat belt requirements.

(a) Except as provided in paragraph (l) of this section, no person may operate an airplane unless it is equipped with passenger information signs that meet the requirements of §25.791 of this chapter. Except as provided in paragraph (l) of this section, the signs must be constructed so that the crewmembers can turn them on and off.

(b) Except as provided in paragraph (l) of this section, the "Fasten Seat Belt" sign shall be turned on during any movement on the surface, for each takeoff, for each landing, and at any other time considered necessary by the pilot in command.

(c) No person may operate an airplane on a flight on which smoking is prohibited by part 252 of this title unless either the "No Smoking" passenger information signs are lighted during the entire flight, or one or more "No Smoking" placards meeting the requirements of §25.1541 of this chapter are posted during the entire flight segment. If both the lighted signs and the placards are used, the signs must remain lighted during the entire flight segment.

(d) No person may operate a passenger-carrying airplane under this part unless at least one legible sign or placard that reads "Fasten Seat Belt While Seated" is visible from each passenger seat. These signs or placards need not meet the requirements of paragraph (a) of this section.

(e) No person may operate an airplane unless there is installed in each lavatory a sign or placard that reads: "Federal law provides for a penalty of up to $2,000 for tampering with the smoke detector installed in this lavatory." These signs or placards need not meet the requirements of paragraph (a) of this section.

(f) Each passenger required by § 121.311(b) to occupy a seat or berth shall fasten his or her safety belt about him or her and keep it fastened while the "Fasten Seat Belt" sign is lighted.

(g) No person may smoke while a "No Smoking" sign is lighted or while "No Smoking" placards are posted, except as follows:

(1) *Supplemental operations.* The pilot in command of an airplane engaged in a supplemental operation may authorize smoking on the flight deck (if it is physically separated from any passenger compartment), but not in any of the following situations:

(i) During airplane movement on the surface or during takeoff or landing;

(ii) During scheduled passenger-carrying public charter operations conducted under part 380 of this title; or

(iii) During any operation where smoking is prohibited by part 252 of this title or by international agreement.

(2) *Certain intrastate domestic operations.* Except during airplane movement on the surface or during takeoff or landing, a pilot in command of an airplane engaged in a domestic operation may authorize smoking on the flight deck (if it is physically separated from the passenger compartment) if—

(i) Smoking on the flight deck is not otherwise prohibited by part 252 of this title;

(ii) The flight is conducted entirely within the same State of the United States (a flight from one place in Hawaii to another place in Hawaii through the airspace over a place outside of Hawaii is not entirely within the same State); and

(iii) The airplane is either not turbojet-powered or the airplane is not capable of carrying at least 30 passengers.

(h) No person may smoke in any airplane lavatory.

(i) No person may tamper with, disable, or destroy any smoke detector installed in any airplane lavatory.

(j) On flight segments other than those described in paragraph (c) of this section, the "No Smoking" sign must be turned on during any movement on the surface, for each takeoff, for each landing, and at any other time considered necessary by the pilot in command.

(k) Each passenger shall comply with instructions given him or her by a crewmember regarding compliance with paragraphs (f), (g), (h), and (l) of this section.

(l) A certificate holder may operate a nontransport category airplane type certificated after December 31, 1964, that is manufactured before December 20, 1997, if it is equipped with at least one placard that is legible to each person seated in the cabin that states "Fasten Seat Belt," and if, during any movement on the surface, for each takeoff, for each landing, and at any other time considered necessary by the pilot in command, a crewmember orally instructs the passengers to fasten their seat belts.

[Doc. No. 25590, 53 FR 12361, Apr. 13, 1988, as amended by Amdt. 121-196, 53 FR 44182, Nov. 2, 1988; Amdt. 121-213, 55 FR 8367, Mar. 7, 1990; Amdt. 121-230, 57 FR 42673, Sept. 15, 1992; Amdt. 121-251, 60 FR 65931, Dec. 20, 1995; Amdt. 121-256, 61 FR 30434, June 14, 1996; Amdt. 121-277, 65 FR 36779, June 9, 2000]

§ 121.318 Public address system.

No person may operate an airplane with a seating capacity of more than 19 passengers unless it is equipped with a public address system which—

(a) Is capable of operation independent of the crewmember interphone system required by § 121.319, except for handsets, headsets, microphones, selector switches, and signaling devices;

(b) Is approved in accordance with § 21.305 of this chapter;

(c) Is accessible for immediate use from each of two flight crewmember stations in the pilot compartment;

(d) For each required floor-level passenger emergency exit which has an adjacent flight attendant seat, has a microphone which is readily accessible to the seated flight attendant, except that one microphone may serve more than one exit, provided the proximity of the exits allows unassisted verbal communication between seated flight attendants;

(e) Is capable of operation within 10 seconds by a flight attendant at each of those stations in the passenger compartment from which its use is accessible;

(f) Is audible at all passenger seats, lavatories, and flight attendant seats and work stations; and

(g) For transport category airplanes manufactured on or after November 27, 1990, meets the requirements of §25.1423 of this chapter.

[Doc. No. 24995, 54 FR 43926, Oct. 27, 1989]

§121.319 Crewmember interphone system.

(a) No person may operate an airplane with a seating capacity of more than 19 passengers unless the airplane is equipped with a crewmember interphone system that:

(1) [Reserved]

(2) Is capable of operation independent of the public address system required by §121.318(a) except for handsets, headsets, microphones, selector switches, and signaling devices, and

(3) Meets the requirements of paragraph (b) of this section.

(b) The crewmember interphone system required by paragraph (a) of this section must be approved in accordance with §21.305 of this chapter and meet the following requirements:

(1) It must provide a means of two-way communication between the pilot compartment and—

(i) Each passenger compartment; and

(ii) Each galley located on other than the main passenger deck level.

(2) It must be accessible for immediate use from each of two flight crewmember stations in the pilot compartment;

(3) It must be accessible for use from at least one normal flight attendant station in each passenger compartment;

(4) It must be capable of operation within 10 seconds by a flight attendant at those stations in each passenger compartment from which its use is accessible; and

(5) For large turbojet-powered airplanes:

(i) It must be accessible for use at enough flight attendant stations so that all floor-level emergency exits (or entryways to those exits in the case of exits located within galleys) in each passenger compartment are observable from one or more of those stations so equipped;

(ii) It must have an alerting system incorporating aural or visual signals for use by flight crewmembers to alert flight attendants and for use by flight attendants to alert flight crewmembers;

(iii) The alerting system required by paragraph (b)(5)(ii) of this section must have a means for the recipient of a call to determine whether it is a normal call or an emergency call; and

(iv) When the airplane is on the ground, it must provide a means of two-way communication between ground personnel and either of at least two flight crewmembers in the pilot compartment. The interphone system station for use by ground personnel must be so located that personnel using the system may avoid visible detection from within the airplane.

[Doc. No. 10865, 38 FR 21494, Aug. 9, 1973, as amended by Amdt. 121–121, 40 FR 42186, Sept. 11, 1975; Amdt. 121–149, 43 FR 50602, Oct. 30, 1978; Amdt. 121–178, 47 FR 13316, Mar. 29, 1982; Amdt. 121–253, 61 FR 2611, Jan. 26, 1996]

§121.321 Operations in icing.

After October 21, 2013, no person may operate an airplane with a certificated maximum takeoff weight less than 60,000 pounds in conditions conducive to airframe icing unless it complies with this section. As used in this section, the phrase "conditions conducive to airframe icing" means visible moisture at or below a static air temperature of 5 °C or a total air temperature of 10 °C, unless the approved Airplane Flight Manual provides another definition.

(a) When operating in conditions conducive to airframe icing, compliance must be shown with paragraph (a)(1), or (2), or (3) of this section.

(1) The airplane must be equipped with a certificated primary airframe ice detection system.

(i) The airframe ice protection system must be activated automatically, or manually by the flightcrew, when the primary ice detection system indicates activation is necessary.

(ii) When the airframe ice protection system is activated, any other procedures in the Airplane Flight Manual for operating in icing conditions must be initiated.

(2) Visual cues of the first sign of ice formation anywhere on the airplane and a certificated advisory airframe ice detection system must be provided.

(i) The airframe ice protection system must be activated when any of the visual cues are observed or when the advisory airframe ice detection system indicates activation is necessary, whichever occurs first.

(ii) When the airframe ice protection system is activated, any other procedures in the Airplane Flight Manual for operating in icing conditions must be initiated.

(3) If the airplane is not equipped to comply with the provisions of paragraph (a)(1) or (2) of this section, then the following apply:

(i) When operating in conditions conducive to airframe icing, the airframe ice protection system must be activated prior to, and operated during, the following phases of flight:

(A) Takeoff climb after second segment,

(B) En route climb,

(C) Go-around climb,

(D) Holding,

(E) Maneuvering for approach and landing, and

(F) Any other operation at approach or holding airspeeds.

(ii) During any other phase of flight, the airframe ice protection system must be activated and operated at the first sign of ice formation anywhere on the airplane, unless the Airplane Flight Manual specifies that the airframe ice protection system should not be used or provides other operational instructions.

(iii) Any additional procedures for operation in conditions conducive to icing specified in the Airplane Flight Manual or in the manual required by § 121.133 must be initiated.

(b) If the procedures specified in paragraph (a)(3)(i) of this section are specifically prohibited in the Airplane Flight Manual, compliance must be shown with the requirements of paragraph (a)(1) or (2) of this section.

(c) Procedures necessary for safe operation of the airframe ice protection system must be established and documented in:

(1) The Airplane Flight Manual for airplanes that comply with paragraph (a)(1) or (2) of this section, or

(2) The Airplane Flight Manual or in the manual required by § 121.133 for airplanes that comply with paragraph (a)(3) of this section.

(d) Procedures for operation of the airframe ice protection system must include initial activation, operation after initial activation, and deactivation. Procedures for operation after initial activation of the ice protection system must address—

(1) Continuous operation,

(2) Automatic cycling,

(3) Manual cycling if the airplane is equipped with an ice detection system that alerts the flightcrew each time the ice protection system must be cycled, or

(4) Manual cycling based on a time interval if the airplane type is not equipped with features necessary to implement (d)(1)–(3) of this section.

(e) System installations used to comply with paragraph (a)(1) or (a)(2) of this section must be approved through an amended or supplemental type certificate in accordance with part 21 of this chapter.

[Doc. No. FAA–2009–0675, 78 FR 15876, Mar. 13, 2013]

§ 121.323 Instruments and equipment for operations at night.

No person may operate an airplane at night under this part unless it is equipped with the following instruments and equipment in addition to those required by §§ 121.305 through 121.321 and 121.803:

(a) Position lights.

(b) An anti-collision light.

(c) Two landing lights, except that only one landing light is required for nontransport category airplanes type certificated after December 31, 1964.

(d) Instrument lights providing enough light to make each required instrument, switch, or similar instrument, easily readable and installed so that the direct rays are shielded from the flight crewmembers' eyes and that no objectionable reflections are visible to them. There must be a means of controlling the intensity of illumination unless it is shown that nondimming instrument lights are satisfactory.

(e) An airspeed-indicating system with heated pitot tube or equivalent means for preventing malfunctioning due to icing.

(f) A sensitive altimeter.

[Doc. No. 6258, 29 FR 19205, Dec. 31, 1964, as amended by Amdt. 121–251, 60 FR 65932, Dec. 20, 1995; Amdt. 121–281, 66 FR 19043, Apr. 12, 2001]

§121.325 Instruments and equipment for operations under IFR or over-the-top.

No person may operate an airplane under IFR or over-the-top conditions under this part unless it is equipped with the following instruments and equipment, in addition to those required by §§121.305 through 121.321 and 121.803:

(a) An airspeed indicating system with heated pitot tube or equivalent means for preventing malfunctioning due to icing.

(b) A sensitive altimeter.

(c) Instrument lights providing enough light to make each required instrument, switch, or similar instrument, easily readable and so installed that the direct rays are shielded from the flight crewmembers' eyes and that no objectionable reflections are visible to them, and a means of controlling the intensity of illumination unless it is shown that nondimming instrument lights are satisfactory.

[Doc. No. 6258, 29 FR 19205, Dec. 31, 1964, as amended at Amdt. 121–281, 66 FR 19043, Apr. 12, 2001]

§121.327 Supplemental oxygen: Reciprocating engine powered airplanes.

(a) *General.* Except where supplemental oxygen is provided in accordance with §121.331, no person may operate an airplane unless supplemental oxygen is furnished and used as set forth in paragraphs (b) and (c) of this section. The amount of supplemental oxygen required for a particular operation is determined on the basis of flight altitudes and flight duration, consistent

with the operation procedures established for each operation and route.

(b) *Crewmembers.* (1) At cabin pressure altitudes above 10,000 feet up to and including 12,000 feet, oxygen must be provided for, and used by, each member of the flight crew on flight deck duty, and must be provided for other crewmembers, for that part of the flight at those altitudes that is of more than 30 minutes duration.

(2) At cabin pressure altitudes above 12,000 feet, oxygen must be provided for, and used by, each member of the flight crew on flight deck duty, and must be provided for other crewmembers, during the entire flight time at those altitudes.

(3) When a flight crewmember is required to use oxygen, he must use it continuously, except when necessary to remove the oxygen mask or other dispenser in connection with his regular duties. Standby crewmembers who are on call or are definitely going to have flight deck duty before completing the flight must be provided with an amount of supplemental oxygen equal to that provided for crewmembers on duty other than on flight deck duty. If a standby crewmember is not on call and will not be on flight deck duty during the remainder of the flight, he is considered to be a passenger for the purposes of supplemental oxygen requirements.

(c) *Passengers.* Each certificate holder shall provide a supply of oxygen, approved for passenger safety, in accordance with the following:

(1) For flights of more than 30 minutes duration at cabin pressure altitudes above 8,000 feet up to and including 14,000 feet, enough oxygen for 30 minutes for 10 percent of the passengers.

(2) For flights at cabin pressure altitudes above 14,000 feet up to and including 15,000 feet, enough oxygen for that part of the flight at those altitudes for 30 percent of the passengers.

(3) For flights at cabin pressure altitudes above 15,000 feet, enough oxygen for each passenger carried during the entire flight at those altitudes.

(d) For the purposes of this subpart *cabin pressure altitude* means the pressure altitude corresponding with the pressure in the cabin of the airplane, and *flight altitude* means the altitude above sea level at which the airplane is operated. For airplanes without pressurized cabins, "cabin pressure altitude" and "flight altitude" mean the same thing.

§ 121.329 Supplemental oxygen for sustenance: Turbine engine powered airplanes.

(a) *General.* When operating a turbine engine powered airplane, each certificate holder shall equip the airplane with sustaining oxygen and dispensing equipment for use as set forth in this section:

(1) The amount of oxygen provided must be at least the quantity necessary to comply with paragraphs (b) and (c) of this section.

(2) The amount of sustaining and first-aid oxygen required for a particular operation to comply with the rules in this part is determined on the basis of cabin pressure altitudes and flight duration, consistent with the operating procedures established for each operation and route.

(3) The requirements for airplanes with pressurized cabins are determined on the basis of cabin pressure altitude and the assumption that a cabin pressurization failure will occur at the altitude or point of flight that is most critical from the standpoint of oxygen need, and that after the failure the airplane will descend in accordance with the emergency procedures specified in the Airplane Flight Manual, without exceeding its operating limitations, to a flight altitude that will allow successful termination of the flight.

(4) Following the failure, the cabin pressure altitude is considered to be the same as the flight altitude unless it is shown that no probable failure of the cabin or pressurization equipment will result in a cabin pressure altitude equal to the flight altitude. Under those circumstances, the maximum cabin pressure altitude attained may be used as a basis for certification or determination of oxygen supply, or both.

(b) *Crewmembers.* Each certificate holder shall provide a supply of oxygen for crewmembers in accordance with the following:

(1) At cabin pressure altitudes above 10,000 feet, up to and including 12,000 feet, oxygen must be provided for and used by each member of the flight crew on flight deck duty and must be provided for other crewmembers for that part of the flight at those altitudes that is of more than 30 minutes duration.

(2) At cabin pressure altitudes above 12,000 feet, oxygen must be provided for, and used by, each member of the flight crew on flight deck duty, and must be provided for other crewmembers during the entire flight at those altitudes.

(3) When a flight crewmember is required to use oxygen, he must use it continuously except when necessary to remove the oxygen mask or other dispenser in connection with his regular duties. Standby crewmembers who are on call or are definitely going to have flight deck duty before completing the flight must be provided with an amount of supplemental oxygen equal to that provided for crewmembers on duty other than on flight duty. If a standby crewmember is not on call and will not be on flight deck duty during the remainder of the flight, he is considered to be a passenger for the purposes of supplemental oxygen requirements.

(c) *Passengers.* Each certificate holder shall provide a supply of oxygen for passengers in accordance with the following:

(1) For flights at cabin pressure altitudes above 10,000 feet, up to and including 14,000 feet, enough oxygen for that part of the flight at those altitudes that is of more than 30 minutes duration, for 10 percent of the passengers.

(2) For flights at cabin pressure altitudes above 14,000 feet, up to and including 15,000 feet, enough oxygen for that part of the flight at those altitudes for 30 percent of the passengers.

(3) For flights at cabin pressure altitudes above 15,000 feet, enough oxygen for each passenger carried during the entire flight at those altitudes.

§ 121.331 Supplemental oxygen requirements for pressurized cabin airplanes: Reciprocating engine powered airplanes.

(a) When operating a reciprocating engine powered airplane pressurized cabin, each certificate holder shall equip the airplane to comply with paragraphs (b) through (d) of this section in the event of cabin pressurization failure.

(b) *For crewmembers.* When operating at flight altitudes above 10,000 feet, the certificate holder shall provide enough oxygen for each crewmember for the entire flight at those altitudes and not less than a two-hour supply for each flight crewmember on flight deck duty. The required two hours supply is that quantity of oxygen necessary for a constant rate of descent from the airplane's maximum certificated operating altitude to 10,000 feet in ten minutes and followed by 110 minutes at 10,000 feet. The oxygen required by § 121.337 may be considered in determining the supplemental breathing supply required for flight crewmembers on flight deck duty in the event of cabin pressurization failure.

(c) *For passengers.* When operating at flight altitudes above 8,000 feet the certificate holder shall provide oxygen as follows:

(1) When an airplane is not flown at a flight altitude above flight level 250, enough oxygen for 30 minutes for 10 percent of the passengers, if at any point along the route to be flown the airplane can safely descend to a flight altitude of 14,000 feet or less within four minutes.

(2) If the airplane cannot descend to a flight altitude of 14,000 feet or less within four minutes, the following supply of oxygen must be provided:

(i) For that part of the flight that is more than four minutes duration at flight altitudes above 15,000 feet, the supply required by § 121.327(c)(3).

(ii) For that part of the flight at flight altitudes above 14,000 feet, up to and including 15,000 feet, the supply required by § 121.327(c)(2).

(iii) For flight at flight altitudes above 8,000 feet up to and including 14,000 feet, enough oxygen for 30 minutes for 10 percent of the passengers.

(3) When an airplane is flown at a flight altitude above flight level 250, enough oxygen for 30 minutes for 10 percent of the passengers for the entire flight (including emergency descent) above 8,000 feet, up to and including 14,000 feet, and to comply with § 121.327(c) (2) and (3) for flight above 14,000 feet.

(d) For the purposes of this section it is assumed that the cabin pressurization failure occurs at a time during flight that is critical from the standpoint of oxygen need and that after the failure the airplane will descend, without exceeding its normal operating limitations, to flight altitudes allowing safe flight with respect to terrain clearance.

[Doc. No. 6258, 29 FR 19205, Dec. 31, 1964, as amended by Amdt. 121–132, 41 FR 55475, Dec. 20, 1976]

§ 121.333 Supplemental oxygen for emergency descent and for first aid; turbine engine powered airplanes with pressurized cabins.

(a) *General.* When operating a turbine engine powered airplane with a pressurized cabin, the certificate holder shall furnish oxygen and dispensing equipment to comply with paragraphs (b) through (e) of this section in the event of cabin pressurization failure.

(b) *Crewmembers.* When operating at flight altitudes above 10,000 feet, the certificate holder shall supply enough oxygen to comply with § 121.329, but not less than a two-hour supply for each flight crewmember on flight deck duty. The required two hours supply is that quantity of oxygen necessary for a constant rate of descent from the airplane's maximum certificated operating altitude to 10,000 feet in ten minutes and followed by 110 minutes at 10,000 feet. The oxygen required in the event of cabin pressurization failure by § 121.337 may be included in determining the supply required for flight crewmembers on flight deck duty.

(c) *Use of oxygen masks by flight crewmembers.* (1) When operating at flight altitudes above flight level 250, each flight crewmember on flight deck duty must be provided with an oxygen mask so designed that it can be rapidly placed on his face from its ready position, properly secured, sealed, and supplying oxygen upon demand; and so designed that after being placed on the face it does not prevent immediate communication between the flight crewmember and other crewmembers over the airplane intercommunication system. When it is not being used at flight altitudes above flight level 250, the oxygen mask must be kept in condition for ready use and located so as to be within the immediate reach of the flight crewmember while at his duty station.

(2) When operating at flight altitudes above flight level 250, one pilot at the controls of the airplane shall at all times wear and use an oxygen mask secured, sealed, and supplying oxygen, in accordance with the following:

(i) The one pilot need not wear and use an oxygen mask at or below the following flight levels if each flight crewmember on flight deck duty has a quick-donning type of oxygen mask that the certificate holder has shown can be placed on the face from its ready position, properly secured, sealed, and supplying oxygen upon demand, with one hand and within five seconds:

(A) For airplanes having a passenger seat configuration of more than 30 seats, excluding any required crewmember seat, or a payload capacity of more than 7,500 pounds, at or below flight level 410.

(B) For airplanes having a passenger seat configuration of less than 31 seats, excluding any required crewmember seat, and a payload capacity of 7,500 pounds or less, at or below flight level 350.

(ii) Whenever a quick-donning type of oxygen mask is to be used under this section, the certificate holder shall also show that the mask can be put on without disturbing eye glasses and without delaying the flight crewmember from proceeding with his assigned emergency duties. The oxygen mask after being put on must not prevent immediate communication between the flight crewmember and other crewmembers over the airplane intercommunication system.

(3) Notwithstanding paragraph (c)(2) of this section, if for any reason at any

time it is necessary for one pilot to leave his station at the controls of the airplane when operating at flight altitudes above flight level 250, the remaining pilot at the controls shall put on and use his oxygen mask until the other pilot has returned to his duty station.

(4) Before the takeoff of a flight, each flight crewmember shall personally preflight his oxygen equipment to insure that the oxygen mask is functioning, fitted properly, and connected to appropriate supply terminals, and that the oxygen supply and pressure are adequate for use.

(d) *Use of portable oxygen equipment by cabin attendants.* After November 28, 2005 each mask used for portable oxygen equipment must be connected to its oxygen supply. Above flight level 250, one of the following is required:

(1) Each attendant shall carry portable oxygen equipment with a 15 minute supply of oxygen; or

(2) There must be sufficient portable oxygen equipment (including masks and spare outlets) distributed throughout the cabin so that such equipment is immediately available to each attendant, regardless of their location in the cabin; or

(3) There are sufficient spare outlets and masks distributed throughout the cabin to ensure immediate availability of oxygen to each cabin attendant, regardless of their location in the cabin.

(e) *Passenger cabin occupants.* When the airplane is operating at flight altitudes above 10,000 feet, the following supply of oxygen must be provided for the use of passenger cabin occupants:

(1) When an airplane certificated to operate at flight altitudes up to and including flight level 250, can at any point along the route to be flown, descend safely to a flight altitude of 14,000 feet or less within four minutes, oxygen must be available at the rate prescribed by this part for a 30-minute period for at least 10 percent of the passenger cabin occupants.

(2) When an airplane is operated at flight altitudes up to and including flight level 250 and cannot descend safely to a flight altitude of 14,000 feet within four minutes, or when an airplane is operated at flight altitudes above flight level 250, oxygen must be

available at the rate prescribed by this part for not less than 10 percent of the passenger cabin occupants for the entire flight after cabin depressurization, at cabin pressure altitudes above 10,000 feet up to and including 14,000 feet and, as applicable, to allow compliance with §121.329(c) (2) and (3), except that there must be not less than a 10-minute supply for the passenger cabin occupants.

(3) For first-aid treatment of occupants who for physiological reasons might require undiluted oxygen following descent from cabin pressure altitudes above flight level 250, a supply of oxygen in accordance with the requirements of §25.1443(d) must be provided for two percent of the occupants for the entire flight after cabin depressurization at cabin pressure altitudes above 8,000 feet, but in no case to less than one person. An appropriate number of acceptable dispensing units, but in no case less than two, must be provided, with a means for the cabin attendants to use this supply.

(f) *Passenger briefing.* Before flight is conducted above flight level 250, a crewmember shall instruct the passengers on the necessity of using oxygen in the event of cabin depressurization and shall point out to them the location and demonstrate the use of the oxygen-dispensing equipment.

[Doc. No. 6258, 29 FR 19205, Dec. 31, 1964, as amended by Amdt. 121–11, 30 FR 12466, Sept. 30, 1965; Amdt. 121–132, 41 FR 55475, Dec. 20, 1976; Amdt. 121–262, 62 FR 13256, Mar. 19, 1997; 62 FR 15570, Apr. 1, 1997; Amdt. 121–306, 69 FR 62789, Oct. 27, 2004]

§121.335 Equipment standards.

(a) *Reciprocating engine powered airplanes.* The oxygen apparatus, the minimum rates of oxygen flow, and the supply of oxygen necessary to comply with §121.327 must meet the standards established in section 4b.651 of the Civil Air Regulations as in effect on July 20, 1950, except that if the certificate holder shows full compliance with those standards to be impracticable, the Administrator may authorize any change in those standards that he finds will provide an equivalent level of safety.

(b) *Turbine engine powered airplanes.* The oxygen apparatus, the minimum rate of oxygen flow, and the supply of oxygen necessary to comply with

§§121.329 and 121.333 must meet the standards established in section 4b.651 of the Civil Air Regulations as in effect on September 1, 1958, except that if the certificate holder shows full compliance with those standards to be impracticable, the Administrator may authorize any changes in those standards that he finds will provide an equivalent level of safety.

§121.337 Protective breathing equipment.

(a) The certificate holder shall furnish approved protective breathing equipment (PBE) meeting the equipment, breathing gas, and communication requirements contained in paragraph (b) of this section.

(b) *Pressurized and nonpressurized cabin airplanes.* Except as provided in paragraph (f) of this section, no person may operate an airplane unless protective breathing equipment meeting the requirements of this section is provided as follows:

(1) *General.* The equipment must protect the flightcrew from the effects of smoke, carbon dioxide or other harmful gases or an oxygen deficient environment caused by other than an airplane depressurization while on flight deck duty and must protect crewmembers from the above effects while combatting fires on board the airplane.

(2) The equipment must be inspected regularly in accordance with inspection guidelines and the inspection periods established by the equipment manufacturer to ensure its condition for continued serviceability and immediate readiness to perform its intended emergency purposes. The inspection periods may be changed upon a showing by the certificate holder that the changes would provide an equivalent level of safety.

(3) That part of the equipment protecting the eyes must not impair the wearer's vision to the extent that a crewmember's duties cannot be accomplished and must allow corrective glasses to be worn without impairment of vision or loss of the protection required by paragraph (b)(1) of this section.

(4) The equipment, while in use, must allow the flightcrew to communicate using the airplane radio equipment and

125

to communicate by interphone with each other while at their assigned duty stations. The equipment, while in use, must also allow crewmember interphone communications between each of two flight crewmember stations in the pilot compartment and at least one normal flight attendant station in each passenger compartment.

(5) The equipment, while in use, must allow any crewmember to use the airplane interphone system at any of the flight attendant stations referred to in paragraph (b)(4) of this section.

(6) The equipment may also be used to meet the supplemental oxygen requirements of this part provided it meets the oxygen equipment standards of § 121.335 of this part.

(7) Protective breathing gas duration and supply system equipment requirements are as follows:

(i) The equipment must supply breathing gas for 15 minutes at a pressure altitude of 8,000 feet for the following:

(A) Flight crewmembers while performing flight deck duties; and

(B) Crewmembers while combatting an in-flight fire.

(ii) The breathing gas system must be free from hazards in itself, in its method of operation, and in its effect upon other components.

(iii) For breathing gas systems other than chemical oxygen generators, there must be a means to allow the crew to readily determine, during the equipment preflight described in paragraph (c) of this section, that the gas supply is fully charged.

(iv) For each chemical oxygen generator, the supply system equipment must meet the requirements of § 25.1450 (b) and (c) of this chapter.

(8) *Smoke and fume protection.* Protective breathing equipment with a fixed or portable breathing gas supply meeting the requirements of this section must be conveniently located on the flight deck and be easily accessible for immediate use by each required flight crewmember at his or her assigned duty station.

(9) *Fire combatting.* Except for nontransport category airplanes type certificated after December 31, 1964, protective breathing equipment with a portable breathing gas supply meeting the requirements of this section must be easily accessible and conveniently located for immediate use by crewmembers in combatting fires as follows:

(i) One PBE is required for each hand fire extinguisher located for use in a galley other than a galley located in a passenger, cargo, or crew compartment.

(ii) One on the flight deck, except that the Administrator may authorize another location for this PBE if special circumstances exist that make compliance impractical and the proposed deviation would provide an equivalent level of safety.

(iii) In each passenger compartment, one for each hand fire extinguisher required by § 121.309 of this part, to be located within 3 feet of each required hand fire extinguisher, except that the Administrator may authorize a deviation allowing locations of PBE more than 3 feet from required hand fire extinguisher locations if special circumstances exist that make compliance impractical and if the proposed deviation provides an equivalent level of safety.

(c) *Equipment preflight.* (1) Before each flight, each item of PBE at flight crewmember duty stations must be checked by the flight crewmember who will use the equipment to ensure that the equipment—

(i) For other than chemical oxygen generator systems, is functioning, is serviceable, fits properly (unless a universal-fit type), and is connected to supply terminals and that the breathing gas supply and pressure are adequate for use; and

(ii) For chemical oxygen generator systems, is serviceable and fits properly (unless a universal-fit type).

(2) Each item of PBE located at other than a flight crewmember duty station must be checked by a designated crewmember to ensure that each is properly stowed and serviceable, and, for other than chemical oxygen generator systems, the breathing gas supply is fully charged. Each certificate holder, in its operations manual, must designate at least one crewmember to perform those checks before he or she takes off in

that airplane for his or her first flight of the day.

[Doc. No. 24792, 52 FR 20957, June 3, 1987, as amended by Amdt. 121–204, 54 FR 22271, May 22, 1989; Amdt. 121–212, 55 FR 5551, Feb 15, 1990; Amdt. 121–218, 55 FR 31565, Aug. 2, 1990; Amdt. 121–230, 57 FR 42674, Sept. 15, 1992; Amdt. 121–251, 60 FR 65932, Dec. 20, 1995; Amdt. 121–261, 61 FR 43921, Aug. 26, 1996]

§121.339 Emergency equipment for extended over-water operations.

(a) Except where the Administrator, by amending the operations specifications of the certificate holder, requires the carriage of all or any specific items of the equipment listed below for any overwater operation, or upon application of the certificate holder, the Administrator allows deviation for a particular extended overwater operation, no person may operate an airplane in extended overwater operations without having on the airplane the following equipment:

(1) A life preserver equipped with an approved survivor locator light, for each occupant of the airplane.

(2) Enough life rafts (each equipped with an approved survivor locator light) of a rated capacity and buoyancy to accommodate the occupants of the airplane. Unless excess rafts of enough capacity are provided, the buoyancy and seating capacity beyond the rated capacity of the rafts must accommodate all occupants of the airplane in the event of a loss of one raft of the largest rated capacity.

(3) At least one pyrotechnic signaling device for each life raft.

(4) An approved survival type emergency locator transmitter. Batteries used in this transmitter must be replaced (or recharged, if the battery is rechargeable) when the transmitter has been in use for more than 1 cumulative hour, or when 50 percent of their useful life (or for rechargeable batteries, 50 percent of their useful life of charge) has expired, as established by the transmitter manufacturer under its approval. The new expiration date for replacing (or recharging) the battery must be legibly marked on the outside of the transmitter. The battery useful life (or useful life of charge) requirements of this paragraph do not apply to batteries (such as water-activated batteries) that are essentially unaffected during probable storage intervals.

(b) The required life rafts, life preservers, and survival type emergency locator transmitter must be easily accessible in the event of a ditching without appreciable time for preparatory procedures. This equipment must be installed in conspicuously marked, approved locations.

(c) A survival kit, appropriately equipped for the route to be flown, must be attached to each required life raft.

[Doc. No. 6258, 29 FR 19205, Dec. 31, 1964, as amended by Amdt. 121–53, 34 FR 15244, Sept. 30, 1969; Amdt. 121–79, 36 FR 18724, Sept. 21, 1971; Amdt. 121–93, 37 FR 14294, June 19, 1972 Amdt. 121–106, 38 FR 22378, Aug. 20, 1973; Amdt. 121–149, 43 FR 50603, Oct. 30, 1978; Amdt. 121–158, 45 FR 38348, June 9, 1980; Amdt. 121–239, 59 FR 32057, June 21, 1994]

§121.340 Emergency flotation means.

(a) Except as provided in paragraph (b) of this section, no person may operate an airplane in any overwater operation unless it is equipped with life preservers in accordance with §121.339(a)(1) or with an approved flotation means for each occupant. This means must be within easy reach of each seated occupant and must be readily removable from the airplane.

(b) Upon application by the air carrier or commercial operator, the Administrator may approve the operation of an airplane over water without the life preservers or flotation means required by paragraph (a) of this section, if the air carrier or commercial operator shows that the water over which the airplane is to be operated is not of such size and depth that life preservers or flotation means would be required for the survival of its occupants in the event the flight terminates in that water.

[Doc. No. 6713, 31 FR 1147, Jan. 28, 1966, as amended by Amdt. 121–25, 32 FR 3223, Feb. 24, 1967; Amdt. 121–251, 60 FR 65932, Dec. 20, 1995]

§121.341 Equipment for operations in icing conditions.

(a) Except as permitted in paragraph (c)(2) of this section, unless an airplane is type certificated under the transport category airworthiness requirements relating to ice protection, or unless an airplane is a non-transport category airplane type certificated after December 31, 1964, that has the ice protection provisions that meet section 34 of appendix A of part 135 of this chapter, no person may operate an airplane in icing conditions unless it is equipped with means for the prevention or removal of ice on windshields, wings, empennage, propellers, and other parts of the airplane where ice formation will adversely affect the safety of the airplane.

(b) No person may operate an airplane in icing conditions at night unless means are provided for illuminating or otherwise determining the formation of ice on the parts of the wings that are critical from the standpoint of ice accumulation. Any illuminating that is used must be of a type that will not cause glare or reflection that would handicap crewmembers in the performance of their duties.

(c) *Non-transport category airplanes type certificated after December 31, 1964.* Except for an airplane that has ice protection provisions that meet section 34 of appendix A of part 135 of this chapter, or those for transport category airplane type certification, no person may operate—

(1) Under IFR into known or forecast light or moderate icing conditions;

(2) Under VFR into known light or moderate icing conditions; unless the airplane has functioning deicing anti-icing equipment protecting each propeller, windshield, wing, stabilizing or control surface, and each airspeed, altimeter, rate of climb, or flight attitude instrument system; or

(3) Into known or forecast severe icing conditions.

(d) If current weather reports and briefing information relied upon by the pilot in command indicate that the forecast icing condition that would otherwise prohibit the flight will not be encountered during the flight because of changed weather conditions since the forecast, the restrictions in paragraph (c) of this section based on forecast conditions do not apply.

[Doc. No. 6258, 29 FR 18205, Dec. 31, 1964, as amended by Amdt. 121–251, 60 FR 65929, Dec. 20, 1995]

§ 121.342   Pitot heat indication systems.

No person may operate a transport category airplane or, after December 20, 1999, a nontransport category airplane type certificated after December 31, 1964, that is equipped with a flight instrument pitot heating system unless the airplane is also equipped with an operable pitot heat indication system that complies § 25.1326 of this chapter in effect on April 12, 1978.

[Doc. No. 28154, 60 FR 65932, Dec. 20, 1995]

§ 121.343   Flight data recorders.

(a) Except as provided in paragraphs (b), (c), (d), (e), and (f) of this section, no person may operate a large airplane that is certificated for operations above 25,000 feet altitude or is turbine-engine powered unless it is equipped with one or more approved flight recorders that record data from which the following may be determined within the ranges, accuracies, and recording intervals specified in appendix B of this part:

(1) Time;

(2) Altitude;

(3) Airspeed;

(4) Vertical acceleration;

(5) Heading; and

(6) Time of each radio transmission either to or from air traffic control.

(b) No person may operate a large airplane type certificated up to and including September 30, 1969, for operations above 25,000 feet altitude, or a turbine-engine powered airplane certificated before the same date, unless it is equipped before May 26, 1989 with one or more approved flight recorders that utilize a digital method of recording and storing data and a method of readily retrieving that data from the storage medium. The following information must be able to be determined within the ranges, accuracies, and recording intervals specified in appendix B of this part:

(1) Time;

(2) Altitude;

(3) Airspeed;

(4) Vertical acceleration;

(5) Heading; and

(6) Time of each radio transmission either to or from air traffic control.

(c) Except as provided in paragraph (1) of this section, no person may operate an airplane specified in paragraph (b) of this section unless it is equipped, before May 26, 1995, with one or more approved flight recorders that utilize a digital method of recording and storing data and a method of readily retrieving that data from the storage medium. The following information must be able to be determined within the ranges, accuracies and recording intervals specified in appendix B of this part:

(1) Time;
(2) Altitude;
(3) Airspeed;
(4) Vertical acceleration;
(5) Heading;
(6) Time of each radio transmission either to or from air traffic control;
(7) Pitch attitude;
(8) Roll attitude;
(9) Longitudinal acceleration;
(10) Control column or pitch control surface position; and
(11) Thrust of each engine.

(d) No person may operate an airplane specified in paragraph (b) of this section that is manufactured after May 26, 1989, as well as airplanes specified in paragraph (a) of this section that have been type certificated after September 30, 1969, unless it is equipped with one or more approved flight recorders that utlitize a digital method of recording and storing data and a method of readily retrieving that data from the storage medium. The following information must be able to be determined within the ranges, accuracies, and recording intervals specified in appendix B of this part:

(1) Time;
(2) Altitude;
(3) Airspeed;
(4) Vertical acceleration;
(5) Heading;
(6) Time of each radio transmission either to or from air traffic control;
(7) Pitch attitude;
(8) Roll attitude;
(9) Longitudinal acceleration;
(10) Pitch trim position;
(11) Control column or pitch control surface position;
(12) Control wheel or lateral control surface position;

(13) Rudder pedal or yaw control surface position;
(14) Thrust of each engine;
(15) Position of each thrust reverser;
(16) Trailing edge flap or cockpit flap control position; and
(17) Leading edge flap or cockpit flap control position.

For the purpose of this section, *manufactured* means the point in time at which the airplane inspection acceptance records reflect that the airplane is complete and meets the FAA-approved type design data.

(e) After October 11, 1991, no person may operate a large airplane equipped with a digital data bus and ARINC 717 digital flight data acquisition unit (DFDAU) or equivalent unless it is equipped with one or more approved flight recorders that utilize a digital method of recording and storing data and a method of readily retrieving that data from the storage medium. Any parameters specified in appendix B of this part that are available on the digital data bus must be recorded within the ranges, accuracies, resolutions, and sampling intervals specified.

(f) After October 11, 1991, no person may operate an airplane specified in paragraph (b) of this section that is manufactured after October 11, 1991, nor an airplane specified in paragraph (a) of this section that has been type certificated after September 30, 1969, and manufactured after October 11, 1991, unless it is equipped with one or more flight recorders that utilize a digital method of recording and storing data and a method of readily retrieving that data from the storage medium. The parameters specified in appendix B of this part must be recorded within the ranges, accuracies, resolutions, and sampling intervals specified.

(g) Whenever a flight recorder required by this section is installed, it must be operated continuously from the instant the airplane begins the takeoff roll until it has completed the landing roll at an airport.

(h) Except as provided in paragraph (i) of this section, and except for recorded data erased as authorized in this paragraph, each certificate holder shall keep the recorded data prescribed in paragraph (a), (b), (c), or (d) of this section, as appropriate, until the airplane has been operated for at least 25 hours of the operating time specified in § 121.359(a). A total of 1 hour of recorded data may be erased for the purpose of testing the flight recorder or the flight recorder system. Any erasure made in accordance with this paragraph must be of the oldest recorded data accumulated at the time of testing. Except as provided in paragraph (i) of this section, no record need be kept more than 60 days.

(i) In the event of an accident or occurrence that requires immediate notification of the National Transportation Safety Board under part 830 of its regulations and that results in termination of the flight, the certificate holder shall remove the recording media from the airplane and keep the recorded data required by paragraph (a), (b), (c), or (d) of this section, as appropriate, for at least 60 days or for a longer period upon the request of the Board or the Administrator.

(j) Each flight recorder required by this section must be installed in accordance with the requirements of § 25.1459 of this chapter in effect on August 31, 1977. The correlation required by § 25.1459(c) of this chapter need be established only on one airplane of any group of airplanes—

(1) That are of the same type;

(2) On which the model flight recorder and its installation are the same; and

(3) On which there is no difference in the type design with respect to the installation of those first pilot's instruments associated with the flight recorder. The most recent instrument calibration, including the recording medium from which this calibration is derived, and the recorder correlation must be retained by the certificate holder.

(k) Each flight recorder required by this section that records the data specified in paragraph (a), (b), (c), or (d) of this section, as appropriate, must have an approved device to assist in locating that recorder under water.

(1) No person may operate an airplane specified in paragraph (b) of this section that meets the Stage 2 noise levels of part 36 of this chapter and is subject to § 91.801(c) of this chapter unless it is

equipped with one or more approved flight data recorders that utilize a digital method of recording and storing data and a method of readily retrieving that data from the storage medium. The information specified in paragraphs (c)(1) through (c)(11) of this section must be able to be determined within the ranges, accuracies and recording intervals specified in appendix B of this part. In addition—

(1) This flight data recorder must be installed at the next heavy maintenance check after May 26, 1994, but no later than May 26, 1995. A heavy maintenance check is considered to be any time an aircraft is scheduled to be out of service for 4 or more days.

(2) By June 23, 1994, each carrier must submit to the FAA Flight Standards Service, Air Transportation Division (AFS–200), documentation listing those airplanes covered under this paragraph and evidence that it has ordered a sufficient number of flight data recorders to meet the May 26, 1995, compliance date for all aircraft on that list.

(3) After May 26, 1994, any aircraft that is modified to meet Stage 3 noise levels must have the flight data recorder described in paragraph (c) of this section installed before operating under this part.

(m) After August 20, 2001, this section applies only to the airplane models listed in § 121.344(1)(2). All other airplanes must comply with the requirements of § 121.344, as applicable.

[Doc. No. 24418, 52 FR 9636, Mar. 25, 1987, as amended by Amdt. 121–197, 53 FR 26147, July 11, 1988; Amdt. 121–238, 59 FR 26900, May 24, 1994; Amdt. 121–338, 73 FR 12565, Mar. 7, 2008]

§ 121.344 Digital flight data recorders for transport category airplanes.

(a) Except as provided in paragraph (1) of this section, no person may operate under this part a turbine-engine-powered transport category airplane unless it is equipped with one or more approved flight recorders that use a digital method of recording and storing data and a method of readily retrieving that data from the storage medium. The operational parameters required to be recorded by digital flight data recorders required by this section are as follows: The phrase "when an information source is installed" following a parameter indicates that recording of that parameter is not intended to require a change in installed equipment:

(1) Time;

(2) Pressure altitude;

(3) Indicated airspeed;

(4) Heading—primary flight crew reference (if selectable, record discrete, true or magnetic);

(5) Normal acceleration (Vertical);

(6) Pitch attitude;

(7) Roll attitude;

(8) Manual radio transmitter keying, or CVR/DFDR synchronization reference;

(9) Thrust/power of each engine—primary flight crew reference;

(10) Autopilot engagement status

(11) Longitudinal acceleration;

(12) Pitch control input;

(13) Lateral control input;

(14) Rudder pedal input;

(15) Primary pitch control surface position;

(16) Primary lateral control surface position;

(17) Primary yaw control surface position;

(18) Lateral acceleration;

(19) Pitch trim surface position or parameters of paragraph (a)(82) of this section if currently recorded;

(20) Trailing edge flap or cockpit flap control selection (except when parameters of paragraph (a)(85) of this section apply);

(21) Leading edge flap or cockpit flap control selection (except when parameters of paragraph (a)(86) of this section apply);

(22) Each Thrust reverser position (or equivalent for propeller airplane);

(23) Ground spoiler position or speed brake selection (except when parameters of paragraph (a)(87) of this section apply);

(24) Outside or total air temperature;

(25) Automatic Flight Control System (AFCS) modes and engagement status, including autothrottle;

(26) Radio altitude (when an information source is installed);

(27) Localizer deviation, MLS Azimuth;

(28) Glideslope deviation, MLS Elevation;

(29) Marker beacon passage;

(30) Master warning;

(31) Air/ground sensor (primary airplane system reference nose or main gear);

(32) Angle of attack (when information source is installed);

(33) Hydraulic pressure low (each system);

(34) Ground speed (when an information source is installed);

(35) Ground proximity warning system;

(36) Landing gear position or landing gear cockpit control selection;

(37) Drift angle (when an information source is installed);

(38) Wind speed and direction (when an information source is installed);

(39) Latitude and longitude (when an information source is installed);

(40) Stick shaker/pusher (when an information source is installed);

(41) Windshear (when an information source is installed);

(42) Throttle/power lever position;

(43) Additional engine parameters (as designated in Appendix M of this part);

(44) Traffic alert and collision avoidance system;

(45) DME 1 and 2 distances;

(46) Nav 1 and 2 selected frequency;

(47) Selected barometric setting (when an information source is installed);

(48) Selected altitude (when an information source is installed);

(49) Selected speed (when an information source is installed);

(50) Selected mach (when an information source is installed);

(51) Selected vertical speed (when an information source is installed);

(52) Selected heading (when an information source is installed);

(53) Selected flight path (when an information source is installed);

(54) Selected decision height (when an information source is installed);

(55) EFIS display format;

(56) Multi-function/engine/alerts display format;

(57) Thrust command (when an information source is installed);

(58) Thrust target (when an information source is installed);

(59) Fuel quantity in CG trim tank (when an information source is installed);

(60) Primary Navigation System Reference;

(61) Icing (when an information source is installed);

(62) Engine warning each engine vibration (when an information source is installed);

(63) Engine warning each engine over temp. (when an information source is installed);

(64) Engine warning each engine oil pressure low (when an information source is installed);

(65) Engine warning each engine over speed (when an information source is installed);

(66) Yaw trim surface position;

(67) Roll trim surface position;

(68) Brake pressure (selected system);

(69) Brake pedal application (left and right);

(70) Yaw or sideslip angle (when an information source is installed);

(71) Engine bleed valve position (when an information source is installed);

(72) De-icing or anti-icing system selection (when an information source is installed);

(73) Computed center of gravity (when an information source is installed);

(74) AC electrical bus status;

(75) DC electrical bus status;

(76) APU bleed valve position (when an information source is installed);

(77) Hydraulic pressure (each system);

(78) Loss of cabin pressure;

(79) Computer failure;

(80) Heads-up display (when an information source is installed);

(81) Para-visual display (when an information source is installed);

(82) Cockpit trim control input position—pitch;

(83) Cockpit trim control input position—roll;

(84) Cockpit trim control input position—yaw;

(85) Trailing edge flap and cockpit flap control position;

(86) Leading edge flap and cockpit flap control position;

(87) Ground spoiler position and speed brake selection;

(88) All cockpit flight control input forces (control wheel, control column, rudder pedal);

(89) Yaw damper status;

(90) Yaw damper command; and

(91) Standby rudder valve status.

(b) For all turbine-engine powered transport category airplanes manufactured on or before October 11, 1991, by August 20, 2001.

(1) For airplanes not equipped as of July 16, 1996, with a flight data acquisition unit (FDAU), the parameters listed in paragraphs (a)(1) through (a)(18) of this section must be recorded within the ranges and accuracies specified in Appendix B of this part, and—

(i) For airplanes with more than two engines, the parameter described in paragraph (a)(18) is not required unless sufficient capacity is available on the existing recorder to record that parameter;

(ii) Parameters listed in paragraphs (a)(12) through (a)(17) each may be recorded from a single source.

(2) For airplanes that were equipped as of July 16, 1996, with a flight data acquisition unit (FDAU), the parameters listed in paragraphs (a)(1) through (a)(22) of this section must be recorded within the ranges, accuracies, and recording intervals specified in Appendix M of this part. Parameters listed in paragraphs (a)(12) through (a)(17) each may be recorded from a single source.

(3) The approved flight recorder required by this section must be installed at the earliest time practicable, but no later than the next heavy maintenance check after August 18, 1999 and no later than August 20, 2001. A heavy maintenance check is considered to be any time an airplane is scheduled to be out of service for 4 or more days and is scheduled to include access to major structural components.

(c) For all turbine-engine powered transport category airplanes manufactured on or before October 11, 1991—

(1) That were equipped as of July 16, 1996, with one or more digital data bus(es) and an ARINC 717 digital flight data acquisition unit (DFDAU) or equivalent, the parameters specified in paragraphs (a)(1) through (a)(22) of this section must be recorded within the ranges, accuracies, resolutions, and sampling intervals specified in Appendix M of this part by August 20, 2001. Parameters listed in paragraphs (a)(12)

through (a)(14) each may be recorded from a single source.

(2) Commensurate with the capacity of the recording system (DFDAU or equivalent and the DFDR), all additional parameters for which information sources are installed and which are connected to the recording system must be recorded within the ranges, accuracies, resolutions, and sampling intervals specified in Appendix M of this part by August 20, 2001.

(3) That were subject to §121.343(e) of this part, all conditions of §121.343(e) must continue to be met until compliance with paragraph (c)(1) of this section is accomplished.

(d) For all turbine-engine-powered transport category airplanes that were manufactured after October 11, 1991—

(1) The parameters listed in paragraph (a)(1) through (a)(34) of this section must be recorded within the ranges, accuracies, resolutions, and recording intervals specified in Appendix M of this part by August 20, 2001. Parameters listed in paragraphs (a)(12) through (a)(14) each may be recorded from a single source.

(2) Commensurate with the capacity of the recording system, all additional parameters for which information sources are installed and which are connected to the recording system must be recorded within the ranges, accuracies, resolutions, and sampling intervals specified in Appendix M of this part by August 20, 2001.

(e) For all turbine-engine-powered transport category airplanes that are manufactured after August 18, 2000—

(1) The parameters listed in paragraph (a)(1) through (57) of this section must be recorded within the ranges, accuracies, resolutions, and recording intervals specified in Appendix M of this part.

(2) Commensurate with the capacity of the recording system, all additional parameters for which information sources are installed and which are connected to the recording system, must be recorded within the ranges, accuracies, resolutions, and sampling intervals specified in Appendix M of this part.

(3) In addition to the requirements of paragraphs (e)(1) and (e)(2) of this section, all Boeing 737 model airplanes

must also comply with the requirements of paragraph (n) of this section, as applicable.

(f) For all turbine-engine-powered transport category airplanes manufactured after August 19, 2002—

(1) The parameters listed in paragraphs (a)(1) through (a)(88) of this section must be recorded within the ranges, accuracies, resolutions, and recording intervals specified in appendix M to this part.

(2) In addition to the requirements of paragraphs (f)(1) of this section, all Boeing 737 model airplanes must also comply with the requirements of paragraph (n) of this section.

(g) Whenever a flight data recorder required by this section is installed, it must be operated continuously from the instant the airplane begins its takeoff roll until it has completed its landing roll.

(h) Except as provided in paragraph (i) of this section, and except for recorded data erased as authorized in this paragraph, each certificate holder shall keep the recorded data prescribed by this section, as appropriate, until the airplane has been operated for at least 25 hours of the operating time specified in §121.359(a) of this part. A total of 1 hour of recorded data may be erased for the purpose of testing the flight recorder or the flight recorder system. Any erasure made in accordance with this paragraph must be of the oldest recorded data accumulated at the time of testing. Except as provided in paragraph (i) of this section, no record need be kept more than 60 days.

(i) In the event of an accident or occurrence that requires immediate notification of the National Transportation Safety Board under 49 CFR 830 of its regulations and that results in termination of the flight, the certificate holder shall remove the recorder from the airplane and keep the recorder data prescribed by this section, as appropriate, for at least 60 days or for a longer period upon the request of the Board or the Administrator.

(j) Each flight data recorder system required by this section must be installed in accordance with the requirements of §25.1459(a) (except paragraphs (a)(3)(ii) and (a)(7)), (b), (d) and (e) of this chapter. A correlation must be established between the values recorded by the flight data recorder and the corresponding values being measured. The correlation must contain a sufficient number of correlation points to accurately establish the conversion from the recorded values to engineering units or discrete state over the full operating range of the parameter. Except for airplanes having separate altitude and airspeed sensors that are an integral part of the flight data recorder system, a single correlation may be established for any group of airplanes—

(1) That are of the same type;

(2) On which the flight recorder system and its installation are the same; and

(3) On which there is no difference in the type design with respect to the installation of those sensors associated with the flight data recorder system. Documentation sufficient to convert recorded data into the engineering units and discrete values specified in the applicable appendix must be maintained by the certificate holder.

(k) Each flight data recorder required by this section must have an approved device to assist in locating that recorder under water.

(l) The following airplanes that were manufactured before August 18, 1997 need not comply with this section, but must continue to comply with applicable paragraphs of § 121.343 of this chapter, as appropriate:

(1) Airplanes that meet the State 2 noise levels of part 36 of this chapter and are subject to § 91.801(c) of this chapter, until January 1, 2000. On and after January 1, 2000, any Stage 2 airplane otherwise allowed to be operated under Part 91 of this chapter must comply with the applicable flight data recorder requirements of this section for that airplane.

(2) British Aerospace 1-11, General Dynamics Convair 580, General Dynamics Convair 600, General Dynamics Convair 640, deHavilland Aircraft Company Ltd. DHC-7, Fairchild Industries FH 227, Fokker F-27 (except Mark 50), F-28 Mark 1000 and Mark 4000, Gulfstream Aerospace G-159, Jetstream 4100 Series, Lockheed Aircraft Corporation Electra 10-A, Lockheed Aircraft Corporation Electra 10-B, Lockheed Aircraft Corporation Electra 10-E, Lockheed Aircraft Corporation Electra L-188, Lockheed Martin Model 382 (L-100) Hercules, Maryland Air Industries, Inc. F27, Mitsubishi Heavy Industries, Ltd. YS-11, Short Bros. Limited SD3-30, Short Bros. Limited SD3-60.

(m) All aircraft subject to the requirements of this section that are manufactured on or after April 7, 2010, must have a digital flight data recorder installed that also—

(1) Meets the requirements of § 25.1459(a)(3), (a)(7), and (a)(8) of this chapter; and

(2) Retains the 25 hours of recorded information required in paragraph (h) of this section using a recorder that meets the standards of TSO-C124a, or later revision.

(n) In addition to all other applicable requirements of this section, all Boeing 737 model airplanes manufactured after August 18, 2000 must record the parameters listed in paragraphs (a)(88) through (a)(91) of this section within the ranges, accuracies, resolutions, and recording intervals specified in Appendix M to this part. Compliance with this paragraph is required no later than February 2, 2011.

[Doc. No. 28109, 62 FR 38378, July 17, 1997; 62 FR 48135, Sept. 12, 1997, as amended by Amdt. 121-300, 68 FR 42936, July 18, 2003; 68 FR 50069, Aug. 20, 2003; Amdt. 121-338, 73 FR 12565, Mar. 7, 2008; Amdt. 121-342, 73 FR 73178, Dec. 2, 2008; Amdt. 121-338, 74 FR 32800, July 9, 2009]

§ 121.344a   Digital flight data recorders for 10-19 seat airplanes.

(a) Except as provided in paragraph (f) of this section, no person may operate under this part a turbine-engine-powered airplane having a passenger seating configuration, excluding any required crewmember seat, of 10 to 19 seats, that was brought onto the U.S. register after, or was registered outside the United States and added to the operator's U.S. operations specifications after, October 11, 1991, unless it is equipped with one or more approved flight recorders that use a digital method of recording and storing data and a method of readily retrieving that data from the storage medium. On or before August 20, 2001, airplanes brought onto the U.S. register after October 11, 1991, must comply with either the requirements in this section or the applicable paragraphs in §135.152 of this chapter. In addition, by August 20, 2001.

(1) The parameters listed in §§121.344(a)(1) through 121.344(a)(18) of this part must be recorded with the ranges, accuracies, and resolutions specified in Appendix B of part 135 of this chapter, except that—

(i) Either the parameter listed in §121.344 (a)(12) or (a)(15) of this part must be recorded; either the parameters listed in §121.344(a)(13) or (a)(16) of this part must be recorded; and either the parameter listed in §121.344(a)(14) or (a)(17) of this part must be recorded.

(ii) For airplanes with more than two engines, the parameter described in §121.344(a)(18) of this part must also be recorded if sufficient capacity is available on the existing recorder to record that parameter;

(iii) Parameters listed in §§121.344(a)(12) through 121.344(a)(17) of this part each may be recorded from a single source;

(iv) Any parameter for which no value is contained in Appendix B of part 135 of this chapter must be recorded within the ranges, accuracies, and resolutions specified in Appendix M of this part.

(2) Commensurate with the capacity of the recording system (FDAU or equivalent and the DFDR), the parameters listed in §§121.344(a)(19) through 121.344(a)(22) of this part also must be recorded within the ranges, accuracies, resolutions, and recording intervals specified in Appendix B of part 135 of this chapter.

(3) The approved flight recorder required by this section must be installed as soon as practicable, but no later than the next heavy maintenance check or equivalent after August 18, 1999. A heavy maintenance check is considered to be any time an airplane is scheduled to be out of service for 4 more days and is scheduled to include access to major structural components.

(b) For a turbine-engine-powered airplanes having a passenger seating configuration, excluding any required crewmember seat, of 10 to 19 seats, that are manufactured after August 18, 2000.

(1) The parameters listed in §§121.344(a)(1) through 121.344(a)(57) of

this part, must be recorded within the ranges, accuracies, resolutions, and recording intervals specified in Appendix M of this part.

(2) Commensurate with the capacity of the recording system, all additional parameters listed in §121.344(a) of this part for which information sources are installed and which are connected to the recording system, must be recorded within the ranges, accuracies, resolutions, and sampling intervals specified in Appendix M of this part by August 20, 2001.

(c) For all turbine-engine-powered airplanes having a passenger seating configuration, excluding any required crewmember seats, of 10 to 19 seats, that are manufactured after August 19, 2002, the parameters listed in §121.344(a)(1) through (a)(88) of this part must be recorded within the ranges, accuracies, resolutions, and recording intervals specified in Appendix M of this part.

(d) Each flight data recorder system required by this section must be installed in accordance with the requirements of §23.1459(a) (except paragraphs (a)(3)(ii) and (6)), (b), (d) and (e) of this chapter. A correlation must be established between the values recorded by the flight data recorder and the corresponding values being measured. The correlation must contain a sufficient number of correlation points to accurately establish the conversion from the recorded values to engineering units or discrete state over the full operating range of the parameter. A single correlation may be established for any group of airplanes—

(1) That are of the same type;

(2) On which the flight recorder system and its installation are the same; and

(3) On which there is no difference in the type design with respect to the installation of those sensors associated with the flight data recorder system. Correlation documentation must be maintained by the certificate holder.

(e) All airplanes subject to this section are also subject to the requirements and exceptions stated in §121.344(g) through (k) and §121.346.

(f) For airplanes that were manufactured before August 18, 1997, the following airplane types need not comply with this section, but must continue to comply with applicable paragraphs of § 135.152 of this chapter, as appropriate: Beech Aircraft-99 Series, Beech Aircraft 1300, Beech Aircraft 1900C, Construcciones Aeronauticas, S.A. (CASA) C-212, deHavilland DHC-6, Dornier 228, HS-748, Embraer EMB 110, Jetstream 3101, Jetstream 3201, Fairchild Aircraft SA-226, Fairchild Metro SA-227.

(g) All airplanes subject to the requirements of this section that are manufactured on or after April 7, 2010, must have a digital flight data recorder installed that also—

(1) Meets the requirements in § 23.1459(a)(3), (a)(6), and (a)(7) or § 25.1459(a)(3), (a)(7), and (a)(8) of this chapter, as applicable; and

(2) Retains the 25 hours of recorded information required in § 121.344(g) using a recorder that meets the standards of TSO-C124a, or later revision.

[Doc. No. 28109, 62 FR 38380, July 17, 1997; 62 FR 48135, Sept. 12, 1997; 62 FR 65202, Dec. 11, 1997, as amended by Amdt. 121-300, 68 FR 42936, July 18, 2003; Amdt. 121-338, 73 FR 12566, Mar. 7, 2008; Amdt. 121-338, 74 FR 32801, July 9, 2009; Amdt. 121-347, 75 FR 7356, Feb. 19, 2010]

§ 121.345 Radio equipment.

(a) No person may operate an airplane unless it is equipped with radio equipment required for the kind of operation being conducted.

(b) Where two independent (separate and complete) radio systems are required by §§ 121.347 and 121.349, each system must have an independent antenna installation except that, where rigidly supported nonwire antennas or other antenna installations of equivalent reliability are used, only one antenna is required.

(c) ATC transponder equipment installed within the time periods indicated below must meet the performance and environmental requirements of the following TSO's:

(1) *Through January 1, 1992:* (i) Any class of TSO-C74b or any class of TSO-C74c as appropriate, provided that the equipment was manufactured before January 1, 1990; or

(ii) The appropriate class of TSO-C112 (Mode S).

(2) *After January 1, 1992:* The appropriate class of TSO-C112 (Mode S). For purposes of paragraph (c) (2) of this section, "installation" does not include—

(i) Temporary installation of TSO-C74b or TSO-C74c substitute equipment, as appropriate, during maintenance of the permanent equipment;

(ii) Reinstallation of equipment after temporary removal for maintenance; or

(iii) For fleet operations, installation of equipment in a fleet aircraft after removal of the equipment for maintenance from another aircraft in the same operator's fleet.

[Doc. No. 6258, 29 FR 19205, Dec. 31, 1964, as amended by Amdt. 121-101, 37 FR 28499, Dec. 27, 1972; Amdt. 121-190, 52 FR 3391, Feb. 3, 1987]

§ 121.346 Flight data recorders: filtered data.

(a) A flight data signal is filtered when an original sensor signal has been changed in any way, other than changes necessary to:

(1) Accomplish analog to digital conversion of the signal;

(2) Format a digital signal to be DFDR compatible; or

(3) Eliminate a high frequency component of a signal that is outside the operational bandwidth of the sensor.

(b) An original sensor signal for any flight recorder parameter required to be recorded under § 121.344 may be filtered only if the recorded signal value continues to meet the requirements of Appendix B or M of this part, as applicable.

(c) For a parameter described in § 121.344(a) (12) through (17), (42), or (88), or the corresponding parameter in Appendix B of this part, if the recorded signal value is filtered and does not meet the requirements of Appendix B or M of this part, as applicable, the certificate holder must:

(1) Remove the filtering and ensure that the recorded signal value meets the requirements of Appendix B or M of this part, as applicable; or

(2) Demonstrate by test and analysis that the original sensor signal value can be reconstructed from the recorded data. This demonstration requires that:

(i) The FAA determine that the procedure and the test results submitted by the certificate holder as its compliance with paragraph (c)(2) of this section are repeatable; and

(ii) The certificate holder maintains documentation of the procedure required to reconstruct the original sensor signal value. This documentation is also subject to the requirements of §121.344(i).

(d) *Compliance.* Compliance is required as follows:

(1) No later than October 20, 2011, each operator must determine, for each airplane on its operations specifications, whether the airplane's DFDR system is filtering any of the parameters listed in paragraph (c) of this section. The operator must create a record of this determination for each airplane it operates, and maintain it as part of the correlation documentation required by §121.344(j)(3) of this part.

(2) For airplanes that are not filtering any listed parameter, no further action is required unless the airplane's DFDR system is modified in a manner that would cause it to meet the definition of filtering on any listed parameter.

(3) For airplanes found to be filtering a parameter listed in paragraph (c) of this section, the operator must either:

(i) No later than April 21, 2014, remove the filtering; or

(ii) No later than April 22, 2013, submit the necessary procedure and test results required by paragraph (c)(2) of this section.

(4) After April 21, 2014, no aircraft flight data recording system may filter any parameter listed in paragraph (c) of this section that does not meet the requirements of Appendix B or M of this part, unless the certificate holder possesses test and analysis procedures and the test results that have been approved by the FAA. All records of tests, analysis and procedures used to comply with this section must be maintained as part of the correlation documentation required by §121.344(j)(3) of this part.

[Doc. No. FAA–2006–26135, 75 FR 7356, Feb. 19, 2010]

§121.347 **Communication and navigation equipment for operations under VFR over routes navigated by pilotage.**

(a) No person may operate an airplane under VFR over routes that can be navigated by pilotage unless the airplane is equipped with the radio communication equipment necessary under normal operating conditions to fulfill the following:

(1) Communicate with at least one appropriate station from any point on the route;

(2) Communicate with appropriate air traffic control facilities from any point within Class B, Class C, or Class D airspace, or within a Class E surface area designated for an airport in which flights are intended; and

(3) Receive meteorological information from any point en route by either of two independent systems. One of the means provided to comply with this subparagraph may be used to comply with paragraphs (a)(1) and (2) of this section.

(b) No person may operate an airplane at night under VFR over routes that can be navigated by pilotage unless that airplane is equipped with—

(1) Radio communication equipment necessary under normal operating conditions to fulfill the functions specified in paragraph (a) of this section; and

(2) Navigation equipment suitable for the route to be flown.

[Doc. No. 6258, 29 FR 19205, Dec. 31, 1964, as amended by Amdt. 121–226, 56 FR 65663, Dec. 17, 1991; Amdt. 121–333, 72 FR 31681, June 7, 2007]

§121.349 **Communication and navigation equipment for operations under VFR over routes not navigated by pilotage or for operations under IFR or over the top.**

(a) *Navigation equipment requirements—General.* No person may conduct operations under VFR over routes that cannot be navigated by pilotage, or operations conducted under IFR or over the top, unless—

(1) The en route navigation aids necessary for navigating the airplane along the route (e.g., ATS routes, arrival and departure routes, and instrument approach procedures, including missed approach procedures if a missed

137

approach routing is specified in the procedure) are available and suitable for use by the aircraft navigation systems required by this section;

(2) The airplane used in those operations is equipped with at least—

(i) Except as provided in paragraph (c) of this section, two approved independent navigation systems suitable for navigating the airplane along the route to be flown within the degree of accuracy required for ATC;

(ii) One marker beacon receiver providing visual and aural signals; and

(iii) One ILS receiver; and

(3) Any RNAV system used to meet the navigation equipment requirements of this section is authorized in the certificate holder's operations specifications.

(b) *Communication equipment requirements.* No person may operate an airplane under VFR over routes that cannot be navigated by pilotage, and no person may operate an airplane under IFR or over the top, unless the airplane is equipped with—

(1) At least two independent communication systems necessary under normal operating conditions to fulfill the functions specified in § 121.347 (a); and

(2) At least one of the communication systems required by paragraph (b)(1) of this section must have two-way voice communication capability.

(c) *Use of a single independent navigation system for operations under VFR over routes that cannot be navigated by pilotage, or operations conducted under IFR or over the top.* Notwithstanding the requirements of paragraph (a)(2)(i) of this section, the airplane may be equipped with a single independent navigation system suitable for navigating the airplane along the route to be flown within the degree of accuracy required for ATC if:

(1) It can be shown that the airplane is equipped with at least one other independent navigation system suitable, in the event of loss of the navigation capability of the single independent navigation system permitted by this paragraph at any point along the route, for proceeding safely to a suitable airport and completing an instrument approach; and

(2) The airplane has sufficient fuel so that the flight may proceed safely to a

suitable airport by use of the remaining navigation system, and complete an instrument approach and land.

(d) *Use of VOR navigation equipment.* If VOR navigation equipment is used to comply with paragraph (a) or (c) of this section, no person may operate an airplane unless it is equipped with at least one approved DME or suitable RNAV system.

(e) *Additional communication system equipment requirements for operators subject to § 121.2.* In addition to the requirements in paragraph (b) of this section, no person may operate an airplane having a passenger seat configuration of 10 to 30 seats, excluding each crewmember seat, and a maximum payload capacity of 7,500 pounds or less, under IFR, over the top, or in extended over-water operations unless it is equipped with at least—

(1) Two microphones; and

(2) Two headsets, or one headset and one speaker.

[Doc. No. FAA–2002–14002, 72 FR 31681, June 7, 2007]

§ 121.351 **Communication and navigation equipment for extended over-water operations and for certain other operations.**

(a) Except as provided in paragraph (c) of this section, no person may conduct an extended over-water operation unless the airplane is equipped with at least two independent long-range navigation systems and at least two independent long-range communication systems necessary under normal operating conditions to fulfill the following functions—

(1) Communicate with at least one appropriate station from any point on the route;

(2) Receive meteorological information from any point on the route by either of two independent communication systems. One of the communication systems used to comply with this paragraph may be used to comply with paragraphs (a)(1) and (a)(3) of this section; and

(3) At least one of the communication systems must have two-way voice communication capability.

(b) No certificate holder conducting a flag or supplemental operation or a domestic operation within the State of

Alaska may conduct an operation without the equipment specified in paragraph (a) of this section, if the Administrator finds that equipment to be necessary for search and rescue operations because of the nature of the terrain to be flown over.

(c) Notwithstanding the requirements of paragraph (a) of this section, installation and use of a single LRNS and a single LRCS may be authorized by the Administrator and approved in the certificate holder's operations specifications for operations and routes in certain geographic areas. The following are among the operational factors the Administrator may consider in granting an authorization:

(1) The ability of the flightcrew to navigate the airplane along the route within the degree of accuracy required for ATC,

(2) The length of the route being flown, and

(3) The duration of the very high frequency communications gap.

[Doc. No. 6258, 29 FR 19205, Dec. 31, 1964, as amended by Amdt. 121–253, 61 FR 2611, Jan. 26, 1996; Amdt. 121–254, 61 FR 7191, Feb. 26, 1996; Amdt. 121–333, 72 FR 31682, June 7, 2007]

§121.353 Emergency equipment for operations over uninhabited terrain areas: Flag, supplemental, and certain domestic operations.

Unless the airplane has the following equipment, no person may conduct a flag or supplemental operation or a domestic operation within the States of Alaska or Hawaii over an uninhabited area or any other area that (in its operations specifications) the Administrator specifies required equipment for search and rescue in case of an emergency:

(a) Suitable pyrotechnic signaling devices.

(b) An approved survival type emergency locator transmitter. Batteries used in this transmitter must be replaced (or recharged, if the battery is rechargeable) when the transmitter has been in use for more than 1 cumulative hour, or when 50 percent of their useful life (or for rechargeable batteries, 50 percent of their useful life of charge) has expired, as established by the transmitter manufacturer under its approval. The new expiration date for re-

placing (or recharging) the battery must be legibly marked on the outside of the transmitter. The battery useful life (or useful life of charge) requirements of this paragraph do not apply to batteries (such as water-activated batteries) that are essentially unaffected during probable storage intervals.

(c) Enough survival kits, appropriately equipped for the route to be flown for the number of occupants of the airplane.

[Doc. No. 6258, 29 FR 19205, Dec. 31, 1964, as amended by Amdt. 121–79, 36 FR 18724, Sept. 21, 1971; Amdt. 121–106, 38 FR 22378 Aug. 20, 1973; Amdt. 121–158, 45 FR 38348, June 9, 1980; Amdt. 121–239, 59 FR 32057, June 21, 1994; Amdt. 121–251, 60 FR 65932, Dec. 20, 1995]

§121.354 Terrain awareness and warning system.

(a) *Airplanes manufactured after March 29, 2002.* No person may operate a turbine-powered airplane unless that airplane is equipped with an approved terrain awareness and warning system that meets the requirements for Class A equipment in Technical Standard Order (TSO)–C151. The airplane must also include an approved terrain situational awareness display.

(b) *Airplanes manufactured on or before March 29, 2002.* No person may operate a turbine-powered airplane after March 29, 2005, unless that airplane is equipped with an approved terrain awareness and warning system that meets the requirements for Class A equipment in Technical Standard Order (TSO)–C151. The airplane must also include an approved terrain situational awareness display.

(Approved by the Office of Management and Budget under control number 2120–0631)

(c) *Airplane Flight Manual.* The Airplane Flight Manual shall contain appropriate procedures for—

(1) The use of the terrain awareness and warning system; and

(2) Proper flight crew reaction in response to the terrain awareness and warning system audio and visual warnings.

[Doc. No. 29312, 65 FR 16755, Mar. 29, 2000]

§ 121.355 Equipment for operations on which specialized means of navigation are used.

(a) No certificate holder may conduct an operation—

(1) Using Doppler Radar or an Inertial Navigation System outside the 48 contiguous States and the District of Columbia, unless such systems have been approved in accordance with appendix G to this part; or

(2) Using Doppler Radar or an Inertial Navigation System within the 48 contiguous States and the District of Columbia, or any other specialized means of navigation, unless it shows that an adequate airborne system is provided for the specialized navigation authorized for the particular operation.

(b) Notwithstanding paragraph (a) of this section, Doppler Radar and Inertial Navigation Systems, and the training programs, maintenance programs, relevant operations manual material, and minimum equipment lists prepared in accordance therewith, approved before April 29, 1972, are not required to be approved in accordance with that paragraph.

[Doc. No. 10204, 37 FR 6464, Mar. 30, 1972]

§ 121.356 Collision avoidance system.

Effective January 1, 2005, any airplane you operate under this part must be equipped and operated according to the following table:

COLLISION AVOIDANCE SYSTEMS

If you operate any—	Then you must operate that airplane with—
(a) Turbine-powered airplane of more than 33,000 pounds maximum certificated takeoff weight.	(1) An appropriate class of Mode S transponder that meets Technical Standard Order (TSO) C–112, or a later version, and one of the following approved units: (i) TCAS II that meets TSO C–119b (version 7.0), or takeoff weight a later version. (ii) TCAS II that meets TSO C–119a (version 6.04A Enhanced) that was installed in that airplane before May 1, 2003. If that TCAS II version 6.04A Enhanced no longer can be repaired to TSO C–119a standards, it must be replaced with a TCAS II that meets TSO C–119b (version 7.0), or a later version. (iii) A collision avoidance system equivalent to TSO C–119b (version 7.0), or a later version, capable of coordinating with units that meet TSO C–119a (version 6.04A Enhanced), or a later version.

COLLISION AVOIDANCE SYSTEMS—Continued

If you operate any—	Then you must operate that airplane with—
(b) Passenger or combination cargo/passenger (combi) airplane that has a passenger seat configuration of 10–30 seats.	(1) TCAS I that meets TSO C–118, or a later version, or (2) A collision avoidance system equivalent to has a TSO C–118, or a later version, or (3) A collision avoidance system and Mode S transponder that meet paragraph (a)(1) of this section.
(c) Piston-powered airplane of more than 33,000 pounds maximum certificated takeoff weight.	(1) TCAS I that meets TSO C–118, or a later version, or (2) A collision avoidance system equivalent to maximum TSO C–118, or a later version, or (3) A collision avoidance system and Mode S transponder that meet paragraph (a)(1) of this section.

[Doc. No. FAA–2001–10910, 68 FR 15902, Apr. 1, 2003]

§ 121.357 Airborne weather radar equipment requirements.

(a) No person may operate any transport category airplane (except C–46 type airplanes) or a nontransport category airplane certificated after December 31, 1964, unless approved airborne weather radar equipment has been installed in the airplane.

(b) [Reserved]

(c) Each person operating an airplane required to have approved airborne weather radar equipment installed shall, when using it under this part, operate it in accordance with the following:

(1) *Dispatch.* No person may dispatch an airplane (or begin the flight of an airplane in the case of a certificate holder, that does not use a dispatch system) under IFR or night VFR conditions when current weather reports indicate that thunderstorms, or other potentially hazardous weather conditions that can be detected with airborne weather radar, may reasonably be expected along the route to be flown, unless the airborne weather radar equipment is in satisfactory operating condition.

(2) If the airborne weather radar becomes inoperative en route, the airplane must be operated in accordance with the approved instructions and procedures specified in the operations manual for such an event.

(d) This section does not apply to airplanes used solely within the State of Hawaii or within the State of Alaska and that part of Canada west of longitude 130 degrees W, between latitude 70 degrees N, and latitude 53 degrees N, or during any training, test, or ferry flight.

(e) Notwithstanding any other provision of this chapter, an alternate electrical power supply is not required for airborne weather radar equipment.

[Doc. No. 6258, 29 FR 19205, Dec. 31, 1964, as amended by Amdt. 121–18, 31 FR 5825, Apr. 15, 1966; Amdt. 121–130, 41 FR 47229, Oct. 28, 1976; Amdt. 121–251, 60 FR 65932, Dec. 20, 1995]

§121.358 Low-altitude windshear system equipment requirements.

(a) *Airplanes manufactured after January 2, 1991.* No person may operate a turbine-powered airplane manufactured after January 2, 1991, unless it is equipped with either an approved airborne windshear warning and flight guidance system, an approved airborne detection and avoidance system, or an approved combination of these systems.

(b) *Airplanes manufactured before January 3, 1991.* Except as provided in paragraph (c) of this section, after January 2, 1991, no person may operate a turbine-powered airplane manufactured before January 3, 1991 unless it meets one of the following requirements as applicable.

(1) The makes/models/series listed below must be equipped with either an approved airborne windshear warning and flight guidance system, an approved airborne detection and avoidance system, or an approved combination of these systems:

(i) A–300–600;
(ii) A–310—all series;
(iii) A–320—all series;
(iv) B–737–300, 400, and 500 series;
(v) B–747–400;
(vi) B–757—all series;
(vii) B–767—all series;
(viii) F–100—all series; and
(ix) MD–11—all series; and
(x) MD–80 series equipped with an EFIS and Honeywell-970 digital flight guidance computer.

(2) All other turbine-powered airplanes not listed above must be equipped with as a minimum requirement, an approved airborne windshear warning system. These airplanes may be equipped with an approved airborne

windshear detection and avoidance system, or an approved combination of these systems.

(c) *Extension of the compliance date.* A certificate holder may obtain an extension of the compliance date in paragraph (b) of this section if it obtains FAA approval of a retrofit schedule. To obtain approval of a retrofit schedule and show continued compliance with that schedule, a certificate holder must do the following:

(1) Submit a request for approval of a retrofit schedule by June 1, 1990, to the appropriate Flight Standards division manager in the responsible Flight Standards office.

(2) Show that all of the certificate holder's airplanes required to be equipped in accordance with this section will be equipped by the final compliance date established for TCAS II retrofit.

(3) Comply with its retrofit schedule and submit status reports containing information acceptable to the Administrator. The initial report must be submitted by January 2, 1991, and subsequent reports must be submitted every six months thereafter until completion of the schedule. The reports must be submitted to the certificate holder's assigned Principal Avionics Inspector.

(d) *Definitions.* For the purposes of this section the following definitions apply—

(1) *Turbine-powered airplane* includes, e.g., turbofan-, turbojet-, propfan-, and ultra-high bypass fan-powered airplanes. The definition specifically excludes turbopropeller-powered airplanes.

(2) An airplane is considered manufactured on the date the inspection acceptance records reflect that the airplane is complete and meets the FAA Approved Type Design data.

[Doc. No. 25954, 55 FR 13242, Apr. 9, 1990, as amended by Docket FAA–2018–0119, Amdt. 121–380, 83 FR 9173, Mar. 5, 2018]

§121.359 Cockpit voice recorders.

(a) No certificate holder may operate a large turbine engine powered airplane or a large pressurized airplane with four reciprocating engines unless an approved cockpit voice recorder is installed in that airplane and is operated continuously from the start of the use of the checklist (before starting engines for the purpose of flight), to completion of the final checklist at the termination of the flight.

(b) [Reserved]

(c) The cockpit voice recorder required by paragraph (a) of this section must meet the following application standards:

(1) The requirements of part 25 of this chapter in affect on August 31, 1977.

(2) After September 1, 1980, each recorder container must—

(i) Be either bright orange or bright yellow;

(ii) Have reflective tape affixed to the external surface to facilitate its location under water; and

(iii) Have an approved underwater locating device on or adjacent to the container which is secured in such a manner that they are not likely to be separated during crash impact, unless the cockpit voice recorder, and the flight recorder required by § 121.343, are installed adjacent to each other in such a manner that they are not likely to be separated during crash impact.

(d) No person may operate a multiengine, turbine-powered airplane having a passenger seat configuration of 10–19 seats unless it is equipped with an approved cockpit voice recorder that:

(1) Is installed in compliance with § 23.1457(a)(1) and (2), (b), (c), (d)(1)(i), (2) and (3), (e), (f), and (g); or § 25.1457(a)(1) and (2), (b), (c), (d)(1)(i), (2) and (3), (e), (f), and (g) of this chapter, as applicable; and

(2) Is operated continuously from the use of the checklist before the flight to completion of the final checklist at the end of the flight.

(e) No person may operate a multiengine, turbine-powered airplane having a passenger seat configuration of 20 to 30 seats unless it is equipped with an approved cockpit voice recorder that—

(1) Is installed in accordance with the requirements of § 23.1457 (except paragraphs (a)(6), (d)(1)(ii), (4), and (5)) or § 25.1457 (except paragraphs (a)(6), (d)(1)(ii), (4), and (5)) of this chapter, as applicable; and

(2) Is operated continuously from the use of the checklist before the flight to completion of the final checklist at the end of the flight.

(f) In complying with this section, an approved cockpit voice recorder having an erasure feature may be used, so that at any time during the operation of the recorder, information recorded more than 30 minutes earlier may be erased or otherwise obliterated.

(g) For those aircraft equipped to record the uninterrupted audio signals received by a boom or a mask microphone, the flight crewmembers are required to use the boom microphone below 18,000 feet mean sea level. No person may operate a large turbine engine powered airplane or a large pressurized airplane with four reciprocating engines manufactured after October 11, 1991, or on which a cockpit voice recorder has been installed after October 11, 1991, unless it is equipped to record the uninterrupted audio signal received by a boom or mask microphone in accordance with § 25.1457(c)(5) of this chapter.

(h) In the event of an accident or occurrence requiring immediate notification of the National Transportation Safety Board under part 830 of its regulations, which results in the termination of the flight, the certificate holder shall keep the recorded information for at least 60 days or, if requested by the Administrator or the Board, for a longer period. Information obtained from the record is used to assist in determining the cause of accidents or occurrences in connection with investigations under part 830. The Administrator does not use the record in any civil penalty or certificate action.

(i) By April 7, 2012, all turbine engine-powered airplanes subject to this section that are manufactured before April 7, 2010, must have a cockpit voice recorder installed that also—

(1) Meets the requirements of § 23.1457(d)(6) or § 25.1457(d)(6) of this chapter, as applicable;

(2) Retains at least the last 2 hours of recorded information using a recorder that meets the standards of TSO–C123a, or later revision; and

(3) Is operated continuously from the use of the checklist before the flight to completion of the final checklist at the end of the flight.

(4) If transport category, meets the requirements in § 25.1457(a)(3), (a)(4), and (a)(5) of this chapter.

(j) All turbine engine-powered airplanes subject to this section that are manufactured on or after April 7, 2010, must have a cockpit voice recorder installed that also—

(1) Is installed in accordance with the requirements of § 23.1457 (except for paragraph (a)(6) or § 25.1457 (except for paragraph (a)(6)) of this chapter, as applicable;

(2) Retains at least the last 2 hours of recorded information using a recorder that meets the standards of TSO–C123a, or later revision; and

(3) Is operated continuously from the use of the checklist before the flight to completion of the final checklist at the end of the flight.

(4) For all airplanes manufactured on or after December 6, 2010, also meets the requirements of § 23.1457(a)(6) or § 25.1457(a)(6) of this chapter, as applicable.

(k) All airplanes required by this part to have a cockpit voice recorder and a flight data recorder, that install datalink communication equipment on or after December 6, 2010, must record all datalink messages as required by the certification rule applicable to the airplane.

[Doc. No. 6258, 29 FR 19205, Dec. 31, 1964]

EDITORIAL NOTE: For FEDERAL REGISTER citations affecting § 121.359, see the List of CFR Sections Affected, which appears in the Finding Aids section of the printed volume and at *www.govinfo.gov*.

§ 121.360 [Reserved]

Subpart L—Maintenance, Preventive Maintenance, and Alterations

SOURCE: Docket No. 6258, 29 FR 19210, Dec. 31, 1964, unless otherwise noted.

§ 121.361 Applicability.

(a) Except as provided by paragraph (b) of this section, this subpart prescribes requirements for maintenance, preventive maintenance, and alterations for all certificate holders.

(b) The Administrator may amend a certificate holder's operations specifications to permit deviation from those provisions of this subpart that would prevent the return to service and

use of airframe components, powerplants, appliances, and spare parts thereof because those items have been maintained, altered, or inspected by persons employed outside the United States who do not hold U.S. airman certificates. Each certificate holder who uses parts under this deviation must provide for surveillance of facilities and practices to assure that all work performed on these parts is accomplished in accordance with the certificate holder's manual.

[Doc. No. 8754, 33 FR 14406, Sept. 25, 1968]

§ 121.363 Responsibility for airworthiness.

(a) Each certificate holder is primarily responsible for—

(1) The airworthiness of its aircraft, including airframes, aircraft engines, propellers, appliances, and parts thereof; and

(2) The performance of the maintenance, preventive maintenance, and alteration of its aircraft, including airframes, aircraft engines, propellers, appliances, emergency equipment, and parts thereof, in accordance with its manual and the regulations of this chapter.

(b) A certificate holder may make arrangements with another person for the performance of any maintenance, preventive maintenance, or alterations. However, this does not relieve the certificate holder of the responsibility specified in paragraph (a) of this section.

[Doc. No. 6258, 29 FR 19210, Dec. 31, 1964, as amended by Amdt. 121–106, 38 FR 22378, Aug. 20, 1973]

§ 121.365 Maintenance, preventive maintenance, and alteration organization.

(a) Each certificate holder that performs any of its maintenance (other than required inspections), preventive maintenance, or alterations, and each person with whom it arranges for the performance of that work must have an organization adequate to perform the work.

(b) Each certificate holder that performs any inspections required by its manual in accordance with § 121.369(b)(2) or (3) (in this subpart referred to as *required inspections*) and each person with whom it arranges for the performance of that work must have an organization adequate to perform that work.

(c) Each person performing required inspections in addition to other maintenance, preventive maintenance, or alterations, shall organize the performance of those functions so as to separate the required inspection functions from the other maintenance, preventive maintenance, and alteration functions. The separation shall be below the level of administrative control at which overall responsibility for the required inspection functions and other maintenance, preventive maintenance, and alteration functions are exercised.

[Doc. No. 6258, 29 FR 19210, Dec. 31, 1964, as amended by Amdt. 121–3, 30 FR 3639, Mar. 19, 1965]

§ 121.367 Maintenance, preventive maintenance, and alterations programs.

Each certificate holder shall have an inspection program and a program covering other maintenance, preventive maintenance, and alterations that ensures that—

(a) Maintenance, preventive maintenance, and alterations performed by it, or by other persons, are performed in accordance with the certificate holder's manual;

(b) Competent personnel and adequate facilities and equipment are provided for the proper performance of maintenance, preventive maintenance, and alterations; and

(c) Each aircraft released to service is airworthy and has been properly maintained for operation under this part.

[Doc. No. 6258, 29 FR 19210, Dec. 31, 1964, as amended by Amdt. 121–100, 37 FR 28053, Dec. 20, 1972]

§ 121.368 Contract maintenance.

(a) A certificate holder may arrange with another person for the performance of maintenance, preventive maintenance, and alterations as authorized in § 121.379(a) only if the certificate holder has met all the requirements in this section. For purposes of this section—

(1) A *maintenance provider* is any person who performs maintenance, preven-

tive maintenance, or an alteration for a certificate holder other than a person who is trained by and employed directly by that certificate holder.

(2) *Covered work* means any of the following:

(i) Essential maintenance that could result in a failure, malfunction, or defect endangering the safe operation of an aircraft if not performed properly or if improper parts or materials are used;

(ii) Regularly scheduled maintenance; or

(iii) A required inspection item on an aircraft.

(3) *Directly in charge* means having responsibility for covered work performed by a maintenance provider. A representative of the certificate holder directly in charge of covered work does not need to physically observe and direct each maintenance provider constantly, but must be available for consultation on matters requiring instruction or decision.

(b) Each certificate holder must be directly in charge of all covered work done for it by a maintenance provider.

(c) Each maintenance provider must perform all covered work in accordance with the certificate holder's maintenance manual.

(d) No maintenance provider may perform covered work unless that work is carried out under the supervision and control of the certificate holder.

(e) Each certificate holder who contracts for maintenance, preventive maintenance, or alterations must develop and implement policies, procedures, methods, and instructions for the accomplishment of all contracted maintenance, preventive maintenance, and alterations. These policies, procedures, methods, and instructions must provide for the maintenance, preventive maintenance, and alterations to be performed in accordance with the certificate holder's maintenance program and maintenance manual.

(f) Each certificate holder who contracts for maintenance, preventive maintenance, or alterations must ensure that its system for the continuing analysis and surveillance of the maintenance, preventive maintenance, and alterations carried out by the maintenance provider, as required by § 121.373(a), contains procedures for oversight of all contracted covered work.

(g) The policies, procedures, methods, and instructions required by paragraphs (e) and (f) of this section must be acceptable to the FAA and included in the certificate holder's maintenance manual as required by §121.369(b)(10).

(h) Each certificate holder who contracts for maintenance, preventive maintenance, or alterations must provide to its responsible Flight Standards office, in a format acceptable to the FAA, a list that includes the name and physical (street) address, or addresses, where the work is carried out for each maintenance provider that performs work for the certificate holder, and a description of the type of maintenance, preventive maintenance, or alteration that is to be performed at each location. The list must be updated with any changes, including additions or deletions, and the updated list provided to the FAA in a format acceptable to the FAA by the last day of each calendar month.

[Docket FAA–2011–1136, Amdt. 121–371, 80 FR 11546, Mar. 4, 2015, as amended by Docket FAA–2018–0119, Amdt. 121–380, 83 FR 9173, Mar. 5, 2018]

§121.369 Manual requirements.

(a) The certificate holder shall put in its manual a chart or description of the certificate holder's organization required by §121.365 and a list of persons with whom it has arranged for the performance of any of its required inspections, other maintenance, preventive maintenance, or alterations, including a general description of that work.

(b) The certificate holder's manual must contain the programs required by §121.367 that must be followed in performing maintenance, preventive maintenance, and alterations of that certificate holder's airplanes, including airframes, aircraft engines, propellers, appliances, emergency equipment, and parts thereof, and must include at least the following:

(1) The method of performing routine and nonroutine maintenance (other than required inspections), preventive maintenance, and alterations.

(2) A designation of the items of maintenance and alteration that must be inspected (required inspections), in-

cluding at least those that could result in a failure, malfunction, or defect endangering the safe operation of the aircraft, if not performed properly or if improper parts or materials are used.

(3) The method of performing required inspections and a designation by occupational title of personnel authorized to perform each required inspection.

(4) Procedures for the reinspection of work performed pursuant to previous required inspection findings (*buy-back procedures*).

(5) Procedures, standards, and limits necessary for required inspections and acceptance or rejection of the items required to be inspected and for periodic inspection and calibration of precision tools, measuring devices, and test equipment.

(6) Procedures to ensure that all required inspections are performed.

(7) Instructions to prevent any person who performs any item of work from performing any required inspection of that work.

(8) Instructions and procedures to prevent any decision of an inspector, regarding any required inspection from being countermanded by persons other than supervisory personnel of the inspection unit, or a person at that level of administrative control that has overall responsibility for the management of both the required inspection functions and the other maintenance, preventive maintenance, and alterations functions.

(9) Procedures to ensure that required inspections, other maintenance, preventive maintenance, and alterations that are not completed as a result of shift changes or similar work interruptions are properly completed before the aircraft is released to service.

(10) Policies, procedures, methods, and instructions for the accomplishment of all maintenance, preventive maintenance, and alterations carried out by a maintenance provider. These policies, procedures, methods, and instructions must be acceptable to the FAA and provide for the maintenance, preventive maintenance, and alterations to be performed in accordance

with the certificate holder's maintenance program and maintenance manual.

(c) The certificate holder must set forth in its manual a suitable system (which may include a coded system) that provides for preservation and retrieval of information in a manner acceptable to the Administrator and that provides—

(1) A description (or reference to data acceptable to the Administrator) of the work performed;

(2) The name of the person performing the work if the work is performed by a person outside the organization of the certificate holder; and

(3) The name or other positive identification of the individual approving the work.

[Doc. No. 6258, 29 FR 19210, Dec. 31, 1964, as amended by Amdt. 121–94, 37 FR 15983, Aug. 9, 1972; Amdt. 121–106, 38 FR 22378, Aug. 20, 1973; Docket FAA–2011–1136, Amdt. 121–371, 80 FR 11546, Mar. 4, 2015]

§§ 121.370–121.370a   [Reserved]

§ 121.371 Required inspection personnel.

(a) No person may use any person to perform required inspections unless the person performing the inspection is appropriately certificated, properly trained, qualified, and authorized to do so.

(b) No person may allow any person to perform a required inspection unless, at that time, the person performing that inspection is under the supervision and control of an inspection unit.

(c) No person may perform a required inspection if he performed the item of work required to be inspected.

(d) Each certificate holder shall maintain, or shall determine that each person with whom it arranges to perform its required inspections maintains, a current listing of persons who have been trained, qualified, and authorized to conduct required inspections. The persons must be identified by name, occupational title, and the inspections they are authorized to perform. The certificate holder (or person with whom it arranges to perform its required inspections) shall give written information to each person so

authorized describing the extent of his responsibilities, authorities, and inspectional limitations. The list shall be made available for inspection by the Administrator upon request.

§ 121.373 Continuing analysis and surveillance.

(a) Each certificate holder shall establish and maintain a system for the continuing analysis and surveillance of the performance and effectiveness of its inspection program and the program covering other maintenance, preventive maintenance, and alterations and for the correction of any deficiency in those programs, regardless of whether those programs are carried out by the certificate holder or by another person.

(b) Whenever the Administrator finds that either or both of the programs described in paragraph (a) of this section does not contain adequate procedures and standards to meet the requirements of this part, the certificate holder shall, after notification by the Administrator, make any changes in those programs that are necessary to meet those requirements.

(c) A certificate holder may petition the Administrator to reconsider the notice to make a change in a program. The petition must be filed with the responsible Flight Standards office charged with the overall inspection of the certificate holder's operations within 30 days after the certificate holder receives the notice. Except in the case of an emergency requiring immediate action in the interest of safety, the filing of the petition stays the notice pending a decision by the Administrator.

[Doc. No. 6258, 29 FR 19210, Dec. 31, 1964, as amended by Amdt. 121–207, 54 FR 39293, Sept. 25, 1989; Amdt. 121–253, 61 FR 2611, Jan. 26, 1996; Docket FAA–2018–0119, Amdt. 121–380, 83 FR 9173, Mar. 5, 2018]

§ 121.374 Continuous airworthiness maintenance program (CAMP) for two-engine ETOPS.

In order to conduct an ETOPS flight using a two-engine airplane, each certificate holder must develop and comply with the ETOPS continuous airworthiness maintenance program, as authorized in the certificate holder's operations specifications, for each airplane-engine combination used in ETOPS. The certificate holder must develop this ETOPS CAMP by supplementing the manufacturer's maintenance program or the CAMP currently approved for the certificate holder. This ETOPS CAMP must include the following elements:

(a) *ETOPS maintenance document.* The certificate holder must have an ETOPS maintenance document for use by each person involved in ETOPS.

(1) The document must—

(i) List each ETOPS significant system,

(ii) Refer to or include all of the ETOPS maintenance elements in this section,

(iii) Refer to or include all supportive programs and procedures,

(iv) Refer to or include all duties and responsibilities, and

(v) Clearly state where referenced material is located in the certificate holder's document system.

(b) *ETOPS pre-departure service check.* Except as provided in Appendix P of this part, the certificate holder must develop a pre-departure check tailored to their specific operation.

(1) The certificate holder must complete a pre-departure service check immediately before each ETOPS flight.

(2) At a minimum, this check must—

(i) Verify the condition of all ETOPS Significant Systems;

(ii) Verify the overall status of the airplane by reviewing applicable maintenance records; and

(iii) Include an interior and exterior inspection to include a determination of engine and APU oil levels and consumption rates.

(3) An appropriately trained maintenance person, who is ETOPS qualified, must accomplish and certify by signature ETOPS specific tasks. Before an ETOPS flight may commence, an ETOPS pre-departure service check (PDSC) Signatory Person, who has been authorized by the certificate holder, must certify by signature, that the ETOPS PDSC has been completed.

(4) For the purposes of this paragraph (b) only, the following definitions apply:

(i) ETOPS qualified person: A person is ETOPS qualified when that person

satisfactorily completes the operator's ETOPS training program and is authorized by the certificate holder.

(ii) ETOPS PDSC Signatory Person: A person is an ETOPS PDSC Signatory Person when that person is ETOPS qualified and that person:

(A) When certifying the completion of the ETOPS PDSC in the United States:

(1) Works for an operator authorized to engage in part 121 operation or works for a part 145 repair station; and

(2) Holds a U.S. Mechanic's Certificate with airframe and powerplant ratings.

(B) When certifying the completion of the ETOPS PDSC outside of the U.S. holds a certificate in accordance with §43.17(c)(1) of this chapter; or

(C) When certifying the completion of the ETOPS PDSC outside the U.S. holds the certificates needed or has the requisite experience or training to return aircraft to service on behalf of an ETOPS maintenance entity.

(iii) ETOPS maintenance entity: An entity authorized to perform ETOPS maintenance and complete ETOPS PDSC and that entity is:

(A) Certificated to engage in part 121 operations;

(B) Repair station certificated under part 145 of this chapter; or

(C) Entity authorized pursuant to §43.17(c)(2) of this chapter.

(c) *Limitations on dual maintenance.* (1) Except as specified in paragraph (c)(2), the certificate holder may not perform scheduled or unscheduled dual maintenance during the same maintenance visit on the same or a substantially similar ETOPS Significant System listed in the ETOPS maintenance document, if the improper maintenance could result in the failure of an ETOPS Significant System.

(2) In the event dual maintenance as defined in paragraph (c)(1) of this section cannot be avoided, the certificate holder may perform maintenance provided:

(i) The maintenance action on each affected ETOPS Significant System is performed by a different technician, or

(ii) The maintenance action on each affected ETOPS Significant System is performed by the same technician under the direct supervision of a second qualified individual; and

(iii) For either paragraph (c)(2)(i) or (ii) of this section, a qualified individual conducts a ground verification test and any in-flight verification test required under the program developed pursuant to paragraph (d) of this section.

(d) *Verification program.* The certificate holder must develop and maintain a program for the resolution of discrepancies that will ensure the effectiveness of maintenance actions taken on ETOPS Significant Systems. The verification program must identify potential problems and verify satisfactory corrective action. The verification program must include ground verification and in-flight verification policy and procedures. The certificate holder must establish procedures to indicate clearly who is going to initiate the verification action and what action is necessary. The verification action may be performed on an ETOPS revenue flight provided the verification action is documented as satisfactorily completed upon reaching the ETOPS Entry Point.

(e) *Task identification.* The certificate holder must identify all ETOPS-specific tasks. An appropriately trained mechanic who is ETOPS qualified must accomplish and certify by signature that the ETOPS-specific task has been completed.

(f) *Centralized maintenance control procedures.* The certificate holder must develop and maintain procedures for centralized maintenance control for ETOPS.

(g) *Parts control program.* The certificate holder must develop an ETOPS parts control program to ensure the proper identification of parts used to maintain the configuration of airplanes used in ETOPS.

(h) *Reliability program.* The certificate holder must have an ETOPS reliability program. This program must be the certificate holder's existing reliability program or its Continuing Analysis and Surveillance System (CASS) supplemented for ETOPS. This program must be event-oriented and include procedures to report the events listed below, as follows:

(1) The certificate holder must report the following events within 96 hours of the occurrence to its responsible Flight Standards office:

(i) IFSDs, except planned IFSDs performed for flight training.

(ii) Diversions and turnbacks for failures, malfunctions, or defects associated with any airplane or engine system.

(iii) Uncommanded power or thrust changes or surges.

(iv) Inability to control the engine or obtain desired power or thrust.

(v) Inadvertent fuel loss or unavailability, or uncorrectable fuel imbalance in flight.

(vi) Failures, malfunctions or defects associated with ETOPS Significant Systems.

(vii) Any event that would jeopardize the safe flight and landing of the airplane on an ETOPS flight.

(2) The certificate holder must investigate the cause of each event listed in paragraph (h)(1) of this section and submit findings and a description of corrective action to its responsible Flight Standards office. The report must include the information specified in § 121.703(e). The corrective action must be acceptable to its responsible Flight Standards office.

(i) *Propulsion system monitoring.* (1) If the IFSD rate (computed on a 12-month rolling average) for an engine installed as part of an airplane-engine combination exceeds the following values, the certificate holder must do a comprehensive review of its operations to identify any common cause effects and systemic errors. The IFSD rate must be computed using all engines of that type in the certificate holder's entire fleet of airplanes approved for ETOPS.

(i) A rate of 0.05 per 1,000 engine hours for ETOPS up to and including 120 minutes.

(ii) A rate of 0.03 per 1,000 engine hours for ETOPS beyond 120-minutes up to and including 207 minutes in the North Pacific Area of Operation and up to and including 180 minutes elsewhere.

(iii) A rate of 0.02 per 1,000 engine hours for ETOPS beyond 207 minutes in the North Pacific Area of Operation and beyond 180 minutes elsewhere.

(2) Within 30 days of exceeding the rates above, the certificate holder must

submit a report of investigation and any necessary corrective action taken to its responsible Flight Standards office.

(j) *Engine condition monitoring.* (1) The certificate holder must have an engine condition monitoring program to detect deterioration at an early stage and to allow for corrective action before safe operation is affected.

(2) This program must describe the parameters to be monitored, the method of data collection, the method of analyzing data, and the process for taking corrective action.

(3) The program must ensure that engine-limit margins are maintained so that a prolonged engine-inoperative diversion may be conducted at approved power levels and in all expected environmental conditions without exceeding approved engine limits. This includes approved limits for items such as rotor speeds and exhaust gas temperatures.

(k) *Oil-consumption monitoring.* The certificate holder must have an engine oil consumption monitoring program to ensure that there is enough oil to complete each ETOPS flight. APU oil consumption must be included if an APU is required for ETOPS. The operator's oil consumption limit may not exceed the manufacturer's recommendation. Monitoring must be continuous and include oil added at each ETOPS departure point. The program must compare the amount of oil added at each ETOPS departure point with the running average consumption to identify sudden increases.

(l) *APU in-flight start program.* If the airplane type certificate requires an APU but does not require the APU to run during the ETOPS portion of the flight, the certificate holder must develop and maintain a program acceptable to the FAA for cold soak in-flight start-and-run reliability.

(m) *Maintenance training.* For each airplane-engine combination, the certificate holder must develop a maintenance training program that provides training adequate to support ETOPS. It must include ETOPS specific training for all persons involved in ETOPS maintenance that focuses on the special nature of ETOPS. This training must be in addition to the operator's

maintenance training program used to qualify individuals to perform work on specific airplanes and engines.

(n) *Configuration, maintenance, and procedures (CMP) document.* If an airplane-engine combination has a CMP document, the certificate holder must use a system that ensures compliance with the applicable FAA-approved document.

(o) *Procedural changes.* Each substantial change to the maintenance or training procedures that were used to qualify the certificate holder for ETOPS, must be submitted to the CHDO for review. The certificate holder cannot implement a change until its responsible Flight Standards office notifies the certificate holder that the review is complete.

[Doc. No. FAA–2002–6717, 72 FR 1880, Jan. 16, 2007, as amended by Amdt. 121–329, 72 FR 7348, Feb. 15, 2007; Amdt. 121–329, 72 FR 26541, May 10, 2007; Amdt. 121–339, 73 FR 33881, June 16, 2008; Docket FAA–2018–0119, Amdt. 121–380, 83 FR 9173, Mar. 5, 2018]

§121.375 Maintenance and preventive maintenance training program.

Each certificate holder or person performing maintenance or preventive maintenance functions for it shall have a training program to ensure that each person (including inspection personnel) who determines the adequacy of work done is fully informed about procedures and techniques and new equipment in use and is competent to perform his duties.

§121.377 Maintenance and preventive maintenance personnel duty time limitations.

Within the United States, each certificate holder (or person performing maintenance or preventive maintenance functions for it) shall relieve each person performing maintenance or preventive maintenance from duty for a period of at least 24 consecutive hours during any seven consecutive days, or the equivalent thereof within any one calendar month.

§121.378 Certificate requirements.

(a) Except for maintenance, preventive maintenance, alterations, and required inspections performed by a certificated repair station that is located outside the United States, each person who is directly in charge of maintenance, preventive maintenance, or alterations, and each person performing required inspections must hold an appropriate airman certificate.

(b) For the purposes of this section, a person *directly in charge* is each person assigned to a position in which he is responsible for the work of a shop or station that performs maintenance, preventive maintenance, alterations, or other functions affecting aircraft airworthiness. A person who is *directly in charge* need not physically observe and direct each worker constantly but must be available for consultation and decision on matters requiring instruction or decision from higher authority than that of the persons performing the work.

[Doc. No. 6258, 29 FR 19210, Dec. 31, 1964, as amended by Amdt. 121–21, 31 FR 10618, Aug. 9, 1966; Amdt. 121–286, 66 FR 41116, Aug. 6, 2001]

§ 121.379 Authority to perform and approve maintenance, preventive maintenance, and alterations.

(a) A certificate holder may perform, or it may make arrangements with other persons to perform, maintenance, preventive maintenance, and alterations as provided in its continuous airworthiness maintenance program and its maintenance manual. In addition, a certificate holder may perform these functions for another certificate holder as provided in the continuous airworthiness maintenance program and maintenance manual of the other certificate holder.

(b) A certificate holder may approve any aircraft, airframe, aircraft engine, propeller, or appliance for return to service after maintenance, preventive maintenance, or alterations that are performed under paragraph (a) of this section. However, in the case of a major repair or major alteration, the work must have been done in accordance with technical data approved by the Administrator.

[Doc. No. 10289, 35 FR 16793, Oct. 30, 1970]

§ 121.380 Maintenance recording requirements.

(a) Each certificate holder shall keep (using the system specified in the manual required in § 121.369) the following

records for the periods specified in paragraph (c) of this section:

(1) All the records necessary to show that all requirements for the issuance of an airworthiness release under § 121.709 have been met.

(2) Records containing the following information:

(i) The total time in service of the airframe.

(ii) Except as provided in paragraph (b) of this section, the total time in service of each engine and propeller.

(iii) The current status of life-limited parts of each airframe, engine, propeller, and appliance.

(iv) The time since last overhaul of all items installed on the aircraft which are required to be overhauled on a specified time basis.

(v) The identification of the current inspection status of the aircraft, including the times since the last inspections required by the inspection program under which the aircraft and its appliances are maintained.

(vi) The current status of applicable airworthiness directives, including the date and methods of compliance, and, if the airworthiness directive involves recurring action, the time and date when the next action is required.

(vii) A list of current major alterations to each airframe, engine, propeller, and appliance.

(b) A certificate holder need not record the total time in service of an engine or propeller on a transport category cargo airplane, a transport category airplane that has a passenger seat configuration of more than 30 seats, or a nontransport category airplane type certificated before January 1, 1958, until the following, whichever occurs first:

(1) March 20, 1997; or

(2) The date of the first overhaul of the engine or propeller, as applicable, after January 19, 1996.

(c) Each certificate holder shall retain the records required to be kept by this section for the following periods:

(1) Except for the records of the last complete overhaul of each airframe, engine, propeller, and appliance, the records specified in paragraph (a)(1) of this section shall be retained until the work is repeated or superseded by

other work or for one year after the work is performed.

(2) The records of the last complete overhaul of each airframe, engine, propeller, and appliance shall be retained until the work is superseded by work of equivalent scope and detail.

(3) The records specified in paragraph (a)(2) of this section shall be retained and transferred with the aircraft at the time the aircraft is sold.

(d) The certificate holder shall make all maintenance records required to be kept by this section available for inspection by the Administrator or any authorized representative of the National Transportation Safety Board (NTSB).

[Doc. No. 10658, 37 FR 15983, Aug. 9, 1972, as amended by Amdt. 121–251, 60 FR 65933, Dec. 20, 1995; Amdt. 121–321, 71 FR 536, Jan. 4, 2006]

§121.380a Transfer of maintenance records.

Each certificate holder who sells a U.S. registered aircraft shall transfer to the purchaser, at the time of sale, the following records of that aircraft, in plain language form or in coded form at the election of the purchaser, if the coded form provides for the preservation and retrieval of information in a manner acceptable to the Administrator:

(a) The record specified in §121.380(a)(2).

(b) The records specified in §121.380(a)(1) which are not included in the records covered by paragraph (a) of this section, except that the purchaser may permit the seller to keep physical custody of such records. However, custody of records in the seller does not relieve the purchaser of his responsibility under §121.380(c) to make the records available for inspection by the Administrator or any authorized representative of the National Transportation Safety Board (NTSB).

[Doc. No. 10658, 37 FR 15984, Aug. 9, 1972]

Subpart M—Airman and Crewmember Requirements

SOURCE: Docket No. 6258, 29 FR 19212, Dec. 31, 1964, unless otherwise noted.

§121.381 Applicability.

This subpart prescribes airman and crewmember requirements for all certificate holders.

§121.383 Airman: Limitations on use of services.

(a) No certificate holder may use any person as an airman nor may any person serve as an airman unless that person—

(1) Holds an appropriate current airman certificate issued by the FAA;

(2) Has in his or her possession while engaged in operations under this part—

(i) Any required appropriate current airman and medical certificates; or

(ii) A temporary document issued in accordance with paragraph (c) of this section; and

(3) Is otherwise qualified for the operation for which he is to be used.

(b) Each airman covered by paragraph (a)(2) of this section shall present his or her certificates or temporary document for inspection upon request of the Administrator.

(c) A certificate holder may obtain approval to provide a temporary document verifying a flightcrew member's airman certificate and medical certificate privileges under an approved certificate verification plan set forth in the certificate holder's operations specifications. A document provided by the certificate holder may be carried as an airman certificate or medical certificate on flights within the United States for up to 72 hours.

(d) No certificate holder may use the services of any person as a pilot on an airplane engaged in operations under this part if that person has reached his or her 65th birthday.

(e) No pilot may serve as a pilot in operations under this part if that person has reached his or her 65th birthday.

[Doc. No. 6258, 29 FR 19212, Dec. 31, 1964, as amended by Amdt. 121–144, 43 FR 22646, May 25, 1978; Amdt. 121–344, 74 FR 34234, July 15, 2009; Amdt. 121–372, 80 FR 33401, June 12, 2015; Amdt. 121–381, 83 FR 30282, June 27, 2018]

§121.385 Composition of flight crew.

(a) No certificate holder may operate an airplane with less than the minimum flight crew in the airworthiness

151

certificate or the airplane Flight Manual approved for that type airplane and required by this part for the kind of operation being conducted.

(b) In any case in which this part requires the performance of two or more functions for which an airman certificate is necessary, that requirement is not satisfied by the performance of multiple functions at the same time by one airman.

(c) The minimum pilot crew is two pilots and the certificate holder shall designate one pilot as pilot in command and the other second in command.

(d) On each flight requiring a flight engineer at least one flight crewmember, other than the flight engineer, must be qualified to provide emergency performance of the flight engineer's functions for the safe completion of the flight if the flight engineer becomes ill or is otherwise incapacitated. A pilot need not hold a flight engineer's certificate to perform the flight engineer's functions in such a situation.

[Doc. No. 6258, 29 FR 19212, Dec. 31, 1964, as amended by Amdt. 121–178, 47 FR 13316, Mar. 29, 1982; Amdt. 121–256, 61 FR 30434, June 14, 1996]

§ 121.387 Flight engineer.

No certificate holder may operate an airplane for which a type certificate was issued before January 2, 1964, having a maximum certificated takeoff weight of more than 80,000 pounds without a flight crewmember holding a current flight engineer certificate. For each airplane type certificated after January 1, 1964, the requirement for a flight engineer is determined under the type certification requirements of § 25.1523.

[Doc. No. 5025, 30 FR 6067, Apr. 29, 1965]

§ 121.389 Flight navigator and specialized navigation equipment.

(a) No certificate holder may operate an airplane outside the 48 contiguous States and the District of Columbia, when its position cannot be reliably fixed for a period of more than 1 hour, without—

(1) A flight crewmember who holds a current flight navigator certificate; or

(2) Specialized means of navigation approved in accordance with § 121.355 which enables a reliable determination to be made of the position of the airplane by each pilot seated at his duty station.

(b) Notwithstanding paragraph (a) of this section, the Administrator may also require a flight navigator or special navigation equipment, or both, when specialized means of navigation are necessary for 1 hour or less. In making this determination, the Administrator considers—

(1) The speed of the airplane;

(2) Normal weather conditions en route;

(3) Extent of air traffic control;

(4) Traffic congestion;

(5) Area of navigational radio coverage at destination;

(6) Fuel requirements;

(7) Fuel available for return to point of departure or alternates;

(8) Predication of flight upon operation beyond the point of no return; and

(9) Any other factors he determines are relevant in the interest of safety.

(c) Operations where a flight navigator or special navigation equipment, or both, are required are specified in the operations specifications of the air carrier or commercial operator.

[Doc. No. 10204, 37 FR 6464, Mar. 30, 1972, as amended by Amdt. 121–178, 47 FR 13316, Mar. 29, 1982]

§ 121.391 Flight attendants.

(a) Except as specified in § 121.393 and § 121.394, each certificate holder must provide at least the following flight attendants on board each passenger-carrying airplane when passengers are on board:

(1) For airplanes having a maximum payload capacity of more than 7,500 pounds and having a seating capacity of more than 9 but less than 51 passengers—one flight attendant.

(2) For airplanes having a maximum payload capacity of 7,500 pounds or less and having a seating capacity of more than 19 but less than 51 passengers—one flight attendant.

(3) For airplanes having a seating capacity of more than 50 but less than 101 passengers—two flight attendants.

(4) For airplanes having a seating capacity of more than 100 passengers—two flight attendants plus one additional flight attendant for each unit (or part of a unit) of 50 passenger seats above a seating capacity of 100 passengers.

(b) If, in conducting the emergency evacuation demonstration required under §121.291 (a) or (b), the certificate holder used more flight attendants than is required under paragraph (a) of this section for the maximum seating capacity of the airplane used in the demonstration, he may not, thereafter, take off that airplane—

(1) In its maximum seating capacity configuration with fewer flight attendants than the number used during the emergency evacuation demonstration; or

(2) In any reduced seating capacity configuration with fewer flight attendants than the number required by paragraph (a) of this section for that seating capacity plus the number of flight attendants used during the emergency evacuation demonstration that were in excess of those required under paragraph (a) of this section.

(c) The number of flight attendants approved under paragraphs (a) and (b) of this section are set forth in the certificate holder's operations specifications.

(d) During takeoff and landing, flight attendants required by this section shall be located as near as practicable to required floor level exits and shall be uniformly distributed throughout the airplane in order to provide the most effective egress of passengers in event of an emergency evacuation. During taxi, flight attendants required by this section must remain at their duty stations with safety belts and shoulder harnesses fastened except to perform duties related to the safety of the airplane and its occupants.

[Doc. No. 2033, 30 FR 3206, Mar. 9, 1965]

EDITORIAL NOTE: For FEDERAL REGISTER citations affecting §121.391, see the List of CFR Sections Affected, which appears in the Finding Aids section of the printed volume and at *www.govinfo.gov*.

§121.392 **Personnel identified as flight attendants.**

(a) Any person identified by the certificate holder as a flight attendant on an aircraft in operations under this part must be trained and qualified in accordance with subparts N and O of this part. This includes:

(1) Flight attendants provided by the certificate holder in excess of the number required by §121.391(a); and

(2) Flight attendants provided by the certificate holder when flight attendants are not required by §121.391(a).

(b) A qualifying flight attendant who is receiving operating experience on an aircraft in operations under subpart O of this part must be identified to passengers as a qualifying flight attendant.

[Doc. No. FAA–2008–0677, 78 FR 67836, Nov. 12, 2013]

§121.393 **Crewmember requirements at stops where passengers remain on board.**

At stops where passengers remain on board, the certificate holder must meet the following requirements:

(a) On each airplane for which a flight attendant is not required by §121.391(a), the certificate holder must ensure that a person who is qualified in the emergency evacuation procedures for the airplane, as required in §121.417, and who is identified to the passengers, remains:

(1) On board the airplane; or

(2) Nearby the airplane, in a position to adequately monitor passenger safety, and:

(i) The airplane engines are shut down; and

(ii) At least one floor level exit remains open to provide for the deplaning of passengers.

(b) On each airplane for which flight attendants are required by §121.391(a), but the number of flight attendants remaining on board is fewer than required by §121.391(a), the certificate holder must meet the following requirements:

(1) The certificate holder shall ensure that:

(i) The airplane engines are shut down;

(ii) At least one floor level exit remains open to provide for the deplaning of passengers; and

(iii) the number of flight attendants on board is at least half the number required by § 121.391(a), rounded down to the next lower number in the case of fractions, but never fewer than one.

(2) The certificate holder may substitute for the required flight attendants other persons qualified in the emergency evacuation procedures for that aircraft as required in § 121.417, if these persons are identified to the passengers.

(3) If only one flight attendant or other qualified person is on board during a stop, that flight attendant or other qualified person shall be located in accordance with the certificate holder's FAA-approved operating procedures. If more than one flight attendant or other qualified person is on board, the flight attendants or other qualified persons shall be spaced throughout the cabin to provide the most effective assistance for the evacuation in case of an emergency.

[Doc. No. 28154, 60 FR 65934, Dec. 20, 1995]

§ 121.394 **Flight attendant requirements during passenger boarding and deplaning.**

(a) During passenger boarding, on each airplane for which more than one flight attendant is required by § 121.391, the certificate holder may:

(1) Reduce the number of required flight attendants by one, provided that:

(i) The flight attendant that leaves the aircraft remains within the immediate vicinity of the door through which passengers are boarding;

(ii) The flight attendant that leaves the aircraft only conducts safety duties related to the flight being boarded;

(iii) The airplane engines are shut down; and

(iv) At least one floor level exit remains open to provide for passenger egress; or

(2) Substitute a pilot or flight engineer employed by the certificate holder and trained and qualified on that type airplane for one flight attendant, provided the certificate holder—

(i) Describes in the manual required by § 121.133:

(A) The necessary functions to be performed by the substitute pilot or flight engineer in an emergency, to include a situation requiring an emergency evacuation. The certificate holder must show those functions are realistic, can be practically accomplished, and will meet any reasonably anticipated emergency; and

(B) How other regulatory functions performed by a flight attendant will be accomplished by the substitute pilot or flight engineer on the airplane.

(ii) Ensures that the following requirements are met:

(A) The substitute pilot or flight engineer is not assigned to operate the flight for which that person is substituting for a required flight attendant.

(B) The substitute pilot or flight engineer is trained in all assigned flight attendant duties regarding passenger handling.

(C) The substitute pilot or flight engineer meets the emergency training requirements for flight attendants in evacuation management and evacuation commands, as appropriate, and frequency of performance drills regarding operation of exits in the normal and emergency modes on that type aircraft.

(D) The substitute pilot or flight engineer is in possession of all items required for duty.

(E) The substitute pilot or flight engineer is located in the passenger cabin.

(F) The substitute pilot or flight engineer is identified to the passengers.

(G) The substitution of a pilot or flight engineer for a required flight attendant does not interfere with the safe operation of the flight.

(H) The airplane engines are shut down.

(I) At least one floor-level exit remains open to provide for passenger egress.

(b) During passenger deplaning, on each airplane for which more than one flight attendant is required by § 121.391, the certificate holder may reduce the number of flight attendants required by that paragraph provided:

(1) The airplane engines are shut down;

(2) At least one floor level exit remains open to provide for passenger egress; and

(3) The number of flight attendants on board is at least half the number required by § 121.391, rounded down to the next lower number in the case of fractions, but never fewer than one.

(c) If only one flight attendant is on the airplane during passenger boarding or deplaning, that flight attendant must be located in accordance with the certificate holder's FAA-approved operating procedures. If more than one flight attendant is on the airplane during passenger boarding or deplaning, the flight attendants must be evenly distributed throughout the airplane cabin, in the vicinity of the floor-level exits, to provide the most effective assistance in the event of an emergency.

(d) The time spent by any crewmember conducting passenger boarding or deplaning duties is considered duty time.

[Doc. No. FAA-2009-0022, 75 FR 68198, Nov. 5, 2010]

§ 121.395 Aircraft dispatcher: Domestic and flag operations.

Each certificate holder conducting domestic or flag operations shall provide enough qualified aircraft dispatchers at each dispatch center to ensure proper operational control of each flight.

[Doc. No. 28154, 61 FR 2611, Jan. 26, 1996]

§ 121.397 Emergency and emergency evacuation duties.

(a) Each certificate holder shall, for each type and model of airplane, assigned to each category of required crewmember, as appropriate, the necessary functions to be performed in an emergency or a situation requiring emergency evacuation. The certificate holder shall show those functions are realistic, can be practically accomplished, and will meet any reasonably anticipated emergency including the possible incapacitation of individual crewmembers or their inability to reach the passenger cabin because of shifting cargo in combination cargo-passenger airplanes.

(b) The certificate holder shall describe in its manual the functions of

each category of required crewmembers under paragraph (a) of this section.

[Doc. No. 2033, 30 FR 3206, Mar. 9, 1965, as amended by Amdt. 121-7, 30 FR 6727, May 18, 1965]

Subpart N—Training Program

SOURCE: Docket No. 9509, 35 FR 90, Jan. 3, 1970, unless otherwise noted.

§ 121.400 Applicability and terms used.

(a) This subpart prescribes the requirements applicable to each certificate holder for establishing and maintaining a training program for crewmembers, aircraft dispatchers, and other operations personnel, and for the approval and use of training devices in the conduct of the program.

(b) For the purpose of this subpart, airplane groups are as follows:

(1) *Group I.* Propeller driven, including—

(i) Reciprocating powered; and

(ii) Turbopropeller powered.

(2) *Group II.* Turbojet powered.

(c) For the purpose of this subpart, the following terms and definitions apply:

(1) *Initial training.* The training required for crewmembers and dispatchers who have not qualified and served in the same capacity on another airplane of the same group.

(2) *Transition training.* The training required for crewmembers and dispatchers who have qualified and served in the same capacity on another airplane of the same group.

(3) *Upgrade training.* The training required for crewmembers who have qualified and served as second in command or flight engineer on a particular airplane type, before they serve as pilot in command or second in command, respectively, on that airplane.

(4) *Differences training.* The training required for crewmembers and dispatchers who have qualified and served on a particular type airplane, when the Administrator finds differences training is necessary before a crewmember serves in the same capacity on a particular variation of that airplane.

(5) *Programmed hours.* The hours of training prescribed in this subpart

which may be reduced by the Administrator upon a showing by the certificate holder that circumstances justify a lesser amount.

(6) *Inflight.* Refers to maneuvers, procedures, or functions that must be conducted in the airplane.

(7) *Training center.* An organization governed by the applicable requirements of part 142 of this chapter that provides training, testing, and checking under contract or other arrangement to certificate holders subject to the requirements of this part.

(8) *Requalification training.* The training required for crewmembers previously trained and qualified, but who have become unqualified due to not having met within the required period the recurrent training requirements of § 121.427 or the proficiency check requirements of § 121.441.

(9) *Related aircraft.* Any two or more aircraft of the same make with either the same or different type certificates that have been demonstrated and determined by the Administrator to have commonality to the extent that credit between those aircraft may be applied for flightcrew member training, checking, recent experience, operating experience, operating cycles, and line operating flight time for consolidation of knowledge and skills.

(10) *Related aircraft differences training.* The flightcrew member training required for aircraft with different type certificates that have been designated as related by the Administrator.

(11) *Base aircraft.* An aircraft identified by a certificate holder for use as a reference to compare differences with another aircraft.

[Doc. No. 9509, 35 FR 90, Jan. 3, 1970; 35 FR 2819, Feb. 11, 1970, as amended by Amdt. 121-104, 38 FR 14915, June 7, 1973; Amdt. 121-259, 61 FR 34560, July 2, 1996; Amdt. 121-366, 78 FR 67836, Nov. 12, 2013]

§ 121.401 Training program: General.

(a) Each certificate holder shall:

(1) Establish and implement a training program that satisfies the requirements of this subpart and appendices E and F of this part and that ensures that each crewmember, aircraft dispatcher, flight instructor and check airman is adequately trained to perform his or her assigned duties. Prior

to implementation, the certificate holder must obtain initial and final FAA approval of the training program.

(2) Provide adequate ground and flight training facilities and properly qualified ground instructors for the training required by this subpart;

(3) Provide and keep current with respect to each airplane type and, if applicable, the particular variations within that airplane type, appropriate training material, examinations, forms, instructions, and procedures for use in conducting the training and checks required by this part; and

(4) Provide enough flight instructors, simulator instructors, and approved check airmen to conduct required flight training and flight checks, and simulator training courses permitted under this part.

(b) Whenever a crewmember or aircraft dispatcher who is required to take recurrent training, a flight check, or a competence check, takes the check or completes the training in the calendar month before or after the calendar month in which that training or check is required, he is considered to have taken or completed it in the calendar month in which it was required.

(c) Each instructor, supervisor, or check airman who is responsible for a particular ground training subject, segment of flight training, course of training, flight check, or competence check under this part shall certify as to the proficiency and knowledge of the crewmember, aircraft dispatcher, flight instructor, or check airman concerned upon completion of that training or check. That certification shall be made a part of the crewmember's or dispatcher's record. When the certification required by this paragraph is made by an entry in a computerized recordkeeping system, the certifying instructor, supervisor, or check airman must be identified with that entry. However, the signature of the certifying instructor, supervisor, or check airman is not required for computerized entries.

(d) Training subjects that are applicable to more than one airplane or crewmember position and that have been satisfactorily completed in connection with prior training for another airplane or another crewmember position, need not be repeated during subsequent training other than recurrent training.

(e) A person who progresses successfully through flight training, is recommended by his instructor or a check airman, and successfully completes the appropriate flight check for a check airman or the Administrator, need not complete the programmed hours of flight training for the particular airplane. However, whenever the Administrator finds that 20 percent of the flight checks given at a particular training base during the previous 6 months under this paragraph are unsuccessful, this paragraph may not be used by the certificate holder at that base until the Administrator finds that the effectiveness of the flight training there has improved.

In the case of a certificate holder using a course of training permitted in §121.409(c), the Administrator may require the programmed hours of inflight training in whole or in part, until he finds the effectiveness of the flight training has improved as provided in paragraph (e) of this section.

[Doc. No. 9509, 35 FR 90, Jan. 3, 1970, as amended by Amdt. 121–104, 38 FR 14915, June 7, 1973; Amdt. 121–108, 38 FR 35446, Dec. 28, 1973; Amdt. 121–143, 43 FR 22642, May 25, 1978; Amdt. 121–316, 70 FR 58823, Oct. 7, 2005]

§121.402 Training program: Special rules.

(a) Other than the certificate holder, only another certificate holder certificated under this part or a flight training center certificated under part 142 of this chapter is eligible under this subpart to provide flight training, testing, and checking under contract or other arrangement to those persons subject to the requirements of this subpart.

(b) A certificate holder may contract with, or otherwise arrange to use the services of, a training center certificated under part 142 of this chapter to provide training, testing, and checking required by this part only if the training center—

(1) Holds applicable training specifications issued under part 142 of this chapter;

(2) Has facilities, training equipment, and courseware meeting the applicable

requirements of part 142 of this chapter;

(3) Has approved curriculums, curriculum segments, and portions of curriculum segments applicable for use in training courses required by this subpart; and

(4) Has sufficient instructor and check airmen qualified under the applicable requirements of §§121.411 or 121.413 to provide training, testing, and checking to persons subject to the requirements of this subpart.

[Doc. No. 26933, 61 FR 34560, July 2, 1996, as amended by Amdt. 121–263, 62 FR 13791, Mar. 21, 1997]

§121.403 Training program: Curriculum.

(a) Each certificate holder must prepare and keep current a written training program curriculum for each type of airplane with respect to dispatchers and each crewmember required for that type airplane. The curriculum must include ground and flight training required by this subpart.

(b) Each training program curriculum must include:

(1) A list of principal ground training subjects, including emergency training subjects, that are provided.

(2) A list of all the training device mockups, systems trainers, procedures trainers, or other training aids that the certificate holder will use. No later than March 12, 2019, a list of all the training equipment approved under §121.408 as well as other training aids that the certificate holder will use.

(3) Detailed descriptions or pictorial displays of the approved normal, abnormal, and emergency maneuvers, procedures and functions that will be performed during each flight training phase or flight check, indicating those maneuvers, procedures and functions that are to be performed during the inflight portions of flight training and flight checks.

(4) A list of airplane simulators or other training devices approved under §121.407, including approvals for particular maneuvers, procedures, or functions.

(5) The programmed hours of training that will be applied to each phase of training.

(6) A copy of each statement issued by the Administrator under § 121.405(d) for reduction of programmed hours of training.

[Doc. No. 9509, 35 FR 90, Jan. 3, 1970, as amended by Amdt. 121–366, 78 FR 67836, Nov. 12, 2013]

§ 121.404   Compliance dates: Crew and dispatcher resource management training.

After March 19, 1998, no certificate holder may use a person as a flight crewmember, and after March 19, 1999, no certificate holder may use a person as a flight attendant or aircraft dispatcher unless that person has completed approved crew resource management (CRM) or dispatcher resource management (DRM) initial training, as applicable, with that certificate holder or with another certificate holder.

[Doc. No. 28154, 61 FR 30435, June 14, 1996]

§ 121.405   Training program and revision: Initial and final approval.

(a) To obtain initial and final approval of a training program, or a revision to an approved training program, each certificate holder must submit to the Administrator—

(1) An outline of the proposed program or revision, including an outline of the proposed or revised curriculum, that provides enough information for a preliminary evaluation of the proposed training program or revised training program; and

(2) Additional relevant information as may be requested by the Administrator.

(b) If the proposed training program or revision complies with this subpart the Administrator grants initial approval in writing after which the certificate holder may conduct the training in accordance with that program. The Administrator then evaluates the effectiveness of the training program and advises the certificate holder of deficiencies, if any, that must be corrected.

(c) The Administrator grants final approval of the training program or revision if the certificate holder shows that the training conducted under the initial approval set forth in paragraph (b) of this section ensures that each person that successfully completes the

training is adequately trained to perform his assigned duties.

(d) In granting initial and final approval of training programs or revisions, including reductions in programmed hours specified in this subpart, the Administrator considers the training aids, devices, methods, and procedures listed in the certificate holder's curriculum as set forth in § 121.403 that increase the quality and effectiveness of the teaching-learning process.

If approval of reduced programmed hours of training is granted, the Administrator provides the certificate holder with a statement of the basis for the approval.

(e) Whenever the Administrator finds that revisions are necessary for the continued adequacy of a training program that has been granted final approval, the certificate holder shall, after notification by the Administrator, make any changes in the program that are found necessary by the Administrator. Within 30 days after the certificate holder receives such notice, it may file a petition to reconsider the notice with the responsible Flight Standards office. The filing of a petition to reconsider stays the notice pending a decision by the Administrator. However, if the Administrator finds that there is an emergency that requires immediate action in the interest of safety in air transportation, he may, upon a statement of the reasons, require a change effective without stay.

(f) Each certificate holder described in § 135.3 (b) and (c) of this chapter must include the material required by § 121.403 in the manual required by § 135.21 of this chapter.

(g) The Administrator may grant a deviation to certificate holders described in § 135.3 (b) and (c) of this chapter to allow reduced programmed hours of ground training required by § 121.419 if it is found that a reduction is warranted based on the certificate holder's operations and the complexity of the make, model, and series of the aircraft used.

[Doc. No. 9509, 35 FR 90, Jan. 3, 1970, as amended by Amdt. 121–207, 54 FR 39293, Sept. 25, 1989; Amdt. 121–250, 60 FR 65948, Dec. 20, 1995; Amdt. 121–253, 61 FR 2612, Jan. 26, 1996; Docket FAA–2018–0119, Amdt. 121–380, 83 FR 9172, Mar. 5, 2018]

§121.406 Credit for previous CRM/DRM training.

(a) For flightcrew members, the Administrator may credit CRM training received before March 19, 1998 toward all or part of the initial ground CRM training required by §121.419.

(b) For flight attendants, the Administrator may credit CRM training received before March 19, 1999 toward all or part of the initial ground CRM training required by §121.421.

(c) For aircraft dispatchers, the Administrator may credit CRM training received before March 19, 1999 toward all or part of the initial ground CRM training required by §121.422.

(d) In granting credit for initial ground CRM or DRM training, the Administrator considers training aids, devices, methods, and procedures used by the certificate holder in a voluntary CRM or DRM program or in an AQP program that effectively meets the quality of an approved CRM or DRM initial ground training program under section 121.419, 121.421, or 121.422 as appropriate.

[Doc. No. 27993, 60 FR 65949, Dec. 20, 1995]

§121.407 Training program: Approval of airplane simulators and other training devices.

(a) Each airplane simulator and other training device used to satisfy a training requirement of this part in an approved training program, must meet all of the following requirements:

(1) Be specifically approved by the Administrator for—

(i) Use in the certificate holder's approved training program;

(ii) The type airplane and, if applicable, the particular variation within type, for which the training or check is being conducted; and

(iii) The particular maneuver, procedure, or flightcrew member function involved.

(2) Maintain the performance, function, and other characteristics that are required for qualification in accordance with part 60 of this chapter or a previously qualified device, as permitted in accordance with §60.17 of this chapter.

(3) Be modified in accordance with part 60 of this chapter to conform with any modification to the airplane being simulated that results in changes to performance, function, or other characteristics required for qualification.

(4) Be given a daily functional preflight check before being used.

(5) Have a daily discrepancy log kept with each discrepancy entered in that log by the appropriate instructor or check airman at the end of each training or check flight.

(b) A particular airplane simulator or other training device may be approved for use by more than one certificate holder.

(c) An airplane simulator may be used instead of the airplane to satisfy the in-flight requirements of §§121.439 and 121.441 and appendices E and F of this part, if the simulator—

(1) Is approved under this section and meets the appropriate simulator requirements of appendix H of this part; and

(2) Is used as part of an approved program that meets the training requirements of §121.424 (a) and (c) and appendix H of this part.

(d) An airplane simulator approved under this section must be used instead of the airplane to satisfy the pilot flight training requirements prescribed in the certificate holder's approved low-altitude windshear flight training program set forth in §121.409(d) of this part.

(e) An airplane simulator approved under this section must be used instead of the airplane to satisfy the pilot flight training requirements prescribed in the extended envelope training set forth in §121.423 of this part. Compliance with this paragraph is required no later than March 12, 2019.

[Doc. No. 9509, 35 FR 90, Jan. 3, 1970, as amended by Amdt. 121–161, 45 FR 44183, June 30, 1980; Amdt. 121–199, 53 FR 37696, Sept. 27, 1988; Amdt. 121–366, 78 FR 67836, Nov. 12, 2013]

§ 121.408 Training equipment other than flight simulation training devices.

(a) The Administrator must approve training equipment used in a training program approved under this part and that functionally replicates aircraft equipment for the certificate holder and the crewmember duty or procedure. Training equipment does not include FSTDs qualified under part 60 of this chapter.

(b) The certificate holder must demonstrate that the training equipment described in paragraph (a) of this section, used to meet the training requirements of this subpart, meets all of the following:

(1) The form, fit, function, and weight, as appropriate, of the aircraft equipment.

(2) Replicates the normal operation (and abnormal and emergency operation, if appropriate) of the aircraft equipment including the following:

(i) The required force, actions and travel of the aircraft equipment.

(ii) Variations in aircraft equipment operated by the certificate holder, if applicable.

(3) Replicates the operation of the aircraft equipment under adverse conditions, if appropriate.

(c) Training equipment must be modified to ensure that it maintains the performance and function of the aircraft type or aircraft equipment replicated.

(d) All training equipment must have a record of discrepancies. The documenting system must be readily available for review by each instructor, check airman or supervisor, prior to conducting training or checking with that equipment.

(1) Each instructor, check airman or supervisor conducting training or checking, and each person conducting an inspection of the equipment who discovers a discrepancy, including any missing, malfunctioning or inoperative components, must record a description of that discrepancy and the date that the discrepancy was identified.

(2) All corrections to discrepancies must be recorded when the corrections are made. This record must include the date of the correction.

(3) A record of a discrepancy must be maintained for at least 60 days.

(e) No person may use, allow the use of, or offer the use of training equipment with a missing, malfunctioning, or inoperative component to meet the crewmember training or checking requirements of this chapter for tasks that require the use of the correctly operating component.

(f) Compliance with this section is required no later than March 12, 2019.

[Doc. No. FAA–2008–0677, 78 FR 67837, Nov. 12, 2013]

§ 121.409 Training courses using airplane simulators and other training devices.

(a) Training courses utilizing airplane simulators and other training devices may be included in the certificate holder's approved training program for use as provided in this section.

(b) Except for the airline transport pilot certification training program approved to satisfy the requirements of § 61.156 of this chapter, a course of training in an airplane simulator may be included for use as provided in § 121.441 if that course—

(1) Provides at least 4 hours of training at the pilot controls of an airplane simulator as well as a proper briefing before and after the training.

(2) Provides training in at least the following:

(i) The procedures and maneuvers set forth in appendix F to this part; or

(ii) Line-oriented flight training (LOFT) that—

(A) Before March 12, 2019,

(1) Utilizes a complete flight crew;

(2) Includes at least the maneuvers and procedures (abnormal and emergency) that may be expected in line operations; and

(3) Is representative of the flight segment appropriate to the operations being conducted by the certificate holder.

(B) Beginning on March 12, 2019—

(1) Utilizes a complete flight crew;

(2) Includes at least the maneuvers and procedures (abnormal and emergency) that may be expected in line operations;

160

(3) Includes scenario-based or maneuver-based stall prevention training before, during or after the LOFT scenario for each pilot;

(4) Is representative of two flight segments appropriate to the operations being conducted by the certificate holder; and

(5) Provides an opportunity to demonstrate workload management and pilot monitoring skills.

(3) Is given by an instructor who meets the applicable requirements of §121.412.

The satisfactory completion of the course of training must be certified by either the Administrator or a qualified check airman.

(c) The programmed hours of flight training set forth in this subpart do not apply if the training program for the airplane type includes—

(1) A course of pilot training in an airplane simulator as provided in §121.424(d); or

(2) A course of flight engineer training in an airplane simulator or other training device as provided in §121.425(c).

(d) Each certificate holder required to comply with §121.358 of this part must use an approved simulator for each airplane type in each of its pilot training courses that provides training in at least the procedures and maneuvers set forth in the certificate holder's approved low-altitude windshear flight training program. The approved low-altitude windshear flight training, if applicable, must be included in each of the pilot flight training courses prescribed in §§121.409(b), 121.418, 121.424, and 121.427 of this part.

[Doc. No. 9509, 35 FR 90, Jan. 3, 1970, as amended by Amdt. 121–130, 41 FR 47229, Oct. 28, 1976; Amdt. 121–144, 43 FR 22646, May 25, 1978; Amdt. 121–199, 53 FR 37696. Sept. 27, 1988; Amdt. 121–264, 62 FR 23120, Apr. 28, 1997; Amdt. 121–365, 78 FR 42377, July 15, 2013; Amdt. 121–366, 78 FR 67837, Nov. 12, 2013]

§121.410 Airline transport pilot certification training program.

(a) A certificate holder may obtain approval to establish and implement a training program to satisfy the requirements of §61.156 of this chapter. The training program must be separate from the air carrier training program required by this part.

(b) No certificate holder may use a person nor may any person serve as an instructor in a training program approved to meet the requirements of §61.156 of this chapter unless the instructor:

(1) Holds an airline transport pilot certificate with an airplane category multiengine class rating;

(2) Has at least 2 years of experience as a pilot in command in operations conducted under §91.1053(a)(2)(i) or §135.243(a)(1) of this chapter, or as a pilot in command or second in command in any operation conducted under this part;

(3) Except for the holder of a flight instructor certificate, receives initial training on the following topics:

(i) The fundamental principles of the learning process;

(ii) Elements of effective teaching, instruction methods, and techniques;

(iii) Instructor duties, privileges, responsibilities, and limitations;

(iv) Training policies and procedures; and

(v) Evaluation.

(4) If providing training in a flight simulation training device, hold an aircraft type rating for the aircraft represented by the flight simulation training device utilized in the training program and have received training within the preceding 12 months from the certificate holder on:

(i) Proper operation of flight simulator and flight training device controls and systems;

(ii) Proper operation of environmental and fault panels;

(iii) Data and motion limitations of simulation;

(iv) Minimum equipment requirements for each curriculum; and

(v) The maneuvers that will be demonstrated in the flight simulation training device.

(c) A certificate holder may not issue a graduation certificate to a student unless that student has completed all the curriculum requirements of the course.

(d) A certificate holder must conduct evaluations to ensure that training techniques, procedures, and standards are acceptable to the Administrator.

[Doc. No. FAA-2010-0100, 78 FR 42377, July 15, 2013]

§ 121.411 Qualifications: Check airmen (airplane) and check airmen (simulator).

(a) For the purposes of this section and § 121.413:

(1) A check airman (airplane) is a person who is qualified, and permitted, to conduct flight checks or instruction in an airplane, in a flight simulator, or in a flight training device for a particular type airplane.

(2) A check airman (simulator) is a person who is qualified to conduct flight checks or instruction, but only in a flight simulator or in a flight training device for a particular type airplane.

(3) Check airmen (airplane) and check airmen (simulator) are those check airmen who perform the functions described in § 121.401(a)(4).

(b) No certificate holder may use a person, nor may any person serve as a check airman (airplane) in a training program established under this subpart unless, with respect to the airplane type involved, that person—

(1) Holds the airman certificates and ratings required to serve as a pilot in command or flight engineer, as applicable, in operations under this part;

(2) Has satisfactorily completed the appropriate training phases for the airplane, including recurrent training, that are required to serve as a pilot in command or flight engineer, as applicable, in operations under this part;

(3) Has satisfactorily completed the appropriate proficiency or flight checks that are required to serve as a pilot in command or flight engineer, as applicable, in operations under this part;

(4) Has satisfactorily completed the applicable training requirements of § 121.413 including in-flight training and practice for initial and transition training;

(5) Holds at least a Class III medical certificate unless serving as a required crewmember, in which case holds a Class I or Class II medical certificate as appropriate;

(6) Has satisfied the recency of experience requirements of § 121.439 of this part, as applicable; and

(7) Has been approved by the Administrator for the check airman duties involved.

(c) No certificate holder may use a person nor may any person serve as a check airman (simulator) in a training program established under this subpart unless, with respect to the airplane type involved, that person meets the provisions of paragraph (b) of this section, or—

(1) Holds the airman certificates and ratings, except medical certificate, required to serve as a pilot in command or a flight engineer, as applicable, in operations under this part;

(2) Has satisfactorily completed the appropriate training phases for the airplane, including recurrent training, that are required to serve as a pilot in command or flight engineer, as applicable, in operations under this part;

(3) Has satisfactorily completed the appropriate proficiency or flight checks that are required to serve as a pilot in command or flight engineer, as applicable, in operations under this part;

(4) Has satisfactorily completed the applicable training requirements of § 121.413; and

(5) Has been approved by the Administrator for the check airman (simulator) duties involved.

(d) Completion of the requirements in paragraphs (b) (2), (3), and (4) or (c) (2), (3), and (4) of this section, as applicable, shall be entered in the individual's training record maintained by the certificate holder.

(e) Check airmen who have reached their 65th birthday or who do not hold an appropriate medical certificate may function as check airmen, but may not serve as pilot flightcrew members in operations under this part.

(f) A check airman (simulator) must accomplish the following—

(1) Fly at least two flight segments as a required crewmember for the type airplane involved within the 12-month period preceding the performance of any check airman duty in a flight simulator; or

(2) Satisfactorily complete an approved line-observation program within the period prescribed by that program and that must precede the performance of any check airman duty in a flight simulator.

(g) The flight segments or line-observation program required in paragraph (f) of this section are considered to be completed in the month required if completed in the calendar month before or in the calendar month after the month in which it is due.

[Doc. No. 28471, 61 FR 30741, June 17, 1996, as amended by Amdt. 121–344, 74 FR 34235, July 15, 2009; Amdt. 121–366, 78 FR 67837, Nov. 12, 2013]

§121.412 Qualifications: Flight instructors (airplane) and flight instructors (simulator).

(a) For the purposes of this section and §121.414:

(1) A flight instructor (airplane) is a person who is qualified to instruct in an airplane, in a flight simulator, or in a flight training device for a particular type airplane.

(2) A flight instructor (simulator) is a person who is qualified to instruct, but only in a flight simulator, in a flight training device, or both, for a particular type airplane.

(3) Flight instructors (airplane) and flight instructors (simulator) are those instructors who perform the functions described in §121.401(a)(4).

(b) No certificate holder may use a person nor may any person serve as a flight instructor (airplane) in a training program established under this subpart unless, with respect to the airplane type involved, that person—

(1) Holds the airman certificates and rating required to serve as a pilot in command or flight engineer, as applicable, in operations under this part;

(2) Has satisfactorily completed the appropriate training phases for the airplane, including recurrent training, that are required to serve as a pilot in command or flight engineer, as applicable, in operations under this part;

(3) Has satisfactorily completed the appropriate proficiency or flight checks that are required to serve as a pilot in command or flight engineer, as applicable, in operations under this part;

(4) Has satisfactorily completed the applicable training requirements of §121.414, including in-flight training and practice for initial and transition training;

(5) Holds at least a Class III medical certificate unless serving as a required crewmember, in which case holds a Class I or a Class II medical certificate as appropriate; and

(6) Has satisfied the recency of experience requirements of §121.439 of this part, as applicable.

(c) No certificate holder may use a person, nor may any person serve as a flight instructor (simulator) in a training program established under this subpart, unless, with respect to the airplane type involved, that person meets the provisions of paragraph (b) of this section, or—

(1) Holds the airman certificates and ratings, except medical certificate, required to serve as a pilot in command or flight engineer, as applicable, in operations under this part;

(2) Has satisfactorily completed the appropriate training phases for the airplane, including recurrent training, that are required to serve as a pilot in command or flight engineer, as applicable, in operations under this part;

(3) Has satisfactorily completed the appropriate proficiency or flight checks that are required to serve as a pilot in command or flight engineer, as applicable, in operations under this part; and

(4) Has satisfactorily completed the applicable training requirements of §121.414.

(d) Completion of the requirements in paragraphs (b) (2), (3), and (4) or (c) (2), (3), and (4) of this section as applicable shall be entered in the individual's training record maintained by the certificate holder.

(e) Flight instructors who have reached their 65th birthday or who do not hold an appropriate medical certificate may function as flight instructors, but may not serve as pilot flightcrew members in operations under this part.

(f) A flight instructor (simulator) must accomplish the following—

(1) Fly at least two flight segments as a required crewmember for the type of airplane within the 12-month period

preceding the performance of any flight instructor duty in a flight simulator (and must hold a Class I or Class II medical certificate as appropriate); or

(2) Satisfactorily complete an approved line-observation program within the period prescribed by that program preceding the performance of any flight instructor duty in a flight simulator.

(g) The flight segments or line-observation program required in paragraph (f) of this section is considered completed in the month required if completed in the calendar month before, or the calendar month after the month in which it is due.

[Doc. No. 28471, 61 FR 30742, June 17, 1996; 61 FR 34927, July 3, 1996; 62 FR 3739, Jan. 24, 1997; Amdt. 121–264, 62 FR 23120, Apr. 28, 1997; Amdt. 121–344, 74 FR 34235, July 15, 2009; Amdt. 121–355, 76 FR 35104, June 16, 2011; Amdt. 121–366, 78 FR 67837, Nov. 12, 2013]

§ 121.413 Initial, transition and recurrent training and checking requirements: Check airmen (airplane), check airmen (simulator).

(a) No certificate holder may use a person nor may any person serve as a check airman unless—

(1) That person has satisfactorily completed initial or transition check airman training; and

(2) Within the preceding 24 calendar months that person satisfactorily conducts a check or supervises operating experience under the observation of an FAA inspector or an aircrew designated examiner employed by the operator. The observation check may be accomplished in part or in full in an airplane, in a flight simulator, or in a flight training device.

(b) The observation check required by paragraph (a)(2) of this section is considered to have been completed in the month required if completed in the calendar month before, or the calendar month after, the month in which it is due.

(c) The initial ground training for check airmen must include the following:

(1) Check airman duties, functions, and responsibilities.

(2) The applicable Code of Federal Regulations and the certificate holder's policies and procedures.

(3) The appropriate methods, procedures, and techniques for conducting the required checks.

(4) Proper evaluation of student performance including the detection of—

(i) Improper and insufficient training; and

(ii) Personal characteristics of an applicant that could adversely affect safety.

(5) The appropriate corrective action in the case of unsatisfactory checks.

(6) The approved methods, procedures, and limitations for performing the required normal, abnormal, and emergency procedures in the airplane.

(7) For check airmen who conduct training or checking in a flight simulator or a flight training device, the following subjects specific to the device(s) for the airplane type:

(i) Proper operation of the controls and systems;

(ii) Proper operation of environmental and fault panels;

(iii) Data and motion limitations of simulation; and

(iv) The minimum airplane simulator equipment required by this part or part 60 of this chapter, for each maneuver and procedure completed in a flight simulator or a flight training device.

(d) The transition ground training for check airmen must include the following:

(1) The approved methods, procedures, and limitations for performing the required normal, abnormal, and emergency procedures applicable to the airplane to which the check airman is transitioning.

(2) For check airmen who conduct training or checking in a flight simulator or a flight training device, the following subjects specific to the device(s) for the airplane type to which the check airman is transitioning:

(i) Proper operation of the controls and systems;

(ii) Proper operation of environmental and fault panels;

(iii) Data and motion limitations of simulation; and

(iv) The minimum airplane simulator equipment required by this part or part 60 of this chapter, for each maneuver and procedure completed in a flight simulator or a flight training device.

(e) The initial and transition flight training for check airmen (airplane) must include the following:

(1) The safety measures for emergency situations that are likely to develop during a check.

(2) The potential results of improper, untimely, or non-execution of safety measures during a check.

(3) For pilot check airman (airplane)—

(i) Training and practice in conducting flight checks from the left and right pilot seats in the required normal, abnormal, and emergency procedures to ensure competence to conduct the pilot flight checks required by this part; and

(ii) The safety measures to be taken from either pilot seat for emergency situations that are likely to develop during a check.

(4) For flight engineer check airmen (airplane), training to ensure competence to perform assigned duties.

(f) The requirements of paragraph (e) of this section may be accomplished in full or in part in flight, in a flight simulator, or in a flight training device, as appropriate.

(g) The initial and transition flight training for check airmen who conduct training or checking in a flight simulator or a flight training device must include the following:

(1) Training and practice in conducting flight checks in the required normal, abnormal, and emergency procedures to ensure competence to conduct the flight checks required by this part. This training and practice must be accomplished in a flight simulator or in a flight training device.

(2) Training in the operation of flight simulators or flight training devices, or both, to ensure competence to conduct the flight checks required by this part.

(h) Recurrent ground training for check airmen who conduct training or checking in a flight simulator or a flight training device must be completed every 12 calendar months and must include the subjects required in paragraph (c)(7) of this section.

(i) Compliance with paragraphs (c)(7), (d)(2), and (h) of this section is required no later than March 12, 2019.

[Doc. No. 28471, 61 FR 30743, June 17, 1996; 62 FR 3739, Jan. 24, 1997; Amdt. 121–264, 62 FR 23120, Apr. 28, 1997; Amdt. 121–366, 78 FR 67838, Nov. 12, 2013]

§ 121.414 Initial, transition and recurrent training and checking requirements: flight instructors (airplane), flight instructors (simulator).

(a) No certificate holder may use a person nor may any person serve as a flight instructor unless—

(1) That person has satisfactorily completed initial or transition flight instructor training; and

(2) Within the preceding 24 calendar months, that person satisfactorily conducts instruction under the observation of an FAA inspector, an operator check airman, or an aircrew designated examiner employed by the operator. The observation check may be accomplished in part or in full in an airplane, in a flight simulator, or in a flight training device.

(b) The observation check required by paragraph (a)(2) of this section is considered to have been completed in the month required if completed in the calendar month before, or the calendar month after, the month in which it is due.

(c) The initial ground training for flight instructors must include the following:

(1) Flight instructor duties, functions, and responsibilities.

(2) The applicable Code of Federal Regulations and the certificate holder's policies and procedures.

(3) The appropriate methods, procedures, and techniques for conducting flight instruction.

(4) Proper evaluation of student performance including the detection of—

(i) Improper and insufficient training; and

(ii) Personal characteristics of an applicant that could adversely affect safety.

(5) The corrective action in the case of unsatisfactory training progress.

(6) The approved methods, procedures, and limitations for performing the required normal, abnormal, and emergency procedures in the airplane.

(7) Except for holders of a flight instructor certificate—

(i) The fundamental principles of the teaching-learning process;

(ii) Teaching methods and procedures; and

(iii) The instructor-student relationship.

(8) For flight instructors who conduct training in a flight simulator or a flight training device, the following subjects specific to the device(s) for the airplane type:

(i) Proper operation of the controls and systems;

(ii) Proper operation of environmental and fault panels;

(iii) Data and motion limitations of simulation; and

(iv) The minimum airplane simulator equipment required by this part or part 60 of this chapter, for each maneuver and procedure completed in a flight simulator or a flight training device.

(d) The transition ground training for flight instructors must include the following:

(1) The approved methods, procedures, and limitations for performing the required normal, abnormal, and emergency procedures applicable to the airplane to which the flight instructor is transitioning.

(2) For flight instructors who conduct training in a flight simulator or a flight training device, the following subjects specific to the device(s) for the airplane type to which the flight instructor is transitioning:

(i) Proper operation of the controls and systems;

(ii) Proper operation of environmental and fault panels;

(iii) Data and motion limitations of simulation; and

(iv) The minimum airplane simulator equipment required by this part or part 60 of this chapter, for each maneuver and procedure completed in a flight simulator or a flight training device.

(e) The initial and transition flight training for flight instructors (airplane) must include the following:

(1) The safety measures for emergency situations that are likely to develop during instruction.

(2) The potential results of improper, untimely, or non-execution of safety measures during instruction.

(3) For pilot flight instructor (airplane)—

(i) In-flight training and practice in conducting flight instruction from the left and right pilot seats in the required normal, abnormal, and emergency procedures to ensure competence as an instructor; and

(ii) The safety measures to be taken from either pilot seat for emergency situations that are likely to develop during instruction.

(4) For flight engineer instructors (airplane), inflight training to ensure competence to perform assigned duties.

(f) The requirements of paragraph (e) of this section may be accomplished in full or in part in flight, in a flight simulator, or in a flight training device, as appropriate.

(g) The initial and transition flight training for flight instructors who conduct training in a flight simulator or a flight training device must include the following:

(1) Training and practice in the required normal, abnormal, and emergency procedures to ensure competence to conduct the flight instruction required by this part. This training and practice must be accomplished in full or in part in a flight simulator or in a flight training device.

(2) Training in the operation of flight simulators or flight training devices, or both, to ensure competence to conduct the flight instruction required by this part.

(h) Recurrent flight instructor ground training for flight instructors who conduct training in a flight simulator or a flight training device must be completed every 12 calendar months and must include the subjects required in paragraph (c)(8) of this section.

(i) Compliance with paragraphs (c)(8), (d)(2), and (h) of this section is required no later than March 12, 2019.

[Doc. No. 28471, 61 FR 30743, June 17, 1996; 62 FR 3739, Jan. 24, 1997, as amended by Amdt. 121–366, 78 FR 67838, Nov. 12, 2013]

§ 121.415 Crewmember and dispatcher training program requirements.

(a) Each training program must provide the following ground training as appropriate to the particular assignment of the crewmember or dispatcher:

(1) Basic indoctrination ground training for newly hired crewmembers or dispatchers including 40 programmed hours of instruction, unless reduced under §121.405 or as specified in §121.401(d), in at least the following—

(i) Duties and responsibilities of crewmembers or dispatchers, as applicable;

(ii) Appropriate provisions of the Federal Aviation Regulations;

(iii) Contents of the certificate holder's operating certificate and operations specifications (not required for flight attendants); and

(iv) Appropriate portions of the certificate holder's operating manual.

(2) The initial and transition ground training specified in §§121.419, 121.421 and 121.422, as applicable.

(3) For crewmembers, emergency training as specified in §§121.417 and 121.805.

(4) After February 15, 2008, training for crewmembers and dispatchers in their roles and responsibilities in the certificate holder's passenger recovery plan, if applicable.

(b) Each training program must provide the flight training specified in §§121.424 through 121.425, as applicable.

(c) Each training program must provide recurrent ground and flight training as provided in §121.427.

(d) Each training program must provide the differences training specified in §121.418(a) if the Administrator finds that, due to differences between airplanes of the same type operated by the certificate holder, additional training is necessary to insure that each crewmember and dispatcher is adequately trained to perform their assigned duties.

(e) Upgrade training as specified in §§121.419 and 121.424 for a particular type airplane may be included in the training program for crewmembers who have qualified and served as second in command pilot or flight engineer on that airplane.

(f) Particular subjects, maneuvers, procedures, or parts thereof specified in §§121.419, 121.421, 121.422, 121.424, and 121.425 for transition or upgrade training, as applicable, may be omitted or the programmed hours of ground instruction or inflight training may be reduced, as provided in §121.405.

(g) In addition to initial, transition, upgrade, recurrent and differences training, each training program must also provide ground and flight training, instruction, and practice as necessary to insure that each crewmember and dispatcher—

(1) Remains adequately trained and currently proficient with respect to each airplane, crewmember position, and type of operation in which he serves; and

(2) Qualifies in new equipment, facilities, procedures, and techniques, including modifications to airplanes.

(h) Each training program must include a process to provide for the regular analysis of individual pilot performance to identify pilots with performance deficiencies during training and checking and multiple failures during checking.

(i) Each training program must include methods for remedial training and tracking of pilots identified in the analysis performed in accordance with paragraph (h) of this section.

(j) Compliance with paragraphs (h) and (i) of this section is required no later than March 12, 2019.

[Doc. No. 9509, 35 FR 90, Jan. 3, 1970, as amended by Amdt. 121–130, 41 FR 47229, Oct. 28, 1976; Amdt. 121–281, 66 FR 19043, Apr. 12, 2001; Amdt. 121–329, 72 FR 1881, Jan. 16, 2007; Amdt. 121–366, 78 FR 67839, Nov. 12, 2013]

§121.417 Crewmember emergency training.

(a) Each training program must provide the emergency training set forth in this section with respect to each airplane type, model, and configuration, each required crewmember, and each kind of operation conducted, insofar as appropriate for each crewmember and the certificate holder.

(b) Emergency training must provide the following:

(1) Instruction in emergency assignments and procedures, including coordination among crewmembers.

(2) Individual instruction in the location, function, and operation of emergency equipment including—

(i) Equipment used in ditching and evacuation;

(ii) [Reserved]

(iii) Portable fire extinguishers, with emphasis on type of extinguisher to be used on different classes of fires; and

(iv) Emergency exits in the emergency mode with the evacuation slide/raft pack attached (if applicable), with training emphasis on the operation of the exits under adverse conditions.

(3) Instruction in the handling of emergency situations including—

(i) Rapid decompression;

(ii) Fire in flight or on the surface, and smoke control procedures with emphasis on electrical equipment and related circuit breakers found in cabin areas including all galleys, service centers, lifts, lavatories and movie screens;

(iii) Ditching and other evacuation, including the evacuation of persons and their attendants, if any, who may need the assistance of another person to move expeditiously to an exit in the event of an emergency.

(iv) [Reserved]

(v) Hijacking and other unusual situations.

(4) Review and discussion of previous aircraft accidents and incidents pertaining to actual emergency situations.

(c) Each crewmember must accomplish the following emergency training during the specified training periods, using those items of installed emergency equipment for each type of airplane in which he or she is to serve (Alternate recurrent training required by § 121.433(c) of this part may be accomplished by approved pictorial presentation or demonstration):

(1) One-time emergency drill requirements to be accomplished during initial training. Each crewmember must perform—

(i) At least one approved protective breathing equipment (PBE) drill in which the crewmember combats an actual or simulated fire using at least one type of installed hand fire extinguisher or approved fire extinguisher that is appropriate for the type of actual fire or simulated fire to be fought while using the type of installed PBE required by § 121.337 or approved PBE simulation device as defined by paragraph (d) of this section for combatting fires aboard airplanes;

(ii) At least one approved firefighting drill in which the crewmember combats an actual fire using at least one type of installed hand fire extinguisher or approved fire extinguisher that is appropriate for the type of fire to be fought. This firefighting drill is not required if the crewmember performs the PBE drill of paragraph (c)(1)(i) by combating an actual fire; and

(iii) An emergency evacuation drill with each person egressing the airplane or approved training device using at least one type of installed emergency evacuation slide. The crewmember may either observe the airplane exits being opened in the emergency mode and the associated exit slide/raft pack being deployed and inflated, or perform the tasks resulting in the accomplishment of these actions.

(2) Additional emergency drill requirements to be accomplished during initial training and once each 24 calendar months during recurrent training. Each crewmember must—

(i) Perform the following emergency drills and operate the following equipment:

(A) Each type of emergency exit in the normal and emergency modes, including the actions and forces required in the deployment of the emergency evacuation slides;

(B) Each type of installed hand fire extinguisher;

(C) Each type of emergency oxygen system to include protective breathing equipment;

(D) Donning, use, and inflation of individual flotation means, if applicable; and

(E) Ditching, if applicable, including but not limited to, as appropriate:

(1) Cockpit preparation and procedures;

(2) Crew coordination;

(3) Passenger briefing and cabin preparation;

(4) Donning and inflation of life preservers;

(5) Use of life-lines; and

(6) Boarding of passengers and crew into raft or a slide/raft pack.

(ii) Observe the following drills:

(A) Removal from the airplane (or training device) and inflation of each type of life raft, if applicable;

(B) Transfer of each type of slide/raft pack from one door to another;

(C) Deployment, inflation, and detachment from the airplane (or training device) of each type of slide/raft pack; and

(D) Emergency evacuation including the use of a slide.

(d) After September 1, 1993, no crewmember may serve in operations under this part unless that crewmember has performed the PBE drill and the firefighting drill described by paragraphs (c)(1)(i) and (c)(1)(ii) of this section, as part of a one-time training requirement of paragraphs (c)(1) or (c)(2) of this section as appropriate. Any crewmember who performs the PBE drill and the firefighting drill prescribed in paragraphs (c)(1)(i) and (c)(1)(ii) of this section after May 26, 1987, is deemed to be in compliance with this regulation upon presentation of information or documentation, in a form and manner acceptable to the Executive Director, Flight Standards Service, showing that the appropriate drills have been accomplished.

(e) Crewmembers who serve in operations above 25,000 feet must receive instruction in the following:

(1) Respiration.

(2) Hypoxia.

(3) Duration of consciousness without supplemental oxygen at altitude.

(4) Gas expansion.

(5) Gas bubble formation.

(6) Physical phenomena and incidents of decompression.

(f) For the purposes of this section the following definitions apply:

(1) *Actual fire* means an ignited combustible material, in controlled conditions, of sufficient magnitude and duration to accomplish the training objectives outlined in paragraphs (c)(1)(i) and (c)(1)(ii) of this section.

(2) *Approved fire extinguisher* means a training device that has been approved by the Administrator for use in meeting the training requirements of §121.417(c).

(3) *Approved PBE simulation device* means a training device that has been approved by the Administrator for use in meeting the training requirements of §121.417(c).

(4) *Combats*, in this context, means to properly fight an actual or simulated

fire using an appropriate type of fire extinguisher until that fire is extinguished.

(5) *Observe* means to watch without participating actively in the drill.

(6) *PBE drill* means an emergency drill in which a crewmember demonstrates the proper use of protective breathing equipment while fighting an actual or simulated fire.

(7) *Perform* means to satisfactorily accomplish a prescribed emergency drill using established procedures that stress the skill of the persons involved in the drill.

(8) *Simulated fire* means an artificial duplication of smoke or flame used to create various aircraft firefighting scenarios, such as lavatory, galley oven, and aircraft seat fires.

[Doc. No. 9509, 35 FR 90, Jan. 3, 1970]

EDITORIAL NOTE: For FEDERAL REGISTER citations affecting §121.417, see the List of CFR Sections Affected, which appears in the Finding Aids section of the printed volume and at *www.govinfo.gov*.

§121.418 Differences training and related aircraft differences training.

(a) *Differences training.* (1) Differences training for crewmembers and dispatchers must consist of at least the following as applicable to their assigned duties and responsibilities:

(i) Instruction in each appropriate subject or part thereof required for initial ground training in the airplane unless the Administrator finds that particular subjects are not necessary.

(ii) Flight training in each appropriate maneuver or procedure required for initial flight training in the airplane unless the Administrator finds that particular maneuvers or procedures are not necessary.

(iii) The number of programmed hours of ground and flight training determined by the Administrator to be necessary for the airplane, the operation, and the crewmember or aircraft dispatcher involved.

(2) Differences training for all variations of a particular type airplane may be included in initial, transition, upgrade, and recurrent training for the airplane.

(b) *Related aircraft differences training.* (1) In order to seek approval of related aircraft differences training for flightcrew members, a certificate holder must submit a request for related aircraft designation to the Administrator, and obtain approval of that request.

(2) If the Administrator determines under paragraph (b)(1) of this section that a certificate holder is operating related aircraft, the certificate holder may submit to the Administrator a request for approval of a training program that includes related aircraft differences training.

(3) A request for approval of a training program that includes related aircraft differences training must include at least the following:

(i) Each appropriate subject required for the ground training for the related aircraft.

(ii) Each appropriate maneuver or procedure required for the flight training and crewmember emergency training for the related aircraft.

(iii) The number of programmed hours of ground training, flight training and crewmember emergency training necessary based on review of the related aircraft and the duty position.

(c) *Approved related aircraft differences training.* Approved related aircraft differences training for flightcrew members may be included in initial, transition, upgrade and recurrent training for the base aircraft. If the certificate holder's approved training program includes related aircraft differences training in accordance with paragraph (b) of this section, the training required by §§ 121.419, 121.424, 121.425, and 121.427, as applicable to flightcrew members, may be modified for the related aircraft.

[Doc. No. 9509, 35 FR 90, Jan. 3, 1970, as amended by Amdt. 121–366, 78 FR 67839, Nov. 12, 2013]

§ 121.419 **Pilots and flight engineers: Initial, transition, and upgrade ground training.**

(a) Except as provided in paragraph (b) of this section, initial, transition, and upgrade ground training for pilots and flight engineers must include instruction in at least the following as applicable to their assigned duties:

(1) General subjects—

(i) The certificate holder's dispatch or flight release procedures;

(ii) Principles and methods for determining weight and balance, and runway limitations for takeoff and landing;

(iii) Enough meteorology to insure a practical knowledge of weather phenomena, including the principles of frontal systems, icing, fog, thunderstorms, and high altitude weather situations;

(iv) Air traffic control systems, procedures, and phraseology;

(v) Navigation and the use of navigation aids, including instrument approach procedures;

(vi) Normal and emergency communication procedures;

(vii) Visual cues prior to and during descent below DA/DH or MDA;

(viii) Approved crew resource management initial training; and

(ix) Other instructions as necessary to ensure pilot and flight engineer competence.

(2) For each airplane type—

(i) A general description;

(ii) Performance characteristics;

(iii) Engines and propellers;

(iv) Major components;

(v) Major airplane systems (e.g., flight controls, electrical, hydraulic); other systems as appropriate; principles of normal, abnormal, and emergency operations; appropriate procedures and limitations;

(vi) Procedures for—

(A) Recognizing and avoiding severe weather situations;

(B) Escaping from severe weather situations, in case of inadvertent encounters, including low-altitude windshear, and

(C) Operating in or near thunderstorms (including best penetrating altitudes), turbulent air (including clear air turbulence), icing, hail, and other potentially hazardous meteorological conditions;

(vii) Operating limitations;

(viii) Fuel consumption and cruise control;

(ix) Flight planning;

(x) Each normal and emergency procedure;

(xi) For pilots, stall prevention and recovery in clean configuration, takeoff and maneuvering configuration, and landing configuration.

(xii) For pilots, upset prevention and recovery; and

(xiii) The approved Airplane Flight Manual.

(b) Initial ground training for pilots who have completed the airline transport pilot certification training program in §61.156 must include instruction in at least the following as applicable to their assigned duties:

(1) Ground training specific to the certificate holder's—

(i) Dispatch or flight release procedures;

(ii) Method for determining weight and balance and runway limitations for takeoff and landing;

(iii) Meteorology hazards applicable to the certificate holder's areas of operation;

(iv) Approved departure, arrival, and approach procedures;

(v) Normal and emergency communication procedures; and

(vi) Approved crew resource management training.

(2) The training required by paragraph (a)(2) of this section for the airplane type.

(c) Initial ground training for pilots and flight engineers must consist of at least the following programmed hours of instruction in the required subjects specified in paragraph (a) of this section and in §121.415(a) unless reduced under §121.405:

(1) Group I airplanes—

(i) Reciprocating powered, 64 hours; and

(ii) Turbopropeller powered, 80 hours.

(2) Group II airplanes, 120 hours.

(d) Initial ground training for pilots who have completed the airline transport pilot certification training program in §61.156 must consist of at least the following programmed hours of instruction in the required subjects specified in paragraph (b) of this section and in §121.415(a) unless reduced under §121.405:

(1) Group I airplanes—

(i) Reciprocating powered, 54 hours; and

(ii) Turbopropeller powered, 70 hours.

(2) Group II airplanes, 110 hours.

(e) *Compliance and pilot programmed hours.* (1) Compliance with the requirements identified in paragraphs

(a)(2)(xi) and (a)(2)(xii) of this section is required no later than March 12, 2019.

(2) Beginning March 12, 2019, initial programmed hours applicable to pilots as specified in paragraphs (c) and (d) of this section must include 2 additional hours.

[Doc. No. FAA–2010–0100, 78 FR 42377, July 15, 2013, as amended by Amdt. 121–366, 78 FR 67839, Nov. 12, 2013]

§121.420 [Reserved]

§121.421 Flight attendants: Initial and transition ground training.

(a) Initial and transition ground training for flight attendants must include instruction in at least the following:

(1) General subjects—

(i) The authority of the pilot in command;

(ii) Passenger handling, including the procedures to be followed in the case of deranged persons or other persons whose conduct might jeopardize safety; and

(iii) Approved crew resource management initial training.

(2) For each airplane type—

(i) A general description of the airplane emphasizing physical characteristics that may have a bearing on ditching, evacuation, and inflight emergency procedures and on other related duties;

(ii) The use of both the public address system and the means of communicating with other flight crewmembers, including emergency means in the case of attempted hijacking or other unusual situations; and

(iii) Proper use of electrical galley equipment and the controls for cabin heat and ventilation.

(b) Initial and transition ground training for flight attendants must include a competence check to determine ability to perform assigned duties and responsibilities.

(c) Initial ground training for flight attendants must consist of at least the following programmed hours of instruction in the subjects specified in paragraph (a) of this section and in §121.415(a) unless reduced under §121.405.

(1) Group I airplanes—

(i) Reciprocating powered, 8 hours; and

(ii) Turbopropeller powered, 8 hours.

(2) Group II airplanes, 16 hours.

[Doc. No. 9509, 35 FR 90, Jan. 3, 1970, as amended by Amdt. 121-250, 60 FR 65949, Dec. 20, 1995]

§ 121.422 Aircraft dispatchers: Initial and transition ground training.

(a) Initial and transition ground training for aircraft dispatchers must include instruction in at least the following:

(1) General subjects—

(i) Use of communications systems including the characteristics of those systems and the appropriate normal and emergency procedures;

(ii) Meteorology, including various types of meteorological information and forecasts, interpretation of weather data (including forecasting of en route and terminal temperatures and other weather conditions), frontal systems, wind conditions, and use of actual and prognostic weather charts for various altitudes;

(iii) The NOTAM system;

(iv) Navigational aids and publications;

(v) Joint dispatcher-pilot responsibilities;

(vi) Characteristics of appropriate airports;

(vii) Prevailing weather phenomena and the available sources of weather information;

(viii) Air traffic control and instrument approach procedures; and

(ix) Approved dispatcher resource management (DRM) initial training.

(2) For each airplane—

(i) A general description of the airplane emphasizing operating and performance characteristics, navigation equipment, instrument approach and communication equipment, emergency equipment and procedures, and other subjects having a bearing on dispatcher duties and responsibilities;

(ii) Flight operation procedures including procedures specified in § 121.419(a)(2)(vi);

(iii) Weight and balance computations;

(iv) Basic airplane performance dispatch requirements and procedures;

(v) Flight planning including track selection, flight time analysis, and fuel requirements; and

(vi) Emergency procedures.

(3) Emergency procedures must be emphasized, including the alerting of proper governmental, company, and private agencies during emergencies to give maximum help to an airplane in distress.

(b) Initial and transition ground training for aircraft dispatchers must include a competence check given by an appropriate supervisor or ground instructor that demonstrates knowledge and ability with the subjects set forth in paragraph (a) of this section.

(c) Initial ground training for aircraft dispatchers must consist of at least the following programmed hours of instruction in the subjects specified in paragraph (a) of this section and in § 121.415(a) unless reduced under § 121.405:

(1) Group I airplanes—

(i) Reciprocating powered, 30 hours; and

(ii) Turbopropeller powered, 40 hours.

(2) Group II airplanes, 40 hours.

[Doc. No. 9509, 35 FR 90, Jan. 3, 1970, as amended by Amdt. 121-250, 60 FR 65949, Dec. 20, 1995]

§ 121.423 Pilot: Extended Envelope Training.

(a) Each certificate holder must include in its approved training program, the extended envelope training set forth in this section with respect to each airplane type for each pilot. The extended envelope training required by this section must be performed in a Level C or higher full flight simulator, approved by the Administrator in accordance with § 121.407 of this part.

(b) Extended envelope training must include the following maneuvers and procedures:

(1) Manually controlled slow flight;

(2) Manually controlled loss of reliable airspeed;

(3) Manually controlled instrument departure and arrival;

(4) Upset recovery maneuvers; and

(5) Recovery from bounced landing.

(c) Extended envelope training must include instructor-guided hands on experience of recovery from full stall and stick pusher activation, if equipped.

(d) Recurrent training: Within 24 calendar months preceding service as a pilot, each person must satisfactorily complete the extended envelope training described in paragraphs (b)(1) through (4) and (c) of this section. Within 36 calendar months preceding service as a pilot, each person must satisfactorily complete the extended envelope training described in paragraph (b)(5) of this section.

(e) Deviation from use of Level C or higher full flight simulator:

(1) A certificate holder may submit a request to the Administrator for approval of a deviation from the requirements of paragraph (a) of this section to conduct the extended envelope training using an alternative method to meet the learning objectives of this section.

(2) A request for deviation from paragraph (a) of this section must include the following information:

(i) A simulator availability assessment, including hours by specific simulator and location of the simulator, and a simulator shortfall analysis that includes the training that cannot be completed in a Level C or higher full flight simulator; and

(ii) Alternative methods for achieving the learning objectives of this section.

(3) A certificate holder may request an extension of a deviation issued under this section.

(4) Deviations or extensions to deviations will be issued for a period not to exceed 12 months.

(f) Compliance with this section is required no later than March 12, 2019. For the recurrent training required in paragraph (d) of this section, each pilot qualified to serve as second in command or pilot in command in operations under this part on March 12, 2019 must complete the recurrent extended envelope training within 12 calendar months after March 12, 2019.

[Doc. No. FAA–2008–0677, 78 FR 67839, Nov. 12, 2013]

§121.424 Pilots: Initial, transition, and upgrade flight training.

(a) Initial, transition, and upgrade training for pilots must include the following:

(1) Flight training and practice in the maneuvers and procedures set forth in the certificate holder's approved low-altitude windshear flight training program and in appendix E to this part, as applicable; and

(2) Extended envelope training set forth in §121.423.

(b) The training required by paragraph (a) of this section must be performed inflight except—

(1) That windshear maneuvers and procedures must be performed in a simulator in which the maneuvers and procedures are specifically authorized to be accomplished;

(2) That the extended envelope training required by §121.423 must be performed in a Level C or higher full flight simulator unless the Administrator has issued to the certificate holder a deviation in accordance with §121.423(e); and

(3) To the extent that certain other maneuvers and procedures may be performed in an airplane simulator, an appropriate training device, or a static airplane as permitted in appendix E to this part.

(c) Except as permitted in paragraph (d) of this section, the initial flight training required by paragraph (a)(1) of this section must include at least the following programmed hours of inflight training and practice unless reduced under §121.405;

(1) Group I airplanes—

(i) *Reciprocating powered.* Pilot in command, 10 hours; second in command, 6 hours; and

(ii) *Turbopropeller powered.* Pilot in command, 15 hours; second in command, 7 hours.

(2) *Group II airplanes.* Pilot in command, 20 hours; second in command, 10 hours.

(d) If the certificate holder's approved training program includes a course of training utilizing an airplane simulator under §121.409 (c) and (d) of this part, each pilot must successfully complete—

(1) With respect to §121.409(c) of this part—

(i) Training and practice in the simulator in at least all of the maneuvers and procedures set forth in appendix E to this part for initial flight training that are capable of being performed in

173

an airplane simulator without a visual system; and

(ii) A flight check in the simulator or the airplane to the level of proficiency of a pilot in command or second in command, as applicable, in at least the maneuvers and procedures set forth in appendix F to this part that are capable of being performed in an airplane simulator without a visual system.

(2) With respect to § 121.409(d) of this part, training and practice in at least the maneuvers and procedures set forth in the certificate holder's approved low-altitude windshear flight training program that are capable of being performed in an airplane simulator in which the maneuvers and procedures are specifically authorized.

(e) Compliance with paragraphs (a)(2) and (b)(2) of this section is required no later than March 12, 2019.

[Doc. No. 9509, 35 FR 90, Jan. 3, 1970, as amended by Amdt. 121–199, 53 FR 37697, Sept. 27, 1988; Amdt. 121–366, 78 FR 67840, Nov. 12, 2013]

§ 121.425 Flight engineers: Initial and transition flight training.

(a) Initial and transition flight training for flight engineers must include at least the following:

(1) Training and practice in procedures related to the carrying out of flight engineer duties and functions. This training and practice may be accomplished either inflight, in an airplane simulator, or in a training device.

(2) A flight check that includes—

(i) Preflight inspection;

(ii) Inflight performance of assigned duties accomplished from the flight engineer station during taxi, runup, takeoff, climb, cruise, descent, approach, and landing;

(iii) Accomplishment of other functions, such as fuel management and preparation of fuel consumption records, and normal and emergency or alternate operation of all airplane flight systems, performed either inflight, in an airplane simulator, or in a training device.

Flight engineers possessing a commercial pilot certificate with an instrument, category and class rating, or pilots already qualified as second in command and reverting to flight engineer,

may complete the entire flight check in an approved airplane simulator.

(b) Except as permitted in paragraph (c) of this section, the initial flight training required by paragraph (a) of this section must include at least the same number of programmed hours of flight training and practice that are specified for a second in command pilot under § 121.424(c) unless reduced under § 121.405.

(c) If the certificate holder's approved training program includes a course of training utilizing an airplane simulator or other training device under § 121.409(c), each flight engineer must successfully complete in the simulator or other training device—

(1) Training and practice in at least all of the assigned duties, procedures, and functions required by paragraph (a) of this section; and

(2) A flight check to a flight engineer level of proficiency in the assigned duties, procedures, and functions.

[Doc. No. 9509, 35 FR 90, Jan. 3, 1970, as amended by Amdt. 121–144, 43 FR 22647, May 25, 1978]

§ 121.426 [Reserved]

§ 121.427 Recurrent training.

(a) Recurrent training must ensure that each crew member or dispatcher is adequately trained and currently proficient with respect to the type airplane (including differences training, if applicable) and crewmember position involved.

(b) Recurrent ground training for crewmembers and dispatchers must include at least the following:

(1) A quiz or other review to determine the state of the crewmember's or dispatcher's knowledge with respect to the airplane and position involved.

(2) Instruction as necessary in the subjects required for initial ground training by §§ 121.415(a) and 121.805, as appropriate, including emergency training (not required for aircraft dispatchers).

(3) For flight attendants and dispatchers, a competence check as required by §§ 121.421(b) and 121.422(b), respectively.

(4) CRM and DRM training. For flightcrew members, CRM training or portions thereof may be accomplished

during an approved simulator line operational flight training (LOFT) session. The recurrent CRM or DRM training requirements do not apply until a person has completed the applicable initial CRM or DRM training required by §§ 121.419, 121.421, or 121.422.

(c) Recurrent ground training for crewmembers and dispatchers must consist of at least the following programmed hours unless reduced under § 121.405:

(1) For pilots and flight engineers—

(i) Group I, reciprocating powered airplanes, 16 hours;

(ii) Group I turbopropeller powered airplanes, 20 hours; and

(iii) Group II airplanes, 25 hours.

(2) For flight attendants—

(i) Group I reciprocating powered airplanes, 4 hours;

(ii) Group I turbopropeller powered airplanes, 5 hours; and

(iii) Group II airplanes, 12 hours.

(3) For aircraft dispatchers—

(i) Group I reciprocating powered airplanes, 8 hours;

(ii) Group I turbopropeller powered airplanes, 10 hours; and

(iii) Group II airplanes, 20 hours.

(d) Recurrent flight training for flightcrew members must include at least the following:

(1) For pilots—

(i) Extended envelope training as required by § 121.423 of this part; and

(ii) Flight training in an approved simulator in maneuvers and procedures set forth in the certificate holder's approved low-altitude windshear flight training program and flight training in maneuvers and procedures set forth in appendix F to this part, or in a flight training program approved by the Administrator, except as follows—

(A) The number of programmed inflight hours is not specified; and

(B) Satisfactory completion of a proficiency check may be substituted for recurrent flight training as permitted in § 121.433(c) and (e) of this part.

(2) For flight engineers, flight training as provided by § 121.425(a) except as follows—

(i) The specified number of inflight hours is not required; and

(ii) The flight check, other than the preflight inspection, may be conducted in an airplane simulator or other train-ing device. The preflight inspection may be conducted in an airplane, or by using an approved pictorial means that realistically portrays the location and detail or preflight inspection items and provides for the portrayal of abnormal conditions. Satisfactory completion of an approved line-oriented simulator training program may be substituted for the flight check.

(e) Compliance and pilot programmed hours:

(1) Compliance with the requirements identified in paragraphs (d)(1)(i) of this section is required no later than March 12, 2019.

(2) After March 12, 2019, recurrent programmed hours applicable to pilots as specified in paragraph (c)(1) of this section must include 30 additional minutes.

[Doc. No. 9509, 35 FR 90, Jan. 30, 1970, as amended by Amdt. 121–80, 36 FR 19362, Oct. 5, 1971; Amdt. 121–144, 43 FR 22647, May 25, 1978; Amdt.121–199, 53 FR 37697, Sept. 27, 1988; Amdt. 121–250, 60 FR 65949, Dec. 20, 1995; Amdt. 121–281, 66 FR 19043, Apr. 12, 2001; Amdt. 121–366, 78 FR 67840, Nov. 12, 2013]

§ 121.429 [Reserved]

Subpart O—Crewmember Qualifications

§ 121.431 Applicability.

(a) This subpart:

(1) Prescribes crewmember qualifications for all certificate holders except where otherwise specified. The qualification requirements of this subpart also apply to each certificate holder that conducts commuter operations under part 135 of this chapter with airplanes for which two pilots are required by the aircraft type certification rules of this chapter. The Administrator may authorize any other certificate holder that conducts operations under part 135 of this chapter to comply with the training and qualification requirements of this subpart instead of subparts E, G, and H of part 135 of this chapter, except that these certificate holders may choose to comply with the operating experience requirements of § 135.244 of this chapter, instead of the requirements of § 121.434. Notwithstanding the requirements of this subpart, a pilot serving under part

135 of this chapter as second in command may meet the requirements of § 135.245 instead of the requirements of § 121.436; and

(2) Permits training center personnel authorized under part 142 of this chapter who meet the requirements of §§ 121.411 through 121.414 to provide training, testing, and checking under contract or other arrangement to those persons subject to the requirements of this subpart.

(b) For the purpose of this subpart, the airplane groups and terms and definitions prescribed in § 121.400 and the following definitions apply:

Consolidation is the process by which a person through practice and practical experience increases proficiency in newly acquired knowledge and skills.

Line operating flight time is flight time performed in operations under this part.

Operating cycle is a complete flight segment consisting of a takeoff, climb, enroute portion, descent, and a landing.

[Doc. No. 10171, 36 FR 12284, June 30, 1971, as amended by Amdt. 121-250, 60 FR 65949, Dec. 20, 1995; Amdt. 121-248, 60 FR 20869, Apr. 27, 1995; Amdt. 121-250, 60 FR 65949, Dec. 20, 1995; Amdt. 121-259, 61 FR 34561, July 2, 1996; Amdt. 121-263, 62 FR 13791, Mar. 21, 1997; Docket FAA-2010-0100, Amdt. 121-365B, 81 FR 2, Jan. 4, 2016]

§ 121.432   General.

(a) Except in the case of operating experience under § 121.434, a pilot who serves as second in command of an operation that requires three or more pilots must be fully qualified to act as pilot in command of that operation.

(b) No certificate holder may conduct a check or any training in operations under this part, except for the following checks and training required by this part or the certificate holder:

(1) Line checks for pilots.

(2) Flight engineer checks (except for emergency procedures), if the person being checked is qualified and current in accordance with § 121.453(a).

(3) Flight attendant training and competence checks.

(c) Except for pilot line checks and flight engineer flight checks, the person being trained or checked may not be used as a required crewmember.

[Doc. No. 9509, 35 FR 95, Jan. 3, 1970, as amended by Amdt. 121-130, 41 FR 47229, Oct. 28, 1976; Amdt. 121-366, 78 FR 67840, Nov. 12, 2013]

§ 121.433   Training required.

(a) *Initial training.* No certificate holder may use any person nor may any person serve as a required crewmember on an airplane unless that person has satisfactorily completed, in a training program approved under subpart N of this part, initial ground and flight training for that type airplane and for the particular crewmember position, except as follows:

(1) Crewmembers who have qualified and served as a crewmember on another type airplane of the same group may serve in the same crewmember capacity upon completion of transition training as provided in § 121.415.

(2) Crewmembers who have qualified and served as second in command or flight engineer on a particular type airplane may serve as pilot in command or second in command, respectively, upon completion of upgrade training for that airplane as provided in § 121.415.

(b) *Differences training.* No certificate holder may use any person nor may any person serve as a required crewmember on an airplane of a type for which differences training is included in the certificate holder's approved training program unless that person has satisfactorily completed, with respect to both the crewmember position and the particular variation of the airplane in which the person serves, either initial or transition ground and flight training, or differences training, as provided in § 121.415.

(c) *Recurrent training.* (1) No certificate holder may use any person nor may any person serve as a required crewmember on an airplane unless, within the preceding 12 calendar months—

(i) For flight crewmembers, the person has satisfactorily completed recurrent ground and flight training for that airplane and crewmember position and a flight check as applicable;

(ii) For flight attendants and dispatchers, the person has satisfactorily completed recurrent ground training and a competence check; and

(iii) In addition, for pilots in command the person has satisfactorily completed, within the preceding 6 calendar months, recurrent flight training in addition to the recurrent flight training required in paragraph (c)(1)(i) of this section, in an airplane in which the person serves as pilot in command in operations under this part.

(2) For pilots, a proficiency check as provided in §121.441 of this part may be substituted for the recurrent flight training required by this paragraph and the approved simulator course of training under §121.409(b) of this part may be substituted for alternate periods of recurrent flight training required in that airplane, except as provided in paragraphs (d) and (e) of this section.

(d) For each airplane in which a pilot serves as pilot in command, the person must satisfactorily complete either recurrent flight training or a proficiency check within the preceding 12 calendar months. The requirement in this paragraph expires on March 12, 2019. After that date, the requirement in §121.441(a)(1)(ii) of this part applies.

(e) Notwithstanding paragraphs (c)(2) and (d) of this section, a proficiency check as provided in §121.441 of this part may not be substituted for the extended envelope training required by §121.423 or training in those maneuvers and procedures set forth in a certificate holder's approved low-altitude windshear flight training program when that program is included in a recurrent flight training course as required by §121.409(d) of this part.

[Doc. No. 9509, 35 FR 95, Jan. 3, 1970, as amended by Amdt. 121–91, 37 FR 10729, May 27, 1972; Amdt. 121–199, 53 FR 37697, Sept. 27, 1988; Amdt. 121–366, 78 FR 67840, Nov. 12, 2013]

§121.434 Operating experience, operating cycles, and consolidation of knowledge and skills.

(a) No certificate holder may use a person nor may any person serve as a required crewmember of an airplane unless the person has satisfactorily completed, on that type airplane and in that crewmember position, the operating experience, operating cycles, and the line operating flight time for consolidation of knowledge and skills, required by this section, except as follows:

(1) Crewmembers other than pilots in command may serve as provided herein for the purpose of meeting the requirements of this section.

(2) Pilots who are meeting the pilot in command requirements may serve as second in command.

(3) Separate operating experience, operating cycles, and line operating flight time for consolidation of knowledge and skills are not required for variations within the same type airplane.

(4) Deviation based upon designation of related aircraft in accordance with §121.418(b).

(i) The Administrator may authorize a deviation from the operating experience, operating cycles, and line operating flight time for consolidation of knowledge and skills required by this section based upon a designation of related aircraft in accordance with §121.418(b) of this part and a determination that the certificate holder can demonstrate an equivalent level of safety.

(ii) A request for deviation from the operating experience, operating cycles, and line operating flight time for consolidation of knowledge and skills required by this section based upon a designation of related aircraft must be submitted to the Administrator. The request must include the following:

(A) Identification of aircraft operated by the certificate holder designated as related aircraft.

(B) Hours of operating experience and number of operating cycles necessary based on review of the related aircraft, the operation, and the duty position.

(C) Consolidation hours necessary based on review of the related aircraft, the operation, and the duty position.

(iii) The administrator may, at any time, terminate a grant of deviation authority issued under this paragraph (a)(4).

(b) In acquiring the operating experience, operating cycles, and line operating flight time for consolidation of knowledge and skills, crewmembers must comply with the following:

(1) In the case of a flight crewmember, the person must hold the appropriate certificates and ratings for the crewmember position and the airplane, except that a pilot who is meeting the pilot in command requirements must hold the appropriate certificates and ratings for a pilot in command in the airplane.

(2) The operating experience, operating cycles, and line operating flight time for consolidation of knowledge and skills must be acquired after satisfactory completion of the appropriate ground and flight training for the particular airplane type and crewmember position.

(3) The experience must be acquired in flight during operations under this part. However, in the case of an aircraft not previously used by the certificate holder in operations under this part, operating experience acquired in the aircraft during proving flights or ferry flights may be used to meet this requirement.

(c) Pilot crewmembers must acquire operating experience and operating cycles as follows:

(1) A pilot in command must—

(i) Perform the duties of a pilot in command under the supervision of a check pilot; and

(ii) In addition, if a qualifying pilot in command is completing initial or upgrade training specified in § 121.424, be observed in the performance of prescribed duties by an FAA inspector during at least one flight leg which includes a takeoff and landing. During the time that a qualifying pilot in command is acquiring the operating experience in paragraphs (c)(1) (i) and (ii) of this section, a check pilot who is also serving as the pilot in command must occupy a pilot station. However, in the case of a transitioning pilot in command the check pilot serving as pilot in command may occupy the observer's seat, if the transitioning pilot has made at least two takeoffs and landings in the type airplane used, and has satisfactorily demonstrated to the check pilot that he is qualified to perform the duties of a pilot in command of that type of airplane.

(2) A second in command pilot must perform the duties of a second in command under the supervision of an appropriately qualified check pilot.

(3) The hours of operating experience and operating cycles for all pilots are as follows:

(i) For initial training, 15 hours in Group I reciprocating powered airplanes, 20 hours in Group I turbopropeller powered airplanes, and 25 hours in Group II airplanes. Operating experience in both airplane groups must include at least 4 operating cycles (at least 2 as the pilot flying the airplane).

(ii) For transition training, except as provided in paragraph (c)(3)(iii) of this section, 10 hours in Group I reciprocating powered airplanes, 12 hours in Group I turbopropeller powered airplanes, 25 hours for pilots in command in Group II airplanes, and 15 hours for second in command pilots in Group II airplanes. Operating experience in both airplane groups must include at least 4 operating cycles (at least 2 as the pilot flying the airplane).

(iii) In the case of transition training where the certificate holder's approved training program includes a course of training in an airplane simulator under § 121.409(c), each pilot in command must comply with the requirements prescribed in paragraph (c)(3)(i) of this section for initial training.

(d) A flight engineer must perform the duties of a flight engineer under the supervision of a check airman or a qualified flight engineer for at least the following number of hours:

(1) Group I reciprocating powered airplanes, 8 hours.

(2) Group I turbopropeller powered airplanes, 10 hours.

(3) Group II airplanes, 12 hours.

(e) A flight attendant must, for at least 5 hours, perform the assigned duties of a flight attendant under the supervision of a flight attendant supervisor qualified under this part who personally observes the performance of these duties. However, operating experience is not required for a flight attendant who has previously acquired such experience on any large passenger carrying airplane of the same group, if the certificate holder shows that the flight attendant has received sufficient ground training for the airplane in which the flight attendant is to serve.

Flight attendants receiving operating experience may not be assigned as a required crewmember. Flight attendants who have satisfactorily completed training time acquired in an approved training program conducted in a full-scale (except for length) cabin training device of the type airplane in which they are to serve may substitute this time for 50 percent of the hours required by this paragraph.

(f) Flight crewmembers may substitute one additional takeoff and landing for each hour of flight to meet the operating experience requirements of this section, up to a maximum reduction of 50% of flight hours, except those in Group II initial training, and second in command pilots in Group II transition training.

(g) Except as provided in paragraph (h) of this section, pilot in command and second in command crewmembers must each acquire at least 100 hours of line operating flight time for consolidation of knowledge and skills (including operating experience required under paragraph (c) of this section) within 120 days after the satisfactory completion of:

(1) Any part of the flight maneuvers and procedures portion of either an airline transport pilot certificate with type rating practical test or an additional type rating practical test, or

(2) A § 121.441 proficiency check.

(h) The following exceptions apply to the consolidation requirement of paragraph (g) of this section:

(1) Pilots who have qualified and served as pilot in command or second in command on a particular type airplane in operations under this part before August 25, 1995 are not required to complete line operating flight time for consolidation of knowledge and skills.

(2) Pilots who have completed the line operating flight time requirement for consolidation of knowledge and skills while serving as second in command on a particular type airplane in operations under this part after August 25, 1995 are not required to repeat the line operating flight time before serving as pilot in command on the same type airplane.

(3) If, before completing the required 100 hours of line operating flight time, a pilot serves as a pilot in another air-

plane type operated by the certificate holder, the pilot may not serve as a pilot in the airplane for which the pilot has newly qualified unless the pilot satifactorily completes refresher training as provided in the certificate holder's approved training program and that training is conducted by an appropriately qualified instructor or check pilot.

(4) If the required 100 hours of line operating flight time are not completed within 120 days, the certificate holder may extend the 120-day period to no more than 150 days if—

(i) The pilot continues to meet all other applicable requirements of subpart O of this part; and

(ii) On or before the 120th day the pilot satisfactorily completes refresher training conducted by an appropriately qualified instructor or check pilot as provided in the certificate holder's approved training program, or a check pilot determines that the pilot has retained an adequate level of proficiency after observing that pilot in a supervised line operating flight.

(5) The Administrator, upon application by the certificate holder, may authorize deviations from the requirements of paragraph (g) of this section, by an appropriate amendment to the operations specifications, to the extent warranted by any of the following circumstances:

(i) A newly certificated certificate holder does not employ any pilots who meet the minimum requirements of paragraph (g) of this section.

(ii) An existing certificate holder adds to its fleet an airplane type not before proven for use in its operations.

(iii) A certificate holder establishes a new domicile to which it assigns pilots who will be required to become qualified on the airplanes operated from that domicile.

(i) Notwithstanding the reductions in programmed hours permitted under §§ 121.405 and 121.409 of subpart N of this part, the hours of operating experience for crewmembers are not subject to reduction other than as provided in accordance with a deviation authorized under paragraph (a) of this section or as provided in paragraphs (e) and (f) of this section.

[Doc. No. 9509, 35 FR 95, Jan. 3, 1970, as amended by Amdt. 121–74, 36 FR 12284, June 30, 1971; Amdt. 121–91, 37 FR 10729, May 27, 1972; Amdt. 121–140, 43 FR 9599, Mar. 9, 1978; Amdt. 121–144, 43 FR 22647, May 25, 1978; Amdt. 121–159, 45 FR 41593, June 19, 1980; Amdt. 121–248, 60 FR 20870, Apr. 27, 1995; Amdt. 121–366, 78 FR 67840, Nov. 12, 2013]

§ 121.435   [Reserved]

§ 121.436   Pilot Qualification: Certificates and experience requirements.

(a) No certificate holder may use nor may any pilot act as pilot in command of an aircraft (or as second in command of an aircraft in a flag or supplemental operation that requires three or more pilots) unless the pilot:

(1) Holds an airline transport pilot certificate not subject to the limitations in § 61.167 of this chapter;

(2) Holds an appropriate aircraft type rating for the aircraft being flown; and

(3) If serving as pilot in command in part 121 operations, has 1,000 hours as second in command in operations under this part, pilot in command in operations under § 91.1053(a)(2)(i) of this chapter, pilot in command in operations under § 135.243(a)(1) of this chapter, or any combination thereof. For those pilots who are employed as pilot in command in part 121 operations on July 31, 2013, compliance with the requirements of this paragraph (a)(3) is not required.

(b) No certificate holder may use nor may any pilot act as second in command unless the pilot holds an airline transport pilot certificate and an appropriate aircraft type rating for the aircraft being flown. A second-in-command type rating obtained under § 61.55 does not satisfy the requirements of this section.

(c) For the purpose of satisfying the flight hour requirement in paragraph (a)(3) of this section, a pilot may credit 500 hours of military flight time obtained as pilot in command of a multi-engine turbine-powered, fixed-wing airplane in an operation requiring more than one pilot.

(d) Compliance with the requirements of this section is required by August 1, 2013. However, for those pilots who are employed as second in command in part 121 operations on July 31, 2013, compliance with the type rating requirement in paragraph (b) of this section is not required until January 1, 2016.

[Doc. No. FAA–2010–0100, 78 FR 42378, July 15, 2013, as amended by Amdt. 121–365A, 78 FR 77574, Dec. 24, 2013]

§ 121.438   Pilot operating limitations and pairing requirements.

(a) If the second in command has fewer than 100 hours of flight time as second in command in operations under this part in the type airplane being flown, and the pilot in command is not an appropriately qualified check pilot, the pilot in command must make all takeoffs and landings in the following situations:

(1) At special airports designated by the Administrator or at special airports designated by the certificate holder; and

(2) In any of the following conditions:

(i) The prevailing visibility value in the latest weather report for the airport is at or below ¾ mile.

(ii) The runway visual range for the runway to be used is at or below 4,000 feet.

(iii) The runway to be used has water, snow, slush or similar conditions that may adversely affect airplane performance.

(iv) The braking action on the runway to be used is reported to be less than "good".

(v) The crosswind component for the runway to be used is in excess of 15 knots.

(vi) Windshear is reported in the vicinity of the airport.

(vii) Any other condition in which the PIC determines it to be prudent to exercise the PIC's prerogative.

(b) No person may conduct operations under this part unless, for that type airplane, either the pilot in command or the second in command has at least 75 hours of line operating flight time, either as pilot in command or second in command. The Administrator may, upon application by the certificate holder, authorize deviations from the requirements of this paragraph (b) by an appropriate amendment to the operations specifications in any of the following circumstances:

(1) A newly certificated certificate holder does not employ any pilots who meet the minimum requirements of this paragraph.

(2) An existing certificate holder adds to its fleet a type airplane not before proven for use in its operations.

(3) An existing certificate holder establishes a new domicile to which it assigns pilots who will be required to become qualified on the airplanes operated from that domicile.

[Doc. No. 27210, 60 FR 20870, Apr. 27, 1995]

§121.439 Pilot qualification: Recent experience.

(a) No certificate holder may use any person nor may any person serve as a required pilot flight crewmember, unless within the preceding 90 days, that person has made at least three takeoffs and landings in the type airplane in which that person is to serve. The takeoffs and landings required by this paragraph may be performed in a visual simulator approved under §121.407 to include takeoff and landing maneuvers. In addition, any person who fails to make the three required takeoffs and landings within any consecutive 90-day period must reestablish recency of experience as provided in paragraph (b) of this section.

(b) In addition to meeting all applicable training and checking requirements of this part, a required pilot flight crewmember who has not met the requirements of paragraph (a) of this section must reestablish recency of experience as follows:

(1) Under the supervision of a check airman, make at least three takeoffs and landings in the type airplane in which that person is to serve or in an advanced simulator or visual simulator. When a visual simulator is used, the requirements of paragraph (c) of this section must be met.

(2) The takeoffs and landings required in paragraph (b)(1) of this section must include—

(i) At least one takeoff with a simulated failure of the most critical powerplant;

(ii) At least one landing from an ILS approach to the lowest ILS minimum authorized for the certificate holder; and

(iii) At least one landing to a full stop.

(c) A required pilot flight crewmember who performs the manuvers prescribed in paragraph (b) of this section in a visual simulator must—

(1) Have previously logged 100 hours of flight time in the same type airplane in which he is to serve;

(2) Be observed on the first two landings made in operations under this part by an approved check airman who acts as pilot in command and occupies a pilot seat. The landings must be made in weather minimums that are not less than those contained in the certificate holder's operations specifications for Category I Operations, and must be made within 45 days following completion of simulator training.

(d) When using a simulator to accomplish any of the requirements of paragraph (a) or (b) of this section, each required flight crewmember position must be occupied by an appropriately qualified person and the simulator must be operated as if in a normal inflight environment without use of the repositioning features of the simulator.

(e) A check airman who observes the takeoffs and landings prescribed in paragraphs (b)(1) and (c) of this section shall certify that the person being observed is proficient and qualified to perform flight duty in operations under this part and may require any additional maneuvers that are determined necessary to make this certifying statement.

(f) Deviation authority based upon designation of related aircraft in accordance with §121.418(b).

(1) The Administrator may authorize a deviation from the requirements of paragraph (a) of this section based upon a designation of related aircraft in accordance with §121.418(b) of this part and a determination that the certificate holder can demonstrate an equivalent level of safety.

(2) A request for deviation from paragraph (a) of this section must be submitted to the Administrator. The request must include the following:

(i) Identification of aircraft operated by the certificate holder designated as related aircraft.

(ii) The number of takeoffs, landings, maneuvers, and procedures necessary to maintain or reestablish recency based on review of the related aircraft, the operation, and the duty position.

(3) The administrator may, at any time, terminate a grant of deviation authority issued under this paragraph (f).

[Doc. No. 16383, 43 FR 22648, May 25, 1978, as amended by Amdt. 121–148, 43 FR 46235, Oct. 5, 1978; Amdt. 121–179, 47 FR 33390, Aug. 2, 1982; Amdt. 121–366, 78 FR 67841, Nov. 12, 2013]

§ 121.440 Line checks.

(a) No certificate holder may use any person nor may any person serve as pilot in command of an airplane unless, within the preceding 12 calendar months, that person has passed a line check in which he satisfactorily performs the duties and responsibilities of a pilot in command in one of the types of airplanes he is to fly.

(b) A pilot in command line check for domestic and flag operations must—

(1) Be given by a pilot check airman who is currently qualified on both the route and the airplane; and

(2) Consist of at least one flight over a typical part of the certificate holder's route, or over a foreign or Federal airway, or over a direct route.

(c) A pilot in command line check for supplemental operations must—

(1) Be given by a pilot check airman who is currently qualified on the airplane; and

(2) Consist of at least one flight over a part of a Federal airway, foreign airway, or advisory route over which the pilot may be assigned.

[Doc. No. 9509, 35 FR 96, Jan. 3, 1970, as amended by Amdt. 121–143, 43 FR 22642, May 25, 1978; Amdt. 121–253, 61 FR 2612, Jan. 26, 1996; Amdt. 121–344, 74 FR 34235, July 15, 2009; Amdt. 121–359, 77 FR 34785, June 12, 2012]

§ 121.441 Proficiency checks.

(a) No certificate holder may use any person nor may any person serve as a required pilot flight crewmember unless that person has satisfactorily completed either a proficiency check, or an approved simulator course of training under § 121.409, as follows:

(1) For a pilot in command—

(i) Before March 12, 2019,

(A) A proficiency check within the preceding 12 calendar months and,

(B) In addition, within the preceding 6 calendar months, either a proficiency check or the approved simulator course of training.

(ii) Beginning on March 12, 2019,

(A) A proficiency check within the preceding 12 calendar months in the aircraft type in which the person is to serve and,

(B) In addition, within the preceding 6 calendar months, either a proficiency check or the approved simulator course of training.

(2) For all other pilots—

(i) Within the preceding 24 calendar months either a proficiency check or the line-oriented simulator training course under § 121.409; and

(ii) Within the preceding 12 calendar months, either a proficiency check or any simulator training course under § 121.409.

(b) Except as provided in paragraphs (c) and (d) of this section, a proficiency check must meet the following requirements:

(1) It must include at least the procedures and maneuvers set forth in appendix F to this part unless otherwise specifically provided in that appendix.

(2) It must be given by the Administrator or a pilot check airman.

(c) An approved airplane simulator or other appropriate training device may be used in the conduct of a proficiency check as provided in appendix F to this part.

(d) A person giving a proficiency check may, in his discretion, waive any of the maneuvers or procedures for which a specific waiver authority is set forth in appendix F to this part if—

(1) The Administrator has not specifically required the particular maneuver or procedure to be performed;

(2) The pilot being checked is, at the time of the check, employed by a certificate holder as a pilot; and

(3) The pilot being checked is currently qualified for operations under this part in the particular type airplane and flight crewmember position or has, within the preceding six calendar months, satisfactorily completed an approved training program for the particular type airplane.

(e) If the pilot being checked fails any of the required maneuvers, the person giving the proficiency check may give additional training to the pilot during the course of the proficiency check. In addition to repeating the maneuvers failed, the person giving the proficiency check may require the pilot being checked to repeat any other maneuvers he finds are necessary to determine the pilot's proficiency. If the pilot being checked is unable to demonstrate satisfactory performance to the person conducting the check, the certificate holder may not use him nor may he serve in operations under this part until he has satisfactorily completed a proficiency check. However the entire proficiency check (other than the initial second-in-command proficiency check) required by this section may be conducted in an approved visual simulator if the pilot being checked accomplishes at least two landings in the appropriate airplane during a line check or other check conducted by a pilot check airman (a pilot-in-command may observe and certify the satisfactory accomplishment of these landings by a second-in-command). If a pilot proficiency check is conducted in accordance with this paragraph, the next required proficiency check for that pilot must be conducted in the same manner, or in accordance with appendix F of this part, or a course of training in an airplane visual simulator under §121.409 may be substituted therefor.

(f) Deviation authority based upon designation of related aircraft in accordance with §121.418(b) of this part.

(1) The Administrator may authorize a deviation from the proficiency check requirements of paragraphs (a), (b)(1), and (c) of this section based upon a designation of related aircraft in accordance with §121.418(b) of this part and a determination that the certificate holder can demonstrate an equivalent level of safety.

(2) A request for deviation from paragraphs (a), (b)(1), and (c) of this section must be submitted to the Administrator. The request must include the following:

(i) Identification of aircraft operated by the certificate holder designated as related aircraft.

(ii) Based on review of the related aircraft, the operation, and the duty position:

(A) For recurrent proficiency checks, the frequency of the related aircraft proficiency check, the maneuvers and procedures to be included in the related aircraft proficiency check, and the level of FSTD to be used for each maneuver and procedure.

(B) For qualification proficiency checks, the maneuvers and procedures to be included in the related aircraft proficiency check and the level of FSTD to be used for each maneuver and procedure.

(3) The administrator may, at any time, terminate a grant of deviation authority issued under this paragraph (f).

[Doc. No. 9509, 35 FR 96, Jan. 3, 1970, as amended by Amdt. 121–103, 38 FR 12203, May 10, 1973, Amdt. 121–108, 38 FR 35446, Dec. 28, 1973; Amdt. 121–144, 43 FR 22648, May 25, 1978; Amdt. 121–263, 62 FR 13791, Mar. 21, 1997; Amdt. 121–366, 78 FR 67841, Nov. 12, 2013; Docket FAA–2016–9526, Amdt. 121–377, 81 FR 90983, Dec. 16, 2016; Amdt. 121–377A, 81 FR 95860, Dec. 29, 2016; Amdt. 121–377B, 83 FR 12475, Mar. 22, 2018]

§121.443   Pilot in command qualification: Route and airports.

(a) Each certificate holder shall provide a system acceptable to the Administrator for disseminating the information required by paragraph (b) of this section to the pilot in command and appropriate flight operation personnel. The system must also provide an acceptable means for showing compliance with §121.445.

(b) No certificate holder may use any person, nor may any person serve, as pilot in command unless the certificate holder has provided that person current information concerning the following subjects pertinent to the areas over which that person is to serve, and to each airport and terminal area into which that person is to operate, and ensures that that person has adequate knowledge of, and the ability to use, the information:

(1) Weather characteristics appropriate to the season.

(2) Navigation facilities.

(3) Communication procedures, including airport visual aids.

(4) Kinds of terrain and obstructions.

(5) Minimum safe flight levels.

(6) En route and terminal area arrival and departure procedures, holding

procedures and authorized instrument approach procedures for the airports involved.

(7) Congested areas and physical layout of each airport in the terminal area in which the pilot will operate.

(8) Notices to Airmen.

[Doc. No. 17897, 45 FR 41594, June 19, 1980; Amdt. 121–159, 45 FR 43154, June 26, 1980]

§ 121.445 Pilot in command airport qualification: Special areas and airports.

(a) The Administrator may determine that certain airports (due to items such as surrounding terrain, obstructions, or complex approach or departure procedures) are special airports requiring special airport qualifications and that certain areas or routes, or both, require a special type of navigation qualification.

(b) Except as provided in paragraph (c) of this section, no certificate holder may use any person, nor may any person serve, as pilot in command to or from an airport determined to require special airport qualifications unless, within the preceding 12 calendar months:

(1) The pilot in command or second in command has made an entry to that airport (including a takeoff and landing) while serving as a pilot flight crewmember; or

(2) The pilot in command has qualified by using pictorial means acceptable to the Administrator for that airport.

(c) Paragraph (b) of this section does not apply when an entry to that airport (including a takeoff or a landing) is being made if the ceiling at that airport is at least 1,000 feet above the lowest MEA or MOCA, or initial approach altitude prescribed for the instrument approach procedure for that airport, and the visibility at that airport is at least 3 miles.

(d) No certificate holder may use any person, nor may any person serve, as pilot in command between terminals over a route or area that requires a special type of navigation qualification unless, within the preceding 12 calendar months, that person has demonstrated qualification on the applicable navigation system in a manner ac-

ceptable to the Administrator, by one of the following methods:

(1) By flying over a route or area as pilot in command using the applicable special type of navigation system.

(2) By flying over a route or area as pilot in command under the supervision of a check airman using the special type of navigation system.

(3) By completing the training program requirements of appendix G of this part.

[Doc. No. 17897, 45 FR 41594, June 19, 1980]

§ 121.447 [Reserved]

§ 121.453 Flight engineer qualifications.

(a) No certificate holder may use any person nor may any person serve as a flight engineer on an airplane unless, within the preceding 6 calendar months, he has had at least 50 hours of flight time as a flight engineer on that type airplane or the certificate holder or the Administrator has checked him on that type airplane and determined that he is familiar and competent with all essential current information and operating procedures.

(b) A flight check given in accordance with § 121.425(a)(2) satisfies the requirements of paragraph (a) of this section.

[Doc. No. 9509, 35 FR 96, Jan. 3, 1970]

§§ 121.455–121.459 [Reserved]

Subpart P—Aircraft Dispatcher Qualifications and Duty Time

Limitations: DOMESTIC AND FLAG OPERATIONS; FLIGHT ATTENDANT DUTY PERIOD LIMITATIONS AND REST REQUIREMENTS: DOMESTIC, FLAG, AND SUPPLEMENTAL OPERATIONS

§ 121.461 Applicability.

This subpart prescribes—

(a) Qualifications and duty time limitations for aircraft dispatchers for certificate holders conducting domestic flag operations; and

(b) Duty period limitations and rest requirements for flight attendants used by certificate holders conducting domestic, flag, or supplemental operations.

[Doc. No. 28154, 61 FR 2612, Jan. 26, 1996]

§121.463 Aircraft dispatcher qualifications.

(a) No certificate holder conducting domestic or flag operations may use any person, nor may any person serve, as an aircraft dispatcher for a particular airplane group unless that person has, with respect to an airplane of that group, satisfactorily completed the following:

(1) Initial dispatcher training, except that a person who has satisfactorily completed such training for another type airplane of the same group need only complete the appropriate transition training.

(2) Operating familiarization consisting of at least 5 hours observing operations under this part from the flight deck or, for airplanes without an observer seat on the flight deck, from a forward passenger seat with headset or speaker. This requirement may be reduced to a minimum of 2½ hours by the substitution of one additional takeoff and landing for an hour of flight. A person may serve as an aircraft dispatcher without meeting the requirement of this paragraph (a) for 90 days after initial introduction of the airplane into operations under this part.

(b) No certificate holder conducting domestic or flag operations may use any person, nor may any person serve, as an aircraft dispatcher for a particular type airplane unless that person has, with respect to that airplane, satisfactorily completed differences training, if applicable.

(c) No certificate holder conducting domestic or flag operations may use any person, nor may any person serve, as an aircraft dispatcher unless within the preceding 12 calendar months the aircraft dispatcher has satisfactorily completed operating familiarization consisting of at least 5 hours observing operations under this part, in one of the types of airplanes in each group to be dispatched. This observation shall be made from the flight deck or, for airplanes without an observer seat on the flight deck, from a forward passenger seat with headset or speaker.

The requirement of paragraph (a) of this section may be reduced to a minimum of 2½ hours by the substitution of one additional takeoff and landing for an hour of flight. The requirement of this paragraph may be satisfied by observation of 5 hours of simulator training for each airplane group in one of the simulators approved under §121.407 for the group. However, if the requirement of paragraph (a) is met by the use of a simulator, no reduction in hours is permitted.

(d) No certificate holder conducting domestic or flag operations may use any person, nor may any person serve as an aircraft dispatcher to dispatch airplanes in operations under this part unless the certificate holder has determined that he is familiar with all essential operating procedures for that segment of the operation over which he exercises dispatch jurisdiction. However, a dispatcher who is qualified to dispatch airplanes through one segment of an operation may dispatch airplanes through other segments of the operation after coordinating with dispatchers who are qualified to dispatch airplanes through those other segments.

(e) For the purposes of this section, the airplane groups, terms, and definitions in §121.400 apply.

[Doc. No. 7325, 37 FR 5607, Mar. 17, 1972, as amended by Amdt. 121–251, 60 FR 65934, Dec. 20, 1995]

§121.465 Aircraft dispatcher duty time limitations: Domestic and flag operations.

(a) Each certificate holder conducting domestic or flag operations shall establish the daily duty period for a dispatcher so that it begins at a time that allows him or her to become thoroughly familiar with existing and anticipated weather conditions along the route before he or she dispatches any airplane. He or she shall remain on duty until each airplane dispatched by him or her has completed its flight, or has gone beyond his or her jurisdiction, or until he or she is relieved by another qualified dispatcher.

(b) Except in cases where circumstances or emergency conditions beyond the control of the certificate holder require otherwise—

185

(1) No certificate holder conducting domestic or flag operations may schedule a dispatcher for more than 10 consecutive hours of duty;

(2) If a dispatcher is scheduled for more than 10 hours of duty in 24 consecutive hours, the certificate holder shall provide him or her a rest period of at least eight hours at or before the end of 10 hours of duty.

(3) Each dispatcher must be relieved of all duty with the certificate holder for at least 24 consecutive hours during any seven consecutive days or the equivalent thereof within any calendar month.

(c) Notwithstanding paragraphs (a) and (b) of this section, a certificate holder conducting flag operations may, if authorized by the Administrator, schedule an aircraft dispatcher at a duty station outside of the 48 contiguous States and the District of Columbia, for more than 10 consecutive hours of duty in a 24-hour period if that aircraft dispatcher is relieved of all duty with the certificate holder for at least eight hours during each 24-hour period.

[Doc. No. 28154, 61 FR 2612, Jan. 26, 1996]

§ 121.467 Flight attendant duty period limitations and rest requirements: Domestic, flag, and supplemental operations.

(a) For purposes of this section—

Calendar day means the period of elapsed time, using Coordinated Universal Time or local time, that begins at midnight and ends 24 hours later at the next midnight.

Duty period means the period of elapsed time between reporting for an assignment involving flight time and release from that assignment by the certificate holder conducting domestic, flag, or supplemental operations. The time is calculated using either Coordinated Universal Time or local time to reflect the total elapsed time.

Flight attendant means an individual, other than a flight crewmember, who is assigned by a certificate holder conducting domestic, flag, or supplemental operations, in accordance with the required minimum crew complement under the certificate holder's operations specifications or in addition to that minimum complement, to duty in an aircraft during flight time and whose duties include but are not necessarily limited to cabin-safety-related responsibilities.

Rest period means the period free of all restraint or duty for a certificate holder conducting domestic, flag, or supplemental operations and free of all responsibility for work or duty should the occasion arise.

(b) Except as provided in paragraph (c) of this section, a certificate holder conducting domestic, flag, or supplemental operations may assign a duty period to a flight attendant only when the applicable duty period limitations and rest requirements of this paragraph are met.

(1) Except as provided in paragraphs (b)(4), (b)(5), and (b)(6) of this section, no certificate holder conducting domestic, flag, or supplemental operations may assign a flight attendant to a scheduled duty period of more than 14 hours.

(2) Except as provided in paragraph (b)(3) of this section, a flight attendant scheduled to a duty period of 14 hours or less as provided under paragraph (b)(1) of this section must be given a scheduled rest period of at least 9 consecutive hours. This rest period must occur between the completion of the scheduled duty period and the commencement of the subsequent duty period.

(3) The rest period required under paragraph (b)(2) of this section may be scheduled or reduced to 8 consecutive hours if the flight attendant is provided a subsequent rest period of at least 10 consecutive hours; this subsequent rest period must be scheduled to begin no later than 24 hours after the beginning of the reduced rest period and must occur between the completion of the scheduled duty period and the commencement of the subsequent duty period.

(4) A certificate holder conducting domestic, flag, or supplemental operations may assign a flight attendant to a scheduled duty period of more than 14 hours, but no more than 16 hours, if the certificate holder has assigned to the flight or flights in that duty period at least one flight attendant in addition to the minimum flight attendant complement required for the flight or flights in that duty period under the

certificate holder's operations specifications.

(5) A certificate holder conducting
domestic, flag, or supplemental operations may assign a flight attendant to
a scheduled duty period of more than 16
hours, but no more than 18 hours, if the
certificate holder has assigned to the
flight or flights in that duty period at
least two flight attendants in addition
to the minimum flight attendant complement required for the flight or
flights in that duty period under the
certificate holder's operations specifications.

(6) A certificate holder conducting
domestic, flag, or supplemental operations may assign a flight attendant to
a scheduled duty period of more than 18
hours, but no more than 20 hours, if the
scheduled duty period includes one or
more flights that land or take off outside the 48 contiguous states and the
District of Columbia, and if the certificate holder has assigned to the flight
or flights in that duty period at least
three flight attendants in addition to
the minimum flight attendant complement required for the flight or
flights in that duty period under the
domestic certificate holder's operations specifications.

(7) Except as provided in paragraph
(b)(8) of this section, a flight attendant
scheduled to a duty period of more
than 14 hours but no more than 20
hours, as provided in paragraphs (b)(4),
(b)(5), and (b)(6) of this section, must be
given a scheduled rest period of at least
12 consecutive hours. This rest period
must occur between the completion of
the scheduled duty period and the commencement of the subsequent duty period.

(8) The rest period required under
paragraph (b)(7) of this section may be
scheduled or reduced to 10 consecutive
hours if the flight attendant is provided a subsequent rest period of at
least 14 consecutive hours; this subsequent rest period must be scheduled to
begin no later than 24 hours after the
beginning of the reduced rest period
and must occur between the completion of the scheduled duty period and
the commencement of the subsequent
duty period.

(9) Notwithstanding paragraphs
(b)(4), (b)(5), and (b)(6) of this section, if

a certificate holder conducting domestic, flag, or supplemental operations
elects to reduce the rest period to 10
hours as authorized by paragraph (b)(8)
of this section, the certificate holder
may not schedule a flight attendant for
a duty period of more than 14 hours
during the 24-hour period commencing
after the beginning of the reduced rest
period.

(10) No certificate holder conducting
domestic, flag, or supplemental operations may assign a flight attendant
any duty period with the certificate
holder unless the flight attendant has
had at least the minimum rest required
under this section.

(11) No certificate holder conducting
domestic, flag, or supplemental operations may assign a flight attendant to
perform any duty with the certificate
holder during any required rest period.

(12) Time spent in transportation,
not local in character, that a certificate holder conducting domestic, flag,
or supplemental operations requires of
a flight attendant and provides to
transport the flight attendant to an
airport at which that flight attendant
is to serve on a flight as a crewmember, or from an airport at which
the flight attendant was relieved from
duty to return to the flight attendant's
home station, is not considered part of
a rest period.

(13) Each certificate holder conducting domestic, flag, or supplemental operations must relieve each
flight attendant engaged in air transportation and each commercial operator must relieve each flight attendant
engaged in air commerce from all further duty for at least 24 consecutive
hours during any 7 consecutive calendar days.

(14) A flight attendant is not considered to be scheduled for duty in excess
of duty period limitations if the flights
to which the flight attendant is assigned are scheduled and normally terminate within the limitations but due
to circumstances beyond the control of
the certificate holder conducting domestic, flag, or supplemental operations (such as adverse weather conditions) are not at the time of departure
expected to reach their destination
within the scheduled time.

(c) Notwithstanding paragraph (b) of this section, a certificate holder conducting domestic, flag, or supplemental operations may apply the flightcrew member flight time and duty limitations and rest requirements of part 117 of this chapter to flight attendants for all operations conducted under this part provided that—

(1) The certificate holder establishes written procedures that—

(i) Apply to all flight attendants used in the certificate holder's operation;

(ii) Include the flightcrew member requirements contained in part 117, as appropriate to the operation being conducted, except that rest facilities on board the aircraft are not required;

(iii) Include provisions to add one flight attendant to the minimum flight attendant complement for each flightcrew member who is in excess of the minimum number required in the aircraft type certificate data sheet and who is assigned to the aircraft under the provisions of part 117, as applicable, of this part;

(iv) Are approved by the Administrator and are described or referenced in the certificate holder's operations specifications; and

(2) Whenever the Administrator finds that revisions are necessary for the continued adequacy of the written procedures that are required by paragraph (c)(1) of this section and that had been granted final approval, the certificate holder must, after notification by the Administrator, make any changes in the procedures that are found necessary by the Administrator. Within 30 days after the certificate holder receives such notice, it may file a petition to reconsider the notice with the responsible Flight Standards office. The filing of a petition to reconsider stays the notice, pending decision by the Administrator. However, if the Administrator finds that an emergency requires immediate action in the interest of safety, the Administrator may, upon a statement of the reasons, require a change effective without stay.

[Amdt. 121-241, 59 FR 42991, Aug. 19, 1994, as amended by Amdt. 121-253, 61 FR 2612, Jan. 26, 1996; Amdt. 121-357, 77 FR 402, Jan. 4, 2012; Amdt. 121-357A, 77 FR 28764, May 16, 2012; Docket FAA-2018-0119, Amdt. 121-380, 83 FR 9172, Mar. 5, 2018]

Subpart Q—Flight Time Limitations and Rest Requirements: Domestic Operations

Source: Docket No. 23634, 50 FR 29319, July 18, 1985, unless otherwise noted.

§ 121.470 Applicability.

This subpart prescribes flight time limitations and rest requirements for domestic all-cargo operations, except that:

(a) Certificate holders conducting operations with airplanes having a passenger seat configuration of 30 seats or fewer, excluding each crewmember seat, and a payload capacity of 7,500 pounds or less, may comply with the applicable requirements of §§ 135.261 through 135.273 of this chapter.

(b) Certificate holders conducting scheduled operations entirely within the States of Alaska or Hawaii with airplanes having a passenger seat configuration of more than 30 seats, excluding each crewmember seat, or a payload capacity of more than 7,500 pounds, may comply with the requirements of this subpart or subpart R of this part for those operations.

(c) A certificate holder may apply the flightcrew member flight time and duty limitations and requirements of part 117 of this chapter. A certificate holder may choose to apply part 117 to its—

(1) Cargo operations conducted under contract to a U.S. government agency.

(2) All-cargo operations not conducted under contract to a U.S. Government agency,

(3) A certificate holder may elect to treat operations in paragraphs (c)(1) and (c)(2) of this section differently but, once having decided to conduct those operations under part 117, may not segregate those operations between this subpart and part 117.

[Doc. No. FAA-2009-1093, 77 FR 402, Jan. 4, 2012; Amdt. 121-357, 78 FR 69288, Nov. 19, 2013]

§ 121.471 Flight time limitations and rest requirements: All flight crewmembers.

(a) No certificate holder conducting domestic operations may schedule any flight crewmember and no flight crewmember may accept an assignment for flight time in scheduled air transportation or in other commercial flying if that crewmember's total flight time in all commercial flying will exceed—

(1) 1,000 hours in any calendar year;

(2) 100 hours in any calendar month;

(3) 30 hours in any 7 consecutive days;

(4) 8 hours between required rest periods.

(b) Except as provided in paragraph (c) of this section, no certificate holder conducting domestic operations may schedule a flight crewmember and no flight crewmember may accept an assignment for flight time during the 24 consecutive hours preceding the scheduled completion of any flight segment without a scheduled rest period during that 24 hours of at least the following:

(1) 9 consecutive hours of rest for less than 8 hours of scheduled flight time.

(2) 10 consecutive hours of rest for 8 or more but less than 9 hours of scheduled flight time.

(3) 11 consecutive hours of rest for 9 or more hours of scheduled flight time.

(c) A certificate holder may schedule a flight crewmember for less than the rest required in paragraph (b) of this section or may reduce a scheduled rest under the following conditions:

(1) A rest required under paragraph (b)(1) of this section may be scheduled for or reduced to a minimum of 8 hours if the flight crewmember is given a rest period of at least 10 hours that must begin no later than 24 hours after the commencement of the reduced rest period.

(2) A rest required under paragraph (b)(2) of this section may be scheduled for or reduced to a minimum of 8 hours if the flight crewmember is given a rest period of at least 11 hours that must begin no later than 24 hours after the commencement of the reduced rest period.

(3) A rest required under paragraph (b)(3) of this section may be scheduled for or reduced to a minimum of 9 hours if the flight crewmember is given a rest period of at least 12 hours that must begin no later than 24 hours after the commencement of the reduced rest period.

(4) No certificate holder may assign, nor may any flight crewmember perform any flight time with the certificate holder unless the flight crewmember has had at least the minimum rest required under this paragraph.

(d) Each certificate holder conducting domestic operations shall relieve each flight crewmember engaged in scheduled air transportation from all further duty for at least 24 consecutive hours during any 7 consecutive days.

(e) No certificate holder conducting domestic operations may assign any flight crewmember and no flight crewmember may accept assignment to any duty with the air carrier during any required rest period.

(f) Time spent in transportation, not local in character, that a certificate holder requires of a flight crewmember and provides to transport the crewmember to an airport at which he is to serve on a flight as a crewmember, or from an airport at which he was relieved from duty to return to his home station, is not considered part of a rest period.

(g) A flight crewmember is not considered to be scheduled for flight time in excess of flight time limitations if the flights to which he is assigned are scheduled and normally terminate within the limitations, but due to circumstances beyond the control of the certificate holder (such as adverse weather conditions), are not at the time of departure expected to reach their destination within the scheduled time.

[Doc. No. 23634, 50 FR 29319, July 18, 1985, as amended by Amdt. 121–253, 61 FR 2612, Jan. 26, 1996]

§121.473 Fatigue risk management system.

(a) No certificate holder may exceed any provision of this subpart unless approved by the FAA under a Fatigue Risk Management System.

(b) The Fatigue Risk Management System must include:

(1) A fatigue risk management policy.

(2) An education and awareness training program.

(3) A fatigue reporting system.

(4) A system for monitoring flightcrew fatigue.

(5) An incident reporting process.

(6) A performance evaluation.

[Doc. No. FAA-2009-1093, 77 FR 403, Jan. 4, 2012]

Subpart R—Flight Time Limitations: Flag Operations

SOURCE: Docket No. 6258, 29 FR 19217, Dec. 31, 1964; 30 FR 3639, Mar. 19, 1965, unless otherwise noted.

§ 121.480 Applicability.

This subpart prescribes flight time limitations and rest requirements for flag all-cargo operations, except that:

(a) Certificate holders conducting operations with airplanes having a passenger seat configuration of 30 seats or fewer, excluding each crewmember seat, and a payload capacity of 7,500 pounds or less, may comply with the applicable requirements of §§ 135.261 through 135.273 of this chapter.

(b) A certificate holder may apply the flightcrew member flight time and duty limitations and requirements of part 117 of this chapter. A certificate holder may choose to apply part 117 to its—

(1) All-cargo operations conducted under contract to a U.S. government agency.

(2) All-cargo operations not conducted under contract to a U.S. Government agency,

(3) A certificate holder may elect to treat operations in paragraphs (b)(1) and (b)(2) of this section differently but, once having decided to conduct those operations under part 117, may not segregate those operations between this subpart and part 117.

[Doc. No. FAA-2009-1093, 77 FR 403, Jan. 4, 2012]

§ 121.481 Flight time limitations: One or two pilot crews.

(a) A certificate holder conducting flag operations may schedule a pilot to fly in an airplane that has a crew of one or two pilots for eight hours or less during any 24 consecutive hours without a rest period during these eight hours.

(b) If a certificate holder conducting flag operations schedules a pilot to fly more than eight hours during any 24 consecutive hours, it shall give him an intervening rest period, at or before the end of eight scheduled hours of flight duty. This rest period must be at least twice the number of hours flown since the preceding rest period, but not less than eight hours. The certificate holder shall relieve that pilot of all duty with it during that rest period.

(c) Each pilot who has flown more than eight hours during 24 consecutive hours must be given at least 18 hours of rest before being assigned to any duty with the certificate holder.

(d) No pilot may fly more than 32 hours during any seven consecutive days, and each pilot must be relieved from all duty for at least 24 consecutive hours at least once during any seven consecutive days.

(e) No pilot may fly as a member of a crew more than 100 hours during any one calendar month.

(f) No pilot may fly as a member of a crew more than 1,000 hours during any 12-calendar-month period.

[Doc. No. 6258, 29 FR 19217, Dec. 31, 1964; 30 FR 3639, Mar. 19, 1965, as amended by Amdt. 121-253, 61 FR 2612, Jan. 26, 1996]

§ 121.483 Flight time limitations: Two pilots and one additional flight crewmember.

(a) No certificate holder conducting flag operations may schedule a pilot to fly, in an airplane that has a crew of two pilots and at least one additional flight crewmember, for a total of more than 12 hours during any 24 consecutive hours.

(b) If a pilot has flown 20 or more hours during any 48 consecutive hours or 24 or more hours during any 72 consecutive hours, he must be given at least 18 hours of rest before being assigned to any duty with the air carrier. In any case, he must be given at least 24 consecutive hours of rest during any seven consecutive days.

(c) No pilot may fly as a flight crewmember more than—

(1) 120 hours during any 30 consecutive days;

(2) 300 hours during any 90 consecutive days; or

(3) 1,000 hours during any 12-calendar-month period.

[Doc. No. 6258, 29 FR 19217, Dec. 31, 1964; 30 FR 3639, Mar. 19, 1965, as amended by Amdt. 121-253, 61 FR 2612, Jan. 26, 1996]

§ 121.485 Flight time limitations: Three or more pilots and an additional flight crewmember.

(a) Each certificate holder conducting flag operations shall schedule its flight hours to provide adequate rest periods on the ground for each pilot who is away from his base and who is a pilot on an airplane that has a crew of three or more pilots and an additional flight crewmember. It shall also provide adequate sleeping quarters on the airplane whenever a pilot is scheduled to fly more than 12 hours during any 24 consecutive hours.

(b) The certificate holder conducting flag operations shall give each pilot, upon return to his base from any flight or series of flights, a rest period that is at least twice the total number of hours he flew since the last rest period at his base. During the rest period required by this paragraph, the air carrier may not require him to perform any duty for it. If the required rest period is more than seven days, that part of the rest period in excess of seven days may be given at any time before the pilot is again scheduled for flight duty on any route.

(c) No pilot may fly as a flight crewmember more than—

(1) 350 hours during any 90 consecutive days; or

(2) 1,000 hours during any 12-calendar-month period.

[Doc. No. 6258, 29 FR 19217, Dec. 31, 1964; 30 FR 3639, Mar. 19, 1965, as amended by Amdt. 121–253, 61 FR 2612, Jan. 26, 1996]

§ 121.487 Flight time limitations: Pilots not regularly assigned.

(a) Except as provided in paragraphs (b) through (e) of this section, a pilot who is not regularly assigned as a flight crewmember for an entire calendar month under § 121.483 or 121.485 may not fly more than 100 hours in any 30 consecutive days.

(b) The monthly flight time limitations for a pilot who is scheduled for duty aloft for more than 20 hours in two-pilot crews in any calendar month, or whose assignment in such a crew is interrupted more than once in that calendar month by assignment to a crew consisting of two or more pilots and an additional flight crewmember, are those set forth in § 121.481.

(c) Except for a pilot covered by paragraph (b) of this section, the monthly and quarterly flight time limitations for a pilot who is scheduled for duty aloft for more than 20 hours in two-pilot and additional flight crewmember crews in any calendar month, or whose assignment in such a crew is interrupted more than once in that calendar month by assignment to a crew consisting of three pilots and additional flight crewmember, are those set forth in § 121.483.

(d) The quarterly flight time limitations for a pilot to whom paragraphs (b) and (c) of this section do not apply and who is scheduled for duty aloft for a total of not more than 20 hours within any calendar month in two-pilot crews (with or without additional flight crewmembers) are those set forth in § 121.485.

(e) The monthly and quarterly flight time limitations for a pilot assigned to each of two-pilot, two-pilot and additional flight crewmember, and three-pilot and additional flight crewmember crews in a given calendar month, and who is not subject to paragraph (b), (c), or (d) of this section, are those set forth in § 121.483.

[Doc. No. 6258, 29 FR 19217, Dec. 31, 1964; Amdt. 121–3, 30 FR 3639, Mar. 19, 1965, as amended by Amdt. 121–137, 42 FR 43973, Sept. 1, 1977]

§ 121.489 Flight time limitations: Other commercial flying.

No pilot that is employed as a pilot by a certificate holder conducting flag operations may do any other commercial flying if that commercial flying plus his flying in air transportation will exceed any flight time limitation in this part.

[Doc. No. 28154, 61 FR 2612, Jan. 26, 1996]

§ 121.491 Flight time limitations: Deadhead transportation.

Time spent in deadhead transportation to or from duty assignment is not considered to be a part of a rest period.

§ 121.493 Flight time limitations: Flight engineers and flight navigators.

(a) In any operation in which one flight engineer or flight navigator is required, the flight time limitations in §121.483 apply to that flight engineer or flight navigator.

(b) In any operation in which more than one flight engineer or flight navigator is required, the flight time limitations in §121.485 apply to those flight engineers or flight navigators.

§ 121.495 Fatigue risk management system.

(a) No certificate holder may exceed any provision of this subpart unless approved by the FAA under a Fatigue Risk Management System.

(b) The Fatigue Risk Management System must include:

(1) A fatigue risk management policy.

(2) An education and awareness training program.

(3) A fatigue reporting system.

(4) A system for monitoring flightcrew fatigue.

(5) An incident reporting process.

(6) A performance evaluation.

[Doc. No. FAA-2009-1093, 77 FR 403, Jan. 4, 2012]

Subpart S—Flight Time Limitations: Supplemental Operations

Source: Docket No. 6258, 29 FR 19218, Dec. 31, 1964; 30 FR 3639, Mar. 19, 1965, unless otherwise noted.

§ 121.500 Applicability.

This subpart prescribes flight time limitations and rest requirements for supplemental all-cargo operations, except that:

(a) Certificate holders conducting operations with airplanes having a passenger seat configuration of 30 seats or fewer, excluding each crewmember seat, and a payload capacity of 7,500 pound or less, may comply with the applicable requirements of §§ 135.261 through 135.273 of this chapter.

(b) A certificate holder may apply the flightcrew member flight time and duty limitations and requirements of part 117 of this chapter. A certificate holder may choose to apply part 117 to its—

(1) All-cargo operations conducted under contract to a U.S. Government agency.

(2) All-cargo operations not conducted under contract to a U.S. Government agency,

(3) A certificate holder may elect to treat operations in paragraphs (b)(1) and (b)(2) of this section differently but, once having decided to conduct those operations under part 117, may not segregate those operations between this subpart and part 117.

[Doc. No. FAA-2009-1093, 77 FR 403, Jan. 4, 2012]

§ 121.503 Flight time limitations: Pilots: airplanes.

(a) A certificate holder conducting supplemental operations may schedule a pilot to fly in an airplane for eight hours or less during any 24 consecutive hours without a rest period during those eight hours.

(b) Each pilot who has flown more than eight hours during any 24 consecutive hours must be given at least 16 hours of rest before being assigned to any duty with the certificate holder.

(c) Each certificate holder conducting supplemental operations shall relieve each pilot from all duty for at least 24 consecutive hours at least once during any seven consecutive days.

(d) No pilot may fly as a crewmember in air transportation more than 100 hours during any 30 consecutive days.

(e) No pilot may fly as a crewmember in air transportation more than 1,000 hours during any calendar year.

(f) Notwithstanding paragraph (a) of this section, the certificate holder may, in conducting a transcontinental nonstop flight, schedule a flight crewmember for more than eight but not more than 10 hours of continuous duty aloft without an intervening rest period, if—

(1) The flight is in an airplane with a pressurization system that is operative at the beginning of the flight;

(2) The flight crew consists of at least two pilots and a flight engineer; and

(3) The certificate holder uses, in conducting the operation, an air/ground communication service that is independent of systems operated by the United States, and a dispatch organization, both of which are approved by the

Administrator as adequate to serve the terminal points concerned.

[Doc. No. 6258, 29 FR 19218, Dec. 31, 1964; 30 FR 3639, Mar. 19, 1965, as amended by Amdt. 121–253, 61 FR 2613, Jan. 26, 1996]

§121.505 Flight time limitations: Two pilot crews: airplanes.

(a) If a certificate holder conducting supplemental operations schedules a pilot to fly more than eight hours during any 24 consecutive hours, it shall give him an intervening rest period at or before the end of eight scheduled hours of flight duty. This rest period must be at least twice the number of hours flown since the preceding rest period, but not less than eight hours. The certificate holder conducting supplemental operations shall relieve that pilot of all duty with it during that rest period.

(b) No pilot of an airplane that has a crew of two pilots may be on duty for more than 16 hours during any 24 consecutive hours.

[Doc. No. 6258, 29 FR 19218, Dec. 31, 1964; 30 FR 3639, Mar. 19, 1965, as amended by Amdt. 121–253, 61 FR 2613, Jan. 26, 1996]

§121.507 Flight time limitations: Three pilot crews: airplanes.

(a) No certificate holder conducting supplemental operations may schedule a pilot—

(1) For flight deck duty in an airplane that has a crew of three pilots for more than eight hours in any 24 consecutive hours; or

(2) To be aloft in an airplane that has a crew of three pilot for more than 12 hours in any 24 consecutive hours.

(b) No pilot of an airplane that has a crew of three pilots may be on duty for more than 18 hours in any 24 consecutive hours.

[Doc. No. 6258, 29 FR 19218, Dec. 31, 1964; 30 FR 3639, Mar. 19, 1965, as amended by Amdt. 121–253, 61 FR 2613, Jan. 26, 1996]

§121.509 Flight time limitations: Four pilot crews: airplanes.

(a) No certificate holder conducting supplemental operations may schedule a pilot—

(1) For flight deck duty in an airplane that has a crew of four pilots for more than eight hours in any 24 consecutive hours; or

(2) To be aloft in an airplane that has a crew of four pilots for more than 16 hours in any 24 consecutive hours.

(b) No pilot of an airplane that has a crew of four pilots may be on duty for more than 20 hours in any 24 consecutive hours.

[Doc. No. 6258, 29 FR 19218, Dec. 31, 1964; 30 FR 3639, Mar. 19, 1965, as amended by Amdt. 121–253, 61 FR 2613, Jan. 26, 1996]

§121.511 Flight time limitations: Flight engineers: airplanes.

(a) In any operation in which one flight engineer is serving the flight time limitations in §§121.503 and 121.505 apply to that flight engineer.

(b) In any operation in which more than one flight engineer is serving and the flight crew contains more than two pilots the flight time limitations in §121.509 apply in place of those in §121.505.

§121.513 Flight time limitations: Overseas and international operations: airplanes.

In place of the flight time limitations in §§121.503 through 121.511, a certificate holder conducting supplemental operations may elect to comply with the flight time limitations of §§121.515 and 121.521 through 121.525 for operations conducted—

(a) Between a place in the 48 contiguous States and the District of Columbia, or Alaska, and any place outside thereof;

(b) Between any two places outside the 48 contiguous States, the District of Columbia, and Alaska; or

(c) Between two places within the State of Alaska or the State of Hawaii.

[Doc. No. 6258, 29 FR 19218, Dec. 31, 1964; 30 FR 3639, Mar. 19, 1965, as amended by Amdt. 121–253, 61 FR 2613, Jan. 26, 1996]

§121.515 Flight time limitations: All airmen: airplanes.

No airman may be aloft as a flight crewmember more than 1,000 hours in any 12-calendar-month period.

§121.517 Flight time limitations: Other commercial flying: airplanes.

No airman who is employed by a certificate holder conducting supplemental operations may do any other commercial flying, if that commercial flying plus his flying in operations under this part will exceed any flight time limitation in this part.

[Doc. No. 28154, 61 FR 2613, Jan. 26, 1996]

§ 121.519 Flight time limitations: Deadhead transportation: airplanes.

Time spent by an airman in deadhead transportation to or from a duty assignment is not considered to be part of any rest period.

§ 121.521 Flight time limitations: Crew of two pilots and one additional airman as required.

(a) No certificate holder conducting supplemental operations may schedule an airman to be aloft as a member of the flight crew in an airplane that has a crew of two pilots and at least one additional flight crewmember for more than 12 hours during any 24 consecutive hours.

(b) If an airman has been aloft as a member of a flight crew for 20 or more hours during any 48 consecutive hours or 24 or more hours during any 72 consecutive hours, he must be given at least 18 hours of rest before being assigned to any duty with the certificate holder. In any case, he must be relieved of all duty for at least 24 consecutive hours during any seven consecutive days.

(c) No airman may be aloft as a flight crewmember more than—

(1) 120 hours during any 30 consecutive days; or

(2) 300 hours during any 90 consecutive days.

[Doc. No. 6258, 29 FR 19218, Dec. 31, 1964, as amended by Amdt. 121–17, 31 FR 1147, Jan. 28, 1966; Amdt. 121–253, 61 FR 2613, Jan. 26, 1996]

§ 121.523 Flight time limitations: Crew of three or more pilots and additional airmen as required.

(a) No certificate holder conducting supplemental operations may schedule an airman for flight deck duty as a flight engineer, or navigator in a crew of three or more pilots and additional airmen for a total of more than 12 hours during any 24 consecutive hours.

(b) Each certificate holder conducting supplemental operations shall schedule its flight hours to provide adequate rest periods on the ground for each airman who is away from his principal operations base. It shall also provide adequate sleeping quarters on the airplane whenever an airman is scheduled to be aloft as a flight crewmember for more than 12 hours during any 24 consecutive hours.

(c) No certificate holder conducting supplemental operations may schedule any flight crewmember to be on continuous duty for more than 30 hours. Such a crewmember is considered to be on continuous duty from the time he reports for duty until the time he is released from duty for a rest period of at least 10 hours on the ground. If a flight crewmember is on continuous duty for more than 24 hours (whether scheduled or not) duty any scheduled duty period, he must be given at least 16 hours for rest on the ground after completing the last flight scheduled for that scheduled duty period before being assigned any further flight duty.

(d) If a flight crewmember is required to engage in deadhead transportation for more than four hours before beginning flight duty, one half of the time spent in deadhead transportation must be treated as duty time for the purpose of complying with duty time limitations, unless he is given at least 10 hours of rest on the ground before being assigned to flight duty.

(e) Each certificate holder conducting supplemental operations shall give each airman, upon return to his operations base from any flight or series of flights, a rest period that is at least twice the total number of hours he was aloft as a flight crewmember since the last rest period at his base, before assigning him to any further duty. If the required rest period is more than seven days, that part of the rest period that is more than seven days may be given at any time before the pilot is again scheduled for flight duty.

(f) No airman may be aloft as a flight crewmember for more than 350 hours in any 90 consecutive days.

[Doc. No. 6258, 29 FR 19218, Dec. 31, 1964; 30 FR 3639, Mar. 19, 1965, as amended by Amdt. 121–253, 61 FR 2613, Jan. 26, 1996]

§121.525 Flight time limitations: Pilots serving in more than one kind of flight crew.

(a) This section applies to each pilot assigned during any 30 consecutive days to more than one type of flight crew.

(b) The flight time limitations for a pilot who is scheduled for duty aloft for more than 20 hours in two-pilot crews in 30 consecutive days, or whose assignment in such a crew is interrupted more than once in any 30 consecutive days by assignment to a crew of two or more pilots and an additional flight crewmember, are those listed in §§121.503 through 121.509, as appropriate.

(c) Except for a pilot covered by paragraph (b) of this section, the flight time limitations for a pilot scheduled for duty aloft for more than 20 hours in two-pilot and additional flight crewmember crews in 30 consecutive days or whose assignment in such a crew is interrupted more than once in any 30 consecutive days by assignment to a crew consisting of three pilots and an additional flight crewmember, are those set forth in §121.521.

(d) The flight time limitations for a pilot to whom paragraphs (b) and (c) of this section do not apply, and who is scheduled for duty aloft for a total of not more than 20 hours within 30 consecutive days in two-pilot crews (with or without additional flight crewmembers) are those set forth in §121.523.

(e) The flight time limitations for a pilot assigned to each of two-pilot, two-pilot and additional flight crewmember, and three-pilot and additional flight crewmember crews in 30 consecutive days, and who is not subject to paragraph (b), (c), or (d) of this section, are those listed in §121.523.

§121.527 Fatigue risk management system.

(a) No certificate holder may exceed any provision of this subpart unless approved by the FAA under a Fatigue Risk Management System.

(b) The Fatigue Risk Management System must include:

(1) A fatigue risk management policy.

(2) An education and awareness training program.

(3) A fatigue reporting system.

(4) A system for monitoring flightcrew fatigue.

(5) An incident reporting process.

(6) A performance evaluation.

[Doc. No. FAA–2009–1093, 77 FR 403, Jan. 4, 2012]

Subpart T—Flight Operations

SOURCE: Docket No. 6258, 29 FR 19219, Dec. 31, 1964, unless otherwise noted.

§121.531 Applicability.

This subpart prescribes requirements for flight operations applicable to all certificate holders, except where otherwise specified.

§121.533 Responsibility for operational control: Domestic operations.

(a) Each certificate holder conducting domestic operations is responsible for operational control.

(b) The pilot in command and the aircraft dispatcher are jointly responsible for the preflight planning, delay, and dispatch release of a flight in compliance with this chapter and operations specifications.

(c) The aircraft dispatcher is responsible for—

(1) Monitoring the progress of each flight;

(2) Issuing necessary information for the safety of the flight; and

(3) Cancelling or redispatching a flight if, in his opinion or the opinion of the pilot in command, the flight cannot operate or continue to operate safely as planned or released.

(d) Each pilot in command of an aircraft is, during flight time, in command of the aircraft and crew and is responsible for the safety of the passengers, crewmembers, cargo, and airplane.

(e) Each pilot in command has full control and authority in the operation of the aircraft, without limitation, over other crewmembers and their duties during flight time, whether or not he holds valid certificates authorizing him to perform the duties of those crewmembers.

[Doc. No. 6258, 29 FR 19219, Dec. 31, 1964, as amended by Amdt. 121–253, 61 FR 2613, Jan. 26, 1996]

§ 121.535 Responsibility for operational control: Flag operations.

(a) Each certificate holder conducting flag operations is responsible for operational control.

(b) The pilot in command and the aircraft dispatcher are jointly responsible for the preflight planning, delay, and dispatch release of a flight in compliance with this chapter and operations specifications.

(c) The aircraft dispatcher is responsible for—

(1) Monitoring the progress of each flight;

(2) Issuing necessary instructions and information for the safety of the flight; and

(3) Cancelling or redispatching a flight if, in his opinion or the opinion of the pilot in command, the flight cannot operate or continue to operate safely as planned or released.

(d) Each pilot in command of an aircraft is, during flight time, in command of the aircraft and crew and is responsible for the safety of the passengers, crewmembers, cargo, and airplane.

(e) Each pilot in command has full control and authority in the operation of the aircraft, without limitation, over other crewmembers and their duties during flight time, whether or not he holds valid certificates authorizing him to perform the duties of those crewmembers.

(f) No pilot may operate an aircraft in a careless or reckless manner so as to endanger life or property.

[Doc. No. 6258, 29 FR 19219, Dec. 31, 1964, as amended by Amdt. 121–253, 61 FR 2613, Jan. 26, 1996]

§ 121.537 Responsibility for operational control: Supplemental operations.

(a) Each certificate holder conducting supplemental operations—

(1) Is responsible for operational control; and

(2) Shall list each person authorized by it to exercise operational control in its operator's manual.

(b) The pilot in command and the director of operations are jointly responsible for the initiation, continuation, diversion, and termination of a flight in compliance with this chapter and the operations specifications. The director of operations may delegate the functions for the initiation, continuation, diversion, and termination of a flight but he may not delegate the responsibility for those functions.

(c) The director of operations is responsible for cancelling, diverting, or delaying a flight if in his opinion or the opinion of the pilot in command the flight cannot operate or continue to operate safely as planned or released. The director of operations is responsible for assuring that each flight is monitored with respect to at least the following:

(1) Departure of the flight from the place of origin and arrival at the place of destination, including intermediate stops and any diversions therefrom.

(2) Maintenance and mechanical delays encountered at places of origin and destination and intermediate stops.

(3) Any known conditions that may adversely affect the safety of flight.

(d) Each pilot in command of an aircraft is, during flight time, in command of the aircraft and crew and is responsible for the safety of the passengers, crewmembers, cargo, and aircraft. The pilot in command has full control and authority in the operation of the aircraft, without limitation, over other crewmembers and their duties during flight time, whether or not he holds valid certificates authorizing him to perform the duties of those crewmembers.

(e) Each pilot in command of an aircraft is responsible for the preflight planning and the operation of the flight in compliance with this chapter and the operations specifications.

(f) No pilot may operate an aircraft, in a careless or reckless manner, so as to endanger life or property.

[Doc. No. 6258, 29 FR 19219, Dec. 31, 1964, as amended by Amdt. 121–253, 61 FR 2613, Jan. 26, 1996]

§121.538 Aircraft security.

Certificate holders conducting operations under this part must comply with the applicable security requirements in 49 CFR chapter XII.

[67 FR 8350, Feb. 22, 2002]

§121.539 Operations notices.

Each certificate holder shall notify its appropriate operations personnel of each change in equipment and operating procedures, including each known change in the use of navigation aids, airports, air traffic control procedures and regulations, local airport traffic control rules, and known hazards to flight, including icing and other potentially hazardous meteorological conditions and irregularities in ground and navigation facilities.

§121.541 Operations schedules: Domestic and flag operations.

In establishing flight operations schedules, each certificate holder conducting domestic or flag operations shall allow enough time for the proper servicing of aircraft at intermediate stops, and shall consider the prevailing winds en route and the cruising speed of the type of aircraft used. This cruising speed may not be more than that resulting from the specified cruising output of the engines.

[Doc. No. 28154, 61 FR 2613, Jan. 26, 1996]

§121.542 Flight crewmember duties.

(a) No certificate holder shall require, nor may any flight crewmember perform, any duties during a critical phase of flight except those duties required for the safe operation of the aircraft. Duties such as company required calls made for such nonsafety related purposes as ordering galley supplies and confirming passenger connections, announcements made to passengers promoting the air carrier or pointing out sights of interest, and filling out company payroll and related records are not required for the safe operation of the aircraft.

(b) No flight crewmember may engage in, nor may any pilot in command permit, any activity during a critical phase of flight which could distract any flight crewmember from the performance of his or her duties or which could interfere in any way with the proper conduct of those duties. Activities such as eating meals, engaging in nonessential conversations within the cockpit and nonessential communications between the cabin and cockpit crews, and reading publications not related to the proper conduct of the flight are not required for the safe operation of the aircraft.

(c) For the purposes of this section, critical phases of flight includes all ground operations involving taxi, takeoff and landing, and all other flight operations conducted below 10,000 feet, except cruise flight.

NOTE: Taxi is defined as "movement of an airplane under its own power on the surface of an airport."

(d) During all flight time as defined in 14 CFR 1.1, no flight crewmember may use, nor may any pilot in command permit the use of, a personal wireless communications device (as defined in 49 U.S.C. 44732(d)) or laptop computer while at a flight crewmember duty station unless the purpose is directly related to operation of the aircraft, or for emergency, safety-related, or employment-related communications, in accordance with air carrier procedures approved by the Administrator.

[Doc. No. 20661, 46 FR 5502, Jan. 19, 1981, as amended by Amdt. 121-369, 79 FR 8263, Feb. 12, 2014]

§121.543 Flight crewmembers at controls.

(a) Except as provided in paragraph (b) of this section, each required flight crewmember on flight deck duty must remain at the assigned duty station with seat belt fastened while the aircraft is taking off or landing, and while it is en route.

(b) A required flight crewmember may leave the assigned duty station—

(1) If the crewmember's absence is necessary for the performance of duties in connection with the operation of the aircraft;

(2) If the crewmember's absence is in connection with physiological needs; or

(3) If the crewmember is taking a rest period, and relief is provided—

(i) In the case of the assigned pilot in command during the en route cruise portion of the flight, by a pilot who holds an airline transport pilot certificate not subject to the limitations in §61.167 of this chapter and an appropriate type rating, is currently qualified as pilot in command or second in command, and is qualified as pilot in command of that aircraft during the en route cruise portion of the flight. A second in command qualified to act as a pilot in command en route need not have completed the following pilot in command requirements: The 6-month recurrent flight training required by §121.433(c)(1)(iii); the operating experience required by §121.434; the takeoffs and landings required by §121.439; the line check required by §121.440; and the 6-month proficiency check or simulator training required by §121.441(a)(1); and

(ii) In the case of the assigned second in command, by a pilot qualified to act as second in command of that aircraft during en route operations. However, the relief pilot need not meet the recent experience requirements of §121.439(b).

[Doc. No. 16383, 43 FR 22648, May 25, 1978, as amended by Amdt. 121-179, 47 FR 33390, Aug. 2, 1982; Amdt. 121-365, 78 FR 42378, July 15, 2013]

§ 121.544 Pilot monitoring.

Each pilot who is seated at the pilot controls of the aircraft, while not flying the aircraft, must accomplish pilot monitoring duties as appropriate in accordance with the certificate holder's procedures contained in the manual required by §121.133 of this part. Compliance with this section is required no later than March 12, 2019.

[Doc. No. FAA-2008-0677, 78 FR 67841, Nov. 12, 2013]

§ 121.545 Manipulation of controls.

No pilot in command may allow any person to manipulate the controls of an aircraft during flight nor may any person manipulate the controls during flight unless that person is—

(a) A qualified pilot of the certificate holder operating that aircraft.

(b) An authorized pilot safety representative of the Administrator or of the National Transportation Safety Board who has the permission of the pilot in command, is qualified in the aircraft, and is checking flight operations; or

(c) A pilot of another certificate holder who has the permission of the pilot in command, is qualified in the aircraft, and is authorized by the certificate holder operating the aircraft.

[Doc. No. 6258, 29 FR 19220, Dec. 31, 1964, as amended by Doc. No. 8084, 32 FR 5769, Apr. 11, 1967; Amdt. 121-144, 43 FR 22648, May 25, 1978]

§ 121.547 Admission to flight deck.

(a) No person may admit any person to the flight deck of an aircraft unless the person being admitted is—

(1) A crewmember;

(2) An FAA air carrier inspector, a DOD commercial air carrier evaluator, or an authorized representative of the National Transportation Safety Board, who is performing official duties;

(3) Any person who—

(i) Has permission of the pilot in command, an appropriate management official of the part 119 certificate holder, and the Administrator; and

(ii) Is an employee of—

(A) The United States, or

(B) A part 119 certificate holder and whose duties are such that admission to the flightdeck is necessary or advantageous for safe operation; or

(C) An aeronautical enterprise certificated by the Administrator and whose duties are such that admission to the flightdeck is necessary or advantageous for safe operation.

(4) Any person who has the permission of the pilot in command, an appropriate management official of the part 119 certificate holder and the Administrator. Paragraph (a)(2) of this section does not limit the emergency authority of the pilot in command to exclude any person from the flightdeck in the interests of safety.

(b) For the purposes of paragraph (a)(3) of this section, employees of the United States who deal responsibly with matters relating to safety and employees of the certificate holder whose efficiency would be increased by familiarity with flight conditions, may be admitted by the certificate holder. However, the certificate holder may not admit employees of traffic, sales, or other departments that are not directly related to flight operations, unless they are eligible under paragraph (a)(4) of this section.

(c) No person may admit any person to the flight deck unless there is a seat available for his use in the passenger compartment, except—

(1) An FAA air carrier inspector, a DOD commercial air carrier evaluator, or authorized representative of the Administrator or National Transportation Safety Board who is checking or observing flight operations;

(2) An air traffic controller who is authorized by the Administrator to observe ATC procedures;

(3) A certificated airman employed by the certificate holder whose duties require an airman certificate;

(4) A certificated airman employed by another part 119 certificate holder whose duties with that part 119 certificate holder require an airman certificate and who is authorized by the part 119 certificate holder operating the aircraft to make specific trips over a route;

(5) An employee of the part 119 certificate holder operating the aircraft whose duty is directly related to the conduct or planning of flight operations or the in-flight monitoring of aircraft equipment or operating procedures, if his presence on the flightdeck is necessary to perform his duties and he has been authorized in writing by a responsible supervisor, listed in the Operations Manual as having that authority; and

(6) A technical representative of the manufacturer of the aircraft or its components whose duties are directly related to the in-flight monitoring of aircraft equipment or operating procedures, if his presence on the flightdeck is necessary to perform his duties and he has been authorized in writing by the Administrator and by a responsible supervisor of the operations department of the part 119 certificate holder, listed in the Operations Manual as having that authority.

[Doc. No. 6258, 29 FR 19220, Dec. 31, 1964 as amended by Doc. No. 8084, 32 FR 5769, Apr. 11, 1967; Amdt. 121–253, 61 FR 2613, Jan. 26, 1996; Amdt. 121–288, 67 FR 2127, Jan. 15, 2002; Amdt. 121–298, 68 FR 41217, July 10, 2003]

§121.548 Aviation safety inspector's credentials: Admission to pilot's compartment.

Whenever, in performing the duties of conducting an inspection, an inspector of the Federal Aviation Administration presents form FAA 110A, "Aviation Safety Inspector's Credential," to the pilot in command of an aircraft operated by a certificate holder, the inspector must be given free and uninterrupted access to the pilot's compartment of that aircraft.

[Doc. No. 28154, 61 FR 2613, Jan. 26, 1996]

§121.548a DOD Commercial Air Carrier Evaluator's Credential.

Whenever, in performing the duties of conducting an evaluation, a DOD commercial air carrier evaluator presents S&A Form 110B, "DOD Commercial Air Carrier Evaluator's Credential," to the pilot in command of an airplane operated by the certificate holder, the evaluator must be given free and uninterrupted access to the pilot's compartment of that airplane.

[Doc. No. FAA–2003–15571, 68 FR 41217, July 10, 2003]

§121.549 Flying equipment.

(a) The pilot in command shall ensure that appropriate aeronautical charts containing adequate information concerning navigation aids and instrument approach procedures are aboard the aircraft for each flight.

(b) Each crewmember shall, on each flight, have readily available for his use a flashlight that is in good working order.

§121.550 Secret Service Agents: Admission to flight deck.

Whenever an Agent of the Secret Service who is assigned the duty of protecting a person aboard an aircraft operated by a certificate holder considers it necessary in the performance of his duty to ride on the flight deck of the aircraft, he must, upon request and presentation of his Secret Service credentials to the pilot in command of the aircraft, be admitted to the flight deck and permitted to occupy an observer seat thereon.

[Doc. No. 9031, 35 FR 12061, July 28, 1970, as amended by Amdt. 121-253, 61 FR 2613, Jan. 26, 1996]

§ 121.551 Restriction or suspension of operation: Domestic and flag operations.

When a certificate holder conducting domestic or flag operations knows of conditions, including airport and runway conditions, that are a hazard to safe operations, it shall restrict or suspend operations until those conditions are corrected.

[Doc. No. 28154, 61 FR 2613, Jan. 26, 1996]

§ 121.553 Restriction or suspension of operation: Supplemental operations.

When a certificate holder conducting supplemental operations or pilot in command knows of conditions, including airport and runway conditions, that are a hazard to safe operations, the certificate holder or pilot in command, as the case may be, shall restrict or suspend operations until those conditions are corrected.

[Doc. No. 28154, 61 FR 2613, Jan. 26, 1996]

§ 121.555 Compliance with approved routes and limitations: Domestic and flag operations.

No pilot may operate an airplane in scheduled air transportation—

(a) Over any route or route segment unless it is specified in the certificate holder's operations specifications; or

(b) Other than in accordance with the limitations in the operations specifications.

[Doc. No. 6258, 29 FR 19219, Dec. 31, 1964, as amended by Amdt. 121-253, 61 FR 2614, Jan. 26, 1996]

§ 121.557 Emergencies: Domestic and flag operations.

(a) In an emergency situation that requires immediate decision and action the pilot in command may take any action that he considers necessary under the circumstances. In such a case he may deviate from prescribed operations procedures and methods, weather minimums, and this chapter, to the extent required in the interests of safety.

(b) In an emergency situation arising during flight that requires immediate decision and action by an aircraft dispatcher, and that is known to him, the aircraft dispatcher shall advise the pilot in command of the emergency, shall ascertain the decision of the pilot in command, and shall have the decision recorded. If the aircraft dispatcher cannot communicate with the pilot, he shall declare an emergency and take any action that he considers necessary under the circumstances.

(c) Whenever a pilot in command or dispatcher exercises emergency authority, he shall keep the appropriate ATC facility and dispatch centers fully informed of the progress of the flight. The person declaring the emergency shall send a written report of any deviation through the certificate holder's operations manager, to the Administrator. A dispatcher shall send his report within 10 days after the date of the emergency, and a pilot in command shall send his report within 10 days after returning to his home base.

[Doc. No. 6258, 29 FR 19219, Dec. 31, 1964, as amended by Amdt. 121-253, 61 FR 2614, Jan. 26, 1996]

§ 121.559 Emergencies: Supplemental operations.

(a) In an emergency situation that requires immediate decision and action, the pilot in command may take any action that he considers necessary under the circumstances. In such a case, he may deviate from prescribed operations, procedures and methods, weather minimums, and this chapter, to the extent required in the interests of safety.

(b) In an emergency situation arising during flight that requires immediate decision and action by appropriate management personnel in the case of operations conducted with a flight following service and which is known to them, those personnel shall advise the pilot in command of the emergency, shall ascertain the decision of the pilot in command, and shall have the decision recorded. If they cannot communicate with the pilot, they shall declare an emergency and take any action that they consider necessary under the circumstances.

(c) Whenever emergency authority is exercised, the pilot in command or the appropriate management personnel shall keep the appropriate communication facility fully informed of the progress of the flight. The person declaring the emergency shall send a written report of any deviation, through the certificate holder's director of operations, to the Administrator within 10 days after the flight is completed or, in the case of operations outside the United States, upon return to the home base.

[Doc. No. 6258, 29 FR 19219, Dec. 31, 1964, as amended by Amdt. 121–253, 61 FR 2614, Jan. 26, 1996; Amdt. 121–333, 72 FR 31682, June 7, 2007]

§121.561 Reporting potentially hazardous meteorological conditions and irregularities of ground facilities or navigation aids.

(a) Whenever he encounters a meteorological condition or an irregularity in a ground facility or navigation aid, in flight, the knowledge of which he considers essential to the safety of other flights, the pilot in command shall notify an appropriate ground station as soon as practicable.

(b) The ground radio station that is notified under paragraph (a) of this section shall report the information to the agency directly responsible for operating the facility.

[Doc. No. 6258, 29 FR 19219, Dec. 31, 1964, as amended by Amdt. 121–333, 72 FR 31682, June 7, 2007]

§121.563 Reporting mechanical irregularities.

The pilot in command shall ensure that all mechanical irregularities occurring during flight time are entered in the maintenance log of the airplane at the end of that flight time. Before each flight the pilot in command shall ascertain the status of each irregu-

larity entered in the log at the end of the preceding flight.

[Doc. No. 17897, 45 FR 41594, June 19, 1980, as amended by Amdt. 121–179, 47 FR 33390, Aug. 2, 1982]

§121.565 Engine inoperative: Landing; reporting.

(a) Except as provided in paragraph (b) of this section, whenever an airplane engine fails or whenever an engine is shutdown to prevent possible damage, the pilot in command must land the airplane at the nearest suitable airport, in point of time, at which a safe landing can be made.

(b) If not more than one engine of an airplane that has three or more engines fails or is shut down to prevent possible damage, the pilot-in-command may proceed to an airport that the pilot selects if, after considering the following, the pilot makes a reasonable decision that proceeding to that airport is as safe as landing at the nearest suitable airport:

(1) The nature of the malfunction and the possible mechanical difficulties that may occur if flight is continued.

(2) The altitude, weight, and useable fuel at the time that the engine is shutdown.

(3) The weather conditions en route and at possible landing points.

(4) The air traffic congestion.

(5) The kind of terrain.

(6) His familiarity with the airport to be used.

(c) The pilot-in-command must report each engine shutdown in flight to the appropriate communication facility as soon as practicable and must keep that facility fully informed of the progress of the flight.

(d) If the pilot in command lands at an airport other than the nearest suitable airport, in point of time, he or she shall (upon completing the trip) send a written report, in duplicate, to his or her director of operations stating the reasons for determining that the selection of an airport, other than the nearest airport, was as safe a course of action as landing at the nearest suitable airport. The director of operations shall, within 10 days after the pilot returns to his or her home base, send a copy of this report with the director of operation's comments to the responsible Flight Standards office.

[Doc. No. 6258, 29 FR 19219, Dec. 31, 1964, as amended by Amdt. 121–207, 54 FR 39293, Sept. 25, 1989; Amdt. 121–253, 61 FR 2614, Jan. 26, 1996; Amdt. 121–329, 72 FR 1881, Jan. 16, 2007; Amdt. 121–333, 72 FR 31682, June 7, 2007; Docket FAA–2018–0119, Amdt. 121–380, 83 FR 9172, Mar. 5, 2018]

§ 121.567 Instrument approach procedures and IFR landing minimums.

No person may make an instrument approach at an airport except in accordance with IFR weather minimums and instrument approach procedures set forth in the certificate holder's operations specifications.

§ 121.569 Equipment interchange: Domestic and flag operations.

(a) Before operating under an interchange agreement, each certificate holder conducting domestic or flag operations shall show that—

(1) The procedures for the interchange operation conform with this chapter and with safe operating practices;

(2) Required crewmembers and dispatchers meet approved training requirements for the airplanes and equipment to be used and are familiar with the communications and dispatch procedures to be used;

(3) Maintenance personnel meet training requirements for the airplanes and equipment, and are familiar with the maintenance procedures to be used;

(4) Flight crewmembers and dispatchers meet appropriate route and airport qualifications; and

(5) The airplanes to be operated are essentially similar to the airplanes of the certificate holder with whom the interchange is effected with respect to the arrangement of flight instruments and the arrangement and motion of controls that are critical to safety unless the Administrator determines that the certificate holder has adequate training programs to insure that any potentially hazardous dissimilarities are safely overcome by flight crew familiarization.

(b) Each certificate holder conducting domestic or flag operations shall include the pertinent provisions and procedures involved in the equipment interchange agreement in its manuals.

[Doc. No. 6258, 29 FR 19219, Dec. 31, 1964, as amended by Amdt. 121–253, 61 FR 2614, Jan. 26, 1996]

§ 121.570 Airplane evacuation capability.

(a) No person may cause an airplane carrying passengers to be moved on the surface, take off, or land unless each automatically deployable emergency evacuation assisting means, installed pursuant to § 121.310(a), is ready for evacuation.

(b) Each certificate holder shall ensure that, at all times passengers are on board prior to airplane movement on the surface, at least one floor-level exit provides for the egress of passengers through normal or emergency means.

[Doc. No. 26142, 57 FR 42674, Sept. 15, 1992]

§ 121.571 Briefing passengers before takeoff.

(a) Each certificate holder operating a passenger-carrying airplane shall insure that all passengers are orally briefed by the appropriate crewmember as follows:

(1) Before each takeoff, on each of the following:

(i) *Smoking.* Each passenger shall be briefed on when, where, and under what conditions smoking is prohibited including, but not limited to, any applicable requirements of part 252 of this title). This briefing shall include a statement that the Federal Aviation Regulations require passenger compliance with the lighted passenger information signs, posted placards, areas designated for safety purposes as no smoking areas, and crewmember instructions with regard to these items. The briefing shall also include a statement that Federal law prohibits tampering with, disabling, or destroying any smoke detector in an airplane lavatory; smoking in lavatories; and, when applicable, smoking in passenger compartments.

(ii) The location of emergency exits.

(iii) The use of safety belts, including instructions on how to fasten and unfasten the safety belts. Each passenger shall be briefed on when, where, and under what conditions the safety belt must be fastened about that passenger. This briefing shall include a statement that the Federal Aviation Regulations require passenger compliance with lighted passenger information signs and crewmember instructions concerning the use of safety belts.

(iv) The location and use of any required emergency flotation means.

(v) On operations that do not use a flight attendant, the following additional information:

(A) The placement of seat backs in an upright position before takeoff and landing.

(B) Location of survival equipment.

(C) If the flight involves operations above 12,000 MSL, the normal and emergency use of oxygen.

(D) Location and operation of fire extinguisher.

(2) After each takeoff, immediately before or immediately after turning the seat belt sign off, an announcement shall be made that passengers should keep their seat belts fastened, while seated, even when the seat belt sign is off.

(3) Except as provided in paragraph (a)(4) of this section, before each takeoff a required crewmember assigned to the flight shall conduct an individual briefing of each person who may need the assistance of another person to move expeditiously to an exit in the event of an emergency. In the briefing the required crewmember shall—

(i) Brief the person and his attendant, if any, on the routes to each appropriate exit and on the most appropriate time to begin moving to an exit in the event of an emergency; and

(ii) Inquire of the person and his attendant, if any, as to the most appropriate manner of assisting the person so as to prevent pain and further injury.

(4) The requirements of paragraph (a)(3) of this section do not apply to a person who has been given a briefing before a previous leg of a flight in the same aircraft when the crewmembers on duty have been advised as to the most appropriate manner of assisting the person so as to prevent pain and further injury.

(b) Each certificate holder must carry on each passenger-carrying airplane, in convenient locations for use of each passenger, printed cards supplementing the oral briefing. Each card must contain information pertinent only to the type and model of airplane used for that flight, including—

(1) Diagrams of, and methods of operating, the emergency exits;

(2) Other instructions necessary for use of emergency equipment; and

(3) No later than June 12, 2005, for Domestic and Flag scheduled passenger-carrying flights, the sentence, "Final assembly of this airplane was completed in [INSERT NAME OF COUNTRY]."

(c) The certificate holder shall describe in its manual the procedure to be followed in the briefing required by paragraph (a) of this section.

[Doc. No. 2033, 30 FR 3206, Mar. 9, 1965]

EDITORIAL NOTE: For FEDERAL REGISTER citations affecting §121.571, see the List of CFR Sections Affected, which appears in the Finding Aids section of the printed volume and at *www.govinfo.gov*.

§121.573 Briefing passengers: Extended overwater operations.

(a) In addition to the oral briefing required by §121.571(a), each certificate holder operating an airplane in extended overwater operations shall ensure that all passengers are orally briefed by the appropriate crewmember on the location and operation of life preservers, liferafts, and other flotation means, including a demonstration of the method of donning and inflating a life preserver.

(b) The certificate holder shall describe in its manual the procedure to be followed in the briefing required by paragraph (a) of this section.

(c) If the airplane proceeds directly over water after takeoff, the briefing required by paragraph (a) of this section must be done before takeoff.

(d) If the airplane does not proceed directly over water after takeoff, no part of the briefing required by paragraph (a) of this section has to be given before takeoff, but the entire briefing must be given before reaching the overwater part of the flight.

[Doc. No. 2033, 30 FR 3206, Mar. 9, 1965, as amended by Amdt. 121–144, 43 FR 22648, May 25, 1978; Amdt. 121–146, 43 FR 28403, June 29, 1978]

§ 121.574 Oxygen and portable oxygen concentrators for medical use by passengers.

(a) A certificate holder may allow a passenger to carry and operate equipment for the storage, generation, or dispensing of oxygen when all of the conditions in paragraphs (a) through (d) of this section are satisfied. Beginning August 22, 2016, a certificate holder may allow a passenger to carry and operate a portable oxygen concentrator when the conditions in paragraphs (b) and (e) of this section are satisfied.

(1) The equipment is—

(i) Furnished by the certificate holder;

(ii) Of an approved type or is in conformity with the manufacturing, packaging, marking, labeling, and maintenance requirements of 49 CFR parts 171, 172, and 173, except § 173.24(a)(1);

(iii) Maintained by the certificate holder in accordance with an approved maintenance program;

(iv) Free of flammable contaminants on all exterior surfaces;

(v) Capable of providing a minimum mass flow of oxygen to the user of four liters per minute;

(vi) Constructed so that all valves, fittings, and gauges are protected from damage; and

(vii) Appropriately secured.

(2) When the oxygen is stored in the form of a liquid, the equipment has been under the certificate holder's approved maintenance program since its purchase new or since the storage container was last purged.

(3) When the oxygen is stored in the form of a compressed gas as defined in 49 CFR 173.115(b)—

(i) The equipment has been under the certificate holder's approved maintenance program since its purchase new or since the last hydrostatic test of the storage cylinder; and

(ii) The pressure in any oxygen cylinder does not exceed the rated cylinder pressure.

(4) Each person using the equipment has a medical need to use it evidenced by a written statement to be kept in that person's possession, signed by a licensed physician which specifies the maximum quantity of oxygen needed each hour and the maximum flow rate needed for the pressure altitude corresponding to the pressure in the cabin of the airplane under normal operating conditions. This paragraph does not apply to the carriage of oxygen in an airplane in which the only passengers carried are persons who may have a medical need for oxygen during flight, no more than one relative or other interested person for each of those persons, and medical attendants.

(5) When a physician's statement is required by paragraph (a)(4) of this section, the total quantity of oxygen carried is equal to the maximum quantity of oxygen needed each hour, as specified in the physician's statement, multiplied by the number of hours used to compute the amount of airplane fuel required by this part.

(6) The pilot in command is advised when the equipment is on board, and when it is intended to be used.

(7) The equipment is stowed, and each person using the equipment is seated, so as not to restrict access to or use of any required emergency, or regular exit or of the aisle in the passenger compartment.

(b) No person may smoke or create an open flame and no certificate holder may allow any person to smoke or create an open flame within 10 feet of oxygen storage and dispensing equipment carried in accordance with paragraph (a) of this section or a portable oxygen concentrator carried and operated in accordance with paragraph (e) of this section.

(c) No certificate holder may allow any person to connect or disconnect oxygen dispensing equipment, to or from a gaseous oxygen cylinder while any passenger is aboard the airplane.

(d) The requirements of this section do not apply to the carriage of supplemental or first-aid oxygen and related equipment required by this chapter.

(e) *Portable oxygen concentrators*—(1) *Acceptance criteria.* A passenger may carry or operate a portable oxygen concentrator for personal use on board an aircraft and a certificate holder may allow a passenger to carry or operate a portable oxygen concentrator on board an aircraft operated under this part during all phases of flight if the portable oxygen concentrator satisfies all of the requirements in this paragraph (e):

(i) Is legally marketed in the United States in accordance with Food and Drug Administration requirements in title 21 of the CFR;

(ii) Does not radiate radio frequency emissions that interfere with aircraft systems;

(iii) Generates a maximum oxygen pressure of less than 200 kPa gauge (29.0 psig/43.8 psia) at 20 °C (68 °F);

(iv) Does not contain any hazardous materials subject to the Hazardous Materials Regulations (49 CFR parts 171 through 180) except as provided in 49 CFR 175.10 for batteries used to power portable electronic devices and that do not require aircraft operator approval; and

(v) Bears a label on the exterior of the device applied in a manner that ensures the label will remain affixed for the life of the device and containing the following certification statement in red lettering: "The manufacturer of this POC has determined this device conforms to all applicable FAA acceptance criteria for POC carriage and use on board aircraft." The label requirements in this paragraph (e)(1)(v) do not apply to the following portable oxygen concentrators approved by the FAA for use on board aircraft prior to May 24, 2016:

(A) AirSep Focus;
(B) AirSep FreeStyle;
(C) AirSep FreeStyle 5;
(D) AirSep LifeStyle;
(E) Delphi RS–00400;
(F) DeVilbiss Healthcare iGo;
(G) Inogen One;
(H) Inogen One G2;
(I) Inogen One G3;
(J) Inova Labs LifeChoice;
(K) Inova Labs LifeChoice Activox;
(L) International Biophysics LifeChoice;
(M) Invacare Solo2;
(N) Invacare XPO2;
(O) Oxlife Independence Oxygen Concentrator;
(P) Oxus RS–00400;
(Q) Precision Medical EasyPulse;
(R) Respironics EverGo;
(S) Respironics SimplyGo;
(T) SeQual Eclipse;
(U) SeQual eQuinox Oxygen System (model 4000);
(V) SeQual Oxywell Oxygen System (model 4000);

(W) SeQual SAROS; and
(X) VBox Trooper Oxygen Concentrator.

(2) *Operating requirements.* Portable oxygen concentrators that satisfy the acceptance criteria identified in paragraph (e)(1) of this section may be carried or operated by a passenger on an aircraft provided the aircraft operator ensures that all of the conditions in this paragraph (e)(2) are satisfied:

(i) *Exit seats.* No person operating a portable oxygen concentrator is permitted to occupy an exit seat.

(ii) *Stowage of device.* During movement on the surface, takeoff and landing, the device must be stowed under the seat in front of the user, or in another approved stowage location so that it does not block the aisle way or the entryway to the row. If the device is to be operated by the user, it must be operated only at a seat location that does not restrict any passenger's access to, or use of, any required emergency or regular exit, or the aisle(s) in the passenger compartment.

[Doc. No. 12169, 39 FR 42677, Dec. 6, 1974, as amended by Amdt. 121–159, 45 FR 41594, June 19, 1980; Docket FAA–2014–0554, Amdt. 121–374, 81 FR 33118, May 24, 2016]

§121.575 Alcoholic beverages.

(a) No person may drink any alcoholic beverage aboard an aircraft unless the certificate holder operating the aircraft has served that beverage to him.

(b) No certificate holder may serve any alcoholic beverage to any person aboard any of its aircraft who—

(1) Appears to be intoxicated;

(2) Is escorting a person or being escorted in accordance with 49 CFR 1544.221; or

(3) Has a deadly or dangerous weapon accessible to him while aboard the aircraft in accordance with 49 CFR 1544.219, 1544.221, or 1544.223.

(c) No certificate holder may allow any person to board any of its aircraft if that person appears to be intoxicated.

(d) Each certificate holder shall, within five days after the incident, report to the Administrator the refusal of any person to comply with paragraph (a) of this section, or of any disturbance caused by a person who appears to be intoxicated aboard any of its aircraft.

[Doc. No. 6258, 29 FR 19219, Dec. 31, 1964, as amended by Amdt. 121–118, 40 FR 17552, Apr. 21, 1975; Amdt. 121–178, 47 FR 13316, Mar. 29, 1982; Amdt. 121–275, 67 FR 31932, May 10, 2002]

§ 121.576 Retention of items of mass in passenger and crew compartments.

The certificate holder must provide and use means to prevent each item of galley equipment and each serving cart, when not in use, and each item of crew baggage, which is carried in a passenger or crew compartment from becoming a hazard by shifting under the appropriate load factors corresponding to the emergency landing conditions under which the airplane was type certificated.

[Doc. No. 16383, 43 FR 22648, May 25, 1978]

§ 121.577 Stowage of food, beverage, and passenger service equipment during airplane movement on the surface, takeoff, and landing.

(a) No certificate holder may move an airplane on the surface, take off, or land when any food, beverage, or tableware furnished by the certificate holder is located at any passenger seat.

(b) No certificate holder may move an airplane on the surface, take off, or land unless each food and beverage tray and seat back tray table is secured in its stowed position.

(c) No certificate holder may permit an airplane to move on the surface, take off, or land unless each passenger serving cart is secured in its stowed position.

(d) No certificate holder may permit an airplane to move on the surface, take off, or land unless each movie screen that extends into an aisle is stowed.

(e) Each passenger shall comply with instructions given by a crewmember with regard to compliance with this section.

[Doc. No. 26142, 57 FR 42674, Sept. 15, 1992]

§ 121.578 Cabin ozone concentration.

(a) For the purpose of this section, the following definitions apply:

(1) *Flight segment* means scheduled nonstop flight time between two airports.

(2) *Sea level equivalent* refers to conditions of 25 °C and 760 millimeters of mercury pressure.

(b) Except as provided in paragraphs (d) and (e) of this section, no certificate holder may operate an airplane above the following flight levels unless it is successfully demonstrated to the Administrator that the concentration of ozone inside the cabin will not exceed—

(1) For flight above flight level 320, 0.25 parts per million by volume, sea level equivalent, at any time above that flight level; and

(2) For flight above flight level 270, 0.1 parts per million by volume, sea level equivalent, time-weighted average for each flight segment that exceeds 4 hours and includes flight above that flight level. (For this purpose, the amount of ozone below flight level 180 is considered to be zero.)

(c) Compliance with this section must be shown by analysis or tests, based on either airplane operational procedures and performance limitations or the certificate holder's operations. The analysis or tests must show either of the following:

(1) Atmospheric ozone statistics indicate, with a statistical confidence of at least 84%, that at the altitudes and locations at which the airplane will be operated cabin ozone concentrations will not exceed the limits prescribed by paragraph (b) of this section.

(2) The airplane ventilation system including any ozone control equipment, will maintain cabin ozone concentrations at or below the limits prescribed by paragraph (b) of this section.

(d) A certificate holder may obtain an authorization to deviate from the requirements of paragraph (b) of this section, by an amendment to its operations specifications, if—

(1) It shows that due to circumstances beyond its control or to unreasonable economic burden it cannot comply for a specified period of time; and

(2) It has submitted a plan acceptable to the Administrator to effect compliance to the extent possible.

(e) A certificate holder need not comply with the requirements of paragraph (b) of this section for an aircraft—

(1) When the only persons carried are flight crewmembers and persons listed in §121.583;

(2) If the aircraft is scheduled for retirement before January 1, 1985; or

(3) If the aircraft is scheduled for re-engining under the provisions of subpart E of part 91, until it is re-engined.

[Doc. No. 121–154, 45 FR 3883, Jan. 21, 1980. Redesignated by Amdt. 121–162, 45 FR 46739, July 10, 1980, and amended by Amdt. 121–181, 47 FR 58489, Dec. 30, 1982; Amdt. 121–251, 60 FR 65935, Dec. 20, 1995]

§121.579 Minimum altitudes for use of autopilot.

(a) *Definitions.* For purpose of this section—

(1) Altitudes for takeoff/initial climb and go-around/missed approach are defined as above the airport elevation.

(2) Altitudes for enroute operations are defined as above terrain elevation.

(3) Altitudes for approach are defined as above the touchdown zone elevation (TDZE), unless the altitude is specifically in reference to DA (H) or MDA, in which case the altitude is defined by reference to the DA(H) or MDA itself.

(b) *Takeoff and initial climb.* No person may use an autopilot for takeoff or initial climb below the higher of 500 feet or an altitude that is no lower than twice the altitude loss specified in the Airplane Flight Manual (AFM), except as follows—

(1) At a minimum engagement altitude specified in the AFM; or

(2) At an altitude specified by the Administrator, whichever is greater.

(c) *Enroute.* No person may use an autopilot enroute, including climb and descent, below the following—

(1) 500 feet;

(2) At an altitude that is no lower than twice the altitude loss specified in the AFM for an autopilot malfunction in cruise conditions; or

(3) At an altitude specified by the Administrator, whichever is greater.

(d) *Approach.* No person may use an autopilot at an altitude lower than 50 feet below the DA(H) or MDA for the instrument procedure being flown, except as follows—

(1) For autopilots with an AFM specified altitude loss for approach operations—

(i) An altitude no lower than twice the specified altitude loss if higher than 50 feet below the MDA or DA(H);

(ii) An altitude no lower than 50 feet higher than the altitude loss specified in the AFM, when the following conditions are met—

(A) Reported weather conditions are less than the basic VFR weather conditions in §91.155 of this chapter;

(B) Suitable visual references specified in §91.175 of this chapter have been established on the instrument approach procedure; and

(C) The autopilot is coupled and receiving both lateral and vertical path references;

(iii) An altitude no lower than the higher of the altitude loss specified in the AFM or 50 feet above the TDZE, when the following conditions are met—

(A) Reported weather conditions are equal to or better than the basic VFR weather conditions in §91.155 of this chapter; and

(B) The autopilot is coupled and receiving both lateral and vertical path references; or

(iv) A greater altitude specified by the Administrator.

(2) For autopilots with AFM specified approach altitude limitations, the greater of—

(i) The minimum use altitude specified for the coupled approach mode selected;

(ii) 50 feet; or

(iii) An altitude specified by Administrator.

(3) For autopilots with an AFM specified negligible or zero altitude loss for an autopilot approach mode malfunction, the greater of—

(i) 50 feet; or

(ii) An altitude specified by Administrator.

(4) If executing an autopilot coupled go-around or missed approach using a certificated and functioning autopilot in accordance with paragraph (e) in this section.

(e) *Go-Around/Missed Approach.* No person may engage an autopilot during a go-around or missed approach below the minimum engagement altitude specified for takeoff and initial climb in paragraph (b) in this section. An autopilot minimum use altitude does not apply to a go-around/missed approach initiated with an engaged autopilot. Performing a go-around or missed approach with an engaged autopilot must not adversely affect safe obstacle clearance.

(f) *Landing.* Notwithstanding paragraph (d) of this section, autopilot minimum use altitudes do not apply to autopilot operations when an approved automatic landing system mode is being used for landing. Automatic landing systems must be authorized in an operations specification issued to the operator.

[Doc. No. FAA–2012–1059, 79 FR 6086, Feb. 3, 2014]

§ 121.580 Prohibition on interference with crewmembers.

No person may assault, threaten, intimidate, or interfere with a crewmember in the performance of the crewmember's duties aboard an aircraft being operated under this part.

[Doc. No. FAA–1998–4954, 64 FR 1080, Jan. 7, 1999]

§ 121.581 Observer's seat: En route inspections.

(a) Except as provided in paragraph (c) of this section, each certificate holder shall make available a seat on the flight deck of each airplane, used by it in air commerce, for occupancy by the Administrator while conducting en route inspections. The location and equipment of the seat, with respect to its suitability for use in conducting en route inspections, is determined by the Administrator.

(b) In each airplane that has more than one observer's seat, in addition to the seats required for the crew complement for which the airplane was certificated, the forward observer's seat or the observer's seat selected by the Administrator must be made available when complying with paragraph (a) of this section.

(c) For any airplane type certificated before December 20, 1995, for not more than 30 passengers that does not have an observer seat on the flightdeck, the certificate holder must provide a forward passenger seat with headset or speaker for occupancy by the Administrator while conducting en route inspections.

[Doc. No. 6258, 29 FR 19219, Dec. 31, 1964, as amended by Amdt. 121–144, 43 FR 22648, May 25, 1978; Amdt. 121–251, 60 FR 65935, Dec. 20, 1995; Amdt. 121–288, 67 FR 2128, Jan. 15, 2002]

§ 121.582 Means to discreetly notify a flightcrew.

Except for all-cargo operations as defined in § 110.2 of this chapter, after October 15, 2007, for all passenger carrying airplanes that require a lockable flightdeck door in accordance with § 121.313(f), the certificate holder must have an approved means by which the cabin crew can discreetly notify the flightcrew in the event of suspicious activity or security breaches in the cabin.

[Doc. No. FAA–2005–22449, 72 FR 45635, Aug. 15, 2007, as amended by Amdt. 121–353, 76 FR 7488, Feb. 10, 2011]

§ 121.583 Carriage of persons without compliance with the passenger-carrying requirements of this part.

(a) When authorized by the certificate holder, the following persons, but no others, may be carried aboard an airplane without complying with the passenger-carrying airplane requirements in §§ 121.309(f), 121.310, 121.391, 121.571, and 121.587; the passenger-carrying operation requirements in part 117 and §§ 121.157(c) and 121.291; the requirements pertaining to passengers in §§ 121.285, 121.313(f), 121.317, 121.547, and 121.573; and the information disclosure requirements in § 121.311(k):

(1) A crewmember.

(2) A company employee.

(3) An FAA air carrier inspector, a DOD commercial air carrier evaluator, or an authorized representative of the National Transportation Safety Board, who is performing official duties.

(4) A person necessary for—

(i) The safety of the flight;

(ii) The safe handling of animals;

(iii) The safe handling of hazardous materials whose carriage is governed by regulations in 49 CFR part 175;

(iv) The security of valuable or confidential cargo;

(v) The preservation of fragile or perishable cargo;

(vi) Experiments on, or testing of, cargo containers or cargo handling devices;

(vii) The operation of special equipment for loading or unloading cargo; and

(viii) The loading or unloading of outsize cargo.

(5) A person described in paragraph (a)(4) of this section, when traveling to or from his assignment.

(6) A person performing duty as an honor guard accompanying a shipment made by or under the authority of the United States.

(7) A military courier, military route supervisor, military cargo contract coordinator, or a flight crewmember of another military cargo contract air carrier or commercial operator, carried by a military cargo contract air carrier or commercial operator in operations under a military cargo contract, if that carriage is specifically authorized by the appropriate armed forces.

(8) A dependent of an employee of the certificate holder when traveling with the employee on company business to or from outlying stations not served by adequate regular passenger flights.

(b) No certificate holder may operate an airplane carrying a person covered by paragraph (a) of this section unless—

(1) Each person has unobstructed access from his seat to the pilot compartment or to a regular or emergency exit;

(2) The pilot in command has a means of notifying each person when smoking is prohibited and when safety belts must be fastened; and

(3) The airplane has an approved seat with an approved safety belt for each person. The seat must be located so that the occupant is not in any position to interfere with the flight crewmembers performing their duties.

(c) Before each takeoff, each certificate holder operating an airplane carrying persons covered by paragraph (a) of this section shall ensure that all such persons have been orally briefed by the appropriate crewmember on—

(1) Smoking;

(2) The use of seat belts;

(3) The location and operation of emergency exits;

(4) The use of oxygen and emergency oxygen equipment; and

(5) For extended overwater operations, the location of life rafts, and the location and operation of life preservers including a demonstration of the method of donning and inflating a life preserver.

(d) Each certificate holder operating an airplane carrying persons covered by paragraph (a) of this section shall incorporate procedures for the safe carriage of such persons into the certificate holder's operations manual.

(e) The pilot in command may authorize a person covered by paragraph (a) of this section to be admitted to the crew compartment of the airplane.

[Doc. No. 10580, 35 FR 14612, Sept. 18, 1970, as amended by Amdt. 121–96, 37 FR 19608, Sept. 21, 1972; Amdt. 121–159, 45 FR 41594, June 19, 1980; Amdt. 121–232, 57 FR 48663, Oct. 27, 1992; Amdt. 121–251, 60 FR 65935, Dec. 20, 1995; Amdt. 121–253, 61 FR 2614, Jan. 26, 1996; Amdt. 121–298, 68 FR 41217, July 10, 2003; Amdt. 121–357, 77 FR 403, Jan. 4, 2012; Amdt. 121–373, 80 FR 58586, Sept. 30, 2015]

§121.584 Requirement to view the area outside the flightdeck door.

From the time the airplane moves in order to initiate a flight segment through the end of that flight segment, no person may unlock or open the flightdeck door unless:

(a) A person authorized to be on the flightdeck uses an approved audio procedure and an approved visual device to verify that:

(1) The area outside the flightdeck door is secure, and;

(2) If someone outside the flightdeck is seeking to have the flightdeck door opened, that person is not under duress, and;

(b) After the requirements of paragraph (a) of this section have been satisfactorily accomplished, the crewmember in charge on the flightdeck authorizes the door to be unlocked and open.

[Amdt. 121–334, 72 FR 45635, Aug. 15, 2007]

§121.585 Exit seating.

(a)(1) Each certificate holder shall determine, to the extent necessary to perform the applicable functions of paragraph (d) of this section, the suitability of each person it permits to occupy an exit seat, in accordance with this section. For the purpose of this section—

(i) *Exit seat* means—

(A) Each seat having direct access to an exit; and,

(B) Each seat in a row of seats through which passengers would have to pass to gain access to an exit, from the first seat inboard of the exit to the first aisle inboard of the exit.

(ii) A passenger seat having "direct access" means a seat from which a passenger can proceed directly to the exit without entering an aisle or passing around an obstruction.

(2) Each certificate holder shall make the passenger exit seating determinations required by this paragraph in a non-discriminatory manner consistent with the requirements of this section, by persons designated in the certificate holder's required operations manual.

(3) Each certificate holder shall designate the exit seats for each passenger seating configuration in its fleet in accordance with the definitions in this paragraph and submit those designations for approval as part of the procedures required to be submitted for approval under paragraphs (n) and (p) of this section.

(b) No certificate holder may seat a person in a seat affected by this section if the certificate holder determines that it is likely that the person would be unable to perform one or more of the applicable functions listed in paragraph (d) of this section because—

(1) The person lacks sufficient mobility, strength, or dexterity in both arms and hands, and both legs:

(i) To reach upward, sideways, and downward to the location of emergency exit and exit-slide operating mechanisms;

(ii) To grasp and push, pull, turn, or otherwise manipulate those mechanisms;

(iii) To push, shove, pull, or otherwise open emergency exits;

(iv) To lift out, hold, deposit on nearby seats, or maneuver over the seatbacks to the next row objects the size and weight of over-wing window exit doors;

(v) To remove obstructions similar in size and weight to over-wing exit doors;

(vi) To reach the emergency exit expeditiously;

(vii) To maintain balance while removing obstructions;

(viii) To exit expeditiously;

(ix) To stabilize an escape slide after deployment; or

(x) To assist others in getting off an escape slide;

(2) The person is less than 15 years of age or lacks the capacity to perform one or more of the applicable functions listed in paragraph (d) of this section without the assistance of an adult companion, parent, or other relative;

(3) The person lacks the ability to read and understand instructions required by this section and related to emergency evacuation provided by the certificate holder in printed or graphic form or the ability to understand oral crew commands.

(4) The person lacks sufficient visual capacity to perform one or more of the applicable functions in paragraph (d) of this section without the assistance of visual aids beyond contact lenses or eyeglasses;

(5) The person lacks sufficient aural capacity to hear and understand instructions shouted by flight attendants, without assistance beyond a hearing aid;

(6) The person lacks the ability adequately to impart information orally to other passengers; or,

(7) The person has:

(i) A condition or responsibilities, such as caring for small children, that might prevent the person from performing one or more of the applicable functions listed in paragraph (d) of this section; or

(ii) A condition that might cause the person harm if he or she performs one or more of the applicable functions listed in paragraph (d) of this section.

(c) Each passenger shall comply with instructions given by a crewmember or other authorized employee of the certificate holder implementing exit seating restrictions established in accordance with this section.

(d) Each certificate holder shall include on passenger information cards, presented in the language in which briefings and oral commands are given by the crew, at each exit seat affected by this section, information that, in the event of an emergency in which a crewmember is not available to assist, a passenger occupying an exit seat may use if called upon to perform the following functions:

(1) Locate the emergency exit;

(2) Recognize the emergency exit opening mechanism;

(3) Comprehend the instructions for operating the emergency exit;

(4) Operate the emergency exit;

(5) Assess whether opening the emergency exit will increase the hazards to which passengers may be exposed;

(6) Follow oral directions and hand signals given by a crewmember;

(7) Stow or secure the emergency exit door so that it will not impede use of the exit;

(8) Assess the condition of an escape slide, activate the slide, and stabilize the slide after deployment to assist others in getting off the slide;

(9) Pass expeditiously through the emergency exit; and

(10) Assess, select, and follow a safe path away from the emergency exit.

(e) Each certificate holder shall include on passenger information cards, at each exit seat—

(1) In the primary language in which emergency commands are given by the crew, the selection criteria set forth in paragraph (b) of this section, and a request that a passenger identify himself or herself to allow reseating if he or she:

(i) Cannot meet the selection criteria set forth in paragraph (b) of this section;

(ii) Has a nondiscernible condition that will prevent him or her from performing the applicable functions listed in paragraph (d) of this section;

(iii) May suffer bodily harm as the result of performing one or more of those functions; or

(iv) Does not wish to perform those functions; and

(2) In each language used by the certificate holder for passenger information cards, a request that a passenger identify himself or herself to allow reseating if he or she lacks the ability to read, speak, or understand the language or the graphic form in which instructions required by this section and related to emergency evacuation are provided by the certificate holder, or the ability to understand the specified

language in which crew commands will be given in an emergency.

(3) May suffer bodily harm as the result of performing one or more of those functions; or,

(4) Does not wish to perform those functions. A certificate holder shall not require the passenger to disclose his or her reason for needing reseating.

(f) Each certificate holder shall make available for inspection by the public at all passenger loading gates and ticket counters at each airport where it conducts passenger operations, written procedures established for making determinations in regard to exit row seating.

(g) No certificate holder may allow taxi or pushback unless at least one required crewmember has verified that no exit seat is occupied by a person the crewmember determines is likely to be unable to perform the applicable functions listed in paragraph (d) of this section.

(h) Each certificate holder shall include in its passenger briefings a reference to the passenger information cards, required by paragraphs (d) and (e), the selection criteria set forth in paragraph (b), and the functions to be performed, set forth in paragraph (d) of this section.

(i) Each certificate holder shall include in its passenger briefings a request that a passenger identify himself or herself to allow reseating if he or she—

(1) Cannot meet the selection criteria set forth in paragraph (b) of this section;

(2) Has a nondiscernible condition that will prevent him or her from performing the applicable functions listed in paragraph (d) of this section;

(3) May suffer bodily harm as the result of performing one or more of those functions listed in paragraph (d) of this section; or,

(4) Does not wish to perform those functions listed in paragraph (d) of this section. A certificate holder shall not require the passenger to disclose his or her reason for needing reseating.

(j) [Reserved]

(k) In the event a certificate holder determines in accordance with this section that it is likely that a passenger assigned to an exit seat would be unable to perform the functions listed in paragraph (d) of this section or a passenger requests a non-exit seat, the certificate holder shall expeditiously relocate the passenger to a non-exit seat.

(l) In the event of full booking in the non-exit seats and if necessary to accommodate a passenger being relocated from an exit seat, the certificate holder shall move a passenger who is willing and able to assume the evacuation functions that may be required, to an exit seat.

(m) A certificate holder may deny transportation to any passenger under this section only because—

(1) The passenger refuses to comply with instructions given by a crewmember or other authorized employee of the certificate holder implementing exit seating restrictions established in accordance with this section, or

(2) The only seat that will physically accommodate the person's handicap is an exit seat.

(n) In order to comply with this section certificate holders shall—

(1) Establish procedures that address:

(i) The criteria listed in paragraph (b) of this section;

(ii) The functions listed in paragraph (d) of this section;

(iii) The requirements for airport information, passenger information cards, crewmember verification of appropriate seating in exit seats, passenger briefings, seat assignments, and denial of transportation as set forth in this section;

(iv) How to resolve disputes arising from implementation of this section, including identification of the certificate holder employee on the airport to whom complaints should be addressed for resolution; and,

(2) Submit their procedures for preliminary review and approval to the principal operations inspectors assigned to them at the responsible Flight Standards office.

(o) Certificate holders shall assign seats prior to boarding consistent with the criteria listed in paragraph (b) and the functions listed in paragraph (d) of this section, to the maximum extent feasible.

(p) The procedures required by paragraph (n) of this section will not become effective until final approval is granted by the Executive Director, Flight Standards Service, Washington, DC. Approval will be based solely upon the safety aspects of the certificate holder's procedures.

[Doc. No. 25821, 55 FR 8072, Mar. 6, 1990, as amended by Amdt. 121–232, 57 FR 48663, Oct. 27, 1992; Amdt. 121–253, 61 FR 2614, Jan. 26, 1996; Docket FAA–2018–0119, Amdt. 121–380, 83 FR 9172, 9173, Mar. 5, 2018]

§ 121.586 Authority to refuse transportation.

(a) No certificate holder may refuse transportation to a passenger on the basis that, because the passenger may need the assistance of another person to move expeditiously to an exit in the event of an emergency, his transportation would or might be inimical to safety of flight unless—

(1) The certificate holder has established procedures (including reasonable notice requirements) for the carriage of passengers who may need the assistance of another person to move expeditiously to an exit in the event of an emergency; and

(2) At least one of the following conditions exist:

(i) The passenger fails to comply with the notice requirements in the certificate holder's procedures.

(ii) The passenger cannot be carried in accordance with the certificate holder's procedures.

(b) Each certificate holder shall provide the responsible Flight Standards office with a copy of each procedure it establishes in accordance with paragraph (a)(2) of this section.

(c) Whenever the Administrator finds that revisions in the procedures described in paragraph (a)(2) of this section are necessary in the interest of safety or in the public interest, the certificate holder, after notification by the Administrator, shall make those revisions in its procedures. Within 30 days after the certificate holder receives such notice, it may file a petition to reconsider the notice with the responsible Flight Standards office. The filing of a petition to reconsider stays the notice pending a decision by the Administrator. However, if the Administrator finds that there is an emergency that requires immediate action in the interest of safety in air commerce, he may, upon a statement of the reasons, require a change effective without stay.

(d) Each certificate holder shall make available to the public at each airport it serves a copy of each procedure it establishes in accordance with paragraph (a)(1) of this section.

[Doc. No. 12881, 42 FR 18394, Apr. 7, 1977, as amended by Amdt. 121–174, 46 FR 38051, July 23, 1981; Amdt. 121–207, 54 FR 39293, Sept. 25, 1989; Amdt. 121–253, 61 FR 2614, Jan. 26, 1996; Docket FAA–2018–0119, Amdt. 121–380, 83 FR 9172, Mar. 5, 2018]

§121.587 Closing and locking of flightcrew compartment door.

(a) Except as provided in paragraph (b) of this section, a pilot in command of an airplane that has a lockable flightcrew compartment door in accordance with §121.313 and that is carrying passengers shall ensure that the door separating the flightcrew compartment from the passenger compartment is closed and locked at all times when the aircraft is being operated

(b) The provisions of paragraph (a) of this section do not apply at any time when it is necessary to permit access and egress by persons authorized in accordance with §121.547 and provided the part 119 operator complies with FAA approved procedures regarding the opening, closing and locking of the flightdeck doors.

[Doc. No. FAA–2001–11032, 67 FR 2128, Jan. 15, 2002]

§121.589 Carry-on baggage.

(a) No certificate holder may allow the boarding of carry-on baggage on an airplane unless each passenger's baggage has been scanned to control the size and amount carried on board in accordance with an approved carry-on baggage program in its operations specifications. In addition, no passenger may board an airplane if his/her carry-on baggage exceeds the baggage allowance prescribed in the carry-on baggage program in the certificate holder's operations specifications.

(b) No certificate holder may allow all passenger entry doors of an airplane to be closed in preparation for taxi or pushback unless at least one required crewmember has verified that each article of baggage is stowed in accordance with this section and §121.285 (c) and (d).

(c) No certificate holder may allow an airplane to take off or land unless each article of baggage is stowed:

(1) In a suitable closet or baggage or cargo stowage compartment placarded for its maximum weight and providing proper restraint for all baggage or cargo stowed within, and in a manner that does not hinder the possible use of any emergency equipment; or

(2) As provided in §121.285 (c) and (d); or

(3) Under a passenger seat.

(d) Baggage, other than articles of loose clothing, may not be placed in an overhead rack unless that rack is equipped with approved restraining devices or doors.

(e) Each passenger must comply with instructions given by crewmembers regarding compliance with paragraphs (a), (b), (c), (d), and (g) of this section.

(f) Each passenger seat under which baggage is allowed to be stowed shall be fitted with a means to prevent articles of baggage stowed under it from sliding forward. In addition, each aisle seat shall be fitted with a means to prevent articles of baggage stowed under it from sliding sideward into the aisle under crash impacts severe enough to induce the ultimate inertia forces specified in the emergency landing condition regulations under which the airplane was type certificated.

(g) In addition to the methods of stowage in paragraph (c) of this section, flexible travel canes carried by blind individuals may be stowed—

(1) Under any series of connected passenger seats in the same row, if the cane does not protrude into an aisle and if the cane is flat on the floor; or

(2) Between a nonemergency exit window seat and the fuselage, if the cane is flat on the floor; or

(3) Beneath any two nonemergency exit window seats, if the cane is flat on the floor; or

(4) In accordance with any other method approved by the Administrator.

[Doc. No. 24996, 52 FR 21476, June 5, 1987, as amended by Amdt. 121–251, 60 FR 65935, Dec. 20, 1995]

§ 121.590 Use of certificated land airports in the United States.

(a) Except as provided in paragraphs (b) or (c) of this section, or unless authorized by the Administrator under 49 U.S.C. 44706(c), no air carrier and no pilot being used by an air carrier may operate, in the conduct of a domestic type operation, flag type operation, or supplemental type operation, an airplane at a land airport in any State of the United States, the District of Columbia, or any territory or possession of the United States unless that airport is certificated under part 139 of this chapter. Further, after June 9, 2005 for Class I airports and after December 9, 2005 for Class II, III, and IV airports, when an air carrier and a pilot being used by the air carrier are required to operate at an airport certificated under part 139 of this chapter, the air carrier and the pilot may only operate at that airport if the airport is classified under part 139 to serve the type airplane to be operated and the type of operation to be conducted.

(b)(1) An air carrier and a pilot being used by the air carrier in the conduct of a domestic type operation, flag type operation, or supplemental type operation may designate and use as a required alternate airport for departure or destination an airport that is not certificated under part 139 of this chapter.

(2) Until December 9, 2005, an air carrier and a pilot being used by the air carrier in the conduct of domestic type operations and flag type operations, may operate an airplane designed for more than 9 but less than 31 passenger seats, at a land airport, in any State of the United States, the District of Columbia, or any territory or possession of the United States, that does not hold an airport operating certificate issued under part 139 of this chapter, and that serves small air carrier aircraft (as defined under "Air carrier aircraft" and "Class III airport" in § 139.5 of this Chapter).

(c) An air carrier and a pilot used by the air carrier in conducting a domestic type operation, flag type operation, or supplemental type operation may operate an airplane at an airport operated by the U.S. Government that is not certificated under part 139 of this chapter, only if that airport meets the equivalent—

(1) Safety standards for airports certificated under part 139 of this chapter; and

(2) Airport classification requirements under part 139 to serve the type airplane to be operated and the type of operation to be conducted.

(d) An air carrier, a commercial operator, and a pilot being used by the air carrier or the commercial operator—when conducting a passenger-carrying airplane operation under this part that is not a domestic type operation, a flag type operation, or a supplemental type operation—may operate at a land airport not certificated under part 139 of this chapter only when the following conditions are met:

(1) The airport is adequate for the proposed operation, considering such items as size, surface, obstructions, and lighting.

(2) For an airplane carrying passengers at night, the pilot may not take off from, or land at, an airport unless—

(i) The pilot has determined the wind direction from an illuminated wind direction indicator or local ground communications or, in the case of takeoff, that pilot's personal observations; and

(ii) The limits of the area to be used for landing or takeoff are clearly shown by boundary or runway marker lights. If the area to be used for takeoff or landing is marked by flare pots or lanterns, their use must be authorized by the Administrator.

(e) A commercial operator and a pilot used by the commercial operator in conducting a domestic type operation, flag type operation, or supplemental type operation may operate an airplane at an airport operated by the U.S. Government that is not certificated under part 139 of this chapter only if that airport meets the equivalent—

(1) Safety standards for airports certificated under part 139 of this chapter; and

(2) Airport classification requirements under part 139 of this chapter to serve the type airplane to be operated and the type of operation to be conducted.

(f) For the purpose of this section, the terms—

Domestic type operation means any domestic operation conducted with—

(1) An airplane designed for at least 31 passenger seats (as determined by the aircraft type certificate issued by a competent civil aviation authority) at any land airport in any State of the United States, the District of Columbia, or any territory or possession of the United States; or

(2) An airplane designed for more than 9 passenger seats but less than 31 passenger seats (as determined by the aircraft type certificate issued by a competent civil aviation authority) at any land airport in any State of the United States (except Alaska), the District of Columbia, or any territory or possession of the United States.

Flag type operation means any flag operation conducted with—

(1) An airplane designed for at least 31 passenger seats (as determined by the aircraft type certificate issued by a competent civil aviation authority) at any land airport in any State of the United States, the District of Columbia, or any territory or possession of the United States; or

(2) An airplane designed for more than 9 passenger seats but less than 31 passenger seats (as determined by the aircraft type certificate issued by a competent civil aviation authority) at any land airport in any State of the United States (except Alaska), the District of Columbia, or any territory or possession of the United States.

Supplemental type operation means any supplemental operation (except an all-cargo operation) conducted with an airplane designed for at least 31 passenger seats (as determined by the aircraft type certificate issued by a competent civil aviation authority) at any land airport in any State of the United States, the District of Columbia, or any territory or possession of the United States.

United States means the States of the United States, the District of Colum

bia, and the territories and possessions of the United States.

NOTE: Special Statutory Requirement to Operate to or From a Part 139 Airport. Each air carrier that provides—in an aircraft (e.g., airplane, rotorcraft, etc.) designed for more than 9 passenger seats—regularly scheduled charter air transportation for which the public is provided in advance a schedule containing the departure location, departure time, and arrival location of the flight must operate to and from an airport certificated under part 139 of this chapter in accordance with 49 U.S.C. 41104(b). That statutory provision contains stand-alone requirements for such air carriers and special exceptions for operations in Alaska and outside the United States. Nothing in §121.590 exempts the air carriers described in this note from the requirements of 49 U.S.C. 41104(b). Certain operations by air carriers that conduct public charter operations under 14 CFR part 380 are covered by the statutory requirements to operate to and from part 139 airports. *See* 49 U.S.C. 41104(b).

[Doc. No. FAA–2000–7479, 69 FR 6424, Feb. 10, 2004; Amdt. 121–304, 69 FR 31522, June 4, 2004]

Subpart U—Dispatching and Flight Release Rules

SOURCE: Docket No. 6258, 29 FR 19222, Dec. 31, 1964, unless otherwise noted.

§121.591 Applicability.

This subpart prescribes dispatching rules for domestic and flag operations and flight release rules for supplemental operations.

[Doc. No. 28154, 61 FR 2614, Jan. 26, 1996]

§121.593 Dispatching authority: Domestic operations.

Except when an airplane lands at an intermediate airport specified in the original dispatch release and remains there for not more than one hour, no person may start a flight unless an aircraft dispatcher specifically authorizes that flight.

§121.595 Dispatching authority: Flag operations.

(a) No person may start a flight unless an aircraft dispatcher specifically authorizes that flight.

(b) No person may continue a flight from an intermediate airport without redispatch if the airplane has been on the ground more than six hours.

§ 121.597　Flight release authority: Supplemental operations.

(a) No person may start a flight under a flight following system without specific authority from the person authorized by the operator to exercise operational control over the flight.

(b) No person may start a flight unless the pilot in command or the person authorized by the operator to exercise operational control over the flight has executed a flight release setting forth the conditions under which the flights will be conducted. The pilot in command may sign the flight release only when he and the person authorized by the operator to exercise operational control believe that the flight can be made with safety.

(c) No person may continue a flight from an intermediate airport without a new flight release if the aircraft has been on the ground more than six hours.

[Doc. No. 6258, 29 FR 19222, Dec. 31, 1964, as amended by Amdt. 121–3, 30 FR 3639, Mar. 19, 1965]

§ 121.599　Familiarity with weather conditions.

(a) *Domestic and flag operations.* No aircraft dispatcher may release a flight unless he is thoroughly familiar with reported and forecast weather conditions on the route to be flown.

(b) *Supplemental operations.* No pilot in command may begin a flight unless he is thoroughly familiar with reported and forecast weather conditions on the route to be flown.

[Doc. No. 6258, 29 FR 19222, Dec. 31, 1964, as amended by Amdt. 121–253, 61 FR 2614, Jan. 26, 1996]

§ 121.601　Aircraft dispatcher information to pilot in command: Domestic and flag operations.

(a) The aircraft dispatcher shall provide the pilot in command all available current reports or information on airport conditions and irregularities of navigation facilities that may affect the safety of the flight.

(b) Before beginning a flight, the aircraft dispatcher shall provide the pilot in command with all available weather reports and forecasts of weather phenomena that may affect the safety of flight, including adverse weather phenomena, such as clear air turbulence, thunderstorms, and low altitude wind shear, for each route to be flown and each airport to be used.

(c) During a flight, the aircraft dispatcher shall provide the pilot in command any additional available information of meteorological conditions (including adverse weather phenomena, such as clear air turbulence, thunderstorms, and low altitude wind shear), and irregularities of facilities and services that may affect the safety of the flight.

[Doc. No. 6258, 29 FR 19222, Dec. 31, 1964, as amended by Amdt. 121–134, 42 FR 27573, May 31, 1977; Amdt. 121–144, 43 FR 22649, May 25, 1978; Amdt. 121–253, 61 FR 2614, Jan. 26, 1996]

§ 121.603　Facilities and services: Supplemental operations.

(a) Before beginning a flight, each pilot in command shall obtain all available current reports or information on airport conditions and irregularities of navigation facilities that may affect the safety of the flight.

(b) During a flight, the pilot in command shall obtain any additional available information of meteorological conditions and irregularities of facilities and services that may affect the safety of the flight.

§ 121.605　Airplane equipment.

No person may dispatch or release an airplane unless it is airworthy and is equipped as prescribed in § 121.303.

§ 121.607　Communication and navigation facilities: Domestic and flag operations.

(a) Except as provided in paragraph (b) of this section for a certificate holder conducting flag operations, no person may dispatch an airplane over an approved route or route segment unless the communication and navigation facilities required by §§ 121.99 and 121.103 for the approval of that route or segment are in satisfactory operating condition.

(b) If, because of technical reasons or other reasons beyond the control of a certificate holder conducting flag operations, the facilities required by §§ 121.99 and 121.103 are not available over a route or route segment outside the United States, the certificate holder may dispatch an airplane over that route or route segment if the pilot in command and dispatcher find that communication and navigation facilities equal to those required are available and are in satisfactory operating condition.

[Doc. No. 6258, 29 FR 19222, Dec. 31, 1964, as amended by Amdt. 121–253, 61 FR 2614, Jan. 26, 1996]

§ 121.609 Communication and navigation facilities: Supplemental operations.

No person may release an aircraft over any route or route segment unless communication and navigation facilities equal to those required by § 121.121 are in satisfactory operating condition.

§ 121.611 Dispatch or flight release under VFR.

No person may dispatch or release an aircraft for VFR operation unless the ceiling and visibility en route, as indicated by available weather reports or forecasts, or any combination thereof, are and will remain at or above applicable VFR minimums until the aircraft arrives at the airport or airports specified in the dispatch or flight release.

§ 121.613 Dispatch or flight release under IFR or over the top.

Except as provided in § 121.615, no person may dispatch or release an aircraft for operations under IFR or over-the-top, unless appropriate weather reports or forecasts, or any combination thereof, indicate that the weather conditions will be at or above the authorized minimums at the estimated time of arrival at the airport or airports to which dispatched or released.

[Doc. No. 6258, 29 FR 19222, Dec. 31, 1964, as amended by Amdt. 121–33, 32 FR 13912, Oct. 6, 1967]

§ 121.615 Dispatch or flight release over water: Flag and supplemental operations.

(a) No person may dispatch or release an aircraft for a flight that involves extended overwater operation unless appropriate weather reports or forecasts or any combination thereof, indicate that the weather conditions will be at or above the authorized minimums at the estimated time of arrival at any airport to which dispatched or released or to any required alternate airport.

(b) Each certificate holder conducting a flag or supplemental operation or a domestic operation within the State of Alaska shall conduct extended overwater operations under IFR unless it shows that operating under IFR is not necessary for safety.

(c) Each certificate holder conducting a flag or supplemental operation or a domestic operation within the State of Alaska shall conduct other overwater operations under IFR if the Administrator determines that operation under IFR is necessary for safety.

(d) Each authorization to conduct extended overwater operations under VFR and each requirement to conduct other overwater operations under IFR will be specified in the certificate holder's operations specifications.

[Doc. No. 6258, 29 FR 19222, Dec. 31, 1964, as amended by Amdt. 121–33, 32 FR 13912, Oct. 6, 1967; Amdt. 121–253, 61 FR 2614, Jan. 26, 1996]

§ 121.617 Alternate airport for departure.

(a) If the weather conditions at the airport of takeoff are below the landing minimums in the certificate holder's operations specifications for that airport, no person may dispatch or release an aircraft from that airport unless the dispatch or flight release specifies an alternate airport located within the following distances from the airport of takeoff:

(1) *Aircraft having two engines.* Not more than one hour from the departure airport at normal cruising speed in still air with one engine inoperative.

(2) *Aircraft having three or more engines.* Not more than two hours from the departure airport at normal cruising speed in still air with one engine inoperative.

(b) For the purpose of paragraph (a) of this section, the alternate airport weather conditions must meet the requirements of the certificate holder's operations specifications.

(c) No person may dispatch or release an aircraft from an airport unless he lists each required alternate airport in the dispatch or flight release.

§ 121.619 Alternate airport for destination: IFR or over-the-top: Domestic operations.

(a) No person may dispatch an airplane under IFR or over-the-top unless he lists at least one alternate airport for each destination airport in the dispatch release. When the weather conditions forecast for the destination and first alternate airport are marginal at least one additional alternate must be designated. However, no alternate airport is required if for at least 1 hour before and 1 hour after the estimated time of arrival at the destination airport the appropriate weather reports or forecasts, or any combination of them, indicate—

(1) The ceiling will be at least 2,000 feet above the airport elevation; and

(2) Visibility will be at least 3 miles.

(b) For the purposes of paragraph (a) of this section, the weather conditions at the alternate airport must meet the requirements of § 121.625.

(c) No person may dispatch a flight unless he lists each required alternate airport in the dispatch release.

[Doc. No. 6258, 29 FR 19222, Dec. 31, 1964, as amended by Amdt. 121–159, 45 FR 41594, June 19, 1980]

§ 121.621 Alternate airport for destination: Flag operations.

(a) No person may dispatch an airplane under IFR or over-the-top unless he lists at least one alternate airport for each destination airport in the dispatch release, unless—

(1) The flight is scheduled for not more than 6 hours and, for at least 1 hour before and 1 hour after the estimated time of arrival at the destination airport, the appropriate weather reports or forecasts, or any combination of them, indicate the ceiling will be:

(i) At least 1,500 feet above the lowest circling MDA, if a circling approach is required and authorized for that airport; or

(ii) At least 1,500 feet above the lowest published instrument approach minimum or 2,000 feet above the airport elevation, whichever is greater; and

(iii) The visibility at that airport will be at least 3 miles, or 2 miles more than the lowest applicable visibility minimums, whichever is greater, for the instrument approach procedures to be used at the destination airport; or

(2) The flight is over a route approved without an available alternate airport for a particular destination airport and the airplane has enough fuel to meet the requirements of § 121.641(b) or § 121.645(c).

(b) For the purposes of paragraph (a) of this section, the weather conditions at the alternate airport must meet the requirements of the certificate holder's operations specifications.

(c) No person may dispatch a flight unless he lists each required alternate airport in the dispatch release.

[Doc. No. 6258, 29 FR 19222, Dec. 31, 1964, as amended by Amdt. 121–159, 45 FR 41594, June 19, 1980; Amdt. 121–253, 61 FR 2614, Jan. 26, 1996]

§ 121.623 Alternate airport for destination: IFR or over-the-top: Supplemental operations.

(a) Except as provided in paragraph (b) of this section, each person releasing an aircraft for operation under IFR or over-the-top shall list at least one alternate airport for each destination airport in the flight release.

(b) An alternate airport need not be designated for IFR or over-the-top operations where the aircraft carries enough fuel to meet the requirements of §§ 121.643 and 121.645 for flights outside the 48 contiguous States and the District of Columbia over routes without an available alternate airport for a particular airport of destination.

(c) For the purposes of paragraph (a) of this section, the weather requirements at the alternate airport must meet the requirements of the certificate holder's operations specifications.

(d) No person may release a flight unless he lists each required alternate airport in the flight release.

[Doc. No. 6258, 29 FR 19222, Dec. 31, 1964, as amended by Amdt. 121–253, 61 FR 2614, Jan. 26, 1996]

§ 121.624 ETOPS Alternate Airports.

(a) No person may dispatch or release an airplane for an ETOPS flight unless enough ETOPS Alternate Airports are listed in the dispatch or flight release such that the airplane remains within the authorized ETOPS maximum diversion time. In selecting these ETOPS Alternate Airports, the certificate holder must consider all adequate airports within the authorized ETOPS diversion time for the flight that meet the standards of this part.

(b) No person may list an airport as an ETOPS Alternate Airport in a dispatch or flight release unless, when it might be used (from the earliest to the latest possible landing time)—

(1) The appropriate weather reports or forecasts, or any combination thereof, indicate that the weather conditions will be at or above the ETOPS Alternate Airport minima specified in the certificate holder's operations specifications; and

(2) The field condition reports indicate that a safe landing can be made.

(c) Once a flight is en route, the weather conditions at each ETOPS Alternate Airport must meet the requirements of §121.631 (c).

(d) No person may list an airport as an ETOPS Alternate Airport in the dispatch or flight release unless that airport meets the public protection requirements of §121.97(b)(1)(ii).

[Doc. No. FAA–2002–6717, 72 FR 1881, Jan. 16, 2007]

§121.625 Alternate Airport weather minima.

Except as provided in §121.624 for ETOPS Alternate Airports, no person may list an airport as an alternate in the dispatch or flight release unless the appropriate weather reports or forecasts, or any combination thereof, indicate that the weather conditions will be at or above the alternate weather minima specified in the certificate holder's operations specifications for that airport when the flight arrives

[Doc. No. FAA–2002–6717, 72 FR 1881, Jan. 16, 2007]

§121.627 Continuing flight in unsafe conditions.

(a) No pilot in command may allow a flight to continue toward any airport to which it has been dispatched or released if, in the opinion of the pilot in command or dispatcher (domestic and flag operations only), the flight cannot be completed safely; unless, in the opinion of the pilot in command, there

is no safer procedure. In that event, continuation toward that airport is an emergency situation as set forth in §121.557.

(b) If any instrument or item of equipment required under this chapter for the particular operation becomes inoperative en route, the pilot in command shall comply with the approved procedures for such an occurrence as specified in the certificate holder's manual.

[Doc. No. 6258, 29 FR 1922, Dec. 31, 1964, as amended by Amdt. 121–222, 56 FR 12310, Mar. 22, 1991; Amdt. 121–253, 61 FR 2615, Jan. 26, 1996]

§121.628 Inoperable instruments and equipment.

(a) No person may take off an airplane with inoperable instruments or equipment installed unless the following conditions are met:

(1) An approved Minimum Equipment List exists for that airplane.

(2) The responsible Flight Standards office has issued the certificate holder operations specifications authorizing operations in accordance with an approved Minimum Equipment List. The flight crew shall have direct access at all times prior to flight to all of the information contained in the approved Minimum Equipment List through printed or other means approved by the Administrator in the certificate holders operations specifications. An approved Minimum Equipment List, as authorized by the operations specifications, constitutes an approved change to the type design without requiring recertification.

(3) The approved Minimum Equipment List must:

(i) Be prepared in accordance with the limitations specified in paragraph (b) of this section.

(ii) Provide for the operation of the airplane with certain instruments and equipment in an inoperable condition.

(4) Records identifying the inoperable instruments and equipment and the information required by paragraph (a)(3)(ii) of this section must be available to the pilot.

(5) The airplane is operated under all applicable conditions and limitations contained in the Minimum Equipment List and the operations specifications

authorizing use of the Minimum Equipment List.

(b) The following instruments and equipment may not be included in the Minimum Equipment List:

(1) Instruments and equipment that are either specifically or otherwise required by the airworthiness requirements under which the airplane is type certificated and which are essential for safe operations under all operating conditions.

(2) Instruments and equipment required by an airworthiness directive to be in operable condition unless the airworthiness directive provides otherwise.

(3) Instruments and equipment required for specific operations by this part.

(c) Notwithstanding paragraphs (b)(1) and (b)(3) of this section, an airplane with inoperable instruments or equipment may be operated under a special flight permit under §§ 21.197 and 21.199 of this chapter.

[Doc. No. 25780, 56 FR 12310, Mar. 22, 1991; Amdt. 121–222, 56 FR 14290, Apr. 8, 1991; Amdt. 121–253, 61 FR 2615, Jan. 26, 1996; Docket FAA–2018–0119, Amdt. 121–380, 83 FR 9172, Mar. 5, 2018]

§ 121.629 Operation in icing conditions.

(a) No person may dispatch or release an aircraft, continue to operate an aircraft en route, or land an aircraft when in the opinion of the pilot in command or aircraft dispatcher (domestic and flag operations only) icing conditions are expected or met that might adversely affect the safety of the flight.

(b) No person may take off an aircraft when frost, ice, or snow is adhering to the wings, control surfaces, propellers, engine inlets, or other critical surfaces of the aircraft or when the takeoff would not be in compliance with paragraph (c) of this section. Takeoffs with frost under the wing in the area of the fuel tanks may be authorized by the Administrator.

(c) Except as provided in paragraph (d) of this section, no person may dispatch, release, or take off an aircraft any time conditions are such that frost, ice, or snow may reasonably be expected to adhere to the aircraft, unless the certificate holder has an approved ground deicing/anti-icing program in its operations specifications and unless the dispatch, release, and takeoff comply with that program. The approved ground deicing/anti-icing program must include at least the following items:

(1) A detailed description of—

(i) How the certificate holder determines that conditions are such that frost, ice, or snow may reasonably be expected to adhere to the aircraft and that ground deicing/anti-icing operational procedures must be in effect;

(ii) Who is responsible for deciding that ground deicing/anti-icing operational procedures must be in effect;

(iii) The procedures for implementing ground deicing/anti-icing operational procedures;

(iv) The specific duties and responsibilities of each operational position or group responsible for getting the aircraft safely airborne while ground deicing/anti-icing operational procedures are in effect.

(2) Initial and annual recurrent ground training and testing for flight crewmembers and qualification for all other affected personnel (e.g., aircraft dispatchers, ground crews, contract personnel) concerning the specific requirements of the approved program and each person's responsibilities and duties under the approved program, specifically covering the following areas:

(i) The use of holdover times.

(ii) Aircraft deicing/anti-icing procedures, including inspection and check procedures and responsibilities.

(iii) Communications procedures.

(iv) Aircraft surface contamination (i.e., adherence of frost, ice, or snow) and critical area identification, and how contamination adversely affects aircraft performance and flight characteristics.

(v) Types and characteristics of deicing/anti-icing fluids.

(vi) Cold weather preflight inspection procedures;

(vii) Techniques for recognizing contamination on the aircraft.

(3) The certificate holder's holdover timetables and the procedures for the use of these tables by the certificate holder's personnel. Holdover time is the estimated time deicing/anti-icing

fluid will prevent the formation of frost or ice and the accumulation of snow on the protected surfaces of an aircraft. Holdover time begins when the final application of deicing/anti-icing fluid commences and expires when the deicing/anti-icing fluid applied to the aircraft loses its effectiveness. The holdover times must be supported by data acceptable to the Administrator. The certificate holder's program must include procedures for flight crewmembers to increase or decrease the determined holdover time in changing conditions. The program must provide that takeoff after exceeding any maximum holdover time in the certificate holder's holdover timetable is permitted only when at least one of the following conditions exists:

(i) A pretakeoff contamination check, as defined in paragraph (c)(4) of this section, determines that the wings, control surfaces, and other critical surfaces, as defined in the certificate holder's program, are free of frost, ice, or snow.

(ii) It is otherwise determined by an alternate procedure approved by the Administrator in accordance with the certificate holder's approved program that the wings, control surfaces, and other critical surfaces, as defined in the certificate holder's program, are free of frost, ice, or snow.

(iii) The wings, control surfaces, and other critical surfaces are redeiced and a new holdover time is determined.

(4) Aircraft deicing/anti-icing procedures and responsibilities, pretakeoff check procedures and responsibilities, and pretakeoff contamination check procedures and responsibilities. A pretakeoff check is a check of the aircraft's wings or representative aircraft surfaces for frost, ice, or snow within the aircraft's holdover time. A pretakeoff contamination check is a check to make sure the wings, control surfaces, and other critical surfaces, as defined in the certificate holder's program, are free of frost, ice, and snow. It must be conducted within five minutes prior to beginning take off. This check must be accomplished from outside the aircraft unless the program specifies otherwise.

(d) A certificate holder may continue to operate under this section without a program as required in paragraph (c) of this section, if it includes in its operations specifications a requirement that, any time conditions are such that frost, ice, or snow may reasonably be expected to adhere to the aircraft, no aircraft will take off unless it has been checked to ensure that the wings, control surfaces, and other critical surfaces are free of frost, ice, and snow. The check must occur within five minutes prior to beginning takeoff. This check must be accomplished from outside the aircraft.

[Doc. No. 6258, 29 FR 19222, Dec. 31, 1964, as amended by Amdt. 121–231, 57 FR 44942, Sept. 29, 1992; Amdt. 121–253, 61 FR 2615, Jan. 26, 1996]

§ 121.631 Original dispatch or flight release, redispatch or amendment of dispatch or flight release.

(a) A certificate holder may specify any regular, provisional, or refueling airport, authorized for the type of aircraft, as a destination for the purpose of original dispatch or release.

(b) No person may allow a flight to continue to an airport to which it has been dispatched or released unless the weather conditions at an alternate airport that was specified in the dispatch or flight release are forecast to be at or above the alternate minimums specified in the operations specifications for that airport at the time the aircraft would arrive at the alternate airport. However, the dispatch or flight release may be amended en route to include any alternate airport that is within the fuel range of the aircraft as specified in §§ 121.639 through 121.647.

(c) No person may allow a flight to continue beyond the ETOPS Entry Point unless—

(1) Except as provided in paragraph (d) of this section, the weather conditions at each ETOPS Alternate Airport required by § 121.624 are forecast to be at or above the operating minima for that airport in the certificate holder's operations specifications when it might be used (from the earliest to the latest possible landing time); and

(2) All ETOPS Alternate Airports within the authorized ETOPS maximum diversion time are reviewed and the flight crew advised of any changes

in conditions that have occurred since dispatch.

(d) If paragraph (c)(1) of this section cannot be met for a specific airport, the dispatch or flight release may be amended to add an ETOPS Alternate Airport within the maximum ETOPS diversion time that could be authorized for that flight with weather conditions at or above operating minima.

(e) Before the ETOPS Entry Point, the pilot in command for a supplemental operator or a dispatcher for a flag operator must use company communications to update the flight plan if needed because of a re-evaluation of aircraft system capabilities.

(f) No person may change an original destination or alternate airport that is specified in the original dispatch or flight release to another airport while the aircraft is en route unless the other airport is authorized for that type of aircraft and the appropriate requirements of §§ 121.593 through 121.661 and 121.173 are met at the time of redispatch or amendment of the flight release.

(g) Each person who amends a dispatch or flight release en route shall record that amendment.

[Doc. No. 628, 29 FR 19222, Dec. 31, 1964, as amended by Amdt. 121–65, 35 FR 12709, Aug. 11, 1970; Amdt. 121–329, 72 FR 1881, Jan. 16, 2007]

§ 121.633 Considering time-limited systems in planning ETOPS alternates.

(a) For ETOPS up to and including 180 minutes, no person may list an airport as an ETOPS Alternate Airport in a dispatch or flight release if the time needed to fly to that airport (at the approved one-engine inoperative cruise speed under standard conditions in still air) would exceed the approved time for the airplane's most limiting ETOPS Significant System (including the airplane's most limiting fire suppression system time for those cargo and baggage compartments required by regulation to have fire-suppression systems) minus 15 minutes.

(b) For ETOPS beyond 180 minutes, no person may list an airport as an ETOPS Alternate Airport in a dispatch or flight release if the time needed to fly to that airport:

(1) at the all engine operating cruise speed, corrected for wind and temperature, exceeds the airplane's most limiting fire suppression system time minus 15 minutes for those cargo and baggage compartments required by regulation to have fire suppression systems (except as provided in paragraph (c) of this section), or

(2) at the one-engine-inoperative cruise speed, corrected for wind and temperature, exceeds the airplane's most limiting ETOPS Significant System time (other than the airplane's most limiting fire suppression system time minus 15 minutes for those cargo and baggage compartments required by regulation to have fire-suppression systems).

(c) For turbine-engine powered airplanes with more than two engines, the certificate holder need not meet paragraph (b)(1) of this section until February 15, 2013.

[Doc. No. FAA–2002–6717, 72 FR 1882, Jan. 16, 2007]

§ 121.635 Dispatch to and from refueling or provisional airports: Domestic and flag operations.

No person may dispatch an airplane to or from a refueling or provisional airport except in accordance with the requirements of this part applicable to dispatch from regular airports and unless that airport meets the requirements of this part applicable to regular airports.

[Doc. No. 16383, 43 FR 22649, May 25, 1978]

§ 121.637 Takeoffs from unlisted and alternate airports: Domestic and flag operations.

(a) No pilot may takeoff an airplane from an airport that is not listed in the operations specifications unless—

(1) The airport and related facilities are adequate for the operation of the airplane;

(2) He can comply with the applicable airplane operating limitations;

(3) The airplane has been dispatched according to dispatching rules applicable to operation from an approved airport; and

(4) The weather conditions at that airport are equal to or better than the following:

(i) *Airports in the United States.* The weather minimums for takeoff prescribed in part 97 of this chapter; or where minimums are not prescribed for the airport, 800–2, 900–1½, or 1,000–1.

(ii) *Airports outside the United States.* The weather minimums for takeoff prescribed or approved by the government of the country in which the airport is located; or where minimums are not prescribed or approved for the airport, 800–2, 900–1½, or 1,000–1.

(b) No pilot may take off from an alternate airport unless the weather conditions are at least equal to the minimums prescribed in the certificate holder's operations specifications for alternate airports.

[Doc. No. 6258, 29 FR 19222, Dec. 31, 1964, as amended by Amdt. 121–33, 32 FR 13912, Oct. 6, 1967; Amdt. 121–253, 61 FR 2615, Jan. 26, 1996]

§ 121.639 Fuel supply: All domestic operations.

No person may dispatch or take off an airplane unless it has enough fuel—

(a) To fly to the airport to which it is dispatched;

(b) Thereafter, to fly to and land at the most distant alternate airport (where required) for the airport to which dispatched; and

(c) Thereafter, to fly for 45 minutes at normal cruising fuel consumption or, for certificate holders who are authorized to conduct day VFR operations in their operations specifications and who are operating nontransport category airplanes type certificated after December 31, 1964, to fly for 30 minutes at normal cruising fuel consumption for day VFR operations.

[Doc. No. 6258, 29 FR 19222, Dec. 31, 1964, as amended by Amdt. 121–251, 60 FR 65935, Dec. 20, 1995]

§ 121.641 Fuel supply: Nonturbine and turbo-propeller-powered airplanes: Flag operations.

(a) No person may dispatch or take off a nonturbine or turbo-propeller-powered airplane unless, considering the wind and other weather conditions expected, it has enough fuel—

(1) To fly to and land at the airport to which it is dispatched;

(2) Thereafter, to fly to and land at the most distant alternate airport specified in the dispatch release; and

(3) Thereafter, to fly for 30 minutes plus 15 percent of the total time required to fly at normal cruising fuel consumption to the airports specified in paragraphs (a) (1) and (2) of this section or to fly for 90 minutes at normal cruising fuel consumption, whichever is less.

(b) No person may dispatch a nonturbine or turbo-propeller-powered airplane to an airport for which an alternate is not specified under § 121.621(a)(2), unless it has enough fuel, considering wind and forecast weather conditions, to fly to that airport and thereafter to fly for three hours at normal cruising fuel consumption.

§ 121.643 Fuel supply: Nonturbine and turbo-propeller-powered airplanes: Supplemental operations.

(a) Except as provided in paragraph (b) of this section, no person may release for flight or takeoff a nonturbine or turbo-propeller-powered airplane unless, considering the wind and other weather conditions expected, it has enough fuel—

(1) To fly to and land at the airport to which it is released;

(2) Thereafter, to fly to and land at the most distant alternate airport specified in the flight release; and

(3) Thereafter, to fly for 45 minutes at normal cruising fuel consumption or, for certificate holders who are authorized to conduct day VFR operations in their operations specifications and who are operating nontransport category airplanes type certificated after December 31, 1964, to fly for 30 minutes at normal cruising fuel consumption for day VFR operations.

(b) If the airplane is released for any flight other than from one point in the contiguous United States to another point in the contiguous United States, it must carry enough fuel to meet the requirements of paragraphs (a) (1) and (2) of this section and thereafter fly for 30 minutes plus 15 percent of the total time required to fly at normal cruising fuel consumption to the airports specified in paragraphs (a) (1) and (2) of this section, or to fly for 90 minutes at normal cruising fuel consumption, whichever is less.

(c) No person may release a nonturbine or turbo-propeller-powered airplane to an airport for which an alternate is not specified under § 121.623(b), unless it has enough fuel, considering wind and other weather conditions expected, to fly to that airport and thereafter to fly for three hours at normal cruising fuel consumption.

[Doc. No. 6258, 29 FR 19222, Dec. 31, 1964, as amended by Amdt. 121–10, 30 FR 10025, Aug. 12, 1965; Amdt. 121–251, 60 FR 65935, Dec. 20, 1995]

§ 121.645 Fuel supply: Turbine-engine powered airplanes, other than turbo propeller: Flag and supplemental operations.

(a) Any flag operation within the 48 contiguous United States and the District of Columbia may use the fuel requirements of § 121.639.

(b) For any certificate holder conducting flag or supplemental operations outside the 48 contiguous United States and the District of Columbia, unless authorized by the Administrator in the operations specifications, no person may release for flight or takeoff a turbine-engine powered airplane (other than a turbo-propeller powered airplane) unless, considering wind and other weather conditions expected, it has enough fuel—

(1) To fly to and land at the airport to which it is released;

(2) After that, to fly for a period of 10 percent of the total time required to fly from the airport of departure to, and land at, the airport to which it was released;

(3) After that, to fly to and land at the most distant alternate airport specified in the flight release, if an alternate is required; and

(4) After that, to fly for 30 minutes at holding speed at 1,500 feet above the alternate airport (or the destination airport if no alternate is required) under standard temperature conditions.

(c) No person may release a turbine-engine powered airplane (other than a turbo-propeller airplane) to an airport for which an alternate is not specified under § 121.621(a)(2) or § 121.623(b) unless it has enough fuel, considering wind and other weather conditions expected, to fly to that airport and thereafter to fly for at least two hours at normal cruising fuel consumption.

(d) The Administrator may amend the operations specifications of a certificate holder conducting flag or supplemental operations to require more fuel than any of the minimums stated in paragraph (a) or (b) of this section if he finds that additional fuel is necessary on a particular route in the interest of safety.

(e) For a supplemental operation within the 48 contiguous States and the District of Columbia with a turbine engine powered airplane the fuel requirements of § 121.643 apply.

[Doc. No. 6258, 29 FR 19222, Dec. 31, 1964, as amended by Amdt. 121–10, 30 FR 10025, Aug. 12, 1965; Amdt. 121–144, 43 FR 22649, May 25, 1978; Amdt. 121–253, 61 FR 2615, Jan. 26, 1996]

§ 121.646 En-route fuel supply: flag and supplemental operations.

(a) No person may dispatch or release for flight a turbine-engine powered airplane with more than two engines for a flight more than 90 minutes (with all engines operating at cruise power) from an Adequate Airport unless the following fuel supply requirements are met:

(1) The airplane has enough fuel to meet the requirements of § 121.645(b);

(2) The airplane has enough fuel to fly to the Adequate Airport—

(i) Assuming a rapid decompression at the most critical point;

(ii) Assuming a descent to a safe altitude in compliance with the oxygen supply requirements of § 121.333; and

(iii) Considering expected wind and other weather conditions.

(3) The airplane has enough fuel to hold for 15 minutes at 1500 feet above field elevation and conduct a normal approach and landing.

(b) No person may dispatch or release for flight an ETOPS flight unless, considering wind and other weather conditions expected, it has the fuel otherwise required by this part and enough fuel to satisfy each of the following requirements:

(1) Fuel to fly to an ETOPS Alternate Airport.

(i) Fuel to account for rapid decompression and engine failure. The airplane must carry the greater of the following amounts of fuel:

(A) Fuel sufficient to fly to an ETOPS Alternate Airport assuming a rapid decompression at the most critical point followed by descent to a safe altitude in compliance with the oxygen supply requirements of § 121.333 of this chapter;

(B) Fuel sufficient to fly to an ETOPS Alternate Airport (at the one-engine-inoperative cruise speed) assuming a rapid decompression and a simultaneous engine failure at the most critical point followed by descent to a safe altitude in compliance with the oxygen requirements of § 121.333 of this chapter; or

(C) Fuel sufficient to fly to an ETOPS Alternate Airport (at the one engine inoperative cruise speed) assuming an engine failure at the most critical point followed by descent to the one engine inoperative cruise altitude.

(ii) Fuel to account for errors in wind forecasting. In calculating the amount of fuel required by paragraph (b)(1)(i) of this section, the certificate holder must increase the actual forecast wind speed by 5% (resulting in an increase in headwind or a decrease in tailwind) to account for any potential errors in wind forecasting. If a certificate holder is not using the actual forecast wind based on a wind model accepted by the FAA, the airplane must carry additional fuel equal to 5% of the fuel required for paragraph (b)(1)(i) of this section, as reserve fuel to allow for errors in wind data.

(iii) Fuel to account for icing. In calculating the amount of fuel required by paragraph (b)(1)(i) of this section (after completing the wind calculation in paragraph (b)(1)(ii) of this section), the certificate holder must ensure that the airplane carries the greater of the following amounts of fuel in anticipation of possible icing during the diversion:

(A) Fuel that would be burned as a result of airframe icing during 10 percent of the time icing is forecast (including the fuel used by engine and wing anti-ice during this period).

(B) Fuel that would be used for engine anti-ice, and if appropriate wing anti-ice, for the entire time during which icing is forecast.

(iv) Fuel to account for engine deterioration. In calculating the amount of fuel required by paragraph (b)(1)(i) of

this section (after completing the wind calculation in paragraph (b)(1)(ii) of this section), the airplane also carries fuel equal to 5% of the fuel specified above, to account for deterioration in cruise fuel burn performance unless the certificate holder has a program to monitor airplane in-service deterioration to cruise fuel burn performance.

(2) Fuel to account for holding, approach, and landing. In addition to the fuel required by paragraph (b)(1) of this section, the airplane must carry fuel sufficient to hold at 1500 feet above field elevation for 15 minutes upon reaching an ETOPS Alternate Airport and then conduct an instrument approach and land.

(3) Fuel to account for APU use. If an APU is a required power source, the certificate holder must account for its fuel consumption during the appropriate phases of flight.

[Doc. No. FAA–2002–6717, 72 FR 1882, Jan. 16, 2007, as amended by Amdt. 121–348, 75 FR 12121, Mar. 15, 2010]

§ 121.647 Factors for computing fuel required.

Each person computing fuel required for the purposes of this subpart shall consider the following:

(a) Wind and other weather conditions forecast.

(b) Anticipated traffic delays.

(c) One instrument approach and possible missed approach at destination.

(d) Any other conditions that may delay landing of the aircraft.

For the purposes of this section, required fuel is in addition to unusable fuel.

§ 121.649 Takeoff and landing weather minimums: VFR: Domestic operations.

(a) Except as provided in paragraph (b) of this section, regardless of any clearance from ATC, no pilot may takeoff or land an airplane under VFR when the reported ceiling or visibility is less than the following:

(1) For day operations—1,000-foot ceiling and one-mile visibility.

(2) For night operations—1,000-foot ceiling and two-mile visibility.

(b) Where a local surface restriction to visibility exists (e.g., smoke, dust, blowing snow or sand) the visibility for day and night operations may be reduced to ½ mile, if all turns after takeoff and prior to landing, and all flight beyond one mile from the airport boundary can be accomplished above or outside the area of local surface visibility restriction.

(c) The weather minimums in this section do not apply to the VFR operation of fixed-wing aircraft at any of the locations where the special weather minimums of § 91.157 of this chapter are not applicable (See part 91, appendix D, section 3 of this chapter). The basic VFR weather minimums of § 91.155 of this chapter apply at those locations.

[Doc. No. 6258, 29 FR 19222, Dec. 31, 1964, as amended by Amdt. 121-39, 33 FR 4097, Mar. 2, 1968; Amdt. 121-206, 54 FR 34331, Aug. 18, 1989; Amdt. 121-226, 56 FR 65663, Dec. 17, 1991]

§ 121.651　Takeoff and landing weather minimums: IFR: All certificate holders.

(a) Notwithstanding any clearance from ATC, no pilot may begin a takeoff in an airplane under IFR when the weather conditions reported by the U.S. National Weather Service, a source approved by that Service, or a source approved by the Administrator, are less than those specified in—

(1) The certificate holder's operations specifications; or

(2) Parts 91 and 97 of this chapter, if the certificate holder's operations specifications do not specify takeoff minimums for the airport.

(b) Except as provided in paragraphs (d) and (e) of this section, no pilot may continue an approach past the final approach fix, or where a final approach fix is not used, begin the final approach segment of an instrument approach procedure—

(1) At any airport, unless the U.S. National Weather Service, a source approved by that Service, or a source approved by the Administrator, issues a weather report for that airport; and

(2) At airports within the United States and its territories or at U.S. military airports, unless the latest weather report for that airport issued by the U.S. National Weather Service, a source approved by that Service, or a source approved by the Administrator, reports the visibility to be equal to or more than the visibility minimums prescribed for that procedure. For the purpose of this section, the term "U.S. military airports" means airports in foreign countries where flight operations are under the control of U.S. military authority.

(c) A pilot who has begun the final approach segment of an instrument approach procedure in accordance with paragraph (b) of this section, and after that receives a later weather report indicating below-minimum conditions, may continue the approach to DA/DH or MDA. Upon reaching DA/DH or at MDA, and at any time before the missed approach point, the pilot may continue the approach below DA/DH or MDA if either the requirements of § 91.176 of this chapter, or the following requirements are met:

(1) The aircraft is continuously in a position from which a descent to a landing on the intended runway can be made at a normal rate of descent using normal maneuvers, and where that descent rate will allow touchdown to occur within the touchdown zone of the runway of intended landing;

(2) The flight visibility is not less than the visibility prescribed in the standard instrument approach procedure being used;

(3) Except for Category II or Category III approaches where any necessary visual reference requirements are specified by authorization of the Administrator, at least one of the following visual references for the intended runway is distinctly visible and identifiable to the pilot:

(i) The approach light system, except that the pilot may not descend below 100 feet above the touchdown zone elevation using the approach lights as a reference unless the red terminating bars or the red side row bars are also distinctly visible and identifiable.

(ii) The threshold.

(iii) The threshold markings.

(iv) The threshold lights.

(v) The runway end identifier lights.

(vi) The visual approach slope indicator.

(vii) The touchdown zone or touchdown zone markings.

(viii) The touchdown zone lights.

(ix) The runway or runway markings.

(x) The runway lights; and

(4) When the aircraft is on a straight-in nonprecision approach procedure which incorporates a visual descent point, the aircraft has reached the visual descent point, except where the aircraft is not equipped for or capable of establishing that point, or a descent to the runway cannot be made using normal procedures or rates of descent if descent is delayed until reaching that point.

(d) A pilot may begin the final approach segment of an instrument approach procedure other than a Category II or Category III procedure at an airport when the visibility is less than the visibility minimums prescribed for that procedure if the airport is served by an operative ILS and an operative PAR, and both are used by the pilot. However, no pilot may continue an approach below the authorized DA/DH unless the requirements of §91.176 of this chapter, or the following requirements are met:

(1) The aircraft is continuously in a position from which a descent to a landing on the intended runway can be made at a normal rate of descent using normal maneuvers and where such a descent rate will allow touchdown to occur within the touchdown zone of the runway of intended landing;

(2) The flight visibility is not less than the visibility prescribed in the standard instrument approach procedure being used; and

(3) Except for Category II or Category III approaches where any necessary visual reference requirements are specified by the authorization of the Administrator, at least one of the following visual references for the intended runway is distinctly visible and identifiable to the pilot:

(i) The approach light system, except that the pilot may not descend below 100 feet above the touchdown zone elevation using the approach lights as a reference unless the red terminating bars or the red side row bars are also distinctly visible and identifiable.

(ii) The threshold.

(iii) The threshold markings.

(iv) The threshold lights.

(v) The runway end identifier lights.

(vi) The visual approach slope indicator.

(vii) The touchdown zone or touchdown zone markings.

(viii) The touchdown zone lights.

(ix) The runway or runway markings.

(x) The runway lights.

(e) A pilot may begin the final approach segment of an instrument approach procedure, or continue that approach procedure, at an airport when the visibility is reported to be less than the visibility minimums prescribed for that procedure if the pilot uses an operable EFVS in accordance with §91.176 of this chapter and the certificate holder's operations specifications for EFVS operations.

(f) For the purpose of this section, the final approach segment begins at the final approach fix or facility prescribed in the instrument approach procedure. When a final approach fix is not prescribed for a procedure that includes a procedure turn, the final approach segment begins at the point where the procedure turn is completed and the aircraft is established inbound toward the airport on the final approach course within the distance prescribed in the procedure.

(g) Unless otherwise authorized in the certificate holder's operations specifications, each pilot making an IFR takeoff, approach, or landing at a foreign airport shall comply with the applicable instrument approach procedures and weather minimums prescribed by the authority having jurisdiction over the airport.

[Doc. No. 20060, 46 FR 2291, Jan. 8, 1981, as amended by Amdt. 121–303, 69 FR 1641, Jan. 9, 2004; Amdt. 121–333, 72 FR 31682, June 7, 2007; Docket FAA–2013–0485, Amdt. 121–376, 81 FR 90175, Dec. 13, 2016]

§121.652 Landing weather minimums: IFR: All certificate holders.

(a) If the pilot in command of an airplane has not served 100 hours as pilot in command in operations under this part in the type of airplane he is operating, the MDA or DA/DH and visibility landing minimums in the certificate holder's operations specification for regular, provisional, or refueling airports are increased by 100 feet and one-half mile (or the RVR equivalent). The MDA or DA/DH and visibility minimums need not be increased above those applicable to the airport when used as an alternate airport, but in no event may the landing minimums be less than 300 and 1. However, a Pilot in command employed by a certificate holder conducting operations in large aircraft under part 135 of this chapter, may credit flight time acquired in operations conducted for that operator under part 91 in the same type airplane for up to 50 percent of the 100 hours of pilot in command experience required by this paragraph.

(b) The 100 hours of pilot in command experience required by paragraph (a) of this section may be reduced (not to exceed 50 percent) by substituting one landing in operations under this part in the type of airplane for 1 required hour of pilot in command experience, if the pilot has at least 100 hours as pilot in command of another type airplane in operations under this part.

(c) Category II minimums and the sliding scale when authorized in the certificate holder's operations specifications do not apply until the pilot in command subject to paragraph (a) of this section meets the requirements of that paragraph in the type of airplane he is operating.

[Doc. No. 7594, 33 FR 10843, July 31, 1968, as amended by Amdt. 121–143, 43 FR 22642, May 25, 1978; Amdt. 121–253, 61 FR 2615, Jan. 26, 1996; Amdt. 121–333, 72 FR 31682, June 7, 2007]

§ 121.653   [Reserved]

§ 121.655   Applicability of reported weather minimums.

In conducting operations under §§ 121.649 through 121.653, the ceiling and visibility values in the main body of the latest weather report control for VFR and IFR takeoffs and landings and for instrument approach procedures on all runways of an airport. However, if the latest weather report, including an oral report from the control tower, contains a visibility value specified as runway visibility or runway visual range for a particular runway of an airport, that specified value controls for VFR and IFR landings and takeoffs and straight-in instrument approaches for that runway.

§ 121.657   Flight altitude rules.

(a) *General.* Notwithstanding § 91.119 or any rule applicable outside the United States, no person may operate an aircraft below the minimums set forth in paragraphs (b) and (c) of this section, except when necessary for takeoff or landing, or except when, after considering the character of the terrain, the quality and quantity of meteorological services, the navigational facilities available, and other flight conditions, the Administrator prescribes other minimums for any route or part of a route where he finds that the safe conduct of the flight requires other altitudes. Outside of the United States the minimums prescribed in this section are controlling unless higher minimums are prescribed in the certificate holder's operations specifications or by the foreign country over which the aircraft is operating.

(b) *Day VFR operations.* No certificate holder conducting domestic operations may operate a passenger-carrying aircraft and no certificate holder conducting flag or supplemental operations may operate any aircraft under VFR during the day at an altitude less than 1,000 feet above the surface or less than 1,000 feet from any mountain, hill, or other obstruction to flight.

(c) *Night VFR, IFR, and over-the-top operations.* No person may operate an aircraft under IFR including over-the-top or at night under VFR at an altitude less than 1,000 feet above the highest obstacle within a horizontal distance of five miles from the center of the intended course, or, in designated mountainous areas, less than 2,000 feet above the highest obstacle within a horizontal distance of five miles from the center of the intended course.

(d) *Day over-the-top operations below minimum en route altitudes.* A person may conduct day over-the-top operations in an airplane at flight altitudes lower than the minimum en route IFR altitudes if—

(1) The operation is conducted at least 1,000 feet above the top of lower broken or overcast cloud cover;

(2) The top of the lower cloud cover is generally uniform and level;

(3) Flight visibility is at least five miles; and

(4) The base of any higher broken or overcast cloud cover is generally uniform and level and is at least 1,000 feet

above the minimum en route IFR altitude for that route segment.

[Doc. No. 6258, 29 FR 19222, Dec. 31, 1964, as amended by Amdt. 121–144, 43 FR 22649 May 25, 1978; Amdt. 121–206, 54 FR 34331, Aug. 18, 1989; Amdt. 121–253, 61 FR 2615, Jan. 26, 1996]

§121.659 Initial approach altitude: Domestic and supplemental operations.

(a) Except as provided in paragraph (b) of this section, when making an initial approach to a radio navigation facility under IFR, no person may descend an aircraft below the pertinent minimum altitude for initial approach (as specified in the instrument approach procedure for that facility) until his arrival over that facility has been definitely established.

(b) When making an initial approach on a flight being conducted under §121.657(d), no pilot may commence an instrument approach until his arrival over the radio facility has definitely been established. In making an instrument approach under these circumstances no person may descend an aircraft lower than 1,000 feet above the top of the lower cloud or the minimum altitude determined by the Administrator for that part of the IFR approach, whichever is lower.

§121.661 Initial approach altitude: Flag operations.

When making an initial approach to a radio navigation facility under IFR, no person may descend below the pertinent minimum altitude for initial approach (as specified in the instrument approach procedure for that facility) until his arrival over that facility has been definitely established.

§121.663 Responsibility for dispatch release: Domestic and flag operations.

Each certificate holder conducting domestic or flag operations shall prepare a dispatch release for each flight between specified points, based on information furnished by an authorized aircraft dispatcher. The pilot in command and an authorized aircraft dispatcher shall sign the release only if they both believe that the flight can be made with safety. The aircraft dispatcher may delegate authority to sign a release for a particular flight, but he may not delegate his authority to dispatch.

[Doc. No. 28154, 61 FR 2615, Jan. 26, 1996]

§121.665 Load manifest.

Each certificate holder is responsible for the preparation and accuracy of a load manifest form before each takeoff. The form must be prepared and signed for each flight by employees of the certificate holder who have the duty of supervising the loading of aircraft and preparing the load manifest forms or by other qualified persons authorized by the certificate holder.

§121.667 Flight plan: VFR and IFR: Supplemental operations.

(a) No person may take off an aircraft unless the pilot in command has filed a flight plan, containing the appropriate information required by part 91, with the nearest FAA communication station or appropriate military station or, when operating outside the United States, with other appropriate authority. However, if communications facilities are not readily available, the pilot in command shall file the flight plan as soon as practicable after the aircraft is airborne. A flight plan must continue in effect for all parts of the flight.

(b) When flights are operated into military airports, the arrival or completion notice required by §§91.153 and 91.169 may be filed with the appropriate airport control tower or aeronautical communication facility used for that airport.

[Doc. No. 6258, 29 FR 19222, Dec. 31, 1964, as amended by Amdt. 121–206, 54 FR 34331, Aug. 18, 1989]

Subpart V—Records and Reports

SOURCE: Docket No. 6258, 29 FR 19226, Dec. 31, 1964, unless otherwise noted.

§121.681 Applicability.

This subpart prescribes requirements for the preparation and maintenance of records and reports for all certificate holders.

§ 121.683 Crewmember and dispatcher record.

(a) Each certificate holder shall—

(1) Maintain current records of each crewmember and each aircraft dispatcher (domestic and flag operations only) that show whether the crewmember or aircraft dispatcher complies with the applicable sections of this chapter, including, but not limited to, proficiency and route checks, airplane and route qualifications, training, any required physical examinations, flight, duty, and rest time records; and

(2) Record each action taken concerning the release from employment or physical or professional disqualification of any flight crewmember or aircraft dispatcher (domestic and flag operations only) and keep the record for at least six months thereafter.

(b) Each certificate holder conducting supplemental operations shall maintain the records required by paragraph (a) of this section at its principal base of operations, or at another location used by it and approved by the Administrator.

(c) Computer record systems approved by the Administrator may be used in complying with the requirements of paragraph (a) of this section.

[Doc. No. 6258, 29 FR 19226, Dec. 31, 1964, as amended by Amdt. 121–144, 43 FR 22649, May 25, 1978; Amdt. 121–241, 59 FR 42993, Aug. 19, 1994; Amdt. 121–253, 61 FR 2615, Jan. 26, 1996]

§ 121.685 Aircraft record: Domestic and flag operations.

Each certificate holder conducting domestic or flag operations shall maintain a current list of each aircraft that it operates in scheduled air transportation and shall send a copy of the record and each change to the responsible Flight Standards office. Airplanes of another certificate holder operated under an interchange agreement may be incorporated by reference.

[Doc. No. 28154, 61 FR 2615, Jan. 26, 1996, as amended by Docket FAA–2018–0119, Amdt. 121–380, 83 FR 9172, Mar. 5, 2018]

§ 121.687 Dispatch release: Flag and domestic operations.

(a) The dispatch release may be in any form but must contain at least the following information concerning each flight:

(1) Identification number of the aircraft.

(2) Trip number.

(3) Departure airport, intermediate stops, destination airports, and alternate airports.

(4) A statement of the type of operation (e.g., IFR, VFR).

(5) Minimum fuel supply.

(6) For each flight dispatched as an ETOPS flight, the ETOPS diversion time for which the flight is dispatched.

(b) The dispatch release must contain, or have attached to it, weather reports, available weather forecasts, or a combination thereof, for the destination airport, intermediate stops, and alternate airports, that are the latest available at the time the release is signed by the pilot in command and dispatcher. It may include any additional available weather reports or forecasts that the pilot in command or the aircraft dispatcher considers necessary or desirable.

[Doc. No. 6258, 29 FR 19226, Dec. 31, 1964, as amended by Amdt. 121–329, 72 FR 1883, Jan. 16, 2007]

§ 121.689 Flight release form: Supplemental operations.

(a) Except as provided in paragraph (c) of this section, the flight release may be in any form but must contain at least the following information concerning each flight:

(1) Company or organization name.

(2) Make, model, and registration number of the aircraft being used.

(3) Flight or trip number, and date of flight.

(4) Name of each flight crewmember, flight attendant, and pilot designated as pilot in command.

(5) Departure airport, destination airports, alternate airports, and route.

(6) Minimum fuel supply (in gallons or pounds).

(7) A statement of the type of operation (e.g., IFR, VFR).

(8) For each flight released as an ETOPS flight, the ETOPS diversion time for which the flight is released.

(b) The aircraft flight release must contain, or have attached to it, weather reports, available weather forecasts, or a combination thereof, for the destination airport, and alternate airports, that are the latest available at the time the release is signed. It may include any additional available weather reports or forecasts that the pilot in command considers necessary or desirable.

(c) Each certificate holder conducting domestic or flag operations under the rules of this part applicable to supplemental operations shall comply with the dispatch or flight release forms required for scheduled operations under this subpart.

[Doc. No. 6258, 29 FR 19226, Dec. 31, 1964, as amended by Amdt. 121–253, 61 FR 2615, Jan. 26, 1996; Amdt. 121–329, 72 FR 1883, Jan. 16, 2007]

§121.691 [Reserved]

§121.693 Load manifest: All certificate holders.

The load manifest must contain the following information concerning the loading of the airplane at takeoff time:

(a) The weight of the aircraft, fuel and oil, cargo and baggage, passengers and crewmembers.

(b) The maximum allowable weight for that flight that must not exceed the least of the following weights:

(1) Maximum allowable takeoff weight for the runway intended to be used (including corrections for altitude and gradient, and wind and temperature conditions existing at the takeoff time).

(2) Maximum takeoff weight considering anticipated fuel and oil consumption that allows compliance with applicable en route performance limitations.

(3) Maximum takeoff weight considering anticipated fuel and oil consumption that allows compliance with the maximum authorized design landing weight limitations on arrival at the destination airport.

(4) Maximum takeoff weight considering anticipated fuel and oil consumption that allows compliance with landing distance limitations on arrival at the destination and alternate airports.

(c) The total weight computed under approved procedures.

(d) Evidence that the aircraft is loaded according to an approved schedule that insures that the center of gravity is within approved limits.

(e) Names of passengers, unless such information is maintained by other means by the certificate holder.

[Doc. No. 6258, 29 FR 19226, Dec. 31, 1964, as amended by Amdt. 121–159, 45 FR 41595, June 19, 1980; Amdt. 121–253, 61 FR 2615, Jan. 26, 1996]

§121.695 Disposition of load manifest, dispatch release, and flight plans: Domestic and flag operations.

(a) The pilot in command of an airplane shall carry in the airplane to its destination—

(1) A copy of the completed load manifest (or information from it, except information concerning cargo and passenger distribution);

(2) A copy of the dispatch release; and

(3) A copy of the flight plan.

(b) The certificate holder shall keep copies of the records required in this section for at least three months.

[Doc. No. 6258, 29 FR 19226, Dec. 31, 1964, as amended by Amdt. 121–178, 47 FR 13316, Mar. 29, 1982; Amdt. 121–253, 61 FR 2616, Jan. 26, 1996]

§121.697 Disposition of load manifest, flight release, and flight plans: Supplemental operations.

(a) The pilot in command of an airplane shall carry in the airplane to its destination the original or a signed copy of the—

(1) Load manifest;

(2) Flight release;

(3) Airworthiness release;

(4) Pilot route certification; and

(5) Flight plan.

(b) If a flight originates at the certificate holder's principal base of operations, it shall retain at that base a signed copy of each document listed in paragraph (a) of this section.

(c) Except as provided in paragraph (d) of this section, if a flight originates at a place other than the certificate holder's principal base of operations, the pilot in command (or another person not aboard the airplane who is authorized by the certificate holder) shall, before or immediately after departure of the flight, mail signed copies of the documents listed in paragraph (a) of this section, to the principal base of operations.

(d) If a flight originates at a place other than the certificate holder's principal base of operations, and there is at that place a person to manage the flight departure for the certificate holder who does not himself or herself depart on the airplane, signed copies of the documents listed in paragraph (a) of this section may be retained at that place for not more than 30 days before being sent to the certificate holder's principal base of operations. However, the documents for a particular flight need not be further retained at that place or be sent to the principal base of operations, if the originals or other copies of them have been previously returned to the principal base of operations.

(e) The certificate holder conducting supplemental operations shall:

(1) Identify in its operations manual the person having custody of the copies of documents retained in accordance with paragraph (d) of this section; and

(2) Retain at its principal base of operations either an original or a copy of the records required by this section for at least three months.

[Doc. No. 6258, 29 FR 19226, Dec. 31, 1964, as amended by Amdt. 121–123, 40 FR 44541, Sept. 29, 1975; Amdt. 121–143, 43 FR 22642, May 25, 1978; Amdt. 121–178, 47 FR 13316, Mar. 29, 1982; Amdt. 121–253, 61 FR 2616, Jan. 26, 1996]

§§ 121.698–121.699   [Reserved]

§ 121.701   Maintenance log: Aircraft.

(a) Each person who takes action in the case of a reported or observed failure or malfunction of an airframe, engine, propeller, or appliance that is critical to the safety of flight shall make, or have made, a record of that action in the airplane's maintenance log.

(b) Each certificate holder shall have an approved procedure for keeping adequate copies of the record required in paragraph (a) of this section in the airplane in a place readily accessible to each flight crewmember and shall put that procedure in the certificate holder's manual.

§ 121.703   Service difficulty reports.

(a) Each certificate holder shall report the occurrence or detection of each failure, malfunction, or defect concerning—

(1) Fires during flight and whether the related fire-warning system functioned properly;

(2) Fires during flight not protected by a related fire-warning system;

(3) False fire warning during flight;

(4) An engine exhaust system that causes damage during flight to the engine, adjacent structure, equipment, or components;

(5) An aircraft component that causes accumulation or circulation of smoke, vapor, or toxic or noxious fumes in the crew compartment or passenger cabin during flight;

(6) Engine shutdown during flight because of flameout;

(7) Engine shutdown during flight when external damage to the engine or airplane structure occurs;

(8) Engine shutdown during flight due to foreign object ingestion or icing;

(9) Engine shutdown during flight of more than one engine;

(10) A propeller feathering system or ability of the system to control overspeed during flight;

(11) A fuel or fuel-dumping system that affects fuel flow or causes hazardous leakage during flight;

(12) An unwanted landing gear extension or retraction, or an unwanted opening or closing of landing gear doors during flight;

(13) Brake system components that result in loss of brake actuating force when the airplane is in motion on the ground;

(14) Aircraft structure that requires major repair;

(15) Cracks, permanent deformation, or corrosion of aircraft structures, if more than the maximum acceptable to the manufacturer or the FAA;

(16) Aircraft components or systems that result in taking emergency actions during flight (except action to shut down an engine); and

(17) Emergency evacuation systems or components including all exit doors, passenger emergency evacuation lighting systems, or evacuation equipment that are found defective, or that fail to perform the intended functions during an actual emergency or during training, testing, maintenance, demonstrations, or inadvertent deployments.

(b) For the purpose of this section *during flight* means the period from the moment the aircraft leaves the surface of the earth on takeoff until it touches down on landing.

(c) In addition to the reports required by paragraph (a) of this section, each certificate holder shall report any other failure, malfunction, or defect in an aircraft that occurs or is detected at any time if, in its opinion, that failure, malfunction, or defect has endangered or may endanger the safe operation of an aircraft used by it.

(d) Each certificate holder shall submit each report required by this section, covering each 24-hour period beginning at 0900 local time of each day and ending at 0900 local time on the next day, to the FAA offices in Oklahoma City, Oklahoma. Each report of occurrences during a 24-hour period shall be submitted to the collection point within the next 96 hours. However, a report due on Saturday or Sunday may be submitted on the following Monday, and a report due on a holiday may be submitted on the next work day.

(e) The certificate holder shall submit the reports required by this section on a form or in another format acceptable to the Administrator. The reports shall include the following information:

(1) Type and identification number of the aircraft.

(2) The name of the operator.

(3) The date, flight number, and stage during which the incident occurred (e.g., preflight, takeoff, climb, cruise, descent landing, and inspection).

(4) The emergency procedure effected (e.g., unscheduled landing and emergency descent).

(5) The nature of the failure, malfunction, or defect.

(6) Identification of the part and system involved, including available information pertaining to type designation of the major component and time since overhaul.

(7) Apparent cause of the failure, malfunction, or defect (e.g., wear, crack, design deficiency, or personnel error).

(8) Whether the part was repaired, replaced, sent to the manufacturer, or other action taken.

(9) Whether the aircraft was grounded.

(10) Other pertinent information necessary for more complete identification, determination of seriousness, or corrective action.

(f) A certificate holder that is also the holder of a Type Certificate (including a Supplemental Type Certificate), a Parts Manufacturer Approval, or a Technical Standard Order Authorization, or that is the licensee of a type certificate holder, need not report a failure, malfunction, or defect under this section if the failure, malfunction, or defect has been reported by it under §21.3 of this chapter or under the accident reporting provisions of 14 CFR part 830.

(g) No person may withhold a report required by this section even though all information required in this section is not available.

(h) When certificate holder gets additional information, including information from the manufacturer or other agency, concerning a report required by this section, it shall expeditiously submit it as a supplement to the first report and reference the date and place of submission of the first report.

[Doc. No. 6258, 29 FR 19226, Dec. 31, 1964, as amended by Doc. No. 8084, 32 FR 5770, Apr. 11, 1967; Amdt. 121-72, 35 FR 18188, Nov. 28, 1970; Amdt. 121-143, 43 FR 22642, May 25, 1978; Amdt. 121-178, 47 FR 13316, Mar. 29, 1982; Amdt. 121-187, 50 FR 32375, Aug. 9, 1985; Amdt. 121-195, 53 FR 8728, Mar. 16, 1988; Amdt. 121-251, 60 FR 65936, Dec. 20, 1995; Amdt. 121-319, 70 FR 76979, Dec. 29, 2005]

§121.705 Mechanical interruption summary report.

Each certificate holder shall submit to the Administrator, before the end of the 10th day of the following month, a summary report for the previous month of:

(a) Each interruption to a flight, unscheduled change of aircraft en route, or unscheduled stop or diversion from a route, caused by known or suspected mechanical difficulties or malfunctions that are not required to be reported under §121.703.

(b) The number of engines removed prematurely because of malfunction, failure or defect, listed by make and model and the aircraft type in which it was installed.

(c) The number of propeller featherings in flight, listed by type of propeller and engine and aircraft on which it was installed. Propeller featherings for training, demonstration, or flight check purposes need not be reported.

[Doc. No. 6258, 29 FR 19226, Dec. 31, 1964, as amended by Amdt. 121-10, 30 FR 10025, Aug. 12, 1965; Amdt. 121-319, 70 FR 76979, Dec. 29, 2005]

§ 121.707 Alteration and repair reports.

(a) Each certificate holder shall, promptly upon its completion, prepare a report of each major alteration or major repair of an airframe, aircraft engine, propeller, or appliance of an aircraft operated by it.

(b) The certificate holder shall submit a copy of each report of a major alteration to, and shall keep a copy of each report of a major repair available for inspection by, the representative of the Administrator who is assigned to it.

§ 121.709 Airworthiness release or aircraft log entry.

(a) No certificate holder may operate an aircraft after maintenance, preventive maintenance or alterations are performed on the aircraft unless the certificate holder, or the person with whom the certificate holder arranges for the performance of the maintenance, preventive maintenance, or alterations, prepares or causes to be prepared—

(1) An airworthiness release; or

(2) An appropriate entry in the aircraft log.

(b) The airworthiness release or log entry required by paragraph (a) of this section must—

(1) Be prepared in accordance with the procedures set forth in the certificate holder's manual;

(2) Include a certification that—

(i) The work was performed in accordance with the requirements of the certificate holder's manual;

(ii) All items required to be inspected were inspected by an authorized person who determined that the work was satisfactorily completed;

(iii) No known condition exists that would make the airplane unairworthy; and

(iv) So far as the work performed is concerned, the aircraft is in condition for safe operation; and

(3) Be signed by an authorized certificated mechanic or repairman except that a certificated repairman may sign the release or entry only for the work for which he is employed and certificated.

(c) Notwithstanding paragraph (b)(3) of this section, after maintenance, preventive maintenance, or alterations performed by a repair station that is located outside the United States, the airworthiness release or log entry required by paragraph (a) of this section may be signed by a person authorized by that repair station.

(d) When an airworthiness release form is prepared the certificate holder must give a copy to the pilot in command and must keep a record thereof for at least 2 months.

(e) Instead of restating each of the conditions of the certification required by paragraph (b) of this section, the air carrier may state in its manual that the signature of an authorized certificated mechanic or repairman constitutes that certification.

[Doc. No. 6258, 29 FR 19226, Dec. 31, 1964, as amended by Amdt. 121-6, 30 FR 6432, May 8, 1965; Amdt. 121-21, 31 FR 10613, Aug. 9, 1966; Amdt. 121-286, 66 FR 41116, Aug. 6, 2001]

§ 121.711 Communication records: Domestic and flag operations.

(a) Each certificate holder conducting domestic or flag operations must record each en route communication between the certificate holder and its pilots using a communication system as required by § 121.99 of this part.

(b) For purposes of this section the term en route means from the time the aircraft pushes back from the departing gate until the time the aircraft reaches the arrival gate at its destination.

(c) The record required in paragraph (a) of this section must contain at least the following information:

(1) The date and time of the contact;

(2) The flight number;

(3) Aircraft registration number;

(4) Approximate position of the aircraft during the contact;

(5) Call sign; and

(6) Narrative of the contact.

(d) The record required in paragraph (a) of this section must be kept for at least 30 days.

[Doc. No. FAA–2008–0677, 78 FR 67841, Nov. 12, 2013]

§ 121.713 Retention of contracts and amendments: Commercial operators who conduct intrastate operations for compensation or hire.

(a) Each commercial operator who conducts intrastate operations for compensation or hire shall keep a copy of each written contract under which it provides services as a commercial operator for a period of at least 1 year after the date of execution of the contract. In the case of an oral contract, it shall keep a memorandum stating its elements, and of any amendments to it, for a period of at least one year after the execution of that contract or change.

(b) Each commercial operator who conducts intrastate operations for compensation or hire shall submit a financial report for the first 6 months of each fiscal year and another financial report for each complete fiscal year. If that person's operating certificate is suspended for more than 29 days, that person shall submit a financial report as of the last day of the month in which the suspension is terminated. The report required to be submitted by this section shall be submitted within 60 days of the last day of the period covered by the report and must include—

(1) A balance sheet that shows assets, liabilities, and net worth on the last day of the reporting period;

(2) The information required by § 119.36 (e)(2), (e)(7), and (e)(8) of this chapter;

(3) An itemization of claims in litigation against the applicant, if any, as of the last day of the period covered by the report;

(4) A profit and loss statement with the separation of items relating to the applicant's commercial operator activities from his other business activities, if any; and

(5) A list of each contract that gave rise to operating income on the profit and loss statement, including the names and addresses of the contracting parties and the nature, scope, date, and duration of each contract.

[Doc. No. 28154, 60 FR 65936, Dec. 20, 1995, as amended by Amdt. 121–262, 62 FR 13257, Mar. 19, 1997]

Subpart W—Crewmember Certificate: International

§ 121.721 Applicability.

This section describes the certificates that were issued to United States citizens who were employed by air carriers at the time of issuance as flight crewmembers on United States registered aircraft engaged in international air commerce. The purpose of the certificate is to facilitate the entry and clearance of those crewmembers into ICAO contracting states. They were issued under Annex 9, as amended, to the Convention on International Civil Aviation.

[Doc. No. 28154, 61 FR 30435, June 14, 1996]

§ 121.723 Surrender of international crewmember certificate.

The holder of a certificate issued under this section, or the air carrier by whom the holder is employed, shall surrender the certificate for cancellation at the responsible Flight Standards office at the termination of the holder's employment with that air carrier.

[Doc. No. 28154, 61 FR 30435, June 14, 1996, as amended by Docket FAA–2018–0119, Amdt. 121–380, 83 FR 9173, Mar. 5, 2018]

Subpart X—Emergency Medical Equipment and Training

SOURCE: Docket No. FAA–2000–7119, 66 FR 19044, Apr. 12, 2001, unless otherwise noted.

§ 121.801 Applicability.

This subpart prescribes the emergency medical equipment and training requirements applicable to all certificate holders operating passenger-carrying airplanes under this part. Nothing in this subpart is intended to require certificate holders or its agents to provide emergency medical care or to establish a standard of care for the provision of emergency medical care.

§ 121.803 Emergency medical equipment.

(a) No person may operate a passenger-carrying airplane under this part unless it is equipped with the emergency medical equipment listed in this section.

(b) Each equipment item listed in this section—

(1) Must be inspected regularly in accordance with inspection periods established in the operations specifications to ensure its condition for continued serviceability and immediate readiness to perform its intended emergency purposes;

(2) Must be readily accessible to the crew and, with regard to equipment located in the passenger compartment, to passengers;

(3) Must be clearly identified and clearly marked to indicate its method of operation; and

(4) When carried in a compartment or container, must be carried in a compartment or container marked as to contents and the compartment or container, or the item itself, must be marked as to date of last inspection.

(c) For treatment of injuries, medical events, or minor accidents that might occur during flight time each airplane must have the following equipment that meets the specifications and requirements of appendix A of this part:

(1) Approved first-aid kits.

(2) In airplanes for which a flight attendant is required, an approved emergency medical kit.

(3) In airplanes for which a flight attendant is required, an approved emergency medical kit as modified effective April 12, 2004.

(4) In airplanes for which a flight attendant is required and with a maximum payload capacity of more than 7,500 pounds, an approved automated external defibrillator as of April 12, 2004.

§ 121.805 Crewmember training for inflight medical events.

(a) Each training program must provide the instruction set forth in this section with respect to each airplane type, model, and configuration, each required crewmember, and each kind of operation conducted, insofar as appropriate for each crewmember and the certificate holder.

(b) Training must provide the following:

(1) Instruction in emergency medical event procedures, including coordination among crewmembers.

(2) Instruction in the location, function, and intended operation of emergency medical equipment.

(3) Instruction to familiarize crewmembers with the content of the emergency medical kit.

(4) Instruction to familiarize crewmembers with the content of the emergency medical kit as modified on April 12, 2004.

(5) For each flight attendant—

(i) Instruction, to include performance drills, in the proper use of automated external defibrillators.

(ii) Instruction, to include performance drills, in cardiopulmonary resuscitation.

(iii) Recurrent training, to include performance drills, in the proper use of an automated external defibrillators and in cardiopulmonary resuscitation at least once every 24 months.

(c) The crewmember instruction, performance drills, and recurrent training required under this section are not required to be equivalent to the expert level of proficiency attained by professional emergency medical personnel.

Subpart Y—Advanced Qualification Program

SOURCE: Docket No. FAA-2005-20750, 70 FR 54815, Sept. 16, 2005, unless otherwise noted.

§ 121.901 Purpose and eligibility.

(a) Contrary provisions of parts 61, 63, 65, 121, 135, and 142 of this chapter notwithstanding, this subpart provides for approval of an alternative method (known as "Advanced Qualification Program" or "AQP") for qualifying, training, certifying, and otherwise ensuring competency of crewmembers, aircraft dispatchers, other operations personnel, instructors, and evaluators who are required to be trained under parts 121 and 135 of this chapter.

(b) A certificate holder is eligible under this subpart if the certificate holder is required or elects to have an approved training program under §§121.401, 135.3(c), or 135.341 of this chapter.

(c) A certificate holder obtains approval of each proposed curriculum under this AQP as specified in §121.909.

§121.903 General requirements for Advanced Qualification Programs.

(a) A curriculum approved under an AQP may include elements of existing training programs under part 121 and part 135 of this chapter. Each curriculum must specify the make, model, series or variant of aircraft and each crewmember position or other positions to be covered by that curriculum. Positions to be covered by the AQP must include all flight crewmember positions, flight instructors, and evaluators and may include other positions, such as flight attendants, aircraft dispatchers, and other operations personnel.

(b) Each certificate holder that obtains approval of an AQP under this subpart must comply with all the requirements of the AQP and this subpart instead of the corresponding provisions of parts 61, 63, 65, 121, or 135 of this chapter. However, each applicable requirement of parts 61, 63, 65, 121, or 135 of this chapter, including but not limited to practical test requirements, that is not specifically addressed in the AQP continues to apply to the certificate holder and to the individuals being trained and qualified by the certificate holder. No person may be trained under an AQP unless that AQP has been approved by the FAA and the person complies with all the requirements of the AQP and this subpart.

(c) No certificate holder that conducts its training program under this subpart may use any person nor may any person serve in any duty position as a required crewmember, an aircraft dispatcher, an instructor, or an evaluator, unless that person has satisfactorily accomplished, in a training program approved under this subpart for the certificate holder, the training and evaluation of proficiency required by the AQP for that type airplane and duty position.

(d) All documentation and data required under this subpart must be submitted in a form and manner acceptable to the FAA.

(e) Any training or evaluation required under an AQP that is satisfactorily completed in the calendar month before or the calendar month after the calendar month in which it is due is considered to have been completed in the calendar month it was due.

§121.905 Confidential commercial information.

(a) Each certificate holder that claims that AQP information or data it is submitting to the FAA is entitled to confidential treatment under 5 U.S.C. 552(b)(4) because it constitutes confidential commercial information as described in 5 U.S.C. 552(b)(4), and should be withheld from public disclosure, must include its request for confidentiality with each submission.

(b) When requesting confidentiality for submitted information or data, the certificate holder must:

(1) If the information or data is transmitted electronically, embed the claim of confidentiality within the electronic record so the portions claimed to be confidential are readily apparent when received and reviewed.

(2) If the information or data is submitted in paper format, place the word "CONFIDENTIAL" on the top of each page containing information or data claimed to be confidential.

(3) Justify the basis for a claim of confidentiality under 5 U.S.C. 552(b)(4).

§121.907 Definitions.

The following definitions apply to this subpart:

Crew Resource Management (CRM) means the effective use of all the resources available to crewmembers, including each other, to achieve a safe and efficient flight.

Curriculum outline means a listing of each segment, module, lesson, and lesson element in a curriculum, or an equivalent listing acceptable to the FAA.

Evaluation of proficiency means a Line Operational Evaluation (LOE) or an equivalent evaluation under an AQP acceptable to the FAA.

Evaluator means a person who assesses or judges the performance of crewmembers, instructors, other evaluators, aircraft dispatchers, or other operations personnel.

First Look means the assessment of performance to determine proficiency on designated flight tasks before any briefing, training, or practice on those tasks is given in the training session for a continuing qualification curriculum. First Look is conducted during an AQP continuing qualification cycle to determine trends of degraded proficiency, if any, due in part to the length of the interval between training sessions.

Instructional systems development means a systematic methodology for developing or modifying qualification standards and associated curriculum content based on a documented analysis of the job tasks, skills, and knowledge required for job proficiency.

Job task listing means a listing of all tasks, subtasks, knowledge, and skills required for accomplishing the operational job.

Line Operational Evaluation (LOE) means a simulated line environment, the scenario content of which is designed to test integrating technical and CRM skills.

Line Operational Simulation (LOS) means a training or evaluation session, as applicable, that is conducted in a simulated line environment using equipment qualified and approved for its intended purpose in an AQP.

Planned hours means the estimated amount of time (as specified in a curriculum outline) that it takes a typical student to complete a segment of instruction (to include all instruction, demonstration, practice, and evaluation, as appropriate, to reach proficiency).

Qualification standard means a statement of a minimum required performance, applicable parameters, criteria, applicable flight conditions, evaluation strategy, evaluation media, and applicable document references.

Qualification standards document means a single document containing all the qualification standards for an AQP together with a prologue that provides a detailed description of all facets of the evaluation process.

Special tracking means assigning a person to an augmented schedule of training, checking, or both.

Training session means a contiguously scheduled period devoted to training activities at a facility approved by the FAA for that purpose.

Variant means a specifically configured aircraft for which the FAA has identified training and qualifications that are significantly different from those applicable to other aircraft of the same make, model, and series.

§ 121.909 Approval of Advanced Qualification Program.

(a) *Approval process.* Application for approval of an AQP curriculum under this subpart is made, through the FAA office responsible for approval of the certificate holder's operations specifications, to the Manager of the Air Transportation Division.

(b) *Approval criteria.* Each AQP must have separate curriculums for indoctrination, qualification, and continuing qualification (including upgrade, transition, and requalification), as specified in §§ 121.911, 121.913, and 121.915. All AQP curriculums must be based on an instructional systems development methodology. This methodology must incorporate a thorough analysis of the certificate holder's operations, aircraft, line environment and job functions. All AQP qualification and continuing qualification curriculums must integrate the training and evaluation of CRM and technical skills and knowledge. An application for approval of an AQP curriculum may be approved if the program meets the following requirements:

(1) The program must meet all the requirements of this subpart.

(2) Each indoctrination, qualification, and continuing qualification AQP, and derivatives must include the following documentation:

(i) Initial application for AQP.

(ii) Initial job task listing.

(iii) Instructional systems development methodology.

(iv) Qualification standards document.

(v) Curriculum outline.

(vi) Implementation and operations plan.

(3) Subject to approval by the FAA, certificate holders may elect, where appropriate, to consolidate information about multiple programs within any of the documents referenced in paragraph (b)(2) of this section.

(4) The Qualification Standards Document must indicate specifically the requirements of the parts 61, 63, 65, 121, or 135 of this chapter, as applicable, that would be replaced by an AQP curriculum. If a practical test requirement of parts 61, 63, 65, 121, or 135 of this chapter is replaced by an AQP curriculum, the certificate holder must establish an initial justification and a continuing process approved by the FAA to show how the AQP curriculum provides an equivalent level of safety for each requirement that is to be replaced.

(c) *Application and transition.* Each certificate holder that applies for one or more advanced qualification curriculums must include as part of its application a proposed transition plan (containing a calendar of events) for moving from its present approved training to the advanced qualification program training.

(d) *Advanced Qualification Program revisions or rescissions of approval.* If after a certificate holder begins training and qualification under an AQP, the FAA finds the certificate holder is not meeting the provisions of its approved AQP, the FAA may require the certificate holder, pursuant to §121.405(e), to make revisions. Or if otherwise warranted, the FAA may withdraw AQP approval and require the certificate holder to submit and obtain approval for a plan (containing a schedule of events) that the certificate holder must comply with and use to transition to an approved training program under subpart N of this part or under subpart H of part 135 of this chapter, as appropriate. The certificate holder may also voluntarily submit and obtain approval for a plan (containing a schedule of events) to transition to an approved training program under subpart N of this part or under subpart H of part 135 of this chapter, as appropriate.

(e) *Approval by the FAA.* Final approval of an AQP by the FAA indicates the FAA has accepted the justification provided under paragraph (b)(4) of this

section and the applicant's initial justification and continuing process establish an equivalent level of safety for each requirement of parts 61, 63, 65, 121, and 135 of this chapter that is being replaced.

[Docket No. FAA–2005–20750, 70 FR 54815, Sept. 16, 2005, as amended by Docket FAA–2018–0119, Amdt. 121–380, 83 FR 9173, Mar. 5, 2018]

§121.911 Indoctrination curriculum.

Each indoctrination curriculum must include the following:

(a) For newly hired persons being trained under an AQP: The certificate holder's policies and operating practices and general operational knowledge.

(b) For newly hired crewmembers and aircraft dispatchers: General aeronautical knowledge appropriate to the duty position.

(c) For instructors: The fundamental principles of the teaching and learning process; methods and theories of instruction; and the knowledge necessary to use aircraft, flight training devices, flight simulators, and other training equipment in advanced qualification curriculums, as appropriate.

(d) For evaluators: General evaluation requirements of the AQP; methods of evaluating crewmembers and aircraft dispatchers and other operations personnel, as appropriate, and policies and practices used to conduct the kinds of evaluations particular to an AQP (e.g., LOE).

§121.913 Qualification curriculum.

Each qualification curriculum must contain training, evaluation, and certification activities, as applicable for specific positions subject to the AQP, as follows:

(a) The certificate holder's planned hours of training, evaluation, and supervised operating experience.

(b) For crewmembers, aircraft dispatchers, and other operations personnel, the following:

(1) Training, evaluation, and certification activities that are aircraft- and equipment-specific to qualify a person for a particular duty position on, or duties related to the operation of, a specific make, model, series, or variant aircraft.

(2) A list of and text describing the knowledge requirements, subject materials, job skills, and qualification standards of each proficiency objective to be trained and evaluated.

(3) The requirements of the certificate holder's approved AQP program that are in addition to or in place of, the requirements of parts 61, 63, 65, 121 or 135 of this chapter, including any applicable practical test requirements.

(4) A list of and text describing operating experience, evaluation/remediation strategies, provisions for special tracking, and how recency of experience requirements will be accomplished.

(c) For flight crewmembers: Initial operating experience and line check.

(d) For instructors, the following as appropriate:

(1) Training and evaluation activities to qualify a person to conduct instruction on how to operate, or on how to ensure the safe operation of a particular make, model, and series aircraft (or variant).

(2) A list of and text describing the knowledge requirements, subject materials, job skills, and qualification standards of each procedure and proficiency objective to be trained and evaluated.

(3) A list of and text describing evaluation/remediation strategies, standardization policies and recency requirements.

(e) For evaluators: The requirements of paragraph (d)(1) of this section plus the following, as appropriate:

(1) Training and evaluation activities that are aircraft and equipment specific to qualify a person to assess the performance of persons who operate or who ensure the safe operation of, a particular make, model, and series aircraft (or variant).

(2) A list of and text describing the knowledge requirements, subject materials, job skills, and qualification standards of each procedure and proficiency objective to be trained and evaluated.

(3) A list of and text describing evaluation/remediation strategies, standardization policies and recency requirements.

§ 121.915 Continuing qualification curriculum.

Each continuing qualification curriculum must contain training and evaluation activities, as applicable for specific positions subject to the AQP, as follows:

(a) *Continuing qualification cycle.* A continuing qualification cycle that ensures that during each cycle each person qualified under an AQP, including instructors and evaluators, will receive a mix that will ensure training and evaluation on all events and subjects necessary to ensure that each person maintains proficiency in knowledge, technical skills, and cognitive skills required for initial qualification in accordance with the approved continuing qualification AQP, evaluation/remediation strategies, and provisions for special tracking. Each continuing qualification cycle must include at least the following:

(1) *Evaluation period.* Initially the continuing qualification cycle is comprised of two or more evaluation periods of equal duration. Each person qualified under an AQP must receive ground training and flight training, as appropriate, and an evaluation of proficiency during each evaluation period at a training facility. The number and frequency of training sessions must be approved by the FAA.

(2) *Training.* Continuing qualification must include training in all tasks, procedures and subjects required in accordance with the approved program documentation, as follows:

(i) For pilots in command, seconds in command, and flight engineers, First Look in accordance with the certificate holder's FAA-approved program documentation.

(ii) For pilots in command, seconds in command, flight engineers, flight attendants, instructors and evaluators: Ground training including a general review of knowledge and skills covered in qualification training, updated information on newly developed procedures, and safety information.

(iii) For crewmembers, instructors, evaluators, and other operational personnel who conduct their duties in flight: Proficiency training in an aircraft, flight training device, flight simulator, or other equipment, as appropriate, on normal, abnormal, and emergency flight procedures and maneuvers.

(iv) For dispatchers and other operational personnel who do not conduct their duties in flight: ground training including a general review of knowledge and skills covered in qualification training, updated information on newly developed procedures, safety related information, and, if applicable, a line observation program.

(v) For instructors and evaluators: Proficiency training in the type flight training device or the type flight simulator, as appropriate, regarding training equipment operation. For instructors and evaluators who are limited to conducting their duties in flight simulators or flight training devices: Training in operational flight procedures and maneuvers (normal, abnormal, and emergency).

(b) *Evaluation of performance.* Continuing qualification must include evaluation of performance on a sample of those events and major subjects identified as diagnostic of competence and approved for that purpose by the FAA. The following evaluation requirements apply:

(1) Evaluation of proficiency as follows:

(i) For pilots in command, seconds in command, and flight engineers: An evaluation of proficiency, portions of which may be conducted in an aircraft, flight simulator, or flight training device as approved in the certificate holder's curriculum that must be completed during each evaluation period.

(ii) For any other persons covered by an AQP, a means to evaluate their proficiency in the performance of their duties in their assigned tasks in an operational setting.

(2) Line checks as follows:

(i) Except as provided in paragraph (b)(2)(ii) of this section, for pilots in command: A line check conducted in an aircraft during actual flight operations under part 121 or part 135 of this chapter or during operationally (line) oriented flights, such as ferry flights or proving flights. A line check must be completed in the calendar month at the midpoint of the evaluation period.

(ii) With the FAA's approval, a no-notice line check strategy may be used in lieu of the line check required by paragraph (b)(2)(i) of this section. The certificate holder who elects to exercise this option must ensure the "no-notice" line checks are administered so the flight crewmembers are not notified before the evaluation. In addition, the AQP certificate holder must ensure that each pilot in command receives at least one "no-notice" line check every 24 months. As a minimum, the number of "no-notice" line checks administered each calendar year must equal at least 50% of the certificate holder's pilot-in-command workforce in accordance with a strategy approved by the FAA for that purpose. In addition, the line checks to be conducted under this paragraph must be conducted over all geographic areas flown by the certificate holder in accordance with a sampling methodology approved by the FAA for that purpose.

(iii) During the line checks required under paragraph (b)(2)(i) and (ii) of this section, each person performing duties as a pilot in command, second in command, or flight engineer for that flight, must be individually evaluated to determine whether the person remains adequately trained and currently proficient with respect to the particular aircraft, crew position, and type of operation in which he or she serves; and the person has sufficient knowledge and skills to operate effectively as part of a crew. The evaluator must be a check airman, an APD, or an FAA inspector and must hold the certificates and ratings required of the pilot in command.

(c) *Recency of experience.* For pilots in command, seconds in command, flight engineers, aircraft dispatchers, instructors, evaluators, and flight attendants, approved recency of experience requirements appropriate to the duty position.

(d) *Duration of cycles and periods.* Initially, the continuing qualification cycle approved for an AQP must not exceed 24 calendar months in duration, and must include two or more evaluation periods of equal duration. After that, upon demonstration by a certificate holder that an extension is warranted, the FAA may approve an extension of the continuing qualification cycle to a maximum of 36 calendar months in duration.

(e) *Requalification.* Each continuing qualification curriculum must include a curriculum segment that covers the requirements for requalifying a crewmember, aircraft dispatcher, other operations personnel, instructor, or evaluator who has not maintained continuing qualification.

§ 121.917 Other requirements.

In addition to the requirements of §§ 121.913 and 121.915, each AQP qualification and continuing qualification curriculum must include the following requirements:

(a) Integrated Crew Resource Management (CRM) or Dispatcher Resource Management (DRM) ground and if appropriate flight training applicable to each position for which training is provided under an AQP.

(b) Approved training on and evaluation of skills and proficiency of each person being trained under AQP to use his or her resource management skills and his or her technical (piloting or other) skills in an actual or simulated operations scenario. For flight crewmembers this training and evaluation must be conducted in an approved flight training device, flight simulator, or, if approved under this subpart, in an aircraft.

(c) Data collection and analysis processes acceptable to the FAA that will ensure the certificate holder provides performance information on its crewmembers, dispatchers, instructors, evaluators, and other operations personnel that will enable the certificate holder and the FAA to determine whether the form and content of training and evaluation activities are satisfactorily accomplishing the overall objectives of the curriculum.

§ 121.919 Certification.

A person subject to an AQP is eligible to receive a commercial or airline transport pilot, flight engineer, or aircraft dispatcher certificate or appropriate rating based on the successful completion of training and evaluation events accomplished under that program if the following requirements are met:

(a) Training and evaluation of required knowledge and skills under the AQP must meet minimum certification and rating criteria established by the FAA in parts 61, 63, or 65 of this chapter. The FAA may approve alternatives to the certification and rating criteria of parts 61, 63, or 65 of this chapter, including practical test requirements, if it can be demonstrated that the newly established criteria or requirements represent an equivalent or better measure of crewmember or dispatcher competence, operational proficiency, and safety.

(b) The applicant satisfactorily completes the appropriate qualification curriculum.

(c) The applicant shows competence in required technical knowledge and skills (e.g., piloting or other) and crew resource management (e.g., CRM or DRM) knowledge and skills in scenarios (*i.e.,* LOE) that test both types of knowledge and skills together.

(d) The applicant is otherwise eligible under the applicable requirements of part 61, 63, or 65 of this chapter.

(e) The applicant has been trained to proficiency on the certificate holder's approved AQP Qualification Standards as witnessed by an instructor, check airman, or APD and has passed an LOE administered by an APD or the FAA.

§ 121.921 Training devices and simulators.

(a) Each flight training device or airplane simulator that will be used in an AQP for one of the following purposes must be evaluated by the FAA for assignment of a flight training device or flight simulator qualification level:

(1) Required evaluation of individual or crew proficiency.

(2) Training to proficiency or training activities that determine if an individual or crew is ready for an evaluation of proficiency.

(3) Activities used to meet recency of experience requirements.

(4) Line Operational Simulations (LOS).

(b) Approval of other training equipment.

(1) Any training equipment that is intended to be used in an AQP for purposes other than those set forth in paragraph (a) of this section must be

approved by the FAA for its intended use.

(2) An applicant for approval of training equipment under this paragraph must identify the device by its nomenclature and describe its intended use.

(3) Each training device approved for use in an AQP must be part of a continuing program to provide for its serviceability and fitness to perform its intended function as approved by the FAA.

§121.923 **Approval of training, qualification, or evaluation by a person who provides training by arrangement.**

(a) A certificate holder operating under part 121 or part 135 of this chapter may arrange to have AQP training, qualification, evaluation, or certification functions performed by another person (a "training provider") if the following requirements are met:

(1) The training provider is certificated under part 119 or 142 of this chapter.

(2) The training provider's AQP training and qualification curriculums, curriculum segments, or portions of curriculum segments must be provisionally approved by the FAA. A training provider may apply for provisional approval independently or in conjunction with a certificate holder's application for AQP approval. Application for provisional approval must be made, through the FAA office directly responsible for oversight of the training provider, to the Manager of the Air Transportation Division.

(3) The specific use of provisionally approved curriculums, curriculum segments, or portions of curriculum segments in a certificate holder's AQP must be approved by the FAA as set forth in §121.909.

(b) An applicant for provisional approval of a curriculum, curriculum segment, or portion of a curriculum segment under this paragraph must show the following requirements are met:

(1) The applicant must have a curriculum for the qualification and continuing qualification of each instructor and evaluator used by the applicant.

(2) The applicant's facilities must be found by the FAA to be adequate for any planned training, qualification, or evaluation for a certificate holder operating under part 121 or part 135 of this chapter.

(3) Except for indoctrination curriculums, the curriculum, curriculum segment, or portion of a curriculum segment must identify the specific make, model, and series aircraft (or variant) and crewmember or other positions for which it is designed.

(c) A certificate holder who wants approval to use a training provider's provisionally approved curriculum, curriculum segment, or portion of a curriculum segment in its AQP, must show the following requirements are met:

(1) Each instructor or evaluator used by the training provider must meet all the qualification and continuing qualification requirements that apply to employees of the certificate holder that has arranged for the training, including knowledge of the certificate holder's operations.

(2) Each provisionally approved curriculum, curriculum segment, or portion of a curriculum segment must be approved by the FAA for use in the certificate holder's AQP. The FAA will either provide approval or require modifications to ensure that each curriculum, curriculum segment, or portion of a curriculum segment is applicable to the certificate holder's AQP.

[Docket No. FAA–2005–20750, 70 FR 54815, Sept. 16, 2005, as amended by Docket FAA–2018–0119, Amdt. 121–380, 83 FR 9173, Mar. 5, 2018]

§121.925 **Recordkeeping requirements.**

Each certificate holder conducting an approved AQP must establish and maintain records in sufficient detail to demonstrate the certificate holder is in compliance with all the requirements of the AQP and this subpart.

Subpart Z—Hazardous Materials Training Program

SOURCE: Docket No. FAA–2003–15085, 70 FR 58823, Oct. 7, 2005, unless otherwise noted.

§ 121.1001 Applicability and definitions.

(a) This subpart prescribes the requirements applicable to each certificate holder for training each crewmember and person performing or directly supervising any of the following job functions involving any item for transport on board an aircraft:

(1) Acceptance;

(2) Rejection;

(3) Handling;

(4) Storage incidental to transport;

(5) Packaging of company material; or

(6) Loading.

(b) *Definitions.* For purposes of this subpart, the following definitions apply:

(1) *Company material (COMAT)*—Material owned or used by a certificate holder.

(2) *Initial hazardous materials training*—The basic training required for each newly hired person, or each person changing job functions, who performs or directly supervises any of the job functions specified in paragraph (a) of this section.

(3) *Recurrent hazardous materials training*—The training required every 24 months for each person who has satisfactorily completed the certificate holder's approved initial hazardous materials training program and performs or directly supervises any of the job functions specified in paragraph (a) of this section.

§ 121.1003 Hazardous materials training: General.

(a) Each certificate holder must establish and implement a hazardous materials training program that:

(1) Satisfies the requirements of Appendix O of this part;

(2) Ensures that each person performing or directly supervising any of the job functions specified in § 121.1001(a) is trained to comply with all applicable parts of 49 CFR parts 171 through 180 and the requirements of this subpart; and

(3) Enables the trained person to recognize items that contain, or may contain, hazardous materials regulated by 49 CFR parts 171 through 180.

(b) Each certificate holder must provide initial hazardous materials training and recurrent hazardous materials training to each crewmember and person performing or directly supervising any of the job functions specified in § 121.1001(a).

(c) Each certificate holder's hazardous materials training program must be approved by the FAA prior to implementation.

§ 121.1005 Hazardous materials training required.

(a) *Training requirement.* Except as provided in paragraphs (b), (c) and (f) of this section, no certificate holder may use any crewmember or person to perform any of the job functions or direct supervisory responsibilities, and no person may perform any of the job functions or direct supervisory responsibilities, specified in § 121.1001(a) unless that person has satisfactorily completed the certificate holder's FAA-approved initial or recurrent hazardous materials training program within the past 24 months.

(b) *New hire or new job function.* A person who is a new hire and has not yet satisfactorily completed the required initial hazardous materials training, or a person who is changing job functions and has not received initial or recurrent training for a job function involving storage incidental to transport, or loading of items for transport on an aircraft, may perform those job functions for not more than 30 days from the date of hire or a change in job function, if the person is under the direct visual supervision of a person who is authorized by the certificate holder to supervise that person and who has successfully completed the certificate holder's FAA-approved initial or recurrent training program within the past 24 months.

(c) *Persons who work for more than one certificate holder.* A certificate holder that uses or assigns a person to perform or directly supervise a job function specified in § 121.1001(a), when that person also performs or directly supervises the same job function for another certificate holder, need only train that person in its own policies and procedures regarding those job functions, if all of the following are met:

(1) The certificate holder using this exception receives written verification

from the person designated to hold the training records representing the other certificate holder that the person has satisfactorily completed hazardous materials training for the specific job function under the other certificate holder's FAA approved hazardous material training program under Appendix O of this part; and

(2) The certificate holder who trained the person has the same operations specifications regarding the acceptance, handling, and transport of hazardous materials as the certificate holder using this exception.

(d) *Recurrent hazardous materials training—Completion date.* A person who satisfactorily completes recurrent hazardous materials training in the calendar month before, or the calendar month after, the month in which the recurrent training is due, is considered to have taken that training during the month in which it is due. If the person completes this training earlier than the month before it is due, the month of the completion date becomes his or her new anniversary month.

(e) *Repair stations.* A certificate holder must ensure that each repair station performing work for, or on the certificate holder's behalf is notified in writing of the certificate holder's policies and operations specification authorization permitting or prohibition against the acceptance, rejection, handling, storage incidental to transport, and transportation of hazardous materials, including company material. This notification requirement applies only to repair stations that are regulated by 49 CFR parts 171 through 180.

(f) *Certificate holders operating at foreign locations.* This exception applies if a certificate holder operating at a foreign location where the country requires the certificate holder to use persons working in that country to load aircraft. In such a case, the certificate holder may use those persons even if they have not been trained in accordance with the certificate holder's FAA approved hazardous materials training program. Those persons, however, must be under the direct visual supervision of someone who has successfully completed the certificate holder's approved initial or recurrent hazardous materials training program in accordance

with this part. This exception applies only to those persons who load aircraft.

§121.1007 **Hazardous materials training records.**

(a) *General requirement.* Each certificate holder must maintain a record of all training required by this part received within the preceding three years for each person who performs or directly supervises a job function specified in §121.1001(a). The record must be maintained during the time that the person performs or directly supervises any of those job functions, and for 90 days thereafter. These training records must be kept for direct employees of the certificate holder, as well as independent contractors, subcontractors, and any other person who performs or directly supervises these job functions for or on behalf of the certificate holder.

(b) *Location of records.* The certificate holder must retain the training records required by paragraph (a) of this section for all initial and recurrent training received within the preceding 3 years for all persons performing or directly supervising the job functions listed in Appendix O at a designated location. The records must be available upon request at the location where the trained person performs or directly supervises the job function specified in §121.1001(a). Records may be maintained electronically and provided on location electronically. When the person ceases to perform or directly supervise a hazardous materials job function, the certificate holder must retain the hazardous materials training records for an additional 90 days and make them available upon request at the last location where the person worked.

(c) *Content of records.* Each record must contain the following:

(1) The individual's name;

(2) The most recent training completion date;

(3) A description, copy or reference to training materials used to meet the training requirement;

(4) The name and address of the organization providing the training; and

(5) A copy of the certification issued when the individual was trained, which

shows that a test has been completed satisfactorily.

(d) *New hire or new job function.* Each certificate holder using a person under the exception in § 121.1005(b) must maintain a record for that person. The records must be available upon request at the location where the trained person performs or directly supervises the job function specified in § 121.1001(a). Records may be maintained electronically and provided on location electronically. The record must include the following:

(1) A signed statement from an authorized representative of the certificate holder authorizing the use of the person in accordance with the exception;

(2) The date of hire or change in job function;

(3) The person's name and assigned job function;

(4) The name of the supervisor of the job function; and

(5) The date the person is to complete hazardous materials training in accordance with appendix O of this part.

Subpart AA—Continued Airworthiness and Safety Improvements

SOURCE: Amdt. 121–336, 72 FR 63411, Nov. 8, 2007, unless otherwise noted.

§ 121.1101 Purpose and definition.

(a) This subpart requires persons holding an air carrier or operating certificate under part 119 of this chapter to support the continued airworthiness of each airplane. These requirements may include, but are not limited to, revising the maintenance program, incorporating design changes, and incorporating revisions to Instructions for Continued Airworthiness.

(b) [Reserved]

[Amdt. 121–336, 72 FR 63411, Nov. 8, 2007, as amended by Docket FAA–2018–0119, Amdt. 121–380, 83 FR 9173, Mar. 5, 2018]

§ 121.1103 [Reserved]

§ 121.1105 Aging airplane inspections and records reviews.

(a) *Applicability.* This section applies to all airplanes operated by a certificate holder under this part, except for those airplanes operated between any point within the State of Alaska and any other point within the State of Alaska.

(b) *Operation after inspection and records review.* After the dates specified in this paragraph, a certificate holder may not operate an airplane under this part unless the Administrator has notified the certificate holder that the Administrator has completed the aging airplane inspection and records review required by this section. During the inspection and records review, the certificate holder must demonstrate to the Administrator that the maintenance of age-sensitive parts and components of the airplane has been adequate and timely enough to ensure the highest degree of safety.

(1) *Airplanes exceeding 24 years in service on December 8, 2003; initial and repetitive inspections and records reviews.* For an airplane that has exceeded 24 years in service on December 8, 2003, no later than December 5, 2007, and thereafter at intervals not to exceed 7 years.

(2) *Airplanes exceeding 14 years in service but not 24 years in service on December 8, 2003; initial and repetitive inspections and records reviews.* For an airplane that has exceeded 14 years in service but not 24 years in service on December 8, 2003, no later than December 4, 2008, and thereafter at intervals not to exceed 7 years.

(3) *Airplanes not exceeding 14 years in service on December 8, 2003; initial and repetitive inspections and records reviews.* For an airplane that has not exceeded 14 years in service on December 8, 2003, no later than 5 years after the start of the airplane's 15th year in service and thereafter at intervals not to exceed 7 years.

(c) *Unforeseen schedule conflict.* In the event of an unforeseen scheduling conflict for a specific airplane, the Administrator may approve an extension of up to 90 days beyond an interval specified in paragraph (b) of this section.

(d) *Airplane and records availability.* The certificate holder must make available to the Administrator each airplane for which an inspection and records review is required under this section, in a condition for inspection specified by the Administrator, together with records containing the following information:

(1) Total years in service of the airplane;

(2) Total time in service of the airframe;

(3) Total flight cycles of the airframe;

(4) Date of the last inspection and records review required by this section;

(5) Current status of life-limited parts of the airframe;

(6) Time since the last overhaul of all structural components required to be overhauled on a specific time basis;

(7) Current inspection status of the airplane, including the time since the last inspection required by the inspection program under which the airplane is maintained;

(8) Current status of applicable airworthiness directives, including the date and methods of compliance, and if the airworthiness directive involves recurring action, the time and date when the next action is required;

(9) A list of major structural alterations; and

(10) A report of major structural repairs and the current inspection status for those repairs.

(e) *Notification to Administrator.* Each certificate holder must notify the Administrator at least 60 days before the date on which the airplane and airplane records will be made available for the inspection and records review.

[Doc. No. FAA–1999–5401, 67 FR 72761, Dec. 6, 2002, as amended by Amdt. 121–284, 70 FR 5532, Feb. 2, 2005; Amdt. 121–310, 70 FR 23936, May 6, 2005. Redesignated by Amdt. 121–336, 72 FR 63412, Nov. 8, 2007]

§ 121.1107 Repairs assessment for pressurized fuselages.

(a) No certificate holder may operate an Airbus Model A300 (excluding the –600 series), British Aerospace Model BAC 1–11, Boeing Model 707, 720, 727, 737, or 747, McDonnell Douglas Model DC–8, DC–9/MD–80 or DC–10, Fokker Model F28, or Lockheed Model L–1011 airplane beyond the applicable flight cycle implementation time specified below, or May 25, 2001, whichever occurs later, unless operations specifications have been issued to reference repair assessment guidelines applicable

to the fuselage pressure boundary (fuselage skin, door skin, and bulkhead webs), and those guidelines are incorporated in its maintenance program. The repair assessment guidelines must be approved by the responsible Aircraft Certification Service office for the type certificate for the affected airplane.

(1) For the Airbus Model A300 (excluding the –600 series), the flight cycle implementation time is:

(i) Model B2: 36,000 flights.

(ii) Model B4–100 (including Model B4–2C): 30,000 flights above the window line, and 36,000 flights below the window line.

(iii) Model B4–200: 25,500 flights above the window line, and 34,000 flights below the window line.

(2) For all models of the British Aerospace BAC 1–11, the flight cycle implementation time is 60,000 flights.

(3) For all models of the Boeing 707, the flight cycle implementation time is 15,000 flights.

(4) For all models of the Boeing 720, the flight cycle implementation time is 23,000 flights.

(5) For all models of the Boeing 727, the flight cycle implementation time is 45,000 flights.

(6) For all models of the Boeing 737, the flight cycle implementation time is 60,000 flights.

(7) For all models of the Boeing 747, the flight cycle implementation time is 15,000 flights.

(8) For all models of the McDonnell Douglas DC–8, the flight cycle implementation time is 30,000 flights.

(9) For all models of the McDonnell Douglas DC–9/MD–80, the flight cycle implementation time is 60,000 flights.

(10) For all models of the McDonnell Douglas DC–10, the flight cycle implementation time is 30,000 flights.

(11) For all models of the Lockheed L–1011, the flight cycle implementation time is 27,000 flights.

(12) For the Fokker F–28 Mark 1000, 2000, 3000, and 4000, the flight cycle implementation time is 60,000 flights.

(b) [Reserved]

[Doc. No. 29104, 65 FR 24125, Apr. 25, 2000; 65 FR 50744, Aug. 21, 2000, as amended by Amdt. 121–282, 66 FR 23130, May 7, 2001; ; Amdt. 121–305, 69 FR 45942, July 30, 2004. Redesignated and amended by Amdt. 121–336, 72 FR 63412, Nov. 8, 2007; Docket FAA–2018–0119, Amdt. 121–380, 83 FR 9173, Mar. 5, 2018]

§ 121.1109 Supplemental inspections.

(a) *Applicability.* Except as specified in paragraph (b) of this section, this section applies to transport category, turbine powered airplanes with a type certificate issued after January 1, 1958, that as a result of original type certification or later increase in capacity have—

(1) A maximum type certificated passenger seating capacity of 30 or more; or

(2) A maximum payload capacity of 7,500 pounds or more.

(b) *Exception.* This section does not apply to an airplane operated by a certificate holder under this part between any point within the State of Alaska and any other point within the State of Alaska.

(c) *General requirements.* After December 20, 2010, a certificate holder may not operate an airplane under this part unless the following requirements have been met:

(1) *Baseline Structure.* The certificate holder's maintenance program for the airplane includes FAA-approved damage-tolerance-based inspections and procedures for airplane structure susceptible to fatigue cracking that could contribute to a catastrophic failure. For the purpose of this section, this structure is termed "fatigue critical structure."

(2) *Adverse effects of repairs, alterations, and modifications.* The maintenance program for the airplane includes a means for addressing the adverse effects repairs, alterations, and modifications may have on fatigue critical structure and on inspections required by paragraph (c)(1) of this section. The means for addressing these adverse effects must be approved by the responsible Aircraft Certification Service office.

(3) *Changes to maintenance program.* The changes made to the maintenance program required by paragraphs (c)(1) and (c)(2) of this section, and any later revisions to these changes, must be submitted to the Principal Mainte-

nance Inspector for review and approval.

[Doc. No. FAA-1999-5401, 70 FR 5532, Feb. 2, 2005. Redesignated by Amdt. 121-336, 72 FR 63412, Nov. 8, 2007; Amdt. 121-337, 72 FR 70508, Dec. 12, 2007; Docket FAA-2018-0119, Amdt. 121-380, 83 FR 9173, Mar. 5, 2018]

§ 121.1111 Electrical wiring interconnection systems (EWIS) maintenance program.

(a) Except as provided in paragraph (f) of this section, this section applies to transport category, turbine-powered airplanes with a type certificate issued after January 1, 1958, that, as a result of original type certification or later increase in capacity, have—

(1) A maximum type-certificated passenger capacity of 30 or more, or

(2) A maximum payload capacity of 7500 pounds or more.

(b) After March 10, 2011, no certificate holder may operate an airplane identified in paragraph (a) of this section unless the maintenance program for that airplane includes inspections and procedures for electrical wiring interconnection systems (EWIS).

(c) The proposed EWIS maintenance program changes must be based on EWIS Instructions for Continued Airworthiness (ICA) that have been developed in accordance with the provisions of Appendix H of part 25 of this chapter applicable to each affected airplane (including those ICA developed for supplemental type certificates installed on each airplane) and that have been approved by the responsible Aircraft Certification Service office.

(1) For airplanes subject to § 26.11 of this chapter, the EWIS ICA must comply with paragraphs H25.5(a)(1) and (b).

(2) For airplanes subject to § 25.1729 of this chapter, the EWIS ICA must comply with paragraph H25.4 and all of paragraph H25.5.

(d) After March 10, 2011, before returning an airplane to service after any alterations for which EWIS ICA are developed, the certificate holder must include in the airplane's maintenance program inspections and procedures for EWIS based on those ICA.

(e) The EWIS maintenance program changes identified in paragraphs (c) and (d) of this section and any later EWIS revisions must be submitted to the Principal Inspector for review and approval.

(f) This section does not apply to the following airplane models:

(1) Lockheed L–188
(2) Bombardier CL–44
(3) Mitsubishi YS–11
(4) British Aerospace BAC 1–11
(5) Concorde
(6) deHavilland D.H. 106 Comet 4C
(7) VFW-Vereinigte Flugtechnische Werk VFW–614
(8) Illyushin Aviation IL 96T
(9) Bristol Aircraft Britannia 305
(10) Handley Page Herald Type 300
(11) Avions Marcel Dassault—Breguet Aviation Mercure 100C
(12) Airbus Caravelle
(13) Lockheed L–300

[Amdt. 121–336, 72 FR 63411, Nov. 8, 2007, as amended by Docket FAA–2018–0119, Amdt. 121–380, 83 FR 9173, Mar. 5, 2018]

§121.1113 Fuel tank system maintenance program.

(a) Except as provided in paragraph (g) of this section, this section applies to transport category, turbine-powered airplanes with a type certificate issued after January 1, 1958, that, as a result of original type certification or later increase in capacity, have—

(1) A maximum type-certificated passenger capacity of 30 or more, or
(2) A maximum payload capacity of 7500 pounds or more.

(b) For each airplane on which an auxiliary fuel tank is installed under a field approval, before June 16, 2008, the certificate holder must submit to the responsible Aircraft Certification Service office proposed maintenance instructions for the tank that meet the requirements of Special Federal Aviation Regulation No. 88 (SFAR 88) of this chapter.

(c) After December 16, 2008, no certificate holder may operate an airplane identified in paragraph (a) of this section unless the maintenance program for that airplane has been revised to include applicable inspections, procedures, and limitations for fuel tanks systems.

(d) The proposed fuel tank system maintenance program revisions must be based on fuel tank system Instructions for Continued Airworthiness (ICA) that have been developed in ac-

cordance with the applicable provisions of SFAR 88 of this chapter or §25.1529 and part 25, Appendix H, of this chapter, in effect on June 6, 2001 (including those developed for auxiliary fuel tanks, if any, installed under supplemental type certificates or other design approval) and that have been approved by the responsible Aircraft Certification Service office.

(e) After December 16, 2008, before returning an aircraft to service after any alteration for which fuel tank ICA are developed under SFAR 88 or under §25.1529 in effect on June 6, 2001, the certificate holder must include in the maintenance program for the airplane inspections and procedures for the fuel tank system based on those ICA.

(f) The fuel tank system maintenance program changes identified in paragraphs (d) and (e) of this section and any later fuel tank system revisions must be submitted to the Principal Inspector for review and approval.

(g) This section does not apply to the following airplane models:

(1) Bombardier CL–44
(2) Concorde
(3) deHavilland D.H. 106 Comet 4C
(4) VFW–Vereinigte Flugtechnische Werk VFW–614
(5) Illyushin Aviation IL 96T
(6) Bristol Aircraft Britannia 305
(7) Handley Page Herald Type 300
(8) Avions Marcel Dassault—Breguet Aviation Mercure 100C
(9) Airbus Caravelle
(10) Lockheed L–300

[Amdt. 121–336, 72 FR 63411, Nov. 8, 2007, as amended by Docket FAA–2018–0119, Amdt. 121–380, 83 FR 9173, Mar. 5, 2018]

§121.1115 Limit of validity.

(a) *Applicability.* This section applies to certificate holders operating any transport category, turbine-powered airplane with a maximum takeoff gross weight greater than 75,000 pounds and a type certificate issued after January 1, 1958, regardless of whether the maximum takeoff gross weight is a result of an original type certificate or a later design change. This section also applies to certificate holders operating any transport category, turbine-powered airplane with a type certificate issued after January 1, 1958, regardless of the maximum takeoff gross weight, for which a limit of validity of the engineering data that supports the structural maintenance program (hereafter referred to as LOV) is required in accordance with § 25.571 or § 26.21 of this chapter after January 14, 2011.

(b) *Limit of validity.* No certificate holder may operate an airplane identified in paragraph (a) of this section after the applicable date identified in Table 1 of this section unless an Airworthiness Limitations section approved under Appendix H to part 25 or § 26.21 of this chapter is incorporated into its maintenance program. The ALS must—

(1) Include an LOV approved under § 25.571 or § 26.21 of this chapter, as applicable, except as provided in paragraph (f) of this section; and

(2) Be clearly distinguishable within its maintenance program.

(c) *Operation of airplanes excluded from § 26.21.* No certificate holder may operate an airplane identified in § 26.21(g) of this chapter after July 14, 2013, unless an Airworthiness Limitations section approved under Appendix H to part 25 or § 26.21 of this chapter is incorporated into its maintenance program. The ALS must—

(1) Include an LOV approved under § 25.571 or § 26.21 of this chapter, as applicable, except as provided in paragraph (f) of this section; and

(2) Be clearly distinguishable within its maintenance program.

(d) *Extended limit of validity.* No certificate holder may operate an airplane beyond the LOV, or extended LOV, specified in paragraph (b)(1), (c), (d), or (f) of this section, as applicable, unless the following conditions are met:

(1) An ALS must be incorporated into its maintenance program that—

(i) Includes an extended LOV and any widespread fatigue damage airworthiness limitation items approved under § 26.23 of this chapter; and

(ii) Is approved under § 26.23 of this chapter.

(2) The extended LOV and the airworthiness limitation items pertaining to widespread fatigue damage must be clearly distinguishable within its maintenance program.

(e) *Principal Maintenance Inspector approval.* Certificate holders must submit the maintenance program revisions required by paragraphs (b), (c), and (d) of this section to the Principal Maintenance Inspector for review and approval.

(f) *Exception.* For any airplane for which an LOV has not been approved as of the applicable compliance date specified in paragraph (c) or Table 1 of this section, instead of including an approved LOV in the ALS, an operator must include the applicable default LOV specified in Table 1 or Table 2 of this section, as applicable, in the ALS.

TABLE 1—AIRPLANES SUBJECT TO § 26.21

Airplane model	Compliance date— months after January 14, 2011	Default LOV [flight cycles (FC) or flight hours (FH)]
Airbus—Existing [1] Models Only:		
A300 B2–1A, B2–1C, B2K–3C, B2–203	30	48,000 FC
A300 B4–2C, B4–103	30	40,000 FC
A300 B4–203	30	34,000 FC
A300–600 Series	60	30,000 FC/67,500 FH
A310–200 Series	60	40,000 FC/60,000 FH
A310–300 Series	60	35,000 FC/60,000 FH
A318 Series	60	48,000 FC/60,000 FH
A319 Series	60	48,000 FC/60,000 FH
A320–100 Series	60	48,000 FC/48,000 FH
A320–200 Series	60	48,000 FC/60,000 FH
A321 Series	60	48,000 FC/60,000 FH
A330–200, –300 Series (except WV050 family) (non enhanced)	60	40,000 FC/60,000 FH
A330–200, –300 Series WV050 family (enhanced)	60	33,000 FC/100,000 FH
A330–200 Freighter Series	60	See NOTE.
A340–200, –300 Series (except WV 027 and WV050 family) (non enhanced).	60	20,000 FC/80,000 FH
A340–200, –300 Series WV 027 (non enhanced)	60	30,000 FC/60,000 FH
A340–300 Series WV050 family (enhanced)	60	20,000 FC/100,000 FH
A340–500, –600 Series	60	16,600 FC/100,000 FH
A380–800 Series	72	See NOTE.
Boeing—Existing [1] Models Only:		

TABLE 1—AIRPLANES SUBJECT TO § 26.21—Continued

Airplane model	Compliance date—months after January 14, 2011	Default LOV [flight cycles (FC) or flight hours (FH)]
717	60	60,000 FC/60,000 FH
727 (all series)	30	60,000 FC
737 (Classics): 737–100, –200, –200C, –300 –400, –500	30	75,000 FC
737 (NG): 737–600, –700, –700C, –800, –900, –900ER	60	75,000 FC
747 (Classics): 747–100, –100B, –100B SUD, –200B, –200C, –200F, –300, 747SP, 747SR.	30	20,000 FC
747–400: 747–400, –400D, –400F	60	20,000 FC
757	60	50,000 FC
767	60	50,000 FC
777–200, –300	60	40,000 FC
777–200LR, 777–300ER	72	40,000 FC
777F	72	11,000 FC
Bombardier—Existing [1] Models Only:		
CL–600: 2D15 (Regional Jet Series 705), 2D24 (Regional Jet Series 900).	72	60,000 FC
Embraer—Existing [1] Models Only:		
ERJ 170	72	See NOTE.
ERJ 190	72	See NOTE.
Fokker—Existing [1] Models Only:		
F.28 Mark 0070, Mark 0100	30	90,000 FC
Lockheed—Existing [1] Models Only:		
L–1011	30	36,000 FC
188	30	26,600 FC
382 (all series)	30	20,000 FC/50,000 FH
McDonnell Douglas—Existing [1] Models Only:		
DC–8, –8F	30	50,000 FC/50,000 FH
DC–9 (except for MD–80 models)	30	100,000 FC/100,000 FH
MD–80 (DC–9–81, –82, –83, –87, MD–88)	30	50,000 FC/50,000 FH
MD–90	60	60,000 FC/90,000 FH
DC–10–10, –15	30	42,000 FC/60,000 FH
DC–10–30, –40, –10F, –30F, –40F	30	30,000 FC/60,000 FH
MD–10–10F	60	42,000 FC/60,000 FH
MD–10–30F	60	30,000 FC/60,000 FH
MD–11, MD–11F	60	20,000 FC/60,000 FH
Maximum Takeoff Gross Weight Changes:		
All airplanes whose maximum takeoff gross weight has been decreased to 75,000 pounds or below after January 14, 2011, or increased to greater than 75,000 pounds at any time by an amended type certificate or supplemental type certificate.	30, or within 12 months after the LOV is approved, or before operating the airplane, whichever occurs latest.	Not applicable.
All Other Airplane Models (TCs and amended TCs) not Listed in Table 2	72, or within 12 months after the LOV is approved, or before operating the airplane, whichever occurs latest.	Not applicable.

[1] Type certificated as of January 14, 2011.
Note: Airplane operation limitation is stated in the Airworthiness Limitation section.

NOTE: Airplane operation limitation is stated in the Airworthiness Limitation section.

TABLE 2—AIRPLANES EXCLUDED FROM § 26.21

Airplane model	Default LOV [flight cycles (FC) or flight hours (FH)]
Airbus:	
Caravelle	15,000 FC/24,000 FH
Avions Marcel Dassault:	
Breguet Aviation Mercure 100C	20,000 FC/16,000 FH
Boeing:	
Boeing 707 (-100 Series and –200 Series)	20,000 FC
Boeing 707 (-300 Series and –400 Series)	20,000 FC

251

TABLE 2—AIRPLANES EXCLUDED FROM § 26.21—Continued

Airplane model	Default LOV [flight cycles (FC) or flight hours (FH)]
Boeing 720	30,000 FC
Bombardier:	
CL–44D4 and CL–44J	20,000 FC
BD–700	15,000 FH
Bristol Aeroplane Company:	
Britannia 305	10,000 FC
British Aerospace Airbus, Ltd.:	
BAC 1–11 (all models)	85,000 FC
British Aerospace (Commercial Aircraft) Ltd.:	
Armstrong Whitworth Argosy A.W. 650 Series 101	20,000 FC
BAE Systems (Operations) Ltd.:	
BAe 146–100A (all models)	50,000 FC
BAe 146–200–07	50,000 FC
BAe 146–200–07 Dev	50,000 FC
BAe 146–200–11	50,000 FC
BAe 146–200–07A	47,000 FC
BAe 146–200–11 Dev	43,000 FC
BAe 146–300 (all models)	40,000 FC
Avro 146–RJ70A (all models)	40,000 FC
Avro 146–RJ85A and 146–RJ100A (all models)	50,000 FC
D & R Nevada, LLC:	
Convair Model 22	1,000 FC/1,000 FH
Convair Model 23M	1,000 FC/1,000 FH
deHavilland Aircraft Company, Ltd.:	
D.H. 106 Comet 4C	8,000 FH
Gulfstream:	
GV	40,000 FH
GV–SP	40,000 FH
Ilyushin Aviation Complex:	
IL–96T	10,000 FC/30,000 FH
Lockheed:	
300–50A01 (USAF C 141A)	20,000 FC

[Doc. No. FAA–2006–24281, 75 FR 69785, Nov. 15, 2010, as amended by Amdt. 121–360, 77 FR 30878, May 24, 2012; Admt. 121–360A, 77 FR 55105, Sept. 7, 2012]

§ 121.1117 Flammability reduction means.

(a) *Applicability.* Except as provided in paragraph (o) of this section, this section applies to transport category, turbine-powered airplanes with a type certificate issued after January 1, 1958, that, as a result of original type certification or later increase in capacity have:

(1) A maximum type-certificated passenger capacity of 30 or more, or

(2) A maximum payload capacity of 7,500 pounds or more.

(b) *New Production Airplanes.* Except in accordance with § 121.628, no certificate holder may operate an airplane identified in Table 1 of this section (including all-cargo airplanes) for which the State of Manufacture issued the original certificate of airworthiness or export airworthiness approval after December 27, 2010 unless an Ignition Mitigation Means (IMM) or Flammability Reduction Means (FRM) meeting the requirements of § 26.33 of this chapter is operational.

TABLE 1

Model—Boeing	Model—Airbus
747 Series 737 Series 777 Series 767 Series	A318, A319, A320, A321 Series A330, A340 Series

(c) *Auxiliary Fuel Tanks.* After the applicable date stated in paragraph (e) of this section, no certificate holder may operate any airplane subject to § 26.33 of this chapter that has an Auxiliary Fuel Tank installed pursuant to a field approval, unless the following requirements are met:

(1) The certificate holder complies with 14 CFR 26.35 by the applicable date stated in that section.

(2) The certificate holder installs Flammability Impact Mitigation

Means (FIMM), if applicable, that is approved by the responsible Aircraft Certification Service office.

(3) Except in accordance with §121.628, the FIMM, if applicable, is operational.

(d) *Retrofit.* Except as provided in paragraphs (j), (k), and (l) of this section, after the dates specified in paragraph (e) of this section, no certificate holder may operate an airplane to which this section applies unless the requirements of paragraphs (d)(1) and (d)(2) of this section are met.

(1) IMM, FRM or FIMM, if required by §§26.33, 26.35, or 26.37 of this chapter, that are approved by the responsible Aircraft Certification Service office, are installed within the compliance times specified in paragraph (e) of this section.

(2) Except in accordance with §121.628, the IMM, FRM or FIMM, as applicable, are operational.

(e) *Compliance Times.* Except as provided in paragraphs (k) and (l) of this section, the installations required by paragraph (d) of this section must be accomplished no later than the applicable dates specified in paragraph (e)(1), (e)(2), or (e)(3) of this section.

(1) Fifty percent of each certificate holder's fleet identified in paragraph (d)(1) of this section must be modified no later than December 26, 2014.

(2) One hundred percent of each certificate holder's fleet identified in paragraph (d)(1) of this section must be modified no later than December 26, 2017.

(3) For those certificate holders that have only one airplane of a model identified in Table 1 of this section, the airplane must be modified no later than December 26, 2017.

(f) *Compliance After Installation.* Except in accordance with §121.628, no certificate holder may—

(1) Operate an airplane on which IMM or FRM has been installed before the dates specified in paragraph (e) of this section unless the IMM or FRM is operational, or

(2) Deactivate or remove an IMM or FRM once installed unless it is replaced by a means that complies with paragraph (d) of this section.

(g) *Maintenance Program Revisions.* No certificate holder may operate an airplane for which airworthiness limitations have been approved by the responsible Aircraft Certification Service office in accordance with §§26.33, 26.35, or 26.37 of this chapter after the airplane is modified in accordance with paragraph (d) of this section unless the maintenance program for that airplane is revised to include those applicable airworthiness limitations.

(h) After the maintenance program is revised as required by paragraph (g) of this section, before returning an airplane to service after any alteration for which airworthiness limitations are required by §§25.981, 26.33, or 26.37 of this chapter, the certificate holder must revise the maintenance program for the airplane to include those airworthiness limitations.

(i) The maintenance program changes identified in paragraphs (g) and (h) of this section must be submitted to the operator's Principal Maintenance Inspector responsible for review and approval prior to incorporation.

(j) The requirements of paragraph (d) of this section do not apply to airplanes operated in all-cargo service, but those airplanes are subject to paragraph (f) of this section.

(k) The compliance dates specified in paragraph (e) of this section may be extended by one year, provided that—

(1) No later than March 26, 2009, the certificate holder notifies its responsible Flight Standards office or Principal Inspector that it intends to comply with this paragraph;

(2) No later than June 24, 2009, the certificate holder applies for an amendment to its operations specification in accordance with §119.51 of this chapter and revises the manual required by §121.133 to include a requirement for the airplane models specified in Table 2 of this section to use ground air conditioning systems for actual gate times of more than 30 minutes, when available at the gate and operational, whenever the ambient temperature exceeds 60 degrees Fahrenheit; and

(3) Thereafter, the certificate holder uses ground air conditioning systems as described in paragraph (k)(2) of this section on each airplane subject to the extension.

TABLE 2

Model—Boeing	Model—Airbus
747 Series	A318, A319, A320, A321 Series
737 Series	A300, A310 Series
777 Series	A330, A340 Series
767 Series	
757 Series	

(l) For any certificate holder for which the operating certificate is issued after December 26, 2008, the compliance date specified in paragraph (e) of this section may be extended by one year, provided that the certificate holder meets the requirements of paragraph (k)(2) of this section when its initial operations specifications are issued and, thereafter, uses ground air conditioning systems as described in paragraph (k)(2) of this section on each airplane subject to the extension.

(m) After the date by which any person is required by this section to modify 100 percent of the affected fleet, no certificate holder may operate in passenger service any airplane model specified in Table 2 of this section unless the airplane has been modified to comply with § 26.33(c) of this chapter.

(n) No certificate holder may operate any airplane on which an auxiliary fuel tank is installed after December 26, 2017 unless the FAA has certified the tank as compliant with § 25.981 of this chapter, in effect on December 26, 2008.

(o) *Exclusions.* The requirements of this section do not apply to the following airplane models:

(1) Convair CV–240, 340, 440, including turbine powered conversions.

(2) Lockheed L–188 Electra.

(3) Vickers VC–10.

(4) Douglas DC–3, including turbine powered conversions.

(5) Bombardier CL–44.

(6) Mitsubishi YS–11.

(7) BAC 1–11.

(8) Concorde.

(9) deHavilland D.H. 106 Comet 4C.

(10) VFW—Vereinigte Flugtechnische VFW–614.

(11) Illyushin Aviation IL 96T.

(12) Bristol Aircraft Britannia 305.

(13) Handley Page Herald Type 300.

(14) Avions Marcel Dassault—Breguet Aviation Mercure 100C.

(15) Airbus Caravelle.

(16) Fokker F–27/Fairchild Hiller FH–227.

(17) Lockheed L–300.

[Doc. No. FAA–2005–22997, 73 FR 42501, July 21, 2008, as amended by Amdt. 121–345, 74 FR 31619, July 2, 2009; Docket FAA–2018–0119, Amdt. 121–380, 83 FR 9173, Mar. 5, 2018]

§ 121.1119 Fuel tank vent explosion protection.

(a) *Applicability.* This section applies to transport category, turbine-powered airplanes with a type certificate issued after January 1, 1958, that have:

(1) A maximum type-certificated passenger capacity of 30 or more; or

(2) A maximum payload capacity of 7,500 pounds or more.

(b) *New production airplanes.* No certificate holder may operate an airplane for which the State of Manufacture issued the original certificate of airworthiness or export airworthiness approval after August 23, 2018 unless means, approved by the Administrator, to prevent fuel tank explosions caused by propagation of flames from outside the fuel tank vents into the fuel tank vapor spaces are installed and operational.

[Docket FAA–2014–0500, Amdt. 121–375, 81 FR 41208, June 24, 2016]

Subpart BB [Reserved]

§§ 121.1200–121.1399 [Reserved]

Subpart CC [Reserved]

§§ 121.1400–121.1499 [Reserved]

Subpart DD—Special Federal Aviation Regulations

§ 121.1500 SFAR No. 111—Lavatory Oxygen Systems.

(a) *Applicability.* This SFAR applies to the following persons:

(1) All operators of transport category airplanes that are required to comply with AD 2012–11–09, but only for airplanes on which the actions required by that AD have not been accomplished.

(2) Applicants for airworthiness certificates.

(3) Holders of production certificates.

(4) Applicants for type certificates, including changes to type certificates.

(b) *Regulatory relief.* Except as noted in paragraph (d) of this section and contrary provisions of 14 CFR part 21, and 14 CFR 25.1447, 119.51, 121.329, 121.333 and 129.13, notwithstanding, for the duration of this SFAR:

(1) A person described in paragraph (a) of this section may conduct flight operations and add airplanes to operations specifications with disabled lavatory oxygen systems, modified in accordance with FAA Airworthiness Directive 2011–04–09, subject to the following limitations:

(i) This relief is limited to regulatory compliance of lavatory oxygen systems.

(ii) Within 30 days of March 29, 2013, all oxygen masks must be removed from affected lavatories, and the mask stowage location must be reclosed.

(iii) Within 60 days of March 29, 2013 each affected operator must verify that crew emergency procedures specifically include a visual check of the lavatory as a priority when checking the cabin following any event where oxygen masks were deployed in the cabin.

(2) An applicant for an airworthiness certificate may obtain an airworthiness certificate for airplanes to be operated by a person described in paragraph (a) of this section, although the airplane lavatory oxygen system is disabled.

(3) A holder of a production certificate may apply for an airworthiness certificate or approval for airplanes to be operated by a person described in paragraph (a) of this section.

(4) An applicant for a type certificate or change to a type certificate may obtain a design approval without showing compliance with § 25.1447(c)(1) of this chapter for lavatory oxygen systems, in accordance with this SFAR.

(5) Each person covered by paragraph (a) of this section may inform passengers that the lavatories are not equipped with supplemental oxygen.

(c) *Return to service documentation.* When a person described in paragraph (a) of this section has modified airplanes as required by Airworthiness Directive 2011–04–09, the affected airplanes must be returned to service with a note in the airplane maintenance records that the modification was done under the provisions of this SFAR.

(d) *Expiration.* This SFAR expires on September 10, 2015, except this SFAR

will continue to apply to any airplane for which the FAA approves an extension of the AD compliance time for the duration of the extension.

[Doc. No. FAA–2011–0186, 78 FR 5710, Jan. 28, 2013]

APPENDIX A TO PART 121—FIRST AID KITS AND EMERGENCY MEDICAL KITS

Approved first-aid kits, at least one approved emergency medical kit, and at least one approved automated external defibrillator required under § 121.803 of this part must be readily accessible to the crew, stored securely, and kept free from dust, moisture, and damaging temperatures.

FIRST-AID KITS

1. The minimum number of first aid kits required is set forth in the following table:

No. of passenger seats	No. of first-aid kits
0–50	1
51–150	2
151–250	3
More than 250	4

2. Except as provided in paragraph (3), each approved first-aid kit must contain at least the following appropriately maintained contents in the specified quantities:

Contents	Quantity
Adhesive bandage compresses, 1-inch	16
Antiseptic swabs	20
Ammonia inhalants	10
Bandage compresses, 4-inch	8
Triangular bandage compresses, 40-inch	5
Arm splint, noninflatable	1
Leg splint, noninflatable	1
Roller bandage, 4-inch	4
Adhesive tape, 1-inch standard roll	2
Bandage scissors	1

3. Arm and leg splints which do not fit within a first-aid kit may be stowed in a readily accessible location that is as near as practicable to the kit.

EMERGENCY MEDICAL KITS

1. Until April 12, 2004, at least one approved emergency medical kit that must contain at least the following appropriately maintained contents in the specified quantities:

Contents	Quantity
Sphygmomanometer	1
Stethoscope	1
Airways, cropharyngeal (3 sizes)	3
Syringes (sizes necessary to administer required drugs).	4

Contents	Quantity
Needles (sizes necessary to administer required drugs).	6
50% Dextrose injection, 50cc	1
Epinephrine 1:1000, single dose ampule or equivalent).	2
Diphenhydramine HC1 injection, single dose ampule or equivalent.	2
Nitroglycerin tablets	10
Basic instructions for use of the drugs in the kit	1
protective nonpermeable gloves or equivalent ...	1 pair

2. As of April 12, 2004, at least one approved emergency medical kit that must contain at least the following appropriately maintained contents in the specified quantities:

Contents	Quantity
Sphygmonanometer	1
Stethoscope	1
Airways, oropharyngeal (3 sizes): 1 pediatric, 1 small adult, 1 large adult or equivalent.	3
Self-inflating manual resuscitation device with 3 masks (1 pediatric, 1 small adult, 1 large adult or equivalent).	1:3 masks
CPR mask (3 sizes), 1 pediatric, 1 small adult, 1 large adult, or equivalent.	3
IV Admin Set: Tubing w/ 2 Y connectors	1
Alcohol sponges	2
Adhesive tape, 1-inch standard roll adhesive.	1
Tape scissors	1 pair
Tourniquet	1
Saline solution, 500 cc	1
Protective nonpermeable gloves or equivalent ...	1 pair
Needles (2–18 ga., 2–20 ga., 2–22 ga., or sizes necessary to administer required medications).	6
Syringes (1–5 cc, 2–10 cc, or sizes necessary to administer required medications).	4
Analgesic, non-narcotic, tablets, 325 mg	4
Antihistamine tablets, 25 mg	4
Antihistamine injectable, 50 mg, (single dose ampule or equivalent).	2
Atropine, 0.5 mg, 5 cc (single dose ampule or equivalent).	2
Aspirin tablets, 325 mg	4

Contents	Quantity
Bronchodilator, inhaled (metered dose inhaler or equivalent).	1
Dextrose, 50%/50 cc injectable, (single dose ampule or equivalent).	1
Epinephrine 1:1000, 1 cc, injectable, (single dose ampule or equivalent).	2
Epinephrine 1:10,000, 2 cc, injectable, (single dose ampule or equivalent).	2
Lidocaine, 5 cc, 20 mg/ml, injectable (single dose ampule or equivalent).	2
Nitroglycerin tablets, 0.4 mg	10
Basic instructions for use of the drugs in the kit	1

3. If all of the above-listed items do not fit into one container, more than one container may be used.

AUTOMATED EXTERNAL DEFIBRILLATORS

At least one approved automated external defibrillator, legally marketed in the United States in accordance with Food and Drug Administration requirements, that must:

1. Be stored in the passenger cabin.

2. After April 30, 2005:

(a) Have a power source that meets FAA Technical Standard Order requirements for power sources for electronic devices used in aviation as approved by the Administrator; or

(b) Have a power source that was manufactured before July 30, 2004, and been found by the FAA to be equivalent to a power source that meets the Technical Standard Order requirements of paragraph (a) of this section.

3. Be maintained in accordance with the manufacturer's specifications.

[Doc. No. FAA–2000–7119, 66 FR 19044, Apr. 12, 2001, as amended by Amdt. 121–280, 69 FR 19762, Apr. 14, 2004; Amdt. 121–309, 70 FR 15196, Mar. 24, 2005]

APPENDIX B TO PART 121—AIRPLANE FLIGHT RECORDER SPECIFICATION

Parameters	Range	Accuracy sensor input to DFDR readout	Sampling interval (per second)	Resolution [4] readout
Time (GMT or Frame Counter) (range 0 to 4095, sampled 1 per frame).	24 Hrs	±0.125% Per Hour	0.25 (1 per 4 seconds).	1 sec.
Altitude	−1,000 ft to max certificated altitude of aircraft.	±100 to ±700 ft (See Table 1, TSO–C51a).	1	5′ to 35′ [1]
Airspeed	50 KIAS to V_{so}, and V_{so} to $1.2V_D$.	±5%, ±3%	1	1 kt.
Heading	360°	±2°	1	0.5°
Normal Acceleration (Vertical)	−3g to + 6g	±1% of max range excluding datum error of ±5%.	8	0.01g.
Pitch Attitude	±75°	±2°	1	0.5°
Roll Attitude	±180°	±2°	1	0.5°
Radio Transmitter Keying	On-Off (Discrete)	±2°	±2%	
Thrust/Power on Each Engine	Full Range Forward	±2°	1 (per engine) ...	0.2% [2]
Trailing Edge Flap or Cockpit Control Selection.	Full Range or Each Discrete Position.	±3° or as Pilot's Indicator	0.5	0.5% [2]
Leading Edge Flap or Cockpit Control Selection.	Full Range or Each Discrete Position.	±3° or as Pilot's Indicator	0.5	0.5% [2]

Parameters	Range	Accuracy sensor input to DFDR readout	Sampling interval (per second)	Resolution [4] readout
Thrust Reverser Position	Stowed, In Transit, and Reverse (Discrete).	....	1 (per 4 seconds per engine).	
Ground Spoiler Position/ Speed Brake Selection.	Full Range or Each Discrete Position.	±2% Unless Higher Accuracy Uniquely Required.	1	0.2% [2].
Marker Beacon Passage	Discrete	....	1	
Autopilot Engagement	Discrete	....	1	
Longitudinal Acceleration	±1g	±1.5% max range excluding datum error of ±5%.	4	0.01g.
Pilot Input and/or Surface Position—Primary Controls (Pitch, Roll, Yaw) [3].	Full Range	±2° Unless Higher Accuracy Uniquely Required.	1	0.2% [2].
Lateral Acceleration	±1g	±1.5% max range excluding datum error of ±5%.	4	0.01g.
Pitch Trim Position	Full Range	±3% Unless Higher Accuracy Uniquely Required.	1	0.3% [2].
Glideslope Deviation	±400 Microamps	±3%	1	0.3% [2].
Localizer Deviation	±400 Microamps	±3%	1	0.3% [2].
AFCS Mode and Engagement Status.	Discrete		1	
Radio Altitude	−20 ft to 2,500 ft	±2 Ft or ±3% Whichever is Greater Below 500 Ft and ±5% Above 500 Ft.	1	1 ft + 5% [2] above 500'.
Master Warning	Discrete		1	
Main Gear Squat Switch Status.	Discrete		1	
Angle of Attack (if recorded directly)..	As installed	As installed	2	0.3% [2]
Outside Air Temperature or Total Air Temperature..	−50 °C to + 90 °C	±2 °c	0.5	0.3 °c
Hydraulics, Each System Low Pressure.	Discrete		0.5	or 0.5% [2]
Groundspeed.	As installed	Most Accurate Systems Installed (IMS Equipped Aircraft Only).	1	0.2% [2]

If additional recording capacity is available, recording of the following parameters is recommended. The parameters are listed in order of significance:

Drift Angle	When available, As installed.	As installed	4	
Wind Speed and Direction	When available, As installed.	As installed	4	
Latitude and Longitude	When available, As installed.	As installed	4	
Brake pressure/Brake pedal position.	As installed	As installed	1	
Additional engine parameters:				
EPR	As installed	As installed	1 (per engine). ..	
N1	As installed	As installed	1 (per engine). ..	
N2	As installed	As installed	1 (per engine). ..	
EGT	As installed	As installed	1 (per engine). ..	
Throttle Lever Position	As installed	As installed	1 (per engine). ..	
Fuel Flow	As installed	As installed	1 (per engine). ..	
TCAS:				
TA	As installed	As installed	1	
RA	As installed	As installed	1	
Sensitivity level (as selected by crew).	As installed	As installed	2	
GPWS (ground proximity warning system).	Discrete		1	
Landing gear or gear selector position.	Discrete		0.25 (1 per 4 seconds).	
DME 1 and 2 Distance	0–200 NM;	As installed	0.25	1 mi.
Nav 1 and 2 Frequency Selection.	Full range	As installed	0.25	

[1] When altitude rate is recorded. Altitude rate must have sufficient resolution and sampling to permit the derivation of altitude to 5 feet.

[2] Per cent of full range.

[3] For airplanes that can demonstrate the capability of deriving either the control input on control movement (one from the other) for all modes of operation and flight regimes, the 'or' applies. For airplanes with non-mechanical control systems (fly-by-wire) the "and" applies. In airplanes with split surfaces, suitable combination of inputs is acceptable in lieu of recording each surface separately.

[4] This column applies to aircraft manufactured after October 11, 1991.

257

[Doc. No. 25530, 53 FR 26147, July 11, 1988; 53 FR 30906, Aug. 16, 1988]

APPENDIX C TO PART 121—C–46
NONTRANSPORT CATEGORY AIRPLANES

Cargo Operations

1. *Required engines.* (a) Except as provided in paragraph (b) of this section, the engines specified in subparagraphs (1) or (2) of this section must be installed in C–46 nontransport category airplanes operated at gross weights exceeding 45,000 pounds:

(1) Pratt and Whitney R2800-51–M1 or R2800-75–M1 engines (engines converted from basic model R2800-51 or R2800-75 engines in accordance with FAA approved data) that—

(i) Conform to Engine Specification 5E–8;

(ii) Conform to the applicable portions of the operator's manual;

(iii) Comply with all the applicable airworthiness directives; and

(iv) Are equipped with high capacity oil pump drive gears in accordance with FAA approved data.

(2) Other engines found acceptable by the Flight Standards office having type certification responsibility for the C–46 airplane.

(b) Upon application by an operator conducting cargo operations with nontransport category C–46 airplanes between points within the State of Alaska, the responsible Flight Standards office may authorize the operation of such airplanes, between points within the State of Alaska, without compliance with paragraph (a) of this section if the operator shows that, in its area of operation, installation of the modified engines is not necessary to provide adequate cooling for single-engine operations. Such authorization and any conditions or limitations therefor is made a part of the Operations Specifications of the operator.

2. *Minimum acceptable means of complying with the special airworthiness requirements.* Unless otherwise authorized under § 121.213, the data set forth in sections 3 through 34 of this appendix, as correlated to the C–46 nontransport category airplane, is the minimum means of compliance with the special airworthiness requirements of §§ 121.215 through 121.281.

3. *Susceptibility of material to fire.* [Deleted as unnecessary]

4. *Cabin interiors.* C–46 crew compartments must meet all the requirements of § 121.215, and, as required in § 121.221, the door between the crew compartment and main cabin (cargo) compartment must be flame resistant.

5. *Internal doors.* Internal doors, including the crew to main cabin door, must meet all the requirements of § 121.217.

6. *Ventilation.* Standard C–46 crew compartments meet the ventilation requirements of § 121.219 if a means of ventilation for control-

ling the flow of air is available between the crew compartment and main cabin. The ventilation requirement may be met by use of a door between the crew compartment and main cabin. The door need not have louvers installed; however, if louvers are installed, they must be controllable.

7. *Fire precautions.* Compliance is required with all the provisions of § 121.221.

(a) In establishing compliance with this section, the C–46 main cabin is considered as a Class A compartment if—

(1) The operator utilizes a standard system of cargo loading and tiedown that allows easy access in flight to all cargo in such compartment, and, such system is included in the appropriate portion of the operator's manual; and

(2) A cargo barrier is installed in the forward end of the main cabin cargo compartment. The barrier must—

(i) Establish the most forward location beyond which cargo cannot be carried;

(ii) Protect the components and systems of the airplane that are essential to its safe operation from cargo damage; and

(iii) Permit easy access, in flight, to cargo in the main cabin cargo compartment.

The barrier may be a cargo net or a network of steel cables or other means acceptable to the Administrator which would provide equivalent protection to that of a cargo net. The barrier need not meet crash load requirements of FAR § 25.561; however, it must be attached to the cargo retention fittings and provide the degree of cargo retention that is required by the operators' standard system of cargo loading and tiedown.

(b) C–46 forward and aft baggage compartments must meet, as a minimum, Class B requirements of this section or be placarded in a manner to preclude their use as cargo or baggage compartments.

8. *Proof of compliance.* The demonstration of compliance required by § 121.223 is not required for C–46 airplanes in which—

(1) The main cabin conforms to Class A cargo compartment requirements of § 121.219; and

(2) Forward and aft baggage compartments conform to Class B requirements of § 121.221, or are placarded to preclude their use as cargo or baggage compartments.

9. *Propeller deicing fluid.* No change from the requirements of § 121.225. Isopropyl alcohol is a combustible fluid within the meaning of this section.

10. *Pressure cross-feed arrangements, location of fuel tanks, and fuel system lines and fittings.* C–46 fuel systems which conform to all applicable Curtiss design specifications and which

comply with the FAA type certification requirements are in compliance with the provisions of §§ 121.227 through 121.231.

11. *Fuel lines and fittings in designated fire zones.* No change from the requirements of § 121.233.

12. *Fuel valves.* Compliance is required with all the provisions of § 121.235. Compliance can be established by showing that the fuel system conforms to all the applicable Curtiss design specifications, the FAA type certification requirements, and, in addition, has explosion-proof fuel booster pump electrical selector switches installed in lieu of the open contact type used originally.

13. *Oil lines and fittings in designated fire zones.* No change from the requirements of § 121.237.

14. *Oil valves.* C–46 oil shutoff valves must conform to the requirements of § 121.239. In addition, C–46 airplanes using Hamilton Standard propellers must provide, by use of stand pipes in the engine oil tanks or other approved means, a positive source of oil for feathering each propeller.

15. *Oil system drains.* The standard C–46 "Y" drains installed in the main oil inlet line for each engine meet the requirements of § 121.241.

16. *Engine breather line.* The standard C–46 engine breather line installation meets the requirements of § 121.243 if the lower breather lines actually extend to the trailing edge of the oil cooler air exit duct.

17. *Firewalls and firewall construction.* Compliance is required with all of the provisions of §§ 121.245 and 121.247. The following requirements must be met in showing compliance with these sections:

(a) *Engine compartment.* The engine firewalls of the C–46 airplane must—

(1) Conform to type design, and all applicable airworthiness directives;

(2) Be constructed of stainless steel or approved equivalent; and

(3) Have fireproof shields over the fairleads used for the engine control cables that pass through each firewall.

(b) *Combustion heater compartment.* C–46 airplanes must have a combustion heater fire extinguishing system which complies with AD–49–18–1 or an FAA approved equivalent.

18. *Cowling.* Standard C–46 engine cowling (cowling of aluminum construction employing stainless steel exhaust shrouds) which conforms to the type design and cowling configurations which conform to the C–46 transport category requirements meet the requirements of § 121.249.

19. *Engine accessory section diaphragm.* C–46 engine nacelles which conform to the C–46 transport category requirements meet the requirements of § 121.251. As provided for in that section, a means of equivalent protection which does not require provision of a diaphragm to isolate the engine power section and exhaust system from the engine accessory compartment is the designation of the entire engine compartment forward of and including the firewall as a designated fire zone, and the installation of adequate fire detection and fire extinguishing systems which meet the requirements of § 121.263 and § 121.273, respectively, in such zone.

20. *Powerplant fire protection.* C–46 engine compartments and combustion heater compartments are considered as designated fire zones within the meaning of § 121.253.

21. *Flammable fluids*—

(a) *Engine compartment.* C–46 engine compartments which conform to the type design and which comply with all applicable airworthiness directives meet the requirements of § 121.255.

(b) *Combustion heater compartment.* C–46 combustion heater compartments which conform to type design and which meet all the requirements of AD–49–18–1 or an FAA approved equivalent meet the requirements of § 121.255.

22. *Shutoff means*—

(a) *Engine compartment.* C–46 engine compartments which comply with AD–62–10–2 or FAA approved equivalent meet the requirements of § 121.257 applicable to engine compartments, if, in addition, a means satisfactory to the Administrator is provided to shut off the flow of hydraulic fluid to the cowl flap cylinder in each engine nacelle. The shutoff means must be located aft of the engine firewall. The operator's manual must include, in the emergency portion, adequate instructions for proper operation of the additional shutoff means to assure correct sequential positioning of engine cowl flaps under emergency conditions. In accordance with § 121.315, this positioning must also be incorporated in the emergency section of the pilot's checklist.

(b) *Combustion heater compartment.* C–46 heater compartments which comply with paragraph (5) of AD–49–18–1 or FAA approved equivalent meet the requirements of § 121.257 applicable to heater compartments if, in addition, a shutoff valve located above the main cabin floor level is installed in the alcohol supply line or lines between the alcohol supply tank and those alcohol pumps located under the main cabin floor. If all of the alcohol pumps are located above the main cabin floor, the alcohol shutoff valve need not be installed. In complying with paragraph (5) of AD–49–18–1, a fail-safe electric fuel shutoff valve may be used in lieu of the manually operated valve.

23. *Lines and fittings*—(a) *Engine compartment.* C–46 engine compartments which comply with all applicable airworthiness directives, including AD–62–10–2, by using FAA approved fire-resistant lines, hoses, and end fittings, and engine compartments which meet the C–46 transport category requirements, meet the requirements of § 121.259.

(b) *Combustion heater compartments* All lines, hoses, and end fittings, and couplings which carry fuel to the heaters and heater controls, must be of FAA approved fire-resistant construction.

24. *Vent and drain lines*—(a) *Enginecompartment.* C-46 engine compartments meet the requirements of § 121.261 if—

(1) The compartments conform to type design and comply with all applicable airworthiness directives or FAA approved equivalent; and

(2) Drain lines from supercharger case, engine-driven fuel pump, and engine-driven hydraulic pump reach into the scupper drain located in the lower cowling segment.

(b) *Combustion heater compartment.* C-46 heater compartments meet the requirements of § 121.261 if they conform to AD-49-18-1 or FAA approved equivalent.

25. *Fire-extinguishing system.* (a) To meet the requirements of § 121.263, C-46 airplanes must have installed fire extinguishing systems to serve all designated fire zones. The fire-extinguishing systems, the quantity of extinguishing agent, and the rate of discharge shall be such as to provide a minimum of one adequate discharge for each designated fire zone. Compliance with this provision requires the installation of a separate fire extinguisher for each engine compartment. Insofar as the engine compartment is concerned, the system shall be capable of protecting the entire compartment against the various types of fires likely to occur in the compartment.

(b) Fire-extinguishing systems which conform to the C-46 transport category requirements meet the requirements set forth in paragraph (a). Furthermore, fire-extinguishing systems for combustion heater compartments which conform to the requirements of AD-49-18-1 or an FAA approved equivalent also meet the requirements in paragraph (a).

In addition, a fire-extinguishing system for C-46 airplanes meets the adequacy requirement of paragraph (a) if it provides the same or equivalent protection to that demonstrated by the CAA in tests conducted in 1941 and 1942, using a CW-20 type engine nacelle (without diaphragm). These tests were conducted at the Bureau of Standards facilities in Washington, DC, and copies of the test reports are available through the FAA Regional Engineering Offices. In this connection, the flow rates and distribution of extinguishing agent substantiated in American Airmotive Report No. 128-52-d, FAA approved February 9, 1953, provides protection equivalent to that demonstrated by the CAA in the CW-20 tests. In evaluating any C-46 fire-extinguishing system with respect to the aforementioned CW-20 tests, the Administration would require data in a narrative form, utilizing drawings or photographs to show at least the following:

Installation of containers; installation and routing of plumbing; type, number, and location of outlets or nozzles; type, total volume, and distribution of extinguishing agent; length of time required for discharging; means for thermal relief, including type and location of discharge indicators; means of discharging, e.g., mechanical cutterheads, electric cartridge, or other method; and whether a one- or two-shot system is used; and if the latter is used, means of cross-feeding or otherwise selecting distribution of extinguishing agent; and types of materials used in makeup of plumbing.

High rate discharge (HRD) systems using agents such as bromotrifluoromethane, dibrodifluoromethane and chlorobromomethane (CB), may also meet the requirements of paragraph (a).

26. *Fire-extinguishing agents, Extinguishing agent container pressure relief, Extinguishing agent container compartment temperatures, and Fire-extinguishing system materials.* No change from the requirements of §§ 121.265 through 121.271.

27. *Fire-detector system.* Compliance with the requirements of § 121.273 requires that C-46 fire detector systems conform to:

(a) AD-62-10-2 or FAA approved equivalent for engine compartments; and

(b) AD-49-18-1 or FAA approved equivalent for combustion heater compartments

28. *Fire detectors.* No change from the requirements of § 121.275.

29. *Protection of other airplane components against fire.* To meet the requirements of § 121.277, C-46 airplanes must—

(a) Conform to the type design and all applicable airworthiness directives; and

(b) Be modified or have operational procedures established to provide additional fire protection for the wheel well door aft of each engine compartment. Modifications may consist of improvements in sealing of the main landing gear wheel well doors. An operational procedure which is acceptable to the Agency is one requiring the landing gear control to be placed in the up position in case of in-flight engine fire. In accordance with § 121.315, such procedure must be set forth in the emergency portion of the operator's emergency checklist pertaining to in-flight engine fire.

30. *Control of engine rotation.* C-46 propeller feathering systems which conform to the type design and all applicable airworthiness directives meet the requirements of § 121.279.

31. *Fuel system independence.* C-46 fuel systems which conform to the type design and all applicable airworthiness directives meet the requirements of § 121.281.

32. *Induction system ice prevention.* The C-46 carburetor anti-icing system which conforms to the type design and all applicable airworthiness directives meets the requirements of § 121.283.

33. *Carriage of cargo in passenger compartments.* Section 121.285 is not applicable to nontransport category C–46 cargo airplanes.

34. *Carriage of cargo in cargo compartments.* A standard cargo loading and tiedown arrangement set forth in the operator's manual and found acceptable to the Administrator must be used in complying with §121.287.

35. *Performance data.* Performance data on Curtiss model C–46 airplane certificated for maximum weight of 45,000 and 48,000 pounds for cargo-only operations.

1. The following performance limitation data, applicable to the Curtiss model C–46 airplane for cargo-only operation, must be used in determining compliance with §§ 121.199 through 121.205. These data are presented in the tables and figures of this appendix.

TABLE 1—TAKEOFF LIMITATIONS

(a) Curtiss C–46 certificated for maximum weight of 45,000 pounds.

(1) *Effective length* of runway required when effective length is determined in accordance with §121.171 (distance to accelerate to 93 knots TIAS and stop, with zero wind and zero gradient). (Factor = 1.00)

[Distance in feet]

Standard altitude in feet	Airplane weight in pounds		
	39,000	42,000	45,000 [1]
S.L	4,110	4,290	4,570
1,000	4,250	4,440	4,720
2,000	4,400	4,600	4,880
3,000	4,650	4,880	5,190
4,000	4,910	5,170	5,500
5,000	5,160	5,450	5,810
6,000	5,420	5,730	6,120
7,000	5,680	6,000	6,440
8,000	5,940	6,280	([1])

[1] Ref. Fig. 1(a)(1) for weight and distance for altitudes above 7,000'.

(2) Actual length of runway required when *effective length,* considering obstacles, is not determined (distance to accelerate to 93 knots TIAS and stop, divided by the factor 0.85).

[Distance in feet]

Standard altitude in feet	Airplane weight in pounds		
	39,000	42,000	45,000 [1]
S.L	4,830	5,050	5,370
1,000	5,000	5,230	5,550
2,000	5,170	5,410	5,740
3,000	5,470	5,740	6,100
4,000	5,770	6,080	6,470
5,000	6,070	6,410	6,830
6,000	6,380	6,740	7,200
7,000	6,680	7,070	7,570
8,000	6,990	7,410	([1])

[1] Ref. Fig. 1(a)(2) for weight and distance for altitudes above 7,000'.

(b) Curtiss C–46 certificated for maximum weight 48,000 pounds.

(1) *Effective length* of runway required when effective length is determined in accordance with §121.171 (distance to accelerate to 93 knots TIAS and stop, with zero wind and zero gradient). (Factor = 1.00)

[Distance in feet]

Standard altitude in feet	Airplane weight in pounds			
	39,000	42,000	45,000	48,000 [1]
S.L	4,110	4,290	4,570	4,950
1,000	4,250	4,440	4,720	5,130
2,000	4,400	4,600	4,880	5,300
3,000	4,650	4,880	5,190	5,670
4,000	4,910	5,170	5,500	6,050
5,000	5,160	5,450	5,810	6,420
6,000	5,420	5,730	6,120	6,800
7,000	5,680	6,000	6,440	([1])
8,000	5,940	6,280	6,750	([1])

[1] Ref. Fig. 1(b)(1) for weight and distance for altitudes above 6,000'.

(2) Actual length of runway required when *effective length,* considering obstacles, is not determined (distance to accelerate to 93 knots TIAS and stop, divided by the factor 0.85).

[Distance in feet]

Standard altitude in feet	Airplane weight in pounds			
	39,000	42,000	45,000	48,000 [1]
S.L	4,830	5,050	5,370	5,830
1,000	5,000	5,230	5,550	6,030
2,000	5,170	5,410	5,740	6,230
3,000	5,470	5,740	6,100	6,670
4,000	5,770	6,080	6,470	7,120
5,000	6,070	6,410	6,830	7,560
6,000	6,380	6,740	7,200	8,010
7,000	6,680	7,070	7,570	([1])
8,000	6,990	7,410	7,940	([1])

[1] Ref. Fig. 1(b)(2) for weight and distance for altitudes above 6,000'.

TABLE 2—EN ROUTE LIMITATIONS

(a) Curtiss model C–46 certificated for maximum weight of 45,000 pounds (based on a climb speed of 113 knots (TIAS)).

Weight (pounds)	Terrain clearance (feet) [1]	Blower setting
45,000	6,450	Low.
44,000	7,000	Do.
43,000	7,500	Do.
42,200	8,000	High.
41,000	9,600	Do.
40,000	11,000	Do.
39,000	12,300	Do.

[1] Highest altitude of terrain over which airplanes may be operated in compliance with § 121.201.
Ref. Fig. 2(a).

(b) Curtiss model C–46 certificated for maximum weight of 48,000 pounds or with engine installation approved for 2,550 revolutions per minute (1,700 brake horsepower). Maximum continuous power in low blower (based on a climb speed of 113 knots (TIAS)).

Weight (pounds)	Terrain clearance (feet) [1]	Blower setting
48,000	5,850	Low.
47,000	6,300	Do.
46,000	6,700	Do.
45,000	7,200	Do.
44,500	7,450	Do.
44,250	8,000	High.
44,000	8,550	Do.
43,000	10,800	Do.
42,000	12,500	Do.

Weight (pounds)	Terrain clearance (feet) [1]	Blower setting
41,000	13,000	Do.

[1] Highest altitude of terrain over which airplanes may be operated in compliance with § 121.201.
Ref. Fig. 2(b).

TABLE 3—LANDING LIMITATIONS

(a) Intended Destination.

Effective length of runway required for intended destination when effective length is determined in accordance with § 121.171 with zero wind and zero gradient.

(1) Curtiss model C–46 certificated for maximum weight of 45,000 pounds. (0.60 factor)

Distance in feet

Standard altitude in feet	Airplane weight in pounds and approach speeds [1] in knots							
	40,000	V_{50}	42,000	V_{50}	44,000	V_{50}	45,000	V_{50}
S.L	4,320	86	4,500	88	4,700	90	4,800	91
1,000	4,440	86	4,620	88	4,830	90	4,930	91
2,000	4,550	86	4,750	88	4,960	90	5,050	91
3,000	4,670	86	4,880	88	5,090	90	5,190	91
4,000	4,800	86	5,000	88	5,220	90	5,320	91
5,000	4,920	86	5,140	88	5,360	90	5,460	91
6,000	5,040	86	5,270	88	5,550	90	5,600	91
7,000	5,170	86	5,410	88	5,650	90	5,750	91
8,000	5,310	86	5,550	88	5,800	90	5,900	91

[1] Steady approach speed through 50–foot height TIAS denoted by symbol V_{50}.
Ref. Fig. 3(a)(1).

(2) Curtiss model C–46 certificated for maximum weight of 48,000 pounds. [1] (0.60 factor.)

Distance in feet

Standard altitude in feet	Airplane weight in pounds and approach speeds [2] in knots							
	42,000	V_{50}	44,000	V_{50}	46,000	V_{50}	43,000	V_{50}
S.L	3,370	80	3,490	82	3,620	84	3,740	86
1,000	3,460	80	3,580	82	3,710	84	3,830	86
2,000	3,540	80	3,670	82	3,800	84	3,920	86
3,000	3,630	80	3,760	82	3,890	84	4,020	86
4,000	3,720	80	3,850	82	3,980	84	4,110	86
5,000	3,800	80	3,940	82	4,080	84	4,220	86
6,000	3,890	80	4,040	82	4,180	84	4,320	86
7,000	3,980	80	4,140	82	4,280	84	4,440	86
8,000	4,080	80	4,240	82	4,390	84	4,550	86

[1] For use with Curtiss model C–46 airplanes when approved for this weight.
[2] Steady approach speed through 50 height knots TIAS denoted by symbol V_{50}3.
Ref. Fig. 3(a)(2).

(b) Alternate Airports.

Effective length of runway required when effective length is determined in accordance with § 121.171 with zero wind and zero gradient.

(1) Curtiss model C–46 certificated for maximum weight of 45,000 pounds. (0.70 factor.)

Distance in feet

Standard altitude in feet	Airplane weight in pounds and approach speeds [1] in knots							
	40,000	V_{50}	42,000	V_{50}	44,000	V_{50}	45,000	V_{50}
S.L	3,700	86	3,860	88	4,030	90	4,110	91
1,000	3,800	86	3,960	88	4,140	90	4,220	91
2,000	3,900	86	4,070	88	4,250	90	4,340	91
3,000	4,000	86	4,180	88	4,360	90	4,450	91
4,000	4,110	86	4,290	88	4,470	90	4,560	91
5,000	4,210	86	4,400	88	4,590	90	4,680	91
6,000	4,330	86	4,510	88	4,710	90	4,800	91
7,000	4,430	86	4,630	88	4,840	90	4,930	91

Distance in feet

Standard altitude in feet	Airplane weight in pounds and approach speeds [1] in knots							
	40,000	V_{50}	42,000	V_{50}	44,000	V_{50}	45,000	V_{50}
8,000	4,550	86	4,750	88	4,970	90	5,060	91

[1] Steady approach speed through 50 foot-height-knots TIAS denoted by symbol V_{50}.
Ref. Fig. 3(b)(1).

(2) Curtiss model C–46 certificated for maximum weight of 48,000 pounds. [1] (0.70 factor.)

Distance in feet

Standard altitude in feet	Airplane weight in pounds and approach speeds [2] in knots							
	42,000	V_{50}	44,000	V_{50}	46,000	V_{50}	48,000	V_{50}
S.L	2,890	80	3,000	82	3,110	84	3,220	86
1,000	2,960	80	3,070	82	3,180	84	3,280	86
2,000	3,040	80	3,150	82	3,260	84	3,360	86
3,000	3,110	80	3,220	82	3,340	84	3,440	86
4,000	3,180	80	3,300	82	3,410	84	3,520	86
5,000	3,260	80	3,380	82	3,500	84	3,610	86
6,000	3,330	80	3,460	82	3,580	84	3,700	86
7,000	3,420	80	3,540	82	3,670	84	3,800	86
8,000	3,500	80	3,630	82	3,760	84	3,900	86

[1] For use with Curtiss model C–46 airplanes when approved for this weight.
[2] Steady approach speed through 50 foot-height-knots TIAS denoted by symbol V_{50}.
Ref. Fig. 3(b)(2).

(c) Actual length of runway required when effective length, considering obstacles, is not determined in accordance with § 121.171.

(1) Curtiss model C–46 certificated for maximum weight of 45,000 pounds. (0.55 factor.)

Distance in feet

Standard altitude in feet	Airplane weight in pounds and approach speeds [1] in knots							
	40,000	V_{50}	42,000	V_{50}	44,000	V_{50}	45,000	V_{50}
S.L	4,710	86	4,910	88	5,130	90	5,230	91
1,000	4,840	86	5,050	88	5,270	90	5,370	91
2,000	4,960	86	5,180	88	5,410	90	5,510	91
3,000	5,090	86	5,320	88	5,550	90	5,660	91
4,000	5,230	86	5,460	88	5,700	90	5,810	91
5,000	5,360	86	5,600	88	5,850	90	5,960	91
6,000	5,500	86	5,740	88	6,000	90	6,110	91
7,000	5,640	86	5,900	88	6,170	90	6,280	91
8,000	5,790	86	6,050	88	6,340	90	6,450	91

[1] Steady approach speed through 50 foot-height-knots TIAS denoted by symbol V_{50}.
Ref. Fig. 3(c)(1).

(2) Curtiss C–46 certificated for maximum weight of 48,000 pounds. [1] (0.55 factor.)

Distance in feet

Standard altitude in feet	Airplane weight in pounds and approach speeds [2] in knots							
	42,000	V_{50}	44,000	V_{50}	46,000	V_{50}	48,000	V_{50}
S.L	3,680	80	3,820	82	3,960	84	4,090	86
1,000	3,770	80	3,910	82	4,050	84	4,180	86
2,000	3,860	80	4,000	82	4,140	84	4,280	86
3,000	3,960	80	4,090	82	4,240	84	4,380	86
4,000	4,050	80	4,190	82	4,340	84	4,490	86
5,000	4,150	80	4,290	82	4,450	84	4,600	86
6,000	4,240	80	4,400	82	4,560	84	4,710	86
7,000	4,350	80	4,510	82	4,670	84	4,840	86
8,000	4,450	80	4,620	82	4,790	84	4,960	86

[1] For use with Curtiss model C–46 airplanes when approved for this weight.
[2] Steady approach speed through 50 foot-height-knots TIAS denoted by symbol V_{50}.
Ref. Fig. 3(c)(2).

CURTISS C-46 MODELS

CERTIFICATED FOR MAX. WEIGHT OF 45,000 LBS.

TAKEOFF LIMITATION.
ZERO WIND AND ZERO GRADIENT.

BASED ON EFFECTIVE TAKEOFF
LENGTH. (1.00 FACTOR)

FAR 121.199

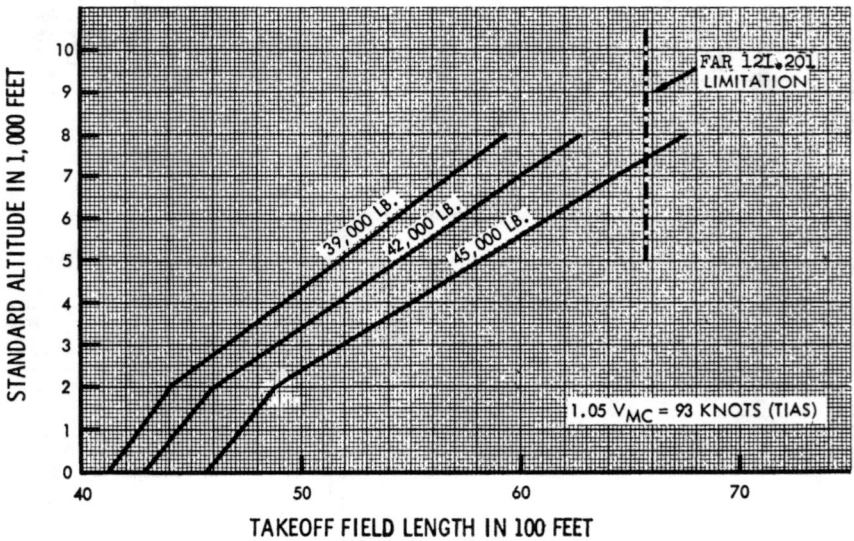

REFERENCE TABLE 1(a) (1)   FIG. 1 (a)(1)

CURTISS C-46 MODELS

CERTIFICATED FOR MAX. WEIGHT OF 45,000 LBS.

TAKEOFF LIMITATION
ZERO WIND AND ZERO GRADIENT

BASED ON ACTUAL TAKEOFF LENGTH
WHEN EFFECTIVE LENGTH IS NOT
DETERMINED.   (0.85 FACTOR)

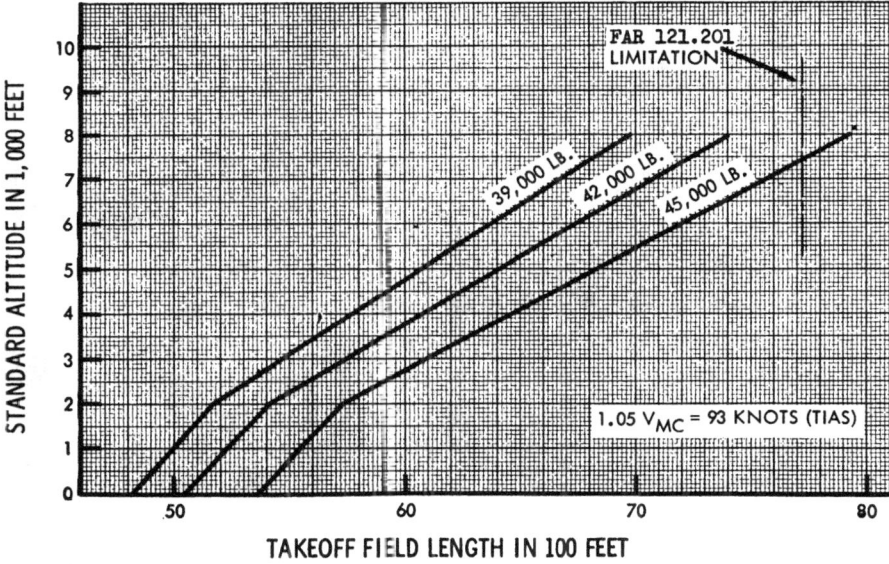

REFERENCE TABLE 1 (a) (2)

FIG. 1(a) (2)

CURTISS C-46 MODELS

CERTIFICATED FOR MAX. WEIGHT OF 48,000 LBS.

TAKEOFF LIMITATION
ZERO WIND AND ZERO GRADIENT

BASED ON EFFECTIVE TAKEOFF
LENGTH. (1.00 FACTOR)

FAR 121.199

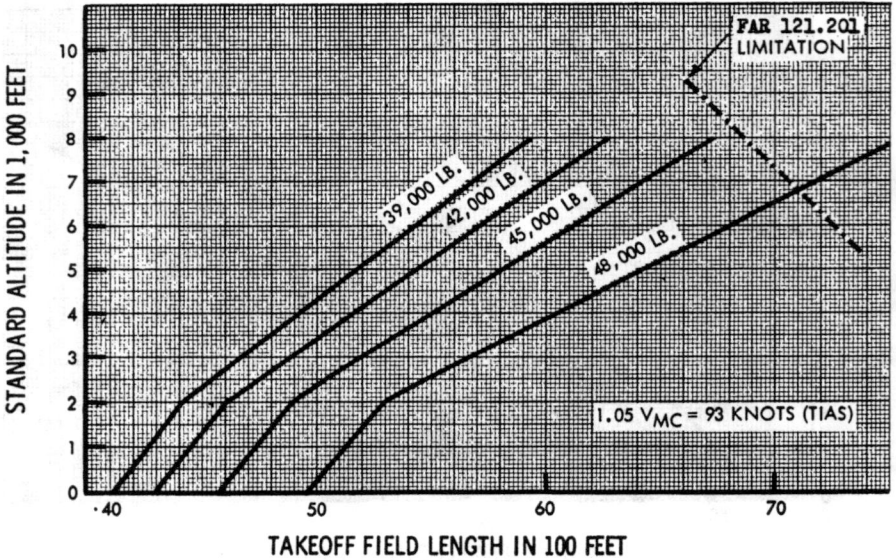

REFERENCE TABLE 1(b) (1)   FIG. 1(b) (1)

CURTISS C-46 MODELS

CERTIFICATED FOR MAX. WEIGHT OF 48,000 LBS.

TAKEOFF LIMITATION
ZERO WIND AND ZERO GRADIENT

BASED ON ACTUAL TAKEOFF LENGTH
WHEN EFFECTIVE LENGTH IS NOT
DETERMINED. (0.85 FACTOR)

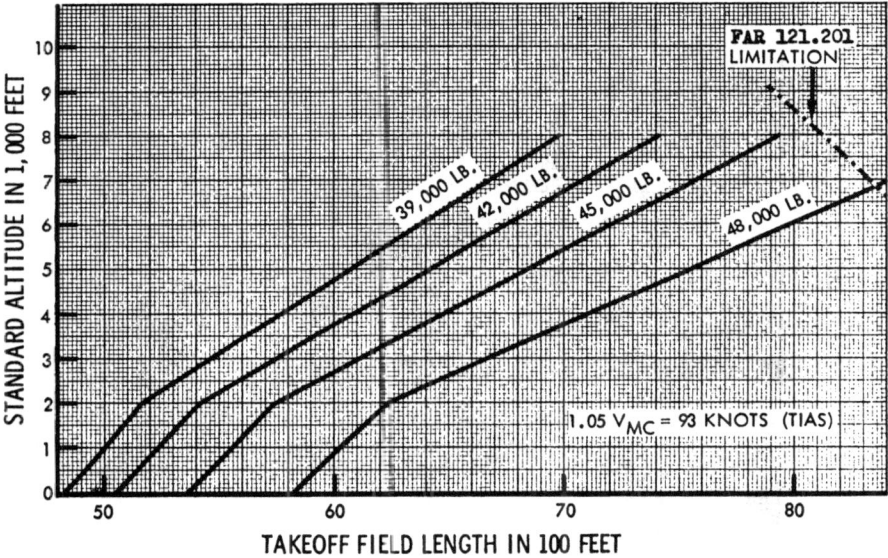

REFERENCE TABLE 1(b) (2)

FIG. 1(b) (2)

267

RUNWAY GRADIENT CORRECTION
FOR ACCELERATE - STOP DISTANCE

FOR C-46 AIRPLANES UNDER FAR 121.199

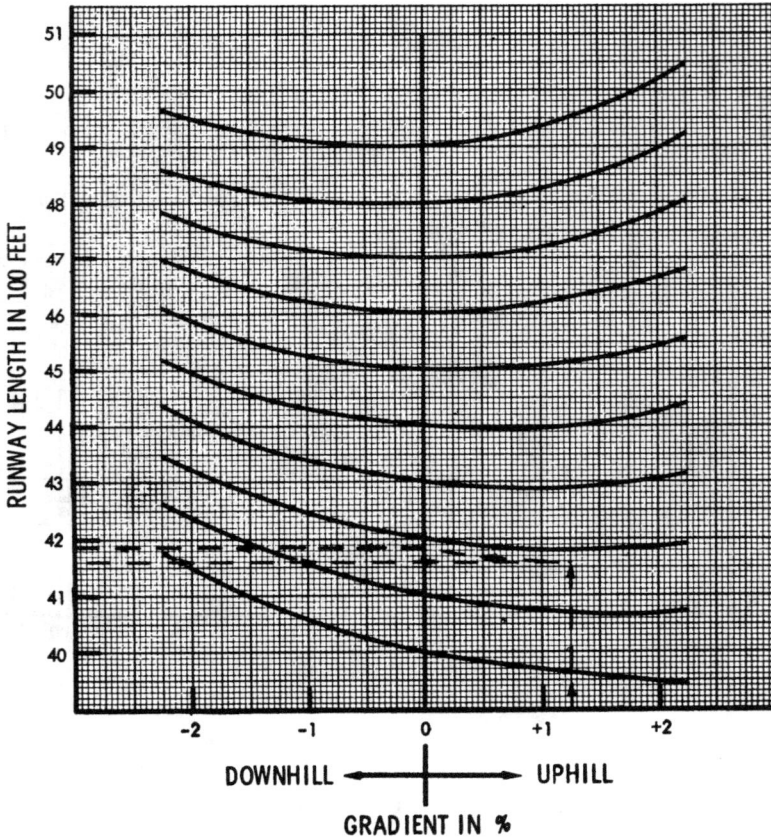

FIG. 1(e)

1-27-64

268

CURTISS C-46 MODELS

ENROUTE LIMITATIONS - ONE ENGINE INOPERATIVE

FAR 121.201

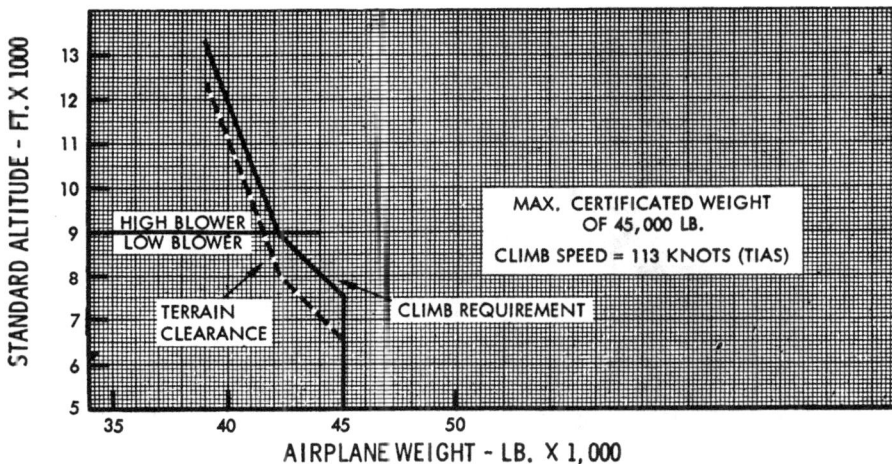

REFERENCE TABLE 2(a)   FIG. 2(a)

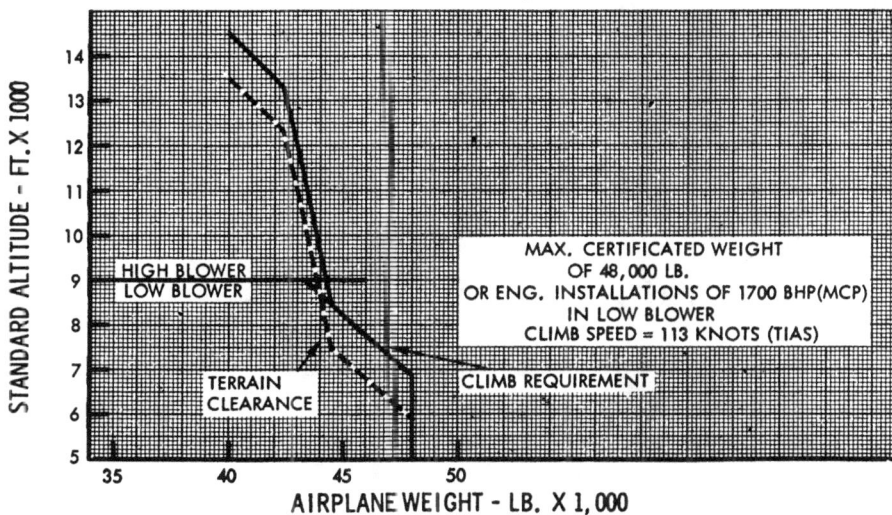

REFERENCE TABLE 2(b)   FIG. 2(b)

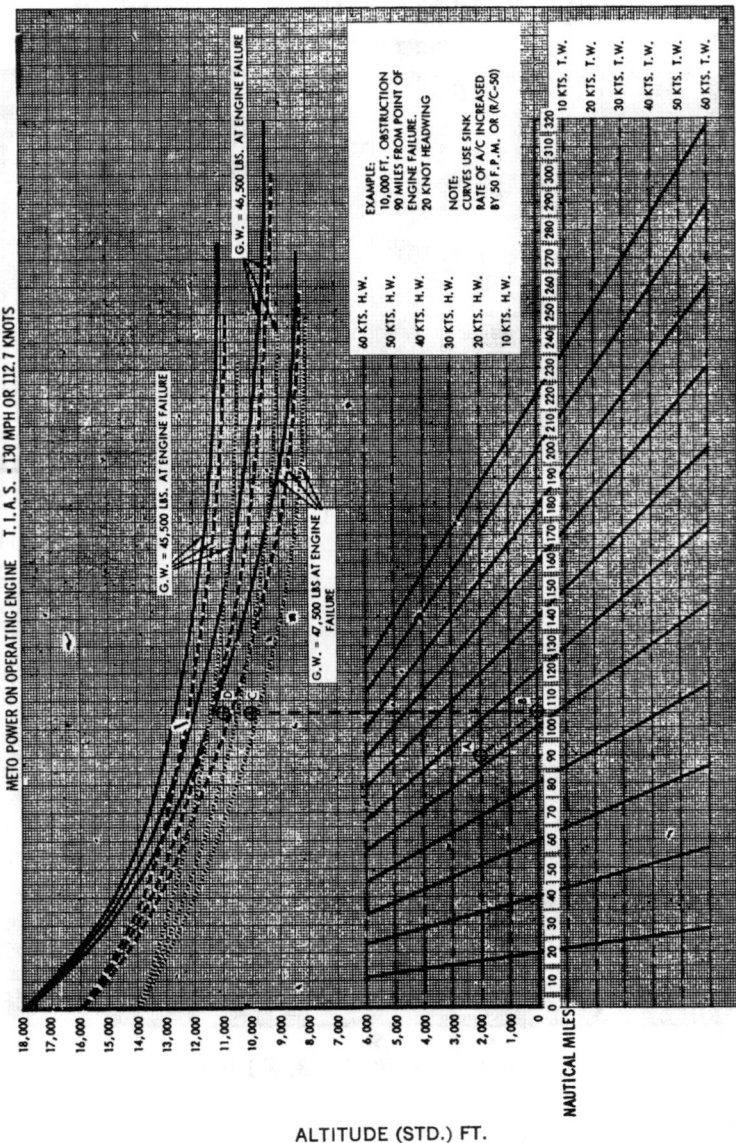

C-46 MAX. CERTIFICATED WEIGHT 48,000 LBS; DRIFT-DOWN CHART FAR 121.201 SINGLE ENGINE ENROUTE OPERATION

METO POWER ON OPERATING ENGINE   T.I.A.S. = 130 MPH OR 112.7 KNOTS

ALTITUDE (STD.) FT.

NAUTICAL MILES

C-46 MAX. CERTIFICATED WEIGHT 48,000 LBS.
ENROUTE CLIMB SUMMARY

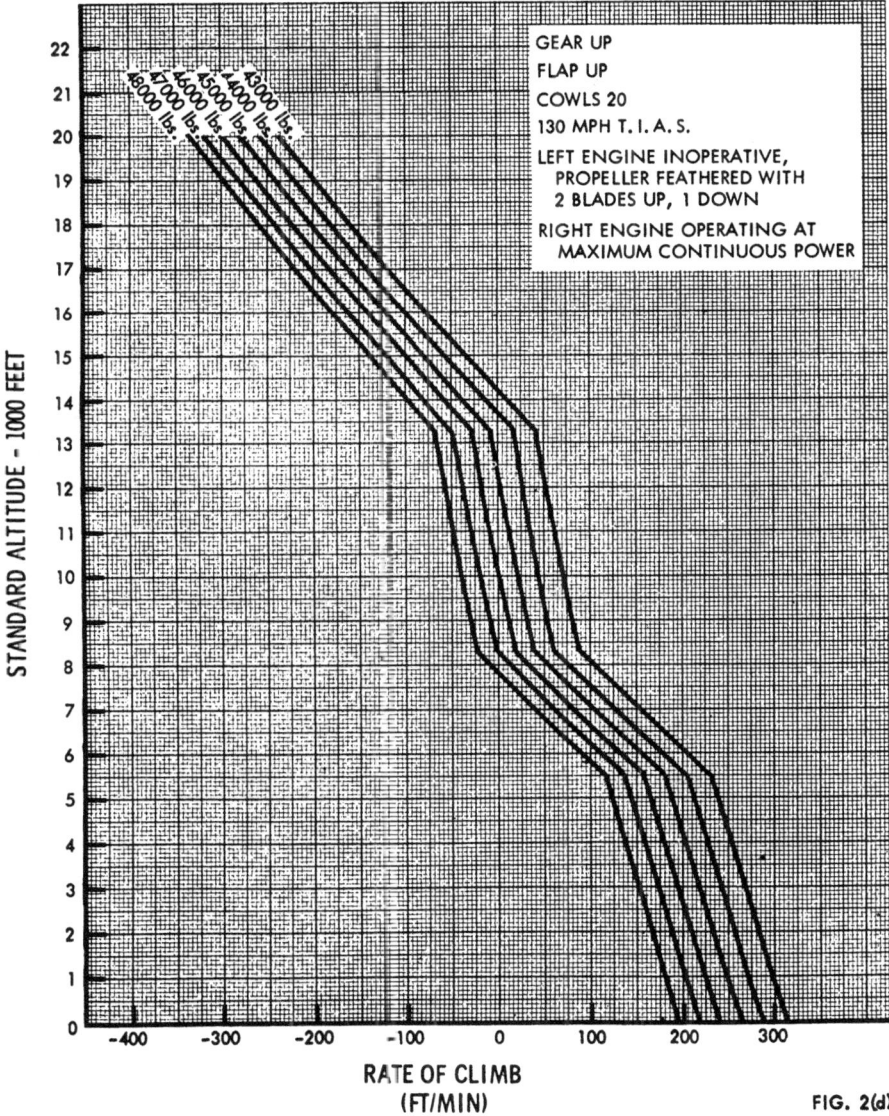

GEAR UP
FLAP UP
COWLS 20
130 MPH T.I.A.S.

LEFT ENGINE INOPERATIVE,
PROPELLER FEATHERED WITH
2 BLADES UP, 1 DOWN

RIGHT ENGINE OPERATING AT
MAXIMUM CONTINUOUS POWER

STANDARD ALTITUDE - 1000 FEET

RATE OF CLIMB
(FT/MIN)

FIG. 2(d)

271

CURTISS C-46 MODELS
CERTIFICATED FOR MAX. WEIGHT OF 45,000 LBS.

LANDING LIMITATIONS.
ZERO WIND AND ZERO GRADIENT

BASED ON EFFECTIVE LANDING LENGTH
AT INTENDED DESTINATION. (0.60 FACTOR)

FAR 121.203

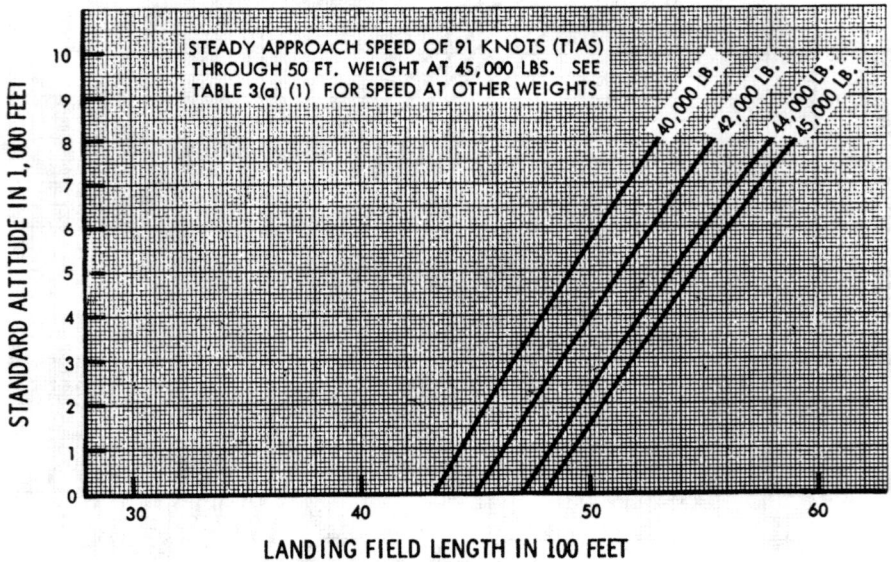

FIG. 3(a) (1)

CURTISS C-46 MODELS

CERTIFICATED FOR MAX. WEIGHT OF 48,000 LBS.

LANDING LIMITATIONS.
ZERO WIND AND ZERO GRADIENT

BASED ON EFFECTIVE LANDING LENGTH
AT INTENDED DESTINATION. (0.60 FACTOR)

FAR 121.203

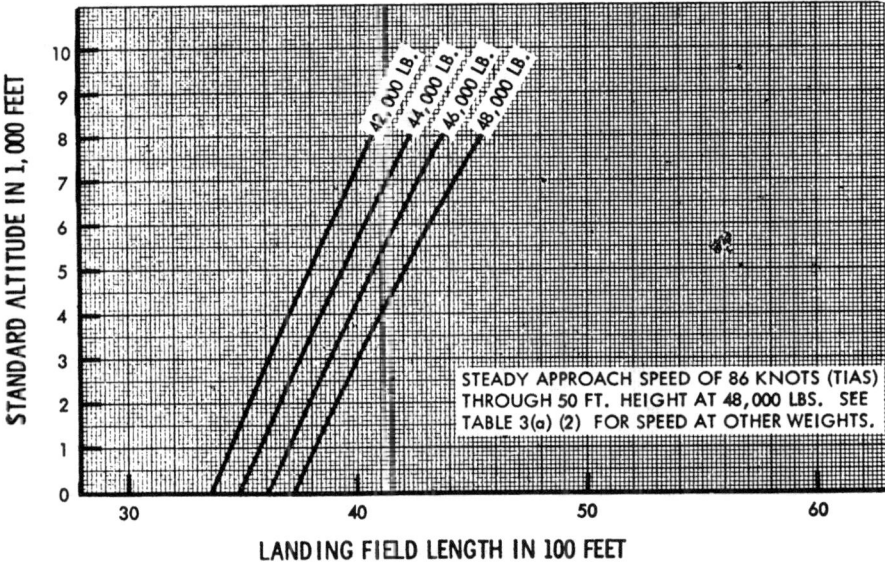

STEADY APPROACH SPEED OF 86 KNOTS (TIAS)
THROUGH 50 FT. HEIGHT AT 48,000 LBS. SEE
TABLE 3(a) (2) FOR SPEED AT OTHER WEIGHTS.

FIG. 3(a) (2)

CURTISS C-46 MODELS

CERTIFICATED FOR MAX. WEIGHT OF 45,000 LBS.

LANDING LIMITATIONS.
ZERO WIND AND ZERO GRADIENT

BASED ON EFFECTIVE LANDING LENGTH
AT ALTERNATE AIRPORTS. (0.70 FACTOR).

FAR 121.205

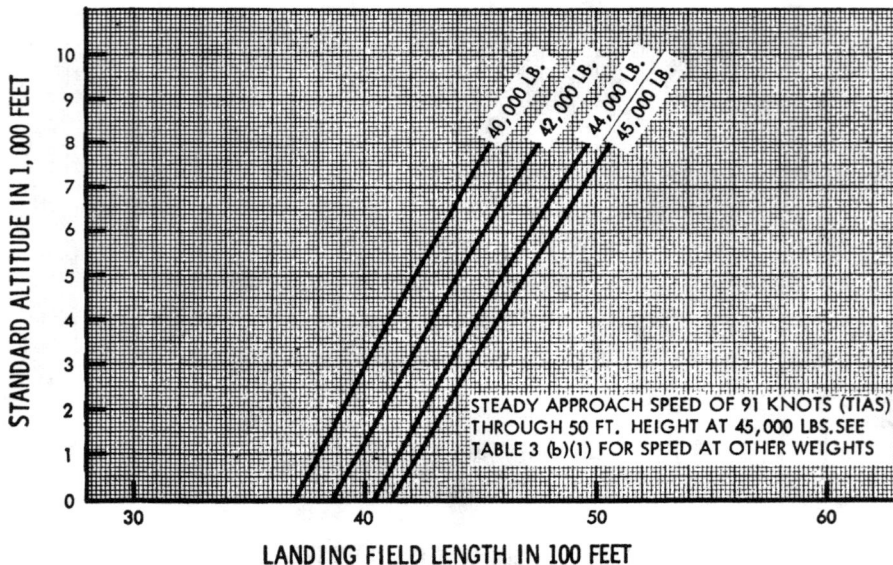

STEADY APPROACH SPEED OF 91 KNOTS (TIAS)
THROUGH 50 FT. HEIGHT AT 45,000 LBS.SEE
TABLE 3 (b)(1) FOR SPEED AT OTHER WEIGHTS

STANDARD ALTITUDE IN 1,000 FEET

LANDING FIELD LENGTH IN 100 FEET

FIG. 3(b) (1)

CURTISS C-46 MODELS

CERTIFICATED FOR MAX. WEIGHT OF 48,000 LBS.

LANDING LIMITATIONS.
ZERO WIND AND ZERO GRADIENT

BASED ON EFFECTIVE LANDING LENGTH
AT ALTERNATE AIRPORTS. (0.70 FACTOR).

FAR 121.205

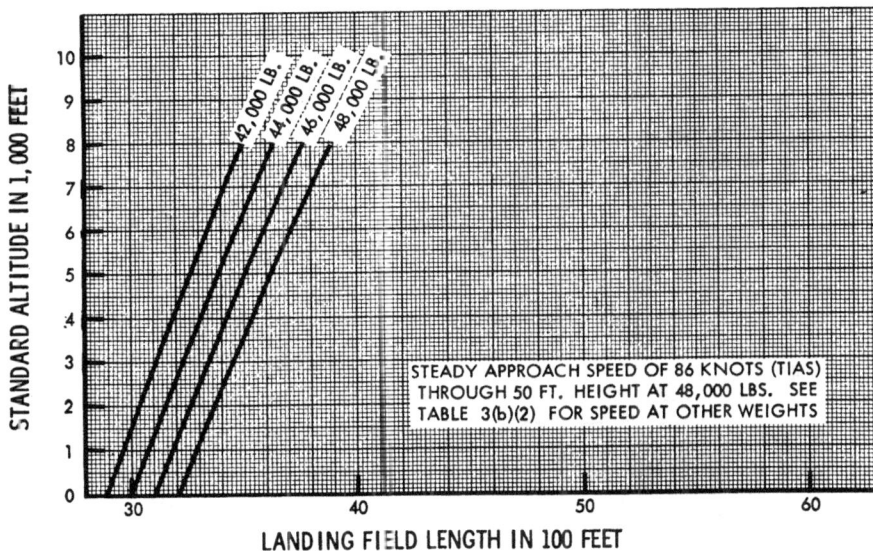

STEADY APPROACH SPEED OF 86 KNOTS (TIAS)
THROUGH 50 FT. HEIGHT AT 48,000 LBS. SEE
TABLE 3(b)(2) FOR SPEED AT OTHER WEIGHTS

FIG. 3(b) (2)

CURTISS C-46 MODELS

CERTIFICATED FOR MAX. WEIGHT OF 45,000 LBS.

LANDING LIMITATIONS.
ZERO WIND AND ZERO GRADIENT

BASED ON ACTUAL LANDING LENGTH
WHEN EFFECTIVE LENGTH IS NOT
DETERMINED. (0.55 FACTOR)

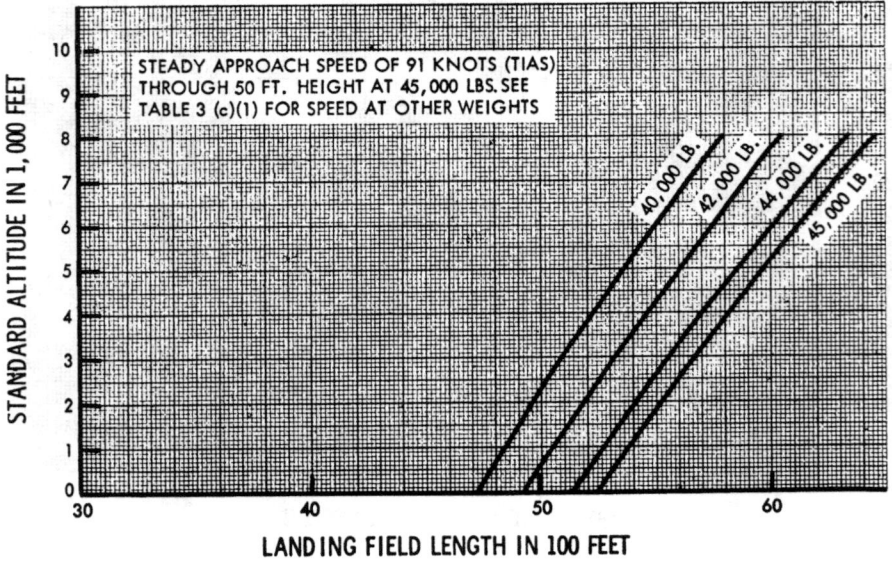

FIG. 3(c) (1)

276

CURTISS C-46 MODELS

CERTIFICATED FOR MAX. WEIGHT OF 48,000 LBS.

LANDING LIMITATIONS,
ZERO WIND AND ZERO GRADIENT

BASED ON ACTUAL LANDING LENGTH
WHEN EFFECTIVE LENGTH IS NOT
DETERMINED. (0.55 FACTOR)

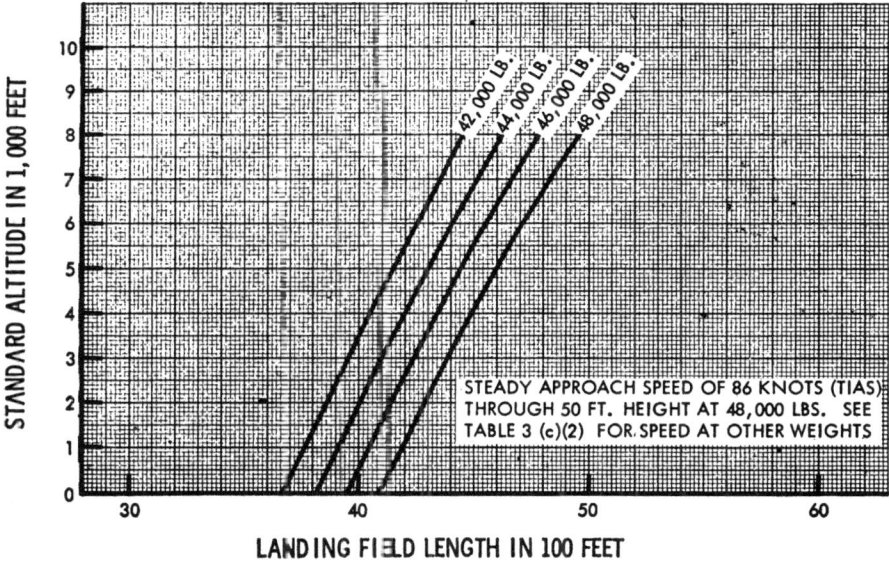

STEADY APPROACH SPEED OF 86 KNOTS (TIAS)
THROUGH 50 FT. HEIGHT AT 48,000 LBS. SEE
TABLE 3 (c)(2) FOR SPEED AT OTHER WEIGHTS

FIG. 3(c) (2)

[Doc. No. 4080, 30 FR 258, Jan. 3, 1965; 30 FR 481, Jan. 14, 1965, as amended by Amdt. 121–207, 54 FR 39293, Sept. 25, 1989; Docket FAA-2018-0119, Amdt. 121–380, 83 FR 9173, Mar. 5, 2018]

APPENDIX D TO PART 121—CRITERIA FOR DEMONSTRATION OF EMERGENCY EVACUATION PROCEDURES UNDER § 121.291

(a) *Aborted takeoff demonstration.* (1) The demonstration must be conducted either during the dark of the night or during daylight with the dark of the night simulated. If the demonstration is conducted indoors during daylight hours, it must be conducted with each window covered and each door closed to minimize the daylight effect. Illumination on the floor or ground may be used, but it must be kept low and shielded against shining into the airplane's windows or doors.

(2) The airplane must be a normal ground attitude with landing gear extended.

(3) Unless the airplane is equipped with an off-wing descent means, stands or ramps may be used for descent from the wing to the ground. Safety equipment such as mats or inverted life rafts may be placed on the floor or ground to protect participants. No other equipment that is not part of the emergency evacuation equipment of the airplane may be used to aid the participants in reaching the ground.

(4) The airplane's normal electrical power sources must be deenergized.

(5) All emergency equipment for the type of passenger-carrying operation involved must be installed in accordance with the certificate holder's manual.

(6) Each external door and exit, and each internal door or curtain must be in position to simulate a normal takeoff.

(7) A representative passenger load of persons in normal health must be used. At least 40 percent of the passenger load must be females. At least 35 percent of the passenger load must be over 50 years of age. At least 15 percent of the passenger load must be female and over 50 year of age. Three life-size dolls, not included as part of the total passenger load, must be carried by passengers to simulate live infants 2 years old or younger. Crewmembers, mechanics, and training personnel, who maintain or operate the airplane in the normal course of their duties, may not be used as passengers.

(8) No passenger may be assigned a specific seat except as the Administrator may require. Except as required by item (12) of this paragraph, no employee of the certificate holder may be seated next to an emergency exit.

(9) Seat belts and shoulder harnesses (as required) must be fastened.

(10) Before the start of the demonstration, approximately one-half of the total average amount of carry-on baggage, blankets, pillows, and other similar articles must be distributed at several locations in the aisles and emergency exit access ways to create minor obstructions.

(11) The seating density and arrangement of the airplane must be representative of the highest capacity passenger version of that airplane the certificate holder operates or proposes to operate.

(12) Each crewmember must be a member of a regularly scheduled line crew, except that flight crewmembers need not be members of a regularly scheduled line crew, provided they have knowledge of the airplane. Each crewmember must be seated in the seat the crewmember is normally assigned for takeoff, and must remain in that seat until the signal for commencement of the demonstration is received.

(13) No crewmember or passenger may be given prior knowledge of the emergency exits available for the demonstration.

(14) The certificate holder may not practice, rehearse, or describe the demonstration for the participants nor may any participant have taken part in this type of demonstration within the preceding 6 months.

(15) The pretakeoff passenger briefing required by § 121.571 may be given in accordance with the certificate holder's manual. The passengers may also be warned to follow directions of crewmembers, but may not be instructed on the procedures to be followed in the demonstration.

(16) If safety equipment as allowed by item (3) of this section is provided, either all passenger and cockpit windows must be blacked out or all of the emergency exits must have safety equipment in order to prevent disclosure of the available emergency exits.

(17) Not more than 50 percent of the emergency exits in the sides of the fuselage of an airplane that meet all of the requirements applicable to the required emergency exits for that airplane may be used for the demonstration. Exits that are not to be used in the demonstration must have the exit handle deactivated or must be indicated by red lights, red tape, or other acceptable means, placed outside the exits to indicate fire or other reason that they are unusable. The exits to be used must be representative of all of the emergency exits on the airplane and must be designated by the certificate holder, subject to approval by the Administrator. At least one floor level exit must be used.

(18) Except as provided in paragraph (a)(3) of this appendix, all evacuees must leave the airplane by a means provided as part of the airplane's equipment.

(19) The certificate holder's approved procedures and all of the emergency equipment that is normally available, including slides, ropes, lights, and megaphones, must be utilized during the demonstration, except that the flightcrew must take no active role in assisting others inside the cabin during the demonstration.

(20) The evacuation time period is completed when the last occupant has evacuated the airplane and is on the ground. Evacuees

using stands or ramps allowed by item (3) above are considered to be on the ground when they are on the stand or ramp: *Provided,* That the acceptance rate of the stand or ramp is no greater than the acceptance rate of the means available on the airplane for descent from the wing during an actual crash situation.

(b) *Ditching demonstration.* The demonstration must assume that daylight hours exist outside the airplane, and that all required crewmembers are available for the demonstration.

(1) If the certificate holder's manual requires the use of passengers to assist in the launching of liferafts, the needed passengers must be aboard the airplane and participate in the demonstration according to the manual.

(2) A stand must be placed at each emergency exit and wing, with the top of the platform at a height simulating the water level of the airplane following a ditching.

(3) After the ditching signal has been received, each evacuee must don a life vest according to the certificate holder's manual.

(4) Each liferaft must be launched and inflated, according to the certificate holder's manual, and all other required emergency equipment must be placed in rafts.

(5) Each evacuee must enter a liferaft, and the crewmembers assigned to each liferaft must indicate the location of emergency equipment aboard the raft and describe its use

(6) Either the airplane, a mockup of the airplane or a floating device simulating a passenger compartment must be used.

(i) If a mockup of the airplane is used, it must be a life-size mockup of the interior and representative of the airplane currently used by or proposed to be used by the certificate holder, and must contain adequate seats for use of the evacuees. Operation of the emergency exits and the doors must closely simulate those on the airplane. Sufficient wing area must be installed outside the over-the-wing exits to demonstrate the evacuation.

(ii) If a floating device simulating a passenger compartment is used, it must be representative, to the extent possible, of the passenger compartment of the airplane used in operations. Operation of the emergency exits and the doors must closely simulate operation on that airplane. Sufficient wing area must be installed outside the over-the-wing exits to demonstrate the evacuation. The device must be equipped with the same survival equipment as is installed on the air-

plane, to accommodate all persons participating in the demonstration.

[Doc. No. 2033, 30 FR 3206, Mar. 9, 1965, as amended by Amdt. 121–30, 32 FR 13268, Sept. 20, 1967; Amdt. 121–41, 33 FR 9067, June 20, 1968; Amdt. 121–46, 34 FR 5545, Mar. 22, 1969; Amdt. 121–47, 34 FR 11489, July 11, 1969; Amdt. 121–233, 58 FR 45230, Aug. 26, 1993]

APPENDIX E TO PART 121—FLIGHT TRAINING REQUIREMENTS

The maneuvers and procedures required by §121.424 of this part for pilot initial, transition, and upgrade flight training are set forth in the certificate holder's approved low-altitude windshear flight training program, §121.423 extended envelope training, and in this appendix. All required maneuvers and procedures must be performed inflight except that windshear and extended envelope training maneuvers and procedures must be performed in an airplane simulator in which the maneuvers and procedures are specifically authorized to be accomplished. Certain other maneuvers and procedures may be performed in an airplane simulator with a visual system (visual simulator), an airplane simulator without a visual system (nonvisual simulator), a training device, or a static airplane as indicated by the appropriate symbol in the respective column opposite the maneuver or procedure.

Whenever a maneuver or procedure is authorized to be performed in a nonvisual simulator, it may be performed in a visual simulator; when authorized in a training device, it may be performed in a visual or nonvisual simulator, and in some cases, a static airplane. Whenever the requirement may be performed in either a training device or a static airplane, the appropriate symbols are entered in the respective columns.

For the purpose of this appendix, the following symbols mean—

P = Pilot in Command (PIC).
S = Second in Command (SIC).
B = PIC and SIC.
F = Flight Engineer.
PJ = PIC transition Jet to Jet.
PP = PIC transition Prop. to Prop.
SJ = SIC transition Jet to Jet.
SP = SIC transition Prop. to Prop.
AT = All transition categories (PJ, PP, SJ, SP).
PS = SIC upgrading to PIC (same airplane).
SF = Flight Engineer upgrading to SIC (same airplane).
BU = Both SIC and Flight Engineer upgrading (same airplane).

FLIGHT TRAINING REQUIREMENTS

Maneuvers/Procedures	Initial training					Transition training					Upgrade training				
	A/P		Simulator			A/P		Simulator			A/P		Simulator		
	Inflight	Static	Visual simulator	Non-visual simulator	Training device	Inflight	Static	Visual simulator	Non-visual simulator	Training device	Inflight	Static	Visual simulator	Non-visual simulator	Training device
As appropriate to the airplane and the operation involved, flight training for pilots must include the following maneuvers and procedures..															
I. Preflight:															
(a) Visual inspection of the exterior and interior of the airplane, the location of each item to be inspected, and the purpose for inspecting it. If a flight engineer is a required crewmember for the particular type of airplane, the visual inspection may be replaced by using an approved pictorial means that realistically portrays the location and detain of preflight inspection items..		B					AT					BU			
(b) Use of the prestart check list, appropriate control system checks, starting procedures, radio and electronic equipment checks, and the selection of proper navigation and communications radio facilities and frequencies prior to flight.				B					AT					BU	
(c)(1) Before March 12, 2019, taxiing, sailing, and docking procedures in compliance with instructions issued by the appropriate Traffic Control Authority or by the person conducting the training.	B					AT					BU				
(2) Taxiing. Beginning March 12, 2019, this maneuver includes the following:.															
(i) Taxiing, sailing, and docking procedures in compliance with instructions issued by the appropriate Traffic Control Authority or by the person conducting the training.	B					AT					BU				
(ii) Use of airport diagram (surface movement chart).															
(iii) Obtaining appropriate clearance before crossing or entering active runways.															

Maneuver/Procedure	1	2	3	4	5	6	7	8
(iv) Observation of all surface movement guidance control markings and lighting.								
(d)(1) Before March 12, 2019, pre-takeoff checks that include power-plant checks.	B	B			AT			BU
(2) Beginning March 12, 2019, pre-takeoff procedures that include power-plant checks, receipt of takeoff clearance and confirmation of aircraft location, and FMS entry (if appropriate) for departure runway prior to crossing hold short line for takeoff.	B				AT			BU
II. Takeoffs:								
(a) Normal takeoffs which, for the purpose of this maneuver, begin when the airplane is taxied into position on the runway to be used.	B	B	AT	BU	AT	BU		BU
(b) Takeoffs with instrument conditions simulated at or before reaching an altitude of 100' above the airport elevation.	B	B	AT	BU	AT	BU		BU
(c)(1) Crosswind takeoffs	B		AT	BU				
(2) Beginning March 12, 2019, crosswind takeoffs including crosswind takeoffs with gusts if practicable under the existing meteorological, airport, and traffic conditions.	B		AT	BU				
(d) Takeoffs with a simulated failure of the most critical powerplant—	B	B	AT		AT	BU		
(1) At a point after V_1 and before V_2 that in the judgment of the person conducting the training is appropriate to the airplane type under the prevailing conditions; or.								
(2) At a point as close as possible after V_1 when V_1 and V_2 or V_1 and V_R are identical; or.								
(3) At the appropriate speed for non-transport category airplanes.								

For transition training in an airplane group with engines mounted in similar positions, or from wing-mounted engines to aft fuselage-mounted engines, the maneuver may be performed in a nonvisual simulator.

281

FLIGHT TRAINING REQUIREMENTS—Continued

Maneuvers/Procedures	Initial training					Transition training					Upgrade training				
	A/P		Simulator			A/P		Simulator			A/P		Simulator		
	Inflight	Static	Visual simulator	Non-visual simulator	Training device	Inflight	Static	Visual simulator	Non-visual simulator	Training device	Inflight	Static	Visual simulator	Non-visual simulator	Training device
(e) Rejected takeoffs accomplished during a normal takeoff run after reaching a reasonable speed determined by giving due consideration to aircraft characteristics, runway length, surface conditions, wind direction and velocity, brake heat energy, and any other pertinent factors that may adversely affect safety or the airplane. Training in at least one of the above takeoffs must be accomplished at night. For transitioning pilots this requirement may be met during the operating experience required under §121.434 of this part by performing a normal takeoff at night when a check airman serving as pilot-in-command is occupying a pilot station.				B					AT					BU	
III. Flight Maneuvers and Procedures:															
(a) Turns with and without spoilers				B	B				AT	AT				BU	BU
(b) Tuck and Mach buffet				B	B				AT	AT				BU	BU
(c) Maximum endurance and maximum range procedures.				B	B				AT	AT				BU	BU
(d) Operation of systems and controls at the flight engineer station.				B					AT					PS	
(e) Runaway and jammed stabilizer				B					AT					BU	
(f) Normal and abnormal or alternate operation of the following systems and procedures:															
(1) Pressurization				B	B				AT	AT				BU	BU
(2) Pneumatic				B	B				AT	AT				BU	BU
(3) Air conditioning				B	B				AT	AT				BU	BU
(4) Fuel and oil		B					AT					BU			
(5) Electrical		B					AT					BU			
(6) Hydraulic		B					AT					BU			
(7) Flight control		B					AT								
(8) Anti-icing and deicing				B					AT					BU	
(9) Auto-pilot				B					AT					BU	
(10) Automatic or other approach aids	B										SF				
(11) Stall warning devices, stall avoidance devices, and stability augmentation devices.	B										SF				

Requirement									
(12) Airborne radar devices									
(13) Any other systems, devices, or aids available.	B	B		AT	AI	AT		BU	BU
(14) Electrical, hydraulic, flight control, and flight instrument system malfunctioning or failure.	B		B	AT		AT	BU		BU
(15) Landing gear and flap systems failure or malfunction.	B	B	B	AT		AT	BU		BU
(16) Failure of navigation or communications equipment.									
(g) Flight emergency procedures that include at least the following:									
(1) Powerplant, heater, cargo compartment, cabin, flight deck, wing, and electrical fires.	B	B	B	AT		AT	BU		BU
(2) Smoke control	B		B	AT		AT	BU		BU
(3) Powerplant failures	B	B	B	B			BU		BU
(4) Fuel jettisoning	B		B	AT		B	BU		BU
(5) Any other emergency procedures outlined in the appropriate flight manual.									
(h) Steep turns in each direction. Each steep turn must involve a bank angle of 45° with a heading change of at least 180° but not more than 360°.	P		PJ				PS		
(i) Stall Prevention. For the purpose of this training the approved recovery procedure must be initiated at the first indication of an impending stall (buffet, stick shaker, aural warning). Stall prevention training must be conducted in at least the following configurations:	B		AT				BU		
(1) Takeoff configuration (except where the airplane uses only a zero-flap takeoff configuration).									
(2) Clean configuration.									
(3) Landing configuration.									
(j) Recovery from specific flight characteristics that are peculiar to the airplane type.	B		AT				BU		
(k) Instrument procedures that include the following:									
(1) Area departure and arrival	B		AT				BU		
(2) Use of navigation systems including adherence to assigned radials.	B		AT				BU		
(3) Holding	B		AT				BU		
(l) ILS instrument approaches that include the following:									
(1) Normal ILS approaches	B	AT	BU						

283

FLIGHT TRAINING REQUIREMENTS—Continued

Maneuvers/Procedures	Initial training					Transition training					Upgrade training				
	A/P		Simulator			A/P		Simulator			A/P		Simulator		
	Inflight	Static	Visual simulator	Non-visual simulator	Training device	Inflight	Static	Visual simulator	Non-visual simulator	Training device	Inflight	Static	Visual simulator	Non-visual simulator	Training device
(2) Manually controlled ILS approaches with a simulated failure of one powerplant which occurs before initiating the final approach course and continues to touchdown or through the missed approach procedure.	B							AT					BU		
(m) Instrument approaches and missed approaches other than ILS which include the following:															
(1) Nonprecision approaches that the trainee is likely to use.			B					AT					BU		
(2) In addition to subparagraph (1) of this paragraph, at least one other nonprecision approach and missed approach procedure that the trainee is likely to use.					B					AT					BU
In connection with paragraphs III(k) and III(l), each instrument approach must be performed according to any procedures and limitations approved for the approach facility used. The instrument approach begins when the airplane is over the initial approach fix for the approach procedure being used (or turned over to the final approach controller in the case of GCA approach) and ends when the airplane touches down on the runway or when transition to a missed approach configuration is completed.															
(n) Circling approaches which include the following:	B					AT					BU				
(1) That portion of the circling approach to the authorized minimum altitude for the procedure being used must be made under simulated instrument conditions.															

(2) The circling approach must be made to the authorized minimum circling approach altitude followed by a change in heading and the necessary maneuvering (by visual reference) to maintain a flight path that permits a normal landing on a runway at least 90° from the final approach course of the simulated instrument portion of the approach.

(3) The circling approach must be performed without excessive maneuvering, and without exceeding the normal operating limits of the airplane. The angle of bank should not exceed 30°.

Training in the circling approach maneuver is not required for a pilot employed by a certificate holder subject to the operating rules of Part 121 of this chapter if the certificate holder's manual prohibits a circling approach in weather conditions below 1000–3 (ceiling and visibility); for a SIC if the certificate holder's manual prohibits the SIC from performing a circling approach in operations under this part.

(o) *Zero-flap approaches.* Training in this maneuver is not required for a particular airplane type if the Administrator has determined that the probability of flap extension failure on that type airplane is extremely remote due to system design. In making this determination, the Administrator determines whether training on slats only and partial flap approaches is necessary.

(p) Missed approaches which include the following:

(1) Missed approaches from ILS approaches.

(2) Other missed approaches ....

(3) Missed approaches that include a complete approved missed approach procedure.

(4) Missed approaches that include a powerplant failure.

IV. Landings and Approaches to Landings:

(a) Normal landings ....

(b) Landing and go around with the horizontal stabilizer out of trim.

Maneuver								
Training in the circling approach	PP, PJ				PS			
(o) Zero-flap approaches	P							
(1) Missed approaches from ILS approaches		B		AT		BU		BU
(2) Other missed approaches		B		AT		BU		BU
(3) Missed approaches that include a complete approved missed approach procedure	B		AT		BU		BU	
(4) Missed approaches that include a powerplant failure	B		AT		BU			
(a) Normal landings	B		PJ, PP	AT		BU		PS
(b) Landing and go around with the horizontal stabilizer out of trim	P							

285

FLIGHT TRAINING REQUIREMENTS—Continued

Maneuvers/Procedures	Initial training					Transition training					Upgrade training				
	A/P		Simulator			A/P		Simulator			A/P		Simulator		
	Inflight	Static	Visual simulator	Non-visual simulator	Training device	Inflight	Static	Visual simulator	Non-visual simulator	Training device	Inflight	Static	Visual simulator	Non-visual simulator	Training device
(c) Landing in sequence from an ILS instrument approach.	B							AT					BU		
(d)(1) Cross wind landing	B					AT					BU				
(2) Beginning March 12, 2019, crosswind landing, including gusts if practicable under the existing meteorological, airport, and traffic conditions.	B					AT					BU				
(e) Maneuvering to a landing with simulated powerplant failure, as follows:															
(1) Except as provided in subparagraph (3) of this paragraph in the case of 3-engine airplanes, maneuvering to a landing with an approved procedure that approximates the loss of two powerplants (center and one outboard engine).	P							PJ, PP.					PS		
(2) Except as provided in subparagraph (3) of this paragraph, in the case of other multiengine airplanes, maneuvering to a landing with a simulated failure of 50 percent of available powerplants with the simulated loss of power on one side of the airplane.	P							PJ, PP.					PS		
(3) Notwithstanding the requirements of subparagraphs (1) and (2) of this paragraph, flight crewmembers who satisfy those requirements in a visual simulator must also:															
(i) Take inflight training in one-engine inoperative landings; and.															
(ii) In the case of a second-in-command up-grading to a pilot-in-command and who has not previously performed the maneuvers required by this paragraph in flight, meet the requirements of this paragraph applicable to initial training for pilots-in-command.															

(4) In the case of flight crewmembers other than the pilot-in-command, perform the maneuver with the simulated loss of power of the most critical powerplant only.							
(f) Landing under simulated circling approach conditions (exceptions under III(n) applicable to this requirement).	B				AT		BU
(g) Rejected landings that include a normal missed approach procedure after the landing is rejected. For the purpose of this maneuver the landing should be rejected at approximately 50 feet and approximately over the runway threshold.	B				AT		BU
(h) Zero-flap landings if the Administrator finds that maneuver appropriate for training in the airplane.	P				PP, PI		PS
(i) Manual reversion (if appropriate)		B		AT			BU
Training in landings and approaches to landings must include the types and conditions provided in IV(a) through (i) but more than one type may be combined where appropriate.					AT		
Training in one of the above landings must be accomplished at night. For transitioning pilots, this requirement may be met during the operating experience required under §121.434 of this part by performing a normal landing when a check pilot serving as pilot-in-command is occupying a pilot station.	B					BU	

[Doc. No. 9509, 35 FR 97, Jan. 3, 1970, as amended by Amdt. 121–91, 37 FR 10730, May 27, 1972; Amdt. 121–108, 38 FR 35446, Dec. 28, 1973; Amdt. 121–159, 45 FR 41595, June 19, 1980; Amdt. 121–199, 53 FR 37697, Sept. 27, 1988; Amdt. 121–366, 78 FR 67841, Nov. 12, 2013]

APPENDIX F TO PART 121—PROFICIENCY
CHECK REQUIREMENTS

The maneuvers and procedures required by
§ 121.441 for pilot proficiency checks are set
forth in this appendix and must be performed
inflight except to the extent that certain
maneuvers and procedures may be performed
in an airplane simulator with a visual system (visual simulator), an airplane simulator without a visual system (nonvisual
simulator), or a training device as indicated
by the appropriate symbol in the respective
column opposite the maneuver or procedure.

Whenever a maneuver or procedure is authorized to be performed in a nonvisual simulator, it may also be performed in a visual
simulator; when authorized in a training device, it may be performed in a visual or nonvisual simulator.

For the purpose of this appendix, the following symbols mean—

P = Pilot in Command.

B = Both Pilot in Command and Second in
Command.

* = A symbol and asterisk (B*) indicates that
a particular condition is specified in the
maneuvers and procedures column.

= When a maneuver is preceded by this
symbol it indicates the maneuver may be
required in the airplane at the discretion
of the person conducting the check.

Throughout the maneuvers prescribed in
this appendix, good judgment commensurate
with a high level of safety must be demonstrated. In determining whether such
judgment has been shown, the person conducting the check considers adherence to approved procedures, actions based on analysis
of situations for which there is no prescribed
procedure or recommended practice, and
qualities of prudence and care in selecting a
course of action.

Maneuvers/Procedures	Required		Permitted			
	Simulated instrument conditions	Inflight	Visual simulator	Non-visual simulator	Training device	Waiver provisions of § 121.441(d)
The procedures and maneuvers set forth in this appendix must be performed in a manner that satisfactorily demonstrates knowledge and skill with respect to—						
(1) The airplane, its systems and components;	....	....	....	....	....	....
(2) Proper control of airspeed, configuration, direction, altitude, and attitude in accordance with procedures and limitations contained in the approved Airplane Flight Manual, the certificate holder's operations Manual, check lists, or other approved material appropriate to the airplane type; and	....	....	....	....	....	....
(3) Compliance with approach, ATC, or other applicable procedures	....	....	....	....	....	....
I. Preflight:						
(a) Equipment examination (oral or written). As part of the practical test the equipment examination must be closely coordinated with, and related to, the flight maneuvers portion but may not be given during the flight maneuvers portion. The equipment examination must cover—	....	....	....	....	B	....
(1) Subjects requiring a practical knowledge of the airplane, its powerplants, systems, components, operational, and performance factors;	....	....	....	....		....
(2) Normal, abnormal, and emergency procedures, and the operations and limitations relating thereto; and	....	....	....	....		....
(3) The appropriate provisions of the approved Airplane Flight Manual	....	....	....	....		....
The person conducting the check may accept, as equal to this equipment test, an equipment test given to the pilot in the certificate holder's ground school within the preceding 6 calendar months						
(b) Preflight inspection. The pilot must—	....	....	....	....	B	B*
(1) Conduct an actual visual inspection of the exterior and interior of the airplane, locating each item and explaining briefly the purpose for inspecting it; and	....	....	....	....		....
(2) Demonstrate the use of the prestart check list, appropriate control system checks, starting procedures, radio and electronic equipment checks, and the selection of proper navigation and communications radio facilities and frequencies prior to flight ...	....	....	....	....		....

Maneuvers/Procedures	Required		Permitted			
	Simulated instrument conditions	Inflight	Visual simulator	Non-visual simulator	Training device	Waiver provisions of §121.441(d)
Except for flight checks required by §121.424(d)(1)(i) an approved pictorial means that realistically portrays the location and detail of preflight inspection items and provides for the portrayal of abnormal conditions may be substituted for the preflight inspection. If a flight engineer is a required flight crewmember for the particular type airplane, the visual inspection may be waived under §121.441(d)						
(c)(1) Taxiing. Before March 12, 2019, this maneuver includes taxiing (in the case of a second in command proficiency check to the extent practical from the second in command crew position), sailing, or docking procedures in compliance with instructions issued by the appropriate traffic control authority or by the person conducting the checks	....	B	....	....	....	
(c)(2) Taxiing. Beginning March 12, 2019, this maneuver includes the following: (i) Taxiing (in the case of a second in command proficiency check to the extent practical from the second in command crew position), sailing, or docking procedures in compliance with instructions issued by the appropriate traffic control authority or by the person conducting the checks. (ii) Use of airport diagram (surface movement chart) (iii) Obtaining appropriate clearance before crossing or entering active runways. (iv) Observation of all surface movement guidance control markings and lighting	....	B	....	....	....	
(d)(1) Power-plant checks. As appropriate to the airplane type	....	....	....	....	B	....
(d)(2) Beginning March 12, 2019, pre-takeoff procedures that include power-plant checks, receipt of takeoff clearance and confirmation of aircraft location, and FMS entry (if appropriate), for departure runway prior to crossing hold short line for takeoff	....	....	B	....	....	
II. Takeoff:						
(a) Normal. One normal takeoff which, for the purpose of this maneuver, begins when the airplane is taxied into position on the runway to be used	....	B*	....	....	....	
(b) Instrument. One takeoff with instrument conditions simulated at or before reaching an altitude of 100′ above the airport elevation	B	....	B*	....	....	
(c)(1) Crosswind. Before March 12, 2019, one crosswind takeoff, if practicable, under the existing meteorological, airport, and traffic conditions	....	B*	....	....	....	
(c)(2) Beginning March 12, 2019, one crosswind takeoff with gusts, if practicable, under the existing meteorological, airport, and traffic conditions	....	B*	....	....	....	
#(d) Powerplant failure. One takeoff with a simulated failure of the most critical powerplant—	....	....	B	....	....	
(1) At a point after V_1 and before V_2 that in the judgment of the person conducting the check is appropriate to the airplane type under the prevailing conditions;	....	....	....	....	....	
(2) At a point as close as possible after V_1 when V_1 and V_2 or V_1 and V_r are identical; or	....	....	....	....	....	
(3) At the appropriate speed for non-transport category airplanes	....	....	....	....	....	
In an airplane group with aft fuselage-mounted engines this maneuver may be performed in a non-visual simulator	....	....	....	....	....	
(e) Rejected. A rejected takeoff may be performed in an airplane during a normal takeoff run after reaching a reasonable speed determined by giving due consideration to aircraft characteristics, runway length, surface conditions wind direction and velocity, brake heat energy, and any other pertinent factors that may adversely affect safety or the airplane	....	....	....	B*	....	B
III. Instrument procedures:						
a) Area departure and area arrival. During each of these maneuvers the applicant must—	B	----	----	B	----	B*
(1) Adhere to actual or simulated ATC clearances (including assigned radials); and	----	----	----	----	----	----

289

Maneuvers/Procedures	Required		Permitted			
	Simulated instrument conditions	Inflight	Visual simu- lator	Non- visual simu- lator	Training device	Waiver provisions of §121.441(d)
(2) Properly use available navigation facilities.	----	----	----	----	----	----
Either area arrival or area departure, but not both, may be waived under §121.441(d).						
(b) Holding. This maneuver includes entering, maintaining, and leaving holding patterns. It may be performed in connection with either area departure or area arrival.	B	----	----	B	----	B
(c) ILS and other instrument approaches. There must be the following:						
(1) At least one normal ILS approach.	B	----	B	----	----	----
(2) At least one manually controlled ILS approach with a simu- lated failure of one powerplant. The simulated failure should occur before initiating the final approach course and must continue to touchdown or through the missed approach pro- cedure.	B	----	----	----	----	----
(3) At least one nonprecision approach procedure that is rep- resentative of the non-precision approach procedures that the certificate holder is likely to use.	B	----	B	----	----	----
(4) Demonstration of at least one nonprecision approach pro- cedure on a letdown aid other than the approach procedure performed under subparagraph (3) of this paragraph that the certificate holder is approved to use.	B	----	----	----	B	----
(5) For each type of EFVS operation the certificate holder is authorized to conduct, at least one instrument approach must be made using an EFVS.	B	B*				
Each instrument approach must be performed according to any procedures and limitations approved for the approach facility used. The instrument approach begins when the airplane is over the initial approach fix for the approach procedure being used (or turned over to the final approach controller in the case of a GCA approach) and ends when the airplane touches down on the runway or when transition to a missed approach configuration is completed. Instrument conditions need not be simulated below 100' above touchdown zone elevation.						
(d) Circling approaches. If the certificate holder is approved for circling minimums below 1000-3, at least one circling ap- proach must be made under the following conditions.	----	----	B*	----	----	B*
(1) The portion of the approach to the authorized minimum cir- cling approach altitude must be made under simulated in- strument conditions.	B	----	----	----	----	----
(2) The approach must be made to the authorized minimum circling approach attitude followed by a change in heading and the necessary maneuvering by visual reference to main- tain a flight path that permits a normal landing on a runway at least 90[degrees] from the final approach course of the simulated instrument portion of the approach.	----	----	----	----	----	----
(3) The circling approach must be performed without excessive maneuvering, and without exceeding the normal operating limits of the airplane. The angle of bank should not exceed 30[degrees]	----	----	----	----	----	----
If local conditions beyond the control of the pilot prohibit the maneuver or prevent it from being performed as required, it may be waived as provided in §121.441(d): Provided, how- ever, that the maneuver may not be waived under this provi- sion for two successive proficiency checks.						

Maneuvers/Procedures	Required		Permitted			
	Simulated instrument conditions	Inflight	Visual simulator	Non-visual simulator	Training device	Waiver provisions of § 121.441(d)
The circling approach maneuver is not required for a second-in-command if the certificate holder's manual prohibits a second-in-command from performing a circling approach in operations under this part.						
(e) Missed Approach	----	----	----	----	----	----
(1) Each pilot must perform at least one missed approach from an ILS approach.	----	----	B*	----	----	----
(2) Each pilot in command must perform at least one additional missed approach. A complete approved missed approach procedure must be accomplished at least once. At the discretion of the person conducting a check a simulated powerplant failure may be required during any of the missed approaches. These maneuvers may be performed either independently or in conjunction with maneuvers required under Sections II or V of this appendix. At least one missed approach must be performed in flight.	----	----	P*	----	----	----
IV. Inflight Maneuvers: (a) Steep turns. At least one steep turn in each direction must be performed. Each steep turn must involve a bank angle of 45° with a heading change of at least 180° but not more than 360°	P	....	....	P	....	P
(b) Stall Prevention. For the purpose of this maneuver the approved recovery procedure must be initiated at the first indication of an impending stall (buffet, stick shaker, aural warning). Except as provided below there must be at least three stall prevention recoveries as follows: .... (1) One in the takeoff configuration (except where the airplane uses only a zero-flap takeoff configuration). (2) One in a clean configuration. (3) One in a landing configuration. At the discretion of the person conducting the check, one stall prevention recovery must be performed in one of the above configurations while in a turn with the bank angle between 15° and 30°. Two out of the three stall prevention recoveries required by this paragraph may be waived. If the certificate holder is authorized to dispatch or flight release the airplane with a stall warning device inoperative the device may not be used during this maneuver	B	....	....	B	....	B*
(c) Specific flight characteristics. Recovery from specific flight characteristics that are peculiar to the airplane type	....	....	....	B	....	B
(d) Powerplant failures. In addition to specific requirements for maneuvers with simulated powerplant failures, the person conducting the check may require a simulated powerplant failure at any time during the check	....	....	....	B	....	....
V. Landings and Approaches to Landings: Notwithstanding the authorizations for combining and waiving maneuvers and for the use of a simulator, at least two actual landings (one to a full stop) must be made for all pilot-in-command and initial second-in-command proficiency checks. Landings and approaches to landings must include the types listed below, but more than one type may be combined where appropriate: (a) Normal landing	....	B	....	....		
(b) Landing in sequence from an ILS instrument approach except that if circumstances beyond the control of the pilot prevent an actual landing, the person conducting the check may accept an approach to a point where in his judgment a landing to a full stop could have been made	....	B*	....	....		
(c)(1) Crosswind landing, if practical under existing meteorological, airport, and traffic conditions	....	B*	....	....		
(c)(2) Beginning March 12, 2019, crosswind landing with gusts, if practical under existing meteorological, airport, and traffic conditions	....	B*	....	....		

Maneuvers/Procedures	Required		Permitted			
	Simulated instrument conditions	Inflight	Visual simulator	Non-visual simulator	Training device	Waiver provisions of § 121.441(d)
(d) Maneuvering to a landing with simulated powerplant failure as follows:						
(1) In the case of 3-engine airplanes, maneuvering to a landing with an approved procedure that approximates the loss of two powerplants (center and one outboard engine); or	....	....	B*	....	....	....
(2) In the case of other multiengine airplanes, maneuvering to a landing with a simulated failure of 50 percent of available powerplants, with the simulated loss of power on one side of the airplane	....	....	B*	....	....	....
Notwithstanding the requirements of subparagraphs (d) (1) and (2) of this paragraph, in a proficiency check for other than a pilot-in-command, the simulated loss of power may be only the most critical powerplant. However, if a pilot satisfies the requirements of subparagraphs (d) (1) or (2) of this paragraph in a visual simulator, he also must maneuver in flight to a landing with a simulated failure of the most critical powerplant. In addition, a pilot-in-command may omit the maneuver required by subparagraph (d)(1) or (d)(2) of this paragraph during a required proficiency check or simulator course of training if he satisfactorily performed that maneuver during the preceding proficiency check, or during the preceding approved simulator course of training under the observation of a check airman, whichever was completed later						
(e) Except as provided in paragraph (f) of this section, if the certificate holder is approved for circling minimums below 1000-3, a landing under simulated circling approach conditions. However, when performed in an airplane, if circumstances beyond the control of the pilot prevent a landing, the person conducting the check may accept an approach to a point where, in his judgment, a landing to a full stop could have been made	....	....	B*	....	....	....
#(f) A rejected landing, including a normal missed approach procedure, that is rejected approximately 50′ over the runway and approximately over the runway threshold. This maneuver may be combined with instrument, circling, or missed approach procedures, but instrument conditions need not be simulated below 100 feet above the runway	....	....	B	....	....	....
(g) If the certificate holder is authorized to conduct EFVS operations to touchdown and rollout, at least one instrument approach to a landing must be made using an EFVS, including the use of enhanced flight vision from 100 feet above the touchdown zone elevation to touchdown and rollout	B	*B				
(h) If the certificate holder is authorized to conduct EFVS operations to 100 feet above the touchdown zone elevation, at least one instrument approach to a landing must be made using an EFVS, including the transition from enhanced flight vision to natural vision at 100 feet above the touchdown zone elevation	B	*B				
VI. Normal and Abnormal Procedures:						
Each applicant must demonstrate the proper use of as many of the systems and devices listed below as the person conducting the check finds are necessary to determine that the person being checked has a practical knowledge of the use of the systems and devices appropriate to the airplane type:						
(a) Anti-icing and de-icing systems	....	....	....	B	....	....
(b) Auto-pilot systems	....	....	....	B	....	....
(c) Automatic or other approach aid systems	....	....	....	B	....	....
(d) Stall warning devices, stall avoidance devices, and stability augmentation devices	....	....	....	B	....	....
(e) Airborne radar devices	....	....	....	B	....	....
(f) Any other systems, devices, or aids available	....	....	....	B	....	....
(g) Hydraulic and electrical system failures and malfunctions	....	....	....	....	B	....
(h) Landing gear and flap systems failure or malfunction ...	....	....	....	....	B	
(i) Failure of navigation or communications equipment	....	....	....	B	....	

292

Maneuvers/Procedures	Required		Permitted			
	Simulated instrument conditions	Inflight	Visual simu-lator	Non-visual simu-lator	Training device	Waiver provisions of §121.441(d)
VII. Emergency Procedures: Each applicant must demonstrate the proper emergency procedures for as many of the emergency situations listed below as the person conducting the check finds are necessary to determine that the person being checked has an adequate knowledge of, and ability to perform, such procedure:						
(a) Fire in flight	....	....	....	B	....	....
(b) Smoke control	....	....	....	B	....	....
(c) Rapid decompression	....	....	....	B	....	....
(d) Emergency descent	....	....	....	B	....	....
(e) Any other emergency procedures outlined in the appropriate approved Airplane Flight Manual	....	....	....	B	....	....

[Doc. No. 9509, 35 FR 99, Jan. 3, 1970, as amended by Amdt. 121–80, 36 FR 19362, Oct. 5, 1971; Amdt. 121–91, 37 FR 10730, May 27, 1972; Amdt. 121–92, 37 FR 12717, June 28, 1972; Amdt. 121–108, 38 FR 35448, Dec. 28, 1973; Amdt. 121–136, 42 FR 43389, Aug. 29, 1977; Amdt. 121–366, 78 FR 67844, Nov. 12, 2013; Docket FAA–2013–0685, Amdt. 121–376, 81 FR 90175, Dec. 13, 2016; Amdt. 121–376B, 83 FR 1187, Jan. 10, 2018; 83 FR 4420, Jan. 31, 2018]

APPENDIX G TO PART 121—DOPPLER RADAR AND INERTIAL NAVIGATION SYSTEM (INS): REQUEST FOR EVALUATION; EQUIPMENT AND EQUIPMENT INSTALLATION; TRAINING PROGRAM; EQUIPMENT ACCURACY AND RELIABILITY; EVALUATION PROGRAM

1. *Application authority.* (a) An applicant for authority to use a Doppler Radar or Inertial Navigation System must submit a request for evaluation of the system to the responsible Flight Standards office charged with the overall inspection of its operations 30 days prior to the start of evaluation flights.

(b) The application must contain:

(1) A summary of experience with the system showing to the satisfaction of the Administrator a history of the accuracy and reliability of the system proposed to be used.

(2) A training program curriculum for initial approval under §121.405.

(3) A maintenance program for compliance with subpart L of this part.

(4) A description of equipment installation.

(5) Proposed revisions to the Operations Manual outlining all normal and emergency procedures relative to use of the proposed system, including detailed methods for continuing the navigational function with partial or complete equipment failure, and methods for determining the most accurate system when an unusually large divergence between systems occurs. For the purpose of this appendix, a large divergence is a divergence that results in a track that falls beyond clearance limits.

(6) Any proposed revisions to the minimum equipment list with adequate justification therefor.

(7) A list of operations to be conducted using the system, containing an analysis of

each with respect to length, magnetic compass reliability, availability of en route aids, and adequacy of gateway and terminal radio facilities to support the system. For the purpose of this appendix, a gateway is a specific navigational fix where use of long range navigation commences or terminates.

2. *Equipment and equipment installation—Inertial Navigation Systems (INS) or Doppler Radar System.* (a) Inertial Navigation and Doppler Radar Systems must be installed in accordance with applicable airworthiness requirements.

(b) Cockpit arrangement must be visible and useable by either pilot seated at his duty station.

(c) The equipment must provide, by visual, mechanical, or electrical output signals, indications of the invalidity of output data upon the occurrence of probable failures or malfunctions within the system.

(d) A probable failure or malfunction within the system must not result in loss of the aircraft's required navigation capability.

(e) The alignment, updating, and navigation computer functions of the system must not be invalidated by normal aircraft power interruptions and transients.

(f) The system must not be the source of cause of objectionable radio frequency interference, and must not be adversely affected by radio frequency interference from other aircraft systems.

(g) The FAA-approved airplane flight manual, or supplement thereto, must include pertinent material as required to define the normal and emergency operating procedures and applicable operating limitations associated with INS and Doppler performance (such as maximum latitude at which ground alignment capability is provided, or deviations between systems).

3. *Equipment and equipment installation—Inertial Navigation Systems (INS).* (a) If an applicant elects to use an Inertial Navigation System it must be at least a dual system (including navigational computers and reference units). At least two systems must be operational at takeoff. The dual system may consist of either two INS units, or one INS unit and one Doppler Radar unit.

(b) Each Inertial Navigation System must incorporate the following:

(1) Valid ground alignment capability at all latitudes appropriate for intended use of the installation.

(2) A display of alignment status or a ready to navigate light showing completed alignment to the flight crew.

(3) The present position of the airplane in suitable coordinates.

(4) Information relative to destinations or waypoint positions:

(i) The information needed to gain and maintain a desired track and to determine deviations from the desired track.

(ii) The information needed to determine distance and time to go to the next waypoint or destination.

(c) For INS installations that do not have memory or other inflight alignment means, a separate electrical power source (independent of the main propulsion system) must be provided which can supply, for at least 5 minutes, enough power (as shown by analysis or as demonstrated in the airplane) to maintain the INS in such condition that its full capability is restored upon the reactivation of the normal electrical supply.

(d) The equipment must provide such visual, mechanical, or electrical output signals as may be required to permit the flight crew to detect probable failures or malfunctions in the system.

4. *Equipment and equipment installation— Doppler Radar Systems.* (a) If an applicant elects to use a Doppler Radar System it must be at least a dual system (including dual antennas or a combined antenna designed for multiple operation), except that:

(1) A single operating transmitter with a standby capable of operation may be used in lieu of two operating transmitters.

(2) Single heading source information to all installations may be utilized, provided a compass comparator system is installed and operational procedures call for frequent cross-checks of all compass heading indicators by crewmembers.

The dual system may consist of either two Doppler Radar units or one Doppler Radar unit and one INS unit.

(b) At least two systems must be operational at takeoff.

(c) As determined by the Administrator and specified in the certificate holder's operations specifications, other navigational aids may be required to update the Doppler Radar for a particular operation. These may include DME, VOR, ADF, ground-based radar, and airborne weather radar. When these aids are required, the cockpit arrangement must be such that all controls are accessible to each pilot seated at his duty station.

5. *Training programs.* The initial training program for Doppler Radar and Inertial Navigation Systems must include the following:

(a) Duties and responsibilities of flight crewmembers, dispatchers, and maintenance personnel.

(b) For pilots, instruction in the following:

(1) Theory and procedures, limitations, detection of malfunctions, preflight and inflight testing, and cross-checking methods.

(2) The use of computers, an explanation of all systems, compass limitations at high latitudes, a review of navigation, flight planning, and applicable meteorology.

(3) The methods for updating by means of reliable fixes.

(4) The actual plotting of fixes.

(c) Abnormal and emergency procedures.

6. *Equipment accuracy and reliability.* (a) Each Inertial Navigation System must meet the following accuracy requirements, as appropriate:

(1) For flights up to 10 hours' duration, no greater than 2 nautical miles per hour of circular error on 95 percent of system flights completed is permitted.

(2) For flights over 10 hours' duration, a tolerance of ±20 miles cross-track and ±25 miles along-track on 95 percent of system flights completed is permitted.

(b) Compass heading information to the Doppler Radar must be maintained to an accuracy of ±1° and total system deviations must not exceed 2°. When free gyro techniques are used, procedures shall be utilized to ensure that an equivalent level of heading accuracy and total system deviation is attained.

(c) Each Doppler Radar System must meet accuracy requirements of ±20 miles cross-track and ±25 miles along-track for 95 percent of the system flights completed. Updating is permitted.

A system that does not meet the requirements of this section will be considered a failed system.

7. *Evaluation program.* (a) Approval by evaluation must be requested as a part of the application for operational approval of a Doppler Radar or Inertial Navigation System.

(b) The applicant must provide sufficient flights which show to the satisfaction of the Administrator the applicant's ability to use cockpit navigation in his operation.

(c) The Administrator bases his evaluation on the following:

(1) Adequacy of operational procedures.

(2) Operational accuracy and reliability of equipment and feasibility of the system with regard to proposed operations.

(3) Availability of terminal, gateway, area, and en route ground-based aids, if required, to support the self-contained system.

(4) Acceptability of cockpit workload.

(5) Adequacy of flight crew qualifications.

(6) Adequacy of maintenance training and availability of spare parts.

After successful completion of evaluation demonstrations, FAA approval is indicated by issuance of amended operations specifications and en route flight procedures defining the new operation. Approval is limited to those operations for which the adequacy of the equipment and the feasibility of cockpit navigation has been satisfactorily demonstrated.

[Doc. No. 10204, 37 FR 6464, Mar. 30, 1972, as amended by Amdt. 121–207, 54 FR 39293, Sept. 25, 1989; Docket FAA–2017–0733, Amdt. 121–379, 82 FR 34398, July 25, 2017; Docket FAA–2018–0119, Amdt. 121–380, 83 FR 9173, Mar. 5, 2018]

APPENDIX H TO PART 121—ADVANCED SIMULATION

This appendix provides guidelines and a means for achieving flightcrew training in advanced airplane simulators. The requirements in this appendix are in addition to the simulator approval requirements in §121.407. Each simulator used under this appendix must be approved as a Level B, C, or D simulator, as appropriate.

ADVANCED SIMULATION TRAINING PROGRAM

For an operator to conduct Level C or D training under this appendix all required simulator instruction and checks must be conducted under an advanced simulation training program approved by the Administrator for the operator. This program must also ensure that all instructors and check airmen used in appendix H training and checking are highly qualified to provide the training required in the training program. The advanced simulation training program must include the following:

1. The operator's initial, transition, upgrade, and recurrent simulator training programs and its procedures for re-establishing recency of experience in the simulator.

2. How the training program will integrate Level B, C, and D simulators with other simulators and training devices to maximize the total training, checking, and certification functions.

3. Documentation that each instructor and check airman has served for at least 1 year in that capacity in a certificate holder's approved program or has served for at least 1 year as a pilot in command or second in command in an airplane of the group in which that pilot is instructing or checking.

4. A procedure to ensure that each instructor and check airman actively participates

in either an approved regularly scheduled line flying program as a flight crewmember or an approved line observation program in the same airplane type for which that person is instructing or checking.

5. A procedure to ensure that each instructor and check airman is given a minimum of 4 hours of training each year to become familiar with the operator's advanced simulation training program, or changes to it, and to emphasize their respective roles in the program. Training for simulator instructors and check airmen must include training policies and procedures, instruction methods and techniques, operation of simulator controls (including environmental and trouble panels), limitations of the simulator, and minimum equipment required for each course of training.

6. A special Line Oriented Flight Training (LOFT) program to facilitate the transition from the simulator to line flying. This LOFT program must consist of at least a 4-hour course of training for each flightcrew. It also must contain at least two representative flight segments of the operator's route. One of the flight segments must contain strictly normal operating procedures from push back at one airport to arrival at another. Another flight segment must contain training in appropriate abnormal and emergency flight operations. After March 12, 2019, the LOFT must provide an opportunity for the pilot to demonstrate workload management and pilot monitoring skills.

LEVEL B

Training and Checking Permitted

1. Recency of experience (§121.439).

2. Night takeoffs and landings (Part 121, Appendix E).

3. Except for EFVS operations, landings in a proficiency check without the landing on the line requirements (§121.441).

LEVEL C

Training and Checking Permitted

1. For all pilots, transition training between airplanes in the same group, and for a pilot in command the certification check required by §61.153 of this chapter.

2. Upgrade to pilot-in-command training and the certification check when the pilot—

a. Has previously qualified as second in command in the equipment to which the pilot is upgrading;

b. Has at least 500 hours of actual flight time while serving as second in command in an airplane of the same group; and

c. Is currently serving as second in command in an airplane in this same group.

3. Initial pilot-in-command training and the certification check when the pilot—

a. Is currently serving as second in command in an airplane of the same group;

b. Has a minimum of 2,500 flight hours as second in command in an airplane of the same group; and

c. Has served as second in command on at least two airplanes of the same group.

4. For all second-in-command pilot applicants who meet the aeronautical experience requirements of § 61.159 of this chapter in the airplane, the initial and upgrade training and checking required by this part, and the certification check requirements of § 61.153 of this chapter.

5. For all pilots, the extended envelope training required by § 121.423 of this part.

LEVEL D

Training and Checking Permitted

Except for the requirements listed in the next sentence, all pilot flight training and checking required by this part and the certification check requirements of § 61.153(h) of this chapter. The line check required by § 121.440, the static airplane requirements of appendix E of this part, and the operating experience requirements of § 121.434 must still be performed in the airplane.

[Doc. No. FAA–2002–12461, 71 FR 63640, Oct. 30, 2006, as amended by Amdt. 121–365, 78 FR 42379, July 15, 2013; Amdt. 121–366, 78 FR 67846, Nov. 12, 2013; Docket FAA–2013–0485, Amdt. 121–376, 81 FR 90176, Dec. 13, 2016]

APPENDIXES I–J TO PART 121
[RESERVED]

APPENDIX K TO PART 121—PERFORM-
ANCE REQUIREMENTS FOR CERTAIN
TURBOPROPELLER POWERED AIR-
PLANES

1. *Applicability.* This appendix specifies requirements for the following turbopropeller powered airplanes that must comply with the Airplane Performance Operating Limitations in §§ 121.189 through 121.197:

a. After December 20, 2010, each airplane manufactured before March 20, 1997 and type certificated in the:

i. Normal category before July 1, 1970, and meets special conditions issued by the Administrator for airplanes intended for use in operations under part 135 of this chapter.

ii. Normal category before July 19, 1970, and meets the additional airworthiness standards in SFAR No. 23 of 14 CFR part 23.

iii. Normal category, and complies with the additional airworthiness standards in appendix A of part 135 of this chapter.

iv. Normal category, and complies with section 1.(a) or 1.(b) of SFAR No. 41 of 14 CFR part 21.

b. After March 20, 1997, each airplane:

i. Type certificated prior to March 29, 1995, in the commuter category.

ii. Manufactured on or after March 20, 1997, and that was type certificated in the normal category, and complies with the requirements described in paragraphs 1.a.i through iii of this appendix.

2. *Background.* Sections 121.157 and 121.173(b) require that the airplanes operated under this part and described in paragraph 1 of this appendix, comply with the Airplane Performance Operating Limitations in §§ 121.189 through 121.197. Airplanes described in § 121.157(f) and paragraph 1.a of this appendix must comply on and after December 20, 2010. Airplanes described in § 121.157(e) and paragraph 1.b of this appendix must comply on and after March 20, 1997. (Airplanes type certificated in the normal category, and in accordance with SFAR No. 41 of 14 CFR part 21, as described in paragraph 1.a.iv of this appendix, may not be produced after October 17, 1991.)

3. *References.* Unless otherwise specified, references in this appendix to sections of part 23 of this chapter are to those sections of 14 CFR part 23, as amended by Amendment No. 23–45 (August 6, 1993, 58 FR 42156).

Performance

4. *Interim Airplane Performance Operating Limitations.*

a. Until December 20, 2010, airplanes described in paragraph 1.a of this appendix may continue to comply with the requirements in subpart I of part 135 and § 135.181(a)(2) of this chapter that apply to small, nontransport category airplanes.

b. Until March 20, 1997, airplanes described in paragraph 1.b.i of this appendix may continue to comply with the requirements in subpart I of part 135 of this chapter that apply to commuter category airplanes.

5. *Final Airplane Performance Operating Limitations.*

a. Through an amended type certification program or a supplemental type certification program, each airplane described in paragraph 1.a and 1.b.ii of this appendix must be shown to comply with the commuter category performance requirements specified in this appendix, which are included in part 23 of this chapter. Each new revision to a current airplane performance operating limitation for an airplane that is or has been demonstrated to comply, must also be approved by the Administrator. An airplane approved to the requirements of section 1.(b) of SFAR No. 41 of 14 CFR part 21, as described in paragraph 1.a.iv of this appendix, and that has been demonstrated to comply with the additional requirements of section 4.(c) of SFAR No. 41 of 14 CFR part 21 and International Civil Aviation Organization Annex 8 (available from the FAA, 800 Independence Avenue SW., Washington, DC 20591), will be considered to be in compliance with the commuter category performance requirements.

b. Each turbopropeller powered airplane subject to this appendix must be demonstrated to comply with the airplane performance operating limitation requirements of this chapter specified as follows:

i. Section 23.45 Performance General.

ii. Section 23.51 Takeoff.

iii. Section 23.53 Takeoff speeds.

iv. Section 23.55 Accelerate stop distance.

v. Section 23.57 Takeoff path.

vi. Section 23.59 Takeoff distance and takeoff run.

vii. Section 23.61 Takeoff flight path.

viii. Section 23.65 Climb: All engines operating.

ix. Section 23.67 Climb: one engine inoperative.

x. Section 23.75 Landing.

xi. Section 23.77 Balked landing.

xii. Sections 23.1581 through 23.1589 Airplane flight manual and approved manual material.

6. *Operation.* After compliance with the final airplane performance operating limitations requirements has been demonstrated and added to the Airplane Flight Manual performance data of the affected airplane, that airplane must be operated in accordance with the performance limitations of §§ 121.189 through 121.197.

[Doc. No. 28154, 60 FR 65936, Dec. 20, 1995, as amended by Doc. No. OST–2002–13435]

APPENDIX L TO PART 121—TYPE CERTIFICATION REGULATIONS MADE PREVIOUSLY EFFECTIVE

Appendix L lists regulations in this part that require compliance with standards contained in superseded type certification regulations that continue to apply to certain transport category airplanes. The tables set out citations to current CFR section, applicable aircraft, superseded type certification regulation and applicable time periods, and the CFR edition and FEDERAL REGISTER documents where the regulation having prior effect is found. Copies of all superseded regulations may be obtained at the Federal Aviation Administration Law Library, Room 924, 800 Independence Avenue SW., Washington, DC.

Part 121 section	Applicable aircraft	Provisions: CFR/FR references
§ 121.312(a)(1)(i)	Transport category; or nontransport category type certificated before January 1, 1965; passenger capacity of 20 or more; manufactured prior to August 20, 1990.	Heat release rate testing. 14 CFR 25.853(d) in effect March 6, 1995: 14 CFR parts 1 to 59, Revised as of January 1, 1995, and amended by Amdt. 25–83, 60 FR 6623, February 2, 1995. Formerly 14 CFR 25.853(a–1) in effect August 20, 1986: 14 CFR parts 1 to 59, Revised as of January 1, 1986.
§ 121.312(a)(1)(ii)	Transport category; or nontransport category type certificated before January 1, 1965; passenger capacity of 20 or more; manufactured after August 19, 1990.	Heat release rate and smoke testing. 14 CFR 25.853(d) in effect March 6, 1995: 14 CFR parts 1 to 59, Revised as of January 1, 1995, and amended by Amdt. 25–83, 60 FR 6623, February 2, 1995. Formerly 14 CFR 25.853(a–1) in effect September 26, 1988: 14 CFR parts 1 to 59, Revised as of January 1, 1988, and amended by Amdt. 25–66, 53 FR 32584, August 25, 1988
§ 121.312(a)(2)(i)	Transport category; or nontransport category type certificate before January 1, 1965; application for type certificate filed prior to May 1, 1972; substantially complete replacement of cabin interior on or after May 1, 1972.	Provisions of 14 CFR 25.853 in effect on April 30, 1972: 14 CFR parts 1 to 59, Revised as of January 1, 1972.
§ 121.312(a)(3)(i)	Transport category type certificated after January 1, 1958; nontransport category type certificated after January 1, 1958, but before January 1, 1965; passenger capacity of 20 or more; substantially complete replacement of the cabin interior on or after March 6, 1995.	Heat release rate testing. 14 CFR 25.853(d) in effect March 6, 1995: 14 CFR parts 1 to 59, Revised as of January 1, 1995; and amended by \n25–83, 60 FR 6623, February 2, 1995. Formerly 14 CFR 25.853(a–1) in effect August 20, 1986: 14 CFR parts 1 to 59, Revised as of January 1, 1986.
§ 121.312(a)(3)(ii)	Transport category type certificated after January 1, 1958; nontransport category type certificated after January 1, 1958, but before January 1, 1965; passenger capacity of 20 or more; substantially complete replacement of the cabin interior on or after August 20, 1990.	Heat release rate and smoke testing. 14 CFR 25.853(d) in effect March 6, 1995: 14 CFR parts 1 to 59, Revised as of January 1, 1995; and amended by \n25–83, 60 FR 6623, February 2, 1995. Formerly 14 CFR § 25.853(a–1) in effect September 26, 1988: CFR, Title 14, Parts 1 to 59, Revised as of January 1, 1988, and amended by \n25–66, 53 FR 32584, August 25, 1988.
§ 121.312(b) (1) and (2)	Transport category airplane type certificated after January 1, 1958; Nontransport category airplane type certificated after December 31, 1964.	Seat cushions. 14 CFR 25.853(c) effective on November 26, 1984: 14 CFR parts 1 to 59, Revised as of January 1, 1984, and amended by \n25–59, 49 FR 43188, October 26, 1984.

Part 121 section	Applicable aircraft	Provisions: CFR/FR references
§ 121.312(c)	Airplane type certificated in accordance with SFAR No. 41; maximum certificated takeoff weight in excess of 12,500 pounds.	Compartment interior requirements. 14 CFR 25.853(a) in effect March 6, 1995: 14 CFR parts 1 to 59, Revised as of January 1, 1995, and amended by \n25–83, 60 FR 6623, February 2, 1995. Formerly 14 CFR 25.853(a), (b–1), (b–2), and (b–3) in effect on September 26, 1978: 14 CFR parts 1 to 59, Revised as of January 1, 1978.
§ 121.314(a)	Transport category airplanes type certificated after January 1, 1958.	Class C or D cargo or baggage compartment definition, 14 CFR 25.857 in effect on June 16, 1986, 14 CFR parts 1 to 59, Revised 1/1/97, and amended by Amendment 25–60, 51 FR 18243, May 16, 1986.

[Doc. No. 28154, 60 FR 65936, Dec. 20, 1995, as amended by Amdt. 121–269, 63 FR 8049, Feb. 17, 1998]

APPENDIX M TO PART 121—AIRPLANE FLIGHT RECORDER SPECIFICATIONS

The recorded values must meet the designated range, resolution and accuracy requirements during static and dynamic conditions. Dynamic condition means the parameter is experiencing change at the maximum rate attainable, including the maximum rate of reversal. All data recorded must be correlated in time to within one second.

Parameters	Range	Accuracy (sensor input)	Seconds per sampling interval	Resolution	Remarks
1. Time or relative times counts. [1]	24 Hrs, 0 to 4095.	±0.125% per hour.	4	1 sec	UTC time preferred when available. Count increments each 4 seconds of system operation.
2. Pressure Altitude.	− 1000 ft to max certificated altitude of aircraft. + 5000 ft.	±100 to ±700 ft (see table, TSO C124a or TSO C51a).	1	5′ to 35′	Data should be obtained from the air data computer when practicable.
3. Indicated airspeed or Calibrated airspeed.	50 KIAS or minimum value to Max V_{so} to 1.2 V_{D}.	±5% and ±3%	1	1 kt	Data should be obtained from the air data computer when practicable.
4. Heading (Primary flight crew reference).	0–360° and Discrete "true" or "mag".	±2°	1	0.5°	When true or magnetic heading can be selected as the primary heading reference, a discrete indicating selection must be recorded.
5. Normal acceleration (vertical) [9].	− 3g to + 6g	±1% of max range excluding datum error of ±5%.	0.125	0.004g.	
6. Pitch Attitude ..	±75°	±2°	1 or 0.25 for airplanes operated under § 121.344(f).	0.5°	A sampling rate of 0.25 is recommended.
7. Roll attitude [2] ...	±180°	±2°	1 or 0.5 for airplanes operated under § 121.344(f).	0.5	A sampling rate of 0.5 is recommended.
8. Manual Radio Transmitter Keying or CVR/ DFDR synchronization reference.	On-Off (Discrete) None	....	1	....	Preferably each crew member but one discrete acceptable for all transmission provided the CVR/ FDR system complies with TSO C124a CVR synchronization requirements (paragraph 4.2.1 ED–55).
9. Thrust/power on each engine—primary flight crew reference.	Full range forward.	±2%	1 (per engine) ...	0.3% of full range.	Sufficient parameters (e.g. EPR, N1 or Torque, NP) as appropriate to the particular engine being recorded to determine power in forward and reverse thrust, including potential overspeed condition.

298

The recorded values must meet the designated range, resolution and accuracy requirements during static and dynamic conditions. Dynamic condition means the parameter is experiencing change at the maximum rate attainable, including the maximum rate of reversal. All data recorded must be correlated in time to within one second.

Parameters	Range	Accuracy (sensor input)	Seconds per sampling interval	Resolution	Remarks
10. Autopilot Engagement.	Discrete "on" or "off".	....	1	....	
11. Longitudinal Acceleration.	±1g	±1.5% max. range excluding datum error of ±5%.	0.25	0.004g	
12a. Pitch control(s) position (nonfly-by-wire systems). [18]	Full Range	±2° unless higher accuracy uniquely required.	0.5 or 0.25 for airplanes operated under § 121.344(f).	0.5% of full range.	For airplanes that have a flight control breakaway capability that allows either pilot to operate the controls independently, record both control inputs. The control inputs may be sampled alternately once per second to produce the sampling interval of 0.5 or 0.25, as applicable.
12b. Pitch control(s) position (fly-by-wire systems). [3] [18]	Full Range	±2° unless higher accuracy uniquely required.	0.5 or 0.25 for airplanes operated under § 121.344(f).	0.2% of full range.	
13a. Lateral control position(s) (nonfly-by-wire). [18]	Full Range	±2° unless higher accuracy uniquely required.	0.5 or 0.25 for airplanes operated under § 121.344(f).	0.2% of full range.	For airplanes that have a flight control breakaway capability that allows either pilot to operate the controls independently, record both control inputs. The control inputs may be sampled alternately once per second to produce the sampling interval of 0.5 or 0.25, as applicable.
13b. Lateral control position(s) (fly-by-wire). [4] [18]	Full Range	±2° unless higher accuracy uniquely required.	0.5 or 0.25 for airplanes operated under § 121.344(f).	0.2% of full range..	
14a. Yaw control position(s) (nonfly-by-wire). [5] [18]	Full Range	±2° unless higher accuracy uniquely required.	0.5	0.3% of full range.	For airplanes that have a flight control breakaway capability that allows either pilot to operate the controls independently, record both control inputs. The control inputs may be sampled alternately once per second to produce the sampling interval of 0.5.
14b. Yaw control position(s) (fly-by-wire). [18]	Full Range	±2° unless higher accuracy uniquely required.	0.5	0.2% of full range.	
15. Pitch control surface(s) position. [6] [18]	Full Range	±2° unless higher accuracy uniquely required.	0.5 or 0.25 for airplanes operated under § 121.344(f).	0.3% of full range.	For airplanes fitted with multiple or split surfaces, a suitable combination of inputs is acceptable in lieu of recording each surface separately. The control surfaces may be sampled alternately once per second to produce the sampling interval of 0.5 or 0.25, as applicable.

The recorded values must meet the designated range, resolution and accuracy requirements during static and dynamic conditions. Dynamic condition means the parameter is experiencing change at the maximum rate attainable, including the maximum rate of reversal. All data recorded must be correlated in time to within one second.

Parameters	Range	Accuracy (sensor input)	Seconds per sampling interval	Resolution	Remarks
16. Lateral control surface(s) position. [7] [18]	Full Range	±2° unless higher accuracy uniquely required.	0.5 or 0.25 for airplanes operated under § 121.344(f).	0.3% of full range.	A suitable combination of surface position sensors is acceptable in lieu of recording each surface separately. The control surfaces may be sampled alternately to produce the sampling interval of 0.5 or 0.25, as applicable.
17. Yaw control surface(s) position. [8] [18]	Full Range	±2° unless higher accuracy uniquely required.	0.5	0.2% of full range.	For airplanes with multiple or split surfaces, a suitable combination of surface position sensors is acceptable in lieu of recording each surface separately. The control surfaces may be sampled alternately to produce the sampling interval of 0.5.
18. Lateral Acceleration.	±1g	±1.5% max. range excluding datum error of ±5%.	0.25	0.004g	
19. Pitch Trim Surface Position.	Full Range	±3° Unless Higher Accuracy Uniquely Required.	1	0.6% of full range.	
20. Trailing Edge Flap or Cockpit Control Selection. [10]	Full Range or Each Position (discrete).	±3° or as Pilot's indicator.	2	0.5% of full range.	Flap position and cockpit control may each be sampled at 4 second intervals, to give a data point every 2 seconds.
21. Leading Edge Flap or Cockpit Control Selection. [11].	Full Range or Each Discrete Position.	±3° or as Pilot's indicator and sufficient to determine each discrete position.	2	0.5% of full range.	Left and right sides, or flap position and cockpit control may each be sampled at 4 second intervals, so as to give a data point every 2 seconds.
22. Each Thrust Reverser Position (or equivalent for propeller airplane).	Stowed, In Transit, and Reverse (Discrete).		1 (per engine)		Turbo-jet—2 discretes enable the 3 states to be determined. Turbo-prop—discrete.
23. Ground spoiler position or brake selection. [12].	Full range or each position (discrete).	±2° Unless higher accuracy uniquely required.	1 or 0.5 for airplanes operated under § 121.344(f).	0.5% of full range.	
24. Outside Air Temperature or Total Air Temperature. [13].	−50 °C to +90 °C.	±2 °C	2	0.3 °C	
25. Autopilot/ Autothrottle/ AFCS Mode and Engagement Status.	A suitable combination of discretes.		1		Discretes should show which systems are engaged and which primary modes are controlling the flight path and speed of the aircraft.
26. Radio Altitude. [14].	−20 ft to 2,500 ft.	±2 ft or ±3% whichever is greater below 500 ft and ±5% above 500 ft.	1	1 ft + 5% above 500 ft.	For autoland/category 3 operations. Each radio altimeter should be recorded, but arranged so that at least one is recorded each second.

The recorded values must meet the designated range resolution and accuracy requirements during static and dynamic conditions. Dynamic condition means the parameter is experiencing change at the maximum rate attainable, including the maximum rate of reversal. All data recorded must be correlated in time to within one second.

Parameters	Range	Accuracy (sensor input)	Seconds per sampling interval	Resolution	Remarks
27. Localizer Deviation, MLS Azimuth, or GPS Latitude Deviation.	±400 Microamps or available sensor range as installed. ±62°	As installed ±2% recommended.	1	0.3% of full range.	For autoland/category 3 operations. Each system should be recorded but arranged so that at least one is recorded each second. It is not necessary to record ILS and MLS at the same time, only the approach aid in use need be recorded.
28. Glideslope Deviation, MLS Elevation, or GPS Vertical Deviation.	±400 Microamps or available sensor range as installed 0.9 to + 30°	As installed + /3 – 3% recommended.	1	0.3% of full range.	For autoland/category 3 operations. Each system should be recorded but arranged so that at least one is recorded each second. It is not necessary to record ILS and MLS at the same time, only the approach aid in use need be recorded.
29. Marker Beacon Passage.	Discrete "on" or "off".	....	1	....	A single discrete is acceptable for all markers.
30. Master Warning.	Discrete	....	1	....	Record the master warning and record each "red" warning that cannot be determined from other parameters or from the cockpit voice recorder.
31. Air/ground sensor (primary airplane system reference nose or main gear).	Discrete "air" or "ground".	....	1 (0.25 recommended).		
32. Angle of Attack (If measured directly).	As installed	As installed	2 or 0.5 for airplanes operated under § 121.344(f).	0.3% of full range.	If left and right sensors are available, each may be recorded at 4 or 1 second intervals, as appropriate, so as to give a data point at 2 seconds or 0.5 second, as required.
33. Hydraulic Pressure Low, Each System.	Discrete or available sensor range, "low" or "normal".	±5%	2	0.5% of full range.	
34. Groundspeed	As Installed	Most Accurate Systems Installed.	1	0.2% of full range.	
35. GPWS (ground proximity warning system).	Discrete "warning" or "off".	....	1	....	A suitable combination of discretes unless recorder capacity is limited in which case a single discrete for all modes is acceptable.
36. Landing Gear Position or Landing gear cockpit control selection.	Discrete	....	4	....	A suitable combination of discretes should be recorded.
37. Drift Angle. [15]	As installed	As installed	4	0.1°	
38. Wind Speed and Direction.	As installed	As installed	4	1 knot, and 1.0°.	
39. Latitude and Longitude.	As installed	As installed	4	0.002°, or as installed.	Provided by the Primary Navigation System Reference. Where capacity permits Latitude/longitude resolution should be 0.0002°.
40. Stick shaker and pusher activation.	Discrete(s) "on" or "off".	....	1	....	A suitable combination of discretes to determine activation.
41. Windshear Detection.	Discrete "warning" or "off".	....	1.		

The recorded values must meet the designated range, resolution and accuracy requirements during static and dynamic conditions. Dynamic condition means the parameter is experiencing change at the maximum rate attainable, including the maximum rate of reversal. All data recorded must be correlated in time to within one second.

Parameters	Range	Accuracy (sensor input)	Seconds per sampling interval	Resolution	Remarks
42. Throttle/power Leverl position. [16].	Full Range	±2%	1 for each lever	2% of full range	For airplanes with non-mechanically linked cockpit engine controls.
43. Additional Engine Parameters.	As installed	As installed	Each engine each second.	2% of full range	Where capacity permits, the preferred priority is indicated vibration level, N2, EGT, Fuel Flow, Fuel Cutoff lever position and N3, unless engine manufacturer recommends otherwise.
44. Traffic Alert and Collision Avoidance System (TCAS).	Discretes	As installed	1		A suitable combination of discretes should be recorded to determine the status of—Combined Control, Vertical Control, Up Advisory, and Down Advisory. (ref. ARINC Characteristic 735 Attachment 6E, TCAS VERTICAL RA DATA OUTPUT WORD.)
45. DME 1 and 2 Distance.	0–200 NM	As installed	4	1 NM	1 mile
46. Nav 1 and 2 Selected Frequency.	Full Range	As installed	4		Sufficient to determine selected frequency
47. Selected barometric setting.	Full Range	±5%	(1 per 64 sec.)	0.2% of full range	
48. Selected Altitude.	Full Range	±5%	1	100 ft	
49. Selected speed.	Full Range	±5%	1	1 knot	
50. Selected Mach.	Full Range	±5%	1	.01	
51. Selected vertical speed.	Full Range	±5%	1	100 ft/min	
52. Selected heading.	Full Range	±5%	1	1°	
53. Selected flight path.	Full Range	±5%	1	1°	
54. Selected decision height.	Full Range	±5%	64	1 ft	
55. EFIS display format.	Discrete(s)		4		Discretes should show the display system status (e.g., off, normal, fail, composite, sector, plan, nav aids, weather radar, range, copy.
56. Multi-function/ Engine Alerts Display format.	Discrete(s)		4		Discretes should show the display system status (e.g., off, normal, fail, and the identity of display pages for emergency procedures, need not be recorded.
57. Thrust command. [17].	Full Range	±2%	2	2% of full range.	
58. Thrust target	Full Range	±2%	4	2% of full range	
59. Fuel quantity in CG trim tank.	Full Range	±5%	(1 per 64 sec.)	1% of full range	
60. Primary Navigation System Reference.	Discrete GPS, INS, VOR/ DME, MLS, Localizer Glideslope.		4		A suitable combination of discretes to determine the Primary Navigation System reference.
61. Ice Detection	Discrete "ice" or "no ice".		4		
62. Engine warning each engine vibration.	Discrete		1		

302

The recorded values must meet the designated range, resolution and accuracy requirements during static and dynamic conditions. Dynamic condition means the parameter is experiencing change at the maximum rate attainable, including the maximum rate of reversal. All data recorded must be correlated in time to within one second.

Parameters	Range	Accuracy (sensor input)	Seconds per sampling interval	Resolution	Remarks
63. Engine warning each engine over temp.	Discrete	....	1		
64. Engine warning each engine oil pressure low.	Discrete	....	1		
65. Engine warning each engine over speed.	Discrete	....	1		
66. Yaw Trim Surface Position.	Full Range	±3% Unless Higher Accuracy Uniquely Required.	2	0.3% of full range.	
67. Roll Trim Surface Position.	Full Range	±3% Unless Higher Accuracy Uniquely Required.	2	0.3% of full range.	
68. Brake Pressure (left and right).	As installed	±5%	1	....	To determine braking effort applied by pilots or by autobrakes.
69. Brake Pedal Application (left and right).	Discrete or Analog "applied" or "off".	±5% (Analog)	1		To determine braking applied by pilots.
70. Yaw or sideslip angle.	Full Range	±5%	1	0.5°	
71. Engine bleed valve position.	Discrete "open" or "closed".	....	4		
72. De-icing or anti-icing system selection.	Discrete "on" or "off".	....	4		
73. Computed center of gravity.	Full Range	±5%	(1 per 64 sec.) ..	1% of full range	
74. AC electrical bus status.	Discrete "power" or "off".	....	4	....	Each bus.
75. DC electrical bus status.	Discrete "power" or "off".	....	4	....	Each bus.
76 APU bleed valve position.	Discrete "open" or "closed".	....	4		
77. Hydraulic Pressure (each system).	Full range	±5%	2	100 psi	
78. Loss of cabin pressure.	Discrete "loss" or "normal".	....	1.		
79. Computer failure (critical flight and engine control systems).	Discrete "fail" or "normal".	....	4.		
80. Heads-up display (when an information source is installed).	Discrete(s) "on" or "off".	....	4		
81. Para-visual display (when an information source is installed).	Discrete(s) "on" or "off".				
82. Cockpit trim control input position—pitch.	Full Range	±5%	1	0.2% of full range.	Where mechanical means for control inputs are not available, cockpit display trim positions should be recorded.
83. Cockpit trim control input position—roll.	Full Range	±5%	1	0.7% of full range.	Where mechanical means for control inputs are not available, cockpit display trim position should be recorded.

The recorded values must meet the designated range, resolution and accuracy requirements during static and dynamic conditions. Dynamic condition means the parameter is experiencing change at the maximum rate attainable, including the maximum rate of reversal. All data recorded must be correlated in time to within one second.

Parameters	Range	Accuracy (sensor input)	Seconds per sampling interval	Resolution	Remarks
84. Cockpit trim control input position—yaw.	Full range	±5%	1	0.3% of full range.	Where mechanical means for control input are not available, cockpit display trim positions should be recorded.
85. Trailing edge flap and cockpit flap control position.	Full Range	±5%	2	0.5% of full range.	Trailing edge flaps and cockpit flap control position may each be sampled alternately at 4 second intervals to provide a sample each 0.5 second.
86. Leading edge flap and cockpit flap control position.	Full Range or Discrete.	±5%	1	0.5% of full range	
87. Ground spoiler position and speed brake selection.	Full range or discrete.	±5%	0.5	0.3% of full range.	
88. All cockpit flight control input forces (control wheel, control column, rudder pedal) [18] [19].	Full range .... Control wheel ±70 lbs. Control column ±85 lbs. Rudder pedal ±165 lbs.	±5%	1	0.3% of full range.	For fly-by-wire flight control systems, where flight control surface position is a function of the displacement of the control input device only, it is not necessary to record this parameter. For airplanes that have a flight control break away capability that allows either pilot to operate the control independently, record both control force inputs. The control force inputs may be sampled alternately once per 2 seconds to produce the sampling interval of 1.
89. Yaw damper status.	Discrete (on/off)	0.5			
90. Yaw damper command.	Full range	As installed	0.5	1% of full range.	
91. Standby rudder valve status.	Discrete	0.5.			

[1] For A300 B2/B4 airplanes, resolution = 6 seconds.
[2] For A330/A340 series airplanes, resolution = 0.703°.
[3] For A318/A319/A320/A321 series airplanes, resolution = 0.275% (0.088°>0.064°). For A330/A340 series airplanes, resolution = 2.20%(0.703°>0.064°).
[4] For A318/A319/A320/A321 series airplanes, resolution = 0.22% (0.088°>0.080°). For A330/A340 series airplanes, resolution = 1.76% (0.703°>0.080°).
[5] For A330/A340 series airplanes, resolution = 1.18% (0.703° >0.120°). For A330/A340 series airplanes, seconds per sampling interval = 1.
[6] For A330/A340 series airplanes, resolution = 0.783% (0.352°>0.090°).
[7] For A330/A340 series airplanes, aileron resolution = 0.704% (0.352°>0.100°). For A330/A340 series airplanes, spoiler resolution = 1.406% (0.703°>0.100°).
[8] For A330/A340 series airplanes, resolution = 0.30% (0.176°>0.12°). For A330/A340 series airplanes, seconds per sampling interval = 1.
[9] For B–717 series airplanes, resolution = .005g. For Dassault F900C/F900EX airplanes, resolution = .007g.
[10] For A330/A340 series airplanes, resolution = 1.05% (0.250°>0.120°).
[11] For A330/A340 series airplanes, resolution = 1.05% (0.250°>0.120°). For A300 B2/B4 series airplanes, resolution = 0.92% (0.230°>0.125°).
[12] For A330/A340 series airplanes, spoiler resolution = 1.406% (0.703°>0.100°).
[13] For A330/A340 series airplanes, resolution = 0.5°C.
[14] For Dassault F900C/F900EX airplanes, Radio altitude resolution = 1.25 ft.
[15] For A330/A340 series airplanes, resolution = 0.352 degrees.
[16] For A318/A319/A320/A321 series airplanes, resolution = 4.32%. For A330/A340 series airplanes, resolution is 3.27% of full range for throttle lever angle (TLA); for reverse thrust, reverse throttle lever angle (RLA) resolution is nonlinear over the active reverse thrust range, which is 51.54 degrees to 96.14 degrees. The resolved element is 2.8 degrees uniformly over the entire active reverse thrust range, or 2.9% of the full range value of 96.14 degrees.
[17] For A318/A319/A320/A321 series airplanes, with IAE engines, resolution = 2.58%.
[18] For all aircraft manufactured on or after December 6, 2010, the seconds per sampling interval is 0.125. Each input must be recorded at this rate. Alternately sampling inputs (interleaving) to meet this sampling interval is prohibited.

[Doc. No. 28109, 62 FR 38382, July 17, 1997; 62 FR 48135, Sept. 12, 1997, as amended by Amdt. 121–271, 64 FR 46120, Aug. 24, 1999; Amdt. 121–278, 65 FR 51745, Aug. 24, 2000; 65 FR 81733, Dec. 27, 2000; Amdt. 121–292, 67 FR 54323, Aug. 21, 2002; Amdt. 121–300, 68 FR 42936, July 18, 2003; 68 FR 50069, Aug. 20, 2003; 68 FR 53877, Sept. 15, 2003; 70 FR 41134, July 18, 2005; Amdt. 125–54, 73 FR 12566, Mar. 7, 2008; Amdt. 121–338, 73 FR 12566, Mar. 7, 2008; Amdt. 121–342, 73 FR 73179, Dec. 2, 2008; Amdt. 121–349, 75 FR 17046, Apr. 5, 2010; Amdt. 121–347, 75 FR 7356, Feb. 19, 2010; Amdt. 121–364, 78 FR 39971, July 3, 2013; Docket FAA–2017–0733, Amdt. 121–379, 82 FR 34398, July 25, 2017]

APPENDIX N TO PART 121 [RESERVED]

APPENDIX O TO PART 121—HAZARDOUS MATERIALS TRAINING REQUIREMENTS FOR CERTIFICATE HOLDERS

This appendix prescribes the requirements for hazardous materials training under part 121, subpart Z, and part 135, subpart K of this chapter. The training requirements for various categories of persons are defined by job function or responsibility. An "X" in a box under a category of persons indicates that the specified category must receive the noted training. All training requirements apply to direct supervisors as well as to persons actually performing the job function. Training requirements for certificate holders

authorized in their operations specifications to transport hazardous materials (will-carry) are prescribed in Table 1. Those certificate holders with a prohibition in their operations specifications against carrying or handling hazardous materials (will-not-carry) must follow the curriculum prescribed in Table 2. The method of delivering the training will be determined by the certificate holder. The certificate holder is responsible for providing a method (may include email, telecommunication, etc.) to answer all questions prior to testing regardless of the method of instruction. The certificate holder must certify that a test has been completed satisfactorily to verify understanding of the regulations and requirements.

TABLE 1—OPERATORS THAT TRANSPORT HAZARDOUS MATERIAL—WILL-CARRY CERTIFICATE HOLDERS

Aspects of transport of hazardous materials by air with which they must be familiar, as a minimum (See note 1)	Shippers (See Note 2) Will-carry	Operators and ground-handling agent's staff accepting hazardous materials (See Note 3) Will-carry	Operators and ground-handling agents staff responsible for the handling, storage, and loading of cargo and baggage Will-carry	Passenger-handling staff Will-carry	Flight crew members and load planners Will-carry	Crew members (other than flight crew members) Will-carry
General philosophy	X	X	X	X	X	X
Limitations	X	X	X	X	X	X
General requirements for shippers	X	X				
Classification	X	X				
List of hazardous materials	X	X			X	
General packing requirements	X	X				
Labeling and marking	X	X	X	X	X	X
Hazardous materials transport document and other relevant documentation	X	X				
Acceptance procedures		X				
Recognition of undeclared hazardous materials	X	X	X	X	X	X
Storage and loading procedures		X	X		X	
Pilots' notification		X	X		X	
Provisions for passengers and crew		X	X	X	X	X

TABLE 1—OPERATORS THAT TRANSPORT HAZARDOUS MATERIAL—WILL-CARRY CERTIFICATE HOLDERS—Continued

Aspects of transport of hazardous materials by air with which they must be familiar, as a minimum (See note 1)	Shippers (See Note 2) Will-carry	Operators and ground-handling agent's staff accepting hazardous materials (See Note 3) Will-carry	Operators and ground-handling agents staff responsible for the handling, storage, and loading of cargo and baggage Will-carry	Passenger-handling staff Will-carry	Flight crew members and load planners Will-carry	Crew members (other than flight crew members) Will-carry
Emergency procedures	X	X	X	X	X	X

Note 1. Depending on the responsibilities of the person, the aspects of training to be covered may vary from those shown in the table.

Note 2. When a person offers a consignment of hazmat, including COMAT, for or on behalf of the certificate holder, then the person must be trained in the certificate holder's training program and comply with shipper responsibilities and training. If offering goods on another certificate holder's equipment, the person must be trained in compliance with the training requirements in 49 CFR. All shippers of hazmat must be trained under 49 CFR. The shipper functions in 49 CFR mirror the training aspects that must be covered for any shipper offering hazmat for transport.

Note 3. When an operator, its subsidiary, or an agent of the operator is undertaking the responsibilities of acceptance staff, such as the passenger handling staff accepting small parcel cargo, the certificate holder, its subsidy, or the agent must be trained in the certificate holder's training program and comply with the acceptance staff training requirements.

TABLE 2—OPERATORS THAT DO NOT TRANSPORT HAZARDOUS MATERIALS—WILL-NOT-CARRY CERTIFICATE HOLDERS

Aspects of transport of hazardous materials by air with which they must be familiar, as a minimum (See Note 1)	Shippers (See Note 2) Will-not-carry	Operators and ground-handling agent's staff accepting cargo other than hazardous materials (See Note 3) Will-not-carry	Operators and ground-handling agents staff responsible for the handling, storage, and loading of cargo and baggage Will-not-carry	Passenger-handling staff Will-not-carry	Flight crew members and load planners Will-not-carry	Crew members (other than flight crew members) Will-not-carry
General philosophy	X	X	X	X	X	X
Limitations	X	X	X	X	X	X
General requirements for shippers	X					
Classification	X					
List of hazardous materials	X					
General packing requirements	X					
Labeling and marking	X	X	X	X	X	X
Hazardous materials transport document and other relevant documentation	X	X				
Acceptance procedures						
Recognition of undeclared hazardous materials	X	X	X	X	X	X
Storage and loading procedures						
Pilots' notification						
Provisions for passengers and Crew		X	X	X	X	X
Emergency procedures	X	X	X	X	X	X

Note 1—Depending on the responsibilities of the person, the aspects of training to be covered may vary from those shown in the table.

Note 2—When a person offers a consignment of hazmat, including COMAT, for air transport for or on behalf of the certificate holder, then that person must be properly trained. All shippers of hazmat must be trained under 49 CFR. The shipper functions in 49 CFR mirror the training aspects that must be covered for any shipper, including a will-not-carry certificate holder offering dangerous goods for transport, with the exception of recognition training. Recognition training is a separate FAA requirement in the certificate holder's training program.

Note 3—When an operator, its subsidiary, or an agent of the operator is undertaking the responsibilities of acceptance staff, such as the passenger handling staff accepting small parcel cargo, the certificate holder, its subsidiary, or the agent must be trained in the certificate holder's training program and comply with the acceptance staff training requirements.

[Doc. No. FAA–2003–15085, 70 FR 58825, Oct. 7, 2005, as amended by Amdt. 121–318, 70 FR 75396, Dec. 20, 2005]

APPENDIX P TO PART 121—REQUIRE-
MENTS FOR ETOPS AND POLAR OP-
ERATIONS

The FAA approves ETOPS in accordance
with the requirements and limitations in
this appendix.

Section I. *ETOPS Approvals: Airplanes with
Two engines.*

(a) *Propulsion system reliability for ETOPS.*
(1) Before the FAA grants ETOPS operational approval, the operator must be able
to demonstrate the ability to achieve and
maintain the level of propulsion system reliability, if any, that is required by §21.4(b)(2)
of this chapter for the ETOPS-approved airplane-engine combination to be used.

(2) Following ETOPS operational approval,
the operator must monitor the propulsion
system reliability for the airplane-engine
combination used in ETOPS, and take action
as required by §121.374(i) for the specified
IFSD rates.

(b) *75 Minutes ETOPS*—(1) *Caribbean/Western
Atlantic Area.* The FAA grants approvals to
conduct
ETOPS with maximum diversion times up
to 75 minutes on Western Atlantic/Caribbean
area routes as follows:

(i) The FAA reviews the airplane-engine
combination to ensure the absence of factors
that could prevent safe operations. The airplane-engine combination need not be type-
design-approved for ETOPS; however, it
must have sufficient favorable experience to
demonstrate to the Administrator a level of
reliability appropriate for 75-minute ETOPS.

(ii) The certificate holder must comply
with the requirements of §121.633 for time-
limited system planning.

(iii) The certificate holder must operate in
accordance with the ETOPS authority as
contained in its operations specifications.

(iv) The certificate holder must comply
with the maintenance program requirements
of §121.374, except that a pre-departure service check before departure of the return
flight is not required.

(2) *Other Areas.* The FAA grants approvals
to conduct ETOPS with maximum diversion
times up to 75 minutes on other than Western Atlantic/Caribbean area routes as follows:

(i) The FAA reviews the airplane-engine
combination to ensure the absence of factors
that could prevent safe operations. The airplane-engine combination need not be type-
design-approved for ETOPS; however, it
must have sufficient favorable experience to
demonstrate to the Administrator a level of
reliability appropriate for 75-minute ETOPS.

(ii) The certificate holder must comply
with the requirements of §121.633 for time-
limited system planning.

(iii) The certificate holder must operate in
accordance with the ETOPS authority as
contained in its operations specifications.

(iv) The certificate holder must comply
with the maintenance program requirements
of §121.374.

(v) The certificate holder must comply
with the MEL in its operations specifications
for 120-minute ETOPS.

(c) *90-minutes ETOPS (Micronesia).* The FAA
grants approvals to conduct ETOPS with
maximum diversion times up to 90 minutes
on Micronesian area routes as follows:

(1) The airplane-engine combination must
be type-design approved for ETOPS of at
least 120-minutes.

(2) The certificate holder must operate in
accordance with the ETOPS authority as
contained in its operations specifications.

(3) The certificate holder must comply
with the maintenance program requirements
of §121.374, except that a pre-departure service check before departure of the return
flight is not required.

(4) The certificate holder must comply
with the MEL requirements in its operations
specifications for 120-minute ETOPS.

(d) *120-minute ETOPS.* The FAA grants approvals to conduct ETOPS with maximum
diversion times up to 120 minutes as follows:

(1) The airplane-engine combination must
be type-design-approved for ETOPS of at
least 120 minutes.

(2) The certificate holder must operate in
accordance with the ETOPS authority as
contained in its operations specifications.

(3) The certificate holder must comply
with the maintenance program requirements
of §121.374.

(4) The certificate holder must comply
with the MEL requirements for 120-minute
ETOPS.

(e) *138-Minute ETOPS.* The FAA grants approval to conduct ETOPS with maximum diversion times up to 138 minutes as follows:

(1) *Operators with 120-minute ETOPS approval.* The FAA grants 138-minute ETOPS
approval as an extension of an existing 120-
minute ETOPS approval as follows:

(i) The authority may be exercised only for
specific flights for which the 120-minute diversion time must be exceeded.

(ii) For these flight-by-flight exceptions,
the airplane-engine combination must be
type-design-approved for ETOPS up to at
least 120 minutes. The capability of the airplane's time-limited systems may not be less
than 138 minutes calculated in accordance
with §121.633.

(iii) The certificate holder must operate in
accordance with the ETOPS authority as
contained in its operations specifications.

(iv) The certificate holder must comply
with the maintenance program requirements
of §121.374.

(v) The certificate holder must comply
with minimum equipment list (MEL) requirements in its operations specifications
for "beyond 120 minutes ETOPS". Operators
without a "beyond 120-minute ETOPS" MEL

307

may apply through their responsible Flight Standards office for a modified MEL which satisfies the master MEL policy for system/component relief in ETOPS beyond 120 minutes.

(vi) The certificate holder must conduct training for maintenance, dispatch, and flight crew personnel regarding differences between 138-minute ETOPS authority and its previously-approved 120-minute ETOPS authority.

(2) *Operators with existing 180-minute ETOPS approval.* The FAA grants approvals to conduct 138-minute ETOPS (without the limitation in paragraph (e)(1)(i) of section I of this appendix) to certificate holders with existing 180-minute ETOPS approval as follows:

(i) The airplane-engine combination must be type-design-approved for ETOPS of at least 180 minutes.

(ii) The certificate holder must operate in accordance with the ETOPS authority as contained in its operations specifications.

(iii) The certificate holder must comply with the maintenance program requirements of § 121.374.

(iv) The certificate holder must comply with the MEL requirements for "beyond 120 minutes ETOPS."

(v) The certificate holder must conduct training for maintenance, dispatch and flight crew personnel for differences between 138-minute ETOPS diversion approval and its previously approved 180-minute ETOPS diversion authority.

(f) *180-minute ETOPS.* The FAA grants approval to conduct ETOPS with diversion times up to 180 minutes as follows:

(1) For these operations the airplane-engine combination must be type-design-approved for ETOPS of at least 180 minutes.

(2) The certificate holder must operate in accordance with the ETOPS authority as contained in its operations specifications.

(3) The certificate holder must comply with the maintenance program requirements of § 121.374.

(4) The certificate holder must comply with the MEL requirements for "beyond 120 minutes ETOPS."

(g) *Greater than 180-minute ETOPS.* The FAA grants approval to conduct ETOPS greater than 180 minutes. The following are requirements for all operations greater than 180 minutes.

(1) The FAA grants approval only to certificate holders with existing 180-minute ETOPS operating authority for the airplane-engine combination to be operated.

(2) The certificate holder must have previous ETOPS experience satisfactory to the Administrator.

(3) In selecting ETOPS Alternate Airports, the operator must make every effort to plan ETOPS with maximum diversion distances of 180 minutes or less, if possible. If conditions necessitate using an ETOPS Alternate Airport beyond 180 minutes, the route may be flown only if the requirements for the specific operating area in paragraph (h) or (i) of section I of this appendix are met.

(4) The certificate holder must inform the flight crew each time an airplane is proposed for dispatch for greater than 180 minutes and tell them why the route was selected.

(5) In addition to the equipment specified in the certificate holder's MEL for 180-minute ETOPS, the following systems must be operational for dispatch:

(i) The fuel quantity indicating system.

(ii) The APU (including electrical and pneumatic supply and operating to the APU's designed capability).

(iii) The auto throttle system.

(iv) The communication system required by § 121.99(d) or § 121.122(c), as applicable.

(v) One-engine-inoperative auto-land capability, if flight planning is predicated on its use.

(6) The certificate holder must operate in accordance with the ETOPS authority as contained in its operations specifications.

(7) The certificate holder must comply with the maintenance program requirements of § 121.374.

(h) *207-minute ETOPS in the North Pacific Area of Operations.* (1) The FAA grants approval to conduct ETOPS with maximum diversion times up to 207 minutes in the North Pacific Area of Operations as an extension to 180-minute ETOPS authority to be used on an exception basis. This exception may be used only on a flight-by-flight basis when an ETOPS Alternate Airport is not available within 180 minutes for reasons such as political or military concerns; volcanic activity; temporary airport conditions; and airport weather below dispatch requirements or other weather related events.

(2) The nearest available ETOPS Alternate Airport within 207 minutes diversion time must be specified in the dispatch or flight release.

(3) In conducting such a flight the certificate holder must consider Air Traffic Service's preferred track.

(4) The airplane-engine combination must be type-design-approved for ETOPS of at least 180 minutes. The approved time for the airplane's most limiting ETOPS significant system and most limiting cargo-fire suppression time for those cargo and baggage compartments required by regulation to have fire-suppression systems must be at least 222 minutes.

(5) The certificate holder must track how many times 207-minute authority is used.

(i) *240-minute ETOPS in the North Polar Area, in the area north of the NOPAC, and in the Pacific Ocean north of the equator.* (1) The FAA grants approval to conduct 240-minute ETOPS authority with maximum diversion times in the North Polar Area, in the area north of the NOPAC area, and the Pacific

Ocean area north of the equator as an extension to 180-minute ETOPS authority to be used on an exception basis. This exception may be used only on a flight-by-flight basis when an ETOPS Alternate Airport is not available within 180 minutes. In that case, the nearest available ETOPS Alternate Airport within 240 minutes diversion time must be specified in the dispatch or flight release.

(2) This exception may be used in the North Polar Area and in the area north of NOPAC only in extreme conditions particular to these areas such as volcanic activity, extreme cold weather at en-route airports, airport weather below dispatch requirements, temporary airport conditions, and other weather related events. The criteria used by the certificate holder to decide that extreme weather precludes using an airport must be established by the certificate holder, accepted by the FAA, and published in the certificate holder's manual for the use of dispatchers and pilots.

(3) This exception may be used in the Pacific Ocean area north of the equator only for reasons such as political or military concern, volcanic activity, airport weather below dispatch requirements, temporary airport conditions and other weather related events.

(4) The airplane-engine combination must be type design approved for ETOPS greater than 180 minutes.

(j) *240-minute ETOPS in areas South of the equator.* (1) The FAA grants approval to conduct ETOPS with maximum diversion times of up to 240 minutes in the following areas:

(i) Pacific oceanic areas between the U.S. West coast and Australia, New Zealand and Polynesia.

(ii) South Atlantic oceanic areas.

(iii) Indian Ocean areas.

(iv) Oceanic areas between Australia and South America.

(2) The operator must designate the nearest available ETOPS Alternate Airports along the planned route of flight.

(3) The airplane-engine combination must be type-design-approved for ETOPS greater than 180 minutes.

(k) *ETOPS beyond 240 minutes.* (1) The FAA grants approval to conduct ETOPS with diversion times beyond 240 minutes for operations between specified city pairs on routes in the following areas:

(i) The Pacific oceanic areas between the U.S. west coast and Australia, New Zealand, and Polynesia;

(ii) The South Atlantic oceanic areas;

(iii) The Indian Oceanic areas; and

(iv) The oceanic areas between Australia and South America, and the South Polar Area.

(2) This approval is granted to certificate holders who have been operating under 180-minute or greater ETOPS authority for at least 24 consecutive months, of which at

least 12 consecutive months must be under 240-minute ETOPS authority with the airplane-engine combination to be used.

(3) The operator must designate the nearest available ETOPS alternate or alternates along the planned route of flight.

(4) For these operations, the airplane-engine combination must be type-design-approved for ETOPS greater than 180 minutes.

Section II. *ETOPS Approval: Passenger-carrying Airplanes With More Than Two Engines.*

(a) The FAA grants approval to conduct ETOPS, as follows:

(1) Except as provided in § 121.162, the airplane-engine combination must be type-design-approved for ETOPS.

(2) The operator must designate the nearest available ETOPS Alternate Airports within 240 minutes diversion time (at one-engine-inoperative cruise speed under standard conditions in still air). If an ETOPS alternate is not available within 240 minutes, operator must designate the nearest available ETOPS Alternate Airports along the planned route of flight.

(3) The MEL limitations for the authorized ETOPS diversion time apply.

(i) The Fuel Quantity Indicating System must be operational.

(ii) The communications systems required by § 121.99(d) or § 121.122(c) must be operational.

(4) The certificate holder must operate in accordance with the ETOPS authority as contained in its operations specifications.

Section III. *Approvals for operations whose airplane routes are planned to traverse either the North Polar or South Polar Areas.*

(a) Except for intrastate operations within the State of Alaska, no certificate holder may operate an aircraft in the North Polar Area or South Polar Area, unless authorized by the FAA.

(b) In addition to any of the applicable requirements of sections I and II of this appendix, the certificate holder's operations specifications must contain the following:

(1) The designation of airports that may be used for en-route diversions and the requirements the airports must meet at the time of diversion.

(2) Except for supplemental all-cargo operations, a recovery plan for passengers at designated diversion airports.

(3) A fuel-freeze strategy and procedures for monitoring fuel freezing.

(4) A plan to ensure communication capability for these operations.

(5) An MEL for these operations.

(6) A training plan for operations in these areas.

(7) A plan for mitigating crew exposure to radiation during solar flare activity.

(8) A plan for providing at least two cold weather anti-exposure suits in the aircraft, to protect crewmembers during outside activity at a diversion airport with extreme

climatic conditions. The FAA may relieve the certificate holder from this requirement if the season of the year makes the equipment unnecessary.

[Doc. No. FAA–2002–6717, 72 FR 1883, Jan. 16, 2007, as amended by Docket FAA–2018–0119, Amdt. 121–380, 83 FR 9173, Mar. 5, 2018]

PART 125—CERTIFICATION AND OPERATIONS: AIRPLANES HAVING A SEATING CAPACITY OF 20 OR MORE PASSENGERS OR A MAXIMUM PAYLOAD CAPACITY OF 6,000 POUNDS OR MORE; AND RULES GOVERNING PERSONS ON BOARD SUCH AIRCRAFT

Special Federal Aviation Regulation No. 89 [Note]
Special Federal Aviation Regulation No. 97 [Note]

Subpart L—Records and Reports

Subpart M—Continued Airworthiness and Safety Improvements

AUTHORITY: 49 U.S.C. 106(f), 106(g), 40113, 44701–44702, 44705, 44710–44711, 44713, 44716–44717, 44722.

SOURCE: Docket No. 19779, 45 FR 67235, Oct. 9, 1980, unless otherwise noted.

SPECIAL FEDERAL AVIATION REGULATION NO. 89

EDITORIAL NOTE: For the text of SFAR No. 89, see part 121 of this chapter.

SPECIAL FEDERAL AVIATION REGULATION NO. 97

EDITORIAL NOTE: For the text of SFAR No. 97, see part 91 of this chapter.

Subpart A—General

§125.1 Applicability.

(a) Except as provided in paragraphs (b), (c) and (d) of this section, this part prescribes rules governing the operations of U.S.-registered civil airplanes which have a seating configuration of 20 or more passengers or a maximum payload capacity of 6,000 pounds or more when common carriage is not involved.

(b) The rules of this part do not apply to the operations of airplanes specified in paragraph (a) of this section, when—

(1) They are required to be operated under part 121, 129, 135, or 137 of this chapter;

(2) They have been issued restricted, limited, or provisional airworthiness certificates, special flight permits, or experimental certificates;

(3) They are being operated by a part 125 certificate holder without carrying passengers or cargo under part 91 for training, ferrying, positioning, or maintenance purposes;

(4) They are being operated under part 91 by an operator certificated to operate those airplanes under the rules of parts 121, 135, or 137 of this chapter, they are being operated under the applicable rules of part 121 or part 135 of this chapter by an applicant for a certificate under part 119 of this chapter or they are being operated by a foreign air carrier or a foreign person engaged in common carriage solely outside the United States under part 91 of this chapter;

(5) They are being operated under a deviation authority issued under §125.3;

(6) They are being operated under part 91, subpart K by a fractional owner as defined in §91.1001 of this chapter; or

(7) They are being operated by a fractional ownership program manager as defined in §91.1001 of this chapter, for training, ferrying, positioning, maintenance, or demonstration purposes under part 91 of this chapter and without carrying passengers or cargo for compensation or hire except as permitted for demonstration flights under §91.501(b)(3) of this chapter.

(c) The rules of this part, except §125.247, do not apply to the operation of airplanes specified in paragraph (a) when they are operated outside the United States by a person who is not a citizen of the United States.

(d) The provisions of this part apply to each person on board an aircraft being operated under this part, unless otherwise specified.

(e) This part also establishes requirements for operators to take actions to support the continued airworthiness of each airplane.

[Doc. No. 19779, 45 FR 67235, Oct. 9, 1980, as amended by Amdt. 125–4, 47 FR 44719, Oct. 12, 1982; Amdt. 125–5, 49 FR 34816, Sept. 4 1984; Amdt. 125–6, 51 FR 873, Jan. 8, 1986; Amdt. 125–9, 52 FR 20028, May 28, 1987; Amdt. 121–251, 60 FR 65937, Dec. 20, 1995; Amdt. 125–31, 64 FR 1080, Jan. 7, 1999; Amdt. 125–44, 68 FR 54585, Sept. 17, 2003; Amdt. 125–53, 72 FR 63412 Nov. 8, 2007]

§ 125.3 Deviation authority.

(a) The Administrator may, upon consideration of the circumstances of a particular operation, issue deviation authority providing relief from specified sections of part 125. This deviation authority will be issued as a Letter of Deviation Authority.

(b) A Letter of Deviation Authority may be terminated or amended at any time by the Administrator.

(c) A request for deviation authority must be submitted to the responsible Flight Standards office, not less than 60 days prior to the date of intended operations. A request for deviation authority must contain a complete statement of the circumstances and justification for the deviation requested.

(d) After February 2, 2012, no deviation authority from the flight data recorder requirements of this part will be granted. Any previously issued deviation from the flight data recorder requirements of this part is no longer valid.

[Doc. No. 19779, 45 FR 67235, Oct. 9, 1980, as amended by Amdt. 125–13, 54 FR 39294, Sept. 25, 1989; Amdt. 125–56, 73 FR 73179, Dec. 2, 2008; Docket FAA–2018–0119, Amdt. 125–68, 83 FR 9173, Mar. 5, 2018]

§ 125.5 Operating certificate and operations specifications required.

(a) After February 3, 1981, no person may engage in operations governed by this part unless that person holds a certificate and operations specification or appropriate deviation authority.

(b) Applicants who file an application before June 1, 1981 shall continue to operate under the rules applicable to their operations on February 2, 1981 until the application for an operating certificate required by this part has been denied or the operating certificate and operations specifications required by this part have been issued.

(c) The rules of this part which apply to a certificate holder also apply to any person who engages in any operation governed by this part without an appropriate certificate and operations specifications required by this part or a Letter of Deviation Authority issued under § 125.3.

[Doc. No. 19779, 45 FR 67235, Oct. 9, 1980, as amended by Amdt. 125–1A, 46 FR 10903, Feb. 5, 1981]

§ 125.7 Display of certificate.

(a) The certificate holder must display a true copy of the certificate in each of its aircraft.

(b) Each operator holding a Letter of Deviation Authority issued under this part must carry a true copy in each of its airplanes.

§ 125.9 Definitions.

(a) For the purposes of this part, *maximum payload capacity* means:

(1) For an airplane for which a maximum zero fuel weight is prescribed in FAA technical specifications, the maximum zero fuel weight, less empty weight, less all justifiable airplane equipment, and less the operating load (consisting of minimum flightcrew, foods and beverages and supplies and equipment related to foods and beverages, but not including disposable fuel or oil):

(2) For all other airplanes, the maximum certificated takeoff weight of an airplane, less the empty weight, less all justifiable airplane equipment, and less the operating load (consisting of minimum fuel load, oil, and flightcrew). The allowance for the weight of the crew, oil, and fuel is as follows:

(i) Crew—200 pounds for each crewmember required under this chapter

(ii) Oil—350 pounds.

(iii) Fuel—the minimum weight of fuel required under this chapter for a flight between domestic points 174 nautical miles apart under VFR weather conditions that does not involve extended overwater operations.

(b) For the purposes of this part, *empty weight* means the weight of the airframe, engines, propellers, and fixed equipment. Empty weight excludes the weight of the crew and payload, but includes the weight of all fixed ballast, unusable fuel supply, undrainable oil, total quantity of engine coolant, and total quantity of hydraulic fluid.

(c) For the purposes of this part, *maximum zero fuel weight* means the maximum permissible weight of an airplane with no disposable fuel or oil. The zero fuel weight figure may be found in either the airplane type certificate data sheet or the approved Airplane Flight Manual, or both.

(d) For the purposes of this section, *justifiable airplane equipment* means any equipment necessary for the operation of the airplane. It does not include equipment or ballast specifically installed, permanently or otherwise, for the purpose of altering the empty weight of an airplane to meet the maximum payload capacity.

§ 125.11 Certificate eligibility and prohibited operations.

(a) No person is eligible for a certificate or operations specifications under this part if the person holds the appropriate operating certificate and/or operations specifications necessary to conduct operations under part 121, 129 or 135 of this chapter.

(b) No certificate holder may conduct any operation which results directly or indirectly from any person's holding out to the public to furnish transportation.

(c) No person holding operations specifications under this part may operate or list on its operations specifications any aircraft listed on any operations specifications or other required aircraft listing under part 121, 129, or 135 of this chapter.

[Doc. No. 19779, 45 FR 67235, Oct. 9, 1980, as amended by Amdt. 125–9, 52 FR 20028, May 28, 1987]

Subpart B—Certification Rules and Miscellaneous Requirements

§ 125.21 Application for operating certificate.

(a) Each applicant for the issuance of an operating certificate must submit an application in a form and manner prescribed by the Administrator to the responsible Flight Standards office in whose area the applicant proposes to establish or has established its principal operations base. The application must be submitted at least 60 days before the date of intended operations.

(b) Each application submitted under paragraph (a) of this section must contain a signed statement showing the following:

(1) The name and address of each director and each officer or person employed or who will be employed in a management position described in § 125.25.

(2) A list of flight crewmembers with the type of airman certificate held, including ratings and certificate numbers.

[Docket No. 19779, 45 FR 67235, Oct. 9, 1980, as amended by Docket FAA–2018–0119, Amdt. 125–68, 83 FR 9173, Mar. 5, 2018]

§ 125.23 Rules applicable to operations subject to this part.

Each person operating an airplane in operations under this part shall—

(a) While operating inside the United States, comply with the applicable rules in part 91 of this chapter; and

(b) While operating outside the United States, comply with Annex 2, Rules of the Air, to the Convention on International Civil Aviation or the regulations of any foreign country, whichever applies, and with any rules of parts 61 and 91 of this chapter and this part that are more restrictive than that Annex or those regulations and that can be complied with without violating that Annex or those regulations. Annex 2 is incorporated by reference in § 91.703(b) of this chapter.

[Doc. No. 19779, 45 FR 67235, Oct. 9, 1980, as amended by Amdt. 125–12, 54 FR 34331, Aug. 18, 1989]

§ 125.25 Management personnel required.

(a) Each applicant for a certificate under this part must show that it has enough management personnel, including at least a director of operations, to assure that its operations are conducted in accordance with the requirements of this part.

(b) Each applicant shall—

(1) Set forth the duties, responsibilities, and authority of each of its management personnel in the general policy section of its manual;

(2) List in the manual the names and addresses of each of its management personnel;

(3) Designate a person as responsible for the scheduling of inspections required by the manual and for the updating of the approved weight and balance system on all airplanes.

(c) Each certificate holder shall notify the responsible Flight Standards office charged with the overall inspection of the certificate holder of any change made in the assignment of persons to the listed positions within 10 days, excluding Saturdays, Sundays, and Federal holidays, of such change.

[Docket No. 19779, 45 FR 67235, Oct. 9, 1980, as amended by Docket FAA–2018–0119, Amdt. 125–68, 83 FR 9173, Mar. 5, 2018]

§ 125.26 Employment of former FAA employees.

(a) Except as specified in paragraph (c) of this section, no certificate holder may knowingly employ or make a contractual arrangement which permits an individual to act as an agent or representative of the certificate holder in any matter before the Federal Aviation Administration if the individual, in the preceding 2 years—

(1) Served as, or was directly responsible for the oversight of, a Flight Standards Service aviation safety inspector; and

(2) Had direct responsibility to inspect, or oversee the inspection of, the operations of the certificate holder.

(b) For the purpose of this section, an individual shall be considered to be acting as an agent or representative of a certificate holder in a matter before the agency if the individual makes any written or oral communication on behalf of the certificate holder to the agency (or any of its officers or employees) in connection with a particular matter, whether or not involving a specific party and without regard to whether the individual has participated in, or had responsibility for, the particular matter while serving as a Flight Standards Service aviation safety inspector.

(c) The provisions of this section do not prohibit a certificate holder from knowingly employing or making a contractual arrangement which permits an individual to act as an agent or rep-

resentative of the certificate holder in any matter before the Federal Aviation Administration if the individual was employed by the certificate holder before October 21, 2011.

[Doc. No. FAA–2008–1154, 76 FR 52235, Aug. 22, 2011]

§ 125.27 Issue of certificate.

(a) An applicant for a certificate under this subpart is entitled to a certificate if the Administrator finds that the applicant is properly and adequately equipped and able to conduct a safe operation in accordance with the requirements of this part and the operations specifications provided for in this part.

(b) The Administrator may deny an application for a certificate under this subpart if the Administrator finds—

(1) That an operating certificate required under this part or part 121, 123, or 135 of this chapter previously issued to the applicant was revoked; or

(2) That a person who was employed in a management position under § 125.25 of this part with (or has exercised control with respect to) any certificate holder under part 121, 123, 125, or 135 of this chapter whose operating certificate has been revoked, will be employed in any of those positions or a similar position with the applicant and that the person's employment or control contributed materially to the reasons for revoking that certificate.

§ 125.29 Duration of certificate.

(a) A certificate issued under this part is effective until surrendered, suspended, or revoked.

(b) The Administrator may suspend or revoke a certificate under section 609 of the Federal Aviation Act of 1958 and the applicable procedures of part 13 of this chapter for any cause that, at the time of suspension or revocation, would have been grounds for denying an application for a certificate.

(c) If the Administrator suspends or revokes a certificate or it is otherwise terminated, the holder of that certificate shall return it to the Administrator.

§ 125.31 Contents of certificate and operations specifications.

(a) Each certificate issued under this part contains the following:

(1) The holder's name.

(2) A description of the operations authorized.

(3) The date it is issued.

(b) The operations specifications issued under this part contain the following:

(1) The kinds of operations authorized.

(2) The types and registration numbers of airplanes authorized for use.

(3) Approval of the provisions of the operator's manual relating to airplane inspections, together with necessary conditions and limitations.

(4) Registration numbers of airplanes that are to be inspected under an approved airplane inspection program under § 125.247.

(5) Procedures for control of weight and balance of airplanes.

(6) Any other item that the Administrator determines is necessary to cover a particular situation.

§ 125.33 Operations specifications not a part of certificate.

Operations specifications are not a part of an operating certificate.

§ 125.35 Amendment of operations specifications.

(a) The responsible Flight Standards office charged with the overall inspection of the certificate holder may amend any operations specifications issued under this part if—

(1) It determines that safety in air commerce requires that amendment; or

(2) Upon application by the holder, the responsible Flight Standards office determines that safety in air commerce allows that amendment.

(b) The certificate holder must file an application to amend operations specifications at least 15 days before the date proposed by the applicant for the amendment to become effective, unless a shorter filing period is approved. The application must be on a form and in a manner prescribed by the Administrator and be submitted to the responsible Flight Standards office charged with the overall inspection of the certificate holder.

(c) Within 30 days after a notice of refusal to approve a holder's application for amendment is received, the holder may petition the Executive Director, Flight Standards Service, to reconsider the refusal to amend.

(d) When the responsible Flight Standards office charged with the overall inspection of the certificate holder amends operations specifications, the responsible Flight Standards office gives notice in writing to the holder of a proposed amendment to the operations specifications, fixing a period of not less than 7 days within which the holder may submit written information, views, and arguments concerning the proposed amendment. After consideration of all relevant matter presented, the responsible Flight Standards office notifies the holder of any amendment adopted, or a rescission of the notice. That amendment becomes effective not less than 30 days after the holder receives notice of the adoption of the amendment, unless the holder petitions the Executive Director, Flight Standards Service, for reconsideration of the amendment. In that case, the effective date of the amendment is stayed pending a decision by the Executive Director. If the Executive Director finds there is an emergency requiring immediate action as to safety in air commerce that makes the provisions of this paragraph impracticable or contrary to the public interest, the Executive Director notifies the certificate holder that the amendment is effective on the date of receipt, without previous notice.

[Doc. No. 19779, 45 FR 67235, Oct. 9, 1980, as amended by Amdt. 125–13, 54 FR 39294, Sept. 25, 1989; Docket FAA–2018–0119, Amdt. 125–68, 83 FR 9173, 9174, Mar. 5, 2018]

§ 125.37 Duty period limitations.

(a) Each flight crewmember and flight attendant must be relieved from all duty for at least 8 consecutive hours during any 24-hour period.

(b) The Administrator may specify rest, flight time, and duty time limitations in the operations specifications that are other than those specified in paragraph (a) of this section.

[Doc. No. 19779, 45 FR 67235, Oct. 9, 1980, as amended by Amdt. 125–21, 59 FR 42993, Aug. 19, 1994]

§125.39 Carriage of narcotic drugs, marihuana, and depressant or stimulant drugs or substances.

If the holder of a certificate issued under this part permits any airplane owned or leased by that holder to be engaged in any operation that the certificate holder knows to be in violation of §91.19(a) of this chapter, that operation is a basis for suspending or revoking the certificate.

[Doc. No. 19779, 45 FR 67235, Oct. 9, 1980, as amended by Amdt. 125–12, 54 FR 34331, Aug. 18, 1989]

§125.41 Availability of certificate and operations specifications.

Each certificate holder shall make its operating certificate and operations specifications available for inspection by the Administrator at its principal operations base.

§125.43 Use of operations specifications.

(a) Each certificate holder shall keep each of its employees informed of the provisions of its operations specifications that apply to the employee's duties and responsibilities.

(b) Each certificate holder shall maintain a complete and separate set of its operations specifications. In addition, each certificate holder shall insert pertinent excerpts of its operations specifications, or reference thereto, in its manual in such a manner that they retain their identity as operations specifications.

§125.45 Inspection authority.

Each certificate holder shall allow the Administrator, at any time or place, to make any inspections or tests to determine its compliance with the Federal Aviation Act of 1958, the Federal Aviation Regulations, its operating certificate and operations specifications, its letter of deviation authority, or its eligibililty to continue to hold its certificate or its letter of deviation authority.

§125.47 Change of address.

Each certificate holder shall notify the responsible Flight Standards office charged with the overall inspection of its operations, in writing, at least 30 days in advance, of any change in the address of its principal business office, its principal operations base, or its principal maintenance base.

[Docket No. 19779, 45 FR 67235, Oct. 9, 1980, as amended by Docket FAA–2018–0119, Amdt. 125–68, 83 FR 9173, Mar. 5, 2018]

§125.49 Airport requirements.

(a) No certificate holder may use any airport unless it is adequate for the proposed operation, considering such items as size, surface, obstructions, and lighting.

(b) No pilot of an airplane carrying passengers at night may take off from, or land on, an airport unless—

(1) That pilot has determined the wind direction from an illuminated wind direction indicator or local ground communications, or, in the case of takeoff, that pilot's personal observations; and

(2) The limits of the area to be used for landing or takeoff are clearly shown by boundary or runway marker lights.

(c) For the purposes of paragraph (b) of this section, if the area to be used for takeoff or landing is marked by flare pots or lanterns, their use must be approved by the Administrator.

§125.51 En route navigation facilities.

(a) Except as provided in paragraph (b) of this section, no certificate holder may conduct any operation over a route (including to any destination, refueling or alternate airports) unless suitable navigation aids are available over the route to navigate the airplane along the route within the degree of accuracy required for ATC. Navigation aids required for routes outside of controlled airspace are listed in the certificate holder's operations specifications except for those aids required for routes to alternate airports.

(b) Navigation aids are not required for any of the following operations—

(1) Day VFR operations that the certificate holder shows can be conducted safely by pilotage because of the characteristics of the terrain;

(2) Night VFR operations on routes that the certificate holder shows have reliably lighted landmarks adequate for safe operations; and

317

(3) Other operations approved by the responsible Flight Standards office.

[Doc. No. FAA–2002–14002, 72 FR 31682, June 7, 2007, as amended by Docket FAA–2018–0119, Amdt. 125–68, 83 FR 9174, Mar. 5, 2018]

§ 125.53 Flight locating requirements.

(a) Each certificate holder must have procedures established for locating each flight for which an FAA flight plan is not filed that—

(1) Provide the certificate holder with at least the information required to be included in a VFR flight plan;

(2) Provide for timely notification of an FAA facility or search and rescue facility, if an airplane is overdue or missing; and

(3) Provide the certificate holder with the location, date, and estimated time for reestablishing radio or telephone communications, if the flight will operate in an area where communications cannot be maintained.

(b) Flight locating information shall be retained at the certificate holder's principal operations base, or at other places designated by the certificate holder in the flight locating procedures, until the completion of the flight.

(c) Each certificate holder shall furnish the representative of the Administrator assigned to it with a copy of its flight locating procedures and any changes or additions, unless those procedures are included in a manual required under this part.

Subpart C—Manual Requirements

§ 125.71 Preparation.

(a) Each certificate holder shall prepare and keep current a manual setting forth the certificate holder's procedures and policies acceptable to the Administrator. This manual must be used by the certificate holder's flight, ground, and maintenance personnel in conducting its operations. However, the Administrator may authorize a deviation from this paragraph if the Administrator finds that, because of the limited size of the operation, all or part of the manual is not necessary for guidance of flight, ground, or maintenance personnel.

(b) Each certificate holder shall maintain at least one copy of the manual at its principal operations base.

(c) The manual must not be contrary to any applicable Federal regulations, foreign regulation applicable to the certificate holder's operations in foreign countries, or the certificate holder's operating certificate or operations specifications.

(d) A copy of the manual, or appropriate portions of the manual (and changes and additions) shall be made available to maintenance and ground operations personnel by the certificate holder and furnished to—

(1) Its flight crewmembers; and

(2) The responsible Flight Standards office charged with the overall inspection of its operations.

(e) Each employee of the certificate holder to whom a manual or appropriate portions of it are furnished under paragraph (d)(1) of this section shall keep it up to date with the changes and additions furnished to them.

(f) For the purpose of complying with paragraph (d) of this section, a certificate holder may furnish the persons listed therein with the maintenance part of its manual in printed form or other form, acceptable to the Administrator, that is retrievable in the English language. If the certificate holder furnishes the maintenance part of the manual in other than printed form, it must ensure there is a compatible reading device available to those persons that provides a legible image of the maintenance information and instructions or a system that is able to retrieve the maintenance information and instructions in the English language.

(g) If a certificate holder conducts airplane inspections or maintenance at specified stations where it keeps the approved inspection program manual, it is not required to carry the manual aboard the airplane en route to those stations.

[Doc. No. 19779, 45 FR 67235, Oct. 9, 1980, as amended by Amdt. 125–28, 62 FR 13257, Mar. 19, 1997; Docket FAA–2018–0119, Amdt. 125–68, 83 FR 9173, Mar. 5, 2018]

§ 125.73 Contents.

Each manual shall have the date of the last revision and revision number on each revised page. The manual must include—

(a) The name of each management person who is authorized to act for the certificate holder, the person's assigned area of responsibility, and the person's duties, responsibilities. and authority;

(b) Procedures for ensuring compliance with airplane weight and balance limitations;

(c) Copies of the certificate holder's operations specifications or appropriate extracted information, including area of operations authorized, category and class of airplane authorized, crew complements, and types of operations authorized;

(d) Procedures for complying with accident notification requirements;

(e) Procedures for ensuring that the pilot in command knows that required airworthiness inspections have been made and that the airplane has been approved for return to service in compliance with applicable maintenance requirements;

(f) Procedures for reporting and recording mechanical irregularities that come to the attention of the pilot in command before, during, and after completion of a flight;

(g) Procedures to be followed by the pilot in command for determining that mechanical irregularities or defects reported for previous flights have been corrected or that correction has been deferred;

(h) Procedures to be followed by the pilot in command to obtain maintenance, preventive maintenance, and servicing of the airplane at a place where previous arrangements have not been made by the operator, when the pilot is authorized to so act for the operator;

(i) Procedures for the release for, or continuation of, flight if any item of equipment required for the particular type of operation becomes inoperative or unserviceable en route;

(j) Procedures for refueling airplanes, eliminating fuel contamination, protecting from fire (including electrostatic protection), and supervising and protecting passengers during refueling;

(k) Procedures to be followed by the pilot in command in the briefing under § 125.327;

(l) Flight locating procedures, when applicable;

(m) Procedures for ensuring compliance with emergency procedures, including a list of the functions assigned each category of required crewmembers in connection with an emergency and emergency evacuation;

(n) The approved airplane inspection program;

(o) Procedures and instructions to enable personnel to recognize hazardous materials, as defined in title 49 CFR, and if these materials are to be carried, stored, or handled, procedures and instructions for—

(1) Accepting shipment of hazardous material required by title 49 CFR, to assure proper packaging, marking, labeling, shipping documents, compatibility of articles, and instructions on their loading, storage, and handling;

(2) Notification and reporting hazardous material incidents as required by title 49 CFR; and

(3) Notification of the pilot in command when there are hazardous materials aboard, as required by title 49 CFR;

(p) Procedures for the evacuation of persons who may need the assistance of another person to move expeditiously to an exit if an emergency occurs;

(q) The identity of each person who will administer tests required by this part, including the designation of the tests authorized to be given by the person; and

(r) Other procedures and policy instructions regarding the certificate holder's operations that are issued by the certificate holder.

§ 125.75 Airplane flight manual.

(a) Each certificate holder shall keep a current approved Airplane Flight Manual or approved equivalent for each type airplane that it operates.

(b) Each certificate holder shall carry the approved Airplane Flight Manual or the approved equivalent aboard each airplane it operates. A certificate holder may elect to carry a combination of the manuals required by this section and § 125.71. If it so elects, the certificate holder may revise the operating procedures sections and modify the presentation of performance from the applicable Airplane Flight Manual if the revised operating procedures and modified performance data presentation are approved by the Administrator.

Subpart D—Airplane Requirements

§ 125.91 Airplane requirements: General.

(a) No certificate holder may operate an airplane governed by this part unless it—

(1) Carries an appropriate current airworthiness certificate issued under this chapter; and

(2) Is in an airworthy condition and meets the applicable airworthiness requirements of this chapter, including those relating to identification and equipment.

(b) No person may operate an airplane unless the current empty weight and center of gravity are calculated from the values established by actual weighing of the airplane within the preceding 36 calendar months.

(c) Paragraph (b) of this section does not apply to airplanes issued an original airworthiness certificate within the preceding 36 calendar months.

§ 125.93 Airplane limitations.

No certificate holder may operate a land airplane (other than a DC-3, C-46, CV-240, CV-340, CV-440, CV-580, CV-600, CV-640, or Martin 404) in an extended overwater operation unless it is certificated or approved as adequate for ditching under the ditching provisions of part 25 of this chapter.

Subpart E—Special Airworthiness Requirements

§ 125.111 General.

(a) Except as provided in paragraph (b) of this section, no certificate holder may use an airplane powered by airplane engines rated at more than 600 horsepower each for maximum continuous operation unless that airplane meets the requirements of §§ 125.113 through 125.181.

(b) If the Administrator determines that, for a particular model of airplane used in cargo service, literal compliance with any requirement under paragraph (a) of this section would be extremely difficult and that compliance would not contribute materially to the objective sought, the Administrator may require compliance with only those requirements that are necessary to accomplish the basic objectives of this part.

(c) This section does not apply to any airplane certificated under—

(1) Part 4b of the Civil Air Regulations in effect after October 31, 1946;

(2) Part 25 of this chapter; or

(3) Special Civil Air Regulation 422, 422A, or 422B.

§ 125.113 Cabin interiors.

(a) Upon the first major overhaul of an airplane cabin or refurbishing of the cabin interior, all materials in each compartment used by the crew or passengers that do not meet the following requirements must be replaced with materials that meet these requirements:

(1) For an airplane for which the application for the type certificate was filed prior to May 1, 1972, § 25.853 in effect on April 30, 1972.

(2) For an airplane for which the application for the type certificate was filed on or after May 1, 1972, the materials requirement under which the airplane was type certificated.

(b) Except as provided in paragraph (a) of this section, each compartment used by the crew or passengers must meet the following requirements:

(1) Materials must be at least flash resistant.

(2) The wall and ceiling linings and the covering of upholstering, floors, and furnishings must be flame resistant.

(3) Each compartment where smoking is to be allowed must be equipped with self-contained ash trays that are completely removable and other compartments must be placarded against smoking.

(4) Each receptacle for used towels, papers, and wastes must be of fire-resistant material and must have a cover or other means of containing possible fires started in the receptacles.

(c) Thermal/acoustic insulation materials. For transport category airplanes type certificated after January 1, 1958:

(1) For airplanes manufactured before September 2, 2005, when thermal/acoustic insulation is installed in the fuselage as replacements after September 2, 2005, the insulation must meet the flame propagation requirements of § 25.856 of this chapter, effective September 2, 2003, if it is:

(i) of a blanket construction or

(ii) Installed around air ducting.

(2) For airplanes manufactured after September 2, 2005, thermal/acoustic insulation materials installed in the fuselage must meet the flame propagation requirements of § 25.856 of this chapter, effective September 2, 2003.

[Doc. No. 19799, 45 FR 67235, Oct. 9, 1980, as amended by Amdt. 125–43, 68 FR 45084, July 31, 2003; Amdt. 125–50, 70 FR 77752, Dec. 30, 2005]

§ 125.115   Internal doors.

In any case where internal doors are equipped with louvres or other ventilating means, there must be a means convenient to the crew for closing the flow of air through the door when necessary.

§ 125.117   Ventilation.

Each passenger or crew compartment must be suitably ventilated. Carbon monoxide concentration may not be more than one part in 20,000 parts of air, and fuel fumes may not be present. In any case where partitions between compartments have louvres or other means allowing air to flow between compartments, there must be a means convenient to the crew for closing the flow of air through the partitions when necessary.

§ 125.119   Fire precautions.

(a) Each compartment must be designed so that, when used for storing cargo or baggage, it meets the following requirements:

(1) No compartment may include controls, wiring, lines, equipment, or accessories that would upon damage or failure, affect the safe operation of the airplane unless the item is adequately shielded, isolated, or otherwise protected so that it cannot be damaged by movement of cargo in the compartment and so that damage to or failure of the item would not create a fire hazard in the compartment.

(2) Cargo or baggage may not interfere with the functioning of the fire-protective features of the compartment.

(3) Materials used in the construction of the compartments, including tie-down equipment, must be at least flame resistant.

(4) Each compartment must include provisions for safeguarding against fires according to the classifications set forth in paragraphs (b) through (f) of this section.

(b) *Class A.* Cargo and baggage compartments are classified in the "A" category if a fire therein would be readily discernible to a member of the crew while at that crewmember's station, and all parts of the compartment are easily accessible in flight. There must be a hand fire extinguisher available for each Class A compartment.

(c) *Class B.* Cargo and baggage compartments are classified in the "B" category if enough access is provided while in flight to enable a member of the crew to effectively reach all of the compartment and its contents with a hand fire extinguisher and the compartment is so designed that, when the access provisions are being used, no hazardous amount of smoke, flames, or extinguishing agent enters any compartment occupied by the crew or passengers. Each Class B compartment must comply with the following:

(1) It must have a separate approved smoke or fire detector system to give warning at the pilot or flight engineer station.

(2) There must be a hand-held fire extinguisher available for the compartment.

(3) It must be lined with fire-resistant material, except that additional service lining of flame-resistant material may be used.

(d) *Class C.* Cargo and baggage compartments are classified in the "C" category if they do not conform with the requirements for the "A", "B", "D", or "E" categories. Each Class C compartment must comply with the following:

(1) It must have a separate approved smoke or fire detector system to give

warning at the pilot or flight engineer station.

(2) It must have an approved built-in fire-extinguishing system controlled from the pilot or flight engineer station.

(3) It must be designed to exclude hazardous quantities of smoke, flames, or extinguishing agents from entering into any compartment occupied by the crew or passengers.

(4) It must have ventilation and draft control so that the extinguishing agent provided can control any fire that may start in the compartment.

(5) It must be lined with fire-resistant material, except that additional service lining of flame-resistant material may be used.

(e) *Class D.* Cargo and baggage compartments are classified in the "D" category if they are so designed and constructed that a fire occurring therein will be completely confined without endangering the safety of the airplane or the occupants. Each Class D compartment must comply with the following:

(1) It must have a means to exclude hazardous quantities of smoke, flames, or noxious gases from entering any compartment occupied by the crew or passengers.

(2) Ventilation and drafts must be controlled within each compartment so that any fire likely to occur in the compartment will not progress beyond safe limits.

(3) It must be completely lined with fire-resistant material.

(4) Consideration must be given to the effect of heat within the compartment on adjacent critical parts of the airplane.

(f) *Class E.* On airplanes used for the carriage of cargo only, the cabin area may be classified as a Class "E" compartment. Each Class E compartment must comply with the following:

(1) It must be completely lined with fire-resistant material.

(2) It must have a separate system of an approved type smoke or fire detector to give warning at the pilot or flight engineer station.

(3) It must have a means to shut off the ventilating air flow to or within the compartment and the controls for

that means must be accessible to the flightcrew in the crew compartment.

(4) It must have a means to exclude hazardous quantities of smoke, flames, or noxious gases from entering the flightcrew compartment.

(5) Required crew emergency exits must be accessible under all cargo loading conditions.

§ 125.121 Proof of compliance with § 125.119.

Compliance with those provisions of § 125.119 that refer to compartment accessibility, the entry of hazardous quantities of smoke or extinguishing agent into compartment occupied by the crew or passengers, and the dissipation of the extinguishing agent in Class "C" compartments must be shown by tests in flight. During these tests it must be shown that no inadvertent operation of smoke or fire detectors in other compartments within the airplane would occur as a result of fire contained in any one compartment, either during the time it is being extinguished, or thereafter, unless the extinguishing system floods those compartments simultaneously.

§ 125.123 Propeller deicing fluid.

If combustible fluid is used for propeller deicing, the certificate holder must comply with § 125.153.

§ 125.125 Pressure cross-feed arrangements.

(a) Pressure cross-feed lines may not pass through parts of the airplane used for carrying persons or cargo unless there is a means to allow crewmembers to shut off the supply of fuel to these lines or the lines are enclosed in a fuel and fume-proof enclosure that is ventilated and drained to the exterior of the airplane. However, such an enclosure need not be used if those lines incorporate no fittings on or within the personnel or cargo areas and are suitably routed or protected to prevent accidental damage.

(b) Lines that can be isolated from the rest of the fuel system by valves at each end must incorporate provisions for relieving excessive pressures that may result from exposure of the isolated line to high temperatures.

§ 125.127 Location of fuel tanks.

(a) Fuel tanks must be located in accordance with § 125.153.

(b) No part of the engine nacelle skin that lies immediately behind a major air outlet from the engine compartment may be used as the wall of an integral tank.

(c) Fuel tanks must be isolated from personnel compartments by means of fume- and fuel-proof enclosures.

§ 125.129 Fuel system lines and fittings.

(a) Fuel lines must be installed and supported so as to prevent excessive vibration and so as to be adequate to withstand loads due to fuel pressure and accelerated flight conditions.

(b) Lines connected to components of the airplane between which there may be relative motion must incorporate provisions for flexibility.

(c) Flexible connections in lines that may be under pressure and subject to axial loading must use flexible hose assemblies rather than hose clamp connections.

(d) Flexible hoses must be of an acceptable type or proven suitable for the particular application.

§ 125.131 Fuel lines and fittings in designated fire zones.

Fuel lines and fittings in each designated fire zone must comply with § 125.157.

§ 125.133 Fuel valves.

Each fuel valve must—

(a) Comply with § 125.155;

(b) Have positive stops or suitable index provisions in the "on" and "off" positions; and

(c) Be supported so that loads resulting from its operation or from accelerated flight conditions are not transmitted to the lines connected to the valve.

§ 125.135 Oil lines and fittings in designated fire zones.

Oil lines and fittings in each designated fire zone must comply with § 125.157.

§ 125.137 Oil valves.

(a) Each oil valve must—

(1) Comply with § 125.155;

(2) Have positive stops or suitable index provisions in the "on" and "off" positions; and

(3) Be supported so that loads resulting from its operation or from accelerated flight conditions are not transmitted to the lines attached to the valve.

(b) The closing of an oil shutoff means must not prevent feathering the propeller, unless equivalent safety provisions are incorporated.

§ 125.139 Oil system drains.

Accessible drains incorporating either a manual or automatic means for positive locking in the closed position must be provided to allow safe drainage of the entire oil system.

§ 125.141 Engine breather lines.

(a) Engine breather lines must be so arranged that condensed water vapor that may freeze and obstruct the line cannot accumulate at any point.

(b) Engine breathers must discharge in a location that does not constitute a fire hazard in case foaming occurs and so that oil emitted from the line does not impinge upon the pilots' windshield.

(c) Engine breathers may not discharge into the engine air induction system.

§ 125.143 Firewalls.

Each engine, auxiliary power unit, fuel-burning heater, or other item of combusting equipment that is intended for operation in flight must be isolated from the rest of the airplane by means of firewalls or shrouds, or by other equivalent means.

§ 125.145 Firewall construction.

Each firewall and shroud must—

(a) Be so made that no hazardous quantity of air, fluids, or flame can pass from the engine compartment to other parts of the airplane;

(b) Have all openings in the firewall or shroud sealed with close-fitting fireproof grommets, bushings, or firewall fittings;

(c) Be made of fireproof material; and

(d) Be protected against corrosion.

§ 125.147 Cowling.

(a) Cowling must be made and supported so as to resist the vibration, inertia, and air loads to which it may be normally subjected.

(b) Provisions must be made to allow rapid and complete drainage of the cowling in normal ground and flight attitudes. Drains must not discharge in locations constituting a fire hazard. Parts of the cowling that are subjected to high temperatures because they are near exhaust system parts or because of exhaust gas impingement must be made of fireproof material. Unless otherwise specified in these regulations, all other parts of the cowling must be made of material that is at least fire resistant.

§ 125.149 Engine accessory section diaphragm.

Unless equivalent protection can be shown by other means, a diaphragm that complies with § 125.145 must be provided on air-cooled engines to isolate the engine power section and all parts of the exhaust system from the engine accessory compartment.

§ 125.151 Powerplant fire protection.

(a) Designated fire zones must be protected from fire by compliance with §§ 125.153 through 125.159.

(b) Designated fire zones are—

(1) Engine accessory sections;

(2) Installations where no isolation is provided between the engine and accessory compartment; and

(3) Areas that contain auxiliary power units, fuel-burning heaters, and other combustion equipment.

§ 125.153 Flammable fluids.

(a) No tanks or reservoirs that are a part of a system containing flammable fluids or gases may be located in designated fire zones, except where the fluid contained, the design of the system, the materials used in the tank, the shutoff means, and the connections, lines, and controls provide equivalent safety.

(b) At least one-half inch of clear airspace must be provided between any tank or reservoir and a firewall or shroud isolating a designated fire zone.

§ 125.155 Shutoff means.

(a) Each engine must have a means for shutting off or otherwise preventing hazardous amounts of fuel, oil, deicer, and other flammable fluids from flowing into, within, or through any designated fire zone. However, means need not be provided to shut off flow in lines that are an integral part of an engine.

(b) The shutoff means must allow an emergency operating sequence that is compatible with the emergency operation of other equipment, such as feathering the propeller, to facilitate rapid and effective control of fires.

(c) Shutoff means must be located outside of designated fire zones, unless equivalent safety is provided, and it must be shown that no hazardous amount of flammable fluid will drain into any designated fire zone after a shutoff.

(d) Adequate provisions must be made to guard against inadvertent operation of the shutoff means and to make it possible for the crew to reopen the shutoff means after it has been closed.

§ 125.157 Lines and fittings.

(a) Each line, and its fittings, that is located in a designated fire zone, if it carries flammable fluids or gases under pressure, or is attached directly to the engine, or is subject to relative motion between components (except lines and fittings forming an integral part of the engine), must be flexible and fire-resistant with fire-resistant, factory-fixed, detachable, or other approved fire-resistant ends.

(b) Lines and fittings that are not subject to pressure or to relative motion between components must be of fire-resistant materials.

§ 125.159 Vent and drain lines.

All vent and drain lines, and their fittings, that are located in a designated fire zone must, if they carry flammable fluids or gases, comply with § 125.157, if the Administrator finds that the rupture or breakage of any vent or drain line may result in a fire hazard.

§125.161 Fire-extinguishing systems.

(a) Unless the certificate holder shows that equivalent protection against destruction of the airplane in case of fire is provided by the use of fireproof materials in the nacelle and other components that would be subjected to flame, fire-extinguishing systems must be provided to serve all designated fire zones.

(b) Materials in the fire-extinguishing system must not react chemically with the extinguishing agent so as to be a hazard.

§125.163 Fire-extinguishing agents.

Only methyl bromide, carbon dioxide, or another agent that has been shown to provide equivalent extinguishing action may be used as a fire-extinguishing agent. If methyl bromide or any other toxic extinguishing agent is used, provisions must be made to prevent harmful concentrations of fluid or fluid vapors from entering any personnel compartment either because of leakage during normal operation of the airplane or because of discharging the fire extinguisher on the ground or in flight when there is a defect in the extinguishing system. If a methyl bromide system is used, the containers must be charged with dry agent and sealed by the fire-extinguisher manufacturer or some other person using satisfactory recharging equipment. If carbon dioxide is used, it must not be possible to discharge enough gas into the personnel compartments to create a danger of suffocating the occupants.

§125.165 Extinguishing agent container pressure relief.

Extinguishing agent containers must be provided with a pressure relief to prevent bursting of the container because of excessive internal pressures. The discharge line from the relief connection must terminate outside the airplane in a place convenient for inspection on the ground. An indicator must be provided at the discharge end of the line to provide a visual indication when the container has discharged.

§125.167 Extinguishing agent container compartment temperature.

Precautions must be taken to ensure that the extinguishing agent containers are installed in places where reasonable temperatures can be maintained for effective use of the extinguishing system.

§125.169 Fire-extinguishing system materials.

(a) Except as provided in paragraph (b) of this section, each component of a fire-extinguishing system that is in a designated fire zone must be made of fireproof materials.

(b) Connections that are subject to relative motion between components of the airplane must be made of flexible materials that are at least fire-resistant and be located so as to minimize the probability of failure.

§125.171 Fire-detector systems.

Enough quick-acting fire detectors must be provided in each designated fire zone to assure the detection of any fire that may occur in that zone.

§125.173 Fire detectors.

Fire detectors must be made and installed in a manner that assures their ability to resist, without failure, all vibration, inertia, and other loads to which they may be normally subjected. Fire detectors must be unaffected by exposure to fumes, oil, water, or other fluids that may be present.

§125.175 Protection of other airplane components against fire.

(a) Except as provided in paragraph (b) of this section, all airplane surfaces aft of the nacelles in the area of one nacelle diameter on both sides of the nacelle centerline must be made of material that is at least fire resistant.

(b) Paragraph (a) of this section does not apply to tail surfaces lying behind nacelles unless the dimensional configuration of the airplane is such that the tail surfaces could be affected readily by heat, flames, or sparks emanating from a designated fire zone or from the engine from a designated fire zone or from the engine compartment of any nacelle.

325

§ 125.177 Control of engine rotation.

(a) Except as provided in paragraph (b) of this section, each airplane must have a means of individually stopping and restarting the rotation of any engine in flight.

(b) In the case of turbine engine installations, a means of stopping rotation need be provided only if the Administrator finds that rotation could jeopardize the safety of the airplane.

§ 125.179 Fuel system independence.

(a) Each airplane fuel system must be arranged so that the failure of any one component does not result in the irrecoverable loss of power of more than one engine.

(b) A separate fuel tank need not be provided for each engine if the certificate holder shows that the fuel system incorporates features that provide equivalent safety.

§ 125.181 Induction system ice prevention.

A means for preventing the malfunctioning of each engine due to ice accumulation in the engine air induction system must be provided for each airplane.

§ 125.183 Carriage of cargo in passenger compartments.

(a) Except as provided in paragraph (b) or (c) of this section, no certificate holder may carry cargo in the passenger compartment of an airplane.

(b) Cargo may be carried aft of the foremost seated passengers if it is carried in an approved cargo bin that meets the following requirements:

(1) The bin must withstand the load factors and emergency landing conditions applicable to the passenger seats of the airplane in which the bin is installed, multiplied by a factor of 1.15, using the combined weight of the bin and the maximum weight of cargo that may be carried in the bin.

(2) The maximum weight of cargo that the bin is approved to carry and any instructions necessary to ensure proper weight distribution within the bin must be conspicuously marked on the bin.

(3) The bin may not impose any load on the floor or other structure of the airplane that exceeds the load limitations of that structure.

(4) The bin must be attached to the seat tracks or to the floor structure of the airplane, and its attachment must withstand the load factors and emergency landing conditions applicable to the passenger seats of the airplane in which the bin is installed, multiplied by either the factor 1.15 or the seat attachment factor specified for the airplane, whichever is greater, using the combined weight of the bin and the maximum weight of cargo that may be carried in the bin.

(5) The bin may not be installed in a position that restricts access to or use of any required emergency exit, or of the aisle in the passenger compartment.

(6) The bin must be fully enclosed and made of material that is at least flame-resistant.

(7) Suitable safeguards must be provided within the bin to prevent the cargo from shifting under emergency landing conditions.

(8) The bin may not be installed in a position that obscures any passenger's view of the "seat belt" sign, "no smoking" sign, or any required exit sign, unless an auxiliary sign or other approved means for proper notification of the passenger is provided.

(c) All cargo may be carried forward of the foremost seated passengers and carry-on baggage may be carried alongside the foremost seated passengers if the cargo (including carry-on baggage) is carried either in approved bins as specified in paragraph (b) of this section or in accordance with the following:

(1) It is properly secured by a safety belt or other tie down having enough strength to eliminate the possibility of shifting under all normally anticipated flight and ground conditions.

(2) It is packaged or covered in a manner to avoid possible injury to passengers.

(3) It does not impose any load on seats or the floor structure that exceeds the load limitation for those components.

(4) Its location does not restrict access to or use of any required emergency or regular exit, or of the aisle in the passenger compartment.

(5) Its location does not obscure any passenger's view of the "seat belt" sign, "no smoking" sign, or required exit sign, unless an auxiliary sign or other approved means for proper notification of the passenger is provided.

§ 125.185 Carriage of cargo in cargo compartments.

When cargo is carried in cargo compartments that are designed to require the physical entry of a crewmember to extinguish any fire that may occur during flight, the cargo must be loaded so as to allow a crewmember to effectively reach all parts of the compartment with the contents of a hand-held fire extinguisher.

§ 125.187 Landing gear: Aural warning device.

(a) Except for airplanes that comply with the requirements of § 25.729 of this chapter on or after January 6, 1992, each airplane must have a landing gear aural warning device that functions continuously under the following conditions:

(1) For airplanes with an established approach wing-flap position, wherever the wing flaps are extended beyond the maximum certificated approach climb configuration position in the Airplane Flight Manual and the landing gear is not fully extended and locked.

(2) For airplanes without an established approach climb wing-flap position, whenever the wing flaps are extended beyond the position at which landing gear extension is normally performed and the landing gear is not fully extended and locked.

(b) The warning system required by paragraph (a) of this section—

(1) May not have a manual shutoff;

(2) Must be in addition to the throttle-actuated device installed under the type certification airworthiness requirements; and

(3) May utilize any part of the throttle-actuated system including the aural warning device.

(c) The flap position sensing unit may be installed at any suitable place in the airplane.

[Doc. No. 19779, 45 FR 67235, Oct. 9, 1980 as amended by Amdt. 125–16, 56 FR 63762, Dec. 5, 1991]

§ 125.189 Demonstration of emergency evacuation procedures.

(a) Each certificate holder must show, by actual demonstration conducted in accordance with paragraph (a) of appendix B of this part, that the emergency evacuation procedures for each type and model of airplane with a seating of more than 44 passengers, that is used in its passenger-carrying operations, allow the evacuation of the full seating capacity, including crewmembers, in 90 seconds or less, in each of the following circumstances:

(1) A demonstration must be conducted by the certificate holder upon the initial introduction of a type and model of airplane into passenger-carrying operations. However, the demonstration need not be repeated for any airplane type or model that has the same number and type of exits, the same cabin configuration, and the same emergency equipment as any other airplane used by the certificate holder in successfully demonstrating emergency evacuation in compliance with this paragraph.

(2) A demonstration must be conducted—

(i) Upon increasing by more than 5 percent the passenger seating capacity for which successful demonstration has been conducted; or

(ii) Upon a major change in the passenger cabin interior configuration that will affect the emergency evacuation of passengers.

(b) If a certificate holder has conducted a successful demonstration required by § 121.291(a) in the same type airplane as a part 121 or part 123 certificate holder, it need not conduct a demonstration under this paragraph in that type airplane to achieve certification under part 125.

(c) Each certificate holder operating or proposing to operate one or more landplanes in extended overwater operations, or otherwise required to have certain equipment under § 125.209, must show, by a simulated ditching conducted in accordance with paragraph (b) of appendix B of this part, that it has the ability to efficiently carry out its ditching procedures.

(d) If a certificate holder has conducted a successful demonstration required by § 121.291(b) in the same type

327

airplane as a part 121 or part 123 certificate holder, it need not conduct a demonstration under this paragraph in that type airplane to achieve certification under part 125.

Subpart F—Instrument and Equipment Requirements

§ 125.201 Inoperable instruments and equipment.

(a) No person may take off an airplane with inoperable instruments or equipment installed unless the following conditions are met:

(1) An approved Minimum Equipment List exists for that airplane.

(2) The responsible Flight Standards office having certification responsibility has issued the certificate holder operations specifications authorizing operations in accordance with an approved Minimum Equipment List. The flight crew shall have direct access at all times prior to flight to all of the information contained in the approved Minimum Equipment List through printed or other means approved by the Administrator in the certificate holders operations specifications. An approved Minimum Equipment List, as authorized by the operations specifications, constitutes an approved change to the type design without requiring recertification.

(3) The approved Minimum Equipment List must:

(i) Be prepared in accordance with the limitations specified in paragraph (b) of this section.

(ii) Provide for the operation of the airplane with certain instruments and equipment in an inoperable condition.

(4) Records identifying the inoperable instruments and equipment and the information required by paragraph (a)(3)(ii) of this section must be available to the pilot.

(5) The airplane is operated under all applicable conditions and limitations contained in the Minimum Equipment List and the operations specifications authorizing use of the Minimum Equipment List.

(b) The following instruments and equipment may not be included in the Minimum Equipment List:

(1) Instruments and equipment that are either specifically or otherwise required by the airworthiness requirements under which the airplane is type certificated and which are essential for safe operations under all operating conditions.

(2) Instruments and equipment required by an airworthiness directive to be in operable condition unless the airworthiness directive provides otherwise.

(3) Instruments and equipment required for specific operations by this part.

(c) Notwithstanding paragraphs (b)(1) and (b)(3) of this section, an airplane with inoperable instruments or equipment may be operated under a special flight permit under §§ 21.197 and 21.199 of this chapter.

[Doc. No. 25780, 56 FR 12310, Mar. 22, 1991, as amended by Docket FAA-2018-0119, Amdt. 125-68, 83 FR 9174, Mar. 5, 2018]

§ 125.203 Communication and navigation equipment.

(a) *Communication equipment—general.* No person may operate an airplane unless it has two-way radio communication equipment able, at least in flight, to transmit to, and receive from, appropriate facilities 22 nautical miles away.

(b) *Navigation equipment for operations over the top.* No person may operate an airplane over the top unless it has navigation equipment suitable for the route to be flown.

(c) *Communication and navigation equipment for IFR or extended over-water operations—General.* Except as provided in paragraph (f) of this section, no person may operate an airplane carrying passengers under IFR or in extended over-water operations unless—

(1) The en route navigation aids necessary for navigating the airplane along the route (e.g., ATS routes, arrival and departure routes, and instrument approach procedures, including missed approach procedures if a missed approach routing is specified in the procedure) are available and suitable for use by the aircraft navigation systems required by this section;

(2) The airplane used in those operations is equipped with at least the following equipment—

(i) Except as provided in paragraph (d) of this section, two approved independent navigation systems suitable for navigating the airplane along the route within the degree of accuracy required for ATC;

(ii) One marker beacon receiver providing visual and aural signals;

(iii) One ILS receiver;

(iv) Two transmitters;

(v) Two microphones;

(vi) Two headsets or one headset and one speaker; and

(vii) Two independent communication systems, one of which must have two-way voice communication capability, capable of transmitting to, and receiving from, at least one appropriate facility from any place on the route to be flown; and

(3) Any RNAV system used to meet the navigation equipment requirements of this section is authorized in the certificate holder's operations specifications.

(d) *Use of a single independent navigation system for operations under IFR—not for extended overwater operations.* Notwithstanding the requirements of paragraph (c)(2)(i) of this section, the airplane may be equipped with a single independent navigation system suitable for navigating the airplane along the route to be flown within the degree of accuracy required for ATC if—

(1) It can be shown that the airplane is equipped with at least one other independent navigation system suitable, in the event of loss of the navigation capability of the single independent navigation system permitted by this paragraph at any point along the route, for proceeding safely to a suitable airport and completing an instrument approach; and

(2) The airplane has sufficient fuel so that the flight may proceed safely to a suitable airport by use of the remaining navigation system, and complete an instrument approach and land.

(e) *Use of VOR navigation equipment.* If VOR navigation equipment is required by paragraph (c) or (d) of this section, no person may operate an airplane unless it is equipped with at least one approved DME or a suitable RNAV system.

(f) *Extended over-water operations.* Notwithstanding the requirements of

paragraph (c) of this section, installation and use of a single long-range navigation system and a single long-range communication system for extended over-water operations in certain geographic areas may be authorized by the Administrator and approved in the certificate holder's operations specifications. The following are among the operational factors the Administrator may consider in granting an authorization:

(1) The ability of the flight crew to navigate the airplane along the route to be flown within the degree of accuracy required for ATC;

(2) The length of the route being flown; and

(3) The duration of the very high frequency communications gap.

[Doc. No. FAA–2002–14002, 72 FR 31682, June 7, 2007]

§125.204 **Portable electronic devices.**

(a) Except as provided in paragraph (b) of this section, no person may operate, nor may any operator or pilot in command of an aircraft allow the operation of, any portable electronic device on any U.S.-registered civil aircraft operating under this part.

(b) Paragraph (a) of this section does not apply to—

(1) Portable voice recorders;

(2) Hearing aids;

(3) Heart pacemakers;

(4) Electric shavers;

(5) Portable oxygen concentrators that comply with the requirements in §125.219; or

(6) Any other portable electronic device that the Part 125 certificate holder has determined will not cause interference with the navigation or communication system of the aircraft on which it is to be used.

(c) The determination required by paragraph (b)(6) of this section shall be made by that Part 125 certificate holder operating the particular device to be used.

[Doc. No. FAA–1998–4954, 64 FR 1080, Jan. 7, 1999, as amended by Docket FAA–2014–0554, Amdt. 125–65, 81 FR 33118, May 24, 2016]

§125.205 **Equipment requirements: Airplanes under IFR.**

No person may operate an airplane under IFR unless it has—

(a) A vertical speed indicator;

(b) A free-air temperature indicator;

(c) A heated pitot tube for each airspeed indicator;

(d) A power failure warning device or vacuum indicator to show the power available for gyroscopic instruments from each power source;

(e) An alternate source of static pressure for the altimeter and the airspeed and vertical speed indicators;

(f) At least two generators each of which is on a separate engine, or which any combination of one-half of the total number are rated sufficiently to supply the electrical loads of all required instruments and equipment necessary for safe emergency operation of the airplane; and

(g) Two independent sources of energy (with means of selecting either), of which at least one is an engine-driven pump or generator, each of which is able to drive all gyroscopic instruments and installed so that failure of one instrument or source does not interfere with the energy supply to the remaining instruments or the other energy source. For the purposes of this paragraph, each engine-driven source of energy must be on a different engine.

(h) For the purposes of paragraph (f) of this section, a continuous inflight electrical load includes one that draws current continuously during flight, such as radio equipment, electrically driven instruments, and lights, but does not include occasional intermittent loads.

(i) An airspeed indicating system with heated pitot tube or equivalent means for preventing malfunctioning due to icing.

(j) A sensitive altimeter.

(k) Instrument lights providing enough light to make each required instrument, switch, or similar instrument easily readable and installed so that the direct rays are shielded from the flight crewmembers' eyes and that no objectionable reflections are visible to them. There must be a means of controlling the intensity of illumination unless it is shown that nondimming instrument lights are satisfactory.

§ 125.206   Pitot heat indication systems.

(a) Except as provided in paragraph (b) of this section, after April 12, 1981, no person may operate a transport category airplane equipped with a flight instrument pitot heating system unless the airplane is equipped with an operable pitot heat indication system that complies with § 25.1326 of this chapter in effect on April 12, 1978.

(b) A certificate holder may obtain an extension of the April 12, 1981, compliance date specified in paragraph (a) of this section, but not beyond April 12, 1983, from the Executive Director, Flight Standards Service if the certificate holder—

(1) Shows that due to circumstances beyond its control it cannot comply by the specified compliance date; and

(2) Submits by the specified compliance date a schedule for compliance acceptable to the Executive Director, indicating that compliance will be achieved at the earliest practicable date.

[Doc. No. 18904, 46 FR 43806, Aug. 31, 1981, as amended by Amdt. 125–13, 54 FR 39294, Sept. 25, 1989; Docket FAA–2018–0119, Amdt. 125–68, 83 FR 9174, Mar. 5, 2018]

§ 125.207   Emergency equipment requirements.

(a) No person may operate an airplane having a seating capacity of 20 or more passengers unless it is equipped with the following emergency equipment:

(1) One approved first aid kit for treatment of injuries likely to occur in flight or in a minor accident, which meets the following specifications and requirements:

(i) Each first aid kit must be dust and moisture proof and contain only materials that either meet Federal Specifications GGK–391a, as revised, or as approved by the Administrator.

(ii) Required first aid kits must be readily accessible to the cabin flight attendants.

(iii) Except as provided in paragraph (a)(1)(iv) of this section, at time of takeoff, each first aid kit must contain at least the following or other contents approved by the Administrator:

Contents	Quantity
Adhesive bandage compressors, 1 in	16

Contents	Quantity
Antiseptic swabs	20
Ammonia inhalants	10
Bandage compressors, 4 in	8
Triangular bandage compressors, 40 in	5
Arm splint, noninflatable	1
Leg splint, noninflatable	1
Roller bandage, 4 in	4
Adhesive tape, 1-in standard roll	2
Bandage scissors	1
Protective latex gloves or equivalent nonpermeable gloves	[1] 1

[1] Pair.

(iv) Protective latex gloves or equivalent nonpermeable gloves may be placed in the first aid kit or in a location that is readily accessible to crewmembers.

(2) A crash axe carried so as to be accessible to the crew but inaccessible to passengers during normal operations.

(3) Signs that are visible to all occupants to notify them when smoking is prohibited and when safety belts should be fastened. The signs must be so constructed that they can be turned on and off by a crewmember. They must be turned on for each takeoff and each landing and when otherwise considered to be necessary by the pilot in command.

(4) The additional emergency equipment specified in appendix A of this part.

(b) *Megaphones.* Each passenger-carrying airplane must have a portable battery-powered megaphone or megaphones readily accessible to the crewmembers assigned to direct emergency evacuation, installed as follows:

(1) One megaphone on each airplane with a seating capacity of more than 60 and less than 100 passengers, at the most rearward location in the passenger cabin where it would be readily accessible to a normal flight attendant seat. However, the Administrator may grant a deviation from the requirements of this paragraph if the Administrator finds that a different location would be more useful for evacuation of persons during an emergency.

(2) Two megaphones in the passenger cabin on each airplane with a seating capacity of more than 99 and less than 200 passengers, one installed at the forward end and the other at the most rearward location where it would be readily accessible to a normal flight attendant seat.

(3) Three megaphones in the passenger cabin on each airplane with a seating capacity of more than 199 passengers, one installed at the forward end, one installed at the most rearward location where it would be readily accessible to a normal flight attendant seat, and one installed in a readily accessible location in the mid-section of the airplane.

[Doc. No. 19779, 45 FR 67235, Oct. 9, 1980, as amended by Amdt. 125–19, 59 FR 1781, Jan. 12, 1994; Amdt. 125–22, 59 FR 52643, Oct. 18, 1994; 59 FR 55208, Nov. 4, 1994]

§125.209 Emergency equipment: Extended overwater operations.

(a) No person may operate an airplane in extended overwater operations unless it carries, installed in conspicuously marked locations easily accessible to the occupants if a ditching occurs, the following equipment:

(1) An approved life preserver equipped with an approved survivor locator light, or an approved flotation means, for each occupant of the aircraft. The life preserver or other flotation means must be easily accessible to each seated occupant. If a flotation means other than a life preserver is used, it must be readily removable from the airplane.

(2) Enough approved life rafts (with proper buoyancy) to carry all occupants of the airplane, and at least the following equipment for each raft clearly marked for easy identification—

(i) One canopy (for sail, sunshade, or rain catcher);

(ii) One radar reflector (or similar device);

(iii) One life raft repair kit;

(iv) One bailing bucket;

(v) One signaling mirror;

(vi) One police whistle;

(vii) One raft knife;

(viii) One CO_2 bottle for emergency inflation;

(ix) One inflation pump;

(x) Two oars;

(xi) One 75-foot retaining line;

(xii) One magnetic compass;

(xiii) One dye marker;

(xiv) One flashlight having at least two size "D" cells or equivalent;

(xv) At least one approved pyrotechnic signaling device;

331

(xvi) A 2-day supply of emergency food rations supplying at least 1,000 calories a day for each person;

(xvii) One sea water desalting kit for each two persons that raft is rated to carry, or two pints of water for each person the raft is rated to carry;

(xviii) One fishing kit; and

(xix) One book on survival appropriate for the area in which the airplane is operated.

(b) No person may operate an airplane in extended overwater operations unless there is attached to one of the life rafts required by paragraph (a) of this section, an approved survival type emergency locator transmitter. Batteries used in this transmitter must be replaced (or recharged, if the batteries are rechargeable) when the transmitter has been in use for more than one cumulative hour, or, when 50 percent of their useful life (or for rechargeable batteries, 50 percent of their useful life of charge) has expired, as established by the transmitter manufacturer under its approval. The new expiration date for replacing (or recharging) the battery must be legibly marked on the outside of the transmitter. The battery useful life (or useful life of charge) requirements of this paragraph do not apply to batteries (such as water-activated batteries) that are essentially unaffected during probable storage intervals.

[Doc. No. 19779, 45 FR 67235, Oct. 9, 1980, as amended by Amdt. 125–20, 59 FR 32058, June 21, 1994]

§ 125.211 Seat and safety belts.

(a) No person may operate an airplane unless there are available during the takeoff, en route flight, and landing—

(1) An approved seat or berth for each person on board the airplane who is at least 2 years old; and

(2) An approved safety belt for separate use by each person on board the airplane who is at least 2 years old, except that two persons occupying a berth may share one approved safety belt and two persons occupying a multiple lounge or divan seat may share one approved safety belt during en route flight only.

(b) Except as provided in paragraphs (b)(1) and (b)(2) of this section, each

person on board an airplane operated under this part shall occupy an approved seat or berth with a separate safety belt properly secured about him or her during movement on the surface, takeoff, and landing. A safety belt provided for the occupant of a seat may not be used for more than one person who has reached his or her second birthday. Notwithstanding the preceding requirements, a child may:

(1) Be held by an adult who is occupying an approved seat or berth, provided the child has not reached his or her second birthday and the child does not occupy or use any restraining device; or

(2) Notwithstanding any other requirement of this chapter, occupy an approved child restraint system furnished by the certificate holder or one of the persons described in paragraph (b)(2)(i) of this section, provided:

(i) The child is accompanied by a parent, guardian, or attendant designated by the child's parent or guardian to attend to the safety of the child during the flight;

(ii) Except as provided in paragraph (b)(2)(ii)(D) of this section, the approved child restraint system bears one or more labels as follows:

(A) Seats manufactured to U.S. standards between January 1, 1981, and February 25, 1985, must bear the label: "This child restraint system conforms to all applicable Federal motor vehicle safety standards";

(B) Seats manufactured to U.S. standards on or after February 26, 1985, must bear two labels:

(1) "This child restraint system conforms to all applicable Federal motor vehicle safety standards"; and

(2) "THIS RESTRAINT IS CERTIFIED FOR USE IN MOTOR VEHICLES AND AIRCRAFT" in red lettering;

(C) Seats that do not qualify under paragraphs (b)(2)(ii)(A) and (b)(2)(ii)(B) of this section must bear a label or markings showing:

(1) That the seat was approved by a foreign government;

(2) That the seat was manufactured under the standards of the United Nations;

(3) That the seat or child restraint device furnished by the certificate

holder was approved by the FAA through Type Certificate or Supplemental Type Certificate; or

(4) That the seat or child restraint device furnished by the certificate holder, or one of the persons described in paragraph (b)(2)(i) of this section, was approved by the FAA in accordance with §21.8(d) of this chapter or Technical Standard Order C–100b, or a later version. The child restraint device manufactured by AmSafe, Inc. (CARES, Part No. 4082) and approved by the FAA in accordance with §21.305(d) (2010 ed.) of this chapter may continue to bear a label or markings showing FAA approval in accordance with §21.305(d) (2010 ed.) of this chapter.

(D) Except as provided in §125.211(b)(2)(ii)(C)(3) and §125.211(b)(2)(ii)(C)(4), booster-type child restraint systems (as defined in Federal Motor Vehicle Safety Standard No. 213 (49 CFR 571.213)), vest- and harness-type child restraint systems, and lap held child restraints are not approved for use in aircraft; and

(iii) The certificate holder complies with the following requirements:

(A) The restraint system must be properly secured to an approved forward-facing seat or berth;

(B) The child must be properly secured in the restraint system and must not exceed the specified weight limit for the restraint system; and

(C) The restraint system must bear the appropriate label(s).

(c) Except as provided in paragraph (c)(3) of this section, the following prohibitions apply to certificate holders:

(1) Except as provided in §125.211(b)(2)(ii)(C)(3) and §125.211(b)(2)(ii)(C)(4), no certificate holder may permit a child, in an aircraft, to occupy a booster-type child restraint system, a vest-type child restraint system, a harness-type child restraint system, or a lap held child restraint system during take off, landing, and movement on the surface.

(2) Except as required in paragraph (c)(1) of this section, no certificate holder may prohibit a child, if requested by the child's parent, guardian, or designated attendant, from occupying a child restraint system furnished by the child's parent, guardian, or designated attendant provided:

(i) The child holds a ticket for an approved seat or berth or such seat or berth is otherwise made available by the certificate holder for the child's use;

(ii) The requirements of paragraph (b)(2)(i) of this section are met;

(iii) The requirements of paragraph (b)(2)(iii) of this section are met; and

(iv) The child restraint system has one or more of the labels described in paragraphs (b)(2)(ii)(A) through (b)(2)(ii)(C) of this section.

(3) This section does not prohibit the certificate holder from providing child restraint systems authorized by this section or, consistent with safe operating practices, determining the most appropriate passenger seat location for the child restraint system.

(d) Each sideward facing seat must comply with the applicable requirements of §25.785(c) of this chapter.

(e) No certificate holder may take off or land an airplane unless each passenger seat back is in the upright position. Each passenger shall comply with instructions given by a crewmember in compliance with this paragraph. This paragraph does not apply to seats on which cargo or persons who are unable to sit erect for a medical reason are carried in accordance with procedures in the certificate holder's manual if the seat back does not obstruct any passenger's access to the aisle or to any emergency exit.

(f) Each occupant of a seat equipped with a shoulder harness must fasten the shoulder harness during takeoff and landing, except that, in the case of crewmembers, the shoulder harness need not be fastened if the crewmember cannot perform his required duties with the shoulder harness fastened.

[Doc. No. 19799, 45 FR 67235, Oct. 9, 1980, as amended by Amdt. 125–17, 57 FR 42674, Sept. 15, 1992; Amdt. 125–26, 61 FR 28422, June 4, 1996; Amdt. 125–48, 70 FR 50907, Aug. 26, 2005; Amdt. 125–51, 71 FR 40009, July 14, 2006; 71 FR 59373, Oct. 10, 2006; Amdt. 125–64, 79 FR 28812, May 20, 2014]

§125.213 Miscellaneous equipment.

No person may conduct any operation unless the following equipment is installed in the airplane:

(a) If protective fuses are installed on an airplane, the number of spare fuses approved for the airplane and appropriately described in the certificate holder's manual.

(b) A windshield wiper or equivalent for each pilot station.

(c) A power supply and distribution system that meets the requirements of §§ 25.1309, 25.1331, 25.1351 (a) and (b) (1) through (4), 25.1353, 25.1355, and 25.1431(b) or that is able to produce and distribute the load for the required instruments and equipment, with use of an external power supply if any one power source or component of the power distribution system fails. The use of common elements in the system may be approved if the Administrator finds that they are designed to be reasonably protected against malfunctioning. Engine-driven sources of energy, when used, must be on separate engines.

(d) A means for indicating the adequacy of the power being supplied to required flight instruments.

(e) Two independent static pressure systems, vented to the outside atmospheric pressure so that they will be least affected by air flow variation or moisture or other foreign matter, and installed so as to be airtight except for the vent. When a means is provided for transferring an instrument from its primary operating system to an alternative system, the means must include a positive positioning control and must be marked to indicate clearly which system is being used.

(f) A placard on each door that is the means of access to a required passenger emergency exit to indicate that it must be open during takeoff and landing.

(g) A means for the crew, in an emergency, to unlock each door that leads to a compartment that is normally accessible to passengers and that can be locked by passengers.

§ 125.215 Operating information required.

(a) The operator of an airplane must provide the following materials, in current and appropriate form, accessible to the pilot at the pilot station, and the pilot shall use them:

(1) A cockpit checklist.

(2) An emergency cockpit checklist containing the procedures required by paragraph (c) of this section, as appropriate.

(3) Pertinent aeronautical charts.

(4) For IFR operations, each pertinent navigational en route, terminal area, and approach and letdown chart;

(5) One-engine-inoperative climb performance data and, if the airplane is approved for use in IFR or over-the-top operations, that data must be sufficient to enable the pilot to determine that the airplane is capable of carrying passengers over-the-top or in IFR conditions at a weight that will allow it to climb, with the critical engine inoperative, at least 50 feet a minute when operating at the MEA's of the route to be flown or 5,000 feet MSL, whichever is higher.

(b) Each cockpit checklist required by paragraph (a)(1) of this section must contain the following procedures:

(1) Before starting engines;

(2) Before take-off;

(3) Cruise;

(4) Before landing;

(5) After landing;

(6) Stopping engines.

(c) Each emergency cockpit checklist required by paragraph (a)(2) of this section must contain the following procedures, as appropriate:

(1) Emergency operation of fuel, hydraulic, electrical, and mechanical systems.

(2) Emergency operation of instruments and controls.

(3) Engine inoperative procedures.

(4) Any other emergency procedures necessary for safety.

§ 125.217 Passenger information.

(a) Except as provided in paragraph (b) of this section, no person may operate an airplane carrying passengers unless it is equipped with signs that meet the requirements of § 25.791 of this chapter and that are visible to passengers and flight attendants to notify them when smoking is prohibited and when safety belts must be fastened. The signs must be so constructed that the crew can turn them on and off. They must be turned on during airplane movement on the surface, for each takeoff, for each landing, and when otherwise considered to be necessary by the pilot in command.

(b) No passenger or crewmember may smoke while any "No Smoking" sign is lighted nor may any passenger or crewmember smoke in any lavatory.

(c) Each passenger required by §125.211(b) to occupy a seat or berth shall fasten his or her safety belt about him or her and keep it fastened while any "Fasten Seat Belt" sign is lighted.

(d) Each passenger shall comply with instructions given him or her by crewmembers regarding compliance with paragraphs (b) and (c) of this section.

[Doc. No. 26142, 57 FR 42675, Sept. 15, 1992]

§125.219 Oxygen and portable oxygen concentrators for medical use by passengers.

(a) Except as provided in paragraphs (d) and (f) of this section, no certificate holder may allow the carriage or operation of equipment for the storage, generation or dispensing of medical oxygen unless the conditions in paragraphs (a) through (c) of this section are satisfied. Beginning August 22, 2016, a certificate holder may allow a passenger to carry and operate a portable oxygen concentrator when the conditions in paragraphs (b) and (f) of this section are satisfied.

(1) The equipment must be—

(i) Of an approved type or in conformity with the manufacturing, packaging, marking, labeling, and maintenance requirements of title 49 CFR parts 171, 172, and 173, except §173.24(a)(1);

(ii) When owned by the certificate holder, maintained under the certificate holder's approved maintenance program;

(iii) Free of flammable contaminants on all exterior surfaces;

(iv) Constructed so that all valves, fittings, and gauges are protected from damage during that carriage or operation; and

(v) Appropriately secured.

(2) When the oxygen is stored in the form of a liquid, the equipment must have been under the certificate holder's approved maintenance program since its purchase new or since the storage container was last purged.

(3) When the oxygen is stored in the form of a compressed gas as defined in title 49 CFR 173.115(b)—

(i) When owned by the certificate holder, it must be maintained under its approved maintenance program; and

(ii) The pressure in any oxygen cylinder must not exceed the rated cylinder pressure.

(4) The pilot in command must be advised when the equipment is on board and when it is intended to be used.

(5) The equipment must be stowed, and each person using the equipment must be seated so as not to restrict access to or use of any required emergency or regular exit or of the aisle in the passenger compartment.

(b) No person may smoke or create an open flame and no certificate holder may allow any person to smoke or create an open flame within 10 feet of oxygen storage and dispensing equipment carried under paragraph (a) of this section or a portable oxygen concentrator carried and operated under paragraph (f) of this section.

(c) No certificate holder may allow any person other than a person trained in the use of medical oxygen equipment to connect or disconnect oxygen bottles or any other ancillary component while any passenger is aboard the airplane.

(d) Paragraph (a)(1)(i) of this section does not apply when that equipment is furnished by a professional or medical emergency service for use on board an airplane in a medical emergency when no other practical means of transportation (including any other properly equipped certificate holder) is reasonably available and the person carried under the medical emergency is accompanied by a person trained in the use of medical oxygen.

(e) Each certificate holder who, under the authority of paragraph (d) of this section, deviates from paragraph (a)(1)(i) of this section under a medical emergency shall, within 10 days, excluding Saturdays, Sundays, and Federal holidays, after the deviation, send to the responsible Flight Standards office charged with the overall inspection of the certificate holder a complete report of the operation involved, including a description of the deviation and the reasons for it.

(f) *Portable oxygen concentrators*—(1) *Acceptance criteria.* A passenger may carry or operate a portable oxygen concentrator for personal use on board an aircraft and a certificate holder may allow a passenger to carry or operate a portable oxygen concentrator on board an aircraft operated under this part during all phases of flight if the portable oxygen concentrator satisfies all of the requirements in this paragraph (f):

(i) Is legally marketed in the United States in accordance with Food and Drug Administration requirements in title 21 of the CFR;

(ii) Does not radiate radio frequency emissions that interfere with aircraft systems;

(iii) Generates a maximum oxygen pressure of less than 200 kPa gauge (29.0 psig/43.8 psia) at 20 °C (68 °F);

(iv) Does not contain any hazardous materials subject to the Hazardous Materials Regulations (49 CFR parts 171 through 180) except as provided in 49 CFR 175.10 for batteries used to power portable electronic devices and that do not require aircraft operator approval; and

(v) Bears a label on the exterior of the device applied in a manner that ensures the label will remain affixed for the life of the device and containing the following certification statement in red lettering: "The manufacturer of this POC has determined this device conforms to all applicable FAA acceptance criteria for POC carriage and use on board aircraft." The label requirements in this paragraph (f)(1)(v) do not apply to the following portable oxygen concentrators approved by the FAA for use on board aircraft prior to May 24, 2016:

(A) AirSep Focus;

(B) AirSep FreeStyle;

(C) AirSep FreeStyle 5;

(D) AirSep LifeStyle;

(E) Delphi RS–00400;

(F) DeVilbiss Healthcare iGo;

(G) Inogen One;

(H) Inogen One G2;

(I) Inogen One G3;

(J) Inova Labs LifeChoice;

(K) Inova Labs LifeChoice Activox;

(L) International Biophysics LifeChoice;

(M) Invacare Solo2;

(N) Invacare XPO2;

(O) Oxlife Independence Oxygen Concentrator;

(P) Oxus RS–00400;

(Q) Precision Medical EasyPulse;

(R) Respironics EverGo;

(S) Respironics SimplyGo;

(T) SeQual Eclipse;

(U) SeQual eQuinox Oxygen System (model 4000);

(V) SeQual Oxywell Oxygen System (model 4000);

(W) SeQual SAROS; and

(X) VBox Trooper Oxygen Concentrator.

(2) *Operating requirements.* Portable oxygen concentrators that satisfy the acceptance criteria identified in paragraph (f)(1) of this section may be carried or used by a passenger on an aircraft provided the aircraft operator ensures that all of the conditions in this paragraph (f)(2) are satisfied:

(i) *Exit seats.* No person operating a portable oxygen concentrator is permitted to occupy an exit seat.

(ii) *Stowage of device.* During movement on the surface, takeoff and landing, the device must be stowed under the seat in front of the user, or in another approved stowage location so that it does not block the aisle way or the entryway to the row. If the device is to be operated by the user, it must be operated only at a seat location that does not restrict any passenger's access to, or use of, any required emergency or regular exit, or the aisle(s) in the passenger compartment.

[Docket No. 19779, 45 FR 67235, Oct. 9, 1980, as amended by Docket FAA–2014–0554, Amdt. 125–65, 81 FR 33119, May 24, 2016; Docket FAA–2018–0119, Amdt. 125–68, 83 FR 9173, Mar. 5, 2018]

§ 125.221   Icing conditions: Operating limitations.

(a) No pilot may take off an airplane that has frost, ice, or snow adhering to any propeller, windshield, stabilizing or control surface; to a powerplant installation; or to an airspeed, altimeter, rate of climb, flight attitude instrument system, or wing, except that takeoffs may be made with frost under the wing in the area of the fuel tanks if authorized by the FAA.

(b) No certificate holder may authorize an airplane to take off and no pilot may take off an airplane any time conditions are such that frost, ice, or snow may reasonably be expected to adhere to the airplane unless the pilot has completed the testing required under §125.287(a)(9) and unless one of the following requirements is met:

(1) A pretakeoff contamination check, that has been established by the certificate holder and approved by the Administrator for the specific airplane type, has been completed within 5 minutes prior to beginning takeoff. A pretakeoff contamination check is a check to make sure the wings and control surfaces are free of frost, ice, or snow.

(2) The certificate holder has an approved alternative procedure and under that procedure the airplane is determined to be free of frost, ice, or snow.

(3) The certificate holder has an approved deicing/anti-icing program that complies with §121.629(c) of this chapter and the takeoff complies with that program.

(c) No pilot may fly under IFR into known or forecast light or moderate icing conditions, or under VFR into known light or moderate icing conditions, unless—

(1) The aircraft has functioning deicing or anti-icing equipment protecting each propeller, windshield, wing, stabilizing or control surface, and each airspeed, altimeter, rate of climb, or flight attitude instrument system;

(2) The airplane has ice protection provisions that meet appendix C of this part; or

(3) The airplane meets transport category airplane type certification provisions, including the requirements for certification for flight in icing conditions.

(d) Except for an airplane that has ice protection provisions that meet appendix C of this part or those for transport category airplane type certification, no pilot may fly an airplane into known or forecast severe icing conditions.

(e) If current weather reports and briefing information relied upon by the pilot in command indicate that the forecast icing condition that would otherwise prohibit the flight will not be encountered during the flight because of changed weather conditions since the forecast, the restrictions in paragraphs (b) and (c) of this section based on forecast conditions do not apply.

[45 FR 67235, Oct. 9, 1980, as amended by Amdt. 125–18, 58 FR 69629, Dec. 30, 1993; Amdt. 125–58, 74 FR 62696, Dec. 1, 2009]

§125.223 Airborne weather radar equipment requirements.

(a) No person may operate an airplane governed by this part in passenger-carrying operations unless approved airborne weather radar equipment is installed in the airplane.

(b) No person may begin a flight under IFR or night VFR conditions when current weather reports indicate that thunderstorms, or other potentially hazardous weather conditions that can be detected with airborne weather radar equipment, may reasonably be expected along the route to be flown, unless the airborne weather radar equipment required by paragraph (a) of this section is in satisfactory operating condition.

(c) If the airborne weather radar equipment becomes inoperative en route, the airplane must be operated under the instructions and procedures specified for that event in the manual required by §125.71.

(d) This section does not apply to airplanes used solely within the State of Hawaii, within the State of Alaska, within that part of Canada west of longitude 130 degrees W, between latitude 70 degrees N, and latitude 53 degrees N, or during any training, test, or ferry flight.

(e) Without regard to any other provision of this part, an alternate electrical power supply is not required for airborne weather radar equipment.

§125.224 Collision avoidance system.

Effective January 1, 2005, any airplane you operate under this part 125 must be equipped and operated according to the following table:

COLLISION AVOIDANCE SYSTEMS

If you operate any . . .	Then you must operate that airplane with:
(a) Turbine-powered airplane of more than 33,000 pounds maximum certificated take-off weight.	(1) An appropriate class of Mode S transponder that meets Technical Standard Order (TSO) C–112, or a later version, and one of the following approved units: (i) TCAS II that meets TSO C–119b (version 7.0), or a later version. (ii) TCAS II that meets TSO C–119a (version 6.04A Enhanced) that was installed in that airplane before May 1, 2003. If that TCAS II version 6.04A Enhanced no longer can be repaired to TSO C–119a standards, it must be replaced with a TCAS II that meets TSO C–119b (version 7.0), or a later version. (iii) A collision avoidance system equivalent to TSO C–119b (version 7.0), or a later version, capable of coordinating with units that meet TSO C–119a (version 6.04A Enhanced), or a later version.
(b) Piston-powered airplane of more than 33,000 pounds maximum certificated take-off weight.	(1) TCAS I that meets TSO C–118, or a later version, or (2) A collision avoidance system equivalent to TSO C–118, or a later version, or (1)(3) A collision avoidance system and Mode S transponder that meet paragraph (a)(1) of this section.

[Doc. No. FAA–2001–10910, 68 FR 15903, Apr. 1, 2003]

§ 125.225 **Flight data recorders.**

(a) Except as provided in paragraph (d) of this section, after October 11, 1991, no person may operate a large airplane type certificated before October 1, 1969, for operations above 25,000 feet altitude, nor a multiengine, turbine powered airplane type certificated before October 1, 1969, unless it is equipped with one or more approved flight recorders that utilize a digital method of recording and storing data and a method of readily retrieving that data from the storage medium. The following information must be able to be determined within the ranges, accuracies, resolution, and recording intervals specified in appendix D of this part:

(1) Time;
(2) Altitude;
(3) Airspeed;
(4) Vertical acceleration;
(5) Heading;
(6) Time of each radio transmission to or from air traffic control;
(7) Pitch attitude;

(8) Roll attitude;
(9) Longitudinal acceleration;
(10) Control column or pitch control surface position; and
(11) Thrust of each engine.

(b) Except as provided in paragraph (d) of this section, after October 11, 1991, no person may operate a large airplane type certificated after September 30, 1969, for operations above 25,000 feet altitude, nor a multiengine, turbine powered airplane type certificated after September 30, 1969, unless it is equipped with one or more approved flight recorders that utilize a digital method of recording and storing data and a method of readily retrieving that data from the storage medium. The following information must be able to be determined within the ranges, accuracies, resolutions, and recording intervals specified in appendix D of this part:

(1) Time;
(2) Altitude;
(3) Airspeed;
(4) Vertical acceleration;
(5) Heading;
(6) Time of each radio transmission either to or from air traffic control;
(7) Pitch attitude;
(8) Roll attitude;
(9) Longitudinal acceleration;
(10) Pitch trim position;
(11) Control column or pitch control surface position;
(12) Control wheel or lateral control surface position;
(13) Rudder pedal or yaw control surface position;
(14) Thrust of each engine;
(15) Position of each trust reverser;
(16) Trailing edge flap or cockpit flap control position; and
(17) Leading edge flap or cockpit flap control position.

(c) After October 11, 1991, no person may operate a large airplane equipped with a digital data bus and ARINC 717 digital flight data acquisition unit (DFDAU) or equivalent unless it is equipped with one or more approved flight recorders that utilize a digital method of recording and storing data and a method of readily retrieving that data from the storage medium. Any parameters specified in appendix D of this part that are available on the digital data bus must be recorded within the ranges, accuracies, resolutions, and sampling intervals specified.

(d) No person may operate under this part an airplane that is manufactured after October 11, 1991, unless it is equipped with one or more approved flight recorders that utilize a digital method of recording and storing data and a method of readily retrieving that data from the storage medium. The parameters specified in appendix D of this part must be recorded within the ranges, accuracies, resolutions and sampling intervals specified. For the purpose of this section, "manufactured" means the point in time at which the airplane inspection acceptance records reflect that the airplane is complete and meets the FAA-approved type design data.

(e) Whenever a flight recorder required by this section is installed, it must be operated continuously from the instant the airplane begins the takeoff roll until it has completed the landing roll at an airport.

(f) Except as provided in paragraph (g) of this section, and except for recorded data erased as authorized in this paragraph, each certificate holder shall keep the recorded data prescribed in paragraph (a), (b), (c), or (d) of this section, as applicable, until the airplane has been operated for at least 25 hours of the operating time specified in §125.227(a) of this chapter. A total of 1 hour of recorded data may be erased for the purpose of testing the flight recorder or the flight recorder system. Any erasure made in accordance with this paragraph must be of the oldest recorded data accumulated at the time of testing. Except as provided in paragraph (g) of this section, no record need be kept more than 60 days.

(g) In the event of an accident or occurrence that requires immediate notification of the National Transportation Safety Board under 49 CFR part 830 and that results in termination of the flight, the certificate holder shall remove the recording media from the airplane and keep the recorded data required by paragraph (a), (b), (c), or (d) of this section, as applicable, for at least 60 days or for a longer period upon the request of the Board or the Administrator.

(h) Each flight recorder required by this section must be installed in accordance with the requirements of §25.1459 of this chapter in effect on August 31, 1977. The correlation required by §25.1459(c) of this chapter need be established only on one airplane of any group of airplanes.

(1) That are of the same type;

(2) On which the flight recorder models and their installations are the same; and

(3) On which there are no differences in the type design with respect to the installation of the first pilot's instruments associated with the flight recorder. The most recent instrument calibration, including the recording medium from which this calibration is derived, and the recorder correlation must be retained by the certificate holder.

(i) Each flight recorder required by this section that records the data specified in paragraphs (a), (b), (c), or (d) of this section must have an approved device to assist in locating that recorder under water.

(j) After August 20, 2001, this section applies only to the airplane models listed in §125.226(l)(2). All other airplanes must comply with the requirements of §125.226.

[Doc. No. 25530, 53 FR 26148, July 11, 1988; 53 FR 30906, Aug. 16, 1988; Amdt. 125–54, 73 FR 12568, Mar. 7, 2008]

§125.226 Digital flight data recorders.

(a) Except as provided in paragraph (l) of this section, no person may operate under this part a turbine-engine-powered transport category airplane unless it is equipped with one or more approved flight recorders that use a digital method of recording and storing data and a method of readily retrieving that data from the storage medium. The operational parameters required to be recorded by digital flight data recorders required by this section are as follows: the phrase "when an information source is installed" following a parameter indicates that recording of that parameter is not intended to require a change in installed equipment:

(1) Time;

(2) Pressure altitude;

(3) Indicated airspeed;

(4) Heading—primary flight crew reference (if selectable, record discrete, true or magnetic);

(5) Normal acceleration (Vertical);

(6) Pitch attitude;

(7) Roll attitude;

(8) Manual radio transmitter keying, or CVR/DFDR synchronization reference;

(9) Thrust/power of each engine—primary flight crew reference;

(10) Autopilot engagement status;

(11) Longitudinal acceleration;

(12) Pitch control input;

(13) Lateral control input;

(14) Rudder pedal input;

(15) Primary pitch control surface position;

(16) Primary lateral control surface position;

(17) Primary yaw control surface position;

(18) Lateral acceleration;

(19) Pitch trim surface position or parameters of paragraph (a)(82) of this section if currently recorded;

(20) Trailing edge flap or cockpit flap control selection (except when parameters of paragraph (a)(85) of this section apply);

(21) Leading edge flap or cockpit flap control selection (except when parameters of paragraph (a)(86) of this section apply);

(22) Each Thrust reverser position (or equivalent for propeller airplane);

(23) Ground spoiler position or speed brake selection (except when parameters of paragraph (a)(87) of this section apply);

(24) Outside or total air temperature;

(25) Automatic Flight Control System (AFCS) modes and engagement status, including autothrottle;

(26) Radio altitude (when an information source is installed);

(27) Localizer deviation, MLS Azimuth;

(28) Glideslope deviation, MLS Elevation;

(29) Marker beacon passage;

(30) Master warning;

(31) Air/ground sensor (primary airplane system reference nose or main gear);

(32) Angle of attack (when information source is installed);

(33) Hydraulic pressure low (each system);

(34) Ground speed (when an information source is installed);

(35) Ground proximity warning system;

(36) Landing gear position or landing gear cockpit control selection;

(37) Drift angle (when an information source is installed);

(38) Wind speed and direction (when an information source is installed);

(39) Latitude and longitude (when an information source is installed);

(40) Stick shaker/pusher (when an information source is installed);

(41) Windshear (when an information source is installed);

(42) Throttle/power lever position;

(43) Additional engine parameters (as designed in appendix E of this part);

(44) Traffic alert and collision avoidance system;

(45) DME 1 and 2 distances;

(46) Nav 1 and 2 selected frequency;

(47) Selected barometric setting (when an information source is installed);

(48) Selected altitude (when an information source is installed);

(49) Selected speed (when an information source is installed);

(50) Selected mach (when an information source is installed);

(51) Selected vertical speed (when an information source is installed);

(52) Selected heading (when an information source is installed);

(53) Selected flight path (when an information source is installed);

(54) Selected decision height (when an information source is installed);

(55) EFIS display format;

(56) Multi-function/engine/alerts display format;

(57) Thrust command (when an information source is installed);

(58) Thrust target (when an information source is installed);

(59) Fuel quantity in CG trim tank (when an information source is installed);

(60) Primary Navigation System Reference;

(61) Icing (when an information source is installed);

(62) Engine warning each engine vibration (when an information source is installed);

340

(63) Engine warning each engine over temp. (when an information source is installed);

(64) Engine warning each engine oil pressure low (when an information source is installed);

(65) Engine warning each engine over speed (when an information source is installed);

(66) Yaw trim surface position;

(67) Roll trim surface position;

(68) Brake pressure (selected system);

(69) Brake pedal application (left and right);

(70) Yaw of sideslip angle (when an information source is installed);

(71) Engine bleed valve position (when an information source is installed);

(72) De-icing or anti-icing system selection (when an information source is installed);

(73) Computed center of gravity (when an information source is installed);

(74) AC electrical bus status;

(75) DC electrical bus status;

(76) APU bleed valve position (when an information source is installed);

(77) Hydraulic pressure (each system);

(78) Loss of cabin pressure;

(79) Computer failure;

(80) Heads-up display (when an information source is installed);

(81) Para-visual display (when an information source is installed);

(82) Cockpit trim control input position-pitch;

(83) Cockpit trim control input position—roll;

(84) Cockpit trim control input position—yaw;

(85) Trailing edge flap and cockpit flap control position;

(86) Leading edge flap and cockpit flap control position;

(87) Ground spoiler position and speed brake selection;

(88) All cockpit flight control input forces (control wheel, control column, rudder pedal);

(89) Yaw damper status;

(90) Yaw damper command; and

(91) Standby rudder valve status.

(b) For all turbine-engine powered transport category airplanes manufactured on or before October 11, 1991, by August 20, 2001—

(1) For airplanes not equipped as of July 16, 1996, with a flight data acquisition unit (FDAU), the parameters listed in paragraphs (a)(1) through (a)(18) of this section must be recorded within the ranges and accuracies specified in Appendix D of this part, and—

(i) For airplanes with more than two engines, the parameter described in paragraph (a)(18) is not required unless sufficient capacity is available on the existing recorder to record that parameter.

(ii) Parameters listed in paragraphs (a)(12) through (a)(17) each may be recorded from a single source.

(2) For airplanes that were equipped as of July 16, 1996, with a flight data acquisition unit (FDAU), the parameters listed in paragraphs (a)(1) through (a)(22) of this section must be recorded within the ranges, accuracies, and recording intervals specified in Appendix E of this part. Parameters listed in paragraphs (a)(12) through (a)(17) each may be recorded from a single source.

(3) The approved flight recorder required by this section must be installed at the earliest time practicable, but no later than the next heavy maintenance check after August 18, 1999 and no later than August 20, 2001. A heavy maintenance check is considered to be any time an airplane is scheduled to be out of service for 4 or more days and is scheduled to include access to major structural components.

(c) For all turbine-engine-powered transport category airplanes manufactured on or before October 11, 1991—

(1) That were equipped as of July 16, 1996, with one or more digital data bus(es) and an ARINC 717 digital flight data acquisition unit (DFDAU) or equivalent, the parameters specified in paragraphs (a)(1) through (a)(22) of this section must be recorded within the ranges, accuracies, resolutions, and sampling intervals specified in Appendix E of this part by August 20, 2001. Parameters listed in paragraphs (a)(12) through (a)(14) each may be recorded from a single source.

(2) Commensurate with the capacity of the recording system (DFDAU or equivalent and the DFDR), all additional parameters for which information sources are installed and which

are connected to the recording system must be recorded within the ranges, accuracies, resolutions, and sampling intervals specified in Appendix E of this part by August 20, 2001.

(3) That were subject to § 125.225(e) of this part, all conditions of § 125.225(c) must continue to be met until compliance with paragraph (c)(1) of this section is accomplished.

(d) For all turbine-engine-powered transport category airplanes that were manufactured after October 11, 1991—

(1) The parameters listed in paragraphs (a)(1) through (a)(34) of this section must be recorded within the ranges, accuracies, resolutions, and recording intervals specified in Appendix E of this part by August 20, 2001. Paramaters listed in paragraphs (a)(12) through (a)(14) each may be recorded from a single source.

(2) Commensurate with the capacity of the recording system, all additional parameters for which information sources are installed and which are connected to the recording system, must be recorded within the ranges, accuracies, resolutions, and sampling intervals specified in Appendix E of this part by August 20, 2001.

(e) For all turbine-engine-powered transport category airplanes that are manufactured after August 18, 2000—

(1) The parameters listed in paragraph (a) (1) through (57) of this section must be recorded within the ranges, accuracies, resolutions, and recording intervals specified in Appendix E of this part.

(2) Commensurate with the capacity of the recording system, all additional parameters for which information sources are installed and which are connected to the recording system, must be recorded within the ranges, accuracies, resolutions, and sampling intervals specified in Appendix E of this part.

(3) In addition to the requirements of paragraphs (e)(1) and (e)(2) of this section, all Boeing 737 model airplanes must also comply with the requirements of paragraph (n) of this section, as applicable.

(f) For all turbine-engine-powered transport category airplanes manufactured after August 19, 2002—

(1) The parameters listed in paragraphs (a)(1) through (a)(88) of this section must be recorded within the ranges, accuracies, resolutions, and recording intervals specified in Appendix E to this part.

(2) In addition to the requirements of paragraphs (f)(1) of this section, all Boeing 737 model airplanes must also comply with the requirements of paragraph (n) of this section.

(g) Whenever a flight data recorder required by this section is installed, it must be operated continuously from the instant the airplane begins its takeoff roll until it has completed its landing roll.

(h) Except as provided in paragraph (i) of this section, and except for recorded data erased as authorized in this paragraph, each certificate holder shall keep the recorded data prescribed by this section, as appropriate, until the airplane has been operated for at least 25 hours of the operating time specified in § 121.359(a) of this part. A total of 1 hour of recorded data may be erased for the purpose of testing the flight recorder or the flight recorder system. Any erasure made in accordance with this paragraph must be of the oldest recorded data accumulated at the time of testing. Except as provided in paragraph (i) of this section, no record need to be kept more than 60 days.

(i) In the event of an accident or occurrence that requires immediate notification of the National Transportation Safety Board under 49 CFR 830 of its regulations and that results in termination of the flight, the certificate holder shall remove the recorder from the airplane and keep the recorder data prescribed by this section, as appropriate, for at least 60 days or for a longer period upon the request of the Board or the Administrator.

(j) Each flight data recorder system required by this section must be installed in accordance with the requirements of § 25.1459(a) (except paragraphs (a)(3)(ii) and (7)), (b), (d) and (e) of this chapter. A correlation must be established between the values recorded by the flight data recorder and the corresponding values being measured. The correlation must contain a sufficient number of correlation points to accurately establish the conversion from the recorded values to engineering units or discrete state over the full operating range of the parameter. Except for airplanes having separate altitude and airspeed sensors that are an integral part of the flight data recorder system, a single correlation may be established for any group of airplanes—

(1) That are of the same type;

(2) On which the flight recorder system and its installation are the same; and

(3) On which there is no difference in the type design with respect to the installation of those sensors associated with the flight data recorder system. Documentation sufficient to convert recorded data into the engineering units and discrete values specified in the applicable appendix must be maintained by the certificate holder.

(k) Each flight data recorder required by this section must have an approved device to assist in locating that recorder under water.

(1) The following airplanes that were manufactured before August 18, 1997 need not comply with this section, but must continue to comply with applicable paragraphs of §125.225 of this chapter, as appropriate:

(1) Airplanes that meet the Stage 2 noise levels of part 36 of this chapter and are subject to §91.801(c) of this chapter, until January 1, 2000. On and after January 1, 2000, any Stage 2 airplane otherwise allowed to be operated under Part 91 of this chapter must comply with the applicable flight data recorder requirements of this section for that airplane.

(2) British Aerospace 1–11, General Dynamics Convair 580, General Dynamics Convair 600, General Dynamics Convair 640, deHavilland Aircraft Company Ltd. DHC–7, Fairchild Industries FH 227, Fokker F–27 (except Mark 50), F–28 Mark 1000 and Mark 4000, Gulfstream Aerospace G–159, Jetstream 4100 Series, Lockheed Aircraft Corporation Electra 10–A, Lockheed Aircraft Corporation Electra 10–B, Lockheed Aircraft Corporation Electra 10–E, Lockheed Aircraft Corporation Electra L–188, Lockheed Martin Model 382 (L–100) Hercules, Maryland Air Industries, Inc. F27, Mitsubishi Heavy Industries, Ltd.

YS–11, Short Bros. Limited SD3–30, Short Bros. Limited SD3–60.

(m) All aircraft subject to the requirements of this section that are manufactured on or after April 7, 2010, must have a flight data recorder installed that also—

(1) Meets the requirements in §25.1459(a)(3), (a)(7), and (a)(8) of this chapter; and

(2) Retains the 25 hours of recorded information required in paragraph (f) of this section using a recorder that meets the standards of TSO–C124a, or later revision.

(n) In addition to all other applicable requirements of this section, all Boeing 737 model airplanes manufactured after August 18, 2000 must record the parameters listed in paragraphs (a)(88) through (a)(91) of this section within the ranges, accuracies, resolutions, and recording intervals specified in Appendix E to this part. Compliance with this paragraph is required no later than February 2, 2011.

[Doc. No. 28109, 62 FR 38387, July 17, 1997; 62 FR 48135, Sept. 12, 1997, as amended by Amdt. 125–42, 68 FR 42937, July 18, 2003; 68 FR 50069, Aug. 20, 2003; Amdt. 125–54, 73 FR 12568, Mar. 7, 2008; Amdt. 125–56, 73 FR 73179, Dec. 2, 2008; Amdt. 125–54, 74 FR 32801, 32804, July 9, 2009]

§125.227 Cockpit voice recorders.

(a) No certificate holder may operate a large turbine engine powered airplane or a large pressurized airplane with four reciprocating engines unless an approved cockpit voice recorder is installed in that airplane and is operated continuously from the start of the use of the checklist (before starting engines for the purpose of flight) to completion of the final checklist at the termination of the flight.

(b) Each certificate holder shall establish a schedule for completion, before the prescribed dates, of the cockpit voice recorder installations required by paragraph (a) of this section. In addition, the certificate holder shall identify any airplane specified in paragraph (a) of this section he intends to discontinue using before the prescribed dates.

(c) The cockpit voice recorder required by this section must also meet the following standards:

(1) The requirements of part 25 of this chapter in effect after October 11, 1991.

(2) After September 1, 1980, each recorder container must—

(i) Be either bright orange or bright yellow;

(ii) Have reflective tape affixed to the external surface to facilitate its location under water; and

(iii) Have an approved underwater locating device on or adjacent to the container which is secured in such a manner that it is not likely to be separated during crash impact, unless the cockpit voice recorder and the flight recorder, required by § 125.225 of this chapter, are installed adjacent to each other in such a manner that they are not likely to be separated during crash impact.

(d) In complying with this section, an approved cockpit voice recorder having an erasure feature may be used so that, at any time during the operation of the recorder, information recorded more than 30 minutes earlier may be erased or otherwise obliterated.

(e) For those aircraft equipped to record the uninterrupted audio signals received by a boom or a mask microphone the flight crewmembers are required to use the boom microphone below 18,000 feet mean sea level. No person may operate a large turbine engine powered airplane or a large pressurized airplane with four reciprocating engines manufactured after October 11, 1991, or on which a cockpit voice recorder has been installed after October 11, 1991, unless it is equipped to record the uninterrupted audio signal received by a boom or mask microphone in accordance with § 25.1457(c)(5) of this chapter.

(f) In the event of an accident or occurrence requiring immediate notification of the National Transportation Safety Board under 49 CFR part 830 of its regulations, which results in the termination of the flight, the certificate holder shall keep the recorded information for at least 60 days or, if requested by the Administrator or the Board, for a longer period. Information obtained from the record is used to assist in determining the cause of accidents or occurrences in connection with investigations under 49 CFR part 830. The Administrator does not use the record in any civil penalty or certificate action.

(g) By April 7, 2012, all turbine engine-powered airplanes subject to this section that are manufactured before April 7, 2010, must have a cockpit voice recorder installed that also—

(1) Meets the requirements of § 25.1457(a)(3), (a)(4), (a)(5), and (d)(6) of this chapter;

(2) Retains at least the last 2 hours of recorded information using a recorder that meets the standards of TSO–C123a, or later revision; and

(3) Is operated continuously from the start of the use of the checklist (before starting the engines for the purpose of flight), to the completion of the final checklist at the termination of the flight.

(h) All turbine engine-powered airplanes subject to this section that are manufactured on or after April 7, 2010, must have a cockpit voice recorder installed that also—

(1) Is installed in accordance with the requirements of § 25.1457 (except for paragraph (a)(6)) of this chapter;

(2) Retains at least the last 2 hours of recorded information using a recorder that meets the standards of TSO–C123a, or later revision; and

(3) Is operated continuously from the start of the use of the checklist (before starting the engines for the purpose of flight), to the completion of the final checklist at the termination of the flight.

(4) For all airplanes manufactured on or after December 6, 2010, also meets the requirements of § 25.1457(a)(6) of this chapter.

(i) All airplanes required by this part to have a cockpit voice recorder and a flight data recorder, that install datalink communication equipment on or after December 6, 2010, must record all datalink messages as required by the certification rule applicable to the airplane.

[Doc. No. 25530, 53 FR 26149, July 11, 1988, as amended by Amdt. 125–54, 73 FR 12568, Mar. 7, 2008; Amdt. 125–54, 74 FR 32801, July 9, 2009; Amdt. 125–60, 75 FR 17046; Apr. 5, 2010]

§ 125.228 Flight data recorders: filtered data.

(a) A flight data signal is filtered when an original sensor signal has been changed in any way, other than changes necessary to:

(1) Accomplish analog to digital conversion of the signal;

(2) Format a digital signal to be DFDR compatible; or

(3) Eliminate a high frequency component of a signal that is outside the operational bandwidth of the sensor.

(b) An original sensor signal for any flight recorder parameter required to be recorded under §125.226 may be filtered only if the recorded signal value continues to meet the requirements of Appendix D or E of this part, as applicable.

(c) For a parameter described in §125.226(a) (12) through (17), (42), or (88), or the corresponding parameter in Appendix D of this part, if the recorded signal value is filtered and does not meet the requirements of Appendix D or E of this part, as applicable, the certificate holder must:

(1) Remove the filtering and ensure that the recorded signal value meets the requirements of Appendix D or E of this part, as applicable; or

(2) Demonstrate by test and analysis that the original sensor signal value can be reconstructed from the recorded data. This demonstration requires that:

(i) The FAA determine that the procedure and the test results submitted by the certificate holder as its compliance with paragraph (c)(2) of this section are repeatable; and

(ii) The certificate holder maintains documentation of the procedure required to reconstruct the original sensor signal value. This documentation is also subject to the requirements of §125.226(i).

(d) *Compliance.* Compliance is required as follows:

(1) No later than October 20, 2011, each operator must determine, for each airplane it operates, whether the airplane's DFDR system is filtering any of the parameters listed in paragraph (c) of this section. The operator must create a record of this determination for each airplane it operates, and maintain it as part of the correlation documentation required by §125.226(j)(3) of this part.

(2) For airplanes that are not filtering any listed parameter, no further

action is required unless the airplane's DFDR system is modified in a manner that would cause it to meet the definition of filtering on any listed parameter.

(3) For airplanes found to be filtering a parameter listed in paragraph (c) of this section, the operator must either:

(i) No later than April 21, 2014, remove the filtering; or

(ii) No later than April 22, 2013, submit the necessary procedure and test results required by paragraph (c)(2) of this section.

(4) After April 21, 2014, no aircraft flight data recording system may filter any parameter listed in paragraph (c) of this section that does not meet the requirements of Appendix D or E of this part, unless the certificate holder possesses test and analysis procedures and the test results that have been approved by the FAA. All records of tests, analysis and procedures used to comply with this section must be maintained as part of the correlation documentation required by §125.226(j)(3) of this part.

[Doc. No. FAA–2006–26135, 75 FR 7356, Feb. 19, 2010]

Subpart G—Maintenance

§125.241 Applicability.

This subpart prescribes rules, in addition to those prescribed in other parts of this chapter, for the maintenance of airplanes, airframes, aircraft engines, propellers, appliances, each item of survival and emergency equipment, and their component parts operated under this part.

§125.243 Certificate holder's responsibilities.

(a) With regard to airplanes, including airframes, aircraft engines, propellers, appliances, and survival and emergency equipment, operated by a certificate holder, that certificate holder is primarily responsible for—

(1) Airworthiness;

(2) The performance of maintenance, preventive maintenance, and alteration in accordance with applicable regulations and the certificate holder's manual;

(3) The scheduling and performance of inspections required by this part; and

(4) Ensuring that maintenance personnel make entries in the airplane maintenance log and maintenance records which meet the requirements of part 43 of this chapter and the certificate holder's manual, and which indicate that the airplane has been approved for return to service after maintenance, preventive maintenance, or alteration has been performed.

§ 125.245   Organization required to perform maintenance, preventive maintenance, and alteration.

The certificate holder must ensure that each person with whom it arranges for the performance of maintenance, preventive maintenance, alteration, or required inspection items identified in the certificate holder's manual in accordance with § 125.249(a)(3)(ii) must have an organization adequate to perform that work.

§ 125.247   Inspection programs and maintenance.

(a) No person may operate an airplane subject to this part unless

(1) The replacement times for life-limited parts specified in the aircraft type certificate data sheets, or other documents approved by the Administrator, are complied with;

(2) Defects disclosed between inspections, or as a result of inspection, have been corrected in accordance with part 43 of this chapter; and

(3) The airplane, including airframe, aircraft engines, propellers, appliances, and survival and emergency equipment, and their component parts, is inspected in accordance with an inspection program approved by the Administrator.

(b) The inspection program specified in paragraph (a)(3) of this section must include at least the following:

(1) Instructions, procedures, and standards for the conduct of inspections for the particular make and model of airplane, including necessary tests and checks. The instructions and procedures must set forth in detail the parts and areas of the airframe, aircraft engines, propellers, appliances,

and survival and emergency equipment required to be inspected.

(2) A schedule for the performance of inspections that must be performed under the program, expressed in terms of the time in service, calendar time, number of system operations, or any combination of these.

(c) No person may be used to perform the inspections required by this part unless that person is authorized to perform maintenance under part 43 of this chapter.

(d) No person may operate an airplane subject to this part unless—

(1) The installed engines have been maintained in accordance with the overhaul periods recommended by the manufacturer or a program approved by the Administrator; and

(2) The engine overhaul periods are specified in the inspection programs required by § 125.247(a)(3).

(e) Inspection programs which may be approved for use under this part include, but are not limited to—

(1) A continuous inspection program which is a part of a current continuous airworthiness program approved for use by a certificate holder under part 121 or part 135 of this chapter;

(2) Inspection programs currently recommended by the manufacturer of the airplane, aircraft engines, propellers, appliances, or survival and emergency equipment; or

(3) An inspection program developed by a certificate holder under this part.

[Doc. No. 19779, 45 FR 67235, Oct. 9, 1980, as amended by Amdt. 125–2, 46 FR 24409, Apr. 30, 1981]

§ 125.248   [Reserved]

§ 125.249   Maintenance manual requirements.

(a) Each certificate holder's manual required by § 125.71 of this part shall contain, in addition to the items required by § 125.73 of this part, at least the following:

(1) A description of the certificate holders maintenance organization, when the certificate holder has such an organization.

(2) A list of those persons with whom the certificate holder has arranged for performance of inspections under this

part. The list shall include the persons' names and addresses.

(3) The inspection programs required by §125.247 of this part to be followed in the performance of inspections under this part including—

(i) The method of performing routine and nonroutine inspections (other than required inspections);

(ii) The designation of the items that must be inspected (required inspections), including at least those which if improperly accomplished could result in a failure, malfunction, or defect endangering the safe operation of the airplane;

(iii) The method of performing required inspections;

(iv) Procedures for the inspection of work performed under previously required inspection findings ("buy-back procedures");

(v) Procedures, standards, and limits necessary for required inspections and acceptance or rejection of the items required to be inspected;

(vi) Instructions to prevent any person who performs any item of work from performing any required inspection of that work; and

(vii) Procedures to ensure that work interruptions do not adversely affect required inspections and to ensure required inspections are properly completed before the airplane is released to service.

(b) In addition, each certificate holder's manual shall contain a suitable system which may include a coded system that provides for the retention of the following:

(1) A description (or reference to data acceptable to the Administrator) of the work performed.

(2) The name of the person performing the work and the person's certificate type and number.

(3) The name of the person approving the work and the person's certificate type and number.

§125.251 Required inspection personnel.

(a) No person may use any person to perform required inspections unless the person performing the inspection is appropriately certificated, properly trained, qualified, and authorized to do so.

(b) No person may perform a required inspection if that person performed the item of work required to be inspected.

Subpart H—Airman and Crewmember Requirements

§125.261 Airman: Limitations on use of services.

(a) No certificate holder may use any person as an airman nor may any person serve as an airman unless that person—

(1) Holds an appropriate current airman certificate issued by the FAA;

(2) Has any required appropriate current airman and medical certificates in that person's possession while engaged in operations under this part; and

(3) Is otherwise qualified for the operation for which that person is to be used.

(b) Each airman covered by paragraph (a) of this section shall present the certificates for inspection upon the request of the Administrator.

§125.263 Composition of flightcrew.

(a) No certificate holder may operate an airplane with less than the minimum flightcrew specified in the type certificate and the Airplane Flight Manual approved for that type airplane and required by this part for the kind of operation being conducted.

(b) In any case in which this part requires the performance of two or more functions for which an airman certificate is necessary, that requirement is not satisfied by the performance of multiple functions at the same time by one airman.

(c) On each flight requiring a flight engineer, at least one flight crewmember, other than the flight engineer, must be qualified to provide emergency performance of the flight engineer's functions for the safe completion of the flight if the flight engineer becomes ill or is otherwise incapacitated. A pilot need not hold a flight engineer's certificate to perform the flight engineer's functions in such a situation.

§ 125.265 Flight engineer requirements.

(a) No person may operate an airplane for which a flight engineer is required by the type certification requirements without a flight crewmember holding a current flight engineer certificate.

(b) No person may serve as a required flight engineer on an airplane unless, within the preceding 6 calendar months, that person has had at least 50 hours of flight time as a flight engineer on that type airplane, or the Administrator has checked that person on that type airplane and determined that person is familiar and competent with all essential current information and operating procedures.

§ 125.267 Flight navigator and long-range navigation equipment.

(a) No certificate holder may operate an airplane outside the 48 conterminous States and the District of Columbia when its position cannot be reliably fixed for a period of more than 1 hour, without—

(1) A flight crewmember who holds a current flight navigator certificate; or

(2) Two independent, properly functioning, and approved long-range means of navigation which enable a reliable determination to be made of the position of the airplane by each pilot seated at that person's duty station.

(b) Operations where a flight navigator or long-range navigation equipment, or both, are required are specified in the operations specifications of the operator.

§ 125.269 Flight attendants.

(a) Each certificate holder shall provide at least the following flight attendants on each passenger-carrying airplane used:

(1) For airplanes having more than 19 but less than 51 passengers—one flight attendant.

(2) For airplanes having more than 50 but less than 101 passengers—two flight attendants.

(3) For airplanes having more than 100 passengers—two flight attendants plus one additional flight attendant for each unit (or part of a unit) of 50 passengers above 100 passengers.

(b) The number of flight attendants approved under paragraphs (a) and (b) of this section are set forth in the certificate holder's operations specifications.

(c) During takeoff and landing, flight attendants required by this section shall be located as near as practicable to required floor level exits and shall be uniformly distributed throughout the airplane to provide the most effective egress of passengers in event of an emergency evacuation.

§ 125.271 Emergency and emergency evacuation duties.

(a) Each certificate holder shall, for each type and model of airplane, assign to each category of required crewmember, as appropriate, the necessary functions to be performed in an emergency or a situation requiring emergency evacuation. The certificate holder shall show those functions are realistic, can be practically accomplished, and will meet any reasonably anticipated emergency, including the possible incapacitation of individual crewmembers or their inability to reach the passenger cabin because of shifting cargo in combination cargo-passenger airplanes.

(b) The certificate holder shall describe in its manual the functions of each category of required crewmembers under paragraph (a) of this section.

Subpart I—Flight Crewmember Requirements

§ 125.281 Pilot-in-command qualifications.

No certificate holder may use any person, nor may any person serve, as pilot in command of an airplane unless that person—

(a) Holds at least a commercial pilot certificate, an appropriate category, class, and type rating, and an instrument rating; and

(b) Has had at least 1,200 hours of flight time as a pilot, including 500 hours of cross-country flight time, 100 hours of night flight time, including at least 10 night takeoffs and landings, and 75 hours of actual or simulated instrument flight time, at least 50 hours of which were actual flight.

§ 125.283 Second-in-command qualifications.

No certificate holder may use any person, nor may any person serve, as second in command of an airplane unless that person—

(a) Holds at least a commercial pilot certificate with appropriate category and class ratings, and an instrument rating; and

(b) For flight under IFR, meets the recent instrument experience requirements prescribed for a pilot in command in part 61 of this chapter.

§ 125.285 Pilot qualifications: Recent experience.

(a) No certificate holder may use any person, nor may any person serve, as a required pilot flight crewmember unless within the preceding 90 calendar days that person has made at least three takeoffs and landings in the type airplane in which that person is to serve. The takeoffs and landings required by this paragraph may be performed in a flight simulator if the flight simulator is qualified and approved by the Administrator for such purpose. However, any person who fails to qualify for a 90-consecutive-day period following the date of that person's last qualification under this paragraph must reestablish recency of experience as provided in paragraph (b) of this section.

(b) A required pilot flight crewmember who has not met the requirements of paragraph (a) of this section may reestablish recency of experience by making at least three takeoffs and landings under the supervision of an authorized check airman, in accordance with the following:

(1) At least one takeoff must be made with a simulated failure of the most critical powerplant.

(2) At least one landing must be made from an ILS approach to the lowest ILS minimums authorized for the certificate holder.

(3) At least one landing must be made to a complete stop.

(c) A required pilot flight crewmember who performs the maneuvers required by paragraph (b) of this section in a qualified and approved flight simulator, as prescribed in paragraph (a) of this section, must—

(1) Have previously logged 100 hours of flight time in the same type airplane in which the pilot is to serve; and

(2) Be observed on the first two landings made in operations under this part by an authorized check airman who acts as pilot in command and occupies a pilot seat. The landings must be made in weather minimums that are not less than those contained in the certificate holder's operations specifications for Category I operations and must be made within 45 days following completion of simulator testing.

(d) An authorized check airman who observes the takeoffs and landings prescribed in paragraphs (b) and (c)(3) of this section shall certify that the person being observed is proficient and qualified to perform flight duty in operations under this part, and may require any additional maneuvers that are determined necessary to make this certifying statement.

[Doc. No. 19779, 45 FR 67235, Oct. 9, 1980, as amended by Amdt. 125–27, 61 FR 34561, July 2, 1996]

§ 125.287 Initial and recurrent pilot testing requirements.

(a) No certificate holder may use any person, nor may any person serve as a pilot, unless, since the beginning of the 12th calendar month before that service, that person has passed a written or oral test, given by the Administrator or an authorized check airman on that person's knowledge in the following areas—

(1) The appropriate provisions of parts 61, 91, and 125 of this chapter and the operations specifications and the manual of the certificate holder;

(2) For each type of airplane to be flown by the pilot, the airplane powerplant, major components and systems, major appliances, performance and operating limitations, standard and emergency operating procedures, and the contents of the approved Airplane Flight Manual or approved equivalent, as applicable;

(3) For each type of airplane to be flown by the pilot, the method of determining compliance with weight and balance limitations for takeoff, landing, and en route operations;

(4) Navigation and use of air navigation aids appropriate to the operation

of pilot authorization, including, when applicable, instrument approach facilities and procedures;

(5) Air traffic control procedures, including IFR procedures when applicable;

(6) Meteorology in general, including the principles of frontal systems, icing, fog, thunderstorms, and windshear, and, if appropriate for the operation of the certificate holder, high altitude weather;

(7) Procedures for avoiding operations in thunderstorms and hail, and for operating in turbulent air or in icing conditions;

(8) New equipment, procedures, or techniques, as appropriate;

(9) Knowledge and procedures for operating during ground icing conditions, (i.e., any time conditions are such that frost, ice, or snow may reasonably be expected to adhere to the airplane), if the certificate holder expects to authorize takeoffs in ground icing conditions, including:

(i) The use of holdover times when using deicing/anti-icing fluids.

(ii) Airplane deicing/anti-icing procedures, including inspection and check procedures and responsibilities.

(iii) Communications.

(iv) Airplane surface contamination (i.e., adherence of frost, ice, or snow) and critical area identification, and knowledge of how contamination adversely affects airplane performance and flight characteristics.

(v) Types and characteristics of deicing/anti-icing fluids, if used by the certificate holder.

(vi) Cold weather preflight inspection procedures.

(vii) Techniques for recognizing contamination on the airplane.

(b) No certificate holder may use any person, nor may any person serve, as a pilot in any airplane unless, since the beginning of the 12th calendar month before that service, that person has passed a competency check given by the Administrator or an authorized check airman in that type of airplane to determine that person's competence in practical skills and techniques in that airplane or type of airplane. The extent of the competency check shall be determined by the Administrator or authorized check airman conducting the competency check. The competency check may include any of the maneuvers and procedures currently required for the original issuance of the particular pilot certificate required for the operations authorized and appropriate to the category, class, and type of airplane involved. For the purposes of this paragraph, type, as to an airplane, means any one of a group of airplanes determined by the Administrator to have a similar means of propulsion, the same manufacturer, and no significantly different handling or flight characteristics.

(c) The instrument proficiency check required by § 125.291 may be substituted for the competency check required by this section for the type of airplane used in the check.

(d) For the purposes of this part, competent performance of a procedure or maneuver by a person to be used as a pilot requires that the pilot be the obvious master of the airplane with the successful outcome of the maneuver never in doubt.

(e) The Administrator or authorized check airman certifies the competency of each pilot who passes the knowledge or flight check in the certificate holder's pilot records.

(f) Portions of a required competency check may be given in an airplane simulator or other appropriate training device, if approved by the Administrator.

(g) If the certificate holder is authorized to conduct EFVS operations, the competency check in paragraph (b) of this section must include tasks appropriate to the EFVS operations the certificate holder is authorized to conduct.

[45 FR 67235, Oct. 9, 1980, as amended by Amdt. 125–18, 58 FR 69629, Dec. 30, 1993; Docket FAA–2013–0485, Amdt. 125–66, 81 FR 90176, Dec. 13, 2016]

§ 125.289 Initial and recurrent flight attendant crewmember testing requirements.

No certificate holder may use any person, nor may any person serve, as a flight attendant crewmember, unless, since the beginning of the 12th calendar month before that service, the certificate holder has determined by appropriate initial and recurrent testing that the person is knowledgeable and competent in the following areas as appropriate to assigned duties and responsibilities:

(a) Authority of the pilot in command;

(b) Passenger handling, including procedures to be followed in handling deranged persons or other persons whose conduct might jeopardize safety;

(c) Crewmember assignments, functions, and responsibilities during ditching and evacuation of persons who may need the assistance of another person to move expeditiously to an exit in an emergency;

(d) Briefing of passengers;

(e) Location and operation of portable fire extinguishers and other items of emergency equipment;

(f) Proper use of cabin equipment and controls;

(g) Location and operation of passenger oxygen equipment;

(h) Location and operation of all normal and emergency exits, including evacuation chutes and escape ropes; and

(i) Seating of persons who may need assistance of another person to move rapidly to an exit in an emergency as prescribed by the certificate holder's operations manual.

§125.291 Pilot in command: Instrument proficiency check requirements.

(a) No certificate holder may use any person, nor may any person serve, as a pilot in command of an airplane under IFR unless, since the beginning of the sixth calendar month before that service, that person has passed an instrument proficiency check and the Administrator or an authorized check airman has so certified in a letter of competency.

(b) No pilot may use any type of precision instrument approach procedure under IFR unless, since the beginning of the sixth calendar month before that use, the pilot has satisfactorily demonstrated that type of approach procedure and has been issued a letter of competency under paragraph (g) of this section. No pilot may use any type of nonprecision approach procedure under IFR unless, since the beginning of the sixth calendar month before that use, the pilot has satisfactorily dem-

onstrated either that type of approach procedure or any other two different types of nonprecision approach procedures and has been issued a letter of competency under paragraph (g) of this section. The instrument approach procedure or procedures must include at least one straight-in approach, one circling approach, and one missed approach. Each type of approach procedure demonstrated must be conducted to published minimums for that procedure.

(c) The instrument proficiency check required by paragraph (a) of this section consists of an oral or written equipment test and a flight check under simulated or actual IFR conditions. The equipment test includes questions on emergency procedures, engine operation, fuel and lubrication systems, power settings, stall speeds, best engine-out speed, propeller and supercharge operations, and hydraulic, mechanical, and electrical systems, as appropriate. The flight check includes navigation by instruments, recovery from simulated emergencies, and standard instrument approaches involving navigational facilities which that pilot is to be authorized to use.

(1) For a pilot in command of an airplane, the instrument proficiency check must include the procedures and maneuvers for a commercial pilot certificate with an instrument rating and, if required, for the appropriate type rating.

(2) The instrument proficiency check must be given by an authorized check airman or by the Administrator.

(d) If the pilot in command is assigned to pilot only one type of airplane, that pilot must take the instrument proficiency check required by paragraph (a) of this section in that type of airplane.

(e) If the pilot in command is assigned to pilot more than one type of airplane, that pilot must take the instrument proficiency check required by paragraph (a) of this section in each type of airplane to which that pilot is assigned, in rotation, but not more than one flight check during each period described in paragraph (a) of this section.

(f) Portions of a required flight check may be given in an airplane simulator or other appropriate training device, if approved by the Administrator.

(g) The Administrator or authorized check airman issues a letter of competency to each pilot who passes the instrument proficiency check. The letter of competency contains a list of the types of instrument approach procedures and facilities authorized.

§ 125.293 Crewmember: Tests and checks, grace provisions, accepted standards.

(a) If a crewmember who is required to take a test or a flight check under this part completes the test or flight check in the calendar month before or after the calendar month in which it is required, that crewmember is considered to have completed the test or check in the calendar month in which it is required.

(b) If a pilot being checked under this subpart fails any of the required maneuvers, the person giving the check may give additional training to the pilot during the course of the check. In addition to repeating the maneuvers failed, the person giving the check may require the pilot being checked to repeat any other maneuvers that are necessary to determine the pilot's proficiency. If the pilot being checked is unable to demonstrate satisfactory performance to the person conducting the check, the certificate holder may not use the pilot, nor may the pilot serve, in the capacity for which the pilot is being checked in operations under this part until the pilot has satisfactorily completed the check.

§ 125.295 Check airman authorization: Application and issue.

Each certificate holder desiring FAA approval of a check airman shall submit a request in writing to the responsible Flight Standards office charged with the overall inspection of the certificate holder. The Administrator may issue a letter of authority to each check airman if that airman passes the appropriate oral and flight test. The letter of authority lists the tests and checks in this part that the check airman is qualified to give, and the category, class and type airplane, where

appropriate, for which the check airman is qualified.

[Docket No. 19779, 45 FR 67235, Oct. 9, 1980, as amended by Docket FAA-2018-0119, Amdt. 125-68, 83 FR 9173, Mar. 5, 2018]

§ 125.296 Training, testing, and checking conducted by training centers: Special rules.

A crewmember who has successfully completed training, testing, or checking in accordance with an approved training program that meets the requirements of this part and that is conducted in accordance with an approved course conducted by a training center certificated under part 142 of this chapter, is considered to meet applicable requirements of this part.

[Doc. No. 26933, 61 FR 34561, July 2, 1996]

§ 125.297 Approval of flight simulators and flight training devices.

(a) Flight simulators and flight training devices approved by the Administrator may be used in training, testing, and checking required by this subpart.

(b) Each flight simulator and flight training device that is used in training, testing, and checking required under this subpart must be used in accordance with an approved training course conducted by a training center certificated under part 142 of this chapter, or meet the following requirements:

(1) It must be specifically approved for—

(i) The certificate holder;

(ii) The type airplane and, if applicable, the particular variation within type for which the check is being conducted; and

(iii) The particular maneuver, procedure, or crewmember function involved.

(2) It must maintain the performance, functional, and other characteristics that are required for approval.

(3) It must be modified to conform with any modification to the airplane being simulated that changes the performance, functional, or other characteristics required for approval.

[Doc. No. 19779, 45 FR 67235, Oct. 9, 1980, as amended by Amdt. 125-27, 61 FR 34561, July 2, 1996]

Subpart J—Flight Operations

§125.311 Flight crewmembers at controls.

(a) Except as provided in paragraph (b) of this section, each required flight crewmember on flight deck duty must remain at the assigned duty station with seat belt fastened while the airplane is taking off or landing and while it is en route.

(b) A required flight crewmember may leave the assigned duty station—

(1) If the crewmember's absence is necessary for the performance of duties in connection with the operation of the airplane;

(2) If the crewmember's absence is in connection with physiological needs; or

(3) If the crewmember is taking a rest period and relief is provided—

(i) In the case of the assigned pilot in command, by a pilot qualified to act as pilot in command.

(ii) In the case of the assigned second in command, by a pilot qualified to act as second in command of that airplane during en route operations. However, the relief pilot need not meet the recent experience requirements of §125.285.

§125.313 Manipulation of controls when carrying passengers.

No pilot in command may allow any person to manipulate the controls of an airplane while carrying passengers during flight, nor may any person manipulate the controls while carrying passengers during flight, unless that person is a qualified pilot of the certificate holder operating that airplane.

§125.315 Admission to flight deck.

(a) No person may admit any person to the flight deck of an airplane unless the person being admitted is—

(1) A crewmember;

(2) An FAA inspector or an authorized representative of the National Transportation Safety Board who is performing official duties; or

(3) Any person who has the permission of the pilot in command.

(b) No person may admit any person to the flight deck unless there is a seat available for the use of that person in the passenger compartment, except—

(1) An FAA inspector or an authorized representative of the Administrator or National Transportation Safety Board who is checking or observing flight operations; or

(2) A certificated airman employed by the certificate holder whose duties require an airman certificate.

§125.317 Inspector's credentials: Admission to pilots' compartment: Forward observer's seat.

(a) Whenever, in performing the duties of conducting an inspection, an FAA inspector presents an Aviation Safety Inspector credential, FAA Form 110A, to the pilot in command of an airplane operated by the certificate holder, the inspector must be given free and uninterrupted access to the pilot compartment of that airplane. However, this paragraph does not limit the emergency authority of the pilot in command to exclude any person from the pilot compartment in the interest of safety.

(b) A forward observer's seat on the flight deck, or forward passenger seat with headset or speaker, must be provided for use by the Administrator while conducting en route inspections. The suitability of the location of the seat and the headset or speaker for use in conducting en route inspections is determined by the Administrator.

§125.319 Emergencies.

(a) In an emergency situation that requires immediate decision and action, the pilot in command may take any action considered necessary under the circumstances. In such a case, the pilot in command may deviate from prescribed operations, procedures and methods, weather minimums, and this chapter, to the extent required in the interests of safety.

(b) In an emergency situation arising during flight that requires immediate decision and action by appropriate management personnel in the case of operations conducted with a flight following service and which is known to them, those personnel shall advise the pilot in command of the emergency, shall ascertain the decision of the pilot

353

in command, and shall have the decision recorded. If they cannot communicate with the pilot, they shall declare an emergency and take any action that they consider necessary under the circumstances.

(c) Whenever emergency authority is exercised, the pilot in command or the appropriate management personnel shall keep the appropriate ground radio station fully informed of the progress of the flight. The person declaring the emergency shall send a written report of any deviation, through the operator's director of operations, to the Administrator within 10 days, exclusive of Saturdays, Sundays, and Federal holidays, after the flight is completed or, in the case of operations outside the United States, upon return to the home base.

§ 125.321 Reporting potentially hazardous meteorological conditions and irregularities of ground and navigation facilities.

Whenever the pilot in command encounters a meteorological condition or an irregularity in a ground facility or navigation aid in flight, the knowledge of which the pilot in command considers essential to the safety of other flights, the pilot in command shall notify an appropriate ground station as soon as practicable.

[Doc. No. 19779, 45 FR 67235, Oct. 9, 1980, as amended by Amdt. 125-52, 72 FR 31683, June 7, 2007]

§ 125.323 Reporting mechanical irregularities.

The pilot in command shall ensure that all mechanical irregularities occurring during flight are entered in the maintenance log of the airplane at the next place of landing. Before each flight, the pilot in command shall ascertain the status of each irregularity entered in the log at the end of the preceding flight.

§ 125.325 Instrument approach procedures and IFR landing minimums.

Except as specified in § 91.176 of this chapter, no person may make an instrument approach at an airport except in accordance with IFR weather minimums and unless the type of instrument approach procedure to be used is listed in the certificate holder's operations specifications.

[Docket FAA-2013-0485, Amdt. 125-66, 81 FR 90176, Dec. 13, 2016]

§ 125.327 Briefing of passengers before flight.

(a) Before each takeoff, each pilot in command of an airplane carrying passengers shall ensure that all passengers have been orally briefed on—

(1) *Smoking.* Each passenger shall be briefed on when, where, and under what conditions smoking is prohibited. This briefing shall include a statement that the Federal Aviation Regulations require passenger compliance with the lighted passenger information signs, posted placards, areas designated for safety purposes as no smoking areas, and crewmember instructions with regard to these items.

(2) *The use of safety belts, including instructions on how to fasten and unfasten the safety belts.* Each passenger shall be briefed on when, where, and under what conditions the safety belt must be fastened about him or her. This briefing shall include a statement that the Federal Aviation Regulations require passenger compliance with lighted passenger information signs and crewmember instructions concerning the use of safety belts.

(3) The placement of seat backs in an upright position before takeoff and landing;

(4) Location and means for opening the passenger entry door and emergency exits;

(5) Location of survival equipment;

(6) If the flight involves extended overwater operation, ditching procedures and the use of required flotation equipment;

(7) If the flight involves operations above 12,000 feet MSL, the normal and emergency use of oxygen; and

(8) Location and operation of fire extinguishers.

(b) Before each takeoff, the pilot in command shall ensure that each person who may need the assistance of another person to move expeditiously to an exit if an emergency occurs and that person's attendant, if any, has received a briefing as to the procedures to be followed if an evacuation occurs.

This paragraph does not apply to a person who has been given a briefing before a previous leg of a flight in the same airplane.

(c) The oral briefing required by paragraph (a) of this section shall be given by the pilot in command or a member of the crew. It shall be supplemented by printed cards for the use of each passenger containing—

(1) A diagram and method of operating the emergency exits; and

(2) Other instructions necessary for the use of emergency equipment on board the airplane.

Each card used under this paragraph must be carried in the airplane in locations convenient for the use of each passenger and must contain information that is appropriate to the airplane on which it is to be used.

(d) The certificate holder shall describe in its manual the procedure to be followed in the briefing required by paragraph (a) of this section.

(e) If the airplane does not proceed directly over water after takeoff, no part of the briefing required by paragraph (a)(6) of this section has to be given before takeoff but the briefing required by paragraph (a)(6) must be given before reaching the overwater part of the flight.

[Doc. No. 19779, 45 FR 67235, Oct. 9, 1980, as amended by Amdt. 125–17, 57 FR 42675, Sept. 15, 1992]

§ 125.328 Prohibition on crew interference.

No person may assault, threaten, intimidate, or interfere with a crewmember in the performance of the crewmember's duties aboard an aircraft being operated under this part.

[Doc. No. FAA–1998–4954, 64 FR 1080, Jan. 7, 1999]

§ 125.329 Minimum altitudes for use of autopilot.

(a) *Definitions.* For purpose of this section—

(1) Altitudes for takeoff/initial climb and go-around/missed approach are defined as above the airport elevation.

(2) Altitudes for enroute operations are defined as above terrain elevation.

(3) Altitudes for approach are defined as above the touchdown zone elevation (TDZE), unless the altitude is specifi-

cally in reference to DA (H) or MDA, in which case the altitude is defined by reference to the DA(H) or MDA itself.

(b) *Takeoff and initial climb.* No person may use an autopilot for takeoff or initial climb below the higher of 500 feet or an altitude that is no lower than twice the altitude loss specified in the Airplane Flight Manual (AFM), except as follows—

(1) At a minimum engagement altitude specified in the AFM; or

(2) At an altitude specified by the Administrator, whichever is greater.

(c) *Enroute.* No person may use an autopilot enroute, including climb and descent, below the following—

(1) 500 feet;

(2) At an altitude that is no lower than twice the altitude loss specified in the AFM for an autopilot malfunction in cruise conditions; or

(3) At an altitude specified by the Administrator, whichever is greater.

(d) *Approach.* No person may use an autopilot at an altitude lower than 50 feet below the DA(H) or MDA for the instrument procedure being flown, except as follows—

(1) For autopilots with an AFM specified altitude loss for approach operations—

(i) An altitude no lower than twice the specified altitude loss if higher than 50 feet below the MDA or DA(H);

(ii) An altitude no lower than 50 feet higher than the altitude loss specified in the AFM, when the following conditions are met—

(A) Reported weather conditions are less than the basic VFR weather conditions in § 91.155 of this chapter;

(B) Suitable visual references specified in § 91.175 of this chapter have been established on the instrument approach procedure; and

(C) The autopilot is coupled and receiving both lateral and vertical path references;

(iii) An altitude no lower than the higher of the altitude loss specified in the AFM or 50 feet above the TDZE, when the following conditions are met—

(A) Reported weather conditions are equal to or better than the basic VFR weather conditions in § 91.155 of this chapter; and

(B) The autopilot is coupled and receiving both lateral and vertical path references; or

(iv) A greater altitude specified by the Administrator.

(2) For autopilots with AFM specified approach altitude limitations, the greater of—

(i) The minimum use altitude specified for the coupled approach mode selected;

(ii) 50 feet; or

(iii) An altitude specified by Administrator.

(3) For autopilots with an AFM specified negligible or zero altitude loss for an autopilot approach mode malfunction, the greater of—

(i) 50 feet; or

(ii) An altitude specified by Administrator.

(4) If executing an autopilot coupled go-around or missed approach using a certificated and functioning autopilot in accordance with paragraph (e) in this section.

(e) *Go-Around/Missed Approach.* No person may engage an autopilot during a go-around or missed approach below the minimum engagement altitude specified for takeoff and initial climb in paragraph (b) in this section. An autopilot minimum use altitude does not apply to a go-around/missed approach initiated with an engaged autopilot. Performing a go-around or missed approach with an engaged autopilot must not adversely affect safe obstacle clearance.

(f) *Landing.* Notwithstanding paragraph (d) of this section, autopilot minimum use altitudes do not apply to autopilot operations when an approved automatic landing system mode is being used for landing. Automatic landing systems must be authorized in an operations specification issued to the operator.

[Doc. No. FAA–2012–1059, 79 FR 6087, Feb. 3, 2014]

§ 125.331 Carriage of persons without compliance with the passenger-carrying provisions of this part.

The following persons may be carried aboard an airplane without complying with the passenger-carrying requirements of this part:

(a) A crewmember.

(b) A person necessary for the safe handling of animals on the airplane.

(c) A person necessary for the safe handling of hazardous materials (as defined in subchapter C of title 49 CFR).

(d) A person performing duty as a security or honor guard accompanying a shipment made by or under the authority of the U.S. Government.

(e) A military courier or a military route supervisor carried by a military cargo contract operator if that carriage is specifically authorized by the appropriate military service.

(f) An authorized representative of the Administrator conducting an en route inspection.

(g) A person authorized by the Administrator.

§ 125.333 Stowage of food, beverage, and passenger service equipment during airplane movement on the surface, takeoff, and landing.

(a) No certificate holder may move an airplane on the surface, take off, or land when any food, beverage, or tableware furnished by the certificate holder is located at any passenger seat.

(b) No certificate holder may move an airplane on the surface, take off, or land unless each food and beverage tray and seat back tray table is secured in its stowed position.

(c) No certificate holder may permit an airplane to move on the surface, take off, or land unless each passenger serving cart is secured in its stowed position.

(d) Each passenger shall comply with instructions given by a crewmember with regard to compliance with this section.

[Doc. No. 26142, 57 FR 42675, Sept. 15, 1992]

Subpart K—Flight Release Rules

§ 125.351 Flight release authority.

(a) No person may start a flight without authority from the person authorized by the certificate holder to exercise operational control over the flight.

(b) No person may start a flight unless the pilot in command or the person authorized by the cetificate holder to exercise operational control over the flight has executed a flight release setting forth the conditions under which the flight will be conducted. The pilot in command may sign the flight release only when both the pilot in command and the person authorized to exercise operational control believe the flight can be made safely, unless the pilot in command is authorized by the certificate holder to exercise operational control and execute the flight release without the approval of any other person.

(c) No person may continue a flight from an intermediate airport without a new flight release if the airplane has been on the ground more than 6 hours.

§125.353 Facilities and services.

During a flight, the pilot in command shall obtain any additional available information of meteorological conditions and irregularities of facilities and services that may affect the safety of the flight.

§125.355 Airplane equipment.

No person may release an airplane unless it is airworthy and is equipped as prescribed.

§125.357 Communication and navigation facilities.

No person may release an airplane over any route or route segment unless communication and navigation facilities equal to those required by §125.51 are in satisfactory operating condition.

§125.359 Flight release under VFR.

No person may release an airplane for VFR operation unless the ceiling and visibility en route, as indicated by available weather reports or forecasts, or any combination thereof, are and will remain at or above applicable VFR minimums until the airplane arrives at the airport or airports specified in the flight release.

§125.361 Flight release under IFR or over-the-top.

Except as provided in §125.363, no person may release an airplane for operations under IFR or over-the-top unless appropriate weather reports or forecasts, or any combination thereof, indicate that the weather conditions will be at or above the authorized minimums at the estimated time of arrival at the airport or airports to which released.

§125.363 Flight release over water.

(a) No person may release an airplane for a flight that involves extended overwater operation unless appropriate weather reports or forecasts, or any combination thereof, indicate that the weather conditions will be at or above the authorized minimums at the estimated time of arrival at any airport to which released or to any required alternate airport.

(b) Each certificate holder shall conduct extended overwater operations under IFR unless it shows that operating under IFR is not necessary for safety.

(c) Each certificate holder shall conduct other overwater operations under IFR if the Administrator determines that operation under IFR is necessary for safety.

(d) Each authorization to conduct extended overwater operations under VFR and each requirement to conduct other overwater operations under IFR will be specified in the operations specifications.

§125.365 Alternate airport for departure.

(a) If the weather conditions at the airport of takeoff are below the landing minimums in the certificate holder's operations specifications for that airport, no person may release an airplane from that airport unless the flight release specifies an alternate airport located within the following distances from the airport of takeoff:

(1) *Airplanes having two engines.* Not more than 1 hour from the departure airport at normal cruising speed in still air with one engine inoperative.

(2) *Airplanes having three or more engines.* Not more than 2 hours from departure airport at normal cruising speed in still air with one engine inoperative.

(b) For the purposes of paragraph (a) of this section, the alternate airport weather conditions must meet the requirements of the certificate holder's operations specifications.

(c) No person may release an airplane from an airport unless that person lists each required alternate airport in the flight release.

§ 125.367   Alternate airport for destination: IFR or over-the-top.

(a) Except as provided in paragraph (b) of this section, each person releasing an airplane for operation under IFR or over-the-top shall list at least one alternate airport for each destination airport in the flight release.

(b) An alternate airport need not be designated for IFR or over-the-top operations where the airplane carries enough fuel to meet the requirements of §§ 125.375 and 125.377 for flights outside the 48 conterminous States and the District of Columbia over routes without an available alternate airport for a particular airport of destination.

(c) For the purposes of paragraph (a) of this section, the weather requirements at the alternate airport must meet the requirements of the operator's operations specifications.

(d) No person may release a flight unless that person lists each required alternate airport in the flight release.

§ 125.369   Alternate airport weather minimums.

No person may list an airport as an alternate airport in the flight release unless the appropriate weather reports or forecasts, or any combination thereof, indicate that the weather conditions will be at or above the alternate weather minimums specified in the certificate holder's operations specifications for that airport when the flight arrives.

§ 125.371   Continuing flight in unsafe conditions.

(a) No pilot in command may allow a flight to continue toward any airport to which it has been released if, in the opinion of the pilot in command, the flight cannot be completed safely, unless, in the opinion of the pilot in command, there is no safer procedure. In that event, continuation toward that airport is an emergency situation.

§ 125.373   Original flight release or amendment of flight release.

(a) A certificate holder may specify any airport authorized for the type of airplane as a destination for the purpose of original release.

(b) No person may allow a flight to continue to an airport to which it has been released unless the weather conditions at an alternate airport that was specified in the flight release are forecast to be at or above the alternate minimums specified in the operations specifications for that airport at the time the airplane would arrive at the alternate airport. However, the flight release may be amended en route to include any alternate airport that is within the fuel range of the airplane as specified in § 125.375 or § 125.377.

(c) No person may change an original destination or alternate airport that is specified in the original flight release to another airport while the airplane is en route unless the other airport is authorized for that type of airplane.

(d) Each person who amends a flight release en route shall record that amendment.

§ 125.375   Fuel supply: Nonturbine and turbopropeller-powered airplanes.

(a) Except as provided in paragraph (b) of this section, no person may release for flight or take off a nonturbine or turbopropeller-powered airplane unless, considering the wind and other weather conditions expected, it has enough fuel—

(1) To fly to and land at the airport to which it is released;

(2) Thereafter, to fly to and land at the most distant alternate airport specified in the flight release; and

(3) Thereafter, to fly for 45 minutes at normal crusing fuel consumption.

(b) If the airplane is released for any flight other than from one point in the conterminous United States to another point in the conterminous United States, it must carry enough fuel to meet the requirements of paragraphs (a) (1) and (2) of this section and thereafter fly for 30 minutes plus 15 percent of the total time required to fly at normal cruising fuel consumption to the airports specified in paragraphs (a) (1) and (2) of this section, or fly for 90 minutes at normal cruising fuel consumption, whichever is less.

(c) No person may release a nonturbine or turbopropeller-powered airplane to an airport for which an alternate is not specified under § 125.367(b) unless it has enough fuel, considering wind and other weather conditions expected, to fly to that airport and thereafter to fly for 3 hours at normal cruising fuel consumption.

§ 125.377 Fuel supply: Turbine-engine-powered airplanes other than turbopropeller.

(a) Except as provided in paragraph (b) of this section, no person may release for flight or takeoff a turbine-powered airplane (other than a turbopropeller-powered airplane) unless, considering the wind and other weather conditions expected, it has enough fuel—

(1) To fly to and land at the airport to which it is released;

(2) Thereafter, to fly to and land at the most distant alternate airport specified in the flight release; and

(3) Thereafter, to fly for 45 minutes at normal cruising fuel consumption.

(b) For any operation outside the 48 conterminous United States and the District of Columbia, unless authorized by the Administrator in the operations specifications, no person may release for flight or take off a turbine-engine powered airplane (other than a turbopropeller-powered airplane) unless, considering wind and other weather conditions expected, it has enough fuel—

(1) To fly and land at the airport to which it is released;

(2) After that, to fly for a period of 10 percent of the total time required to fly from the airport of departure and land at the airport to which it was released;

(3) After that, to fly to and land at the most distant alternate airport specified in the flight release, if an alternate is required; and

(4) After that, to fly for 30 minutes at holding speed at 1,500 feet above the alternate airport (or the destination airport if no alternate is required) under standard temperature conditions.

(c) No person may release a turbine-engine-powered airplane (other than a turbopropeller airplane) to an airport for which an alternate is not specified under § 125.367(b) unless it has enough fuel, considering wind and other weather conditions expected, to fly to that airport and thereafter to fly for at

least 2 hours at normal cruising fuel consumption.

(d) The Administrator may amend the operations specifications of a certificate holder to require more fuel than any of the minimums stated in paragraph (a) or (b) of this section if the Administrator finds that additional fuel is necessary on a particular route in the interest of safety.

§ 125.379 Landing weather minimums: IFR.

(a) If the pilot in command of an airplane has not served 100 hours as pilot in command in the type of airplane being operated, the MDA or DA/DH and visibility landing minimums in the certificate holder's operations specification are increased by 100 feet and one-half mile (or the RVR equivalent). The MDA or DA/DH and visibility minimums need not be increased above those applicable to the airport when used as an alternate airport, but in no event may the landing minimums be less than a 300-foot ceiling and 1 mile of visibility.

(b) The 100 hours of pilot-in-command experience required by paragraph (a) may be reduced (not to exceed 50 percent) by substituting one landing in operations under this part in the type of airplane for 1 required hour of pilot-in-command experience if the pilot has at least 100 hours as pilot in command of another type airplane in operations under this part.

(c) Category II minimums, when authorized in the certificate holder's operations specifications, do not apply until the pilot in command subject to paragraph (a) of this section meets the requirements of that paragraph in the type of airplane the pilot is operating.

[Doc. No. 19779, 45 FR 67235, Oct. 9, 1980, as amended by Amdt. 125–52, 72 FR 31683, June 7, 2007]

§ 125.381 Takeoff and landing weather minimums: IFR.

(a) Regardless of any clearance from ATC, if the reported weather conditions are less than that specified in the certificate holder's operations specifications, no pilot may—

(1) Take off an airplane under IFR; or

(2) Except as provided in paragraphs (c) and (d) of this section, land an airplane under IFR.

(b) Except as provided in paragraphs (c) and (d) of this section, no pilot may execute an instrument approach procedure if the latest reported visibility is less than the landing minimums specified in the certificate holder's operations specifications.

(c) A pilot who initiates an instrument approach procedure based on a weather report that indicates that the specified visibility minimums exist and subsequently receives another weather report that indicates that conditions are below the minimum requirements, may continue the approach only if either the requirements of § 91.176 of this chapter, or the following conditions are met—

(1) The later weather report is received when the airplane is in one of the following approach phases:

(i) The airplane is on a ILS approach and has passed the final approach fix;

(ii) The airplane is on an ASR or PAR final approach and has been turned over to the final approach controller; or

(iii) The airplane is on a nonprecision final approach and the airplane—

(A) Has passed the appropriate facility or final approach fix; or

(B) Where a final approach fix is not specified, has completed the procedure turn and is established inbound toward the airport on the final approach course within the distance prescribed in the procedure; and

(2) The pilot in command finds, on reaching the authorized MDA, or DA/DH, that the actual weather conditions are at or above the minimums prescribed for the procedure being used.

(d) A pilot may execute an instrument approach procedure, or continue the approach, at an airport when the visibility is reported to be less than the visibility minimums prescribed for that procedure if the pilot uses an operable EFVS in accordance with § 91.176 of this chapter and the certificate holder's operations specifications for EFVS operations, or for a holder of a part 125 letter of deviation authority, a letter of authorization for the use of EFVS.

[Doc. No. 19779, 45 FR 67235, Oct. 9, 1980, as amended by Amdt. 125-2, 46 FR 24409, Apr. 30, 1981; Amdt. 125-45, 69 FR 1641, Jan. 9, 2004; Amdt. 125-52, 72 FR 31683, June 7, 2007; Docket FAA-2013-0485, Amdt. 125-66, 81 FR 90177, Dec. 13, 2016]

§ 125.383 Load manifest.

(a) Each certificate holder is responsible for the preparation and accuracy of a load manifest in duplicate containing information concerning the loading of the airplane. The manifest must be prepared before each takeoff and must include—

(1) The number of passengers;

(2) The total weight of the loaded airplane;

(3) The maximum allowable takeoff and landing weights for that flight;

(4) The center of gravity limits;

(5) The center of gravity of the loaded airplane, except that the actual center of gravity need not be computed if the airplane is loaded according to a loading schedule or other approved method that ensures that the center of gravity of the loaded airplane is within approved limits. In those cases, an entry shall be made on the manifest indicating that the center of gravity is within limits according to a loading schedule or other approved method:

(6) The registration number of the airplane;

(7) The origin and destination ; and

(8) Names of passengers.

(b) The pilot in command of an airplane for which a load manifest must be prepared shall carry a copy of the completed load manifest in the airplane to its destination. The certificate holder shall keep copies of completed load manifests for at least 30 days at its principal operations base, or at another location used by it and approved by the Administrator.

Subpart L—Records and Reports

§ 125.401 Crewmember record.

(a) Each certificate holder shall—

(1) Maintain current records of each crewmember that show whether or not that crewmember complies with this chapter (e.g., proficiency checks, airplane qualifications, any required

physical examinations, and flight time records); and

(2) Record each action taken concerning the release from employment or physical or professional disqualification of any flight crewmember and keep the record for at least 6 months thereafter.

(b) Each certificate holder shall maintain the records required by paragraph (a) of this section at its principal operations base, or at another location used by it and approved by the Administrator.

(c) Computer record systems approved by the Administrator may be used in complying with the requirements of paragraph (a) of this section.

§ 125.403 Flight release form.

(a) The flight release may be in any form but must contain at least the following information concerning each flight:

(1) Company or organization name.

(2) Make, model, and registration number of the airplane being used.

(3) Date of flight.

(4) Name and duty assignment of each crewmember.

(5) Departure airport, destination airports, alternate airports, and route.

(6) Minimum fuel supply (in gallons or pounds).

(7) A statement of the type of operation (e.g., IFR, VFR).

(b) The airplane flight release must contain, or have attached to it, weather reports, available weather forecasts, or a combination thereof.

§ 125.405 Disposition of load manifest, flight release, and flight plans.

(a) The pilot in command of an airplane shall carry in the airplane to its destination the original or a signed copy of the—

(1) Load manifest required by § 125.383;

(2) Flight release;

(3) Airworthiness release; and

(4) Flight plan, including route.

(b) If a flight originates at the principal operations base of the certificate holder, it shall retain at that base a signed copy of each document listed in paragraph (a) of this section.

(c) Except as provided in paragraph (d) of this section, if a flight originates

at a place other than the principal operations base of the certificate holder, the pilot in command (or another person not aboard the airplane who is authorized by the operator) shall, before or immediately after departure of the flight, mail signed copies of the documents listed in paragraph (a) of this section to the principal operations base.

(d) If a flight originates at a place other than the principal operations base of the certificate holder and there is at that place a person to manage the flight departure for the operator who does not depart on the airplane, signed copies of the documents listed in paragraph (a) of this section may be retained at that place for not more than 30 days before being sent to the principal operations base of the certificate holder. However, the documents for a particular flight need not be further retained at that place or be sent to the principal operations base, if the originals or other copies of them have been previously returned to the principal operations base.

(e) The certificate holder shall:

(1) Identify in its operations manual the person having custody of the copies of documents retained in accordance with paragraph (d) of this section; and

(2) Retain at its principal operations base either the original or a copy of the records required by this section for at least 30 days.

§ 125.407 Maintenance log: Airplanes.

(a) Each person who takes corrective action or defers action concerning a reported or observed failure or malfunction of an airframe, aircraft engine, propeller, or appliance shall record the action taken in the airplane maintenance log in accordance with part 43 of this chapter.

(b) Each certificate holder shall establish a procedure for keeping copies of the airplane maintenance log required by this section in the airplane for access by appropriate personnel and shall include that procedure in the manual required by § 125.249.

§ 125.409 Service difficulty reports.

(a) Each certificate holder shall report the occurrence or detection of each failure, malfunction, or defect, in a form and manner prescribed by the Administrator.

(b) Each certificate holder shall submit each report required by this section, covering each 24-hour period beginning at 0900 local time of each day and ending at 0900 local time on the next day, to the FAA office in Oklahoma City, Oklahoma. Each report of occurrences during a 24-hour period shall be submitted to the collection point within the next 96 hours. However, a report due on Saturday or Sunday may be submitted on the following Monday, and a report due on a holiday may be submitted on the next work day.

[Doc. No. 19779, 45 FR 67235, Oct. 9, 1980, as amended by Amdt. 125–49, 70 FR 76979, Dec. 29, 2005]

§ 125.411 Airworthiness release or maintenance record entry.

(a) No certificate holder may operate an airplane after maintenance, preventive maintenance, or alteration is performed on the airplane unless the person performing that maintenance, preventive maintenance, or alteration prepares or causes to be prepared—

(1) An airworthiness release; or

(2) An entry in the aircraft maintenance records in accordance with the certificate holder's manual.

(b) The airworthiness release or maintenance record entry required by paragraph (a) of this section must—

(1) Be prepared in accordance with the procedures set forth in the certificate holder's manual;

(2) Include a certification that—

(i) The work was performed in accordance with the requirements of the certificate holder's manual;

(ii) All items required to be inspected were inspected by an authorized person who determined that the work was satisfactorily completed;

(iii) No known condition exists that would make the airplane unairworthy; and

(iv) So far as the work performed is concerned, the airplane is in condition for safe operation; and

(3) Be signed by a person authorized in part 43 of this chapter to perform maintenance, preventive maintenance, and alteration.

(c) When an airworthiness release form is prepared, the certificate holder must give a copy to the pilot in command and keep a record of it for at least 60 days.

(d) Instead of restating each of the conditions of the certification required by paragraph (b) of this section, the certificate holder may state in its manual that the signature of a person authorized in part 43 of this chapter constitutes that certification.

Subpart M—Continued Airworthiness and Safety Improvements

SOURCE: Amdt. 125–53, 72 FR 63412, Nov. 8, 2007, unless otherwise noted.

§ 125.501 Purpose and definition.

(a) This subpart requires operators to support the continued airworthiness of each airplane. These requirements may include, but are not limited to, revising the inspection program, incorporating design changes, and incorporating revisions to Instructions for Continued Airworthiness.

(b) [Reserved]

[Amdt. 125–53, 72 FR 63412, Nov. 8, 2007, as amended by Docket FAA–2018–0119, Amdt. 125–68, 83 FR 9174, Mar. 5, 2018]

§ 125.503 [Reserved]

§ 125.505 Repairs assessment for pressurized fuselages.

(a) No person may operate an Airbus Model A300 (excluding the –600 series), British Aerospace Model BAC 1–11, Boeing Model 707, 720, 727, 737 or 747, McDonnell Douglas Model DC–8, DC–9/MD–80 or DC–10, Fokker Model F28, or Lockheed Model L–1011 beyond the applicable flight cycle implementation time specified below, or May 25, 2001, whichever occurs later, unless operations specifications have been issued to reference repair assessment guidelines applicable to the fuselage pressure boundary (fuselage skin, door skin, and bulkhead webs), and those guidelines are incorporated in its maintenance program. The repair assessment guidelines must be approved by the responsible Aircraft Certification Service office for the type certificate for the affected airplane.

(1) For the Airbus Model A300 (excluding the –600 series), the flight cycle implementation time is:

(i) Model B2: 36,000 flights.

(ii) Model B4–100 (including Model B4–2C): 30,000 flights above the window line, and 36,000 flights below the window line.

(iii) Model B4–200: 25,500 flights above the window line, and 34,000 flights below the window line.

(2) For all models of the British Aerospace BAC 1–11, the flight cycle implementation time is 60,000 flights.

(3) For all models of the Boeing 707, the flight cycle implementation time is 15,000 flights.

(4) For all models of the Boeing 720, the flight cycle implementation time is 23,000 flights.

(5) For all models of the Boeing 727, the flight cycle implementation time is 45,000 flights.

(6) For all models of the Boeing 737, the flight cycle implementation time is 60,000 flights.

(7) For all models of the Boeing 747, the flight cycle implementation time is 15,000 flights.

(8) For all models of the McDonnell Douglas DC–8, the flight cycle implementation time is 30,000 flights.

(9) For all models of the McDonnell Douglas DC–9/MD–80, the flight cycle implementation time is 60,000 flights.

(10) For all models of the McDonnell Douglas DC–10, the flight cycle implementation time is 30,000 flights.

(11) For all models of the Lockheed L–1011, the flight cycle implementation time is 27,000 flights.

(12) For the Fokker F–28 Mark, 1000, 2000, 3000, and 4000, the flight cycle implementation time is 60,000 flights.

(b) [Reserved]

[Doc. No. 29104, 65 FR 24126, Apr. 25, 2000; 65 FR 50744, Aug. 21, 2000, as amended by Amdt. 125–36, 66 FR 23131, May 7, 2001; Amdt. 125–40, 37 FR 72834, Dec. 9, 2002; Amdt. 125–46, 69 FR 45942, July 30, 2004. Redesignated by Amdt. 125–53, 72 FR 63412, Nov. 8, 2007; Docket FAA–2018–0119, Amdt. 125–68, 83 FR 9174, Mar. 5, 2018]

§125.507 Fuel tank system inspection program.

(a) Except as provided in paragraph (g) of this section, this section applies to transport category, turbine-powered airplanes with a type certificate issued after January 1, 1958, that, as a result of original type certification or later increase in capacity, have—

(1) A maximum type-certificated passenger capacity of 30 or more, or

(2) A maximum payload capacity of 7500 pounds or more.

(b) For each airplane on which an auxiliary fuel tank is installed under a field approval, before June 16, 2008, the certificate holder must submit to the responsible Aircraft Certification Service office proposed maintenance instructions for the tank that meet the requirements of Special Federal Aviation Regulation No. 88 (SFAR 88) of this chapter.

(c) After December 16, 2008, no certificate holder may operate an airplane identified in paragraph (a) of this section unless the inspection program for that airplane has been revised to include applicable inspections, procedures, and limitations for fuel tank systems.

(d) The proposed fuel tank system inspection program revisions must be based on fuel tank system Instructions for Continued Airworthiness (ICA) that have been developed in accordance with the applicable provisions of SFAR 88 of this chapter or §25.1529 and part 25, Appendix H, of this chapter, in effect on June 6, 2001 (including those developed for auxiliary fuel tanks, if any, installed under supplemental type certificates or other design approval) and that have been approved by the responsible Aircraft Certification Service office.

(e) After December 16, 2008, before returning an aircraft to service after any alteration for which fuel tank ICA are developed under SFAR 88, or under §25.1529 in effect on June 6, 2001, the certificate holder must include in the inspection program for the airplane inspections and procedures for the fuel tank system based on those ICA.

(f) The fuel tank system inspection program changes identified in paragraphs (d) and (e) of this section and any later fuel tank system revisions must be submitted to the Principal Inspector for review and approval.

(g) This section does not apply to the following airplane models:

(1) Bombardier CL–44

(2) Concorde

(3) deHavilland D.H. 106 Comet 4C

(4) VFW–Vereinigte Flugtechnische Werk VFW–614

(5) Illyushin Aviation IL 96T

(6) Bristol Aircraft Britannia 305

(7) Handley Page Herald Type 300

(8) Avions Marcel Dassault—Breguet Aviation Mercure 100C

(9) Airbus Caravelle

(10) Lockheed L–300

[Amdt. 125–53, 72 FR 63412, Nov. 8, 2007, as amended by Docket FAA–2018–0119, Amdt. 125–68, 83 FR 9174, Mar. 5, 2018]

§ 125.509 Flammability reduction means.

(a) *Applicability.* Except as provided in paragraph (m) of this section, this section applies to transport category, turbine-powered airplanes with a type certificate issued after January 1, 1958, that, as a result of original type certification or later increase in capacity have:

(1) A maximum type-certificated passenger capacity of 30 or more, or

(2) A maximum payload capacity of 7,500 pounds or more.

(b) *New Production Airplanes.* Except in accordance with § 125.201, no person may operate an airplane identified in Table 1 of this section (including all-cargo airplanes) for which the State of Manufacture issued the original certificate of airworthiness or export airworthiness approval after December 27, 2010 unless an Ignition Mitigation Means (IMM) or Flammability Reduction Means (FRM) meeting the requirements of § 26.33 of this chapter is operational.

TABLE 1

Model—Boeing	Model—Airbus
747 Series	A318, A319, A320, A321 Series
737 Series	A330, A340 Series
777 Series	
767 Series	

(c) *Auxiliary Fuel Tanks.* After the applicable date stated in paragraph (e) of this section, no person may operate any airplane subject to § 26.33 of this chapter that has an Auxiliary Fuel Tank installed pursuant to a field approval, unless the following requirements are met:

(1) The person complies with 14 CFR 26.35 by the applicable date stated in that section.

(2) The person installs Flammability Impact Mitigation Means (FIMM), if applicable, that is approved by the responsible Aircraft Certification Service office.

(3) Except in accordance with § 125.201, the FIMM, if applicable, are operational.

(d) *Retrofit.* Except as provided in paragraph (j) of this section, after the dates specified in paragraph (e) of this section, no person may operate an airplane to which this section applies unless the requirements of paragraphs (d)(1) and (d)(2) of this section are met.

(1) Ignition Mitigation Means (IMM), Flammability Reduction Means (FRM), or FIMM, if required by §§ 26.33, 26.35, or 26.37 of this chapter, that are approved by the responsible Aircraft Certification Service office, are installed within the compliance times specified in paragraph (e) of this section.

(2) Except in accordance with § 125.201 of this part, the IMM, FRM or FIMM, as applicable, are operational.

(e) *Compliance Times.* The installations required by paragraph (d) of this section must be accomplished no later than the applicable dates specified in paragraph (e)(1), (e)(2) or (e)(3) of this section.

(1) Fifty percent of each person's fleet of airplanes subject to paragraph (d)(1) of this section must be modified no later than December 26, 2014.

(2) One hundred percent of each person's fleet of airplanes subject to paragraph (d)(1) of this section must be modified no later than December 26, 2017.

(3) For those persons that have only one airplane of a model identified in Table 1 of this section, the airplane must be modified no later than December 26, 2017.

(f) *Compliance after Installation.* Except in accordance with § 125.201, no person may—

(1) Operate an airplane on which IMM or FRM has been installed before the dates specified in paragraph (e) of this section unless the IMM or FRM is operational, or

(2) Deactivate or remove an IMM or FRM once installed unless it is replaced by a means that complies with paragraph (d) of this section.

(g) *Inspection Program Revisions.* No person may operate an airplane for which airworthiness limitations have been approved by the responsible Aircraft Certification Service office in accordance with §§ 26.33, 26.35, or 26.37 of this chapter after the airplane is modified in accordance with paragraph (d) of this section unless the inspection program for that airplane is revised to include those applicable airworthiness limitations.

(h) After the inspection program is revised as required by paragraph (g) of this section, before returning an airplane to service after any alteration for which airworthiness limitations are required by §§ 25.981, 26.33, 26.35, or 26.37 of this chapter, the person must revise the inspection program for the airplane to include those airworthiness limitations.

(i) The inspection program changes identified in paragraphs (g) and (h) of this section must be submitted to the operator's assigned Flight Standards office responsible for review and approval prior to incorporation.

(j) The requirements of paragraph (d) of this section do not apply to airplanes operated in all-cargo service, but those airplanes are subject to paragraph (f) of this section.

(k) After the date by which any person is required by this section to modify 100 percent of the affected fleet, no person may operate in passenger service any airplane model specified in Table 2 of this section unless the airplane has been modified to comply with § 26.33(c) of this chapter.

TABLE 2

Model—Boeing	Model—Airbus
747 Series	A318, A319, A320, A321 Series.
737 Series	A300, A310 Series.
777 Series	A330, A340 Series.
767 Series.	
757 Series.	

(1) No person may operate any airplane on which an auxiliary fuel tank is installed after December 26, 2017 unless the FAA has certified the tank as compliant with § 25.981 of this chapter, in effect on December 26, 2008.

(m) *Exclusions.* The requirements of this section do not apply to the following airplane models:

(1) Convair CV–240, 340, 440, including turbine powered conversions.

(2) Lockheed L–188 Electra.

(3) Vickers VC–10.

(4) Douglas DC–3, including turbine powered conversions.

(5) Bombardier CL–44.

(6) Mitsubishi YS–11.

(7) BAC 1–11.

(8) Concorde.

(9) deHavilland D.H. 106 Comet 4C.

(10) VFW—Vereinigte Flugtechnische VFW–614.

(11) Illyushin Aviation IL 96T.

(12) Bristol Aircraft Britannia 305.

(13) Handley Page Herald Type 300.

(14) Avions Marcel Dassault—Breguet Aviation Mercure 100C.

(15) Airbus Caravelle.

(16) Fokker F–27/Fairchild Hiller FH–227.

(17) Lockheed L–300.

[Doc. No. FAA–2005–22997, 73 FR 42502, July 21, 2008, as amended by Amdt. 125–57, 74 FR 31619, July 2, 2009; Docket FAA–2018–0119, Amdt. 125–68, 83 FR 9174, Mar. 5, 2018]

APPENDIX A TO PART 125—ADDITIONAL EMERGENCY EQUIPMENT

(a) *Means for emergency evacuation.* Each passenger-carrying landplane emergency exit (other than over-the-wing) that is more that 6 feet from the ground with the airplane on the ground and the landing gear extended must have an approved means to assist the occupants in descending to the ground. The assisting means for a floor level emergency exit must meet the requirements of § 25.809(f)(1) of this chapter in effect on April 30, 1972, except that, for any airplane for which the application for the type certificate was filed after that date, it must meet the requirements under which the airplane was type certificated. An assisting means that deploys automatically must be armed during taxiing, takeoffs, and landings. However, if the Administrator finds that the design of the exit makes compliance impractical, the Administrator may grant a deviation from the requirement of automatic deployment if the assisting means automatically erects upon deployment and, with respect to required emergency exits, if an emergency evacuation demonstration is conducted in accordance with §125.189. This paragraph does not apply to the rear window emergency exit of DC–3 airplanes operated with less than 36 occupants, including crewmembers, and less than five exits authorized for passenger use.

(b) *Interior emergency exit marking.* The following must be complied with for each passenger-carrying airplane:

(1) Each passenger emergency exit, its means of access, and means of opening must be conspicuously marked. The identity and location of each passenger emergency exit must be recognizable from a distance equal to the width of the cabin. The location of each passenger emergency exit must be indicated by a sign visible to occupants approaching along the main passenger aisle. There must be a locating sign—

(i) Above the aisle near each over-the-wing passenger emergency exit, or at another ceiling location if it is more practical because of low headroom;

(ii) Next to each floor level passenger emergency exit, except that one sign may serve two such exits if they both can be seen readily from that sign; and

(iii) On each bulkhead or divider that prevents fore and aft vision along the passenger cabin, to indicate emergency exits beyond and obscured by it, except that if this is not possible the sign may be placed at another appropriate location.

(2) Each passenger emergency exit marking and each locating sign must meet the following:

(i) For an airplane for which the application for the type certificate was filed prior to May 1, 1972, each passenger emergency exit marking and each locating sign must be manufactured to meet the requirements of §25.812(b) of this chapter in effect on April 30, 1972. On these airplanes, no sign may continue to be used if its luminescence (brightness) decreases to below 100 microlamberts. The colors may be reversed if it increases the emergency illumination of the passenger compartment. However, the Administrator may authorize deviation from the 2-inch background requirements if the Administrator finds that special circumstances exist that make compliance impractical and that the proposed deviation provides an equivalent level of safety.

(ii) For an airplane for which the application for the type certificate was filed on or after May 1, 1972, each passenger emergency exit marking and each locating sign must be manufactured to meet the interior emergency exit marking requirements under which the airplane was type certificated. On these airplanes, no sign may continue to be used if its luminescence (brightness) decreases to below 250 microlamberts.

(c) *Lighting for interior emergency exit markings.* Each passenger-carrying airplane must have an emergency lighting system, independent of the main lighting system. However, sources of general cabin illumination may be common to both the emergency and the main lighting systems if the power supply to the emergency lighting system is independent of the power supply to the main lighting system. The emergency lighting system must—

(1) Illuminate each passenger exit marking and locating sign; and

(2) Provide enough general lighting in the passenger cabin so that the average illumination, when measured at 40-inch intervals at seat armrest height, on the centerline of the main passenger aisle, is at least 0.05 foot-candles.

(d) *Emergency light operation.* Except for lights forming part of emergency lighting subsystems provided in compliance with §25.812(g) of this chapter (as prescribed in paragraph (h) of this section) that serve no more than one assist means, are independent of the airplane's main emergency lighting systems, and are automatically activated when the assist means is deployed, each light required by paragraphs (c) and (h) must comply with the following:

(1) Each light must be operable manually and must operate automatically from the independent lighting system—

(i) In a crash landing; or

(ii) Whenever the airplane's normal electric power to the light is interrupted.

(2) Each light must—

(i) Be operable manually from the flightcrew station and from a point in the passenger compartment that is readily accessible to a normal flight attendant seat;

(ii) Have a means to prevent inadvertent operation of the manual controls; and

(iii) When armed or turned on at either station, remain lighted or become lighted upon interruption of the airplane's normal electric power.

Each light must be armed or turned on during taxiing, takeoff, and landing. In showing compliance with this paragraph, a transverse vertical separation of the fuselage need not be considered.

(3) Each light must provide the required level of illumination for at least 10 minutes at the critical ambient conditions after emergency landing.

(e) *Emergency exit operating handles.* (1) For a passenger-carrying airplane for which the application for the type certificate was filed prior to May 1, 1972, the location of each passenger emergency exit operating handle and instructions for opening the exit must be shown by a marking on or near the exit that is readable from a distance of 30 inches. In addition, for each Type I and Type II emergency exit with a locking mechanism released by rotary motion of the handle, the instructions for opening must be shown by—

(1) A red arrow with a shaft at least ¾ inch wide and a head twice the width of the shaft,

extending along at least 70 degrees of arc at a radius approximately equal to ¾ of the handle length; and

(ii) The word "open" in red letters 1 inch high placed horizontally near the head of the arrow.

(2) For a passenger-carrying airplane for which the application for the type certificate was filed on or after May 1, 1972, the location of each passenger emergency exit operating handle and instructions for opening the exit must be shown in accordance with the requirements under which the airplane was type certificated. On these airplanes, no operating handle or operating handle cover may continue to be used if its luminescence (brightness) decreases to below 100 microlamberts.

(f) *Emergency exit access.* Access to emergency exits must be provided as follows for each passenger-carrying airplane:

(1) Each passageway between individual passenger areas, or leading to a Type I or Type II emergency exit, must be unobstructed and at least 20 inches wide.

(2) There must be enough space next to each Type I or Type II emergency exit to allow a crewmember to assist in the evacuation of passengers without reducing the unobstructed width of the passageway below that required in paragraph (f)(1) of this section. However, the Administrator may authorize deviation from this requirement for an airplane certificated under the provisions of part 4b of the Civil Air Regulations in effect before December 20, 1951, if the Administrator finds that special circumstances exist that provide an equivalent level of safety.

(3) There must be access from the main aisle to each Type III and Type IV exit. The access from the aisle to these exits must not be obstructed by seats, berths, or other protrusions in a manner that would reduce the effectiveness of the exit. In addition—

(i) For an airplane for which the application for the type certificate was filed prior to May 1, 1972, the access must meet the requirements of § 25.813(c) of this chapter in effect on April 30, 1972; and

(ii) For an airplane for which the application for the type certificate was filed on or after May 1, 1972, the access must meet the emergency exit access requirements under which the airplane was certificated.

(4) If it is necessary to pass through a passageway between passenger compartments to reach any required emergency exit from any seat in the passenger cabin, the passageway must not be obstructed. However, curtains may be used if they allow free entry through the passageway.

(5) No door may be installed in any partition between passenger compartments.

(6) If it is necessary to pass through a doorway separating the passenger cabin from other areas to reach any required emergency exit from any passenger seat, the door must

have a means to latch it in open position, and the door must be latched open during each takeoff and landing. The latching means must be able to withstand the loads imposed upon it when the door is subjected to the ultimate interia forces, relative to the surrounding structure, listed in § 25.561(b) of this chapter.

(g) *Exterior exit markings.* Each passenger emergency exit and the means of opening that exit from the outside must be marked on the outside of the airplane. There must be a 2-inch colored band outlining each passenger emergency exit on the side of the fuselage. Each outside marking, including the band, must be readily distinguishable from the surrounding fuselage area by contrast in color. The markings must comply with the following:

(1) If the reflectance of the darker color is 15 percent or less, the reflectance of the lighter color must be at least 45 percent. "Reflectance" is the ratio of the luminous flux reflected by a body to the luminous flux it receives.

(2) If the reflectance of the darker color is greater than 15 percent, at least a 30 percent difference between its reflectance and the reflectance of the lighter color must be provided.

(3) Exits that are not in the side of the fuselage must have the external means of opening and applicable instructions marked conspicuously in red or, if red is inconspicuous against the background color, in bright chrome yellow and, when the opening means for such an exit is located on only one side of the fuselage, a conspicuous marking to that effect must be provided on the other side.

(h) *Exterior emergency lighting and escape route.* (1) Each passenger-carrying airplane must be equipped with exterior lighting that meets the following requirements:

(i) For an airplane for which the application for the type certificate was filed prior to May 1, 1972, the requirements of § 25.812(f) and (g) of this chapter in effect on April 30, 1972.

(ii) For an airplane for which the application for the type certificate was filed on or after May 1, 1972, the exterior emergency lighting requirements under which the airplane was type certificated.

(2) Each passenger-carrying airplane must be equipped with a slip-resistant escape route that meets the following requirements:

(i) For an airplane for which the application for the type certificate was filed prior to May 1, 1972, the requirements of § 25.803(e) of this chapter in effect on April 30, 1972.

(ii) For an airplane for which the application for the type certificate was filed on or after May 1, 1972, the slip-resistant escape route requirements under which the airplane was type certificated.

(i) *Floor level exits.* Each floor level door or exit in the side of the fuselage (other than those leading into a cargo or baggage compartment that is not accessible from the passenger cabin) that is 44 or more inches high and 20 or more inches wide, but not wider than 46 inches, each passenger ventral exit (except the ventral exits on M-404 and CV-240 airplanes) and each tail cone exit must meet the requirements of this section for floor level emergency exits. However, the Administrator may grant a deviation from this paragraph if the Administrator finds that circumstances make full compliance impractical and that an acceptable level of safety has been achieved.

(j) *Additional emergency exits.* Approved emergency exits in the passenger compartments that are in excess of the minimum number of required emergency exits must meet all of the applicable provisions of this section except paragraph (f), (1), (2), and (3) and must be readily accessible.

(k) On each large passenger-carrying turbojet-powered airplane, each ventral exit and tailcone exit must be—

(1) Designed and constructed so that it cannot be opened during flight; and

(2) Marked with a placard readable from a distance of 30 inches and installed at a conspicuous location near the means of opening the exit, stating that the exit has been designed and constructed so that it cannot be opened during flight.

APPENDIX B TO PART 125—CRITERIA FOR DEMONSTRATION OF EMERGENCY EVACUATION PROCEDURES UNDER § 125.189

(a) *Aborted takeoff demonstration.* (1) The demonstration must be conducted either during the dark of the night or during daylight with the dark of the night simulated. If the demonstration is conducted indoors during daylight hours, it must be conducted with each window covered and each door closed to minimize the daylight effect. Illumination on the floor or ground may be used, but it must be kept low and shielded against shining into the airplane's windows or doors.

(2) The airplane must be in a normal ground attitude with landing gear extended.

(3) Stands or ramps may be used for descent from the wing to the ground. Safety equipment such as mats or inverted life rafts may be placed on the ground to protect participants. No other equipment that is not part of the airplane's emergency evacuation equipment may be used to aid the participants in reaching the ground.

(4) The airplane's normal electric power sources must be deenergized.

(5) All emergency equipment for the type of passenger-carrying operation involved must be installed in accordance with the certificate holder's manual.

(6) Each external door and exit and each internal door or curtain must be in position to simulate a normal takeoff.

(7) A representative passenger load of persons in normal health must be used. At least 30 percent must be females. At least 5 percent must be over 60 years of age with a proportionate number of females. At least 5 percent, but not more than 10 percent, must be children under 12 years of age, prorated through that age group. Three life-size dolls, not included as part of the total passenger load, must be carried by passengers to simulate live infants 2 years old or younger. Crewmembers, mechanics, and training personnel who maintain or operate the airplane in the normal course of their duties may not be used as passengers.

(8) No passenger may be assigned a specific seat except as the Administrator may require. Except as required by item (12) of this paragraph, no employee of the certificate holder may be seated next to an emergency exit.

(9) Seat belts and shoulder harnesses (as required) must be fastened.

(10) Before the start of the demonstration, approximately one-half of the total average amount of carry-on baggage, blankets, pillows, and other similar articles must be distributed at several locations in the aisles and emergency exit access ways to create minor obstructions.

(11) The seating density and arrangement of the airplane must be representative of the highest capacity passenger version of that airplane the certificate holder operates or proposes to operate.

(12) Each crewmember must be a member of a regularly scheduled line crew, must be seated in that crewmember's normally assigned seat for takeoff, and must remain in that seat until the signal for commencement of the demonstration is received.

(13) No crewmember or passenger may be given prior knowledge of the emergency exits available for the demonstration.

(14) The certificate holder may not practice, rehearse, or describe the demonstration for the participants nor may any participant have taken part in this type of demonstration within the preceding 6 months.

(15) The pretakeoff passenger briefing required by § 125.327 may be given in accordance with the certificate holder's manual. The passengers may also be warned to follow directions of crewmembers, but may not be instructed on the procedures to be followed in the demonstration.

(16) If safety equipment as allowed by item (3) of this section is provided, either all passenger and cockpit windows must be blacked out or all of the emergency exits must have safety equipment to prevent disclosure of the available emergency exits.

(17) Not more than 50 percent of the emergency exits in the sides of the fuselage of an

airplane that meet all of the requirements applicable to the required emergency exits for that airplane may be used for the demonstration. Exits that are not to be used in the demonstration must have the exit handle deactivated or must be indicated by red lights, red tape or other acceptable means, placed outside the exits to indicate fire or other reason that they are unusable. The exits to be used must be representative of all of the emergency exits on the airplane and must be designated by the certificate holder, subject to approval by the Administrator. At least one floor level exit must be used.

(18) All evacuees, except those using an over-the-wing exit, must leave the airplane by a means provided as part of the airplane's equipment.

(19) The certificate holder's approved procedures and all of the emergency equipment that is normally available, including slides, ropes, lights, and megaphones, must be fully utilized during the demonstration.

(20) The evacuation time period is completed when the last occupant has evacuated the airplane and is on the ground. Evacuees using stands or ramps allowed by item (3) above are considered to be on the ground when they are on the stand or ramp: *Provided,* That the acceptance rate of the stand or ramp is no greater than the acceptance rate of the means available on the wing for descent from the wing during an actual crash situation.

(b) *Ditching demonstration.* The demonstration must assume that daylight hours exist outside the airplane and that all required crewmembers are available for the demonstration.

(1) If the certificate holder's manual requires the use of passengers to assist in the launching of liferafts, the needed passengers must be aboard the airplane and participate in the demonstration according to the manual.

(2) A stand must be placed at each emergency exit and wing with the top of the platform at a height simulating the water level of the airplane following a ditching.

(3) After the ditching signal has been received, each evacuee must don a life vest according to the certificate holder's manual.

(4) Each liferaft must be launched and inflated according to the certificate holder's manual and all other required emergency equipment must be placed in rafts.

(5) Each evacuee must enter a liferaft and the crewmembers assigned to each liferaft must indicate the location of emergency equipment aboard the raft and describe its use.

(6) Either the airplane, a mockup of the airplane, or a floating device simulating a passenger compartment must be used.

(i) If a mockup of the airplane is used, it must be a life-size mockup of the interior and representative of the airplane currently used by or proposed to be used by the certificate holder and must contain adequate seats for use of the evacuees. Operation of the emergency exits and the doors must closely simulate that on the airplane. Sufficient wing area must be installed outside the over-the-wing exits to demonstrate the evacuation.

(ii) If a floating device simulating a passenger compartment is used, it must be representative, to the extent possible, of the passenger compartment of the airplane used in operations. Operation of the emergency exits and the doors must closely simulate operation on that airplane. Sufficient wing area must be installed outside the over-the-wing exits to demonstrate the evacuation. The device must be equipped with the same survival equipment as is installed on the airplane, to accommodate all persons participating in the demonstration.

APPENDIX C TO PART 125—ICE PROTECTION

If certification with ice protection provisions is desired, compliance with the following must be shown:

(a) The recommended procedures for the use of the ice protection equipment must be set forth in the Airplane Flight Manual.

(b) An analysis must be performed to establish, on the basis of the airplane's operational needs, the adequacy of the ice protection system for the various components of the airplane. In addition, tests of the ice protection system must be conducted to demonstrate that the airplane is capable of operating safely in continuous maximum and intermittent maximum icing conditions as described in appendix C of part 25 of this chapter.

(c) Compliance with all or portions of this section may be accomplished by reference, where applicable because of similarity of the designs, to analyses and tests performed by the applicant for a type certificated model.

APPENDIX D TO PART 125—AIRPLANE FLIGHT RECORDER SPECIFICATION

Parameters	Range	Accuracy sensor input to DFDR readout	Sampling interval (per second)	Resolution [4] read out
Time (GMT or Frame Counter) (range 0 to 4095, sampled 1 per frame).	24 Hrs	±0.125% Per Hour	0.25 (1 per 4 seconds).	1 sec.

Parameters	Range	Accuracy sensor input to DFDR readout	Sampling interval (per second)	Resolution [4] read out
Altitude	−1,000 ft to max certificated altitude of aircraft.	±100 to ±700 ft (See Table 1, TSO-C51a).	1	5′ to 35′ [1]
Airspeed	50 KIAS to V_{so}, and V_{so} to 1.2 V_D.	±5%, ±3%	1	1 kt.
Heading	360°	±2°	1	0.5°
Normal Acceleration (Vertical)	−3g to + 6g	±1% of max range excluding datum error of ±5%.	8	0.01g.
Pitch Attitude	±75°	±2°	1	0.5°.
Roll Attitude	±180°	±2°	1	0.5°.
Radio Transmitter Keying	On-Off (Discrete)		1	
Thrust/Power on Each Engine	Full range forward	±2%	1	0.2% [2]
Trailing Edge Flap or Cockpit Control Selection.	Full range or each discrete position.	±3° or as pilot's Indicator	0.5	0.5% [2]
Leading Edge Flap or Cockpit Control Selection.	Full range or each discrete position.	±3° or as pilot's indicator	0.5	0.5% [2]
Thrust Reverser Position	Stowed, in transit, and reverse (Discrete).		1 (per 4 seconds per engine).	
Ground Spoiler Position/Speed Brake Selection.	Full range or each discrete position.	±2% unless higher accuracy uniquely required.	1	0.2% [2].
Marker Beacon Passage	Discrete		1	
Autopilot Engagement	Discrete		1	
Longitudinal Acceleration	±1g	±1.5% max range excluding datum error of ±5%.	4	0.01g
Pilot Input and/or Surface Position-Primary Controls (Pitch, Roll, Yaw) [3].	Full range	±2° unless higher accuracy uniquely required.	1	0.2% [2].
Lateral Acceleration	±1g	±1.5% max range excluding datum error of ±5%.	4	0.01g.
Pitch Trim Position	Full range	±3% unless higher accuracy uniquely required.	1	0.3% [2]
Glideslope Deviation	±400 Microamps	±3%	1	0.3% [2]
Localizer Deviation	±400 Microamps	±3%	1	0.3% [2].
AFCS Mode and Engagement Status.	Discrete		1	
Radio Altitude	−20 ft to 2,500 ft	±2 Ft or ±3% Whichever is Greater Below 500 Ft and ±5% Above 500 Ft.		1 ft + 5% [2] above 500′.
Master Warning	Discrete		1	
Main Gear Squat Switch Status	Discrete		1	
Angle of Attack (if recorded directly).	As installed	As installed	2	0.3% [2].
Outside Air Temperature or Total Air Temperature.	−50 °C to + 90 °C	±2 °C	0.5	0.3 °C
Hydraulics, Each System Low Pressure.	Discrete		0.5	or 0.5% [2].
Groundspeed	As Installed	Most Accurate Systems Installed (IMS Equipped Aircraft Only).	1	0.2% [2].

If additional recording capacity is available, recording of the following parameters is recommended. The parameters are listed in order of significance:

Parameters	Range	Accuracy sensor input to DFDR readout	Sampling interval (per second)	Resolution read out
Drift Angle	When available. As installed.	As installed	4	
Wind Speed and Direction	When available. As installed.	As installed	4	
Latitude and Longitude	When available. As installed.	As installed	4	
Brake pressure/Brake pedal position.	As installed	As installed	1	
Additional engine parameters:				
EPR	As installed	As installed	1 (per engine)	
N [1]	As installed	As installed	1 (per engine)	
N [2]	As installed	As installed	1 (per engine)	
EGT	As installed	As installed	1 (per engine)	
Throttle Lever Position	As installed	As installed	1 (per engine)	
Fuel Flow	As installed	As installed	1 (per engine)	
TCAS:				
TA	As installed	As installed	1	
RA	As installed	As installed	1	
Sensitivity level (as selected by crew).	As installed	As installed	2	

Parameters	Range	Accuracy sensor input to DFDR readout	Sampling interval (per second)	Resolution [4] read out
GPWS (ground proximity warning system).	Discrete	....	1	
Landing gear or gear selector position.	Discrete	....	0.25 (1 per 4 seconds).	
DME 1 and 2 Distance	0–200 NM; ....__......	As installed	0.25	1 mi.
Nav 1 and 2 Frequency Selection.	Full range ...._......	As installed	0.25	

[1] When altitude rate is recorded. Altitude rate must have sufficient resolution and sampling to permit the derivation of altitude to 5 feet.
[2] Percent of full range.
[3] For airplanes that can demonstrate the capability of deriving either the control input on control movement (one from the other) for all modes of operation and flight regimes, the "or" applies. For airplanes with non-mechanical control systems (fly-by-wire) the "and" applies. In airplanes with split surfaces, suitable combination of inputs is acceptable in lieu of recording each surface separately.
[4] This column applies to aircraft manufactured after October 11, 1991.

[Doc. No. 25530, 53 FR 26150, July 11, 1988; 53 FR 30906, Aug. 16, 1988]

APPENDIX E TO PART 125—AIRPLANE FLIGHT RECORDER SPECIFICATIONS

The recorded values must meet the designated range, resolution and accuracy requirements during static and dynamic conditions. Dynamic condition means the parameter is experiencing change at the maximum rate attainable, including the maximum rate of reversal. All data recorded must be correlated in time to within one second.

Parameters	Range	Accuracy (sensor input)	Seconds per sampling interval	Resolution	Remarks
1. Time or Relative Times Counts. [1].	24 Hrs, 0 to 4095.	±0.125% Per Hour.	4	1 sec	UTC time preferred when available. Count increments each 4 seconds of system operation.
2. Pressure Altitude.	−1000 ft to max certificated altitude of aircraft. +5000 ft.	±100 to ±700 ft (see table, TSO C124a or TSO C51a).	1	5′ to 35′	Data should be obtained from the air data computer when practicable.
3. Indicated airspeed or Calibrated airspeed.	50 KIAS or minimum value to Max V_{so}, to 1.2 V_{D}.	±5% and ±3%	1	1 kt	Data should be obtained from the air data computer when practicable.
4. Heading (Primary flight crew reference).	0–360° and Discrete "true" or "mag".	±2°	1	0.5°	When true or magnetic heading can be selected as the primary heading reference, a discrete indicating selection must be recorded.
5. Normal Acceleration (Vertical) [9].	−3g to +6g	±1% of max range excluding datum error of ±5%.	0.125	0.004g.	
6. Pitch Attitude ..	±75°	±2°	1 or 0.25 for airplanes operated under § 125.226(f).	0.5°	A sampling rate of 0.25 is recommended.
7. Roll Attitude [2] ..	±180°	±2°	1 or 0.5 for airplanes operated under § 121.344(f).	0.5°	A sampling rate of 0.5 is recommended.
8. Manual Radio Transmitter Keying or CVR/ DFDR synchronization reference	On-Off (Discrete) None.	....	1		Preferably each crew member but one discrete acceptable for all transmission provided the CVR/ FDR system complies with TSO C124a CVR synchronization requirements (paragraph 4.2.1 ED–55).
9. Thrust/Power on each engine—primary flight crew reference.	Full Range Forward.	±2%	1 (per engine) ...	0.3% of full range.	Sufficient parameters (e.g., EPR, N1 or Torque, NP) as appropriate to the particular engine being recorded to determine power in forward and reverse thrust, including potential overspeed condition.
10. Autopilot Engagement.	Discrete "on" or "off".	....	1.		

371

The recorded values must meet the designated range, resolution and accuracy requirements during static and dynamic conditions. Dynamic condition means the parameter is experiencing change at the maximum rate attainable, including the maximum rate of reversal. All data recorded must be correlated in time to within one second.

Parameters	Range	Accuracy (sensor input)	Seconds per sampling interval	Resolution	Remarks
11. Longitudinal Acceleration.	±1g	±1.5% max. range excluding datum error of ±5%.	0.25	0.004g.	
12a. Pitch control(s) position (nonfly-by-wire systems) [18].	Full range	±2° unless higher accuracy uniquely required.	0.5 or 0.25 for airplanes operated under § 125.226(f).	0.5% of full range.	For airplanes that have a flight control breakaway capability that allows either pilot to operate the controls independently, record both control inputs. The control inputs may be sampled alternately once per second to produce the sampling interval of 0.5 or 0.25, as applicable.
12b. Pitch control(s) position (fly-by-wire systems) [3] [18].	Full range	±2° unless higher accuracy uniquely required.	0.5 or 0.25 for airplanes operated under § 125.226(f).	0.2% of full range.	
13a. Lateral control position(s) (nonfly-by-wire) [18].	Full range	±2° unless higher accuracy uniquely required.	0.5 or 0.25 for airplanes operated under § 125.226(f).	0.2% of full range.	For airplanes that have a flight control break away capability that allows either pilot to operate the controls independently, record both control inputs. The control inputs may be sampled alternately once per second to produce the sampling interval of 0.5 or 0.25, as applicable.
13b. Lateral control position(s) (fly-by-wire) [4] [18].	Full range	±2° unless higher accuracy uniquely required.	0.5 or 0.25 for airplanes operated under § 125.226(f).	0.2% of full range.	
14a. Yaw control position(s) (nonfly-by-wire) [5] [18].	Full range	±2° unless higher accuracy uniquely required.	0.5	0.3% of full range.	For airplanes that have a flight control breakaway capability that allows either pilot to operate the controls independently, record both control inputs. The control inputs may be sampled alternately once per second to produce the sampling interval of 0.5.
14b. Yaw control position(s) (fly-by-wire) [18].	Full range	±2° unless higher accuracy uniquely required.	0.5	0.2% of full range.	
15. Pitch control surface(s) position [6] [18].	Full range	±2° unless higher accuracy uniquely required.	0.5 or 0.25 for airplanes operated under § 125.226(f).	0.3% of full range.	For airplanes fitted with multiple or split surfaces, a suitable combination of inputs is acceptable in lieu of recording each surface separately. The control surfaces may be sampled alternately to produce the sampling interval of 0.5 or 0.25, as applicable.
16. Lateral control surface(s) position [7] [18].	Full Range	±2° unless higher accuracy uniquely required.	0.5 or 0.25 for airplanes operated under § 125.226(f).	0.2% of full range.	A suitable combination of surface position sensors is acceptable in lieu of recording each surface separately. The control surfaces may be sampled alternately to produce the sampling interval of 0.5 or 0.25, as applicable.

The recorded values must meet the designated range, resolution and accuracy requirements during static and dynamic conditions. Dynamic condition means the parameter is experiencing change at the maximum rate attainable, including the maximum rate of reversal. All data recorded must be correlated in time to within one second.

Parameters	Range	Accuracy (sensor input)	Seconds per sampling interval	Resolution	Remarks
17. Yaw control surface(s) position [8] [18].	Full range	±2° unless higher accuracy uniquely required.	0.5	0.2% of full range.	For airplanes fitted with multiple or split surfaces, a suitable combination of surface position sensors is acceptable in lieu of recording each surface separately. The control surfaces may be sampled alternately to produce the sampling interval of 0.5.
18. Lateral Acceleration.	±1g	±1.5% max. range excluding datum error of ±5%.	0.25	0.004g.	
19. Pitch Trim Surface Position.	Full Range	±3° Unless Higher Accuracy Uniquely Required.	1	0.6% of full range	
20. Trailing Edge Flap or Cockpit Control Selection. [10].	Full Range or Each Position (discrete).	±3° or as Pilot's indicator.	2	0.5% of full range.	Flap position and cockpit control may each be sampled at 4 second intervals, to give a data point every 2 seconds.
21. Leading Edge Flap or Cockpit Control Selection. [11].	Full Range or Each Discrete Position.	±3° or as Pilot's indicator and sufficient to determine each discrete position.	2	0.5% of full range.	Left and right sides, or flap position and cockpit control may each be sampled at 4 second intervals, so as to give a data point every 2 seconds.
22. Each Thrust Reverser Position (or equivalent for propeller airplane).	Stowed, In Transit, and Reverse (Discrete).	....	1 (per engine). ..	....	Turbo-jet—2 discretes enable the 3 states to be determined. Turbo-prop—1 discrete.
23. Ground Spoiler Position or Speed Brake Selection [12].	Full Range or Each Position (discrete).	±2° Unless higher accuracy uniquely required.	1 or 0.5 for airplanes operated under § 125.226(f).	0.2% of full range.	
24. Outside Air Temperature or Total Air Temperature. [13].	−50 °C to +90 °C.	±2 °C	2	0.3 °C..	
25. Autopilot/ Autothrottle/ AFCS Mode and Engagement Status.	A suitable combination of discretes.	....	1	....	Discretes should show which systems are engaged and which primary modes are controlling the flight path and speed of the aircraft.
26. Radio Altitude [14].	−20 ft to 2,500 ft.	±2 ft or ±3% Whichever is Greater Below 500 ft and ±5% above 500 ft.	1	1 ft + 5% Above 500 ft.	For autoland/category 3 operations. Each radio altimeter should be recorded, but arranged so that at least one is recorded each second.
27. Localizer Deviation, MLS Azimuth, or GPS Lateral Deviation.	±400 Microamps or available sensor range as installed ±62°.	As installed. ±3% recommended .	1	0.3% of full range.	For autoland/category 3 operations. each system should be recorded but arranged so that at least one is recorded each second. It is not necessary to record ILS and MLS at the same time, only the approach aid in use need be recorded.

The recorded values must meet the designated range, resolution and accuracy requirements during static and dynamic conditions. Dynamic condition means the parameter is experiencing change at the maximum rate attainable, including the maximum rate of reversal. All data recorded must be correlated in time to within one second.

Parameters	Range	Accuracy (sensor input)	Seconds per sampling interval	Resolution	Remarks
28. Glideslope Deviation, MLS Elevation, or GPS Vertical Deviation.	±400 Microamps or available sensor range as installed. 0.9 to + 30°	As installed ±3% recommended ...	1	0.3% of full range.	For autoland/category 3 operations. each system should be recorded but arranged so that at least one is recorded each second. It is not necessary to record ILS and MLS at the same time, only the approach aid in use need be recorded.
29. Marker Beacon Passage.	Discrete "on" or "off".	....	1	....	A single discrete is acceptable for all markers.
30. Master Warning.	Discrete	....	1	....	Record the master warning and record each 'red' warning that cannot be determined from other parameters or from the cockpit voice recorder.
31. Air/ground sensor (primary airplane system reference nose or main gear).	Discrete "air" or "ground".	....	1 (0.25 recommended).		
32. Angle of Attack (If measured directly).	As installed	As Installed	2 or 0.5 for airplanes operated under § 125.226(f).	0.3% of full range.	If left and right sensors are available, each may be recorded at 4 or 1 second intervals, as appropriate, so as to give a data point at 2 seconds or 0.5 second, as required.
33. Hydraulic Pressure Low, Each System.	Discrete or available sensor range, "low" or "normal".	±5%	2	0.5% of full range.	
34. Groundspeed	As Installed	Most Accurate Systems Installed.	1	0.2% of full range.	
35. GPWS (ground proximity warning system).	Discrete "warning" or "off".	....	1	....	A suitable combination of discretes unless recorder capacity is limited in which case a single discrete for all modes is acceptable.
36. Landing Gear Position or Landing gear cockpit control selection.	Discrete	....	4	....	A suitable combination of discretes should be recorded.
37. Drift Angle. [15]	As installed	As installed	4	0.1%.	
38. Wind Speed and Direction.	As installed	As installed	4	1 knot, and 1.0°.	
39. Latitude and Longitude.	As installed	As installed	4	0.002°, or as installed.	Provided by the Primary Navigation System Reference. Where capacity permits Latitude/longtitude resolution should be 0.0002°.
40. Stick shaker and pusher activation.	Discrete(s) "on" or "off".	....	1	....	A suitable combination of discretes to determine activation.
41. Windshear Detection.	Discrete "warning" or "off".	....	1		
42. Throttle/power lever position. [16].	Full Range	±2%	1 for each lever	2% of full range	For airplanes with non-mechanically linked cockpit engine controls.

The recorded values must meet the designated range, resolution and accuracy requirements during static and dynamic conditions. Dynamic condition means the parameter is experiencing change at the maximum rate attainable, including the maximum rate of reversal. All data recorded must be correlated in time to within one second.

Parameters	Range	Accuracy (sensor input)	Seconds per sampling interval	Resolution	Remarks
43. Additional Engine Parameters.	As installed	As installed	Each engine each second.	2% of full range	Where capacity permits, the preferred priority is indicated vibration level, N2, EGT, Fuel Flow, Fuel Cutoff lever position and N3, unless engine manufacturer recommends otherwise.
44. Traffic Alert and Collision Avoidance System (TCAS).	Discretes	As installed	1		A suitable combination of discretes should be recorded to determine the status of-Combined Control, Vertical Control, Up Advisory, and Down Advisory. (ref. ARINC Characteristic 735 Attachment 6E, TCAS VERTICAL RA DATA OUTPUT WORD.)
45. DME 1 and 2 Distance.	0–200 NM	As installed	4	1 NM	1 mile.
46. Nav 1 and 2 Selected Frequency.	Full range	As installed	4		Sufficient to determine selected frequency
47. Selected barometric setting.	Full range	±5%	(1 per 64 sec.)	0.2% of full range.	
48. Selected Altitude.	Full range	±5%	1	100 ft.	
49. Selected speed.	Full range	±5%	1	1 knot.	
50. Selected Mach.	Full range	±5%	1	.01.	
51. Selected vertical speed.	Full range	±5%	1	100 ft/min.	
52. Selected heading.	Full range	±5%	1	1°.	
53. Selected flight path.	Full range	±5%	1	1°.	
54. Selected decision height.	Full range	±5%	64	1 ft.	
55. EFIS display format.	Discrete(s)		4		Discretes should show the display system status (e.g., off, normal, fail, composite, sector, plan, nav aids, weather radar, range, copy).
56. Multi-function/ Engine Alerts Display format.	Discrete(s)		4		Discretes should show the display system status (e.g., off, normal, fail, and the identity of display pages for emergency procedures, need not be recorded).
57. Thrust command. [17].	Full Range	±2%	2	2% of full range	
58. Thrust target.	Full range	±2%	4	2% of full range.	
59. Fuel quantity in CG trim tank.	Full range	±5%	(1 per 64 sec.)	1% of full range.	
60. Primary Navigation System Reference.	Discrete GPS, INS, VOR/ DME, MLS, Localizer Glideslope.		4		A suitable combination of discretes to determine the Primary Navigation System reference.
61. Ice Detection	Discrete "ice" or "no ice".		4		
62. Engine warning each engine vibration.	Discrete		1		
63. Engine warning each engine over temp.	Discrete		1		

The recorded values must meet the designated range, resolution and accuracy requirements during static and dynamic conditions. Dynamic condition means the parameter is experiencing change at the maximum rate attainable, including the maximum rate of reversal. All data recorded must be correlated in time to within one second.

Parameters	Range	Accuracy (sensor input)	Seconds per sampling interval	Resolution	Remarks
64. Engine warning each engine oil pressure low.	Discrete	....	1		
65. Engine warning each engine over speed.	Discrete	....	1		
66. Yaw Trim Surface Position.	Full Range	±3% Unless Higher Accuracy Uniquely Required.	2	0.3% of full range..	
67. Roll Trim Surface Position.	Full Range	±3% Unless Higher Accuracy Uniquely Required.	2	0.3% of full range..	
68. Brake Pressure (left and right).	As installed	±5%	1	....	To determine braking effort applied by pilots or by autobrakes.
69. Brake Pedal Application (left and right).	Discrete or Analog "applied" or "off".	±5% (Analog)	1	....	To determine braking applied by pilots.
70. Yaw or side-slip angle.	Full Range	±5%	1	0,5°.	
71. Engine bleed valve position.	Decrete "open" or "closed".	....	4	....	
72. De-icing or anti-icing system selection.	Discrete "on" or "off".	....	4	....	
73. Computed center of gravity.	Full Range	±5%	(1 per 64 sec.) ..	1% of full range.	
74. AC electrical bus status.	Discrete "power" or "off".	....	4	....	Each bus.
75. DC electrical bus status.	Discrete "power" or "off".	....	4	....	Each bus.
76. APU bleed valve position.	Discrete "open" or "closed.	....	4.	....	
77. Hydraulic Pressure (each system).	Full range	±5%	2	100 psi.	
78. Loss of cabin pressure.	Discrete "loss" or "normal".	....	1.		
79. Computer failure (critical flight and engine control systems).	Discrete "fail" or "normal".	....	4.		
80. Heads-up display (when an information source is installed).	Discrete(s) "on" or "off".	....	4.		
81. Para-visual display (when an information source is installed).	Discrete(s) "on" or "off".	....	1.		
82. Cockpit trim control input position—pitch.	Full Range	±5%	1	0.2% of full range.	Where mechanical means for control inputs are not available, cockpit display trim positions should be recorded.
83. Cockpit trim control input position—roll.	Full Range	±5%	1	0.7% of full range.	Where mechanical means for control inputs are not available, cockpit display trim position should be recorded.

The recorded values must meet the designated range, resolution and accuracy requirements during static and dynamic conditions. Dynamic condition means the parameter is experiencing change at the maximum rate attainable, including the maximum rate of reversal. All data recorded must be correlated in time to within one second.

Parameters	Range	Accuracy (sensor input)	Seconds per sampling interval	Resolution	Remarks
84. Cockpit trim control input position—yaw.	Full Range	±5% .... _ ...	1	0.3% of full range.	Where mechanical means for control input are not available, cockpit display trim positions should be recorded.
85. Trailing edge flap and cockpit flap control position.	Full Range	±5% .... _ ...	2	0.5% of full range.	Trailing edge flaps and cockpit flap control position may each be sampled alternately at 4 second intervals to provide a sample each 0.5 second.
86. Leading edge flap and cockpit flap control position.	Full Range or Discrete.	±5%	1	0.5% of full range.	
87. Ground spoiler position and speed brake selection.	Full Range or Discrete.	±5% .... _ ...	0.5	0.3% of full range	
88. All cockpit flight control input forces (control wheel, control column, rudder pedal) [18] [19].	Full range Control wheel ±70 lbs. Control column ±85 lbs. Rudder pedal ±165 lbs.	±5% .... _ ...	1	0.3% of full range.	For fly-by-wire flight control systems, where flight control surface position is a function of the displacement of the control input device only, it is not necessary to record this parameter. For airplanes that have a flight control break away capability that allows either pilot to operate the control independently, record both control force inputs. The control force inputs may be sampled alternately once per 2 seconds to produce the sampling interval of 1.
89. Yaw damper status.	Discrete (on/off)	0.5			
90. Yaw damper command.	Full range	As installed	0.5	1% of full range.	
91. Standby rudder valve status.	Discrete	0.5 .... _ ...			

[1] For A300 B2/B4 airplanes, resolution = 6 seconds.
[2] For A330/A340 series airplanes, resolution = 0.703°.
[3] For A318/A319/A320/A321 series airplanes, resolution = 0.275% (0.088°>0.064°)
  For A330/A340 series airplanes, resolution = 2.20% (0.703°>0.064°)
[4] For A318/A319/A320/A321 series airplanes, resolution = 0.22% (0.088°>0.080°)
  For A330/A340 series airplanes, resolution = 1.76% (0.703°>0.080°)
[5] For A330/A340 series airplanes, resolution = 1.18% (0.703° >0.120°).
  For A330/A340 series airplanes, seconds per sampling interval = 1.
[6] For A330/A340 series airplanes, resolution = 0.783% (0.352°>0.090°)
[7] For A330/A340 series airplanes, aileron resolution = 0.704% (0.352°>0.100°). For A330/A340 series airplanes, spoiler resolution = 1.406% (0.703°>0.100°).
[8] For A330/A340 series airplanes, resolution = 0.30% (0.176°>0.12°)
  For A330/A340 series airplanes, seconds per sampling interval = 1
[9] For B–717 series airplanes, resolution = .005g. For Dassault F900C/F900EX airplanes, resolution = .007g.
[10] For A330/A340 series airplanes, resolution = 1.05% (0.250°>0.120°)
[11] For A330/A340 series airplanes, resolution = 1.05% (0.250°>0.120°). For A330 B2/B4 series airplanes, resolution = 0.92% (0.230°>0.125°).
[12] For A330/A340 series airplanes, spoiler resolution = 1.406% (0.703°>0.100°).
[13] For A330/A340 series airplanes, resolution = 0.5°C
[14] For Dassault F900C/F900EX airplanes, Radio Altitude resolution = 1.25 ft.
[15] For A330/A340 series airplanes, resolution = 0.352 degrees.
[16] For A318/A319/A320/A321 series airplanes, resolution = 4.32%. For A330/A340 series airplanes, resolution is 3.27% of full range for throttle lever angle (TLA); for reverse thrust, reverse throttle lever angle (RLA) resolution is nonlinear over the active reverse thrust range, which is 51.54 degrees to 96.14 degrees. The resolved element is 2.8 degrees uniformly over the entire active reverse thrust range, or 2.9% of the full range value of 96.14 degrees.
[17] For A318/A319/A320/A321 series airplanes, with IAE engines, resolution = 2.58%.
[18] For all aircraft manufactured on or after December 6, 2010, the seconds per sampling interval is 0.125. Each input must be recorded at this rate. Alternately sampling inputs (interleaving) to meet this sampling interval is prohibited.

[19] For all 737 model airplanes manufactured between August 19, 2000, and April 6, 2010: The seconds per sampling interval is 0.5 per control input; the remarks regarding the sampling rate do not apply; a single control wheel force transducer installed on the left cable control is acceptable provided the left and right control wheel positions also are recorded.

[Doc. No. 28109, 62 FR 38390, July 17, 1997; 62 FR 48135, Sept. 12, 1997, as amended by Amdt. 125-32, 64 FR 46121, Aug. 24, 1999; 65 FR 2295, Jan. 14, 2000; Amdt. 125-32, 65 FR 2295, Jan. 14, 2000; Amdt. 125-34, 65 FR 51745, Aug. 24, 2000; 65 FR 81735, Dec. 27, 2000; Amdt. 125-39, 67 FR 54323, Aug. 21, 2002; Amdt. 125-42, 68 FR 42937, July 18, 2003; 68 FR 50069, Aug. 20, 2003; 68 FR 53877, Sept. 15, 2003; Amdt. 125-54, 73 FR 12568, Mar. 7, 2008; Amdt. 125-56, 73 FR 73180, Dec. 2, 2008; Amdt. 125-60, 75 FR 17046, Apr. 5, 2010; Amdt. 125-59, 75 FR 7357, Feb. 19, 2010; Amdt. 125-62, 78 FR 39971, July 3, 2013; Docket FAA-2017-0733, Amdt. 125-67, 82 FR 34399, July 25, 2017]

PART 129—OPERATIONS: FOREIGN AIR CARRIERS AND FOREIGN OPERATORS OF U.S.-REGISTERED AIRCRAFT ENGAGED IN COMMON CARRIAGE

Sec.
SPECIAL FEDERAL AVIATION REGULATION NO. 97 [NOTE]

AUTHORITY: 49 U.S.C. 1372, 40113, 40119, 44101, 44701-44702, 44705, 44709-44711, 44713, 44716-44717, 44722, 44901-44904, 44906, 44912, 46105, Pub. L. 107-71 sec. 104.

SOURCE: Docket No. 1994, 29 FR 1720, Feb. 5, 1964, unless otherwise noted.

SPECIAL FEDERAL AVIATION REGULATION NO. 97

EDITORIAL NOTE: For the text of SFAR No. 97, see part 91 of this chapter.

Subpart A—General

§ 129.1   Applicability and definitions.

(a) *Foreign air carrier operations in the United States.* This part prescribes rules governing the operation within the United States of each foreign air carrier holding the following:

(1) A permit issued by the U.S. Department of Transportation under 49 U.S.C. 41301 through 41306, or

(2) Other appropriate economic or exemption authority issued by the U.S. Department of Transportation.

(b) *Operations of U.S.-registered aircraft solely outside the United States.* In addition to the operations specified under paragraph (a) of this section, §§ 129.5, 129.7, 129.9, 129.11, 129.14, 129.20

and 129.24, and subpart B of this part also apply to operations of U.S.-registered aircraft operated solely outside the United States in common carriage by a foreign person or foreign air carrier.

(c) *Definitions.* For the purpose of this part—

(1) *Foreign person* means any person who is not a citizen of the United States and who operates a U.S-registered aircraft in common carriage solely outside the United States.

(2) *Years in service* means the calendar time elapsed since an aircraft was issued its first U.S. or first foreign airworthiness certificate.

[Doc. No. FAA–1999–5401, 67 FR 72762, Dec. 6, 2002, as amended by Amdt. 129–43, 72 FR 63413, Nov. 8, 2007; Amdt. 129–45, 73 FR 12570, Mar. 7, 2008; Amdt. 129–45, 74 FR 32801, July 9, 2009; Amdt. 129–49, 76 FR 7489, Feb. 10, 2011]

§129.5 Operations specifications.

(a) Each foreign air carrier conducting operations within the United States, and each foreign air carrier or foreign person operating U.S.-registered aircraft solely outside the United States in common carriage must conduct its operations in accordance with operations specifications issued by the Administrator under this part.

(b) Each foreign air carrier conducting operations within the United States must conduct its operations in accordance with the Standards contained in Annex 1 (Personnel Licensing), Annex 6 (Operation of Aircraft), Part I (International Commercial Air Transport—Aeroplanes) or Part III (International Operations—Helicopters), as appropriate, and in Annex 8 (Airworthiness of Aircraft) to the Convention on International Civil Aviation.

(c) No foreign air carrier may operate to or from locations within the United States without, or in violation of, appropriate operations specifications.

(d) No foreign air carrier or foreign person shall operate U.S.-registered aircraft solely outside the United States in common carriage without, or in violation of, appropriate operations specifications.

(e) Each foreign air carrier must keep each of its employees and other persons used in its operations informed of the provisions of its operations specifications that apply to that employee's or person's duties and responsibilities.

(f) Operations specifications issued under this part are effective until—

(1) The foreign air carrier or foreign person surrenders them to the FAA;

(2) The Administrator suspends or terminates the operations specifications; or

(3) The operations specifications are amended as provided in §129.11.

(g) Within 30 days after a foreign air carrier or foreign person terminates operations under part 129 of this subchapter, the operations specifications must be surrendered by the foreign air carrier or foreign person to the responsible Flight Standards office.

(h) No person operating under this part may operate or list on its operations specifications any airplane listed on operations specifications issued under part 125 of this chapter.

[Doc. No. FAA–2009–0140; 76 FR 7489, Feb. 10, 2011, as amended by Docket FAA–2018–0119, Amdt. 129–53, 83 FR 9174, Mar. 5, 2018]

§129.7 Application, issuance, or denial of operations specifications.

(a) A foreign air carrier or foreign person applying to the FAA for operations specifications under this part must submit an application—

(1) In a form and manner prescribed by the Administrator; and

(2) At least 90 days before the intended date of operation.

(b) An authorized officer or employee of the applicant, having knowledge of the matters stated in the application, must sign the application and certify in writing that the statements in the application are true. The application must include two copies of the appropriate written authority issued to that officer or employee by the applicant.

(c) A foreign applicant may be issued operations specifications, if after review, the Administrator finds the applicant—

(1) Meets the applicable requirements of this part;

(2) Holds the economic or exemption authority required by the Department of Transportation, applicable to the operations to be conducted;

(3) Complies with the applicable security requirements of 49 CFR chapter XII;

(4) Is properly and adequately equipped to conduct the operations described in the operations specifications; and

(5) Holds a valid air operator certificate issued by the State of the Operator.

(d) An application may be denied if the Administrator finds that the applicant is not properly or adequately equipped to conduct the operations to be described in the operations specifications.

[Doc. No. FAA–2009–0140; 76 FR 7489, Feb. 10, 2011]

§ 129.9 Contents of operations specifications.

(a) The contents of operations specifications issued to a foreign air carrier conducting operations within the United States under § 129.1(a) shall include:

(1) The specific location and mailing address of the applicant's principal place of business in the State of the Operator and, if different, the address that will serve as the primary point of contact for correspondence between the FAA and the foreign air carrier;

(2) Within 1 year after February 10, 2011, the designation of an agent for service within the United States, including the agent's full name and office address or usual place of residence;

(3) The certificate number and validity of the foreign air carrier's Air Operator Certificate issued by the State of the Operator;

(4) Each regular and alternate airport to be used in scheduled operations;

(5) The type of aircraft and registration markings of each aircraft;

(6) The approved maintenance program and minimum equipment list for United States registered aircraft authorized for use; and

(7) Any other item the Administrator determines is necessary.

(b) The contents of operations specifications issued to a foreign air carrier or foreign person operating U.S.-registered aircraft solely outside the United States in common carriage in accordance with § 129.1(b) shall include—

(1) The specific location and mailing address of the principal place of business in the State of the Operator and, if different, the address that will serve as the primary point of contact for correspondence between the FAA and the foreign air carrier or foreign person;

(2) Within 1 year after February 10, 2011, the designation of an agent for service within the United States, including the agent's full name and office address or usual place of residence;

(3) In the case of a foreign air carrier, the certificate number and validity of the foreign air carrier's Air Operator Certificate issued by the State of the Operator;

(4) Any other business names under which the foreign air carrier or foreign person may operate;

(5) The type, registration markings, and serial number of each United States registered aircraft authorized for use;

(6) The approved maintenance program and minimum equipment list for United States registered aircraft authorized for use; and

(7) Any other item the Administrator determines is necessary.

[Doc. No. FAA–2009–0140; 76 FR 7489, Feb. 10, 2011; Amdt. 129–49–A, 76 FR 15212, Mar. 21, 2011]

§ 129.11 Amendment, suspension and termination of operations specifications.

(a) The Administrator may amend any operations specifications issued under this part if—

(1) The Administrator determines that safety in air commerce and the public interest require the amendment; or

(2) The foreign air carrier or foreign person applies for an amendment, and the Administrator determines that safety in air commerce and the public interest allows the amendment.

(b) The Administrator may suspend or terminate any operations specifications issued under this part if the Administrator determines that safety in air commerce and the public interest require the suspension or termination;

(c) Except as provided in paragraphs (f) and (g) of this section, when the Administrator initiates an action to amend, suspend or terminate a foreign air carrier or foreign person's operations specifications, the following procedure applies:

(1) The responsible Flight Standards office notifies the foreign air carrier or foreign person in writing of the proposed amendment, suspension or termination.

(2) The responsible Flight Standards office sets a reasonable period (but not less than 7 days) within which the foreign air carrier or foreign person may submit written information, views, and arguments on the amendment, suspension or termination.

(3) After considering all material presented, the responsible Flight Standards office notifies the foreign air carrier or foreign person of—

(i) The adoption of the proposed amendment, suspension or termination;

(ii) The partial adoption of the proposed amendment, suspension or termination; or

(iii) The withdrawal of the proposed amendment, suspension or termination.

(4) If the responsible Flight Standards Office issues an action to amend, suspend or terminate the operations specifications, it becomes effective not less than 30 days after the foreign air carrier or foreign person receives notice of it unless—

(i) The responsible Flight Standards office finds under paragraph (g) of this section that there is an emergency requiring immediate action with respect to safety in air commerce; or

(ii) The foreign air carrier or foreign person petitions for reconsideration of the amendment, suspension or termination under paragraph (e) of this section.

(d) When the foreign air carrier or foreign person applies for an amendment to its operations specifications, the following procedure applies:

(1) The foreign air carrier or foreign person must file an application to amend its operations specifications—

(i) At least 90 days before the date proposed by the applicant for the amendment to become effective in cases of mergers; acquisitions of airline operational assets that require an additional showing to Department of Transportation for economic author-

ity; major changes in the type of operation; and resumption of operations following a suspension of operations as a result of bankruptcy actions, unless a shorter time is approved by the Administrator.

(ii) At least 30 days before the date proposed by the applicant for the amendment to become effective in all other cases.

(2) The application must be submitted to the responsible Flight Standards office in a form and manner prescribed by the Administrator.

(3) After considering all material presented, the responsible Flight Standards office notifies the foreign air carrier or foreign person of—

(i) The adoption of the applied for amendment;

(ii) The partial adoption of the applied for amendment; or

(iii) The denial of the applied for amendment.

(4) If the responsible Flight Standards office approves the amendment, following coordination with the foreign air carrier or foreign person regarding its implementation, the amendment is effective on the date the responsible Flight Standards office approves it.

(e) The foreign air carrier or foreign person may petition for reconsideration of a full or partial adoption of an amendment, a denial of an amendment or a suspension or termination of operations specifications.

(f) When a foreign air carrier or foreign person seeks reconsideration of a decision from the responsible Flight Standards office concerning the amendment, suspension or termination of operations specifications, the following procedure applies:

(1) The foreign air carrier or foreign person must petition for reconsideration of that decision within 30 days after the date that the foreign air carrier or foreign person receives a notice of the decision.

(2) The foreign air carrier or foreign person must address its petition to the Executive Director, Flight Standards Service.

(3) A petition for reconsideration, if filed within the 30-day period, suspends the effectiveness of any amendment, suspension or termination issued by the responsible Flight Standards office

unless the responsible Flight Standards office has found, under paragraph (g) of this section, that an emergency exists requiring immediate action with respect to safety in air transportation or air commerce.

(g) If the responsible Flight Standards office finds that an emergency exists requiring immediate action with respect to safety in air commerce or air transportation that makes the procedures set out in this section impracticable or contrary to the public interest, that office may make the amendment, suspension or termination effective on the day the foreign air carrier or foreign person receives notice of it. In the notice to the foreign air carrier or foreign person, the responsible Flight Standards office will articulate the reasons for its finding that an emergency exists requiring immediate action with respect to safety in air transportation or air commerce or that makes it impracticable or contrary to the public interest to stay the effectiveness of the amendment, suspension or termination.

[Doc. No. FAA-2009-0140, 76 FR 7490, Feb. 10, 2011, as amended by Docket FAA-2018-0119, Amdt. 129-53, 83 FR 9174, Mar. 5, 2018]

§ 129.13 Airworthiness and registration certificates.

(a) No foreign air carrier may operate any aircraft within the United States unless that aircraft carries a current registration certificate and displays the nationality and registration markings of the State of Registry, and an airworthiness certificate issued or validated by:

(1) The State of Registry; or

(2) The State of the Operator, provided that the State of the Operator and the State of Registry have entered into an agreement under Article 83bis of the Convention on International Civil Aviation that covers the aircraft.

(b) No foreign air carrier may operate a foreign aircraft within the United States except in accordance with the limitations on maximum certificated weights prescribed for that aircraft and that operation by the country of manufacture of the aircraft.

[Doc. No. 1994, 29 FR 1720, Feb. 5, 1964, as amended by Amdt. 129-33, 67 FR 42455, June 21, 2002; Amdt. 129-49, 76 FR 7490, Feb. 10, 2011]

§ 129.14 Maintenance program and minimum equipment list requirements for U.S.-registered aircraft.

(a) Each foreign air carrier and each foreign person operating a U.S.-registered aircraft within or outside the United States in common carriage must ensure that each aircraft is maintained in accordance with a program approved by the Administrator in the operations specifications.

(b) No foreign air carrier or foreign person may operate a U.S.-registered aircraft with inoperable instruments or equipment unless the following conditions are met:

(1) A master minimum equipment list exists for the aircraft type.

(2) The foreign operator submits for review and approval its aircraft minimum equipment list based on the master minimum equipment list, to the responsible Flight Standards office for the operator. The foreign operator must show, before minimum equipment list approval can be obtained, that the maintenance procedures used under its maintenance program are adequate to support the use of its minimum equipment list.

(3) For leased aircraft maintained and operated under a U.S. operator's continuous airworthiness maintenance program and FAA-approved minimum equipment list, the foreign operator submits the U.S. operator's approved continuous airworthiness maintenance program and approved aircraft minimum equipment list to the FAA office prescribed in paragraph (b)(2) of this section for review and evaluation. The foreign operator must show that it is capable of operating under the lessor's approved maintenance program and that it is also capable of meeting the maintenance and operational requirements specified in the lessor's approved minimum equipment list.

(4) The FAA operations specification permitting the operator to use an approved minimum equipment list is carried aboard the aircraft. An approved

minimum equipment list, as authorized by the operations specifications, constitutes an approved change to the type design without requiring recertification.

(5) The approved minimum equipment list provides for the operation of the aircraft with certain instruments and equipment in an inoperable condition.

(6) The aircraft records available to the pilot must include an entry describing the inoperable instruments and equipment.

(7) The aircraft is operated under all applicable conditions and limitations contained in the minimum equipment list and the operations specification authorizing the use of the list.

[Doc. No. 24856, 52 FR 20029, May 28, 1987, as amended by Amdt. 129–49, 76 FR 7490, Feb. 10, 2011; Docket FAA–2018–0119, Amdt. 129–53, 83 FR 9174, Mar. 5, 2018]

§129.15 Flightcrew member certificates.

Each person acting as a flightcrew member must hold a certificate or license that shows the person's ability to perform duties in connection with the operation of the aircraft. The certificate or license must have been issued or rendered valid by:

(a) The State in which the aircraft is registered; or

(b) The State of the Operator, provided that the State of the Operator and the State of Registry have entered into an agreement under Article 33*bis* of the Convention on International Civil Aviation that covers the aircraft.

[Doc. No. FAA–2009–0140; 76 FR 7491, Feb. 10, 2011]

§129.17 Aircraft communication and navigation equipment for operations under IFR or over the top.

(a) *Aircraft navigation equipment requirements—General.* No foreign air carrier may conduct operations under IFR or over the top unless—

(1) The en route navigation aids necessary for navigating the aircraft along the route (e.g., ATS routes, arrival and departure routes, and instrument approach procedures, including missed approach procedures if a missed approach routing is specified in the procedure) are available and suitable for use by the aircraft navigation equipment required by this section;

(2) The aircraft used in those operations is equipped with at least the following—

(i) Except as provided in paragraph (c) of this section, two approved independent navigation systems suitable for navigating the aircraft along the route to be flown within the degree of accuracy required for ATC;

(ii) One marker beacon receiver providing visual and aural signals; and

(iii) One ILS receiver; and

(3) Any RNAV system used to meet the navigation equipment requirements of this section is authorized in the foreign air carrier's operations specifications.

(b) *Aircraft communication equipment requirements.* No foreign air carrier may operate an aircraft under IFR or over the top, unless it is equipped with—

(1) At least two independent communication systems necessary under normal operating conditions to fulfill the functions specified in §121.347(a) of this chapter; and

(2) At least one of the communication systems required by paragraph (b)(1) of this section must have two-way voice communication capability.

(c) *Use of a single independent navigation system for operations under IFR or over the top.* Notwithstanding the requirements of paragraph (a)(2)(i) of this section, the aircraft may be equipped with a single independent navigation system suitable for navigating the aircraft along the route to be flown within the degree of accuracy required for ATC if:

(1) It can be shown that the aircraft is equipped with at least one other independent navigation system suitable, in the event of loss of the navigation capability of the single independent navigation system permitted by this paragraph at any point along the route, for proceeding safely to a suitable airport and completing an instrument approach; and

(2) The aircraft has sufficient fuel so that the flight may proceed safely to a suitable airport by use of the remaining navigation system, and complete an instrument approach and land.

(d) *VOR navigation equipment.* If VOR navigation equipment is required by paragraph (a) or (c) of this section, no foreign air carrier may operate an aircraft unless it is equipped with at least one approved DME or suitable RNAV system.

[Doc. No. FAA–2002–14002, 72 FR 31683, June 7, 2007]

§ 129.18   Collision avoidance system.

Effective January 1, 2005, any airplane you, as a foreign air carrier, operate under part 129 must be equipped and operated according to the following table:

COLLISION AVOIDANCE SYSTEMS

If you operate in the United States any	Then you must operate that airplane with:
(a) Turbine-powered airplane of more than 33,000 pounds maximum certificated take-off weight.	(1) An appropriate class of Mode S transponder that meets Technical Standard Order (TSO) C–112, or a later version, and one of the followign approved units; (i) TCAS II that meets TSO C–119b (version 7.0), or takeoff weight a later version. (ii) TCAS II that meets TSO C–119a (version 6.04A Enhanced) that was installed in that airplane before May 1, 2003. If that TCAS II version 6.04A Enhanced no longer can be repaired to TSO C–119a standards, it must be replaced with a TCAS II that meets TSO C–119b (version 7.0), or a later version. (iii) A collision avoidance system equivalent to TSO C–119b (version 7.0), or a later version, capable of coordinating with units that meet TSO C–119a (version 6.04A Enhanced), or a later version.
(b) Turbine-powered airplane with a passenger-seat configuration, excluding any pilot seat, or 10–30 seats.	(1) TCAS I that meets TSO C–118, or a later version, or (2) A collision avoidance system equivalent to excluding any TSO C–118, or a later version, or (3) A collision avoidance system and Mode S transponder that meet paragraph (a)(1) of this section.

[Doc. No. FAA–2001–10910, 68 FR 15903, Apr. 1, 2003]

§ 129.19   Air traffic rules and procedures.

(a) Each pilot must be familiar with the applicable rules, the navigational and communications facilities, and the air traffic control and other procedures, of the areas to be traversed by him within the United States.

(b) Each foreign air carrier shall establish procedures to assure that each of its pilots has the knowledge required

by paragraph (a) of this section and shall check the ability of each of its pilots to operate safely according to applicable rules and procedures.

(c) Each foreign air carrier shall conform to the practices, procedures, and other requirements prescribed by the Administrator for U.S. air carriers for the areas to be operated in.

§ 129.20   Digital flight data recorders.

No person may operate an aircraft under this part that is registered in the United States unless it is equipped with one or more approved flight recorders that use a digital method of recording and storing data and a method of readily retrieving that data from the storage medium. The flight data recorder must record the parameters that would be required to be recorded if the aircraft were operated under part 121, 125, or 135 of this chapter, and must be installed by the compliance times required by those parts, as applicable to the aircraft.

[Doc. No. 28109, 62 FR 38396, July 17, 1997]

§ 129.21   Control of traffic.

(a) Subject to applicable immigration laws and regulations, each foreign air carrier must furnish sufficient personnel necessary to provide two-way voice communications between its aircraft and stations at places where the FAA finds that communication is necessary but cannot be maintained in a language with which station operators are familiar.

(b) Each person furnished by a foreign air carrier under paragraph (a) of this section must be able to speak English and the language necessary to maintain communications with its aircraft and must assist station operators in directing traffic.

[Doc. No. FAA–2002–14002, 72 FR 31683, June 7, 2007]

§ 129.22   Communication and navigation equipment for rotorcraft operations under VFR over routes navigated by pilotage.

(a) No foreign air carrier may operate a rotorcraft under VFR over routes that can be navigated by pilotage unless the rotorcraft is equipped with the radio communication equipment necessary under normal operating conditions to fulfill the following:

(1) Communicate with at least one appropriate station from any point on the route;

(2) Communicate with appropriate air traffic control facilities from any point within Class B, Class C, or Class D airspace, or within a Class E surface area designated for an airport in which flights are intended; and

(3) Receive meteorological information from any point en route.

(b) No foreign air carrier may operate a rotorcraft at night under VFR over routes that can be navigated by pilotage unless that rotorcraft is equipped with—

(1) Radio communication equipment necessary under normal operating conditions to fulfill the functions specified in paragraph (a) of this section; and

(2) Navigation equipment suitable for the route to be flown.

[Doc. No. FAA–2002–14002, 72 FR 31683, June 7, 2007]

§129.23 Transport category cargo service airplanes: Increased zero fuel and landing weights.

(a) Notwithstanding the applicable structural provisions of the transport category airworthiness regulations, but subject to paragraphs (b) through (g) of this section, a foreign air carrier may operate (for cargo service only) any of the following transport category airplanes (certificated under part 4b of the Civil Air Regulations effective before March 13, 1956) at increased zero fuel and landing weights—

(1) DC–6A, DC–6B, and DC–7B, and DC–7C; and

(2) L–1049 B, C, D, E, F, G, and H, and the L–1649A when modified in accordance with supplemental type certificate SA 4–1402.

(b) The zero fuel weight (maximum weight of the airplane with no disposable fuel and oil) and the structural landing weight may be increased beyond the maximum approved in full compliance with applicable rules only if the Administrator finds that—

(1) The increase is not likely to reduce seriously the structural strength;

(2) The probability of sudden fatigue failure is not noticeably increased;

(3) The flutter, deformation, and vibration characteristics do not fall below those required by applicable regulations; and

(4) All other applicable weight limitations will be met.

(c) No zero fuel weight may be increased by more than five percent, and the increase in the structural landing weight may not exceed the amount, in pounds, of the increase in zero fuel weight.

(d) Each airplane must be inspected in accordance with the approved special inspection procedures, for operations at increased weights, established and issued by the manufacturer of the type of airplane.

(e) A foreign air carrier may not operate an airplane under this section unless the country of registry requires the airplane to be operated in accordance with the passenger-carrying transport category performance operating limitations in part 121 or the equivalent.

(f) The Airplane Flight Manual for each airplane operated under this section must be appropriately revised to include the operating limitations and information needed for operation at the increased weights.

(g) Each airplane operated at an increased weight under this section must, before it is used in passenger service, be inspected under the special inspection procedures for return to passenger service established and issued by the manufacturer and approved by the Administrator.

[Doc. No. 6403, 29 FR 19098, Dec. 30, 1964]

§129.24 Cockpit voice recorders.

No person may operate an aircraft under this part that is registered in the United States unless it is equipped with an approved cockpit voice recorder that meets the standards of TSO–C123a, or later revision. The cockpit voice recorder must record the information that would be required to be recorded if the aircraft were operated under part 121, 125, or 135 of this chapter, and must be installed by the compliance times required by that part, as applicable to the aircraft.

[Doc. No. FAA–2005–20245, 73 FR 12570, Mar. 7, 2008]

§ 129.25   Airplane security.

Foreign air carriers conducting operations under this part must comply with the applicable security requirements in 49 CFR chapter XII.

[67 FR 8350, Feb. 22, 2002]

§ 129.28   Flightdeck security.

(a) After August 20, 2002, except for a newly manufactured airplane on a non-revenue delivery flight, no foreign air carrier covered by § 129.1(a), may operate:

(1) A passenger carrying transport category airplane within the United States, except for overflights, unless the airplane is equipped with a door between the passenger and pilot compartment that incorporates features to restrict the unwanted entry of persons into the flightdeck that are operable from the flightdeck only; or

(2) A transport category all-cargo airplane within the United States, except for overflights, that has a door installed between the pilot compartment and any other occupied compartment on or after June 21, 2002, unless the door incorporates features to restrict the unwanted entry of persons into the flightdeck that are operable from the flightdeck only.

(b) To the extent necessary to meet the requirements of paragraph (a) of this section, the requirements of § 129.13(a) to maintain airworthiness certification are waived until April 9, 2003. After that date, the requirements of § 129.13(a) apply in full.

(c) After April 9, 2003, except for a newly manufactured airplane on a non-revenue delivery flight, no foreign air carrier covered by § 129.1(a) may operate a passenger carrying transport category airplane, or a transport category all-cargo airplane that has a door installed between the pilot compartment and any other occupied compartment on or after June 21, 2002, within the United States, except for overflights, unless the airplane's flightdeck door installation meets the requirements of paragraphs (c)(1) and(2) of this section or an alternative standard found acceptable to the Administrator.

(1) Except for a newly manufactured airplane on a non-revenue delivery flight, no foreign air carrier covered by § 129.1(a) may operate:

(i) After April 9, 2003, a passenger carrying transport category airplane within the United States, except on overflights, unless the airplane's flightdeck door installation meets the requirements of paragraphs (c)(2) and (c)(3) of this section or an alternative standard found acceptable to the Administrator.

(ii) After October 1, 2003, a transport category all-cargo airplane that had a door installed between the pilot compartment and any other occupied compartment on or after June 21, 2002, within the United States, except on overflights, unless the airplane's flightdeck door installation meets the requirements of paragraphs (c)(2) and (c)(3) of this section or an alternative standard found acceptable to the Administrator; or the operator must implement a security program approved by the Transportation Security Administration (TSA) for the operation of all airplanes in that operator's fleet.

(2) The door must resist forcible intrusion by unauthorized persons and be capable of withstanding impacts of 300 joules (221.3 foot-pounds) at the critical locations on the door, as well as a 1,113-newton (250 pounds) constant tensile load on the knob or handle, and

(3) The door must resist penetration by small arms fire and fragmentation devices to a level equivalent to Level IIIa of the National Institute of Justice Standard (NIJ) 0101.04.

(d) After August 20, 2002, no foreign air carrier covered by § 129.1 may operate a passenger carrying transport category airplane, or a transport category all-cargo airplane that has a door installed between the pilot compartment and any other occupied compartment on or after June 21, 2002, within the United States, except for overflights, unless the carrier has procedures in place that are acceptable to the civil aviation authority responsible for oversight of the foreign air carriers operating under this part to prevent access to the flightdeck except as authorized as follows:

(1) No person other than a person who is assigned to perform duty on the flight deck may have a key to the

flight deck door that will provide access to the flightdeck.

(2) Except when it is necessary to permit access and egress by persons authorized in accordance with paragraph (d)(3) of this section, a pilot in command of an airplane that has a lockable flight deck door in accordance with §129.28(a) and that is carrying passengers shall ensure that the door separating the flight crew compartment from the passenger compartment is closed and locked at all times when the airplane is being operated.

(3) No person may admit any person to the flight deck of an airplane unless the person being admitted is—

(i) A crewmember,

(ii) An inspector of the civil aviation authority responsible for oversight of the part 129 operator, or

(iii) Any other person authorized by the civil aviation authority responsible for oversight of the part 129 operator.

(e) The requirements of paragraph (a) through (d) except (d)(3), do not apply to transport category passenger carrying airplanes originally type certificated with a maximum passenger seating configuration of 19 seats or less, or to all-cargo airplanes with a payload capacity of 7,500 pounds or less.

[Doc. No. FAA–2002–12504, 67 FR 79824, Dec. 30, 2002, as amended by Amdt. 129–38, 68 FR 42882, July 18, 2003]

§129.29   Smoking prohibitions.

(a) No person may smoke and no operator may permit smoking in any aircraft lavatory.

(b) Unless otherwise authorized by the Secretary of Transportation, no person may smoke and no operator may permit smoking anywhere on the aircraft (including the passenger cabin and the flight deck) during scheduled passenger foreign air transportation or during any scheduled passenger interstate or intrastate air transportation.

[Doc. No. FAA–2000–7467, 65 FR 36780, June 9, 2000]

Subpart B—Continued Airworthiness and Safety Improvements

§129.101   Purpose and definition.

(a) This subpart requires a foreign person or foreign air carrier operating a U.S. registered airplane in common carriage to support the continued airworthiness of each airplane. These requirements may include, but are not limited to, revising the maintenance program, incorporating design changes, and incorporating revisions to Instructions for Continued Airworthiness.

(b) [Reserved]

[Amdt. 129–43, 72 FR 63413, Nov. 8, 2007, as amended by Docket FAA–2018–0119, Amdt. 129–53, 83 FR 9174, Mar. 5, 2018]

§129.103   [Reserved]

§129.105   Aging airplane inspections and records reviews for U.S.-registered multiengine aircraft.

(a) *Operation after inspection and records review.* After the dates specified in this paragraph, a foreign air carrier or foreign person may not operate a U.S.-registered multiengine airplane under this part unless the Administrator has notified the foreign air carrier or foreign person that the Administrator has completed the aging airplane inspection and records review required by this section. During the inspection and records review, the foreign air carrier or foreign person must demonstrate to the Administrator that the maintenance of age sensitive parts and components of the airplane has been adequate and timely enough to ensure the highest degree of safety.

(1) *Airplanes exceeding 24 years in service on* December 8, 2003; *initial and repetitive inspections and records reviews.* For an airplane that has exceeded 24 years in service on December 8, 2003, no later than December 5, 2007, and thereafter at intervals not to exceed 7 years.

(2) *Airplanes exceeding 14 years in service but not 24 years in service on* December 8, 2003; *initial and repetitive inspections and records reviews.* For an airplane that has exceeded 14 years in service, but not 24 years in service, on December 8, 2003, no later than December 4, 2008, and thereafter at intervals not to exceed 7 years.

(3) *Airplanes not exceeding 14 years in service on* December 8, 2003; *initial and repetitive inspections and records reviews.* For an airplane that has not exceeded 14 years in service on December 8, 2003, no later than 5 years after the start of the airplane's 15th year in service and thereafter at intervals not to exceed 7 years.

(b) *Unforeseen schedule conflict.* In the event of an unforeseen scheduling conflict for a specific airplane, the Administrator may approve an extension of up to 90 days beyond an interval specified in paragraph (b) of this section.

(c) *Airplane and records availability.* The foreign air carrier or foreign person must make available to the Administrator each U.S.-registered multiengine airplane for which an inspection and records review is required under this section, in a condition for inspection specified by the Administrator, together with the records containing the following information:

(1) Total years in service of the airplane;

(2) Total time in service of the airframe;

(3) Total flight cycles of the airframe;

(4) Date of the last inspection and records review required by this section;

(5) Current status of life-limited parts of the airframe;

(6) Time since the last overhaul of all structural components required to be overhauled on a specific time basis;

(7) Current inspection status of the airplane, including the time since the last inspection required by the inspection program under which the airplane is maintained;

(8) Current status of applicable airworthiness directives, including the date and methods of compliance, and if the airworthiness directive involves recurring action, the time and date when the next action is required;

(9) A list of major structural alterations; and

(10) A report of major structural repairs and the current inspection status for those repairs.

(d) *Notification to Administrator.* Each foreign air carrier or foreign person must notify the Administrator at least 60 days before the date on which the airplane and airplane records will be made available for the inspection and records review.

[Doc. No. FAA–1999–5401, 67 FR 72763, Dec. 6, 2002, as amended by Amdt. 129–34, 70 FR 5533, Feb. 2, 2005; Amdt. 129–41, 70 FR 23936, May 6, 2005. Redesignated by Amdt. 129–43, 72 FR 63413, Nov. 8, 2007]

§ 129.107 Repairs assessment for pressurized fuselages.

(a) No foreign air carrier or foreign persons operating a U.S. registered airplane may operate an Airbus Model A300 (excluding −600 series), British Aerospace Model BAC 1–11, Boeing Model 707, 720, 727, 737, or 747, McDonnell Douglas Model DC–8, DC–9/MD–80 or DC–10, Fokker Model F28, or Lockheed Model L–1011 beyond the applicable flight cycle implementation time specified below, or May 25, 2001, whichever occurs later, unless operations specifications have been issued to reference repair assessment guidelines applicable to the fuselage pressure boundary (fuselage skin, door skin, and bulkhead webs), and those guidelines are incorporated in its maintenance program. The repair assessment guidelines must be approved by the responsible Aircraft Certification Service office for the type certificate for the affected airplane.

(1) For the Airbus Model A300 (excluding the –600 series), the flight cycle implementation time is:

(i) Model B2: 36,000 flights.

(ii) Model B4–100 (including Model B4–2C): 30,000 flights above the window line, and 36,000 flights below the window line.

(iii) Model B4–200: 25,500 flights above the window line, and 34,000 flights below the window line.

(2) For all models of the British Aerospace BAC 1–11, the flight cycle implementation time is 60,000 flights.

(3) For all models of the Boeing 707, the flight cycle implementation time is 15,000 flights.

(4) For all models of the Boeing 720, the flight cycle implementation time is 23,000 flights.

(5) For all models of the Boeing 727, the flight cycle implementation time is 45,000 flights.

(6) For all models of the Boeing 737, the flight cycle implementation time is 60,00 flights.

(7) For all models of the Boeing 747, the flight cycle implementation time is 15,000 flights.

(8) For all models of the McDonnell Douglas DC–8, the flight cycle implementation time is 30,000 flights.

(9) For all models of the McDonnell Douglas DC–9/MD–80, the flight cycle implementation time is 60,000 flights.

(10) For all models of the McDonnell Douglas DC–10, the flight cycle implementation time is 30,000 flights.

(11) For all models of the Lockheed L–1011, the flight cycle implementation time is 27,000 flights.

(12) For the Fokker F–28 Mark 1000, 2000, 3000, and 4000, the flight cycle implementation time is 60,000 flights.

(b) [Reserved]

[Doc. No. 29104, 65 FR 24126, Apr. 25, 2000; 65 FR 35703, June 5, 2000, as amended by Amdt. 129–30, 66 FR 23131, May 7, 2001; Amdt. 129–35, 67 FR 72834, Dec. 9, 2002; Amdt. 129–39, 69 FR 45942, July 30, 2004. Redesignated and amended by Amdt. 129–43, 72 FR 63413, Nov. 8, 2007; Docket FAA–2018–0119, Amdt. 129–53, 83 FR 9174, Mar. 5, 2018]

§ 129.109 Supplemental inspections for U.S.-registered aircraft.

(a) *Applicability.* This section applies to U.S.-registered, transport category, turbine powered airplanes with a type certificate issued after January 1, 1958 that as a result of original type certification or later increase in capacity have—

(1) A maximum type certificated passenger seating capacity of 30 or more; or

(2) A maximum payload capacity of 7,500 pounds or more.

(b) *General requirements.* After December 20, 2010, a certificate holder may not operate an airplane under this part unless the following requirements have been met:

(1) *Baseline Structure.* The certificate holder's maintenance program for the airplane includes FAA-approved damage-tolerance-based inspections and procedures for airplane structure susceptible to fatigue cracking that could contribute to a catastrophic failure. For the purpose of this section, this structure is termed "fatigue critical structure."

(2) *Adverse effects of repairs, alterations, and modifications.* The maintenance program for the airplane includes a means for addressing the adverse effects repairs, alterations, and modifications may have on fatigue critical structure and on inspections required by paragraph (b)(1) of this section. The means for addressing these adverse effects must be approved by the responsible Aircraft Certification Service office.

(3) *Changes to maintenance program.* The changes made to the maintenance program required by paragraph (b)(1) and (b)(2) of this section, and any later revisions to these changes, must be submitted to the Principal Maintenance Inspector for review and approval.

[Doc. No. FAA–1999–5401, 70 FR 5532, Feb. 2, 2005. Redesignated by Amdt. 129–43, 72 FR 63413, Nov. 8, 2007; Amdt. 129–44, 72 FR 70508, Dec. 12, 2007; Docket FAA–2018–0119, Amdt. 129–53, 83 FR 9174, Mar. 5, 2018]

§ 129.111 Electrical wiring interconnection systems (EWIS) maintenance program.

(a) Except as provided in paragraph (f) of this section, this section applies to transport category, turbine-powered airplanes with a type certificate issued after January 1, 1958, that, as a result of original type certification or later increase in capacity, have—

(1) A maximum type-certificated passenger capacity of 30 or more, or

(2) A maximum payload capacity of 7500 pounds or more.

(b) After March 10, 2011, no foreign person or foreign air carrier may operate a U.S.-registered airplane identified in paragraph (a) of this section unless the maintenance program for that airplane includes inspections and procedures for EWIS.

(c) The proposed EWIS maintenance program changes must be based on EWIS Instructions for Continued Airworthiness (ICA) that have been developed in accordance with the provisions of Appendix H of part 25 of this chapter applicable to each affected airplane (including those ICA developed for supplemental type certificates installed on each airplane) and that have been approved by the responsible Aircraft Certification Service office.

(1) For airplanes subject to § 26.11 of this chapter, the EWIS ICA must comply with paragraphs H25.5(a)(1) and (b).

389

(2) For airplanes subject to § 25.1729 of this chapter, the EWIS ICA must comply with paragraph H25.4 and all of paragraph H25.5.

(d) After March 10, 2011, before returning a U.S.-registered airplane to service after any alterations for which EWIS ICA are developed, the foreign person or foreign air carrier must include in the maintenance program for that airplane inspections and procedures for EWIS based on those ICA.

(e) The EWIS maintenance program changes identified in paragraphs (c) and (d) of this section and any later EWIS revisions must be submitted to the Principal Inspector or Flight Standards office responsible for review and approval.

(f) This section does not apply to the following airplane models:

(1) Lockheed L–188

(2) Bombardier CL–44

(3) Mitsubishi YS–11

(4) British Aerospace BAC 1–11

(5) Concorde

(6) deHavilland D.H. 106 Comet 4C

(7) VFW–Vereinigte Flugtechnische Werk VFW–614

(8) Illyushin Aviation IL 96T

(9) Bristol Aircraft Britannia 305

(10) Handley Page Herald Type 300

(11) Avions Marcel Dassault—Breguet Aviation Mercure 100C

(12) Airbus Caravelle

(13) Lockheed L–300

[Amdt. 129–43, 72 FR 63413, Nov. 8, 2007, as amended by Docket FAA–2018–0119, Amdt. 129–53, 83 FR 9174, Mar. 5, 2018]

§ 129.113 Fuel tank system maintenance program.

(a) Except as provided in paragraph (g) of this section, this section applies to transport category, turbine-powered airplanes with a type certificate issued after January 1, 1958, that, as a result of original type certification or later increase in capacity, have—

(1) A maximum type-certificated passenger capacity of 30 or more, or

(2) A maximum payload capacity of 7500 pounds or more.

(b) For each U.S.-registered airplane on which an auxiliary fuel tank is installed under a field approval, before June 16, 2008, the foreign person or foreign air carrier operating the airplane must submit to the responsible Aircraft Certification Service office proposed maintenance instructions for the tank that meet the requirements of Special Federal Aviation Regulation No. 88 (SFAR 88) of this chapter.

(c) After December 16, 2008, no foreign person or foreign air carrier may operate a U.S.-registered airplane identified in paragraph (a) of this section unless the maintenance program for that airplane has been revised to include applicable inspections, procedures, and limitations for fuel tank systems.

(d) The proposed fuel tank system maintenance program revisions must be based on fuel tank system Instructions for Continued Airworthiness (ICA) that have been developed in accordance with the applicable provisions of SFAR 88 of this chapter or § 25.1529 and part 25, Appendix H, of this chapter, in effect on June 6, 2001 (including those developed for auxiliary fuel tanks, if any, installed under supplemental type certificates or other design approval) and that have been approved by the responsible Aircraft Certification Service office.

(e) After December 16, 2008, before returning a U.S.-registered airplane to service after any alteration for which fuel tank ICA are developed under SFAR 88, or under § 25.1529 in effect on June 6, 2001, the foreign person or foreign air carrier must include in the maintenance program for the airplane inspections and procedures for the fuel tank system based on those ICA.

(f) The fuel tank system maintenance program changes identified in paragraphs (d) and (e) of this section and any later fuel tank system revisions must be submitted to the Principal Inspector or Flight Standards office responsible for review and approval.

(g) This section does not apply to the following airplane models:

(1) Bombardier CL–44

(2) Concorde

(3) deHavilland D.H. 106 Comet 4C

(4) VFW–Vereinigte Flugtechnische Werk VFW–614

(5) Illyushin Aviation IL 96T

(6) Bristol Aircraft Britannia 305

(7) Handley Page Herald Type 300

(8) Avions Marcel Dassault—Breguet Aviation Mercure 100C

(9) Airbus Caravelle

(10) Lockheed L–300

[Amdt. 129–43, 72 FR 63413, Nov. 8, 2007, as amended by Docket FAA–2018–0119, Amdt. 129–53, 83 FR 9174, Mar. 5, 2018]

§129.115 Limit of validity.

(a) *Applicability.* This section applies to foreign air carriers or foreign persons operating any U.S.-registered transport category, turbine-powered airplane with a maximum takeoff gross weight greater than 75,000 pounds and a type certificate issued after January 1, 1958, regardless of whether the maximum takeoff gross weight is a result of an original type certificate or a later design change. This section also applies to foreign air carriers or foreign persons operating any other U.S.-registered transport category, turbine-powered airplane with a type certificate issued after January 1, 1958, regardless of the maximum takeoff gross weight, for which a limit of validity of the engineering data that supports the structural maintenance program (hereafter referred to as LOV) is required in accordance with §25.571 or §26.21 of this chapter after January 14, 2011.

(b) *Limit of validity.* No foreign air carrier or foreign person may operate a U.S.-registered airplane identified in paragraph (a) of this section after the applicable date identified in Table 1 of this section, unless an Airworthiness Limitations section (ALS) approved under Appendix H to part 25 or §26.21 of this chapter is incorporated into its maintenance program. The ALS must—

(1) Include an LOV approved under §25.571 or §26.21 of this chapter, as applicable, except as provided in paragraph (f) of this section; and

(2) Be clearly distinguishable within its maintenance program.

(c) *Operation of airplanes excluded from §26.21.* No certificate holder may operate an airplane identified in §26.21(g) of this chapter after July 14, 2013, unless an ALS approved under Appendix H to part 25 or §26.21 of this chapter is incorporated into its maintenance program. The ALS must—

(1) Include an LOV approved under §25.571 or §26.21 of this chapter, as applicable, except as provided in paragraph (f) of this section; and

(2) Be clearly distinguishable within its maintenance program

(d) *Extended limit of validity.* No foreign air carrier or foreign person may operate an airplane beyond the LOV or extended LOV specified in paragraph (b)(1), (c), (d), or (f) of this section, as applicable, unless the following conditions are met:

(1) An ALS must be incorporated into its maintenance program that—

(i) Includes an extended LOV and any widespread fatigue damage airworthiness limitation items (ALIs) approved under §26.23 of this chapter; and

(ii) Is approved under §26.23 of this chapter;

(2) The extended LOV and the airworthiness limitation items pertaining to widespread fatigue damage must be clearly distinguishable within its maintenance program.

(e) *Principal Maintenance Inspector approval.* Foreign air carriers or foreign persons must submit the maintenance program revisions required by paragraphs (b), (c), and (d) of this section to the Principal Maintenance Inspector or Flight Standards office for review and approval.

(f) *Exception.* For any airplane for which an LOV has not been approved as of the applicable compliance date specified in paragraph (c) or Table 1 of this section, instead of including an approved LOV in the ALS, an operator must include the applicable default LOV specified in Table 1 or Table 2 of this section, as applicable, in the ALS.

TABLE 1—AIRPLANES SUBJECT TO §26.21

Airplane model	Compliance Date— months after January 14, 2011	Default LOV [flight cycles (FC) or flight hours (FH)]
Airbus—Existing [1] Models Only:		
A300 B2–1A, B2–1C, B2K–3C, B2–203	30	48,000 FC
A300 B4–2C, B4–103	30	40,000 FC
A300 B4–203	30	34,000 FC
A300–600 Series	60	30,000 FC/67,500 FH
A310–200 Series	60	40,000 FC/60,000 FH
A310–300 Series	60	35,000 FC/60,000 FH

391

TABLE 1—AIRPLANES SUBJECT TO § 26.21—Continued

Airplane model	Compliance Date— months after January 14, 2011	Default LOV [flight cycles (FC) or flight hours (FH)]
A318 Series	60	48,000 FC/60,000 FH
A319 Series	60	48,000 FC/60,000 FH
A320–100 Series	60	48,000 FC/48,000 FH
A320–200 Series	60	48,000 FC/60,000 FH
A321 Series	60	48,000 FC/60,000 FH
A330–200, –300 Series (except WV050 family) (non enhanced)	60	40,000 FC/60,000 FH
A330–200, –300 Series WV050 family (enhanced)	60	33,000 FC/100,000 FH
A330–200 Freighter Series	60	See NOTE.
A340–200, –300 Series (except WV 027 and WV050 family) (non enhanced).	60	20,000 FC/80,000 FH
A340–200, –300 Series WV 027 (non enhanced)	60	30,000 FC/60,000 FH
A340–300 Series WV050 family (enhanced)	60	20,000 FC/100,000 FH
A340–500, –600 Series	60	16,600 FC/100,000 FH
A380–800 Series	72	See NOTE.
Boeing—Existing [1] Models Only:		
717	60	60,000 FC/60,000 FH
727 (all series)	30	60,000 FC
737 (Classics): 737–100, –200, –200C, –300, –400, –500	30	75,000 FC
737 (NG): 737–600, –700, –700C, –800, –900, –900ER	60	75,000 FC
747 (Classics): 747–100, –100B, –100B SUD, –200B, –200C, –200F, –300, 747SP, 747SR.	30	20,000 FC
747–400: 747–400, –400D, –400F	60	20,000 FC
757	60	50,000 FC
767	60	50,000 FC
777–200, –300	60	40,000 FC
777–200LR, 777–300ER	72	40,000 FC
777F	72	11,000 FC
Bombardier—Existing [1] Models Only:		
CL–600: 2D15 (Regional Jet Series 705), 2D24 (Regional Jet Series 900).	72	60,000 FC
Embraer—Existing [1] Models Only:		
ERJ 170	72	See NOTE.
ERJ 190	72	See NOTE.
Fokker—Existing [1] Models Only:		
F.28 Mark 0070, Mark 0100	30	90,000 FC
Lockheed—Existing [1] Models Only:		
L–1011	30	36,000 FC
188	30	26,600 FC
382 (all series)	30	20,000 FC/50,000 FH
McDonnell Douglas—Existing [1] Models Only:		
DC–8, –8F	30	50,000 FC/50,000 FH
DC–9 (except for MD–80 models)	30	100,000 FC/100,000 FH
MD–80 (DC–9–81, –82, –83, –87, MD–88)	30	50,000 FC/50,000 FH
MD–90	60	60,000 FC/90,000 FH
DC–10–10, –15	30	42,000 FC/60,000 FH
DC–10–30, –40, –10F, –30F, –40F	30	30,000 FC/60,000 FH
MD–10–10F	60	42,000 FC/60,000 FH
MD–10–30F	60	30,000 FC/60,000 FH
MD–11, MD–11F	60	20,000 FC/60,000 FH
Maximum Takeoff Gross Weight Changes:		
All airplanes whose maximum takeoff gross weight has been decreased to 75,000 pounds or below after January 14, 2011, or increased to greater than 75,000 pounds at any time by an amended type certificate or supplemental type certificate.	30, or within 12 months after the LOV is approved, or before operating the airplane, whichever occurs latest.	Not applicable.
All Other Airplane Models (TCs and amended TCs) not Listed in Table 2.	72, or within 12 months after the LOV is approved, or before operating the airplane, whichever occurs latest.	Not applicable.

[1] Type certificated as of January 14, 2011.
Note: Airplane operation limitation is stated in the Airworthiness Limitation section.

NOTE: Airplane operation limitation is stated in the Airworthiness Limitation section.

TABLE 2—AIRPLANES EXCLUDED FROM §26.21

Airplane model	Default LOV [flight cycles (FC) or flight hours (FH)]
Airbus:	
Caravelle	15,000 FC/24,000 FH
Avions Marcel Dassault:	
Breguet Aviation Mercure 100C	20,000 FC/16,000 FH
Boeing:	
Boeing 707 (–100 Series and –200 Series)	20,000 FC
Boeing 707 (–300 Series and –400 Series)	20,000 FC
Boeing 720	30,000 FC
Bombardier:	
CL–44D4 and CL–44J	20,000 FC
BD–700	15,000 FH
Bristol Aeroplane Company:	
Britannia 305	10,000 FC
British Aerospace Airbus, Ltd.:	
BAC 1–11 (all models)	85,000 FC
British Aerospace (Commercial Aircraft) Ltd.:	
Armstrong Whitworth Argosy A.W. 650 Series 101	20,000 FC
BAE Systems (Operations) Ltd.:	
BAe 146–100A (all models)	50,000 FC
BAe 146–200–07	50,000 FC
BAe 146–200–07 Dev	50,000 FC
BAe 146–200–11	50,000 FC
BAe 146–200–07A	47,000 FC
BAe 146–200–11 Dev	43,000 FC
BAe 146–300 (all models)	40,000 FC
Avro 146–RJ70A (all models)	40,000 FC
Avro 146–RJ85A and 146–RJ100A (all models)	50,000 FC
D & R Nevada, LLC:	
Convair Model 22	1,000 FC/1,000 FH
Convair Model 23M	1,000 FC/1,000 FH
deHavilland Aircraft Company, Ltd.:	
D.H. 106 Comet 4C	8,000 FH
Gulfstream:	
GV	40,000 FH
GV–SP	40,000 FH
Ilyushin Aviation Complex:	
IL–96T	10,000 FC/30,000 FH
Lockheed:	
300–50A01 (USAF C 141A)	20,000 FC

[Doc. No. FAA–2006–24281, 75 FR 69787, Nov. 15, 2010, as amended by Amdt. 129–51, 77 FR 30878, May 24, 2012; Amdt. 129–51A, 77 FR 55107, Sept. 7, 2012; Docket FAA–2018–0119, Amdt. 129–53, 83 FR 9174, Mar. 5, 2018]

§129.117 Flammability reduction means.

(a) *Applicability.* Except as provided in paragraph (o) of this section, this section applies to U.S.-registered transport category, turbine-powered airplanes with a type certificate issued after January 1, 1958, that as a result of original type certification or later increase in capacity have:

(1) A maximum type-certificated passenger capacity of 30 or more, or

(2) A maximum payload capacity of 7,500 pounds or more.

(b) *New Production Airplanes.* Except in accordance with §129.14, no foreign air carrier or foreign person may operate an airplane identified in Table 1 of this section (including all-cargo airplanes) for which application is made for original certificate of airworthiness or export airworthiness approval after December 27, 2010 unless an Ignition Mitigation Means (IMM) or Flammability Reduction Means (FRM) meeting the requirements of §26.33 of this chapter is operational.

TABLE 1

Model—Boeing	Model—Airbus
747 Series	A318, A319, A320, A321 Series
737 Series	A330, A340 Series
777 Series	
767 Series	

393

(c) *Auxiliary Fuel Tanks.* After the applicable date stated in paragraph (e) of this section, no foreign air carrier or foreign person may operate any airplane subject § 26.33 of this chapter that has an Auxiliary Fuel Tank installed pursuant to a field approval, unless the following requirements are met:

(1) The foreign air carrier or foreign person complies with 14 CFR 26.35 by the applicable date stated in that section.

(2) The foreign air carrier or foreign person installs Flammability Impact Mitigation Means (FIMM), if applicable, that are approved by the responsible Aircraft Certification Service office.

(3) Except in accordance with § 129.14, the FIMM, if applicable, are operational.

(d) *Retrofit.* After the dates specified in paragraph (e) of this section, no foreign air carrier or foreign person may operate an airplane to which this section applies unless the requirements of paragraphs (d)(1) and (d)(2) of this section are met.

(1) IMM, FRM or FIMM, if required by §§ 26.33, 26.35, or 26.37 of this chapter, that are approved by the responsible Aircraft Certification Service office, are installed within the compliance times specified in paragraph (e) of this section.

(2) Except in accordance with § 129.14, the IMM, FRM or FIMM, as applicable, are operational.

(e) *Compliance Times.* Except as provided in paragraphs (k) and (l) of this section, the installations required by paragraph (d) of this section must be accomplished no later than the applicable dates specified in paragraph (e)(1) or (e)(2) of this section.

(1) Fifty percent of each foreign air carrier or foreign person's fleet identified in paragraph (d)(1) of this section must be modified no later than December 26, 2014.

(2) One hundred percent of each foreign air carrier or foreign person's fleet of airplanes subject to paragraph (d)(1) or this section must be modified no later than December 26, 2017.

(3) For those foreign air carriers or foreign persons that have only one airplane for a model identified in Table 1,

the airplane must be modified no later than December 26, 2017.

(f) *Compliance after Installation.* Except in accordance with § 129.14, no person may—

(1) Operate an airplane on which IMM or FRM has been installed before the dates specified in paragraph (e) of this section unless the IMM or FRM is operational.

(2) Deactivate or remove an IMM or FRM once installed unless it is replaced by a means that complies with paragraph (d) of this section.

(g) *Maintenance Program Revisions.* No foreign air carrier or foreign person may operate an airplane for which airworthiness limitations have been approved by the responsible Aircraft Certification Service office in accordance with §§ 26.33, 26.35, or 26.37 of this chapter after the airplane is modified in accordance with paragraph (d) of this section unless the maintenance program for that airplane is revised to include those applicable airworthiness limitations.

(h) After the maintenance program is revised as required by paragraph (g) of this section, before returning an airplane to service after any alteration for which airworthiness limitations are required by §§ 25.981, 26.33, 26.35, or 26.37 of this chapter, the foreign person or foreign air carrier must revise the maintenance program for the airplane to include those airworthiness limitations.

(i) The maintenance program changes identified in paragraphs (g) and (h) of this section must be submitted to the operator's responsible Flight Standards office or Principal Inspector for review and approval prior to incorporation.

(j) The requirements of paragraph (d) of this section do not apply to airplanes operated in all-cargo service, but those airplanes are subject to paragraph (f) of this section.

(k) The compliance dates specified in paragraph (e) of this section may be extended by one year, provided that—

(1) No later than March 26, 2009, the foreign air carrier or foreign person notifies its responsible Flight Standards office or Principal Inspector that it intends to comply with this paragraph;

(2) No later than June 24, 2009, the foreign air carrier or foreign person applies for an amendment to its operations specifications in accordance with §129.11 to include a requirement for the airplane models specified in Table 2 of this section to use ground air conditioning systems for actual gate times of more than 30 minutes, when available at the gate and operational, whenever the ambient temperature exceeds 60 degrees Fahrenheit; and

(3) Thereafter, the certificate holder uses ground air conditioning systems as described in paragraph (k)(2) of this section on each airplane subject to the extension.

TABLE 2

Model—Boeing	Model—Airbus
747 Series	A318, A319, A320, A321 Series
737 Series	A300, A310 Series
777 Series	A330, A340 Series
767 Series	
757 Series	

(1) For any foreign air carrier or foreign person for which the operating certificate is issued after December 26, 2008, the compliance date specified in paragraph (e) of this section may be extended by one year, provided that the foreign air carrier or foreign person meets the requirements of paragraph (k)(2) of this section when its initial operations specifications are issued and, thereafter, uses ground air conditioning systems as described in paragraph (k)(2) of this section on each airplane subject to the extension.

(m) After the date by which any person is required by this section to modify 100 percent of the affected fleet, no person may operate in passenger service any airplane model specified in Table 2 of this section unless the airplane has been modified to comply with §26.33(c) of this chapter.

TABLE 3

Model—Boeing	Model—Airbus
747 Series	A318, A319, A320, A321 Series
737 Series	A300, A310 Series
777 Series	A330, A340 Series
767 Series	
757 Series	

(n) No foreign air carrier or foreign person may operate any airplane on which an auxiliary fuel tank is installed after December 26, 2017 unless the FAA has certified the tank as compliant with §25.981 of this chapter, in effect on December 26, 2008.

(o) *Exclusions.* The requirements of this section do not apply to the following airplane models:

(1) Convair CV–240, 340, 440, including turbine powered conversions.

(2) Lockheed L–188 Electra.

(3) Vickers VC–10.

(4) Douglas DC–3, including turbine powered conversions.

(5) Bombardier CL–44.

(6) Mitsubishi YS–11.

(7) BAC 1–11.

(8) Concorde.

(9) deHavilland D.H. 106 Comet 4C.

(10) VFW—Vereinigte Flugtechnische VFW–614.

(11) Illyushin Aviation IL 96T.

(12) Bristol Aircraft Britannia 305.

(13) Handley Page Herald Type 300.

(14) Avions Marcel Dassault—Breguet Aviation Mercure 100C.

(15) Airbus Caravelle.

(16) Fokker F–27/Fairchild Hiller FH–227.

(17) Lockheed L–300.

[Doc. No. FAA–2005–22997, 73 FR 42503, July 21, 2008, as amended by Amdt. 129–47, 74 FR 31620, July 2, 2009; Docket FAA–2018–0119, Amdt. 129–53, 83 FR 9174, Mar. 5, 2018]

§ 129.119   Fuel tank vent explosion protection.

(a) *Applicability.* This section applies to transport category, turbine-powered airplanes with a type certificate issued after January 1, 1958, that have:

(1) A maximum type-certificated passenger capacity of 30 or more; or

(2) A maximum payload capacity of 7,500 pounds or more.

(b) *New production airplanes.* No certificate holder may operate an airplane for which the State of Manufacture issued the original certificate of airworthiness or export airworthiness approval after August 23, 2018 unless means, approved by the Administrator, to prevent fuel tank explosions caused by propagation of flames from outside the fuel tank vents into the fuel tank vapor spaces are installed and operational.

[Docket FAA–2014–0500, Amdt. 129–52, 81 FR 41208, June 24, 2016]

Subpart C—Special Federal Aviation Regulations

§ 129.201   SFAR No. 111—Lavatory Oxygen Systems.

The requirements of § 121.1500 of this chapter also apply to this part.

[Doc. No. FAA–2011–0186, 76 FR 12556, Mar. 8, 2011]

APPENDIX A TO PART 129 [RESERVED]

PART 133—ROTORCRAFT EXTERNAL-LOAD OPERATIONS

Subpart A—Applicability

Sec.
133.1   Applicability.

Subpart B—Certification Rules

133.11   Certificate required.
133.13   Duration of certificate.
133.14   Carriage of narcotic drugs, marihuana, and depressant or stimulant drugs or substances.
133.15   Application for certificate issuance or renewal.
133.17   Requirements for issuance of a rotorcraft external-load operator certificate.
133.19   Rotorcraft.
133.21   Personnel.
133.22   Employment of former FAA employees.
133.23   Knowledge and skill.
133.25   Amendment of certificate.
133.27   Availability, transfer, and surrender of certificate.

Subpart C—Operating Rules and Related Requirements

133.31   Emergency operations.
133.33   Operating rules.
133.35   Carriage of persons.
133.37   Crewmember training, currency, and testing requirements.
133.39   Inspection authority.

Subpart D—Airworthiness Requirements

133.41   Flight characteristics requirements.
133.43   Structures and design.
133.45   Operating limitations.
133.47   Rotorcraft-load combination flight manual.
133.49   Markings and placards.
133.51   Airworthiness certification.

AUTHORITY: 49 U.S.C. 106(g), 40113, 44701–44702.

SOURCE: Docket No. 1529, 29 FR 603, Jan. 24, 1964, unless otherwise noted.

Subpart A—Applicability

§ 133.1   Applicability.

Except for aircraft subject to part 107 of this chapter, this part prescribes—

(a) Airworthiness certification rules for rotorcraft used in; and

(b) Operating and certification rules governing the conduct of rotorcraft external-load operations in the United States by any person.

(c) The certification rules of this part do not apply to—

(1) Rotorcraft manufacturers when developing external-load attaching means;

(2) Rotorcraft manufacturers demonstrating compliance of equipment utilized under this part or appropriate portions of part 27 or 29 of this chapter;

(3) Operations conducted by a person demonstrating compliance for the issuance of a certificate or authorization under this part;

(4) Training flights conducted in preparation for the demonstration of compliance with this part; or

(5) A Federal, State, or local government conducting operations with public aircraft.

(d) For the purpose of this part, a person other than a crewmember or a person who is essential and directly connected with the external-load operation may be carried only in approved Class D rotorcraft-load combinations.

[Doc. No. 15176, 42 FR 24198, May 12, 1977, as amended by Amdt. 133–9, 51 FR 40707, Nov. 7, 1986; Docket FAA–2015–0150, Amdt. 133–15, 81 FR 42214, June 28, 2016]

Subpart B—Certification Rules

§ 133.11   Certificate required.

(a) No person subject to this part may conduct rotorcraft external-load operations within the United States without, or in violation of the terms of, a Rotorcraft External-Load Operator Certificate issued by the Administrator under § 133.17.

(b) No person holding a Rotorcraft External-Load Operator Certificate may conduct rotorcraft external-load operations subject to this part under a business name that is not on that certificate.

[Doc. No. 15176, 42 FR 24198, May 12, 1977, as amended by Amdt. 133–7, 42 FR 32531, June 27, 1977; Amdt. 133–9, 51 FR 40707, Nov. 7, 1986]

§ 133.13 Duration of certificate.

Unless sooner surrendered, suspended, or revoked, a Rotorcraft External-Load Operator Certificate expires at the end of the twenty-fourth month after the month in which it is issued or renewed.

[Doc. No. 15176, 42 FR 24198, May 12, 1977, as amended by Amdt. 133–7, 42 FR 32531, June 27, 1977; Amdt. 133–9, 51 FR 40707, Nov. 7 1986]

§ 133.14 Carriage of narcotic drugs, marihuana, and depressant or stimulant drugs or substances.

If the holder of a certificate issued under this part permits any aircraft owned or leased by that holder to be engaged in any operation that the certificate holder knows to be in violation of § 91.19(a) of this chapter, that operation is a basis for suspending or revoking the certificate.

[Doc. No. 12035, 38 FR 17493, July 2, 1973, as amended by Amdt. 133–10, 54 FR 34332, Aug. 18, 1989]

§ 133.15 Application for certificate issuance or renewal.

Application for an original certificate or renewal of a certificate issued under this part is made on a form, and in a manner, prescribed by the Administrator. The form may be obtained from a Flight Standards office. The completed application is sent to the responsible Flight Standards office for the area in which the applicant's home base of operation is located.

[Doc. No. 15176, 42 FR 24198, May 12, 1977, as amended by Amdt. 133–11, 54 FR 39294, Sept. 25, 1989; Docket FAA–2018–0119, Amdt. 133–16, 83 FR 9174, Mar. 5, 2018]

§ 133.17 Requirements for issuance of a rotorcraft external-load operator certificate.

If an applicant shows that he complies with §§ 133.19, 133.21, and 133.23, the Administrator issues a Rotorcraft External-Load Operator Certificate to him with an authorization to operate specified rotorcraft with those classes of rotorcraft-load combinations for

which he complies with the applicable provisions of subpart D of this part.

§ 133.19 Rotorcraft.

(a) The applicant must have the exclusive use of at least one rotorcraft that—

(1) Was type certificated under, and meets the requirements of, part 27 or 29 of this chapter (but not necessarily with external-load-carrying attaching means installed) or of § 21.25 of this chapter for the special purpose of rotorcraft external-load operations;

(2) Complies with the certification provisions in subpart D of this part that apply to the rotorcraft-load combinations for which authorization is requested; and

(3) Has a valid standard or restricted category airworthiness certificate.

(b) For the purposes of paragraph (a) of this section, a person has exclusive use of a rotorcraft if he has the sole possession, control, and use of it for flight, as owner, or has a written agreement (including arrangements for the performance of required maintenance) giving him that possession, control, and use for at least six consecutive months.

[Doc. No. 15176, 42 FR 24198, May 12, 1977]

§ 133.21 Personnel.

(a) The applicant must hold, or have available the services of at least one person who holds, a current commercial or airline transport pilot certificate, with a rating appropriate for the rotorcraft prescribed in § 133.19, issued by the Administrator.

(b) The applicant must designate one pilot, who may be the applicant, as chief pilot for rotorcraft external-load operations. The applicant also may designate qualified pilots as assistant chief pilots to perform the functions of the chief pilot when the chief pilot is not readily available. The chief pilot and assistant chief pilots must be acceptable to the Administrator and each must hold a current Commercial or Airline Transport Pilot Certificate, with a rating appropriate for the rotorcraft prescribed in § 133.19.

(c) The holder of a Rotorcraft External-Load Operator Certificate shall report any change in designation of chief pilot or assistant chief pilot immediately to the responsible Flight Standards office. The new chief pilot must be designated and must comply with § 133.23 within 30 days or the operator may not conduct further operations under the Rotorcraft External-Load Operator Certificate unless otherwise authorized by the responsible Flight Standards office.

[Doc. No. 1529, 29 FR 603, Jan. 24, 1964, as amended by Amdt. 133–9, 51 FR 40707, Nov. 7, 1986; Docket FAA–2018–0119, Amdt. 133–16, 83 FR 9174, Mar. 5, 2018]

§ 133.22 Employment of former FAA employees.

(a) Except as specified in paragraph (c) of this section, no certificate holder may knowingly employ or make a contractual arrangement which permits an individual to act as an agent or representative of the certificate holder in any matter before the Federal Aviation Administration if the individual, in the preceding 2 years—

(1) Served as, or was directly responsible for the oversight of, a Flight Standards Service aviation safety inspector; and

(2) Had direct responsibility to inspect, or oversee the inspection of, the operations of the certificate holder.

(b) For the purpose of this section, an individual shall be considered to be acting as an agent or representative of a certificate holder in a matter before the agency if the individual makes any written or oral communication on behalf of the certificate holder to the agency (or any of its officers or employees) in connection with a particular matter, whether or not involving a specific party and without regard to whether the individual has participated in, or had responsibility for, the particular matter while serving as a Flight Standards Service aviation safety inspector.

(c) The provisions of this section do not prohibit a certificate holder from knowingly employing or making a contractual arrangement which permits an individual to act as an agent or representative of the certificate holder in any matter before the Federal Aviation Administration if the individual was

employed by the certificate holder before October 21, 2011.

[Doc. No. FAA–2008–1154, 76 FR 52236, Aug. 22, 2011]

§ 133.23 Knowledge and skill.

(a) Except as provided in paragraph (d) of this section, the applicant, or the chief pilot designated in accordance with § 133.21(b), must demonstrate to the Administrator satisfactory knowledge and skill regarding rotorcraft external-load operations as set forth in paragraphs (b) and (c) of this section.

(b) The test of knowledge (which may be oral or written, at the option of the applicant) covers the following subjects:

(1) Steps to be taken before starting operations, including a survey of the flight area.

(2) Proper method of loading, rigging, or attaching the external load.

(3) Performance capabilities, under approved operating procedures and limitations, of the rotorcraft to be used.

(4) Proper instructions of flight crew and ground workers.

(5) Appropriate rotorcraft-load combination flight manual.

(c) The test of skill requires appropriate maneuvers for each class requested. The appropriate maneuvers for each load class must be demonstrated in the rotorcraft prescribed in § 133.19.

(1) Takeoffs and landings.

(2) Demonstration of directional control while hovering.

(3) Acceleration from a hover.

(4) Flight at operational airspeeds.

(5) Approaches to landing or working area.

(6) Maneuvering the external load into the release position.

(7) Demonstration of winch operation, if a winch is installed to hoist the external load.

(d) Compliance with paragraphs (b) and (c) of this section need not be shown if the Administrator finds, on the basis of the applicant's (or his designated chief pilot's) previous experience and safety record in rotorcraft external-load operations, that his knowledge and skill are adequate.

[Doc. No. 1529, 29 FR 603, Jan. 24, 1964, as amended by Amdt. 133–9, 51 FR 40707, Nov. 7, 1986]

§ 133.25 Amendment of certificate.

(a) The holder of a Rotorcraft External-Load Certificate may apply to the responsible Flight Standards office for the area in which the applicant's home base of operation is located, or to the responsible Flight Standards office for the area in which operations are to be conducted, for an amendment of the applicant's certificate, to add or delete a rotorcraft-load combination authorization, by executing the appropriate portion of the form used in applying for a Rotorcraft External-Load Operator Certificate. If the applicant for the amendment shows compliance with §§ 133.19 and 133.49, the responsible Flight Standards office issues an amended Rotorcraft External-Load Operator Certificate to the applicant with authorization to operate with those classes of rotorcraft-load combinations for which the applicant complies with the applicable provisions of subpart D of this part.

(b) The holder of a rotorcraft external-load certificate may apply for an amendment to add or delete a rotorcraft authorization by submitting to the responsible Flight Standards office a new list of rotorcraft, by registration number, with the classes of rotorcraft-load combinations for which authorization is requested.

[Doc. No. 18434, 43 FR 52206, Nov. 9, 1973, as amended by Amdt. 133–9, 51 FR 40707, Nov. 7, 1986; Amdt. 133–11, 54 FR 39294, Sept. 25, 1989; Docket FAA–2018–0119, Amdt. 133–16, 83 FR 9174, Mar. 5, 2018]

§ 133.27 Availability, transfer, and surrender of certificate.

(a) Each holder of a rotorcraft external-load operator certificate shall keep that certificate and a list of authorized rotorcraft at the home base of operations and shall make it available for inspection by the Administrator upon request.

(b) Each person conducting a rotorcraft external-load operation shall carry a facsimile of the Rotorcraft External-Load Operator Certificate in each rotorcraft used in the operation.

(c) If the Administrator suspends or revokes a Rotorcraft External-Load Operator Certificate, the holder of that certificate shall return it to the Administrator. If the certificate holder,

for any other reason, discontinues operations under his certificate, and does not resume operations within two years, he shall return the certificate to the responsible Flight Standards office.

[Doc. No. 1529, 29 FR 603, Jan. 24, 1964, as amended by Amdt. 133–9, 51 FR 40708, Nov. 7, 1986; Amdt. 133–11, 54 FR 39294, Sept. 25, 1989; Docket FAA–2018–0119, Amdt. 133–16, 83 FR 9174, Mar. 5, 2018]

Subpart C—Operating Rules and Related Requirements

§ 133.31 Emergency operations.

(a) In an emergency involving the safety of persons or property, the certificate holder may deviate from the rules of this part to the extent required to meet that emergency.

(b) Each person who, under the authority of this section, deviates from a rule of this part shall notify the Administrator within 10 days after the deviation. Upon the request of the Administrator, that person shall provide the responsible Flight Standards office a complete report of the aircraft operation involved, including a description of the deviation and reasons for it.

[Doc. No. 24550, 51 FR 40708, Nov. 7, 1986, as amended by Amdt. 133–11, 54 FR 39294, Sept. 25, 1989; Docket FAA–2018–0119, Amdt. 133–16, 83 FR 9175, Mar. 5, 2018]

§ 133.33 Operating rules.

(a) No person may conduct a rotorcraft external-load operation without, or contrary to, the Rotorcraft-Load Combination Flight Manual prescribed in § 133.47.

(b) No person may conduct a rotorcraft external-load operation unless—

(1) The rotorcraft complies with § 133.19; and

(2) The rotorcraft and rotorcraft-load combination is authorized under the Rotorcraft External-Load Operator Certificate.

(c) Before a person may operate a rotorcraft with an external-load configuration that differs substantially from any that person has previously carried with that type of rotorcraft (whether or not the rotorcraft-load combination is of the same class), that person must conduct, in a manner that will not endanger persons or property on the surface, such of the following flight-operational checks as the Administrator determines are appropriate to the rotorcraft-load combination:

(1) A determination that the weight of the rotorcraft-load combination and the location of its center of gravity are within approved limits, that the external load is securely fastened, and that the external load does not interfere with devices provided for its emergency release.

(2) Make an initial liftoff and verify that controllability is satisfactory.

(3) While hovering, verify that directional control is adequate.

(4) Accelerate into forward flight to verify that no attitude (whether of the rotorcraft or of the external load) is encountered in which the rotorcraft is uncontrollable or which is otherwise hazardous.

(5) In forward flight, check for hazardous oscillations of the external load, but if the external load is not visible to the pilot, other crewmembers or ground personnel may make this check and signal the pilot.

(6) Increase the forward airspeed and determine an operational airspeed at which no hazardous oscillation or hazardous aerodynamic turbulence is encountered.

(d) Notwithstanding the provisions of part 91 of this chapter, the holder of a Rotorcraft External-Load Operator Certificate may conduct (in rotorcraft type certificated under and meeting the requirements of part 27 or 29 of this chapter, including the external-load attaching means) rotorcraft external-load operations over congested areas if those operations are conducted without hazard to persons or property on the surface and comply with the following:

(1) The operator must develop a plan for each complete operation, coordinate this plan with the responsible Flight Standards office for the area in which the operation will be conducted, and obtain approval for the operation from that office. The plan must include an agreement with the appropriate political subdivision that local officials will exclude unauthorized persons from the area in which the operation will be conducted, coordination with air traffic control, if necessary, and a detailed chart depicting the flight routes and altitudes.

(2) Each flight must be conducted at an altitude, and on a route, that will allow a jettisonable external load to be released, and the rotorcraft landed, in an emergency without hazard to persons or property on the surface.

(e) Notwithstanding the provisions of part 91 of this chapter, and except as provided in § 133.45(d), the holder of a Rotorcraft External-Load Operator Certificate may conduct external-load operations, including approaches, departures, and load positioning maneuvers necessary for the operation, below 500 feet above the surface and closer than 500 feet to persons, vessels, vehicles, and structures, if the operations are conducted without creating a hazard to persons or property on the surface.

(f) No person may conduct rotorcraft external-load operations under IFR unless specifically approved by the Administrator. However, under no circumstances may a person be carried as part of the external-load under IFR.

[Doc. No. 24550, 51 FR 40708, Nov. 7, 1986, as amended by Amdt. 133–11, 54 FR 39294, Sept. 25, 1989; Docket FAA–2018–0119, Amdt. 133–16, 83 FR 9175, Mar. 5, 2018]

§ 133.35   Carriage of persons.

(a) No certificate holder may allow a person to be carried during rotorcraft external-load operations unless that person—

(1) Is a flight crewmember;

(2) Is a flight crewmember trainee;

(3) Performs an essential function in connection with the external-load operation; or

(4) Is necessary to accomplish the work activity directly associated with that operation.

(b) The pilot in command shall ensure that all persons are briefed before takeoff on all pertinent procedures to be followed (including normal, abnormal, and emergency procedures) and equipment to be used during the external-load operation.

[Doc. No. 24550, 51 FR 40708, Nov. 7, 1986]

§ 133.37   Crewmember training, currency, and testing requirements.

(a) No certificate holder may use, nor may any person serve, as a pilot in operations conducted under this part unless that person—

(1) Has successfully demonstrated, to the Administrator knowledge and skill with respect to the rotorcraft-load combination in accordance with §133.23 (in the case of a pilot other than the chief pilot or an assistant chief pilot who has been designated in accordance with §133.21(b), this demonstration may be made to the chief pilot or assistant chief pilot); and

(2) Has in his or her personal possession a letter of competency or an appropriate logbook entry indicating compliance with paragraph (a)(1) of this section.

(b) No certificate holder may use, nor may any person serve as, a crewmember or other operations personnel in Class D operations conducted under this part unless, within the preceding 12 calendar months, that person has successfully completed either an approved initial or a recurrent training program.

(c) Notwithstanding the provisions of paragraph (b) of this section, a person who has performed a rotorcraft external-load operation of the same class and in an aircraft of the same type within the past 12 calendar months need not undergo recurrent training.

[Doc. No. 24550, 51 FR 40708, Nov. 7, 1986]

§133.39 Inspection authority.

Each person conducting an operation under this part shall allow the Administrator to make any inspections or tests that he considers necessary to determine compliance with the Federal Aviation Regulations and the Rotorcraft External-Load Operator Certificate.

[Doc. No. 1529, 29 FR 603, Jan. 24, 1964. Redesignated by Amdt. 133–9, 51 FR 40708, Nov. 7, 1986]

Subpart D—Airworthiness Requirements

§133.41 Flight characteristics requirements.

(a) The applicant must demonstrate to the Administrator, by performing the operational flight checks prescribed in paragraphs (b), (c), and (d) of this section, as applicable, that the rotorcraft-load combination has satisfactory flight characteristics, unless

these operational flight checks have been demonstrated previously and the rotorcraft-load combination flight characteristics were satisfactory. For the purposes of this demonstration, the external-load weight (including the external-load attaching means) is the maximum weight for which authorization is requested.

(b) Class A rotorcraft-load combinations: The operational flight check must consist of at least the following maneuvers:

(1) Take off and landing.

(2) Demonstration of adequate directional control while hovering.

(3) Acceleration from a hover.

(4) Horizontal flight at airspeeds up to the maximum airspeed for which authorization is requested.

(c) *Class B and D rotorcraft-load combinations:* The operational flight check must consist of at least the following maneuvers:

(1) Pickup of the external load.

(2) Demonstration of adequate directional control while hovering.

(3) Acceleration from a hover.

(4) Horizontal flight at airspeeds up to the maximum airspeed for which authorization is requested.

(5) Demonstrating appropriate lifting device operation.

(6) Maneuvering of the external load into release position and its release, under probable flight operation conditions, by means of each of the quick-release controls installed on the rotorcraft.

(d) Class C rotorcraft-load combinations: For Class C rotorcraft-load combinations used in wire-stringing, cable-laying, or similar operations, the operational flight check must consist of the maneuvers, as applicable, prescribed in paragraph (c) of this section.

[Doc. No. 1529, 29 FR 603, Jan. 24, 1964, as amended by Amdt. 133–5, 41 FR 55475, Dec. 20, 1976; Amdt. 133–9, 51 FR 40709, Nov. 7, 1986]

§133.43 Structures and design.

(a) *External-load attaching means.* Each external-load attaching means must have been approved under—

(1) Part 8 of the Civil Air Regulations on or before January 17, 1964;

(2) Part 133, before February 1, 1977;

(3) Part 27 or 29 of this chapter, as applicable, irrespective of the date of approval; or

(4) Section 21.25 of this chapter.

(b) *Quick release devices.* Each quick release device must have been approved under—

(1) Part 27 or 29 of this chapter, as applicable;

(2) Part 133, before February 1, 1977; or

(3) Section 21.25 of this chapter, except the device must comply with §§ 27.865(b) and 29.865(b), as applicable, of this chapter.

(c) *Weight and center of gravity*—

(1) *Weight.* The total weight of the rotorcraft-load combination must not exceed the total weight approved for the rotorcraft during its type certification.

(2) *Center of gravity.* The location of the center of gravity must, for all loading conditions, be within the range established for the rotorcraft during its type certification. For Class C rotorcraft-load combinations, the magnitude and direction of the loading force must be established at those values for which the effective location of the center of gravity remains within its established range.

[Doc. No. 14324, 41 FR 55475, Dec. 20, 1976, as amended by Amdt. 133–12, 55 FR 8006, Mar. 6, 1990]

§ 133.45   Operating limitations.

In addition to the operating limitations set forth in the approved Rotorcraft Flight Manual, and to any other limitations the Administrator may prescribe, the operator shall establish at least the following limitations and set them forth in the Rotorcraft-Load Combination Flight Manual for rotorcraft-load combination operations:

(a) The rotorcraft-load combination may be operated only within the weight and center of gravity limitations established in accordance with § 133.43(c).

(b) The rotorcraft-load combination may not be operated with an external load weight exceeding that used in showing compliance with §§ 133.41 and 133.43.

(c) The rotorcraft-load combination may not be operated at airspeeds greater than those established in accordance with § 133.41 (b), (c), and (d).

(d) No person may conduct an external-load operation under this part with a rotorcraft type certificated in the restricted category under § 21.25 of this chapter over a densely populated area, in a congested airway, or near a busy airport where passenger transport operations are conducted.

(e) The rotorcraft-load combination of Class D may be conducted only in accordance with the following:

(1) The rotorcraft to be used must have been type certificated under transport Category A for the operating weight and provide hover capability with one engine inoperative at that operating weight and altitude.

(2) The rotorcraft must be equipped to allow direct radio intercommunication among required crewmembers.

(3) The personnel lifting device must be FAA approved.

(4) The lifting device must have an emergency release requiring two distinct actions.

[Doc. No. 1529, 29 FR 603, Jan. 24, 1964, as amended by Amdt. 133–1, 30 FR 883, Jan. 28, 1965; Amdt. 133–5, 41 FR 55476, Dec. 20, 1976; Amdt. 133–6, 42 FR 24198, May 12, 1977; Amdt. 133–9, 51 FR 40709, Nov. 7, 1986]

§ 133.47   Rotorcraft-load   combination flight manual.

The applicant must prepare a Rotorcraft-Load Combination Flight Manual and submit it for approval by the Administrator. The manual must be prepared in accordance with the rotorcraft flight manual provisions of subpart G of part 27 or 29 of this chapter, whichever is applicable. The limiting height-speed envelope data need not be listed as operating limitations. The manual must set forth—

(a) Operating limitations, procedures (normal and emergency), performance, and other information established under this subpart;

(b) The class of rotorcraft-load combinations for which the airworthiness of the rotorcraft has been demonstrated in accordance with §§ 133.41 and 133.43; and

(c) In the information section of the Rotorcraft-Load Combination Flight Manual—

(1) Information on any peculiarities discovered when operating particular rotorcraft-load combinations;

(2) Precautionary advice regarding static electricity discharges for Class B, Class C, and Class D rotorcraft-load combinations; and

(3) Any other information essential for safe operation with external loads.

[Doc. No. 1529, 29 FR 603, Jan. 24, 1964, as amended by Amdt. 133–9, 51 FR 40709, Nov. 7, 1986]

§ 133.49 Markings and placards.

The following markings and placards must be displayed conspicuously and must be such that they cannot be easily erased, disfigured, or obscured:

(a) A placard (displayed in the cockpit or cabin) stating the class of rotorcraft-load combination for which the rotorcraft has been approved and the occupancy limitation prescribed in § 133.35(a).

(b) A placard, marking, or instruction (displayed next to the external-load attaching means) stating the maximum external load prescribed as an operating limitation in § 133.45(b).

[Docket 1529, Amdt. 133–9A, 81 FR 85138, Nov. 25, 2016]

§ 133.51 Airworthiness certification.

A Rotorcraft External-Load Operator Certificate is a current and valid airworthiness certificate for each rotorcraft type certificated under part 27 or 29 of this chapter (or their predecessor parts) and listed by registration number on a list attached to the certificate, when the rotorcraft is being used in operations conducted under this part.

[Doc. No. 24550, 51 FR 40709, Nov. 7, 1986]

PART 135—OPERATING REQUIRE-MENTS: COMMUTER AND ON DE-MAND OPERATIONS AND RULES GOVERNING PERSONS ON BOARD SUCH AIRCRAFT

Special Federal Aviation Regulation No. 50–2 [Note]

Special Federal Aviation Regulation No. 71 [Note]

Special Federal Aviation Regulation No. 89 [Note]

Special Federal Aviation Regulation No. 97 [Note]

Subpart A—General

Subpart B—Flight Operations

AUTHORITY: 49 U.S.C. 106(f), 106(g), 40113, 41706, 44701–44702, 44705, 44709, 44711–44713, 44715–44717, 44722, 44730, 45101–45105; Pub. L. 112–95, 126 Stat. 58 (49 U.S.C. 44730).

SOURCE: Docket No. 16097, 43 FR 46783, Oct. 10, 1978, unless otherwise noted.

SPECIAL FEDERAL AVIATION REGULATION
No. 50–2

EDITORIAL NOTE: For the text of SFAR No. 50–2, see part 91 of this chapter.

SPECIAL FEDERAL AVIATION REGULATION
No. 71

EDITORIAL NOTE: For the text of SFAR No. 71, see part 91 of this chapter.

SPECIAL FEDERAL AVIATION REGULATION
No. 89

EDITORIAL NOTE: For the text of SFAR No. 89, see part 121 of this chapter.

SPECIAL FEDERAL AVIATION REGULATION
No. 97

EDITORIAL NOTE: For the text of SFAR No. 97, see part 91 of this chapter.

Subpart A—General

§ 135.1 Applicability.

(a) This part prescribes rules governing—

(1) The commuter or on-demand operations of each person who holds or is required to hold an Air Carrier Certificate or Operating Certificate under part 119 of this chapter.

(2) Each person employed or used by a certificate holder conducting operations under this part including the maintenance, preventative maintenance and alteration of an aircraft.

(3) The transportation of mail by aircraft conducted under a postal service contract awarded under 39 U.S.C. 5402c.

(4) Each person who applies for provisional approval of an Advanced Qualification Program curriculum, curriculum segment, or portion of a curriculum segment under subpart Y of part 121 of this chapter of 14 CFR part 121 and each person employed or used by an air carrier or commercial operator under this part to perform training, qualification, or evaluation functions under an Advanced Qualification Program under subpart Y of part 121 of this chapter of 14 CFR part 121.

(5) Nonstop Commercial Air Tour flights conducted for compensation or hire in accordance with § 119.1(e)(2) of this chapter that begin and end at the same airport and are conducted within a 25-statute-mile radius of that airport; provided further that these operations must comply only with the drug and alcohol testing requirements in §§ 120.31, 120.33, 120.35, 120.37, and 120.39 of this chapter; and with the provisions of part 136, subpart A, and § 91.147 of this chapter by September 11, 2007.

(6) Each person who is on board an aircraft being operated under this part.

(7) Each person who is an applicant for an Air Carrier Certificate or an Operating Certificate under 119 of this chapter, when conducting proving tests.

(8) Commercial Air tours conducted by holders of operations specifications issued under this part must comply with the provisions of part 136, Subpart A of this chapter by September 11, 2007.

(9) Helicopter air ambulance operations as defined in § 135.601(b)(1).

(b) [Reserved]

(c) An operator who does not hold a part 119 certificate and who operates under the provisions of § 91.147 of this chapter is permitted to use a person who is otherwise authorized to perform aircraft maintenance or preventive maintenance duties and who is not subject to anti-drug and alcohol misuse prevent programs to perform—

(1) Aircraft maintenance or preventive maintenance on the operator's aircraft if the operator would otherwise be required to transport the aircraft more than 50 nautical miles further than the repair point closest to operator's principal place of operation to obtain these services; or

(2) Emergency repairs on the operator's aircraft if the aircraft cannot be safely operated to a location where an employee subject to FAA-approved programs can perform the repairs.

[Doc. No. 16097, 43 FR 46783, Oct. 10, 1978]

EDITORIAL NOTE: For FEDERAL REGISTER citations affecting § 135.1, see the List of CFR Sections Affected, which appears in the Finding Aids section of the printed volume and at *www.govinfo.gov*.

§ 135.2 Compliance schedule for operators that transition to part 121 of this chapter; certain new entrant operators.

(a) *Applicability.* This section applies to the following:

(1) Each certificate holder that was issued an air carrier or operating certificate and operations specifications under the requirements of part 135 of this chapter or under SFAR No. 38–2 of 14 CFR part 121 before January 19, 1996, and that conducts scheduled passenger-carrying operations with:

(i) Nontransport category turbopropeller powered airplanes type certificated after December 31, 1964, that have a passenger seat configuration of 10–19 seats;

(ii) Transport category turbopropeller powered airplanes that have a passenger seat configuration of 20–30 seats; or

(iii) Turbojet engine powered airplanes having a passenger seat configuration of 1–30 seats.

(2) Each person who, after January 19, 1996, applies for or obtains an initial air carrier or operating certificate and operations specifications to conduct

scheduled passenger-carrying operations in the kinds of airplanes described in paragraphs (a)(1)(i), (a)(1)(ii), or paragraph (a)(1)(iii) of this section.

(b) *Obtaining operations specifications.* A certificate holder described in paragraph (a)(1) of this section may not, after March 20, 1997, operate an airplane described in paragraphs (a)(1)(i), (a)(1)(ii), or (a)(1)(iii) of this section in scheduled passenger-carrying operations, unless it obtains operations specifications to conduct its scheduled operations under part 121 of this chapter on or before March 20, 1997.

(c) *Regular or accelerated compliance.* Except as provided in paragraphs (d), and (e) of this section, each certificate holder described in paragraph (a)(1) of this section shall comply with each applicable requirement of part 121 of this chapter on and after March 20, 1997 or on and after the date on which the certificate holder is issued operations specifications under this part, whichever occurs first. Except as provided in paragraphs (d) and (e) of this section, each person described in paragraph (a)(2) of this section shall comply with each applicable requirement of part 121 of this chapter on and after the date on which that person is issued a certificate and operations specifications under part 121 of this chapter.

(d) *Delayed compliance dates.* Unless paragraph (e) of this section specifies an earlier compliance date, no certificate holder that is covered by paragraph (a) of this section may operate an airplane in 14 CFR part 121 operations on or after a date listed in this paragraph unless that airplane meets the applicable requirement of this paragraph:

(1) *Nontransport category turbopropeller powered airplanes type certificated after December 31, 1964, that have a passenger seat configuration of 10–19 seats.* No certificate holder may operate under this part an airplane that is described in paragraph (a)(1)(i) of this section on or after a date listed in paragraph (d)(1) of this section unless that airplane meets the applicable requirement listed in paragraph (d)(1) of this section:

(i) December 20, 1997:
(A) Section 121.289, Landing gear aural warning.

(B) Section 121.308, Lavatory fire protection.

(C) Section 121.310(e), Emergency exit handle illumination.

(D) Section 121.337(b)(8), Protective breathing equipment.

(E) Section 121.340, Emergency flotation means.

(ii) December 20, 1999: Section 121.342, Pitot heat indication system.

(iii) December 20, 2010:
(A) For airplanes described in § 121.157(f), the Airplane Performance Operating Limitations in §§ 121.189 through 121.197.

(B) Section 121.161(b), Ditching approval.

(C) Section 121.305(j), Third attitude indicator.

(D) Section 121.312(c), Passenger seat cushion flammability.

(iv) March 12, 1999: Section 121.310(b)(1), Interior emergency exit locating sign.

(2) *Transport category turbopropeller powered airplanes that have a passenger seat configuration of 20–30 seats.* No certificate holder may operate under this part an airplane that is described in paragraph (a)(1)(ii) of this section on or after a date listed in paragraph (d)(2) of this section unless that airplane meets the applicable requirement listed in paragraph (d)(2) of this section:

(i) December 20, 1997:
(A) Section 121.308, Lavatory fire protection.

(B) Section 121.337(b) (8) and (9), Protective breathing equipment.

(C) Section 121.340, Emergency flotation means.

(ii) December 20, 2010: Section 121.305(j), Third attitude indicator.

(e) *Newly manufactured airplanes.* No certificate holder that is described in paragraph (a) of this section may operate under part 121 of this chapter an airplane manufactured on or after a date listed in this paragraph (e) unless that airplane meets the applicable requirement listed in this paragraph (e).

(1) For nontransport category turbopropeller powered airplanes type certificated after December 31, 1964, that have a passenger seat configuration of 10–19 seats:

(i) Manufactured on or after March 20, 1997:

(A) Section 121.305(j), Third attitude indicator.

(B) Section 121.311(f), Safety belts and shoulder harnesses.

(ii) Manufactured on or after December 20, 1997: Section 121.317(a), Fasten seat belt light.

(iii) Manufactured on or after December 20, 1999: Section 121.293, Takeoff warning system.

(iv) Manufactured on or after March 12, 1999: Section 121.310(b)(1), Interior emergency exit locating sign.

(2) For transport category turbopropeller powered airplanes that have a passenger seat configuration of 20–30 seats manufactured on or after March 20, 1997: Section 121.305(j), Third attitude indicator.

(f) *New type certification requirements.* No person may operate an airplane for which the application for a type certificate was filed after March 29, 1995, in 14 CFR part 121 operations unless that airplane is type certificated under part 25 of this chapter.

(g) *Transition plan.* Before March 19, 1996 each certificate holder described in paragraph (a)(1) of this section must submit to the FAA a transition plan (containing a calendar of events) for moving from conducting its scheduled operations under the commuter requirements of part 135 of this chapter to the requirements for domestic or flag operations under part 121 of this chapter. Each transition plan must contain details on the following:

(1) Plans for obtaining new operations specifications authorizing domestic or flag operations;

(2) Plans for being in compliance with the applicable requirements of part 121 of this chapter on or before March 20, 1997; and

(3) Plans for complying with the compliance date schedules contained in paragraphs (d) and (e) of this section.

[Doc. No. 28154, 60 FR 65938, Dec. 20, 1995, as amended by Amdt. 135–65, 61 FR 30435, June 14, 1996; Amdt. 135–66, 62 FR 13257, Mar. 19, 1997]

§ 135.3 Rules applicable to operations subject to this part.

(a) Each person operating an aircraft in operations under this part shall—

(1) While operating inside the United States, comply with the applicable rules of this chapter; and

(2) While operating outside the United States, comply with Annex 2, Rules of the Air, to the Convention on International Civil Aviation or the regulations of any foreign country, whichever applies, and with any rules of parts 61 and 91 of this chapter and this part that are more restrictive than that Annex or those regulations and that can be complied with without violating that Annex or those regulations. Annex 2 is incorporated by reference in § 91.703(b) of this chapter.

(b) Each certificate holder that conducts commuter operations under this part with airplanes in which two pilots are required by the type certification rules of this chapter shall comply with subparts N and O of part 121 of this chapter instead of the requirements of subparts E, G, and H of this part. Notwithstanding the requirements of this paragraph, a pilot serving under this part as second in command in a commuter operation with airplanes in which two pilots are required by the type certification rules of this chapter may meet the requirements of § 135.245 instead of the requirements of § 121.436.

(c) If authorized by the Administrator upon application, each certificate holder that conducts operations under this part to which paragraph (b) of this section does not apply, may comply with the applicable sections of subparts N and O of part 121 instead of the requirements of subparts E, G, and H of this part, except that those authorized certificate holders may choose to comply with the operating experience requirements of § 135.244, instead of the requirements of § 121.434 of this chapter. Notwithstanding the requirements of this paragraph, a pilot serving under this part as second in command may meet the requirements of § 135.245 instead of the requirements of § 121.436.

[Doc. No. 27993, 60 FR 65949, Dec. 20, 1995, as amended by Amdt. 135–65, 61 FR 30435, June 14, 1996; Amdt. 135–127A, 78 FR 77574, Dec. 24, 2013; Docket FAA–2010–0100, Amdt. 135–127B, 81 FR 2, Jan. 4, 2016]

§ 135.4 Applicability of rules for eligible on-demand operations.

(a) An "eligible on-demand operation" is an on-demand operation conducted under this part that meets the following requirements:

(1) *Two-pilot crew.* The flightcrew must consist of at least two qualified pilots employed or contracted by the certificate holder.

(2) *Flight crew experience.* The crewmembers must have met the applicable requirements of part 61 of this chapter and have the following experience and ratings:

(i) Total flight time for all pilots:

(A) Pilot in command—A minimum of 1,500 hours.

(B) Second in command—A minimum of 500 hours.

(ii) For multi-engine turbine-powered fixed-wing and powered-lift aircraft, the following FAA certification and ratings requirements:

(A) Pilot in command—Airline transport pilot and applicable type ratings.

(B) Second in command—Commercial pilot and instrument ratings.

(iii) For all other aircraft, the following FAA certification and rating requirements:

(A) Pilot in command—Commercial pilot and instrument ratings.

(B) Second in command—Commercial pilot and instrument ratings.

(3) *Pilot operating limitations.* If the second in command of a fixed-wing aircraft has fewer than 100 hours of flight time as second in command flying in the aircraft make and model and, if a type rating is required, in the type aircraft being flown, and the pilot in command is not an appropriately qualified check pilot, the pilot in command shall make all takeoffs and landings in any of the following situations:

(i) Landings at the destination airport when a Destination Airport Analysis is required by § 135.385(f); and

(ii) In any of the following conditions:

(A) The prevailing visibility for the airport is at or below ¾ mile.

(B) The runway visual range for the runway to be used is at or below 4,000 feet.

(C) The runway to be used has water, snow, slush, ice, or similar contamina-

tion that may adversely affect aircraft performance.

(D) The braking action on the runway to be used is reported to be less than "good."

(E) The crosswind component for the runway to be used is in excess of 15 knots.

(F) Windshear is reported in the vicinity of the airport.

(G) Any other condition in which the pilot in command determines it to be prudent to exercise the pilot in command's authority.

(4) *Crew pairing.* Either the pilot in command or the second in command must have at least 75 hours of flight time in that aircraft make or model and, if a type rating is required, for that type aircraft, either as pilot in command or second in command.

(b) The Administrator may authorize deviations from paragraphs (a)(2)(i) or (a)(4) of this section if the responsible Flight Standards office that issued the certificate holder's operations specifications finds that the crewmember has comparable experience, and can effectively perform the functions associated with the position in accordance with the requirements of this chapter. The Administrator may, at any time, terminate any grant of deviation authority issued under this paragraph. Grants of deviation under this paragraph may be granted after consideration of the size and scope of the operation, the qualifications of the intended personnel and the following circumstances:

(1) A newly authorized certificate holder does not employ any pilots who meet the minimum requirements of paragraphs (a)(2)(i) or (a)(4) of this section.

(2) An existing certificate holder adds to its fleet a new category and class aircraft not used before in its operation.

(3) An existing certificate holder establishes a new base to which it assigns pilots who will be required to become qualified on the aircraft operated from that base.

(c) An eligible on-demand operation may comply with alternative requirements specified in §§ 135.225(b), 135.385(f), and 135.387(b) instead of the requirements that apply to other on-demand operations.

[Doc. No. FAA–2001–10047, 68 FR 54585, Sept. 17, 2003, as amended by Docket FAA–2018–0119, Amdt. 135–139, 83 FR 9175, Mar. 5, 2018]

§135.7 Applicability of rules to unauthorized operators.

The rules in this part which apply to a person certificated under part 119 of this chapter also apply to a person who engages in any operation governed by this part without an appropriate certificate and operations specifications required by part 119 of this chapter.

[Doc. No. 16097, 43 FR 46783, Oct. 10, 1978, as amended by Amdt. 135–58, 60 FR 65939, Dec. 20, 1995]

§135.12 Previously trained crewmembers.

A certificate holder may use a crewmember who received the certificate holder's training in accordance with subparts E, G, and H of this part before March 19, 1997 without complying with initial training and qualification requirements of subparts N and O of part 121 of this chapter. The crewmember must comply with the applicable recurrent training requirements of part 121 of this chapter.

[Doc. No. 27993, 60 FR 65950, Dec. 20, 1995]

§135.19 Emergency operations.

(a) In an emergency involving the safety of persons or property, the certificate holder may deviate from the rules of this part relating to aircraft and equipment and weather minimums to the extent required to meet that emergency.

(b) In an emergency involving the safety of persons or property, the pilot in command may deviate from the rules of this part to the extent required to meet that emergency.

(c) Each person who, under the authority of this section, deviates from a rule of this part shall, within 10 days, excluding Saturdays, Sundays, and Federal holidays, after the deviation, send to the responsible Flight Standards office charged with the overall inspection of the certificate holder a complete report of the aircraft oper-

ation involved, including a description of the deviation and reasons for it.

[Docket No. 16097, 43 FR 46783, Oct. 10, 1978, as amended by Docket FAA–2018–0119, Amdt. 135–139, 83 FR 9175, Mar. 5, 2018]

§135.21 Manual requirements.

(a) Each certificate holder, other than one who uses only one pilot in the certificate holder's operations, shall prepare and keep current a manual setting forth the certificate holder's procedures and policies acceptable to the Administrator. This manual must be used by the certificate holder's flight, ground, and maintenance personnel in conducting its operations. However, the Administrator may authorize a deviation from this paragraph if the Administrator finds that, because of the limited size of the operation, all or part of the manual is not necessary for guidance of flight, ground, or maintenance personnel.

(b) Each certificate holder shall maintain at least one copy of the manual at its principal base of operations.

(c) The manual must not be contrary to any applicable Federal regulations, foreign regulation applicable to the certificate holder's operations in foreign countries, or the certificate holder's operating certificate or operations specifications.

(d) A copy of the manual, or appropriate portions of the manual (and changes and additions) shall be made available to maintenance and ground operations personnel by the certificate holder and furnished to—

(1) Its flight crewmembers; and

(2) Representatives of the Administrator assigned to the certificate holder.

(e) Each employee of the certificate holder to whom a manual or appropriate portions of it are furnished under paragraph (d)(1) of this section shall keep it up to date with the changes and additions furnished to them.

(f) Except as provided in paragraph (h) of this section, each certificate holder must carry appropriate parts of the manual on each aircraft when away from the principal operations base. The appropriate parts must be available for use by ground or flight personnel.

(g) For the purpose of complying with paragraph (d) of this section, a certificate holder may furnish the persons listed therein with all or part of its manual in printed form or other form, acceptable to the Administrator, that is retrievable in the English language. If the certificate holder furnishes all or part of the manual in other than printed form, it must ensure there is a compatible reading device available to those persons that provides a legible image of the information and instructions, or a system that is able to retrieve the information and instructions in the English language.

(h) If a certificate holder conducts aircraft inspections or maintenance at specified stations where it keeps the approved inspection program manual, it is not required to carry the manual aboard the aircraft en route to those stations.

[Doc. No. 16097, 43 FR 46783, Oct. 10, 1978, as amended by Amdt. 135–18, 47 FR 33396, Aug. 2, 1982; Amdt. 135–58, 60 FR 65939, Dec. 20, 1995; Amdt. 135–66, 62 FR 13257, Mar. 19, 1997; Amdt. 135–91, 68 FR 54585, Sept. 17, 2003]

§ 135.23   Manual contents.

Each manual shall have the date of the last revision on each revised page. The manual must include—

(a) The name of each management person required under § 119.69(a) of this chapter who is authorized to act for the certificate holder, the person's assigned area of responsibility, the person's duties, responsibilities, and authority, and the name and title of each person authorized to exercise operational control under § 135.77;

(b) Procedures for ensuring compliance with aircraft weight and balance limitations and, for multiengine aircraft, for determining compliance with § 135.185;

(c) Copies of the certificate holder's operations specifications or appropriate extracted information, including area of operations authorized, category and class of aircraft authorized, crew complements, and types of operations authorized;

(d) Procedures for complying with accident notification requirements;

(e) Procedures for ensuring that the pilot in command knows that required airworthiness inspections have been made and that the aircraft has been approved for return to service in compliance with applicable maintenance requirements;

(f) Procedures for reporting and recording mechanical irregularities that come to the attention of the pilot in command before, during, and after completion of a flight;

(g) Procedures to be followed by the pilot in command for determining that mechanical irregularities or defects reported for previous flights have been corrected or that correction has been deferred;

(h) Procedures to be followed by the pilot in command to obtain maintenance, preventive maintenance, and servicing of the aircraft at a place where previous arrangements have not been made by the operator, when the pilot is authorized to so act for the operator;

(i) Procedures under § 135.179 for the release for, or continuation of, flight if any item of equipment required for the particular type of operation becomes inoperative or unserviceable en route;

(j) Procedures for refueling aircraft, eliminating fuel contamination, protecting from fire (including electrostatic protection), and supervising and protecting passengers during refueling;

(k) Procedures to be followed by the pilot in command in the briefing under § 135.117;

(l) Flight locating procedures, when applicable;

(m) Procedures for ensuring compliance with emergency procedures, including a list of the functions assigned each category of required crewmembers in connection with an emergency and emergency evacuation duties under § 135.123;

(n) En route qualification procedures for pilots, when applicable;

(o) The approved aircraft inspection program, when applicable;

(p)(1) Procedures and information, as described in paragraph (p)(2) of this section, to assist each crewmember and person performing or directly supervising the following job functions involving items for transport on an aircraft:

(i) Acceptance;

(ii) Rejection;

(iii) Handling;

(iv) Storage incidental to transport;

(v) Packaging of company material; or

(vi) Loading.

(2) Ensure that the procedures and information described in this paragraph are sufficient to assist a person in identifying packages that are marked or labeled as containing hazardous materials or that show signs of containing undeclared hazardous materials. The procedures and information must include:

(i) Procedures for rejecting packages that do not conform to the Hazardous Materials Regulations in 49 CFR parts 171 through 180 or that appear to contain undeclared hazardous materials;

(ii) Procedures for complying with the hazardous materials incident reporting requirements of 49 CFR 171.15 and 171.16 and discrepancy reporting requirements of 49 CFR 175.31.

(iii) The certificate holder's hazmat policies and whether the certificate holder is authorized to carry, or is prohibited from carrying, hazardous materials; and

(iv) If the certificate holder's operations specifications permit the transport of hazardous materials, procedures and information to ensure the following:

(A) That packages containing hazardous materials are properly offered and accepted in compliance with 49 CFR parts 171 through 180;

(B) That packages containing hazardous materials are properly handled, stored, packaged, loaded and carried on board an aircraft in compliance with 49 CFR parts 171 through 180;

(C) That the requirements for Notice to the Pilot in Command (49 CFR 175.33) are complied with; and

(D) That aircraft replacement parts, consumable materials or other items regulated by 49 CFR parts 171 through 180 are properly handled, packaged, and transported.

(q) Procedures for the evacuation of persons who may need the assistance of another person to move expeditiously to an exit if an emergency occurs; and

(r) If required by §135.385, an approved Destination Airport Analysis establishing runway safety margins at destination airports, taking into account the following factors as supported by published aircraft performance data supplied by the aircraft manufacturer for the appropriate runway conditions—

(1) Pilot qualifications and experience;

(2) Aircraft performance data to include normal, abnormal and emergency procedures as supplied by the aircraft manufacturer;

(3) Airport facilities and topography;

(4) Runway conditions (including contamination);

(5) Airport or area weather reporting;

(6) Appropriate additional runway safety margins, if required;

(7) Airplane inoperative equipment;

(8) Environmental conditions; and

(9) Other criteria affecting aircraft performance.

(s) Other procedures and policy instructions regarding the certificate holder's operations issued by the certificate holder.

[Doc. No. 16097, 43 FR 46783, Oct. 10, 1978, as amended by Amdt. 135–20, 51 FR 40709, Nov. 7, 1986; Amdt. 135–58, 60 FR 65939, Dec. 20, 1995; Amdt. 135–91, 68 FR 54586, Sept. 17, 2003; Amdt. 135–101, 70 FR 58829, Oct. 7, 2005]

§135.25 Aircraft requirements.

(a) Except as provided in paragraph (d) of this section, no certificate holder may operate an aircraft under this part unless that aircraft—

(1) Is registered as a civil aircraft of the United States and carries an appropriate and current airworthiness certificate issued under this chapter; and

(2) Is in an airworthy condition and meets the applicable airworthiness requirements of this chapter, including those relating to identification and equipment.

(b) Each certificate holder must have the exclusive use of at least one aircraft that meets the requirements for at least one kind of operation authorized in the certificate holder's operations specifications. In addition, for each kind of operation for which the certificate holder does not have the exclusive use of an aircraft, the certificate holder must have available for use under a written agreement (including arrangements for performing required maintenance) at least one aircraft that meets the requirements for that kind of operation. However, this paragraph does not prohibit the operator from using or authorizing the use of the aircraft for other than operations under this part and does not require the certificate holder to have exclusive use of all aircraft that the certificate holder uses.

(c) For the purposes of paragraph (b) of this section, a person has exclusive use of an aircraft if that person has the sole possession, control, and use of it for flight, as owner, or has a written agreement (including arrangements for performing required maintenance), in effect when the aircraft is operated, giving the person that possession, control, and use for at least 6 consecutive months.

(d) A certificate holder may operate in common carriage, and for the carriage of mail, a civil aircraft which is leased or chartered to it without crew and is registered in a country which is a party to the Convention on International Civil Aviation if—

(1) The aircraft carries an appropriate airworthiness certificate issued by the country of registration and meets the registration and identification requirements of that country;

(2) The aircraft is of a type design which is approved under a U.S. type certificate and complies with all of the requirements of this chapter (14 CFR chapter I) that would be applicable to that aircraft were it registered in the United States, including the requirements which must be met for issuance of a U.S. standard airworthiness certificate (including type design conformity, condition for safe operation, and the noise, fuel venting, and engine emission requirements of this chapter), except that a U.S. registration certificate and a U.S. standard airworthiness certificate will not be issued for the aircraft;

(3) The aircraft is operated by U.S.-certificated airmen employed by the certificate holder; and

(4) The certificate holder files a copy of the aircraft lease or charter agreement with the FAA Aircraft Registry, Department of Transportation, 6400 South MacArthur Boulevard, Okla-

homa City, OK (Mailing address: P.O. Box 25504, Oklahoma City, OK 73125).

[Doc. No. 16097, 43 FR 46783, Oct. 10, 1978, as amended by Amdt. 135–8, 45 FR 68649, Oct. 16, 1980; Amdt. 135–66, 62 FR 13257, Mar. 19, 1997]

§ 135.41 Carriage of narcotic drugs, marihuana, and depressant or stimulant drugs or substances.

If the holder of a certificate operating under this part allows any aircraft owned or leased by that holder to be engaged in any operation that the certificate holder knows to be in violation of § 91.19(a) of this chapter, that operation is a basis for suspending or revoking the certificate.

[Doc. No. 28154, 60 FR 65939, Dec. 20, 1995]

§ 135.43 Crewmember certificates: International operations.

(a) This section describes the certificates that were issued to United States citizens who were employed by air carriers at the time of issuance as flight crewmembers on United States registered aircraft engaged in international air commerce. The purpose of the certificate is to facilitate the entry and clearance of those crewmembers into ICAO contracting states. They were issued under Annex 9, as amended, to the Convention on International Civil Aviation.

(b) The holder of a certificate issued under this section, or the air carrier by whom the holder is employed, shall surrender the certificate for cancellation at the responsible Flight Standards office at the termination of the holder's employment with that air carrier.

[Doc. No. 28154, 61 FR 30435, June 14, 1996, as amended by Docket FAA–2018–0119, Amdt. 135–139, 83 FR 9175, Mar. 5, 2018]

Subpart B—Flight Operations

§ 135.61 General.

This subpart prescribes rules, in addition to those in part 91 of this chapter, that apply to operations under this part.

§ 135.63 Recordkeeping requirements.

(a) Each certificate holder shall keep at its principal business office or at other places approved by the Administrator, and shall make available for inspection by the Administrator the following—

(1) The certificate holder's operating certificate;

(2) The certificate holder's operations specifications;

(3) A current list of the aircraft used or available for use in operations under this part and the operations for which each is equipped;

(4) An individual record of each pilot used in operations under this part, including the following information:

(i) The full name of the pilot.

(ii) The pilot certificate (by type and number) and ratings that the pilot holds.

(iii) The pilot's aeronautical experience in sufficient detail to determine the pilot's qualifications to pilot aircraft in operations under this part

(iv) The pilot's current duties and the date of the pilot's assignment to those duties.

(v) The effective date and class of the medical certificate that the pilot holds.

(vi) The date and result of each of the initial and recurrent competency tests and proficiency and route checks required by this part and the type of aircraft flown during that test or check.

(vii) The pilot's flight time in sufficient detail to determine compliance with the flight time limitations of this part.

(viii) The pilot's check pilot authorization, if any.

(ix) Any action taken concerning the pilot's release from employment for physical or professional disqualification.

(x) The date of the completion of the initial phase and each recurrent phase of the training required by this part; and

(5) An individual record for each flight attendant who is required under this part, maintained in sufficient detail to determine compliance with the applicable portions of § 135.273 of this part.

(b) Each certificate holder must keep each record required by paragraph (a)(3) of this section for at least 6 months, and must keep each record re-

quired by paragraphs (a)(4) and (a)(5) of this section for at least 12 months.

(c) For multiengine aircraft, each certificate holder is responsible for the preparation and accuracy of a load manifest in duplicate containing information concerning the loading of the aircraft. The manifest must be prepared before each takeoff and must include:

(1) The number of passengers;

(2) The total weight of the loaded aircraft;

(3) The maximum allowable takeoff weight for that flight;

(4) The center of gravity limits;

(5) The center of gravity of the loaded aircraft, except that the actual center of gravity need not be computed if the aircraft is loaded according to a loading schedule or other approved method that ensures that the center of gravity of the loaded aircraft is within approved limits. In those cases, an entry shall be made on the manifest indicating that the center of gravity is within limits according to a loading schedule or other approved method;

(6) The registration number of the aircraft or flight number;

(7) The origin and destination; and

(8) Identification of crew members and their crew position assignments.

(d) The pilot in command of an aircraft for which a load manifest must be prepared shall carry a copy of the completed load manifest in the aircraft to its destination. The certificate holder shall keep copies of completed load manifests for at least 30 days at its principal operations base, or at another location used by it and approved by the Administrator.

[Doc. No. 16097, 43 FR 46783, Oct. 10, 1978, as amended by Amdt. 135–52, 59 FR 42993, Aug. 19, 1994]

§ 135.64 Retention of contracts and amendments: Commercial operators who conduct intrastate operations for compensation or hire.

Each commercial operator who conducts intrastate operations for compensation or hire shall keep a copy of each written contract under which it provides services as a commercial operator for a period of at least one year after the date of execution of the contract. In the case of an oral contract, it shall keep a memorandum stating its elements, and of any amendments to it, for a period of at least one year after the execution of that contract or change.

[Doc. No. 28154, 60 FR 65939, Dec. 20, 1995, as amended by Amdt. 135–65, 61 FR 30435, June 14, 1996; Amdt. 135–66, 62 FR 13257, Mar. 19, 1997]

§ 135.65 Reporting mechanical irregularities.

(a) Each certificate holder shall provide an aircraft maintenance log to be carried on board each aircraft for recording or deferring mechanical irregularities and their correction.

(b) The pilot in command shall enter or have entered in the aircraft maintenance log each mechanical irregularity that comes to the pilot's attention during flight time. Before each flight, the pilot in command shall, if the pilot does not already know, determine the status of each irregularity entered in the maintenance log at the end of the preceding flight.

(c) Each person who takes corrective action or defers action concerning a reported or observed failure or malfunction of an airframe, powerplant, propeller, rotor, or appliance, shall record the action taken in the aircraft maintenance log under the applicable maintenance requirements of this chapter.

(d) Each certificate holder shall establish a procedure for keeping copies of the aircraft maintenance log required by this section in the aircraft for access by appropriate personnel and shall include that procedure in the manual required by § 135.21.

§ 135.67 Reporting potentially hazardous meteorological conditions and irregularities of ground facilities or navigation aids.

Whenever a pilot encounters a potentially hazardous meteorological condition or an irregularity in a ground facility or navigation aid in flight, the knowledge of which the pilot considers essential to the safety of other flights, the pilot shall notify an appropriate ground radio station as soon as practicable.

[Doc. No. 16097, 43 FR 46783, Oct. 1, 1978, as amended at Amdt. 135–1, 44 FR 26737, May 7, 1979; Amdt. 135–110, 72 FR 31684, June 7, 2007]

§ 135.69 Restriction or suspension of operations: Continuation of flight in an emergency.

(a) During operations under this part, if a certificate holder or pilot in command knows of conditions, including airport and runway conditions, that are a hazard to safe operations, the certificate holder or pilot in command, as the case may be, shall restrict or suspend operations as necessary until those conditions are corrected.

(b) No pilot in command may allow a flight to continue toward any airport of intended landing under the conditions set forth in paragraph (a) of this section, unless, in the opinion of the pilot in command, the conditions that are a hazard to safe operations may reasonably be expected to be corrected by the estimated time of arrival or, unless there is no safer procedure. In the latter event, the continuation toward that airport is an emergency situation under § 135.19.

§ 135.71 Airworthiness check.

The pilot in command may not begin a flight unless the pilot determines that the airworthiness inspections required by § 91.409 of this chapter, or § 135.419, whichever is applicable, have been made.

[Doc. No. 16097, 43 FR 46783, Oct. 10, 1978, as amended by Amdt. 135–32, 54 FR 34332, Aug. 18, 1989]

§ 135.73 Inspections and tests.

Each certificate holder and each person employed by the certificate holder shall allow the Administrator, at any time or place, to make inspections or tests (including en route inspections) to determine the holder's compliance with the Federal Aviation Act of 1958, applicable regulations, and the certificate holder's operating certificate, and operations specifications.

§ 135.75 Inspectors credentials: Admission to pilots' compartment: Forward observer's seat.

(a) Whenever, in performing the duties of conducting an inspection, an FAA inspector presents an Aviation Safety Inspector credential, FAA Form 110A, to the pilot in command of an aircraft operated by the certificate holder, the inspector must be given free and uninterrupted access to the pilot compartment of that aircraft. However, this paragraph does not limit the emergency authority of the pilot in command to exclude any person from the pilot compartment in the interest of safety.

(b) A forward observer's seat on the flight deck, or forward passenger seat with headset or speaker must be provided for use by the Administrator while conducting en route inspections. The suitability of the location of the seat and the headset or speaker for use in conducting en route inspections is determined by the Administrator.

§135.76 DOD Commercial Air Carrier Evaluator's Credentials: Admission to pilots compartment: Forward observer's seat.

(a) Whenever, in performing the duties of conducting an evaluation, a DOD commercial air carrier evaluator presents S&A Form 110B, "DOD Commercial Air Carrier Evaluator's Credential," to the pilot in command of an aircraft operated by the certificate holder, the evaluator must be given free and uninterrupted access to the pilot's compartment of that aircraft. However, this paragraph does not limit the emergency authority of the pilot in command to exclude any person from the pilot compartment in the interest of safety.

(b) A forward observer's seat on the flight deck or forward passenger seat with headset or speaker must be provided for use by the evaluator while conducting en route evaluations. The suitability of the location of the seat and the headset or speaker for use in conducting en route evaluations is determined by the FAA.

[Doc. No. FAA–2003–15571, 68 FR 41218, July 10, 2003]

§135.77 Responsibility for operational control.

Each certificate holder is responsible for operational control and shall list, in the manual required by §135.21, the name and title of each person authorized by it to exercise operational control.

§135.78 Instrument approach procedures and IFR landing minimums.

No person may make an instrument approach at an airport except in accordance with IFR weather minimums and instrument approach procedures set forth in the certificate holder's operations specifications.

[Doc. No. FAA–2002–14002, 72 FR 31684, June 7, 2007]

§135.79 Flight locating requirements.

(a) Each certificate holder must have procedures established for locating each flight, for which an FAA flight plan is not filed, that—

(1) Provide the certificate holder with at least the information required to be included in a VFR flight plan;

(2) Provide for timely notification of an FAA facility or search and rescue facility, if an aircraft is overdue or missing; and

(3) Provide the certificate holder with the location, date, and estimated time for reestablishing communications, if the flight will operate in an area where communications cannot be maintained.

(b) Flight locating information shall be retained at the certificate holder's principal place of business, or at other places designated by the certificate holder in the flight locating procedures, until the completion of the flight.

(c) Each certificate holder shall furnish the representative of the Administrator assigned to it with a copy of its flight locating procedures and any changes or additions, unless those procedures are included in a manual required under this part.

[Doc. No. 16097, 43 FR 46783, Oct. 10, 1978, as amended by Amdt. 135–110, 72 FR 31684, June 7, 2007]

§135.81 Informing personnel of operational information and appropriate changes.

Each certificate holder shall inform each person in its employment of the operations specifications that apply to that person's duties and responsibilities and shall make available to each pilot in the certificate holder's employ the following materials in current form:

(a) Airman's Information Manual (Alaska Supplement in Alaska and Pacific Chart Supplement in Pacific-Asia Regions) or a commercial publication that contains the same information.

(b) This part and part 91 of this chapter.

(c) Aircraft Equipment Manuals, and Aircraft Flight Manual or equivalent.

(d) For foreign operations, the International Flight Information Manual or a commercial publication that contains the same information concerning the pertinent operational and entry requirements of the foreign country or countries involved.

§ 135.83 Operating information required.

(a) The operator of an aircraft must provide the following materials, in current and appropriate form, accessible to the pilot at the pilot station, and the pilot shall use them:

(1) A cockpit checklist.

(2) For multiengine aircraft or for aircraft with retractable landing gear, an emergency cockpit checklist containing the procedures required by paragraph (c) of this section, as appropriate.

(3) Pertinent aeronautical charts.

(4) For IFR operations, each pertinent navigational en route, terminal area, and approach and letdown chart.

(5) For multiengine aircraft, one-engine-inoperative climb performance data and if the aircraft is approved for use in IFR or over-the-top operations, that data must be sufficient to enable the pilot to determine compliance with § 135.181(a)(2).

(b) Each cockpit checklist required by paragraph (a)(1) of this section must contain the following procedures:

(1) Before starting engines;

(2) Before takeoff;

(3) Cruise;

(4) Before landing;

(5) After landing;

(6) Stopping engines.

(c) Each emergency cockpit checklist required by paragraph (a)(2) of this section must contain the following procedures, as appropriate:

(1) Emergency operation of fuel, hydraulic, electrical, and mechanical systems.

(2) Emergency operation of instruments and controls.

(3) Engine inoperative procedures.

(4) Any other emergency procedures necessary for safety.

§ 135.85 Carriage of persons without compliance with the passenger-carrying provisions of this part.

The following persons may be carried aboard an aircraft without complying with the passenger-carrying requirements of this part:

(a) A crewmember or other employee of the certificate holder.

(b) A person necessary for the safe handling of animals on the aircraft.

(c) A person necessary for the safe handling of hazardous materials (as defined in subchapter C of title 49 CFR).

(d) A person performing duty as a security or honor guard accompanying a shipment made by or under the authority of the U.S. Government.

(e) A military courier or a military route supervisor carried by a military cargo contract air carrier or commercial operator in operations under a military cargo contract, if that carriage is specifically authorized by the appropriate military service.

(f) An authorized representative of the Administrator conducting an en route inspection.

(g) A person, authorized by the Administrator, who is performing a duty connected with a cargo operation of the certificate holder.

(h) A DOD commercial air carrier evaluator conducting an en route evaluation.

[Doc. No. 16097, 43 FR 46783, Oct. 10, 1978, as amended by Amdt. 135–88, 68 FR 41218, July 10, 2003]

§ 135.87 Carriage of cargo including carry-on baggage.

No person may carry cargo, including carry-on baggage, in or on any aircraft unless—

(a) It is carried in an approved cargo rack, bin, or compartment installed in or on the aircraft;

(b) It is secured by an approved means; or

(c) It is carried in accordance with each of the following:

(1) For cargo, it is properly secured by a safety belt or other tie-down having enough strength to eliminate the possibility of shifting under all normally anticipated flight and ground conditions, or for carry-on baggage, it is restrained so as to prevent its movement during air turbulence.

(2) It is packaged or covered to avoid possible injury to occupants.

(3) It does not impose any load on seats or on the floor structure that exceeds the load limitation for those components.

(4) It is not located in a position that obstructs the access to, or use of, any required emergency or regular exit, or the use of the aisle between the crew and the passenger compartment, or located in a position that obscures any passenger's view of the "seat belt" sign, "no smoking" sign, or any required exit sign, unless an auxiliary sign or other approved means for proper notification of the passengers is provided.

(5) It is not carried directly above seated occupants.

(6) It is stowed in compliance with this section for takeoff and landing.

(7) For cargo only operations, paragraph (c)(4) of this section does not apply if the cargo is loaded so that at least one emergency or regular exit is available to provide all occupants of the aircraft a means of unobstructed exit from the aircraft if an emergency occurs.

(d) Each passenger seat under which baggage is stowed shall be fitted with a means to prevent articles of baggage stowed under it from sliding under crash impacts severe enough to induce the ultimate inertia forces specified in the emergency landing condition regulations under which the aircraft was type certificated.

(e) When cargo is carried in cargo compartments that are designed to require the physical entry of a crewmember to extinguish any fire that may occur during flight, the cargo must be loaded so as to allow a crewmember to effectively reach all parts of the compartment with the contents of a hand fire extinguisher.

§ 135.89 **Pilot requirements: Use of oxygen.**

(a) *Unpressurized aircraft.* Each pilot of an unpressurized aircraft shall use oxygen continuously when flying—

(1) At altitudes above 10,000 feet through 12,000 feet MSL for that part of the flight at those altitudes that is of more than 30 minutes duration; and

(2) Above 12,000 feet MSL.

(b) *Pressurized aircraft.* (1) Whenever a pressurized aircraft is operated with the cabin pressure altitude more than 10,000 feet MSL, each pilot shall comply with paragraph (a) of this section.

(2) Whenever a pressurized aircraft is operated at altitudes above 25,000 feet through 35,000 feet MSL, unless each pilot has an approved quick-donning type oxygen mask—

(i) At least one pilot at the controls shall wear, secured and sealed, an oxygen mask that either supplies oxygen at all times or automatically supplies oxygen whenever the cabin pressure altitude exceeds 12,000 feet MSL; and

(ii) During that flight, each other pilot on flight deck duty shall have an oxygen mask, connected to an oxygen supply, located so as to allow immediate placing of the mask on the pilot's face sealed and secured for use.

(3) Whenever a pressurized aircraft is operated at altitudes above 35,000 feet MSL, at least one pilot at the controls shall wear, secured and sealed, an oxygen mask required by paragraph (b)(2)(i) of this section.

(4) If one pilot leaves a pilot duty station of an aircraft when operating at altitudes above 25,000 feet MSL, the remaining pilot at the controls shall put on and use an approved oxygen mask until the other pilot returns to the pilot duty station of the aircraft.

§ 135.91 **Oxygen and portable oxygen concentrators for medical use by passengers.**

(a) Except as provided in paragraphs (d) and (e) of this section, no certificate holder may allow the carriage or operation of equipment for the storage, generation or dispensing of medical oxygen unless the conditions in paragraphs (a) through (c) of this section are satisfied. Beginning August 22, 2016, a certificate holder may allow a passenger to carry and operate a portable oxygen concentrator when the conditions in paragraphs (b) and (f) of this section are satisfied.

(1) The equipment must be—

(i) Of an approved type or in conformity with the manufacturing, packaging, marking, labeling, and maintenance requirements of title 49 CFR parts 171, 172, and 173, except § 173.24(a)(1);

(ii) When owned by the certificate holder, maintained under the certificate holder's approved maintenance program;

(iii) Free of flammable contaminants on all exterior surfaces;

(iv) Constructed so that all valves, fittings, and gauges are protected from damage during carriage or operation; and

(v) Appropriately secured.

(2) When the oxygen is stored in the form of a liquid, the equipment must have been under the certificate holder's approved maintenance program since its purchase new or since the storage container was last purged.

(3) When the oxygen is stored in the form of a compressed gas as defined in title 49 CFR 173.115(b)—

(i) When owned by the certificate holder, it must be maintained under its approved maintenance program; and

(ii) The pressure in any oxygen cylinder must not exceed the rated cylinder pressure.

(4) The pilot in command must be advised when the equipment is on board, and when it is intended to be used.

(5) The equipment must be stowed, and each person using the equipment must be seated, so as not to restrict access to or use of any required emergency or regular exit, or of the aisle in the passenger compartment.

(b) No person may smoke or create an open flame and no certificate holder may allow any person to smoke or create an open flame within 10 feet of oxygen storage and dispensing equipment carried under paragraph (a) of this section or a portable oxygen concentrator carried and operated under paragraph (f) of this section.

(c) No certificate holder may allow any person other than a person trained in the use of medical oxygen equipment to connect or disconnect oxygen bottles or any other ancillary compo-

nent while any passenger is aboard the aircraft.

(d) Paragraph (a)(1)(i) of this section does not apply when that equipment is furnished by a professional or medical emergency service for use on board an aircraft in a medical emergency when no other practical means of transportation (including any other properly equipped certificate holder) is reasonably available and the person carried under the medical emergency is accompanied by a person trained in the use of medical oxygen.

(e) Each certificate holder who, under the authority of paragraph (d) of this section, deviates from paragraph (a)(1)(i) of this section under a medical emergency shall, within 10 days, excluding Saturdays, Sundays, and Federal holidays, after the deviation, send to the responsible Flight Standards office a complete report of the operation involved, including a description of the deviation and the reasons for it.

(f) *Portable oxygen concentrators*—(1) *Acceptance criteria.* A passenger may carry or operate a portable oxygen concentrator for personal use on board an aircraft and a certificate holder may allow a passenger to carry or operate a portable oxygen concentrator on board an aircraft operated under this part during all phases of flight if the portable oxygen concentrator satisfies all of the requirements of this paragraph (f):

(i) Is legally marketed in the United States in accordance with Food and Drug Administration requirements in title 21 of the CFR;

(ii) Does not radiate radio frequency emissions that interfere with aircraft systems;

(iii) Generates a maximum oxygen pressure of less than 200 kPa gauge (29.0 psig/43.8 psia) at 20 °C (68 °F);

(iv) Does not contain any hazardous materials subject to the Hazardous Materials Regulations (49 CFR parts 171 through 180) except as provided in 49 CFR 175.10 for batteries used to power portable electronic devices and that do not require aircraft operator approval; and

(v) Bears a label on the exterior of the device applied in a manner that ensures the label will remain affixed for the life of the device and containing the following certification statement in red lettering: "The manufacturer of this POC has determined this device conforms to all applicable FAA acceptance criteria for POC carriage and use on board aircraft." The label requirements in this paragraph (f)(1)(v) do not apply to the following portable oxygen concentrators approved by the FAA for use on board aircraft prior to May 24, 2016:

(A) AirSep Focus;
(B) AirSep FreeStyle;
(C) AirSep FreeStyle 5;
(D) AirSep LifeStyle;
(E) Delphi RS–00400;
(F) DeVilbiss Healthcare iGo;
(G) Inogen One;
(H) Inogen One G2;
(I) Inogen One G3;
(J) Inova Labs LifeChoice;
(K) Inova Labs LifeChoice Activox;
(L) International Biophysics LifeChoice;
(M) Invacare Solo2;
(N) Invacare XPO2;
(O) Oxlife Independence Oxygen Concentrator;
(P) Oxus RS–00400;
(Q) Precision Medical EasyPulse;
(R) Respironics EverGo;
(S) Respironics SimplyGo;
(T) SeQual Eclipse;
(U) SeQual eQuinox Oxygen System (model 4000);
(V) SeQual Oxywell Oxygen System (model 4000);
(W) SeQual SAROS; and
(X) VBox Trooper Oxygen Concentrator.

(2) *Operating requirements.* Portable oxygen concentrators that satisfy the acceptance criteria identified in paragraph (f)(1) of this section may be carried on or operated by a passenger on board an aircraft provided the aircraft operator ensures that all of the conditions in this paragraph (f)(2) are satisfied:

(i) *Exit seats.* No person operating a portable oxygen concentrator is permitted to occupy an exit seat.

(ii) *Stowage of device.* During movement on the surface, takeoff and landing, the device must be stowed under the seat in front of the user, or in another approved stowage location so that it does not block the aisle way or the entryway to the row. If the device

is to be operated by the user, it must be operated only at a seat location that does not restrict any passenger's access to, or use of, any required emergency or regular exit, or the aisle(s) in the passenger compartment.

[Doc. No. 16097, 43 FR 46783, Oct. 10, 1978, as amended by Amdt. 135–60, 61 FR 2616, Jan. 26, 1996; Docket FAA–2014–0554, Amdt. 135–133, 81 FR 33119, May 24, 2016; Docket FAA–2018–0119, Amdt. 135–139, 83 FR 9175, Mar. 5, 2018]

§135.93 Minimum altitudes for use of autopilot.

(a) *Definitions.* For purpose of this section—

(1) Altitudes for takeoff/initial climb and go-around/missed approach are defined as above the airport elevation.

(2) Altitudes for enroute operations are defined as above terrain elevation.

(3) Altitudes for approach are defined as above the touchdown zone elevation (TDZE), unless the altitude is specifically in reference to DA (H) or MDA, in which case the altitude is defined by reference to the DA(H) or MDA itself.

(b) *Takeoff and initial climb.* No person may use an autopilot for takeoff or initial climb below the higher of 500 feet or an altitude that is no lower than twice the altitude loss specified in the Airplane Flight Manual (AFM), except as follows—

(1) At a minimum engagement altitude specified in the AFM; or

(2) At an altitude specified by the Administrator, whichever is greater.

(c) *Enroute.* No person may use an autopilot enroute, including climb and descent, below the following—

(1) 500 feet;

(2) At an altitude that is no lower than twice the altitude loss specified in the AFM for an autopilot malfunction in cruise conditions; or

(3) At an altitude specified by the Administrator, whichever is greater.

(d) *Approach.* No person may use an autopilot at an altitude lower than 50 feet below the DA(H) or MDA for the instrument procedure being flown, except as follows—

(1) For autopilots with an AFM specified altitude loss for approach operations—

(i) An altitude no lower than twice the specified altitude loss if higher than 50 feet below the MDA or DA(H);

(ii) An altitude no lower than 50 feet higher than the altitude loss specified in the AFM, when the following conditions are met—

(A) Reported weather conditions are less than the basic VFR weather conditions in § 91.155 of this chapter;

(B) Suitable visual references specified in § 91.175 of this chapter have been established on the instrument approach procedure; and

(C) The autopilot is coupled and receiving both lateral and vertical path references;

(iii) An altitude no lower than the higher of the altitude loss specified in the AFM or 50 feet above the TDZE, when the following conditions are met—

(A) Reported weather conditions are equal to or better than the basic VFR weather conditions in § 91.155 of this chapter; and

(B) The autopilot is coupled and receiving both lateral and vertical path references; or

(iv) A greater altitude specified by the Administrator.

(2) For autopilots with AFM specified approach altitude limitations, the greater of—

(i) The minimum use altitude specified for the coupled approach mode selected;

(ii) 50 feet; or

(iii) An altitude specified by Administrator.

(3) For autopilots with an AFM specified negligible or zero altitude loss for an autopilot approach mode malfunction, the greater of—

(i) 50 feet; or

(ii) An altitude specified by Administrator.

(4) If executing an autopilot coupled go-around or missed approach using a certificated and functioning autopilot in accordance with paragraph (e) in this section.

(e) *Go-Around/Missed Approach.* No person may engage an autopilot during a go-around or missed approach below the minimum engagement altitude specified for takeoff and initial climb in paragraph (b) in this section. An autopilot minimum use altitude does not apply to a go-around/missed approach initiated with an engaged autopilot. Performing a go-around or missed approach with an engaged autopilot must not adversely affect safe obstacle clearance.

(f) *Landing.* Notwithstanding paragraph (d) of this section, autopilot minimum use altitudes do not apply to autopilot operations when an approved automatic landing system mode is being used for landing. Automatic landing systems must be authorized in an operations specification issued to the operator.

(g) This section does not apply to operations conducted in rotorcraft.

[Doc. No. FAA–2012–1059, 79 FR 6088, Feb. 3, 2014]

§ 135.95   Airmen: Limitations on use of services.

(a) No certificate holder may use the services of any person as an airman unless the person performing those services—

(1) Holds an appropriate and current airman certificate; and

(2) Is qualified, under this chapter, for the operation for which the person is to be used.

(b) A certificate holder may obtain approval to provide a temporary document verifying a flightcrew member's airman certificate and medical certificate privileges under an approved certificate verification plan set forth in the certificate holder's operations specifications. A document provided by the certificate holder may be carried as an airman certificate or medical certificate on flights within the United States for up to 72 hours.

[Amdt. No. 135–140, 83 FR 30282, June 27, 2018]

§ 135.97   Aircraft and facilities for recent flight experience.

Each certificate holder shall provide aircraft and facilities to enable each of its pilots to maintain and demonstrate the pilot's ability to conduct all operations for which the pilot is authorized.

§ 135.98   Operations in the North Polar Area.

After August 13, 2008, no certificate holder may operate an aircraft in the region north of 78° N latitude ("North Polar Area"), other than intrastate operations wholly within the state of

Alaska, unless authorized by the FAA. The certificate holder's operation specifications must include the following:

(a) The designation of airports that may be used for en-route diversions and the requirements the airports must meet at the time of diversion.

(b) Except for all-cargo operations, a recovery plan for passengers at designated diversion airports.

(c) A fuel-freeze strategy and procedures for monitoring fuel freezing for operations in the North Polar Area.

(d) A plan to ensure communication capability for operations in the North Polar Area.

(e) An MEL for operations in the North Polar Area.

(f) A training plan for operations in the North Polar Area.

(g) A plan for mitigating crew exposure to radiation during solar flare activity.

(h) A plan for providing at least two cold weather anti-exposure suits in the aircraft, to protect crewmembers during outside activity at a diversion airport with extreme climatic conditions. The FAA may relieve the certificate holder from this requirement if the season of the year makes the equipment unnecessary.

[Doc. No. FAA–2002–6717, 72 FR 1885, Jan. 16, 2007, as amended by Amdt. 135–112, 73 FR 8798, Feb. 15, 2008]

§135.99 Composition of flight crew.

(a) No certificate holder may operate an aircraft with less than the minimum flight crew specified in the aircraft operating limitations or the Aircraft Flight Manual for that aircraft and required by this part for the kind of operation being conducted.

(b) No certificate holder may operate an aircraft without a second in command if that aircraft has a passenger seating configuration, excluding any pilot seat, of ten seats or more.

(c) Except as provided in paragraph (d) of this section, a certificate holder authorized to conduct operations under instrument flight rules may receive authorization from the Administrator through its operations specifications to establish a second-in-command professional development program. As part of that program, a pilot employed by the certificate holder may log time as sec-

ond in command in operations conducted under this part and part 91 of this chapter that do not require a second pilot by type certification of the aircraft or the regulation under which the flight is being conducted, provided the flight operation is conducted in accordance with the certificate holder's operations specifications for second-in-command professional development program; and—

(1) The certificate holder:

(i) Maintains records for each assigned second in command consistent with the requirements in §135.63;

(ii) Provides a copy of the records required by §135.63(a)(4)(vi) and (x) to the assigned second in command upon request and within a reasonable time; and

(iii) Establishes and maintains a data collection and analysis process that will enable the certificate holder and the FAA to determine whether the second-in-command professional development program is accomplishing its objectives.

(2) The aircraft is a multiengine airplane or a single-engine turbine-powered airplane. The aircraft must have an independent set of controls for a second pilot flightcrew member, which may not include a throwover control wheel. The aircraft must also have the following equipment and independent instrumentation for a second pilot:

(i) An airspeed indicator;

(ii) Sensitive altimeter adjustable for barometric pressure;

(iii) Gyroscopic bank and pitch indicator;

(iv) Gyroscopic rate-of-turn indicator combined with an integral slip-skid indicator;

(v) Gyroscopic direction indicator;

(vi) For IFR operations, a vertical speed indicator;

(vii) For IFR operations, course guidance for en route navigation and instrument approaches; and

(viii) A microphone, transmit switch, and headphone or speaker.

(3) The pilot assigned to serve as second in command satisfies the following requirements:

(i) The second in command qualifications in §135.245;

(ii) The flight time and duty period limitations and rest requirements in subpart F of this part;

(iii) The crewmember testing requirements for second in command in subpart G of this part; and

(iv) The crewmember training requirements for second in command in subpart H of this part.

(4) The pilot assigned to serve as pilot in command satisfies the following requirements:

(i) Has been fully qualified to serve as a pilot in command for the certificate holder for at least the previous 6 calendar months; and

(ii) Has completed mentoring training, including techniques for reinforcing the highest standards of technical performance, airmanship and professionalism within the preceding 36 calendar months.

(d) The following certificate holders are not eligible to receive authorization for a second-in-command professional development program under paragraph (c) of this section:

(1) A certificate holder that uses only one pilot in its operations; and

(2) A certificate holder that has been approved to deviate from the requirements in § 135.21(a), § 135.341(a), or § 119.69(a) of this chapter.

[Doc. No. 16097, 43 FR 46783, Oct. 10, 1978, as amended at 83 FR 30282, June 27, 2018]

§ 135.100 Flight crewmember duties.

(a) No certificate holder shall require, nor may any flight crewmember perform, any duties during a critical phase of flight except those duties required for the safe operation of the aircraft. Duties such as company required calls made for such nonsafety related purposes as ordering galley supplies and confirming passenger connections, announcements made to passengers promoting the air carrier or pointing out sights of interest, and filling out company payroll and related records are not required for the safe operation of the aircraft.

(b) No flight crewmember may engage in, nor may any pilot in command permit, any activity during a critical phase of flight which could distract any flight crewmember from the performance of his or her duties or which could interfere in any way with the proper conduct of those duties. Activities such as eating meals, engaging in nonessential conversations within the cockpit and nonessential communications between the cabin and cockpit crews, and reading publications not related to the proper conduct of the flight are not required for the safe operation of the aircraft.

(c) For the purposes of this section, critical phases of flight includes all ground operations involving taxi, takeoff and landing, and all other flight operations conducted below 10,000 feet, except cruise flight.

NOTE: Taxi is defined as "movement of an airplane under its own power on the surface of an airport."

[Doc. No. 20661, 46 FR 5502, Jan. 19, 1981]

§ 135.101 Second in command required under IFR.

Except as provided in § 135.105, no person may operate an aircraft carrying passengers under IFR unless there is a second in command in the aircraft.

[Doc. No. 28743, 62 FR 42374, Aug. 6, 1997]

§ 135.103 [Reserved]

§ 135.105 Exception to second in command requirement: Approval for use of autopilot system.

(a) Except as provided in §§ 135.99 and 135.111, unless two pilots are required by this chapter for operations under VFR, a person may operate an aircraft without a second in command, if it is equipped with an operative approved autopilot system and the use of that system is authorized by appropriate operations specifications. No certificate holder may use any person, nor may any person serve, as a pilot in command under this section of an aircraft operated in a commuter operation, as defined in part 119 of this chapter unless that person has at least 100 hours pilot in command flight time in the make and model of aircraft to be flown and has met all other applicable requirements of this part.

(b) The certificate holder may apply for an amendment of its operations specifications to authorize the use of an autopilot system in place of a second in command.

(c) The Administrator issues an amendment to the operations specifications authorizing the use of an autopilot system, in place of a second in command, if—

(1) The autopilot is capable of operating the aircraft controls to maintain flight and maneuver it about the three axes; and

(2) The certificate holder shows, to the satisfaction of the Administrator, that operations using the autopilot system can be conducted safely and in compliance with this part.

The amendment contains any conditions or limitations on the use of the autopilot system that the Administrator determines are needed in the interest of safety.

[Doc. No. 16097, 43 FR 46783, Oct. 10, 1978, as amended by Amdt. 135–3, 45 FR 7542, Feb. 4, 1980; Amdt. 135–58, 60 FR 65939, Dec. 20 1995]

§135.107 Flight attendant crewmember requirement.

No certificate holder may operate an aircraft that has a passenger seating configuration, excluding any pilot seat, of more than 19 unless there is a flight attendant crewmember on board the aircraft.

§135.109 Pilot in command or second in command: Designation required.

(a) Each certificate holder shall designate a—

(1) Pilot in command for each flight; and

(2) Second in command for each flight requiring two pilots.

(b) The pilot in command, as designated by the certificate holder, shall remain the pilot in command at all times during that flight.

§135.111 Second in command required in Category II operations.

No person may operate an aircraft in a Category II operation unless there is a second in command of the aircraft.

§135.113 Passenger occupancy of pilot seat.

No certificate holder may operate an aircraft type certificated after October 15, 1971, that has a passenger seating configuration, excluding any pilot seat, of more than eight seats if any person other than the pilot in command, a sec-

ond in command, a company check airman, or an authorized representative of the Administrator, the National Transportation Safety Board, or the United States Postal Service occupies a pilot seat.

§135.115 Manipulation of controls.

No pilot in command may allow any person to manipulate the flight controls of an aircraft during flight conducted under this part, nor may any person manipulate the controls during such flight unless that person is—

(a) A pilot employed by the certificate holder and qualified in the aircraft; or

(b) An authorized safety representative of the Administrator who has the permission of the pilot in command, is qualified in the aircraft, and is checking flight operations.

§135.117 Briefing of passengers before flight.

(a) Before each takeoff each pilot in command of an aircraft carrying passengers shall ensure that all passengers have been orally briefed on—

(1) *Smoking.* Each passenger shall be briefed on when, where, and under what conditions smoking is prohibited (including, but not limited to, any applicable requirements of part 252 of this title). This briefing shall include a statement that the Federal Aviation Regulations require passenger compliance with the lighted passenger information signs (if such signs are required), posted placards, areas designated for safety purposes as no smoking areas, and crewmember instructions with regard to these items. The briefing shall also include a statement (if the aircraft is equipped with a lavatory) that Federal law prohibits: tampering with, disabling, or destroying any smoke detector installed in an aircraft lavatory; smoking in lavatories; and, when applicable, smoking in passenger compartments.

(2) The use of safety belts, including instructions on how to fasten and unfasten the safety belts. Each passenger shall be briefed on when, where, and under what conditions the safety belt must be fastened about that passenger. This briefing shall include a statement that the Federal Aviation Regulations

require passenger compliance with lighted passenger information signs and crewmember instructions concerning the use of safety belts.

(3) The placement of seat backs in an upright position before takeoff and landing;

(4) Location and means for opening the passenger entry door and emergency exits;

(5) Location of survival equipment;

(6) If the flight involves extended overwater operation, ditching procedures and the use of required flotation equipment;

(7) If the flight involves operations above 12,000 feet MSL, the normal and emergency use of oxygen; and

(8) Location and operation of fire extinguishers.

(9) If a rotorcraft operation involves flight beyond autorotational distance from the shoreline, as defined in § 135.168(a), use of life preservers, ditching procedures and emergency exit from the rotorcraft in the event of a ditching; and the location and use of life rafts and other life preserver devices if applicable.

(b) Before each takeoff the pilot in command shall ensure that each person who may need the assistance of another person to move expeditiously to an exit if an emergency occurs and that person's attendant, if any, has received a briefing as to the procedures to be followed if an evacuation occurs. This paragraph does not apply to a person who has been given a briefing before a previous leg of a flight in the same aircraft.

(c) The oral briefing required by paragraph (a) of this section shall be given by the pilot in command or a crewmember.

(d) Notwithstanding the provisions of paragraph (c) of this section, for aircraft certificated to carry 19 passengers or less, the oral briefing required by paragraph (a) of this section shall be given by the pilot in command, a crewmember, or other qualified person designated by the certificate holder and approved by the Administrator.

(e) The oral briefing required by paragraph (a) of this section must be supplemented by printed cards which must be carried in the aircraft in locations convenient for the use of each passenger. The cards must—

(1) Be appropriate for the aircraft on which they are to be used;

(2) Contain a diagram of, and method of operating, the emergency exits;

(3) Contain other instructions necessary for the use of emergency equipment on board the aircraft; and

(4) No later than June 12, 2005, for scheduled Commuter passenger-carrying flights, include the sentence, "Final assembly of this aircraft was completed in [INSERT NAME OF COUNTRY]."

(f) The briefing required by paragraph (a) may be delivered by means of an approved recording playback device that is audible to each passenger under normal noise levels.

[Doc. No. 16097, 43 FR 46783, Oct. 10, 1978, as amended by Amdt. 135–9, 51 FR 40709, Nov. 7, 1986; Amdt. 135–25, 53 FR 12362, Apr. 13, 1988; Amdt. 135–44, 57 FR 42675, Sept. 15, 1992; 57 FR 43776, Sept. 22, 1992; 69 FR 39294, June 29, 2004; Amdt. 135–129, 79 FR 9973, Feb. 21, 2014]

§ 135.119   Prohibition against carriage of weapons.

No person may, while on board an aircraft being operated by a certificate holder, carry on or about that person a deadly or dangerous weapon, either concealed or unconcealed. This section does not apply to—

(a) Officials or employees of a municipality or a State, or of the United States, who are authorized to carry arms; or

(b) Crewmembers and other persons authorized by the certificate holder to carry arms.

§ 135.120   Prohibition on interference with crewmembers.

No person may assault, threaten, intimidate, or interfere with a crewmember in the performance of the crewmember's duties aboard an aircraft being operated under this part.

[Doc. No. FAA–1998–4954, 64 FR 1080, Jan. 7, 1999]

§ 135.121   Alcoholic beverages.

(a) No person may drink any alcoholic beverage aboard an aircraft unless the certificate holder operating the aircraft has served that beverage.

(b) No certificate holder may serve any alcoholic beverage to any person aboard its aircraft if that person appears to be intoxicated.

(c) No certificate holder may allow any person to board any of its aircraft if that person appears to be intoxicated.

§135.122 Stowage of food, beverage, and passenger service equipment during aircraft movement on the surface, takeoff, and landing.

(a) No certificate holder may move an aircraft on the surface, take off, or land when any food, beverage, or tableware furnished by the certificate holder is located at any passenger seat.

(b) No certificate holder may move an aircraft on the surface, take off, or land unless each food and beverage tray and seat back tray table is secured in its stowed position.

(c) No certificate holder may permit an aircraft to move on the surface, take off, or land unless each passenger serving cart is secured in its stowed position.

(d) Each passenger shall comply with instructions given by a crewmember with regard to compliance with this section.

[Doc. No. 26142, 57 FR 42675, Sept. 15, 1992]

§135.123 Emergency and emergency evacuation duties.

(a) Each certificate holder shall assign to each required crewmember for each type of aircraft as appropriate, the necessary functions to be performed in an emergency or in a situation requiring emergency evacuation. The certificate holder shall ensure that those functions can be practicably accomplished, and will meet any reasonably anticipated emergency including incapacitation of individual crewmembers or their inability to reach the passenger cabin because of shifting cargo in combination cargo-passenger aircraft.

(b) The certificate holder shall describe in the manual required under §135.21 the functions of each category of required crewmembers assigned under paragraph (a) of this section.

§135.125 Aircraft security.

Certificate holders conducting operations under this part must comply with the applicable security requirements in 49 CFR chapter XII.

[67 FR 8350, Feb. 22, 2002]

§135.127 Passenger information requirements and smoking prohibitions.

(a) No person may conduct a scheduled flight on which smoking is prohibited by part 252 of this title unless the "No Smoking" passenger information signs are lighted during the entire flight, or one or more "No Smoking" placards meeting the requirements of §25.1541 of this chapter are posted during the entire flight. If both the lighted signs and the placards are used, the signs must remain lighted during the entire flight segment.

(b) No person may smoke while a "No Smoking" sign is lighted or while "No Smoking" placards are posted, except as follows:

(1) *On-demand operations.* The pilot in command of an aircraft engaged in an on-demand operation may authorize smoking on the flight deck (if it is physically separated from any passenger compartment), except in any of the following situations:

(i) During aircraft movement on the surface or during takeoff or landing;

(ii) During scheduled passenger-carrying public charter operations conducted under part 380 of this title;

(iii) During on-demand operations conducted interstate that meet paragraph (2) of the definition "On-demand operation" in §110.2 of this chapter, unless permitted under paragraph (b)(2) of this section; or

(iv) During any operation where smoking is prohibited by part 252 of this title or by international agreement.

(2) *Certain intrastate commuter operations and certain intrastate on-demand operations.* Except during aircraft movement on the surface or during takeoff or landing, a pilot in command of an aircraft engaged in a commuter operation or an on-demand operation that meets paragraph (2) of the definition of "On-demand operation" in

§ 110.2 of this chapter may authorize smoking on the flight deck (if it is physically separated from the passenger compartment, if any) if—

(i) Smoking on the flight deck is not otherwise prohibited by part 252 of this title;

(ii) The flight is conducted entirely within the same State of the United States (a flight from one place in Hawaii to another place in Hawaii through the airspace over a place outside Hawaii is not entirely within the same State); and

(iii) The aircraft is either not turbojet-powered or the aircraft is not capable of carrying at least 30 passengers.

(c) No person may smoke in any aircraft lavatory.

(d) No person may operate an aircraft with a lavatory equipped with a smoke detector unless there is in that lavatory a sign or placard which reads: "Federal law provides for a penalty of up to $2,000 for tampering with the smoke detector installed in this lavatory."

(e) No person may tamper with, disable, or destroy any smoke detector installed in any aircraft lavatory.

(f) On flight segments other than those described in paragraph (a) of this section, the "No Smoking" sign required by § 135.177(a)(3) of this part must be turned on during any movement of the aircraft on the surface, for each takeoff or landing, and at any other time considered necessary by the pilot in command.

(g) The passenger information requirements prescribed in § 91.517 (b) and (d) of this chapter are in addition to the requirements prescribed in this section.

(h) Each passenger shall comply with instructions given him or her by crewmembers regarding compliance with paragraphs (b), (c), and (e) of this section.

[Doc. No. 25590, 55 FR 8367, Mar. 7, 1990, as amended by Amdt. 135–35, 55 FR 20135, May 15, 1990; Amdt. 135–44, 57 FR 42675, Sept. 15, 1992; Amdt. 135–60, 61 FR 2616, Jan. 26, 1996; Amdt. 135–76, 65 FR 36780, June 9, 2000; Amdt. 135–124, 76 FR 7491, Feb. 10, 2011]

§ 135.128 Use of safety belts and child restraint systems.

(a) Except as provided in this paragraph, each person on board an aircraft operated under this part shall occupy an approved seat or berth with a separate safety belt properly secured about him or her during movement on the surface, takeoff, and landing. For seaplane and float equipped rotorcraft operations during movement on the surface, the person pushing off the seaplane or rotorcraft from the dock and the person mooring the seaplane or rotorcraft at the dock are excepted from the preceding seating and safety belt requirements. A safety belt provided for the occupant of a seat may not be used by more than one person who has reached his or her second birthday. Notwithstanding the preceding requirements, a child may:

(1) Be held by an adult who is occupying an approved seat or berth, provided the child has not reached his or her second birthday and the child does not occupy or use any restraining device; or

(2) Notwithstanding any other requirement of this chapter, occupy an approved child restraint system furnished by the certificate holder or one of the persons described in paragraph (a)(2)(i) of this section, provided:

(i) The child is accompanied by a parent, guardian, or attendant designated by the child's parent or guardian to attend to the safety of the child during the flight;

(ii) Except as provided in paragraph (a)(2)(ii)(D) of this section, the approved child restraint system bears one or more labels as follows:

(A) Seats manufactured to U.S. standards between January 1, 1981, and February 25, 1985, must bear the label: "This child restraint system conforms to all applicable Federal motor vehicle safety standards";

(B) Seats manufactured to U.S. standards on or after February 26, 1985, must bear two labels:

(1) "This child restraint system conforms to all applicable Federal motor vehicle safety standards"; and

(2) "THIS RESTRAINT IS CERTIFIED FOR USE IN MOTOR VEHICLES AND AIRCRAFT" in red lettering;

(C) Seats that do not qualify under paragraphs (a)(2)(ii)(A) and (a)(2)(ii)(B) of this section must bear a label or markings showing:

(1) That the seat was approved by a foreign government;

(2) That the seat was manufactured under the standards of the United Nations;

(3) That the seat or child restraint device furnished by the certificate holder was approved by the FAA through Type Certificate or Supplemental Type Certificate; or

(4) That the seat or child restraint device furnished by the certificate holder, or one of the persons described in paragraph (a)(2)(i) of this section, was approved by the FAA in accordance with §21.8(d) of this chapter or Technical Standard Order C–100b, or a later version. The child restraint device manufactured by AmSafe, Inc. (CARES, Part No. 4082) and approved by the FAA in accordance with §21.305(d) (2010 ed.) of this chapter may continue to bear a label or markings showing FAA approval in accordance with §21.305(d) (2010 ed.) of this chapter.

(D) Except as provided in §135.128(a)(2)(ii)(C)(3) and §135.128(a)(2)(ii)(C)(4), booster-type child restraint systems (as defined in Federal Motor Vehicle Safety Standard No. 213 (49 CFR 571.213)), vest- and harness-type child restraint systems, and lap held child restraints are not approved for use in aircraft; and

(iii) The certificate holder complies with the following requirements:

(A) The restraint system must be properly secured to an approved forward-facing seat or berth;

(B) The child must be properly secured in the restraint system and must not exceed the specified weight limit for the restraint system; and

(C) The restraint system must bear the appropriate label(s).

(b) Except as provided in paragraph (b)(3) of this section, the following prohibitions apply to certificate holders:

(1) Except as provided in §135.128(a)(2)(ii)(C)(3) and §135.128(a)(2)(ii)(C)(4), no certificate holder may permit a child, in an aircraft, to occupy a booster-type child restraint system, a vest-type child restraint system, a harness-type child restraint system, or a lap held child restraint system during take off, landing, and movement on the surface.

(2) Except as required in paragraph (b)(1) of this section, no certificate holder may prohibit a child, if requested by the child's parent, guardian, or designated attendant, from occupying a child restraint system furnished by the child's parent, guardian, or designated attendant provided:

(i) The child holds a ticket for an approved seat or berth or such seat or berth is otherwise made available by the certificate holder for the child's use;

(ii) The requirements of paragraph (a)(2)(i) of this section are met;

(iii) The requirements of paragraph (a)(2)(iii) of this section are met; and

(iv) The child restraint system has one or more of the labels described in paragraphs (a)(2)(ii)(A) through (a)(2)(ii)(C) of this section.

(3) This section does not prohibit the certificate holder from providing child restraint systems authorized by this or, consistent with safe operating practices, determining the most appropriate passenger seat location for the child restraint system.

[Doc. No. 26142, 57 FR 42676, Sept. 15, 1992, as amended by Amdt. 135–62, 61 FR 28422, June 4, 1996; Amdt. 135–100, 70 FR 50907, Aug. 26, 2005; Amdt. 135–106, 71 FR 40010, July 14, 2006; 71 FR 59374, Oct. 10, 2006; Amdt. 135–130, 79 FR 28812, May 20, 2014]

§ 135.129 Exit seating.

(a)(1) *Applicability.* This section applies to all certificate holders operating under this part, except for on-demand operations with aircraft having 19 or fewer passenger seats and commuter operations with aircraft having 9 or fewer passenger seats.

(2) *Duty to make determination of suitability.* Each certificate holder shall determine, to the extent necessary to perform the applicable functions of paragraph (d) of this section, the suitability of each person it permits to occupy an exit seat. For the purpose of this section—

(i) *Exit seat* means—

(A) Each seat having direct access to an exit; and

(B) Each seat in a row of seats through which passengers would have to pass to gain access to an exit, from the first seat inboard of the exit to the first aisle inboard of the exit.

(ii) A passenger seat having *direct access* means a seat from which a passenger can proceed directly to the exit without entering an aisle or passing around an obstruction.

(3) *Persons designated to make determination.* Each certificate holder shall make the passenger exit seating determinations required by this paragraph in a non-discriminatory manner consistent with the requirements of this section, by persons designated in the certificate holder's required operations manual.

(4) *Submission of designation for approval.* Each certificate holder shall designate the exit seats for each passenger seating configuration in its fleet in accordance with the definitions in this paragraph and submit those designations for approval as part of the procedures required to be submitted for approval under paragraphs (n) and (p) of this section.

(b) No certificate holder may seat a person in a seat affected by this section if the certificate holder determines that it is likely that the person would be unable to perform one or more of the applicable functions listed in paragraph (d) of this section because—

(1) The person lacks sufficient mobility, strength, or dexterity in both arms and hands, and both legs:

(i) To reach upward, sideways, and downward to the location of emergency exit and exit-slide operating mechanisms;

(ii) To grasp and push, pull, turn, or otherwise manipulate those mechanisms;

(iii) To push, shove, pull, or otherwise open emergency exits;

(iv) To lift out, hold, deposit on nearby seats, or maneuver over the seatbacks to the next row objects the size and weight of over-wing window exit doors;

(v) To remove obstructions of size and weight similar over-wing exit doors;

(vi) To reach the emergency exit expeditiously;

(vii) To maintain balance while removing obstructions;

(viii) To exit expeditiously;

(ix) To stabilize an escape slide after deployment; or

(x) To assist others in getting off an escape slide;

(2) The person is less than 15 years of age or lacks the capacity to perform one or more of the applicable functions listed in paragraph (d) of this section without the assistance of an adult companion, parent, or other relative;

(3) The person lacks the ability to read and understand instructions required by this section and related to emergency evacuation provided by the certificate holder in printed or graphic form or the ability to understand oral crew commands.

(4) The person lacks sufficient visual capacity to perform one or more of the applicable functions in paragraph (d) of this section without the assistance of visual aids beyond contact lenses or eyeglasses;

(5) The person lacks sufficient aural capacity to hear and understand instructions shouted by flight attendants, without assistance beyond a hearing aid;

(6) The person lacks the ability adequately to impart information orally to other passengers; or,

(7) The person has:

(i) A condition or responsibilities, such as caring for small children, that might prevent the person from performing one or more of the applicable functions listed in paragraph (d) of this section; or

(ii) A condition that might cause the person harm if he or she performs one or more of the applicable functions listed in paragraph (d) of this section.

(c) Each passenger shall comply with instructions given by a crewmember or other authorized employee of the certificate holder implementing exit seating restrictions established in accordance with this section.

(d) Each certificate holder shall include on passenger information cards, presented in the language in which briefings and oral commands are given by the crew, at each exit seat affected by this section, information that, in the event of an emergency in which a crewmember is not available to assist, a passenger occupying an exit seat may use if called upon to perform the following functions:

(1) Locate the emergency exit;

(2) Recognize the emergency exit opening mechanism;

(3) Comprehend the instructions for operating the emergency exit;

(4) Operate the emergency exit;

(5) Assess whether opening the emergency exit will increase the hazards to which passengers may be exposed;

(6) Follow oral directions and hand signals given by a crewmember;

(7) Stow or secure the emergency exit door so that it will not impede use of the exit;

(8) Assess the condition of an escape slide, activate the slide, and stabilize the slide after deployment to assist others in getting off the slide;

(9) Pass expeditiously through the emergency exit; and

(10) Assess, select, and follow a safe path away from the emergency exit.

(e) Each certificate holder shall include on passenger information cards, at each exit seat—

(1) In the primary language in which emergency commands are given by the crew, the selection criteria set forth in paragraph (b) of this section, and a request that a passenger identify himself or herself to allow reseating if he or she—

(i) Cannot meet the selection criteria set forth in paragraph (b) of this section;

(ii) Has a nondiscernible condition that will prevent him or her from performing the applicable functions listed in paragraph (d) of this section;

(iii) May suffer bodily harm as the result of performing one or more of those functions; or

(iv) Does not wish to perform those functions; and,

(2) In each language used by the certificate holder for passenger information cards, a request that a passenger identify himself or herself to allow reseating if he or she lacks the ability to read, speak, or understand the language or the graphic form in which instructions required by this section and related to emergency evacuation are provided by the certificate holder, or the ability to understand the specified language in which crew commands will be given in an emergency;

(3) May suffer bodily harm as the result of performing one or more of those functions; or,

(4) Does not wish to perform those functions.

A certificate holder shall not require the passenger to disclose his or her reason for needing reseating.

(f) Each certificate holder shall make available for inspection by the public at all passenger loading gates and ticket counters at each airport where it conducts passenger operations, written procedures established for making determinations in regard to exit row seating.

(g) No certificate holder may allow taxi or pushback unless at least one required crewmember has verified that no exit seat is occupied by a person the crewmember determines is likely to be unable to perform the applicable functions listed in paragraph (d) of this section.

(h) Each certificate holder shall include in its passenger briefings a reference to the passenger information cards, required by paragraphs (d) and (e), the selection criteria set forth in paragraph (b), and the functions to be performed, set forth in paragraph (d) of this section.

(i) Each certificate holder shall include in its passenger briefings a request that a passenger identify himself or herself to allow reseating if he or she—

(1) Cannot meet the selection criteria set forth in paragraph (b) of this section;

(2) Has a nondiscernible condition that will prevent him or her from performing the applicable functions listed in paragraph (d) of this section;

(3) May suffer bodily harm as the result of performing one or more of those functions; or,

(4) Does not wish to perform those functions.

A certificate holder shall not require the passenger to disclose his or her reason for needing reseating.

(j) [Reserved]

(k) In the event a certificate holder determines in accordance with this section that it is likely that a passenger assigned to an exit seat would be unable to perform the functions listed in paragraph (d) of this section or a passenger requests a non-exit seat, the certificate holder shall expeditiously relocate the passenger to a non-exit seat.

(l) In the event of full booking in the non-exit seats and if necessary to accommodate a passenger being relocated from an exit seat, the certificate holder shall move a passenger who is willing and able to assume the evacuation functions that may be required, to an exit seat.

(m) A certificate holder may deny transportation to any passenger under this section only because—

(1) The passenger refuses to comply with instructions given by a crewmember or other authorized employee of the certificate holder implementing exit seating restrictions established in accordance with this section, or

(2) The only seat that will physically accommodate the person's handicap is an exit seat.

(n) In order to comply with this section certificate holders shall—

(1) Establish procedures that address:

(i) The criteria listed in paragraph (b) of this section;

(ii) The functions listed in paragraph (d) of this section;

(iii) The requirements for airport information, passenger information cards, crewmember verification of appropriate seating in exit seats, passenger briefings, seat assignments, and denial of transportation as set forth in this section;

(iv) How to resolve disputes arising from implementation of this section, including identification of the certificate holder employee on the airport to whom complaints should be addressed for resolution; and,

(2) Submit their procedures for preliminary review and approval to the principal operations inspectors assigned to them at the responsible Flight Standards office.

(o) Certificate holders shall assign seats prior to boarding consistent with the criteria listed in paragraph (b) and the functions listed in paragraph (d) of this section, to the maximum extent feasible.

(p) The procedures required by paragraph (n) of this section will not become effective until final approval is granted by the Executive Director, Flight Standards Service, Washington, DC. Approval will be based solely upon the safety aspects of the certificate holder's procedures.

[Doc. No. 25821, 55 FR 8073, Mar. 6, 1990, as amended by Amdt. 135–45, 57 FR 48664, Oct. 27, 1992; Amdt. 135–50, 59 FR 33603, June 29, 1994; Amdt. 135–60, 61 FR 2616, Jan. 26, 1996; Docket FAA–2018–0119, Amdt. 135–139, 83 FR 9175, Mar. 5, 2018]

Subpart C—Aircraft and Equipment

§ 135.141   Applicability.

This subpart prescribes aircraft and equipment requirements for operations under this part. The requirements of this subpart are in addition to the aircraft and equipment requirements of part 91 of this chapter. However, this part does not require the duplication of any equipment required by this chapter.

§ 135.143   General requirements.

(a) No person may operate an aircraft under this part unless that aircraft and its equipment meet the applicable regulations of this chapter.

(b) Except as provided in § 135.179, no person may operate an aircraft under this part unless the required instruments and equipment in it have been approved and are in an operable condition.

(c) ATC transponder equipment installed within the time periods indicated below must meet the performance and environmental requirements of the following TSO's:

(1) *Through January 1, 1992:* (i) Any class of TSO-C74b or any class of TSO-C74c as appropriate, provided that the equipment was manufactured before January 1, 1990; or

(ii) The appropriate class of TSO-C112 (Mode S).

(2) *After January 1, 1992:* The appropriate class of TSO-C112 (Mode S). For purposes of paragraph (c)(2) of this section, "installation" does not include—

(i) Temporary installation of TSO-C74b or TSO-C74c substitute equipment, as appropriate, during maintenance of the permanent equipment;

(ii) Reinstallation of equipment after temporary removal for maintenance; or

(iii) For fleet operations, installation of equipment in a fleet aircraft after removal of the equipment for maintenance from another aircraft in the same operator's fleet.

[Doc. No. 16097, 43 FR 46783, Oct. 10, 1978, as amended by Amdt. 135–22, 52 FR 3392, Feb. 3, 1987]

§ 135.144 Portable electronic devices.

(a) Except as provided in paragraph (b) of this section, no person may operate, nor may any operator or pilot in command of an aircraft allow the operation of, any portable electronic device on any U.S.-registered civil aircraft operating under this part.

(b) Paragraph (a) of this section does not apply to—

(1) Portable voice recorders;

(2) Hearing aids;

(3) Heart pacemakers;

(4) Electric shavers;

(5) Portable oxygen concentrators that comply with the requirements in § 135.91; or

(6) Any other portable electronic device that the part 119 certificate holder has determined will not cause interference with the navigation or communication system of the aircraft on which it is to be used.

(c). The determination required by paragraph (b)(6) of this section shall be made by that part 119 certificate holder operating the aircraft on which the particular device is to be used.

[Doc. No. FAA–1998–4954, 64 FR 1080, Jan. 7, 1999, as amended by Docket FAA–2014–0554, Amdt. 135–133, 81 FR 33120, May 24, 2016]

§ 135.145 Aircraft proving and validation tests.

(a) No certificate holder may operate an aircraft, other than a turbojet aircraft, for which two pilots are required by this chapter for operations under VFR, if it has not previously proved such an aircraft in operations under this part in at least 25 hours of proving tests acceptable to the Administrator including—

(1) Five hours of night time, if night flights are to be authorized;

(2) Five instrument approach procedures under simulated or actual conditions, if IFR flights are to be authorized; and

(3) Entry into a representative number of en route airports as determined by the Administrator.

(b) No certificate holder may operate a turbojet airplane if it has not previously proved a turbojet airplane in operations under this part in at least 25 hours of proving tests acceptable to the Administrator including—

(1) Five hours of night time, if night flights are to be authorized;

(2) Five instrument approach procedures under simulated or actual conditions, if IFR flights are to be authorized; and

(3) Entry into a representative number of en route airports as determined by the Administrator.

(c) No certificate holder may carry passengers in an aircraft during proving tests, except those needed to make the tests and those designated by the Administrator to observe the tests. However, pilot flight training may be conducted during the proving tests.

(d) Validation testing is required to determine that a certificate holder is capable of conducting operations safely and in compliance with applicable regulatory standards. Validation tests are required for the following authorizations:

(1) The addition of an aircraft for which two pilots are required for operations under VFR or a turbojet airplane, if that aircraft or an aircraft of the same make or similar design has not been previously proved or validated in operations under this part.

(2) Operations outside U.S. airspace.

(3) Class II navigation authorizations.

(4) Special performance or operational authorizations.

(e) Validation tests must be accomplished by test methods acceptable to the Administrator. Actual flights may not be required when an applicant can demonstrate competence and compliance with appropriate regulations without conducting a flight.

(f) Proving tests and validation tests may be conducted simultaneously when appropriate.

(g) The Administrator may authorize deviations from this section if the Administrator finds that special circumstances make full compliance with this section unnecessary.

[Doc. No. FAA-2001-10047, 68 FR 54586, Sept. 17, 2003]

§ 135.147   Dual controls required.

No person may operate an aircraft in operations requiring two pilots unless it is equipped with functioning dual controls. However, if the aircraft type certification operating limitations do not require two pilots, a throwover control wheel may be used in place of two control wheels.

§ 135.149   Equipment requirements: General.

No person may operate an aircraft unless it is equipped with—

(a) A sensitive altimeter that is adjustable for barometric pressure;

(b) Heating or deicing equipment for each carburetor or, for a pressure carburetor, an alternate air source;

(c) For turbojet airplanes, in addition to two gyroscopic bank-and-pitch indicators (artificial horizons) for use at the pilot stations, a third indicator that is installed in accordance with the instrument requirements prescribed in § 121.305(j) of this chapter.

(d) [Reserved]

(e) For turbine powered aircraft, any other equipment as the Administrator may require.

[Doc. No. 16097, 43 FR 46783, Oct. 10, 1978, as amended at Amdt. 135-1, 44 FR 26737, May 7, 1979; Amdt. 135-34, 54 FR 43926, Oct. 27, 1989; Amdt. 135-38, 55 FR 43310, Oct. 26, 1990]

§ 135.150   Public address and crewmember interphone systems.

No person may operate an aircraft having a passenger seating configuration, excluding any pilot seat, of more than 19 unless it is equipped with—

(a) A public address system which—

(1) Is capable of operation independent of the crewmember interphone system required by paragraph (b) of this section, except for handsets, headsets, microphones, selector switches, and signaling devices;

(2) Is approved in accordance with § 21.305 of this chapter;

(3) Is accessible for immediate use from each of two flight crewmember stations in the pilot compartment;

(4) For each required floor-level passenger emergency exit which has an adjacent flight attendant seat, has a microphone which is readily accessible to the seated flight attendant, except that one microphone may serve more than one exit, provided the proximity of the exits allows unassisted verbal communication between seated flight attendants;

(5) Is capable of operation within 10 seconds by a flight attendant at each of those stations in the passenger compartment from which its use is accessible;

(6) Is audible at all passenger seats, lavatories, and flight attendant seats and work stations; and

(7) For transport category airplanes manufactured on or after November 27, 1990, meets the requirements of § 25.1423 of this chapter.

(b) A crewmember interphone system which—

(1) Is capable of operation independent of the public address system required by paragraph (a) of this section, except for handsets, headsets, microphones, selector switches, and signaling devices;

(2) Is approved in accordance with § 21.305 of this chapter;

(3) Provides a means of two-way communication between the pilot compartment and—

(i) Each passenger compartment; and

(ii) Each galley located on other than the main passenger deck level;

(4) Is accessible for immediate use from each of two flight crewmember stations in the pilot compartment;

(5) Is accessible for use from at least one normal flight attendant station in each passenger compartment;

(6) Is capable of operation within 10 seconds by a flight attendant at each of those stations in each passenger compartment from which its use is accessible; and

(7) For large turbojet-powered airplanes—

(i) Is accessible for use at enough flight attendant stations so that all floor-level emergency exits (or entryways to those exits in the case of exits located within galleys) in each passenger compartment are observable from one or more of those stations so equipped;

(ii) Has an alerting system incorporating aural or visual signals for use by flight crewmembers to alert flight attendants and for use by flight attendants to alert flight crewmembers;

(iii) For the alerting system required by paragraph (b)(7)(ii) of this section, has a means for the recipient of a call to determine whether it is a normal call or an emergency call; and

(iv) When the airplane is on the ground, provides a means of two-way communication between ground personnel and either of at least two flight crewmembers in the pilot compartment. The interphone system station for use by ground personnel must be so located that personnel using the system may avoid visible detection from within the airplane.

[Doc. No. 24995, 54 FR 43926, Oct. 27, 1989]

§135.151 Cockpit voice recorders.

(a) No person may operate a multiengine, turbine-powered airplane or rotorcraft having a passenger seating configuration of six or more and for which two pilots are required by certification or operating rules unless it is equipped with an approved cockpit voice recorder that:

(1) Is installed in compliance with §23.1457(a)(1) and (2), (b), (c), (d)(1)(i), (2) and (3), (e), (f), and (g); §25.1457(a)(1) and (2), (b), (c), (d)(1)(i), (2) and (3), (e), (f), and (g), §27.1457(a)(1) and (2), (b), (c), (d)(1)(i), (2) and (3), (e), (f), and (g); or §29.1457(a)(1) and (2), (b), (c), (d)(1)(i), (2) and (3), (e), (f), and (g) of this chapter, as applicable; and

(2) Is operated continuously from the use of the check list before the flight to completion of the final check list at the end of the flight.

(b) No person may operate a multiengine, turbine-powered airplane or rotorcraft having a passenger seating configuration of 20 or more seats unless it is equipped with an approved cockpit voice recorder that—

(1) Is installed in accordance with the requirements of §23.1457 (except paragraphs (a)(6), (d)(1)(ii), (4), and (5)); §25.1457 (except paragraphs (a)(6), (d)(1)(ii), (4), and (5)); §27.1457 (except paragraphs (a)(6), (d)(1)(ii), (4), and (5));

or §29.1457 (except paragraphs (a)(6), (d)(1)(ii), (4), and (5)) of this chapter, as applicable; and

(2) Is operated continuously from the use of the check list before the flight to completion of the final check list at the end of the flight.

(c) In the event of an accident, or occurrence requiring immediate notification of the National Transportation Safety Board which results in termination of the flight, the certificate holder shall keep the recorded information for at least 60 days or, if requested by the Administrator or the Board, for a longer period. Information obtained from the record may be used to assist in determining the cause of accidents or occurrences in connection with investigations. The Administrator does not use the record in any civil penalty or certificate action.

(d) For those aircraft equipped to record the uninterrupted audio signals received by a boom or a mask microphone the flight crewmembers are required to use the boom microphone below 18,000 feet mean sea level. No person may operate a large turbine engine powered airplane manufactured after October 11, 1991, or on which a cockpit voice recorder has been installed after October 11, 1991, unless it is equipped to record the uninterrupted audio signal received by a boom or mask microphone in accordance with §25.1457(c)(5) of this chapter.

(e) In complying with this section, an approved cockpit voice recorder having an erasure feature may be used, so that during the operation of the recorder, information:

(1) Recorded in accordance with paragraph (a) of this section and recorded more than 15 minutes earlier; or

(2) Recorded in accordance with paragraph (b) of this section and recorded more than 30 minutes earlier; may be erased or otherwise obliterated.

(f) By April 7, 2012, all airplanes subject to paragraph (a) or paragraph (b) of this section that are manufactured before April 7, 2010, and that are required to have a flight data recorder installed in accordance with §135.152, must have a cockpit voice recorder that also—

(1) Meets the requirements in §23.1457(d)(6) or §25.1457(d)(6) of this chapter, as applicable; and

(2) If transport category, meet the requirements in §25.1457(a)(3), (a)(4), and (a)(5) of this chapter.

(g)(1) No person may operate a multi-engine, turbine-powered airplane or rotorcraft that is manufactured on or after April 7, 2010, that has a passenger seating configuration of six or more seats, for which two pilots are required by certification or operating rules, and that is required to have a flight data recorder under §135.152, unless it is equipped with an approved cockpit voice recorder that also—

(i) Is installed in accordance with the requirements of §23.1457 (except for paragraph (a)(6)); §25.1457 (except for paragraph (a)(6)); §27.1457 (except for paragraph (a)(6)); or §29.1457 (except for paragraph (a)(6)) of this chapter, as applicable; and

(ii) Is operated continuously from the use of the check list before the flight, to completion of the final check list at the end of the flight; and

(iii) Retains at least the last 2 hours of recorded information using a recorder that meets the standards of TSO–C123a, or later revision.

(iv) For all airplanes or rotorcraft manufactured on or after December 6, 2010, also meets the requirements of §23.1457(a)(6);   §25.1457(a)(6); §27.1457(a)(6); or §29.457(a)(6) of this chapter, as applicable.

(2) No person may operate a multien-gine, turbine-powered airplane or rotorcraft that is manufactured on or after April 7, 2010, has a passenger seating configuration of 20 or more seats, and that is required to have a flight data recorder under §135.152, unless it is equipped with an approved cockpit voice recorder that also—

(i) Is installed in accordance with the requirements of §23.1457 (except for paragraph (a)(6)); §25.1457 (except for paragraph (a)(6)); §27.1457 (except for paragraph (a)(6)); or §29.1457 (except for paragraph (a)(6)) of this chapter, as applicable; and

(ii) Is operated continuously from the use of the check list before the flight, to completion of the final check list at the end of the flight; and

(iii) Retains at least the last 2 hours of recorded information using a recorder that meets the standards of TSO–C123a, or later revision.

(iv) For all airplanes or rotorcraft manufactured on or after December 6, 2010, also meets the requirements of §23.1457(a)(6);   §25.1457(a)(6); §27.1457(a)(6); or §29.457(a)(6) of this chapter, as applicable.

(h) All airplanes or rotorcraft required by this part to have a cockpit voice recorder and a flight data recorder, that install datalink communication equipment on or after December 6, 2010, must record all datalink messages as required by the certification rule applicable to the aircraft.

[Doc. No. 16097, 43 FR 46783, Oct. 10, 1978, as amended by Amdt. 135–23, 52 FR 9637, Mar. 25, 1987; Amdt. 135–26, 53 FR 26151, July 11, 1988; Amdt. 135–60, 61 FR 2616, Jan. 26, 1996; Amdt. 135–113, 73 FR 12570, Mar. 7, 2008; Amdt. 135–113, 74 FR 32801, July 9, 2009; Amdt. 135–121, 75 FR 17046, Apr. 5, 2010]

§ 135.152   Flight data recorders.

(a) Except as provided in paragraph (k) of this section, no person may operate under this part a multi-engine, tur-bine-engine powered airplane or rotor-craft having a passenger seating configuration, excluding any required crewmember seat, of 10 to 19 seats, that was either brought onto the U.S. register after, or was registered outside the United States and added to the operator's U.S. operations specifications after, October 11, 1991, unless it is equipped with one or more approved flight recorders that use a digital method of recording and storing data and a method of readily retrieving that data from the storage medium. The parameters specified in either Appendix B or C of this part, as applicable must be recorded within the range, accuracy, resolution, and recording intervals as specified. The recorder shall retain no less than 25 hours of aircraft operation.

(b) After October 11, 1991, no person may operate a multiengine, turbine-powered airplane having a passenger seating configuration of 20 to 30 seats or a multiengine, turbine-powered rotorcraft having a passenger seating configuration of 20 or more seats unless it is equipped with one or more approved flight recorders that utilize a digital method of recording and storing data, and a method of readily retrieving that data from the storage medium. The parameters in appendix D or E of this part, as applicable, that are set forth below, must be recorded within the ranges, accuracies, resolutions, and sampling intervals as specified.

(1) Except as provided in paragraph (b)(3) of this section for aircraft type certificated before October 1, 1969, the following parameters must be recorded:

(i) Time;

(ii) Altitude;

(iii) Airspeed;

(iv) Vertical acceleration;

(v) Heading;

(vi) Time of each radio transmission to or from air traffic control;

(vii) Pitch attitude;

(viii) Roll attitude;

(ix) Longitudinal acceleration;

(x) Control column or pitch control surface position; and

(xi) Thrust of each engine.

(2) Except as provided in paragraph (b)(3) of this section for aircraft type certificated after September 30, 1969, the following parameters must be recorded:

(i) Time;

(ii) Altitude;

(iii) Airspeed;

(iv) Vertical acceleration;

(v) Heading;

(vi) Time of each radio transmission either to or from air traffic control;

(vii) Pitch attitude;

(viii) Roll attitude;

(ix) Longitudinal acceleration;

(x) Pitch trim position;

(xi) Control column or pitch control surface position;

(xii) Control wheel or lateral control surface position;

(xiii) Rudder pedal or yaw control surface position;

(xiv) Thrust of each engine;

(xv) Position of each thrust reverser;

(xvi) Trailing edge flap or cockpit flap control position; and

(xvii) Leading edge flap or cockpit flap control position.

(3) For aircraft manufactured after October 11, 1991, all of the parameters listed in appendix D or E of this part, as applicable, must be recorded.

(c) Whenever a flight recorder required by this section is installed, it must be operated continuously from the instant the airplane begins the takeoff roll or the rotorcraft begins the lift-off until the airplane has completed the landing roll or the rotorcraft has landed at its destination.

(d) Except as provided in paragraph (c) of this section, and except for recorded data erased as authorized in this paragraph, each certificate holder shall keep the recorded data prescribed in paragraph (a) of this section until the aircraft has been operating for at least 25 hours of the operating time specified in paragraph (c) of this section. In addition, each certificate holder shall keep the recorded data prescribed in paragraph (b) of this section for an airplane until the airplane has been operating for at least 25 hours, and for a rotorcraft until the rotorcraft has been operating for at least 10 hours, of the operating time specified in paragraph (c) of this section. A total of 1 hour of recorded data may be erased for the purpose of testing the flight recorder or the flight recorder system. Any erasure made in accordance with this paragraph must be of the oldest recorded data accumulated at the time of testing. Except as provided in paragraph (c) of this section, no record need be kept more than 60 days.

(e) In the event of an accident or occurrence that requires the immediate notification of the National Transportation Safety Board under 49 CFR part 830 of its regulations and that results in termination of the flight, the certificate holder shall remove the recording media from the aircraft and keep the recorded data required by paragraphs (a) and (b) of this section for at least 60 days or for a longer period upon request of the Board or the Administrator.

(f)(1) For airplanes manufactured on or before August 18, 2000, and all other aircraft, each flight recorder required by this section must be installed in accordance with the requirements of § 23.1459 (except paragraphs (a)(3)(ii) and (6)), § 25.1459 (except paragraphs (a)(3)(ii) and (7)), § 27.1459 (except paragraphs (a)(3)(ii) and (6)), or § 29.1459 (except paragraphs (a)(3)(ii) and (6)), as appropriate, of this chapter. The correlation required by paragraph (c) of

§§ 23.1459, 25.1459, 27.1459, or 29.1459 of this chapter, as appropriate, need be established only on one aircraft of a group of aircraft:

(i) That are of the same type;

(ii) On which the flight recorder models and their installations are the same; and

(iii) On which there are no differences in the type designs with respect to the installation of the first pilot's instruments associated with the flight recorder. The most recent instrument calibration, including the recording medium from which this calibration is derived, and the recorder correlation must be retained by the certificate holder.

(2) For airplanes manufactured after August 18, 2000, each flight data recorder system required by this section must be installed in accordance with the requirements of § 23.1459(a) (except paragraphs (a)(3)(ii) and (6)), (b), (d) and (e), or § 25.1459(a) (except paragraphs (a)(3)(ii) and (7)), (b), (d) and (e) of this chapter. A correlation must be established between the values recorded by the flight data recorder and the corresponding values being measured. The correlation must contain a sufficient number of correlation points to accurately establish the conversion from the recorded values to engineering units or discrete state over the full operating range of the parameter. Except for airplanes having separate altitude and airspeed sensors that are an integral part of the flight data recorder system, a single correlation may be established for any group of airplanes—

(i) That are of the same type;

(ii) On which the flight recorder system and its installation are the same; and

(iii) On which there is no difference in the type design with respect to the installation of those sensors associated with the flight data recorder system. Documentation sufficient to convert recorded data into the engineering units and discrete values specified in the applicable appendix must be maintained by the certificate holder.

(g) Each flight recorder required by this section that records the data specified in paragraphs (a) and (b) of this section must have an approved device

to assist in locating that recorder under water.

(h) The operational parameters required to be recorded by digital flight data recorders required by paragraphs (i) and (j) of this section are as follows, the phrase "when an information source is installed" following a parameter indicates that recording of that parameter is not intended to require a change in installed equipment.

(1) Time;

(2) Pressure altitude;

(3) Indicated airspeed;

(4) Heading—primary flight crew reference (if selectable, record discrete, true or magnetic);

(5) Normal acceleration (Vertical);

(6) Pitch attitude;

(7) Roll attitude;

(8) Manual radio transmitter keying, or CVR/DFDR synchronization reference;

(9) Thrust/power of each engine—primary flight crew reference;

(10) Autopilot engagement status;

(11) Longitudinal acceleration;

(12) Pitch control input;

(13) Lateral control input;

(14) Rudder pedal input;

(15) Primary pitch control surface position;

(16) Primary lateral control surface position;

(17) Primary yaw control surface position;

(18) Lateral acceleration;

(19) Pitch trim surface position or parameters of paragraph (h)(82) of this section if currently recorded;

(20) Trailing edge flap or cockpit flap control selection (except when parameters of paragraph (h)(85) of this section apply);

(21) Leading edge flap or cockpit flap control selection (except when parameters of paragraph (h)(86) of this section apply);

(22) Each Thrust reverser position (or equivalent for propeller airplane);

(23) Ground spoiler position or speed brake selection (except when parameters of paragraph (h)(87) of this section apply);

(24) Outside or total air temperature;

(25) Automatic Flight Control System (AFCS) modes and engagement status, including autothrottle;

(26) Radio altitude (when an information source is installed);

(27) Localizer deviation, MLS Azimuth;

(28) Glideslope deviation, MLS Elevation;

(29) Marker beacon passage;

(30) Master warning;

(31) Air/ground sensor (primary airplane system reference nose or main gear);

(32) Angle of attack (when information source is installed);

(33) Hydraulic pressure low (each system);

(34) Ground speed (when an information source is installed);

(35) Ground proximity warning system;

(36) Landing gear position or landing gear cockpit control selection;

(37) Drift angle (when an information source is installed);

(38) Wind speed and direction (when an information source is installed);

(39) Latitude and longitude (when an information source is installed);

(40) Stick shaker/pusher (when an information source is installed);

(41) Windshear (when an information source is installed);

(42) Throttle/power lever position;

(43) Additional engine parameters (as designated in appendix F of this part);

(44) Traffic alert and collision avoidance system;

(45) DME 1 and 2 distances;

(46) Nav 1 and 2 selected frequency;

(47) Selected barometric setting (when an information source is installed);

(48) Selected altitude (when an information source is installed);

(49) Selected speed (when an information source is installed);

(50) Selected mach (when an information source is installed);

(51) Selected vertical speed (when an information source is installed);

(52) Selected heading (when an information source is installed);

(53) Selected flight path (when an information source is installed);

(54) Selected decision height (when an information source is installed);

(55) EFIS display format;

(56) Multi-function/engine/alerts display format;

(57) Thrust command (when an information source is installed);

(58) Thrust target (when an information source is installed);

(59) Fuel quantity in CG trim tank (when an information source is installed);

(60) Primary Navigation System Reference;

(61) Icing (when an information source is installed);

(62) Engine warning each engine vibration (when an information source is installed);

(63) Engine warning each engine over temp. (when an information source is installed);

(64) Engine warning each engine oil pressure low (when an information source is installed);

(65) Engine warning each engine over speed (when an information source is installed);

(66) Yaw trim surface position;

(67) Roll trim surface position;

(68) Brake pressure (selected system);

(69) Brake pedal application (left and right);

(70) Yaw or sideslip angle (when an information source is installed);

(71) Engine bleed valve position (when an information source is installed);

(72) De-icing or anti-icing system selection (when an information source is installed);

(73) Computed center of gravity (when an information source is installed);

(74) AC electrical bus status;

(75) DC electrical bus status;

(76) APU bleed valve position (when an information source is installed);

(77) Hydraulic pressure (each system);

(78) Loss of cabin pressure;

(79) Computer failure;

(80) Heads-up display (when an information source is installed);

(81) Para-visual display (when an information source is installed);

(82) Cockpit trim control input position—pitch;

(83) Cockpit trim control input position—roll;

(84) Cockpit trim control input position—yaw;

(85) Trailing edge flap and cockpit flap control position;

(86) Leading edge flap and cockpit flap control position;

(87) Ground spoiler position and speed brake selection; and

(88) All cockpit flight control input forces (control wheel, control column, rudder pedal).

(i) For all turbine-engine powered airplanes with a seating configuration, excluding any required crewmember seat, of 10 to 30 passenger seats, manufactured after August 18, 2000—

(1) The parameters listed in paragraphs (h)(1) through (h)(57) of this section must be recorded within the ranges, accuracies, resolutions, and recording intervals specified in Appendix F of this part.

(2) Commensurate with the capacity of the recording system, all additional parameters for which information sources are installed and which are connected to the recording system must be recorded within the ranges, accuracies, resolutions, and sampling intervals specified in Appendix F of this part.

(j) For all turbine-engine-powered airplanes with a seating configuration, excluding any required crewmember seat, of 10 to 30 passenger seats, that are manufactured after August 19, 2002 the parameters listed in paragraph (a)(1) through (a)(88) of this section must be recorded within the ranges, accuracies, resolutions, and recording intervals specified in Appendix F of this part.

(k) For aircraft manufactured before August 18, 1997, the following aircraft types need not comply with this section: Bell 212, Bell 214ST, Bell 412, Bell 412SP, Boeing Chinook (BV-234), Boeing/Kawasaki Vertol 107 (BV/KV-107-II), deHavilland DHC-6, Eurocopter Puma 330J, Sikorsky 58, Sikorsky 61N, Sikorsky 76A.

(l) By April 7, 2012, all aircraft manufactured before April 7, 2010, must also meet the requirements in §23.1459(a)(7), §25.1459(a)(8), §27.1459(e), or §29.1459(e) of this chapter, as applicable.

(m) All aircraft manufactured on or after April 7, 2010, must have a flight data recorder installed that also—

(1) Meets the requirements of §23.1459(a)(3), (a)(6), and (a)(7), §25.1459(a)(3), (a)(7), and (a)(8), §27.1459(a)(3), (a)(6), and (e), or §29.1459(a)(3), (a)(6), and (e) of this chapter, as applicable; and

(2) Retains the 25 hours of recorded information required in paragraph (d) of this section using a recorder that meets the standards of TSO–C124a, or later revision.

[Doc. No. 25530, 53 FR 26151, July 11, 1988, as amended by Amdt. 135–69, 62 FR 38396, July 17, 1997; 62 FR 48135, Sept. 12, 1997; Amdt. 135–89, 68 FR 42939, July 18, 2003; Amdt. 135–113, 73 FR 12570, Mar. 7, 2008; Amdt. 135–113, 74 FR 32801, July 9, 2009]

§ 135.153   [Reserved]

§ 135.154   Terrain awareness and warning system.

(a) *Airplanes manufactured after March 29, 2002:*

(1) No person may operate a turbine-powered airplane configured with 10 or more passenger seats, excluding any pilot seat, unless that airplane is equipped with an approved terrain awareness and warning system that meets the requirements for Class A equipment in Technical Standard Order (TSO)–C151. The airplane must also include an approved terrain situational awareness display.

(2) No person may operate a turbine-powered airplane configured with 6 to 9 passenger seats, excluding any pilot seat, unless that airplane is equipped with an approved terrain awareness and warning system that meets as a minimum the requirements for Class B equipment in Technical Standard Order (TSO)–C151.

(b) *Airplanes manufactured on or before March 29, 2002:*

(1) No person may operate a turbine-powered airplane configured with 10 or more passenger seats, excluding any pilot seat, after March 29, 2005, unless that airplane is equipped with an approved terrain awareness and warning system that meets the requirements for Class A equipment in Technical Standard Order (TSO)–C151. The airplane must also include an approved terrain situational awareness display.

(2) No person may operate a turbine-powered airplane configured with 6 to 9 passenger seats, excluding any pilot seat, after March 29, 2005, unless that airplane is equipped with an approved terrain awareness and warning system

that meets as a minimum the requirements for Class B equipment in Technical Standard Order (TSO)–C151.

(Approved by the Office of Management and Budget under control number 2120–0631)

(c) *Airplane Flight Manual.* The Airplane Flight Manual shall contain appropriate procedures for—

(1) The use of the terrain awareness and warning system; and

(2) Proper flight crew reaction in response to the terrain awareness and warning system audio and visual warnings.

[Doc. No. 29312, 65 FR 16755, Mar. 29, 2000]

§135.155 Fire extinguishers: Passenger-carrying aircraft.

No person may operate an aircraft carrying passengers unless it is equipped with hand fire extinguishers of an approved type for use in crew and passenger compartments as follows—

(a) The type and quantity of extinguishing agent must be suitable for the kinds of fires likely to occur;

(b) At least one hand fire extinguisher must be provided and conveniently located on the flight deck for use by the flight crew; and

(c) At least one hand fire extinguisher must be conveniently located in the passenger compartment of each aircraft having a passenger seating configuration, excluding any pilot seat, of at least 10 seats but less than 31 seats.

§135.156 Flight data recorders: filtered data.

(a) A flight data signal is filtered when an original sensor signal has been changed in any way, other than changes necessary to:

(1) Accomplish analog to digital conversion of the signal;

(2) Format a digital signal to be DFDR compatible; or

(3) Eliminate a high frequency component of a signal that is outside the operational bandwidth of the sensor.

(b) An original sensor signal for any flight recorder parameter required to be recorded under §135.152 may be filtered only if the recorded signal value continues to meet the requirements of Appendix D or F of this part, as applicable.

(c) For a parameter described in §135.152(h)(12) through (17), (42), or (88), or the corresponding parameter in Appendix D of this part, if the recorded signal value is filtered and does not meet the requirements of Appendix D or F of this part, as applicable, the certificate holder must:

(1) Remove the filtering and ensure that the recorded signal value meets the requirements of Appendix D or F of this part, as applicable; or

(2) Demonstrate by test and analysis that the original sensor signal value can be reconstructed from the recorded data. This demonstration requires that:

(i) The FAA determine that the procedure and test results submitted by the certificate holder as its compliance with paragraph (c)(2) of this section are repeatable; and

(ii) The certificate holder maintains documentation of the procedure required to reconstruct the original sensor signal value. This documentation is also subject to the requirements of §135.152(e).

(d) *Compliance.* Compliance is required as follows:

(1) No later than October 20, 2011, each operator must determine, for each aircraft on its operations specifications, whether the aircraft's DFDR system is filtering any of the parameters listed in paragraph (c) of this section. The operator must create a record of this determination for each aircraft it operates, and maintain it as part of the correlation documentation required by §135.152 (f)(1)(iii) or (f)(2)(iii) of this part as applicable.

(2) For aircraft that are not filtering any listed parameter, no further action is required unless the aircraft's DFDR system is modified in a manner that would cause it to meet the definition of filtering on any listed parameter.

(3) For aircraft found to be filtering a parameter listed in paragraph (c) of this section the operator must either:

(i) No later than April 21, 2014, remove the filtering; or

(ii) No later than April 22, 2013, submit the necessary procedure and test results required by paragraph (c)(2) of this section.

(4) After April 21, 2014, no aircraft flight data recording system may filter

any parameter listed in paragraph (c) of this section that does not meet the requirements of Appendix D or F of this part, unless the certificate holder possesses test and analysis procedures and the test results that have been approved by the FAA. All records of tests, analysis and procedures used to comply with this section must be maintained as part of the correlation documentation required by § 135.152 (f)(1)(iii) or (f)(2)(iii) of this part as applicable.

[Doc. No. FAA–2006–26135, 75 FR 7357, Feb. 19, 2010]

§ 135.157 Oxygen equipment requirements.

(a) *Unpressurized aircraft.* No person may operate an unpressurized aircraft at altitudes prescribed in this section unless it is equipped with enough oxygen dispensers and oxygen to supply the pilots under § 135.89(a) and to supply, when flying—

(1) At altitudes above 10,000 feet through 15,000 feet MSL, oxygen to at least 10 percent of the occupants of the aircraft, other than the pilots, for that part of the flight at those altitudes that is of more than 30 minutes duration; and

(2) Above 15,000 feet MSL, oxygen to each occupant of the aircraft other than the pilots.

(b) *Pressurized aircraft.* No person may operate a pressurized aircraft—

(1) At altitudes above 25,000 feet MSL, unless at least a 10-minute supply of supplemental oxygen is available for each occupant of the aircraft, other than the pilots, for use when a descent is necessary due to loss of cabin pressurization; and

(2) Unless it is equipped with enough oxygen dispensers and oxygen to comply with paragraph (a) of this section whenever the cabin pressure altitude exceeds 10,000 feet MSL and, if the cabin pressurization fails, to comply with § 135.89 (a) or to provide a 2-hour supply for each pilot, whichever is greater, and to supply when flying—

(i) At altitudes above 10,000 feet through 15,000 feet MSL, oxygen to at least 10 percent of the occupants of the aircraft, other than the pilots, for that part of the flight at those altitudes

that is of more than 30 minutes duration; and

(ii) Above 15,000 feet MSL, oxygen to each occupant of the aircraft, other than the pilots, for one hour unless, at all times during flight above that altitude, the aircraft can safely descend to 15,000 feet MSL within four minutes, in which case only a 30-minute supply is required.

(c) The equipment required by this section must have a means—

(1) To enable the pilots to readily determine, in flight, the amount of oxygen available in each source of supply and whether the oxygen is being delivered to the dispensing units; or

(2) In the case of individual dispensing units, to enable each user to make those determinations with respect to that person's oxygen supply and delivery; and

(3) To allow the pilots to use undiluted oxygen at their discretion at altitudes above 25,000 feet MSL.

§ 135.158 Pitot heat indication systems.

(a) Except as provided in paragraph (b) of this section, after April 12, 1981, no person may operate a transport category airplane equipped with a flight instrument pitot heating system unless the airplane is also equipped with an operable pitot heat indication system that complies with § 25.1326 of this chapter in effect on April 12, 1978.

(b) A certificate holder may obtain an extension of the April 12, 1981, compliance date specified in paragraph (a) of this section, but not beyond April 12, 1983, from the Executive Director, Flight Standards Service if the certificate holder—

(1) Shows that due to circumstances beyond its control it cannot comply by the specified compliance date; and

(2) Submits by the specified compliance date a schedule for compliance, acceptable to the Executive Director, indicating that compliance will be achieved at the earliest practicable date.

[Doc. No. 18094, Amdt. 135–17, 46 FR 48306, Aug. 31, 1981, as amended by Amdt. 135–33, 54 FR 39294, Sept. 25, 1989; Docket FAA–2018–0119, Amdt. 135–139, 83 FR 9175, Mar. 5, 2018]

§135.159 Equipment requirements: Carrying passengers under VFR at night or under VFR over-the-top conditions.

No person may operate an aircraft carrying passengers under VFR at night or under VFR over-the-top, unless it is equipped with—

(a) A gyroscopic rate-of-turn indicator except on the following aircraft:

(1) Airplanes with a third attitude instrument system usable through flight attitudes of 360 degrees of pitch-and-roll and installed in accordance with the instrument requirements prescribed in §121.305(j) of this chapter.

(2) Helicopters with a third attitude instrument system usable through flight attitudes of ±80 degrees of pitch and ±120 degrees of roll and installed in accordance with §29.1303(g) of this chapter.

(3) Helicopters with a maximum certificated takeoff weight of 6,000 pounds or less.

(b) A slip skid indicator.

(c) A gyroscopic bank-and-pitch indicator.

(d) A gyroscopic direction indicator.

(e) A generator or generators able to supply all probable combinations of continuous in-flight electrical loads for required equipment and for recharging the battery.

(f) For night flights—

(1) An anticollision light system;

(2) Instrument lights to make all instruments, switches, and gauges easily readable, the direct rays of which are shielded from the pilots' eyes; and

(3) A flashlight having at least two size "D" cells or equivalent.

(g) For the purpose of paragraph (e) of this section, a continuous in-flight electrical load includes one that draws current continuously during flight, such as radio equipment and electrically driven instruments and lights, but does not include occasional intermittent loads.

(h) Notwithstanding provisions of paragraphs (b), (c), and (d), helicopters having a maximum certificated takeoff weight of 6,000 pounds or less may be operated until January 6, 1988, under visual flight rules at night without a slip skid indicator, a gyroscopic bank-and-pitch indicator, or a gyroscopic direction indicator.

[Doc. No. 24550, 51 FR 40709, Nov. 7, 1986, as amended by Amdt. 135–38, 55 FR 43310, Oct. 26, 1990]

§135.160 Radio altimeters for rotorcraft operations.

(a) After April 24, 2017, no person may operate a rotorcraft unless that rotorcraft is equipped with an operable FAA-approved radio altimeter, or an FAA-approved device that incorporates a radio altimeter, unless otherwise authorized in the certificate holder's approved minimum equipment list.

(b) *Deviation authority.* The Administrator may authorize deviations from paragraph (a) of this section for rotorcraft that are unable to incorporate a radio altimeter. This deviation will be issued as a Letter of Deviation Authority. The deviation may be terminated or amended at any time by the Administrator. The request for deviation authority is applicable to rotorcraft with a maximum gross takeoff weight no greater than 2,950 pounds. The request for deviation authority must contain a complete statement of the circumstances and justification, and must be submitted to the responsible Flight Standards office, not less than 60 days prior to the date of intended operations.

[Doc. No. FAA–2010–0982, 79 FR 9973, Feb. 21, 2014, as amended by Docket FAA–2018–0119, Amdt. 135–139, 83 FR 9175, Mar. 5, 2018]

§135.161 Communication and navigation equipment for aircraft operations under VFR over routes navigated by pilotage.

(a) No person may operate an aircraft under VFR over routes that can be navigated by pilotage unless the aircraft is equipped with the two-way radio communication equipment necessary under normal operating conditions to fulfill the following:

(1) Communicate with at least one appropriate station from any point on the route, except in remote locations and areas of mountainous terrain where geographical constraints make such communication impossible.

(2) Communicate with appropriate air traffic control facilities from any point

within Class B, Class C, or Class D airspace, or within a Class E surface area designated for an airport in which flights are intended; and

(3) Receive meteorological information from any point en route, except in remote locations and areas of mountainous terrain where geographical constraints make such communication impossible.

(b) No person may operate an aircraft at night under VFR over routes that can be navigated by pilotage unless that aircraft is equipped with—

(1) Two-way radio communication equipment necessary under normal operating conditions to fulfill the functions specified in paragraph (a) of this section; and

(2) Navigation equipment suitable for the route to be flown.

[Doc. No. FAA–2002–14002, 72 FR 31684, June 7, 2007, as amended by Amdt. 135–116, 74 FR 20205, May 1, 2009]

§ 135.163 Equipment requirements: Aircraft carrying passengers under IFR.

No person may operate an aircraft under IFR, carrying passengers, unless it has—

(a) A vertical speed indicator;

(b) A free-air temperature indicator;

(c) A heated pitot tube for each airspeed indicator;

(d) A power failure warning device or vacuum indicator to show the power available for gyroscopic instruments from each power source;

(e) An alternate source of static pressure for the altimeter and the airspeed and vertical speed indicators;

(f) For a single-engine aircraft:

(1) Two independent electrical power generating sources each of which is able to supply all probable combinations of continuous inflight electrical loads for required instruments and equipment; or

(2) In addition to the primary electrical power generating source, a standby battery or an alternate source of electric power that is capable of supplying 150% of the electrical loads of all required instruments and equipment necessary for safe emergency operation of the aircraft for at least one hour;

(g) For multi-engine aircraft, at least two generators or alternators each of which is on a separate engine, of which any combination of one-half of the total number are rated sufficiently to supply the electrical loads of all required instruments and equipment necessary for safe emergency operation of the aircraft except that for multi-engine helicopters, the two required generators may be mounted on the main rotor drive train; and

(h) Two independent sources of energy (with means of selecting either) of which at least one is an engine-driven pump or generator, each of which is able to drive all required gyroscopic instruments powered by, or to be powered by, that particular source and installed so that failure of one instrument or source, does not interfere with the energy supply to the remaining instruments or the other energy source unless, for single-engine aircraft in all cargo operations only, the rate of turn indicator has a source of energy separate from the bank and pitch and direction indicators. For the purpose of this paragraph, for multi-engine aircraft, each engine-driven source of energy must be on a different engine.

(i) For the purpose of paragraph (f) of this section, a continuous inflight electrical load includes one that draws current continuously during flight, such as radio equipment, electrically driven instruments, and lights, but does not include occasional intermittent loads.

[Doc. No. 16097, 43 FR 46783, Oct. 10, 1978, as amended by Amdt. 135–70, 62 FR 42374, Aug. 6, 1997; Amdt. 135–72, 63 FR 25573, May 8, 1998]

§ 135.165 Communication and navigation equipment: Extended over-water or IFR operations.

(a) *Aircraft navigation equipment requirements—General.* Except as provided in paragraph (g) of this section, no person may conduct operations under IFR or extended over-water unless—

(1) The en route navigation aids necessary for navigating the aircraft along the route (e.g., ATS routes, arrival and departure routes, and instrument approach procedures, including missed approach procedures if a missed approach routing is specified in the procedure) are available and suitable for

use by the navigation systems required by this section:

(2) The aircraft used in extended over-water operations is equipped with at least two-approved independent navigation systems suitable for navigating the aircraft along the route to be flown within the degree of accuracy required for ATC.

(3) The aircraft used for IFR operations is equipped with at least—

(i) One marker beacon receiver providing visual and aural signals; and

(ii) One ILS receiver.

(4) Any RNAV system used to meet the navigation equipment requirements of this section is authorized in the certificate holder's operations specifications.

(b) *Use of a single independent navigation system for IFR operations.* The aircraft may be equipped with a single independent navigation system suitable for navigating the aircraft along the route to be flown within the degree of accuracy required for ATC if:

(1) It can be shown that the aircraft is equipped with at least one other independent navigation system suitable, in the event of loss of the navigation capability of the single independent navigation system permitted by this paragraph at any point along the route, for proceeding safely to a suitable airport and completing an instrument approach; and

(2) The aircraft has sufficient fuel so that the flight may proceed safely to a suitable airport by use of the remaining navigation system, and complete an instrument approach and land.

(c) *VOR navigation equipment.* Whenever VOR navigation equipment is required by paragraph (a) or (b) of this section, no person may operate an aircraft unless it is equipped with at least one approved DME or suitable RNAV system.

(d) *Airplane communication equipment requirements.* Except as permitted in paragraph (e) of this section, no person may operate a turbojet airplane having a passenger seat configuration, excluding any pilot seat, of 10 seats or more, or a multiengine airplane in a commuter operation, as defined in part 119 of this chapter, under IFR or in extended over-water operations unless the airplane is equipped with—

(1) At least two independent communication systems necessary under normal operating conditions to fulfill the functions specified in § 121.347(a) of this chapter; and

(2) At least one of the communication systems required by paragraph (d)(1) of this section must have two-way voice communication capability.

(e) *IFR or extended over-water communications equipment requirements.* A person may operate an aircraft other than that specified in paragraph (d) of this section under IFR or in extended over-water operations if it meets all of the requirements of this section, with the exception that only one communication system transmitter is required for operations other than extended over-water operations.

(f) *Additional aircraft communication equipment requirements.* In addition to the requirements in paragraphs (d) and (e) of this section, no person may operate an aircraft under IFR or in extended over-water operations unless it is equipped with at least:

(1) Two microphones; and

(2) Two headsets or one headset and one speaker.

(g) *Extended over-water exceptions.* Notwithstanding the requirements of paragraphs (a), (d), and (e) of this section, installation and use of a single long-range navigation system and a single long-range communication system for extended over-water operations in certain geographic areas may be authorized by the Administrator and approved in the certificate holder's operations specifications. The following are among the operational factors the Administrator may consider in granting an authorization:

(1) The ability of the flight crew to navigate the airplane along the route within the degree of accuracy required for ATC;

(2) The length of the route being flown; and

(3) The duration of the very high frequency communications gap.

[Doc. No. FAA–2002–14002, 72 FR 31684, June 7, 2007]

§ 135.167 Emergency equipment: Extended overwater operations.

(a) Except where the Administrator, by amending the operations specifications of the certificate holder, requires the carriage of all or any specific items of the equipment listed below for any overwater operation, or, upon application of the certificate holder, the Administrator allows deviation for a particular extended overwater operation, no person may operate an aircraft in extended overwater operations unless it carries, installed in conspicuously marked locations easily accessible to the occupants if a ditching occurs, the following equipment:

(1) An approved life preserver equipped with an approved survivor locator light for each occupant of the aircraft. The life preserver must be easily accessible to each seated occupant.

(2) Enough approved liferafts of a rated capacity and buoyancy to accommodate the occupants of the aircraft.

(b) Each liferaft required by paragraph (a) of this section must be equipped with or contain at least the following:

(1) One approved survivor locator light.

(2) One approved pyrotechnic signaling device.

(3) Either—

(i) One survival kit, appropriately equipped for the route to be flown; or

(ii) One canopy (for sail, sunshade, or rain catcher);

(iii) One radar reflector;

(iv) One liferaft repair kit;

(v) One bailing bucket;

(vi) One signaling mirror;

(vii) One police whistle;

(viii) One raft knife;

(ix) One CO_2 bottle for emergency inflation;

(x) One inflation pump;

(xi) Two oars;

(xii) One 75-foot retaining line;

(xiii) One magnetic compass;

(xiv) One dye marker;

(xv) One flashlight having at least two size "D" cells or equivalent;

(xvi) A 2-day supply of emergency food rations supplying at least 1,000 calories per day for each person;

(xvii) For each two persons the raft is rated to carry, two pints of water or one sea water desalting kit;

(xviii) One fishing kit; and

(xix) One book on survival appropriate for the area in which the aircraft is operated.

(c) No person may operate an airplane in extended overwater operations unless there is attached to one of the life rafts required by paragraph (a) of this section, an approved survival type emergency locator transmitter. Batteries used in this transmitter must be replaced (or recharged, if the batteries are rechargeable) when the transmitter has been in use for more than 1 cumulative hour, or, when 50 percent of their useful life (or for rechargeable batteries, 50 percent of their useful life of charge) has expired, as established by the transmitter manufacturer under its approval. The new expiration date for replacing (or recharging) the battery must be legibly marked on the outside of the transmitter. The battery useful life (or useful life of charge) requirements of this paragraph do not apply to batteries (such as water-activated batteries) that are essentially unaffected during probable storage intervals.

[Doc. No. 16097, 43 FR 46783, Oct. 10, 1978, as amended by Amdt. 135-4, 45 FR 38348, June 30, 1980; Amdt. 135-20, 51 FR 40710, Nov. 7, 1986; Amdt. 135-49, 59 FR 32058, June 21, 1994; Amdt. 135-91, 68 FR 54586, Sept. 17, 2003]

§ 135.168 Emergency equipment: Overwater rotorcraft operations.

(a) *Definitions.* For the purposes of this section, the following definitions apply—

Autorotational distance refers to the distance a rotorcraft can travel in autorotation as described by the manufacturer in the approved Rotorcraft Flight Manual.

Shoreline means that area of the land adjacent to the water of an ocean, sea, lake, pond, river, or tidal basin that is above the high-water mark at which a rotorcraft could be landed safely. This does not include land areas which are unsuitable for landing such as vertical cliffs or land intermittently under water.

(b) *Required equipment.* Except when authorized by the certificate holder's operations specifications, or when necessary only for takeoff or landing, no person may operate a rotorcraft beyond autorotational distance from the shoreline unless it carries:

(1) An approved life preserver equipped with an approved survivor locator light for each occupant of the rotorcraft. The life preserver must be worn by each occupant while the rotorcraft is beyond autorotational distance from the shoreline, except for a patient transported during a helicopter air ambulance operation, as defined in § 135.601(b)(1), when wearing a life preserver would be inadvisable for medical reasons; and

(2) An approved and installed 406 MHz emergency locator transmitter (ELT) with 121.5 MHz homing capability Batteries used in ELTs must be maintained in accordance with the following—

(i) Non-rechargeable batteries must be replaced when the transmitter has been in use for more than 1 cumulative hour or when 50% of their useful lives have expired, as established by the transmitter manufacturer under its approval. The new expiration date for replacing the batteries must be legibly marked on the outside of the transmitter. The battery useful life requirements of this paragraph (b)(2) do not apply to batteries (such as water-activated batteries) that are essentially unaffected during probable storage intervals; or

(ii) Rechargeable batteries used in the transmitter must be recharged when the transmitter has been in use for more than 1 cumulative hour or when 50% of their useful-life-of-charge has expired, as established by the transmitter manufacturer under its approval. The new expiration date for recharging the batteries must be legibly marked on the outside of the transmitter. The battery useful-life-of-charge requirements of this paragraph (b)(2) do not apply to batteries (such as water-activated batteries) that are essentially unaffected during probable storage intervals.

(c) [Reserved]

(d) *ELT standards.* The ELT required by paragraph (b)(2) of this section must meet the requirements in:

(1) TSO–C126, TSO–C126a, or TSO–C126b; and

(2) Section 2 of either RTCA DO–204 or RTCA DO–204A, as specified by the TSO complied with in paragraph (d)(1) of this section.

(e) *ELT alternative compliance.* Operators with an ELT required by paragraph (b)(2) of this section, or an ELT with an approved deviation under § 21.618 of this chapter, are in compliance with this section.

(f) *Incorporation by reference.* The standards required in this section are incorporated by reference into this section with the approval of the Director of the Federal Register under 5 U.S.C. 552(a) and 1 CFR part 51. To enforce any edition other than that specified in this section, the FAA must publish notice of change in the FEDERAL REGISTER and the material must be available to the public. All approved material is available for inspection at the FAA's Office of Rulemaking (ARM–1), 800 Independence Avenue SW., Washington, DC 20591 (telephone (202) 267–9677) and from the sources indicated below. It is also available for inspection at the National Archives and Records Administration (NARA). For information on the availability of this material at NARA, call (202) 741–6030 or go to *http://www.archives.gov/ federal_register/ code_of_federal_regulations/ ibr_locations.html.*

(1) U.S. Department of Transportation, Subsequent Distribution Office, DOT Warehouse M30, Ardmore East Business Center, 3341 Q 75th Avenue, Landover, MD 20785; telephone (301) 322–5377. Copies are also available on the FAA's Web site. Use the following link and type the TSO number in the search box: *http://www.airweb.faa.gov/ Regulatory_and_Guidance_Library/ rgTSO.nsf/Frameset?OpenPage.*

(i) TSO–C126, 406 MHz Emergency Locator Transmitter (ELT), Dec. 23, 1992,

(ii) TSO–C126a, 406 MHz Emergency Locator Transmitter (ELT), Dec. 17, 2008, and

(iii) TSO–C126b, 406 MHz Emergency Locator Transmitter (ELT), Nov. 26, 2012.

(2) RTCA, Inc., 1150 18th Street NW., Suite 910, Washington, DC 20036, telephone (202) 833–9339, and are also available on RTCA's Web site at *http:// www.rtca.org/onlinecart/index.cfm.*

(i) RTCA DO–204, Minimum Operational Performance Standards (MOPS) 406 MHz Emergency Locator Transmitters (ELTs), Sept. 29, 1989, and

(ii) RTCA DO–204A, Minimum Operational Performance Standards (MOPS) 406 MHz Emergency Locator Transmitters (ELT), Dec. 6, 2007.

[Doc. No. FAA–2010–0982, 79 FR 9973, Feb. 21, 2014, as amended by Amdt. 135–138, 83 FR 1189, Jan. 10, 2018]

§ 135.169 Additional airworthiness requirements.

(a) Except for commuter category airplanes, no person may operate a large airplane unless it meets the additional airworthiness requirements of §§ 121.213 through 121.283 and 121.307 of this chapter.

(b) No person may operate a small airplane that has a passenger-seating configuration, excluding pilot seats, of 10 seats or more unless it is type certificated—

(1) In the transport category;

(2) Before July 1, 1970, in the normal category and meets special conditions issued by the Administrator for airplanes intended for use in operations under this part;

(3) Before July 19, 1970, in the normal category and meets the additional airworthiness standards in Special Federal Aviation Regulation No. 23;

(4) In the normal category and meets the additional airworthiness standards in appendix A;

(5) In the normal category and complies with section 1.(a) of Special Federal Aviation Regulation No. 41;

(6) In the normal category and complies with section 1.(b) of Special Federal Aviation Regulation No. 41;

(7) In the commuter category; or

(8) In the normal category, as a multi-engine certification level 4 airplane as defined in part 23 of this chapter.

(c) No person may operate a small airplane with a passenger seating configuration, excluding any pilot seat, of 10 seats or more, with a seating configuration greater than the maximum seating configuration used in that type airplane in operations under this part before August 19, 1977. This paragraph does not apply to—

(1) An airplane that is type certificated in the transport category; or

(2) An airplane that complies with—

(i) Appendix A of this part provided that its passenger seating configuration, excluding pilot seats, does not exceed 19 seats; or

(ii) Special Federal Aviation Regulation No. 41.

(d) Cargo or baggage compartments:

(1) After March 20, 1991, each Class C or D compartment, as defined in § 25.857 of part 25 of this chapter, greater than 200 cubic feet in volume in a transport category airplane type certificated after January 1, 1958, must have ceiling and sidewall panels which are constructed of:

(i) Glass fiber reinforced resin;

(ii) Materials which meet the test requirements of part 25, appendix F, part III of this chapter; or

(iii) In the case of liner installations approved prior to March 20, 1989, aluminum.

(2) For compliance with this paragraph, the term "liner" includes any design feature, such as a joint or fastener, which would affect the capability of the liner to safely contain a fire.

[Doc. No. 16097, 43 FR 46783, Oct. 10, 1978, as amended by Amdt. 135–2, 44 FR 53731, Sept. 17, 1979; Amdt. 135–21, 52 FR 1836, Jan. 15, 1987; 52 FR 34745, Sept. 14, 1987; Amdt. 135–31, 54 FR 7389, Feb. 17, 1989; Amdt. 135–55, 60 FR 6628, Feb. 2, 1995; Docket FAA–2015–1621, Amdt. 135–136, 81 FR 96701, Dec. 30, 2016]

§ 135.170 Materials for compartment interiors.

(a) No person may operate an airplane that conforms to an amended or supplemental type certificate issued in accordance with SFAR No. 41 for a maximum certificated takeoff weight in excess of 12,500 pounds unless within one year after issuance of the initial airworthiness certificate under that SFAR, the airplane meets the compartment interior requirements set forth in § 25.853(a) in effect March 6, 1995 (formerly § 25.853 (a), (b), (b–1), (b–2), and (b–3) of this chapter in effect on September 26, 1978).

(b) Except for commuter category airplanes and airplanes certificated under Special Federal Aviation Regulation No. 41, no person may operate a large airplane unless it meets the following additional airworthiness requirements:

(1) Except for those materials covered by paragraph (b)(2) of this section, all materials in each compartment used by the crewmembers or passengers must meet the requirements of §25.853 of this chapter in effect as follows or later amendment thereto:

(i) Except as provided in paragraph (b)(1)(iv) of this section, each airplane with a passenger capacity of 20 or more and manufactured after August 19, 1988, but prior to August 20, 1990, must comply with the heat release rate testing provisions of §25.853(d) in effect March 6, 1995 (formerly §25.853(a–1) in effect on August 20, 1986), except that the total heat release over the first 2 minutes of sample exposure rate must not exceed 100 kilowatt minutes per square meter and the peak heat release rate must not exceed 100 kilowatts per square meter.

(ii) Each airplane with a passenger capacity of 20 or more and manufactured after August 19, 1990, must comply with the heat release rate and smoke testing provisions of §25.853(d) in effect March 6, 1995 (formerly §25.83(a–1) in effect on September 26, 1988).

(iii) Except as provided in paragraph (b)(1) (v) or (vi) of this section, each airplane for which the application for type certificate was filed prior to May 1, 1972, must comply with the provisions of §25.853 in effect on April 30, 1972, regardless of the passenger capacity, if there is a substantially complete replacement of the cabin interior after April 30, 1972.

(iv) Except as provided in paragraph (b)(1) (v) or (vi) of this section, each airplane for which the application for type certificate was filed after May 1, 1972, must comply with the material requirements under which the airplane was type certificated regardless of the passenger capacity if there is a substantially complete replacement of the cabin interior after that date.

(v) Except as provided in paragraph (b)(1)(vi) of this section, each airplane that was type certificated after January 1, 1958, must comply with the heat release testing provisions of §25.853(d) in effect March 6, 1995 (formerly

§25.853(a–1) in effect on August 20, 1986), if there is a substantially complete replacement of the cabin interior components identified in that paragraph on or after that date, except that the total heat release over the first 2 minutes of sample exposure shall not exceed 100 kilowatt-minutes per square meter and the peak heat release rate shall not exceed 100 kilowatts per square meter.

(vi) Each airplane that was type certificated after January 1, 1958, must comply with the heat release rate and smoke testing provisions of §25.853(d) in effect March 6, 1995 (formerly §25.853(a–1) in effect on August 20, 1986), if there is a substantially complete replacement of the cabin interior components identified in that paragraph after August 19, 1990.

(vii) Contrary provisions of this section notwithstanding, the Director of the division of the Aircraft Certification Service responsible for the airworthiness rules may authorize deviation from the requirements of paragraph (b)(1)(i), (b)(1)(ii), (b)(1)(v), or (b)(1)(vi) of this section for specific components of the cabin interior that do not meet applicable flammability and smoke emission requirements, if the determination is made that special circumstances exist that make compliance impractical. Such grants of deviation will be limited to those airplanes manufactured within 1 year after the applicable date specified in this section and those airplanes in which the interior is replaced within 1 year of that date. A request for such grant of deviation must include a thorough and accurate analysis of each component subject to §25.853(d) in effect March 6, 1995 (formerly §25.853(a–1) in effect on August 20, 1986), the steps being taken to achieve compliance, and, for the few components for which timely compliance will not be achieved, credible reasons for such noncompliance.

(viii) Contrary provisions of this section notwithstanding, galley carts and standard galley containers that do not meet the flammability and smoke emission requirements of §25.853(d) in effect March 6, 1995 (formerly §25.853(a–1) in effect on August 20, 1986), may be used in airplanes that must meet the requirements of paragraph (b)(1)(i), (b)(1)(ii), (b)(1)(iv) or (b)(1)(vi) of this section provided the galley carts or standard containers were manufactured prior to March 6, 1995.

(2) For airplanes type certificated after January 1, 1958, seat cushions, except those on flight crewmember seats, in any compartment occupied by crew or passengers must comply with the requirements pertaining to fire protection of seat cushions in § 25.853(c) effective November 26, 1984.

(c) Thermal/acoustic insulation materials. For transport category airplanes type certificated after January 1, 1958:

(1) For airplanes manufactured before September 2, 2005, when thermal/acoustic insulation is installed in the fuselage as replacements after September 2, 2005, the insulation must meet the flame propagation requirements of § 25.856 of this chapter, effective September 2, 2003, if it is:

(i) Of a blanket construction, or

(ii) Installed around air ducting.

(2) For airplanes manufactured after September 2, 2005, thermal/acoustic insulation materials installed in the fuselage must meet the flame propagation requirements of § 25.856 of this chapter, effective September 2, 2003.

[Doc. No. 26192, 60 FR 6628, Feb. 2, 1995; Amdt. 135–55, 60 FR 11194, Mar. 1, 1995; Amdt. 135–56, 60 FR 13011, Mar. 9, 1995; Amdt. 135–90, 68 FR 45084, July 31, 2003; Amdt. 135–103, 70 FR 77752, Dec. 30, 2005; Docket FAA–2018–0119, Amdt. 135–139, 83 FR 9175, Mar. 5, 2018]

§ 135.171 Shoulder harness installation at flight crewmember stations.

(a) No person may operate a turbojet aircraft or an aircraft having a passenger seating configuration, excluding any pilot seat, of 10 seats or more unless it is equipped with an approved shoulder harness installed for each flight crewmember station.

(b) Each flight crewmember occupying a station equipped with a shoulder harness must fasten the shoulder harness during takeoff and landing, except that the shoulder harness may be unfastened if the crewmember cannot perform the required duties with the shoulder harness fastened.

§ 135.173 Airborne thunderstorm detection equipment requirements.

(a) No person may operate an aircraft that has a passenger seating configuration, excluding any pilot seat, of 10 seats or more in passenger-carrying operations, except a helicopter operating under day VFR conditions, unless the aircraft is equipped with either approved thunderstorm detection equipment or approved airborne weather radar equipment.

(b) No person may operate a helicopter that has a passenger seating configuration, excluding any pilot seat, of 10 seats or more in passenger-carrying operations, under night VFR when current weather reports indicate that thunderstorms or other potentially hazardous weather conditions that can be detected with airborne thunderstorm detection equipment may reasonably be expected along the route to be flown, unless the helicopter is equipped with either approved thunderstorm detection equipment or approved airborne weather radar equipment.

(c) No person may begin a flight under IFR or night VFR conditions when current weather reports indicate that thunderstorms or other potentially hazardous weather conditions that can be detected with airborne thunderstorm detection equipment, required by paragraph (a) or (b) of this section, may reasonably be expected along the route to be flown, unless the airborne thunderstorm detection equipment is in satisfactory operating condition.

(d) If the airborne thunderstorm detection equipment becomes inoperative en route, the aircraft must be operated under the instructions and procedures specified for that event in the manual required by § 135.21.

(e) This section does not apply to aircraft used solely within the State of Hawaii, within the State of Alaska, within that part of Canada west of longitude 130 degrees W, between latitude 70 degrees N, and latitude 53 degrees N, or during any training, test, or ferry flight.

(f) Without regard to any other provision of this part, an alternate electrical power supply is not required for airborne thunderstorm detection equipment.

[Doc. No. 16097, 43 FR 46783, Oct. 10, 1978, as amended by Amdt. 135–20, 51 FR 40710, Nov. 7, 1986; Amdt. 135–60, 61 FR 2616, Jan. 26, 1996]

§135.175 Airborne weather radar equipment requirements.

(a) No person may operate a large, transport category aircraft in passenger-carrying operations unless approved airborne weather radar equipment is installed in the aircraft.

(b) No person may begin a flight under IFR or night VFR conditions when current weather reports indicate that thunderstorms, or other potentially hazardous weather conditions that can be detected with airborne weather radar equipment, may reasonably be expected along the route to be flown, unless the airborne weather radar equipment required by paragraph (a) of this section is in satisfactory operating condition.

(c) If the airborne weather radar equipment becomes inoperative en route, the aircraft must be operated under the instructions and procedures specified for that event in the manual required by §135.21.

(d) This section does not apply to aircraft used solely within the State of Hawaii, within the State of Alaska, within that part of Canada west of longitude 130 degrees W, between latitude 70 degrees N, and latitude 53 degrees N, or during any training, test, or ferry flight.

(e) Without regard to any other provision of this part, an alternate electrical power supply is not required for airborne weather radar equipment.

§135.177 Emergency equipment requirements for aircraft having a passenger seating configuration of more than 19 passengers.

(a) No person may operate an aircraft having a passenger seating configuration, excluding any pilot seat, of more than 19 seats unless it is equipped with the following emergency equipment:

(1) At least one approved first-aid kit for treatment of injuries likely to occur in flight or in a minor accident that must:

(i) Be readily accessible to crewmembers.

(ii) Be stored securely and kept free from dust, moisture, and damaging temperatures.

(iii) Contain at least the following appropriately maintained contents in the specified quantities:

Contents	Quantity
Adhesive bandage compresses, 1-inch	16
Antiseptic swabs	20
Ammonia inhalants	10
Bandage compresses, 4-inch	8
Triangular bandage compresses, 40-inch	5
Arm splint, noninflatable	1
Leg splint, noninflatable	1
Roller bandage, 4-inch	4
Adhesive tape, 1-inch standard roll	2
Bandage scissors	1
Protective nonpermeable gloves or equivalent	1 pair

(2) A crash axe carried so as to be accessible to the crew but inaccessible to passengers during normal operations.

(3) Signs that are visible to all occupants to notify them when smoking is prohibited and when safety belts must be fastened. The signs must be constructed so that they can be turned on during any movement of the aircraft on the surface, for each takeoff or landing, and at other times considered necessary by the pilot in command. "No smoking" signs shall be turned on when required by §135.127.

(4) [Reserved]

(b) Each item of equipment must be inspected regularly under inspection periods established in the operations specifications to ensure its condition for continued serviceability and immediate readiness to perform its intended emergency purposes.

[Doc. No. 16097, 43 FR 46783, Oct. 10, 1978, as amended by Amdt. 135–25, 53 FR 12362, Apr. 13, 1988; Amdt. 135–43, 57 FR 19245, May 4, 1992; Amdt. 135–44, 57 FR 42676, Sept. 15, 1992; Amdt. 135–47, 59 FR 1781, Jan. 12, 1994; Amdt. 135–53, 59 FR 52643, Oct. 18, 1994; 59 FR 55208, Nov. 4, 1994; Amdt. 121–281, 66 FR 19045, Apr. 12, 2001]

§135.178 Additional emergency equipment.

No person may operate an airplane having a passenger seating configuration of more than 19 seats, unless it has the additional emergency equipment specified in paragraphs (a) through (l) of this section.

(a) *Means for emergency evacuation.* Each passenger-carrying landplane emergency exit (other than over-the-wing) that is more than 6 feet from the ground, with the airplane on the ground and the landing gear extended, must have an approved means to assist the occupants in descending to the ground. The assisting means for a floor-level emergency exit must meet the requirements of § 25.809(f)(1) of this chapter in effect on April 30, 1972, except that, for any airplane for which the application for the type certificate was filed after that date, it must meet the requirements under which the airplane was type certificated. An assisting means that deploys automatically must be armed during taxiing, take-offs, and landings; however, the Administrator may grant a deviation from the requirement of automatic deployment if he finds that the design of the exit makes compliance impractical, if the assisting means automatically erects upon deployment and, with respect to required emergency exits, if an emergency evacuation demonstration is conducted in accordance with § 121.291(a) of this chapter. This paragraph does not apply to the rear window emergency exit of Douglas DC–3 airplanes operated with fewer than 36 occupants, including crewmembers, and fewer than five exits authorized for passenger use.

(b) *Interior emergency exit marking.* The following must be complied with for each passenger-carrying airplane:

(1) Each passenger emergency exit, its means of access, and its means of opening must be conspicuously marked. The identity and locating of each passenger emergency exit must be recognizable from a distance equal to the width of the cabin. The location of each passenger emergency exit must be indicated by a sign visible to occupants approaching along the main passenger aisle. There must be a locating sign—

(i) Above the aisle near each over-the-wing passenger emergency exit, or at another ceiling location if it is more practical because of low headroom;

(ii) Next to each floor level passenger emergency exit, except that one sign may serve two such exits if they both can be seen readily from that sign; and

(iii) On each bulkhead or divider that prevents fore and aft vision along the passenger cabin, to indicate emergency exits beyond and obscured by it, except

that if this is not possible, the sign may be placed at another appropriate location.

(2) Each passenger emergency exit marking and each locating sign must meet the following:

(i) For an airplane for which the application for the type certificate was filed prior to May 1, 1972, each passenger emergency exit marking and each locating sign must be manufactured to meet the requirements of § 25.812(b) of this chapter in effect on April 30, 1972. On these airplanes, no sign may continue to be used if its luminescence (brightness) decreases to below 100 microlamberts. The colors may be reversed if it increases the emergency illumination of the passenger compartment. However, the Administrator may authorize deviation from the 2-inch background requirements if he finds that special circumstances exist that make compliance impractical and that the proposed deviation provides an equivalent level of safety.

(ii) For an airplane for which the application for the type certificate was filed on or after May 1, 1972, each passenger emergency exit marking and each locating sign must be manufactured to meet the interior emergency exit marking requirements under which the airplane was type certificated. On these airplanes, no sign may continue to be used if its luminescence (brightness) decreases to below 250 microlamberts.

(c) *Lighting for interior emergency exit markings.* Each passenger-carrying airplane must have an emergency lighting system, independent of the main lighting system; however, sources of general cabin illumination may be common to both the emergency and the main lighting systems if the power supply to the emergency lighting system is independent of the power supply to the main lighting system. The emergency lighting system must—

(1) Illuminate each passenger exit marking and locating sign;

(2) Provide enough general lighting in the passenger cabin so that the average illumination when measured at 40-inch intervals at seat armrest height, on the centerline of the main passenger aisle, is at least 0.05 foot-candles; and

(3) For airplanes type certificated after January 1, 1958, include floor proximity emergency escape path marking which meets the requirements of §25.812(e) of this chapter in effect on November 26, 1984.

(d) *Emergency light operation.* Except for lights forming part of emergency lighting subsystems provided in compliance with §25.812(h) of this chapter (as prescribed in paragraph (h) of this section) that serve no more than one assist means, are independent of the airplane's main emergency lighting systems, and are automatically activated when the assist means is deployed, each light required by paragraphs (c) and (h) of this section must:

(1) Be operable manually both from the flightcrew station and from a point in the passenger compartment that is readily accessible to a normal flight attendant seat;

(2) Have a means to prevent inadvertent operation of the manual controls;

(3) When armed or turned on at either station, remain lighted or become lighted upon interruption of the airplane's normal electric power;

(4) Be armed or turned on during taxiing, takeoff, and landing. In showing compliance with this paragraph, a transverse vertical separation of the fuselage need not be considered;

(5) Provide the required level of illumination for at least 10 minutes at the critical ambient conditions after emergency landing; and

(6) Have a cockpit control device that has an "on," "off," and "armed" position.

(e) *Emergency exit operating handles.* (1) For a passenger-carrying airplane for which the application for the type certificate was filed prior to May 1, 1972, the location of each passenger emergency exit operating handle, and instructions for opening the exit, must be shown by a marking on or near the exit that is readable from a distance of 30 inches. In addition, for each Type I and Type II emergency exit with a locking mechanism released by rotary motion of the handle, the instructions for opening must be shown by—

(i) A red arrow with a shaft at least three-fourths inch wide and a head twice the width of the shaft, extending along at least 70° of arc at a radius approximately equal to three-fourths of the handle length; and

(ii) The word "open" in red letters 1 inch high placed horizontally near the head of the arrow.

(2) For a passenger-carrying airplane for which the application for the type certificate was filed on or after May 1, 1972, the location of each passenger emergency exit operating handle and instructions for opening the exit must be shown in accordance with the requirements under which the airplane was type certificated. On these airplanes, no operating handle or operating handle cover may continue to be used if its luminescence (brightness) decreases to below 100 microlamberts.

(f) *Emergency exit access.* Access to emergency exits must be provided as follows for each passenger-carrying airplane:

(1) Each passageway between individual passenger areas, or leading to a Type I or Type II emergency exit, must be unobstructed and at least 20 inches wide.

(2) There must be enough space next to each Type I or Type II emergency exit to allow a crewmember to assist in the evacuation of passengers without reducing the unobstructed width of the passageway below that required in paragraph (f)(1) of this section; however, the Administrator may authorize deviation from this requirement for an airplane certificated under the provisions of part 4b of the Civil Air Regulations in effect before December 20, 1951, if he finds that special circumstances exist that provide an equivalent level of safety.

(3) There must be access from the main aisle to each Type III and Type IV exit. The access from the aisle to these exits must not be obstructed by seats, berths, or other protrusions in a manner that would reduce the effectiveness of the exit. In addition, for a transport category airplane type certificated after January 1, 1958, there must be placards installed in accordance with §25.813(c)(3) of this chapter for each Type III exit after December 3, 1992.

(4) If it is necessary to pass through a passageway between passenger compartments to reach any required emergency exit from any seat in the passenger cabin, the passageway must not be obstructed. Curtains may, however, be used if they allow free entry through the passageway.

(5) No door may be installed in any partition between passenger compartments.

(6) If it is necessary to pass through a doorway separating the passenger cabin from other areas to reach a required emergency exit from any passenger seat, the door must have a means to latch it in the open position, and the door must be latched open during each takeoff and landing. The latching means must be able to withstand the loads imposed upon it when the door is subjected to the ultimate inertia forces, relative to the surrounding structure, listed in § 25.561(b) of this chapter.

(g) *Exterior exit markings.* Each passenger emergency exit and the means of opening that exit from the outside must be marked on the outside of the airplane. There must be a 2-inch colored band outlining each passenger emergency exit on the side of the fuselage. Each outside marking, including the band, must be readily distinguishable from the surrounding fuselage area by contrast in color. The markings must comply with the following:

(1) If the reflectance of the darker color is 15 percent or less, the reflectance of the lighter color must be at least 45 percent.

(2) If the reflectance of the darker color is greater than 15 percent, at least a 30 percent difference between its reflectance and the reflectance of the lighter color must be provided.

(3) Exits that are not in the side of the fuselage must have the external means of opening and applicable instructions marked conspicuously in red or, if red is inconspicuous against the background color, in bright chrome yellow and, when the opening means for such an exit is located on only one side of the fuselage, a conspicuous marking to that effect must be provided on the other side. "Reflectance" is the ratio of the luminous flux reflected by a body to the luminous flux it receives.

(h) *Exterior emergency lighting and escape route.* (1) Each passenger-carrying airplane must be equipped with exterior lighting that meets the following requirements:

(i) For an airplane for which the application for the type certificate was filed prior to May 1, 1972, the requirements of § 25.812 (f) and (g) of this chapter in effect on April 30, 1972.

(ii) For an airplane for which the application for the type certificate was filed on or after May 1, 1972, the exterior emergency lighting requirements under which the airplane was type certificated.

(2) Each passenger-carrying airplane must be equipped with a slip-resistant escape route that meets the following requirements:

(i) For an airplane for which the application for the type certificate was filed prior to May 1, 1972, the requirements of § 25.803(e) of this chapter in effect on April 30, 1972.

(ii) For an airplane for which the application for the type certificate was filed on or after May 1, 1972, the slip-resistant escape route requirements under which the airplane was type certificated.

(i) *Floor level exits.* Each floor level door or exit in the side of the fuselage (other than those leading into a cargo or baggage compartment that is not accessible from the passenger cabin) that is 44 or more inches high and 20 or more inches wide, but not wider than 46 inches, each passenger ventral exit (except the ventral exits on Martin 404 and Convair 240 airplanes), and each tail cone exit, must meet the requirements of this section for floor level emergency exits. However, the Administrator may grant a deviation from this paragraph if he finds that circumstances make full compliance impractical and that an acceptable level of safety has been achieved.

(j) *Additional emergency exits.* Approved emergency exits in the passenger compartments that are in excess of the minimum number of required emergency exits must meet all of the applicable provisions of this section, except paragraphs (f) (1), (2), and

(3) of this section, and must be readily accessible.

(k) On each large passenger-carrying turbojet-powered airplane, each ventral exit and tailcone exit must be—

(1) Designed and constructed so that it cannot be opened during flight; and

(2) Marked with a placard readable from a distance of 30 inches and installed at a conspicuous location near the means of opening the exit, stating that the exit has been designed and constructed so that it cannot be opened during flight.

(1) *Portable lights.* No person may operate a passenger-carrying airplane unless it is equipped with flashlight stowage provisions accessible from each flight attendant seat.

[Doc. No. 26530, 57 FR 19245, May 4, 1992; 57 FR 29120, June 30, 1992, as amended at 57 FR 34682, Aug. 6, 1992]

§ 135.179 Inoperable instruments and equipment.

(a) No person may take off an aircraft with inoperable instruments or equipment installed unless the following conditions are met:

(1) An approved Minimum Equipment List exists for that aircraft.

(2) The responsible Flight Standards office has issued the certificate holder operations specifications authorizing operations in accordance with an approved Minimum Equipment List. The flight crew shall have direct access at all times prior to flight to all of the information contained in the approved Minimum Equipment List through printed or other means approved by the Administrator in the certificate holders operations specifications. An approved Minimum Equipment List, as authorized by the operations specifications, constitutes an approved change to the type design without requiring recertification.

(3) The approved Minimum Equipment List must:

(i) Be prepared in accordance with the limitations specified in paragraph (b) of this section.

(ii) Provide for the operation of the aircraft with certain instruments and equipment in an inoperable condition.

(4) Records identifying the inoperable instruments and equipment and the information required by (a)(3)(ii) of this section must be available to the pilot.

(5) The aircraft is operated under all applicable conditions and limitations contained in the Minimum Equipment List and the operations specifications authorizing use of the Minimum Equipment List.

(b) The following instruments and equipment may not be included in the Minimum Equipment List:

(1) Instruments and equipment that are either specifically or otherwise required by the airworthiness requirements under which the airplane is type certificated and which are essential for safe operations under all operating conditions.

(2) Instruments and equipment required by an airworthiness directive to be in operable condition unless the airworthiness directive provides otherwise.

(3) Instruments and equipment required for specific operations by this part.

(c) Notwithstanding paragraphs (b)(1) and (b)(3) of this section, an aircraft with inoperable instruments or equipment may be operated under a special flight permit under §§ 21.197 and 21.199 of this chapter.

[Doc. No. 25780, 56 FR 12311, Mar. 22, 1991; 56 FR 14920, Apr. 8, 1991, as amended by Amdt. 135–60, 61 FR 2616, Jan. 26, 1996; Amdt. 135–91, 68 FR 54586, Sept. 17, 2003; Docket FAA–2018–0119, Amdt. 135–139, 83 FR 9175, Mar. 5, 2018]

§ 135.180 Traffic Alert and Collision Avoidance System.

(a) Unless otherwise authorized by the Administrator, after December 31, 1995, no person may operate a turbine powered airplane that has a passenger seat configuration, excluding any pilot seat, of 10 to 30 seats unless it is equipped with an approved traffic alert and collision avoidance system. If a TCAS II system is installed, it must be capable of coordinating with TCAS units that meet TSO C–119.

(b) The airplane flight manual required by § 135.21 of this part shall contain the following information on the TCAS I system required by this section:

(1) Appropriate procedures for—

(i) The use of the equipment; and

(ii) Proper flightcrew action with respect to the equipment operation.

(2) An outline of all input sources that must be operating for the TCAS to function properly.

[Doc. No. 25355, 54 FR 951, Jan. 10, 1989, as amended by Amdt. 135–54, 59 FR 67587, Dec. 29, 1994]

§ 135.181 Performance requirements: Aircraft operated over-the-top or in IFR conditions.

(a) Except as provided in paragraphs (b) and (c) of this section, no person may—

(1) Operate a single-engine aircraft carrying passengers over-the-top; or

(2) Operate a multiengine aircraft carrying passengers over-the-top or in IFR conditions at a weight that will not allow it to climb, with the critical engine inoperative, at least 50 feet a minute when operating at the MEAs of the route to be flown or 5,000 feet MSL, whichever is higher.

(b) Notwithstanding the restrictions in paragraph (a)(2) of this section, multiengine helicopters carrying passengers offshore may conduct such operations in over-the-top or in IFR conditions at a weight that will allow the helicopter to climb at least 50 feet per minute with the critical engine inoperative when operating at the MEA of the route to be flown or 1,500 feet MSL, whichever is higher.

(c) Without regard to paragraph (a) of this section, if the latest weather reports or forecasts, or any combination of them, indicate that the weather along the planned route (including takeoff and landing) allows flight under VFR under the ceiling (if a ceiling exists) and that the weather is forecast to remain so until at least 1 hour after the estimated time of arrival at the destination, a person may operate an aircraft over-the-top.

(d) Without regard to paragraph (a) of this section, a person may operate an aircraft over-the-top under conditions allowing—

(1) For multiengine aircraft, descent or continuance of the flight under VFR if its critical engine fails; or

(2) For single-engine aircraft, descent under VFR if its engine fails.

[Doc. No. 16097, 43 FR 46783, Oct. 10, 1978, as amended by Amdt. 135–20, 51 FR 40710, Nov. 7, 1986; Amdt. 135–70, 62 FR 42374, Aug. 6, 1997]

§ 135.183 Performance requirements: Land aircraft operated over water.

No person may operate a land aircraft carrying passengers over water unless—

(a) It is operated at an altitude that allows it to reach land in the case of engine failure;

(b) It is necessary for takeoff or landing;

(c) It is a multiengine aircraft operated at a weight that will allow it to climb, with the critical engine inoperative, at least 50 feet a minute, at an altitude of 1,000 feet above the surface; or

(d) It is a helicopter equipped with helicopter flotation devices.

§ 135.185 Empty weight and center of gravity: Currency requirement.

(a) No person may operate a multiengine aircraft unless the current empty weight and center of gravity are calculated from values established by actual weighing of the aircraft within the preceding 36 calendar months.

(b) Paragraph (a) of this section does not apply to—

(1) Aircraft issued an original airworthiness certificate within the preceding 36 calendar months; and

(2) Aircraft operated under a weight and balance system approved in the operations specifications of the certificate holder.

Subpart D—VFR/IFR Operating Limitations and Weather Requirements

§ 135.201 Applicability.

This subpart prescribes the operating limitations for VFR/IFR flight operations and associated weather requirements for operations under this part.

§ 135.203 VFR: Minimum altitudes.

Except when necessary for takeoff and landing, no person may operate under VFR—

(a) An airplane—

(1) During the day, below 500 feet above the surface or less than 500 feet horizontally from any obstacle; or

(2) At night, at an altitude less than 1,000 feet above the highest obstacle within a horizontal distance of 5 miles from the course intended to be flown or, in designated mountainous terrain, less than 2,000 feet above the highest obstacle within a horizontal distance of 5 miles from the course intended to be flown; or

(b) A helicopter over a congested area at an altitude less than 300 feet above the surface.

§135.205 VFR: Visibility requirements.

(a) No person may operate an airplane under VFR in uncontrolled airspace when the ceiling is less than 1,000 feet unless flight visibility is at least 2 miles.

(b) No person may operate a helicopter under VFR in Class G airspace at an altitude of 1,200 feet or less above the surface or within the lateral boundaries of the surface areas of Class B, Class C, Class D, or Class E airspace designated for an airport unless the visibility is at least—

(1) During the day—½ mile; or

(2) At night—1 mile.

[Doc. No. 16097, 43 FR 46783, Oct. 10, 1978, as amended by Amdt. 135–41, 56 FR 65663, Dec. 17, 1991]

§135.207 VFR: Helicopter surface reference requirements.

No person may operate a helicopter under VFR unless that person has visual surface reference or, at night, visual surface light reference, sufficient to safely control the helicopter.

§135.209 VFR: Fuel supply.

(a) No person may begin a flight operation in an airplane under VFR unless, considering wind and forecast weather conditions, it has enough fuel to fly to the first point of intended landing and, assuming normal cruising fuel consumption—

(1) During the day, to fly after that for at least 30 minutes; or

(2) At night, to fly after that for at least 45 minutes.

(b) No person may begin a flight operation in a helicopter under VFR unless, considering wind and forecast

weather conditions, it has enough fuel to fly to the first point of intended landing and, assuming normal cruising fuel consumption, to fly after that for at least 20 minutes.

§135.211 VFR: Over-the-top carrying passengers: Operating limitations.

Subject to any additional limitations in §135.181, no person may operate an aircraft under VFR over-the-top carrying passengers, unless—

(a) Weather reports or forecasts, or any combination of them, indicate that the weather at the intended point of termination of over-the-top flight—

(1) Allows descent to beneath the ceiling under VFR and is forecast to remain so until at least 1 hour after the estimated time of arrival at that point; or

(2) Allows an IFR approach and landing with flight clear of the clouds until reaching the prescribed initial approach altitude over the final approach facility, unless the approach is made with the use of radar under §91.175(i) of this chapter; or

(b) It is operated under conditions allowing—

(1) For multiengine aircraft, descent or continuation of the flight under VFR if its critical engine fails; or

(2) For single-engine aircraft, descent under VFR if its engine fails.

[Doc. No. 16097, 43 FR 46783, Oct. 10, 1978, as amended by Amdt. 135–32, 54 FR 34332, Aug. 18, 1989; 73 FR 20164, Apr. 15, 2008]

§135.213 Weather reports and forecasts.

(a) Whenever a person operating an aircraft under this part is required to use a weather report or forecast, that person shall use that of the U.S. National Weather Service, a source approved by the U.S. National Weather Service, or a source approved by the Administrator. However, for operations under VFR, the pilot in command may, if such a report is not available, use weather information based on that pilot's own observations or on those of other persons competent to supply appropriate observations.

(b) For the purposes of paragraph (a) of this section, weather observations made and furnished to pilots to conduct IFR operations at an airport must be taken at the airport where those IFR operations are conducted, unless the Administrator issues operations specifications allowing the use of weather observations taken at a location not at the airport where the IFR operations are conducted. The Administrator issues such operations specifications when, after investigation by the U.S. National Weather Service and the responsible Flight Standards office, it is found that the standards of safety for that operation would allow the deviation from this paragraph for a particular operation for which an air carrier operating certificate or operating certificate has been issued.

[Doc. No. 16097, 43 FR 46783, Oct. 10, 1978, as amended by Amdt. 135–60, 61 FR 2616, Jan. 26, 1996; Docket FAA–2018–0119, Amdt. 135–139, 83 FR 9175, Mar. 5, 2018]

§ 135.215   IFR: Operating limitations.

(a) Except as provided in paragraphs (b), (c) and (d) of this section, no person may operate an aircraft under IFR outside of controlled airspace or at any airport that does not have an approved standard instrument approach procedure.

(b) The Administrator may issue operations specifications to the certificate holder to allow it to operate under IFR over routes outside controlled airspace if—

(1) The certificate holder shows the Administrator that the flight crew is able to navigate, without visual reference to the ground, over an intended track without deviating more than 5 degrees or 5 miles, whichever is less, from that track; and

(2) The Administrator determines that the proposed operations can be conducted safely.

(c) A person may operate an aircraft under IFR outside of controlled airspace if the certificate holder has been approved for the operations and that operation is necessary to—

(1) Conduct an instrument approach to an airport for which there is in use a current approved standard or special instrument approach procedure; or

(2) Climb into controlled airspace during an approved missed approach procedure; or

(3) Make an IFR departure from an airport having an approved instrument approach procedure.

(d) The Administrator may issue operations specifications to the certificate holder to allow it to depart at an airport that does not have an approved standard instrument approach procedure when the Administrator determines that it is necessary to make an IFR departure from that airport and that the proposed operations can be conducted safely. The approval to operate at that airport does not include an approval to make an IFR approach to that airport.

§ 135.217   IFR: Takeoff limitations.

No person may takeoff an aircraft under IFR from an airport where weather conditions are at or above takeoff minimums but are below authorized IFR landing minimums unless there is an alternate airport within 1 hour's flying time (at normal cruising speed, in still air) of the airport of departure.

§ 135.219   IFR: Destination airport weather minimums.

No person may take off an aircraft under IFR or begin an IFR or over-the-top operation unless the latest weather reports or forecasts, or any combination of them, indicate that weather conditions at the estimated time of arrival at the next airport of intended landing will be at or above authorized IFR landing minimums.

§ 135.221   IFR: Alternate airport weather minimums.

(a) *Aircraft other than rotorcraft.* No person may designate an alternate airport unless the weather reports or forecasts, or any combination of them, indicate that the weather conditions will be at or above authorized alternate airport landing minimums for that airport at the estimated time of arrival.

(b) *Rotorcraft.* Unless otherwise authorized by the Administrator, no person may include an alternate airport in an IFR flight plan unless appropriate weather reports or weather forecasts, or a combination of them, indicate that, at the estimated time of arrival at the alternate airport, the ceiling and visibility at that airport will be at or above the following weather minimums—

(1) If, for the alternate airport, an instrument approach procedure has been published in part 97 of this chapter or a special instrument approach procedure has been issued by the FAA to the certificate holder, the ceiling is 200 feet above the minimum for the approach to be flown, and visibility is at least 1 statute mile but never less than the minimum visibility for the approach to be flown.

(2) If, for the alternate airport, no instrument approach procedure has been published in part 97 of this chapter and no special instrument approach procedure has been issued by the FAA to the certificate holder, the ceiling and visibility minimums are those allowing descent from the minimum enroute altitude (MEA), approach, and landing under basic VFR.

[Doc. No. FAA-2010-0982, 79 FR 9974, Feb. 21, 2014]

§135.223 IFR: Alternate airport requirements.

(a) Except as provided in paragraph (b) of this section, no person may operate an aircraft in IFR conditions unless it carries enough fuel (considering weather reports or forecasts or any combination of them) to—

(1) Complete the flight to the first airport of intended landing;

(2) Fly from that airport to the alternate airport; and

(3) Fly after that for 45 minutes at normal cruising speed or, for helicopters, fly after that for 30 minutes at normal cruising speed.

(b) Paragraph (a)(2) of this section does not apply if part 97 of this chapter prescribes a standard instrument approach procedure for the first airport of intended landing and, for at least one hour before and after the estimated time of arrival, the appropriate weather reports or forecasts, or any combination of them, indicate that—

(1) The ceiling will be at least 1,500 feet above the lowest circling approach MDA; or

(2) If a circling instrument approach is not authorized for the airport, the ceiling will be at least 1,500 feet above the lowest published minimum or 2,000 feet above the airport elevation, whichever is higher; and

(3) Visibility for that airport is forecast to be at least three miles, or two miles more than the lowest applicable visibility minimums, whichever is the greater, for the instrument approach procedure to be used at the destination airport.

[Doc. No. 16097, 43 FR 46783, Oct. 10, 1978, as amended by Amdt. 135-20, 51 FR 40710, Nov. 7, 1986]

§135.225 IFR: Takeoff, approach and landing minimums.

(a) Except to the extent permitted by paragraphs (b) and (j) of this section, no pilot may begin an instrument approach procedure to an airport unless—

(1) That airport has a weather reporting facility operated by the U.S. National Weather Service, a source approved by U.S. National Weather Service, or a source approved by the Administrator; and

(2) The latest weather report issued by that weather reporting facility indicates that weather conditions are at or above the authorized IFR landing minimums for that airport.

(b) A pilot conducting an eligible on-demand operation may begin and conduct an instrument approach procedure to an airport that does not have a weather reporting facility operated by the U.S. National Weather Service, a source approved by the U.S. National Weather Service, or a source approved by the Administrator if—

(1) The alternate airport has a weather reporting facility operated by the U.S. National Weather Service, a source approved by the U.S. National Weather Service, or a source approved by the Administrator; and

(2) The latest weather report issued by the weather reporting facility includes a current local altimeter setting for the destination airport. If no local altimeter setting for the destination airport is available, the pilot may use the current altimeter setting provided by the facility designated on the approach chart for the destination airport.

(c) Except as provided in paragraph (j) of this section, no pilot may begin the final approach segment of an instrument approach procedure to an airport unless the latest weather reported by the facility described in paragraph (a)(1) of this section indicates that weather conditions are at or above the authorized IFR landing minimums for that procedure.

(d) Except as provided in paragraph (j) of this section, a pilot who has begun the final approach segment of an instrument approach to an airport under paragraph (c) of this section, and receives a later weather report indicating that conditions have worsened to below the minimum requirements, may continue the approach only if the following conditions are met—

(1) The later weather report is received when the aircraft is in one of the following approach phases:

(i) The aircraft is on an ILS final approach and has passed the final approach fix;

(ii) The aircraft is on an ASR or PAR final approach and has been turned over to the final approach controller; or

(iii) The aircraft is on a non-precision final approach and the aircraft—

(A) Has passed the appropriate facility or final approach fix; or

(B) Where a final approach fix is not specified, has completed the procedure turn and is established inbound toward the airport on the final approach course within the distance prescribed in the procedure; and

(2) The pilot in command finds, on reaching the authorized MDA or DA/DH, that the actual weather conditions are at or above the minimums prescribed for the procedure being used.

(e) The MDA or DA/DH and visibility landing minimums prescribed in part 97 of this chapter or in the operator's operations specifications are increased by 100 feet and ½ mile respectively, but not to exceed the ceiling and visibility minimums for that airport when used as an alternate airport, for each pilot in command of a turbine-powered airplane who has not served at least 100 hours as pilot in command in that type of airplane.

(f) Each pilot making an IFR takeoff or approach and landing at a military or foreign airport shall comply with applicable instrument approach procedures and weather minimums prescribed by the authority having jurisdiction over that airport. In addition, unless authorized by the certificate holder's operations specifications, no pilot may, at that airport—

(1) Take off under IFR when the visibility is less than 1 mile; or

(2) Make an instrument approach when the visibility is less than ½ mile.

(g) If takeoff minimums are specified in part 97 of this chapter for the takeoff airport, no pilot may take off an aircraft under IFR when the weather conditions reported by the facility described in paragraph (a)(1) of this section are less than the takeoff minimums specified for the takeoff airport in part 97 or in the certificate holder's operations specifications.

(h) Except as provided in paragraph (i) of this section, if takeoff minimums are not prescribed in part 97 of this chapter for the takeoff airport, no pilot may takeoff an aircraft under IFR when the weather conditions reported by the facility described in paragraph (a)(1) of this section are less than that prescribed in part 91 of this chapter or in the certificate holder's operations specifications.

(i) At airports where straight-in instrument approach procedures are authorized, a pilot may takeoff an aircraft under IFR when the weather conditions reported by the facility described in paragraph (a)(1) of this section are equal to or better than the lowest straight-in landing minimums, unless otherwise restricted, if—

(1) The wind direction and velocity at the time of takeoff are such that a straight-in instrument approach can be made to the runway served by the instrument approach;

(2) The associated ground facilities upon which the landing minimums are predicated and the related airborne equipment are in normal operation; and

(3) The certificate holder has been approved for such operations.

(j) A pilot may begin an instrument approach procedure, or continue an approach, at an airport when the visibility is reported to be less than the visibility minimums prescribed for that procedure if the pilot uses an operable EFVS in accordance with § 91.176

of this chapter and the certificate holder's operations specifications for EFVS operations.

[Doc. No. 16097, 43 FR 46783, Oct. 10, 1978, as amended by Amdt. 135–91, 68 FR 54586 Sept. 17, 2003; Amdt. 135–93, 69 FR 1641, Jan. 9, 2004; Amdt. 135–110, 72 FR 31685, June 7 2007; Amdt. 135–126, 77 FR 1632, Jan. 11, 2012; Docket FAA–2013–0485, Amdt. 135–135, 81 FR 90177, Dec. 13, 2016]

§ 135.227 Icing conditions: Operating limitations.

(a) No pilot may take off an aircraft that has frost, ice, or snow adhering to any rotor blade, propeller, windshield, stabilizing or control surface; to a powerplant installation; or to an airspeed, altimeter, rate of climb, flight attitude instrument system, or wing, except that takeoffs may be made with frost under the wing in the area of the fuel tanks if authorized by the FAA.

(b) No certificate holder may authorize an airplane to take off and no pilot may take off an airplane any time conditions are such that frost, ice, or snow may reasonably be expected to adhere to the airplane unless the pilot has completed all applicable training as required by § 135.341 and unless one of the following requirements is met:

(1) A pretakeoff contamination check, that has been established by the certificate holder and approved by the Administrator for the specific airplane type, has been completed within 5 minutes prior to beginning takeoff. A pretakeoff contamination check is a check to make sure the wings and control surfaces are free of frost, ice, or snow.

(2) The certificate holder has an approved alternative procedure and under that procedure the airplane is determined to be free of frost, ice, or snow.

(3) The certificate holder has an approved deicing/anti-icing program that complies with § 121.629(c) of this chapter and the takeoff complies with that program.

(c) No pilot may fly under IFR into known or forecast light or moderate icing conditions or under VFR into known light or moderate icing conditions, unless—

(1) The aircraft has functioning deicing or anti-icing equipment protecting each rotor blade, propeller, windshield, wing, stabilizing or control surface,

and each airspeed, altimeter, rate of climb, or flight attitude instrument system;

(2) The airplane has ice protection provisions that meet section 34 of appendix A of this part; or

(3) The airplane meets transport category airplane type certification provisions, including the requirements for certification for flight in icing conditions.

(d) No pilot may fly a helicopter under IFR into known or forecast icing conditions or under VFR into known icing conditions unless it has been type certificated and appropriately equipped for operations in icing conditions.

(e) Except for an airplane that has ice protection provisions that meet section 34 of appendix A, or those for transport category airplane type certification, no pilot may fly an aircraft into known or forecast severe icing conditions.

(f) If current weather reports and briefing information relied upon by the pilot in command indicate that the forecast icing condition that would otherwise prohibit the flight will not be encountered during the flight because of changed weather conditions since the forecast, the restrictions in paragraphs (c), (d), and (e) of this section based on forecast conditions do not apply.

[Doc. No. 16097, 43 FR 46783, Oct. 10, 1978, as amended by Amdt. 133–20, 51 FR 40710, Nov. 7, 1986; Amdt. 135–46, 58 FR 69629, Dec. 30, 1993; Amdt. 135–60, 61 FR 2616, Jan. 26, 1996; Amdt. 135–119, 74 FR 62696, Dec. 1, 2009]

§ 135.229 Airport requirements.

(a) No certificate holder may use any airport unless it is adequate for the proposed operation, considering such items as size, surface, obstructions, and lighting.

(b) No pilot of an aircraft carrying passengers at night may takeoff from, or land on, an airport unless—

(1) That pilot has determined the wind direction from an illuminated wind direction indicator or local ground communications or, in the case of takeoff, that pilot's personal observations; and

(2) The limits of the area to be used for landing or takeoff are clearly shown—

(i) For airplanes, by boundary or runway marker lights;

(ii) For helicopters, by boundary or runway marker lights or reflective material.

(c) For the purpose of paragraph (b) of this section, if the area to be used for takeoff or landing is marked by flare pots or lanterns, their use must be approved by the Administrator.

Subpart E—Flight Crewmember Requirements

§ 135.241 Applicability.

Except as provided in § 135.3, this subpart prescribes the flight crewmember requirements for operations under this part.

[Doc. No. 16097, 43 FR 46783, Oct. 10, 1978, as amended by Amdt. 121–250, 60 FR 65950, Dec. 20, 1995]

§ 135.243 Pilot in command qualifications.

(a) No certificate holder may use a person, nor may any person serve, as pilot in command in passenger-carrying operations—

(1) Of a turbojet airplane, of an airplane having a passenger-seat configuration, excluding each crewmember seat, of 10 seats or more, or of a multiengine airplane in a commuter operation as defined in part 119 of this chapter, unless that person holds an airline transport pilot certificate with appropriate category and class ratings and, if required, an appropriate type rating for that airplane.

(2) Of a helicopter in a scheduled interstate air transportation operation by an air carrier within the 48 contiguous states unless that person holds an airline transport pilot certificate, appropriate type ratings, and an instrument rating.

(b) Except as provided in paragraph (a) of this section, no certificate holder may use a person, nor may any person serve, as pilot in command of an aircraft under VFR unless that person—

(1) Holds at least a commercial pilot certificate with appropriate category and class ratings and, if required, an appropriate type rating for that aircraft; and

(2) Has had at least 500 hours time as a pilot, including at least 100 hours of cross-country flight time, at least 25 hours of which were at night; and

(3) For an airplane, holds an instrument rating or an airline transport pilot certificate with an airplane category rating; or

(4) For helicopter operations conducted VFR over-the-top, holds a helicopter instrument rating, or an airline transport pilot certificate with a category and class rating for that aircraft, not limited to VFR.

(c) Except as provided in paragraph (a) of this section, no certificate holder may use a person, nor may any person serve, as pilot in command of an aircraft under IFR unless that person—

(1) Holds at least a commercial pilot certificate with appropriate category and class ratings and, if required, an appropriate type rating for that aircraft; and

(2) Has had at least 1,200 hours of flight time as a pilot, including 500 hours of cross country flight time, 100 hours of night flight time, and 75 hours of actual or simulated instrument time at least 50 hours of which were in actual flight; and

(3) For an airplane, holds an instrument rating or an airline transport pilot certificate with an airplane category rating; or

(4) For a helicopter, holds a helicopter instrument rating, or an airline transport pilot certificate with a category and class rating for that aircraft, not limited to VFR.

(d) Paragraph (b)(3) of this section does not apply when—

(1) The aircraft used is a single reciprocating-engine-powered airplane;

(2) The certificate holder does not conduct any operation pursuant to a published flight schedule which specifies five or more round trips a week between two or more points and places between which the round trips are performed, and does not transport mail by air under a contract or contracts with the United States Postal Service having total amount estimated at the beginning of any semiannual reporting period (January 1–June 30; July 1–December 31) to be in excess of $20,000 over the 12 months commencing with the beginning of the reporting period;

(3) The area, as specified in the certificate holder's operations specifications, is an isolated area, as determined by the Flight Standards office, if it is shown that—

(i) The primary means of navigation in the area is by pilotage, since radio navigational aids are largely ineffective; and

(ii) The primary means of transportation in the area is by air;

(4) Each flight is conducted under day VFR with a ceiling of not less than 1,000 feet and visibility not less than 3 statute miles;

(5) Weather reports or forecasts, or any combination of them, indicate that for the period commencing with the planned departure and ending 30 minutes after the planned arrival at the destination the flight may be conducted under VFR with a ceiling of not less than 1,000 feet and visibility of not less than 3 statute miles, except that if weather reports and forecasts are not available, the pilot in command may use that pilot's observations or those of other persons competent to supply weather observations if those observations indicate the flight may be conducted under VFR with the ceiling and visibility required in this paragraph;

(6) The distance of each flight from the certificate holder's base of operation to destination does not exceed 250 nautical miles for a pilot who holds a commercial pilot certificate with an airplane rating without an instrument rating, provided the pilot's certificate does not contain any limitation to the contrary; and

(7) The areas to be flown are approved by the responsible Flight Standards office and are listed in the certificate holder's operations specifications.

[Doc. No. 16097, 43 FR 46783, Oct. 10, 1978; Amdt. 135–1, 43 FR 49975, Oct. 26, 1978, as amended by Amdt. 135–15, 46 FR 30971, June 11, 1981; Amdt. 135–58, 60 FR 65939, Dec. 20, 1995; Docket FAA–2018–0119, Amdt. 135–139, 83 FR 9175, Mar. 5, 2018]

§ 135.244 Operating experience.

(a) No certificate holder may use any person, nor may any person serve, as a pilot in command of an aircraft operated in a commuter operation, as defined in part 119 of this chapter unless that person has completed, prior to

designation as pilot in command, on that make and basic model aircraft and in that crewmember position, the following operating experience in each make and basic model of aircraft to be flown:

(1) Aircraft, single engine—10 hours.

(2) Aircraft multiengine, reciprocating engine-powered—15 hours.

(3) Aircraft multiengine, turbine engine-powered—20 hours.

(4) Airplane, turbojet-powered—25 hours.

(b) In acquiring the operating experience, each person must comply with the following:

(1) The operating experience must be acquired after satisfactory completion of the appropriate ground and flight training for the aircraft and crewmember position. Approved provisions for the operating experience must be included in the certificate holder's training program.

(2) The experience must be acquired in flight during commuter passenger-carrying operations under this part. However, in the case of an aircraft not previously used by the certificate holder in operations under this part, operating experience acquired in the aircraft during proving flights or ferry flights may be used to meet this requirement.

(3) Each person must acquire the operating experience while performing the duties of a pilot in command under the supervision of a qualified check pilot.

(4) The hours of operating experience may be reduced to not less than 50 percent of the hours required by this section by the substitution of one additional takeoff and landing for each hour of flight.

[Doc. No. 20011, 45 FR 7541, Feb. 4, 1980, as amended by Amdt. 135–9, 45 FR 80461, Dec. 14, 1980; Amdt. 135–58, 60 FR 65940, Dec. 20, 1995]

§ 135.245 Second in command qualifications.

(a) Except as provided in paragraph (b) of this section, no certificate holder may use any person, nor may any person serve, as second in command of an aircraft unless that person holds at least a commercial pilot certificate with appropriate category and class ratings and an instrument rating.

(b) A second in command of a helicopter operated under VFR, other than over-the-top, must have at least a commercial pilot certificate with an appropriate aircraft category and class rating.

(c) No certificate holder may use any person, nor may any person serve, as second in command under IFR unless that person meets the following instrument experience requirements:

(1) *Use of an airplane or helicopter for maintaining instrument experience.* Within the 6 calendar months preceding the month of the flight, that person performed and logged at least the following tasks and iterations in-flight in an airplane or helicopter, as appropriate, in actual weather conditions, or under simulated instrument conditions using a view-limiting device:

(i) Six instrument approaches;

(ii) Holding procedures and tasks; and

(iii) Intercepting and tracking courses through the use of navigational electronic systems.

(2) *Use of an FSTD for maintaining instrument experience.* A person may accomplish the requirements in paragraph (c)(1) of this section in an approved FSTD, or a combination of aircraft and FSTD, provided:

(i) The FSTD represents the category of aircraft for the instrument rating privileges to be maintained;

(ii) The person performs the tasks and iterations in simulated instrument conditions; and

(iii) A flight instructor qualified under § 135.338 or a check pilot qualified under § 135.337 observes the tasks and iterations and signs the person's logbook or training record to verify the time and content of the session.

(d) A second in command who has failed to meet the instrument experience requirements of paragraph (c) of this section for more than six calendar months must reestablish instrument recency under the supervision of a flight instructor qualified under § 135.338 or a check pilot qualified under § 135.337. To reestablish instrument recency, a second in command must complete at least the following areas of operation required for the instrument rating practical test in an aircraft or FSTD that represents the category of

aircraft for the instrument experience requirements to be reestablished:

(1) Air traffic control clearances and procedures;

(2) Flight by reference to instruments;

(3) Navigation systems;

(4) Instrument approach procedures;

(5) Emergency operations; and

(6) Postflight procedures.

[44 FR 26738, May 7, 1979, as amended by Doc. No. FAA-2016-6142, 83 FR 30283, June 27, 2018]

§ 135.247 Pilot qualifications: Recent experience.

(a) No certificate holder may use any person, nor may any person serve, as pilot in command of an aircraft carrying passengers unless, within the preceding 90 days, that person has—

(1) Made three takeoffs and three landings as the sole manipulator of the flight controls in an aircraft of the same category and class and, if a type rating is required, of the same type in which that person is to serve; or

(2) For operation during the period beginning 1 hour after sunset and ending 1 hour before sunrise (as published in the Air Almanac), made three takeoffs and three landings during that period as the sole manipulator of the flight controls in an aircraft of the same category and class and, if a type rating is required, of the same type in which that person is to serve.

A person who complies with paragraph (a)(2) of this section need not comply with paragraph (a)(1) of this section.

(3) Paragraph (a)(2) of this section does not apply to a pilot in command of a turbine-powered airplane that is type certificated for more than one pilot crewmember, provided that pilot has complied with the requirements of paragraph (a)(3)(i) or (ii) of this section:

(i) The pilot in command must hold at least a commercial pilot certificate with the appropriate category, class, and type rating for each airplane that is type certificated for more than one pilot crewmember that the pilot seeks to operate under this alternative, and:

(A) That pilot must have logged at least 1,500 hours of aeronautical experience as a pilot;

(B) In each airplane that is type certificated for more than one pilot crewmember that the pilot seeks to operate under this alternative, that pilot must have accomplished and logged the daytime takeoff and landing recent flight experience of paragraph (a) of this section, as the sole manipulator of the flight controls;

(C) Within the preceding 90 days prior to the operation of that airplane that is type certificated for more than one pilot crewmember, the pilot must have accomplished and logged at least 15 hours of flight time in the type of airplane that the pilot seeks to operate under this alternative; and

(D) That pilot has accomplished and logged at least 3 takeoffs and 3 landings to a full stop, as the sole manipulator of the flight controls, in a turbine-powered airplane that requires more than one pilot crewmember. The pilot must have performed the takeoffs and landings during the period beginning 1 hour after sunset and ending 1 hour before sunrise within the preceding 6 months prior to the month of the flight.

(ii) The pilot in command must hold at least a commercial pilot certificate with the appropriate category, class, and type rating for each airplane that is type certificated for more than one pilot crewmember that the pilot seeks to operate under this alternative, and:

(A) That pilot must have logged at least 1,500 hours of aeronautical experience as a pilot;

(B) In each airplane that is type certificated for more than one pilot crewmember that the pilot seeks to operate under this alternative, that pilot must have accomplished and logged the daytime takeoff and landing recent flight experience of paragraph (a) of this section, as the sole manipulator of the flight controls;

(C) Within the preceding 90 days prior to the operation of that airplane that is type certificated for more than one pilot crewmember, the pilot must have accomplished and logged at least 15 hours of flight time in the type of airplane that the pilot seeks to operate under this alternative; and

(D) Within the preceding 12 months prior to the month of the flight, the pilot must have completed a training

program that is approved under part 142 of this chapter. The approved training program must have required and the pilot must have performed, at least 6 takeoffs and 6 landings to a full stop as the sole manipulator of the controls in a flight simulator that is representative of a turbine-powered airplane that requires more than one pilot crewmember. The flight simulator's visual system must have been adjusted to represent the period beginning 1 hour after sunset and ending 1 hour before sunrise.

(b) For the purpose of paragraph (a) of this section, if the aircraft is a tailwheel airplane, each takeoff must be made in a tailwheel airplane and each landing must be made to a full stop in a tailwheel airplane.

[Doc. No. 16097, 43 FR 46783, Oct. 10, 1978, as amended by Amdt. 135–91, 68 FR 54587, Sept. 17, 2003]

§§ 135.249–135.255 [Reserved]

Subpart F—Crewmember Flight Time and Duty Period Limitations and Rest Requirements

SOURCE: Docket No. 23634, 50 FR 29320, July 18, 1985, unless otherwise noted.

§ 135.261 Applicability.

Sections 135.263 through 135.273 of this part prescribe flight time limitations, duty period limitations, and rest requirements for operations conducted under this part as follows:

(a) Section 135.263 applies to all operations under this subpart.

(b) Section 135.265 applies to:

(1) Scheduled passenger-carrying operations except those conducted solely within the state of Alaska. "Scheduled passenger-carrying operations" means passenger-carrying operations that are conducted in accordance with a published schedule which covers at least five round trips per week on at least one route between two or more points, includes dates or times (or both), and is openly advertised or otherwise made readily available to the general public, and

(2) Any other operation under this part, if the operator elects to comply

with § 135.265 and obtains an appropriate operations specification amendment.

(c) Sections 135.267 and 135.269 apply to any operation that is not a scheduled passenger-carrying operation and to any operation conducted solely within the State of Alaska, unless the operator elects to comply with § 135.265 as authorized under paragraph (b)(2) of this section.

(d) Section 135.271 contains special daily flight time limits for operations conducted under the helicopter emergency medical evacuation service (HEMES).

(e) Section 135.273 prescribes duty period limitations and rest requirements for flight attendants in all operations conducted under this part.

[Doc. No. 23634, 50 FR 29320, July 18, 1985, as amended by Amdt. 135–52, 59 FR 42993, Aug. 19, 1994]

§ 135.263 Flight time limitations and rest requirements: All certificate holders.

(a) A certificate holder may assign a flight crewmember and a flight crewmember may accept an assignment for flight time only when the applicable requirements of §§ 135.263 through 135.271 are met.

(b) No certificate holder may assign any flight crewmember to any duty with the certificate holder during any required rest period.

(c) Time spent in transportation, not local in character, that a certificate holder requires of a flight crewmember and provides to transport the crewmember to an airport at which he is to serve on a flight as a crewmember, or from an airport at which he was relieved from duty to return to his home station, is not considered part of a rest period.

(d) A flight crewmember is not considered to be assigned flight time in excess of flight time limitations if the flights to which he is assigned normally terminate within the limitations, but due to circumstances beyond the control of the certificate holder or flight crewmember (such as adverse weather conditions), are not at the time of departure expected to reach their destination within the planned flight time.

§ 135.265 Flight time limitations and rest requirements: Scheduled operations.

(a) No certificate holder may schedule any flight crewmember, and no flight crewmember may accept an assignment, for flight time in scheduled operations or in other commercial flying if that crewmember's total flight time in all commercial flying will exceed—

(1) 1,200 hours in any calendar year.

(2) 120 hours in any calendar month.

(3) 34 hours in any 7 consecutive days.

(4) 8 hours during any 24 consecutive hours for a flight crew consisting of one pilot.

(5) 8 hours between required rest periods for a flight crew consisting of two pilots qualified under this part for the operation being conducted.

(b) Except as provided in paragraph (c) of this section, no certificate holder may schedule a flight crewmember, and no flight crewmember may accept an assignment, for flight time during the 24 consecutive hours preceding the scheduled completion of any flight segment without a scheduled rest period during that 24 hours of at least the following:

(1) 9 consecutive hours of rest for less than 8 hours of scheduled flight time.

(2) 10 consecutive hours of rest for 8 or more but less than 9 hours of scheduled flight time.

(3) 11 consecutive hours of rest for 9 or more hours of scheduled flight time.

(c) A certificate holder may schedule a flight crewmember for less than the rest required in paragraph (b) of this section or may reduce a scheduled rest under the following conditions:

(1) A rest required under paragraph (b)(1) of this section may be scheduled for or reduced to a minimum of 8 hours if the flight crewmember is given a rest period of at least 10 hours that must begin no later than 24 hours after the commencement of the reduced rest period.

(2) A rest required under paragraph (b)(2) of this section may be scheduled for or reduced to a minimum of 8 hours if the flight crewmember is given a rest period of at least 11 hours that must begin no later than 24 hours after the commencement of the reduced rest period.

466

(3) A rest required under paragraph (b)(3) of this section may be scheduled for or reduced to a minimum of 9 hours if the flight crewmember is given a rest period of at least 12 hours that must begin no later than 24 hours after the commencement of the reduced rest period.

(d) Each certificate holder shall relieve each flight crewmember engaged in scheduled air transportation from all further duty for at least 24 consecutive hours during any 7 consecutive days.

§ 135.267 Flight time limitations and rest requirements: Unscheduled one- and two-pilot crews.

(a) No certificate holder may assign any flight crewmember, and no flight crewmember may accept an assignment, for flight time as a member of a one- or two-pilot crew if that crewmember's total flight time in all commercial flying will exceed—

(1) 500 hours in any calendar quarter.

(2) 800 hours in any two consecutive calendar quarters.

(3) 1,400 hours in any calendar year.

(b) Except as provided in paragraph (c) of this section, during any 24 consecutive hours the total flight time of the assigned flight when added to any other commercial flying by that flight crewmember may not exceed—

(1) 8 hours for a flight crew consisting of one pilot; or

(2) 10 hours for a flight crew consisting of two pilots qualified under this part for the operation being conducted.

(c) A flight crewmember's flight time may exceed the flight time limits of paragraph (b) of this section if the assigned flight time occurs during a regularly assigned duty period of no more than 14 hours and—

(1) If this duty period is immediately preceded by and followed by a required rest period of at least 10 consecutive hours of rest;

(2) If flight time is assigned during this period, that total flight time when added to any other commercial flying by the flight crewmember may not exceed—

(i) 8 hours for a flight crew consisting of one pilot; or

(ii) 10 hours for a flight crew consisting of two pilots; and

(3) If the combined duty and rest periods equal 24 hours.

(d) Each assignment under paragraph (b) of this section must provide for at least 10 consecutive hours of rest during the 24-hour period that precedes the planned completion time of the assignment.

(e) When a flight crewmember has exceeded the daily flight time limitations in this section, because of circumstances beyond the control of the certificate holder or flight crewmember (such as adverse weather conditions), that flight crewmember must have a rest period before being assigned or accepting an assignment for flight time of at least—

(1) 11 consecutive hours of rest if the flight time limitation is exceeded by not more than 30 minutes;

(2) 12 consecutive hours of rest if the flight time limitation is exceeded by more than 30 minutes, but not more than 60 minutes; and

(3) 16 consecutive hours of rest if the flight time limitation is exceeded by more than 60 minutes.

(f) The certificate holder must provide each flight crewmember at least 13 rest periods of at least 24 consecutive hours each in each calendar quarter.

[Doc. No. 23634, 50 FR 29320, July 18, 1985, as amended by Amdt. 135–33, 54 FR 39294, Sept. 25, 1989; Amdt. 135–60, 61 FR 2616, Jan. 26, 1996]

§ 135.269 Flight time limitations and rest requirements: Unscheduled three- and four-pilot crews.

(a) No certificate holder may assign any flight crewmember, and no flight crewmember may accept an assignment, for flight time as a member of a three- or four-pilot crew if that crewmember's total flight time in all commercial flying will exceed—

(1) 500 hours in any calendar quarter.

(2) 800 hours in any two consecutive calendar quarters.

(3) 1,400 hours in any calendar year.

(b) No certificate holder may assign any pilot to a crew of three or four pilots, unless that assignment provides—

(1) At least 10 consecutive hours of rest immediately preceding the assignment;

(2) No more than 8 hours of flight deck duty in any 24 consecutive hours;

(3) No more than 18 duty hours for a three-pilot crew or 20 duty hours for a four-pilot crew in any 24 consecutive hours;

(4) No more than 12 hours aloft for a three-pilot crew or 16 hours aloft for a four-pilot crew during the maximum duty hours specified in paragraph (b)(3) of this section;

(5) Adequate sleeping facilities on the aircraft for the relief pilot;

(6) Upon completion of the assignment, a rest period of at least 12 hours;

(7) For a three-pilot crew, a crew which consists of at least the following:

(i) A pilot in command (PIC) who meets the applicable flight crewmember requirements of subpart E of part 135;

(ii) A PIC who meets the applicable flight crewmember requirements of subpart E of part 135, except those prescribed in §§ 135.244 and 135.247; and

(iii) A second in command (SIC) who meets the SIC qualifications of § 135.245.

(8) For a four-pilot crew, at least three pilots who meet the conditions of paragraph (b)(7) of this section, plus a fourth pilot who meets the SIC qualifications of § 135.245.

(c) When a flight crewmember has exceeded the daily flight deck duty limitation in this section by more than 60 minutes, because of circumstances beyond the control of the certificate holder or flight crewmember, that flight crewmember must have a rest period before the next duty period of at least 16 consecutive hours.

(d) A certificate holder must provide each flight crewmember at least 13 rest periods of at least 24 consecutive hours each in each calendar quarter.

§ 135.271 Helicopter hospital emergency medical evacuation service (HEMES).

(a) No certificate holder may assign any flight crewmember, and no flight crewmember may accept an assignment for flight time if that crewmember's total flight time in all commercial flight will exceed—

(1) 500 hours in any calendar quarter.

(2) 800 hours in any two consecutive calendar quarters.

(3) 1,400 hours in any calendar year.

(b) No certificate holder may assign a helicopter flight crewmember, and no flight crewmember may accept an assignment, for hospital emergency medical evacuation service helicopter operations unless that assignment provides for at least 10 consecutive hours of rest immediately preceding reporting to the hospital for availability for flight time.

(c) No flight crewmember may accrue more than 8 hours of flight time during any 24-consecutive hour period of a HEMES assignment, unless an emergency medical evacuation operation is prolonged. Each flight crewmember who exceeds the daily 8 hour flight time limitation in this paragraph must be relieved of the HEMES assignment immediately upon the completion of that emergency medical evacuation operation and must be given a rest period in compliance with paragraph (h) of this section.

(d) Each flight crewmember must receive at least 8 consecutive hours of rest during any 24 consecutive hour period of a HEMES assignment. A flight crewmember must be relieved of the HEMES assignment if he or she has not or cannot receive at least 8 consecutive hours of rest during any 24 consecutive hour period of a HEMES assignment.

(e) A HEMES assignment may not exceed 72 consecutive hours at the hospital.

(f) An adequate place of rest must be provided at, or in close proximity to, the hospital at which the HEMES assignment is being performed.

(g) No certificate holder may assign any other duties to a flight crewmember during a HEMES assignment.

(h) Each pilot must be given a rest period upon completion of the HEMES assignment and prior to being assigned any further duty with the certificate holder of—

(1) At least 12 consecutive hours for an assignment of less than 48 hours.

(2) At least 16 consecutive hours for an assignment of more than 48 hours.

(i) The certificate holder must provide each flight crewmember at least 13 rest periods of at least 24 consecutive hours each in each calendar quarter.

§135.273 Duty period limitations and rest time requirements.

(a) For purposes of this section—

Calendar day means the period of elapsed time, using Coordinated Universal Time or local time, that begins at midnight and ends 24 hours later at the next midnight.

Duty period means the period of elapsed time between reporting for an assignment involving flight time and release from that assignment by the certificate holder. The time is calculated using either Coordinated Universal Time or local time to reflect the total elapsed time.

Flight attendant means an individual, other than a flight crewmember, who is assigned by the certificate holder, in accordance with the required minimum crew complement under the certificate holder's operations specifications or in addition to that minimum complement, to duty in an aircraft during flight time and whose duties include but are not necessarily limited to cabin-safety-related responsibilities.

Rest period means the period free of all responsibility for work or duty should the occasion arise.

(b) Except as provided in paragraph (c) of this section, a certificate holder may assign a duty period to a flight attendant only when the applicable duty period limitations and rest requirements of this paragraph are met.

(1) Except as provided in paragraphs (b)(4), (b)(5), and (b)(6) of this section, no certificate holder may assign a flight attendant to a scheduled duty period of more than 14 hours.

(2) Except as provided in paragraph (b)(3) of this section, a flight attendant scheduled to a duty period of 14 hours or less as provided under paragraph (b)(1) of this section must be given a scheduled rest period of at least 9 consecutive hours. This rest period must occur between the completion of the scheduled duty period and the commencement of the subsequent duty period.

(3) The rest period required under paragraph (b)(2) of this section may be scheduled or reduced to 8 consecutive hours if the flight attendant is provided a subsequent rest period of at least 10 consecutive hours; this subsequent rest period must be scheduled to begin no later than 24 hours after the beginning of the reduced rest period and must occur between the completion of the scheduled duty period and the commencement of the subsequent duty period.

(4) A certificate holder may assign a flight attendant to a scheduled duty period of more than 14 hours, but no more than 16 hours, if the certificate holder has assigned to the flight or flights in that duty period at least one flight attendant in addition to the minimum flight attendant complement required for the flight or flights in that duty period under the certificate holder's operations specifications.

(5) A certificate holder may assign a flight attendant to a scheduled duty period of more than 16 hours, but no more than 18 hours, if the certificate holder has assigned to the flight or flights in that duty period at least two flight attendants in addition to the minimum flight attendant complement required for the flight or flights in that duty period under the certificate holder's operations specifications.

(6) A certificate holder may assign a flight attendant to a scheduled duty period of more than 18 hours, but no more than 20 hours, if the scheduled duty period includes one or more flights that land or take off outside the 48 contiguous states and the District of Columbia, and if the certificate holder has assigned to the flight or flights in that duty period at least three flight attendants in addition to the minimum flight attendant complement required for the flight or flights in that duty period under the certificate holder's operations specifications.

(7) Except as provided in paragraph (b)(8) of this section, a flight attendant scheduled to a duty period of more than 14 hours but no more than 20 hours, as provided in paragraphs (b)(4), (b)(5), and (b)(6) of this section, must be given a scheduled rest period of at least 12 consecutive hours. This rest period must occur between the completion of the scheduled duty period and the commencement of the subsequent duty period.

(8) The rest period required under paragraph (b)(7) of this section may be scheduled or reduced to 10 consecutive

hours if the flight attendant is provided a subsequent rest period of at least 14 consecutive hours; this subsequent rest period must be scheduled to begin no later than 24 hours after the beginning of the reduced rest period and must occur between the completion of the scheduled duty period and the commencement of the subsequent duty period.

(9) Notwithstanding paragraphs (b)(4), (b)(5), and (b)(6) of this section, if a certificate holder elects to reduce the rest period to 10 hours as authorized by paragraph (b)(8) of this section, the certificate holder may not schedule a flight attendant for a duty period of more than 14 hours during the 24-hour period commencing after the beginning of the reduced rest period.

(10) No certificate holder may assign a flight attendant any duty period with the certificate holder unless the flight attendant has had at least the minimum rest required under this section.

(11) No certificate holder may assign a flight attendant to perform any duty with the certificate holder during any required rest period.

(12) Time spent in transportation, not local in character, that a certificate holder requires of a flight attendant and provides to transport the flight attendant to an airport at which that flight attendant is to serve on a flight as a crewmember, or from an airport at which the flight attendant was relieved from duty to return to the flight attendant's home station, is not considered part of a rest period.

(13) Each certificate holder must relieve each flight attendant engaged in air transportation from all further duty for at least 24 consecutive hours during any 7 consecutive calendar days.

(14) A flight attendant is not considered to be scheduled for duty in excess of duty period limitations if the flights to which the flight attendant is assigned are scheduled and normally terminate within the limitations but due to circumstances beyond the control of the certificate holder (such as adverse weather conditions) are not at the time of departure expected to reach their destination within the scheduled time.

(c) Notwithstanding paragraph (b) of this section, a certificate holder may apply the flight crewmember flight time and duty limitations and rest requirements of this part to flight attendants for all operations conducted under this part provided that—

(1) The certificate holder establishes written procedures that—

(i) Apply to all flight attendants used in the certificate holder's operation;

(ii) Include the flight crewmember requirements contained in subpart F of this part, as appropriate to the operation being conducted, except that rest facilities on board the aircraft are not required; and

(iii) Include provisions to add one flight attendant to the minimum flight attendant complement for each flight crewmember who is in excess of the minimum number required in the aircraft type certificate data sheet and who is assigned to the aircraft under the provisions of subpart F of this part, as applicable.

(iv) Are approved by the Administrator and described or referenced in the certificate holder's operations specifications; and

(2) Whenever the Administrator finds that revisions are necessary for the continued adequacy of duty period limitation and rest requirement procedures that are required by paragraph (c)(1) of this section and that had been granted final approval, the certificate holder must, after notification by the Administrator, make any changes in the procedures that are found necessary by the Administrator. Within 30 days after the certificate holder receives such notice, it may file a petition to reconsider the notice with the responsible Flight Standards office. The filing of a petition to reconsider stays the notice, pending decision by the Administrator. However, if the Administrator finds that there is an emergency that requires immediate action in the interest of safety, the Administrator may, upon a statement of the reasons, require a change effective without stay.

[Amdt. 135–52, 59 FR 42993, Aug. 19, 1994, as amended by Amdt. 135–60, 61 FR 2616, Jan. 26, 1996; Docket FAA–2018–0119, Amdt. 135–139, 83 FR 9175, Mar. 5, 2018]

Subpart G—Crewmember Testing Requirements

§ 135.291 Applicability.

Except as provided in § 135.3, this subpart—

(a) Prescribes the tests and checks required for pilot and flight attendant crewmembers and for the approval of check pilots in operations under this part; and

(b) Permits training center personnel authorized under part 142 of this chapter who meet the requirements of §§ 135.337 and 135.339 to conduct training, testing, and checking under contract or other arrangement to those persons subject to the requirements of this subpart.

[Doc. No. 26933, 61 FR 34561, July 2, 1996, as amended by Amdt. 135–91, 68 FR 54587, Sept. 17, 2003]

§ 135.293 Initial and recurrent pilot testing requirements.

(a) No certificate holder may use a pilot, nor may any person serve as a pilot, unless, since the beginning of the 12th calendar month before that service, that pilot has passed a written or oral test, given by the Administrator or an authorized check pilot, on that pilot's knowledge in the following areas—

(1) The appropriate provisions of parts 61, 91, and 135 of this chapter and the operations specifications and the manual of the certificate holder;

(2) For each type of aircraft to be flown by the pilot, the aircraft powerplant, major components and systems, major appliances, performance and operating limitations, standard and emergency operating procedures, and the contents of the approved Aircraft Flight Manual or equivalent, as applicable;

(3) For each type of aircraft to be flown by the pilot, the method of determining compliance with weight and balance limitations for takeoff, landing and en route operations;

(4) Navigation and use of air navigation aids appropriate to the operation or pilot authorization, including, when applicable, instrument approach facilities and procedures;

(5) Air traffic control procedures, including IFR procedures when applicable;

(6) Meteorology in general, including the principles of frontal systems, icing, fog, thunderstorms, and windshear, and, if appropriate for the operation of the certificate holder, high altitude weather;

(7) Procedures for—

(i) Recognizing and avoiding severe weather situations;

(ii) Escaping from severe weather situations, in case of inadvertent encounters, including low-altitude windshear (except that rotorcraft pilots are not required to be tested on escaping from low-altitude windshear);

(iii) Operating in or near thunderstorms (including best penetrating altitudes), turbulent air (including clear air turbulence), icing, hail, and other potentially hazardous meteorological conditions; and

(8) New equipment, procedures, or techniques, as appropriate; and

(9) For rotorcraft pilots, procedures for aircraft handling in flat-light, whiteout, and brownout conditions, including methods for recognizing and avoiding those conditions.

(b) No certificate holder may use a pilot, nor may any person serve as a pilot, in any aircraft unless, since the beginning of the 12th calendar month before that service, that pilot has passed a competency check given by the Administrator or an authorized check pilot in that class of aircraft, if single-engine airplane other than turbojet, or that type of aircraft, if helicopter, multiengine airplane, or turbojet airplane, to determine the pilot's competence in practical skills and techniques in that aircraft or class of aircraft. The extent of the competency check shall be determined by the Administrator or authorized check pilot conducting the competency check. The competency check may include any of the maneuvers and procedures currently required for the original issuance of the particular pilot certificate required for the operations authorized and appropriate to the category, class and type of aircraft involved. For the purposes of this paragraph, type, as to an airplane, means

471

any one of a group of airplanes determined by the Administrator to have a similar means of propulsion, the same manufacturer, and no significantly different handling or flight characteristics. For the purposes of this paragraph, type, as to a helicopter, means a basic make and model.

(c) Each competency check given in a rotorcraft must include a demonstration of the pilot's ability to maneuver the rotorcraft solely by reference to instruments. The check must determine the pilot's ability to safely maneuver the rotorcraft into visual meteorological conditions following an inadvertent encounter with instrument meteorological conditions. For competency checks in non-IFR-certified rotorcraft, the pilot must perform such maneuvers as are appropriate to the rotorcraft's installed equipment, the certificate holder's operations specifications, and the operating environment.

(d) The instrument proficiency check required by § 135.297 may be substituted for the competency check required by this section for the type of aircraft used in the check.

(e) For the purpose of this part, competent performance of a procedure or maneuver by a person to be used as a pilot requires that the pilot be the obvious master of the aircraft, with the successful outcome of the maneuver never in doubt.

(f) The Administrator or authorized check pilot certifies the competency of each pilot who passes the knowledge or flight check in the certificate holder's pilot records.

(g) Portions of a required competency check may be given in an aircraft simulator or other appropriate training device, if approved by the Administrator.

(h) Rotorcraft pilots must be tested on the subjects in paragraph (a)(9) of this section when taking a written or oral knowledge test after April 22, 2015. Rotorcraft pilots must be checked on the maneuvers and procedures in paragraph (c) of this section when taking a competency check after April 22, 2015.

(i) If the certificate holder is authorized to conduct EFVS operations, the competency check in paragraph (b) of this section must include tasks appropriate to the EFVS operations the cer-

tificate holder is authorized to conduct.

[Doc. No. 16097, 43 FR 46783, Oct. 10, 1978, as amended by Amdt. 135–27, 53 FR 37697, Sept. 27, 1988; Amdt. 135–129, 79 FR 9974, Feb. 21, 2014; 79 FR 22012, Apr. 21, 2014; Docket FAA–2013–0485, Amdt. 135–135, 81 FR 90177, Dec. 13, 2016]

§ 135.295 Initial and recurrent flight attendant crewmember testing requirements.

No certificate holder may use a flight attendant crewmember, nor may any person serve as a flight attendant crewmember unless, since the beginning of the 12th calendar month before that service, the certificate holder has determined by appropriate initial and recurrent testing that the person is knowledgeable and competent in the following areas as appropriate to assigned duties and responsibilities—

(a) Authority of the pilot in command;

(b) Passenger handling, including procedures to be followed in handling deranged persons or other persons whose conduct might jeopardize safety;

(c) Crewmember assignments, functions, and responsibilities during ditching and evacuation of persons who may need the assistance of another person to move expeditiously to an exit in an emergency;

(d) Briefing of passengers;

(e) Location and operation of portable fire extinguishers and other items of emergency equipment;

(f) Proper use of cabin equipment and controls;

(g) Location and operation of passenger oxygen equipment;

(h) Location and operation of all normal and emergency exits, including evacuation chutes and escape ropes; and

(i) Seating of persons who may need assistance of another person to move rapidly to an exit in an emergency as prescribed by the certificate holder's operations manual.

§ 135.297 Pilot in command: Instrument proficiency check requirements.

(a) No certificate holder may use a pilot, nor may any person serve, as a pilot in command of an aircraft under IFR unless, since the beginning of the

6th calendar month before that service, that pilot has passed an instrument proficiency check under this section administered by the Administrator or an authorized check pilot.

(b) No pilot may use any type of precision instrument approach procedure under IFR unless, since the beginning of the 6th calendar month before that use, the pilot satisfactorily demonstrated that type of approach procedure. No pilot may use any type of nonprecision approach procedure under IFR unless, since the beginning of the 6th calendar month before that use, the pilot has satisfactorily demonstrated either that type of approach procedure or any other two different types of nonprecision approach procedures. The instrument approach procedure or procedures must include at least one straight-in approach, one circling approach, and one missed approach. Each type of approach procedure demonstrated must be conducted to published minimums for that procedure.

(c) The instrument proficiency check required by paragraph (a) of this section consists of an oral or written equipment test and a flight check under simulated or actual IFR conditions. The equipment test includes questions on emergency procedures, engine operation, fuel and lubrication systems, power settings, stall speeds, best engine-out speed, propeller and supercharger operations, and hydraulic, mechanical, and electrical systems, as appropriate. The flight check includes navigation by instruments, recovery from simulated emergencies, and standard instrument approaches involving navigational facilities which that pilot is to be authorized to use. Each pilot taking the instrument proficiency check must show that standard of competence required by §135.293(e).

(1) The instrument proficiency check must—

(i) For a pilot in command of an airplane under §135.243(a), include the procedures and maneuvers for an airline transport pilot certificate in the particular type of airplane, if appropriate; and

(ii) For a pilot in command of an airplane or helicopter under §135.243(c), include the procedures and maneuvers

for a commercial pilot certificate with an instrument rating and, if required, for the appropriate type rating.

(2) The instrument proficiency check must be given by an authorized check airman or by the Administrator.

(d) If the pilot in command is assigned to pilot only one type of aircraft, that pilot must take the instrument proficiency check required by paragraph (a) of this section in that type of aircraft.

(e) If the pilot in command is assigned to pilot more than one type of aircraft, that pilot must take the instrument proficiency check required by paragraph (a) of this section in each type of aircraft to which that pilot is assigned, in rotation, but not more than one flight check during each period described in paragraph (a) of this section.

(f) If the pilot in command is assigned to pilot both single-engine and multiengine aircraft, that pilot must initially take the instrument proficiency check required by paragraph (a) of this section in a multiengine aircraft, and each succeeding check alternately in single-engine and multiengine aircraft, but not more than one flight check during each period described in paragraph (a) of this section. Portions of a required flight check may be given in an aircraft simulator or other appropriate training device, if approved by the Administrator.

(g) If the pilot in command is authorized to use an autopilot system in place of a second in command, that pilot must show, during the required instrument proficiency check, that the pilot is able (without a second in command) both with and without using the autopilot to—

(1) Conduct instrument operations competently; and

(2) Properly conduct air-ground communications and comply with complex air traffic control instructions.

(3) Each pilot taking the autopilot check must show that, while using the autopilot, the airplane can be operated as proficiently as it would be if a second in command were present to handle air-ground communications and air traffic control instructions. The autopilot check need only be demonstrated once every 12 calendar months during

the instrument proficiency check required under paragraph (a) of this section.

[Doc. No. 16097, 43 FR 46783, Oct. 10, 1978, as amended by Amdt. 135–15, 46 FR 30971, June 11, 1981; Amdt. 135–129, 79 FR 9975, Feb. 21, 2014]

§ 135.299　Pilot in command: Line checks: Routes and airports.

(a) No certificate holder may use a pilot, nor may any person serve, as a pilot in command of a flight unless, since the beginning of the 12th calendar month before that service, that pilot has passed a flight check in one of the types of aircraft which that pilot is to fly. The flight check shall—

(1) Be given by an approved check pilot or by the Administrator;

(2) Consist of at least one flight over one route segment; and

(3) Include takeoffs and landings at one or more representative airports. In addition to the requirements of this paragraph, for a pilot authorized to conduct IFR operations, at least one flight shall be flown over a civil airway, an approved off-airway route, or a portion of either of them.

(b) The pilot who conducts the check shall determine whether the pilot being checked satisfactorily performs the duties and responsibilities of a pilot in command in operations under this part, and shall so certify in the pilot training record.

(c) Each certificate holder shall establish in the manual required by § 135.21 a procedure which will ensure that each pilot who has not flown over a route and into an airport within the preceding 90 days will, before beginning the flight, become familiar with all available information required for the safe operation of that flight.

§ 135.301　Crewmember: Tests and checks, grace provisions, training to accepted standards.

(a) If a crewmember who is required to take a test or a flight check under this part, completes the test or flight check in the calendar month before or after the calendar month in which it is required, that crewmember is considered to have completed the test or check in the calendar month in which it is required.

(b) If a pilot being checked under this subpart fails any of the required maneuvers, the person giving the check may give additional training to the pilot during the course of the check. In addition to repeating the maneuvers failed, the person giving the check may require the pilot being checked to repeat any other maneuvers that are necessary to determine the pilot's proficiency. If the pilot being checked is unable to demonstrate satisfactory performance to the person conducting the check, the certificate holder may not use the pilot, nor may the pilot serve, as a flight crewmember in operations under this part until the pilot has satisfactorily completed the check.

Subpart H—Training

§ 135.321　Applicability and terms used.

(a) Except as provided in § 135.3, this subpart prescribes the requirements applicable to—

(1) A certificate holder under this part which contracts with, or otherwise arranges to use the services of a training center certificated under part 142 to perform training, testing, and checking functions;

(2) Each certificate holder for establishing and maintaining an approved training program for crewmembers, check airmen and instructors, and other operations personnel employed or used by that certificate holder; and

(3) Each certificate holder for the qualification, approval, and use of aircraft simulators and flight training devices in the conduct of the program.

(b) For the purposes of this subpart, the following terms and definitions apply:

(1) *Initial training.* The training required for crewmembers who have not qualified and served in the same capacity on an aircraft.

(2) *Transition training.* The training required for crewmembers who have qualified and served in the same capacity on another aircraft.

(3) *Upgrade training.* The training required for crewmembers who have qualified and served as second in command on a particular aircraft type, before they serve as pilot in command on that aircraft.

(4) *Differences training.* The training required for crewmembers who have qualified and served on a particular type aircraft, when the Administrator finds differences training is necessary before a crewmember serves in the same capacity on a particular variation of that aircraft.

(5) *Recurrent training.* The training required for crewmembers to remain adequately trained and currently proficient for each aircraft, crewmember position, and type of operation in which the crewmember serves.

(6) *In flight.* The maneuvers, procedures, or functions that must be conducted in the aircraft.

(7) *Training center.* An organization governed by the applicable requirements of part 142 of this chapter that conducts training, testing, and checking under contract or other arrangement to certificate holders subject to the requirements of this part.

(8) *Requalification training.* The training required for crewmembers previously trained and qualified, but who have become unqualified due to not having met within the required period the—

(i) Recurrent pilot testing requirements of § 135.293;

(ii) Instrument proficiency check requirements of § 135.297; or

(iii) Line checks required by § 135.299.

[Doc. No. 16097, 43 FR 46783, Oct. 10, 1978, as amended by Amdt. 121–250, 60 FR 65950, Dec. 20, 1995; Amdt. 135–63, 61 FR 34561, July 2, 1996; Amdt. 135–91, 68 FR 54588 Sept. 17, 2003]

§ 135.323 Training program: General.

(a) Each certificate holder required to have a training program under § 135.341 shall:

(1) Establish and implement a training program that satisfies the requirements of this subpart and that ensures that each crewmember, aircraft dispatcher, flight instructor and check airman is adequately trained to perform his or her assigned duties. Prior to implementation, the certificate holder must obtain initial and final FAA approval of the training program.

(2) Provide adequate ground and flight training facilities and properly qualified ground instructors for the training required by this subpart.

(3) Provide and keep current for each aircraft type used and, if applicable, the particular variations within the aircraft type, appropriate training material, examinations, forms, instructions, and procedures for use in conducting the training and checks required by this subpart.

(4) Provide enough flight instructors, check airmen, and simulator instructors to conduct required flight training and flight checks, and simulator training courses allowed under this subpart.

(b) Whenever a crewmember who is required to take recurrent training under this subpart completes the training in the calendar month before, or the calendar month after, the month in which that training is required, the crewmember is considered to have completed it in the calendar month in which it was required.

(c) Each instructor, supervisor, or check airman who is responsible for a particular ground training subject, segment of flight training, course of training, flight check, or competence check under this part shall certify as to the proficiency and knowledge of the crewmember, flight instructor, or check airman concerned upon completion of that training or check. That certification shall be made a part of the crewmember's record. When the certification required by this paragraph is made by an entry in a computerized recordkeeping system, the certifying instructor, supervisor, or check airman, must be identified with that entry. However, the signature of the certifying instructor, supervisor, or check airman, is not required for computerized entries.

(d) Training subjects that apply to more than one aircraft or crewmember position and that have been satisfactorily completed during previous training while employed by the certificate holder for another aircraft or another crewmember position, need not be repeated during subsequent training other than recurrent training.

(e) Aircraft simulators and other training devices may be used in the certificate holder's training program if approved by the Administrator.

[Doc. No. 16097, 43 FR 46783, Oct. 10, 1978, as amended by Amdt. 135–101, 70 FR 58829, Oct. 7, 2005]

§ 135.324 Training program: Special rules.

(a) Other than the certificate holder, only another certificate holder certificated under this part or a training center certificated under part 142 of this chapter is eligible under this subpart to conduct training, testing, and checking under contract or other arrangement to those persons subject to the requirements of this subpart.

(b) A certificate holder may contract with, or otherwise arrange to use the services of, a training center certificated under part 142 of this chapter to conduct training, testing, and checking required by this part only if the training center—

(1) Holds applicable training specifications issued under part 142 of this chapter;

(2) Has facilities, training equipment, and courseware meeting the applicable requirements of part 142 of this chapter;

(3) Has approved curriculums, curriculum segments, and portions of curriculum segments applicable for use in training courses required by this subpart; and

(4) Has sufficient instructor and check airmen qualified under the applicable requirements of §§ 135.337 through 135.340 to provide training, testing, and checking to persons subject to the requirements of this subpart.

[Doc. No. 26933, 61 FR 34562, July 2, 1996, as amended by Amdt. 135–67, 62 FR 13791, Mar. 21, 1997; Amdt. 135–91, 68 FR 54588, Sept. 17, 2003]

§ 135.325 Training program and revision: Initial and final approval.

(a) To obtain initial and final approval of a training program, or a revision to an approved training program, each certificate holder must submit to the Administrator—

(1) An outline of the proposed or revised curriculum, that provides enough information for a preliminary evaluation of the proposed training program or revision; and

(2) Additional relevant information that may be requested by the Administrator.

(b) If the proposed training program or revision complies with this subpart, the Administrator grants initial approval in writing after which the certificate holder may conduct the training under that program. The Administrator then evaluates the effectiveness of the training program and advises the certificate holder of deficiencies, if any, that must be corrected.

(c) The Administrator grants final approval of the proposed training program or revision if the certificate holder shows that the training conducted under the initial approval in paragraph (b) of this section ensures that each person who successfully completes the training is adequately trained to perform that person's assigned duties.

(d) Whenever the Administrator finds that revisions are necessary for the continued adequacy of a training program that has been granted final approval, the certificate holder shall, after notification by the Administrator, make any changes in the program that are found necessary by the Administrator. Within 30 days after the certificate holder receives the notice, it may file a petition to reconsider the notice with the Administrator. The filing of a petition to reconsider stays the notice pending a decision by the Administrator. However, if the Administrator finds that there is an emergency that requires immediate action in the interest of safety, the Administrator may, upon a statement of the reasons, require a change effective without stay.

§ 135.327 Training program: Curriculum.

(a) Each certificate holder must prepare and keep current a written training program curriculum for each type of aircraft for each crewmember required for that type aircraft. The curriculum must include ground and flight training required by this subpart.

(b) Each training program curriculum must include the following:

(1) A list of principal ground training subjects, including emergency training subjects, that are provided.

(2) A list of all the training devices, mockups, systems trainers, procedures trainers, or other training aids that the certificate holder will use.

(3) Detailed descriptions or pictorial displays of the approved normal, abnormal, and emergency maneuvers, procedures and functions that will be performed during each flight training phase or flight check, indicating those maneuvers, procedures and functions that are to be performed during the inflight portions of flight training and flight checks.

§ 135.329 Crewmember training requirements.

(a) Each certificate holder must include in its training program the following initial and transition ground training as appropriate to the particular assignment of the crewmember:

(1) Basic indoctrination ground training for newly hired crewmembers including instruction in at least the—

(i) Duties and responsibilities of crewmembers as applicable;

(ii) Appropriate provisions of this chapter;

(iii) Contents of the certificate holder's operating certificate and operations specifications (not required for flight attendants); and

(iv) Appropriate portions of the certificate holder's operating manual.

(2) The initial and transition ground training in §§ 135.345 and 135.349, as applicable.

(3) Emergency training in § 135.331.

(4) Crew resource management training in § 135.330.

(b) Each training program must provide the initial and transition flight training in § 135.347, as applicable.

(c) Each training program must provide recurrent ground and flight training in § 135.351.

(d) Upgrade training in §§ 135.345 and 135.347 for a particular type aircraft may be included in the training program for crewmembers who have qualified and served as second in command on that aircraft.

(e) In addition to initial, transition, upgrade and recurrent training, each training program must provide ground and flight training, instruction, and practice necessary to ensure that each crewmember—

(1) Remains adequately trained and currently proficient for each aircraft, crewmember position, and type of oper-

ation in which the crewmember serves; and

(2) Qualifies in new equipment, facilities, procedures, and techniques, including modifications to aircraft.

[Doc. No. 16097, 43 FR 46783, Oct. 10, 1978, as amended by Amdt. 135–122, 76 FR 3837, Jan. 21, 2011]

§ 135.330 Crew resource management training.

(a) Each certificate holder must have an approved crew resource management training program that includes initial and recurrent training. The training program must include at least the following:

(1) Authority of the pilot in command;

(2) Communication processes, decisions, and coordination, to include communication with Air Traffic Control, personnel performing flight locating and other operational functions, and passengers;

(3) Building and maintenance of a flight team;

(4) Workload and time management;

(5) Situational awareness;

(6) Effects of fatigue on performance, avoidance strategies and countermeasures;

(7) Effects of stress and stress reduction strategies; and

(8) Aeronautical decision-making and judgment training tailored to the operator's flight operations and aviation environment.

(b) After March 22, 2013, no certificate holder may use a person as a flightcrew member or flight attendant unless that person has completed approved crew resource management initial training with that certificate holder.

(c) For flightcrew members and flight attendants, the Administrator, at his or her discretion, may credit crew resource management training completed with that certificate holder before March 22, 2013, toward all or part of the initial CRM training required by this section.

(d) In granting credit for initial CRM training, the Administrator considers training aids, devices, methods and procedures used by the certificate holder in a voluntary CRM program included in a training program required by § 135.341, § 135.345, or § 135.349.

[Doc. No. FAA–2009–0023, 76 FR 3837, Jan. 21, 2011]

§ 135.331 Crewmember emergency training.

(a) Each training program must provide emergency training under this section for each aircraft type, model, and configuration, each crewmember, and each kind of operation conducted, as appropriate for each crewmember and the certificate holder.

(b) Emergency training must provide the following:

(1) Instruction in emergency assignments and procedures, including coordination among crewmembers.

(2) Individual instruction in the location, function, and operation of emergency equipment including—

(i) Equipment used in ditching and evacuation;

(ii) First aid equipment and its proper use; and

(iii) Portable fire extinguishers, with emphasis on the type of extinguisher to be used on different classes of fires.

(3) Instruction in the handling of emergency situations including—

(i) Rapid decompression;

(ii) Fire in flight or on the surface and smoke control procedures with emphasis on electrical equipment and related circuit breakers found in cabin areas;

(iii) Ditching and evacuation;

(iv) Illness, injury, or other abnormal situations involving passengers or crewmembers; and

(v) Hijacking and other unusual situations.

(4) Review of the certificate holder's previous aircraft accidents and incidents involving actual emergency situations.

(c) Each crewmember must perform at least the following emergency drills, using the proper emergency equipment and procedures, unless the Administrator finds that, for a particular drill, the crewmember can be adequately trained by demonstration:

(1) Ditching, if applicable.

(2) Emergency evacuation.

(3) Fire extinguishing and smoke control.

(4) Operation and use of emergency exits, including deployment and use of evacuation chutes, if applicable.

(5) Use of crew and passenger oxygen.

(6) Removal of life rafts from the aircraft, inflation of the life rafts, use of life lines, and boarding of passengers and crew, if applicable.

(7) Donning and inflation of life vests and the use of other individual flotation devices, if applicable.

(d) Crewmembers who serve in operations above 25,000 feet must receive instruction in the following:

(1) Respiration.

(2) Hypoxia.

(3) Duration of consciousness without supplemental oxygen at altitude.

(4) Gas expansion.

(5) Gas bubble formation.

(6) Physical phenomena and incidents of decompression.

§ 135.335 Approval of aircraft simulators and other training devices.

(a) Training courses using aircraft simulators and other training devices may be included in the certificate holder's training program if approved by the Administrator.

(b) Each aircraft simulator and other training device that is used in a training course or in checks required under this subpart must meet the following requirements:

(1) It must be specifically approved for—

(i) The certificate holder; and

(ii) The particular maneuver, procedure, or crewmember function involved.

(2) It must maintain the performance, functional, and other characteristics that are required for approval.

(3) Additionally, for aircraft simulators, it must be—

(i) Approved for the type aircraft and, if applicable, the particular variation within type for which the training or check is being conducted; and

(ii) Modified to conform with any modification to the aircraft being simulated that changes the performance, functional, or other characteristics required for approval.

(c) A particular aircraft simulator or other training device may be used by more than one certificate holder.

(d) In granting initial and final approval of training programs or revisions to them, the Administrator considers the training devices, methods and procedures listed in the certificate holder's curriculum under §135.327.

[Doc. No. 16907, 43 FR 46783, Oct. 10, 1978, as amended by Amdt. 135–1, 44 FR 26738, May 7, 1979]

§135.336 Airline transport pilot certification training program.

(a) A certificate holder may obtain approval to establish and implement a training program to satisfy the requirements of §61.156 of this chapter. The training program must be separate from the air carrier training program required by this part.

(b) No certificate holder may use a person nor may any person serve as an instructor in a training program approved to meet the requirements of §61.156 of this chapter unless the instructor:

(1) Holds an airline transport pilot certificate with an airplane category multiengine class rating;

(2) Has at least 2 years of experience as a pilot in command in operations conducted under §91.1053(a)(2)(i) of this chapter, §135.243(a)(1) of this part, or as a pilot in command or second in command in any operation conducted under part 121 of this chapter;

(3) Except for the holder of a flight instructor certificate, receives initial training on the following topics:

(i) The fundamental principles of the learning process;

(ii) Elements of effective teaching, instruction methods, and techniques;

(iii) Instructor duties, privileges, responsibilities, and limitations;

(iv) Training policies and procedures; and

(v) Evaluation.

(4) If providing training in a flight simulation training device, holds an aircraft type rating for the aircraft represented by the flight simulation training device utilized in the training program and have received training and evaluation within the preceding 12 months from the certificate holder on:

(i) Proper operation of flight simulator and flight training device controls and systems;

(ii) Proper operation of environmental and fault panels;

(iii) Data and motion limitations of simulation;

(iv) Minimum equipment requirements for each curriculum; and

(v) The maneuvers that will be demonstrated in the flight simulation training device.

(c) A certificate holder may not issue a graduation certificate to a student unless that student has completed all the curriculum requirements of the course.

(d) A certificate holder must conduct evaluations to ensure that training techniques, procedures, and standards are acceptable to the Administrator.

[Doc. No. FAA–2010–0100, 78 FR 42379, July 15, 2013]

§135.337 Qualifications: Check airmen (aircraft) and check airmen (simulator).

(a) For the purposes of this section and §135.339:

(1) A check airman (aircraft) is a person who is qualified to conduct flight checks in an aircraft, in a flight simulator, or in a flight training device for a particular type aircraft.

(2) A check airman (simulator) is a person who is qualified to conduct flight checks, but only in a flight simulator, in a flight training device, or both, for a particular type aircraft.

(3) Check airmen (aircraft) and check airmen (simulator) are those check airmen who perform the functions described in §§135.321 (a) and 135.323(a)(4) and (c).

(b) No certificate holder may use a person, nor may any person serve as a check airman (aircraft) in a training program established under this subpart unless, with respect to the aircraft type involved, that person—

(1) Holds the airman certificates and ratings required to serve as a pilot in command in operations under this part;

(2) Has satisfactorily completed the training phases for the aircraft, including recurrent training, that are required to serve as a pilot in command in operations under this part;

479

(3) Has satisfactorily completed the proficiency or competency checks that are required to serve as a pilot in command in operations under this part;

(4) Has satisfactorily completed the applicable training requirements of § 135.339;

(5) Holds at least a Class III medical certificate unless serving as a required crewmember, in which case holds a Class I or Class II medical certificate as appropriate.

(6) Has satisfied the recency of experience requirements of § 135.247; and

(7) Has been approved by the Administrator for the check airman duties involved.

(c) No certificate holder may use a person, nor may any person serve as a check airman (simulator) in a training program established under this subpart unless, with respect to the aircraft type involved, that person meets the provisions of paragraph (b) of this section, or—

(1) Holds the applicable airman certificates and ratings, except medical certificate, required to serve as a pilot in command in operations under this part;

(2) Has satisfactorily completed the appropriate training phases for the aircraft, including recurrent training, that are required to serve as a pilot in command in operations under this part;

(3) Has satisfactorily completed the appropriate proficiency or competency checks that are required to serve as a pilot in command in operations under this part;

(4) Has satisfactorily completed the applicable training requirements of § 135.339; and

(5) Has been approved by the Administrator for the check airman (simulator) duties involved.

(d) Completion of the requirements in paragraphs (b) (2), (3), and (4) or (c) (2), (3), and (4) of this section, as applicable, shall be entered in the individual's training record maintained by the certificate holder.

(e) Check airmen who do not hold an appropriate medical certificate may function as check airmen (simulator), but may not serve as flightcrew members in operations under this part.

(f) A check airman (simulator) must accomplish the following—

(1) Fly at least two flight segments as a required crewmember for the type, class, or category aircraft involved within the 12-month preceding the performance of any check airman duty in a flight simulator; or

(2) Satisfactorily complete an approved line-observation program within the period prescribed by that program and that must precede the performance of any check airman duty in a flight simulator.

(g) The flight segments or line-observation program required in paragraph (f) of this section are considered to be completed in the month required if completed in the calendar month before or the calendar month after the month in which they are due.

[Doc. No. 28471, 61 FR 30744, June 17, 1996]

§ 135.338   Qualifications: Flight instructors (aircraft) and flight instructors (simulator).

(a) For the purposes of this section and § 135.340:

(1) A flight instructor (aircraft) is a person who is qualified to instruct in an aircraft, in a flight simulator, or in a flight training device for a particular type, class, or category aircraft.

(2) A flight instructor (simulator) is a person who is qualified to instruct in a flight simulator, in a flight training device, or in both, for a particular type, class, or category aircraft.

(3) Flight instructors (aircraft) and flight instructors (simulator) are those instructors who perform the functions described in § 135.321(a) and 135.323 (a)(4) and (c).

(b) No certificate holder may use a person, nor may any person serve as a flight instructor (aircraft) in a training program established under this subpart unless, with respect to the type, class, or category aircraft involved, that person—

(1) Holds the airman certificates and ratings required to serve as a pilot in command in operations under this part;

(2) Has satisfactorily completed the training phases for the aircraft, including recurrent training, that are required to serve as a pilot in command in operations under this part;

(3) Has satisfactorily completed the proficiency or competency checks that are required to serve as a pilot in command in operations under this part;

(4) Has satisfactorily completed the applicable training requirements of §135.340;

(5) Holds at least a Class III medical certificate; and

(6) Has satisfied the recency of experience requirements of §135.247.

(c) No certificate holder may use a person, nor may any person serve as a flight instructor (simulator) in a training program established under this subpart, unless, with respect to the type, class, or category aircraft involved, that person meets the provisions of paragraph (b) of this section, or—

(1) Holds the airman certificates and ratings, except medical certificate, required to serve as a pilot in command in operations under this part except before March 19, 1997 that person need not hold a type rating for the type, class, or category of aircraft involved.

(2) Has satisfactorily completed the appropriate training phases for the aircraft, including recurrent training, that are required to serve as a pilot in command in operations under this part;

(3) Has satisfactorily completed the appropriate proficiency or competency checks that are required to serve as a pilot in command in operations under this part; and

(4) Has satisfactorily completed the applicable training requirements of §135.340.

(d) Completion of the requirements in paragraphs (b) (2), (3), and (4) or (c) (2), (3), and (4) of this section, as applicable, shall be entered in the individual's training record maintained by the certificate holder.

(e) An airman who does not hold a medical certificate may function as a flight instructor in an aircraft if functioning as a non-required crewmember, but may not serve as a flightcrew member in operations under this part.

(f) A flight instructor (simulator) must accomplish the following—

(1) Fly at least two flight segments as a required crewmember for the type, class, or category aircraft involved within the 12-month period preceding

the performance of any flight instructor duty in a flight simulator; or

(2) Satisfactorily complete an approved line-observation program within the period prescribed by that program preceding the performance of any flight instructor duty in a flight simulator.

(g) The flight segments or line-observation program required in paragraph (f) of this section are considered completed in the month required if completed in the calendar month before, or in the calendar month after, the month in which they are due.

[Doc. No. 28471, 61 FR 30744, June 17, 1996; 62 FR 3739, Jan. 24, 1997, as amended by Amdt. 135–125, 76 FR 35104, June 16, 2011]

§135.339 Initial and transition training and checking: Check airmen (aircraft), check airmen (simulator).

(a) No certificate holder may use a person nor may any person serve as a check airman unless—

(1) That person has satisfactorily completed initial or transition check airman training; and

(2) Within the preceding 24 calendar months, that person satisfactorily conducts a proficiency or competency check under the observation of an FAA inspector or an aircrew designated examiner employed by the operator. The observation check may be accomplished in part or in full in an aircraft, in a flight simulator, or in a flight training device. This paragraph applies after March 19, 1997.

(b) The observation check required by paragraph (a)(2) of this section is considered to have been completed in the month required if completed in the calendar month before or the calendar month after the month in which it is due.

(c) The initial ground training for check airmen must include the following:

(1) Check airman duties, functions, and responsibilities.

(2) The applicable Code of Federal Regulations and the certificate holder's policies and procedures.

(3) The applicable methods, procedures, and techniques for conducting the required checks.

(4) Proper evaluation of student performance including the detection of—

(i) Improper and insufficient training; and

(ii) Personal characteristics of an applicant that could adversely affect safety.

(5) The corrective action in the case of unsatisfactory checks.

(6) The approved methods, procedures, and limitations for performing the required normal, abnormal, and emergency procedures in the aircraft.

(d) The transition ground training for check airmen must include the approved methods, procedures, and limitations for performing the required normal, abnormal, and emergency procedures applicable to the aircraft to which the check airman is in transition.

(e) The initial and transition flight training for check airmen (aircraft) must include the following—

(1) The safety measures for emergency situations that are likely to develop during a check;

(2) The potential results of improper, untimely, or nonexecution of safety measures during a check;

(3) Training and practice in conducting flight checks from the left and right pilot seats in the required normal, abnormal, and emergency procedures to ensure competence to conduct the pilot flight checks required by this part; and

(4) The safety measures to be taken from either pilot seat for emergency situations that are likely to develop during checking.

(f) The requirements of paragraph (e) of this section may be accomplished in full or in part in flight, in a flight simulator, or in a flight training device, as appropriate.

(g) The initial and transition flight training for check airmen (simulator) must include the following:

(1) Training and practice in conducting flight checks in the required normal, abnormal, and emergency procedures to ensure competence to conduct the flight checks required by this part. This training and practice must be accomplished in a flight simulator or in a flight training device.

(2) Training in the operation of flight simulators, flight training devices, or both, to ensure competence to conduct the flight checks required by this part.

[Doc. No. 28471, 61 FR 30745, June 17, 1996; 62 FR 3739, Jan. 24, 1997]

§ 135.340 Initial and transition training and checking: Flight instructors (aircraft), flight instructors (simulator).

(a) No certificate holder may use a person nor may any person serve as a flight instructor unless—

(1) That person has satisfactorily completed initial or transition flight instructor training; and

(2) Within the preceding 24 calendar months, that person satisfactorily conducts instruction under the observation of an FAA inspector, an operator check airman, or an aircrew designated examiner employed by the operator. The observation check may be accomplished in part or in full in an aircraft, in a flight simulator, or in a flight training device. This paragraph applies after March 19, 1997.

(b) The observation check required by paragraph (a)(2) of this section is considered to have been completed in the month required if completed in the calendar month before, or the calendar month after, the month in which it is due.

(c) The initial ground training for flight instructors must include the following:

(1) Flight instructor duties, functions, and responsibilities.

(2) The applicable Code of Federal Regulations and the certificate holder's policies and procedures.

(3) The applicable methods, procedures, and techniques for conducting flight instruction.

(4) Proper evaluation of student performance including the detection of—

(i) Improper and insufficient training; and

(ii) Personal characteristics of an applicant that could adversely affect safety.

(5) The corrective action in the case of unsatisfactory training progress.

(6) The approved methods, procedures, and limitations for performing the required normal, abnormal, and emergency procedures in the aircraft.

(7) Except for holders of a flight instructor certificate—

(i) The fundamental principles of the teaching-learning process;

(ii) Teaching methods and procedures; and

(iii) The instructor-student relationship.

(d) The transition ground training for flight instructors must include the approved methods, procedures, and limitations for performing the required normal, abnormal, and emergency procedures applicable to the type, class, or category aircraft to which the flight instructor is in transition.

(e) The initial and transition flight training for flight instructors (aircraft) must include the following—

(1) The safety measures for emergency situations that are likely to develop during instruction;

(2) The potential results of improper or untimely safety measures during instruction;

(3) Training and practice from the left and right pilot seats in the required normal, abnormal, and emergency maneuvers to ensure competence to conduct the flight instruction required by this part; and

(4) The safety measures to be taken from either the left or right pilot seat for emergency situations that are likely to develop during instruction.

(f) The requirements of paragraph (e) of this section may be accomplished in full or in part in flight, in a flight simulator, or in a flight training device, as appropriate.

(g) The initial and transition flight training for a flight instructor (simulator) must include the following:

(1) Training and practice in the required normal, abnormal, and emergency procedures to ensure competence to conduct the flight instruction required by this part. These maneuvers and procedures must be accomplished in full or in part in a flight simulator or in a flight training device.

(2) Training in the operation of flight simulators, flight training devices, or both, to ensure competence to conduct the flight instruction required by this part.

[Doc. No. 28471, 61 FR 30745, June 17, 1993; 61 FR 34927, July 3, 1996; 62 FR 3739, Jan 24, 1997]

§135.341 Pilot and flight attendant crewmember training programs.

(a) Each certificate holder, other than one who uses only one pilot in the certificate holder's operations, shall establish and maintain an approved pilot training program, and each certificate holder who uses a flight attendant crewmember shall establish and maintain an approved flight attendant training program, that is appropriate to the operations to which each pilot and flight attendant is to be assigned, and will ensure that they are adequately trained to meet the applicable knowledge and practical testing requirements of §§135.293 through 135.301. However, the Administrator may authorize a deviation from this section if the Administrator finds that, because of the limited size and scope of the operation, safety will allow a deviation from these requirements. This deviation authority does not extend to the training provided under §135.336.

(b) Each certificate holder required to have a training program by paragraph (a) of this section shall include in that program ground and flight training curriculums for—

(1) Initial training;

(2) Transition training;

(3) Upgrade training;

(4) Differences training; and

(5) Recurrent training.

(c) Each certificate holder required to have a training program by paragraph (a) of this section shall provide current and appropriate study materials for use by each required pilot and flight attendant.

(d) The certificate holder shall furnish copies of the pilot and flight attendant crewmember training program, and all changes and additions, to the assigned representative of the Administrator. If the certificate holder uses training facilities of other persons, a copy of those training programs or appropriate portions used for those facilities shall also be furnished. Curricula that follow FAA published curricula may be cited by reference in the copy of the training program furnished to the representative of the Administrator and need not be furnished with the program.

[Doc. No. 16097, 43 FR 46783, Oct. 10, 1978, as amended by Amdt. 135–18, 47 FR 33396, Aug. 2, 1982; Amdt. 135–127, 78 FR 42379, July 15, 2013; Amdt. 135–127A, 78 FR 77574, Dec. 24, 2013]

§ 135.343 Crewmember initial and recurrent training requirements.

No certificate holder may use a person, nor may any person serve, as a crewmember in operations under this part unless that crewmember has completed the appropriate initial or recurrent training phase of the training program appropriate to the type of operation in which the crewmember is to serve since the beginning of the 12th calendar month before that service. This section does not apply to a certificate holder that uses only one pilot in the certificate holder's operations.

[Doc. No. 16097, 43 FR 46783, Oct. 10, 1978, as amended by Amdt. 135–18, 47 FR 33396, Aug. 2, 1982]

§ 135.345 Pilots: Initial, transition, and upgrade ground training.

Initial, transition, and upgrade ground training for pilots must include instruction in at least the following, as applicable to their duties:

(a) General subjects—

(1) The certificate holder's flight locating procedures;

(2) Principles and methods for determining weight and balance, and runway limitations for takeoff and landing;

(3) Enough meteorology to ensure a practical knowledge of weather phenomena, including the principles of frontal systems, icing, fog, thunderstorms, windshear and, if appropriate, high altitude weather situations;

(4) Air traffic control systems, procedures, and phraseology;

(5) Navigation and the use of navigational aids, including instrument approach procedures;

(6) Normal and emergency communication procedures;

(7) Visual cues before and during descent below DA/DH or MDA;

(8) ETOPS, if applicable;

(9) After August 13, 2008, passenger recovery plan for any passenger-carrying operation (other than intrastate operations wholly within the state of Alaska) in the North Polar area; and

(10) Other instructions necessary to ensure the pilot's competence.

(b) For each aircraft type—

(1) A general description;

(2) Performance characteristics;

(3) Engines and propellers;

(4) Major components;

(5) Major aircraft systems (i.e., flight controls, electrical, and hydraulic), other systems, as appropriate, principles of normal, abnormal, and emergency operations, appropriate procedures and limitations;

(6) Knowledge and procedures for—

(i) Recognizing and avoiding severe weather situations;

(ii) Escaping from severe weather situations, in case of inadvertent encounters, including low-altitude windshear (except that rotorcraft pilots are not required to be trained in escaping from low-altitude windshear);

(iii) Operating in or near thunderstorms (including best penetrating altitudes), turbulent air (including clear air turbulence), icing, hail, and other potentially hazardous meteorological conditions; and

(iv) Operating airplanes during ground icing conditions, (i.e., any time conditions are such that frost, ice, or snow may reasonably be expected to adhere to the airplane), if the certificate holder expects to authorize takeoffs in ground icing conditions, including:

(A) The use of holdover times when using deicing/anti-icing fluids;

(B) Airplane deicing/anti-icing procedures, including inspection and check procedures and responsibilities;

(C) Communications;

(D) Airplane surface contamination (i.e., adherence of frost, ice, or snow) and critical area identification, and knowledge of how contamination adversely affects airplane performance and flight characteristics;

(E) Types and characteristics of deicing/anti-icing fluids, if used by the certificate holder;

(F) Cold weather preflight inspection procedures;

(G) Techniques for recognizing contamination on the airplane;

(7) Operating limitations;

(8) Fuel consumption and cruise control;

(9) Flight planning;

(10) Each normal and emergency procedure; and

(11) The approved Aircraft Flight Manual, or equivalent.

[Doc. No. 16097, 43 FR 46783, Oct. 10, 1978, as amended by Amdt. 135–27, 53 FR 37697, Sept. 27, 1988; Amdt. 135–46, 58 FR 69630, Dec. 30, 1993; Amdt. 135–108, 72 FR 1885, Jan. 16, 2007; Amdt. 135–110, 72 FR 31685, June 7, 2007; Amdt. 135–112, 73 FR 8798, Feb. 15, 2008]

§135.347 Pilots: Initial, transition, upgrade, and differences flight training.

(a) Initial, transition, upgrade, and differences training for pilots must include flight and practice in each of the maneuvers and procedures in the approved training program curriculum.

(b) The maneuvers and procedures required by paragraph (a) of this section must be performed in flight, except to the extent that certain maneuvers and procedures may be performed in an aircraft simulator, or an appropriate training device, as allowed by this subpart.

(c) If the certificate holder's approved training program includes a course of training using an aircraft simulator or other training device, each pilot must successfully complete—

(1) Training and practice in the simulator or training device in at least the maneuvers and procedures in this subpart that are capable of being performed in the aircraft simulator or training device; and

(2) A flight check in the aircraft or a check in the simulator or training device to the level of proficiency of a pilot in command or second in command, as applicable, in at least the maneuvers and procedures that are capable of being performed in an aircraft simulator or training device.

§135.349 Flight attendants: Initial and transition ground training.

Initial and transition ground training for flight attendants must include instruction in at least the following—

(a) General subjects—

(1) The authority of the pilot in command; and

(2) Passenger handling, including procedures to be followed in handling deranged persons or other persons whose conduct might jeopardize safety.

(b) For each aircraft type—

(1) A general description of the aircraft emphasizing physical characteristics that may have a bearing on ditching, evacuation, and inflight emergency procedures and on other related duties;

(2) The use of both the public address system and the means of communicating with other flight crewmembers, including emergency means in the case of attempted hijacking or other unusual situations; and

(3) Proper use of electrical galley equipment and the controls for cabin heat and ventilation.

§135.351 Recurrent training.

(a) Each certificate holder must ensure that each crewmember receives recurrent training and is adequately trained and currently proficient for the type aircraft and crewmember position involved.

(b) Recurrent ground training for crewmembers must include at least the following:

(1) A quiz or other review to determine the crewmember's knowledge of the aircraft and crewmember position involved.

(2) Instruction as necessary in the subjects required for initial ground training by this subpart, as appropriate, including low-altitude windshear training and training on operating during ground icing conditions as prescribed in §135.341 and described in §135.345, crew resource management training as prescribed in §135.330, and emergency training as prescribed in §135.331.

(c) Recurrent flight training for pilots must include, at least, flight training in the maneuvers or procedures in this subpart, except that satisfactory completion of the check required by §135.293 within the preceding 12 calendar months may be substituted for recurrent flight training.

[Doc. No. 16097, 43 FR 46783, Oct. 10, 1978, as amended by Amdt. 135–27, 53 FR 37698, Sept. 27, 1988; Amdt. 135–46, 58 FR 69630, Dec. 30, 1993; Amdt. 135–122, 76 FR 3837, Jan. 21, 2011]

§ 135.353   [Reserved]

Subpart I—Airplane Performance Operating Limitations

§ 135.361   Applicability.

(a) This subpart prescribes airplane performance operating limitations applicable to the operation of the categories of airplanes listed in § 135.363 when operated under this part.

(b) For the purpose of this subpart, *effective length of the runway*, for landing means the distance from the point at which the obstruction clearance plane associated with the approach end of the runway intersects the centerline of the runway to the far end of the runway.

(c) For the purpose of this subpart, *obstruction clearance plane* means a plane sloping upward from the runway at a slope of 1:20 to the horizontal, and tangent to or clearing all obstructions within a specified area surrounding the runway as shown in a profile view of that area. In the plan view, the centerline of the specified area coincides with the centerline of the runway, beginning at the point where the obstruction clearance plane intersects the centerline of the runway and proceeding to a point at least 1,500 feet from the beginning point. After that the centerline coincides with the takeoff path over the ground for the runway (in the case of takeoffs) or with the instrument approach counterpart (for landings), or, where the applicable one of these paths has not been established, it proceeds consistent with turns of at least 4,000-foot radius until a point is reached beyond which the obstruction clearance plane clears all obstructions. This area extends laterally 200 feet on each side of the centerline at the point where the obstruction clearance plane intersects the runway and continues at this width to the end of the runway; then it increases uniformly to 500 feet on each side of the centerline at a point 1,500 feet from the intersection of the obstruction clearance plane with the runway; after that it extends laterally 500 feet on each side of the centerline.

§ 135.363   General.

(a) Each certificate holder operating a reciprocating engine powered large

transport category airplane shall comply with §§ 135.365 through 135.377.

(b) Each certificate holder operating a turbine engine powered large transport category airplane shall comply with §§ 135.379 through 135.387, except that when it operates a turbopropeller-powered large transport category airplane certificated after August 29, 1959, but previously type certificated with the same number of reciprocating engines, it may comply with §§ 135.365 through 135.377.

(c) Each certificate holder operating a large nontransport category airplane shall comply with §§ 135.389 through 135.395 and any determination of compliance must be based only on approved performance data. For the purpose of this subpart, a large nontrans- port category airplane is an airplane that was type certificated before July 1, 1942.

(d) Each certificate holder operating a small transport category airplane shall comply with § 135.397.

(e) Each certificate holder operating a small nontransport category airplane shall comply with § 135.399.

(f) The performance data in the Airplane Flight Manual applies in determining compliance with §§ 135.365 through 135.387. Where conditions are different from those on which the performance data is based, compliance is determined by interpolation or by computing the effects of change in the specific variables, if the results of the interpolation or computations are substantially as accurate as the results of direct tests.

(g) No person may take off a reciprocating engine powered large transport category airplane at a weight that is more than the allowable weight for the runway being used (determined under the runway takeoff limitations of the transport category operating rules of this subpart) after taking into account the temperature operating correction factors in section 4a.749a-T or section 4b.117 of the Civil Air Regulations in effect on January 31, 1965, and in the applicable Airplane Flight Manual.

(h) The Administrator may authorize in the operations specifications deviations from this subpart if special circumstances make a literal observance of a requirement unnecessary for safety.

(i) The 10-mile width specified in §§ 135.369 through 135.373 may be reduced to 5 miles, for not more than 20 miles, when operating under VFR or where navigation facilities furnish reliable and accurate identification of high ground and obstructions located outside of 5 miles, but within 10 miles, on each side of the intended track.

(j) Each certificate holder operating a commuter category airplane shall comply with § 135.398.

[Doc. No. 16097, 43 FR 46783, Oct. 10, 1978, as amended by Amdt. 135–21, 52 FR 1836, Jan. 15, 1987]

§ 135.364 Maximum flying time outside the United States.

After August 13, 2008, no certificate holder may operate an airplane, other than an all-cargo airplane with more than two engines, on a planned route that exceeds 180 minutes flying time (at the one-engine-inoperative cruise speed under standard conditions in still air) from an Adequate Airport outside the continental United States unless the operation is approved by the FAA in accordance with Appendix G of this part, Extended Operations (ETOPS).

[Doc. No. FAA–1999–6717, 73 FR 8798, Feb. 15, 2008]

§ 135.365 Large transport category airplanes: Reciprocating engine powered: Weight limitations.

(a) No person may take off a reciprocating engine powered large transport category airplane from an airport located at an elevation outside of the range for which maximum takeoff weights have been determined for that airplane.

(b) No person may take off a reciprocating engine powered large transport category airplane for an airport of intended destination that is located at an elevation outside of the range for which maximum landing weights have been determined for that airplane.

(c) No person may specify, or have specified, an alternate airport that is located at an elevation outside of the range for which maximum landing weights have been determined for the reciprocating engine powered large transport category airplane concerned.

(d) No person may take off a reciprocating engine powered large transport category airplane at a weight more than the maximum authorized takeoff weight for the elevation of the airport.

(e) No person may take off a reciprocating engine powered large transport category airplane if its weight on arrival at the airport of destination will be more than the maximum authorized landing weight for the elevation of that airport, allowing for normal consumption of fuel and oil en route.

§ 135.367 Large transport category airplanes: Reciprocating engine powered: Takeoff limitations.

(a) No person operating a reciprocating engine powered large transport category airplane may take off that airplane unless it is possible—

(1) To stop the airplane safely on the runway, as shown by the accelerate-stop distance data, at any time during takeoff until reaching critical-engine failure speed;

(2) If the critical engine fails at any time after the airplane reaches critical-engine failure speed V_1, to continue the takeoff and reach a height of 50 feet, as indicated by the takeoff path data, before passing over the end of the runway; and

(3) To clear all obstacles either by at least 50 feet vertically (as shown by the takeoff path data) or 200 feet horizontally within the airport boundaries and 300 feet horizontally beyond the boundaries, without banking before reaching a height of 50 feet (as shown by the takeoff path data) and after that without banking more than 15 degrees.

(b) In applying this section, corrections must be made for any runway gradient. To allow for wind effect, takeoff data based on still air may be corrected by taking into account not more than 50 percent of any reported headwind component and not less than 150 percent of any reported tailwind component.

§ 135.369 Large transport category airplanes: Reciprocating engine powered: En route limitations: All engines operating.

(a) No person operating a reciprocating engine powered large transport category airplane may take off that airplane at a weight, allowing for normal consumption of fuel and oil, that does not allow a rate of climb (in feet per minute), with all engines operating, of at least 6.90 Vs$_0$ (that is, the number of feet per minute obtained by multiplying the number of knots by 6.90) at an altitude of a least 1,000 feet above the highest ground or obstruction within ten miles of each side of the intended track.

(b) This section does not apply to large transport category airplanes certificated under part 4a of the Civil Air Regulations.

§ 135.371 **Large transport category airplanes: Reciprocating engine powered: En route limitations: One engine inoperative.**

(a) Except as provided in paragraph (b) of this section, no person operating a reciprocating engine powered large transport category airplane may take off that airplane at a weight, allowing for normal consumption of fuel and oil, that does not allow a rate of climb (in feet per minute), with one engine inoperative, of at least $(0.079 - 0.106/N)$ Vs$_0$2 (where N is the number of engines installed and Vs$_0$ is expressed in knots) at an altitude of least 1,000 feet above the highest ground or obstruction within 10 miles of each side of the intended track. However, for the purposes of this paragraph the rate of climb for transport category airplanes certificated under part 4a of the Civil Air Regulations is 0.026 Vs$_0$2.

(b) In place of the requirements of paragraph (a) of this section, a person may, under an approved procedure, operate a reciprocating engine powered large transport category airplane at an all-engines-operating altitude that allows the airplane to continue, after an engine failure, to an alternate airport where a landing can be made under § 135.377, allowing for normal consumption of fuel and oil. After the assumed failure, the flight path must clear the ground and any obstruction within five miles on each side of the intended track by at least 2,000 feet.

(c) If an approved procedure under paragraph (b) of this section is used, the certificate holder shall comply with the following:

(1) The rate of climb (as prescribed in the Airplane Flight Manual for the appropriate weight and altitude) used in calculating the airplane's flight path shall be diminished by an amount in feet per minute, equal to $(0.079 - 0.106/N)$ Vs$_0$2 (when N is the number of engines installed and Vs$_0$ is expressed in knots) for airplanes certificated under part 25 of this chapter and by 0.026 Vs$_0$2 for airplanes certificated under part 4a of the Civil Air Regulations.

(2) The all-engines-operating altitude shall be sufficient so that in the event the critical engine becomes inoperative at any point along the route, the flight will be able to proceed to a predetermined alternate airport by use of this procedure. In determining the takeoff weight, the airplane is assumed to pass over the critical obstruction following engine failure at a point no closer to the critical obstruction than the nearest approved navigational fix, unless the Administrator approves a procedure established on a different basis upon finding that adequate operational safeguards exist.

(3) The airplane must meet the provisions of paragraph (a) of this section at 1,000 feet above the airport used as an alternate in this procedure.

(4) The procedure must include an approved method of accounting for winds and temperatures that would otherwise adversely affect the flight path.

(5) In complying with this procedure, fuel jettisoning is allowed if the certificate holder shows that it has an adequate training program, that proper instructions are given to the flight crew, and all other precautions are taken to ensure a safe procedure.

(6) The certificate holder and the pilot in command shall jointly elect an alternate airport for which the appropriate weather reports or forecasts, or any combination of them, indicate that weather conditions will be at or above the alternate weather minimum specified in the certificate holder's operations specifications for that airport when the flight arrives.

[Doc. No. 16097, 43 FR 46783, Oct. 10, 1978, as amended by Amdt. 135–110, 72 FR 31685, June 7, 2007]

§135.373 Part 25 transport category airplanes with four or more engines: Reciprocating engine powered: En route limitations: Two engines inoperative.

(a) No person may operate an airplane certificated under part 25 and having four or more engines unless—

(1) There is no place along the intended track that is more than 90 minutes (with all engines operating at cruising power) from an airport that meets §135.377; or

(2) It is operated at a weight allowing the airplane, with the two critical engines inoperative, to climb at 0.013 Vs_o2 feet per minute (that is, the number of feet per minute obtained by multiplying the number of knots squared by 0.013) at an altitude of 1,000 feet above the highest ground or obstruction within 10 miles on each side of the intended track, or at an altitude of 5,000 feet, whichever is higher.

(b) For the purposes of paragraph (a)(2) of this section, it is assumed that—

(1) The two engines fail at the point that is most critical with respect to the takeoff weight;

(2) Consumption of fuel and oil is normal with all engines operating up to the point where the two engines fail with two engines operating beyond that point;

(3) Where the engines are assumed to fail at an altitude above the prescribed minimum altitude, compliance with the prescribed rate of climb at the prescribed minimum altitude need not be shown during the descent from the cruising altitude to the prescribed minimum altitude, if those requirements can be met once the prescribed minimum altitude is reached, and assuming descent to be along a net flight path and the rate of descent to be 0.013 Vs_o2 greater than the rate in the approved performance data; and

(4) If fuel jettisoning is provided, the airplane's weight at the point where the two engines fail is considered to be not less than that which would include enough fuel to proceed to an airport meeting §135.377 and to arrive at an altitude of at least 1,000 feet directly over that airport.

§135.375 Large transport category airplanes: Reciprocating engine powered: Landing limitations: Destination airports.

(a) Except as provided in paragraph (b) of this section, no person operating a reciprocating engine powered large transport category airplane may take off that airplane, unless its weight on arrival, allowing for normal consumption of fuel and oil in flight, would allow a full stop landing at the intended destination within 60 percent of the effective length of each runway described below from a point 50 feet directly above the intersection of the obstruction clearance plane and the runway. For the purposes of determining the allowable landing weight at the destination airport the following is assumed:

(1) The airplane is landed on the most favorable runway and in the most favorable direction in still air.

(2) The airplane is landed on the most suitable runway considering the probable wind velocity and direction (forecast for the expected time of arrival), the ground handling characteristics of the type of airplane, and other conditions such as landing aids and terrain, and allowing for the effect of the landing path and roll of not more than 50 percent of the headwind component or not less than 150 percent of the tailwind component.

(b) An airplane that would be prohibited from being taken off because it could not meet paragraph (a)(2) of this section may be taken off if an alternate airport is selected that meets all of this section except that the airplane can accomplish a full stop landing within 70 percent of the effective length of the runway.

§135.377 Large transport category airplanes: Reciprocating engine powered: Landing limitations: Alternate airports.

No person may list an airport as an alternate airport in a flight plan unless the airplane (at the weight anticipated at the time of arrival at the airport), based on the assumptions in §135.375(a) (1) and (2), can be brought to a full stop landing within 70 percent of the effective length of the runway.

§ 135.379 Large transport category airplanes: Turbine engine powered: Takeoff limitations.

(a) No person operating a turbine engine powered large transport category airplane may take off that airplane at a weight greater than that listed in the Airplane Flight Manual for the elevation of the airport and for the ambient temperature existing at take- off.

(b) No person operating a turbine engine powered large transport category airplane certificated after August 26, 1957, but before August 30, 1959 (SR422, 422A), may take off that airplane at a weight greater than that listed in the Airplane Flight Manual for the minimum distance required for takeoff. In the case of an airplane certificated after September 30, 1958 (SR422A, 422B), the takeoff distance may include a clearway distance but the clearway distance included may not be greater than one-half of the takeoff run.

(c) No person operating a turbine engine powered large transport category airplane certificated after August 29, 1959 (SR422B), may take off that airplane at a weight greater than that listed in the Airplane Flight Manual at which compliance with the following may be shown:

(1) The accelerate-stop distance, as defined in § 25.109 of this chapter, must not exceed the length of the runway plus the length of any stopway.

(2) The takeoff distance must not exceed the length of the runway plus the length of any clearway except that the length of any clearway included must not be greater than one-half the length of the runway.

(3) The takeoff run must not be greater than the length of the runway.

(d) No person operating a turbine engine powered large transport category airplane may take off that airplane at a weight greater than that listed in the Airplane Flight Manual—

(1) For an airplane certificated after August 26, 1957, but before October 1, 1958 (SR422), that allows a takeoff path that clears all obstacles either by at least (35 + 0.01 D) feet vertically (D is the distance along the intended flight path from the end of the runway in feet), or by at least 200 feet horizontally within the airport boundaries

and by at least 300 feet horizontally after passing the boundaries; or

(2) For an airplane certificated after September 30, 1958 (SR422A, 422B), that allows a net takeoff flight path that clears all obstacles either by a height of at least 35 feet vertically, or by at least 200 feet horizontally within the airport boundaries and by at least 300 feet horizontally after passing the boundaries.

(e) In determining maximum weights, minimum distances, and flight paths under paragraphs (a) through (d) of this section, correction must be made for the runway to be used, the elevation of the airport, the effective runway gradient, the ambient temperature and wind component at the time of takeoff, and, if operating limitations exist for the minimum distances required for takeoff from wet runways, the runway surface condition (dry or wet). Wet runway distances associated with grooved or porous friction course runways, if provided in the Airplane Flight Manual, may be used only for runways that are grooved or treated with a porous friction course (PFC) overlay, and that the operator determines are designed, constructed, and maintained in a manner acceptable to the Administrator.

(f) For the purposes of this section, it is assumed that the airplane is not banked before reaching a height of 50 feet, as shown by the takeoff path or net takeoff flight path data (as appropriate) in the Airplane Flight Manual, and after that the maximum bank is not more than 15 degrees.

(g) For the purposes of this section, the terms, *takeoff distance, takeoff run, net takeoff flight path,* have the same meanings as set forth in the rules under which the airplane was certificated.

[Doc. No. 16097, 43 FR 46783, Oct. 10, 1978, as amended by Amdt. 135–71, 63 FR 8321, Feb. 18, 1998]

§ 135.381 Large transport category airplanes: Turbine engine powered: En route limitations: One engine inoperative.

(a) No person operating a turbine engine powered large transport category airplane may take off that airplane at a weight, allowing for normal consumption of fuel and oil, that is greater than that which (under the approved, one engine inoperative, en route net flight path data in the Airplane Flight Manual for that airplane) will allow compliance with paragraph (a) (1) or (2) of this section, based on the ambient temperatures expected en route.

(1) There is a positive slope at an altitude of at least 1,000 feet above all terrain and obstructions within five statute miles on each side of the intended track, and, in addition, if that airplane was certificated after August 29, 1958 (SR422B), there is a positive slope at 1,500 feet above the airport where the airplane is assumed to land after an engine fails.

(2) The net flight path allows the airplane to continue flight from the cruising altitude to an airport where a landing can be made under § 135.387 clearing all terrain and obstructions within five statute miles of the intended track by at least 2,000 feet vertically and with a positive slope at 1,000 feet above the airport where the airplane lands after an engine fails, or, if that airplane was certificated after September 30, 1958 (SR422A, 422B), with a positive slope at 1,500 feet above the airport where the airplane lands after an engine fails.

(b) For the purpose of paragraph (a)(2) of this section, it is assumed that—

(1) The engine fails at the most critical point en route;

(2) The airplane passes over the critical obstruction, after engine failure at a point that is no closer to the obstruction than the approved navigation fix, unless the Administrator authorizes a different procedure based on adequate operational safeguards;

(3) An approved method is used to allow for adverse winds;

(4) Fuel jettisoning will be allowed if the certificate holder shows that the crew is properly instructed, that the training program is adequate, and that all other precautions are taken to ensure a safe procedure;

(5) The alternate airport is selected and meets the prescribed weather minimums; and

(6) The consumption of fuel and oil after engine failure is the same as the consumption that is allowed for in the

approved net flight path data in the Airplane Flight Manual.

[Doc. No. 16097, 43 FR 46783, Oct. 10, 1978, as amended by Amdt. 135–110, 72 FR 31685, June 7, 2007]

§ 135.383 Large transport category airplanes: Turbine engine powered: En route limitations: Two engines inoperative.

(a) Airplanes certificated after August 26, 1957, but before October 1, 1958 (SR422). No person may operate a turbine engine powered large transport category airplane along an intended route unless that person complies with either of the following:

(1) There is no place along the intended track that is more than 90 minutes (with all engines operating at cruising power) from an airport that meets § 135.387.

(2) Its weight, according to the two-engine-inoperative, en route, net flight path data in the Airplane Flight Manual, allows the airplane to fly from the point where the two engines are assumed to fail simultaneously to an airport that meets § 135.387, with a net flight path (considering the ambient temperature anticipated along the track) having a positive slope at an altitude of at least 1,000 feet above all terrain and obstructions within five statute miles on each side of the intended track, or at an altitude of 5,000 feet, whichever is higher.

For the purposes of paragraph (a)(2) of this section, it is assumed that the two engines fail at the most critical point en route, that if fuel jettisoning is provided, the airplane's weight at the point where the engines fail includes enough fuel to continue to the airport and to arrive at an altitude of at least 1,000 feet directly over the airport, and that the fuel and oil consumption after engine failure is the same as the consumption allowed for in the net flight path data in the Airplane Flight Manual.

(b) Airplanes certificated after September 30, 1958, but before August 30, 1959 (SR422A). No person may operate a turbine engine powered large transport category airplane along an intended route unless that person complies with either of the following:

491

(1) There is no place along the intended track that is more than 90 minutes (with all engines operating at cruising power) from an airport that meets § 135.387.

(2) Its weight, according to the two-engine-inoperative, en route, net flight path data in the Airplane Flight Manual allows the airplane to fly from the point where the two engines are assumed to fail simultaneously to an airport that meets § 135.387 with a net flight path (considering the ambient temperatures anticipated along the track) having a positive slope at an altitude of at least 1,000 feet above all terrain and obstructions within five statute miles on each side of the intended track, or at an altitude of 2,000 feet, whichever is higher.

For the purpose of paragraph (b)(2) of this section, it is assumed that the two engines fail at the most critical point en route, that the airplane's weight at the point where the engines fail includes enough fuel to continue to the airport, to arrive at an altitude of at least 1,500 feet directly over the airport, and after that to fly for 15 minutes at cruise power or thrust, or both, and that the consumption of fuel and oil after engine failure is the same as the consumption allowed for in the net flight path data in the Airplane Flight Manual.

(c) Aircraft certificated after August 29, 1959 (SR422B). No person may operate a turbine engine powered large transport category airplane along an intended route unless that person complies with either of the following:

(1) There is no place along the intended track that is more than 90 minutes (with all engines operating at cruising power) from an airport that meets § 135.387.

(2) Its weight, according to the two-engine-inoperative, en route, net flight path data in the Airplane Flight Manual, allows the airplane to fly from the point where the two engines are assumed to fail simultaneously to an airport that meets § 135.387, with the net flight path (considering the ambient temperatures anticipated along the track) clearing vertically by at least 2,000 feet all terrain and obstructions within five statute miles on each side

of the intended track. For the purposes of this paragraph, it is assumed that—

(i) The two engines fail at the most critical point en route;

(ii) The net flight path has a positive slope at 1,500 feet above the airport where the landing is assumed to be made after the engines fail;

(iii) Fuel jettisoning will be approved if the certificate holder shows that the crew is properly instructed, that the training program is adequate, and that all other precautions are taken to ensure a safe procedure;

(iv) The airplane's weight at the point where the two engines are assumed to fail provides enough fuel to continue to the airport, to arrive at an altitude of at least 1,500 feet directly over the airport, and after that to fly for 15 minutes at cruise power or thrust, or both; and

(v) The consumption of fuel and oil after the engines fail is the same as the consumption that is allowed for in the net flight path data in the Airplane Flight Manual.

§ 135.385 Large transport category airplanes: Turbine engine powered: Landing limitations: Destination airports.

(a) No person operating a turbine engine powered large transport category airplane may take off that airplane at a weight that (allowing for normal consumption of fuel and oil in flight to the destination or alternate airport) the weight of the airplane on arrival would exceed the landing weight in the Airplane Flight Manual for the elevation of the destination or alternate airport and the ambient temperature anticipated at the time of landing.

(b) Except as provided in paragraph (c), (d), (e), or (f) of this section, no person operating a turbine engine powered large transport category airplane may take off that airplane unless its weight on arrival, allowing for normal consumption of fuel and oil in flight (in accordance with the landing distance in the Airplane Flight Manual for the elevation of the destination airport and the wind conditions expected there at the time of landing), would allow a full stop landing at the intended destination airport within 60 percent of the effective length of each runway described below from a point 50 feet above the intersection of the obstruction clearance plane and the runway. For the purpose of determining the allowable landing weight at the destination airport the following is assumed:

(1) The airplane is landed on the most favorable runway and in the most favorable direction, in still air.

(2) The airplane is landed on the most suitable runway considering the probable wind velocity and direction and the ground handling characteristics of the airplane, and considering other conditions such as landing aids and terrain.

(c) A turbopropeller powered airplane that would be prohibited from being taken off because it could not meet paragraph (b)(2) of this section, may be taken off if an alternate airport is selected that meets all of this section except that the airplane can accomplish a full stop landing within 70 percent of the effective length of the runway.

(d) Unless, based on a showing of actual operating landing techniques on wet runways, a shorter landing distance (but never less than that required by paragraph (b) of this section) has been approved for a specific type and model airplane and included in the Airplane Flight Manual, no person may take off a turbojet airplane when the appropriate weather reports or forecasts, or any combination of them, indicate that the runways at the destination airport may be wet or slippery at the estimated time of arrival unless the effective runway length at the destination airport is at least 115 percent of the runway length required under paragraph (b) of this section.

(e) A turbojet airplane that would be prohibited from being taken off because it could not meet paragraph (b)(2) of this section may be taken off if an alternate airport is selected that meets all of paragraph (b) of this section.

(f) An eligible on-demand operator may take off a turbine engine powered large transport category airplane on an on-demand flight if all of the following conditions exist:

(1) The operation is permitted by an approved Destination Airport Analysis in that person's operations manual.

(2) The airplane's weight on arrival, allowing for normal consumption of fuel and oil in flight (in accordance with the landing distance in the Airplane Flight Manual for the elevation of the destination airport and the wind conditions expected there at the time of landing), would allow a full stop landing at the intended destination airport within 80 percent of the effective length of each runway described below from a point 50 feet above the intersection of the obstruction clearance plane and the runway. For the purpose of determining the allowable landing weight at the destination airport, the following is assumed:

(i) The airplane is landed on the most favorable runway and in the most favorable direction, in still air.

(ii) The airplane is landed on the most suitable runway considering the probable wind velocity and direction and the ground handling characteristics of the airplane, and considering other conditions such as landing aids and terrain.

(3) The operation is authorized by operations specifications.

[Doc. No. 16097, 43 FR 46783, Oct. 10, 1978, as amended by Amdt. 135-91, 68 FR 54588, Sept. 17, 2003]

§ 135.387 Large transport category airplanes: Turbine engine powered: Landing limitations: Alternate airports.

(a) Except as provided in paragraph (b) of this section, no person may select an airport as an alternate airport for a turbine engine powered large transport category airplane unless (based on the assumptions in § 135.385(b)) that airplane, at the weight expected at the time of arrival, can be brought to a full stop landing within 70 percent of the effective length of the runway for turbo-propeller-powered airplanes and 60 percent of the effective length of the runway for turbojet airplanes, from a point 50 feet above the intersection of the obstruction clearance plane and the runway.

(b) Eligible on-demand operators may select an airport as an alternate airport for a turbine engine powered large transport category airplane if (based on the assumptions in § 135.385(f)) that airplane, at the weight expected at the

493

time of arrival, can be brought to a full stop landing within 80 percent of the effective length of the runway from a point 50 feet above the intersection of the obstruction clearance plane and the runway.

[Doc. No. FAA–2001–10047, 68 FR 54588, Sept. 17, 2003]

§ 135.389 **Large nontransport category airplanes: Takeoff limitations.**

(a) No person operating a large nontransport category airplane may take off that airplane at a weight greater than the weight that would allow the airplane to be brought to a safe stop within the effective length of the runway, from any point during the takeoff before reaching 105 percent of minimum control speed (the minimum speed at which an airplane can be safely controlled in flight after an engine becomes inoperative) or 115 percent of the power off stalling speed in the takeoff configuration, whichever is greater.

(b) For the purposes of this section—

(1) It may be assumed that takeoff power is used on all engines during the acceleration;

(2) Not more than 50 percent of the reported headwind component, or not less than 150 percent of the reported tailwind component, may be taken into account;

(3) The average runway gradient (the difference between the elevations of the endpoints of the runway divided by the total length) must be considered if it is more than one-half of one percent;

(4) It is assumed that the airplane is operating in standard atmosphere; and

(5) For takeoff, *effective length of the runway* means the distance from the end of the runway at which the takeoff is started to a point at which the obstruction clearance plane associated with the other end of the runway intersects the runway centerline.

§ 135.391 **Large nontransport category airplanes: En route limitations: One engine inoperative.**

(a) Except as provided in paragraph (b) of this section, no person operating a large nontransport category airplane may take off that airplane at a weight that does not allow a rate of climb of at least 50 feet a minute, with the crit-

ical engine inoperative, at an altitude of at least 1,000 feet above the highest obstruction within five miles on each side of the intended track, or 5,000 feet, whichever is higher.

(b) Without regard to paragraph (a) of this section, if the Administrator finds that safe operations are not impaired, a person may operate the airplane at an altitude that allows the airplane, in case of engine failure, to clear all obstructions within five miles on each side of the intended track by 1,000 feet. If this procedure is used, the rate of descent for the appropriate weight and altitude is assumed to be 50 feet a minute greater than the rate in the approved performance data. Before approving such a procedure, the Administrator considers the following for the route, route segment, or area concerned:

(1) The reliability of wind and weather forecasting.

(2) The location and kinds of navigation aids.

(3) The prevailing weather conditions, particularly the frequency and amount of turbulence normally encountered.

(4) Terrain features.

(5) Air traffic problems.

(6) Any other operational factors that affect the operations.

(c) For the purposes of this section, it is assumed that—

(1) The critical engine is inoperative;

(2) The propeller of the inoperative engine is in the minimum drag position;

(3) The wing flaps and landing gear are in the most favorable position;

(4) The operating engines are operating at the maximum continuous power available;

(5) The airplane is operating in standard atmosphere; and

(6) The weight of the airplane is progressively reduced by the anticipated consumption of fuel and oil.

§ 135.393 **Large nontransport category airplanes: Landing limitations: Destination airports.**

(a) No person operating a large nontransport category airplane may take off that airplane at a weight that—

(1) Allowing for anticipated consumption of fuel and oil, is greater than the

weight that would allow a full stop landing within 60 percent of the effective length of the most suitable runway at the destination airport; and

(2) Is greater than the weight allowable if the landing is to be made on the runway—

(i) With the greatest effective length in still air; and

(ii) Required by the probable wind, taking into account not more than 50 percent of the headwind component or not less than 150 percent of the tailwind component.

(b) For the purpose of this section, it is assumed that—

(1) The airplane passes directly over the intersection of the obstruction clearance plane and the runway at a height of 50 feet in a steady gliding approach at a true indicated airspeed of at least 1.3 V_{so};

(2) The landing does not require exceptional pilot skill; and

(3) The airplane is operating in standard atmosphere.

§135.395 Large nontransport category airplanes: Landing limitations: Alternate airports.

No person may select an airport as an alternate airport for a large nontransport category airplane unless that airplane (at the weight anticipated at the time of arrival), based on the assumptions in §135.393(b), can be brought to a full stop landing within 70 percent of the effective length of the runway.

§135.397 Small transport category airplane performance operating limitations.

(a) No person may operate a reciprocating engine powered small transport category airplane unless that person complies with the weight limitations in §135.365, the takeoff limitations in §135.367 (except paragraph (a)(3)), and the landing limitations in §§135.375 and 135.377.

(b) No person may operate a turbine engine powered small transport category airplane unless that person complies with the takeoff limitations in §135.379 (except paragraphs (d) and (f)) and the landing limitations in §§135.385 and 135.387.

§135.398 Commuter category airplanes performance operating limitations.

(a) No person may operate a commuter category airplane unless that person complies with the takeoff weight limitations in the approved Airplane Flight Manual.

(b) No person may take off an airplane type certificated in the commuter category at a weight greater than that listed in the Airplane Flight Manual that allows a net takeoff flight path that clears all obstacles either by a height of at least 35 feet vertically, or at least 200 feet horizontally within the airport boundaries and by at least 300 feet horizontally after passing the boundaries.

(c) No person may operate a commuter category airplane unless that person complies with the landing limitations prescribed in §§135.385 and 135.387 of this part. For purposes of this paragraph, §§135.385 and 135.387 are applicable to all commuter category airplanes notwithstanding their stated applicability to turbine-engine-powered large transport category airplanes.

(d) In determining maximum weights, minimum distances and flight paths under paragraphs (a) through (c) of this section, correction must be made for the runway to be used, the elevation of the airport, the effective runway gradient, and ambient temperature, and wind component at the time of takeoff.

(e) For the purposes of this section, the assumption is that the airplane is not banked before reaching a height of 50 feet as shown by the net takeoff flight path data in the Airplane Flight Manual and thereafter the maximum bank is not more than 15 degrees.

[Doc. No. 23516, 52 FR 1836, Jan. 15, 1987]

§135.399 Small nontransport category airplane performance operating limitations.

(a) No person may operate a reciprocating engine or turbopropeller-powered small airplane that is certificated under §135.169(b) (2), (3), (4), (5), or (6) unless that person complies with the takeoff weight limitations in the approved Airplane Flight Manual or equivalent for operations under this part, and, if the airplane is certificated under §135.169(b) (4) or (5) with the landing weight limitations in the Approved Airplane Flight Manual or equivalent for operations under this part.

(b) No person may operate an airplane that is certificated under § 135.169(b)(6) unless that person complies with the landing limitations prescribed in §§ 135.385 and 135.387 of this part. For purposes of this paragraph, §§ 135.385 and 135.387 are applicable to reciprocating and turbopropeller-powered small airplanes notwithstanding their stated applicability to turbine engine powered large transport category airplanes.

[44 FR 53731, Sept. 17, 1979]

Subpart J—Maintenance, Preventive Maintenance, and Alterations

§ 135.411   Applicability.

(a) This subpart prescribes rules in addition to those in other parts of this chapter for the maintenance, preventive maintenance, and alterations for each certificate holder as follows:

(1) Aircraft that are type certificated for a passenger seating configuration, excluding any pilot seat, of nine seats or less, shall be maintained under parts 91 and 43 of this chapter and §§ 135.415, 135.417, 135.421 and 135.422. An approved aircraft inspection program may be used under § 135.419.

(2) Aircraft that are type certificated for a passenger seating configuration, excluding any pilot seat, of ten seats or more, shall be maintained under a maintenance program in §§ 135.415, 135.417, 135.423 through 135.443.

(b) A certificate holder who is not otherwise required, may elect to maintain its aircraft under paragraph (a)(2) of this section.

(c) Single engine aircraft used in passenger-carrying IFR operations shall also be maintained in accordance with § 135.421 (c), (d), and (e).

(d) A certificate holder who elects to operate in accordance with § 135.364 must maintain its aircraft under paragraph (a)(2) of this section and the ad-

ditional requirements of Appendix G of this part.

[Doc. No. 16097, 43 FR 46783, Oct. 10, 1978, as amended by Amdt. 135–70, 62 FR 42374, Aug. 6, 1997; Amdt. 135–78, 65 FR 60556, Oct. 11, 2000; Amdt. 135–92, 68 FR 69308, Dec. 12, 2003; Amdt. 135–81, 70 FR 5533, Feb. 2, 2005; Amdt. 135–108, 72 FR 1885, Jan. 16, 2007; 72 FR 53114, Sept. 18, 2007]

§ 135.413   Responsibility for airworthiness.

(a) Each certificate holder is primarily responsible for the airworthiness of its aircraft, including airframes, aircraft engines, propellers, rotors, appliances, and parts, and shall have its aircraft maintained under this chapter, and shall have defects repaired between required maintenance under part 43 of this chapter.

(b) Each certificate holder who maintains its aircraft under § 135.411(a)(2) shall—

(1) Perform the maintenance, preventive maintenance, and alteration of its aircraft, including airframe, aircraft engines, propellers, rotors, appliances, emergency equipment and parts, under its manual and this chapter; or

(2) Make arrangements with another person for the performance of maintenance, preventive maintenance, or alteration. However, the certificate holder shall ensure that any maintenance, preventive maintenance, or alteration that is performed by another person is performed under the certificate holder's manual and this chapter.

§ 135.415   Service difficulty reports.

(a) Each certificate holder shall report the occurrence or detection of each failure, malfunction, or defect in an aircraft concerning—

(1) Fires during flight and whether the related fire-warning system functioned properly;

(2) Fires during flight not protected by related fire-warning system;

(3) False fire-warning during flight;

(4) An exhaust system that causes damage during flight to the engine, adjacent structure, equipment, or components;

(5) An aircraft component that causes accumulation or circulation of smoke, vapor, or toxic or noxious

fumes in the crew compartment or passenger cabin during flight;

(6) Engine shutdown during flight because of flameout;

(7) Engine shutdown during flight when external damage to the engine or aircraft structure occurs

(8) Engine shutdown during flight due to foreign object ingestion or icing;

(9) Shutdown of more than one engine during flight;

(10) A propeller feathering system or ability of the system to control overspeed during flight;

(11) A fuel or fuel-dumping system that affects fuel flow or causes hazardous leakage during flight;

(12) An unwanted landing gear extension or retraction or opening or closing of landing gear doors during flight;

(13) Brake system components that result in loss of brake actuating force when the aircraft is in motion on the ground;

(14) Aircraft structure that requires major repair;

(15) Cracks, permanent deformation, or corrosion of aircraft structures, if more than the maximum acceptable to the manufacturer or the FAA; and

(16) Aircraft components or systems that result in taking emergency actions during flight (except action to shut-down an engine).

(b) For the purpose of this section, *during flight* means the period from the moment the aircraft leaves the surface of the earth on takeoff until it touches down on landing.

(c) In addition to the reports required by paragraph (a) of this section, each certificate holder shall report any other failure, malfunction, or defect in an aircraft that occurs or is detected at any time if, in its opinion, the failure, malfunction, or defect has endangered or may endanger the safe operation of the aircraft.

(d) Each certificate holder shall submit each report required by this section, covering each 24-hour period beginning at 0900 local time of each day and ending at 0900 local time on the next day, to the FAA offices in Oklahoma City, Oklahoma. Each report of occurrences during a 24-hour period shall be submitted to the collection point within the next 96 hours. However, a report due on Saturday or Sunday may be submitted on the following Monday, and a report due on a holiday may be submitted on the next workday.

(e) The certificate holder shall transmit the reports required by this section on a form and in a manner prescribed by the Administrator, and shall include as much of the following as is available:

(1) The type and identification number of the aircraft.

(2) The name of the operator.

(3) The date.

(4) The nature of the failure, malfunction, or defect.

(5) Identification of the part and system involved, including available information pertaining to type designation of the major component and time since last overhaul, if known.

(6) Apparent cause of the failure, malfunction or defect (e.g., wear, crack, design deficiency, or personnel error).

(7) Other pertinent information necessary for more complete identification, determination of seriousness, or corrective action.

(f) A certificate holder that is also the holder of a type certificate (including a supplemental type certificate), a Parts Manufacturer Approval, or a Technical Standard Order Authorization, or that is the licensee of a type certificate need not report a failure, malfunction, or defect under this section if the failure, malfunction, or defect has been reported by it under §21.3 or §37.17 of this chapter or under the accident reporting provisions of part 830 of the regulations of the National Transportation Safety Board.

(g) No person may withhold a report required by this section even though all information required by this section is not available.

(h) When the certificate holder gets additional information, including information from the manufacturer or other agency, concerning a report required by this section, it shall expeditiously submit it as a supplement to the first report and reference the date and place of submission of the first report.

[Doc. No. 16097, 43 FR 46783, Oct. 10, 1978, as amended by Amdt. 135–102, 70 FR 76979, Dec. 29, 2005]

§ 135.417 Mechanical interruption summary report.

Each certificate holder shall mail or deliver, before the end of the 10th day of the following month, a summary report of the following occurrences in multiengine aircraft for the preceding month to the responsible Flight Standards office:

(a) Each interruption to a flight, unscheduled change of aircraft en route, or unscheduled stop or diversion from a route, caused by known or suspected mechanical difficulties or malfunctions that are not required to be reported under § 135.415.

(b) The number of propeller featherings in flight, listed by type of propeller and engine and aircraft on which it was installed. Propeller featherings for training, demonstration, or flight check purposes need not be reported.

[Doc. No. 16097, 43 FR 46783, Oct. 10, 1978, as amended by Amdt. 135–60, 61 FR 2616, Jan. 26, 1996; Docket FAA–2018–0119, Amdt. 135–139, 83 FR 9175, Mar. 5, 2018]

§ 135.419 Approved aircraft inspection program.

(a) Whenever the Administrator finds that the aircraft inspections required or allowed under part 91 of this chapter are not adequate to meet this part, or upon application by a certificate holder, the Administrator may amend the certificate holder's operations specifications under § 119.51, to require or allow an approved aircraft inspection program for any make and model aircraft of which the certificate holder has the exclusive use of at least one aircraft (as defined in § 135.25(b)).

(b) A certificate holder who applies for an amendment of its operations specifications to allow an approved aircraft inspection program must submit that program with its application for approval by the Administrator.

(c) Each certificate holder who is required by its operations specifications to have an approved aircraft inspection program shall submit a program for approval by the Administrator within 30 days of the amendment of its operations specifications or within any other period that the Administrator may prescribe in the operations specifications.

(d) The aircraft inspection program submitted for approval by the Administrator must contain the following:

(1) Instructions and procedures for the conduct of aircraft inspections (which must include necessary tests and checks), setting forth in detail the parts and areas of the airframe, engines, propellers, rotors, and appliances, including emergency equipment, that must be inspected.

(2) A schedule for the performance of the aircraft inspections under paragraph (d)(1) of this section expressed in terms of the time in service, calendar time, number of system operations, or any combination of these.

(3) Instructions and procedures for recording discrepancies found during inspections and correction or deferral of discrepancies including form and disposition of records.

(e) After approval, the certificate holder shall include the approved aircraft inspection program in the manual required by § 135.21.

(f) Whenever the Administrator finds that revisions to an approved aircraft inspection program are necessary for the continued adequacy of the program, the certificate holder shall, after notification by the Administrator, make any changes in the program found by the Administrator to be necessary. The certificate holder may petition the Administrator to reconsider the notice to make any changes in a program. The petition must be filed with the representatives of the Administrator assigned to it within 30 days after the certificate holder receives the notice. Except in the case of an emergency requiring immediate action in the interest of safety, the filing of the petition stays the notice pending a decision by the Administrator.

(g) Each certificate holder who has an approved aircraft inspection program shall have each aircraft that is subject to the program inspected in accordance with the program.

(h) The registration number of each aircraft that is subject to an approved aircraft inspection program must be included in the operations specifications of the certificate holder.

[Doc. No. 16097, 43 FR 46783, Oct. 10, 1978, as amended by Amdt. 135–104, 71 FR 536, Jan. 4, 2006]

§135.421 Additional maintenance requirements.

(a) Each certificate holder who operates an aircraft type certificated for a passenger seating configuration, excluding any pilot seat, of nine seats or less, must comply with the manufacturer's recommended maintenance programs, or a program approved by the Administrator, for each aircraft engine, propeller, rotor, and each item of emergency equipment required by this chapter.

(b) For the purpose of this section, a manufacturer's maintenance program is one which is contained in the maintenance manual or maintenance instructions set forth by the manufacturer as required by this chapter for the aircraft, aircraft engine, propeller, rotor or item of emergency equipment.

(c) For each single engine aircraft to be used in passenger-carrying IFR operations, each certificate holder must incorporate into its maintenance program either:

(1) The manufacturer's recommended engine trend monitoring program, which includes an oil analysis, if appropriate, or

(2) An FAA approved engine trend monitoring program that includes an oil analysis at each 100 hour interval or at the manufacturer's suggested interval, whichever is more frequent.

(d) For single engine aircraft to be used in passenger-carrying IFR operations, written maintenance instructions containing the methods, techniques, and practices necessary to maintain the equipment specified in §§135.105, and 135.163 (f) and (h) are required.

(e) No certificate holder may operate a single engine aircraft under IFR, carrying passengers, unless the certificate holder records and maintains in the engine maintenance records the results of each test, observation, and inspection required by the applicable engine trend monitoring program specified in (c) (1) and (2) of this section.

[Doc. No. 16097, 43 FR 46783, Oct. 10, 1978, as amended by Amdt. 135–70, 62 FR 42374, Aug. 6, 1997]

§135.422 Aging airplane inspections and records reviews for multiengine airplanes certificated with nine or fewer passenger seats.

(a) *Applicability.* This section applies to multiengine airplanes certificated with nine or fewer passenger seats, operated by a certificate holder in a scheduled operation under this part, except for those airplanes operated by a certificate holder in a scheduled operation between any point within the State of Alaska and any other point within the State of Alaska.

(b) *Operation after inspections and records review.* After the dates specified in this paragraph, a certificate holder may not operate a multiengine airplane in a scheduled operation under this part unless the Administrator has notified the certificate holder that the Administrator has completed the aging airplane inspection and records review required by this section. During the inspection and records review, the certificate holder must demonstrate to the Administrator that the maintenance of age-sensitive parts and components of the airplane has been adequate and timely enough to ensure the highest degree of safety.

(1) *Airplanes exceeding 24 years in service on December 8, 2003; initial and repetitive inspections and records reviews.* For an airplane that has exceeded 24 years in service on December 8, 2003, no later than December 5, 2007, and thereafter at intervals not to exceed 7 years.

(2) *Airplanes exceeding 14 years in service but not 24 years in service on December 8, 2003; initial and repetitive inspections and records reviews.* For an airplane that has exceeded 14 years in service, but not 24 years in service, on December 8, 2003, no later than December 4, 2008, and thereafter at intervals not to exceed 7 years.

(3) *Airplanes not exceeding 14 years in service on December 8, 2003; initial and repetitive inspections and records reviews.* For an airplane that has not exceeded 14 years in service on December 8, 2003, no later than 5 years after the start of the airplane's 15th year in service and thereafter at intervals not to exceed 7 years.

(c) *Unforeseen schedule conflict.* In the event of an unforeseen scheduling conflict for a specific airplane, the Administrator may approve an extension of up to 90 days beyond an interval specified in paragraph (b) of this section.

(d) *Airplane and records availability.* The certificate holder must make available to the Administrator each airplane for which an inspection and records review is required under this section, in a condition for inspection specified by the Administrator, together with the records containing the following information:

(1) Total years in service of the airplane;

(2) Total time in service of the airframe;

(3) Date of the last inspection and records review required by this section;

(4) Current status of life-limited parts of the airframe;

(5) Time since the last overhaul of all structural components required to be overhauled on a specific time basis;

(6) Current inspection status of the airplane, including the time since the last inspection required by the inspection program under which the airplane is maintained;

(7) Current status of applicable airworthiness directives, including the date and methods of compliance, and, if the airworthiness directive involves recurring action, the time and date when the next action is required;

(8) A list of major structural alterations; and

(9) A report of major structural repairs and the current inspection status for these repairs.

(e) *Notification to the Administrator.* Each certificate holder must notify the Administrator at least 60 days before the date on which the airplane and airplane records will be made available for the inspection and records review.

[Doc. No. FAA-1999-5401, 70 FR 5533, Feb. 2, 2005]

§ 135.423 Maintenance, preventive maintenance, and alteration organization.

(a) Each certificate holder that performs any of its maintenance (other than required inspections), preventive maintenance, or alterations, and each person with whom it arranges for the performance of that work, must have an organization adequate to perform the work.

(b) Each certificate holder that performs any inspections required by its manual under § 135.427(b) (2) or (3), (in this subpart referred to as *required inspections*), and each person with whom it arranges for the performance of that work, must have an organization adequate to perform that work.

(c) Each person performing required inspections in addition to other maintenance, preventive maintenance, or alterations, shall organize the performance of those functions so as to separate the required inspection functions from the other maintenance, preventive maintenance, and alteration functions. The separation shall be below the level of administrative control at which overall responsibility for the required inspection functions and other maintenance, preventive maintenance, and alteration functions is exercised.

[Doc. No. 16097, 43 FR 46783, Oct. 10, 1978. Redesignated by Amdt. 135–81, 67 FR 72765, Dec. 6, 2002. Redesignated by Amdt. 135–81, 70 FR 5533, Feb. 2, 2005]

§ 135.425 Maintenance, preventive maintenance, and alteration programs.

Each certificate holder shall have an inspection program and a program covering other maintenance, preventive maintenance, and alterations, that ensures that—

(a) Maintenance, preventive maintenance, and alterations performed by it, or by other persons, are performed under the certificate holder's manual;

(b) Competent personnel and adequate facilities and equipment are provided for the proper performance of maintenance, preventive maintenance, and alterations; and

(c) Each aircraft released to service is airworthy and has been properly maintained for operation under this part.

§ 135.426 Contract maintenance.

(a) A certificate holder may arrange with another person for the performance of maintenance, preventive maintenance, and alterations as authorized in § 135.437(a) only if the certificate holder has met all the requirements in this section. For purposes of this section—

(1) A *maintenance provider* is any person who performs maintenance, preventive maintenance, or an alteration for a certificate holder other than a person who is trained by and employed directly by that certificate holder.

(2) *Covered work* means any of the following:

(i) Essential maintenance that could result in a failure, malfunction, or defect endangering the safe operation of an aircraft if not performed properly or if improper parts or materials are used;

(ii) Regularly scheduled maintenance; or

(iii) A required inspection item on an aircraft.

(3) *Directly in charge* means having responsibility for covered work performed by a maintenance provider. A representative of the certificate holder directly in charge of covered work does not need to physically observe and direct each maintenance provider constantly, but must be available for consultation on matters requiring instruction or decision.

(b) Each certificate holder must be directly in charge of all covered work done for it by a maintenance provider.

(c) Each maintenance provider must perform all covered work in accordance with the certificate holder's maintenance manual.

(d) No maintenance provider may perform covered work unless that work is carried out under the supervision and control of the certificate holder.

(e) Each certificate holder who contracts for maintenance, preventive maintenance, or alterations must develop and implement policies, procedures, methods, and instructions for the accomplishment of all contracted maintenance, preventive maintenance, and alterations. These policies, procedures, methods, and instructions must provide for the maintenance, preventive maintenance, and alterations to be performed in accordance with the certificate holder's maintenance program and maintenance manual.

(f) Each certificate holder who contracts for maintenance, preventive maintenance, or alterations must ensure that its system for the continuing analysis and surveillance of the main-

tenance, preventive maintenance, and alterations carried out by a maintenance provider, as required by §135.431(a), contains procedures for oversight of all contracted covered work.

(g) The policies, procedures, methods, and instructions required by paragraphs (e) and (f) of this section must be acceptable to the FAA and included in the certificate holder's maintenance manual, as required by §135.427(b)(10).

(h) Each certificate holder who contracts for maintenance, preventive maintenance, or alterations must provide to its responsible Flight Standards office, in a format acceptable to the FAA, a list that includes the name and physical (street) address, or addresses, where the work is carried out for each maintenance provider that performs work for the certificate holder, and a description of the type of maintenance, preventive maintenance, or alteration that is to be performed at each location. The list must be updated with any changes, including additions or deletions, and the updated list provided to the FAA in a format acceptable to the FAA by the last day of each calendar month.

[Docket FAA–2011–1136, Amdt. 135–132, 80 FR 11547, Mar. 4, 2015, as amended by Docket FAA–2018–0119, Amdt. 135–139, 83 FR 9175, Mar. 5, 2018]

§135.427 Manual requirements.

(a) Each certificate holder shall put in its manual the chart or description of the certificate holder's organization required by §135.423 and a list of persons with whom it has arranged for the performance of any of its required inspections, other maintenance, preventive maintenance, or alterations, including a general description of that work.

(b) Each certificate holder shall put in its manual the programs required by §135.425 that must be followed in performing maintenance, preventive maintenance, and alterations of that certificate holder's aircraft, including airframes, aircraft engines, propellers, rotors, appliances, emergency equipment, and parts, and must include at least the following:

(1) The method of performing routine and nonroutine maintenance (other

than required inspections), preventive maintenance, and alterations.

(2) A designation of the items of maintenance and alteration that must be inspected (required inspections) including at least those that could result in a failure, malfunction, or defect endangering the safe operation of the aircraft, if not performed properly or if improper parts or materials are used.

(3) The method of performing required inspections and a designation by occupational title of personnel authorized to perform each required inspection.

(4) Procedures for the reinspection of work performed under previous required inspection findings (*buy-back procedures*).

(5) Procedures, standards, and limits necessary for required inspections and acceptance or rejection of the items required to be inspected and for periodic inspection and calibration of precision tools, measuring devices, and test equipment.

(6) Procedures to ensure that all required inspections are performed.

(7) Instructions to prevent any person who performs any item of work from performing any required inspection of that work.

(8) Instructions and procedures to prevent any decision of an inspector regarding any required inspection from being countermanded by persons other than supervisory personnel of the inspection unit, or a person at the level of administrative control that has overall responsibility for the management of both the required inspection functions and the other maintenance, preventive maintenance, and alterations functions.

(9) Procedures to ensure that required inspections, other maintenance, preventive maintenance, and alterations that are not completed as a result of work interruptions are properly completed before the aircraft is released to service.

(10) Policies, procedures, methods, and instructions for the accomplishment of all maintenance, preventive maintenance, and alterations carried out by a maintenance provider. These policies, procedures, methods, and instructions must be acceptable to the FAA and ensure that, when followed by the maintenance provider, the maintenance, preventive maintenance, and alterations are performed in accordance with the certificate holder's maintenance program and maintenance manual.

(c) Each certificate holder shall put in its manual a suitable system (which may include a coded system) that provides for the retention of the following information—

(1) A description (or reference to data acceptable to the Administrator) of the work performed;

(2) The name of the person performing the work if the work is performed by a person outside the organization of the certificate holder; and

(3) The name or other positive identification of the individual approving the work.

(d) For the purposes of this part, the certificate holder must prepare that part of its manual containing maintenance information and instructions, in whole or in part, in printed form or other form, acceptable to the Administrator, that is retrievable in the English language.

[Doc. No. 16097, 43 FR 46783, Oct. 10, 1978, as amended by Amdt. 135–66, 62 FR 13257, Mar. 19, 1997; 69 FR 18472, Apr. 8, 2004; Amdt. 135–118, 74 FR 38522, Aug. 4, 2009; Docket FAA–2011–1136, Amdt. 135–132, 80 FR 11547, Mar. 4, 2015]

§ 135.429 Required inspection personnel.

(a) No person may use any person to perform required inspections unless the person performing the inspection is appropriately certificated, properly trained, qualified, and authorized to do so.

(b) No person may allow any person to perform a required inspection unless, at the time, the person performing that inspection is under the supervision and control of an inspection unit.

(c) No person may perform a required inspection if that person performed the item of work required to be inspected.

(d) In the case of rotorcraft that operate in remote areas or sites, the Administrator may approve procedures for the performance of required inspection items by a pilot when no other

qualified person is available, provided—

(1) The pilot is employed by the certificate holder;

(2) It can be shown to the satisfaction
of the Administrator that each pilot
authorized to perform required inspections is properly trained and qualified;

(3) The required inspection is a result
of a mechanical interruption and is not
a part of a certificate holder's continuous airworthiness maintenance program;

(4) Each item is inspected after each
flight until the item has been inspected
by an appropriately certificated mechanic other than the one who originally performed the item of work; and

(5) Each item of work that is a required inspection item that is part of
the flight control system shall be flight
tested and reinspected before the aircraft is approved for return to service.

(e) Each certificate holder shall
maintain, or shall determine that each
person with whom it arranges to perform its required inspections maintains, a current listing of persons who
have been trained, qualified, and authorized to conduct required inspections. The persons must be identified
by name, occupational title and the inspections that they are authorized to
perform. The certificate holder (or person with whom it arranges to perform
its required inspections) shall give
written information to each person so
authorized, describing the extent of
that person's responsibilities, authorities, and inspectional limitations. The
list shall be made available for inspection by the Administrator upon request.

[Doc. No. 16097, 43 FR 46783, Oct. 10, 1973, as
amended by Amdt. 135–20, 51 FR 40710, Nov. 7,
1986]

§135.431 **Continuing analysis and surveillance.**

(a) Each certificate holder shall establish and maintain a system for the
continuing analysis and surveillance of
the performance and effectiveness of
its inspection program and the program covering other maintenance, preventive maintenance, and alterations
and for the correction of any deficiency
in those programs, regardless of whether those programs are carried out by

the certificate holder or by another
person.

(b) Whenever the Administrator finds
that either or both of the programs described in paragraph (a) of this section
does not contain adequate procedures
and standards to meet this part, the
certificate holder shall, after notification by the Administrator, make
changes in those programs requested
by the Administrator.

(c) A certificate holder may petition
the Administrator to reconsider the
notice to make a change in a program.
The petition must be filed with the responsible Flight Standards office within 30 days after the certificate holder
receives the notice. Except in the case
of an emergency requiring immediate
action in the interest of safety, the filing of the petition stays the notice
pending a decision by the Administrator.

[Doc. No. 16097, 43 FR 46783, Oct. 10, 1978, as
amended by Amdt. 135–60, 61 FR 2617, Jan. 26,
1996; Docket FAA–2018–0119, Amdt. 135–139, 83
FR 9175, Mar. 5, 2018]

§135.433 **Maintenance and preventive
maintenance training program.**

Each certificate holder or a person
performing maintenance or preventive
maintenance functions for it shall have
a training program to ensure that each
person (including inspection personnel)
who determines the adequacy of work
done is fully informed about procedures
and techniques and new equipment in
use and is competent to perform that
person's duties.

§135.435 **Certificate requirements.**

(a) Except for maintenance, preventive maintenance, alterations, and required inspections performed by a certificated repair station that is located
outside the United States, each person
who is directly in charge of maintenance, preventive maintenance, or alterations, and each person performing
required inspections must hold an appropriate airman certificate.

(b) For the purpose of this section, a
person *directly in charge* is each person
assigned to a position in which that
person is responsible for the work of a

503

shop or station that performs maintenance, preventive maintenance, alterations, or other functions affecting airworthiness. A person who is *directly in charge* need not physically observe and direct each worker constantly but must be available for consultation and decision on matters requiring instruction or decision from higher authority than that of the person performing the work.

[Doc. No. 16097, 43 FR 46783, Oct. 10, 1978, as amended by Amdt. 135–82, 66 FR 41117, Aug. 6, 2001]

§ 135.437 Authority to perform and approve maintenance, preventive maintenance, and alterations.

(a) A certificate holder may perform or make arrangements with other persons to perform maintenance, preventive maintenance, and alterations as provided in its maintenance manual. In addition, a certificate holder may perform these functions for another certificate holder as provided in the maintenance manual of the other certificate holder.

(b) A certificate holder may approve any airframe, aircraft engine, propeller, rotor, or appliance for return to service after maintenance, preventive maintenance, or alterations that are performed under paragraph (a) of this section. However, in the case of a major repair or alteration, the work must have been done in accordance with technical data approved by the Administrator.

§ 135.439 Maintenance recording requirements.

(a) Each certificate holder shall keep (using the system specified in the manual required in § 135.427) the following records for the periods specified in paragraph (b) of this section:

(1) All the records necessary to show that all requirements for the issuance of an airworthiness release under § 135.443 have been met.

(2) Records containing the following information:

(i) The total time in service of the airframe, engine, propeller, and rotor.

(ii) The current status of life-limited parts of each airframe, engine, propeller, rotor, and appliance.

(iii) The time since last overhaul of each item installed on the aircraft which are required to be overhauled on a specified time basis.

(iv) The identification of the current inspection status of the aircraft, including the time since the last inspections required by the inspection program under which the aircraft and its appliances are maintained.

(v) The current status of applicable airworthiness directives, including the date and methods of compliance, and, if the airworthiness directive involves recurring action, the time and date when the next action is required.

(vi) A list of current major alterations and repairs to each airframe, engine, propeller, rotor, and appliance.

(b) Each certificate holder shall retain the records required to be kept by this section for the following periods:

(1) Except for the records of the last complete overhaul of each airframe, engine, propeller, rotor, and appliance the records specified in paragraph (a)(1) of this section shall be retained until the work is repeated or superseded by other work or for one year after the work is performed.

(2) The records of the last complete overhaul of each airframe, engine, propeller, rotor, and appliance shall be retained until the work is superseded by work of equivalent scope and detail.

(3) The records specified in paragraph (a)(2) of this section shall be retained and transferred with the aircraft at the time the aircraft is sold.

(c) The certificate holder shall make all maintenance records required to be kept by this section available for inspection by the Administrator or any representative of the National Transportation Safety Board.

[Doc. No. 16097, 43 FR 46783, Oct. 10, 1978; 43 FR 49975, Oct. 26, 1978]

§ 135.441 Transfer of maintenance records.

Each certificate holder who sells a United States registered aircraft shall transfer to the purchaser, at the time of the sale, the following records of that aircraft, in plain language form or in coded form which provides for the preservation and retrieval of information in a manner acceptable to the Administrator:

(a) The records specified in §135.439(a)(2).

(b) The records specified in §135.439(a)(1) which are not included in the records covered by paragraph (a) of this section, except that the purchaser may allow the seller to keep physical custody of such records. However, custody of records by the seller does not relieve the purchaser of its responsibility under §135.439(c) to make the records available for inspection by the Administrator or any representative of the National Transportation Safety Board.

§135.443 Airworthiness release or aircraft maintenance log entry.

(a) No certificate holder may operate an aircraft after maintenance, preventive maintenance, or alterations are performed on the aircraft unless the certificate holder prepares, or causes the person with whom the certificate holder arranges for the performance of the maintenance, preventive maintenance, or alterations, to prepare—

(1) An airworthiness release; or

(2) An appropriate entry in the aircraft maintenance log.

(b) The airworthiness release or log entry required by paragraph (a) of this section must—

(1) Be prepared in accordance with the procedure in the certificate holder's manual;

(2) Include a certification that—

(i) The work was performed in accordance with the requirements of the certificate holder's manual;

(ii) All items required to be inspected were inspected by an authorized person who determined that the work was satisfactorily completed;

(iii) No known condition exists that would make the aircraft unairworthy; and

(iv) So far as the work performed is concerned, the aircraft is in condition for safe operation; and

(3) Be signed by an authorized certificated mechanic or repairman, except that a certificated repairman may sign the release or entry only for the work for which that person is employed and for which that person is certificated.

(c) Notwithstanding paragraph (b)(3) of this section, after maintenance, preventive maintenance, or alterations performed by a repair station located outside the United States , the airworthiness release or log entry required by paragraph (a) of this section may be signed by a person authorized by that repair station.

(d) Instead of restating each of the conditions of the certification required by paragraph (b) of this section, the certificate holder may state in its manual that the signature of an authorized certificated mechanic or repairman constitutes that certification.

[Doc. No. 16097, 43 FR 46783, Oct. 10, 1978, as amended by Amdt. 135–29, 53 FR 47375, Nov. 22, 1988; Amdt. 135–82, 66 FR 41117, Aug. 6, 2001]

Subpart K—Hazardous Materials Training Program

SOURCE: Docket No. FAA–2003–15085, 70 FR 58829, Oct. 7, 2005, unless otherwise noted.

§135.501 Applicability and definitions.

(a) This subpart prescribes the requirements applicable to each certificate holder for training each crewmember and person performing or directly supervising any of the following job functions involving any item for transport on board an aircraft:

(1) Acceptance;

(2) Rejection;

(3) Handling;

(4) Storage incidental to transport;

(5) Packaging of company material; or

(6) Loading.

(b) *Definitions.* For purposes of this subpart, the following definitions apply:

(1) *Company material (COMAT)*—Material owned or used by a certificate holder.

(2) *Initial hazardous materials training*—The basic training required for each newly hired person, or each person changing job functions, who performs or directly supervises any of the job functions specified in paragraph (a) of this section.

(3) *Recurrent hazardous materials training*—The training required every 24 months for each person who has satisfactorily completed the certificate holder's approved initial hazardous materials training program and performs or directly supervises any of the job

functions specified in paragraph (a) of this section.

§ 135.503 Hazardous materials training: General.

(a) Each certificate holder must establish and implement a hazardous materials training program that:

(1) Satisfies the requirements of Appendix O of part 121 of this part;

(2) Ensures that each person performing or directly supervising any of the job functions specified in § 135.501(a) is trained to comply with all applicable parts of 49 CFR parts 171 through 180 and the requirements of this subpart; and

(3) Enables the trained person to recognize items that contain, or may contain, hazardous materials regulated by 49 CFR parts 171 through 180.

(b) Each certificate holder must provide initial hazardous materials training and recurrent hazardous materials training to each crewmember and person performing or directly supervising any of the job functions specified in § 135.501(a).

(c) Each certificate holder's hazardous materials training program must be approved by the FAA prior to implementation.

§ 135.505 Hazardous materials training required.

(a) *Training requirement.* Except as provided in paragraphs (b), (c) and (f) of this section, no certificate holder may use any crewmember or person to perform any of the job functions or direct supervisory responsibilities, and no person may perform any of the job functions or direct supervisory responsibilities, specified in § 135.501(a) unless that person has satisfactorily completed the certificate holder's FAA-approved initial or recurrent hazardous materials training program within the past 24 months.

(b) *New hire or new job function.* A person who is a new hire and has not yet satisfactorily completed the required initial hazardous materials training, or a person who is changing job functions and has not received initial or recurrent training for a job function involving storage incidental to transport, or loading of items for transport on an aircraft, may perform those job func-

tions for not more than 30 days from the date of hire or a change in job function, if the person is under the direct visual supervision of a person who is authorized by the certificate holder to supervise that person and who has successfully completed the certificate holder's FAA-approved initial or recurrent training program within the past 24 months.

(c) *Persons who work for more than one certificate holder.* A certificate holder that uses or assigns a person to perform or directly supervise a job function specified in § 135.501(a), when that person also performs or directly supervises the same job function for another certificate holder, need only train that person in its own policies and procedures regarding those job functions, if all of the following are met:

(1) The certificate holder using this exception receives written verification from the person designated to hold the training records representing the other certificate holder that the person has satisfactorily completed hazardous materials training for the specific job function under the other certificate holder's FAA approved hazardous material training program under appendix O of part 121 of this chapter; and

(2) The certificate holder who trained the person has the same operations specifications regarding the acceptance, handling, and transport of hazardous materials as the certificate holder using this exception.

(d) *Recurrent hazardous materials training—Completion date.* A person who satisfactorily completes recurrent hazardous materials training in the calendar month before, or the calendar month after, the month in which the recurrent training is due, is considered to have taken that training during the month in which it is due. If the person completes this training earlier than the month before it is due, the month of the completion date becomes his or her new anniversary month.

(e) *Repair stations.* A certificate holder must ensure that each repair station performing work for, or on the certificate holder's behalf is notified in writing of the certificate holder's policies and operations specification authorization permitting or prohibition against the acceptance, rejection, handling, storage incidental to transport, and transportation of hazardous materials, including company material. This notification requirement applies only to repair stations that are regulated by 49 CFR parts 171 through 180.

(f) *Certificate holders operating at foreign locations.* This exception applies if a certificate holder operating at a foreign location where the country requires the certificate holder to use persons working in that country to load aircraft. In such a case, the certificate holder may use those persons even if they have not been trained in accordance with the certificate holder's FAA approved hazardous materials training program. Those persons, however, must be under the direct visual supervision of someone who has successfully completed the certificate holder's approved initial or recurrent hazardous materials training program in accordance with this part. This exception applies only to those persons who load aircraft.

§135.507 **Hazardous materials training records.**

(a) *General requirement.* Each certificate holder must maintain a record of all training required by this part received within the preceding three years for each person who performs or directly supervises a job function specified in §135.501(a). The record must be maintained during the time that the person performs or directly supervises any of those job functions, and for 90 days thereafter. These training records must be kept for direct employees of the certificate holder, as well as independent contractors, subcontractors, and any other person who performs or directly supervises these job functions for the certificate holder.

(b) *Location of records.* The certificate holder must retain the training records required by paragraph (a) of this section for all initial and recurrent training received within the preceding 3 years for all persons performing or directly supervising the job functions listed in Appendix O of part 121 of this chapter at a designated location. The records must be available upon request at the location where the trained person performs or directly supervises the job function specified in §135.501(a).

Records may be maintained electronically and provided on location electronically. When the person ceases to perform or directly supervise a hazardous materials job function, the certificate holder must retain the hazardous materials training records for an additional 90 days and make them available upon request at the last location where the person worked.

(c) *Content of records.* Each record must contain the following:

(1) The individual's name;

(2) The most recent training completion date;

(3) A description, copy or reference to training materials used to meet the training requirement;

(4) The name and address of the organization providing the training; and

(5) A copy of the certification issued when the individual was trained, which shows that a test has been completed satisfactorily.

(d) *New hire or new job function.* Each certificate holder using a person under the exception in §135.505(b) must maintain a record for that person. The records must be available upon request at the location where the trained person performs or directly supervises the job function specified in §135.501(a). Records may be maintained electronically and provided on location electronically. The record must include the following:

(1) A signed statement from an authorized representative of the certificate holder authorizing the use of the person in accordance with the exception;

(2) The date of hire or change in job function;

(3) The person's name and assigned job function;

(4) The name of the supervisor of the job function; and

(5) The date the person is to complete hazardous materials training in accordance with Appendix O of part 121 of this chapter.

Subpart L—Helicopter Air Ambulance Equipment, Operations, and Training Requirements

SOURCE: Docket No. FAA–2010–0982, 79 FR 9975, Feb. 21, 2014, unless otherwise noted.

§ 135.601 Applicability and definitions.

(a) *Applicability.* This subpart prescribes the requirements applicable to each certificate holder conducting helicopter air ambulance operations.

(b) *Definitions.* For purposes of this subpart, the following definitions apply:

(1) *Helicopter air ambulance operation* means a flight, or sequence of flights, with a patient or medical personnel on board, for the purpose of medical transportation, by a part 135 certificate holder authorized by the Administrator to conduct helicopter air ambulance operations. A helicopter air ambulance operation includes, but is not limited to—

(i) Flights conducted to position the helicopter at the site at which a patient or donor organ will be picked up.

(ii) Flights conducted to reposition the helicopter after completing the patient, or donor organ transport.

(iii) Flights initiated for the transport of a patient or donor organ that are terminated due to weather or other reasons.

(2) *Medical personnel* means a person or persons with medical training, including but not limited to flight physicians, flight nurses, or flight paramedics, who are carried aboard a helicopter during helicopter air ambulance operations in order to provide medical care.

(3) *Mountainous* means designated mountainous areas as listed in part 95 of this chapter.

(4) *Nonmountainous* means areas other than mountainous areas as listed in part 95 of this chapter.

§ 135.603 Pilot-in-command instrument qualifications.

After April 24, 2017, no certificate holder may use, nor may any person serve as, a pilot in command of a helicopter air ambulance operation unless that person meets the requirements of § 135.243 and holds a helicopter instrument rating or an airline transport pilot certificate with a category and class rating for that aircraft, that is not limited to VFR.

§ 135.605 Helicopter terrain awareness and warning system (HTAWS).

(a) After April 24, 2017, no person may operate a helicopter in helicopter air ambulance operations unless that helicopter is equipped with a helicopter terrain awareness and warning system (HTAWS) that meets the requirements in TSO–C194 and Section 2 of RTCA DO–309.

(b) The certificate holder's Rotorcraft Flight Manual must contain appropriate procedures for—

(1) The use of the HTAWS; and

(2) Proper flight crew response to HTAWS audio and visual warnings.

(c) Certificate holders with HTAWS required by this section with an approved deviation under § 21.618 of this chapter are in compliance with this section.

(d) The standards required in this section are incorporated by reference into this section with the approval of the Director of the Federal Register under 5 U.S.C. 552(a) and 1 CFR part 51. To enforce any edition other than that specified in this section, the FAA must publish notice of change in the FEDERAL REGISTER and the material must be available to the public. All approved material is available for inspection at the FAA's Office of Rulemaking (ARM–1), 800 Independence Avenue SW., Washington, DC 20591 (telephone (202) 267–9677) and from the sources indicated below. It is also available for inspection at the National Archives and Records Administration (NARA). For information on the availability of this material at NARA, call (202) 741–6030 or go to *http://www.archives.gov/ federal_register/ code_of_federal_regulations/ ibr_locations.html.*

(1) U.S. Department of Transportation, Subsequent Distribution Office, DOT Warehouse M30, Ardmore East Business Center, 3341 Q 75th Avenue, Landover, MD 20785; telephone (301) 322–5377. Copies are also available on the FAA's Web site. Use the following link and type the TSO number in the search box: *http://rgl.faa.gov/ Regulatory_and_Guidance_Library/ rgTSO.nsf/Frameset?OpenPage.*

(i) TSO C–194, Helicopter Terrain Awareness and Warning System (HTAWS), Dec. 17, 2008.

(ii) [Reserved]

(2) RTCA, Inc., 1150 18th Street NW., Suite 910, Washington, DC 20036, telephone (202) 833–9339, and are also available on RTCA's Web site at *http://www.rtca.org/onlinecart/index.cfm.*

(i) RTCA DO–309, Minimum Operational Performance Standards (MOPS) for Helicopter Terrain Awareness and Warning System (HTAWS) Airborne Equipment, Mar. 13, 2008

(ii) [Reserved]

§135.607 Flight Data Monitoring System.

After April 23, 2018, no person may operate a helicopter in air ambulance operations unless it is equipped with an approved flight data monitoring system capable of recording flight performance data. This system must:

(a) Receive electrical power from the bus that provides the maximum reliability for operation without jeopardizing service to essential or emergency loads, and

(b) Be operated from the application of electrical power before takeoff until the removal of electrical power after termination of flight.

§135.609 VFR ceiling and visibility requirements for Class G airspace.

(a) Unless otherwise specified in the certificate holder's operations specifications, when conducting VFR helicopter air ambulance operations in Class G airspace, the weather minimums in the following table apply:

Location	Day		Night		Night using an Approved NVIS or HTAWS	
	Ceiling	Flight Visibility	Ceiling	Flight Visibility	Ceiling	Flight Visibility
Nonmountainous local flying areas	800-feet	2 statute miles	1,000-feet	3 statute miles	800-feet	3 statute miles
Nonmountainous non-local flying areas	800-feet	3 statute miles	1,000-feet	5 statute miles	1,000-feet	3 statute miles
Mountainous local flying areas	800-feet	3 statute miles	1,500-feet	3 statute miles	1,000-feet	3 statute miles
Mountainous non-local flying areas	1,000-feet	3 statute miles	1,500-feet	5 statute miles	1,000-feet	5 statute miles

(b) A certificate holder may designate local flying areas in a manner acceptable to the Administrator, that must—

(1) Not exceed 50 nautical miles in any direction from each designated location;

(2) Take into account obstacles and terrain features that are easily identifiable by the pilot in command and from which the pilot in command may visually determine a position; and

(3) Take into account the operating environment and capabilities of the certificate holder's helicopters.

(c) A pilot must demonstrate a level of familiarity with the local flying area by passing an examination given by the certificate holder within the 12 calendar months prior to using the local flying area.

[Doc. No. FAA–2010–0982, 79 FR 9975, Feb. 21, 2014; Amdt. 135–129A, 79 FR 41126, July 15, 2014]

§ 135.611 IFR operations at locations without weather reporting.

(a) If a certificate holder is authorized to conduct helicopter IFR operations, the Administrator may authorize the certificate holder to conduct IFR helicopter air ambulance operations at airports with an instrument approach procedure and at which a weather report is not available from the U.S. National Weather Service (NWS), a source approved by the NWS, or a source approved by the FAA, subject to the following limitations:

(1) The certificate holder must obtain a weather report from a weather reporting facility operated by the NWS, a source approved by the NWS, or a source approved by the FAA, that is located within 15 nautical miles of the airport. If a weather report is not available, the certificate holder may obtain the area forecast from the NWS, a source approved by the NWS, or a source approved by the FAA, for information regarding the weather observed in the vicinity of the airport;

(2) Flight planning for IFR flights conducted under this paragraph must include selection of an alternate airport that meets the requirements of §§ 135.221 and 135.223;

(3) In Class G airspace, IFR departures with visual transitions are authorized only after the pilot in command determines that the weather conditions at the departure point are at or above takeoff minimums depicted in the published Obstacle Departure Procedure or VFR minimum ceilings and visibilities in accordance with § 135.609.

(4) All approaches must be conducted at Category A approach speeds as established in part 97 or those required for the type of approach being used.

(b) Each helicopter air ambulance operated under this section must be equipped with functioning severe weather detection equipment.

(c) Pilots conducting operations pursuant to this section may use the weather information obtained in paragraph (a) to satisfy the weather report and forecast requirements of § 135.213 and § 135.225(a).

(d) After completing a landing at the airport at which a weather report is not available, the pilot in command is authorized to determine if the weather meets the takeoff requirements of part 97 of this chapter or the certificate holder's operations specification, as applicable.

[Doc. No. FAA–2010–0982, 79 FR 9975, Feb. 21, 2014, as amended by Amdt. 135–131, 79 FR 43622, July 28, 2014]

§ 135.613 Approach/departure IFR transitions.

(a) *Approaches.* When conducting an authorized instrument approach and transitioning from IFR to VFR flight, upon transitioning to VFR flight the following weather minimums apply—

(1) For Point-in-Space (PinS) Copter Instrument approaches annotated with a "Proceed VFR" segment, if the distance from the missed approach point to the landing area is 1 NM or less, flight visibility must be at least 1 statute mile and the ceiling on the approach chart applies;

(2) For all instrument approaches, including PinS when paragraph (a)(1) of this section does not apply, if the distance from the missed approach point to the landing area is 3 NM or less, the applicable VFR weather minimums are—

(i) For Day Operations: No less than a 600-foot ceiling and 2 statute miles flight visibility;

(ii) For Night Operations: No less than a 600-foot ceiling and 3 statute miles flight visibility; or

(3) For all instrument approaches, including PinS, if the distance from the missed approach point to the landing area is greater than 3 NM, the VFR weather minimums required by the class of airspace.

(b) *Departures.* For transitions from VFR to IFR upon departure—

(1) The VFR weather minimums of paragraph (a) of this section apply if—

(i) An FAA-approved obstacle departure procedure is followed; and

(ii) An IFR clearance is obtained on or before reaching a predetermined location that is not more than 3 NM from the departure location.

(2) If the departure does not meet the requirements of paragraph (b)(1) of this section, the VFR weather minimums required by the class of airspace apply.

§135.615 VFR flight planning.

(a) *Pre-flight.* Prior to conducting VFR operations, the pilot in command must—

(1) Determine the minimum safe cruise altitude by evaluating the terrain and obstacles along the planned route of flight;

(2) Identify and document the highest obstacle along the planned route of flight; and

(3) Using the minimum safe cruise altitudes in paragraphs (b)(1)–(2) of this section, determine the minimum required ceiling and visibility to conduct the planned flight by applying the weather minimums appropriate to the class of airspace for the planned flight.

(b) *Enroute.* While conducting VFR operations, the pilot in command must ensure that all terrain and obstacles along the route of flight are cleared vertically by no less than the following:

(1) 300 feet for day operations.

(2) 500 feet for night operations.

(c) *Rerouting the planned flight path.* A pilot in command may deviate from the planned flight path for reasons such as weather conditions or operational considerations. Such deviations do not relieve the pilot in command of the weather requirements or the requirements for terrain and obstacle clearance contained in this part and in part 91 of this chapter. Rerouting, change in destination, or other changes to the planned flight that occur while the helicopter is on the ground at an intermediate stop require evaluation of the new route in accordance with paragraph (a) of this section.

(d) *Operations manual.* Each certificate holder must document its VFR flight planning procedures in its operations manual.

§135.617 Pre-flight risk analysis.

(a) Each certificate holder conducting helicopter air ambulance operations must establish, and document in its operations manual, an FAA-approved preflight risk analysis that includes at least the following—

(1) Flight considerations, to include obstacles and terrain along the planned route of flight, landing zone conditions, and fuel requirements;

(2) Human factors, such as crew fatigue, life events, and other stressors;

(3) Weather, including departure, en route, destination, and forecasted;

(4) A procedure for determining whether another helicopter air ambulance operator has refused or rejected a flight request; and

(5) Strategies and procedures for mitigating identified risks, including procedures for obtaining and documenting approval of the certificate holder's management personnel to release a flight when a risk exceeds a level predetermined by the certificate holder.

(b) Each certificate holder must develop a preflight risk analysis worksheet to include, at a minimum, the items in paragraph (a) of this section.

(c) Prior to the first leg of each helicopter air ambulance operation, the pilot in command must conduct a preflight risk analysis and complete the preflight risk analysis worksheet in accordance with the certificate holder's FAA-approved procedures. The pilot in command must sign the preflight risk analysis worksheet and specify the date and time it was completed.

(d) The certificate holder must retain the original or a copy of each completed preflight risk analysis worksheet at a location specified in its operations manual for at least 90 days from the date of the operation.

§135.619 Operations control centers.

(a) *Operations control center.* After April 22, 2016, certificate holders authorized to conduct helicopter air ambulance operations, with 10 or more helicopter air ambulances assigned to the certificate holder's operations specifications, must have an operations control center. The operations control center must be staffed by operations control specialists who, at a minimum—

(1) Provide two-way communications with pilots;

(2) Provide pilots with weather briefings, to include current and forecasted weather along the planned route of flight;

(3) Monitor the progress of the flight; and

511

(4) Participate in the preflight risk analysis required under § 135.617 to include the following:

(i) Ensure the pilot has completed all required items on the preflight risk analysis worksheet;

(ii) Confirm and verify all entries on the preflight risk analysis worksheet;

(iii) Assist the pilot in mitigating any identified risk prior to takeoff; and

(iv) Acknowledge in writing, specifying the date and time, that the preflight risk analysis worksheet has been accurately completed and that, according to their professional judgment, the flight can be conducted safely.

(b) *Operations control center staffing.* Each certificate holder conducting helicopter air ambulance operations must provide enough operations control specialists at each operations control center to ensure the certificate holder maintains operational control of each flight.

(c) *Documentation of duties and responsibilities.* Each certificate holder must describe in its operations manual the duties and responsibilities of operations control specialists, including preflight risk mitigation strategies and control measures, shift change checklist, and training and testing procedures to hold the position, including procedures for retesting.

(d) *Training requirements.* No certificate holder may use, nor may any person perform the duties of, an operations control specialist unless the operations control specialist has satisfactorily completed the training requirements of this paragraph.

(1) *Initial training.* Before performing the duties of an operations control specialist, each person must satisfactorily complete the certificate holder's FAA-approved operations control specialist initial training program and pass an FAA-approved knowledge and practical test given by the certificate holder. Initial training must include a minimum of 80 hours of training on the topics listed in paragraph (f) of this section. A certificate holder may reduce the number of hours of initial training to a minimum of 40 hours for persons who have obtained, at the time of beginning initial training, a total of at least 2 years of experience during the last 5 years in any one or in any combination of the following areas—

(i) In military aircraft operations as a pilot, flight navigator, or meteorologist;

(ii) In air carrier operations as a pilot, flight engineer, certified aircraft dispatcher, or meteorologist; or

(iii) In aircraft operations as an air traffic controller or a flight service specialist.

(2) *Recurrent training.* Every 12 months after satisfactory completion of the initial training, each operations control specialist must complete a minimum of 40 hours of recurrent training on the topics listed in paragraph (f) of this section and pass an FAA-approved knowledge and practical test given by the certificate holder on those topics.

(e) *Training records.* The certificate holder must maintain a training record for each operations control specialist employed by the certificate holder for the duration of that individual's employment and for 90 days thereafter. The training record must include a chronological log for each training course, including the number of training hours and the examination dates and results.

(f) *Training topics.* Each certificate holder must have an FAA-approved operations control specialist training program that covers at least the following topics—

(1) Aviation weather, including:

(i) General meteorology;

(ii) Prevailing weather;

(iii) Adverse and deteriorating weather;

(iv) Windshear;

(v) Icing conditions;

(vi) Use of aviation weather products;

(vii) Available sources of information; and

(viii) Weather minimums;

(2) Navigation, including:

(i) Navigation aids;

(ii) Instrument approach procedures;

(iii) Navigational publications; and

(iv) Navigation techniques;

(3) Flight monitoring, including:

(i) Available flight-monitoring procedures; and

(ii) Alternate flight-monitoring procedures;

(4) Air traffic control, including:

(i) Airspace;

(ii) Air traffic control procedures;

(iii) Aeronautical charts; and

(iv) Aeronautical data sources;

(5) Aviation communication, including:

(i) Available aircraft communications systems;

(ii) Normal communication procedures;

(iii) Abnormal communication procedures; and

(iv) Emergency communication procedures;

(6) Aircraft systems, including:

(i) Communications systems;

(ii) Navigation systems;

(iii) Surveillance systems;

(iv) Fueling systems;

(v) Specialized systems;

(vi) General maintenance requirements; and

(vii) Minimum equipment lists;

(7) Aircraft limitations and performance, including:

(i) Aircraft operational limitations;

(ii) Aircraft performance;

(iii) Weight and balance procedures and limitations; and

(iv) Landing zone and landing facility requirements;

(8) Aviation policy and regulations, including:

(i) 14 CFR Parts 1, 27, 29, 61, 71, 91, and 135;

(ii) 49 CFR Part 830;

(iii) Company operations specifications;

(iv) Company general operations policies;

(v) Enhanced operational control policies;

(vi) Aeronautical decision making and risk management;

(vii) Lost aircraft procedures; and

(viii) Emergency and search and rescue procedures, including plotting coordinates in degrees, minutes, seconds format, and degrees, decimal minutes format;

(9) Crew resource management, including:

(i) Concepts and practical application;

(ii) Risk management and risk mitigation; and

(iii) Pre-flight risk analysis procedures required under §135.617;

(10) Local flying area orientation, including:

(i) Terrain features;

(ii) Obstructions;

(iii) Weather phenomena for local area;

(iv) Airspace and air traffic control facilities;

(v) Heliports, airports, landing zones, and fuel facilities;

(vi) Instrument approaches;

(vii) Predominant air traffic flow;

(viii) Landmarks and cultural features, including areas prone to flatlight, whiteout, and brownout conditions; and

(ix) Local aviation and safety resources and contact information; and

(11) Any other requirements as determined by the Administrator to ensure safe operations.

(g) *Operations control specialist duty time limitations.* (1) Each certificate holder must establish the daily duty period for an operations control specialist so that it begins at a time that allows that person to become thoroughly familiar with operational considerations, including existing and anticipated weather conditions in the area of operations, helicopter operations in progress, and helicopter maintenance status, before performing duties associated with any helicopter air ambulance operation. The operations control specialist must remain on duty until relieved by another qualified operations control specialist or until each helicopter air ambulance monitored by that person has completed its flight or gone beyond that person's jurisdiction.

(2) Except in cases where circumstances or emergency conditions beyond the control of the certificate holder require otherwise—

(i) No certificate holder may schedule an operations control specialist for more than 10 consecutive hours of duty;

(ii) If an operations control specialist is scheduled for more than 10 hours of duty in 24 consecutive hours, the certificate holder must provide that person a rest period of at least 8 hours at or before the end of 10 hours of duty;

(iii) If an operations control specialist is on duty for more than 10 consecutive hours, the certificate holder must provide that person a rest period of at least 8 hours before that person's next duty period;

(iv) Each operations control specialist must be relieved of all duty with the certificate holder for at least 24 consecutive hours during any 7 consecutive days.

(h) *Drug and alcohol testing.* Operations control specialists must be tested for drugs and alcohol according to the certificate holder's Drug and Alcohol Testing Program administered under part 120 of this chapter.

§ 135.621 Briefing of medical personnel.

(a) Except as provided in paragraph (b) of this section, prior to each helicopter air ambulance operation, each pilot in command, or other flight crewmember designated by the certificate holder, must ensure that all medical personnel have been briefed on the following—

(1) Passenger briefing requirements in § 135.117(a) and (b); and

(2) Physiological aspects of flight;

(3) Patient loading and unloading;

(4) Safety in and around the helicopter;

(5) In-flight emergency procedures;

(6) Emergency landing procedures;

(7) Emergency evacuation procedures;

(8) Efficient and safe communications with the pilot; and

(9) Operational differences between day and night operations, if appropriate.

(b) The briefing required in paragraphs (a)(2) through (9) of this section may be omitted if all medical personnel on board have satisfactorily completed the certificate holder's FAA-approved medical personnel training program within the preceding 24 calendar months. Each training program must include a minimum of 4 hours of ground training, and 4 hours of training in and around an air ambulance helicopter, on the topics set forth in paragraph (a)(2) through (9) of this section.

(c) Each certificate holder must maintain a record for each person trained under this section that—

(1) Contains the individual's name, the most recent training completion date, and a description, copy, or reference to training materials used to meet the training requirement.

(2) Is maintained for 24 calendar months following the individual's completion of training.

[Doc. No. FAA–2010–0982, 79 FR 9975, Feb. 21, 2014; Amdt. 135–129A, 79 FR 41126, July 15, 2014]

APPENDIX A TO PART 135—ADDITIONAL AIRWORTHINESS STANDARDS FOR 10 OR MORE PASSENGER AIRPLANES

Applicability

1. *Applicability.* This appendix prescribes the additional airworthiness standards required by § 135.169.

2. *References.* Unless otherwise provided, references in this appendix to specific sections of part 23 of the Federal Aviation Regulations (FAR part 23) are to those sections of part 23 in effect on March 30, 1967.

Flight Requirements

3. *General.* Compliance must be shown with the applicable requirements of subpart B of FAR part 23, as supplemented or modified in §§ 4 through 10.

Performance

4. *General.* (a) Unless otherwise prescribed in this appendix, compliance with each applicable performance requirement in sections 4 through 7 must be shown for ambient atmospheric conditions and still air.

(b) The performance must correspond to the propulsive thrust available under the particular ambient atmospheric conditions and the particular flight condition. The available propulsive thrust must correspond to engine power or thrust, not exceeding the approved power or thrust less—

(1) Installation losses; and

(2) The power or equivalent thrust absorbed by the accessories and services appropriate to the particular ambient atmospheric conditions and the particular flight condition.

(c) Unless otherwise prescribed in this appendix, the applicant must select the takeoff, en route, and landing configurations for the airplane.

(d) The airplane configuration may vary with weight, altitude, and temperature, to the extent they are compatible with the operating procedures required by paragraph (e) of this section.

(e) Unless otherwise prescribed in this appendix, in determining the critical engine inoperative takeoff performance, the accelerate-stop distance, takeoff distance, changes in the airplane's configuration, speed, power, and thrust must be made under procedures established by the applicant for operation in service.

(f) Procedures for the execution of balked landings must be established by the applicant and included in the Airplane Flight Manual.

(g) The procedures established under paragraphs (e) and (f) of this section must—

(1) Be able to be consistently executed in service by a crew of average skill;

(2) Use methods or devices that are safe and reliable; and

(3) Include allowance for any time delays, in the execution of the procedures, that may reasonably be expected in service.

5. *Takeoff.* (a) *General.* Takeoff speeds, the accelerate-stop distance, the takeoff distance, and the one-engine-inoperative takeoff flight path data (described in paragraphs (b), (c), (d), and (f) of this section), must be determined for—

(1) Each weight, altitude, and ambient temperature within the operational limits selected by the applicant;

(2) The selected configuration for takeoff;

(3) The center of gravity in the most unfavorable position;

(4) The operating engine within approved operating limitations; and

(5) Takeoff data based on smooth, dry, hard-surface runway.

(b) *Takeoff speeds.* (1) The decision speed V_1 is the calibrated airspeed on the ground at which, as a result of engine failure or other reasons, the pilot is assumed to have made a decision to continue or discontinue the takeoff. The speed V_1 must be selected by the applicant but may not be less than—

(i) $1.10V_{S1}$;

(ii) $1.10V_{MC}$;

(iii) A speed that allows acceleration to V_1 and stop under paragraph (c) of this section; or

(iv) A speed at which the airplane can be rotated for takeoff and shown to be adequate to safely continue the takeoff, using normal piloting skill, when the critical engine is suddenly made inoperative.

(2) The initial climb out speed V_2, in terms of calibrated airspeed, must be selected by the applicant so as to allow the gradient of climb required in section 6(b)(2), but it must not be less than V_1 or less than $1.2V_{S1}$.

(3) Other essential take off speeds necessary for safe operation of the airplane.

(c) *Accelerate-stop distance.* (1) The accelerate-stop distance is the sum of the distances necessary to—

(i) Accelerate the airplane from a starting start to V_1; and

(ii) Come to a full stop from the point at which V_1 is reached assuming that in the case of engine failure, failure of the critical engine is recognized by the pilot at the speed V_1.

(2) Means other than wheel brakes may be used to determine the accelerate-stop distance if that means is available with the critical engine inoperative and—

(i) Is safe and reliable;

(ii) Is used so that consistent results can be expected under normal operating conditions; and

(iii) Is such that exceptional skill is not required to control the airplane.

(d) *All engines operating takeoff distance.* The all engine operating takeoff distance is the horizontal distance required to takeoff and climb to a height of 50 feet above the takeoff surface under the procedures in FAR 23.51(a).

(e) *One-engine-inoperative takeoff.* Determine the weight for each altitude and temperature within the operational limits established for the airplane, at which the airplane has the capability, after failure of the critical engine at V_1 determined under paragraph (b) of this section, to take off and climb at not less than V_2, to a height 1,000 feet above the takeoff surface and attain the speed and configuration at which compliance is shown with the en route one-engine-inoperative gradient of climb specified in section 6(c).

(f) *One-engine-inoperative takeoff flight path data.* The one-engine-inoperative takeoff flight path data consist of takeoff flight paths extending from a standing start to a point in the takeoff at which the airplane reaches a height 1,000 feet above the takeoff surface under paragraph (e) of this section.

6. *Climb.* (a) *Landing climb: All-engines-operating.* The maximum weight must be determined with the airplane in the landing configuration, for each altitude, and ambient temperature within the operational limits established for the airplane, with the most unfavorable center of gravity, and out-of-ground effect in free air, at which the steady gradient of climb will not be less than 3.3 percent, with:

(1) The engines at the power that is available 8 seconds after initiation of movement of the power or thrust controls from the minimum flight idle to the takeoff position.

(2) A climb speed not greater than the approach speed established under section 7 and not less than the greater of $1.05V_{MC}$ or $1.10V_{S1}$.

(b) *Takeoff climb: one-engine-inoperative.* The maximum weight at which the airplane meets the minimum climb performance specified in paragraphs (1) and (2) of this paragraph must be determined for each altitude and ambient temperature within the operational limits established for the airplane, out of ground effect in free air, with the airplane in the takeoff configuration, with the most unfavorable center of gravity, the critical engine inoperative, the remaining engines at the maximum takeoff power or thrust, and the propeller of the inoperative engine windmilling with the propeller controls in the normal position except that, if an approved automatic feathering system is installed, the propellers may be in the feathered position:

(1) *Takeoff: landing gear extended.* The minimum steady gradient of climb must be measurably positive at the speed V_1.

(2) *Takeoff: landing gear retracted.* The minimum steady gradient of climb may not be less than 2 percent at speed V_2. For airplanes with fixed landing gear this requirement must be met with the landing gear extended.

(c) *En route climb: one-engine-inoperative.* The maximum weight must be determined for each altitude and ambient temperature within the operational limits established for the airplane, at which the steady gradient of climb is not less 1.2 percent at an altitude 1,000 feet above the takeoff surface, with the airplane in the en route configuration, the critical engine inoperative, the remaining engine at the maximum continuous power or thrust, and the most unfavorable center of gravity.

7. *Landing.* (a) The landing field length described in paragraph (b) of this section must be determined for standard atmosphere at each weight and altitude within the operational limits established by the applicant.

(b) The landing field length is equal to the landing distance determined under FAR 23.75(a) divided by a factor of 0.6 for the destination airport and 0.7 for the alternate airport. Instead of the gliding approach specified in FAR 23.75(a)(1), the landing may be preceded by a steady approach down to the 50-foot height at a gradient of descent not greater than 5.2 percent (3°) at a calibrated airspeed not less than $1.3V_{S1}$.

Trim

8. *Trim.* (a) *Lateral and directional trim.* The airplane must maintain lateral and directional trim in level flight at a speed of V_H or V_{MO}/M_{MO}, whichever is lower, with landing gear and wing flaps retracted.

(b) *Longitudinal trim.* The airplane must maintain longitudinal trim during the following conditions, except that it need not maintain trim at a speed greater than V_{MO}/M_{MO}:

(1) In the approach conditions specified in FAR 23.161(c) (3) through (5), except that instead of the speeds specified in those paragraphs, trim must be maintained with a stick force of not more than 10 pounds down to a speed used in showing compliance with section 7 or $1.4V_{S1}$ whichever is lower.

(2) In level flight at any speed from V_H or V_{MO}/M_{MO}, whichever is lower, to either V_x or $1.4V_{S1}$, with the landing gear and wing flaps retracted.

Stability

9. *Static longitudinal stability.* (a) In showing compliance with FAR 23.175(b) and with paragraph (b) of this section, the airspeed must return to within ±7½ percent of the trim speed.

(b) *Cruise stability.* The stick force curve must have a stable slope for a speed range of ±50 knots from the trim speed except that the speeds need not exceed V_{FC}/M_{FC} or be less than $1.4V_{S1}$. This speed range will be considered to begin at the outer extremes of the friction band and the stick force may not exceed 50 pounds with—

(1) Landing gear retracted;

(2) Wing flaps retracted;

(3) The maximum cruising power as selected by the applicant as an operating limitation for turbine engines or 75 percent of maximum continuous power for reciprocating engines except that the power need not exceed that required at V_{MO}/M_{MO};

(4) Maximum takeoff weight; and

(5) The airplane trimmed for level flight with the power specified in paragraph (3) of this paragraph.

V_{FC}/M_{FC} may not be less than a speed midway between V_{MO}/M_{MO} and V_{DF}/M_{DF}, except that, for altitudes where Mach number is the limiting factor, M_{FC} need not exceed the Mach number at which effective speed warning occurs.

(c) *Climb stability (turbopropeller powered airplanes only).* In showing compliance with FAR 23.175(a), an applicant must, instead of the power specified in FAR 23.175(a)(4), use the maximum power or thrust selected by the applicant as an operating limitation for use during climb at the best rate of climb speed, except that the speed need not be less than $1.4V_{S1}$.

Stalls

10. *Stall warning.* If artificial stall warning is required to comply with FAR 23.207, the warning device must give clearly distinguishable indications under expected conditions of flight. The use of a visual warning device that requires the attention of the crew within the cockpit is not acceptable by itself.

Control Systems

11. *Electric trim tabs.* The airplane must meet FAR 23.677 and in addition it must be shown that the airplane is safely controllable and that a pilot can perform all the maneuvers and operations necessary to effect a safe landing following any probable electric trim tab runaway which might be reasonably expected in service allowing for appropriate time delay after pilot recognition of the runaway. This demonstration must be conducted at the critical airplane weights and center of gravity positions.

Instruments: Installation

12. *Arrangement and visibility.* Each instrument must meet FAR 23.1321 and in addition:

(a) Each flight, navigation, and powerplant instrument for use by any pilot must be plainly visible to the pilot from the pilot's station with the minimum practicable deviation from the pilot's normal position and line of vision when the pilot is looking forward along the flight path.

(b) The flight instruments required by FAR 23.1303 and by the applicable operating rules must be grouped on the instrument panel and centered as nearly as practicable about the vertical plane of each pilot's forward vision. In addition—

(1) The instrument that most effectively indicates the attitude must be in the panel in the top center position;

(2) The instrument that most effectively indicates the airspeed must be on the panel directly to the left of the instrument in the top center position;

(3) The instrument that most effectively indicates altitude must be adjacent to and directly to the right of the instrument in the top center position; and

(4) The instrument that most effectively indicates direction of flight must be adjacent to and directly below the instrument in the top center position.

13. *Airspeed indicating system.* Each airspeed indicating system must meet FAR 23.1323 and in addition:

(a) Airspeed indicating instruments must be of an approved type and must be calibrated to indicate true airspeed at sea level in the standard atmosphere with a minimum practicable instrument calibration error when the corresponding pitot and static pressures are supplied to the instruments.

(b) The airspeed indicating system must be calibrated to determine the system error, i.e., the relation between IAS and CAS, in flight and during the accelerate-takeoff ground run. The ground run calibration must be obtained between 0.8 of the minimum value of V_1 and 1.2 times the maximum value of V_1, considering the approved ranges of altitude and weight. The ground run calibration is determined assuming an engine failure at the minimum value of V_1.

(c) The airspeed error of the installation excluding the instrument calibration error, must not exceed 3 percent or 5 knots whichever is greater, throughout the speed range from V_{MO} to $1.3V_{S1}$ with flaps retracted and from $1.3V_{SO}$ to V_{FE} with flaps in the landing position.

(d) Information showing the relationship between IAS and CAS must be shown in the Airplane Flight Manual.

14. *Static air vent system.* The static air vent system must meet FAR 23.1325. The altimeter system calibration must be determined and shown in the Airplane Flight Manual.

Operating Limitations and Information

15. *Maximum operating limit speed V_{MO}/M_{MO}.* Instead of establishing operating limitations based on V_{NE} and V_{NO}, the applicant must establish a maximum operating limit speed V_{MO}/M_{MO} as follows:

(a) The maximum operating limit speed must not exceed the design cruising speed V_C and must be sufficiently below V_D/M_D or V_{DF}/M_{DF} to make it highly improbable that the latter speeds will be inadvertently exceeded in flight.

(b) The speed V_{MO} must not exceed $0.8V_D/M_D$ or $0.8V_{DF}/M_{DF}$ unless flight demonstrations involving upsets as specified by the Administrator indicates a lower speed margin will not result in speeds exceeding V_D/M_D or V_{DF}. Atmospheric variations, horizontal gusts, system and equipment errors, and airframe production variations are taken into account.

16. *Minimum flight crew.* In addition to meeting FAR 23.1523, the applicant must establish the minimum number and type of qualified flight crew personnel sufficient for safe operation of the airplane considering—

(a) Each kind of operation for which the applicant desires approval;

(b) The workload on each crewmember considering the following:

(1) Flight path control.

(2) Collision avoidance.

(3) Navigation.

(4) Communications.

(5) Operation and monitoring of all essential aircraft systems.

(6) Command decisions; and

(c) The accessibility and ease of operation of necessary controls by the appropriate crewmember during all normal and emergency operations when at the crewmember flight station.

17. *Airspeed indicator.* The airspeed indicator must meet FAR 23.1545 except that, the airspeed notations and markings in terms of V_{NO} and V_{NH} must be replaced by the V_{MO}/M_{MO} notations. The airspeed indicator markings must be easily read and understood by the pilot. A placard adjacent to the airspeed indicator is an acceptable means of showing compliance with FAR 23.1545(c).

Airplane Flight Manual

18. *General.* The Airplane Flight Manual must be prepared under FARs 23.1583 and 23.1587, and in addition the operating limitations and performance information in sections 19 and 20 must be included.

19. *Operating limitations.* The Airplane Flight Manual must include the following limitations—

(a) *Airspeed limitations.* (1) The maximum operating limit speed V_{MO}/M_{MO} and a statement that this speed limit may not be deliberately exceeded in any regime of flight (climb, cruise, or descent) unless a higher speed is authorized for flight test or pilot training;

(2) If an airspeed limitation is based upon compressibility effects, a statement to this effect and information as to any symptoms, the probable behavior of the airplane, and the recommended recovery procedures; and

(3) The airspeed limits, shown in terms of V_{MO}/M_{MO} instead of V_{NO} and $V_{NE.}$

(b) *Takeoff weight limitations.* The maximum takeoff weight for each airport elevation ambient temperature and available takeoff runway length within the range selected by the applicant may not exceed the weight at which—

(1) The all-engine-operating takeoff distance determined under section 5(b) or the accelerate-stop distance determined under section 5(c), whichever is greater, is equal to the available runway length;

(2) The airplane complies with the one-engine-inoperative takeoff requirements specified in section 5(e); and

(3) The airplane complies with the one-engine-inoperative takeoff and en route climb requirements specified in sections 6 (b) and (c).

(c) *Landing weight limitations.* The maximum landing weight for each airport elevation (standard temperature) and available landing runway length, within the range selected by the applicant. This weight may not exceed the weight at which the landing field length determined under section 7(b) is equal to the available runway length. In showing compliance with this operating limitation, it is acceptable to assume that the landing weight at the destination will be equal to the takeoff weight reduced by the normal consumption of fuel and oil en route.

20. *Performance information.* The Airplane Flight Manual must contain the performance information determined under the performance requirements of this appendix. The information must include the following:

(a) Sufficient information so that the takeoff weight limits specified in section 19(b) can be determined for all temperatures and altitudes within the operation limitations selected by the applicant.

(b) The conditions under which the performance information was obtained, including the airspeed at the 50-foot height used to determine landing distances.

(c) The performance information (determined by extrapolation and computed for the range of weights between the maximum landing and takeoff weights) for—

(1) Climb in the landing configuration; and

(2) Landing distance.

(d) Procedure established under section 4 related to the limitations and information required by this section in the form of guidance material including any relevant limitations or information.

(e) An explanation of significant or unusual flight or ground handling characteristics of the airplane.

(f) Airspeeds, as indicated airspeeds, corresponding to those determined for takeoff under section 5(b).

21. *Maximum operating altitudes.* The maximum operating altitude to which operation is allowed, as limited by flight, structural, powerplant, functional, or equipment characteristics, must be specified in the Airplane Flight Manual.

22. *Stowage provision for airplane flight manual.* Provision must be made for stowing the Airplane Flight Manual in a suitable fixed container which is readily accessible to the pilot.

23. *Operating procedures.* Procedures for restarting turbine engines in flight (including the effects of altitude) must be set forth in the Airplane Flight Manual.

Airframe Requirements

Flight Loads

24. *Engine torque.* (a) Each turbopropeller engine mount and its supporting structure must be designed for the torque effects of:

(1) The conditions in FAR 23.361(a).

(2) The limit engine torque corresponding to takeoff power and propeller speed multiplied by a factor accounting for propeller control system malfunction, including quick feathering action, simultaneously with $1g$ level flight loads. In the absence of a rational analysis, a factor of 1.6 must be used.

(b) The limit torque is obtained by multiplying the mean torque by a factor of 1.25.

25. *Turbine engine gyroscopic loads.* Each turbopropeller engine mount and its supporting structure must be designed for the gyroscopic loads that result, with the engines at maximum continuous r.p.m., under either—

(a) The conditions in FARs 23.351 and 23.423; or

(b) All possible combinations of the following:

(1) A yaw velocity of 2.5 radians per second.

(2) A pitch velocity of 1.0 radians per second.

(3) A normal load factor of 2.5.

(4) Maximum continuous thrust.

26. *Unsymmetrical loads due to engine failure.* (a) Turbopropeller powered airplanes must be designed for the unsymmet- rical loads resulting from the failure of the critical engine including the following conditions in combination with a single malfunction of the propeller drag limiting system, considering the probable pilot corrective action on the flight controls:

(1) At speeds between V_{mo} and $V_{D,}$ the loads resulting from power failure because of fuel flow interruption are considered to be limit loads.

(2) At speeds between V_{mo} and V_c, the loads resulting from the disconnection of the engine compressor from the turbine or from loss of the turbine blades are considered to be ultimate loads.

(3) The time history of the thrust decay and drag buildup occurring as a result of the prescribed engine failures must be substantiated by test or other data applicable to the particular engine-propeller combination.

(4) The timing and magnitude of the probable pilot corrective action must be conservatively estimated, considering the characteristics of the particular engine-propeller-airplane combination.

(b) Pilot corrective action may be assumed to be initiated at the time maximum yawing velocity is reached, but not earlier than 2 seconds after the engine failure. The magnitude of the corrective action may be based on the control forces in FAR 23.397 except that lower forces may be assumed where it is shown by analysis or test that these forces can control the yaw and roll resulting from the prescribed engine failure conditions.

Ground Loads

27. *Dual wheel landing gear units.* Each dual wheel landing gear unit and its supporting structure must be shown to comply with the following:

(a) *Pivoting.* The airplane must be assumed to pivot about one side of the main gear with the brakes on that side locked. The limit vertical load factor must be 1.0 and the coefficient of friction 0.8. This condition need apply only to the main gear and its supporting structure.

(b) *Unequal tire inflation.* A 60–40 percent distribution of the loads established under FAR 23.471 through FAR 23.483 must be applied to the dual wheels.

(c) *Flat tire.* (1) Sixty percent of the loads in FAR 23.471 through FAR 23.483 must be applied to either wheel in a unit.

(2) Sixty percent of the limit drag and side loads and 100 percent of the limit vertical load established under FARs 23.493 and 23.485 must be applied to either wheel in a unit except that the vertical load need not exceed the maximum vertical load in paragraph (c)(1) of this section.

Fatigue Evaluation

28. *Fatigue evaluation of wing and associated structure.* Unless it is shown that the structure, operating stress levels, materials and expected use are comparable from a fatigue standpoint to a similar design which has had substantial satisfactory service experience, the strength, detail design, and the fabrication of those parts of the wing, wing carry-through, and attaching structure whose failure would be catastrophic must be evaluated under either—

(a) A fatigue strength investigation in which the structure is shown by analysis, tests, or both to be able to withstand the repeated loads of variable magnitude expected in service; or

(b) A fail-safe strength investigation in which it is shown by analysis, tests, or both that catastrophic failure of the structure is not probable after fatigue, or obvious partial failure, of a principal structural element, and that the remaining structure is able to withstand a static ultimate load factor of 75 percent of the critical limit load factor at V_C. These loads must be multiplied by a factor of 1.15 unless the dynamic effects of failure under static load are otherwise considered.

Design and Construction

29. *Flutter.* For multiengine turbopropeller powered airplanes, a dynamic evaluation must be made and must include—

(a) The significant elastic, inertia, and aerodynamic forces associated with the rotations and displacements of the plane of the propeller; and

(b) Engine-propeller-nacelle stiffness and damping variations appropriate to the particular configuration.

Landing Gear

30. *Flap operated landing gear warning device.* Airplanes having retractable landing gear and wing flaps must be equipped with a warning device that functions continuously when the wing flaps are extended to a flap position that activates the warning device to give adequate warning before landing, using normal landing procedures, if the landing gear is not fully extended and locked. There may not be a manual shut off for this warning device. The flap position sensing unit may be installed at any suitable location. The system for this device may use any part of the system (including the aural warning device) provided for other landing gear warning devices.

Personnel and Cargo Accommodations

31. *Cargo and baggage compartments.* Cargo and baggage compartments must be designed to meet FAR 23.787 (a) and (b), and in addition means must be provided to protect passengers from injury by the contents of any cargo or baggage compartment when the ultimate forward inertia force is 9*g*.

32. *Doors and exits.* The airplane must meet FAR 23.783 and FAR 23.807 (a)(3), (b), and (c), and in addition:

(a) There must be a means to lock and safeguard each external door and exit against opening in flight either inadvertently by persons, or as a result of mechanical failure. Each external door must be operable from both the inside and the outside.

(b) There must be means for direct visual inspection of the locking mechanism by crewmembers to determine whether external doors and exits, for which the initial opening movement is outward, are fully locked. In addition, there must be a visual means to signal to crewmembers when normally used external doors are closed and fully locked.

(c) The passenger entrance door must qualify as a floor level emergency exit. Each additional required emergency exit except floor level exits must be located over the wing or must be provided with acceptable means to assist the occupants in descending to the ground. In addition to the passenger entrance door:

(1) For a total seating capacity of 15 or less, an emergency exit as defined in FAR 23.807(b) is required on each side of the cabin.

(2) For a total seating capacity of 16 through 23, three emergency exits as defined in FAR 23.807(b) are required with one on the same side as the door and two on the side opposite the door.

(d) An evacuation demonstration must be conducted utilizing the maximum number of occupants for which certification is desired. It must be conducted under simulated night conditions utilizing only the emergency exits on the most critical side of the aircraft. The participants must be representative of average airline passengers with no previous practice or rehearsal for the demonstration. Evacuation must be completed within 90 seconds.

(e) Each emergency exit must be marked with the word "Exit" by a sign which has white letters 1 inch high on a red background 2 inches high, be self-illuminated or independently internally electrically illuminated, and have a minimum luminescence (brightness) of at least 160 microlamberts. The colors may be reversed if the passenger compartment illumination is essentially the same.

(f) Access to window type emergency exits must not be obstructed by seats or seat backs.

(g) The width of the main passenger aisle at any point between seats must equal or exceed the values in the following table:

Total seating capacity	Minimum main passenger aisle width	
	Less than 25 inches from floor	25 inches and more from floor
10 through 23	9 inches	15 inches.

Miscellaneous

33. *Lightning strike protection.* Parts that are electrically insulated from the basic airframe must be connected to it through lightning arrestors unless a lightning strike on the insulated part—

(a) Is improbable because of shielding by other parts; or

(b) Is not hazardous.

34. *Ice protection.* If certification with ice protection provisions is desired, compliance with the following must be shown:

(a) The recommended procedures for the use of the ice protection equipment must be set forth in the Airplane Flight Manual.

(b) An analysis must be performed to establish, on the basis of the airplane's operational needs, the adequacy of the ice protection system for the various components of the airplane. In addition, tests of the ice protection system must be conducted to demonstrate that the airplane is capable of operating safely in continuous maximum and intermittent maximum icing conditions as described in appendix C of part 25 of this chapter.

(c) Compliance with all or portions of this section may be accomplished by reference, where applicable because of similarity of the designs, to analysis and tests performed by the applicant for a type certificated model.

35. *Maintenance information.* The applicant must make available to the owner at the time of delivery of the airplane the information the applicant considers essential for the proper maintenance of the airplane. That information must include the following:

(a) Description of systems, including electrical, hydraulic, and fuel controls.

(b) Lubrication instructions setting forth the frequency and the lubricants and fluids which are to be used in the various systems.

(c) Pressures and electrical loads applicable to the various systems.

(d) Tolerances and adjustments necessary for proper functioning.

(e) Methods of leveling, raising, and towing.

(f) Methods of balancing control surfaces.

(g) Identification of primary and secondary structures.

(h) Frequency and extent of inspections necessary to the proper operation of the airplane.

(i) Special repair methods applicable to the airplane.

(j) Special inspection techniques, such as X-ray, ultrasonic, and magnetic particle inspection.

(k) List of special tools.

Propulsion

General

36. *Vibration characteristics.* For turbopropeller powered airplanes, the engine installation must not result in vibration characteristics of the engine exceeding those established during the type certification of the engine.

37. *In flight restarting of engine.* If the engine on turbopropeller powered airplanes cannot be restarted at the maximum cruise altitude, a determination must be made of the altitude below which restarts can be consistently accomplished. Restart information

must be provided in the Airplane Flight Manual.

38. *Engines.* (a) *For turbopropeller powered airplanes.* The engine installation must comply with the following:

(1) *Engine isolation.* The powerplants must be arranged and isolated from each other to allow operation, in at least one configuration, so that the failure or malfunction of any engine, or of any system that can affect the engine, will not—

(i) Prevent the continued safe operation of the remaining engines; or

(ii) Require immediate action by any crewmember for continued safe operation.

(2) *Control of engine rotation* There must be a means to individually stop and restart the rotation of any engine in flight except that engine rotation need not be stopped if continued rotation could not jeopardize the safety of the airplane. Each component of the stopping and restarting system on the engine side of the firewall, and that might be exposed to fire, must be at least fire resistant. If hydraulic propeller feathering systems are used for this purpose, the feathering lines must be at least fire resistant under the operating conditions that may be expected to exist during feathering.

(3) *Engine speed and gas temperature control devices.* The powerplant systems associated with engine control devices, systems, and instrumentation must provide reasonable assurance that those engine operating limitations that adversely affect turbine rotor structural integrity will not be exceeded in service.

(b) *For reciprocating engine powered airplanes.* To provide engine isolation, the powerplants must be arranged and isolated from each other to allow operation, in at least one configuration, so that the failure or malfunction of any engine, or of any system that can affect that engine, will not—

(1) Prevent the continued safe operation of the remaining engines; or

(2) Require immediate action by any crewmember for continued safe operation.

39. *Turbopropeller reversing systems.* (a) Turbopropeller reversing systems intended for ground operation must be designed so that no single failure or malfunction of the system will result in unwanted reverse thrust under any expected operating condition. Failure of structural elements need not be considered if the probability of this kind of failure is extremely remote.

(b) Turbopropeller reversing systems intended for in flight use must be designed so that no unsafe condition will result during normal operation of the system, or from any failure (or reasonably likely combination of failures) of the reversing system, under any anticipated condition of operation of the airplane. Failure of structural elements need not be considered if the probability of this kind of failure is extremely remote.

(c) Compliance with this section may be shown by failure analysis, testing, or both for propeller systems that allow propeller blades to move from the flight low-pitch position to a position that is substantially less than that at the normal flight low-pitch position. The analysis may include or be supported by the analysis made to show compliance with the type certification of the propeller and associated installation components. Credit will be given for pertinent analysis and testing completed by the engine and propeller manufacturers.

40. *Turbopropeller drag-limiting systems.* Turbopropeller drag-limiting systems must be designed so that no single failure or malfunction of any of the systems during normal or emergency operation results in propeller drag in excess of that for which the airplane was designed. Failure of structural elements of the drag-limiting systems need not be considered if the probability of this kind of failure is extremely remote.

41. *Turbine engine powerplant operating characteristics.* For turbopropeller powered airplanes, the turbine engine powerplant operating characteristics must be investigated in flight to determine that no adverse characteristics (such as stall, surge, or flameout) are present to a hazardous degree, during normal and emergency operation within the range of operating limitations of the airplane and of the engine.

42. *Fuel flow.* (a) For turbopropeller powered airplanes—

(1) The fuel system must provide for continuous supply of fuel to the engines for normal operation without interruption due to depletion of fuel in any tank other than the main tank; and

(2) The fuel flow rate for turbopropeller engine fuel pump systems must not be less than 125 percent of the fuel flow required to develop the standard sea level atmospheric conditions takeoff power selected and included as an operating limitation in the Airplane Flight Manual.

(b) For reciprocating engine powered airplanes, it is acceptable for the fuel flow rate for each pump system (main and reserve supply) to be 125 percent of the takeoff fuel consumption of the engine.

Fuel System Components

43. *Fuel pumps.* For turbopropeller powered airplanes, a reliable and independent power source must be provided for each pump used with turbine engines which do not have provisions for mechanically driving the main pumps. It must be demonstrated that the pump installations provide a reliability and durability equivalent to that in FAR 23.991(a).

44. *Fuel strainer or filter.* For turbopropeller powered airplanes, the following apply:

(a) There must be a fuel strainer or filter between the tank outlet and the fuel metering device of the engine. In addition, the fuel strainer or filter must be—

(1) Between the tank outlet and the engine-driven positive displacement pump inlet, if there is an engine-driven positive displacement pump;

(2) Accessible for drainage and cleaning and, for the strainer screen, easily removable; and

(3) Mounted so that its weight is not supported by the connecting lines or by the inlet or outlet connections of the strainer or filter itself.

(b) Unless there are means in the fuel system to prevent the accumulation of ice on the filter, there must be means to automatically maintain the fuel-flow if ice-clogging of the filter occurs; and

(c) The fuel strainer or filter must be of adequate capacity (for operating limitations established to ensure proper service) and of appropriate mesh to insure proper engine operation, with the fuel contaminated to a degree (for particle size and density) that can be reasonably expected in service. The degree of fuel filtering may not be less than that established for the engine type certification.

45. *Lightning strike protection.* Protection must be provided against the ignition of flammable vapors in the fuel vent system due to lightning strikes.

Cooling

46. *Cooling test procedures for turbopropeller powered airplanes.* (a) Turbopropeller powered airplanes must be shown to comply with FAR 23.1041 during takeoff, climb, en route, and landing stages of flight that correspond to the applicable performance requirements. The cooling tests must be conducted with the airplane in the configuration, and operating under the conditions that are critical relative to cooling during each stage of flight. For the cooling tests a temperature is "stabilized" when its rate of change is less than 2 °F. per minute.

(b) Temperatures must be stabilized under the conditions from which entry is made into each stage of flight being investigated unless the entry condition is not one during which component and engine fluid temperatures would stabilize, in which case, operation through the full entry condition must be conducted before entry into the stage of flight being investigated to allow temperatures to reach their natural levels at the time of entry. The takeoff cooling test must be preceded by a period during which the powerplant component and engine fluid temperatures are stabilized with the engines at ground idle.

(c) Cooling tests for each stage of flight must be continued until—

(1) The component and engine fluid temperatures stabilize;

(2) The stage of flight is completed; or

(3) An operating limitation is reached.

Induction System

47. *Air induction.* For turbopropeller powered airplanes—

(a) There must be means to prevent hazardous quantities of fuel leakage or overflow from drains, vents, or other components of flammable fluid systems from entering the engine intake systems; and

(b) The air inlet ducts must be located or protected so as to minimize the ingestion of foreign matter during takeoff, landing, and taxiing.

48. *Induction system icing protection.* For turbopropeller powered airplanes, each turbine engine must be able to operate throughout its flight power range without adverse effect on engine operation or serious loss of power or thrust, under the icing conditions specified in appendix C of part 25 of this chapter. In addition, there must be means to indicate to appropriate flight crewmembers the functioning of the powerplant ice protection system.

49. *Turbine engine bleed air systems.* Turbine engine bleed air systems of turbopropeller powered airplanes must be investigated to determine—

(a) That no hazard to the airplane will result if a duct rupture occurs. This condition must consider that a failure of the duct can occur anywhere between the engine port and the airplane bleed service; and

(b) That, if the bleed air system is used for direct cabin pressurization, it is not possible for hazardous contamination of the cabin air system to occur in event of lubrication system failure.

Exhaust System

50. *Exhaust system drains.* Turbopropeller engine exhaust systems having low spots or pockets must incorporate drains at those locations. These drains must discharge clear of the airplane in normal and ground attitudes to prevent the accumulation of fuel after the failure of an attempted engine start.

Powerplant Controls and Accessories

51. *Engine controls.* If throttles or power levers for turbopropeller powered airplanes are such that any position of these controls will reduce the fuel flow to the engine(s) below that necessary for satisfactory and safe idle operation of the engine while the airplane is in flight, a means must be provided to prevent inadvertent movement of the control into this position. The means provided must incorporate a positive lock or stop at this idle position and must require a separate and distinct operation by the crew to displace

the control from the normal engine operating range.

52. *Reverse thrust controls.* For turbopropeller powered airplanes, the propeller reverse thrust controls must have a means to prevent their inadvertent operation. The means must have a positive lock or stop at the idle position and must require a separate and distinct operation by the crew to displace the control from the flight regime.

53. *Engine ignition systems.* Each turbopropeller airplane ignition system must be considered an essential electrical load.

54. *Powerplant accessories.* The powerplant accessories must meet FAR 23.1163, and if the continued rotation of any accessory remotely driven by the engine is hazardous when malfunctioning occurs, there must be means to prevent rotation without interfering with the continued operation of the engine.

Powerplant Fire Protection

55. *Fire detector system.* For turbopropeller powered airplanes, the following apply:

(a) There must be a means that ensures prompt detection of fire in the engine compartment. An overtemperature switch in each engine cooling air exit is an acceptable method of meeting this requirement.

(b) Each fire detector must be constructed and installed to withstand the vibration, inertia, and other loads to which it may be subjected in operation.

(c) No fire detector may be affected by any oil, water, other fluids, or fumes that might be present.

(d) There must be means to allow the flight crew to check, in flight, the functioning of each fire detector electric circuit.

(e) Wiring and other components of each fire detector system in a fire zone must be at least fire resistant.

56. *Fire protection, cowling and nacelle skin.* For reciprocating engine powered airplanes, the engine cowling must be designed and constructed so that no fire originating in the engine compartment can enter either through openings or by burn through, any other region where it would create additional hazards.

57. *Flammable fluid fire protection.* If flammable fluids or vapors might be liberated by the leakage of fluid systems in areas other than engine compartments, there must be means to—

(a) Prevent the ignition of those fluids or vapors by any other equipment; or

(b) Control any fire resulting from that ignition.

Equipment

58. *Powerplant instruments.* (a) The following are required for turbopropeller airplanes:

(1) The instruments required by FAR 23.1305 (a) (1) through (4), (b) (2) and (4).

(2) A gas temperature indicator for each engine.

(3) Free air temperature indicator.

(4) A fuel flowmeter indicator for each engine.

(5) Oil pressure warning means for each engine.

(6) A torque indicator or adequate means for indicating power output for each engine.

(7) Fire warning indicator for each engine.

(8) A means to indicate when the propeller blade angle is below the low-pitch position corresponding to idle operation in flight.

(9) A means to indicate the functioning of the ice protection system for each engine.

(b) For turbopropeller powered airplanes, the turbopropeller blade position indicator must begin indicating when the blade has moved below the flight low-pitch position.

(c) The following instruments are required for reciprocating engine powered airplanes:

(1) The instruments required by FAR 23.1305.

(2) A cylinder head temperature indicator for each engine.

(3) A manifold pressure indicator for each engine.

Systems and Equipments

General

59. *Function and installation.* The systems and equipment of the airplane must meet FAR 23.1301, and the following:

(a) Each item of additional installed equipment must—

(1) Be of a kind and design appropriate to its intended function;

(2) Be labeled as to its identification, function, or operating limitations, or any applicable combination of these factors, unless misuse or inadvertent actuation cannot create a hazard;

(3) Be installed according to limitations specified for that equipment; and

(4) Function properly when installed.

(b) Systems and installations must be designed to safeguard against hazards to the aircraft in the event of their malfunction or failure.

(c) Where an installation, the functioning of which is necessary in showing compliance with the applicable requirements, requires a power supply, that installation must be considered an essential load on the power supply, and the power sources and the distribution system must be capable of supplying the following power loads in probable operation combinations and for probable durations:

(1) All essential loads after failure of any prime mover, power converter, or energy storage device.

(2) All essential loads after failure of any one engine on two-engine airplanes.

(3) In determining the probable operating combinations and durations of essential loads for the power failure conditions described in paragraphs (1) and (2) of this paragraph, it is permissible to assume that the power loads are reduced in accordance with a monitoring procedure which is consistent with safety in the types of operations authorized.

60. *Ventilation.* The ventilation system of the airplane must meet FAR 23.831, and in addition, for pressurized aircraft, the ventilating air in flight crew and passenger compartments must be free of harmful or hazardous concentrations of gases and vapors in normal operation and in the event of reasonably probable failures or malfunctioning of the ventilating, heating, pressurization, or other systems, and equipment. If accumulation of hazardous quantities of smoke in the cockpit area is reasonably probable, smoke evacuation must be readily accomplished.

Electrical Systems and Equipment

61. *General.* The electrical systems and equipment of the airplane must meet FAR 23.1351, and the following:

(a) *Electrical system capacity.* The required generating capacity, and number and kinds of power sources must—

(1) Be determined by an electrical load analysis; and

(2) Meet FAR 23.1301.

(b) *Generating system.* The generating system includes electrical power sources, main power busses, transmission cables, and associated control, regulation and protective devices. It must be designed so that—

(1) The system voltage and frequency (as applicable) at the terminals of all essential load equipment can be maintained within the limits for which the equipment is designed, during any probable operating conditions;

(2) System transients due to switching, fault clearing, or other causes do not make essential loads inoperative, and do not cause a smoke or fire hazard;

(3) There are means, accessible in flight to appropriate crewmembers, for the individual and collective disconnection of the electrical power sources from the system; and

(4) There are means to indicate to appropriate crewmembers the generating system quantities essential for the safe operation of the system, including the voltage and current supplied by each generator.

62. *Electrical equipment and installation.* Electrical equipment, controls, and wiring must be installed so that operation of any one unit or system of units will not adversely affect the simultaneous operation of any other electrical unit or system essential to the safe operation.

63. *Distribution system.* (a) For the purpose of complying with this section, the distribution system includes the distribution busses, their associated feeders, and each control and protective device.

(b) Each system must be designed so that essential load circuits can be supplied in the event of reasonably probable faults or open circuits, including faults in heavy current carrying cables.

(c) If two independent sources of electrical power for particular equipment or systems are required under this appendix, their electrical energy supply must be ensured by means such as duplicate electrical equipment, throwover switching, or multichannel or loop circuits separately routed.

64. *Circuit protective devices.* The circuit protective devices for the electrical circuits of the airplane must meet FAR 23.1357, and in addition circuits for loads which are essential to safe operation must have individual and exclusive circuit protection.

APPENDIX B TO PART 135—AIRPLANE FLIGHT RECORDER SPECIFICATIONS

Parameters	Range	Installed system [1] minimum accuracy (to recovered data)	Sampling interval (per second)	Resolution [4] read out
Relative time (from recorded on prior to takeoff).	25 hr minimum	±0.125% per hour	1	1 sec.
Indicated airspeed	V$_{so}$ to V$_D$ (KIAS)	±5% or ±10 kts., whichever is greater. Resolution 2 kts. below 175 KIAS.	1	1% [3].
Altitude	−1,000 ft. to max cert. alt. of A/C.	±100 to ±700 ft. (see Table 1, TSO C51–a).	1	25 to 150
Magnetic heading	360°	±5°	1	1°
Vertical acceleration	−3g to + 6g	±0.2g in addition to ±0.3g maximum datum.	4 (or 1 per second where peaks, ref. to 1g are recorded).	0.03g.
Longitudinal acceleration	±1.0g	±1.5% max. range excluding datum error of ±5%.	2	0.01g.
Pitch attitude	100% of usable	±2°	1	0.8°

Parameters	Range	Installed system[1] minimum accuracy (to recovered data)	Sampling interval (per second)	Resolution[4] read out
Roll attitude	±60° or 100% of usable range, whichever is greater.	±2°	1	0.8°
Stabilizer trim position	Full range	±3% unless higher uniquely required.	1	1%[3].
Or				
Pitch control position	Full range	±3% unless higher uniquely required.	1	1%[3].
Engine Power, Each Engine				
Fan or N_1 speed or EPR or cockpit indications used for aircraft certification.	Maximum range	±5%	1	1%[3].
Or				
Prop. speed and torque (sample once/sec as close together as practicable).			1 (prop speed), 1 (torque).	
Altitude rate[2] (need depends on altitude resolution).	±8,000 fpm	±10%. Resolution 250 fpm below 12,000 ft. indicated.	1	250 fpm Below 12,000
Angle of attack[2] (need depends on altitude resolution).	−20° to 40° or of usable range.	±2°	1	0.8%[3]
Radio transmitter keying (discrete).	On/off		1.	
TE flaps (discrete or analog)	Each discrete position (U, D, T/O, AAP). Or.		1.	
	Analog 0–100% range	±3°	1	1%[3]
LE flaps (discrete or analog)	Each discrete position (U, D, T/O, AAP). Or.		1.	
	Analog 0–100% range	±3°	1	1%[3].
Thrust reverser, each engine (Discrete).	Stowed or full reverse		1.	
Spoiler/speedbrake (discrete)	Stowed or out		1.	
Autopilot engaged (discrete)	Engaged or disengaged		1.	

[1] When data sources are aircraft instruments (except altimeters) of acceptable quality to fly the aircraft the recording system excluding these sensors (but including all other characteristics of the recording system) shall contribute no more than half of the values in this column.
[2] If data from the altitude encoding altimeter (100 ft. resolution) is used, then either one of these parameters should also be recorded. If however, altitude is recorded at a minimum resolution of 25 feet, then these two parameters can be omitted.
[3] Per cent of full range.
[4] This column applies to aircraft manufacturing after October 11, 1991.

[Doc. No. 25530, 53 FR 26152, July 11, 1988; 53 FR 30906, Aug. 16, 1988, as amended by Amdt. 135–69, 62 FR 38397, July 17, 1997]

APPENDIX C TO PART 135—HELICOPTER FLIGHT RECORDER SPECIFICATIONS

Parameters	Range	Installed system[1] minimum accuracy (to recovered data)	Sampling interval (per second)	Resolution[3] read out
Relative time (from recorded on prior to takeoff).	25 hr minimum	±0.125% per hour	1	1 sec.
Indicated airspeed	V_m in to V_D (KIAS) (minimum airspeed signal attainable with installed pilot-static system).	±5% or ±10 kts., whichever is greater.	1	1 kt.
Altitude	−1,000 ft to 20,000 ft. pressure altitude.	±100 to ±700 ft. (see Table 1, TSO C51–a).	1	25 to 150 ft.
Magnetic heading	360°	±5°	1	1°.
Vertical acceleration	−3g to +6g	±0.2g in addition to ±0.3g maximum datum.	4 (or 1 per second where peaks, ref. to 1g are recorded).	0.05g.
Longitudinal acceleration	±1.0g	±1.5% max. range excluding datum error of ±5%.	2	0.03g.
Pitch attitude	100% of usable range	±2°	1	0.8°.
Roll attitude	±60° or 100% of usable range, whichever is greater.	±2°	1	0.8°.

525

Parameters	Range	Installed system [1] minimum accuracy (to recovered data)	Sampling interval (per second)	Resolution [3] read out
Altitude rate	±8,000 fpm	±10% Resolution 250 fpm below 12,000 ft. indicated.	1	250 fpm below 12,000.
Engine Power, Each Engine				
Main rotor speed	Maximum range	±5%	1	1% [2]
Free or power turbine	Maximum range	+ 5%	1	1% [2]
Engine torque	Maximum range	±5%	1	1% [2]
Flight Control—Hydraulic Pressure				
Primary (discrete)	High/low		1.	
Secondary—if applicable (discrete).	High/low		1.	
Radio transmitter keying (discrete).	On/off		1.	
Autopilot engaged (discrete) ..	Engaged or disengaged		1.	
SAS status—engaged (discrete).	Engaged/disengaged		1.	
SAS fault status (discrete)	Fault/OK		1.	
Flight Controls				
Collective [4]	Full range	±3%	2	1% [2]
Pedal Position [4]	Full range	±3%	2	1% [2]
Lat. Cyclic [4]	Full range	±3%	2	1% [2]
Long. Cyclic [4]	Full range	±3%	2	1% [2]
Controllable Stabilator Position [4].	Full range	±3%	2	1% [2]

[1] When data sources are aircraft instruments (except altimeters) of acceptable quality to fly the aircraft the recording system excluding these sensors (but including all other characteristics of the recording system) shall contribute no more than half of the values in this column.

[2] Per cent of full range.

[3] This column applies to aircraft manufactured after October 11, 1991.

[4] For all aircraft manufactured on or after December 6, 2010, the sampling interval per second is 4.

[Doc. No. 25530, 53 FR 26152, July 11, 1988; 53 FR 30906, Aug. 16, 1988, as amended by Amdt. 135–69, 62 FR 38397, July 17, 1997; Amdt. 135–113, 73 FR 12570, Mar. 7, 2008; 73 FR 15281, Mar. 21, 2008; Amdt. 135–121, 75 FR 17047, Apr. 5, 2010]

APPENDIX D TO PART 135—AIRPLANE FLIGHT RECORDER SPECIFICATION

Parameters	Range	Accuracy sensor input to DFDR readout	Sampling interval (per second)	resolution [4] read out
Time (GMT or Frame Counter) (range 0 to 4095, sampled 1 per frame).	24 Hrs	±0.125% Per Hour	0.25 (1 per 4 seconds).	1 sec.
Altitude	−1,000 ft to max certificated altitude of aircraft.	±100 to ±700 ft (See Table 1, TSO–C51a).	1	5′ to 35′ [1].
Airspeed	50 KIAS to V_{so}, and V_{so} to 1.2 V_D.	±5%, ±3%	1	1kt
Heading	360°	±2°	1	0.5°
Normal Acceleration (Vertical)	−3g to + 6g	±1% of max range excluding datum error of ±5%.	8	0.01g
Pitch Attitude	±75°	±2°	1	0.5°
Roll Attitude	±180°	±2°	1	0.5°.
Radio Transmitter Keying	On-Off (Discrete)		1	
Thrust/Power on Each Engine	Full range forward	±2%	1 (per engine) ...	0.2% [2].
Trailing Edge Flap or Cockpit Control Selection.	Full range or each discrete position.	±3° or as pilot's indicator	0.5	0.5% [2].
Leading Edge Flap on or Cockpit Control Selection.	Full range or each discrete position.	±3° or as pilot's indicator	0.5	0.5% [2].
Thrust Reverser Position	Stowed, in transit, and reverse (discretion).		1 (per 4 seconds per engine).	
Ground Spoiler Position/ Speed Brake Selection.	Full range or each discrete position.	±2% unless higher accuracy uniquely required.	1	0.22 [2].
Marker Beacon Passage	Discrete		1	
Autopilot Engagement	Discrete		1	
Longitudinal Acceleration	±1g	±1.5% max range excluding datum error of ±5%.	4	0.01g.
Pilot Input And/or Surface Position-Primary Controls (Pitch, Roll, Yaw) [3].	Full range	±2° unless higher accuracy uniquely required.	1	0.2% [2].

Parameters	Range	Accuracy sensor input to DFDR readout	Sampling interval (per second)	resolution [4] read out
Lateral Acceleration	±1g	±1.5% max range excluding datum error of ±5%.	4	0.01g.
Pitch Trim Position	Full range	±3% unless higher accuracy uniquely required.	1	0.3% [2].
Glideslope Deviation	±400 Microamps	±3%	1	0.3% [2].
Localizer Deviation	±400 Microamps	±3%	1	0.3% [2].
AFCS Mode And Engagement Status.	Discrete		1	
Radio Altitude	−20 ft to 2,500 ft	±2 Ft or ±3% whichever is greater below 500 ft and ±5% above 500 ft.	1	1 ft + 5% [2] above 500'.
Master Warning	Discrete		1	
Main Gear Squat Switch Status.	Discrete		1	
Angle of Attack (if recorded directly).	As installed	As installed	2	0.3% [2].
Outside Air Temperature or Total Air Temperature.	−50 °C to +90 °C	±2° c	0.5	0.3° c
Hydraulics, Each System Low Pressure.	Discrete		0.5	or 0.5% [2].
Groundspeed	As installed	Most accurate systems installed (IMS equipped aircraft only).	1	0.2% [2].

If additional recording capacity is available, recording of the following parameters is recommended. The parameters are listed in order of significance:

Drift Angle	When available. As installed.	As installed	4	
Wind Speed and Direction	When available. As installed.	As installed	4	
Latitude and Longitude	When available. As installed.	As installed	4	
Brake pressure/Brake pedal position.	As installed	As installed	1	
Additional engine parameters:				
EPR	As installed	As installed	1 (per engine)	
N [1]	As installed	As installed	1 (per engine)	
N [2]	As installed	As installed	1 (per engine)	
EGT	As installed	As installed	1 (per engine)	
Throttle Lever Position	As installed	As installed	1 (per engine)	
Fuel Flow	As installed	As installed	1 (per engine)	
TCAS:				
TA	As installed	As installed	1	
RA	As installed	As installed	1	
Sensitivity level (as selected by crew).	As installed	As installed	2	
GPWS (ground proximity warning system).	Discrete		1	
Landing gear or gear selector position.	Discrete		0.25 (1 per 4 seconds).	
DME 1 and 2 Distance	0–200 NM;	As installed	0.25	1mi.
Nav 1 and 2 Frequency Selection.	Full range	As installed	0.25.	

[1] When altitude rate is recorded. Altitude rate must have sufficient resolution and sampling to permit the derivation of altitude to 5 feet.

[2] Per cent of full range.

[3] For airplanes that can demonstrate the capability of deriving either the control input on control movement (one from the other) for all modes of operation and flight regimes, the "or" applies. For airplanes with non-mechanical control systems (fly-by-wire) the "and" applies. In airplanes with split surfaces, suitable combination of inputs is acceptable in lieu of recording each surface separately.

[4] This column applies to aircraft manufactured after October 11, 1991.

[Doc. No. 25530, 53 FR 26153, July 11, 1988; 53 FR 30906, Aug. 16, 1988]

APPENDIX E TO PART 135—HELICOPTER FLIGHT RECORDER SPECIFICATIONS

Parameters	Range	Accuracy sensor input to DFDR readout	Sampling interval (per second)	Resolution [2] read out
Time (GMT)	24 Hrs	±0.125% Per Hour	0.25 (1 per 4 seconds).	1 sec

Parameters	Range	Accuracy sensor input to DFDR readout	Sampling interval (per second)	Resolution[2] read out
Altitude	−1,000 ft to max certificated altitude of aircraft.	±100 to ±700 ft (See Table 1, TSO-C51a).	1	5′ to 30′.
Airspeed	As the installed measuring system.	±3%	1	1 kt
Heading	360°	±2°	1	0.5°.
Normal Acceleration (Vertical)	−3g to + 6g	±1% of max range excluding datum error of ±5%.	8	0.01g
Pitch Attitude	±75°	±2°	2	0.5°
Roll Attitude	±180°	±2°	2	0.5°.
Radio Transmitter Keying	On-Off (Discrete)		1	0.25 sec
Power in Each Engine: Free Power Turbine Speed *and* Engine Torque.	0–130% (power Turbine Speed) Full range (Torque).	±2%	1 speed 1 torque (per engine).	0.2%[1] to 0.4%[1]
Main Rotor Speed	0–130%	±2%	2	0.3%[1]
Altitude Rate	±6,000 ft/min	As installed	2	0.2%[1]
Pilot Input—Primary Controls (Collective, Longitudinal Cyclic, Lateral Cyclic, Pedal)[3].	Full range	±3%	2	0.5%[1]
Flight Control Hydraulic Pressure Low.	Discrete, each circuit		1	
Flight Control Hydraulic Pressure Selector Switch Position, 1st and 2nd stage.	Discrete		1	
AFCS Mode and Engagement Status.	Discrete (5 bits necessary).		1	
Stability Augmentation System Engage.	Discrete		1	
SAS Fault Status	Discrete		0.25	
Main Gearbox Temperature Low.	As installed	As installed	0.25	0.5%[1]
Main Gearbox Temperature High.	As installed	As installed	0.5	0.5%[1]
Controllable Stabilator Position.	Full Range	±3%	2	0.4%[1].
Longitudinal Acceleration	±1g	±1.5% max range excluding datum error of ±5%.	4	0.01g.
Lateral Acceleration	±1g	±1.5% max range excluding datum of ±5%.	4	0.01g.
Master Warning	Discrete		1	
Nav 1 and 2 Frequency Selection.	Full range	As installed	0.25	
Outside Air Temperature	−50 °C to + 90 °C	±2° c	0.5	0.3° c

[1] Per cent of full range.
[2] This column applies to aircraft manufactured after October 11, 1991.
[3] For all aircraft manufactured on or after December 6, 2010, the sampling interval per second is 4.

[Doc. No. 25530, 53 FR 26154, July 11, 1988; 53 FR 30906, Aug. 16, 1988; Amdt. 135–113, 73 FR 12571, Mar. 7, 2008; 73 FR 15281, Mar. 21, 2008; Amdt. 135–121, 75 FR 17047, Apr. 5, 2010]

APPENDIX F TO PART 135—AIRPLANE FLIGHT RECORDER SPECIFICATION

The recorded values must meet the designated range, resolution and accuracy requirements during static and dynamic conditions. Dynamic condition means the parameter is experiencing change at the maximum rate attainable, including the maximum rate of reversal. All data recorded must be correlated in time to within one second.

Parameters	Range	Accuracy (sensor input)	Seconds per sampling interval	Resolution	Remarks
1. Time or Relative Time Counts[1].	24 Hrs, 0 to 4095.	±0.125% Per Hour.	4	1 sec	UTC time preferred when available. Counter increments each 4 seconds of system operation.
2. Pressure Altitude.	−1000 ft to max certificated altitude of aircraft. + 5000 ft.	±100 to ±700 ft (see table, TSO C124a or TSO C51a).	1	5′ to 35″	Data should be obtained from the air data computer when practicable.
3. Indicated airspeed or Calibrated airspeed.	50 KIAS or minimum value to Max V_{so+} and V_{so} to 1.2 $V_{.D.}$	±5% and ±3%	1	1 kt	Data should be obtained from the air data computer when practicable.

528

The recorded values must meet the designated range, resolution and accuracy requirements during static and dynamic conditions. Dynamic condition means the parameter is experiencing change at the maximum rate attainable, including the maximum rate of reversal. All data recorded must be correlated in time to within one second.

Parameters	Range	Accuracy (sensor input)	Seconds per sampling interval	Resolution	Remarks
4. Heading (Primary flight crew reference).	0–360° and Discrete "true" or "mag".	±2°	1	0.5°	When true or magnetic heading can be selected as the primary heading reference, a discrete indicating selection must be recorded.
5. Normal Acceleration (Vertical)[9].	−3g to +6g	±1% of max range excluding datum error of ±5%.	0.125	0.004g	
6. Pitch Attitude ..	±75%	±2°	1 or 0.25 for airplanes operated under § 135.152(j).	0.5°	A sampling rate of 0.25 is recommended.
7. Roll Attitude[2] ..	±180°	±2°	1 or 0.5 0.5 airplanes operated under § 135.152(j).	0.5°	A sampling rate of 0.5 is recommended.
8. Manual Radio Transmitter Keying or CVR/DFDR synchronization reference.	On-Off (Discrete) None		1		Preferably each crew member but one discrete acceptable for all transmission provided the CVR/FDR system complies with TSO C124a CVR synchronization requirements (paragraph 4.2.1 ED–55).
9. Thrust/Power on each engine—primary flight crew reference.	Full Range Forward.	±2%	1 (per engine)	0.3% of full range.	Sufficient parameters (e.g. EPR, N1 or Torque, NP) as appropriate to the particular engine being recorded to determine power in forward and reverse thrust, including potential overspeed condition.
10. Autopilot Engagement.	Discrete "on" or "off".		1		
11. Longitudinal Acceleration.	±1g	±1.5% max. range excluding datum error of ±5%.	0.25	0.004g.	
12a. Pitch control(s) position (nonfly-by-wire systems)[18].	Full Range	±2° unless higher accuracy uniquely required.	0.5 or 0.25 for airplanes operated under § 135.152(j).	0.5% of full range.	For airplanes that have a flight control breakaway capability that allows either pilot to operate the controls independently, record both control inputs. The control inputs may be sampled alternately once per second to produce the sampling interval of 0.5 or 0.25, as applicable.
12b. Pitch control(s) position (fly-by-wire systems)[3][18].	Full Range	±2° unless higher accuracy uniquely required.	0.5 or 0.25 for airplanes operated under § 135.152(j).	0.2% of full range.	
13a. Lateral control position(s) (nonfly-by-wire)[18].	Full Range	±2° unless higher accuracy uniquely required.	0.5 or 0.25 for airplanes operated under § 135.152(j).	0.2% of full range.	For airplanes that have a flight control breakaway capability that allows either pilot to operate the controls independently, record both control inputs. The control inputs may be sampled alternately once per second to produce the sampling interval of 0.5 or 0.25, as applicable.
13b. Lateral control position(s) (fly-by-wire)[4][18].	Full Range	±2° unless higher accuracy uniquely required.	0.5 or 0.25 for airplanes operated under § 135.152(j).	0.2% of full range.	

529

The recorded values must meet the designated range, resolution and accuracy requirements during static and dynamic conditions. Dynamic condition means the parameter is experiencing change at the maximum rate attainable, including the maximum rate of reversal. All data recorded must be correlated in time to within one second.

Parameters	Range	Accuracy (sensor input)	Seconds per sampling interval	Resolution	Remarks
14a. Yaw control position(s) (nonfly-by-wire) [5] [18].	Full Range	±2° unless higher accuracy uniquely required.	0.5	0.3% of full range.	For airplanes that have a flight control breakaway capability that allows either pilot to operate the controls independently, record both control inputs. The control inputs may be sampled alternately once per second to produce the sampling of 0.5 or 0.25, as applicable.
14b. Yaw control position(s) (fly-by-wire) [18].	Full Range	±2° unless higher accuracy uniquely required.	0.5	0.2% of full range.	
15. Pitch control surface(s) position [6] [18].	Full Range	±2° unless higher accuracy uniquely required.	0.5 or 0.25 for airplanes operated under § 135.152(j)..	0.3% of full range.	For airplanes fitted with multiple or split surfaces, a suitable combination of inputs is acceptable in lieu of recording each surface separately. The control surfaces may be sampled alternately to produce the sampling interval of 0.5 or 0.25, as applicable.
16. Lateral control surface(s) position [7] [18].	Full Range	±2° unless higher accuracy uniquely required.	0.5 or 0.25 for airplanes operated under § 135.152(j).	0.2% of full range.	A suitable combination of surface position sensors is acceptable in lieu of recording each surface separately. The control surfaces may be sampled alternately to produce the sampling interval of 0.5 or 0.25, as applicable.
17. Yaw control surface(s) position [8] [18].	Full Range	±2° unless higher accuracy uniquely required.	0.5	0.2% of full range.	For airplanes with multiple or split surfaces, a suitable combination of surface position sensors is acceptable in lieu of recording each surface separately. The control surfaces may be sampled alternately to produce the sampling interval of 0.5.
18. Lateral Acceleration.	±1g	±1.5% max. range excluding datum error of ±5%.	0.25	0.004g.	
19. Pitch Trim Surface Position.	Full Range	±3° Unless Higher Accuracy Uniquely Required.	1	0.6% of full range	
20. Trailing Edge Flap or Cockpit Control Selection [10].	Full Range or Each Position (discrete).	±3° or as Pilot's Indicator.	2	0.5% of full range.	Flap position and cockpit control may each be sampled alternately at 4 second intervals, to give a data point every 2 seconds.
21. Leading Edge Flap or Cockpit Control Selection [11].	Full Range or Each Discrete Position.	±3° or as Pilot's Indicator and sufficient to determine each discrete position.	2	0.5% of full range.	Left and right sides, of flap position and cockpit control may each be sampled at 4 second intervals, so as to give a data point to every 2 seconds.
22. Each Thrust reverser Position (or equivalent for propeller airplane).	Stowed, In Transit, and reverse (Discrete).		1 (per engine)		Turbo-jet—2 discretes enable the 3 states to be determined. Turbo-prop—1 discrete

The recorded values must meet the designated range, resolution and accuracy requirements during static and dynamic conditions. Dynamic condition means the parameter is experiencing change at the maximum rate attainable, including the maximum rate of reversal. All data recorded must be correlated in time to within one second.

Parameters	Range	Accuracy (sensor input)	Seconds per sampling interval	Resolution	Remarks
23. Ground Spoiler Position or Speed Brake Selection [12].	Full Range or Each Position (discrete).	±2° Unless Higher Accuracy Uniquely Required.	1 or 0.5 for airplanes operated under § 135.152(j).	0.5% of full range	
24. Outside Air Temperature or Total Air Temperature [13].	−50 °C to + 90 °C.	±2 °C	2	0.3 °C	
25. Autopilot/ Autothrottle/ AFCS Mode and Engagement Status.	A suitable combination of discretes.		1		Discretes should show which systems are engaged and which primary modes are controlling the flight path and speed of the aircraft.
26. Radio Altitude [14].	−20 ft to 2,500 ft.	±2 ft or ±3% Whichever is Greater Below 500 ft and ±5% Above 500 ft.	1	1 ft + 5% above 500 ft.	For autoland/category 3 operations. Each radio altimeter should be recorded, but arranged so that at least one is recorded each second.
27. Localizer Deviation, MLS Azimuth, or GPS Lateral Deviation.	±400 Microamps or available sensor range as installed ±62°.	As installed ±3% recommended.	1	0.3% of full range.	For autoland/category 3 operations. Each system should be recorded but arranged so that at least one is recorded each second. It is not necessary to record ILS and MLS at the same time, only the approach aid in use need be recorded.
28. Glideslope Deviation, MLS Elevation, or GPS Vertical Deviation.	±400 Microamps or available sensor range as installed. 0.9 to + 30°	As installed ±3% recommended.	1	0.3% of full range.	For autoland/category 3 operations. Each system should be recorded but arranged so that at least one is recorded each second. It is not necessary to record ILS and MLS at the same time, only the approach aid in use need be recorded.
29. Marker Beacon Passage.	Discrete "on" or "off".		1		A single discrete is acceptable for all markers.
30. Master Warning.	Discrete		1		Record the master warning and record each "red" warning that cannot be determined from other parameters or from the cockpit voice recorder.
31. Air/ground sensor (primary airplane system reference nose or main gear).	Discrete "air" or "ground".		1 (0.25 recommended.).		
32. Angle of Attack (If measured directly).	As installed	As installed	2 or 0.5 for airplanes operated under § 135.152(j).	0.3% of full range.	If left and right sensors are available, each may be recorded at 4 or 1 second intervals, as appropriate, so as to give a data point at 2 seconds or 0.5 second, as required.
33. Hydraulic Pressure Low, Each System.	Discrete or available sensor range, "low" or "normal".	±5%	2	0.5% of full range.	
34. Groundspeed	As installed	Most Accurate Systems Installed.	1	0.2% of full range.	
35. GPWS (ground proximity warning system).	Discrete "warning" or "off".		1		A suitable combination of discretes unless recorder capacity is limited in which case a single discrete for all modes is acceptable.

531

The recorded values must meet the designated range, resolution and accuracy requirements during static and dynamic conditions. Dynamic condition means the parameter is experiencing change at the maximum rate attainable, including the maximum rate of reversal. All data recorded must be correlated in time to within one second.

Parameters	Range	Accuracy (sensor input)	Seconds per sampling interval	Resolution	Remarks
36. Landing Gear Position or Landing gear cockpit control selection.	Discrete	....	4	....	A suitable combination of discretes should be recorded.
37. Drift Angle [15]	As installed	As installed	4	0.1°	
38. Wind Speed and Direction.	As installed	As installed	4	1 knot, and 1.0°.	
39. Latitude and Longitude.	As installed	As installed	4	0.002°, or as installed.	Provided by the Primary Navigation System Reference. Where capacity permits latitude/longitude resolution should be 0.0002°.
40. Stick shaker and pusher activation.	Discrete(s) "on" or "off".	....	1	....	A suitable combination of discretes to determine activation.
41. Windshear Detection.	Discrete "warning" or "off".	....	1.		
42. Throttle/power lever position [16].	Full Range	±2%	1 for each lever	2% of full range	For airplanes with non-mechanically linked cockpit engine controls.
43. Additional Engine Parameters.	As installed	As installed	Each engine each second.	2% of full range	Where capacity permits, the preferred priority is indicated vibration level, N2, EGT, Fuel Flow, Fuel Cutoff lever position and N3, unless engine manufacturer recommends otherwise.
44. Traffic Alert and Collision Avoidance System (TCAS).	Discretes	As installed	1	....	A suitable combination of discretes should be recorded to determine the status of—Combined Control, Vertical Control, Up Advisory, and down advisory. (ref. ARINC Characteristic 735 Attachment 6E, TCAS VERTICAL RA DATA OUTPUT WORD.)
45. DME 1 and 2 Distance.	0–200 NM;	As installed	4	1 NM	1 mile.
46. Nav 1 and 2 Selected Frequency.	Full range	As installed	4	....	Sufficient to determine selected frequency.
47. Selected barometric setting.	Full Range	±5%	(1 per 64 sec.) ..	0.2% of full range.	
48. Selected altitude.	Full Range	±5%	1	100 ft.	
49. Selected speed.	Full Range	±5%	1	1 knot.	
50. Selected Mach.	Full Range	±5%	1	.01.	
51. Selected vertical speed.	Full Range	±5%	1	100 ft./min.	
52. Selected heading.	Full Range	±5%	1	1°.	
53. Selected flight path.	Full Range	±5%	1	1°.	
54. Selected decision height.	Full Range	±5%	64	1 ft.	
55. EFIS display format.	Discrete(s)		4	....	Discretes should show the display system status (e.g., off, normal, fail, composite, sector, plan, nav aids, weather radar, range, copy.

The recorded values must meet the designated range, resolution and accuracy requirements during static and dynamic conditions. Dynamic condition means the parameter is experiencing change at the maximum rate attainable, including the maximum rate of reversal. All data recorded must be correlated in time to within one second.

Parameters	Range	Accuracy (sensor input)	Seconds per sampling interval	Resolution	Remarks
56. Multi-function/ Engine Alerts Display format.	Discrete(s)	....	4	....	Discretes should show the display system status (e.g., off, normal, fail, and the identity of display pages for emergency procedures, need not be recorded.
57. Thrust comand [17].	Full Range	±2%	2	2% of full range	
58. Thrust target	Full Range	±2%	4	2% of full range.	
59. Fuel quantity in CG trim tank.	Full Range	±5%	(1 per 64 sec.) ..	1% of full range.	
60. Primary Navigation System Reference.	Discrete GPS, INS, VOR/ DME, MLS, Localizer Glideslope.	....	4	....	A suitable combination of discretes to determine the Primary Navigation System reference.
61. Ice Detection	Discrete "ice" or "no ice".	....	4.		
62. Engine warning each engine vibration.	Discrete	....	1.		
63. Engine warning each engine over temp..	Discrete	....	1.		
64. Engine warning each engine oil pressure low.	Discrete	....	1.		
65. Engine warning each engine over speed.	Discrete	....	1.		
66. Yaw Trim Surface Position.	Full Range	±3% Unless Higher Accuracy Uniquely Required.	2	0.3% of full range.	
67. Roll Trim Surface Position.	Full Range	±3% Unless Higher Accuracy Uniquely Required.	2	0.3% of full range.	
68. Brake Pressure (left and right).	As installed	±5%	1	....	To determine braking effort applied by pilots or by autobrakes.
69. Brake Pedal Application (left and right).	Discrete or Analog "applied" or "off".	±5% (Analog)	1	....	To determine braking applied by pilots.
70. Yaw or sideslip angle.	Full Range	±5%	1	0.5°.	
71. Engine bleed valve position.	Discrete "open" or "closed".	....	4.		
72. De-icing or anti-icing system selection.	Discrete "on" or "off".	....	4.		
73. Computed center of gravity.	Full Range	±5%	(1 per 64 sec.) ..	1% of full range.	
74. AC electrical bus status.	Discrete "power" or "off".	....	4	....	Each bus.
75. DC electrical bus status.	Discrete "power" or "off".	....	4	....	Each bus.
76. APU bleed valve position.	Discrete "open" or "closed".	....	4.		
77. Hydraulic Pressure (each system).	Full range	±5%	2	100 psi.	
78. Loss of cabin pressure.	Discrete "loss" or "normal".	....	1.		
79. Computer failure (critical flight and engine control systems).	Discrete "fail" or "normal".	....	4.		

The recorded values must meet the designated range, resolution and accuracy requirements during static and dynamic conditions. Dynamic condition means the parameter is experiencing change at the maximum rate attainable, including the maximum rate of reversal. All data recorded must be correlated in time to within one second.

Parameters	Range	Accuracy (sensor input)	Seconds per sampling interval	Resolution	Remarks
80. Heads-up display (when an information source is installed).	Discrete(s) "on" or "off".	....	4.		
81. Para-visual display (when an information source is installed).	Discrete(s) "on" or "off".	....	1.		
82. Cockpit trim control input position—pitch.	Full Range	±5%	1	0.2% of full range.	Where mechanical means for control inputs are not available, cockpit display trim positions should be recorded.
83. Cockpit trim control input position—roll.	Full Range	±5%	1	0.7% of full range.	Where mechanical means for control inputs are not available, cockpit display trim position should be recorded.
84. Cockpit trim control input position—yaw.	Full Range	±5%	1	0.3% of full range.	Where mechanical means for control input are not available, cockpit display trim positions should be recorded.
85. Trailing edge flap and cockpit flap control position.	Full Range	±5%	2	0.5% of full range.	Trailing edge flaps and cockpit flap control position may each be sampled alternately at 4 second intervals to provide a sample each 0.5 second.
86. Leading edge flap and cockpit flap control position.	Full Range or Discrete.	±5%	1	0.5% of full range.	
87. Ground spoiler position and speed brake selection.	Full Range or Discrete.	±5%	0.5	0.3% of full range	
88. All cockpit flight control input forces (control wheel, control column, rudder pedal) [18].	Full Range Control wheel ±70 lbs. Control column ±85 lbs. Rudder pedal ±165 lbs.	±5°	1	0.3% of full range.	For fly-by-wire flight control systems, where flight control surface position is a function of the displacement of the control input device only, it is not necessary to record this parameter. For airplanes that have a flight control breakaway capability that allows either pilot to operate the control independently, record both control force inputs. The control force inputs may be sampled alternately once per 2 seconds to produce the sampling interval of 1.

[1] For A300 B2/B4 airplanes, resolution = 6 seconds.
[2] For A330/A340 series airplanes, resolution = 0.703°.
[3] For A318/A319/A320/A321 series airplanes, resolution = 0.275% (0.088°>0.064°). For A330/A340 series airplanes, resolution = 2.20% (0.703°>0.064°).
[4] For A318/A319/A320/A321 series airplanes, resolution = 0.22% (0.088°>0.080°). For A330/A340 series airplanes, resolution = 1.76% (0.703°>0.080°).
[5] For A330/A340 series airplanes, resolution = 1.18% (0.703°>0.120°).
[6] For A330/A340 series airplanes, resolution = 0.783% (0.352°>0.090°).
[7] For A330/A340 series airplanes, aileron resolution = 0.704% (0.352°>0.100°). For A330/A340 series airplanes, spoiler resolution = 1.406% (0.703°>0.100°).
[8] For A330/A340 series airplanes, resolution = 0.30% (0.176°>0.12°). For A330/A340 series airplanes, seconds per sampling interval = 1.
[9] For B–717 series airplanes, resolution = .005g. For Dassault F900C/F900EX airplanes, resolution = .007g.
[10] For A330/A340 series airplanes, resolution = 1.05% (0.250°>0.120°).

¹¹ For A330/A340 series airplanes, resolution = 1.05% (0.250°>0.120°). For A300 B2/B4 series airplanes, resolution = 0.92% (0.230°>0.125°).
¹² For A330/A340 series airplanes, spoiler resolution = 1.406% (0.703°>0.100°).
¹³ For A330/A340 series airplanes, resolution = 3.5 °C.
¹⁴ For Dassault F900C/F900EX airplanes, Radic Altitude resolution = 1.25 ft.
¹⁵ For A330/A340 series airplanes, resolution = 3.352 degrees.
¹⁶ For A318/A319/A320/A321 series airplanes, resolution = 4.32%. For A330/A340 series airplanes, resolution is 3.27% of full range for throttle lever angle (TLA); for reverse thrust, reverse throttle lever angle (RLA) resolution is nonlinear over the active reverse thrust range, which is 51.54 degrees to 96.14 degrees. The resolved element is 2.8 degrees uniformly over the entire active reverse thrust range, or 2.9% of the full range value of 96.14 degrees.
¹⁷ For A318/A319/A320/A321 series airplanes, with IAE engines, resolution = 2.58%.
¹⁸ For all aircraft manufactured on or after December 6, 2010, the seconds per sampling interval is 0.125. Each input must be recorded at this rate. Alternately sampling inputs (interleaving) to meet this sampling interval is prohibited.

[Doc. No. 28109, 62 FR 38398, July 17, 1997; 62 FR 48135, Sept. 12, 1997; Amdt. 135–85, 67 FR 54323, Aug. 21, 2002; Amdt. 135–89, 68 FR 42339, July 18, 2003; 68 FR 50069, Aug. 20, 2003; Amdt. 135–113, 73 FR 12570, Mar. 7, 2008; Amdt. 135–121, 75 FR 17047, Apr. 5, 2010; Amdt. 135–120, 75 FR 7357, Feb. 19, 2010; Docket FAA–2017–0733, Amdt. 135–137, 82 FR 34399, July 25, 2017]

APPENDIX G TO PART 135—EXTENDED OPERATIONS (ETOPS)

G135.1 *Definitions.*

G135.1.1 *Adequate Airport* means an airport that an airplane operator may list with approval from the FAA because that airport meets the landing limitations of §135.385 or is a military airport that is active and operational.

G135.1.2 *ETOPS Alternate Airport* means an adequate airport that is designated in a dispatch or flight release for use in the event of a diversion during ETOPS. This definition applies to flight planning and does not in any way limit the authority of the pilot in command during flight.

G135.1.3 *ETOPS Entry Point* means the first point on the route of an ETOPS flight, determined using a one-engine inoperative cruise speed under standard conditions in still air, that is more than 180 minutes from an adequate airport.

G135.1.4 *ETOPS Qualified Person* means a person, performing maintenance for the certificate holder, who has satisfactorily completed the certificate holder's ETOPS training program.

G135.2 *Requirements.*

G135.2.1 *General.* After August 13, 2008, no certificate holder may operate an airplane, other than an all-cargo airplane with more than two engines, outside the continental United States more than 180 minutes flying time (at the one-engine-inoperative cruise speed under standard conditions in still air) from an airport described in §135.364 unless—

(a) The certificate holder receives ETOPS approval from the FAA;

(b) The operation is conducted in a multi-engine transport category turbine-powered airplane;

(c) The operation is planned to be no more than 240 minutes flying time (at the one engine inoperative cruise speed under standard conditions in still air) from an airport described in §135.364; and

(d) The certificate holder meets the requirements of this appendix.

G135.2.2 *Required certificate holder experience prior to conducting ETOPS.*

Before applying for ETOPS approval, the certificate holder must have at least 12 months experience conducting international operations (excluding Canada and Mexico) with multi-engine transport category turbine-engine powered airplanes. The certificate holder may consider the following experience as international operations:

(a) Operations to or from the State of Hawaii.

(b) For certificate holders granted approval to operate under part 135 or part 121 before February 15, 2007, up to 6 months of domestic operating experience and operations in Canada and Mexico in multi-engine transport category turbojet-powered airplanes may be credited as part of the required 12 months of international experience required by paragraph G135.2.2(a) of this appendix.

(c) ETOPS experience with other aircraft types to the extent authorized by the FAA.

G135.2.3 *Airplane requirements.* No certificate holder may conduct ETOPS in an airplane that was manufactured after February 17, 2015 unless the airplane meets the standards of §25.1535.

G135.2.4 *Crew information requirements.* The certificate holder must ensure that flight crews have in-flight access to current weather and operational information needed to comply with §135.83, §135.225, and §135.229. This includes information on all ETOPS Alternate Airports, all destination alternates, and the destination airport proposed for each ETOPS flight.

G135.2.5 *Operational Requirements.*

(a) No person may allow a flight to continue beyond its ETOPS Entry Point unless—

(1) The weather conditions at each ETOPS Alternate Airport are forecast to be at or above the operating minima in the certificate holder's operations specifications for that airport when it might be used (from the earliest to the latest possible landing time), and

(3) All ETOPS Alternate Airports within the authorized ETOPS maximum diversion time are reviewed for any changes in conditions that have occurred since dispatch.

(b) In the event that an operator cannot comply with paragraph G135.2.5(a)(1) of this appendix for a specific airport, another ETOPS Alternate Airport must be substituted within the maximum ETOPS diversion time that could be authorized for that flight with weather conditions at or above operating minima.

(c) Pilots must plan and conduct ETOPS under instrument flight rules.

(d) *Time-Limited Systems.* (1) Except as provided in paragraph G135.2.5(d)(3) of this appendix, the time required to fly the distance to each ETOPS Alternate Airport (at the all-engines-operating cruise speed, corrected for wind and temperature) may not exceed the time specified in the Airplane Flight Manual for the airplane's most limiting fire suppression system time required by regulation for any cargo or baggage compartments (if installed), minus 15 minutes.

(2) Except as provided in G135.2.5(d)(3) of this appendix, the time required to fly the distance to each ETOPS Alternate Airport (at the approved one-engine-inoperative cruise speed, corrected for wind and temperature) may not exceed the time specified in the Airplane Flight Manual for the airplane's most time limited system time (other than the airplane's most limiting fire suppression system time required by regulation for any cargo or baggage compartments), minus 15 minutes.

(3) A certificate holder operating an airplane without the Airplane Flight Manual information needed to comply with paragraphs G135.2.5(d)(1) and (d)(2) of this appendix, may continue ETOPS with that airplane until February 17, 2015.

G135.2.6 *Communications Requirements.*

(a) No person may conduct an ETOPS flight unless the following communications equipment, appropriate to the route to be flown, is installed and operational:

(1) Two independent communication transmitters, at least one of which allows voice communication.

(2) Two independent communication receivers, at least one of which allows voice communication.

(3) Two headsets, or one headset and one speaker.

(b) In areas where voice communication facilities are not available, or are of such poor quality that voice communication is not possible, communication using an alternative system must be substituted.

G135.2.7 *Fuel Requirements.* No person may dispatch or release for flight an ETOPS flight unless, considering wind and other weather conditions expected, it has the fuel otherwise required by this part and enough

fuel to satisfy each of the following requirements:

(a) *Fuel to fly to an ETOPS Alternate Airport.* (1) Fuel to account for rapid decompression and engine failure. The airplane must carry the greater of the following amounts of fuel:

(i) Fuel sufficient to fly to an ETOPS Alternate Airport assuming a rapid decompression at the most critical point followed by descent to a safe altitude in compliance with the oxygen supply requirements of § 135.157;

(ii) Fuel sufficient to fly to an ETOPS Alternate Airport (at the one-engine-inoperative cruise speed under standard conditions in still air) assuming a rapid decompression and a simultaneous engine failure at the most critical point followed by descent to a safe altitude in compliance with the oxygen requirements of § 135.157; or

(iii) Fuel sufficient to fly to an ETOPS Alternate Airport (at the one-engine-inoperative cruise speed under standard conditions in still air) assuming an engine failure at the most critical point followed by descent to the one engine inoperative cruise altitude.

(2) Fuel to account for errors in wind forecasting. In calculating the amount of fuel required by paragraph G135.2.7(a)(1) of this appendix, the certificate holder must increase the actual forecast wind speed by 5% (resulting in an increase in headwind or a decrease in tailwind) to account for any potential errors in wind forecasting. If a certificate holder is not using the actual forecast wind based on a wind model accepted by the FAA, the airplane must carry additional fuel equal to 5% of the fuel required by paragraph G135.2.7(a) of this appendix, as reserve fuel to allow for errors in wind data.

(3) Fuel to account for icing. In calculating the amount of fuel required by paragraph G135.2.7(a)(1) of this appendix, (after completing the wind calculation in G135.2.7(a)(2) of this appendix), the certificate holder must ensure that the airplane carries the greater of the following amounts of fuel in anticipation of possible icing during the diversion:

(i) Fuel that would be burned as a result of airframe icing during 10 percent of the time icing is forecast (including the fuel used by engine and wing anti-ice during this period).

(ii) Fuel that would be used for engine anti-ice, and if appropriate wing anti-ice, for the entire time during which icing is forecast.

(4) Fuel to account for engine deterioration. In calculating the amount of fuel required by paragraph G135.2.7(a)(1) of this appendix (after completing the wind calculation in paragraph G135.2.7(a)(2) of this appendix), the certificate holder must ensure the airplane also carries fuel equal to 5% of the fuel specified above, to account for deterioration in cruise fuel burn performance unless the certificate holder has a program to monitor airplane in-service deterioration to cruise fuel burn performance.

(b) *Fuel to account for holding, approach, and landing.* In addition to the fuel required by paragraph G135.2.7 (a) of this appendix, the airplane must carry fuel sufficient to hold at 1500 feet above field elevation for 15 minutes upon reaching the ETOPS Alternate Airport and then conduct an instrument approach and land.

(c) *Fuel to account for APU use.* If an APU is a required power source, the certificate holder must account for its fuel consumption during the appropriate phases of flight.

G135.2.8 *Maintenance Program Requirements.* In order to conduct an ETOPS flight under § 135.364, each certificate holder must develop and comply with the ETOPS maintenance program as authorized in the certificate holder's operations specifications for each two-engine airplane-engine combination used in ETOPS. This provision does not apply to operations using an airplane with more than two engines. The certificate holder must develop this ETOPS maintenance program to supplement the maintenance program currently approved for the operator. This ETOPS maintenance program must include the following elements:

(a) *ETOPS maintenance document.* The certificate holder must have an ETOPS maintenance document for use by each person involved in ETOPS. The document must—

(1) List each ETOPS Significant System,

(2) Refer to or include all of the ETOPS maintenance elements in this section,

(3) Refer to or include all supportive programs and procedures,

(4) Refer to or include all duties and responsibilities, and

(5) Clearly state where referenced material is located in the certificate holder's document system.

(b) *ETOPS pre-departure service check.* The certificate holder must develop a pre-departure check tailored to their specific operation.

(1) The certificate holder must complete a pre-departure service check immediately before each ETOPS flight.

(2) At a minimum, this check must:

(i) Verify the condition of all ETOPS Significant Systems;

(ii) Verify the overall status of the airplane by reviewing applicable maintenance records; and

(iii) Include an interior and exterior inspection to include a determination of engine and APU oil levels and consumption rates.

(3) An appropriately trained maintenance person, who is ETOPS qualified must accomplish and certify by signature ETOPS specific tasks. Before an ETOPS flight may commence, an ETOPS pre-departure service check (PDSC) Signatory Person, who has been authorized by the certificate holder, must certify by signature, that the ETOPS PDSC has been completed.

(4) For the purposes of this paragraph (b) only, the following definitions apply:

(i) ETOPS qualified person: A person is ETOPS qualified when that person satisfactorily completes the operator's ETOPS training program and is authorized by the certificate holder.

(ii) ETOPS PDSC Signatory Person: A person is an ETOPS PDSC Signatory Person when that person is ETOPS Qualified and that person:

(A) When certifying the completion of the ETOPS PDSC in the United States:

(1) Works for an operator authorized to engage in part 135 or 121 operation or works for a part 145 repair station; and

(2) Holds a U.S. Mechanic's Certificate with airframe and powerplant ratings.

(B) When certifying the completion of the ETOPS PDSC outside of the U.S. holds a certificate in accordance with § 43.17(c)(1) of this chapter; or

(C) When certifying the completion of the ETOPS PDSC outside the U.S. holds the certificates needed or has the requisite experience or training to return aircraft to service on behalf of an ETOPS maintenance entity.

(iii) ETOPS maintenance entity: An entity authorized to perform ETOPS maintenance and complete ETOPS pre-departure service checks and that entity is:

(A) Certificated to engage in part 135 or 121 operations;

(B) Repair station certificated under part 145 of this title; or

(C) Entity authorized pursuant to § 43.17(c)(2) of this chapter.

(c) *Limitations on dual maintenance.* (1) Except as specified in paragraph G135.2.8(c)(2) of this appendix, the certificate holder may not perform scheduled or unscheduled dual maintenance during the same maintenance visit on the same or a substantially similar ETOPS Significant System listed in the ETOPS maintenance document, if the improper maintenance could result in the failure of an ETOPS Significant System.

(2) In the event dual maintenance as defined in paragraph G135.2.8(c)(1) of this appendix cannot be avoided, the certificate holder may perform maintenance provided:

(i) The maintenance action on each affected ETOPS Significant System is performed by a different technician, or

(ii) The maintenance action on each affected ETOPS Significant System is performed by the same technician under the direct supervision of a second qualified individual; and

(iii) For either paragraph G135.2.8(c)(2)(i) or (ii) of this appendix, a qualified individual conducts a ground verification test and any in-flight verification test required under the program developed pursuant to paragraph G135.2.8(d) of this appendix.

(d) *Verification program.* The certificate holder must develop a program for the resolution of discrepancies that will ensure the effectiveness of maintenance actions taken on ETOPS Significant Systems. The verification program must identify potential problems and verify satisfactory corrective action. The verification program must include ground verification and in-flight verification policy and procedures. The certificate holder must establish procedures to clearly indicate who is going to initiate the verification action and what action is necessary. The verification action may be performed on an ETOPS revenue flight provided the verification action is documented as satisfactorily completed upon reaching the ETOPS entry point.

(e) *Task identification.* The certificate holder must identify all ETOPS-specific tasks. An ETOPS qualified person must accomplish and certify by signature that the ETOPS-specific task has been completed.

(f) *Centralized maintenance control procedures.* The certificate holder must develop procedures for centralized maintenance control for ETOPS.

(g) *ETOPS parts control program.* The certificate holder must develop an ETOPS parts control program to ensure the proper identification of parts used to maintain the configuration of airplanes used in ETOPS.

(h) *Enhanced Continuing Analysis and Surveillance System (E–CASS) program.* A certificate holder's existing CASS must be enhanced to include all elements of the ETOPS maintenance program. In addition to the reporting requirements of §135.415 and §135.417, the program includes reporting procedures, in the form specified in §135.415(e), for the following significant events detrimental to ETOPS within 96 hours of the occurrence to the responsible Flight Standards office:

(1) IFSDs, except planned IFSDs performed for flight training.

(2) Diversions and turnbacks for failures, malfunctions, or defects associated with any airplane or engine system.

(3) Uncommanded power or thrust changes or surges.

(4) Inability to control the engine or obtain desired power or thrust.

(5) Inadvertent fuel loss or unavailability, or uncorrectable fuel imbalance in flight.

(6) Failures, malfunctions or defects associated with ETOPS Significant Systems.

(7) Any event that would jeopardize the safe flight and landing of the airplane on an ETOPS flight.

(i) *Propulsion system monitoring.* The certificate holder, in coordination with the responsible Flight Standards office, must—

(1) Establish criteria as to what action is to be taken when adverse trends in propulsion system conditions are detected, and

(2) Investigate common cause effects or systemic errors and submit the findings to the responsible Flight Standards office within 30 days.

(j) *Engine condition monitoring.* (1) The certificate holder must establish an engine-condition monitoring program to detect deterioration at an early stage and to allow for corrective action before safe operation is affected.

(2) This program must describe the parameters to be monitored, the method of data collection, the method of analyzing data, and the process for taking corrective action.

(3) The program must ensure that engine limit margins are maintained so that a prolonged engine-inoperative diversion may be conducted at approved power levels and in all expected environmental conditions without exceeding approved engine limits. This includes approved limits for items such as rotor speeds and exhaust gas temperatures.

(k) *Oil consumption monitoring.* The certificate holder must develop an engine oil consumption monitoring program to ensure that there is enough oil to complete each ETOPS flight. APU oil consumption must be included if an APU is required for ETOPS. The operator's consumption limit may not exceed the manufacturer's recommendation. Monitoring must be continuous and include oil added at each ETOPS departure point. The program must compare the amount of oil added at each ETOPS departure point with the running average consumption to identify sudden increases.

(l) *APU in-flight start program.* If an APU is required for ETOPS, but is not required to run during the ETOPS portion of the flight, the certificate holder must have a program acceptable to the FAA for cold soak in-flight start and run reliability.

(m) *Maintenance training.* For each airplane-engine combination, the certificate holder must develop a maintenance training program to ensure that it provides training adequate to support ETOPS. It must include ETOPS specific training for all persons involved in ETOPS maintenance that focuses on the special nature of ETOPS. This training must be in addition to the operator's maintenance training program used to qualify individuals for specific airplanes and engines.

(n) *Configuration, maintenance, and procedures (CMP) document.* The certificate holder must use a system to ensure compliance with the minimum requirements set forth in the current version of the CMP document for each airplane-engine combination that has a CMP.

(o) *Reporting.* The certificate holder must report quarterly to the responsible Flight Standards office and the airplane and engine manufacturer for each airplane authorized for ETOPS. The report must provide the operating hours and cycles for each airplane.

G135.2.9 *Delayed compliance date for all airplanes.* A certificate holder need not comply with this appendix for any airplane until August 13, 2008.

[Doc. No. FAA–2002–6717, 72 FR 1885, Jan. 16, 2007, as amended by Amdt. 135–108, 72 FR 7348, Feb. 15, 2007; 72 FR 26542, May 10, 2007; Amdt. 135–112, 73 FR 8798, Feb. 15, 2008; Amdt. 135–115, 73 FR 33882, June 16, 2008; Docket FAA–2018–0119, Amdt. 135–139, 83 FR 9175, Mar. 5, 2018]

PART 136—COMMERCIAL AIR TOURS AND NATIONAL PARKS AIR TOUR MANAGEMENT

Subpart A—National Air Tour Safety Standards

Subpart B—National Parks Air Tour Management

Subpart C—Grand Canyon National Park

AUTHORITY: 49 U.S.C. 106(g), 40113, 40119, 44101, 44701, 44701–44702, 44705, 44709–44711, 44713, 44716–44717, 44722, 44901, 44903–44904, 44912, 46105.

SOURCE: Docket No. FAA–2001–8690, 67 FR 65667, Oct. 25, 2002, unless otherwise noted.

Subpart A—National Air Tour Safety Standards

SOURCE: Docket No. FAA–1998–4521, 72 FR 6912, Feb. 13, 2007, unless otherwise noted.

§136.1 Applicability and definitions.

(a) This subpart applies to each person operating or intending to operate a commercial air tour in an airplane or helicopter and, when applicable, to all occupants of the airplane or helicopter engaged in a commercial air tour. When any requirement of this subpart is more stringent than any other requirement of this chapter, the person operating the commercial air tour must comply with the requirement in this subpart.

(b) As of September 11, 2007, this subpart is applicable to:

(1) Part 121 or 135 operators conducting a commercial air tour and holding a part 119 certificate;

(2) Part 91 operators conducting flights as described in §119.1(e)(2); and

(3) Part 91 operators conducting flights as described in 14 CFR 91.146

(c) This subpart is not applicable to operations conducted in balloons, gliders (powered or un-powered), parachutes (powered or un-powered), gyroplanes, or airships.

(d) For the purposes of this subpart the following definitions apply:

Commercial Air Tour means a flight conducted for compensation or hire in an airplane or helicopter where a purpose of the flight is sightseeing. The FAA may consider the following factors in determining whether a flight is a commercial air tour for purposes of this subpart:

(1) Whether there was a holding out to the public of willingness to conduct a sightseeing flight for compensation or hire;

(2) Whether the person offering the flight provided a narrative that referred to areas or points of interest on the surface below the route of the flight;

(3) The area of operation;

(4) How often the person offering the flight conducts such flights;

(5) The route of the flight;

(6) The inclusion of sightseeing flights as part of any travel arrangement package;

(7) Whether the flight in question would have been canceled based on poor visibility of the surface below the route of the flight; and

(8) Any other factors that the FAA considers appropriate.

Commercial Air Tour operator means any person who conducts a commercial air tour.

Life preserver means a flotation device used by an aircraft occupant if the aircraft ditches in water. If an inflatable device, it must be un-inflated and ready for its intended use once inflated. In evaluating whether a non-inflatable life preserver is acceptable to the FAA, the operator must demonstrate to the FAA that such a preserver can be used during an evacuation and will allow all passengers to exit the aircraft without blocking the exit. Each occupant must have the physical capacity to wear and inflate the type of device used once briefed by the commercial air tour operator. Seat cushions do not meet this definition.

Raw terrain means any area on the surface, including water, devoid of any person, structure, vehicle, or vessel.

Shoreline means that area of the land adjacent to the water of an ocean, sea, lake, pond, river or tidal basin that is above the high water mark and excludes land areas unsuitable for landing such as vertical cliffs or land intermittently under water during the particular flight.

Suitable landing area for helicopters means an area that provides the operator reasonable capability to land without damage to equipment or injury to persons. Suitable landing areas must be site-specific, designated by the operator, and accepted by the FAA. These site-specific areas would provide an emergency landing area for a single-engine helicopter or a multiengine helicopter that does not have the capability to reach a safe landing area after an engine power loss.

(e) In an in-flight emergency requiring immediate action, the pilot in command may deviate from any rule of this subpart to the extent required to meet that emergency.

§ 136.3 Letters of Authorization.

Operators subject to this subpart who have Letters of Authorization may use the procedures described in 14 CFR 119.51 to amend or have the FAA reconsider those Letters of Authorization.

§ 136.5 Additional requirements for Hawaii.

No person may conduct a commercial air tour in the State of Hawaii unless they comply with the additional requirements and restrictions in appendix A to part 136.

§ 136.7 Passenger briefings.

(a) Before takeoff each pilot in command shall ensure that each passenger has been briefed on the following:

(1) Procedures for fastening and unfastening seatbelts;

(2) Prohibition on smoking; and

(3) Procedures for opening exits and exiting the aircraft.

(b) For flight segments over water beyond the shoreline, briefings must also include:

(1) Procedures for water ditching;

(2) Use of required life preservers; and

(3) Procedures for emergency exit from the aircraft in the event of a water landing.

§ 136.9 Life preservers for over water.

(a) Except as provided in paragraphs (b) or (c) of this section, the operator and pilot in command of commercial air tours over water beyond the shoreline must ensure that each occupant is wearing a life preserver from before takeoff until flight is no longer over water.

(b) The operator and pilot in command of a commercial air tour over water beyond the shoreline must ensure that a life preserver is readily available for its intended use and easily accessible to each occupant if:

(1) The aircraft is equipped with floats; or

(2) The airplane is within power-off gliding distance to the shoreline for the duration of the time that the flight is over water.

(3) The aircraft is a multi engine that can be operated with the critical engine inoperative at a weight that will allow it to climb, at least 50 feet a minute, at an altitude of 1,000 feet above the surface, as provided in the Airplane Flight Manual or the Rotorcraft Flight Manual, as appropriate.

(c) No life preserver is required if the overwater operation is necessary only for takeoff or landing.

§136.11 Helicopter floats for over water.

(a) A helicopter used in commercial air tours over water beyond the shoreline must be equipped with fixed floats or an inflatable flotation system adequate to accomplish a safe emergency ditching, if—

(1) It is a single-engine helicopter; or

(2) It is a multi-engine helicopter that cannot be operated with the critical engine inoperative at a weight that will allow it to climb, at least 50 feet a minute, at an altitude of 1,000 feet above the surface, as provided in the Rotorcraft Flight Manual (RFM).

(b) Each helicopter that is required to be equipped with an inflatable flotation system must have:

(1) The activation switch for the flotation system on one of the primary flight controls, and

(2) The flotation system armed when the helicopter is over water and is flying at a speed that does not exceed the maximum speed prescribed in the Rotorcraft Flight Manual for flying with the flotation system armed.

(c) Fixed floats or an inflatable flotation system is not required for a helicopter under this section if:

(1) The helicopter is over water only during the takeoff or landing portion of the flight, or

(2) The helicopter is operated within power-off gliding distance to the shoreline for the duration of the flight and each occupant is wearing a life preserver from before takeoff until the aircraft is no longer over water.

(d) Air tour operators required to comply with paragraphs (a) and/or (b) of this section must meet these requirements on or before September 5, 2008.

§136.13 Helicopter performance plan and operations.

(a) Each operator must complete a performance plan before each helicopter commercial air tour, or flight operated under 14 CFR 91.146 or 91.147. The pilot in command must review for accuracy and comply with the performance plan on the day the flight is flown. The performance plan must be based on the information in the Rotorcraft Flight Manual (RFM) for that helicopter, taking into consideration the maximum density altitude for which the operation is planned, in order to determine:

(1) Maximum gross weight and center of gravity (CG) limitations for hovering in ground effect;

(2) Maximum gross weight and CG limitations for hovering out of ground effect; and

(3) Maximum combination of weight, altitude, and temperature for which height/velocity information in the RFM is valid.

(b) Except for the approach to and transition from a hover for the purpose of takeoff and landing, or during takeoff and landing, the pilot in command must make a reasonable plan to operate the helicopter outside of the caution/warning/avoid area of the limiting height/velocity diagram.

(c) Except for the approach to and transition from a hover for the purpose of takeoff and landing, during takeoff and landing, or when necessary for safety of flight, the pilot in command must operate the helicopter in compliance with the plan described in paragraph (b) of this section.

§§136.15–136.29 [Reserved]

Subpart B—National Parks Air Tour Management

SOURCE: Docket No. FAA–1998–4521, 72 FR 6912, Feb. 13, 2007, unless otherwise noted.

§136.31 Applicability.

(a) This part restates and paraphrases several sections of the National Parks Air Tour Management Act of 2000, including section 803 (codified at 49 U.S.C. 40128) and sections 806 and 809. This subpart clarifies the requirements for the development of an air tour management plan for each park in the national park system where commercial air tour operations are flown.

(b) Except as provided in paragraph (c) of this section, this subpart applies to each commercial air tour operator who conducts a commercial air tour operation over—

(1) A unit of the national park system;

(2) Tribal lands as defined in this subpart; or

(3) Any area within one-half mile outside the boundary of any unit of the national park system.

(c) This subpart does not apply to a commercial air tour operator conducting a commercial air tour operation—

(1) Over the Grand Canyon National Park;

(2) Over that portion of tribal lands within or abutting the Grand Canyon National Park;

(3) Over any land or waters located in the State of Alaska; or

(4) While flying over or near the Lake Mead Recreation Area, solely as a transportation route, to conduct a commercial air tour over the Grand Canyon National Park.

[Doc. No. FAA–2001–8690, 67 FR 65667, Oct. 25, 2002. Redesignated and amended by Amdt. 136–1, 72 FR 6912, Feb. 13, 2007]

§ 136.33 Definitions.

For purposes of this subpart—

(a) *Commercial air tour operator* means any person who conducts a commercial air tour operation.

(b) *Existing commercial air tour operator* means a commercial air tour operator that was actively engaged in the business of providing commercial air tour operations over a national park at any time during the 12-month period ending on April 5, 2000.

(c) *New entrant commercial air tour operator* means a commercial air tour operator that—

(1) Applies for operating authority as a commercial air tour operator for a national park or tribal lands; and

(2) Has not engaged in the business of providing commercial air tour operations over the national park or tribal lands for the 12-month period preceding enactment.

(d) *Commercial air tour operation*—

(1) Means any flight, conducted for compensation or hire in a powered aircraft where a purpose of the flight is sightseeing over a national park, within ½ mile outside the boundary of any national park, or over tribal lands, during which the aircraft flies—

(i) Below 5,000 feet above ground level (except for the purpose of takeoff or landing, or as necessary for the safe operation of an aircraft as determined under the rules and regulations of the

Federal Aviation Administration requiring the pilot-in-command to take action to ensure the safe operation of the aircraft);

(ii) Less than 1 mile laterally from any geographic feature within the park (unless more than ½ mile outside the boundary); or

(iii) Except as provided in § 136.35.

(2) The Administrator may consider the following factors in determining whether a flight is a commercial air tour operation for purposes of this subpart—

(i) Whether there was a holding out to the public of willingness to conduct a sightseeing flight for compensation or hire;

(ii) Whether a narrative that referred to areas or points of interest on the surface below the route of the flight was provided by the person offering the flight;

(iii) The area of operation;

(iv) The frequency of flights conducted by the person offering the flight;

(v) The route of flight;

(vi) The inclusion of sightseeing flights as part of any travel arrangement package offered by the person offering the flight;

(vii) Whether the flight would have been canceled based on poor visibility of the surface below the route of the flight; and

(viii) Any other factors that the Administrator and Director consider appropriate.

(3) For purposes of § 136.35, means any flight conducted for compensation or hire in a powered aircraft where a purpose of the flight is sightseeing over a national park.

(e) *National park* means any unit of the national park system. (See title 16 of the U.S. Code, section 1, *et seq.*)

(f) *Tribal lands* means that portion of Indian country (as that term is defined in section 1151 of title 18 of the U.S. Code) that is within or abutting a national park.

(g) *Administrator* means the Administrator of the Federal Aviation Administration.

(h) *Director* means the Director of the National Park Service.

(i) *Superintendent* means the duly appointed representative of the National

Park Service for a particular unit of the national park system.

[Doc. No. FAA–2001–8690, 67 FR 65667, Oct. 25, 2002. Redesignated and amended by Amdt. 136–1, 72 FR 6912, Feb. 13, 2007; Amdt. 133–1, 72 FR 31450, June 7, 2007]

§136.35 Prohibition of commercial air tour operations over the Rocky Mountain National Park.

All commercial air tour operations in the airspace over the Rocky Mountain National Park are prohibited regardless of altitude.

[Doc. No. FAA–2001–8690, 67 FR 65667, Oct. 25, 2002. Redesignated by Amdt. 136–1, 72 FR 6912, Feb. 13, 2007]

§136.37 Overflights of national parks and tribal lands.

(a) *General.* A commercial air tour operator may not conduct commercial air tour operations over a national park or tribal land except—

(1) In accordance with this section;

(2) In accordance with conditions and limitations prescribed for that operator by the Administrator; and

(3) In accordance with any applicable air tour management plan for the park or tribal lands.

(b) *Application for operating authority.* Before commencing commercial air tour operations over a national park or tribal lands, a commercial air tour operator shall apply to the Administrator for authority to conduct the operations over the park or tribal lands.

(c) *Number of operations authorized.* In determining the number of authorizations to issue to provide commercial air tour operations over a national park, the Administrator, in cooperation with the Director, shall take into consideration the provisions of the air tour management plan, the number of existing commercial air tour operators and current level of service and equipment provided by any such operators, and the financial viability of each commercial air tour operation.

(d) *Cooperation with National Park Service.* Before granting an application under this subpart, the Administrator, in cooperation with the Director, shall develop an air tour management plan in accordance with §136.39 and implement such a plan.

(e) *Time limit on response to applications.* Every effort will be made to act on any application under this subpart and issue a decision on the application not later than 24 months after it is received or amended.

(f) *Priority.* In acting on applications under this paragraph to provide commercial air tour operations over a national park, the Administrator shall give priority to an application under this paragraph in any case where a new entrant commercial air tour operator is seeking operating authority with respect to that national park.

(g) *Exception.* Notwithstanding this section, commercial air tour operators may conduct commercial air tour operations over a national park under part 91 of this chapter if—

(1) Such activity is permitted under part 119 of this chapter;

(2) The operator secures a letter of agreement from the Administrator and the Superintendent for that park describing the conditions under which the operations will be conducted; and

(3) The number of operations under this exception is limited to not more than a total of 5 flights by all operators in any 30-day period over a particular park.

(h) *Special rule for safety requirement.* Notwithstanding §136.41, an existing commercial air tour operator shall apply, not later than January 23, 2003 for operating authority under part 119 of this chapter, for certification under part 121 or part 135 of this chapter. A new entrant commercial air tour operator shall apply for such authority before conducting commercial air tour operations over a national park or tribal lands that are within or abut a national park. The Administrator shall make every effort to act on such application for a new entrant and issue a decision on the application not later than 24 months after it is received or amended.

[Doc. No. FAA–2001–8690, 67 FR 65667, Oct. 25, 2002. Redesignated and amended by Amdt. 136–1, 72 FR 6912, Feb. 13, 2007; Amdt. 136–1, 72 FR 31450, June 7, 2007]

§136.39 Air tour management plans (ATMP).

(a) *Establishment.* The Administrator, in cooperation with the Director, shall establish an air tour management plan for any national park or tribal land for which such a plan is not in effect whenever a person applies for authority to conduct a commercial air tour operation over the park. The air tour management plan shall be developed by means of a public process in accordance with paragraph (d) of this section. The objective of any air tour management plan is to develop acceptable and effective measures to mitigate or prevent the significant adverse impacts, if any, of commercial air tour operations upon the natural and cultural resources, visitor experiences, and tribal lands.

(b) *Environmental determination.* In establishing an air tour management plan under this section, the Administrator and the Director shall each sign the environmental decision document required by section 102 of the National Environmental Policy Act of 1969 (42 U.S.C. 4332) which may include a finding of no significant impact, an environmental assessment, or an environmental impact statement and the record of decision for the air tour management plan.

(c) *Contents.* An air tour management plan for a park—

(1) May prohibit commercial air tour operations in whole or in part;

(2) May establish conditions for the conduct of commercial air tour operations, including, but not limited to, commercial air tour routes, maximum number of flights per unit of time, maximum and minimum altitudes, time of day restrictions, restrictions for particular events, intrusions on privacy on tribal lands, and mitigation of noise, visual, or other impacts;

(3) Shall apply to all commercial air tour operations within ½ mile outside the boundary of a national park;

(4) Shall include incentives (such as preferred commercial air tour routes and altitudes, and relief from caps and curfews) for the adoption of quiet technology aircraft by commercial air tour operators conducting commercial air tour operations at the park;

(5) Shall provide for the initial allocation of opportunities to conduct commercial air tour operations if the plan includes a limitation on the number of commercial air tour operations for any time period; and

(6) Shall justify and document the need for measures taken pursuant to paragraphs (c)(1) through (c)(5) of this section and include such justification in the record of decision.

(d) *Procedure.* In establishing an ATMP for a national park or tribal lands, the Administrator and Director shall—

(1) Hold at least one public meeting with interested parties to develop the air tour management plan;

(2) Publish the proposed plan in the FEDERAL REGISTER for notice and comment and make copies of the proposed plan available to the public;

(3) Comply with the regulations set forth in 40 CFR 1501.3 and 1501.5 through 1501.8 (for the purposes of complying with 40 CFR 1501.3 and 1501.5 through 1501.8, the Federal Aviation Administration is the lead agency and the National Park Service is a cooperating agency); and

(4) Solicit the participation of any Indian tribe whose tribal lands are, or may be, overflown by aircraft involved in a commercial air tour operation over the park or tribal lands to which the plan applies, as a cooperating agency under the regulations referred to in paragraph (d)(3) of this section.

(e) *Amendments.* The Administrator, in cooperation with the Director, may make amendments to an air tour management plan. Any such amendments will be published in the FEDERAL REGISTER for notice and comment. A request for amendment of an ATMP will be made in accordance with § 11.25 of this chapter as a petition for rulemaking.

[Doc. No. FAA-2001-8690, 67 FR 65667, Oct. 25, 2002. Redesignated by Amdt. 136-1, 72 FR 6912, Feb. 13, 2007]

§ 136.41   Interim operating authority.

(a) *General.* Upon application for operating authority, the Administrator shall grant interim operating authority under this section to a commercial air tour operator for commercial air tour operations over a national park or tribal land for which the operator is an existing commercial air tour operator.

(b) *Requirements and limitations.* Interim operating authority granted under this section—

(1) Shall provide annual authorization only for the greater of—

(i) The number of flights used by the operator to provide the commercial air tour operations within the 12-month period prior to April 5, 2000; or

(ii) The average number of flights per 12-month period used by the operator to provide such operations within the 36-month period prior to April 5, 2000, and for seasonal operations, the number of flights so used during the season or seasons covered by that 12-month period;

(2) May not provide for an increase in the number of commercial air tour operations conducted during any time period by the commercial air tour operator above the number the air tour operator was originally granted unless such an increase is agreed to by the Administrator and the Director;

(3) Shall be published in the FEDERAL REGISTER to provide notice and opportunity for comment;

(4) May be revoked by the Administrator for cause;

(5) Shall terminate 180 days after the date on which an air tour management plan is established for the park and tribal lands;

(6) Shall promote protection of national park resources, visitor experiences, and tribal lands;

(7) Shall promote safe commercial air tour operations;

(8) Shall promote the adoption of quiet technology, as appropriate, and

(9) Shall allow for modifications of the interim operating authority based on experience if the modification improves protection of national park resources and values and of tribal lands.

(c) *New entrant operators.* The Administrator, in cooperation with the Director, may grant interim operating authority under this paragraph (c) to an air tour operator for a national park or tribal lands for which that operator is a new entrant air tour operator if the Administrator determines the authority is necessary to ensure competition in the provision of commercial air tour operations over the park or tribal lands.

(1) *Limitation.* The Administrator may not grant interim operating authority under this paragraph (c) if the Administrator determines that it would create a safety problem at the park or on the tribal lands, or if the Director determines that it would create a noise problem at the park or on the tribal lands.

(2) *ATMP limitation.* The Administrator may grant interim operating authority under this paragraph (c) only if the ATMP for the park or tribal lands to which the application relates has not been developed within 24 months after April 5, 2000.

[Doc. No. FAA–2001–8690, 67 FR 65667, Oct. 25, 2002. Redesignated by Amdt. 136–1, 72 FR 6912, Feb. 13, 2007]

§§ 136.43–136.49 [Reserved]

Subpart C—Grand Canyon National Park

§§ 136.51–136.69 [Reserved]

APPENDIX A TO PART 136—SPECIAL OPERATING RULES FOR AIR TOUR OPERATORS IN THE STATE OF HAWAII

Section 1. Applicability. This appendix prescribes operating rules for airplane and helicopter visual flight rules air tour flights conducted in the State of Hawaii under 14 CFR parts 91, 121, and 135. This appendix does not apply to:

(a) Operations conducted under 14 CFR part 121 in airplanes with a passenger seating configuration of more than 30 seats or a payload capacity of more than 7,500 pounds.

(b) Flights conducted in gliders or hot air balloons.

Section 2. Definitions. For the purposes of this appendix:

"Air tour" means any sightseeing flight conducted under visual flight rules in an airplane or helicopter for compensation or hire.

"Air tour operator" means any person who conducts an air tour.

Section 3. Helicopter flotation equipment. No person may conduct an air tour in Hawaii in a single-engine helicopter beyond the shore of any island, regardless of whether the helicopter is within gliding distance of the shore, unless:

(a) The helicopter is amphibious or is equipped with floats adequate to accomplish a safe emergency ditching and approved flotation gear is easily accessible for each occupant; or

(b) Each person on board the helicopter is wearing approved flotation gear.

Section 4. Helicopter performance plan. Each operator must complete a performance plan before each helicopter air tour flight. The performance plan must be based on the information in the Rotorcraft Flight Manual (RFM), considering the maximum density altitude for which the operation is planned for the flight to determine the following:

(a) Maximum gross weight and center of gravity (CG) limitations for hovering in ground effect;

(b) Maximum gross weight and CG limitations for hovering out of ground effect; and,

(c) Maximum combination of weight, altitude, and temperature for which height-velocity information in the RFM is valid.

The pilot in command (PIC) must comply with the performance plan.

Section 5. Helicopter Operating Limitations. Except for approach to and transition from a hover, and except for the purpose of takeoff and landing, the PIC shall operate the helicopter at a combination of height and forward speed (including hover) that would permit a safe landing in event of engine power loss, in accordance with the height-speed envelope for that helicopter under current weight and aircraft altitude.

Section 6. Minimum flight altitudes. Except when necessary for takeoff and landing, or operating in compliance with an air traffic control clearance, or as otherwise authorized by the Administrator, no person may conduct an air tour in Hawaii:

(a) Below an altitude of 1,500 feet above the surface over all areas of the State of Hawaii, and,

(b) Closer than 1,500 feet to any person or property; or,

(c) Below any altitude prescribed by federal statute or regulation.

Section 7. Passenger briefing. Before takeoff, each PIC of an air tour flight of Hawaii with a flight segment beyond the ocean shore of any island shall ensure that each passenger has been briefed on the following, in addition to requirements set forth in 14 CFR 91.107, 121.571, or 135.117:

(a) Water ditching procedures;

(b) Use of required flotation equipment; and

(c) Emergency egress from the aircraft in event of a water landing.

[Doc. No. FAA-1998-4521, 72 FR 6914, Feb. 13, 2007]

PART 137—AGRICULTURAL AIRCRAFT OPERATIONS

Subpart A—General

Sec.
137.1   Applicability.
137.3   Definition of terms.

Subpart B—Certification Rules

137.11   Certificate required.
137.15   Application for certificate.
137.17   Amendment of certificate.
137.19   Certification requirements.
137.21   Duration of certificate.
137.23   Carriage of narcotic drugs, marihuana, and depressant or stimulant drugs or substances.

Subpart C—Operating Rules

137.29   General.
137.31   Aircraft requirements.
137.33   Carrying of certificate.
137.35   Limitations on private agricultural aircraft operator.
137.37   Manner of dispensing.
137.39   Economic poison dispensing.
137.40   Employment of former FAA employees.
137.41   Personnel.
137.42   Fastening of safety belts and shoulder harnesses.
137.43   Operations in controlled airspace designated for an airport.
137.45   Nonobservance of airport traffic pattern.
137.47   Operation without position lights.
137.49   Operations over other than congested areas.
137.51   Operation over congested areas: General.
137.53   Operation over congested areas: Pilots and aircraft.
137.55   Business name: Commercial agricultural aircraft operator.
137.57   Availability of certificate.
137.59   Inspection authority.

Subpart D—Records and Reports

137.71   Records: Commercial agricultural aircraft operator.
137.75   Change of address.
137.77   Termination of operations.

AUTHORITY: 49 U.S.C. 106(g), 40103, 40113, 44701–44702.

SOURCE: Docket No. 1464, 30 FR 8106, June 24, 1965, unless otherwise noted.

Subpart A—General

§ 137.1   Applicability.

(a) This part prescribes rules governing—

(1) Agricultural aircraft operations within the United States; and

(2) The issue of commercial and private agricultural aircraft operator certificates for those operations.

(b) In a public emergency, a person conducting agricultural aircraft operations under this part may, to the extent necessary, deviate from the operating rules of this part for relief and welfare activities approved by an agency of the United States or of a State or local government.

(c) Each person who, under the authority of this section, deviates from a rule of this part shall, within 10 days after the deviation send to the responsible Flight Standards office a complete report of the aircraft operation involved, including a description of the operation and the reasons for it.

[Doc. No. 1464, 30 FR 8106, June 24, 1965, as amended by Amdt. 137–13, 54 FR 39294, Sept. 25, 1989; Docket FAA–2018–0119, Amdt. 137–17, 83 FR 9175, Mar. 5, 2018]

§ 137.3 Definition of terms.

For the purposes of this part—

Agricultural aircraft operation means the operation of an aircraft for the purpose of (1) dispensing any economic poison, (2) dispensing any other substance intended for plant nourishment, soil treatment, propagation of plant life, or pest control, or (3) engaging in dispensing activities directly affecting agriculture, horticulture, or forest preservation, but not including the dispensing of live insects.

Economic poison means (1) any substance or mixture of substances intended for preventing, destroying, repelling, or mitigating any insects, rodents, nematodes, fungi, weeds, and other forms of plant or animal life or viruses, except viruses on or in living man or other animals, which the Secretary of Agriculture shall declare to be a pest, and (2) any substance or mixture of substances intended for use as a plant regulator, defoliant or desiccant.

[Doc. No. 1464, 30 FR 8106, June 24, 1965, as amended by Amdt. 137–3, 33 FR 9601, July 2, 1968]

Subpart B—Certification Rules

§ 137.11 Certificate required.

(a) Except as provided in paragraphs (c) and (d) of this section, no person may conduct agricultural aircraft operations without, or in violation of, an agricultural aircraft operator certificate issued under this part.

(b) Notwithstanding part 133 of this chapter, an operator may, if he complies with this part, conduct agricultural aircraft operations with a rotorcraft with external dispensing equipment in place without a rotorcraft external-load operator certificate.

(c) A Federal, State, or local government conducting agricultural aircraft operations with public aircraft need not comply with this subpart.

(d) The holder of a rotorcraft external-load operator certificate under part 133 of this chapter conducting an agricultural aircraft operation, involving only the dispensing of water on forest fires by rotorcraft external-load means, need not comply with this subpart.

[Doc. No. 1464, 30 FR 8106, June 24, 1965, as amended by Amdt. 137–3, 33 FR 9601, July 2, 1968; Amdt. 137–6, 41 FR 35060, Aug. 19, 1976]

§ 137.15 Application for certificate.

An application for an agricultural aircraft operator certificate is made on a form and in a manner prescribed by the Administrator, and filed with the responsible Flight Standards office for the area in which the applicant's home base of operations is located.

[Doc. No. 1464, 30 FR 8106, June 24, 1965, as amended by Amdt. 137–13, 54 FR 39294, Sept. 25, 1989; Docket FAA–2018–0119, Amdt. 137–17, 83 FR 9175, Mar. 5, 2018]

§ 137.17 Amendment of certificate.

(a) An agricultural aircraft operator certificate may be amended—

(1) On the Administrator's own initiative, under section 609 of the Federal Aviation Act of 1958 (49 U.S.C. 1429) and part 13 of this chapter; or

(2) Upon application by the holder of that certificate.

(b) An application to amend an agricultural aircraft operator certificate is submitted on a form and in a manner prescribed by the Administrator. The applicant must file the application with the responsible Flight Standards office for the area in which the applicant's home base of operations is located at least 15 days before the date that it proposes the amendment become effective, unless a shorter filing period is approved by that office.

(c) The responsible Flight Standards office grants a request to amend a certificate if it determines that safety in air commerce and the public interest so allow.

(d) Within 30 days after receiving a refusal to amend, the holder may petition the Executive Director, Flight Standards Service, to reconsider the refusal.

[Doc. No. 1464, 30 FR 8106, June 24, 1965, as amended by Amdt. 137–9, 43 FR 52206, Nov. 9, 1978; Amdt. 137–11, 45 FR 47838, July 17, 1980; Amdt. 137–13, 54 FR 39294, Sept. 25, 1989; Docket FAA–2018–0119, Amdt. 137–17, 83 FR 9175, Mar. 5, 2018]

§ 137.19   Certification requirements.

(a) *General.* An applicant for a private agricultural aircraft operator certificate is entitled to that certificate if he shows that he meets the requirements of paragraphs (b), (d), and (e) of this section. An applicant for a commercial agricultural aircraft operator certificate is entitled to that certificate if he shows that he meets the requirements of paragraphs (c), (d), and (e) of this section. However, if an applicant applies for an agricultural aircraft operator certificate containing a prohibition against the dispensing of economic poisons, that applicant is not required to demonstrate the knowledge required in paragraphs (e)(1) (ii) through (iv) of this section.

(b) *Private operator—pilot.* The applicant must hold a current U.S. private, commercial, or airline transport pilot certificate and be properly rated for the aircraft to be used.

(c) *Commercial operator—pilots.* The applicant must have available the services of at least one person who holds a current U.S. commercial or airline transport pilot certificate and who is properly rated for the aircraft to be used. The applicant himself may be the person available.

(d) *Aircraft.* The applicant must have at least one certificated and airworthy aircraft, equipped for agricultural operation.

(e) *Knowledge and skill tests.* The applicant must show, or have the person who is designated as the chief supervisor of agricultural aircraft operations for him show, that he has satisfactory knowledge and skill regarding agricultural aircraft operations, as described in paragraphs (e) (1) and (2) of this section.

(1) The test of knowledge consists of the following:

(i) Steps to be taken before starting operations, including survey of the area to be worked.

(ii) Safe handling of economic poisons and the proper disposal of used containers for those poisons.

(iii) The general effects of economic poisons and agricultural chemicals on plants, animals, and persons, with emphasis on those normally used in the areas of intended operations; and the precautions to be observed in using poisons and chemicals.

(iv) Primary symptoms of poisoning of persons from economic poisons, the appropriate emergency measures to be taken, and the location of poison control centers.

(v) Performance capabilities and operating limitations of the aircraft to be used.

(vi) Safe flight and application procedures.

(2) The test of skill consists of the following maneuvers that must be shown in any of the aircraft specified in paragraph (d) of this section, and at that aircraft's maximum certificated take-off weight, or the maximum weight established for the special purpose load, whichever is greater:

(i) Short-field and soft-field takeoffs (airplanes and gyroplanes only).

(ii) Approaches to the working area.

(iii) Flare-outs.

(iv) Swath runs.

(v) Pullups and turnarounds.

(vi) Rapid deceleration (quick stops) in helicopters only.

[Doc. No. 1464, 30 FR 8106, June 24, 1965, as amended by Amdt. 137–1, 30 FR 15143, Dec. 8, 1965; Amdt. 137–7, 43 FR 22643, May 25, 1978]

§ 137.21   Duration of certificate.

An agricultural aircraft operator certificate is effective until it is surrendered, suspended, or revoked. The holder of an agricultural aircraft operator certificate that is suspended or revoked shall return it to the Administrator.

§137.23 Carriage of narcotic drugs, marihuana, and depressant or stimulant drugs or substances.

If the holder of a certificate issued under this part permits any aircraft owned or leased by that holder to be engaged in any operation that the certificate holder knows to be in violation of §91.19(a) of this chapter, that operation is a basis for suspending or revoking the certificate.

[Doc. No. 12035, 38 FR 17493, July 2, 1973, as amended by Amdt. 137-12, 54 FR 34332, Aug. 18, 1989]

Subpart C—Operating Rules

§137.29 General.

(a) Except as provided in paragraphs (d) and (e) of this section, this subpart prescribes rules that apply to persons and aircraft used in agricultural aircraft operations conducted under this part.

(b) [Reserved]

(c) The holder of an agricultural aircraft operator certificate may deviate from the provisions of part 91 of this chapter without a certificate of waiver, as authorized in this subpart for dispensing operations, when conducting nondispensing aerial work operations related to agriculture, horticulture, or forest preservation in accordance with the operating rules of this subpart.

(d) Sections 137.31 through 137.35, §§137.41, and 137.53 through 137.59 do not apply to persons and aircraft used in agricultural aircraft operations conducted with public aircraft.

(e) Sections 137.31 through 137.35, §§137.39, 137.41, 137.51 through 137.59, and subpart D do not apply to persons and rotorcraft used in agricultural aircraft operations conducted by a person holding a certificate under part 133 of this chapter and involving only the dispensing of water on forest fires by rotorcraft external-load means. However, the operation shall be conducted in accordance with—

(1) The rules of part 133 of this chapter governing rotorcraft external-load operations; and

(2) The operating rules of this subpart contained in §§137.29, 137.37, and §§137.43 through 137.49.

[Doc. No. 1464, 30 FR 8106, June 24, 1965, as amended by Amdt. 137-3, 33 FR 9601, July 2, 1968; Amdt. 137-6, 41 FR 35060, Aug. 19, 1976]

§137.31 Aircraft requirements.

No person may operate an aircraft unless that aircraft—

(a) Meets the requirements of §137.19(d); and

(b) Is equipped with a suitable and properly installed shoulder harness for use by each pilot.

§137.33 Carrying of certificate.

(a) No person may operate an aircraft unless a facsimile of the agricultural aircraft operator certificate, under which the operation is conducted, is carried on that aircraft. The facsimile shall be presented for inspection upon the request of the Administrator or any Federal, State, or local law enforcement officer.

(b) Notwithstanding part 91 of this chapter, the registration and airworthiness certificates issued for the aircraft need not be carried in the aircraft. However, when those certificates are not carried in the aircraft they shall be kept available for inspection at the base from which the dispensing operation is conducted.

[Doc. No. 1464, 30 FR 8106, June 24, 1965, as amended by Amdt. 137-3, 33 FR 9601, July 2, 1968]

§137.35 Limitations on private agricultural aircraft operator.

No person may conduct an agricultural aircraft operation under the authority of a private agricultural aircraft operator certificate—

(a) For compensation or hire;

(b) Over a congested area; or

(c) Over any property unless he is the owner or lessee of the property, or has ownership or other property interest in the crop located on that property.

§137.37 Manner of dispensing.

No persons may dispense, or cause to be dispensed, from an aircraft, any material or substance in a manner that creates a hazard to persons or property on the surface.

[Doc. No. 1464, 30 FR 8106, June 24, 1965, as amended by Amdt. 137–3, 33 FR 9601, July 2, 1968]

§ 137.39 Economic poison dispensing.

(a) Except as provided in paragraph (b) of this section, no person may dispense or cause to be dispensed from an aircraft, any economic poison that is registered with the U.S. Department of Agriculture under the Federal Insecticide, Fungicide, and Rodenticide Act (7 U.S.C. 135–135k)—

(1) For a use other than that for which it is registered;

(2) Contrary to any safety instructions or use limitations on its label; or

(3) In violation of any law or regulation of the United States.

(b) This section does not apply to any person dispensing economic poisons for experimental purposes under—

(1) The supervision of a Federal or State agency authorized by law to conduct research in the field of economic poisons; or

(2) A permit from the U.S. Department of Agriculture issued pursuant to the Federal Insecticide, Fungicide, and Rodenticide Act (7 U.S.C. 135–135k).

[Amdt. 137–2, 31 FR 6686, May 5, 1966]

§ 137.40 Employment of former FAA employees.

(a) Except as specified in paragraph (c) of this section, no certificate holder may knowingly employ or make a contractual arrangement which permits an individual to act as an agent or representative of the certificate holder in any matter before the Federal Aviation Administration if the individual, in the preceding 2 years—

(1) Served as, or was directly responsible for the oversight of, a Flight Standards Service aviation safety inspector; and

(2) Had direct responsibility to inspect, or oversee the inspection of, the operations of the certificate holder.

(b) For the purpose of this section, an individual shall be considered to be acting as an agent or representative of a certificate holder in a matter before the agency if the individual makes any written or oral communication on behalf of the certificate holder to the agency (or any of its officers or employees) in connection with a particular matter, whether or not involving a specific party and without regard to whether the individual has participated in, or had responsibility for, the particular matter while serving as a Flight Standards Service aviation safety inspector.

(c) The provisions of this section do not prohibit a certificate holder from knowingly employing or making a contractual arrangement which permits an individual to act as an agent or representative of the certificate holder in any matter before the Federal Aviation Administration if the individual was employed by the certificate holder before October 21, 2011.

[Doc. No. FAA–2008–1154, 76 FR 52236, Aug. 22, 2011]

§ 137.41 Personnel.

(a) *Information.* The holder of an agricultural aircraft operator certificate shall insure that each person used in the holder's agricultural aircraft operation is informed of that person's duties and responsibilities for the operation.

(b) *Supervisors.* No person may supervise an agricultural aircraft operation unless he has met the knowledge and skill requirements of § 137.19(e).

(c) *Pilot in command.* No person may act as pilot in command of an aircraft unless he holds a pilot certificate and rating prescribed by § 137.19 (b) or (c), as appropriate to the type of operation conducted. In addition, he must demonstrate to the holder of the Agricultural Aircraft Operator Certificate conducting the operation that he has met the knowledge and skill requirements of § 137.19(e). If the holder of that certificate has designated a person under § 137.19(e) to supervise his agricultural aircraft operations the demonstration must be made to the person so designated. However, a demonstration of the knowledge and skill requirement is not necessary for any pilot in command who—

(1) Is, at the time of the filing of an application by an agricultural aircraft operator, working as a pilot in command for that operator; and

(2) Has a record of operation under that applicant that does not disclose

any question regarding the safety of his flight operations or his competence in dispensing agricultural materials or chemicals.

§137.42 Fastening of safety belts and shoulder harnesses.

No person may operate an aircraft in operations required to be conducted under part 137 without a safety belt and shoulder harness properly secured about that person except that the shoulder harness need not be fastened if that person would be unable to perform required duties with the shoulder harness fastened.

[Amdt. 137–10, 44 FR 61325, Oct. 25, 1979]

§137.43 Operations in controlled airspace designated for an airport.

(a) Except for flights to and from a dispensing area, no person may operate an aircraft within the lateral boundaries of the surface area of Class D airspace designated for an airport unless authorization for that operation has been obtained from the ATC facility having jurisdiction over that area.

(b) No person may operate an aircraft in weather conditions below VFR minimums within the lateral boundaries of a Class E airspace area that extends upward from the surface unless authorization for that operation has been obtained from the ATC facility having jurisdiction over that area.

(c) Notwithstanding §91.157(b)(4) of this chapter, an aircraft may be operated under the special VFR weather minimums without meeting the requirements prescribed therein.

[Amdt. 137–14, 56 FR 65664, Dec. 17, 1991, as amended by Amdt. 137–14, 58 FR 32840, June 14, 1993; 74 FR 13099, Mar. 26, 2009]

§137.45 Nonobservance of airport traffic pattern.

Notwithstanding part 91 of this chapter, the pilot in command of an aircraft may deviate from an airport traffic pattern when authorized by the control tower concerned. At an airport without a functioning control tower, the pilot in command may deviate from the traffic pattern if—

(a) Prior coordination is made with the airport management concerned;

(b) Deviations are limited to the agricultural aircraft operation;

(c) Except in an emergency, landing and takeoffs are not made on ramps, taxiways, or other areas of the airport not intended for such use; and

(d) The aircraft at all times remains clear of, and gives way to, aircraft conforming to the traffic pattern for the airport.

§137.47 Operation without position lights.

Notwithstanding part 91 of this chapter, an aircraft may be operated without position lights if prominent unlighted objects are visible for at least 1 mile and takeoffs and landings at—

(a) Airports with a functioning control tower are made only as authorized by the control tower operator; and

(b) Other airports are made only with the permission of the airport management and no other aircraft operations requiring position lights are in progress at that airport.

§137.49 Operations over other than congested areas.

Notwithstanding part 91 of this chapter, during the actual dispensing operation, including approaches, departures, and turnarounds reasonably necessary for the operation, an aircraft may be operated over other than congested areas below 500 feet above the surface and closer than 500 feet to persons, vessels, vehicles, and structures, if the operations are conducted without creating a hazard to persons or property on the surface.

[Amdt. 137–3, 33 FR 9601, July 2, 1968]

§137.51 Operation over congested areas: General.

(a) Notwithstanding part 91 of this chapter, an aircraft may be operated over a congested area at altitudes required for the proper accomplishment of the agricultural aircraft operation if the operation is conducted—

(1) With the maximum safety to persons and property on the surface, consistent with the operation; and

(2) In accordance with the requirements of paragraph (b) of this section.

(b) No person may operate an aircraft over a congested area except in accordance with the requirements of this paragraph.

(1) Prior written approval must be obtained from the appropriate official or governing body of the political subdivision over which the operations are conducted.

(2) Notice of the intended operation must be given to the public by some effective means, such as daily newspapers, radio, television, or door-to-door notice.

(3) A plan for each complete operation must be submitted to, and approved by appropriate personnel of the responsible Flight Standards office for the area where the operation is to be conducted. The plan must include consideration of obstructions to flight; the emergency landing capabilities of the aircraft to be used; and any necessary coordination with air traffic control.

(4) Single engine aircraft must be operated as follows:

(i) Except for helicopters, no person may take off a loaded aircraft, or make a turnaround over a congested area.

(ii) No person may operate an aircraft over a congested area below the altitudes prescribed in part 91 of this chapter except during the actual dispensing operation, including the approaches and departures necessary for that operation.

(iii) No person may operate an aircraft over a congested area during the actual dispensing operation, including the approaches and departures for that operation, unless it is operated in a pattern and at such an altitude that the aircraft can land, in an emergency, without endangering persons or property on the surface.

(5) Multiengine aircraft must be operated as follows:

(i) No person may take off a multiengine airplane over a congested area except under conditions that will allow the airplane to be brought to a safe stop within the effective length of the runway from any point on takeoff up to the time of attaining, with all engines operating at normal takeoff power, 105 percent of the minimum control speed with the critical engine inoperative in the takeoff configuration or 115 percent of the power-off stall speed in the takeoff configuration, whichever is greater, as shown by the accelerate stop distance data. In applying this requirement, takeoff data is based upon still-air conditions, and no correction is made for any uphill gradient of 1 percent or less when the percentage is measured as the difference between elevation at the end points of the runway divided by the total length. For uphill gradients greater than 1 percent, the effective takeoff length of the runway is reduced 20 percent for each 1-percent grade.

(ii) No person may operate a multiengine airplane at a weight greater than the weight that, with the critical engine inoperative, would permit a rate of climb of at least 50 feet per minute at an altitude of at least 1,000 feet above the elevation of the highest ground or obstruction within the area to be worked or at an altitude of 5,000 feet, whichever is higher. For the purposes of this subdivision, it is assumed that the propeller of the inoperative engine is in the minimum drag position; that the wing flaps and landing gear are in the most favorable positions; and that the remaining engine or engines are operating at the maximum continuous power available.

(iii) No person may operate any multiengine aircraft over a congested area below the altitudes prescribed in part 91 of this chapter except during the actual dispensing operation, including the approaches, departures, and turnarounds necessary for that operation.

[Doc. No. 1464, 30 FR 8106, June 24, 1965, as amended by Doc. No. 8084, 32 FR 5769, Apr. 11, 1967; Amdt. 137–13, 54 FR 39294, Sept. 25, 1989; Docket FAA–2018–0119, Amdt. 137–17, 83 FR 9175, Mar. 5, 2018]

§ 137.53 Operation over congested areas: Pilots and aircraft.

(a) *General.* No person may operate an aircraft over a congested area except in accordance with the pilot and aircraft rules of this section.

(b) *Pilots.* Each pilot in command must have at least—

(1) 25 hours of pilot-in-command flight time in the make and basic model of the aircraft, at least 10 hours of which must have been acquired within the preceding 12 calendar months; and

(2) 100 hours of flight experience as pilot in command in dispensing agricultural materials or chemicals.

(c) *Aircraft.* (1) Each aircraft must—

(i) If it is an aircraft not specified in paragraph (c)(1)(ii) of this section, have had within the preceding 100 hours of time in service a 100-hour or annual inspection by a person authorized by part 65 or 145 of this chapter, or have been inspected under a progressive inspection system; and

(ii) If it is a large or turbine-powered multiengine civil airplane of U.S. registry, have been inspected in accordance with the applicable inspection program requirements of §91.409 of this chapter.

(2) If other than a helicopter, it must be equipped with a device capable of jettisoning at least one-half of the aircraft's maximum authorized load of agricultural material within 45 seconds. If the aircraft is equipped with a device for releasing the tank or hopper as a unit, there must be a means to prevent inadvertent release by the pilot or other crewmember.

[Doc. No. 1464, 30 FR 8106, June 24, 1965, as amended by Amdt. 137–5, 41 FR 16796, Apr. 22, 1976; Amdt. 137–12, 54 FR 34332, Aug. 18, 1989]

§ 137.55 Business name: Commercial agricultural aircraft operator.

No person may operate under a business name that is not shown on his commercial agricultural aircraft operator certificate.

§ 137.57 Availability of certificate.

Each holder of an agricultural aircraft operator certificate shall keep that certificate at his home base of operations and shall present it for inspection on the request of the Administrator or any Federal, State, or local law enforcement officer.

§ 137.59 Inspection authority.

Each holder of an agricultural aircraft operator certificate shall allow the Administrator at any time and place to make inspections, including on-the-job inspections, to determine compliance with applicable regulations and his agricultural aircraft operator certificate.

Subpart D—Records and Reports

§ 137.71 Records: Commercial agricultural aircraft operator.

(a) Each holder of a commercial agricultural aircraft operator certificate shall maintain and keep current, at the home base of operations designated in his application, the following records:

(1) The name and address of each person for whom agricultural aircraft services were provided;

(2) The date of the service;

(3) The name and quantity of the material dispensed for each operation conducted; and

(4) The name, address, and certificate number of each pilot used in agricultural aircraft operations and the date that pilot met the knowledge and skill requirements of § 137.19(e).

(b) The records required by this section must be kept at least 12 months and made available for inspection by the Administrator upon request.

§ 137.75 Change of address.

Each holder of an agricultural aircraft operator certificate shall notify the FAA in writing in advance of any change in the address of his home base of operations.

§ 137.77 Termination of operations.

Whenever a person holding an agricultural aircraft operator certificate ceases operations under this part, he shall surrender that certificate to the responsible Flight Standards office last having jurisdiction over his operation.

[Doc. No. 1464, 30 FR 8106, June 24, 1965, as amended by Amdt. 137–13, 54 FR 39294, Sept. 25, 1989; 54 FR 52872, Dec. 22, 1989; Docket FAA–2018–0119, Amdt. 137–17, 83 FR 9175, Mar. 5, 2018]

PART 139—CERTIFICATION OF AIRPORTS

Subpart A—General

AUTHORITY: 49 U.S.C. 106(g), 40113, 44701–44706, 44709, 44719.

SOURCE: Docket No. FAA–2000–7479, 69 FR 6424, Feb. 10, 2004, unless otherwise noted.

EDITORIAL NOTE: Nomenclature changes to part 139 appear at 69 FR 24069, May 3, 2004.

Subpart A—General

§ 139.1 Applicability.

(a) This part prescribes rules governing the certification and operation of airports in any State of the United States, the District of Columbia, or any territory or possession of the United States serving any—

(1) Scheduled passenger-carrying operations of an air carrier operating aircraft configured for more than 9 passenger seats, as determined by the regulations under which the operation is conducted or the aircraft type certificate issued by a competent civil aviation authority; and

(2) Unscheduled passenger-carrying operations of an air carrier operating aircraft configured for at least 31 passenger seats, as determined by the regulations under which the operation is conducted or the aircraft type certificate issued by a competent civil aviation authority.

(b) This part applies to those portions of a joint-use or shared-use airport that are within the authority of a person serving passenger-carrying operations defined in paragraphs (a)(1) and (a)(2) of this section.

(c) This part does not apply to—

(1) Airports serving scheduled air carrier operations only by reason of being designated as an alternate airport;

(2) Airports operated by the United States;

(3) Airports located in the State of Alaska that only serve scheduled operations of small air carrier aircraft and do not serve scheduled or unscheduled operations of large air carrier aircraft;

(4) Airports located in the State of Alaska during periods of time when not serving operations of large air carrier aircraft; or

(5) Heliports.

[Doc. No. FAA–2000–7479, 69 FR 6424, Feb. 10, 2004, as amended by Amdt. 139–27, 78 FR 3316, Jan. 16, 2013]

§ 139.3 Delegation of authority.

The authority of the Administrator to issue, deny, and revoke Airport Operating Certificates is delegated to the Associate Administrator for Airports, Director of Airport Safety and Standards, and Regional Airports Division Managers.

§ 139.5 Definitions.

The following are definitions of terms used in this part:

AFFF means aqueous film forming foam agent.

Air carrier aircraft means an aircraft that is being operated by an air carrier and is categorized as either a large air carrier aircraft if designed for at least 31 passenger seats or a small air carrier aircraft if designed for more than 9 passenger seats but less than 31 passenger seats, as determined by the aircraft type certificate issued by a competent civil aviation authority.

Air carrier operation means the takeoff or landing of an air carrier aircraft and includes the period of time from 15 minutes before until 15 minutes after the takeoff or landing.

Airport means an area of land or other hard surface, excluding water, that is used or intended to be used for the landing and takeoff of aircraft, including any buildings and facilities.

Airport Operating Certificate means a certificate, issued under this part, for operation of a Class I, II, III, or IV airport.

Average daily departures means the average number of scheduled departures per day of air carrier aircraft computed on the basis of the busiest 3 consecutive calendar months of the immediately preceding 12 consecutive calendar months. However, if the average daily departures are expected to increase, then "average daily departures" may be determined by planned rather than current activity, in a manner authorized by the Administrator.

Certificate holder means the holder of an Airport Operating Certificate issued under this part.

Class I airport means an airport certificated to serve scheduled operations of large air carrier aircraft that can also serve unscheduled passenger operations of large air carrier aircraft and/ or scheduled operations of small air carrier aircraft.

Class II airport means an airport certificated to serve scheduled operations of small air carrier aircraft and the unscheduled passenger operations of large air carrier aircraft. A Class II airport cannot serve scheduled large air carrier aircraft.

Class III airport means an airport certificated to serve scheduled operations of small air carrier aircraft. A Class III airport cannot serve scheduled or unscheduled large air carrier aircraft.

Class IV airport means an airport certificated to serve unscheduled passenger operations of large air carrier aircraft. A Class IV airport cannot serve scheduled large or small air carrier aircraft.

Clean agent means an electrically nonconducting volatile or gaseous fire extinguishing agent that does not leave a residue upon evaporation and has been shown to provide extinguishing action equivalent to halon 1211 under test protocols of FAA Technical Report DOT/FAA/AR–95/87.

Heliport means an airport, or an area of an airport, used or intended to be used for the landing and takeoff of helicopters.

Index means the type of aircraft rescue and firefighting equipment and quantity of fire extinguishing agent that the certificate holder must provide in accordance with §139.315.

Joint-use airport means an airport owned by the Department of Defense, at which both military and civilian aircraft make shared use of the airfield.

Movement area means the runways, taxiways, and other areas of an airport that are used for taxiing, takeoff, and landing of aircraft, exclusive of loading ramps and aircraft parking areas.

Regional Airports Division Manager means the airports division manager for the FAA region in which the airport is located.

Safety area means a defined area comprised of either a runway or taxiway and the surrounding surfaces that is prepared or suitable for reducing the risk of damage to aircraft in the event of an undershoot, overshoot, or excursion from a runway or the unintentional departure from a taxiway.

Scheduled operation means any common carriage passenger-carrying operation for compensation or hire conducted by an air carrier for which the air carrier or its representatives offers in advance the departure location, departure time, and arrival location. It does not include any operation that is conducted as a supplemental operation under 14 CFR part 121 or public charter operations under 14 CFR part 380.

Shared-use airport means a U.S. Government-owned airport that is co-located with an airport specified under §139.1(a) and at which portions of the movement areas and safety areas are shared by both parties.

Unscheduled operation means any common carriage passenger-carrying operation for compensation or hire, using aircraft designed for at least 31 passenger seats, conducted by an air carrier for which the departure time, departure location, and arrival location are specifically negotiated with the customer or the customer's representative. It includes any passenger-carrying supplemental operation conducted under 14 CFR part 121 and any passenger-carrying public charter operation conducted under 14 CFR part 380.

Wildlife hazard means a potential for a damaging aircraft collision with wildlife on or near an airport. As used in this part, "wildlife" includes feral animals and domestic animals out of the control of their owners.

NOTE: *Special Statutory Requirement To Operate to or From a Part 139 Airport.* Each air carrier that provides—in an aircraft designed for more than 9 passenger seats—regularly scheduled charter air transportation for which the public is provided in advance a schedule containing the departure location, departure time, and arrival location of the flight must operate to and from an airport certificated under part 139 of this chapter in accordance with 49 U.S.C. 41104(b). That statutory provision contains stand-alone requirements for such air carriers and special exceptions for operations in Alaska and outside the United States. Certain operations by air carriers that conduct public charter operations under 14 CFR part 380 are covered by the statutory requirements to operate to and from part 139 airports. See 49 U.S.C. 41104(b).

[Doc. No. FAA–2000–7479, 69 FR 6424, Feb. 10, 2004, as amended by Amdt. 139–27, 78 FR 3316, Jan. 16, 2013]

§ 139.7 Methods and procedures for compliance.

Certificate holders must comply with requirements prescribed by subparts C and D of this part in a manner authorized by the Administrator. FAA Advisory Circulars contain methods and procedures for compliance with this part that are acceptable to the Administrator.

Subpart B—Certification

§ 139.101 General requirements.

(a) Except as otherwise authorized by the Administrator, no person may operate an airport specified under § 139.1 of this part without an Airport Operating Certificate or in violation of that certificate, the applicable provisions, or the approved Airport Certification Manual.

(b) Each certificate holder shall adopt and comply with an Airport Certification Manual as required under § 139.203.

(c) Persons required to have an Airport Operating Certificate under this part shall submit their Airport Certification Manual to the FAA for approval, in accordance with the following schedule:

(1) Class I airports—6 months after June 9, 2004.

(2) Class II, III, and IV airports—12 months after June 9, 2004.

§ 139.103 Application for certificate.

Each applicant for an Airport Operating Certificate must—

(a) Prepare and submit an application, in a form and in the manner prescribed by the Administrator, to the Regional Airports Division Manager.

(b) Submit with the application, two copies of an Airport Certification Manual prepared in accordance with subpart C of this part.

§ 139.105 Inspection authority.

Each applicant for, or holder of, an Airport Operating Certificate must allow the Administrator to make any inspections, including unannounced inspections, or tests to determine compliance with 49 U.S.C. 44706 and the requirements of this part.

§ 139.107 Issuance of certificate.

An applicant for an Airport Operating Certificate is entitled to a certificate if—

(a) The applicant provides written documentation that air carrier service will begin on a date certain.

(b) The applicant meets the provisions of § 139.103.

(c) The Administrator, after investigation, finds the applicant is properly and adequately equipped and able to provide a safe airport operating environment in accordance with—

(1) Any limitation that the Administrator finds necessary to ensure safety in air transportation.

(2) The requirements of the Airport Certification Manual, as specified under §139.203.

(3) Any other provisions of this part that the Administrator finds necessary to ensure safety in air transportation.

(d) The Administrator approves the Airport Certification Manual.

§139.109 Duration of certificate.

An Airport Operating Certificate issued under this part is effective until the certificate holder surrenders it or the certificate is suspended or revoked by the Administrator.

§139.111 Exemptions.

(a) An applicant or a certificate holder may petition the Administrator under 14 CFR part 11, General Rulemaking Procedures, of this chapter for an exemption from any requirement of this part.

(b) Under 49 U.S.C. 44706(c), the Administrator may exempt an applicant or a certificate holder that enplanes annually less than one-quarter of 1 percent of the total number of passengers enplaned at all air carrier airports from all, or part, of the aircraft rescue and firefighting equipment requirements of this part on the grounds that compliance with those requirements is, or would be, unreasonably costly, burdensome, or impractical.

(1) Each petition filed under this paragraph must—

(i) Be submitted in writing at least 120 days before the proposed effective date of the exemption;

(ii) Set forth the text of §§139.317 or 139.319 from which the exemption is sought;

(iii) Explain the interest of the certificate holder in the action requested, including the nature and extent of relief sought; and

(iv) Contain information, views, or arguments that demonstrate that the requirements of §§139.317 or 139.319 would be unreasonably costly, burdensome, or impractical.

(2) Information, views, or arguments provided under paragraph (b)(1) of this section shall include the following information pertaining to the airport for which the Airport Operating Certificate is held:

(i) An itemized cost to comply with the requirement from which the exemption is sought;

(ii) Current staffing levels;

(iii) The current annual financial report, such as a single audit report or FAA Form 5100–127, Operating and Financial Summary;

(iv) Annual passenger enplanement data for the previous 12 calendar months;

(v) The type and frequency of air carrier operations served;

(vi) A history of air carrier service;

(vii) Anticipated changes to air carrier service;

(c) Each petition filed under this section must be submitted in duplicate to the—

(1) Regional Airports Division Manager and

(2) Federal Docket Management System, as specified under 14 CFR part 11.

[Doc. No. FAA–2000–7479, 69 FR 6424, Feb. 10, 2004; 72 FR 68475, Dec. 5, 2007]

§139.113 Deviations.

In emergency conditions requiring immediate action for the protection of life or property, the certificate holder may deviate from any requirement of subpart D of this part, or the Airport Certification Manual, to the extent required to meet that emergency. Each certificate holder who deviates from a requirement under this section must, within 14 days after the emergency, notify the Regional Airports Division Manager of the nature, extent, and duration of the deviation. When requested by the Regional Airports Division Manager, the certificate holder must provide this notification in writing.

§139.115 Falsification, reproduction, or alteration of applications, certificates, reports, or records.

(a) No person shall make or cause to be made:

(1) Any fraudulent or intentionally false statement on any application for a certificate or approval under this part.

(2) Any fraudulent or intentionally false entry in any record or report that

is required to be made, kept, or used to show compliance with any requirement under this part.

(3) Any reproduction, for a fraudulent purpose, of any certificate or approval issued under this part.

(4) Any alteration, for a fraudulent purpose, of any certificate or approval issued under this part.

(b) The commission by any owner, operator, or other person acting on behalf of a certificate holder of an act prohibited under paragraph (a) of this section is a basis for suspending or revoking any certificate or approval issued under this part and held by that certificate holder and any other certificate issued under this title and held by the person committing the act.

[Doc. No. FAA–2010–0247, 78 FR 3316, Jan. 16, 2013]

Subpart C—Airport Certification Manual

§ 139.201 General requirements.

(a) No person may operate an airport subject to this part unless that person adopts and complies with an Airport Certification Manual, as required under this part, that—

(1) Has been approved by the Administrator;

(2) Contains only those items authorized by the Administrator;

(3) Is in printed form and signed by the certificate holder acknowledging the certificate holder's responsibility to operate the airport in compliance with the Airport Certification Manual approved by the Administrator; and

(4) Is in a form that is easy to revise and organized in a manner helpful to the preparation, review, and approval processes, including a revision log. In addition, each page or attachment must include the date of the Adminis-

trator's initial approval or approval of the latest revision.

(b) Each holder of an Airport Operating Certificate must—

(1) Keep its Airport Certification Manual current at all times;

(2) Maintain at least one complete and current copy of its approved Airport Certification Manual on the airport, which will be available for inspection by the Administrator; and

(3) Furnish the applicable portions of the approved Airport Certification Manual to airport personnel responsible for its implementation.

(c) Each certificate holder must ensure that the Regional Airports Division Manager is provided a complete copy of its most current approved Airport Certification Manual, as specified under paragraph (b)(2) of this section, including any amendments approved under § 139.205.

(d) FAA Advisory Circulars contain methods and procedures for the development of Airport Certification Manuals that are acceptable to the Administrator.

§ 139.203 Contents of Airport Certification Manual.

(a) Except as otherwise authorized by the Administrator, each certificate holder must include in the Airport Certification Manual a description of operating procedures, facilities and equipment, responsibility assignments, and any other information needed by personnel concerned with operating the airport in order to comply with applicable provisions of subpart D of this part and paragraph (b) of this section.

(b) Except as otherwise authorized by the Administrator, the certificate holder must include in the Airport Certification Manual the following elements, as appropriate for its class:

REQUIRED AIRPORT CERTIFICATION MANUAL ELEMENTS

Manual elements	Airport certificate class			
	Class I	Class II	Class III	Class IV
1. Lines of succession of airport operational responsibility	X	X	X	X
2. Each current exemption issued to the airport from the requirements of this part	X	X	X	X
3. Any limitations imposed by the Administrator	X	X	X	X
4. A grid map or other means of identifying locations and terrain features on and around the airport that are significant to emergency operations	X	X	X	X
5. The location of each obstruction required to be lighted or marked within the airport's area of authority	X	X	X	X

REQUIRED AIRPORT CERTIFICATION MANUAL ELEMENTS—Continued

Manual elements	Airport certificate class			
	Class I	Class II	Class III	Class IV
6. A description of each movement area available for air carriers and its safety areas, and each road described in § 139.319(k) that serves it	X	X	X	X
7. Procedures for avoidance of interruption or failure during construction work of utilities serving facilities or NAVAIDS that support air carrier operations	X	X	X	
8. A description of the system for maintaining records as required under § 139.301	X	X	X	X
9. A description of personnel training, as required under § 139.303	X	X	X	X
10. Procedures for maintaining the paved areas, as required under § 139.305	X	X	X	X
11. Procedures for maintaining the unpaved areas, as required under § 139.307	X	X	X	X
12. Procedures for maintaining the safety areas, as required under § 139.309	X	X	X	X
13. A plan showing the runway and taxiway identification system, including the location and inscription of signs, runway markings, and holding position markings, as required under § 139.311	X	X	X	X
14. A description of, and procedures for maintaining, the marking, signs, and lighting systems, as required under § 139.311	X	X	X	X
15. A snow and ice control plan, as required under § 139.313	X	X	X	
16. A description of the facilities, equipment, personnel, and procedures for meeting the aircraft rescue and firefighting requirements, in accordance with §§ 139.315, 139.317 and 139.319	X	X	X	X
17. A description of any approved exemption to aircraft rescue and firefighting requirements, as authorized under § 139.111	X	X	X	X
18. Procedures for protecting persons and property during the storing, dispensing, and handling of fuel and other hazardous substances and materials, as required under § 139.321	X	X	X	X
19. A description of, and procedures for maintaining, the traffic and wind direction indicators, as required under § 139.323	X	X	X	X
20. An emergency plan as required under § 139.325	X	X	X	X
21. Procedures for conducting the self-inspection program, as required under § 139.327	X	X	X	X
22. Procedures for controlling pedestrians and ground vehicles in movement areas and safety areas, as required under § 139.329	X	X	X	X
23. Procedures for obstruction removal, marking, or lighting, as required under § 139.331	X	X	X	X
24. Procedures for protection of NAVAIDS, as required under § 139.333	X	X	X	
25. A description of public protection, as required under § 139.335	X	X	X	
26. Procedures for wildlife hazard management, as required under § 139.337	X	X	X	
27. Procedures for airport condition reporting, as required under § 139.339	X	X	X	X
28. Procedures for identifying, marking, and lighting construction and other unserviceable areas, as required under § 139.341	X	X	X	
29. Any other item that the Administrator finds is necessary to ensure safety in air transportation	X	X	X	X

[Doc. No. FAA-2000-7479, 69 FR 6424, Feb. 10, 2004; Amdt. 139–26, 69 FR 31522, June 4, 2004, as amended by Amdt. 139–27, 78 FR 3316, Jan. 16, 2013]

§139.205 Amendment of Airport Certification Manual.

(a) Under §139.3, the Regional Airports Division Manager may amend any Airport Certification Manual approved under this part, either—

(1) Upon application by the certificate holder or

(2) On the Regional Airports Division Manager's own initiative if the Regional Airports Division Manager determines that safety in air transportation requires the amendment.

(b) A certificate holder must submit in writing a proposed amendment to its Airport Certification Manual to the Regional Airports Division Manager at least 30 days before the proposed effective date of the amendment, unless a shorter filing period is allowed by the Regional Airports Division Manager.

(c) At any time within 30 days after receiving a notice of refusal to approve the application for amendment, the certificate holder may petition the Associate Administrator for Airports to reconsider the refusal to amend.

(d) In the case of amendments initiated by the FAA, the Regional Airports Division Manager notifies the certificate holder of the proposed amendment, in writing, fixing a reasonable period (but not less than 7 days) within which the certificate holder may submit written information, views, and arguments on the amendment. After considering all relevant material presented, the Regional Airports Division Manager notifies the certificate holder within 30 days of any amendment adopted or rescinds the notice. The amendment becomes effective not less than 30 days after the certificate holder receives notice of it, except that, prior to the effective date, the certificate holder may petition the Associate Administrator for Airports to reconsider the amendment, in which case its effective date is stayed pending a decision by the Associate Administrator for Airports.

(e) Notwithstanding the provisions of paragraph (d) of this section, if the Regional Airports Division Manager finds there is an emergency requiring immediate action with respect to safety in air transportation, the Regional Airports Division Manager may issue an amendment, effective without stay on the date the certificate holder receives notice of it. In such a case, the Regional Airports Division Manager incorporates the finding of the emergency and a brief statement of the reasons for the finding in the notice of the amendment. Within 30 days after the issuance of such an emergency amendment, the certificate holder may petition the Associate Administrator for Airports to reconsider either the finding of an emergency, the amendment itself, or both. This petition does not automatically stay the effectiveness of the emergency amendment.

Subpart D—Operations

§ 139.301   Records.

In a manner authorized by the Administrator, each certificate holder must—

(a) Furnish upon request by the Administrator all records required to be maintained under this part.

(b) Maintain records required under this part as follows:

(1) *Personnel training.* Twenty-four consecutive calendar months for personnel training records, as required under §§ 139.303 and 139.327.

(2) *Emergency personnel training.* Twenty-four consecutive calendar months for aircraft rescue and firefighting and emergency medical service personnel training records, as required under § 139.319.

(3) *Airport fueling agent inspection.* Twelve consecutive calendar months for records of inspection of airport fueling agents, as required under § 139.321.

(4) *Fueling personnel training.* Twelve consecutive calendar months for training records of fueling personnel, as required under § 139.321.

(5) *Self-inspection.* Twelve consecutive calendar months for self-inspection records, as required under § 139.327.

(6) *Movement areas and safety areas training.* Twenty-four consecutive calendar months for records of training given to pedestrians and ground vehicle operators with access to movement areas and safety areas, as required under § 139.329.

(7) *Accident and incident.* Twelve consecutive calendar months for each accident or incident in movement areas and safety areas involving an air carrier aircraft and/or ground vehicle, as required under § 139.329.

(8) *Airport condition.* Twelve consecutive calendar months for records of airport condition information dissemination, as required under § 139.339.

(c) Make and maintain any additional records required by the Administrator, this part, and the Airport Certification Manual.

§ 139.303   Personnel.

In a manner authorized by the Administrator, each certificate holder must—

(a) Provide sufficient and qualified personnel to comply with the requirements of its Airport Certification Manual and the requirements of this part.

(b) Equip personnel with sufficient resources needed to comply with the requirements of this part.

(c) Train all persons who access movement areas and safety areas and perform duties in compliance with the requirements of the Airport Certification Manual and the requirements of this part. This training must be completed prior to the initial performance of such duties and at least once every 12 consecutive calendar months. The curriculum for initial and recurrent training must include at least the following areas:

(1) Airport familiarization, including airport marking, lighting, and signs system.

(2) Procedures for access to, and operation in, movement areas and safety areas, as specified under § 139.329.

(3) Airport communications, including radio communication between the air traffic control tower and personnel, use of the common traffic advisory frequency if there is no air traffic control tower or the tower is not in operation, and procedures for reporting unsafe airport conditions.

(4) Duties required under the Airport Certification Manual and the requirements of this part.

(5) Any additional subject areas required under §§ 139.319, 139.321, 139.327, 139.329, 139.337, and 139.339, as appropriate.

(d) Make a record of all training completed after June 9, 2004 by each individual in compliance with this section that includes, at a minimum, a description and date of training received. Such records must be maintained for 24 consecutive calendar months after completion of training.

(e) As appropriate, comply with the following training requirements of this part:

(1) § 139.319, Aircraft rescue and firefighting: Operational requirements;

(2) § 139.321, Handling and storage of hazardous substances and materials;

(3) § 139.327, Self-inspection program;

(4) § 139.329, Pedestrians and Ground Vehicles;

(5) § 139.337, Wildlife hazard management; and

(6) § 139.339, Airport condition reporting.

(f) Use an independent organization, or designee, to comply with the requirements of its Airport Certification Manual and the requirements of this part only if—

(1) Such an arrangement is authorized by the Administrator;

(2) A description of responsibilities and duties that will be assumed by an independent organization or designee is specified in the Airport Certification Manual; and

(3) The independent organization or designee prepares records required under this part in sufficient detail to assure the certificate holder and the Administrator of adequate compliance

with the Airport Certification Manual and the requirements of this part.

[Doc. No. FAA-2000-7479, 69 FR 6424, Feb. 10, 2004; Amdt. 139-26, 69 FR 31522, June 4, 2004, as amended by Amdt. 139-27, 78 FR 3316, Jan. 16, 2013]

§ 139.305 Paved areas.

(a) In a manner authorized by the Administrator, each certificate holder must maintain, and promptly repair the pavement of, each runway, taxiway, loading ramp, and parking area on the airport that is available for air carrier use as follows:

(1) The pavement edges must not exceed 3 inches difference in elevation between abutting pavement sections and between pavement and abutting areas.

(2) The pavement must have no hole exceeding 3 inches in depth nor any hole the slope of which from any point in the hole to the nearest point at the lip of the hole is 45 degrees or greater, as measured from the pavement surface plane, unless, in either case, the entire area of the hole can be covered by a 5-inch diameter circle.

(3) The pavement must be free of cracks and surface variations that could impair directional control of air carrier aircraft, including any pavement crack or surface deterioration that produces loose aggregate or other contaminants.

(4) Except as provided in paragraph (b) of this section, mud, dirt, sand, loose aggregate, debris, foreign objects, rubber deposits, and other contaminants must be removed promptly and as completely as practicable.

(5) Except as provided in paragraph (b) of this section, any chemical solvent that is used to clean any pavement area must be removed as soon as possible, consistent with the instructions of the manufacturer of the solvent.

(6) The pavement must be sufficiently drained and free of depressions to prevent ponding that obscures markings or impairs safe aircraft operations.

(b) Paragraphs (a)(4) and (a)(5) of this section do not apply to snow and ice accumulations and their control, including the associated use of materials, such as sand and deicing solutions.

(c) FAA Advisory Circulars contain methods and procedures for the maintenance and configuration of paved areas that are acceptable to the Administrator.

[Doc. No. FAA-2000-7479, 69 FR 6424, Feb. 10, 2004; Amdt. 139-26, 69 FR 31522, June 4, 2004]

§ 139.307 Unpaved areas.

(a) In a manner authorized by the Administrator, each certificate holder must maintain and promptly repair the surface of each gravel, turf, or other unpaved runway, taxiway, or loading ramp and parking area on the airport that is available for air carrier use as follows:

(1) No slope from the edge of the full-strength surfaces downward to the existing terrain must be steeper than 2:1.

(2) The full-strength surfaces must have adequate crown or grade to assure sufficient drainage to prevent ponding.

(3) The full-strength surfaces must be adequately compacted and sufficiently stable to prevent rutting by aircraft or the loosening or build-up of surface material, which could impair directional control of aircraft or drainage.

(4) The full-strength surfaces must have no holes or depressions that exceed 3 inches in depth and are of a breadth capable of impairing directional control or causing damage to an aircraft.

(5) Debris and foreign objects must be promptly removed from the surface.

(b) FAA Advisory Circulars contain methods and procedures for the maintenance and configuration of unpaved areas that are acceptable to the Administrator.

§ 139.309 Safety areas.

(a) In a manner authorized by the Administrator, each certificate holder must provide and maintain, for each runway and taxiway that is available for air carrier use, a safety area of at least the dimensions that—

(1) Existed on December 31, 1987, if the runway or taxiway had a safety area on December 31, 1987, and if no reconstruction or significant expansion of the runway or taxiway was begun on or after January 1, 1988; or

(2) Are authorized by the Administrator at the time the construction, reconstruction, or expansion began if construction, reconstruction, or significant expansion of the runway or taxiway began on or after January 1, 1988.

(b) Each certificate holder must maintain its safety areas as follows:

(1) Each safety area must be cleared and graded and have no potentially hazardous ruts, humps, depressions, or other surface variations.

(2) Each safety area must be drained by grading or storm sewers to prevent water accumulation.

(3) Each safety area must be capable under dry conditions of supporting snow removal and aircraft rescue and firefighting equipment and of supporting the occasional passage of aircraft without causing major damage to the aircraft.

(4) No objects may be located in any safety area, except for objects that need to be located in a safety area because of their function. These objects must be constructed, to the extent practical, on frangibly mounted structures of the lowest practical height, with the frangible point no higher than 3 inches above grade.

(c) FAA Advisory Circulars contain methods and procedures for the configuration and maintenance of safety areas acceptable to the Administrator.

§ 139.311 Marking, signs, and lighting.

(a) *Marking.* Each certificate holder must provide and maintain marking systems for air carrier operations on the airport that are authorized by the Administrator and consist of at least the following:

(1) Runway markings meeting the specifications for takeoff and landing minimums for each runway.

(2) A taxiway centerline.

(3) Taxiway edge markings, as appropriate.

(4) Holding position markings.

(5) Instrument landing system (ILS) critical area markings.

(b) *Signs.* (1) Each certificate holder must provide and maintain sign systems for air carrier operations on the airport that are authorized by the Administrator and consist of at least the following:

(i) Signs identifying taxiing routes on the movement area.

(ii) Holding position signs.

(iii) Instrument landing system (ILS) critical area signs.

(2) Unless otherwise authorized by the Administrator, the signs required by paragraph (b)(1) of this section must be internally illuminated at each Class I, II, and IV airport.

(3) Unless otherwise authorized by the Administrator, the signs required by paragraphs (b)(1)(ii) and (b)(1)(iii) of this section must be internally illuminated at each Class III airport.

(c) *Lighting.* Each certificate holder must provide and maintain lighting systems for air carrier operations when the airport is open at night, during conditions below visual flight rules (VFR) minimums, or in Alaska, during periods in which a prominent unlighted object cannot be seen from a distance of 3 statute miles or the sun is more than six degrees below the horizon. These lighting systems must be authorized by the Administrator and consist of at least the following:

(1) Runway lighting that meets the specifications for takeoff and landing minimums, as authorized by the Administrator, for each runway.

(2) One of the following taxiway lighting systems:

(i) Centerline lights.

(ii) Centerline reflectors.

(iii) Edge lights.

(iv) Edge reflectors.

(3) An airport beacon.

(4) Approach lighting that meets the specifications for takeoff and landing minimums, as authorized by the Administrator, for each runway, unless provided and/or maintained by an entity other than the certificate holder

(5) Obstruction marking and lighting, as appropriate, on each object within its authority that has been determined by the FAA to be an obstruction.

(d) *Maintenance.* Each certificate holder must properly maintain each marking, sign, or lighting system installed and operated on the airport. As used in this section, to "properly maintain" includes cleaning, replacing, or repairing any faded, missing, or nonfunctional item; keeping each item unobscured and clearly visible; and ensuring that each item provides an accurate reference to the user.

(e) *Lighting interference.* Each certificate holder must ensure that all light-

ing on the airport, including that for aprons, vehicle parking areas, roadways, fuel storage areas, and buildings, is adequately adjusted or shielded to prevent interference with air traffic control and aircraft operations.

(f) *Standards.* FAA Advisory Circulars contain methods and procedures for the equipment, material, installation, and maintenance of marking, sign, and lighting systems listed in this section that are acceptable to the Administrator.

(g) *Implementation.* The sign systems required under paragraph (b)(3) of this section must be implemented by each holder of a Class III Airport Operating Certificate not later than 36 consecutive calendar months after June 9, 2004.

§ 139.313 Snow and ice control.

(a) As determined by the Administrator, each certificate holder whose airport is located where snow and icing conditions occur must prepare, maintain, and carry out a snow and ice control plan in a manner authorized by the Administrator.

(b) The snow and ice control plan required by this section must include, at a minimum, instructions and procedures for—

(1) Prompt removal or control, as completely as practical, of snow, ice, and slush on each movement area;

(2) Positioning snow off the movement area surfaces so all air carrier aircraft propellers, engine pods, rotors, and wing tips will clear any snowdrift and snowbank as the aircraft's landing gear traverses any portion of the movement area;

(3) Selection and application of authorized materials for snow and ice control to ensure that they adhere to snow and ice sufficiently to minimize engine ingestion;

(4) Timely commencement of snow and ice control operations; and

(5) Prompt notification, in accordance with § 139.339, of all air carriers using the airport when any portion of the movement area normally available to them is less than satisfactorily cleared for safe operation by their aircraft.

(c) FAA Advisory Circulars contain methods and procedures for snow and ice control equipment, materials, and removal that are acceptable to the Administrator.

§ 139.315 Aircraft rescue and firefighting: Index determination.

(a) An index is required by paragraph (c) of this section for each certificate holder. The Index is determined by a combination of—

(1) The length of air carrier aircraft and

(2) Average daily departures of air carrier aircraft.

(b) For the purpose of Index determination, air carrier aircraft lengths are grouped as follows:

(1) Index A includes aircraft less than 90 feet in length.

(2) Index B includes aircraft at least 90 feet but less than 126 feet in length.

(3) Index C includes aircraft at least 126 feet but less than 159 feet in length.

(4) Index D includes aircraft at least 159 feet but less than 200 feet in length.

(5) Index E includes aircraft at least 200 feet in length.

(c) Except as provided in § 139.319(c), if there are five or more average daily departures of air carrier aircraft in a single Index group serving that airport, the longest aircraft with an average of five or more daily departures determines the Index required for the airport. When there are fewer than five average daily departures of the longest air carrier aircraft serving the airport, the Index required for the airport will be the next lower Index group than the Index group prescribed for the longest aircraft.

(d) The minimum designated index shall be Index A.

(e) A holder of a Class III Airport Operating Certificate may comply with this section by providing a level of safety comparable to Index A that is approved by the Administrator. Such alternate compliance must be described in the ACM and must include:

(1) Pre-arranged firefighting and emergency medical response procedures, including agreements with responding services.

(2) Means for alerting firefighting and emergency medical response personnel.

(3) Type of rescue and firefighting equipment to be provided.

(4) Training of responding firefighting and emergency medical personnel on airport familiarization and communications.

[Doc. No. FAA-2000-7479, 69 FR 6424, Feb. 10, 2004; Amdt. 139-26, 69 FR 31522, June 4, 2004]

§ 139.317 Aircraft rescue and firefighting: Equipment and agents.

Unless otherwise authorized by the Administrator, the following rescue and firefighting equipment and agents are the minimum required for the Indexes referred to in § 139.315:

(a) *Index A.* One vehicle carrying at least—

(1) 500 pounds of sodium-based dry chemical, halon 1211, or clean agent; or

(2) 450 pounds of potassium-based dry chemical and water with a commensurate quantity of AFFF to total 100 gallons for simultaneous dry chemical and AFFF application.

(b) *Index B.* Either of the following:

(1) One vehicle carrying at least 500 pounds of sodium-based dry chemical, halon 1211, or clean agent and 1,500 gallons of water and the commensurate quantity of AFFF for foam production.

(2) Two vehicles—

(i) One vehicle carrying the extinguishing agents as specified in paragraphs (a)(1) or (a)(2) of this section; and

(ii) One vehicle carrying an amount of water and the commensurate quantity of AFFF so the total quantity of water for foam production carried by both vehicles is at least 1,500 gallons.

(c) *Index C.* Either of the following:

(1) Three vehicles—

(i) One vehicle carrying the extinguishing agents as specified in paragraph (a)(1) or (a)(2) of this section; and

(ii) Two vehicles carrying an amount of water and the commensurate quantity of AFFF so the total quantity of water for foam production carried by all three vehicles is at least 3,000 gallons.

(2) Two vehicles—

(i) One vehicle carrying the extinguishing agents as specified in paragraph (b)(1) of this section; and

(ii) One vehicle carrying water and the commensurate quantity of AFFF so the total quantity of water for foam production carried by both vehicles is at least 3,000 gallons.

(d) *Index D.* Three vehicles—
(1) One vehicle carrying the extinguishing agents as specified in paragraphs (a)(1) or (a)(2) of this section; and
(2) Two vehicles carrying an amount of water and the commensurate quantity of AFFF so the total quantity of water for foam production carried by all three vehicles is at least 4,000 gallons.

(e) *Index E.* Three vehicles—
(1) One vehicle carrying the extinguishing agents as specified in paragraphs (a)(1) or (a)(2) of this section; and
(2) Two vehicles carrying an amount of water and the commensurate quantity of AFFF so the total quantity of water for foam production carried by all three vehicles is at least 6,000 gallons.

(f) *Foam discharge capacity.* Each aircraft rescue and firefighting vehicle used to comply with Index B, C, D, or E requirements with a capacity of at least 500 gallons of water for foam production must be equipped with a turret. Vehicle turret discharge capacity must be as follows:
(1) Each vehicle with a minimum-rated vehicle water tank capacity of at least 500 gallons, but less than 2,000 gallons, must have a turret discharge rate of at least 500 gallons per minute, but not more than 1,000 gallons per minute.
(2) Each vehicle with a minimum-rated vehicle water tank capacity of at least 2,000 gallons must have a turret discharge rate of at least 600 gallons per minute, but not more than 1,200 gallons per minute.

(g) *Agent discharge capacity.* Each aircraft rescue and firefighting vehicle that is required to carry dry chemical, halon 1211, or clean agent for compliance with the Index requirements of this section must meet one of the following minimum discharge rates for the equipment installed:
(1) Dry chemical, halon 1211, or clean agent through a hand line—5 pounds per second.
(2) Dry chemical, halon 1211, or clean agent through a turret—16 pounds per second.

(h) *Extinguishing agent substitutions.* Other extinguishing agent substi-

tutions authorized by the Administrator may be made in amounts that provide equivalent firefighting capability.

(i) *AFFF quantity requirements.* In addition to the quantity of water required, each vehicle required to carry AFFF must carry AFFF in an appropriate amount to mix with twice the water required to be carried by the vehicle.

(j) *Methods and procedures.* FAA Advisory Circulars contain methods and procedures for ARFF equipment and extinguishing agents that are acceptable to the Administrator.

(k) *Implementation.* Each holder of a Class II, III, or IV Airport Operating Certificate must implement the requirements of this section no later than 36 consecutive calendar months after June 9, 2004.

[Doc. No. FAA–2000–7479, 69 FR 6424, Feb. 10, 2004; Amdt. 139–26, 69 FR 31523, June 4, 2004]

§139.319 Aircraft rescue and firefighting: Operational requirements.

(a) *Rescue and firefighting capability.* Except as provided in paragraph (c) of this section, each certificate holder must provide on the airport, during air carrier operations at the airport, at least the rescue and firefighting capability specified for the Index required by §139.317 in a manner authorized by the Administrator.

(b) *Increase in Index.* Except as provided in paragraph (c) of this section, if an increase in the average daily departures or the length of air carrier aircraft results in an increase in the Index required by paragraph (a) of this section, the certificate holder must comply with the increased requirements.

(c) *Reduction in rescue and firefighting.* During air carrier operations with only aircraft shorter than the Index aircraft group required by paragraph (a) of this section, the certificate holder may reduce the rescue and firefighting to a lower level corresponding to the Index group of the longest air carrier aircraft being operated.

(d) *Procedures for reduction in capability.* Any reduction in the rescue and firefighting capability from the Index required by paragraph (a) of this section, in accordance with paragraph (c) of this section, must be subject to the following conditions:

(1) Procedures for, and the persons having the authority to implement, the reductions must be included in the Airport Certification Manual.

(2) A system and procedures for recall of the full aircraft rescue and firefighting capability must be included in the Airport Certification Manual.

(3) The reductions may not be implemented unless notification to air carriers is provided in the Airport/Facility Directory or Notices to Airmen (NOTAM), as appropriate, and by direct notification of local air carriers.

(e) *Vehicle communications.* Each vehicle required under § 139.317 must be equipped with two-way voice radio communications that provide for contact with at least—

(1) All other required emergency vehicles;

(2) The air traffic control tower;

(3) The common traffic advisory frequency when an air traffic control tower is not in operation or there is no air traffic control tower, and

(4) Fire stations, as specified in the airport emergency plan.

(f) *Vehicle marking and lighting.* Each vehicle required under § 139.317 must—

(1) Have a flashing or rotating beacon and

(2) Be painted or marked in colors to enhance contrast with the background environment and optimize daytime and nighttime visibility and identification.

(g) *Vehicle readiness.* Each vehicle required under § 139.317 must be maintained as follows:

(1) The vehicle and its systems must be maintained so as to be operationally capable of performing the functions required by this subpart during all air carrier operations.

(2) If the airport is located in a geographical area subject to prolonged temperatures below 33 degrees Fahrenheit, the vehicles must be provided with cover or other means to ensure equipment operation and discharge under freezing conditions.

(3) Any required vehicle that becomes inoperative to the extent that it cannot perform as required by paragraph (g)(1) of this section must be replaced immediately with equipment having at least equal capabilities. If replacement

equipment is not available immediately, the certificate holder must so notify the Regional Airports Division Manager and each air carrier using the airport in accordance with § 139.339. If the required Index level of capability is not restored within 48 hours, the airport operator, unless otherwise authorized by the Administrator, must limit air carrier operations on the airport to those compatible with the Index corresponding to the remaining operative rescue and firefighting equipment.

(h) *Response requirements.* (1) With the aircraft rescue and firefighting equipment required under this part and the number of trained personnel that will assure an effective operation, each certificate holder must—

(i) Respond to each emergency during periods of air carrier operations; and

(ii) When requested by the Administrator, demonstrate compliance with the response requirements specified in this section.

(2) The response required by paragraph (h)(1)(ii) of this section must achieve the following performance criteria:

(i) Within 3 minutes from the time of the alarm, at least one required aircraft rescue and firefighting vehicle must reach the midpoint of the farthest runway serving air carrier aircraft from its assigned post or reach any other specified point of comparable distance on the movement area that is available to air carriers, and begin application of extinguishing agent.

(ii) Within 4 minutes from the time of alarm, all other required vehicles must reach the point specified in paragraph (h)(2)(i) of this section from their assigned posts and begin application of an extinguishing agent.

(i) *Personnel.* Each certificate holder must ensure the following:

(1) All rescue and firefighting personnel are equipped in a manner authorized by the Administrator with protective clothing and equipment needed to perform their duties.

(2) All rescue and firefighting personnel are properly trained to perform their duties in a manner authorized by the Administrator. Such personnel must be trained prior to initial performance of rescue and firefighting duties and receive recurrent instruction

every 12 consecutive calendar months. The curriculum for initial and recurrent training must include at least the following areas:

(i) Airport familiarization, including airport signs, marking, and lighting.

(ii) Aircraft familiarization.

(iii) Rescue and firefighting personnel safety.

(iv) Emergency communications systems on the airport, including fire alarms.

(v) Use of the fire hoses, nozzles, turrets, and other appliances required for compliance with this part.

(vi) Application of the types of extinguishing agents required for compliance with this part.

(vii) Emergency aircraft evacuation assistance.

(viii) Firefighting operations.

(ix) Adapting and using structural rescue and firefighting equipment for aircraft rescue and firefighting.

(x) Aircraft cargo hazards, including hazardous materials/dangerous goods incidents.

(xi) Familiarization with firefighters' duties under the airport emergency plan.

(3) All rescue and firefighting personnel must participate in at least one live-fire drill prior to initial performance of rescue and firefighting duties and every 12 consecutive calendar months thereafter.

(4) At least one individual, who has been trained and is current in basic emergency medical services, is available during air carrier operations. This individual must be trained prior to initial performance of emergency medical services. Training must be at a minimum 40 hours in length and cover the following topics:

(i) Bleeding.

(ii) Cardiopulmonary resuscitation.

(iii) Shock.

(iv) Primary patient survey.

(v) Injuries to the skull, spine, chest, and extremities.

(vi) Internal injuries.

(vii) Moving patients.

(viii) Burns.

(ix) Triage.

(5) A record is maintained of all training given to each individual under this section for 24 consecutive calendar months after completion of training.

Such records must include, at a minimum, a description and date of training received.

(6) Sufficient rescue and firefighting personnel are available during all air carrier operations to operate the vehicles, meet the response times, and meet the minimum agent discharge rates required by this part.

(7) Procedures and equipment are established and maintained for alerting rescue and firefighting personnel by siren, alarm, or other means authorized by the Administrator to any existing or impending emergency requiring their assistance.

(j) *Hazardous materials guidance.* Each aircraft rescue and firefighting vehicle responding to an emergency on the airport must be equipped with, or have available through a direct communications link, the "North American Emergency Response Guidebook" published by the U.S. Department of Transportation or similar response guidance to hazardous materials/dangerous goods incidents. Information on obtaining the "North American Emergency Response Guidebook" is available from the Regional Airports Division Manager.

(k) *Emergency access roads.* Each certificate holder must ensure that roads designated for use as emergency access roads for aircraft rescue and firefighting vehicles are maintained in a condition that will support those vehicles during all-weather conditions.

(l) *Methods and procedures.* FAA Advisory Circulars contain methods and procedures for aircraft rescue and firefighting and emergency medical equipment and training that are acceptable to the Administrator.

(m) *Implementation.* Each holder of a Class II, III, or IV Airport Operating Certificate must implement the requirements of this section no later than 36 consecutive calendar months after June 9, 2004.

[Doc. No. FAA–2000–7479, 69 FR 6424, Feb. 10, 2004; Amdt. 139–26, 69 FR 31523, June 4, 2004]

§139.321 Handling and storing of hazardous substances and materials.

(a) Each certificate holder who acts as a cargo handling agent must establish and maintain procedures for the protection of persons and property on the airport during the handling and storing of any material regulated by the Hazardous Materials Regulations (49 CFR 171 through 180) that is, or is intended to be, transported by air. These procedures must provide for at least the following:

(1) Designated personnel to receive and handle hazardous substances and materials.

(2) Assurance from the shipper that the cargo can be handled safely, including any special handling procedures required for safety.

(3) Special areas for storage of hazardous materials while on the airport.

(b) Each certificate holder must establish and maintain standards authorized by the Administrator for protecting against fire and explosions in storing, dispensing, and otherwise handling fuel (other than articles and materials that are, or are intended to be, aircraft cargo) on the airport. These standards must cover facilities, procedures, and personnel training and must address at least the following:

(1) Bonding.

(2) Public protection.

(3) Control of access to storage areas.

(4) Fire safety in fuel farm and storage areas.

(5) Fire safety in mobile fuelers, fueling pits, and fueling cabinets.

(6) Training of fueling personnel in fire safety in accordance with paragraph (e) of this section. Such training at Class III airports must be completed within 12 consecutive calendar months after June 9, 2004.

(7) The fire code of the public body having jurisdiction over the airport.

(c) Each certificate holder must, as a fueling agent, comply with, and require all other fueling agents operating on the airport to comply with, the standards established under paragraph (b) of this section and must perform reasonable surveillance of all fueling activities on the airport with respect to those standards.

(d) Each certificate holder must inspect the physical facilities of each airport tenant fueling agent at least once every 3 consecutive months for compliance with paragraph (b) of this section and maintain a record of that inspection for at least 12 consecutive calendar months.

(e) The training required in paragraph (b)(6) of this section must include at least the following:

(1) At least one supervisor with each fueling agent must have completed an aviation fuel training course in fire safety that is authorized by the Administrator. Such an individual must be trained prior to initial performance of duties, or enrolled in an authorized aviation fuel training course that will be completed within 90 days of initiating duties, and receive recurrent instruction at least every 24 consecutive calendar months.

(2) All other employees who fuel aircraft, accept fuel shipments, or otherwise handle fuel must receive at least initial on-the-job training and recurrent instruction every 24 consecutive calendar months in fire safety from the supervisor trained in accordance with paragraph (e)(1) of this section.

(f) Each certificate holder must obtain a written confirmation once every 12 consecutive calendar months from each airport tenant fueling agent that the training required by paragraph (e) of this section has been accomplished. This written confirmation must be maintained for 12 consecutive calendar months.

(g) Unless otherwise authorized by the Administrator, each certificate holder must require each tenant fueling agent to take immediate corrective action whenever the certificate holder becomes aware of noncompliance with a standard required by paragraph (b) of this section. The certificate holder must notify the appropriate FAA Regional Airports Division Manager immediately when noncompliance is discovered and corrective action cannot be accomplished within a reasonable period of time.

(h) FAA Advisory Circulars contain methods and procedures for the handling and storage of hazardous substances and materials that are acceptable to the Administrator.

§ 139.323   Traffic and wind direction indicators.

In a manner authorized by the Administrator, each certificate holder must provide and maintain the following on its airport:

(a) A wind cone that visually provides surface wind direction information to pilots. For each runway available for air carrier use, a supplemental wind cone must be installed at the end of the runway or at least at one point visible to the pilot while on final approach and prior to takeoff. If the airport is open for air carrier operations at night, the wind direction indicators, including the required supplemental indicators, must be lighted.

(b) For airports serving any air carrier operation when there is no control tower operating, a segmented circle, a landing strip indicator and a traffic pattern indicator must be installed around a wind cone for each runway with a right-hand traffic pattern.

(c) FAA Advisory Circulars contain methods and procedures for the installation, lighting, and maintenance of traffic and wind indicators that are acceptable to the Administrator.

§ 139.325 Airport emergency plan.

(a) In a manner authorized by the Administrator, each certificate holder must develop and maintain an airport emergency plan designed to minimize the possibility and extent of personal injury and property damage on the airport in an emergency. The plan must—

(1) Include procedures for prompt response to all emergencies listed in paragraph (b) of this section, including a communications network;

(2) Contain sufficient detail to provide adequate guidance to each person who must implement these procedures; and

(3) To the extent practicable, provide for an emergency response for the largest air carrier aircraft in the Index group required under § 139.315.

(b) The plan required by this section must contain instructions for response to—

(1) Aircraft incidents and accidents;

(2) Bomb incidents, including designation of parking areas for the aircraft involved;

(3) Structural fires;

(4) Fires at fuel farms or fuel storage areas;

(5) Natural disaster;

(6) Hazardous materials/dangerous goods incidents;

(7) Sabotage, hijack incidents, and other unlawful interference with operations;

(8) Failure of power for movement area lighting; and

(9) Water rescue situations, as appropriate.

(c) The plan required by this section must address or include—

(1) To the extent practicable, provisions for medical services, including transportation and medical assistance for the maximum number of persons that can be carried on the largest air carrier aircraft that the airport reasonably can be expected to serve;

(2) The name, location, telephone number, and emergency capability of each hospital and other medical facility and the business address and telephone number of medical personnel on the airport or in the communities it serves who have agreed to provide medical assistance or transportation;

(3) The name, location, and telephone number of each rescue squad, ambulance service, military installation, and government agency on the airport or in the communities it serves that agrees to provide medical assistance or transportation;

(4) An inventory of surface vehicles and aircraft that the facilities, agencies, and personnel included in the plan under paragraphs (c)(2) and (3) of this section will provide to transport injured and deceased persons to locations on the airport and in the communities it serves;

(5) A list of each hangar or other building on the airport or in the communities it serves that will be used to accommodate uninjured, injured, and deceased persons;

(6) Plans for crowd control, including the name and location of each safety or security agency that agrees to provide assistance for the control of crowds in the event of an emergency on the airport; and

(7) Procedures for removing disabled aircraft, including, to the extent practical, the name, location, and telephone numbers of agencies with aircraft removal responsibilities or capabilities.

(d) The plan required by this section must provide for—

(1) The marshalling, transportation, and care of ambulatory injured and uninjured accident survivors;

(2) The removal of disabled aircraft;

(3) Emergency alarm or notification systems; and

(4) Coordination of airport and control tower functions relating to emergency actions, as appropriate.

(e) The plan required by this section must contain procedures for notifying the facilities, agencies, and personnel who have responsibilities under the plan of the location of an aircraft accident, the number of persons involved in that accident, or any other information necessary to carry out their responsibilities, as soon as that information becomes available.

(f) The plan required by this section must contain provisions, to the extent practicable, for the rescue of aircraft accident victims from significant bodies of water or marsh lands adjacent to the airport that are crossed by the approach and departure flight paths of air carriers. A body of water or marshland is significant if the area exceeds one-quarter square mile and cannot be traversed by conventional land rescue vehicles. To the extent practicable, the plan must provide for rescue vehicles with a combined capacity for handling the maximum number of persons that can be carried on board the largest air carrier aircraft in the Index group required under § 139.315.

(g) Each certificate holder must—

(1) Coordinate the plan with law enforcement agencies, rescue and firefighting agencies, medical personnel and organizations, the principal tenants at the airport, and all other persons who have responsibilities under the plan;

(2) To the extent practicable, provide for participation by all facilities, agencies, and personnel specified in paragraph (g)(1) of this section in the development of the plan;

(3) Ensure that all airport personnel having duties and responsibilities under the plan are familiar with their assignments and are properly trained; and

(4) At least once every 12 consecutive calendar months, review the plan with all of the parties with whom the plan is coordinated, as specified in paragraph

(g)(1) of this section, to ensure that all parties know their responsibilities and that all of the information in the plan is current.

(h) Each holder of a Class I Airport Operating Certificate must hold a full-scale airport emergency plan exercise at least once every 36 consecutive calendar months.

(i) Each airport subject to applicable FAA and Transportation Security Administration security regulations must ensure that instructions for response to paragraphs (b)(2) and (b)(7) of this section in the airport emergency plan are consistent with its approved airport security program.

(j) FAA Advisory Circulars contain methods and procedures for the development of an airport emergency plan that are acceptable to the Administrator.

(k) The emergency plan required by this section must be submitted by each holder of a Class II, III, or IV Airport Operating Certificate no later than 24 consecutive calendar months after June 9, 2004.

§ 139.327 Self-inspection program.

(a) In a manner authorized by the Administrator, each certificate holder must inspect the airport to assure compliance with this subpart according to the following schedule:

(1) Daily, except as otherwise required by the Airport Certification Manual;

(2) When required by any unusual condition, such as construction activities or meteorological conditions, that may affect safe air carrier operations; and

(3) Immediately after an accident or incident.

(b) Each certificate holder must provide the following:

(1) Equipment for use in conducting safety inspections of the airport;

(2) Procedures, facilities, and equipment for reliable and rapid dissemination of information between the certificate holder's personnel and air carriers; and

(3) Procedures to ensure qualified personnel perform the inspections. Such procedures must ensure personnel are trained, as specified under § 139.303,

and receive initial and recurrent instruction every 12 consecutive calendar months in at least the following areas:

(i) Airport familiarization, including airport signs, marking and lighting.

(ii) Airport emergency plan.

(iii) Notice to Airmen (NOTAM) notification procedures.

(iv) Procedures for pedestrians and ground vehicles in movement areas and safety areas.

(v) Discrepancy reporting procedures; and

(4) A reporting system to ensure prompt correction of unsafe airport conditions noted during the inspection, including wildlife strikes.

(c) Each certificate holder must—

(1) Prepare, and maintain for at least 12 consecutive calendar months, a record of each inspection prescribed by this section, showing the conditions found and all corrective actions taken.

(2) Prepare records of all training given after June 9, 2004 to each individual in compliance with this section that includes, at a minimum, a description and date of training received. Such records must be maintained for 24 consecutive calendar months after completion of training.

(d) FAA Advisory Circulars contain methods and procedures for the conduct of airport self-inspections that are acceptable to the Administrator.

§139.329 Pedestrians and ground vehicles.

In a manner authorized by the Administrator, each certificate holder must—

(a) Limit access to movement areas and safety areas only to those pedestrians and ground vehicles necessary for airport operations;

(b) Establish and implement procedures for the safe and orderly access to and operation in movement areas and safety areas by pedestrians and ground vehicles, including provisions identifying the consequences of noncompliance with the procedures by all persons;

(c) When an air traffic control tower is in operation, ensure that each pedestrian and ground vehicle in movement areas or safety areas is controlled by one of the following:

(1) Two-way radio communications between each pedestrian or vehicle and the tower;

(2) An escort with two-way radio communications with the tower accompanying any pedestrian or vehicle without a radio; or

(3) Measures authorized by the Administrator for controlling pedestrians and vehicles, such as signs, signals, or guards, when it is not operationally practical to have two-way radio communications between the tower and the pedestrian, vehicle, or escort;

(d) When an air traffic control tower is not in operation, or there is no air traffic control tower, provide adequate procedures to control pedestrians and ground vehicles in movement areas or safety areas through two-way radio communications or prearranged signs or signals;

(e) Ensure that all persons are trained on procedures required under paragraph (b) of this section prior to the initial performance of such duties and at least once every 12 consecutive calendar months, including consequences of noncompliance, prior to moving on foot, or operating a ground vehicle, in movement areas or safety areas; and

(f) Maintain the following records:

(1) A description and date of training completed after June 9, 2004 by each individual in compliance with this section. A record for each individual must be maintained for 24 consecutive months after the termination of an individual's access to movement areas and safety areas.

(2) A description and date of any accidents or incidents in the movement areas and safety areas involving air carrier aircraft, a ground vehicle or a pedestrian. Records of each accident or incident occurring after the June 9, 2004 must be maintained for 12 consecutive calendar months from the date of the accident or incident.

[Doc. No. FAA–2000–7479, 69 FR 6424, Feb. 10, 2004, as amended by Amdt. 139–27, 78 FR 3316, Jan. 16, 2013]

§139.331 Obstructions.

In a manner authorized by the Administrator, each certificate holder must ensure that each object in each area within its authority that has been determined by the FAA to be an obstruction is removed, marked, or lighted, unless determined to be unnecessary by an FAA aeronautical study. FAA Advisory Circulars contain methods and procedures for the lighting of obstructions that are acceptable to the Administrator.

§ 139.333 Protection of NAVAIDS.

In a manner authorized by the Administrator, each certificate holder must—

(a) Prevent the construction of facilities on its airport that, as determined by the Administrator, would derogate the operation of an electronic or visual NAVAID and air traffic control facilities on the airport;

(b) Protect—or if the owner is other than the certificate holder, assist in protecting—all NAVAIDS on its airport against vandalism and theft; and

(c) Prevent, insofar as it is within the airport's authority, interruption of visual and electronic signals of NAVAIDS.

§ 139.335 Public protection.

(a) In a manner authorized by the Administrator, each certificate holder must provide—

(1) Safeguards to prevent inadvertent entry to the movement area by unauthorized persons or vehicles; and

(2) Reasonable protection of persons and property from aircraft blast.

(b) Fencing that meets the requirements of applicable FAA and Transportation Security Administration security regulations in areas subject to these regulations is acceptable for meeting the requirements of paragraph (a)(1) of this section.

§ 139.337 Wildlife hazard management.

(a) In accordance with its Airport Certification Manual and the requirements of this section, each certificate holder must take immediate action to alleviate wildlife hazards whenever they are detected.

(b) In a manner authorized by the Administrator, each certificate holder must ensure that a wildlife hazard assessment is conducted when any of the following events occurs on or near the airport:

(1) An air carrier aircraft experiences multiple wildlife strikes;

(2) An air carrier aircraft experiences substantial damage from striking wildlife. As used in this paragraph, substantial damage means damage or structural failure incurred by an aircraft that adversely affects the structural strength, performance, or flight characteristics of the aircraft and that would normally require major repair or replacement of the affected component;

(3) An air carrier aircraft experiences an engine ingestion of wildlife; or

(4) Wildlife of a size, or in numbers, capable of causing an event described in paragraphs (b)(1), (b)(2), or (b)(3) of this section is observed to have access to any airport flight pattern or aircraft movement area.

(c) The wildlife hazard assessment required in paragraph (b) of this section must be conducted by a wildlife damage management biologist who has professional training and/or experience in wildlife hazard management at airports or an individual working under direct supervision of such an individual. The wildlife hazard assessment must contain at least the following:

(1) An analysis of the events or circumstances that prompted the assessment.

(2) Identification of the wildlife species observed and their numbers, locations, local movements, and daily and seasonal occurrences.

(3) Identification and location of features on and near the airport that attract wildlife.

(4) A description of wildlife hazards to air carrier operations.

(5) Recommended actions for reducing identified wildlife hazards to air carrier operations.

(d) The wildlife hazard assessment required under paragraph (b) of this section must be submitted to the Administrator for approval and determination of the need for a wildlife hazard management plan. In reaching this determination, the Administrator will consider—

(1) The wildlife hazard assessment;

(2) Actions recommended in the wildlife hazard assessment to reduce wildlife hazards;

(3) The aeronautical activity at the airport, including the frequency and size of air carrier aircraft;

(4) The views of the certificate holder;

(5) The views of the airport users; and

(6) Any other known factors relating to the wildlife hazard of which the Administrator is aware.

(e) When the Administrator determines that a wildlife hazard management plan is needed, the certificate holder must formulate and implement a plan using the wildlife hazard assessment as a basis. The plan must—

(1) Provide measures to alleviate or eliminate wildlife hazards to air carrier operations;

(2) Be submitted to, and approved by, the Administrator prior to implementation; and

(3) As authorized by the Administrator, become a part of the Airport Certification Manual.

(f) The plan must include at least the following:

(1) A list of the individuals having authority and responsibility for implementing each aspect of the plan.

(2) A list prioritizing the following actions identified in the wildlife hazard assessment and target dates for their initiation and completion:

(i) Wildlife population management;

(ii) Habitat modification; and

(iii) Land use changes.

(3) Requirements for and, where applicable, copies of local, State, and Federal wildlife control permits.

(4) Identification of resources that the certificate holder will provide to implement the plan.

(5) Procedures to be followed during air carrier operations that at a minimum includes—

(i) Designation of personnel responsible for implementing the procedures;

(ii) Provisions to conduct physical inspections of the aircraft movement areas and other areas critical to successfully manage known wildlife hazards before air carrier operations begin;

(iii) Wildlife hazard control measures; and

(iv) Ways to communicate effectively between personnel conducting wildlife control or observing wildlife hazards and the air traffic control tower.

(6) Procedures to review and evaluate the wildlife hazard management plan every 12 consecutive months or following an event described in paragraphs (b)(1), (b)(2), and (b)(3) of this section, including:

(i) The plan's effectiveness in dealing with known wildlife hazards on and in the airport's vicinity and

(ii) Aspects of the wildlife hazards described in the wildlife hazard assessment that should be reevaluated.

(7) A training program conducted by a qualified wildlife damage management biologist to provide airport personnel with the knowledge and skills needed to successfully carry out the wildlife hazard management plan required by paragraph (d) of this section.

(g) FAA Advisory Circulars contain methods and procedures for wildlife hazard management at airports that are acceptable to the Administrator.

§139.339 Airport condition reporting.

In a manner authorized by the Administrator, each certificate holder must—

(a) Provide for the collection and dissemination of airport condition information to air carriers.

(b) In complying with paragraph (a) of this section, use the NOTAM system, as appropriate, and other systems and procedures authorized by the Administrator.

(c) In complying with paragraph (a) of this section, provide information on the following airport conditions that may affect the safe operations of air carriers:

(1) Construction or maintenance activity on movement areas, safety areas, or loading ramps and parking areas.

(2) Surface irregularities on movement areas, safety areas, or loading ramps and parking areas.

(3) Snow, ice, slush, or water on the movement area or loading ramps and parking areas.

(4) Snow piled or drifted on or near movement areas contrary to §139.313.

(5) Objects on the movement area or safety areas contrary to §139.309.

(6) Malfunction of any lighting system, holding position signs, or ILS critical area signs required by §139.311.

(7) Unresolved wildlife hazards as identified in accordance with §139.337.

(8) Nonavailability of any rescue and firefighting capability required in §§ 139.317 or 139.319.

(9) Any other condition as specified in the Airport Certification Manual or that may otherwise adversely affect the safe operations of air carriers.

(d) Each certificate holder must prepare and keep, for at least 12 consecutive calendar months, a record of each dissemination of airport condition information to air carriers prescribed by this section.

(e) FAA Advisory Circulars contain methods and procedures for using the NOTAM system and the dissemination of airport information that are acceptable to the Administrator.

§ 139.341 Identifying, marking, and lighting construction and other unserviceable areas.

(a) In a manner authorized by the Administrator, each certificate holder must—

(1) Mark and, if appropriate, light in a manner authorized by the Administrator—

(i) Each construction area and unserviceable area that is on or adjacent to any movement area or any other area of the airport on which air carrier aircraft may be operated;

(ii) Each item of construction equipment and each construction roadway, which may affect the safe movement of aircraft on the airport; and

(iii) Any area adjacent to a NAVAID that, if traversed, could cause derogation of the signal or the failure of the NAVAID; and

(2) Provide procedures, such as a review of all appropriate utility plans prior to construction, for avoiding damage to existing utilities, cables, wires, conduits, pipelines, or other underground facilities.

(b) FAA Advisory Circulars contain methods and procedures for identifying and marking construction areas that are acceptable to the Administrator.

§ 139.343 Noncomplying conditions.

Unless otherwise authorized by the Administrator, whenever the requirements of subpart D of this part cannot be met to the extent that uncorrected unsafe conditions exist on the airport, the certificate holder must limit air carrier operations to those portions of the airport not rendered unsafe by those conditions.

SUBCHAPTER H—SCHOOLS AND OTHER CERTIFICATED AGENCIES

PART 140 [RESERVED]

PART 141—PILOT SCHOOLS

AUTHORITY: 49 U.S.C. 106(f), 106(g), 40113, 44701–44703, 44707, 44709, 44711, 45102–45103, 45301–45302.

575

SOURCE: Docket No. 25910, 62 FR 16347, Apr. 4, 1997, unless otherwise noted.

Subpart A—General

§ 141.1 Applicability.

This part prescribes the requirements for issuing pilot school certificates, provisional pilot school certificates, and associated ratings, and the general operating rules applicable to a holder of a certificate or rating issued under this part.

§ 141.3 Certificate required.

No person may operate as a certificated pilot school without, or in violation of, a pilot school certificate or provisional pilot school certificate issued under this part.

§ 141.5 Requirements for a pilot school certificate.

The FAA may issue a pilot school certificate with the appropriate ratings if, within the 24 calendar months before the date application is made, the applicant—

(a) Completes the application for a pilot school certificate on the form and in the manner prescribed by the FAA;

(b) Has held a provisional pilot school certificate;

(c) Meets the applicable requirements under subparts A through C of this part for the school certificate and associated ratings sought;

(d) Has established a pass rate of 80 percent or higher on the first attempt for all:

(1) Knowledge tests leading to a certificate or rating;

(2) Practical tests leading to a certificate or rating;

(3) End-of-course tests for an approved training course specified in appendix K of this part; and

(4) End-of-course tests for special curricula courses approved under § 141.57.

(e) Has graduated at least 10 different people from the school's approved training courses.

[Doc. No. FAA–2006–26661, 74 FR 42563, Aug. 21, 2009, as amended by Amdt. 141–14, 75 FR 56858, Sept. 17, 2010; Doc. No. FAA–2016–6142, Amdt. 141–20, 83 FR 30283, June 27, 2018]

§ 141.7 Provisional pilot school certificate.

An applicant that meets the applicable requirements of subparts A, B, and C of this part, but does not meet the recent training activity requirements of § 141.5(d) of this part, may be issued a provisional pilot school certificate with ratings.

§ 141.9 Examining authority.

The FAA issues examining authority to a pilot school for a training course if the pilot school and its training course meet the requirements of subpart D of this part.

[Doc. No. FAA–2006–26661, 74 FR 42563, Aug. 21, 2009]

§ 141.11 Pilot school ratings.

(a) The ratings listed in paragraph (b) of this section may be issued to an applicant for:

(1) A pilot school certificate, provided the applicant meets the requirements of § 141.5 of this part; or

(2) A provisional pilot school certificate, provided the applicant meets the requirements of § 141.7 of this part.

(b) An applicant may be authorized to conduct the following courses:

(1) *Certification and rating courses.* (Appendixes A through J).

(i) Recreational pilot course.

(ii) Private pilot course.

(iii) Commercial pilot course.

(iv) Instrument rating course.

(v) Airline transport pilot course.

(vi) Flight instructor course.

(vii) Flight instructor instrument course.

(viii) Ground instructor course.

(ix) Additional aircraft category or class rating course.

(x) Aircraft type rating course.

(2) *Special preparation courses.* (Appendix K).

(i) Pilot refresher course.

(ii) Flight instructor refresher course.

(iii) Ground instructor refresher course.

(iv) Agricultural aircraft operations course.

(v) Rotorcraft external-load operations course.

(vi) Special operations course.

(vii) Test pilot course.

(viii) Airline transport pilot certification training program.

(3) *Pilot ground school course.* (Appendix L).

[Doc. No. 25910, 62 FR 16347, Apr. 4, 1997, as amended by Amdt. 141–17, 78 FR 42379, July 15, 2013; Amdt. 141–17A, 78 FR 53026, Aug. 28, 2013]

§141.13 Application for issuance, amendment, or renewal.

(a) Application for an original certificate and rating, an additional rating, or the renewal of a certificate under this part must be made on a form and in a manner prescribed by the Administrator.

(b) Application for the issuance or amendment of a certificate or rating must be accompanied by two copies of each proposed training course curriculum for which approval is sought.

§141.17 Duration of certificate and examining authority.

(a) Unless surrendered, suspended, or revoked, a pilot school's certificate or a provisional pilot school's certificate expires:

(1) On the last day of the 24th calendar month from the month the certificate was issued;

(2) Except as provided in paragraph (b) of this section, on the date that any change in ownership of the school occurs;

(3) On the date of any change in the facilities upon which the school's certificate is based occurs; or

(4) Upon notice by the Administrator that the school has failed for more than 60 days to maintain the facilities, aircraft, or personnel required for any one of the school's approved training courses.

(b) A change in the ownership of a pilot school or provisional pilot school does not terminate that school's certificate if, within 30 days after the date that any change in ownership of the school occurs:

(1) Application is made for an appropriate amendment to the certificate; and

(2) No change in the facilities personnel, or approved training courses is involved.

(c) An examining authority issued to the holder of a pilot school certificate

expires on the date that the pilot school certificate expires, or is surrendered, suspended, or revoked.

§141.18 Carriage of narcotic drugs, marijuana, and depressant or stimulant drugs or substances.

If the holder of a certificate issued under this part permits any aircraft owned or leased by that holder to be engaged in any operation that the certificate holder knows to be in violation of §91.19(a) of this chapter, that operation is a basis for suspending or revoking the certificate.

§141.19 Display of certificate.

(a) Each holder of a pilot school certificate or a provisional pilot school certificate must display that certificate in a place in the school that is normally accessible to the public and is not obscured.

(b) A certificate must be made available for inspection upon request by:

(1) The Administrator;

(2) An authorized representative of the National Transportation Safety Board; or

(3) A Federal, State, or local law enforcement officer.

§141.21 Inspections.

Each holder of a certificate issued under this part must allow the Administrator to inspect its personnel, facilities, equipment, and records to determine the certificate holder's:

(a) Eligibility to hold its certificate;

(b) Compliance with 49 U.S.C. 40101 *et seq.*, formerly the Federal Aviation Act of 1958, as amended; and

(c) Compliance with the Federal Aviation Regulations.

§141.23 Advertising limitations.

(a) The holder of a pilot school certificate or a provisional pilot school certificate may not make any statement relating to its certification and ratings that is false or designed to mislead any person contemplating enrollment in that school.

(b) The holder of a pilot school certificate or a provisional pilot school certificate may not advertise that the school is certificated unless it clearly differentiates between courses that have been approved under part 141 of

§ 141.25

14 CFR Ch. I (1-1-19 Edition)

this chapter and those that have not been approved under part 141 of this chapter.

(c) The holder of a pilot school certificate or a provisional pilot school certificate must promptly remove:

(1) From vacated premises, all signs indicating that the school was certificated by the Administrator; or

(2) All indications (including signs), wherever located, that the school is certificated by the Administrator when its certificate has expired or has been surrendered, suspended, or revoked.

§ 141.25 Business office and operations base.

(a) Each holder of a pilot school or a provisional pilot school certificate must maintain a principal business office with a mailing address in the name shown on its certificate.

(b) The facilities and equipment at the principal business office must be adequate to maintain the files and records required to operate the business of the school.

(c) The principal business office may not be shared with, or used by, another pilot school.

(d) Before changing the location of the principal business office or the operations base, each certificate holder must notify the responsible Flight Standards office for the area of the new location, and the notice must be:

(1) Submitted in writing at least 30 days before the change of location; and

(2) Accompanied by any amendments needed for the certificate holder's approved training course outline.

(e) A certificate holder may conduct training at an operations base other than the one specified in its certificate, if:

(1) The Administrator has inspected and approved the base for use by the certificate holder; and

(2) The course of training and any needed amendments have been approved for use at that base.

[Docket No. 25910, 62 FR 16347, Apr. 4, 1997, as amended by Docket FAA–2018–0119, Amdt. 141–19, 83 FR 9175, Mar. 5, 2018]

§ 141.26 Training agreements.

(a) A training center certificated under part 142 of this chapter may provide the training, testing, and checking for pilot schools certificated under this part and is considered to meet the requirements of this part, provided—

(1) There is a training agreement between the certificated training center and the pilot school;

(2) The training, testing, and checking provided by the certificated training center is approved and conducted under part 142;

(3) The pilot school certificated under this part obtains the Administrator's approval for a training course outline that includes the training, testing, and checking to be conducted under this part and the training, testing, and checking to be conducted under part 142; and

(4) Upon completion of the training, testing, and checking conducted under part 142, a copy of each student's training record is forwarded to the part 141 school and becomes part of the student's permanent training record.

(b) A pilot school that provides flight training for an institution of higher education that holds a letter of authorization under § 61.169 of this chapter must have a training agreement with that institution of higher education.

[Doc. No. FAA–2010–0100, 78 FR 42379, July 15, 2013]

§ 141.27 Renewal of certificates and ratings.

(a) *Pilot school.* (1) A pilot school may apply for renewal of its school certificate and ratings within 30 days preceding the month the pilot school's certificate expires, provided the school meets the requirements prescribed in paragraph (a)(2) of this section for renewal of its certificate and ratings.

(2) A pilot school may have its school certificate and ratings renewed for an additional 24 calendar months if the Administrator determines the school's personnel, aircraft, facility and airport, approved training courses, training records, and recent training ability and quality meet the requirements of this part.

(3) A pilot school that does not meet the renewal requirements in paragraph (a)(2) of this section, may apply for a provisional pilot school certificate if the school meets the requirements of § 141.7 of this part.

578

(b) *Provisional pilot school.* (1) Except as provided in paragraph (b)(3) of this section, a provisional pilot school may not have its provisional pilot school certificate or the ratings on that certificate renewed.

(2) A provisional pilot school may apply for a pilot school certificate and associated ratings provided that school meets the requirements of §141.5 of this part.

(3) A former provisional pilot school may apply for another provisional pilot school certificate, provided 180 days have elapsed since its last provisional pilot school certificate expired.

§141.29 [Reserved]

Subpart B—Personnel, Aircraft, and Facilities Requirements

§141.31 Applicability.

(a) This subpart prescribes:

(1) The personnel and aircraft requirements for a pilot school certificate or a provisional pilot school certificate; and

(2) The facilities that a pilot school or provisional pilot school must have available on a continuous basis.

(b) As used in this subpart, to have continuous use of a facility, including an airport, the school must have:

(1) Ownership of the facility or airport for at least 6 calendar months after the date the application for initial certification and on the date of renewal of the school's certificate is made; or

(2) A written lease agreement for the facility or airport for at least 6 calendar months after the date the application for initial certification and on the date of renewal of the school's certificate is made.

[Doc. No. 25910, 62 FR 16347, Apr. 4, 1997; Amdt. 141–9, 62 FR 40907, July 30, 1997]

§141.33 Personnel.

(a) An applicant for a pilot school certificate or for a provisional pilot school certificate must meet the following personnel requirements:

(1) Each applicant must have adequate personnel, including certificated flight instructors, certificated ground instructors, or holders of a commercial pilot certificate with a lighter-than-air rating, and a chief instructor for each approved course of training who is qualified and competent to perform the duties to which that instructor is assigned.

(2) If the school employs dispatchers, aircraft handlers, and line and service personnel, then it must instruct those persons in the procedures and responsibilities of their employment.

(3) Each instructor to be used for ground or flight training must hold a flight instructor certificate, ground instructor certificate, or commercial pilot certificate with a lighter-than-air rating, as appropriate, with ratings for the approved course of training and any aircraft used in that course.

(4) In addition to meeting the requirements of paragraph (a)(3) of this section, each instructor used for the airline transport pilot certification training program in §61.156 of this chapter must:

(i) Hold an airline transport pilot certificate with an airplane category multiengine class rating;

(ii) Have at least 2 years of experience as a pilot in command in operations conducted under §91.1053(a)(2)(i) or §135.243(a)(1) of this chapter, or as a pilot in command or second in command in any operation conducted under part 121 of this chapter; and

(iii) If providing training in a flight simulation training device, have received training and evaluation within the preceding 12 months from the certificate holder on—

(A) Proper operation of flight simulator and flight training device controls and systems;

(B) Proper operation of environmental and fault panels,

(C) Data and motion limitations of simulation;

(D) Minimum equipment requirements for each curriculum; and

(E) The maneuvers that will be demonstrated in the flight simulation training device.

(b) An applicant for a pilot school certificate or for a provisional pilot school certificate must designate a chief instructor for each of the school's approved training courses, who must meet the requirements of §141.35 of this part.

(c) When necessary, an applicant for a pilot school certificate or for a provisional pilot school certificate may designate a person to be an assistant chief instructor for an approved training course, provided that person meets the requirements of § 141.36 of this part.

(d) A pilot school and a provisional pilot school may designate a person to be a check instructor for conducting student stage checks, end-of-course tests, and instructor proficiency checks, provided:

(1) That person meets the requirements of § 141.37 of this part; and

(2) The school has an enrollment of at least 10 students at the time designation is sought.

(e) A person, as listed in this section, may serve in more than one position for a school, provided that person is qualified for each position.

[Doc. No. 25910, 62 FR 16347, Apr. 4, 1997; Amdt. 141–9, 62 FR 40907, July 30, 1997; Amdt. 141–12, 74 FR 42563, Aug. 21, 2009; Amdt. 141–17, 78 FR 42379, July 15, 2013; Amdt. 141–17A, 78 FR 53026, Aug. 28, 2013]

§ 141.34 Employment of former FAA employees.

(a) Except as specified in paragraph (c) of this section, no holder of a pilot school certificate or a provisional pilot school certificate may knowingly employ or make a contractual arrangement which permits an individual to act as an agent or representative of the certificate holder in any matter before the Federal Aviation Administration if the individual, in the preceding 2 years—

(1) Served as, or was directly responsible for the oversight of, a Flight Standards Service aviation safety inspector; and

(2) Had direct responsibility to inspect, or oversee the inspection of, the operations of the certificate holder.

(b) For the purpose of this section, an individual shall be considered to be acting as an agent or representative of a certificate holder in a matter before the agency if the individual makes any written or oral communication on behalf of the certificate holder to the agency (or any of its officers or employees) in connection with a particular matter, whether or not involving a specific party and without regard to whether the individual has participated in, or had responsibility for, the particular matter while serving as a Flight Standards Service aviation safety inspector.

(c) The provisions of this section do not prohibit a holder of a pilot school certificate or a provisional pilot school certificate from knowingly employing or making a contractual arrangement which permits an individual to act as an agent or representative of the certificate holder in any matter before the Federal Aviation Administration if the individual was employed by the certificate holder before October 21, 2011.

[Doc. No. FAA–2008–1154, 76 FR 52236, Aug. 22, 2011]

§ 141.35 Chief instructor qualifications.

(a) To be eligible for designation as a chief instructor for a course of training, a person must meet the following requirements:

(1) Hold a commercial pilot certificate or an airline transport pilot certificate, and, except for a chief instructor for a course of training solely for a lighter-than-air rating, a current flight instructor certificate. The certificates must contain the appropriate aircraft category and class ratings for the category and class of aircraft used in the course and an instrument rating, if an instrument rating is required for enrollment in the course of training;

(2) Meet the pilot-in-command recent flight experience requirements of § 61.57 of this chapter;

(3) Pass a knowledge test on—

(i) Teaching methods;

(ii) Applicable provisions of the "Aeronautical Information Manual";

(iii) Applicable provisions of parts 61, 91, and 141 of this chapter; and

(iv) The objectives and approved course completion standards of the course for which the person seeks to obtain designation.

(4) Pass a proficiency test on instructional skills and ability to train students on the flight procedures and maneuvers appropriate to the course;

(5) Except for a course of training for gliders, balloons, or airships, the chief instructor must meet the applicable requirements in paragraphs (b), (c), and (d) of this section; and

(6) A chief instructor for a course of training for gliders, balloons or airships is only required to have 40 percent of the hours required in paragraphs (b) and (d) of this section.

(b) For a course of training leading to the issuance of a recreational or private pilot certificate or rating, a chief instructor must have:

(1) At least 1,000 hours as pilot in command; and

(2) Primary flight training experience, acquired as either a certificated flight instructor or an instructor in a military pilot flight training program, or a combination thereof, consisting of at least—

(i) 2 years and a total of 500 flight hours; or

(ii) 1,000 flight hours.

(c) For a course of training leading to the issuance of an instrument rating or a rating with instrument privileges, a chief instructor must have:

(1) At least 100 hours of flight time under actual or simulated instrument conditions;

(2) At least 1,000 hours as pilot in command; and

(3) Instrument flight instructor experience, acquired as either a certificated flight instructor-instrument or an instructor in a military pilot flight training program, or a combination thereof, consisting of at least—

(i) 2 years and a total of 250 flight hours; or

(ii) 400 flight hours.

(d) For a course of training other than one leading to the issuance of a recreational or private pilot certificate or rating, or an instrument rating or a rating with instrument privileges, a chief instructor must have:

(1) At least 2,000 hours as pilot in command; and

(2) Flight training experience, acquired as either a certificated flight instructor or an instructor in a military pilot flight training program, or a combination thereof, consisting of at least—

(i) 3 years and a total of 1,000 flight hours; or

(ii) 1,500 flight hours.

(e) To be eligible for designation as chief instructor for a ground school course, a person must have 1 year of experience as a ground school instructor at a certificated pilot school.

[Doc. No. 25910, 62 FR 16347, Apr. 4, 1997; Amdt. 141–9, 62 FR 40907, July 30, 1997, as amended by Amdt. 141–10, 63 FR 20289, Apr. 23, 1998]

§ 141.36 Assistant chief instructor qualifications.

(a) To be eligible for designation as an assistant chief instructor for a course of training, a person must meet the following requirements:

(1) Hold a commercial pilot or an airline transport pilot certificate and, except for the assistant chief instructor for a course of training solely for a lighter-than-air rating, a current flight instructor certificate. The certificates must contain the appropriate aircraft category, class, and instrument ratings if an instrument rating is required by the course of training for the category and class of aircraft used in the course;

(2) Meet the pilot-in-command recent flight experience requirements of § 61.57 of this chapter;

(3) Pass a knowledge test on—

(i) Teaching methods;

(ii) Applicable provisions of the "Aeronautical Information Manual";

(iii) Applicable provisions of parts 61, 91, and 141 of this chapter; and

(iv) The objectives and approved course completion standards of the course for which the person seeks to obtain designation.

(4) Pass a proficiency test on the flight procedures and maneuvers appropriate to that course; and

(5) Meet the applicable requirements in paragraphs (b), (c), and (d) of this section. However, an assistant chief instructor for a course of training for gliders, balloons, or airships is only required to have 40 percent of the hours required in paragraphs (b) and (d) of this section.

(b) For a course of training leading to the issuance of a recreational or private pilot certificate or rating, an assistant chief instructor must have:

(1) At least 500 hours as pilot in command; and

(2) Flight training experience, acquired as either a certificated flight instructor or an instructor in a military

581

pilot flight training program, or a combination thereof, consisting of at least—

(i) 1 year and a total of 250 flight hours; or

(ii) 500 flight hours.

(c) For a course of training leading to the issuance of an instrument rating or a rating with instrument privileges, an assistant chief flight instructor must have:

(1) At least 50 hours of flight time under actual or simulated instrument conditions;

(2) At least 500 hours as pilot in command; and

(3) Instrument flight instructor experience, acquired as either a certificated flight instructor-instrument or an instructor in a military pilot flight training program, or a combination thereof, consisting of at least—

(i) 1 year and a total of 125 flight hours; or

(ii) 200 flight hours.

(d) For a course of training other than one leading to the issuance of a recreational or private pilot certificate or rating, or an instrument rating or a rating with instrument privileges, an assistant chief instructor must have:

(1) At least 1,000 hours as pilot in command; and

(2) Flight training experience, acquired as either a certificated flight instructor or an instructor in a military pilot flight training program, or a combination thereof, consisting of at least—

(i) 1½ years and a total of 500 flight hours; or

(ii) 750 flight hours.

(e) To be eligible for designation as an assistant chief instructor for a ground school course, a person must have 6 months of experience as a ground school instructor at a certificated pilot school.

[Doc. No. 25910, 62 FR 16347, Apr. 4, 1997; Amdt. 141-9, 62 FR 40907, July 30, 1997, as amended by Amdt. 141-10, 63 FR 20289, Apr. 23, 1998]

§ 141.37 Check instructor qualifications.

(a) To be designated as a check instructor for conducting student stage checks, end-of-course tests, and instructor proficiency checks under this part, a person must meet the eligibility requirements of this section:

(1) For checks and tests that relate to either flight or ground training, the person must pass a test, given by the chief instructor, on—

(i) Teaching methods;

(ii) Applicable provisions of the "Aeronautical Information Manual";

(iii) Applicable provisions of parts 61, 91, and 141 of this chapter; and

(iv) The objectives and course completion standards of the approved training course for the designation sought.

(2) For checks and tests that relate to a flight training course, the person must—

(i) Meet the requirements in paragraph (a)(1) of this section;

(ii) Hold a commercial pilot certificate or an airline transport pilot certificate and, except for a check instructor for a course of training for a lighter-than-air rating, a current flight instructor certificate. The certificates must contain the appropriate aircraft category, class, and instrument ratings for the category and class of aircraft used in the course;

(iii) Meet the pilot-in-command recent flight experience requirements of § 61.57 of this chapter; and

(iv) Pass a proficiency test, given by the chief instructor or assistant chief instructor, on the flight procedures and maneuvers of the approved training course for the designation sought.

(3) For checks and tests that relate to ground training, the person must—

(i) Meet the requirements in paragraph (a)(1) of this section;

(ii) Except for a course of training for a lighter-than-air rating, hold a current flight instructor certificate or ground instructor certificate with ratings appropriate to the category and class of aircraft used in the course; and

(iii) For a course of training for a lighter-than-air rating, hold a commercial pilot certificate with a lighter-than-air category rating and the appropriate class rating.

(b) A person who meets the eligibility requirements in paragraph (a) of this section must:

(1) Be designated, in writing, by the chief instructor to conduct student

stage checks, end-of-course tests, and instructor proficiency checks; and

(2) Be approved by the responsible Flight Standards office for the school.

(c) A check instructor may not conduct a stage check or an end-of-course test of any student for whom the check instructor has:

(1) Served as the principal instructor; or

(2) Recommended for a stage check or end-of-course test.

[Doc. No. 25910, 62 FR 16347, Apr. 4 1997; Amdt. 141–9, 62 FR 40907, July 30, 1997, as amended by Docket FAA–2018–0119, Amdt. 141–19, 83 FR 9175, Mar. 5, 2018]

§141.38 Airports.

(a) An applicant for a pilot school certificate or a provisional pilot school certificate must show that he or she has continuous use of each airport at which training flights originate.

(b) Each airport used for airplanes and gliders must have at least one runway or takeoff area that allows training aircraft to make a normal takeoff or landing under the following conditions at the aircraft's maximum certificated takeoff gross weight:

(1) Under wind conditions of not more than 5 miles per hour;

(2) At temperatures in the operating area equal to the mean high temperature for the hottest month of the year;

(3) If applicable, with the powerplant operation, and landing gear and flap operation recommended by the manufacturer; and

(4) In the case of a takeoff—

(i) With smooth transition from liftoff to the best rate of climb speed without exceptional piloting skills or techniques; and

(ii) Clearing all obstacles in the takeoff flight path by at least 50 feet.

(c) Each airport must have a wind direction indicator that is visible from the end of each runway at ground level;

(d) Each airport must have a traffic direction indicator when:

(1) The airport does not have an operating control tower; and

(2) UNICOM advisories are not available.

(e) Except as provided in paragraph (f) of this section, each airport used for night training flights must have permanent runway lights;

(f) An airport or seaplane base used for night training flights in seaplanes is permitted to use adequate non-permanent lighting or shoreline lighting, if approved by the Administrator.

[Doc. No. 25910, 62 FR 16347, Apr. 4, 1997; Amdt. 141–9, 62 FR 40907, July 30, 1997]

§141.39 Aircraft.

(a) When the school's training facility is located within the U.S., an applicant for a pilot school certificate or provisional pilot school certificate must show that each aircraft used by the school for flight training and solo flights:

(1) Is a civil aircraft of the United States;

(2) Is certificated with a standard airworthiness certificate, a primary airworthiness certificate, or a special airworthiness certificate in the light-sport category unless the FAA determines otherwise because of the nature of the approved course;

(3) Is maintained and inspected in accordance with the requirements for aircraft operated for hire under part 91, subpart E, of this chapter;

(4) Has two pilot stations with engine-power controls that can be easily reached and operated in a normal manner from both pilot stations (for flight training); and

(5) Is equipped and maintained for IFR operations if used in a course involving IFR en route operations and instrument approaches. For training in the control and precision maneuvering of an aircraft by reference to instruments, the aircraft may be equipped as provided in the approved course of training.

(b) When the school's training facility is located outside the U.S. and the training will be conducted outside the U.S., an applicant for a pilot school certificate or provisional pilot school certificate must show that each aircraft used by the school for flight training and solo flights:

(1) Is either a civil aircraft of the United States or a civil aircraft of foreign registry;

(2) Is certificated with a standard or primary airworthiness certificate or an equivalent certification from the foreign aviation authority;

(3) Is maintained and inspected in accordance with the requirements for aircraft operated for hire under part 91, subpart E of this chapter, or in accordance with equivalent maintenance and inspection from the foreign aviation authority's requirements;

(4) Has two pilot stations with engine-power controls that can be easily reached and operated in a normal manner from both pilot stations (for flight training); and

(5) Is equipped and maintained for IFR operations if used in a course involving IFR en route operations and instrument approaches. For training in the control and precision maneuvering of an aircraft by reference to instruments, the aircraft may be equipped as provided in the approved course of training.

[Doc. No. FAA–2006–26661, 74 FR 42563, Aug. 21, 2009, as amended by Amdt. 141–13, 75 FR 5223, Feb. 1, 2010]

§ 141.41 Full flight simulators, flight training devices, aviation training devices, and training aids.

An applicant for a pilot school certificate or a provisional pilot school certificate must show that its full flight simulators, flight training devices, aviation training devices, training aids, and equipment meet the following requirements:

(a) *Full flight simulators and flight training devices.* Each full flight simulator and flight training device used to obtain flight training credit in an approved pilot training course curriculum must be:

(1) Qualified under part 60 of this chapter, or a previously qualified device, as permitted in accordance with § 60.17 of this chapter; and

(2) Approved by the Administrator for the tasks and maneuvers.

(b) *Aviation training devices.* Each basic or advanced aviation training device used to obtain flight training credit in an approved pilot training course curriculum must be evaluated, qualified, and approved by the Administrator.

(c) *Training aids and equipment.* Each training aid, including any audiovisual aid, projector, mockup, chart, or aircraft component listed in the approved training course outline, must be accu-

rate and relevant to the course for which it is used.

[Docket FAA–2015–1846, Amdt. 141–18, 81 FR 21460, Apr. 12, 2016]

§ 141.43 Pilot briefing areas.

(a) An applicant for a pilot school certificate or provisional pilot school certificate must show that the applicant has continuous use of a briefing area located at each airport at which training flights originate that is:

(1) Adequate to shelter students waiting to engage in their training flights;

(2) Arranged and equipped for the conduct of pilot briefings; and

(3) Except as provided in paragraph (c) of this section, for a school with an instrument rating or commercial pilot course, equipped with private landline or telephone communication to the nearest FAA Flight Service Station.

(b) A briefing area required by paragraph (a) of this section may not be used by the applicant if it is available for use by any other pilot school during the period it is required for use by the applicant.

(c) The communication equipment required by paragraph (a)(3) of this section is not required if the briefing area and the flight service station are located on the same airport, and are readily accessible to each other.

§ 141.45 Ground training facilities.

An applicant for a pilot school or provisional pilot school certificate must show that:

(a) Except as provided in paragraph (c) of this section, each room, training booth, or other space used for instructional purposes is heated, lighted, and ventilated to conform to local building, sanitation, and health codes.

(b) Except as provided in paragraph (c) of this section, the training facility is so located that the students in that facility are not distracted by the training conducted in other rooms, or by flight and maintenance operations on the airport.

(c) If a training course is conducted through an internet-based medium, the holder of a pilot school certificate or provisional pilot school certificate that provides such training need not comply with paragraphs (a) and (b) of this section but must maintain in current status a permanent business location and business telephone number.

[Doc. No. FAA–2008–0938, 76 FR 54107, Aug. 31, 2011]

Subpart C—Training Course Outline and Curriculum

§ 141.51 Applicability.

This subpart prescribes the curriculum and course outline requirements for the issuance of a pilot school certificate or provisional pilot school certificate and ratings.

§ 141.53 Approval procedures for a training course: General.

(a) *General.* An applicant for a pilot school certificate or provisional pilot school certificate must obtain the Administrator's approval of the outline of each training course for which certification and rating is sought.

(b) *Application.* (1) An application for the approval of an initial or amended training course must be submitted in duplicate to the responsible Flight Standards office for the area where the school is based.

(2) An application for the approval of an initial or amended training course must be submitted at least 30 days before any training under that course, or any amendment thereto, is scheduled to begin.

(3) An application for amending a training course must be accompanied by two copies of the amendment.

(c) *Training courses.* An applicant for a pilot school certificate or provisional pilot school certificate may request approval for the training courses specified under § 141.11(b).

(d) *Additional rules for internet based training courses.* An application for an initial or amended training course offered through an internet based medium must comply with the following:

(1) All amendments must be identified numerically by page, date, and screen. Minor editorial and typographical changes do not require FAA approval, provided the school notifies the FAA within 30 days of their insertion.

(2) For monitoring purposes, the school must provide the FAA an acceptable means to log-in and log-off from a remote location to review all elements of the course as viewed by attendees and to by-pass the normal attendee restrictions.

(3) The school must incorporate adequate security measures into its internet-based courseware information system and into its operating and maintenance procedures to ensure the following fundamental areas of security and protection:

(i) Integrity.

(ii) Identification/Authentication.

(iii) Confidentiality.

(iv) Availability.

(v) Access control.

[Doc. No. 25910, 62 FR 16347, Apr. 4, 1997; Amdt. 141–9, 62 FR 40908, July 30, 1997; Amdt. 141–12, 74 FR 42563, Aug. 21, 2009; Amdt. 141–15, 76 FR 54107, Aug. 31, 2011, as amended by Docket FAA–2018–0119, Amdt. 141–19, 83 FR 9175, Mar. 5, 2018]

§ 141.55 Training course: Contents.

(a) Each training course for which approval is requested must meet the minimum curriculum requirements in accordance with the appropriate appendix of this part.

(b) Except as provided in paragraphs (d) and (e) of this section, each training course for which approval is requested must meet the minimum ground and flight training time requirements in accordance with the appropriate appendix of this part.

(c) Each training course for which approval is requested must contain:

(1) A description of each room used for ground training, including the room's size and the maximum number of students that may be trained in the room at one time, unless the course is provided via an internet-based training medium;

(2) A description of each type of audiovisual aid, projector, tape recorder, mockup, chart, aircraft component, and other special training aids used for ground training;

(3) A description of each flight simulator or flight training device used for training;

(4) A listing of the airports at which training flights originate and a description of the facilities, including pilot

briefing areas that are available for use by the school's students and personnel at each of those airports;

(5) A description of the type of aircraft including any special equipment used for each phase of training;

(6) The minimum qualifications and ratings for each instructor assigned to ground or flight training; and

(7) A training syllabus that includes the following information—

(i) The prerequisites for enrolling in the ground and flight portion of the course that include the pilot certificate and rating (if required by this part), training, pilot experience, and pilot knowledge;

(ii) A detailed description of each lesson, including the lesson's objectives, standards, and planned time for completion;

(iii) A description of what the course is expected to accomplish with regard to student learning;

(iv) The expected accomplishments and the standards for each stage of training; and

(v) A description of the checks and tests to be used to measure a student's accomplishments for each stage of training.

(d) A pilot school may request and receive initial approval for a period of not more than 24 calendar months for any training course under this part that does not meet the minimum ground and flight training time requirements, provided the following provisions are met:

(1) The school holds a pilot school certificate issued under this part and has held that certificate for a period of at least 24 consecutive calendar months preceding the month of the request;

(2) In addition to the information required by paragraph (c) of this section, the training course specifies planned ground and flight training time requirements for the course;

(3) The school does not request the training course to be approved for examining authority, nor may that school hold examining authority for that course; and

(4) The practical test or knowledge test for the course is to be given by—

(i) An FAA inspector; or

(ii) An examiner who is not an employee of the school.

(e) A pilot school may request and receive final approval for any training course under this part that does not meet the minimum ground and flight training time requirements, provided the following conditions are met:

(1) The school has held initial approval for that training course for at least 24 calendar months.

(2) The school has—

(i) Trained at least 10 students in that training course within the preceding 24 calendar months and recommended those students for a pilot, flight instructor, or ground instructor certificate or rating; and

(ii) At least 80 percent of those students passed the practical or knowledge test, as appropriate, on the first attempt, and that test was given by—

(A) An FAA inspector; or

(B) An examiner who is not an employee of the school.

(3) In addition to the information required by paragraph (c) of this section, the training course specifies planned ground and flight training time requirements for the course.

(4) The school does not request that the training course be approved for examining authority nor may that school hold examining authority for that course.

[Doc. No. 25910, 62 FR 16347, Apr. 4, 1997, as amended by Amdt. 141–12, 74 FR 42563, Aug. 21, 2009; Amdt. 141–15, 76 FR 54107, Aug. 31, 2011]

§ 141.57   Special curricula.

An applicant for a pilot school certificate or provisional pilot school certificate may apply for approval to conduct a special course of airman training for which a curriculum is not prescribed in the appendixes of this part, if the applicant shows that the training course contains features that could achieve a level of pilot proficiency equivalent to that achieved by a training course prescribed in the appendixes of this part or the requirements of part 61 of this chapter.

Subpart D—Examining Authority

§141.61 Applicability.

This subpart prescribes the requirements for the issuance of examining authority to the holder of a pilot school certificate, and the privileges and limitations of that examining authority.

§141.63 Examining authority qualification requirements.

(a) A pilot school must meet the following prerequisites to receive initial approval for examining authority:

(1) The school must complete the application for examining authority on a form and in a manner prescribed by the Administrator;

(2) The school must hold a pilot school certificate and rating issued under this part;

(3) The school must have held the rating in which examining authority is sought for at least 24 consecutive calendar months preceding the month of application for examining authority;

(4) The training course for which examining authority is requested may not be a course that is approved without meeting the minimum ground and flight training time requirements of this part; and

(5) Within 24 calendar months before the date of application for examining authority, that school must meet the following requirements—

(i) The school must have trained at least 10 students in the training course for which examining authority is sought and recommended those students for a pilot, flight instructor, or ground instructor certificate or rating; and

(ii) At least 90 percent of those students passed the required practical or knowledge test, or any combination thereof, for the pilot, flight instructor, or ground instructor certificate or rating on the first attempt, and that test was given by—

(A) An FAA inspector; or

(B) An examiner who is not an employee of the school.

(b) A pilot school must meet the following requirements to retain approval of its examining authority:

(1) The school must complete the application for renewal of its examining authority on a form and in a manner prescribed by the Administrator;

(2) The school must hold a pilot school certificate and rating issued under this part;

(3) The school must have held the rating for which continued examining authority is sought for at least 24 calendar months preceding the month of application for renewal of its examining authority; and

(4) The training course for which continued examining authority is requested may not be a course that is approved without meeting the minimum ground and flight training time requirements of this part.

[Doc. No. 25910, 62 FR 16347, Apr. 4, 1997; Amdt. 141–9, 62 FR 40908, July 30, 1997]

§141.65 Privileges.

A pilot school that holds examining authority may recommend a person who graduated from its course for the appropriate pilot, flight instructor, or ground instructor certificate or rating without taking the FAA knowledge test or practical test in accordance with the provisions of this subpart.

§141.67 Limitations and reports.

A pilot school that holds examining authority may only recommend the issuance of a pilot, flight instructor, or ground instructor certificate and rating to a person who does not take an FAA knowledge test or practical test, if the recommendation for the issuance of that certificate or rating is in accordance with the following requirements:

(a) The person graduated from a training course for which the pilot school holds examining authority.

(b) Except as provided in this paragraph, the person satisfactorily completed all the curriculum requirements of that pilot school's approved training course. A person who transfers from one part 141 approved pilot school to another part 141 approved pilot school may receive credit for that previous training, provided the following requirements are met:

(1) The maximum credited training time does not exceed one-half of the receiving school's curriculum requirements;

(2) The person completes a knowledge and proficiency test conducted by the receiving school for the purpose of determining the amount of pilot experience and knowledge to be credited;

(3) The receiving school determines (based on the person's performance on the knowledge and proficiency test required by paragraph (b)(2) of this section) the amount of credit to be awarded, and records that credit in the person's training record;

(4) The person who requests credit for previous pilot experience and knowledge obtained the experience and knowledge from another part 141 approved pilot school and training course; and

(5) The receiving school retains a copy of the person's training record from the previous school.

(c) Tests given by a pilot school that holds examining authority must be approved by the Administrator and be at least equal in scope, depth, and difficulty to the comparable knowledge and practical tests prescribed by the Administrator under part 61 of this chapter.

(d) A pilot school that holds examining authority may not use its knowledge or practical tests if the school:

(1) Knows, or has reason to believe, the test has been compromised; or

(2) Is notified by the responsible Flight Standards office that there is reason to believe or it is known that the test has been compromised.

(e) A pilot school that holds examining authority must maintain a record of all temporary airman certificates it issues, which consist of the following information:

(1) A chronological listing that includes—

(i) The date the temporary airman certificate was issued;

(ii) The student to whom the temporary airman certificate was issued, and that student's permanent mailing address and telephone number;

(iii) The training course from which the student graduated;

(iv) The name of person who conducted the knowledge or practical test;

(v) The type of temporary airman certificate or rating issued to the student; and

(vi) The date the student's airman application file was sent to the FAA for processing for a permanent airman certificate.

(2) A copy of the record containing each student's graduation certificate, airman application, temporary airman certificate, superseded airman certificate (if applicable), and knowledge test or practical test results; and

(3) The records required by paragraph (e) of this section must be retained for 1 year and made available to the Administrator upon request. These records must be surrendered to the Administrator when the pilot school ceases to have examining authority.

(f) Except for pilot schools that have an airman certification representative, when a student passes the knowledge test or practical test, the pilot school that holds examining authority must submit that student's airman application file and training record to the FAA for processing for the issuance of a permanent airman certificate.

[Doc. No. 25910, 62 FR 16347, Apr. 4, 1997; Amdt. 141-9, 62 FR 40908, July 30, 1997, as amended by Docket FAA-2018-0119, Amdt. 141-19, 83 FR 9176, Mar. 5, 2018]

Subpart E—Operating Rules

§ 141.71　Applicability.

This subpart prescribes the operating rules applicable to a pilot school or provisional pilot school certificated under the provisions of this part.

§ 141.73　Privileges.

(a) The holder of a pilot school certificate or a provisional pilot school certificate may advertise and conduct approved pilot training courses in accordance with the certificate and any ratings that it holds.

(b) A pilot school that holds examining authority for an approved training course may recommend a graduate of that course for the issuance of an appropriate pilot, flight instructor, or ground instructor certificate and rating, without taking an FAA knowledge test or practical test, provided the training course has been approved and meets the minimum ground and flight training time requirements of this part.

§ 141.75 Aircraft requirements.

The following items must be carried on each aircraft used for flight training and solo flights:

(a) A pretakeoff and prelanding checklist; and

(b) The operator's handbook for the aircraft, if one is furnished by the manufacturer, or copies of the handbook if furnished to each student using the aircraft.

[Doc. No. 25910, 62 FR 40908, July 30, 1997]

§ 141.77 Limitations.

(a) The holder of a pilot school certificate or a provisional pilot school certificate may not issue a graduation certificate to a student, or recommend a student for a pilot certificate or rating, unless the student has:

(1) Completed the training specified in the pilot school's course of training; and

(2) Passed the required final tests.

(b) Except as provided in paragraph (c) of this section, the holder of a pilot school certificate or a provisional pilot school certificate may not graduate a student from a course of training unless the student has completed all of the curriculum requirements of that course;

(c) A student may be given credit towards the curriculum requirements of a course for previous training under the following conditions:

(1) If the student completed a proficiency test and knowledge test that was conducted by the receiving pilot school and the previous training was based on a part 141- or a part 142-approved flight training course, the credit is limited to not more than 50 percent of the flight training requirements of the curriculum.

(2) If the student completed a knowledge test that was conducted by the receiving pilot school and the previous training was based on a part 141- or a part 142-approved aeronautical knowledge training course, the credit is limited to not more than 50 percent of the aeronautical knowledge training requirements of the curriculum.

(3) If the student completed a proficiency test and knowledge test that was conducted by the receiving pilot school and the training was received

from other than a part 141- or a part 142-approved flight training course, the credit is limited to not more than 25 percent of the flight training requirements of the curriculum.

(4) If the student completed a knowledge test that was conducted by the receiving pilot school and the previous training was received from other than a part 141- or a part 142-approved aeronautical knowledge training course, the credit is limited to not more than 25 percent of the aeronautical knowledge training requirements of the curriculum.

(5) Completion of previous training must be certified in the student's training record by the training provider or a management official within the training provider's organization, and must contain—

(i) The kind and amount of training provided; and

(ii) The result of each stage check and end-of-course test, if appropriate.

[Doc. No. 25910, 62 FR 16347, Apr. 4, 1997; Amdt. 141–9, 62 FR 40908, July 30, 1997; Amdt. 141–12, 74 FR 42564, Aug. 21, 2009]

§ 141.79 Flight training.

(a) No person other than a certificated flight instructor or commercial pilot with a lighter-than-air rating who has the ratings and the minimum qualifications specified in the approved training course outline may give a student flight training under an approved course of training.

(b) No student pilot may be authorized to start a solo practice flight from an airport until the flight has been approved by a certificated flight instructor or commercial pilot with a lighter-than-air rating who is present at that airport.

(c) Each chief instructor and assistant chief instructor assigned to a training course must complete, at least once every 12 calendar months, an approved syllabus of training consisting of ground or flight training, or both, or an approved flight instructor refresher course.

(d) Each certificated flight instructor or commercial pilot with a lighter-than-air rating who is assigned to a flight training course must satisfactorily complete the following tasks, which must be administered by the school's chief instructor, assistant chief instructor, or check instructor:

(1) Prior to receiving authorization to train students in a flight training course, must—

(i) Accomplish a review of and receive a briefing on the objectives and standards of that training course; and

(ii) Accomplish an initial proficiency check in each make and model of aircraft used in that training course in which that person provides training; and

(2) Every 12 calendar months after the month in which the person last complied with the requirements of paragraph (d)(1)(ii) of this section, accomplish a recurrent proficiency check in one of the aircraft in which the person trains students.

[Doc. No. 25910, 62 FR 16347, Apr. 4, 1997; Amdt. 141-9, 62 FR 40908, July 30, 1997]

§ 141.81   Ground training.

(a) Except as provided in paragraph (b) of this section, each instructor who is assigned to a ground training course must hold a flight or ground instructor certificate, or a commercial pilot certificate with a lighter-than-air rating, with the appropriate rating for that course of training.

(b) A person who does not meet the requirements of paragraph (a) of this section may be assigned ground training duties in a ground training course, if:

(1) The chief instructor who is assigned to that ground training course finds the person qualified to give that training; and

(2) The training is given while under the supervision of the chief instructor or the assistant chief instructor who is present at the facility when the training is given.

(c) An instructor may not be used in a ground training course until that instructor has been briefed on the objectives and standards of that course by the chief instructor, assistant chief instructor, or check instructor.

[Doc. No. 25910, 62 FR 16347, Apr. 4, 1997; Amdt. 141-9, 62 FR 40908, July 30, 1997]

§ 141.83   Quality of training.

(a) Each pilot school or provisional pilot school must meet the following requirements:

(1) Comply with its approved training course; and

(2) Provide training of such quality that meets the requirements of § 141.5(d) of this part.

(b) The failure of a pilot school or provisional pilot school to maintain the quality of training specified in paragraph (a) of this section may be the basis for suspending or revoking that school's certificate.

(c) When requested by the Administrator, a pilot school or provisional pilot school must allow the FAA to administer any knowledge test, practical test, stage check, or end-of-course test to its students.

(d) When a stage check or end-of-course test is administered by the FAA under the provisions of paragraph (c) of this section, and the student has not completed the training course, then that test will be based on the standards prescribed in the school's approved training course.

(e) When a practical test or knowledge test is administered by the FAA under the provisions of paragraph (c) of this section, to a student who has completed the school's training course, that test will be based upon the areas of operation approved by the Administrator.

[Doc. No. 25910, 62 FR 16347, Apr. 4, 1997; Amdt. 141-9, 62 FR 40908, July 30, 1997]

§ 141.85   Chief instructor responsibilities.

(a) A chief instructor designated for a pilot school or provisional pilot school is responsible for:

(1) Certifying each student's training record, graduation certificate, stage check and end-of-course test reports, and recommendation for course completion, unless the duties are delegated by the chief instructor to an assistant chief instructor or recommending instructor;

(2) Ensuring that each certificated flight instructor, certificated ground instructor, or commercial pilot with a lighter-than-air rating passes an initial

proficiency check prior to that instructor being assigned instructing duties in the school's approved training course, and thereafter that the instructor passes a recurrent proficiency check every 12 calendar months after the month in which the initial test was accomplished;

(3) Ensuring that each student accomplishes the required stage checks and end-of-course tests in accordance with the school's approved training course; and

(4) Maintaining training techniques, procedures, and standards for the school that are acceptable to the Administrator.

(b) The chief instructor or an assistant chief instructor must be available at the pilot school or, if away from the pilot school, be available by telephone, radio, or other electronic means during the time that training is given for an approved training course.

(c) The chief instructor may delegate authority for conducting stage checks, end-of-course tests, and flight instructor proficiency checks to the assistant chief instructor or a check instructor.

[Doc. No. 25910, 62 FR 16347, Apr. 4, 1997; Amdt. 141–9, 62 FR 40908, July 30, 1997; Amdt. 141–12, 74 FR 42564, Aug. 21, 2009]

§141.87 Change of chief instructor.

Whenever a pilot school or provisional pilot school makes a change of designation of its chief instructor, that school:

(a) Must immediately provide the FAA responsible Flight Standards office in which the school is located with written notification of the change;

(b) May conduct training without a chief instructor for that training course for a period not to exceed 60 days while awaiting the designation and approval of another chief instructor;

(c) May, for a period not to exceed 60 days, have the stage checks and end-of-course tests administered by:

(1) The training course's assistant chief instructor, if one has been designated;

(2) The training course's check instructor, if one has been designated;

(3) An FAA inspector; or

(4) An examiner.

(d) Must, after 60 days without a chief instructor, cease operations and surrender its certificate to the Administrator; and

(e) May have its certificate reinstated, upon:

(1) Designating and approving another chief instructor;

(2) Showing it meets the requirements of §141.27(a)(2) of this part; and

(3) Applying for reinstatement on a form and in a manner prescribed by the Administrator.

[Docket No. 25910, 62 FR 16347, Apr. 4, 1997, as amended by Docket FAA–2018–0119, Amdt. 141–19, 83 FR 9176, Mar. 5, 2018]

§141.89 Maintenance of personnel, facilities, and equipment.

The holder of a pilot school certificate or provisional pilot school certificate may not provide training to a student who is enrolled in an approved course of training unless:

(a) Each airport, aircraft, and facility necessary for that training meets the standards specified in the holder's approved training course outline and the appropriate requirements of this part; and

(b) Except as provided in §141.87 of this part, each chief instructor, assistant chief instructor, check instructor, or instructor meets the qualifications specified in the holder's approved course of training and the appropriate requirements of this part.

§141.91 Satellite bases.

The holder of a pilot school certificate or provisional pilot school certificate may conduct ground training or flight training in an approved course of training at a base other than its main operations base if:

(a) An assistant chief instructor is designated for each satellite base, and that assistant chief instructor is available at that base or, if away from the premises, by telephone, radio, or other electronic means during the time that training is provided for an approved training course;

(b) The airport, facilities, and personnel used at the satellite base meet the appropriate requirements of subpart B of this part and its approved training course outline;

(c) The instructors are under the direct supervision of the chief instructor or assistant chief instructor for the appropriate training course, who is readily available for consultation in accordance with § 141.85(b) of this part; and

(d) The responsible Flight Standards office for the area in which the school is located is notified in writing if training is conducted at a base other than the school's main operations base for more than 7 consecutive days.

[Doc. No. 25910, 62 FR 16347, Apr. 4, 1997; Amdt. 141–9, 62 FR 40908, July 30, 1997, as amended by Docket FAA–2018–0119, Amdt. 141–19, 83 FR 9175, Mar. 5, 2018]

§ 141.93 Enrollment.

(a) The holder of a pilot school certificate or a provisional pilot school certificate must, at the time a student is enrolled in an approved training course, furnish that student with a copy of the following:

(1) A certificate of enrollment containing—

(i) The name of the course in which the student is enrolled; and

(ii) The date of that enrollment.

(2) A copy of the student's training syllabus.

(3) Except for a training course offered through an internet based medium, a copy of the safety procedures and practices developed by the school that describe the use of the school's facilities and the operation of its aircraft. Those procedures and practices shall include training on at least the following information—

(i) The weather minimums required by the school for dual and solo flights;

(ii) The procedures for starting and taxiing aircraft on the ramp;

(iii) Fire precautions and procedures;

(iv) Redispatch procedures after unprogrammed landings, on and off airports;

(v) Aircraft discrepancies and approval for return-to-service determinations;

(vi) Securing of aircraft when not in use;

(vii) Fuel reserves necessary for local and cross-country flights;

(viii) Avoidance of other aircraft in flight and on the ground;

(ix) Minimum altitude limitations and simulated emergency landing instructions; and

(x) A description of and instructions regarding the use of assigned practice areas.

(b) The holder of a pilot school certificate or provisional pilot school certificate must maintain a monthly listing of persons enrolled in each training course offered by the school.

[Doc. No. 25910, 62 FR 16347, Apr. 4, 1997; Amdt. 141–9, 62 FR 40908, July 30, 1997; Amdt. 141–15, 76 FR 54107, Aug. 31, 2011]

§ 141.95 Graduation certificate.

(a) The holder of a pilot school certificate or provisional pilot school certificate must issue a graduation certificate to each student who completes its approved course of training.

(b) The graduation certificate must be issued to the student upon completion of the course of training and contain at least the following information:

(1) The name of the school and the certificate number of the school;

(2) The name of the graduate to whom it was issued;

(3) The course of training for which it was issued;

(4) The date of graduation;

(5) A statement that the student has satisfactorily completed each required stage of the approved course of training including the tests for those stages;

(6) A certification of the information contained on the graduation certificate by the chief instructor for that course of training; and

(7) A statement showing the cross-country training that the student received in the course of training.

(8) Certificates issued upon graduating from a course based on internet media must be uniquely identified using an alphanumeric code that is specific to the student graduating from that course.

[Doc. No. 25910, 62 FR 16347, Apr. 4, 1997; Amdt. 141–9, 62 FR 40908, July 30, 1997, as amended by Amdt. 141–15, 76 FR 54108, Aug. 31, 2011]

Subpart F—Records

§ 141.101 Training records.

(a) Each holder of a pilot school certificate or provisional pilot school certificate must establish and maintain a current and accurate record of the participation of each student enrolled in an approved course of training conducted by the school that includes the following information:

(1) The date the student was enrolled in the approved course;

(2) A chronological log of the student's course attendance, subjects, and flight operations covered in the student's training, and the names and grades of any tests taken by the student; and

(3) The date the student graduated, terminated training, or transferred to another school. In the case of graduation from a course based on internet media, the school must maintain the identifying graduation certificate code required by § 141.95(b)(8).

(b) The records required to be maintained in a student's logbook will not suffice for the record required by paragraph (a) of this section.

(c) Whenever a student graduates, terminates training, or transfers to another school, the student's record must be certified to that effect by the chief instructor.

(d) The holder of a pilot school certificate or a provisional pilot school certificate must retain each student record required by this section for at least 1 year from the date that the student:

(1) Graduates from the course to which the record pertains;

(2) Terminates enrollment in the course to which the record pertains; or

(3) Transfers to another school.

(e) The holder of a pilot school certificate or a provisional pilot school certificate must make a copy of the student's training record available upon request by the student.

[Doc. No. 25910, 62 FR 16347, Apr. 4, 1997; Amdt. 141–9, 62 FR 40908, July 30, 1997, as amended by Amdt. 141–15, 76 FR 54108, Aug. 31, 2011]

APPENDIX A TO PART 141—RECREATIONAL PILOT CERTIFICATION COURSE

1. *Applicability.* This appendix prescribes the minimum curriculum required for a recreational pilot certification course under this part, for the following ratings:

(a) Airplane single-engine.

(b) Rotorcraft helicopter.

(c) Rotorcraft gyroplane.

2. *Eligibility for enrollment.* A person must hold a student pilot certificate prior to enrolling in the flight portion of the recreational pilot certification course.

3. *Aeronautical knowledge training.* Each approved course must include at least 20 hours of ground training on the following aeronautical knowledge areas, appropriate to the aircraft category and class for which the course applies:

(a) Applicable Federal Aviation Regulations for recreational pilot privileges, limitations, and flight operations;

(b) Accident reporting requirements of the National Transportation Safety Board;

(c) Applicable subjects in the "Aeronautical Information Manual" and the appropriate FAA advisory circulars;

(d) Use of aeronautical charts for VFR navigation using pilotage with the aid of a magnetic compass;

(e) Recognition of critical weather situations from the ground and in flight, windshear avoidance, and the procurement and use of aeronautical weather reports and forecasts;

(f) Safe and efficient operation of aircraft, including collision avoidance, and recognition and avoidance of wake turbulence;

(g) Effects of density altitude on takeoff and climb performance;

(h) Weight and balance computations;

(i) Principles of aerodynamics, powerplants, and aircraft systems;

(j) Stall awareness, spin entry, spins, and spin recovery techniques, if applying for an airplane single-engine rating;

(k) Aeronautical decision making and judgment; and

(l) Preflight action that includes—

(1) How to obtain information on runway lengths at airports of intended use, data on takeoff and landing distances, weather reports and forecasts, and fuel requirements; and

(2) How to plan for alternatives if the planned flight cannot be completed or delays are encountered.

4. *Flight training.* (a) Each approved course must include at least 30 hours of flight training (of which 15 hours must be with a certificated flight instructor and 3 hours must be solo flight training as provided in section No. 5 of this appendix) on the approved areas of operation listed in paragraph (c) of this section that are appropriate to the aircraft

category and class rating for which the course applies, including:

(1) Except as provided in §61.100 of this chapter, 2 hours of dual flight training to and at an airport that is located more than 25 nautical miles from the airport where the applicant normally trains, with at least three takeoffs and three landings; and

(2) 3 hours of dual flight training in an aircraft that is appropriate to the aircraft category and class for which the course applies, in preparation for the practical test within 60 days preceding the date of the test.

(b) Each training flight must include a pre-flight briefing and a postflight critique of the student by the flight instructor assigned to that flight.

(c) Flight training must include the following approved areas of operation appropriate to the aircraft category and class rating—

(1) *For an airplane single-engine course:* (i) Preflight preparation;

(ii) Preflight procedures;

(iii) Airport operations;

(iv) Takeoffs, landings, and go-arounds;

(v) Performance maneuvers;

(vi) Ground reference maneuvers;

(vii) Navigation;

(viii) Slow flight and stalls;

(ix) Emergency operations; and

(x) Postflight procedures.

(2) *For a rotorcraft helicopter course:* (i) Preflight preparation;

(ii) Preflight procedures;

(iii) Airport and heliport operations;

(iv) Hovering maneuvers;

(v) Takeoffs, landings, and go-arounds;

(vi) Performance maneuvers;

(vii) Navigation;

(viii) Emergency operations; and

(ix) Postflight procedures.

(3) *For a rotorcraft gyroplane course:* (i) Preflight preparation;

(ii) Preflight procedures;

(iii) Airport operations;

(iv) Takeoffs, landings, and go-arounds;

(v) Performance maneuvers;

(vi) Ground reference maneuvers;

(vii) Navigation;

(viii) Flight at slow airspeeds;

(ix) Emergency operations; and

(x) Postflight procedures.

5. *Solo flight training.* Each approved course must include at least 3 hours of solo flight training on the approved areas of operation listed in paragraph (c) of section No. 4 of this appendix that are appropriate to the aircraft category and class rating for which the course applies.

6. *Stage checks and end-of-course tests.* (a) Each student enrolled in a recreational pilot course must satisfactorily accomplish the stage checks and end-of-course tests, in accordance with the school's approved training course, consisting of the approved areas of operation listed in paragraph (c) of section

No. 4 of this appendix that are appropriate to the aircraft category and class rating for which the course applies.

(b) Each student must demonstrate satisfactory proficiency prior to receiving an endorsement to operate an aircraft in solo flight.

[Doc. No. 25910, 62 FR 16347, Apr. 4, 1997; Amdt. 141-9, 62 FR 40908, July 30, 1997]

APPENDIX B TO PART 141—PRIVATE
PILOT CERTIFICATION COURSE

1. *Applicability.* This appendix prescribes the minimum curriculum for a private pilot certification course required under this part, for the following ratings:

(a) Airplane single-engine.

(b) Airplane multiengine.

(c) Rotorcraft helicopter.

(d) Rotorcraft gyroplane.

(e) Powered-lift.

(f) Glider.

(g) Lighter-than-air airship.

(h) Lighter-than-air balloon.

2. *Eligibility for enrollment.* A person must hold either a recreational pilot certificate, sport pilot certificate, or student pilot certificate before enrolling in the solo flight phase of the private pilot certification course.

3. *Aeronautical knowledge training.*

(a) Each approved course must include at least the following ground training on the aeronautical knowledge areas listed in paragraph (b) of this section, appropriate to the aircraft category and class rating:

(1) 35 hours of training if the course is for an airplane, rotorcraft, or powered-lift category rating.

(2) 15 hours of training if the course is for a glider category rating.

(3) 10 hours of training if the course is for a lighter-than-air category with a balloon class rating.

(4) 35 hours of training if the course is for a lighter-than-air category with an airship class rating.

(b) Ground training must include the following aeronautical knowledge areas:

(1) Applicable Federal Aviation Regulations for private pilot privileges, limitations, and flight operations;

(2) Accident reporting requirements of the National Transportation Safety Board;

(3) Applicable subjects of the "Aeronautical Information Manual" and the appropriate FAA advisory circulars;

(4) Aeronautical charts for VFR navigation using pilotage, dead reckoning, and navigation systems;

(5) Radio communication procedures;

(6) Recognition of critical weather situations from the ground and in flight, windshear avoidance, and the procurement and use of aeronautical weather reports and forecasts;

(7) Safe and efficient operation of aircraft, including collision avoidance, and recognition and avoidance of wake turbulence;

(8) Effects of density altitude on takeoff and climb performance;

(9) Weight and balance computations;

(10) Principles of aerodynamics, powerplants, and aircraft systems;

(11) If the course of training is for an airplane category or glider category rating, stall awareness, spin entry, spins, and spin recovery techniques;

(12) Aeronautical decision making and judgment; and

(13) Preflight action that includes—

(i) How to obtain information on runway lengths at airports of intended use, data on takeoff and landing distances, weather reports and forecasts, and fuel requirements; and

(ii) How to plan for alternatives if the planned flight cannot be completed or delays are encountered.

4. *Flight training.* (a) Each approved course must include at least the following flight training, as provided in this section and section No. 5 of this appendix, on the approved areas of operation listed in paragraph (d) of this section, appropriate to the aircraft category and class rating:

(1) 35 hours of training if the course is for an airplane, rotorcraft, powered-lift, or airship rating.

(2) 6 hours of training if the course is for a glider rating.

(3) 8 hours of training if the course is for a balloon rating.

(b) Each approved course must include at least the following flight training:

(1) *For an airplane single-engine course:* 20 hours of flight training from a certificated flight instructor on the approved areas of operation in paragraph (d)(1) of this section that includes at least—

(i) Except as provided in §61.111 of this chapter, 3 hours of cross-country flight training in a single-engine airplane;

(ii) 3 hours of night flight training in a single-engine airplane that includes—

(A) One cross-country flight of more than 100-nautical-miles total distance; and

(B) 10 takeoffs and 10 landings to a full stop (with each landing involving a flight in the traffic pattern) at an airport.

(iii) Three hours of flight training in a single engine airplane on the control and maneuvering of a single engine airplane solely by reference to instruments, including straight and level flight, constant airspeed climbs and descents, turns to a heading, recovery from unusual flight attitudes, radio communications, and the use of navigation systems/facilities and radar services appropriate to instrument flight; and

(iv) 3 hours of flight training in a single-engine airplane in preparation for the practical test within 60 days preceding the date of the test.

(2) *For an airplane multiengine course:* 20 hours of flight training from a certificated flight instructor on the approved areas of operation in paragraph (d)(2) of this section that includes at least—

(i) Except as provided in §61.111 of this chapter, 3 hours of cross-country flight training in a multiengine airplane;

(ii) 3 hours of night flight training in a multiengine airplane that includes—

(A) One cross-country flight of more than 100-nautical-miles total distance; and

(B) 10 takeoffs and 10 landings to a full stop (with each landing involving a flight in the traffic pattern) at an airport.

(iii) Three hours of flight training in a multiengine airplane on the control and maneuvering of a multiengine airplane solely by reference to instruments, including straight and level flight, constant airspeed climbs and descents, turns to a heading, recovery from unusual flight attitudes, radio communications, and the use of navigation systems/facilities and radar services appropriate to instrument flight; and

(iv) 3 hours of flight training in a multiengine airplane in preparation for the practical test within 60 days preceding the date of the test.

(3) *For a rotorcraft helicopter course:* 20 hours of flight training from a certificated flight instructor on the approved areas of operation in paragraph (d)(3) of this section that includes at least—

(i) Except as provided in §61.111 of this chapter, 3 hours of cross-country flight training in a helicopter.

(ii) 3 hours of night flight training in a helicopter that includes—

(A) One cross-country flight of more than 50-nautical-miles total distance; and

(B) 10 takeoffs and 10 landings to a full stop (with each landing involving a flight in the traffic pattern) at an airport.

(iii) 3 hours of flight training in a helicopter in preparation for the practical test within 60 days preceding the date of the test.

(4) *For a rotorcraft gyroplane course:* 20 hours of flight training from a certificated flight instructor on the approved areas of operation in paragraph (d)(4) of this section that includes at least—

(i) Except as provided in §61.111 of this chapter, 3 hours of cross-country flight training in a gyroplane.

(ii) 3 hours of night flight training in a gyroplane that includes—

(A) One cross-country flight over 50-nautical-miles total distance; and

(B) 10 takeoffs and 10 landings to a full stop (with each landing involving a flight in the traffic pattern) at an airport.

(iii) 3 hours of flight training in a gyroplane in preparation for the practical test within 60 days preceding the date of the test.

(5) *For a powered-lift course:* 20 hours of flight training from a certificated flight instructor on the approved areas of operation in paragraph (d)(5) of this section that includes at least—

(i) Except as provided in §61.111 of this chapter, 3 hours of cross-country flight training in a powered-lift;

(ii) 3 hours of night flight training in a powered-lift that includes—

(A) One cross-country flight of more than 100-nautical-miles total distance; and

(B) 10 takeoffs and 10 landings to a full stop (with each landing involving a flight in the traffic pattern) at an airport.

(iii) Three hours of flight training in a powered-lift on the control and maneuvering of a powered-lift solely by reference to instruments, including straight and level flight, constant airspeed climbs and descents, turns to a heading, recovery from unusual flight attitudes, radio communications, and the use of navigation systems/facilities and radar services appropriate to instrument flight; and

(iv) 3 hours of flight training in a powered-lift in preparation for the practical test, within 60 days preceding the date of the test.

(6) *For a glider course:* 4 hours of flight training from a certificated flight instructor on the approved areas of operation in paragraph (d)(6) of this section that includes at least—

(i) Five training flights in a glider with a certificated flight instructor on the launch/tow procedures approved for the course and on the appropriate approved areas of operation listed in paragraph (d)(6) of this section; and

(ii) Three training flights in a glider with a certificated flight instructor in preparation for the practical test within 60 days preceding the date of the test.

(7) *For a lighter-than-air airship course:* 20 hours of flight training from a commercial pilot with an airship rating on the approved areas of operation in paragraph (d)(7) of this section that includes at least—

(i) Except as provided in §61.111 of this chapter, 3 hours of cross-country flight training in an airship;

(ii) 3 hours of night flight training in an airship that includes—

(A) One cross-country flight over 25-nautical-miles total distance; and

(B) Five takeoffs and five landings to a full stop (with each landing involving a flight in the traffic pattern) at an airport.

(iii) 3 hours of instrument training in an airship; and

(iv) 3 hours of flight training in an airship in preparation for the practical test within 60 days preceding the date of the test.

(8) *For a lighter-than-air balloon course:* 8 hours of flight training, including at least five training flights, from a commercial pilot with a balloon rating on the approved areas

of operation in paragraph (d)(8) of this section, that includes—

(i) If the training is being performed in a gas balloon—

(A) Two flights of 1 hour each;

(B) One flight involving a controlled ascent to 3,000 feet above the launch site; and

(C) Two flights in preparation for the practical test within 60 days preceding the date of the test.

(ii) If the training is being performed in a balloon with an airborne heater—

(A) Two flights of 30 minutes each;

(B) One flight involving a controlled ascent to 2,000 feet above the launch site; and

(C) Two flights in preparation for the practical test within 60 days preceding the date of the test.

(c) For use of full flight simulators or flight training devices:

(1) The course may include training in a full flight simulator or flight training device, provided it is representative of the aircraft for which the course is approved, meets the requirements of this paragraph, and the training is given by an authorized instructor.

(2) Training in a full flight simulator that meets the requirements of §141.41(a) may be credited for a maximum of 20 percent of the total flight training hour requirements of the approved course, or of this section, whichever is less.

(3) Training in a flight training device that meets the requirements of §141.41(a) may be credited for a maximum of 15 percent of the total flight training hour requirements of the approved course, or of this section, whichever is less.

(4) Training in full flight simulators or flight training devices described in paragraphs (c)(2) and (3) of this section, if used in combination, may be credited for a maximum of 20 percent of the total flight training hour requirements of the approved course, or of this section, whichever is less. However, credit for training in a flight training device that meets the requirements of §141.41(a) cannot exceed the limitation provided for in paragraph (c)(3) of this section.

(d) Each approved course must include the flight training on the approved areas of operation listed in this paragraph that are appropriate to the aircraft category and class rating—

(1) *For a single-engine airplane course:* (i) Preflight preparation;

(ii) Preflight procedures;

(iii) Airport and seaplane base operations;

(iv) Takeoffs, landings, and go-arounds;

(v) Performance maneuvers;

(vi) Ground reference maneuvers;

(vii) Navigation;

(viii) Slow flight and stalls;

(ix) Basic instrument maneuvers;

(x) Emergency operations;

(xi) Night operations, and

(xii) Postflight procedures.

(2) *For a multiengine airplane course:* (i) Preflight preparation;

(ii) Preflight procedures;

(iii) Airport and seaplane base operations;

(iv) Takeoffs, landings, and go-arounds;

(v) Performance maneuvers;

(vi) Ground reference maneuvers;

(vii) Navigation;

(viii) Slow flight and stalls;

(ix) Basic instrument maneuvers;

(x) Emergency operations;

(xi) Multiengine operations;

(xii) Night operations; and

(xiii) Postflight procedures.

(3) *For a rotorcraft helicopter course:* (i) Preflight preparation;

(ii) Preflight procedures;

(iii) Airport and heliport operations;

(iv) Hovering maneuvers;

(v) Takeoffs, landings, and go-arounds;

(vi) Performance maneuvers;

(vii) Navigation;

(viii) Emergency operations;

(ix) Night operations; and

(x) Postflight procedures.

(4) *For a rotorcraft gyroplane course:*

(i) Preflight preparation;

(ii) Preflight procedures;

(iii) Airport operations;

(iv) Takeoffs, landings, and go-arounds;

(v) Performance maneuvers;

(vi) Ground reference maneuvers;

(vii) Navigation;

(viii) Flight at slow airspeeds;

(ix) Emergency operations;

(x) Night operations; and

(xi) Postflight procedures.

(5) *For a powered-lift course:* (i) Preflight preparation;

(ii) Preflight procedures;

(iii) Airport and heliport operations;

(iv) Hovering maneuvers;

(v) Takeoffs, landings, and go-arounds;

(vi) Performance maneuvers;

(vii) Ground reference maneuvers;

(viii) Navigation;

(ix) Slow flight and stalls;

(x) Basic instrument maneuvers;

(xi) Emergency operations;

(xii) Night operations; and

(xiii) Postflight procedures.

(6) *For a glider course:* (i) Preflight preparation;

(ii) Preflight procedures;

(iii) Airport and gliderport operations

(iv) Launches/tows, as appropriate, and landings;

(v) Performance speeds;

(vi) Soaring techniques;

(vii) Performance maneuvers;

(viii) Navigation;

(ix) Slow flight and stalls;

(x) Emergency operations; and

(xi) Postflight procedures.

(7) *For a lighter-than-air airship course:* (i) Preflight preparation;

(ii) Preflight procedures;

(iii) Airport operations;

(iv) Takeoffs, landings, and go-arounds;

(v) Performance maneuvers;

(vi) Ground reference maneuvers;

(vii) Navigation;

(viii) Emergency operations; and

(ix) Postflight procedures.

(8) *For a lighter-than-air balloon course:* (i) Preflight preparation;

(ii) Preflight procedures;

(iii) Airport operations;

(iv) Launches and landings;

(v) Performance maneuvers;

(vi) Navigation;

(vii) Emergency operations; and

(viii) Postflight procedures.

5. *Solo flight training.* Each approved course must include at least the following solo flight training:

(a) *For an airplane single-engine course:* 5 hours of solo flight training in a single-engine airplane on the approved areas of operation in paragraph (d)(1) of section No. 4 of this appendix that includes at least—

(1) One solo 100 nautical miles cross country flight with landings at a minimum of three points and one segment of the flight consisting of a straight-line distance of more than 50 nautical miles between the takeoff and landing locations; and

(2) Three takeoffs and three landings to a full stop (with each landing involving a flight in the traffic pattern) at an airport with an operating control tower.

(b) *For an airplane multiengine course:* 5 hours of flight training in a multiengine airplane performing the duties of a pilot in command while under the supervision of a certificated flight instructor. The training must consist of the approved areas of operation in paragraph (d)(2) of section No. 4 of this appendix, and include at least—

(1) One 100 nautical miles cross country flight with landings at a minimum of three points and one segment of the flight consisting of a straight-line distance of more than 50 nautical miles between the takeoff and landing locations; and

(2) Three takeoffs and three landings to a full stop (with each landing involving a flight in the traffic pattern) at an airport with an operating control tower.

(c) *For a rotorcraft helicopter course:* 5 hours of solo flight training in a helicopter on the approved areas of operation in paragraph (d)(3) of section No. 4 of this appendix that includes at least—

(1) One solo 100 nautical miles cross country flight with landings at a minimum of three points and one segment of the flight consisting of a straight-line distance of more than 25 nautical miles between the takeoff and landing locations; and

(2) Three takeoffs and three landings to a full stop (with each landing involving a

flight in the traffic pattern) at an airport with an operating control tower.

(d) *For a rotorcraft gyroplane course:* 5 hours of solo flight training in gyroplanes on the approved areas of operation in paragraph (d)(4) of section No. 4 of this appendix that includes at least—

(1) One solo 100 nautical miles cross country flight with landings at a minimum of three points and one segment of the flight consisting of a straight-line distance of more than 25 nautical miles between the takeoff and landing locations; and

(2) Three takeoffs and three landings to a full stop (with each landing involving a flight in the traffic pattern) at an airport with an operating control tower.

(e) *For a powered-lift course:* 5 hours of solo flight training in a powered-lift on the approved areas of operation in paragraph (d)(5) of section No. 4 of this appendix that includes at least—

(1) One solo 100 nautical miles cross country flight with landings at a minimum of three points and one segment of the flight consisting of a straight-line distance of more than 50 nautical miles between the takeoff and landing locations; and

(2) Three takeoffs and three landings to a full stop (with each landing involving a flight in the traffic pattern) at an airport with an operating control tower.

(f) *For a glider course:* Two solo flights in a glider on the approved areas of operation in paragraph (d)(6) of section No. 4 of this appendix, and the launch and tow procedures appropriate for the approved course.

(g) *For a lighter-than-air airship course:* 5 hours of flight training in an airship performing the duties of pilot in command while under the supervision of a commercial pilot with an airship rating. The training must consist of the approved areas of operation in paragraph (d)(7) of section No. 4 of this appendix.

(h) *For a lighter-than-air balloon course:* Two solo flights in a balloon with an airborne heater if the course involves a balloon with an airborne heater or, if the course involves a gas balloon, at least two flights in a gas balloon performing the duties of pilot in command while under the supervision of a commercial pilot with a balloon rating. The training must consist of the approved areas of operation in paragraph (d)(8) of section No. 4 of this appendix, in the kind of balloon for which the course applies.

6. *Stage checks and end-of-course tests.*

(a) Each student enrolled in a private pilot course must satisfactorily accomplish the stage checks and end-of-course tests in accordance with the school's approved training course, consisting of the approved areas of operation listed in paragraph (d) of section No. 4 of this appendix that are appropriate to the aircraft category and class rating for which the course applies.

(b) Each student must demonstrate satisfactory proficiency prior to receiving an endorsement to operate an aircraft in solo flight.

[Doc. No. 25910, 62 FR 16347, Apr. 4, 1997; Amdt. 141–9, 62 FR 40908, July 30, 1997, as amended by Amdt. 141–10, 63 FR 20289, Apr. 23, 1998; Amdt. 141–12, 74 FR 42564, Aug. 21, 2009; Docket FAA–2015–1846, Amdt. 141–18, 81 FR 21460, Apr. 12, 2016]

APPENDIX C TO PART 141—INSTRUMENT RATING COURSE

1. *Applicability.* This appendix prescribes the minimum curriculum for an instrument rating course and an additional instrument rating course, required under this part, for the following ratings:

(a) Instrument—airplane.

(b) Instrument—helicopter.

(c) Instrument—powered-lift.

2. *Eligibility for enrollment.* A person must hold at least a private pilot certificate with an aircraft category and class rating appropriate to the instrument rating for which the course applies prior to enrolling in the flight portion of the instrument rating course.

3. *Aeronautical knowledge training.* (a) Each approved course must include at least the following ground training on the aeronautical knowledge areas listed in paragraph (b) of this section appropriate to the instrument rating for which the course applies:

(1) 30 hours of training if the course is for an initial instrument rating.

(2) 20 hours of training if the course is for an additional instrument rating.

(b) Ground training must include the following aeronautical knowledge areas:

(1) Applicable Federal Aviation Regulations for IFR flight operations;

(2) Appropriate information in the "Aeronautical Information Manual";

(3) Air traffic control system and procedures for instrument flight operations;

(4) IFR navigation and approaches by use of navigation systems;

(5) Use of IFR en route and instrument approach procedure charts;

(6) Procurement and use of aviation weather reports and forecasts, and the elements of forecasting weather trends on the basis of that information and personal observation of weather conditions;

(7) Safe and efficient operation of aircraft under instrument flight rules and conditions;

(8) Recognition of critical weather situations and windshear avoidance;

(9) Aeronautical decision making and judgment; and

(10) Crew resource management, to include crew communication and coordination.

4. *Flight training.* (a) Each approved course must include at least the following flight training on the approved areas of operation

listed in paragraph (d) of this section, appropriate to the instrument-aircraft category and class rating for which the course applies:

(1) 35 hours of instrument training if the course is for an initial instrument rating.

(2) 15 hours of instrument training if the course is for an additional instrument rating.

(b) For the use of full flight simulators, flight training devices, or aviation training devices—

(1) The course may include training in a full flight simulator, flight training device, or aviation training device, provided it is representative of the aircraft for which the course is approved, meets the requirements of this paragraph, and the training is given by an authorized instructor.

(2) Credit for training in a full flight simulator that meets the requirements of §141.41(a) cannot exceed 50 percent of the total flight training hour requirements of the course or of this section, whichever is less.

(3) Credit for training in a flight training device that meets the requirements of §141.41(a), an advanced aviation training device that meets the requirements of §141.41(b), or a combination of these devices cannot exceed 40 percent of the total flight training hour requirements of the course or of this section, whichever is less. Credit for training in a basic aviation training device that meets the requirements of §141.41(b) cannot exceed 25 percent of the total training hour requirements permitted under this paragraph.

(4) Credit for training in full flight simulators, flight training devices, and aviation training devices if used in combination cannot exceed 50 percent of the total flight training hour requirements of the course or of this section, whichever is less. However, credit for training in a flight training device or aviation training device cannot exceed the limitation provided for in paragraph (b)(3) of this section.

(c) Each approved course must include the following flight training—

(1) *For an instrument airplane course:* Instrument training time from a certificated flight instructor with an instrument rating on the approved areas of operation in paragraph (d) of this section including at least one cross-country flight that—

(i) Is in the category and class of airplane that the course is approved for, and is performed under IFR;

(ii) Is a distance of at least 250 nautical miles along airways or ATC-directed routing with one segment of the flight consisting of at least a straight-line distance of 100 nautical miles between airports;

(iii) Involves an instrument approach at each airport; and

(iv) Involves three different kinds of approaches with the use of navigation systems.

(2) *For an instrument helicopter course:* Instrument training time from a certificated flight instructor with an instrument rating on the approved areas of operation in paragraph (d) of this section including at least one cross-country flight that—

(i) Is in a helicopter and is performed under IFR;

(ii) Is a distance of at least 100 nautical miles along airways or ATC-directed routing with one segment of the flight consisting of at least a straight-line distance of 50 nautical miles between airports;

(iii) Involves an instrument approach at each airport; and

(iv) Involves three different kinds of approaches with the use of navigation systems.

(3) *For an instrument powered-lift course:* Instrument training time from a certificated flight instructor with an instrument rating on the approved areas of operation in paragraph (d) of this section including at least one cross-country flight that—

(i) Is in a powered-lift and is performed under IFR;

(ii) Is a distance of at least 250 nautical miles along airways or ATC-directed routing with one segment of the flight consisting of at least a straight-line distance of 100 nautical miles between airports;

(iii) Involves an instrument approach at each airport; and

(iv) Involves three different kinds of approaches with the use of navigation systems.

(d) Each course must include flight training on the areas of operation listed under this paragraph appropriate to the instrument aircraft category and class rating (if a class rating is appropriate) for which the course applies:

(1) Preflight preparation;

(2) Preflight procedures;

(3) Air traffic control clearances and procedures;

(4) Flight by reference to instruments;

(5) Navigation systems;

(6) Instrument approach procedures;

(7) Emergency operations; and

(8) Postflight procedures.

5. *Stage checks and end-of-course tests.* Each student enrolled in an instrument rating course must satisfactorily accomplish the stage checks and end-of-course tests, in accordance with the school's approved training course, consisting of the approved areas of operation listed in paragraph (d) of section No. 4 of this appendix that are appropriate to the aircraft category and class rating for which the course applies.

[Doc. No. 25910, 62 FR 16347, Apr. 4, 1997; Amdt. 141–9, 62 FR 40909, July 30, 1997; Amdt. 141–12, 74 FR 42564, Aug. 21, 2009; Docket FAA–2015–1846, Amdt. 141–18, 81 FR 21460, Apr. 12, 2016]

APPENDIX D TO PART 141—COMMERCIAL
PILOT CERTIFICATION COURSE

1. *Applicability.* This appendix prescribes
the minimum curriculum for a commercial
pilot certification course required under this
part, for the following ratings:

(a) Airplane single-engine.

(b) Airplane multiengine.

(c) Rotorcraft helicopter.

(d) Rotorcraft gyroplane.

(e) Powered-lift.

(f) Glider.

(g) Lighter-than-air airship.

(h) Lighter-than-air balloon.

2. *Eligibility for enrollment.* A person must
hold the following prior to enrolling in the
flight portion of the commercial pilot certification course:

(a) At least a private pilot certificate; and

(b) If the course is for a rating in an airplane or a powered-lift category, then the
person must:

(1) Hold an instrument rating in the aircraft that is appropriate to the aircraft category rating for which the course applies; or

(2) Be concurrently enrolled in an instrument rating course that is appropriate to the
aircraft category rating for which the course
applies, and pass the required instrument
rating practical test prior to completing the
commercial pilot certification course.

3. *Aeronautical knowledge training.* (a) Each
approved course must include at least the
following ground training on the aeronautical knowledge areas listed in paragraph
(b) of this section, appropriate to the aircraft
category and class rating for which the
course applies:

(1) 35 hours of training if the course is for
an airplane category rating or a powered-lift
category rating.

(2) 65 hours of training if the course is for
a lighter-than-air category with an airship
class rating.

(3) 30 hours of training if the course is for
a rotorcraft category rating.

(4) 20 hours of training if the course is for
a glider category rating.

(5) 20 hours of training if the course is for
lighter-than-air category with a balloon
class rating.

(b) Ground training must include the following aeronautical knowledge areas:

(1) Federal Aviation Regulations that
apply to commercial pilot privileges, limitations, and flight operations;

(2) Accident reporting requirements of the
National Transportation Safety Board;

(3) Basic aerodynamics and the principles
of flight;

(4) Meteorology, to include recognition of
critical weather situations, windshear recognition and avoidance, and the use of aeronautical weather reports and forecasts;

(5) Safe and efficient operation of aircraft;

(6) Weight and balance computations;

(7) Use of performance charts;

(8) Significance and effects of exceeding
aircraft performance limitations;

(9) Use of aeronautical charts and a magnetic compass for pilotage and dead reckoning;

(10) Use of air navigation facilities;

(11) Aeronautical decision making and
judgment;

(12) Principles and functions of aircraft
systems;

(13) Maneuvers, procedures, and emergency
operations appropriate to the aircraft;

(14) Night and high-altitude operations;

(15) Descriptions of and procedures for operating within the National Airspace System; and

(16) Procedures for flight and ground training for lighter-than-air ratings.

4. *Flight training.* (a) Each approved course
must include at least the following flight
training, as provided in this section and section No. 5 of this appendix, on the approved
areas of operation listed in paragraph (d) of
this section that are appropriate to the aircraft category and class rating for which the
course applies:

(1) 120 hours of training if the course is for
an airplane or powered-lift rating.

(2) 155 hours of training if the course is for
an airship rating.

(3) 115 hours of training if the course is for
a rotorcraft rating.

(4) 6 hours of training if the course is for a
glider rating.

(5) 10 hours of training and 8 training
flights if the course is for a balloon rating.

(b) Each approved course must include at
least the following flight training:

(1) *For an airplane single-engine course:* 55
hours of flight training from a certificated
flight instructor on the approved areas of operation listed in paragraph (d)(1) of this section that includes at least—

(i) Ten hours of instrument training using
a view-limiting device including attitude instrument flying, partial panel skills, recovery from unusual flight attitudes, and intercepting and tracking navigational systems.
Five hours of the 10 hours required on instrument training must be in a single engine airplane;

(ii) Ten hours of training in a complex airplane, a turbine-powered airplane, or a tech-
nically advanced airplane that meets the requirements of §61.129(j) of this chapter, or
any combination thereof. The airplane must
be appropriate to land or sea for the rating
sought;

(iii) One 2-hour cross country flight in daytime conditions in a single engine airplane
that consists of a total straight-line distance
of more than 100 nautical miles from the
original point of departure;

(iv) One 2-hour cross country flight in
nighttime conditions in a single engine airplane that consists of a total straight-line

distance of more than 100 nautical miles from the original point of departure; and

(v) 3 hours in a single-engine airplane in preparation for the practical test within 60 days preceding the date of the test.

(2) *For an airplane multiengine course:* 55 hours of flight training from a certificated flight instructor on the approved areas of operation listed in paragraph (d)(2) of this section that includes at least—

(i) Ten hours of instrument training using a view-limiting device including attitude instrument flying, partial panel skills, recovery from unusual flight attitudes, and intercepting and tracking navigational systems. Five hours of the 10 hours required on instrument training must be in a multiengine airplane;

(ii) 10 hours of training in a multiengine complex or turbine-powered airplane or any combination thereof;

(iii) One 2-hour cross country flight in daytime conditions in a multiengine airplane that consists of a total straight-line distance of more than 100 nautical miles from the original point of departure;

(iv) One 2-hour cross country flight in nighttime conditions in a multiengine airplane that consists of a total straight-line distance of more than 100 nautical miles from the original point of departure; and

(v) 3 hours in a multiengine airplane in preparation for the practical test within 60 days preceding the date of the test.

(3) *For a rotorcraft helicopter course:* 30 hours of flight training from a certificated flight instructor on the approved areas of operation listed in paragraph (d)(3) of this section that includes at least—

(i) Five hours on the control and maneuvering of a helicopter solely by reference to instruments, including using a view-limiting device for attitude instrument flying partial panel skills, recovery from unusual flight attitudes, and intercepting and tracking navigational systems. This aeronautical experience may be performed in an aircraft, full flight simulator, flight training device, or an aviation training device;

(ii) One 2-hour cross country flight in daytime conditions in a helicopter that consists of a total straight-line distance of more than 50 nautical miles from the original point of departure;

(iii) One 2-hour cross country flight in nighttime conditions in a helicopter that consists of a total straight-line distance of more than 50 nautical miles from the original point of departure; and

(iv) 3 hours in a helicopter in preparation for the practical test within 60 days preceding the date of the test.

(4) *For a rotorcraft gyroplane course:* 30 hours of flight training from a certificated flight instructor on the approved areas of operation listed in paragraph (d)(4) of this section that includes at least—

(i) 2.5 hours on the control and maneuvering of a gyroplane solely by reference to instruments, including using a view-limiting device for attitude instrument flying, partial panel skills, recovery from unusual flight attitudes, and intercepting and tracking navigational systems. This aeronautical experience may be performed in an aircraft, full flight simulator, flight training device, or an aviation training device;

(ii) One 2-hour cross country flight in daytime conditions in a gyroplane that consists of a total straight-line distance of more than 50 nautical miles from the original point of departure;

(iii) Two hours of flight training in nighttime conditions in a gyroplane at an airport, that includes 10 takeoffs and 10 landings to a full stop (with each landing involving a flight in the traffic pattern); and

(iv) 3 hours in a gyroplane in preparation for the practical test within 60 days preceding the date of the test.

(5) *For a powered-lift course:* 55 hours of flight training from a certificated flight instructor on the approved areas of operation listed in paragraph (d)(5) of this section that includes at least—

(i) Ten hours of instrument training using a view-limiting device including attitude instrument flying, partial panel skills, recovery from unusual flight attitudes, and intercepting and tracking navigational systems. Five hours of the 10 hours required on instrument training must be in a powered-lift;

(ii) One 2-hour cross country flight in daytime conditions in a powered-lift that consists of a total straight-line distance of more than 100 nautical miles from the original point of departure;

(iii) One 2-hour cross country flight in nighttime conditions in a powered-lift that consists of a total straight-line distance of more than 100 nautical miles from the original point of departure; and

(iv) 3 hours in a powered-lift in preparation for the practical test within 60 days preceding the date of the test.

(6) *For a glider course:* 4 hours of flight training from a certificated flight instructor on the approved areas of operation in paragraph (d)(6) of this section, that includes at least—

(i) Five training flights in a glider with a certificated flight instructor on the launch/tow procedures approved for the course and on the appropriate approved areas of operation listed in paragraph (d)(6) of this section; and

(ii) Three training flights in a glider with a certificated flight instructor in preparation for the practical test within 60 days preceding the date of the test.

(7) *For a lighter-than-air airship course:* 55 hours of flight training in airships from a commercial pilot with an airship rating on

the approved areas of operation in paragraph (d)(7) of this section that includes at least—

(i) Three hours of instrument training in an airship, including using a view-limiting device for attitude instrument flying, partial panel skills, recovery from unusual flight attitudes, and intercepting and tracking navigational systems;

(ii) One hour cross country flight in daytime conditions in an airship that consists of a total straight-line distance of more than 25 nautical miles from the original point of departure;

(iii) One hour cross country flight in nighttime conditions in an airship that consists of a total straight-line distance of more than 25 nautical miles from the original point of departure; and

(iv) 3 hours in an airship, in preparation for the practical test within 60 days preceding the date of the test.

(8) *For a lighter-than-air balloon course:* Flight training from a commercial pilot with a balloon rating on the approved areas of operation in paragraph (d)(8) of this section that includes at least—

(i) If the course involves training in a gas balloon:

(A) Two flights of 1 hour each;

(B) One flight involving a controlled ascent to at least 5,000 feet above the launch site; and

(C) Two flights in preparation for the practical test within 60 days preceding the date of the test.

(ii) If the course involves training in a balloon with an airborne heater:

(A) Two flights of 30 minutes each;

(B) One flight involving a controlled ascent to at least 3,000 feet above the launch site; and

(C) Two flights in preparation for the practical test within 60 days preceding the date of the test.

(c) For the use of full flight simulators or flight training devices:

(1) The course may include training in a full flight simulator or flight training device, provided it is representative of the aircraft for which the course is approved, meets the requirements of this paragraph, and is given by an authorized instructor.

(2) Training in a full flight simulator that meets the requirements of §141.41(a) may be credited for a maximum of 30 percent of the total flight training hour requirements of the approved course, or of this section, whichever is less.

(3) Training in a flight training device that meets the requirements of §141.41(a) may be credited for a maximum of 20 percent of the total flight training hour requirements of the approved course, or of this section, whichever is less.

(4) Training in the flight training devices described in paragraphs (c)(2) and (3) of this section, if used in combination, may be credited for a maximum of 30 percent of the total flight training hour requirements of the approved course, or of this section, whichever is less. However, credit for training in a flight training device that meets the requirements of §141.41(a) cannot exceed the limitation provided for in paragraph (c)(3) of this section.

(d) Each approved course must include the flight training on the approved areas of operation listed in this paragraph that are appropriate to the aircraft category and class rating—

(1) *For an airplane single-engine course:* (i) Preflight preparation;

(ii) Preflight procedures;

(iii) Airport and seaplane base operations;

(iv) Takeoffs, landings, and go-arounds;

(v) Performance maneuvers;

(vi) Navigation;

(vii) Slow flight and stalls;

(viii) Emergency operations;

(ix) High-altitude operations; and

(x) Postflight procedures.

(2) *For an airplane multiengine course:* (i) Preflight preparation;

(ii) Preflight procedures;

(iii) Airport and seaplane base operations;

(iv) Takeoffs, landings, and go-arounds;

(v) Performance maneuvers;

(vi) Navigation;

(vii) Slow flight and stalls;

(viii) Emergency operations;

(ix) Multiengine operations;

(x) High-altitude operations; and

(xi) Postflight procedures.

(3) *For a rotorcraft helicopter course:* (i) Preflight preparation;

(ii) Preflight procedures;

(iii) Airport and heliport operations;

(iv) Hovering maneuvers;

(v) Takeoffs, landings, and go-arounds;

(vi) Performance maneuvers;

(vii) Navigation;

(viii) Emergency operations;

(ix) Special operations; and

(x) Postflight procedures.

(4) *For a rotorcraft gyroplane course:* (i) Preflight preparation;

(ii) Preflight procedures;

(iii) Airport operations;

(iv) Takeoffs, landings, and go-arounds;

(v) Performance maneuvers;

(vi) Ground reference maneuvers;

(vii) Navigation;

(viii) Flight at slow airspeeds;

(ix) Emergency operations; and

(x) Postflight procedures.

(5) *For a powered-lift course:* (i) Preflight preparation;

(ii) Preflight procedures;

(iii) Airport and heliport operations;

(iv) Hovering maneuvers;

(v) Takeoffs, landings, and go-arounds;

(vi) Performance maneuvers;

(vii) Navigation;

(viii) Slow flight and stalls;

(ix) Emergency operations
(x) High altitude operations;
(xi) Special operations; and
(xii) Postflight procedures.
(6) *For a glider course:* (i) Preflight preparation;
(ii) Preflight procedures;
(iii) Airport and gliderport operations;
(iv) Launches/tows, as appropriate, and
landings;
(v) Performance speeds;
(vi) Soaring techniques;
(vii) Performance maneuvers;
(viii) Navigation;
(ix) Slow flight and stalls;
(x) Emergency operations; and
(xi) Postflight procedures.
(7) *For a lighter-than-air airship course:* (i)
Fundamentals of instructing;
(ii) Technical subjects;
(iii) Preflight preparation;
(iv) Preflight lessons on a maneuver to be
performed in flight;
(v) Preflight procedures;
(vi) Airport operations;
(vii) Takeoffs, landings, and go-arounds;
(viii) Performance maneuvers;
(ix) Navigation;
(x) Emergency operations; and
(xi) Postflight procedures.
(8) *For a lighter-than-air balloon course:* (i)
Fundamentals of instructing;
(ii) Technical subjects;
(iii) Preflight preparation;
(iv) Preflight lesson on a maneuver to be
performed in flight;
(v) Preflight procedures;
(vi) Airport operations;
(vii) Launches and landings;
(viii) Performance maneuvers;
(ix) Navigation;
(x) Emergency operations; and
(xi) Postflight procedures.
5. *Solo training.* Each approved course must
include at least the following solo flight
training:
(a) *For an airplane single engine course* Ten
hours of solo flight time in a single engine
airplane, or 10 hours of flight time while performing the duties of pilot in command in a
single engine airplane with an authorized instructor on board. The training must consist
of the approved areas of operation under
paragraph (d)(1) of section 4 of this appendix,
and include—
(1) One cross-country flight, if the training
is being performed in the State of Hawaii,
with landings at a minimum of three points,
and one of the segments consisting of a
straight-line distance of at least 150 nautical
miles;
(2) One cross-country flight, if the training
is being performed in a State other than Hawaii, with landings at a minimum of three
points, and one segment of the flight consisting of a straight-line distance of at least
250 nautical miles; and

(3) 5 hours in night VFR conditions with 10
takeoffs and 10 landings (with each landing
involving a flight with a traffic pattern) at
an airport with an operating control tower.
(b) *For an airplane multiengine course.* Ten
hours of solo flight time in a multiengine
airplane, or 10 hours of flight time while performing the duties of pilot in command in a
multiengine airplane with an authorized instructor on board. The training must consist
of the approved areas of operation under
paragraph (d)(2) of section 4 of this appendix,
and include—
(1) One cross-country flight, if the training
is being performed in the State of Hawaii,
with landings at a minimum of three points,
and one of the segments consisting of a
straight-line distance of at least 150 nautical
miles;
(2) One cross-country flight, if the training
is being performed in a State other than Hawaii, with landings at a minimum of three
points and one segment of the flight consisting of straight-line distance of at least
250 nautical miles; and
(3) 5 hours in night VFR conditions with 10
takeoffs and 10 landings (with each landing
involving a flight with a traffic pattern) at
an airport with an operating control tower.
(c) *For a rotorcraft helicopter course.* Ten
hours of solo flight time in a helicopter, or 10
hours of flight time while performing the duties of pilot in command in a helicopter with
an authorized instructor on board. The training must consist of the approved areas of operation under paragraph (d)(3) of section 4 of
this appendix, and include—
(1) One cross-country flight with landings
at a minimum of three points and one segment of the flight consisting of a straight-
line distance of at least 50 nautical miles
from the original point of departure; and
(2) 5 hours in night VFR conditions with 10
takeoffs and 10 landings (with each landing
involving a flight with a traffic pattern) at
an airport with an operating control tower.
(d) *For a rotorcraft-gyroplane course.* Ten
hours of solo flight time in a gyroplane, or 10
hours of flight time while performing the duties of pilot in command in a gyroplane with
an authorized instructor on board. The training must consist of the approved areas of operation under paragraph (d)(4) of section 4 of
this appendix, and include—
(1) One cross-country flight with landings
at a minimum of three points, and one segment of the flight consisting of a straight-
line distance of at least 50 nautical miles
from the original point of departure; and
(2) 5 hours in night VFR conditions with 10
takeoffs and 10 landings (with each landing
involving a flight with a traffic pattern) at
an airport with an operating control tower.
(e) *For a powered-lift course.* Ten hours of
solo flight time in a powered-lift, or 10 hours
of flight time while performing the duties of
pilot in command in a powered-lift with an

authorized instructor on board. The training must consist of the approved areas of operation under paragraph (d)(5) of section No. 4 of this appendix, and include—

(1) One cross-country flight, if the training is being performed in the State of Hawaii, with landings at a minimum of three points, and one segment of the flight consisting of a straight-line distance of at least 150 nautical miles;

(2) One cross-country flight, if the training is being performed in a State other than Hawaii, with landings at a minimum of three points, and one segment of the flight consisting of a straight-line distance of at least 250 nautical miles; and

(3) 5 hours in night VFR conditions with 10 takeoffs and 10 landings (with each landing involving a flight with a traffic pattern) at an airport with an operating control tower.

(f) *For a glider course:* 5 solo flights in a glider on the approved areas of operation in paragraph (d)(6) of section No. 4 of this appendix.

(g) *For a lighter-than-air airship course:* 10 hours of flight training in an airship performing the duties of pilot in command while under the supervision of a commercial pilot with an airship rating. The training must consist of the approved areas of operation in paragraph (d)(7) of section No. 4 of this appendix and include at least—

(1) One cross-country flight with landings at a minimum of three points, and one segment of the flight consisting of a straight-line distance of at least 25 nautical miles from the original point of departure; and

(2) 5 hours in night VFR conditions with 10 takeoffs and 10 landings (with each landing involving a flight with a traffic pattern).

(h) *For a lighter-than-air balloon course:* Two solo flights if the course is for a hot air balloon rating, or, if the course is for a gas balloon rating, at least two flights in a gas balloon, while performing the duties of pilot in command under the supervision of a commercial pilot with a balloon rating. The training shall consist of the approved areas of operation in paragraph (d)(8) of section No. 4 of this appendix, in the kind of balloon for which the course applies.

6. *Stage checks and end-of-course tests.* (a) Each student enrolled in a commercial pilot course must satisfactorily accomplish the stage checks and end-of-course tests, in accordance with the school's approved training course, consisting of the approved areas of operation listed in paragraph (d) of section No. 4 of this appendix that are appropriate to aircraft category and class rating for which the course applies.

(b) Each student must demonstrate satisfactory proficiency prior to receiving an en-

dorsement to operate an aircraft in solo flight.

[Doc. No. 25910, 62 FR 16347, Apr. 4, 1997; Amdt. 141–9, 62 FR 40909, July 30, 1997, as amended by Amdt. 141–10, 63 FR 20290, Apr. 23, 1998; Amdt. 141–12, 74 FR 42565, Aug. 21, 2009; Docket FAA–2015–1846, Amdt. 141–18, 81 FR 21461, Apr. 12, 2016; 83 FR 30283, June 27, 2018]

APPENDIX E TO PART 141—AIRLINE TRANSPORT PILOT CERTIFICATION COURSE

1. *Applicability.* This appendix prescribes the minimum curriculum for an airline transport pilot certification course under this part, for the following ratings:

(a) Airplane single-engine.
(b) Airplane multiengine.
(c) Rotorcraft helicopter.
(d) Powered-lift.

2. *Eligibility for enrollment.* Before completing the flight portion of the airline transport pilot certification course, a person must meet the aeronautical experience requirements for an airline transport pilot certificate under part 61, subpart G of this chapter that is appropriate to the aircraft category and class rating for which the course applies, and:

(a) Hold a commercial pilot certificate and an instrument rating, or an airline transport pilot certificate with instrument privileges;

(b) Meet the military experience requirements under §61.73 of this chapter to qualify for a commercial pilot certificate and an instrument rating, if the person is a rated military pilot or former rated military pilot of an Armed Force of the United States; or

(c) Hold either a foreign airline transport pilot license or foreign commercial pilot license and an instrument rating, if the person holds a pilot license issued by a contracting State to the Convention on International Civil Aviation.

3. *Aeronautical knowledge areas.* (a) Each approved course must include at least 40 hours of ground training on the aeronautical knowledge areas listed in paragraph (b) of this section, appropriate to the aircraft category and class rating for which the course applies.

(b) Ground training must include the following aeronautical knowledge areas:

(1) Applicable Federal Aviation Regulations of this chapter that relate to airline transport pilot privileges, limitations, and flight operations;

(2) Meteorology, including knowledge of and effects of fronts, frontal characteristics, cloud formations, icing, and upper-air data;

(3) General system of weather and NOTAM collection, dissemination, interpretation, and use;

(4) Interpretation and use of weather charts, maps, forecasts, sequence reports, abbreviations, and symbols;

(5) National Weather Service functions as they pertain to operations in the National Airspace System;

(6) Windshear and microburst awareness, identification, and avoidance;

(7) Principles of air navigation under instrument meteorological conditions in the National Airspace System;

(8) Air traffic control procedures and pilot responsibilities as they relate to en route operations, terminal area and radar operations, and instrument departure and approach procedures;

(9) Aircraft loading; weight and balance; use of charts, graphs, tables, formulas, and computations; and the effects on aircraft performance;

(10) Aerodynamics relating to an aircraft's flight characteristics and performance in normal and abnormal flight regimes;

(11) Human factors;

(12) Aeronautical decision making and judgment; and

(13) Crew resource management to include crew communication and coordination.

4. *Flight training.* (a) Each approved course must include at least 25 hours of flight training on the approved areas of operation listed in paragraph (c) of this section appropriate to the aircraft category and class rating for which the course applies. At least 15 hours of this flight training must be instrument flight training.

(b) For the use of full flight simulators or flight training devices—

(1) The course may include training in a full flight simulator or flight training device, provided it is representative of the aircraft for which the course is approved, meets the requirements of this paragraph, and the training is given by an authorized instructor.

(2) Training in a full flight simulator that meets the requirements of §141.41(a) may be credited for a maximum of 50 percent of the total flight training hour requirements of the approved course, or of this section, whichever is less.

(3) Training in a flight training device that meets the requirements of §141.41(a) may be credited for a maximum of 25 percent of the total flight training hour requirements of the approved course, or of this section, whichever is less.

(4) Training in full flight simulators or flight training devices described in paragraphs (b)(2) and (3) of this section, if used in combination, may be credited for a maximum of 50 percent of the total flight training hour requirements of the approved course, or of this section, whichever is less. However, credit for training in a flight training device that meets the requirements of

§141.41(a) cannot exceed the limitation provided for in paragraph (b)(3) of this section.

(c) Each approved course must include flight training on the approved areas of operation listed in this paragraph appropriate to the aircraft category and class rating for which the course applies:

(1) Preflight preparation;

(2) Preflight procedures;

(3) Takeoff and departure phase;

(4) In-flight maneuvers;

(5) Instrument procedures;

(6) Landings and approaches to landings;

(7) Normal and abnormal procedures;

(8) Emergency procedures; and

(9) Postflight procedures.

5. *Stage checks and end-of-course tests.* (a) Each student enrolled in an airline transport pilot course must satisfactorily accomplish the stage checks and end-of-course tests, in accordance with the school's approved training course, consisting of the approved areas of operation listed in paragraph (c) of section No. 4 of this appendix that are appropriate to the aircraft category and class rating for which the course applies.

(b) Each student must demonstrate satisfactory proficiency prior to receiving an endorsement to operate an aircraft in solo flight.

[Doc. No. 25910, 62 FR 16347, Apr. 4, 1997; Amdt. 141–9, 62 FR 40909, July 30, 1997; Amdt. 141–12, 74 FR 42565, Aug. 21, 2009; Docket FAA–2015–1846, Amdt. 141–18, 81 FR 21461, Apr. 12, 2016]

APPENDIX F TO PART 141—FLIGHT INSTRUCTOR CERTIFICATION COURSE

1. *Applicability.* This appendix prescribes the minimum curriculum for a flight instructor certification course and an additional flight instructor rating course required under this part, for the following ratings:

(a) Airplane single-engine.

(b) Airplane multiengine.

(c) Rotorcraft helicopter.

(d) Rotorcraft gyroplane.

(e) Powered-lift.

(f) Glider category.

2. *Eligibility for enrollment.* A person must hold the following prior to enrolling in the flight portion of the flight instructor or additional flight instructor rating course:

(a) A commercial pilot certificate or an airline transport pilot certificate, with an aircraft category and class rating appropriate to the flight instructor rating for which the course applies; and

(b) An instrument rating or privilege in an aircraft that is appropriate to the aircraft category and class rating for which the course applies, if the course is for a flight instructor airplane or powered-lift instrument rating.

3. *Aeronautical knowledge training.* (a) Each approved course must include at least the following ground training in the aeronautical knowledge areas listed in paragraph (b) of this section:

(1) 40 hours of training if the course is for an initial issuance of a flight instructor certificate; or

(2) 20 hours of training if the course is for an additional flight instructor rating.

(b) Ground training must include the following aeronautical knowledge areas:

(1) The fundamentals of instructing including—

(i) The learning process;

(ii) Elements of effective teaching;

(iii) Student evaluation and testing;

(iv) Course development;

(v) Lesson planning; and

(vi) Classroom training techniques.

(2) The aeronautical knowledge areas in which training is required for—

(i) A recreational, private, and commercial pilot certificate that is appropriate to the aircraft category and class rating for which the course applies; and

(ii) An instrument rating that is appropriate to the aircraft category and class rating for which the course applies, if the course is for an airplane or powered-lift aircraft rating.

(c) A student who satisfactorily completes 2 years of study on the principles of education at a college or university may be credited with no more than 20 hours of the training required in paragraph (a)(1) of this section.

4. *Flight training.* (a) Each approved course must include at least the following flight training on the approved areas of operation of paragraph (c) of this section appropriate to the flight instructor rating for which the course applies:

(1) 25 hours, if the course is for an airplane, rotorcraft, or powered-lift rating; and

(2) 10 hours, which must include 10 flights, if the course is for a glider category rating.

(b) For the use of flight simulators or flight training devices:

(1) The course may include training in a full flight simulator or flight training device, provided it is representative of the aircraft for which the course is approved, meets the requirements of this paragraph, and the training is given by an authorized instructor.

(2) Training in a full flight simulator that meets the requirements of §141.41(a), may be credited for a maximum of 10 percent of the total flight training hour requirements of the approved course, or of this section, whichever is less.

(3) Training in a flight training device that meets the requirements of §141.41(a), may be credited for a maximum of 5 percent of the total flight training hour requirements of

the approved course, or of this section, whichever is less.

(4) Training in full flight simulators or flight training devices described in paragraphs (b)(2) and (3) of this section, if used in combination, may be credited for a maximum of 10 percent of the total flight training hour requirements of the approved course, or of this section, whichever is less. However, credit for training in a flight training device that meets the requirements of §141.41(a) cannot exceed the limitation provided for in paragraph (b)(3) of this section.

(c) Each approved course must include flight training on the approved areas of operation listed in this paragraph that are appropriate to the aircraft category and class rating for which the course applies—

(1) *For an airplane—single-engine course:* (i) Fundamentals of instructing;

(ii) Technical subject areas;

(iii) Preflight preparation;

(iv) Preflight lesson on a maneuver to be performed in flight;

(v) Preflight procedures;

(vi) Airport and seaplane base operations;

(vii) Takeoffs, landings, and go-arounds;

(viii) Fundamentals of flight;

(ix) Performance maneuvers;

(x) Ground reference maneuvers;

(xi) Slow flight, stalls, and spins;

(xii) Basic instrument maneuvers;

(xiii) Emergency operations; and

(xiv) Postflight procedures.

(2) *For an airplane—multiengine course:* (i) Fundamentals of instructing;

(ii) Technical subject areas;

(iii) Preflight preparation;

(iv) Preflight lesson on a maneuver to be performed in flight;

(v) Preflight procedures;

(vi) Airport and seaplane base operations;

(vii) Takeoffs, landings, and go-arounds;

(viii) Fundamentals of flight;

(ix) Performance maneuvers;

(x) Ground reference maneuvers;

(xi) Slow flight and stalls;

(xii) Basic instrument maneuvers;

(xiii) Emergency operations;

(xiv) Multiengine operations; and

(xv) Postflight procedures.

(3) *For a rotorcraft—helicopter course:* (i) Fundamentals of instructing;

(ii) Technical subject areas;

(iii) Preflight preparation;

(iv) Preflight lesson on a maneuver to be performed in flight;

(v) Preflight procedures;

(vi) Airport and heliport operations;

(vii) Hovering maneuvers;

(viii) Takeoffs, landings, and go-arounds;

(ix) Fundamentals of flight;

(x) Performance maneuvers;

(xi) Emergency operations;

(xii) Special operations; and

(xiii) Postflight procedures.

(4) *For a rotorcraft—gyroplane course:* (i) Fundamentals of instructing;

(ii) Technical subject areas;

(iii) Preflight preparation;

(iv) Preflight lesson on a maneuver to be performed in flight;

(v) Preflight procedures;

(vi) Airport operations;

(vii) Takeoffs, landings, and go-arounds;

(viii) Fundamentals of flight;

(ix) Performance maneuvers;

(x) Flight at slow airspeeds;

(xi) Ground reference maneuvers;

(xii) Emergency operations; and

(xiii) Postflight procedures.

(5) *For a powered-lift course:* (i) Fundamentals of instructing;

(ii) Technical subject areas;

(iii) Preflight preparation;

(iv) Preflight lesson on a maneuver to be performed in flight;

(v) Preflight procedures;

(vi) Airport and heliport operations;

(vii) Hovering maneuvers;

(viii) Takeoffs, landings, and go-arounds;

(ix) Fundamentals of flight;

(x) Performance maneuvers;

(xi) Ground reference maneuvers;

(xii) Slow flight and stalls;

(xiii) Basic instrument maneuvers;

(xiv) Emergency operations;

(xv) Special operations; and

(xvi) Postflight procedures.

(6) *For a glider course:* (i) Fundamentals of instructing;

(ii) Technical subject areas;

(iii) Preflight preparation;

(iv) Preflight lesson on a maneuver to be performed in flight;

(v) Preflight procedures;

(vi) Airport and gliderport operations;

(vii) Tows or launches, landings, and go-arounds, if applicable;

(viii) Fundamentals of flight;

(ix) Performance speeds;

(x) Soaring techniques;

(xi) Performance maneuvers;

(xii) Slow flight, stalls, and spins;

(xiii) Emergency operations; and

(xiv) Postflight procedures.

5. *Stage checks and end-of-course tests.* (a) Each student enrolled in a flight instructor course must satisfactorily accomplish the stage checks and end-of-course tests, in accordance with the school's approved training course, consisting of the appropriate approved areas of operation listed in paragraph (c) of section No. 4 of this appendix appropriate to the flight instructor rating for which the course applies.

(b) In the case of a student who is enrolled in a flight instructor-airplane rating or flight instructor-glider rating course, that student must have:

(1) Received a logbook endorsement from a certificated flight instructor certifying the student received ground and flight training

on stall awareness, spin entry, spins, and spin recovery procedures in an aircraft that is certificated for spins and is appropriate to the rating sought; and

(2) Demonstrated instructional proficiency in stall awareness, spin entry, spins, and spin recovery procedures.

[Doc. No. 25910, 62 FR 16347, Apr. 4, 1997; Amdt. 141–9, 62 FR 40909, July 30, 1997, as amended by Docket FAA–2015–1846, Amdt. 141–18, 81 FR 21461, Apr. 12, 2016]

APPENDIX G TO PART 141—FLIGHT INSTRUCTOR INSTRUMENT (FOR AN AIRPLANE, HELICOPTER, OR POWERED-LIFT INSTRUMENT INSTRUCTOR RATING, AS APPROPRIATE) CERTIFICATION COURSE

1. *Applicability.* This appendix prescribes the minimum curriculum for a flight instructor instrument certification course required under this part, for the following ratings:

(a) Flight Instructor Instrument—Airplane.

(b) Flight Instructor Instrument—Helicopter.

(c) Flight Instructor Instrument—Powered-lift aircraft.

2. *Eligibility for enrollment.* A person must hold the following prior to enrolling in the flight portion of the flight instructor instrument course:

(a) A commercial pilot certificate or airline transport pilot certificate with an aircraft category and class rating appropriate to the flight instructor category and class rating for which the course applies; and

(b) An instrument rating or privilege on that flight instructor applicant's pilot certificate that is appropriate to the flight instructor instrument rating (for an airplane-, helicopter-, or powered-lift-instrument rating, as appropriate) for which the course applies.

3. *Aeronautical knowledge training.* (a) Each approved course must include at least 15 hours of ground training on the aeronautical knowledge areas listed in paragraph (b) of this section, appropriate to the flight instructor instrument rating (for an airplane-, helicopter-, or powered-lift-instrument rating, as appropriate) for which the course applies:

(b) Ground training must include the following aeronautical knowledge areas:

(1) The fundamentals of instructing including:

(i) The learning process;

(ii) Elements of effective teaching;

(iii) Student evaluation and testing;

(iv) Course development;

(v) Lesson planning; and

(vi) Classroom training techniques.

(2) The aeronautical knowledge areas in which training is required for an instrument rating that is appropriate to the aircraft category and class rating for the course which applies.

4. *Flight training.* (a) Each approved course must include at least 15 hours of flight training in the approved areas of operation of paragraph (c) of this section appropriate to the flight instructor rating for which the course applies.

(b) For the use of full flight simulators or flight training devices:

(1) The course may include training in a full flight simulator or flight training device, provided it is representative of the aircraft for which the course is approved for, meets requirements of this paragraph, and the training is given by an instructor.

(2) Training in a full flight simulator that meets the requirements of §141.41(a), may be credited for a maximum of 10 percent of the total flight training hour requirements of the approved course, or of this section, whichever is less.

(3) Training in a flight training device that meets the requirements of §141.41(a), may be credited for a maximum of 5 percent of the total flight training hour requirements of the approved course, or of this section, whichever is less.

(4) Training in full flight simulators or flight training devices described in paragraphs (b)(2) and (3) of this section, if used in combination, may be credited for a maximum of 10 percent of the total flight training hour requirements of the approved course, or of this section, whichever is less. However, credit for training in a flight training device that meets the requirements of §141.41(b) cannot exceed the limitation provided for in paragraph (b)(3) of this section.

(c) An approved course for the flight instructor-instrument rating must include flight training on the following approved areas of operation that are appropriate to the instrument-aircraft category and class rating for which the course applies:

(1) Fundamentals of instructing;
(2) Technical subject areas;
(3) Preflight preparation;
(4) Preflight lesson on a maneuver to be performed in flight;
(5) Air traffic control clearances and procedures;
(6) Flight by reference to instruments;
(7) Navigation systems;
(8) Instrument approach procedures;
(9) Emergency operations; and
(10) Postflight procedures.

5. *Stage checks and end-of-course tests.* Each student enrolled in a flight instructor instrument course must satisfactorily accomplish the stage checks and end-of-course tests, in accordance with the school's approved training course, consisting of the approved areas of operation listed in paragraph (c) of section

No. 4 of this appendix that are appropriate to the flight instructor instrument rating (for an airplane-, helicopter-, or powered-lift-instrument rating, as appropriate) for which the course applies.

[Doc. No. 25910, 62 FR 16347, Apr. 4, 1997; Amdt. 141-9, 62 FR 40909, July 30, 1997, as amended by Docket FAA-2015-1846, Amdt. 141-18, 81 FR 21461, Apr. 12, 2016]

APPENDIX H TO PART 141—GROUND INSTRUCTOR CERTIFICATION COURSE

1. *Applicability.* This appendix prescribes the minimum curriculum for a ground instructor certification course and an additional ground instructor rating course, required under this part, for the following ratings:

(a) Ground Instructor—Basic.
(b) Ground Instructor—Advanced.
(c) Ground Instructor—Instrument.

2. *Aeronautical knowledge training.* (a) Each approved course must include at least the following ground training on the knowledge areas listed in paragraphs (b), (c), (d), and (e) of this section, appropriate to the ground instructor rating for which the course applies:

(1) 20 hours of training if the course is for an initial issuance of a ground instructor certificate; or

(2) 10 hours of training if the course is for an additional ground instructor rating.

(b) Ground training must include the following aeronautical knowledge areas:

(1) Learning process;
(2) Elements of effective teaching;
(3) Student evaluation and testing;
(4) Course development;
(5) Lesson planning; and
(6) Classroom training techniques.

(c) Ground training for a basic ground instructor certificate must include the aeronautical knowledge areas applicable to a recreational and private pilot.

(d) Ground training for an advanced ground instructor rating must include the aeronautical knowledge areas applicable to a recreational, private, commercial, and airline transport pilot.

(e) Ground training for an instrument ground instructor rating must include the aeronautical knowledge areas applicable to an instrument rating.

(f) A student who satisfactorily completed 2 years of study on the principles of education at a college or university may be credited with 10 hours of the training required in paragraph (a)(1) of this section.

3. *Stage checks and end-of-course tests.* Each student enrolled in a ground instructor course must satisfactorily accomplish the stage checks and end-of-course tests, in accordance with the school's approved training course, consisting of the approved knowledge areas in paragraph (b), (c), (d), and (e) of section No. 2 of this appendix appropriate to the

ground instructor rating for which the course applies.

APPENDIX I TO PART 141—ADDITIONAL AIRCRAFT CATEGORY AND/OR CLASS RATING COURSE

1. *Applicability.* This appendix prescribes the minimum curriculum for an additional aircraft category rating course or an additional aircraft class rating course required under this part, for the following ratings:

(a) Airplane single-engine.
(b) Airplane multiengine.
(c) Rotorcraft helicopter.
(d) Rotorcraft gyroplane.
(e) Powered-lift.
(f) Glider.
(g) Lighter-than-air airship.
(h) Lighter-than-air balloon.

2. *Eligibility for enrollment.* A person must hold the level of pilot certificate for the additional aircraft category and class rating for which the course applies prior to enrolling in the flight portion of an additional aircraft category or additional aircraft class rating course.

3. *Aeronautical knowledge training.*

(a) For a recreational pilot certificate, the following aeronautical knowledge areas must be included in a 10-hour ground training course for an additional aircraft category and/or class rating:

(1) Applicable regulations issued by the Federal Aviation Administration for recreational pilot privileges, limitations, and flight operations;

(2) Safe and efficient operation of aircraft, including collision avoidance, and recognition and avoidance of wake turbulence;

(3) Effects of density altitude on takeoff and climb performance;

(4) Weight and balance computations;

(5) Principles of aerodynamics, powerplants, and aircraft systems;

(6) Stall awareness, spin entry, spins and spin recovery techniques if applying for an airplane single engine rating; and

(7) Preflight action that includes how to obtain information on runway lengths at airports of intended use, data on takeoff and landing distances, weather reports and forecasts, and fuel requirements.

(b) For a private pilot certificate, the following aeronautical knowledge areas must be included in a 10-hour ground training course for an additional class rating or a 15-hour ground training course for an additional aircraft category and class rating:

(1) Applicable regulations issued by the Federal Aviation Administration for private pilot privileges, limitations, and flight operations;

(2) Safe and efficient operation of aircraft, including collision avoidance, and recognition and avoidance of wake turbulence;

(3) Effects of density altitude on takeoff and climb performance;

(4) Weight and balance computations;

(5) Principles of aerodynamics, powerplants, and aircraft systems;

(6) Stall awareness, spin entry, spins, and spin recovery techniques if applying for an airplane single engine rating; and

(7) Preflight action that includes how to obtain information on runway lengths at airports of intended use, data on takeoff and landing distances, weather reports and forecasts, and fuel requirements.

(c) For a commercial pilot certificate, the following aeronautical knowledge areas must be included in a 15-hour ground training course for an additional class rating or a 20-hour ground training course for an additional aircraft category and class rating:

(1) Applicable regulations issued by the Federal Aviation Administration for commercial pilot privileges, limitations, and flight operations;

(2) Basic aerodynamics and the principles of flight;

(3) Safe and efficient operation of aircraft;

(4) Weight and balance computations;

(5) Use of performance charts;

(6) Significance and effects of exceeding aircraft performance limitations;

(7) Principles and functions of aircraft systems;

(8) Maneuvers, procedures, and emergency operations appropriate to the aircraft;

(9) Nighttime and high-altitude operations; and

(10) Procedures for flight and ground training for lighter-than-air ratings.

(d) For an airline transport pilot certificate, the following aeronautical knowledge areas must be included in a 25-hour ground training course for an additional aircraft category and/or class rating:

(1) Applicable regulations issued by the Federal Aviation Administration for airline transport pilot privileges, limitations, and flight operations;

(2) Meteorology, including knowledge and effects of fronts, frontal characteristics, cloud formations, icing, and upper-air data;

(3) General system of weather and NOTAM collection, dissemination, interpretation, and use;

(4) Interpretation and use of weather charts, maps, forecasts, sequence reports, abbreviations, and symbols;

(5) National Weather Service functions as they pertain to operations in the National Airspace System;

(6) Windshear and microburst awareness, identification, and avoidance;

(7) Principles of air navigation under instrument meteorological conditions in the National Airspace System;

(8) Air traffic control procedures and pilot responsibilities as they relate to en route operations, terminal area and radar operations,

and instrument departure and approach procedures;

(9) Aircraft loading; weight and balance; use of charts, graphs, tables, formulas, and computations; and the effects on aircraft performance;

(10) Aerodynamics relating to an aircraft's flight characteristics and performance in normal and abnormal flight regimes;

(11) Human factors;

(12) Aeronautical decision making and judgment; and

(13) Crew resource management to include crew communication and coordination.

4. Flight training.

(a) Course for an additional airplane category and single engine class rating.

(1) For the recreational pilot certificate, the course must include 15 hours of flight training on the areas of operations under part 141, appendix A, paragraph 4(c)(1) that include—

(i) Two hours of flight training to an airport and at an airport that is located more than 25 nautical miles from the airport where the applicant normally trains, with three takeoffs and three landings, except as provided under §61.100 of this chapter; and

(ii) Three hours of flight training in an aircraft with the airplane category and single engine class within 2 calendar months before the date of the practical test.

(2) For the private pilot certificate, the course must include 20 hours of flight training on the areas of operations under part 141, appendix B, paragraph 4(d)(1). A flight simulator and flight training device cannot be used to meet more than 4 hours of the training requirements, and the use of the flight training device is limited to 3 hours of the 4 hours permitted. The course must include—

(i) Three hours of cross country training in a single engine airplane, except as provided under §61.111 of this chapter;

(ii) Three hours of nighttime flight training in a single engine airplane that includes one cross country flight of more than 100 nautical miles total distance, and 10 takeoffs and 10 landings to a full stop (with each landing involving a flight in the traffic pattern) at an airport;

(iii) Three hours of flight training in a single engine airplane on the control and maneuvering of the airplane solely by reference to instruments, including straight and level flight, constant airspeed climbs and descents, turns to a heading, recovery from unusual flight attitudes, radio communications, and the use of navigation systems/facilities and radar services appropriate to instrument flight; and

(iv) Three hours of flight training in a single engine airplane within 2 calendar months before the date of the practical test.

(3) For the commercial pilot certificate, the course must include 55 hours of flight training on the areas of operations under

part 141, appendix D, paragraph 4(d)(1). A flight simulator and flight training device cannot be used to meet more than 16.5 hours of the training requirements, and the use of the flight training device is limited to 11 hours of the 16.5 hours permitted. The course must include—

(i) Five hours of instrument training in a single engine airplane that includes training using a view-limiting device on attitude instrument flying, partial panel skills, recovery from unusual flight attitudes, and intercepting and tracking navigational systems;

(ii) Ten hours of training in an airplane that has retractable landing gear, flaps, and a controllable pitch propeller, or is turbine-powered;

(iii) One 2-hour cross country flight during daytime conditions in a single engine airplane, a total straight-line distance of more than 100 nautical miles from the original point of departure;

(iv) One 2-hour cross country flight during nighttime conditions in a single engine airplane, a total straight-line distance of more than 100 nautical miles from the original point of departure; and

(v) Three hours in a single engine airplane within 2 calendar months before the date of the practical test.

(4) For the airline transport pilot certificate, the course must include 25 hours flight training, including 15 hours of instrument training, in a single engine airplane on the areas of operation under part 141, appendix E, paragraph 4.(c). A flight simulator and flight training device cannot be used to meet more than 12.5 hours of the training requirements; and the use of the flight training device is limited to 6.25 hours of the 12.5 hours permitted.

(b) Course for an additional airplane category and multiengine class rating.

(1) For the private pilot certificate, the course requires 20 hours flight training on the areas of operations under part 141, appendix B, paragraph 4.(d)(2). A flight simulator and flight training device cannot be used more than 4 hours to meet the training requirements, and use of the flight training device is limited to 3 hours of the 4 hours permitted. The course must include—

(i) Three hours of cross country training in a multiengine airplane, except as provided under §61.111 of this chapter;

(ii) Three hours of nighttime flight training in a multiengine airplane that includes one cross country flight of more than 100 nautical miles total distance, and 10 takeoffs and 10 landings to a full stop (with each landing involving a flight in the traffic pattern) at an airport;

(iii) Three hours of flight training in a multiengine airplane on the control and maneuvering of a multiengine airplane solely by reference to instruments, including straight and level flight, constant airspeed climbs and descents, turns to a heading, recovery from unusual flight attitudes, radio communications, and the use of navigation systems/facilities and radar services appropriate to instrument flight; and

(iv) Three hours of flight training in a multiengine airplane in preparation for the practical test within 2 calendar months before the date of the test.

(2) For the commercial pilot certificate, the course requires 55 hours flight training on the areas of operations under part 141, appendix D, paragraph 4.(d)(2). A flight simulator and flight training device cannot be used more than 16.5 hours to meet the training requirements, and use of the flight training device is limited to 11 hours of the 16.5 hours permitted. The course must include—

(i) Five hours of instrument training in a multiengine airplane including training using a view-limiting device for attitude instrument flying, partial panel skills, recovery from unusual flight attitudes, and intercepting and tracking navigational systems;

(ii) Ten hours of training in a multiengine airplane that has retractable landing gear, flaps, and a controllable pitch propeller, or is turbine-powered;

(iii) One 2-hour cross country flight during daytime conditions in a multiengine airplane, and a total straight-line distance of more than 100 nautical miles from the original point of departure;

(iv) One 2-hour cross country flight during nighttime conditions in a multiengine airplane, and a total straight-line distance of more than 100 nautical miles from the original point of departure; and

(v) Three hours in a multiengine airplane within 2 calendar months before the date of the practical test.

(3) For the airline transport pilot certificate, the course requires 25 hours of flight training in a multiengine airplane on the areas of operation under part 141, appendix E, paragraph 4.(c) that includes 15 hours of instrument training. A flight simulator and flight training device cannot be used more than 12.5 hours to meet the training requirements, and use of the flight training device is limited to 6.25 hours of the 12.5 hours permitted.

(c) Course for an additional rotorcraft category and helicopter class rating.

(1) For the recreational pilot certificate, the course requires 15 hours of flight training on the areas of operations under part 141, appendix A, paragraph 4.(c)(2) that includes—

(i) Two hours of flight training to and at an airport that is located more than 25 nautical miles from the airport where the applicant normally trains, with three takeoffs and three landings, except as provided under §61.100 of this chapter; and

(ii) Three hours of flight training in a rotorcraft category and a helicopter class

aircraft within 2 calendar months before the date of the practical test.

(2) For the private pilot certificate, the course requires 20 hours flight training on the areas of operations under part 141, appendix B, paragraph 4.(d)(3). A flight simulator and flight training device cannot be used more than 4 hours to meet the training requirements, and use of the flight training device is limited to 3 hours of the 4 hours permitted. The course must include—

(i) Except as provided under §61.111 of this chapter, 3 hours of cross country flight training in a helicopter;

(ii) Three hours of nighttime flight training in a helicopter that includes one cross country flight of more than 50 nautical miles total distance, and 10 takeoffs and 10 landings to a full stop (with each landing involving a flight in the traffic pattern) at an airport; and

(iii) Three hours of flight training in a helicopter within 2 calendar months before the date of the practical test.

(3) The commercial pilot certificate level requires 30 hours flight training on the areas of operations under appendix D of part 141, paragraph 4.(d)(3). A flight simulator and flight training device cannot be used more than 9 hours to meet the training requirements, and use of the flight training device is limited to 6 hours of the 9 hours permitted. The course must include—

(i) Five hours on the control and maneuvering of a helicopter solely by reference to instruments, and must include training using a view-limiting device for attitude instrument flying, partial panel skills, recovery from unusual flight attitudes, and intercepting and tracking navigational systems. This aeronautical experience may be performed in an aircraft, flight simulator, flight training device, or an aviation training device;

(ii) One 2-hour cross country flight during daytime conditions in a helicopter, a total straight-line distance of more than 50 nautical miles from the original point of departure;

(iii) One 2-hour cross country flight during nighttime conditions in a helicopter, a total straight-line distance of more than 50 nautical miles from the original point of departure; and

(iv) Three hours in a helicopter within 2 calendar months before the date of the practical test.

(4) For the airline transport pilot certificate, the course requires 25 hours of flight training, including 15 hours of instrument training, in a helicopter on the areas of operation under part 141, appendix E, paragraph 4.(c). A flight simulator and flight training device cannot be used more than 12.5 hours to meet the training requirements, and use of the flight training device is limited to 6.25 hours of the 12.5 hours permitted.

(d) Course for an additional rotorcraft category and a gyroplane class rating.

(1) For the recreational pilot certificate, the course requires 15 hours flight training on the areas of operations under part 141, appendix A, paragraph 4.(c)(3) that includes—

(i) Two hours of flight training to and at an airport that is located more than 25 nautical miles from the airport where the applicant normally trains, with three takeoffs and three landings, except as provided under § 61.100 of this chapter; and

(ii) Three hours of flight training in a gyroplane class within 2 calendar months before the date of the practical test.

(2) For the private pilot certificate, the course requires 20 hours flight training on the areas of operations under part 141, appendix B, paragraph 4.(d)(4). A flight simulator and flight training device cannot be used more than 4 hours to meet the training requirements, and use of the flight training device is limited to 3 hours of the 4 hours permitted. The course must include—

(i) Three hours of cross country flight training in a gyroplane, except as provided under § 61.111 of this chapter;

(ii) Three hours of nighttime flight training in a gyroplane that includes one cross country flight of more than 50 nautical miles total distance, and 10 takeoffs and 10 landings to a full stop (with each landing involving a flight in the traffic pattern) at an airport; and

(iii) Three hours of flight training in a gyroplane within 2 calendar months before the date of the practical test.

(3) For the commercial pilot certificate, the course requires 30 hours flight training on the areas of operations of appendix D to part 141, paragraph 4.(d)(4). A flight simulator and flight training device cannot be used more than 6 hours to meet the training requirements, and use of the flight training device is limited to 6 hours of the 9 hours permitted. The course must include—

(i) 2.5 hours on the control and maneuvering of a gyroplane solely by reference to instruments, and must include training using a view-limiting device for attitude instrument flying, partial panel skills, recovery from unusual flight attitudes, and intercepting and tracking navigational systems. This aeronautical experience may be performed in an aircraft, flight simulator, flight training device, or an aviation training device.

(ii) One 2-hour cross country flight during daytime conditions in a gyroplane, a total straight-line distance of more than 50 nautical miles from the original point of departure;

(iii) Two hours of flight training during nighttime conditions in a gyroplane at an airport, that includes 10 takeoffs and 10 landings to a full stop (with each landing involving a flight in the traffic pattern); and

(iv) Three hours in a gyroplane within 2 calendar months before the date of the practical test.

(e) Course for an additional lighter-than-air category and airship class rating.

(1) For the private pilot certificate, the course requires 20 hours of flight training on the areas of operation under part 141, appendix B, paragraph 4.(d)(7). A flight simulator and flight training device cannot be used more than 4 hours to meet the training requirements, and use of the flight training device is limited to 3 hours of the 4 hours permitted. The course must include—

(i) Three hours of cross country flight training in an airship, except as provided under § 61.111 of this chapter;

(ii) Three hours of nighttime flight training in an airship that includes one cross country flight of more than 25 nautical miles total distance and 5 takeoffs and 5 landings to a full stop (with each landing involving a flight in the traffic pattern) at an airport;

(iii) Three hours of flight training in an airship on the control and maneuvering of an airship solely by reference to instruments, including straight and level flight, constant airspeed climbs and descents, turns to a heading, recovery from unusual flight attitudes, radio communications, and the use of navigation systems/facilities and radar services appropriate to instrument flight; and

(iv) Three hours of flight training in an airship within 2 calendar months before the date of the practical test.

(2) For the commercial pilot certificate, the course requires 55 hours of flight training on the areas of operation under part 141, appendix D, paragraph 4.(d)(7). A flight simulator and flight training device cannot be used more than 16.5 hours to meet the training requirements, and use of the flight training device is limited to 11 hours of the 16.5 hours permitted. The course must include—

(i) Three hours of instrument training in an airship that must include training using a view-limiting device for attitude instrument flying, partial panel skills, recovery from unusual flight attitudes, and intercepting and tracking navigational systems;

(ii) One hour cross country flight during daytime conditions in an airship that consists of, a total straight-line distance of more than 25 nautical miles from the original point of departure;

(iii) One hour cross country flight during nighttime conditions in an airship that consists of a total straight-line distance of more than 25 nautical miles from the original point of departure; and

(iv) Three hours of flight training in an airship within 2 calendar months before the date of the practical test.

(f) Course for an additional lighter-than-air category and a gas balloon class rating.

(1) For the private pilot certificate, the course requires eight hours of flight training

that includes 5 training flights on the areas of operations under part 141, appendix B, paragraph 4(d)(8). A flight simulator and flight training device cannot be used more than 1.6 hours to meet the training requirements, and use of the flight training device is limited to 1.2 hours of the 1.6 hours permitted. The course must include—

(i) Two flights of 1 hour each;

(ii) One flight involving a controlled ascent to 3,000 feet above the launch site; and

(iii) Two flights within 2 calendar months before the date of the practical test.

(2) For the commercial pilot certificate, the course requires 10 hours of flight training that includes eight training flights on the areas of operations under part 141, appendix D, paragraph 4(d)(8). A flight simulator and flight training device cannot be used more than 3 hours to meet the training requirements, and use of the flight training device is limited to 2 hours of the 3 hours permitted. The course must include—

(i) Two flights of 1 hour each;

(ii) One flight involving a controlled ascent to 5,000 feet above the launch site; and

(iii) Two flights within 2 calendar months before the date of the practical test.

(g) Course for an additional lighter-than-air category and a hot air balloon class rating.

(1) For the private pilot certificate, the course requires eight hours of flight training that includes 5 training flights on the areas of operations under part 141, appendix B, paragraph 4(d)(8). A flight simulator and flight training device cannot be used more than 1.6 hours to meet the training requirements, and use of the flight training device is limited to 1.2 hours of the 1.6 hours permitted. The course must include—

(i) Two flights of 30 minutes each;

(ii) One flight involving a controlled ascent to 2,000 feet above the launch site; and

(iii) Two flights within 2 calendar months before the date of the practical test.

(2) For the commercial pilot certificate, the course requires 10 hours of flight training that includes eight training flights on the areas of operation under part 141, appendix D, paragraph 4(d)(8). A flight simulator and flight training device cannot be used more than 3 hours to meet the training requirements, and use of the flight training device is limited to 2 hours of the 3 hours permitted. The course must include—

(i) Two flights of 30 minutes each;

(ii) One flight involving a controlled ascent to 3,000 feet above the launch site; and

(iii) Two flights within 2 calendar months before the date of the practical test.

(h) Course for an additional powered-lift category rating.

(1) For the private pilot certificate, the course requires 20 hours flight training on the areas of operations under part 141, appendix B, paragraph 4(d)(5). A flight simulator and flight training device cannot be used more than 4 hours to meet the training requirements, and use of the flight training device is limited to 3 hours of the 4 hours permitted. The course must include—

(i) Three hours of cross country flight training in a powered-lift except as provided under §61.111 of this chapter;

(ii) Three hours of nighttime flight training in a powered-lift that includes one cross-country flight of more than 100 nautical miles total distance, and 10 takeoffs and 10 landings to a full stop (with each landing involving a flight in the traffic pattern) at an airport;

(iii) Three hours of flight training in a powered-lift on the control and maneuvering of a powered-lift solely by reference to instruments, including straight and level flight, constant airspeed climbs and descents, turns to a heading, recovery from unusual flight attitudes, radio communications, and the use of navigation systems/facilities and radar services appropriate to instrument flight;

(iv) Three hours of flight training in a powered-lift within 2 calendar months before the date of the practical test.

(2) For the commercial pilot certificate, the course requires 55 hours flight training on the areas of operations under part 141, appendix D, paragraph 4(d)(5). A flight simulator and flight training device cannot be used more than 16.5 hours to meet the training requirements, and use of the flight training device is limited to 11 hours of the 16.5 hours permitted. The course includes—

(i) Five hours of instrument training in a powered-lift that must include training using a view-limiting device for attitude instrument flying, partial panel skills, recovery from unusual flight attitudes, and intercepting and tracking navigational systems;

(ii) One 2-hour cross country flight during daytime conditions in a powered-lift, a total straight-line distance of more than 100 nautical miles from the original point of departure;

(iii) One 2-hour cross country flight during nighttime conditions in a powered-lift, a total straight-line distance of more than 100 nautical miles from the original point of departure; and

(iv) Three hours of flight training in a powered-lift within 2 calendar months before the date of the practical test.

(3) For the airline transport pilot certificate, the course requires 25 hours flight training in a powered-lift on the areas of operation under part 141, appendix E, paragraph 4(c) that includes 15 hours of instrument training. A flight simulator and flight training device cannot be used more than 12.5 hours to meet the training requirements, and use of the flight training device is limited to 6.25 hours of the 12.5 hours permitted.

(i) Course for an additional glider category rating.

(1) For the private pilot certificate, the course requires 4 hours of flight training in a glider on the areas of operations under part 141, appendix B, paragraph 4(d)(6). A flight simulator and flight training device cannot be used more than 0.8 hours to meet the training requirements, and use of the flight training device is limited to 0.6 hours of the 0.8 hours permitted. The course must include—

(i) Five training flights in a glider with a certificated flight instructor on the launch/tow procedures approved for the course and on the appropriate approved areas of operation listed under appendix B, paragraph 4(d)(6) of this part; and

(ii) Three training flights in a glider with a certificated flight instructor within 2 calendar months before the date of the practical test.

(2) The commercial pilot certificate level requires 4 hours of flight training in a glider on the areas of operation under part 141, appendix D, paragraph 4.(d)(6). A flight simulator and flight training device cannot be used more than 0.8 hours to meet the training requirements, and use of the flight training device is limited to 0.6 hours of the 0.8 hours permitted. The course must include—

(j) Course for an airplane additional single engine class rating.

(1) For the private pilot certificate, the course requires 3 hours of flight training in the areas of operations under part 141, appendix B, paragraph 4.(d)(1). A flight simulator and flight training device cannot be used more than 0.6 hours to meet the training requirements, and use of the flight training device is limited to 0.4 hours of the 0.6 hours permitted. The course must include—

(i) Three hours of cross country training in a single engine airplane, except as provided under §61.111 of this chapter;

(ii) Three hours of nighttime flight training in a single engine airplane that includes one cross country flight of more than 100 nautical miles total distance in a single engine airplane and 10 takeoffs and 10 landings to a full stop (with each landing involving a flight in the traffic pattern) at an airport;

(iii) Three hours of flight training in a single engine airplane on the control and maneuvering of a single engine airplane solely by reference to instruments, including straight and level flight, constant airspeed climbs and descents, turns to a heading, recovery from unusual flight attitudes, radio communications, and the use of navigation systems/facilities and radar services appropriate to instrument flight; and

(iv) Three hours of flight training in a single engine airplane within 2 calendar months before the date of the practical test.

(2) For the commercial pilot certificate, the course requires 10 hours of flight training on the areas of operations under part 141, appendix D, paragraph 4.(d)(1).

(i) Five hours of instrument training in a single engine airplane that must include training using a view-limiting device for attitude instrument flying, partial panel skills, recovery from unusual flight attitudes, and intercepting and tracking navigational systems.

(ii) Ten hours of flight training in an airplane that has retractable landing gear, flaps, and a controllable pitch propeller, or is turbine-powered.

(iii) One 2-hour cross country flight during daytime conditions in a single engine airplane and a total straight-line distance of more than 100 nautical miles from the original point of departure;

(iv) One 2-hour cross country flight during nighttime conditions in a single engine airplane and a total straight-line distance of more than 100 nautical miles from the original point of departure; and

(v) Three hours of flight training in a single engine airplane within 2 calendar months before the date of the practical test.

(3) For the airline transport pilot certificate, the course requires 25 hours flight training in a single engine airplane on the areas of operation under appendix E to part 141, paragraph 4.(c), that includes 15 hours of instrument training. A flight simulator and flight training device cannot be used more than 12.5 hours to meet the training requirements, and use of the flight training device is limited to 6.25 hours of the 12.5 hours permitted.

(k) Course for an airplane additional multiengine class rating.

(1) For the private pilot certificate, the course requires 3 hours of flight training on the areas of operations of appendix B to part 141, paragraph 4(d)(2). A flight simulator and flight training device cannot be used more than 0.6 hours to meet the training requirements, and use of the flight training device is limited to 0.4 hours of the 0.6 hours permitted. The course must include—

(i) Three hours of cross country training in a multiengine airplane, except as provided under §61.111 of this chapter;

(ii) Three hours of nighttime flight training in a multiengine airplane that includes one cross country flight of more than 100 nautical miles total distance in a multiengine airplane, and 10 takeoffs and 10 landings to a full stop (with each landing involving a flight in the traffic pattern) at an airport;

(iii) Three hours of flight training in a multiengine airplane on the control and maneuvering of a multiengine airplane solely by reference to instruments, including straight and level flight, constant airspeed climbs and descents, turns to a heading, recovery from unusual flight attitudes, radio communications, and the use of navigation systems/facilities and radar services appropriate to instrument flight; and

(iv) Three hours of flight training in a multiengine airplane within 2 calendar months before the date of the practical test.

(2) For the commercial pilot certificate, the course requires 10 hours of training on the areas of operations under appendix D of part 141, paragraph 4(d)(2). A flight simulator and flight training device cannot be used more than 3 hours to meet the training requirements, and use of the flight training device is limited to 2 hours of the 3 hours permitted. The course must include—

(i) Five hours of instrument training in a multiengine airplane that must include training using a view-limiting device on for attitude instrument flying, partial panel skills, recovery from unusual flight attitudes, and intercepting and tracking navigational systems;

(ii) Ten hours of training in a multiengine airplane that has retractable landing gear, flaps, and a controllable pitch propeller or is turbine-powered;

(iii) One 2-hour cross country flight during daytime conditions in a multiengine airplane and, a total straight-line distance of more than 100 nautical miles from the original point of departure;

(iv) One 2-hour cross country flight during nighttime conditions in a multiengine airplane and, a total straight-line distance of more than 100 nautical miles from the original point of departure; and

(v) Three hours of flight training in a multiengine airplane within 2 calendar months before the date of the practical test.

(3) For the airline transport pilot certificate, the course requires 25 hours of training in a multiengine airplane on the areas of operation of appendix E to part 141, paragraph 4.(c) that includes 15 hours of instrument training. A flight simulator and flight training device cannot be used more than 12.5 hours to meet the training requirements, and use of the flight training device is limited to 6.25 hours of the 12.5 hours permitted.

(l) Course for a rotorcraft additional helicopter class rating.

(1) For the recreational pilot certificate, the course requires 3 hours of flight training on the areas of operations under appendix A of part 141, paragraph 4.(c)(2) that includes—

(i) Two hours of flight training to and at an airport that is located more than 25 nautical miles from the airport where the applicant normally trains, with three takeoffs and three landings, except as provided under §61.100 of this chapter; and

(ii) Three hours of flight training in a helicopter within 2 calendar months before the date of the practical test.

(2) For the private pilot certificate, the course requires 3 hours flight training on the areas of operations under appendix B of part 141, paragraph 4.(d)(3). A flight simulator and

flight training device cannot be used more than 0.6 hours to meet the training requirements, and use of the flight training device is limited to 0.4 hours of the 0.6 hours permitted. The course must include—

(i) Three hours of cross country training in a helicopter, except as provided under §61.111 of this chapter;

(ii) Three hours of nighttime flight training in a helicopter that includes one cross country flight of more than 50 nautical miles total distance, and 10 takeoffs and 10 landings to a full stop (with each landing involving a flight in the traffic pattern) at an airport; and

(iii) Three hours of flight training in a helicopter within 2 calendar months before the date of the practical test.

(3) For the commercial pilot certificate, the course requires 5 hours flight training on the areas of operations under appendix D of part 141, paragraph 4.(d)(3). Use of a flight simulator and flight training device in the approved training course cannot exceed 1 hour; however, use of the flight training device cannot exceed 0.7 of the one hour. The course must include—

(i) Five hours on the control and maneuvering of a helicopter solely by reference to instruments, and must include training using a view-limiting device for attitude instrument flying, partial panel skills, recovery from unusual flight attitudes, and intercepting and tracking navigational systems. This aeronautical experience may be performed in an aircraft, flight simulator, flight training device, or an aviation training device;

(ii) One 2-hour cross country flight during daytime conditions in a helicopter and, a total straight-line distance of more than 50 nautical miles from the original point of departure;

(iii) One 2-hour cross country flight during nighttime conditions in a helicopter and a total straight-line distance of more than 50 nautical miles from the original point of departure; and

(iv) Three hours of flight training in a helicopter within 2 calendar months before the date of the practical test.

(4) For the airline transport pilot certificate, the course requires 25 hours of flight training in a helicopter on the areas of operation under appendix E of part 141, paragraph 4.(c) that includes 15 hours of instrument training. A flight simulator and flight training device cannot be used more than 12.5 hours to meet the training requirements, and use of the flight training device is limited to 6.25 hours of the 12.5 hours permitted.

(m) Course for a rotorcraft additional gyroplane class rating.

(1) For the recreational pilot certificate, the course requires 3 hours flight training on the areas of operations of appendix A to part 141, paragraph 4.(c)(3) that includes—

(i) Except as provided under § 61.100 of this chapter, 2 hours of flight training to and at an airport that is located more than 25 nautical miles from the airport where the applicant normally trains, with three takeoffs and three landings; and

(ii) Within 2 calendar months before the date of the practical test, 3 hours of flight training in a gyroplane.

(2) For the private pilot certificate, the course requires 3 hours flight training on the areas of operations of appendix B to part 141, paragraph 4.(d)(4). A flight simulator and flight training device cannot be used more than 0.6 hours to meet the training requirements, and use of the flight training device is limited to 0.4 hours of the 0.6 hours permitted. The course must include—

(i) Three hours of cross country training in a gyroplane;

(ii) Three hours of nighttime flight training in a gyroplane that includes one cross country flight of more than 50 nautical miles total distance, and 10 takeoffs and 10 landings to a full stop (with each landing involving a flight in the traffic pattern) at an airport; and

(iii) Three hours of flight training in a gyroplane within 2 calendar months before the date of the practical test.

(3) For the commercial pilot certificate, the course requires 5 hours flight training on the areas of operations of appendix D to part 141, paragraph 4.(d)(4). A flight simulator and flight training device cannot be used more than 1 hour to meet the training requirements, and use of the flight training device is limited to 0.7 hours of the 1 hour permitted. The course must include—

(i) 2.5 hours on the control and maneuvering of a gyroplane solely by reference to instruments, and must include training using a view-limiting device for attitude instrument flying, partial panel skills, recovery from unusual flight attitudes, and intercepting and tracking navigational systems. This aeronautical experience may be performed in an aircraft, flight simulator, flight training device, or an aviation training device.

(ii) Three hours of cross country flight training in a gyroplane, except as provided under § 61.111 of this chapter;

(iii) Two hours of flight training during nighttime conditions in a gyroplane at an airport that includes 10 takeoffs and 10 landings to a full stop (with each landing involving a flight in the traffic pattern); and

(iv) Three hours of flight training in a gyroplane within 2 calendar months before the date of the practical test.

(n) Course for a lighter-than-air additional airship class rating.

(1) For the private pilot certificate, the course requires 20 hours of flight training on the areas of operation under appendix B of part 141, paragraph 4.(d)(7). A flight simu-

lator and flight training device cannot be used more than 4 hours to meet the training requirements, and use of the flight training device is limited to 3 hours of the 4 hours permitted. The course must include—

(i) Three hours of cross country training in an airship, except as provided under § 61.111 of this chapter;

(ii) Three hours of nighttime flight training in an airship that includes one cross country flight of more than 25 nautical miles total distance, and 5 takeoffs and 5 landings to a full stop (with each landing involving a flight in the traffic pattern) at an airport;

(iii) Three hours of flight training in an airship on the control and maneuvering of an airship solely by reference to instruments, including straight and level flight, constant airspeed climbs and descents, turns to a heading, recovery from unusual flight attitudes, radio communications, and the use of navigation systems/facilities and radar services appropriate to instrument flight; and

(iv) Three hours of flight training in an airship within 2 calendar months before the date of the practical test.

(2) For the commercial pilot certificate, the course requires 55 hours of flight training on the areas of operation under appendix D of part 141, paragraph 4.(d)(7). A flight simulator and flight training device cannot be used more than 16.5 hours to meet the training requirements, and use of the flight training device is limited to 11 hours of the 16.5 hours permitted. The course must include—

(i) Three hours of instrument training in an airship that must include training using a view-limiting device for attitude instrument flying, partial panel skills, recovery from unusual flight attitudes, and intercepting and tracking navigational systems;

(ii) One hour cross country flight during daytime conditions in an airship that consists of a total straight-line distance of more than 25 nautical miles from the original point of departure;

(iii) One hour cross country flight during nighttime conditions in an airship that consists of a total straight-line distance of more than 25 nautical miles from the original point of departure; and

(iv) Three hours of flight training in an airship within 2 calendar months before the date of the practical test.

(o) Course for a lighter-than-air additional gas balloon class rating.

(1) For the private pilot certificate, the course requires eight hours of flight training that includes 5 training flights on the areas of operations under appendix B of part 141, paragraph 4.(d)(8). A flight simulator and flight training device cannot be used more than 1.6 hours to meet the training requirements, and use of the flight training device is limited to 1.2 hours of the 1.6 hours permitted. The course must include—

(i) Two flights of 1 hour each;

(ii) One flight involving a controlled ascent to 3,000 feet above the launch site; and

(iii) Two flights within 2 calendar months before the date of the practical test.

(2) For the commercial pilot certificate, the course requires 10 hours of flight training that includes eight training flights on the areas of operations of appendix D to part 141, paragraph 4.(d)(8). A flight simulator and flight training device cannot be used more than 3 hours to meet the training requirements, and use of the flight training device is limited to 2 hours of the 3 hours permitted. The course must include—

(i) Two flights of 1 hour each;

(ii) One flight involving a controlled ascent to 5,000 feet above the launch site; and

(iii) Two flights within 2 calendar months before the date of the practical test.

(p) Course for a lighter-than-air additional hot air balloon class rating.

(1) For the private pilot certificate, the course requires 8 hours of flight training that includes 5 training flights on the areas of operations of appendix B to part 141, paragraph 4.(d)(8). A flight simulator and flight training device cannot be used more than 1.6 hours to meet the training requirements, and use of the flight training device is limited to 1.2 hours of the 1.6 hours permitted. The course must include—

(i) Two flights of 30 minutes each;

(ii) One flight involving a controlled ascent to 2,000 feet above the launch site; and

(iii) Two flights within 2 calendar months before the date of the practical test.

(2) For the commercial pilot certificate, the course requires 10 hours of flight training that includes eight training flight on the areas of operation of appendix D to part 141, paragraph 4.(d)(8). A flight simulator and flight training device cannot be used more than 3 hours to meet the training requirements, and use of the flight training device is limited to 2 hours of the 3 hours permitted. The course must include—

(i) Two flights of 30 minutes each.

(ii) One flight involving a controlled ascent to 3,000 feet above the launch site; and

(iii) Two flights within 2 calendar months before the date of the practical test.

5. *Stage checks and end-of-course tests.* (a) Each student enrolled in an additional aircraft category rating course or an additional aircraft class rating course must satisfactorily accomplish the stage checks and end-of-course tests, in accordance with the school's approved training course, consisting of the approved areas of operation in section No. 4 of this appendix that are appropriate to the aircraft category and class rating for which the course applies at the appropriate pilot certificate level.

(b) Each student must demonstrate satisfactory proficiency prior to receiving an endorsement to operate an aircraft in solo flight.

[Doc. No. 25910, 62 FR 16347, Apr. 4, 1997; Amdt. 141–9, 62 FR 40909, July 30, 1997; Amdt. 141–12, 74 FR 42566, Aug. 21, 2009; Doc. No. FAA–2016–6142, Amdt. 141–20, 83 FR 30284, June 27, 2018]

APPENDIX J TO PART 141—AIRCRAFT TYPE RATING COURSE, FOR OTHER THAN AN AIRLINE TRANSPORT PILOT CERTIFICATE

1. *Applicability.* This appendix prescribes the minimum curriculum for an aircraft type rating course other than an airline transport pilot certificate, for:

(a) A type rating in an airplane category—single-engine class.

(b) A type rating in an airplane category—multiengine class.

(c) A type rating in a rotorcraft category—helicopter class.

(d) A type rating in a powered-lift category.

(e) Other aircraft type ratings specified by the Administrator through the aircraft type certificate procedures.

2. *Eligibility for enrollment.* Prior to enrolling in the flight portion of an aircraft type rating course, a person must hold at least a private pilot certificate and:

(a) An instrument rating in the category and class of aircraft that is appropriate to the aircraft type rating for which the course applies, provided the aircraft's type certificate does not have a VFR limitation; or

(b) Be concurrently enrolled in an instrument rating course in the category and class of aircraft that is appropriate to the aircraft type rating for which the course applies, and pass the required instrument rating practical test concurrently with the aircraft type rating practical test.

3. *Aeronautical knowledge training.* (a) Each approved course must include at least 10 hours of ground training on the aeronautical knowledge areas listed in paragraph (b) of this section, appropriate to the aircraft type rating for which the course applies.

(b) Ground training must include the following aeronautical areas:

(1) Proper control of airspeed, configuration, direction, altitude, and attitude in accordance with procedures and limitations contained in the aircraft's flight manual, checklists, or other approved material appropriate to the aircraft type;

(2) Compliance with approved en route, instrument approach, missed approach, ATC, or other applicable procedures that apply to the aircraft type;

(3) Subjects requiring a practical knowledge of the aircraft type and its powerplant, systems, components, operational, and performance factors;

(4) The aircraft's normal, abnormal, and emergency procedures, and the operations and limitations relating thereto;

(5) Appropriate provisions of the approved aircraft's flight manual;

(6) Location of and purpose for inspecting each item on the aircraft's checklist that relates to the exterior and interior preflight; and

(7) Use of the aircraft's prestart checklist, appropriate control system checks, starting procedures, radio and electronic equipment checks, and the selection of proper navigation and communication radio facilities and frequencies.

4. *Flight training.* (a) Each approved course must include at least:

(1) Flight training on the approved areas of operation of paragraph (c) of this section in the aircraft type for which the course applies; and

(2) 10 hours of training of which at least 5 hours must be instrument training in the aircraft for which the course applies.

(b) For the use of full flight simulators or flight training devices:

(1) The course may include training in a full flight simulator or flight training device, provided it is representative of the aircraft for which the course is approved, meets requirements of this paragraph, and the training is given by an authorized instructor.

(2) Training in a full flight simulator that meets the requirements of § 141.41(a), may be credited for a maximum of 50 percent of the total flight training hour requirements of the approved course, or of this section, whichever is less.

(3) Training in a flight training device that meets the requirements of § 141.41(a), may be credited for a maximum of 25 percent of the total flight training hour requirements of the approved course, or of this section, whichever is less.

(4) Training in the full flight simulators or flight training devices described in paragraphs (b)(2) and (3) of this section, if used in combination, may be credited for a maximum of 50 percent of the total flight training hour requirements of the approved course, or of this section, whichever is less. However, credit training in a flight training device that meets the requirements of § 141.41(a) cannot exceed the limitation provided for in paragraph (b)(3) of this section.

(c) Each approved course must include the flight training on the areas of operation listed in this paragraph, that are appropriate to the aircraft category and class rating for which the course applies:

(1) *A type rating for an airplane—single-engine course:* (i) Preflight preparation;

(ii) Preflight procedures;

(iii) Takeoff and departure phase;

(iv) In-flight maneuvers;

(v) Instrument procedures;

(vi) Landings and approaches to landings;

(vii) Normal and abnormal procedures;

(viii) Emergency procedures; and

(ix) Postflight procedures.

(2) *A type rating for an airplane—multiengine course:* (i) Preflight preparation;

(ii) Preflight procedures;

(iii) Takeoff and departure phase;

(iv) In-flight maneuvers;

(v) Instrument procedures;

(vi) Landings and approaches to landings;

(vii) Normal and abnormal procedures;

(viii) Emergency procedures; and

(ix) Postflight procedures.

(3) *A type rating for a powered-lift course:* (i) Preflight preparation;

(ii) Preflight procedures;

(iii) Takeoff and departure phase;

(iv) In-flight maneuvers;

(v) Instrument procedures;

(vi) Landings and approaches to landings;

(vii) Normal and abnormal procedures;

(viii) Emergency procedures; and

(ix) Postflight procedures.

(4) *A type rating for a rotorcraft—helicopter course:* (i) Preflight preparation;

(ii) Preflight procedures;

(iii) Takeoff and departure phase;

(iv) In-flight maneuvers;

(v) Instrument procedures;

(vi) Landings and approaches to landings;

(vii) Normal and abnormal procedures;

(viii) Emergency procedures; and

(ix) Postflight procedures.

(5) *Other aircraft type ratings specified by the Administrator through aircraft type certificate procedures:* (i) Preflight preparation;

(ii) Preflight procedures;

(iii) Takeoff and departure phase;

(iv) In-flight maneuvers;

(v) Instrument procedures;

(vi) Landings and approaches to landings;

(vii) Normal and abnormal procedures;

(viii) Emergency procedures; and

(ix) Postflight procedures.

5. *Stage checks and end-of-course tests.* (a) Each student enrolled in an aircraft type rating course must satisfactorily accomplish the stage checks and end-of-course tests, in accordance with the school's approved training course, consisting of the approved areas of operation that are appropriate to the aircraft type rating for which the course applies at the airline transport pilot certificate level; and

(b) Each student must demonstrate satisfactory proficiency prior to receiving an endorsement to operate an aircraft in solo flight.

[Doc. No. 25910, 62 FR 16347, Apr. 4, 1997; Amdt. 141–9, 62 FR 40910, July 30, 1997, as amended by Docket FAA–2015–1846, Amdt. 141–18, 81 FR 21461, Apr. 12, 2016]

APPENDIX K TO PART 141—SPECIAL
PREPARATION COURSES

1. *Applicability.* This appendix prescribes
the minimum curriculum for the special
preparation courses that are listed in §141.11
of this part.

2. *Eligibility for enrollment.* Prior to enrolling in the flight portion of a special preparation course, a person must hold a pilot certificate, flight instructor certificate, or
ground instructor certificate that is appropriate for the exercise of the operating privileges or authorizations sought.

3. *General requirements.* (a) To be approved,
a special preparation course must:

(1) Meet the appropriate requirements of
this appendix; and

(2) Prepare the graduate with the necessary skills, competency, and proficiency to
exercise safely the privileges of the certificate, rating, or authorization for which the
course is established.

(b) An approved special preparation course
must include ground and flight training on
the operating privileges or authorization
sought, for developing competency, proficiency, resourcefulness, self-confidence,
and self-reliance in the student.

4. *Use of full flight simulators or flight training devices.* (a) The approved special preparation course may include training in a full
flight simulator or flight training device,
provided it is representative of the aircraft
for which the course is approved, meets requirements of this paragraph, and the training is given by an authorized instructor.

(b) Except for the airline transport pilot
certification program in section 13 of this appendix, training in a full flight simulator
that meets the requirements of §141.41(a),
may be credited for a maximum of 10 percent
of the total flight training hour requirements of the approved course, or of this section, whichever is less.

(c) Except for the airline transport pilot
certification program in section 13 of this appendix, training in a flight training device
that meets the requirements of §141.41(a),
may be credited for a maximum of 5 percent
of the total flight training hour requirements of the approved course, or of this section, whichever is less.

(d) Training in the full flight simulators or
flight training devices described in paragraphs (b) and (c) of this section, if used in
combination, may be credited for a maximum of 10 percent of the total flight training hour requirements of the approved
course, or of this section, whichever is less.
However, credit for training in a flight training device that meets the requirements of
§141.41(a) cannot exceed the limitation provided for in paragraph (c) of this section.

5. *Stage check and end-of-course tests.* Each
person enrolled in a special preparation
course must satisfactorily accomplish the

stage checks and end-of-course tests, in accordance with the school's approved training
course, consisting of the approved areas of
operation that are appropriate to the operating privileges or authorization sought, and
for which the course applies.

6. *Agricultural aircraft operations course.* An
approved special preparation course for pilots in agricultural aircraft operations must
include at least the following—

(a) 25 hours of training on:

(1) Agricultural aircraft operations;

(2) Safe piloting and operating practices
and procedures for handling, dispensing, and
disposing agricultural and industrial chemicals, including operating in and around congested areas; and

(3) Applicable provisions of part 137 of this
chapter.

(b) 15 hours of flight training on agricultural aircraft operations.

7. *Rotorcraft external-load operations course.*
An approved special preparation course for
pilots of external-load operations must include at least the following—

(a) 10 hours of training on:

(1) Rotorcraft external-load operations;

(2) Safe piloting and operating practices
and procedures for external-load operations,
including operating in and around congested
areas; and

(3) Applicable provisions of part 133 of this
chapter.

(b) 15 hours of flight training on external-
load operations.

8. *Test pilot course.* An approved special
preparation course for pilots in test pilot duties must include at least the following—

(a) Aeronautical knowledge training on:

(1) Performing aircraft maintenance, quality assurance, and certification test flight
operations;

(2) Safe piloting and operating practices
and procedures for performing aircraft maintenance, quality assurance, and certification
test flight operations;

(3) Applicable parts of this chapter that
pertain to aircraft maintenance, quality assurance, and certification tests; and

(4) Test pilot duties and responsibilities.

(b) 15 hours of flight training on test pilot
duties and responsibilities.

9. *Special operations course.* An approved
special preparation course for pilots in special operations that are mission-specific for
certain aircraft must include at least the following—

(a) Aeronautical knowledge training on:

(1) Performing that special flight operation;

(2) Safe piloting operating practices and
procedures for performing that special flight
operation;

(3) Applicable parts of this chapter that
pertain to that special flight operation; and

(4) Pilot in command duties and responsibilities for performing that special flight operation.

(b) Flight training:

(1) On that special flight operation; and

(2) To develop skills, competency, proficiency, resourcefulness, self-confidence, and self-reliance in the student for performing that special flight operation in a safe manner.

10. *Pilot refresher course.* An approved special preparation pilot refresher course for a pilot certificate, aircraft category and class rating, or an instrument rating must include at least the following—

(a) 4 hours of aeronautical knowledge training on:

(1) The aeronautical knowledge areas that are applicable to the level of pilot certificate, aircraft category and class rating, or instrument rating, as appropriate, that pertain to that course;

(2) Safe piloting operating practices and procedures; and

(3) Applicable provisions of parts 61 and 91 of this chapter for pilots.

(b) 6 hours of flight training on the approved areas of operation that are applicable to the level of pilot certificate, aircraft category and class rating, or instrument rating, as appropriate, for performing pilot-in-command duties and responsibilities.

11. *Flight instructor refresher course.* An approved special preparation flight instructor refresher course must include at least a combined total of 16 hours of aeronautical knowledge training, flight training, or any combination of ground and flight training on the following—

(a) Aeronautical knowledge training on:

(1) The aeronautical knowledge areas of part 61 of this chapter that apply to student, recreational, private, and commercial pilot certificates and instrument ratings;

(2) The aeronautical knowledge areas of part 61 of this chapter that apply to flight instructor certificates;

(3) Safe piloting operating practices and procedures, including airport operations and operating in the National Airspace System; and

(4) Applicable provisions of parts 61 and 91 of this chapter that apply to pilots and flight instructors.

(b) Flight training to review:

(1) The approved areas of operations applicable to student, recreational, private, and commercial pilot certificates and instrument ratings; and

(2) The skills, competency, and proficiency for performing flight instructor duties and responsibilities.

12. *Ground instructor refresher course.* An approved special preparation ground instructor refresher course must include at least 16 hours of aeronautical knowledge training on:

(a) The aeronautical knowledge areas of part 61 of this chapter that apply to student, recreational, private, and commercial pilots and instrument rated pilots;

(b) The aeronautical knowledge areas of part 61 of this chapter that apply to ground instructors;

(c) Safe piloting operating practices and procedures, including airport operations and operating in the National Airspace System; and

(d) Applicable provisions of parts 61 and 91 of this chapter that apply to pilots and ground instructors.

13. Airline transport pilot certification training program. An approved airline transport pilot certification training program must include the academic and FSTD training set forth in §61.156 of this chapter. The FAA will not approve a course with fewer hours than those prescribed in §61.156 of this chapter.

[Doc. No. 25910, 62 FR 16347, Apr. 4, 1997; Amdt. 141–9, 62 FR 40910, July 30, 1997, as amended by Amdt. 141–17, 78 FR 42380, July 15, 2013; Amdt. 141–17A, 78 FR 53026, Aug. 28, 2013; Docket FAA–2015–1846, Amdt. 141–18, 81 FR 21462, Apr. 12, 2016]

APPENDIX L TO PART 141—PILOT
GROUND SCHOOL COURSE

1. *Applicability.* This appendix prescribes the minimum curriculum for a pilot ground school course required under this part.

2. *General requirements.* An approved course of training for a pilot ground school must include training on the aeronautical knowledge areas that are:

(a) Needed to safely exercise the privileges of the certificate, rating, or authority for which the course is established; and

(b) Conducted to develop competency, proficiency, resourcefulness, self-confidence, and self-reliance in each student.

3. *Aeronautical knowledge training requirements.* Each approved pilot ground school course must include:

(a) The aeronautical knowledge training that is appropriate to the aircraft rating and pilot certificate level for which the course applies; and

(b) An adequate number of total aeronautical knowledge training hours appropriate to the aircraft rating and pilot certificate level for which the course applies.

4. *Stage checks and end-of-course tests.* Each person enrolled in a pilot ground school course must satisfactorily accomplish the stage checks and end-of-course tests, in accordance with the school's approved training course, consisting of the approved areas of operation that are appropriate to the operating privileges or authorization that graduation from the course will permit and for which the course applies.

APPENDIX M TO PART 141—COMBINED PRIVATE PILOT CERTIFICATION AND INSTRUMENT RATING COURSE

1. *Applicability.* This appendix prescribes the minimum curriculum for a combined private pilot certification and instrument rating course required under this part, for the following ratings:

(a) Airplane.

(1) Airplane single-engine.

(2) Airplane multiengine.

(b) Rotorcraft helicopter.

(c) Powered-lift.

2. *Eligibility for enrollment.* A person must hold a sport pilot, recreational, or student pilot certificate prior to enrolling in the flight portion of a combined private pilot certification and instrument rating course.

3. *Aeronautical knowledge training.*

(a) Each approved course must include at least 65 hours of ground training on the aeronautical knowledge areas listed in paragraph (b) of this section that are appropriate to the aircraft category and class rating of the course:

(b) Ground training must include the following aeronautical knowledge areas:

(1) Applicable Federal Aviation Regulations for private pilot privileges, limitations, flight operations, and instrument flight rules (IFR) flight operations.

(2) Accident reporting requirements of the National Transportation Safety Board.

(3) Applicable subjects of the "Aeronautical Information Manual" and the appropriate FAA advisory circulars.

(4) Aeronautical charts for visual flight rules (VFR) navigation using pilotage, dead reckoning, and navigation systems.

(5) Radio communication procedures.

(6) Recognition of critical weather situations from the ground and in flight, windshear avoidance, and the procurement and use of aeronautical weather reports and forecasts.

(7) Safe and efficient operation of aircraft under instrument flight rules and conditions.

(8) Collision avoidance and recognition and avoidance of wake turbulence.

(9) Effects of density altitude on takeoff and climb performance.

(10) Weight and balance computations.

(11) Principles of aerodynamics, powerplants, and aircraft systems.

(12) If the course of training is for an airplane category, stall awareness, spin entry, spins, and spin recovery techniques.

(13) Air traffic control system and procedures for instrument flight operations.

(14) IFR navigation and approaches by use of navigation systems.

(15) Use of IFR en route and instrument approach procedure charts.

(16) Aeronautical decision making and judgment.

(17) Preflight action that includes—

(i) How to obtain information on runway lengths at airports of intended use, data on takeoff and landing distances, weather reports and forecasts, and fuel requirements.

(ii) How to plan for alternatives if the planned flight cannot be completed or delays are encountered.

(iii) Procurement and use of aviation weather reports and forecasts, and the elements of forecasting weather trends on the basis of that information and personal observation of weather conditions.

4. *Flight training.*

(a) Each approved course must include at least 70 hours of training, as described in section 4 and section 5 of this appendix, on the approved areas of operation listed in paragraph (d) of section 4 of this appendix that are appropriate to the aircraft category and class rating of the course:

(b) Each approved course must include at least the following flight training:

(1) *For an airplane single engine course:* 70 hours of flight training from an authorized instructor on the approved areas of operation in paragraph (d)(1) of this section that includes at least—

(i) Except as provided in §61.111 of this chapter, 3 hours of cross-country flight training in a single engine airplane.

(ii) 3 hours of night flight training in a single-engine airplane that includes—

(A) One cross-country flight of more than 100 nautical miles total distance.

(B) 10 takeoffs and 10 landings to a full stop (with each landing involving a flight in the traffic pattern) at an airport.

(iii) 35 hours of instrument flight training in a single-engine airplane that includes at least one cross-country flight that is performed under IFR and—

(A) Is a distance of at least 250 nautical miles along airways or air traffic control-directed (ATC-directed) routing with one segment of the flight consisting of at least a straight-line distance of 100 nautical miles between airports.

(B) Involves an instrument approach at each airport.

(C) Involves three different kinds of approaches with the use of navigation systems.

(iv) 3 hours of flight training in a single-engine airplane in preparation for the practical test within 60 days preceding the date of the test.

(2) *For an airplane multiengine course:* 70 hours of training from an authorized instructor on the approved areas of operation in paragraph (d)(2) of this section that includes at least—

(i) Except as provided in §61.111 of this chapter, 3 hours of cross-country flight training in a multiengine airplane.

(ii) 3 hours of night flight training in a multiengine airplane that includes—

(A) One cross-country flight of more than 100 nautical miles total distance.

(B) 10 takeoffs and 10 landings to a full stop (with each landing involving a flight in the traffic pattern) at an airport.

(iii) 35 hours of instrument flight training in a multiengine airplane that includes at least one cross-country flight that is performed under IFR and—

(A) Is a distance of at least 250 nautical miles along airways or ATC-directed routing with one segment of the flight consisting of at least a straight-line distance of 100 nautical miles between airports.

(B) Involves an instrument approach at each airport.

(C) Involves three different kinds of approaches with the use of navigation systems.

(iv) 3 hours of flight training in a multiengine airplane in preparation for the practical test within 60 days preceding the date of the test.

(3) *For a rotorcraft helicopter course:* 70 hours of training from an authorized instructor on the approved areas of operation in paragraph (d)(3) of this section that includes at least—

(i) Except as provided in §61.111 of this chapter, 3 hours of cross-country flight training in a helicopter.

(ii) 3 hours of night flight training in a helicopter that includes—

(A) One cross-country flight of more than 50 nautical miles total distance.

(B) 10 takeoffs and 10 landings to a full stop (with each landing involving a flight in the traffic pattern) at an airport.

(iii) 35 hours of instrument flight training in a helicopter that includes at least one cross-country flight that is performed under IFR and—

(A) Is a distance of at least 100 nautical miles along airways or ATC-directed routing with one segment of the flight consisting of at least a straight-line distance of 50 nautical miles between airports.

(B) Involves an instrument approach at each airport.

(C) Involves three different kinds of approaches with the use of navigation systems.

(iv) 3 hours of flight training in a helicopter in preparation for the practical test within 60 days preceding the date of the test.

(4) *For a powered-lift course:* 70 hours of training from an authorized instructor on the approved areas of operation in paragraph (d)(4) of this section that includes at least—

(i) Except as provided in §61.111 of this chapter, 3 hours of cross-country flight training in a powered-lift.

(ii) 3 hours of night flight training in a powered-lift that includes—

(A) One cross-country flight of more than 100 nautical miles total distance.

(B) 10 takeoffs and 10 landings to a full stop (with each landing involving a flight in the traffic pattern) at an airport.

(iii) 35 hours of instrument flight training in a powered-lift that includes at least one cross-country flight that is performed under IFR and—

(A) Is a distance of at least 250 nautical miles along airways or ATC-directed routing with one segment of the flight consisting of at least a straight-line distance of 100 nautical miles between airports.

(B) Involves an instrument approach at each airport.

(C) Involves three different kinds of approaches with the use of navigation systems.

(iv) 3 hours of flight training in a powered-lift in preparation for the practical test, within 60 days preceding the date of the test.

(c) For use of full flight simulators or flight training devices:

(1) The course may include training in a combination of full flight simulators, flight training devices, and aviation training devices, provided it is representative of the aircraft for which the course is approved, meets the requirements of this section, and the training is given by an authorized instructor.

(2) Training in a full flight simulator that meets the requirements of §141.41(a) may be credited for a maximum of 35 percent of the total flight training hour requirements of the approved course, or of this section, whichever is less.

(3) Training in a flight training device that meets the requirements of §141.41(a) or an aviation training device that meets the requirements of §141.41(b) may be credited for a maximum of 25 percent of the total flight training hour requirements of the approved course, or of this section, whichever is less.

(4) Training in a combination of flight simulators, flight training devices, or aviation training devices, described in paragraphs (c)(2) and (3) of this section, may be credited for a maximum of 35 percent of the total flight training hour requirements of the approved course, or of this section, whichever is less. However, credit for training in a flight training device and aviation training device, that meets the requirements of §141.41(b), cannot exceed the limitation provided for in paragraph (c)(3) of this section.

(d) Each approved course must include the flight training on the approved areas of operation listed in this section that are appropriate to the aircraft category and class rating course—

(1) *For a combined private pilot certification and instrument rating course involving a single-engine airplane:*

(i) Preflight preparation.

(ii) Preflight procedures.

(iii) Airport and seaplane base operations.

(iv) Takeoffs, landings, and go-arounds.

(v) Performance maneuvers.

(vi) Ground reference maneuvers.

(vii) Navigation and navigation systems.

(viii) Slow flight and stalls.

(ix) Basic instrument maneuvers and flight by reference to instruments.

(x) Instrument approach procedures.

(xi) Air traffic control clearances and procedures.

(xii) Emergency operations.

(xiii) Night operations.

(xiv) Postflight procedures.

(2) *For a combined private pilot certification and instrument rating course involving a multiengine airplane:*

(i) Preflight preparation.

(ii) Preflight procedures.

(iii) Airport and seaplane base operations.

(iv) Takeoffs, landings, and go-arounds.

(v) Performance maneuvers.

(vi) Ground reference maneuvers.

(vii) Navigation and navigation systems.

(viii) Slow flight and stalls.

(ix) Basic instrument maneuvers and flight by reference to instruments.

(x) Instrument approach procedures.

(xi) Air traffic control clearances and procedures.

(xii) Emergency operations.

(xiii) Multiengine operations.

(xiv) Night operations.

(xv) Postflight procedures.

(3) *For a combined private pilot certification and instrument rating course involving a rotorcraft helicopter:*

(i) Preflight preparation.

(ii) Preflight procedures.

(iii) Airport and heliport operations.

(iv) Hovering maneuvers.

(v) Takeoffs, landings, and go-arounds.

(vi) Performance maneuvers.

(vii) Navigation and navigation systems.

(viii) Basic instrument maneuvers and flight by reference to instruments.

(ix) Instrument approach procedures.

(x) Air traffic control clearances and procedures.

(xi) Emergency operations.

(xii) Night operations.

(xiii) Postflight procedures.

(4) *For a combined private pilot certification and instrument rating course involving a powered-lift:*

(i) Preflight preparation.

(ii) Preflight procedures.

(iii) Airport and heliport operations.

(iv) Hovering maneuvers.

(v) Takeoffs, landings, and go-arounds.

(vi) Performance maneuvers

(vii) Ground reference maneuvers.

(viii) Navigation and navigation systems.

(ix) Slow flight and stalls.

(x) Basic instrument maneuvers and flight by reference to instruments.

(xi) Instrument approach procedures.

(xii) Air traffic control clearances and procedures.

(xiii) Emergency operations.

(xiv) Night operations.

(xv) Postflight procedures.

5. *Solo flight training.* Each approved course must include at least the following solo flight training:

(a) *For a combined private pilot certification and instrument rating course involving an airplane single engine:* Five hours of flying solo in a single-engine airplane on the appropriate areas of operation in paragraph (d)(1) of section 4 of this appendix that includes at least—

(1) One solo cross-country flight of at least 100 nautical miles with landings at a minimum of three points, and one segment of the flight consisting of a straight-line distance of at least 50 nautical miles between the takeoff and landing locations.

(2) Three takeoffs and three landings to a full stop (with each landing involving a flight in the traffic pattern) at an airport with an operating control tower.

(b) *For a combined private pilot certification and instrument rating course involving an airplane multiengine:* Five hours of flying solo in a multiengine airplane or 5 hours of performing the duties of a pilot in command while under the supervision of an authorized instructor. The training must consist of the appropriate areas of operation in paragraph (d)(2) of section 4 of this appendix, and include at least—

(1) One cross-country flight of at least 100 nautical miles with landings at a minimum of three points, and one segment of the flight consisting of a straight-line distance of at least 50 nautical miles between the takeoff and landing locations.

(2) Three takeoffs and three landings to a full stop (with each landing involving a flight in the traffic pattern) at an airport with an operating control tower.

(c) *For a combined private pilot certification and instrument rating course involving a helicopter:* Five hours of flying solo in a helicopter on the appropriate areas of operation in paragraph (d)(3) of section 4 of this appendix that includes at least—

(1) One solo cross-country flight of more than 50 nautical miles with landings at a minimum of three points, and one segment of the flight consisting of a straight-line distance of at least 25 nautical miles between the takeoff and landing locations.

(2) Three takeoffs and three landings to a full stop (with each landing involving a flight in the traffic pattern) at an airport with an operating control tower.

(d) *For a combined private pilot certification and instrument rating course involving a powered-lift:* Five hours of flying solo in a powered-lift on the appropriate areas of operation in paragraph (d)(4) of section 4 of this appendix that includes at least—

(1) One solo cross-country flight of at least 100 nautical miles with landings at a minimum of three points, and one segment of the flight consisting of a straight-line distance of at least 50 nautical miles between the takeoff and landing locations.

(2) Three takeoffs and three landings to a full stop (with each landing involving a

flight in the traffic pattern) at an airport with an operating control tower.

6. *Stage checks and end-of-course tests.*

(a) Each student enrolled in a private pilot course must satisfactorily accomplish the stage checks and end-of-course tests in accordance with the school's approved training course that consists of the approved areas of operation listed in paragraph (d) of section 4 of this appendix that are appropriate to the aircraft category and class rating for which the course applies.

(b) Each student must demonstrate satisfactory proficiency prior to receiving an endorsement to operate an aircraft in solo flight.

[Doc. No. FAA–2008–0938, 76 FR 54108, Aug. 31, 2011, as amended by Docket FAA–2015–1846, Amdt. 141–18, 81 FR 21462, Apr. 12, 2016]

PART 142—TRAINING CENTERS

Subpart A—General

AUTHORITY: 49 U.S.C. 106(f), 106(g), 40113, 40119, 44101, 44701–44703, 44705, 44707, 44709–44711, 45102–45103, 45301–45302.

SOURCE: Docket No. 26933, 61 FR 34562, July 2, 1996, unless otherwise noted.

Subpart A—General

§142.1 Applicability.

(a) This subpart prescribes the requirements governing the certification and operation of training centers. Except as provided in paragraph (b) of this section, this part provides an alternative means to accomplish training required by parts 61, 63, 65, 91, 121, 125, 135, or 137 of this chapter.

(b) Certification under this part is not required for training that is—

(1) Approved under the provisions of parts 63, 91, 121, 127, 135, or 137 of this chapter;

(2) Approved under subpart Y of part 121 of this chapter, Advanced Qualification Programs, for the authorization holder's own employees;

(3) Conducted under part 61 unless that part requires certification under this part;

(4) Conducted by a part 121 certificate holder for another part 121 certificate holder;

(5) Conducted by a part 135 certificate holder for another part 135 certificate holder; or

(6) Conducted by a part 91 fractional ownership program manager for another part 91 fractional ownership program manager.

(c) Except as provided in paragraph (b) of this section, after August 3 1998, no person may conduct training, testing, or checking in advanced flight training devices or flight simulators without, or in violation of, the certificate and training specifications required by this part.

[Doc. No. 26933, 61 FR 34562, July 2, 1996, as amended by Amdt. 142–4, 66 FR 21067, Apr. 27, 2001; Amdt. 142–5, 68 FR 54588, Sept. 17, 2003; Amdt. 142–9, 78 FR 42380, July 15, 2013]

§ 142.3 Definitions.

As used in this part:

Advanced Flight Training Device as used in this part, means a flight training device as defined in part 61 of this chapter that has a cockpit that accurately replicates a specific make, model, and type aircraft cockpit, and handling characteristics that accurately model the aircraft handling characteristics.

Core Curriculum means a set of courses approved by the Administrator, for use by a training center and its satellite training centers. The core curriculum consists of training which is required for certification. It does not include training for tasks and circumstances unique to a particular user.

Course means—

(1) A program of instruction to obtain pilot certification, qualification, authorization, or currency;

(2) A program of instruction to meet a specified number of requirements of a program for pilot training, certification, qualification, authorization, or currency; or

(3) A curriculum, or curriculum segment, as defined in subpart Y of part 121 of this chapter.

Courseware means instructional material developed for each course or curriculum, including lesson plans, flight event descriptions, computer software programs, audiovisual programs, workbooks, and handouts.

Evaluator means a person employed by a training center certificate holder who performs tests for certification, added ratings, authorizations, and proficiency checks that are authorized by the certificate holder's training specification, and who is authorized by the

Administrator to administer such checks and tests.

Flight training equipment means full flight simulators, as defined in § 1.1 of this chapter, flight training devices, as defined in § 1.1 of this chapter, and aircraft.

Instructor means a person employed by a training center and designated to provide instruction in accordance with subpart C of this part.

Line-Operational Simulation means simulation conducted using operational-oriented flight scenarios that accurately replicate interaction among flightcrew members and between flightcrew members and dispatch facilities, other crewmembers, air traffic control, and ground operations. Line operational simulation simulations are conducted for training and evaluation purposes and include random, abnormal, and emergency occurrences. Line operational simulation specifically includes line-oriented flight training, special purpose operational training, and line operational evaluation.

Specialty Curriculum means a set of courses that is designed to satisfy a requirement of the Federal Aviation Regulations and that is approved by the Administrator for use by a particular training center or satellite training center. The specialty curriculum includes training requirements unique to one or more training center clients.

Training center means an organization governed by the applicable requirements of this part that provides training, testing, and checking under contract or other arrangement to airmen subject to the requirements of this chapter.

Training program consists of courses, courseware, facilities, flight training equipment, and personnel necessary to accomplish a specific training objective. It may include a core curriculum and a specialty curriculum.

Training specifications means a document issued to a training center certificate holder by the Administrator that prescribes that center's training, checking, and testing authorizations and limitations, and specifies training program requirements.

[Doc. No. 26933, 61 FR 34562, July 2, 1996, as amended by Amdt. 142–2, 62 FR 68137, Dec. 30, 1997; Amdt. 142–7, 76 FR 54110, Aug. 31, 2011; Amdt. 142–9, 78 FR 42380, July 15, 2013]

§ 142.5 Certificate and training specifications required.

(a) No person may operate a certificated training center without, or in violation of, a training center certificate and training specifications issued under this part.

(b) An applicant will be issued a training center certificate and training specifications with appropriate limitations if the applicant shows that it has adequate facilities, equipment, personnel, and courseware required by § 142.11 to conduct training approved under § 142.37.

§ 142.7 Duration of a certificate.

(a) Except as provided in paragraph (b) of this section, a training center certificate issued under this part is effective until the certificate is surrendered or until the Administrator suspends, revokes, or terminates it.

(b) Unless sooner surrendered, suspended, or revoked, a certificate issued under this part for a training center located outside the United States expires at the end of the twelfth month after the month in which it is issued or renewed.

(c) If the Administrator suspends, revokes, or terminates a training center certificate, the holder of that certificate shall return the certificate to the Administrator within 5 working days after being notified that the certificate is suspended, revoked, or terminated.

§ 142.9 Deviations or waivers.

(a) The Administrator may issue deviations or waivers from any of the requirements of this part.

(b) A training center applicant requesting a deviation or waiver under this section must provide the Administrator with information acceptable to the Administrator that shows—

(1) Justification for the deviation or waiver; and

(2) That the deviation or waiver will not adversely affect the quality of instruction or evaluation.

§ 142.11 Application for issuance or amendment.

(a) An application for a training center certificate and training specifications shall—

(1) Be made on a form and in a manner prescribed by the Administrator;

(2) Be filed with the responsible Flight Standards office for the area in which the applicant's principal business office is located; and

(3) Be made at least 120 calendar days before the beginning of any proposed training or 60 calendar days before effecting an amendment to any approved training, unless a shorter filing period is approved by the Administrator.

(b) Each application for a training center certificate and training specification shall provide—

(1) A statement showing that the minimum qualification requirements for each management position are met or exceeded;

(2) A statement acknowledging that the applicant shall notify the Administrator within 10 working days of any change made in the assignment of persons in the required management positions;

(3) The proposed training authorizations and training specifications requested by the applicant;

(4) The proposed evaluation authorization;

(5) A description of the flight training equipment that the applicant proposes to use;

(6) A description of the applicant's training facilities, equipment, qualifications of personnel to be used, and proposed evaluation plans;

(7) A training program curriculum, including syllabi, outlines, courseware, procedures, and documentation to support the items required in subpart B of this part, upon request by the Administrator;

(8) A description of a recordkeeping system that will identify and document the details of training, qualification, and certification of students, instructors, and evaluators;

(9) A description of quality control measures proposed; and

(10) A method of demonstrating the applicant's qualification and ability to provide training for a certificate or rating in fewer than the minimum

hours prescribed in part 61 of this chapter if the applicant proposes to do so.

(c) The facilities and equipment described in paragraph (b)(6) of this section shall—

(1) Be available for inspection and evaluation prior to approval; and

(2) Be in place and operational at the location of the proposed training center prior to issuance of a certificate under this part.

(d) An applicant who meets the requirements of this part and is approved by the Administrator is entitled to—

(1) A training center certificate containing all business names included on the application under which the certificate holder may conduct operations and the address of each business office used by the certificate holder; and

(2) Training specifications, issued by the Administrator to the certificate holder, containing—

(i) The type of training authorized, including approved courses;

(ii) The category, class, and type of aircraft that may be used for training, testing, and checking;

(iii) For each flight simulator or flight training device, the make, model, and series of airplane or the set of airplanes being simulated and the qualification level assigned, or the make, model, and series of rotorcraft, or set of rotorcraft being simulated and the qualification level assigned;

(iv) For each flight simulator and flight training device subject to qualification evaluation by the Administrator, the identification number assigned by the FAA;

(v) The name and address of all satellite training centers, and the approved courses offered at each satellite training center;

(vi) Authorized deviations or waivers from this part; and

(vii) Any other items the Administrator may require or allow.

(e) The Administrator may deny, suspend, revoke, or terminate a certificate under this part if the Administrator finds that the applicant or the certificate holder—

(1) Held a training center certificate that was revoked, suspended, or terminated within the previous 5 years; or

(2) Employs or proposes to employ a person who—

(i) Was previously employed in a management or supervisory position by the holder of a training center certificate that was revoked, suspended, or terminated within the previous 5 years;

(ii) Exercised control over any certificate holder whose certificate has been revoked, suspended, or terminated within the last 5 years; and

(iii) Contributed materially to the revocation, suspension, or termination of that certificate and who will be employed in a management or supervisory position, or who will be in control of or have a substantial ownership interest in the training center.

(3) Has provided incomplete, inaccurate, fraudulent, or false information for a training center certificate;

(4) Should not be granted a certificate if the grant would not foster aviation safety.

(f) At any time, the Administrator may amend a training center certificate—

(1) On the Administrator's own initiative, under section 609 of the Federal Aviation Act of 1958 (49 U.S.C. 1429), as amended, and part 13 of this chapter; or

(2) Upon timely application by the certificate holder.

(g) The certificate holder must file an application to amend a training center certificate at least 60 calendar days prior to the applicant's proposed effective amendment date unless a different filing period is approved by the Administrator.

[Doc. No. 26933, 61 FR 34562, July 2, 1996, as amended by Amdt. 142–1, 62 FR 13791, Mar. 21, 1997; Docket FAA–2018–0119, Amdt. 142–10, 83 FR 9176, Mar. 5, 2018]

§ 142.13 Management and personnel requirements.

An applicant for a training center certificate must show that—

(a) For each proposed curriculum, the training center has, and shall maintain, a sufficient number of instructors who are qualified in accordance with subpart C of this part to perform the duties to which they are assigned;

(b) The training center has designated, and shall maintain, a sufficient number of approved evaluators to provide required checks and tests to graduation candidates within 7 calendar days of training completion for any curriculum leading to airman certificates or ratings, or both;

(c) The training center has, and shall maintain, a sufficient number of management personnel who are qualified and competent to perform required duties; and

(d) A management representative, and all personnel who are designated by the training center to conduct direct student training, are able to understand, read, write, and fluently speak the English language.

§ 142.14 Employment of former FAA employees.

(a) Except as specified in paragraph (c) of this section, no holder of a training center certificate may knowingly employ or make a contractual arrangement which permits an individual to act as an agent or representative of the certificate holder in any matter before the Federal Aviation Administration if the individual, in the preceding 2 years—

(1) Served as, or was directly responsible for the oversight of, a Flight Standards Service aviation safety inspector; and

(2) Had direct responsibility to inspect, or oversee the inspection of, the operations of the certificate holder.

(b) For the purpose of this section, an individual shall be considered to be acting as an agent or representative of a certificate holder in a matter before the agency if the individual makes any written or oral communication on behalf of the certificate holder to the agency (or any of its officers or employees) in connection with a particular matter, whether or not involving a specific party and without regard to whether the individual has participated in, or had responsibility for, the particular matter while serving as a Flight Standards Service aviation safety inspector.

(c) The provisions of this section do not prohibit a holder of a training center certificate from knowingly employing or making a contractual arrangement which permits an individual to act as an agent or representative of the certificate holder in any matter before the Federal Aviation Administration if the individual was employed by the

certificate holder before October 21, 2011.

[Doc. No. FAA–2008–1154, 76 FR 52237, Aug. 22, 2011]

§ 142.15 Facilities.

(a) An applicant for, or holder of, a training center certificate shall ensure that—

(1) Each room, training booth, or other space used for instructional purposes is heated, lighted, and ventilated to conform to local building, sanitation, and health codes; and

(2) The facilities used for instruction are not routinely subject to significant distractions caused by flight operations and maintenance operations at the airport.

(b) An applicant for, or holder of, a training center certificate shall establish and maintain a principal business office that is physically located at the address shown on its training center certificate.

(c) The records required to be maintained by this part must be located in facilities adequate for that purpose.

(d) An applicant for, or holder of, a training center certificate must have available exclusively, for adequate periods of time and at a location approved by the Administrator, adequate flight training equipment and courseware, including at least one flight simulator or advanced flight training device.

[Doc. No. 26933, 61 FR 34562, July 2, 1996, as amended by Amdt. 142–3, 63 FR 53537, Oct. 5, 1998]

§ 142.17 Satellite training centers.

(a) The holder of a training center certificate may conduct training in accordance with an approved training program at a satellite training center if—

(1) The facilities, equipment, personnel, and course content of the satellite training center meet the applicable requirements of this part;

(2) The instructors and evaluators at the satellite training center are under the direct supervision of management personnel of the principal training center;

(3) The Administrator is notified in writing that a particular satellite is to begin operations at least 60 days prior

to proposed commencement of operations at the satellite training center; and

(4) The certificate holder's training specifications reflect the name and address of the satellite training center and the approved courses offered at the satellite training center.

(b) The certificate holder's training specifications shall prescribe the operations required and authorized at each satellite training center.

[Doc. No. 26933, 61 FR 34562, July 2, 1996, as amended by Amdt. 142–3, 63 FR 53537, Oct. 5, 1998]

§§142.21–142.25 [Reserved]

§142.27 Display of certificate.

(a) Each holder of a training center certificate must prominently display that certificate in a place accessible to the public in the principal business office of the training center.

(b) A training center certificate and training specifications must be made available for inspection upon request by—

(1) The Administrator;

(2) An authorized representative of the National Transportation Safety Board; or

(3) Any Federal, State, or local law enforcement agency.

§142.29 Inspections.

Each certificate holder must allow the Administrator to inspect training center facilities, equipment, and records at any reasonable time and in any reasonable place in order to determine compliance with or to determine initial or continuing eligibility under 49 U.S.C. 44701, 44707, formerly the Federal Aviation Act of 1958, as amended, and the training center's certificate and training specifications.

§142.31 Advertising limitations.

(a) A certificate holder may not conduct, and may not advertise to conduct, any training, testing, and checking that is not approved by the Administrator if that training is designed to satisfy any requirement of this chapter.

(b) A certificate holder whose certificate has been surrendered, suspended, revoked, or terminated must—

(1) Promptly remove all indications, including signs, wherever located, that the training center was certificated by the Administrator; and

(2) Promptly notify all advertising agents, or advertising media, or both, employed by the certificate holder to cease all advertising indicating that the training center is certificated by the Administrator.

§142.33 Training agreements.

A pilot school certificated under part 141 of this chapter may provide training, testing, and checking for a training center certificated under this part if—

(a) There is a training, testing, and checking agreement between the certificated training center and the pilot school;

(b) The training, testing, and checking provided by the certificated pilot school is approved and conducted in accordance with this part;

(c) The pilot school certificated under part 141 obtains the Administrator's approval for a training course outline that includes the portion of the training, testing, and checking to be conducted under part 141; and

(d) Upon completion of training, testing, and checking conducted under part 141, a copy of each student's training record is forwarded to the part 142 training center and becomes part of the student's permanent training record.

Subpart B—Aircrew Curriculum and Syllabus Requirements

§142.35 Applicability.

This subpart prescribes the curriculum and syllabus requirements for the issuance of a training center certificate and training specifications for training, testing, and checking conducted to meet the requirements of part 61 of this chapter.

§142.37 Approval of flight aircrew training program.

(a) Except as provided in paragraph (b) of this section, each applicant for, or holder of, a training center certificate must apply to the Administrator for training program approval.

(b) A curriculum approved under SFAR 58 of part 121 of this chapter is

629

approved under this part without modifications.

(c) Application for training program approval shall be made in a form and in a manner acceptable to the Administrator.

(d) Each application for training program approval must indicate—

(1) Which courses are part of the core curriculum and which courses are part of the specialty curriculum;

(2) Which requirements of part 61 of this chapter would be satisfied by the curriculum or curriculums; and

(3) Which requirements of part 61 of this chapter would not be satisfied by the curriculum or curriculums.

(e) If, after a certificate holder begins operations under an approved training program, the Administrator finds that the certificate holder is not meeting the provisions of its approved training program, the Administrator may require the certificate holder to make revisions to that training program.

(f) If the Administrator requires a certificate holder to make revisions to an approved training program and the certificate holder does not make those required revisions, within 30 calendar days, the Administrator may suspend, revoke, or terminate the training center certificate under the provisions of § 142.11(e).

§ 142.39 Training program curriculum requirements.

Each training program curriculum submitted to the Administrator for approval must meet the applicable requirements of this part and must contain—

(a) A syllabus for each proposed curriculum;

(b) Minimum aircraft and flight training equipment requirements for each proposed curriculum;

(c) Minimum instructor and evaluator qualifications for each proposed curriculum;

(d) A curriculum for initial training and continuing training of each instructor or evaluator employed to instruct in a proposed curriculum; and

(e) For each curriculum that provides for the issuance of a certificate or rating in fewer than the minimum hours prescribed by part 61 of this chapter—

(1) A means of demonstrating the ability to accomplish such training in the reduced number of hours; and

(2) A means of tracking student performance.

Subpart C—Personnel and Flight Training Equipment Requirements

§ 142.45 Applicability.

This subpart prescribes the personnel and flight training equipment requirements for a certificate holder that is training to meet the requirements of part 61 of this chapter.

§ 142.47 Training center instructor eligibility requirements.

(a) A certificate holder may not employ a person as an instructor in a flight training course that is subject to approval by the Administrator unless that person—

(1) Is at least 18 years of age;

(2) Is able to read, write, and speak and understand in the English language;

(3) If instructing in an aircraft in flight, is qualified in accordance with subpart H of this chapter;

(4) Satisfies the requirements of paragraph (c) of this section; and

(5) Meets at least one of the following requirements—

(i) Except as allowed by paragraph (a)(5)(ii) of this section, meets the aeronautical experience requirements of § 61.129 (a), (b), (c), or (e) of this chapter, as applicable, excluding the required hours of instruction in preparation for the commercial pilot practical test;

(ii) If instructing in flight simulator or flight training device that represents an airplane requiring a type rating or if instructing in a curriculum leading to the issuance of an airline transport pilot certificate or an added rating to an airline transport pilot certificate, meets the aeronautical experience requirements of § 61.159, § 61.161, or § 61.163 of this chapter, as applicable; or

(iii) Is employed as a flight simulator instructor or a flight training device instructor for a training center providing instruction and testing to meet the requirements of part 61 of this chapter on August 1, 1996.

(b) A training center must designate each instructor in writing to instruct in each approved course, prior to that person functioning as an instructor in that course.

(c) Prior to initial designation, each instructor shall:

(1) Complete at least 8 hours of ground training on the following subject matter:

(i) Instruction methods and techniques.

(ii) Training policies and procedures.

(iii) The fundamental principles of the learning process.

(iv) Instructor duties, privileges, responsibilities, and limitations.

(v) Proper operation of simulation controls and systems.

(vi) Proper operation of environmental control and warning or caution panels.

(vii) Limitations of simulation.

(viii) Minimum equipment requirements for each curriculum.

(ix) Revisions to the training courses.

(x) Cockpit resource management and crew coordination.

(2) Satisfactorily complete a written test—

(i) On the subjects specified in paragraph (c)(1) of this section; and

(ii) That is accepted by the Administrator as being of equivalent difficulty, complexity, and scope as the tests provided by the Administrator for the flight instructor airplane and instrument flight instructor knowledge tests.

[Doc. No. 26933, 61 FR 34562, July 2, 1996, as amended by Amdt. 142–2, 62 FR 68137, Dec. 30, 1997]

§ 142.49 Training center instructor and evaluator privileges and limitations.

(a) A certificate holder may allow an instructor to provide:

(1) Instruction for each curriculum for which that instructor is qualified.

(2) Testing and checking for which that instructor is qualified.

(3) Instruction, testing, and checking intended to satisfy the requirements of any part of this chapter.

(b) A training center whose instructor or evaluator is designated in accordance with the requirements of this subpart to conduct training, testing, or checking in qualified and approved flight training equipment, may allow its instructor or evaluator to give endorsements required by part 61 of this chapter if that instructor or evaluator is authorized by the Administrator to instruct or evaluate in a part 142 curriculum that requires such endorsements.

(c) A training center may not allow an instructor to—

(1) Excluding briefings and debriefings, conduct more than 8 hours of instruction in any 24-consecutive-hour period;

(2) Provide flight training equipment instruction unless that instructor meets the requirements of § 142.53 (a)(1) through (a)(4), and § 142.53(b), as applicable; or

(3) Provide flight instruction in an aircraft unless that instructor—

(i) Meets the requirements of § 142.53(a)(1), (a)(2), and (a)(5);

(ii) Is qualified and authorized in accordance with subpart H of part 61 of this chapter;

(iii) Holds certificates and ratings specified by part 61 of this chapter appropriate to the category, class, and type aircraft in which instructing;

(iv) If instructing or evaluating in an aircraft in flight while serving as a required crewmember, holds at least a valid second class medical certificate; and

(v) Meets the recency of experience requirements of part 61 of this chapter.

[Doc. No. 26933, 61 FR 34562, July 2, 1996, as amended by Amdt. 142–2, 62 FR 68137, Dec. 30, 1997; Amdt. 142–9, 78 FR 42380, July 15, 2013]

§ 142.51 [Reserved]

§ 142.53 Training center instructor training and testing requirements.

(a) Except as provided in paragraph (c) of this section, prior to designation and every 12 calendar months beginning the first day of the month following an instructor's initial designation, a certificate holder must ensure that each of its instructors meets the following requirements:

(1) Each instructor must satisfactorily demonstrate to an authorized evaluator knowledge of, and proficiency in, instructing in a representative segment of each curriculum for

which that instructor is designated to instruct under this part.

(2) Each instructor must satisfactorily complete an approved course of ground instruction in at least—

(i) The fundamental principles of the learning process;

(ii) Elements of effective teaching, instruction methods, and techniques;

(iii) Instructor duties, privileges, responsibilities, and limitations;

(iv) Training policies and procedures;

(v) Cockpit resource management and crew coordination; and

(vi) Evaluation.

(3) Each instructor who instructs in a qualified and approved flight simulator or flight training device must satisfactorily complete an approved course of training in the operation of the flight simulator, and an approved course of ground instruction, applicable to the training courses the instructor is designated to instruct.

(4) The flight simulator training course required by paragraph (a)(3) of this section which must include—

(i) Proper operation of flight simulator and flight training device controls and systems;

(ii) Proper operation of environmental and fault panels;

(iii) Limitations of simulation; and

(iv) Minimum equipment requirements for each curriculum.

(5) Each flight instructor who provides training in an aircraft must satisfactorily complete an approved course of ground instruction and flight training in an aircraft, flight simulator, or flight training device.

(6) The approved course of ground instruction and flight training required by paragraph (a)(5) of this section which must include instruction in—

(i) Performance and analysis of flight training procedures and maneuvers applicable to the training courses that the instructor is designated to instruct;

(ii) Technical subjects covering aircraft subsystems and operating rules applicable to the training courses that the instructor is designated to instruct;

(iii) Emergency operations;

(iv) Emergency situations likely to develop during training; and

(v) Appropriate safety measures.

(7) Each instructor who instructs in qualified and approved flight training equipment must pass a written test and annual proficiency check—

(i) In the flight training equipment in which the instructor will be instructing; and

(ii) On the subject matter and maneuvers of a representative segment of each curriculum for which the instructor will be instructing.

(b) In addition to the requirements of paragraphs (a)(1) through (a)(7) of this section, each certificate holder must ensure that each instructor who instructs in a flight simulator that the Administrator has approved for all training and all testing for the airline transport pilot certification test, aircraft type rating test, or both, has met at least one of the following three requirements:

(1) Each instructor must have performed 2 hours in flight, including three takeoffs and three landings as the sole manipulator of the controls of an aircraft of the same category and class, and, if a type rating is required, of the same type replicated by the approved flight simulator in which that instructor is designated to instruct;

(2) Each instructor must have participated in an approved line-observation program under part 121 or part 135 of this chapter, and that—

(i) Was accomplished in the same airplane type as the airplane represented by the flight simulator in which that instructor is designated to instruct; and

(ii) Included line-oriented flight training of at least 1 hour of flight during which the instructor was the sole manipulator of the controls in a flight simulator that replicated the same type aircraft for which that instructor is designated to instruct; or

(3) Each instructor must have participated in an approved in-flight observation training course that—

(i) Consisted of at least 2 hours of flight time in an airplane of the same type as the airplane replicated by the flight simulator in which the instructor is designated to instruct; and

(ii) Included line-oriented flight training of at least 1 hour of flight during which the instructor was the sole manipulator of the controls in a flight simulator that replicated the same type aircraft for which that instructor is designated to instruct

(c) An instructor who satisfactorily completes a curriculum required by paragraph (a) or (b) of this section in the calendar month before or after the month in which it is due is considered to have taken it in the month in which it was due for the purpose of computing when the next training is due.

(d) The Administrator may give credit for the requirements of paragraph (a) or (b) of this section to an instructor who has satisfactorily completed an instructor training course for a part 121 or part 135 certificate holder if the Administrator finds such a course equivalent to the requirements of paragraph (a) or (b) of this section.

[Doc. No. 26933, 61 FR 34562, July 2, 1996, as amended by Amdt. 142–1, 62 FR 13791, Mar. 21, 1997]

§142.54 Airline transport pilot certification training program.

No certificate holder may use a person nor may any person serve as an instructor in a training program approved to meet the requirements of §61.156 of this chapter unless the instructor:

(a) Holds an airline transport pilot certificate with an airplane category multiengine class rating;

(b) Has at least 2 years of experience as a pilot in command in operations conducted under §91.1053(a)(2)(i) or §135.243(a)(1) of this chapter, or as a pilot in command or second in command in any operation conducted under part 121 of this chapter;

(c) Except for the holder of a flight instructor certificate, receives initial training on the following topics:

(1) The fundamental principles of the learning process;

(2) Elements of effective teaching, instruction methods, and techniques;

(3) Instructor duties, privileges, responsibilities, and limitations;

(4) Training policies and procedures; and

(5) Evaluation.

(d) If providing training in a flight simulation training device—

(1) Holds an aircraft type rating for the aircraft represented by the flight simulation training device utilized in

the training program and have received training and evaluation within the preceding 12 months from the certificate holder on the maneuvers that will be demonstrated in the flight simulation training device; and

(2) Satisfies the requirements of §142.53(a)(4).

(e) A certificate holder may not issue a graduation certificate to a student unless that student has completed all the curriculum requirements of the course.

(f) A certificate holder must conduct evaluations to ensure that training techniques, procedures, and standards are acceptable to the Administrator.

[Doc. No. FAA–2010–0100, 78 FR 42380, July 15, 2013]

§142.55 Training center evaluator requirements.

(a) Except as provided by paragraph (d) of this section, a training center must ensure that each person authorized as an evaluator—

(1) Is approved by the Administrator;

(2) Is in compliance with §§142.47, 142.49, and 142.53 and applicable sections of part 183 of this chapter; and

(3) Prior to designation, and except as provided in paragraph (b) of this section, every 12-calendar-month period following initial designation, the certificate holder must ensure that the evaluator satisfactorily completes a curriculum that includes the following:

(i) Evaluator duties, functions, and responsibilities;

(ii) Methods, procedures, and techniques for conducting required tests and checks;

(iii) Evaluation of pilot performance; and

(iv) Management of unsatisfactory tests and subsequent corrective action; and

(4) If evaluating in qualified and approved flight training equipment must satisfactorily pass a written test and annual proficiency check in a flight simulator or aircraft in which the evaluator will be evaluating.

(b) An evaluator who satisfactorily completes a curriculum required by paragraph (a) of this section in the calendar month before or the calendar month after the month in which it is due is considered to have taken it in the month is which it was due for the purpose of computing when the next training is due.

(c) The Administrator may give credit for the requirements of paragraph (a)(3) of this section to an evaluator who has satisfactorily completed an evaluator training course for a part 121 or part 135 certificate holder if the Administrator finds such a course equivalent to the requirements of paragraph (a)(3) of this section.

(d) An evaluator who is qualified under subpart Y of part 121 of this chapter shall be authorized to conduct evaluations under the Advanced Qualification Program without complying with the requirements of this section.

[Doc. No. 26933, 61 FR 34562, July 2, 1996, as amended by Amdt. 142-9, 78 FR 42380, July 15, 2013]

§ 142.57 Aircraft requirements.

(a) An applicant for, or holder of, a training center certificate must ensure that each aircraft used for flight instruction and solo flights meets the following requirements:

(1) Except for flight instruction and solo flights in a curriculum for agricultural aircraft operations, external load operations, and similar aerial work operations, the aircraft must have an FAA standard airworthiness certificate or a foreign equivalent of an FAA standard airworthiness certificate, acceptable to the Administrator.

(2) The aircraft must be maintained and inspected in accordance with—

(i) The requirements of part 91, subpart E, of this chapter; and

(ii) An approved program for maintenance and inspection.

(3) The aircraft must be equipped as provided in the training specifications for the approved course for which it is used.

(b) Except as provided in paragraph (c) of this section, an applicant for, or holder of, a training center certificate must ensure that each aircraft used for flight instruction is at least a two-place aircraft with engine power controls and flight controls that are easily reached and that operate in a conventional manner from both pilot stations.

(c) Airplanes with controls such as nose-wheel steering, switches, fuel selectors, and engine air flow controls that are not easily reached and operated in a conventional manner by both pilots may be used for flight instruction if the certificate holder determines that the flight instruction can be conducted in a safe manner considering the location of controls and their nonconventional operation, or both.

§ 142.59 Flight simulators and flight training devices.

(a) An applicant for, or holder of, a training center certificate must show that each flight simulator and flight training device used for training, testing, and checking (except AQP) will be or is specifically qualified and approved by the Administrator for—

(1) Each maneuver and procedure for the make, model, and series of aircraft, set of aircraft, or aircraft type simulated, as applicable; and

(2) Each curriculum or training course in which the flight simulator or flight training device is used, if that curriculum or course is used to satisfy any requirement of 14 CFR chapter I.

(b) The approval required by paragraph (a)(2) of this section must include—

(1) The set of aircraft, or type aircraft;

(2) If applicable, the particular variation within type, for which the training, testing, or checking is being conducted; and

(3) The particular maneuver, procedure, or crewmember function to be performed.

(c) Each qualified and approved flight simulator or flight training device used by a training center must—

(1) Be maintained to ensure the reliability of the performances, functions, and all other characteristics that were required for qualification;

(2) Be modified to conform with any modification to the aircraft being simulated if the modification results in changes to performance, function, or other characteristics required for qualification;

(3) Be given a functional preflight check each day before being used; and

(4) Have a discrepancy log in which the instructor or evaluator, at the end of each training session, enters each discrepancy.

(d) Unless otherwise authorized by the Administrator, each component on a qualified and approved flight simulator or flight training device used by a training center must be operative if the component is essential to, or involved in, the training, testing, or checking of airmen.

(e) Training centers shall not be restricted to specific—

(1) Route segments during line-oriented flight training scenarios; and

(2) Visual data bases replicating a specific customer's bases of operation.

(f) Training centers may request evaluation, qualification, and continuing evaluation for qualification of flight simulators and flight training devices without—

(1) Holding an air carrier certificate; or

(2) Having a specific relationship to an air carrier certificate holder.

Subpart D—Operating Rules

§ 142.61 Applicability.

This subpart prescribes the operating rules applicable to a training center certificated under this part and operating a course or training program curriculum approved in accordance with subpart B of this part.

§ 142.63 Privileges.

A certificate holder may allow flight simulator instructors and evaluators to meet recency of experience requirements through the use of a qualified and approved flight simulator or qualified and approved flight training device if that flight simulator or flight training device is—

(a) Used in a course approved in accordance with subpart B of this part; or

(b) Approved under the Advanced Qualification Program for meeting recency of experience requirements.

§ 142.65 Limitations.

(a) A certificate holder shall—

(1) Ensure that a flight simulator or flight training device freeze, slow motion, or repositioning feature is not used during testing or checking; and

(2) Ensure that a repositioning feature is used during line operational simulation for evaluation and line-oriented flight training only to advance along a flight route to the point where the descent and approach phase of the flight begins.

(b) When flight testing, flight checking, or line operational simulation is being conducted, the certificate holder must ensure that one of the following occupies each crewmember position:

(1) A crewmember qualified in the aircraft category, class, and type, if a type rating is required, provided that no flight instructor who is giving instruction may occupy a crewmember position.

(2) A student, provided that no student may be used in a crewmember position with any other student not in the same specific course.

(c) The holder of a training center certificate may not recommend a trainee for a certificate or rating, unless the trainee—

(1) Has satisfactorily completed the training specified in the course approved under § 142.37; and

(2) Has passed the final tests required by § 142.37.

(d) The holder of a training center certificate may not graduate a student from a course unless the student has satisfactorily completed the curriculum requirements of that course.

Subpart E—Recordkeeping

§ 142.71 Applicability.

This subpart prescribes the training center recordkeeping requirements for trainees enrolled in a course, and instructors and evaluators designated to instruct a course, approved in accordance with subpart B of this part.

§ 142.73 Recordkeeping requirements.

(a) A certificate holder must maintain a record for each trainee that contains—

(1) The name of the trainee;

(2) A copy of the trainee's pilot certificate, if any, and medical certificate;

(3) The name of the course and the make and model of flight training equipment used;

(4) The trainee's prerequisite experience and course time completed;

(5) The trainee's performance on each lesson and the name of the instructor providing instruction;

(6) The date and result of each end-of-course practical test and the name of the evaluator conducting the test; and

(7) The number of hours of additional training that was accomplished after any unsatisfactory practical test.

(b) A certificate holder shall maintain a record for each instructor or evaluator designated to instruct a course approved in accordance with subpart B of this part that indicates that the instructor or evaluator has complied with the requirements of §§ 142.13, 142.45, 142.47, 142.49, and 142.53, as applicable.

(c) The certificate holder shall—

(1) Maintain the records required by paragraphs (a) of this section for at least 1 year following the completion of training, testing or checking;

(2) Maintain the qualification records required by paragraph (b) of this section while the instructor or evaluator is in the employ of the certificate holder and for 1 year thereafter; and

(3) Maintain the recurrent demonstration of proficiency records required by paragraph (b) of this section for at least 1 year.

(d) The certificate holder must provide the records required by this section to the Administrator, upon request and at a reasonable time, and shall keep the records required by—

(1) Paragraph (a) of this section at the training center, or satellite training center where the training, testing, or checking, if appropriate, occurred; and

(2) Paragraph (b) of this section at the training center or satellite training center where the instructor or evaluator is primarily employed.

(e) The certificate holder shall provide to a trainee, upon request and at a reasonable time, a copy of his or her training records.

Subpart F—Other Approved Courses

§ 142.81 Conduct of other approved courses.

(a) An applicant for, or holder of, a training center certificate may apply for approval to conduct a course for which a curriculum is not prescribed by this part.

(b) The course for which application is made under paragraph (a) of this section may be for flight crewmembers other than pilots, airmen other than flight crewmembers, material handlers, ground servicing personnel, and security personnel, and others approved by the Administrator.

(c) An applicant for course approval under this subpart must comply with the applicable requirements of subpart A through subpart F of this part.

(d) The Administrator approves the course for which the application is made if the training center or training center applicant shows that the course contains a curriculum that will achieve a level of competency equal to, or greater than, that required by the appropriate part of this chapter.

PART 143 [RESERVED]

PART 145—REPAIR STATIONS

Subpart A—General

145.159 Recommendation of a person for certification as a repairman.
145.160 Employment of former FAA employees.
145.161 Records of management, supervisory, and inspection personnel.
145.163 Training requirements.
145.165 Hazardous materials training.

Subpart E—Operating Rules

145.201 Privileges and limitations of certificate.
145.203 Work performed at another location.
145.205 Maintenance, preventive maintenance, and alterations performed for certificate holders under parts 121, 125, and 135, and for foreign air carriers or foreign persons operating a U.S.-registered aircraft in common carriage under part 129.
145.206 Notification of hazardous materials authorizations.
145.207 Repair station manual.
145.209 Repair station manual contents.
145.211 Quality control system.
145.213 Inspection of maintenance, preventive maintenance, or alterations.
145.215 Capability list.
145.217 Contract maintenance.
145.219 Recordkeeping.
145.221 Service difficulty reports.
145.223 FAA inspections.

AUTHORITY: 49 U.S.C. 106(g), 40113, 44701–44702, 44707, 44709, 44717.

Subpart A—General

SOURCE: Docket No. FAA-1999–5836, 66 FR 41117, Aug. 6, 2001, unless otherwise noted.

§145.1 Applicability.

This part describes how to obtain a repair station certificate. This part also contains the rules a certificated repair station must follow related to its performance of maintenance, preventive maintenance, or alterations of an aircraft, airframe, aircraft engine, propeller, appliance, or component part to which part 43 applies. It also applies to any person who holds, or is required to hold, a repair station certificate issued under this part.

§145.3 Definition of terms.

For the purposes of this part, the following definitions apply:

(a) *Accountable manager* means the person designated by the certificated repair station who is responsible for and has the authority over all repair station operations that are conducted under part 145, including ensuring that repair station personnel follow the regulations and serving as the primary contact with the FAA.

(b) *Article* means an aircraft, airframe, aircraft engine, propeller, appliance, or component part.

(c) *Directly in charge* means having the responsibility for the work of a certificated repair station that performs maintenance, preventive maintenance, alterations, or other functions affecting aircraft airworthiness. A person directly in charge does not need to physically observe and direct each worker constantly but must be available for consultation on matters requiring instruction or decision from higher authority.

(d) *Line maintenance means—*

(1) Any unscheduled maintenance resulting from unforeseen events; or

(2) Scheduled checks that contain servicing and/or inspections that do not require specialized training, equipment, or facilities.

§145.5 Certificate and operations specifications requirements.

(a) No person may operate as a certificated repair station without, or in violation of, a repair station certificate, ratings, or operations specifications issued under this part.

(b) The certificate and operations specifications issued to a certificated repair station must be available on the premises for inspection by the public and the FAA.

§145.12 Repair station records: Falsification, reproduction, alteration, or omission.

(a) No person may make or cause to be made:

(1) Any fraudulent or intentionally false entry in:

(i) Any application for a repair station certificate or rating (including in any document used in support of that application); or

(ii) Any record or report that is made, kept, or used to show compliance with any requirement under this part;

(2) Any reproduction, for fraudulent purpose, of any application (including any document used in support of that

application), record, or report under this part; or

(3) Any alteration, for fraudulent purpose, of any application (including any document used in support of that application), record, or report under this part.

(b) No person may, by omission, knowingly conceal or cause to be concealed, a material fact in:

(1) Any application for a repair station certificate or rating (including in any document used in support of that application); or

(2) Any record or report that is made, kept, or used to show compliance with any requirement under this part.

(c) The commission by any person of an act prohibited under paragraphs (a) or (b) of this section is a basis for any one or any combination of the following:

(1) Suspending or revoking the repair station certificate and any certificate, approval, or authorization issued by the FAA and held by that person.

(2) A civil penalty.

(3) The denial of an application under this part.

[Doc. No. FAA-2006-26408, 79 FR 46984, Aug. 12, 2014]

Subpart B—Certification

SOURCE: Docket No. FAA-1999-5836, 66 FR 41117, Aug. 6, 2001, unless otherwise noted.

§ 145.51 Application for certificate.

(a) An application for a repair station certificate and rating must be made in a format acceptable to the FAA and must include the following:

(1) A repair station manual acceptable to the FAA as required by § 145.207;

(2) A quality control manual acceptable to the FAA as required by § 145.211(c);

(3) A list by type, make, or model, as appropriate, of each article for which the application is made;

(4) An organizational chart of the repair station and the names and titles of managing and supervisory personnel;

(5) A description of the housing and facilities, including the physical address, in accordance with § 145.103;

(6) A list of the maintenance functions, for approval by the FAA, to be performed for the repair station under

contract by another person in accordance with § 145.217; and

(7) A training program for approval by the FAA in accordance with § 145.163.

(b) The equipment, personnel, technical data, and housing and facilities required for the certificate and rating, or for an additional rating, must be in place for inspection at the time of certification or rating approval by the FAA. However, the requirement to have the equipment in place at the time of initial certification or rating approval may be met if the applicant has a contract acceptable to the FAA with another person to make the equipment available to the repair station at any time it is necessary when the relevant work is being performed.

(c) In addition to meeting the other applicable requirements for a repair station certificate and rating, an applicant for a repair station certificate and rating located outside the United States must meet the following requirements:

(1) The applicant must show that the repair station certificate and/or rating is necessary for maintaining or altering the following:

(i) U.S.-registered aircraft and articles for use on U.S.-registered aircraft, or

(ii) Foreign-registered aircraft operated under the provisions of part 121 or part 135, and articles for use on these aircraft.

(2) The applicant must show that the fee prescribed by the FAA has been paid.

(d) An application for an additional rating, amended repair station certificate, or renewal of a repair station certificate must be made in a format acceptable to the FAA. The application must include only that information necessary to substantiate the change or renewal of the certificate.

(e) The FAA may deny an application for a repair station certificate if the FAA finds that:

(1) The applicant holds a repair station certificate in the process of being revoked, or previously held a repair station certificate that was revoked;

(2) The applicant intends to fill or fills a management position with an individual who exercised control over or

who held the same or a similar position with a certificate holder whose repair station certificate was revoked, or is in the process of being revoked, and that individual materially contributed to the circumstances causing the revocation or causing the revocation process; or

(3) An individual who will have control over or substantial ownership interest in the applicant had the same or similar control or interest in a certificate holder whose repair station certificate was revoked, or is in the process of being revoked, and that individual materially contributed to the circumstances causing the revocation or causing the revocation process.

(f) If the FAA revokes a repair station certificate, an individual described in paragraphs (e)(2) and (3) of this section is subject to an order under the procedures set forth in 14 CFR 13.20, finding that the individual materially contributed to the circumstances causing the revocation or causing the revocation process.

[Doc. No. FAA–1999–5836, 66 FR 41117, Aug. 6, 2001, as amended by Amdt. 145–30, 79 FR 46984, Aug. 12, 2014]

§ 145.53 Issue of certificate.

(a) Except as provided in § 145.51(e) or paragraph (b), (c), or (d) of this section, a person who meets the requirements of subparts A through E of this part is entitled to a repair station certificate with appropriate ratings prescribing such operations specifications and limitations as are necessary in the interest of safety.

(b) If the person is located in a country with which the United States has a bilateral aviation safety agreement, the FAA may find that the person meets the requirements of this part based on a certification from the civil aviation authority of that country. This certification must be made in accordance with implementation procedures signed by the Administrator or the Administrator's designee.

(c) Before a repair station certificate can be issued for a repair station that is located within the United States, the applicant shall certify in writing that all "hazmat employees" (see 49 CFR 171.8) for the repair station, its contractors, or subcontractors are trained as required in 49 CFR part 172 subpart H.

(d) Before a repair station certificate can be issued for a repair station that is located outside the United States, the applicant shall certify in writing that all employees for the repair station, its contractors, or subcontractors performing a job function concerning the transport of dangerous goods (hazardous material) are trained as outlined in the most current edition of the International Civil Aviation Organization Technical Instructions for the Safe Transport of Dangerous Goods by Air.

[Doc. No. FAA–2003–15085, 70 FR 58831, Oct. 7, 2005, as amended by Amdt. 145–30, 79 FR 46984, Aug. 12, 2014]

§ 145.55 Duration and renewal of certificate.

(a) A certificate or rating issued to a repair station located in the United States is effective from the date of issue until the repair station surrenders the certificate and the FAA accepts it for cancellation, or the FAA suspends or revokes it.

(b) A certificate or rating issued to a repair station located outside the United States is effective from the date of issue until the last day of the 12th month after the date of issue unless the repair station surrenders the certificate and the FAA accepts it for cancellation, or the FAA suspends or revokes it. The FAA may renew the certificate or rating for 24 months if the repair station has operated in compliance with the applicable requirements of part 145 within the preceding certificate duration period.

(c) A certificated repair station located outside the United States that applies for a renewal of its repair station certificate must—

(1) Submit its request for renewal no later than 30 days before the repair station's current certificate expires. If a request for renewal is not made within this period, the repair station must follow the application procedures in § 145.51.

(2) Send its request for renewal to the FAA office that has jurisdiction over the certificated repair station.

(3) Show that the fee prescribed by the FAA has been paid.

(d) The holder of an expired, surrendered, suspended, or revoked certificate must return it to the FAA.

[Doc. No. FAA–1999–5836, 66 FR 41117, Aug. 6, 2001, as amended by Amdt. 145–30, 79 FR 46984, Aug. 12, 2014]

§ 145.57 Amendment to or transfer of certificate.

(a) A repair station certificate holder applying for a change to its certificate must submit a request in a format acceptable to the Administrator. A change to the certificate must include certification in compliance with § 145.53(c) or (d), if not previously submitted. A certificate change is necessary if the certificate holder—

(1) Changes the name or location of the repair station, or

(2) Requests to add or amend a rating.

(b) If the holder of a repair station certificate sells or transfers its assets and the new owner chooses to operate as a repair station, the new owner must apply for an amended or new certificate in accordance with § 145.51.

[Doc. No. FAA–2006–26408, 79 FR 46984, Aug. 12, 2014]

§ 145.59 Ratings.

The following ratings are issued under this subpart:

(a) *Airframe ratings.* (1) *Class 1:* Composite construction of small aircraft.

(2) *Class 2:* Composite construction of large aircraft.

(3) *Class 3:* All-metal construction of small aircraft.

(4) *Class 4:* All-metal construction of large aircraft.

(b) *Powerplant ratings.* (1) *Class 1:* Reciprocating engines of 400 horsepower or less.

(2) *Class 2:* Reciprocating engines of more than 400 horsepower.

(3) *Class 3:* Turbine engines.

(c) *Propeller ratings.* (1) *Class 1:* Fixed-pitch and ground-adjustable propellers of wood, metal, or composite construction.

(2) *Class 2:* Other propellers, by make.

(d) *Radio ratings.* (1) *Class 1:* Communication equipment. Radio transmitting and/or receiving equipment used in an aircraft to send or receive communications in flight, regardless of carrier frequency or type of modulation used.

This equipment includes auxiliary and related aircraft interphone systems, amplifier systems, electrical or electronic intercrew signaling devices, and similar equipment. This equipment does not include equipment used for navigating or aiding navigation of aircraft, equipment used for measuring altitude or terrain clearance, other measuring equipment operated on radio or radar principles, or mechanical, electrical, gyroscopic, or electronic instruments that are a part of communications radio equipment.

(2) *Class 2:* Navigational equipment. A radio system used in an aircraft for en route or approach navigation. This does not include equipment operated on radar or pulsed radio frequency principles, or equipment used for measuring altitude or terrain clearance.

(3) *Class 3:* Radar equipment. An aircraft electronic system operated on radar or pulsed radio frequency principles.

(e) *Instrument ratings.* (1) *Class 1:* Mechanical. A diaphragm, bourdon tube, aneroid, optical, or mechanically driven centrifugal instrument used on aircraft or to operate aircraft, including tachometers, airspeed indicators, pressure gauges drift sights, magnetic compasses, altimeters, or similar mechanical instruments.

(2) *Class 2:* Electrical. Self-synchronous and electrical-indicating instruments and systems, including remote indicating instruments, cylinder head temperature gauges, or similar electrical instruments.

(3) *Class 3:* Gyroscopic. An instrument or system using gyroscopic principles and motivated by air pressure or electrical energy, including automatic pilot control units, turn and bank indicators, directional gyros, and their parts, and flux gate and gyrosyn compasses.

(4) *Class 4:* Electronic. An instrument whose operation depends on electron tubes, transistors, or similar devices, including capacitance type quantity gauges, system amplifiers, and engine analyzers.

(f) *Accessory ratings.* (1) *Class 1:* A mechanical accessory that depends on friction, hydraulics, mechanical linkage, or pneumatic pressure for operation, including aircraft wheel brakes, mechanically driven pumps, carburetors, aircraft wheel assemblies, shock absorber struts and hydraulic servo units.

(2) *Class 2:* An electrical accessory that depends on electrical energy for its operation, and a generator, including starters, voltage regulators electric motors, electrically driven fuel pumps magnetos, or similar electrical accessories.

(3) *Class 3:* An electronic accessory that depends on the use of an electron tube transistor, or similar device, including supercharger, temperature, air conditioning controls, or similar electronic controls.

§145.61 Limited ratings.

(a) The FAA may issue a limited rating to a certificated repair station that maintains or alters only a particular type of airframe, powerplant, propeller, radio, instrument, or accessory, or part thereof, or performs only specialized maintenance requiring equipment and skills not ordinarily performed under other repair station ratings. Such a rating may be limited to a specific model aircraft, engine, or constituent part, or to any number of parts made by a particular manufacturer.

(b) The FAA issues limited ratings for—

(1) Airframes of a particular make and model;

(2) Engines of a particular make and model;

(3) Propellers of a particular make and model;

(4) Instruments of a particular make and model;

(5) Radio equipment of a particular make and model;

(6) Accessories of a particular make and model;

(7) Landing gear components;

(8) Floats, by make;

(9) Nondestructive inspection, testing, and processing;

(10) Emergency equipment;

(11) Rotor blades, by make and model;

(12) Aircraft fabric work;

(13) Any other purpose for which the FAA finds the applicant's request is appropriate.

(c) For a limited rating for specialized services, the operations specifications of the repair station must contain the specification used to perform the specialized service. The specification may be—

(1) A civil or military specification currently used by industry and approved by the FAA, or

(2) A specification developed by the applicant and approved by the FAA.

[Docket No. FAA–1999–5836, 66 FR 41117, Aug. 6, 2001, as amended by Docket FAA–2016–8744, Amdt. 145–31, 81 FR 49163, July 27, 2016]

Subpart C—Housing, Facilities, Equipment, Materials, and Data

SOURCE: Docket No. FAA–1999–5836, 66 FR 41117, Aug. 6, 2001, unless otherwise noted.

§145.101 General.

A certificated repair station must provide housing, facilities, equipment, materials, and data that meet the applicable requirements for the issuance of the certificate and ratings the repair station holds.

§145.103 Housing and facilities requirements.

(a) Each certificated repair station must provide—

(1) Housing for the facilities, equipment, materials, and personnel consistent with its ratings and limitations.

(2) Facilities for properly performing the maintenance, preventive maintenance, or alterations of articles or the specialized service for which it is rated. Facilities must include the following:

(i) Sufficient work space and areas for the proper segregation and protection of articles during all maintenance, preventive maintenance, or alterations;

(ii) Segregated work areas enabling environmentally hazardous or sensitive operations such as painting, cleaning, welding, avionics work, electronic work, and machining to be done properly and in a manner that does not adversely affect other maintenance or alteration articles or activities;

(iii) Suitable racks, hoists, trays, stands, and other segregation means for the storage and protection of all articles undergoing maintenance, preventive maintenance, or alterations, and;

(iv) Space sufficient to segregate articles and materials stocked for installation from those articles undergoing maintenance, preventive maintenance, or alterations to the standards required by this part.

(v) Ventilation, lighting, and control of temperature, humidity, and other climatic conditions sufficient to ensure personnel perform maintenance, preventive maintenance, or alterations to the standards required by this part.

(b) A certificated repair station may perform maintenance, preventive maintenance, or alterations on articles outside of its housing if it provides suitable facilities that are acceptable to the FAA and meet the requirements of § 145.103(a) so that the work can be done in accordance with the requirements of part 43 of this chapter.

[Docket FAA–2016–8744, Amdt. 145–31, 81 FR 49163, July 27, 2016]

§ 145.105 Change of location, housing, or facilities.

(a) A certificated repair station may not change the location of its housing without written approval from the FAA.

(b) A certificated repair station may not make any changes to its housing or facilities required by § 145.103 that could have a significant effect on its ability to perform the maintenance, preventive maintenance, or alterations under its repair station certificate and operations specifications without written approval from the FAA.

(c) The FAA may prescribe the conditions, including any limitations, under which a certificated repair station must operate while it is changing its location, housing, or facilities.

§ 145.107 Satellite repair stations.

(a) A certificated repair station under the managerial control of another certificated repair station may operate as a satellite repair station with its own certificate issued by the FAA. A satellite repair station—

(1) May not hold a rating not held by the certificated repair station with managerial control;

(2) Must meet the requirements for each rating it holds;

(3) Must submit a repair station manual acceptable to the FAA as required by § 145.207; and

(4) Must submit a quality control manual acceptable to the FAA as required by § 145.211(c).

(b) Unless the FAA indicates otherwise, personnel and equipment from the certificated repair station with managerial control and from each of the satellite repair stations may be shared. However, inspection personnel must be designated for each satellite repair station and available at the satellite repair station any time a determination of airworthiness or return to service is made. In other circumstances, inspection personnel may be away from the premises but must be available by telephone, radio, or other electronic means.

(c) A satellite repair station may not be located in a country other than the domicile country of the certificated repair station with managerial control.

§ 145.109 Equipment, materials, and data requirements.

(a) Except as otherwise prescribed by the FAA, a certificated repair station must have the equipment, tools, and materials necessary to perform the maintenance, preventive maintenance, or alterations under its repair station certificate and operations specifications in accordance with part 43. The equipment, tools, and material must be located on the premises and under the repair station's control when the work is being done.

(b) A certificated repair station must ensure all test and inspection equipment and tools used to make airworthiness determinations on articles are calibrated to a standard acceptable to the FAA.

(c) The equipment, tools, and material must be those recommended by the manufacturer of the article or must be at least equivalent to those recommended by the manufacturer and acceptable to the FAA.

(d) A certificated repair station must maintain, in a format acceptable to the FAA, the documents and data required for the performance of maintenance, preventive maintenance, or alterations under its repair station certificate and operations specifications in accordance with part 43. The following documents and data must be current and accessible when the relevant work is being done:

(1) Airworthiness directives,

(2) Instructions for continued airworthiness,

(3) Maintenance manuals,

(4) Overhaul manuals,

(5) Standard practice manuals,

(6) Service bulletins, and

(7) Other applicable data acceptable to or approved by the FAA.

Subpart D—Personnel

SOURCE: Docket No. FAA–1999–5836, 66 FR 41117, Aug. 6, 2001, unless otherwise noted.

§145.151 Personnel requirements.

Each certificated repair station must—

(a) Designate a repair station employee as the accountable manager;

(b) Provide qualified personnel to plan, supervise, perform, and approve for return to service the maintenance, preventive maintenance, or alterations performed under the repair station certificate and operations specifications;

(c) Ensure it has a sufficient number of employees with the training or knowledge and experience in the performance of maintenance, preventive maintenance, or alterations authorized by the repair station certificate and operations specifications to ensure all work is performed in accordance with part 43; and

(d) Determine the abilities of its noncertificated employees performing maintenance functions based on training, knowledge, experience, or practical tests.

§145.153 Supervisory personnel requirements.

(a) A certificated repair station must ensure it has a sufficient number of supervisors to direct the work performed under the repair station certificate and operations specifications. The supervisors must oversee the work performed by any individuals who are unfamiliar with the methods, techniques, practices, aids, equipment, and tools used to perform the maintenance, preventive maintenance, or alterations.

(b) Each supervisor must—

(1) If employed by a repair station located inside the United States, be appropriately certificated as a mechanic or repairman under part 65 of this chapter for the work being supervised.

(2) If employed by a repair station located outside the United States—

(i) Have a minimum of 18 months of practical experience in the work being performed; or

(ii) Be trained in or thoroughly familiar with the methods, techniques, practices, aids, equipment, and tools used to perform the maintenance, preventive maintenance, or alterations.

(c) A certificated repair station must ensure its supervisors understand, read, and write English.

[Doc. No. FAA–1999–5836, 66 FR 41117, Aug. 6, 2001, as amended by Amdt. 145–30, 79 FR 46984, Aug. 12, 2014]

§145.155 Inspection personnel requirements.

(a) A certificated repair station must ensure that persons performing inspections under the repair station certificate and operations specifications are—

(1) Thoroughly familiar with the applicable regulations in this chapter and with the inspection methods, techniques, practices, aids, equipment, and tools used to determine the airworthiness of the article on which maintenance, preventive maintenance, or alterations are being performed; and

(2) Proficient in using the various types of inspection equipment and visual inspection aids appropriate for the article being inspected.

(b) A certificated repair station must ensure its inspectors understand, read, and write English.

[Doc. No. FAA–1999–5836, 66 FR 41117, Aug. 6, 2001, as amended by Amdt. 145–30, 79 FR 46985, Aug. 12, 2014]

§145.157 Personnel authorized to approve an article for return to service.

(a) A certificated repair station located inside the United States must ensure each person authorized to approve an article for return to service under the repair station certificate and operations specifications is appropriately certificated as a mechanic or repairman under part 65.

(b) A certificated repair station located outside the United States must ensure each person authorized to approve an article for return to service under the repair station certificate and operations specifications is—

(1) Trained in or has 18 months practical experience with the methods, techniques, practices, aids, equipment, and tools used to perform the maintenance, preventive maintenance, or alterations; and

(2) Thoroughly familiar with the applicable regulations in this chapter and proficient in the use of the various inspection methods, techniques, practices, aids, equipment, and tools appropriate for the work being performed and approved for return to service.

(c) A certificated repair station must ensure each person authorized to approve an article for return to service understands, reads, and writes English.

[Doc. No. FAA–1999–5836, 66 FR 41117, Aug. 6, 2001, as amended by Amdt. 145–30, 79 FR 46985, Aug. 12, 2014]

§ 145.159 Recommendation of a person for certification as a repairman.

A certificated repair station that chooses to use repairmen to meet the applicable personnel requirements of this part must certify in a format acceptable to the FAA that each person recommended for certification as a repairman—

(a) Is employed by the repair station, and

(b) Meets the eligibility requirements of § 65.101.

§ 145.160 Employment of former FAA employees.

(a) Except as specified in paragraph (c) of this section, no holder of a repair station certificate may knowingly employ or make a contractual arrangement which permits an individual to act as an agent or representative of the certificate holder in any matter before the Federal Aviation Administration if the individual, in the preceding 2 years—

(1) Served as, or was directly responsible for the oversight of, a Flight Standards Service aviation safety inspector; and

(2) Had direct responsibility to inspect, or oversee the inspection of, the operations of the certificate holder.

(b) For the purpose of this section, an individual shall be considered to be acting as an agent or representative of a certificate holder in a matter before the agency if the individual makes any written or oral communication on behalf of the certificate holder to the agency (or any of its officers or employees) in connection with a particular matter, whether or not involving a specific party and without regard to whether the individual has participated in, or had responsibility for, the particular matter while serving as a Flight Standards Service aviation safety inspector.

(c) The provisions of this section do not prohibit a holder of a repair station certificate from knowingly employing or making a contractual arrangement which permits an individual to act as an agent or representative of the certificate holder in any matter before the Federal Aviation Administration if the individual was employed by the certificate holder before October 21, 2011.

[Doc. No. FAA–2008–1154, 76 FR 52237, Aug. 22, 2011]

§ 145.161 Records of management, supervisory, and inspection personnel.

(a) A certificated repair station must maintain and make available in a format acceptable to the FAA the following:

(1) A roster of management and supervisory personnel that includes the names of the repair station officials who are responsible for its management and the names of its supervisors who oversee maintenance functions.

(2) A roster with the names of all inspection personnel.

(3) A roster of personnel authorized to sign a maintenance release for approving a maintained or altered article for return to service.

(4) A summary of the employment of each individual whose name is on the personnel rosters required by paragraphs (a)(1) through (a)(3) of this section. The summary must contain enough information on each individual listed on the roster to show compliance with the experience requirements of

this part and must include the following:

(i) Present title,

(ii) Total years of experience and the type of maintenance work performed,

(iii) Past relevant employment with names of employers and periods of employment,

(iv) Scope of present employment, and

(v) The type of mechanic or repairman certificate held and the ratings on that certificate, if applicable.

(b) Within 5 business days of the change, the rosters required by this section must reflect changes caused by termination, reassignment, change in duties or scope of assignment, or addition of personnel.

§ 145.163 Training requirements.

(a) A certificated repair station must have and use an employee training program approved by the FAA that consists of initial and recurrent training. An applicant for a repair station certificate must submit a training program for approval by the FAA as required by § 145.51(a)(7).

(b) The training program must ensure each employee assigned to perform maintenance, preventive maintenance, or alterations, and inspection functions is capable of performing the assigned task.

(c) A certificated repair station must document, in a format acceptable to the FAA, the individual employee training required under paragraph (a) of this section. These training records must be retained for a minimum of 2 years.

(d) A certificated repair station must submit revisions to its training program to its responsible Flight Standards office in accordance with the procedures required by § 145.209(e).

[Doc. No. FAA–1999–5836, 66 FR 41117, Aug. 6, 2001, as amended at 70 FR 15581, Mar. 28, 2005; Amdt. 145–30, 79 FR 46985, Aug. 12, 2014; Docket FAA–2018–0119, Amdt. 145–32, 83 FR 9176, Mar. 5, 2018]

§ 145.165 Hazardous materials training.

(a) Each repair station that meets the definition of a hazmat employer under 49 CFR 171.8 must have a hazardous materials training program

that meets the training requirements of 49 CFR part 172 subpart H.

(b) A repair station employee may not perform or directly supervise a job function listed in § 121.1001 or § 135.501 for, or on behalf of the part 121 or 135 operator including loading of items for transport on an aircraft operated by a part 121 or part 135 certificate holder unless that person has received training in accordance with the part 121 or part 135 operator's FAA approved hazardous materials training program.

[Doc. No. FAA–2003–15085, 70 FR 58831, Oct. 7, 2005]

Subpart E—Operating Rules

SOURCE: Docket No. FAA–1999–5836, 66 FR 41117, Aug. 6, 2001, unless otherwise noted.

§ 145.201 Privileges and limitations of certificate.

(a) A certificated repair station may—

(1) Perform maintenance, preventive maintenance, or alterations in accordance with part 43 on any article for which it is rated and within the limitations in its operations specifications.

(2) Arrange for another person to perform the maintenance, preventive maintenance, or alterations of any article for which the certificated repair station is rated. If that person is not certificated under part 145, the certificated repair station must ensure that the noncertificated person follows a quality control system equivalent to the system followed by the certificated repair station.

(3) Approve for return to service any article for which it is rated after it has performed maintenance, preventive maintenance, or an alteration in accordance with part 43.

(b) A certificated repair station may not maintain or alter any article for which it is not rated, and may not maintain or alter any article for which it is rated if it requires special technical data, equipment, or facilities that are not available to it.

(c) A certificated repair station may not approve for return to service'

(1) Any article unless the maintenance, preventive maintenance, or alteration was performed in accordance

with the applicable approved technical data or data acceptable to the FAA.

(2) Any article after a major repair or major alteration unless the major repair or major alteration was performed in accordance with applicable approved technical data; and

(3) Any experimental aircraft after a major repair or major alteration performed under § 43.1(b) unless the major repair or major alteration was performed in accordance with methods and applicable technical data acceptable to the FAA.

§ 145.203 Work performed at another location.

A certificated repair station may temporarily transport material, equipment, and personnel needed to perform maintenance, preventive maintenance, alterations, or certain specialized services on an article for which it is rated to a place other than the repair station's fixed location if the following requirements are met:

(a) The work is necessary due to a special circumstance, as determined by the FAA; or

(b) It is necessary to perform such work on a recurring basis, and the repair station's manual includes the procedures for accomplishing maintenance, preventive maintenance, alterations, or specialized services at a place other than the repair station's fixed location.

§ 145.205 Maintenance, preventive maintenance, and alterations performed for certificate holders under parts 121, 125, and 135, and for foreign air carriers or foreign persons operating a U.S.-registered aircraft in common carriage under part 129.

(a) A certificated repair station that performs maintenance, preventive maintenance, or alterations for an air carrier or commercial operator that has a continuous airworthiness maintenance program under part 121 or part 135 must follow the air carrier's or commercial operator's program and applicable sections of its maintenance manual.

(b) A certificated repair station that performs inspections for a certificate holder conducting operations under part 125 must follow the operator's FAA-approved inspection program.

(c) A certificated repair station that performs maintenance, preventive maintenance, or alterations for a foreign air carrier or foreign person operating a U.S.-registered aircraft under part 129 must follow the operator's FAA-approved maintenance program.

(d) The FAA may grant approval for a certificated repair station to perform line maintenance for an air carrier certificated under part 121 or part 135 of this chapter, or a foreign air carrier or foreign person operating a U.S.-registered aircraft in common carriage under part 129 of this chapter on any aircraft of that air carrier or person, provided-

(1) The certificated repair station performs such line maintenance in accordance with the operator's manual, if applicable, and approved maintenance program;

(2) The certificated repair station has the necessary equipment, trained personnel, and technical data to perform such line maintenance; and

(3) The certificated repair station's operations specifications include an authorization to perform line maintenance.

[Docket No. FAA-1999-5836, 66 FR 41117, Aug. 6, 2001, as amended by Docket FAA-2016-8744, Amdt. 145-31, 81 FR 49163, July 27, 2016]

§ 145.206 Notification of hazardous materials authorizations.

(a) Each repair station must acknowledge receipt of the part 121 or part 135 operator notification required under §§ 121.1005(e) and 135.505(e) of this chapter prior to performing work for, or on behalf of that certificate holder.

(b) Prior to performing work for or on behalf of a part 121 or part 135 operator, each repair station must notify its employees, contractors, or subcontractors that handle or replace aircraft components or other items regulated by 49 CFR parts 171 through 180 of each certificate holder's operations specifications authorization permitting, or prohibition against, carrying hazardous materials. This notification must be provided subsequent to the notification by the part 121 or part 135 operator of such operations specifications authorization/designation.

[Doc. No. FAA–2003–15085, 70 FR 58831. Oct. 7, 2005, as amended by Amdt. 145–25, 70 FR 75397, Dec. 20, 2005]

§145.207 Repair station manual.

(a) A certificated repair station must prepare and follow a repair station manual acceptable to the FAA.

(b) A certificated repair station must maintain a current repair station manual.

(c) A certificated repair station's current repair station manual must be accessible for use by repair station personnel required by subpart D of this part.

(d) A certificated repair station must provide to its responsible Flight Standards office the current repair station manual in a format acceptable to the FAA.

(e) A certificated repair station must notify its responsible Flight Standards office of each revision of its repair station manual in accordance with the procedures required by §145.209(j).

[Docket No. FAA–1999–5836, 66 FR 41117, Aug. 6, 2001, as amended by Docket FAA–2018–0119, Amdt. 145–32, 83 FR 9176, Mar. 5, 2018]

§145.209 Repair station manual contents.

A certificated repair station's manual must include the following:

(a) An organizational chart identifying—

(1) Each management position with authority to act on behalf of the repair station,

(2) The area of responsibility assigned to each management position, and

(3) The duties, responsibilities, and authority of each management position;

(b) Procedures for maintaining and revising the rosters required by §145.161;

(c) A description of the certificated repair station's operations, including the housing, facilities, equipment, and materials as required by subpart C of this part;

(d) Procedures for—

(1) Revising the capability list provided for in §145.215 and notifying the responsible Flight Standards office of revisions to the list, including how often the responsible Flight Standards office will be notified of revisions; and

(2) The self-evaluation required under §145.215(c) for revising the capability list, including methods and frequency of such evaluations, and procedures for reporting the results to the appropriate manager for review and action;

(e) Procedures for revising the training program required by §145.163 and submitting revisions to the responsible Flight Standards office for approval;

(f) Procedures to govern work performed at another location in accordance with §145.203;

(g) Procedures for maintenance, preventive maintenance, or alterations performed under §145.205;

(h) Procedures for—

(1) Maintaining and revising the contract maintenance information required by §145.217(a)(2)(i), including submitting revisions to the responsible Flight Standards office for approval; and

(2) Maintaining and revising the contract maintenance information required by §145.217(a)(2)(ii) and notifying the responsible Flight Standards office of revisions to this information, including how often the responsible Flight Standards office will be notified of revisions;

(i) A description of the required records and the recordkeeping system used to obtain, store, and retrieve the required records;

(j) Procedures for revising the repair station's manual and notifying its responsible Flight Standards office of revisions to the manual, including how often the responsible Flight Standards office will be notified of revisions; and

(k) A description of the system used to identify and control sections of the repair station manual.

[Docket No. FAA–1999–5836, 66 FR 41117, Aug. 6, 2001, as amended by Docket FAA–2018–0119, Amdt. 145–32, 83 FR 9176, Mar. 5, 2018]

§145.211 Quality control system.

(a) A certificated repair station must establish and maintain a quality control system acceptable to the FAA that ensures the airworthiness of the articles on which the repair station or any of its contractors performs maintenance, preventive maintenance, or alterations.

(b) Repair station personnel must follow the quality control system when performing maintenance, preventive maintenance, or alterations under the repair station certificate and operations specifications.

(c) A certificated repair station must prepare and keep current a quality control manual in a format acceptable to the FAA that includes the following:

(1) A description of the system and procedures used for—

(i) Inspecting incoming raw materials to ensure acceptable quality;

(ii) Performing preliminary inspection of all articles that are maintained;

(iii) Inspecting all articles that have been involved in an accident for hidden damage before maintenance, preventive maintenance, or alteration is performed;

(iv) Establishing and maintaining proficiency of inspection personnel;

(v) Establishing and maintaining current technical data for maintaining articles;

(vi) Qualifying and surveilling noncertificated persons who perform maintenance, prevention maintenance, or alterations for the repair station;

(vii) Performing final inspection and return to service of maintained articles;

(viii) Calibrating measuring and test equipment used in maintaining articles, including the intervals at which the equipment will be calibrated; and

(ix) Taking corrective action on deficiencies;

(2) References, where applicable, to the manufacturer's inspection standards for a particular article, including reference to any data specified by that manufacturer;

(3) A sample of the inspection and maintenance forms and instructions for completing such forms or a reference to a separate forms manual; and

(4) Procedures for revising the quality control manual required under this section and notifying the responsible Flight Standards office of the revisions, including how often the respon-

sible Flight Standards office will be notified of revisions.

(d) A certificated repair station must notify its responsible Flight Standards office of revisions to its quality control manual.

[Docket No. FAA-1999-5836, 66 FR 41117, Aug. 6, 2001, as amended by Docket FAA-2018-0119, Amdt. 145-32, 83 FR 9176, Mar. 5, 2018]

§ 145.213 Inspection of maintenance, preventive maintenance, or alterations.

(a) A certificated repair station must inspect each article upon which it has performed maintenance, preventive maintenance, or alterations as described in paragraphs (b) and (c) of this section before approving that article for return to service.

(b) A certificated repair station must certify on an article's maintenance release that the article is airworthy with respect to the maintenance, preventive maintenance, or alterations performed after—

(1) The repair station performs work on the article; and

(2) An inspector inspects the article on which the repair station has performed work and determines it to be airworthy with respect to the work performed.

(c) For the purposes of paragraphs (a) and (b) of this section, an inspector must meet the requirements of § 145.155.

(d) Except for individuals employed by a repair station located outside the United States, only an employee appropriately certificated as a mechanic or repairman under part 65 is authorized to sign off on final inspections and maintenance releases for the repair station.

[Doc. No. FAA-1999-5836, 66 FR 41117, Aug. 6, 2001, as amended by Amdt. 145-30, 79 FR 46985, Aug. 12, 2014]

§ 145.215 Capability list.

(a) A certificated repair station with a limited rating may perform maintenance, preventive maintenance, or alterations on an article if the article is listed on a current capability list acceptable to the FAA or on the repair station's operations specifications.

(b) The capability list must identify each article by make and model or other nomenclature designated by the article's manufacturer and be available in a format acceptable to the FAA.

(c) An article may be listed on the capability list only if the article is within the scope of the ratings of the repair station's certificate, and only after the repair station has performed a self-evaluation in accordance with the procedures under § 145.209(d)(2). The repair station must perform this self-evaluation to determine that the repair station has all of the housing, facilities, equipment, material, technical data, processes, and trained personnel in place to perform the work on the article as required by part 145. The repair station must retain on file documentation of the evaluation.

(d) Upon listing an additional article on its capability list, the repair station must provide its responsible Flight Standards office with a copy of the revised list in accordance with the procedures required in § 145.209(d)(1).

[Docket No. FAA–1999–5836, 66 FR 41117 Aug. 6, 2001, as amended by Docket FAA–2018–0119, Amdt. 145–32, 83 FR 9176, Mar. 5, 2018]

§ 145.217 Contract maintenance.

(a) A certificated repair station may contract a maintenance function pertaining to an article to an outside source provided—

(1) The FAA approves the maintenance function to be contracted to the outside source; and

(2) The repair station maintains and makes available to its responsible Flight Standards office, in a format acceptable to the FAA, the following information:

(i) The maintenance functions contracted to each outside facility; and

(ii) The name of each outside facility to whom the repair station contracts maintenance functions and the type of certificate and ratings, if any, held by each facility.

(b) A certificated repair station may contract a maintenance function pertaining to an article to a noncertificated person provided—

(1) The noncertificated person follows a quality control system equivalent to the system followed by the certificated repair station;

(2) The certificated repair station remains directly in charge of the work

performed by the noncertificated person; and

(3) The certificated repair station verifies, by test and/or inspection, that the work has been performed satisfactorily by the noncertificated person and that the article is airworthy before approving it for return to service.

(c) A certificated repair station may not provide only approval for return to service of a complete type-certificated product following contract maintenance, preventive maintenance, or alterations.

[Docket No. FAA–1999–5836, 66 FR 41117, Aug. 6, 2001, as amended by Docket FAA–2018–0119, Amdt. 145–32, 83 FR 9176, Mar. 5, 2018]

§ 145.219 Recordkeeping.

(a) A certificated repair station must retain records in English that demonstrate compliance with the requirements of part 43. The records must be retained in a format acceptable to the FAA.

(b) A certificated repair station must provide a copy of the maintenance release to the owner or operator of the article on which the maintenance, preventive maintenance, or alteration was performed.

(c) A certificated repair station must retain the records required by this section for at least 2 years from the date the article was approved for return to service.

(d) A certificated repair station must make all required records available for inspection by the FAA and the National Transportation Safety Board.

§ 145.221 Service difficulty reports.

(a) A certificated repair station must report to the FAA within 96 hours after it discovers any serious failure, malfunction, or defect of an article. The report must be in a format acceptable to the FAA.

(b) The report required under paragraph (a) of this section must include as much of the following information as is available:

(1) Aircraft registration number;

(2) Type, make, and model of the article;

(3) Date of the discovery of the failure, malfunction, or defect;

(4) Nature of the failure, malfunction, or defect;

(5) Time since last overhaul, if applicable;

(6) Apparent cause of the failure, malfunction, or defect; and

(7) Other pertinent information that is necessary for more complete identification, determination of seriousness, or corrective action.

(c) The holder of a repair station certificate that is also the holder of a part 121, 125, or 135 certificate; type certificate (including a supplemental type certificate); parts manufacturer approval; or technical standard order authorization, or that is the licensee of a type certificate holder, does not need to report a failure, malfunction, or defect under this section if the failure, malfunction, or defect has been reported under parts 21, 121, 125, or 135 of this chapter.

(d) A certificated repair station may submit a service difficulty report for the following:

(1) A part 121 certificate holder, provided the report meets the requirements of part 121 of this chapter, as appropriate.

(2) A part 125 certificate holder, provided the report meets the requirements of part 125 of this chapter, as appropriate.

(3) A part 135 certificate holder, provided the report meets the requirements of part 135 of the chapter, as appropriate.

(e) A certificated repair station authorized to report a failure, malfunction, or defect under paragraph (d) of this section must not report the same failure, malfunction, or defect under paragraph (a) of this section. A copy of the report submitted under paragraph (d) of this section must be forwarded to the certificate holder.

[Doc. No. FAA–1999–5836, 66 FR 41117, Aug. 6, 2001, as amended by Amdt. 22, 68 FR 75382, Dec. 30, 2003; Amdt. 145–26, 70 FR 76979, Dec. 29, 2005; Amdt. 145–30, 79 FR 46985, Aug. 12, 2014; Amdt. 145–30A, 79 FR 66607, Nov. 10, 2014]

§ 145.223 FAA inspections.

(a) A certificated repair station must allow the FAA to inspect that repair station at any time to determine compliance with this chapter.

(b) A certificated repair station may not contract for the performance of a maintenance function on an article

with a noncertificated person unless it provides in its contract with the noncertificated person that the FAA may make an inspection and observe the performance of the noncertificated person's work on the article.

(c) A certificated repair station may not return to service any article on which a maintenance function was performed by a noncertificated person if the noncertificated person does not permit the FAA to make the inspection described in paragraph (b) of this section.

PART 147—AVIATION MAINTENANCE TECHNICIAN SCHOOLS

Subpart A—General

APPENDIX C TO PART 147—AIRFRAME CURRICULUM SUBJECTS
APPENDIX D TO PART 147—POWERPLANT CURRICULUM SUBJECTS

AUTHORITY: 49 U.S.C. 106(g), 40113, 44701–44702, 44707–44709.

SOURCE: Docket No. 1157, 27 FR 6669 July 13, 1962, unless otherwise noted.

Subpart A—General

§ 147.1 Applicability.

This part prescribes the requirements for issuing aviation maintenance technician school certificates and associated ratings and the general operating rules for the holders of those certificates and ratings.

§ 147.3 Certificate required.

No person may operate as a certificated aviation maintenance technician school without, or in violation of, an aviation maintenance technician school certificate issued under this part.

[Doc. No. 15196, 41 FR 47230, Oct. 28, 1976]

§ 147.5 Application and issue.

(a) An application for a certificate and rating, or for an additional rating, under this part is made on a form and in a manner prescribed by the Administrator, and submitted with—

(1) A description of the proposed curriculum;

(2) A list of the facilities and materials to be used;

(3) A list of its instructors, including the kind of certificate and ratings held and the certificate numbers; and

(4) A statement of the maximum number of students it expects to teach at any one time.

(b) An applicant who meets the requirements of this part is entitled to an aviation maintenance technician school certificate and associated ratings prescribing such operations specifications and limitations as are necessary in the interests of safety.

[Doc. No. 1157, 27 FR 6669, July 13, 1962, as amended by Amdt. 147–5, 57 FR 28959, June 29, 1992]

§ 147.7 Duration of certificates.

(a) An aviation maintenance technician school certificate or rating is effective until it is surrendered, suspended, or revoked.

(b) The holder of a certificate that is surrendered, suspended, or revoked, shall return it to the Administrator.

[Doc. No. 1157, 27 FR 6669, July 19, 1962, as amended by Amdt. 147–3, 41 FR 47230, Oct. 28, 1976]

§ 147.8 Employment of former FAA employees.

(a) Except as specified in paragraph (c) of this section, no holder of an aviation maintenance technician certificate may knowingly employ or make a contractual arrangement which permits an individual to act as an agent or representative of the certificate holder in any matter before the Federal Aviation Administration if the individual, in the preceding 2 years—

(1) Served as, or was directly responsible for the oversight of, a Flight Standards Service aviation safety inspector; and

(2) Had direct responsibility to inspect, or oversee the inspection of, the operations of the certificate holder.

(b) For the purpose of this section, an individual shall be considered to be acting as an agent or representative of a certificate holder in a matter before the agency if the individual makes any written or oral communication on behalf of the certificate holder to the agency (or any of its officers or employees) in connection with a particular matter, whether or not involving a specific party and without regard to whether the individual has participated in, or had responsibility for, the particular matter while serving as a Flight Standards Service aviation safety inspector.

(c) The provisions of this section do not prohibit a holder of an aviation maintenance technician school certificate from knowingly employing or making a contractual arrangement which permits an individual to act as an agent or representative of the certificate holder in any matter before the Federal Aviation Administration if the individual was employed by the certificate holder before October 21, 2011.

[Doc. No. FAA–2008–1154, 76 FR 52237, Aug. 22, 2011]

Subpart B—Certification Requirements

§ 147.11 Ratings.

The following ratings are issued under this part:

(a) Airframe.

(b) Powerplant.

(c) Airframe and powerplant.

§ 147.13 Facilities, equipment, and material requirements.

An applicant for an aviation maintenance technician school certificate and rating, or for an additional rating, must have at least the facilities, equipment, and materials specified in §§ 147.15 to 147.19 that are appropriate to the rating he seeks.

§ 147.15 Space requirements.

An applicant for an aviation maintenance technician school certificate and rating, or for an additional rating, must have such of the following properly heated, lighted, and ventilated facilities as are appropriate to the rating he seeks and as the Administrator determines are appropriate for the maximum number of students expected to be taught at any time:

(a) An enclosed classroom suitable for teaching theory classes.

(b) Suitable facilities, either central or located in training areas, arranged to assure proper separation from the working space, for parts, tools, materials, and similar articles.

(c) Suitable area for application of finishing materials, including paint spraying.

(d) Suitable areas equipped with washtank and degreasing equipment with air pressure or other adequate cleaning equipment.

(e) Suitable facilities for running engines.

(f) Suitable area with adequate equipment, including benches, tables, and test equipment, to disassemble, service, and inspect.

(1) Ignition, electrical equipment, and appliances;

(2) Carburetors and fuel systems; and

(3) Hydraulic and vacuum systems for aircraft, aircraft engines, and their appliances.

(g) Suitable space with adequate equipment, including tables, benches, stands, and jacks, for disassembling, inspecting, and rigging aircraft.

(h) Suitable space with adequate equipment for disassembling, inspecting, assembling, troubleshooting, and timing engines.

[Amdt. 147-2, 35 FR 5533, Apr. 3, 1970, as amended by Amdt. 147-5, 57 FR 28959, June 29, 1992]

§ 147.17 Instructional equipment requirements.

(a) An applicant for a mechanic school certificate and rating, or for an additional rating, must have such of the following instructional equipment as is appropriate to the rating he seeks:

(1) Various kinds of airframe structures, airframe systems and components, powerplants, and powerplant systems and components (including propellers), of a quantity and type suitable to complete the practical projects required by its approved curriculums.

(2) At least one aircraft of a type currently certificated by FAA for private or commercial operation, with powerplant, propeller, instruments, navigation and communications equipment, landing lights, and other equipment and accessories on which a maintenance technician might be required to work and with which the technician should be familiar.

(b) The equipment required by paragraph (a) of this section need not be in an airworthy condition. However, if it was damaged, it must have been repaired enough for complete assembly.

(c) Airframes, powerplants, propellers, appliances, and components thereof, on which instruction is to be given, and from which practical working experience is to be gained, must be so diversified as to show the different methods of construction, assembly, inspection, and operation when installed in an aircraft for use. There must be enough units so that not more than eight students will work on any one unit at a time.

(d) If the aircraft used for instructional purposes does not have retractable landing gear and wing flaps, the school must provide training aids, or operational mock-ups of them.

[Doc. No. 1157, 27 FR 6669, July 19, 1962, as amended by Amdt. 147-5, 57 FR 28959, June 29, 1992]

§ 147.19 Materials, special tools, and shop equipment requirements.

An applicant for an aviation maintenance technician school certificate and rating, or for an additional rating, must have an adequate supply of material, special tools, and such of the shop equipment as are appropriate to the approved curriculum of the school and are used in constructing and maintaining aircraft, to assure that each student will be properly instructed. The special tools and shop equipment must be in satisfactory working condition for the purpose for which they are to be used.

[Amdt. 147-5, 57 FR 28959, June 29, 1992]

§ 147.21 General curriculum requirements.

(a) An applicant for an aviation maintenance technician school certificate and rating, or for an additional rating, must have an approved curriculum that is designed to qualify his students to perform the duties of a mechanic for a particular rating or ratings.

(b) The curriculum must offer at least the following number of hours of instruction for the rating shown, and the instruction unit hour shall not be less than 50 minutes in length—

(1) Airframe—1,150 hours (400 general plus 750 airframe).

(2) Powerplant—1,150 hours (400 general plus 750 powerplant).

(3) Combined airframe and powerplant—1,900 hours (400 general plus 750 airframe and 750 powerplant).

(c) The curriculum must cover the subjects and items prescribed in appendixes B, C, or D, as applicable. Each item must be taught to at least the indicated level of proficiency, as defined in appendix A.

(d) The curriculum must show—

(1) The required practical projects to be completed;

(2) For each subject, the proportions of theory and other instruction to be given; and

(3) A list of the minimum required school tests to be given.

(e) Notwithstanding the provisions of paragraphs (a) through (d) of this section and § 147.11, the holder of a certificate issued under subpart B of this part may apply for and receive approval of special courses in the performance of special inspection and preventive maintenance programs for a primary category aircraft type certificated under § 21.24(b) of this chapter. The school may also issue certificates of competency to persons successfully completing such courses provided that all other requirements of this part are met and the certificate of competency specifies the aircraft make and model to which the certificate applies.

[Doc. No. 1157, 27 FR 6669, July 13, 1962, as amended by Amdt. 147-1, 32 FR 5770 Apr. 11, 1967; Amdt. 147-5, 57 FR 28959, June 29, 1992; Amdt. 147-6, 57 FR 41370, Sept. 9, 1992]

§ 147.23 Instructor requirements.

An applicant for an aviation maintenance technician school certificate and rating, or for an additional rating, must provide the number of instructors holding appropriate mechanic certificates and ratings that the Administrator determines necessary to provide adequate instruction and supervision of the students, including at least one such instructor for each 25 students in each shop class. However, the applicant may provide specialized instructors, who are not certificated mechanics, to teach mathematics, physics, basic electricity, basic hydraulics, drawing, and similar subjects. The applicant is required to maintain a list of the names and qualifications of specialized instructors, and upon request, provide a copy of the list to the FAA.

[Amdt. 147-5, 57 FR 28959, June 29, 1992]

Subpart C—Operating Rules

§ 147.31 Attendance and enrollment, tests, and credit for prior instruction or experience.

(a) A certificated aviation maintenance technician school may not require any student to attend classes of instruction more than 8 hours in any day or more than 6 days or 40 hours in any 7-day period.

(b) Each school shall give an appropriate test to each student who completes a unit of instruction as shown in that school's approved curriculum.

(c) A school may not graduate a student unless he has completed all of the appropriate curriculum requirements. However, the school may credit a student with instruction or previous experience as follows:

(1) A school may credit a student with instruction satisfactorily completed at—

(i) An accredited university, college, junior college;

(ii) An accredited vocational, technical, trade or high school;

(iii) A military technical school;

(iv) A certificated aviation maintenance technician school.

(2) A school may determine the amount of credit to be allowed—

(i) By an entrance test equal to one given to the students who complete a comparable required curriculum subject at the crediting school;

(ii) By an evaluation of an authenticated transcript from the student's former school; or

(iii) In the case of an applicant from a military school, only on the basis of an entrance test.

(3) A school may credit a student with previous aviation maintenance experience comparable to required curriculum subjects. It must determine the amount of credit to be allowed by documents verifying that experience, and by giving the student a test equal to the one given to students who complete the comparable required curriculum subject at the school.

(4) A school may credit a student seeking an additional rating with previous satisfactory completion of the general portion of an AMTS curriculum.

(d) A school may not have more students enrolled than the number stated in its application for a certificate, unless it amends its application and has it approved.

(e) A school shall use an approved system for determining final course grades and for recording student attendance. The system must show hours of absence allowed and show how the missed material will be made available to the student.

[Amdt. 147–2, 35 FR 5534, Apr. 3, 1970, as amended by Amdt. 147–4, 43 FR 22643, May 25, 1978; Amdt. 147–5, 57 FR 28959, June 29, 1992]

§ 147.33   Records.

(a) Each certificated aviation maintenance technician school shall keep a current record of each student enrolled, showing—

(1) His attendance, tests, and grades received on the subjects required by this part;

(2) The instruction credited to him under § 147.31(c), if any; and

(3) The authenticated transcript of his grades from that school.

It shall retain the record for at least two years after the end of the student's enrollment, and shall make each record available for inspection by the Administrator during that period.

(b) Each school shall keep a current progress chart or individual progress record for each of its students, showing the practical projects or laboratory work completed, or to be completed, by the student in each subject.

[Doc. No. 1157, 27 FR 6669, July 13, 1962]

§ 147.35   Transcripts and graduation certificates.

(a) Upon request, each certificated aviation maintenance technician school shall provide a transcript of the student's grades to each student who is graduated from that school or who leaves it before being graduated. An official of the school shall authenticate the transcript. The transcript must state the curriculum in which the student was enrolled, whether the student satisfactorily completed that curriculum, and the final grades the student received.

(b) Each school shall give a graduation certificate or certificate of completion to each student that it graduates. An official of the school shall authenticate the certificate. The certificate must show the date of graduation and the approved curriculum title.

[Doc. No. 1157, 27 FR 6669, July 13, 1962, as amended by Amdt. 147–5, 57 FR 28959, June 29, 1992]

§ 147.36 Maintenance of instructor requirements.

Each certificated aviation maintenance technician school shall, after certification or addition of a rating, continue to provide the number of instructors holding appropriate mechanic certificates and ratings that the Administrator determines necessary to provide adequate instruction to the students, including at least one such instructor for each 25 students in each shop class. The school may continue to provide specialized instructors who are not certificated mechanics to teach mathematics, physics, drawing, basic electricity, basic hydraulics, and similar subjects.

[Amdt. 147–5, 57 FR 28959, June 29, 1992]

§ 147.37 Maintenance of facilities, equipment, and material.

(a) Each certificated aviation maintenance technician school shall provide facilities, equipment, and material equal to the standards currently required for the issue of the certificate and rating that it holds.

(b) A school may not make a substantial change in facilities, equipment, or material that have been approved for a particular curriculum, unless that change is approved in advance.

§ 147.38 Maintenance of curriculum requirements.

(a) Each certificated aviation maintenance technician school shall adhere to its approved curriculum. With FAA approval, curriculum subjects may be taught at levels exceeding those shown in appendix A of this part.

(b) A school may not change its approved curriculum unless the change is approved in advance.

[Amdt. 147–2, 35 FR 5534, Apr. 3, 1970, as amended by Amdt. 147–5, 57 FR 28960, June 29, 1992]

§ 147.38a Quality of instruction.

Each certificated aviation maintenance technician school shall provide instruction of such quality that, of its graduates of a curriculum for each rating who apply for a mechanic certificate or additional rating within 60 days after they are graduated, the percentage of those passing the applicable FAA written tests on their first attempt during any period of 24 calendar months is at least the percentage figured as follows:

(a) For a school graduating fewer than 51 students during that period—the national passing norm minus the number 20.

(b) For a school graduating at least 51, but fewer than 201, students during that period—the national passing norm minus the number 15.

(c) For a school graduating more than 200 students during that period—the national passing norm minus the number 10.

As used in this section, "national passing norm" is the number representing the percentage of all graduates (of a curriculum for a particular rating) of all certificated aviation maintenance technician schools who apply for a mechanic certificate or additional rating within 60 days after they are graduated and pass the applicable FAA written tests on their first attempt during the period of 24 calendar months described in this section.

[Amdt. 147–2, 35 FR 5534, Apr. 3, 1970, as amended by Amdt. 147–3, 41 FR 47230, Oct. 28, 1976]

§ 147.39 Display of certificate.

Each holder of an aviation maintenance technician school certificate and ratings shall display them at a place in the school that is normally accessible to the public and is not obscured. The certificate must be available for inspection by the Administrator.

§ 147.41 Change of location.

The holder of an aviation maintenance technician school certificate may not make any change in the school's location unless the change is approved in advance. If the holder desires to change the location he shall notify the Administrator, in writing, at least 30 days before the date the change is contemplated. If he changes its location without approval, the certificate is revoked.

§ 147.43 Inspection.

The Administrator may, at any time, inspect an aviation maintenance technician school to determine its compliance with this part. Such an inspection is normally made once each six months to determine if the school continues to meet the requirements under which it was originally certificated. After such an inspection is made, the school is notified, in writing, of any deficiencies found during the inspection. Other informal inspections may be made from time to time.

§ 147.45 Advertising.

(a) A certificated aviation maintenance technician school may not make any statement relating to itself that is false or is designed to mislead any person considering enrollment therein.

(b) Whenever an aviation maintenance technician school indicates in advertising that it is a certificated school, it shall clearly distinguish between its approved courses and those that are not approved.

APPENDIX A TO PART 147—CURRICULUM REQUIREMENTS

This appendix defines terms used in appendices B, C, and D of this part, and describes the levels of proficiency at which items under each subject in each curriculum must be taught, as outlined in appendices B, C, and D.

(a) *Definitions.* As used in appendices B, C, and D:

(1) *Inspect* means to examine by sight and touch.

(2) *Check* means to verify proper operation.

(3) *Troubleshoot* means to analyze and identify malfunctions.

(4) *Service* means to perform functions that assure continued operation.

(5) *Repair* means to correct a defective condition. Repair of an airframe or powerplant system includes component replacement and adjustment, but not component repair.

(6) *Overhaul* means to disassemble, inspect, repair as necessary, and check.

(b) *Teaching levels.* (1) Level 1 requires:

(i) Knowledge of general principles, but no practical application.

(ii) No development of manipulative skill.

(iii) Instruction by lecture, demonstration, and discussion.

(2) Level 2 requires:

(i) Knowledge of general principles, and limited practical application.

(ii) Development of sufficient manipulative skill to perform basic operations.

(iii) Instruction by lecture, demonstration, discussion, and limited practical application.

(3) Level 3 requires:

(i) Knowledge of general principles, and performance of a high degree of practical application.

(ii) Development of sufficient manipulative skills to simulate return to service.

(iii) Instruction by lecture, demonstration, discussion, and a high degree of practical application.

(c) *Teaching materials and equipment.* The curriculum may be presented utilizing currently accepted educational materials and equipment, including, but not limited to: calculators, computers, and audio-visual equipment.

[Amdt. 147-2, 35 FR 5534, Apr. 3, 1970, as amended by Amdt. 147-5, 57 FR 28960, June 29, 1992]

APPENDIX B TO PART 147—GENERAL CURRICULUM SUBJECTS

This appendix lists the subjects required in at least 400 hours in general curriculum subjects.

The number in parentheses before each item listed under each subject heading indicates the level of proficiency at which that item must be taught.

Teaching level		
	A. BASIC ELECTRICITY	
(2)	1.	Calculate and measure capacitance and inductance.
(2)	2.	Calculate and measure electrical power.
(3)	3.	Measure voltage, current, resistance, and continuity.
(3)	4.	Determine the relationship of voltage, current, and resistance in electrical circuits.
(3)	5.	Read and interpret aircraft electrical circuit diagrams, including solid state devices and logic functions.
(3)	6.	Inspect and service batteries.
	B. AIRCRAFT DRAWINGS	
(2)	7.	Use aircraft drawings, symbols, and system schematics.
(3)	8.	Draw sketches of repairs and alterations.
(3)	9.	Use blueprint information.
(3)	10.	Use graphs and charts.
	C. WEIGHT AND BALANCE	
(2)	11.	Weigh aircraft.
(3)	12.	Perform complete weight-and-balance check and record data.
	D. FLUID LINES AND FITTINGS	
(3)	13.	Fabricate and install rigid and flexible fluid lines and fittings.
	E. MATERIALS AND PROCESSES	
(1)	14.	Identify and select appropriate nondestructive testing methods.

Teach-
ing
level

(2) 15. Perform dye penetrant, eddy current, ultrasonic, and magnetic particle inspections.
(1) 16. Perform basic heat-treating processes.
(3) 17. Identify and select aircraft hardware and materials.
(3) 18. Inspect and check welds.
(3) 19. Perform precision measurements.

F. GROUND OPERATION AND SERVICING

(2) 20. Start, ground operate, move, service, and secure aircraft and identify typical ground operation hazards.
(2) 21. Identify and select fuels.

G. CLEANING AND CORROSION CONTROL

(3) 22. Identify and select cleaning materials.
(3) 23. Inspect, identify, remove, and treat aircraft corrosion and perform aircraft cleaning.

H. MATHEMATICS

(3) 24. Extract roots and raise numbers to a given power.
(3) 25. Determine areas and volumes of various geometrical shapes.
(3) 26. Solve ratio, proportion, and percentage problems.
(3) 27. Perform algebraic operations involving addition, subtraction, multiplication, and division of positive and negative numbers.

I. MAINTENANCE FORMS AND RECORDS

(3) 28. Write descriptions of work performed including aircraft discrepancies and corrective actions using typical aircraft maintenance records.
(3) 29. Complete required maintenance forms, records, and inspection reports.

J. BASIC PHYSICS

(2) 30. Use and understand the principles of simple machines; sound, fluid, and heat dynamics; basic aerodynamics; aircraft structures; and theory of flight.

K. MAINTENANCE PUBLICATIONS

(3) 31. Demonstrate ability to read, comprehend, and apply information contained in FAA and manufacturers' aircraft maintenance specifications, data sheets, manuals, publications, and related Federal Aviation Regulations, Airworthiness Directives, and Advisory material.
(3) 32. Read technical data.

L. MECHANIC PRIVILEGES AND LIMITATIONS

(3) 33. Exercise mechanic privileges within the limitations prescribed by part 65 of this chapter

[Amdt. 147–2, 35 FR 5534, Apr. 3, 1970, as amended by Amdt. 147–5, 57 FR 28960, June 29, 1992]

APPENDIX C TO PART 147—AIRFRAME CURRICULUM SUBJECTS

This appendix lists the subjects required in at least 750 hours of each airframe curriculum, in addition to at least 400 hours in general curriculum subjects.

The number in parentheses before each item listed under each subject heading indicates the level of proficiency at which that item must be taught.

I. AIRFRAME STRUCTURES

Teach-
ing
level

A. WOOD STRUCTURES

(1) 1. Service and repair wood structures.
(1) 2. Identify wood defects.
(1) 3. Inspect wood structures.

B. AIRCRAFT COVERING

(1) 4. Select and apply fabric and fiberglass covering materials.
(1) 5. Inspect, test, and repair fabric and fiberglass.

C. AIRCRAFT FINISHES

(1) 6. Apply trim, letters, and touchup paint.
(2) 7. Identify and select aircraft finishing materials.
(2) 8. Apply finishing materials.
(2) 9. Inspect finishes and identify defects.

D. SHEET METAL AND NON-METALLIC STRUCTURES

(2) 10. Select, install, and remove special fasteners for metallic, bonded, and composite structures.
(2) 11. Inspect bonded structures.
(2) 12. Inspect, test, and repair fiberglass, plastics, honeycomb, composite, and laminated primary and secondary structures.
(2) 13. Inspect, check, service, and repair windows, doors, and interior furnishings.
(3) 14. Inspect and repair sheet-metal structures.
(3) 15. Install conventional rivets.
(3) 16. Form, lay out, and bend sheet metal.

E. WELDING

(1) 17. Weld magnesium and titanium.
(1) 18. Solder stainless steel.
(1) 19. Fabricate tubular structures.
(2) 20. Solder, braze, gas-weld, and arc-weld steel.
(1) 21. Weld aluminum and stainless steel.

F. ASSEMBLY AND RIGGING

(1) 22. Rig rotary-wing aircraft.
(2) 23. Rig fixed-wing aircraft.
(2) 24. Check alignment of structures.
(3) 25. Assemble aircraft components, including flight control surfaces.
(3) 26. Balance, rig, and inspect movable primary and secondary flight control surfaces.
(3) 27. Jack aircraft.

G. AIRFRAME INSPECTION

(3) 28. Perform airframe conformity and airworthiness inspections.

II. AIRFRAME SYSTEMS AND COMPONENTS

Teach-
ing
level

A. AIRCRAFT LANDING GEAR SYSTEMS

(3) 29. Inspect, check, service, and repair landing gear, retraction systems, shock struts, brakes, wheels, tires, and steering systems.

B. HYDRAULIC AND PNEUMATIC POWER SYSTEMS

(2) 30. Repair hydraulic and pneumatic power systems components.
(3) 31. Identify and select hydraulic fluids.
(3) 32. Inspect, check, service, troubleshoot, and repair hydraulic and pneumatic power systems.

C. CABIN ATMOSPHERE CONTROL SYSTEMS

(1) 33. Inspect, check, troubleshoot, service, and repair heating, cooling, air conditioning, pressurization systems, and air cycle machines.

II. AIRFRAME SYSTEMS AND COMPONENTS— Continued

Teach-
ing
level

(1) 34. Inspect, check, troubleshoot, service, and repair heating, cooling, air-conditioning, and pressurization systems.
(2) 35. Inspect, check, troubleshoot, service and repair oxygen systems.

D. AIRCRAFT INSTRUMENT SYSTEMS

(1) 36. Inspect, check, service, troubleshoot, and repair electronic flight instrument systems and both mechanical and electrical heading, speed, altitude, temperature, pressure, and position indicating systems to include the use of built-in test equipment.
(2) 37. Install instruments and perform a static pressure system leak test.

E. COMMUNICATION AND NAVIGATION SYSTEMS

(1) 38. Inspect, check, and troubleshoot autopilot, servos and approach coupling systems.
(1) 39. Inspect, check, and service aircraft electronic communication and navigation systems, including VHF passenger address interphones and static discharge devices, aircraft VOR, ILS, Radar beacon transponders, flight management computers, and GPWS.
(2) 40. Inspect and repair antenna and electronic equipment installations.

F. AIRCRAFT FUEL SYSTEMS

(1) 41. Check and service fuel dump systems.
(1) 42. Perform fuel management transfer, and defueling.
(1) 43. Inspect, check, and repair pressure fueling systems.
(2) 44. Repair aircraft fuel system components.
(2) 45. Inspect and repair fluid quantity indicating systems.
(2) 46. Troubleshoot, service, and repair fluid pressure and temperature warning systems.
(3) 47. Inspect, check, service, troubleshoot, and repair aircraft fuel systems.

G. AIRCRAFT ELECTRICAL SYSTEMS

(2) 48. Repair and inspect aircraft electrical system components; crimp and splice wiring to manufacturers' specifications; and repair pins and sockets of aircraft connectors.
(3) 49. Install, check, and service airframe electrical wiring, controls, switches, indicators, and protective devices.
(3) 50.a. Inspect, check, troubleshoot, service, and repair alternating and direct current electrical systems.
(1) 50.b. Inspect, check, and troubleshoot constant speed and integrated speed drive generators.

H. POSITION AND WARNING SYSTEMS

(2) 51. Inspect, check, and service speed and configuration warning systems, electrical brake controls, and anti-skid systems.
(3) 52. Inspect, check, troubleshoot, and service landing gear position indicating and warning systems.

I. ICE AND RAIN CONTROL SYSTEMS

(2) 53. Inspect, check, troubleshoot, service, and repair airframe ice and rain control systems.

J. FIRE PROTECTION SYSTEMS

(1) 54. Inspect, check, and service smoke and carbon monoxide detection systems.
(3) 55. Inspect, check, troubleshoot, and repair aircraft fire detection and extinguishing systems.

[Amdt. 147-2, 35 FR 5535, Apr. 3, 1970, as amended by Amdt. 147-5, 57 FR 28960, June 29, 1992; Docket FAA-2017-0733, Amdt. 147-8, 82 FR 34399, July 25, 2017]

APPENDIX D TO PART 147—POWERPLANT CURRICULUM SUBJECTS

This appendix lists the subjects required in at least 750 hours of each powerplant curriculum, in addition to at least 400 hours in general curriculum subjects.

The number in parentheses before each item listed under each subject heading indicates the level of proficiency at which that item must be taught.

I. POWERPLANT THEORY AND MAINTENANCE

Teach-
ing
level

A. RECIPROCATING ENGINES

(1) 1. Inspect and repair a radial engine.
(2) 2. Overhaul reciprocating engine.
(3) 3. Inspect, check, service, and repair reciprocating engines and engine installations.
(3) 4. Install, troubleshoot, and remove reciprocating engines.

B. TURBINE ENGINES

(2) 5. Overhaul turbine engine.
(3) 6. Inspect, check, service, and repair turbine engines and turbine engine installations.
(3) 7. Install, troubleshoot, and remove turbine engines.

C. ENGINE INSPECTION

(3) 8. Perform powerplant conformity and air worthiness inspections.

II. POWERPLANT SYSTEMS AND COMPONENTS

Teach-
ing
level

A. ENGINE INSTRUMENT SYSTEMS

(2) 9. Troubleshoot, service, and repair electrical and mechanical fluid rate-of-flow indicating systems.
(3) 10. Inspect, check, service, troubleshoot, and repair electrical and mechanical engine temperature, pressure, and r.p.m. indicating systems.

B. ENGINE FIRE PROTECTION SYSTEMS

(3) 11. Inspect, check, service, troubleshoot, and repair engine fire detection and extinguishing systems.

C. ENGINE ELECTRICAL SYSTEMS

(2) 12. Repair engine electrical system components.
(3) 13. Install, check, and service engine electrical wiring, controls, switches, indicators, and protective devices.

D. LUBRICATION SYSTEMS

(2) 14. Identify and select lubricants.
(2) 15. Repair engine lubrication system components.
(3) 16. Inspect, check, service, troubleshoot, and repair engine lubrication systems.

E. IGNITION AND STARTING SYSTEMS

(2) 17. Overhaul magneto and ignition harness.
(2) 18. Inspect, service, troubleshoot, and repair reciprocating and turbine engine ignition systems and components.
(3) 19.a. Inspect, service, troubleshoot, and repair turbine engine electrical starting systems.

II. POWERPLANT SYSTEMS AND COMPONENTS—
Continued

II. POWERPLANT SYSTEMS AND COMPONENTS—
Continued

Teach-ing level	
(1)	19.b. Inspect, service, and troubleshoot turbine engine pneumatic starting systems.
	F. FUEL METERING SYSTEMS
(1)	20. Troubleshoot and adjust turbine engine fuel metering systems and electronic engine fuel controls.
(2)	21. Overhaul carburetor.
(2)	22. Repair engine fuel metering system components.
(3)	23. Inspect, check, service, troubleshoot, and repair reciprocating and turbine engine fuel metering systems.
	G. ENGINE FUEL SYSTEMS
(2)	24. Repair engine fuel system components.
(3)	25. Inspect, check, service, troubleshoot, and repair engine fuel systems.
	H. INDUCTION AND ENGINE AIRFLOW SYSTEMS
(2)	26. Inspect, check, troubleshoot, service, and repair engine ice and rain control systems.
(1)	27. Inspect, check, service, troubleshoot and repair heat exchangers, superchargers, and turbine engine airflow and temperature control systems.
(3)	28. Inspect, check, service, and repair carburetor air intake and induction manifolds.
	I. ENGINE COOLING SYSTEMS
(2)	29. Repair engine cooling system components.
(3)	30. Inspect, check, troubleshoot, service, and repair engine cooling systems.
	J. ENGINE EXHAUST AND REVERSER SYSTEMS
(2)	31. Repair engine exhaust system components.

Teach-ing level	
(3)	32.a. Inspect, check, troubleshoot, service, and repair engine exhaust systems.
(1)	32.b. Troubleshoot and repair engine thrust reverser systems and related components.
	K. PROPELLERS
(1)	33. Inspect, check, service, and repair propeller synchronizing and ice control systems.
(2)	34. Identify and select propeller lubricants.
(1)	35. Balance propellers.
(2)	36. Repair propeller control system components.
(3)	37. Inspect, check, service, and repair fixed-pitch, constant-speed, and feathering propellers, and propeller governing systems.
(3)	38. Install, troubleshoot, and remove propellers.
(3)	39. Repair aluminum alloy propeller blades.
	L. UNDUCTED FANS
(1)	40. Inspect and troubleshoot unducted fan systems and components.
	M. AUXILIARY POWER UNITS
(1)	41. Inspect, check, service, and troubleshoot turbine-driven auxiliary power units.

(Sec. 6(c), Dept. of Transportation Act; 49 U.S.C. 1655(c))

[Amdt. 147–2, 35 FR 5535, Apr. 3, 1970, as amended by Amdt. 147–5, 57 FR 28961, June 29, 1992]

SUBCHAPTER I—AIRPORTS

PART 150—AIRPORT NOISE COMPATIBILITY PLANNING

Subpart A—General Provisions

AUTHORITY: 49 U.S.C. 106(g), 40113, 44715, 47101, 47501–47504.

SOURCE: Docket No. 18691, 49 FR 49269, Dec. 18, 1984, unless otherwise noted.

Subpart A—General Provisions

§ 150.1 Scope and purpose.

This part prescribes the procedures, standards, and methodology governing the development, submission, and review of airport noise exposure maps and airport noise compatibility programs, including the process for evaluating and approving or disapproving those programs. It prescribes single systems for—(a) measuring noise at airports and surrounding areas that generally provides a highly reliable relationship between projected noise exposure and surveyed reaction of people to noise; and (b) determining exposure of individuals to noise that results from the operations of an airport. This part also identifies those land uses which are normally compatible with various levels of exposure to noise by individuals. It provides technical assistance to airport operators, in conjunction with other local, State, and Federal authorities, to prepare and execute appropriate noise compatibility planning and implementation programs.

§ 150.3 Applicability.

This part applies to the airport noise compatibility planning activities of the operators of "public use airports," including heliports, as that term is used in section 47501(2) as amended (49 U.S.C. 47501 et seq.) and as defined in section 47102(17) of 49 U.S.C.

[Doc. No. FAA–2004–19158, 69 FR 57625, Sept. 24, 2004]

§ 150.5 Limitations of this part.

(a) Pursuant to 49 U.S.C. 47501 et seq., this part provides for airport noise compatibility planning and land use programs necessary to the purposes of those provisions. No submittal of a map, or approval or disapproval, in whole or part, of any map or program submitted under this part is a determination concerning the acceptability or unacceptability of that land use under Federal, State, or local law.

(b) Approval of a noise compatibility program under this part is neither a commitment by the FAA to financially assist in the implementation of the program, nor a determination that all measures covered by the program are eligible for grant-in-aid funding from the FAA.

(c) Approval of a noise compatibility program under this part does not by itself constitute an FAA implementing action. A request for Federal action or approval to implement specific noise compatibility measures may be required, and an FAA decision on the request may require an environmental assessment of the proposed action, pursuant to the National Environmental Policy Act (42 U.S.C. 4332 et seq.) and guidelines.

(d) Acceptance of a noise exposure map does not constitute an FAA determination that any specific parcel of land lies within a particular noise contour. Responsibility for interpretation of the effects of noise contours upon subjacent land uses, including the relationship between noise contours and specific properties, rests with the sponsor or with other state or local government.

[Doc. No. 18691, 49 FR 49269, Dec. 18, 1984, as amended by Amdt. 150–4, 69 FR 57625, Sept. 24, 2004]

§150.7 **Definitions.**

As used in this part, unless the context requires otherwise, the following terms have the following meanings.

Airport means any public use airport, including heliports, as defined by the ASNA Act, including: (a) Any airport which is used or to be used for public purposes, under the control of a public agency, the landing area of which is publicly owned; (b) any privately owned reliever airport; and (c) any privately owned airport which is determined by the Secretary to enplane annually 2,500 or more passengers and receive scheduled passenger service of aircraft, which is used or to be used for public purposes.

Airport noise compatibility program and *program* mean that program, and all revisions thereto, reflected in documents (and revised documents) developed in accordance with appendix B of this part, including the measures proposed or taken by the airport operator to reduce existing noncompatible land uses and to prevent the introduction of additional noncompatible land uses within the area.

Airport Operator means, the operator of an airport as defined in the ASNA Act.

ASNA Act means 49 U.S.C. 47501 et seq.

Average sound level means the level, in decibels, of the mean-square, A-weighted sound pressure during a specified period, with reference to the square of the standard reference sound pressure of 20 micropascals.

Compatible land use means the use of land that is identified under this part as normally compatible with the outdoor noise environment (or an adequately attenuated noise level reduc-

tion for any indoor activities involved) at the location because the yearly day-night average sound level is at or below that identified for that or similar use under appendix A (Table 1) of this part.

Day-night average sound level (DNL) means the 24-hour average sound level, in decibels, for the period from midnight to midnight, obtained after the addition of ten decibels to sound levels for the periods between midnight and 7 a.m., and between 10 p.m., and midnight, local time. The symbol for DNL is L_{dn}.

Noise exposure map means a scaled, geographic depiction of an airport, its noise contours, and surrounding area developed in accordance with section A150.1 of Appendix A of this part, including the accompanying documentation setting forth the required descriptions of forecast aircraft operations at that airport during the fifth calendar year (or later) beginning after submission of the map, together with the ways, if any, those operations will affect the map (including noise contours and the forecast land uses).

Noise level reduction (NLR) means the amount of noise level reduction in decibels achieved through incorporation of noise attenuation (between outdoor and indoor levels) in the design and construction of a structure.

Noncompatible land use means the use of land that is identified under this part as normally not compatible with the outdoor noise environment (or an adequately attenuated noise reduction level for the indoor activities involved at the location) because the yearly day-night average sound level is above that identified for that or similar use under appendix A (Table 1) of this part.

Regional Airports Division Manager means the Airports Division Manager having responsibility for the geographic area in which the airport in question is located.

Restriction affecting flight procedures means any requirement, limitation, or other action affecting the operation of aircraft, in the air or on the ground.

Sound exposure level means the level, in decibels, of the time integral of squared A-weighted sound pressure during a specified period or event, with reference to the square of the standard reference sound pressure of 20 micropascals and a duration of one second.

Yearly day-night average sound level (YDNL) means the 365-day average, in decibels, day-night average sound level. The symbol for YDNL is also L_{dn}.

[Doc. No. 18691, 49 FR 49269, Dec. 18, 1984, as amended by Amdt. 150–1, 53 FR 8724, Mar. 16, 1988; 53 FR 9726, Mar. 24, 1988; Amdt. 150–2, 54 FR 39295, Sept. 25, 1989; Amdt. 150–4, 69 FR 57625, Sept. 24, 2004]

§ 150.9 Designation of noise systems.

For purposes of this part, the following designations apply:

(a) The noise at an airport and surrounding areas covered by a noise exposure map must be measured in A-weighted sound pressure level (L_A) in units of decibels (dBA) in accordance with the specifications and methods prescribed under appendix A of this part.

(b) The exposure of individuals to noise resulting from the operation of an airport must be established in terms of yearly day-night average sound level (YDNL) calculated in accordance with the specifications and methods prescribed under appendix A of this part.

(c) Uses of computer models to create noise contours must be in accordance with the criteria prescribed under appendix A of this part.

§ 150.11 Identification of land uses.

For the purposes of this part, uses of land which are normally compatible or noncompatible with various noise exposure levels to individuals around airports must be identified in accordance with the criteria prescribed under appendix A of this part. Determination of land use must be based on professional planning criteria and procedures utilizing comprehensive, or master, land use planning, zoning, and building and site designing, as appropriate. If more than one current or future land use is permissible, determination of compatibility must be based on that use most adversely affected by noise.

§ 150.13 Incorporations by reference.

(a) *General.* This part prescribes certain standards and procedures which are not set forth in full text in the rule. Those standards and procedures are hereby incorporated by reference

and were approved for incorporation by reference by the Director of the Federal Register under 5 U.S.C. 552(a) and 1 CFR part 51.

(b) *Changes to incorporated matter.* Incorporated matter which is subject to subsequent change is incorporated by reference according to the specific reference and to the identification statement. Adoption of any subsequent change in incorporated matter that affects compliance with standards and procedures of this part will be made under 14 CFR part 11 and 1 CFR part 51.

(c) *Identification statement.* The complete title or description which identifies each published matter incorporated by reference in this part is as follows:

International Electrotechnical Commission (IEC) Publication No. 179, entitled "Precision Sound Level Meters," dated 1973.

(d) *Availability for purchase.* Published material incorporated by reference in this part may be purchased at the price established by the publisher or distributor at the following mailing addresses.

IEC publications:

(1) The Bureau Central de la Commission Electrotechnique, Internationale, 1, rue de Varembe, Geneva, Switzerland.

(2) American National Standards Institute, 1430 Broadway, New York, NY 10018.

(e) *Availability for inspection.* A copy of each publication incorporated by reference in this part is available for public inspection at the following locations:

(1) FAA Office of the Chief Counsel, Rules Docket, AGC–200, Federal Aviation Administration Headquarters Building, 800 Independence Avenue, SW., Washington, DC 20591.

(2) The respective Regional Offices of the Federal Aviation Administration as follows. The most current mailing address, phone numbers, and States covered by each region are available on the FAA's Web site at *http://www.faa.gov/arp/index.cfm?nav = hq.*

(i) New England Regional Office, 12 New England Executive Park, Burlington, Massachusetts 01803.

(ii) Eastern Regional Office, Airports Division, 1 Aviation Plaza, Jamaica, NY 11434–4809.

(iii) Southern Regional Office, Federal Aviation Administration, ATTN: ASO–600, P.O. Box 20636, Atlanta, GA 30320–0631.

(iv) Great Lakes Regional Office. 2300 East Devon, Des Plaines, Illinois 60018.

(v) Central Regional Office, Federal Aviation Administration, ACE–6C0, 901 Locust, Kansas City, MO 64106–2325.

(vi) Southwest Regional Office. Federal Aviation Administration, 2601 Meacham Blvd., Fort Worth, TX 76137–4298.

(vii) Northwest Mountain Regional Office, Federal Aviation Administration, Airports Division, 1601 Lind Avenue SW., Suite 315, Renton, WA 98055–4056.

(viii) Western Pacific Regional Office, 15000 Aviation Boulevard, Hawthorne, California (P.O. Box 92007, Worldway Postal Center, Los Angeles) 90009.

(ix) Alaskan Regional Office, 222 W. 7th Avenue #14, Anchorage, AK 9951.

(3) National Archives and Records Administration (NARA). For information on the availability of this material at NARA, call 202–741–6030, or go to: *http://www.archives.gov/ federal_register/ code_of_federal_regulations/ ibr_locations.html.*

[Doc. No. 18691, 49 FR 49269, Dec. 18, 1984, as amended by Amdt. 150–2, 54 FR 39295, Sept. 25, 1989; 69 FR 18803, Apr. 9, 2004; Amdt. 150–4, 69 FR 57625, Sept. 24, 2004; 72 FR 68475, Dec. 5, 2007]

Subpart B—Development of Noise Exposure Maps and Noise Compatibility Programs

§ 150.21 Noise exposure maps and related descriptions.

(a) Each airport operator may after completion of the consultations and public procedure specified under paragraph (b) of this section submit to the Regional Airports Division Manager five copies of the noise exposure map (or revised map) which identifies each noncompatible land use in each area depicted on the map, as of the date of submission, and five copies of a map each with accompanying documentation setting forth—

(1) The noise exposure based on forecast aircraft operations at the airport

for a forecast period that is at least 5 years in the future, beginning after the date of submission (based on reasonable assumptions concerning future type and frequency of aircraft operations, number of nighttime operations, flight patterns, airport layout including any planned airport development, planned land use changes, and demographic changes in the surrounding areas); and

(2) The nature and extent, if any, to which those forecast operations will affect the compatibility and land uses depicted on the map.

(b) Each map, and related documentation submitted under this section must be developed and prepared in accordance with appendix A of this part, or an FAA approved equivalent, and in consultation with states, and public agencies and planning agencies whose area, or any portion of whose area, of jurisdiction is within the L_{dn} 65 dB contour depicted on the map, FAA regional officials, and other Federal officials having local responsibility for land uses depicted on the map. This consultation must include regular aeronautical users of the airport. The airport operator shall certify that it has afforded interested persons adequate opportunity to submit their views, data, and comments concerning the correctness and adequacy of the draft noise exposure map and descriptions of forecast aircraft operations. Each map and revised map must be accompanied by documentation describing the consultation accomplished under this paragraph and the opportunities afforded the public to review and comment during the development of the map. One copy of all written comments received during consultation shall also be filed with the Regional Airports Division Manager.

(c) The Regional Airports Division Manager acknowledges receipt of noise exposure maps and descriptions and indicates whether they are in compliance with the applicable requirements. The Regional Airports Division Manager publishes in the FEDERAL REGISTER a notice of compliance for each such noise exposure map and description, identifying the airport involved. Such notice includes information as to when and where the map and related documentation are available for public inspection.

(d) The airport operator shall, in accordance with this section, promptly prepare and submit a revised noise exposure map.

(1) If, after submission of a noise exposure map under paragraph (a) of this section, any change in the operation of the airport would create any "substantial, new noncompatible use" in any area depicted on the map beyond that which is forecast for a period of at least five years after the date of submission, the airport operator shall, in accordance with this section, promptly prepare and submit a revised noise exposure map. A change in the operation of an airport creates a substantial new noncompatible use if that change results in an increase in the yearly day-night average sound level of 1.5 dB or greater in either a land area which was formerly compatible but is thereby made noncompatible under Appendix A (Table 1), or in a land area which was previously determined to be noncompatible under that Table and whose noncompatibility is now significantly increased.

(2) If, after submission of a noise exposure map under paragraph (a) of this section, any change in the operation of the airport would significantly reduce noise over existing noncompatible uses that is not reflected in either the existing conditions or forecast noise exposure map on file with the FAA, the airport operator shall, in accordance with this section, promptly prepare and submit a revised noise exposure map. A change in the operation of the airport creates a significant reduction in noise over existing noncompatible uses if that change results in a decrease in the yearly day-night average sound level of 1.5 dB or greater in a land area which was formerly noncompatible but is thereby made compatible under Appendix A (Table 1).

(3) Such updating of the map shall include a reassessment of those areas excluded under section A150.101(e)(5) of Appendix A because of high ambient noise levels.

(4) If the forecast map is based on assumptions involving recommendations in a noise compatibility program which are subsequently disapproved by the FAA, a revised map must be submitted if revised assumptions would create a substantial, new noncompatible use not indicated on the forecast map. Revised noise exposure maps are subject to the same requirements and procedures as initial submissions of noise exposure maps under this part.

(e) Each map, or revised map, and description of consultation and opportunity for public comment, submitted to the FAA, must be certified as true and complete under penalty of 18 U.S.C. 1001.

(f)(1) Title 49, section 47506 provides that no person who acquires property or an interest therein after the date of enactment of the Act in an area surrounding an airport with respect to which a noise exposure map has been submitted under section 47503 of the Act shall be entitled to recover damages with respect to the noise attributable to such airport if such person had actual or constructive knowledge of the existence of such noise exposure map unless, in addition to any other elements for recovery of damages, such person can show that—

No person who acquires property or an interest therein after the date of enactment of the Act in an area surrounding an airport with respect to which a noise exposure map has been submitted under section 103 of the Act shall be entitled to recover damages with respect to the noise attributable to such airport if such person had actual or constructive knowledge of the existence of such noise exposure map unless, in addition to any other elements for recovery of damages, such person can show that—

(i) A significant change in the type or frequency of aircraft operations at the airport; or

(ii) A significant change in the airport layout; or

(iii) A significant change in the flight patterns; or

(iv) A significant increase in nighttime operations; occurred after the date of the acquisition of such property or interest therein and that the damages for which recovery is sought have resulted from any such change or increase."

(f)(2) Title 49 section 47506(b) further provides:

That for this purpose, "constructive knowledge" shall be imputed, at a minimum, to any person who acquires property or an interest therein in an area surrounding an airport after the date of enactment of the Act if—

(i) Prior to the date of such acquisition, notice of the existence of a noise exposure map for such area was published at least three times in a newspaper of general circulation in the county in which such property is located; or

(ii) A copy of such noise exposure map is furnished to such person at the time of such acquisition.

(g) For this purpose, the term *significant* in paragraph (f) of this section means that change or increase in one or more of the four factors which results in a "substantial new noncompatible use" as defined in § 150.21(d), affecting the property in issue. Responsibility for applying or interpreting this provision with respect to specific properties rests with local government.

[Doc. No. 18691, 49 FR 49269, Dec. 1, 1984; 50 FR 5063, Feb. 6, 1985; Amdt. 150–2, 54 FR 39295, Sept. 25, 1989; Amdt. 150–4, 69 FR 57626, Sept. 24, 2004]

§ 150.23 Noise compatibility programs.

(a) Any airport operator who has submitted an acceptable noise exposure map under § 150.21 may, after FAA notice of acceptability and other consultation and public procedure specified under paragraphs (b) and (c) of this section, as applicable, submit to the Regional Airports Division Manager five copies of a noise compatibility program.

(b) An airport operator may submit the noise compatibility program at the same time as the noise exposure map. In this case, the Regional Airports Division Manager will not begin the statutory 180-day review period (for the program) until after FAA reviews the noise exposure map and finds that it and its supporting documentation are in compliance with the applicable requirements.

(c) Each noise compatibility program must be developed and prepared in accordance with appendix B of this part, or an FAA approved equivalent, and in consultation with FAA regional officials, the officials of the state and of any public agencies and planning agencies whose area, or any portion or whose area, of jurisdiction within the L_{dn} 65 dB noise contours is depicted on

the noise exposure map, and other Federal officials having local responsibility of land uses depicted on the map. Consultation with FAA regional officials shall include, to the extent practicable, informal agreement from FAA on proposed new or modified flight procedures. For air carrier airports, consultation must include any air carriers and, to the extent practicable, other aircraft operators using the airport. For other airports, consultation must include, to the extent practicable, aircraft operators using the airport.

(d) Prior to and during the development of a program, and prior to submission of the resulting draft program to the FAA, the airport operator shall afford adequate opportunity for the active and direct participation of the States, public agencies and planning agencies in the areas surrounding the airport, aeronautical users of the airport, the airport operator, and the general public to submit their views, data, and comments on the formulation and adequacy of that program. Prior to submitting the program to the FAA, the airport operator shall also provide notice and the opportunity for a public hearing.

(e) Each noise compatibility program submitted to the FAA must consist of at least the following:

(1) A copy of the noise exposure map and its supporting documentation as found in compliance with the applicable requirements by the FAA, per § 150.21(c).

(2) A description and analysis of the alternative measures considered by the airport operator in developing the program, together with a discussion of why each rejected measure was not included in the program.

(3) Program measures proposed to reduce or eliminate present and future noncompatible land uses and a description of the relative contribution of each of the proposed measures to the overall effectiveness of the program.

(4) A description of public participation and the consultation with officials of public agencies and planning agencies in areas surrounding the airport, FAA regional officials and other Federal officials having local responsibility for land uses depicted on the

map, any air carriers and other users of the airport.

(5) The actual or anticipated effect of the program on reducing noise exposure to individuals and noncompatible land uses and preventing the introduction of additional noncompatible uses within the area covered by the noise exposure map. The effects must be based on expressed assumptions concerning the type and frequency of aircraft operations, number of nighttime operations, flight patterns, airport layout including planned airport development, planned land use changes, and demographic changes within the L_{dn} 65 dB noise contours.

(6) A description of how the proposed future actions may change any noise control or compatibility plans or actions previously adopted by the airport proprietor.

(7) A summary of the comments at any public hearing on the program and a copy of all written material submitted to the operator under paragraphs (c) and (d) of this section, together with the operator's response and disposition of those comments and materials to demonstrate the program is feasible and reasonably consistent with obtaining the objectives of airport noise compatibility planning under this part.

(8) The period covered by the program, the schedule for implementation of the program, the persons responsible for implementation of each measure in the program, and, for each measure, documentation supporting the feasibility of implementation, including any essential governmental actions, costs, and anticipated sources of funding, that will demonstrate that the program is reasonably consistent with achieving the goals of airport noise compatibility planning under this part.

(9) Provision for revising the program if made necessary by revision of the noise exposure map.

[Doc. No. 18691, 49 FR 49269, Dec. 18, 1984; 50 FR 5063, Feb. 6, 1985; Amdt. 150-2, 54 FR 39295, Sept. 25, 1989; Amdt. 150-4, 69 FR 57626, Sept. 24, 2004]

Subpart C—Evaluations and Determinations of Effects of Noise Compatibility Programs

§ 150.31 Preliminary review: Acknowledgments.

(a) Upon receipt of a noise compatibility program submitted under § 150.23, the Regional Airports Division Manager acknowledges to the airport operator receipt of the program and conducts a preliminary review of the submission.

(b) If, based on the preliminary review, the Regional Airports Division Manager finds that the submission does not conform to the requirements of this part, he disapproves and returns the unacceptable program to the airport operator for reconsideration and development of a program in accordance with this part.

(c) If, based on the preliminary review, the Regional Airports Division Manager finds that the program conforms to the requirements of this part, the Regional Airports Division Manager publishes in the FEDERAL REGISTER a notice of receipt of the program for comment which indicates the following:

(1) The airport covered by the program, and the date of receipt.

(2) The availability of the program for examination in the offices of the Regional Airports Division Manager and the airport operator.

(3) That comments on the program are invited and, will be considered by the FAA.

(d) The date of signature of the published notice of receipt starts the 180-day approval period for the program.

[Doc. No. 18691, 49 FR 49269, Dec. 18, 1984, as amended by Amdt. 150-2, 54 FR 39295, Sept. 25, 1989]

§ 150.33 Evaluation of programs.

(a) The FAA conducts an evaluation of each noise compatibility program and, based on that evaluation, either approves or disapproves the program. The evaluation includes consideration of proposed measures to determine whether they—

(1) May create an undue burden on interstate or foreign commerce (including unjust discrimination);

(2) Are reasonably consistent with obtaining the goal of reducing existing noncompatible land uses and preventing the introduction of additional noncompatible land uses; and

(3) Include the use of new or modified flight procedures to control the operation of aircraft for purposes of noise control, or affect flight procedures in any way.

(b) The evaluation may also include an evaluation of those proposed measures to determine whether they may adversely affect the exercise of the authority and responsibilities of the Administrator under the Federal Aviation Act of 1958, as amended.

(c) To the extent considered necessary, the FAA may—

(1) Confer with the airport operator and other persons known to have information and views material to the evaluation;

(2) Explore the objectives of the program and the measures, and any alternative measures, for achieving the objectives.

(3) Examine the program for developing a range of alternatives that would eliminate the reasons, if any, for disapproving the program.

(4) Convene an informal meeting with the airport operator and other persons involved in developing or implementing the program for the purposes of gathering all facts relevant to the determination of approval or disapproval of the program and of discussing any needs to accommodate or modify the program as submitted.

(d) If requested by the FAA, the airport operator shall furnish all information needed to complete FAA's review under (c).

(e) An airport operator may, at any time before approval or disapproval of a program, withdraw or revise the program. If the airport operator withdraws or revises the program or indicates to the Regional Airports Division Manager, in writing, the intention to revise the program, the Regional Airports Division Manager terminates the evaluation and notifies the airport operator of that action. That termination cancels the 180-day review period. The FAA does not evaluate a second program for any airport until any previously submitted program has been

withdrawn or a determination on it is issued. A new evaluation is commenced upon receipt of a revised program, and a new 180-day approval period is begun, unless the Regional Airports Division Manager finds that the modification made, in light of the overall revised program, can be integrated into the unmodified portions of the revised program without exceeding the original 180-day approval period or causing undue expense to the government.

[Doc. No. 18691, 49 FR 49269, Dec. 18, 1984, as amended by Amdt. 150–2, 54 FR 39295, Sept. 25, 1989]

§ 150.35 Determinations; publications; effectivity.

(a) The FAA issues a determination approving or disapproving each airport noise compatibility program (and revised program). Portions of a program may be individually approved or disapproved. No conditional approvals will be issued. A determination on a program acceptable under this part is issued within 180 days after the program is received under § 150.23 of this part or it may be considered approved, except that this time period may be exceeded for any portion of a program relating to the use of flight procedures for noise control purposes. A determination on portions of a program covered by the exceptions to the 180-day review period for approval will be issued within a reasonable time after receipt of the program. Determinations relating to the use of any flight procedure for noise control purposes may be issued either in connection with the determination on other portions of the program or separately. Except as provided by this paragraph, no approval of any noise compatibility program, or any portion of a program, may be implied in the absence of the FAA's express approval.

(b) The Administrator approves programs under this part, if—

(1) It is found that the program measures to be implemented would not create an undue burden on interstate or foreign commerce (including any unjust discrimination) and are reasonably consistent with achieving the goals of reducing existing noncompatible land

uses around the airport and of preventing the introduction of additional noncompatible land uses;

(2) The program provides for revision if made necessary by the revision of the noise map; and

(3) Those aspects of programs relating to the use of flight procedures for noise control can be implemented within the period covered by the program and without—

(i) Reducing the level of aviation safety provided;

(ii) Derogating the requisite level of protection for aircraft, their occupants and persons and property on the ground;

(iii) Adversely affecting the efficient use and management of the Navigable Airspace and Air Traffic Control Systems; or

(iv) Adversely affecting any other powers and responsibilities of the Administrator prescribed by law or any other program, standard, or requirement established in accordance with law.

(c) When a determination is issued, the Regional Airports Division Manager notifies the airport operator and publishes a notice of approval or disapproval in the FEDERAL REGISTER identifying the nature and extent of the determination.

(d) Approvals issued under this part for a program or portion thereof become effective as specified therein and may be withdrawn when one of the following occurs:

(1) The program or portion thereof is required to be revised under this part or under its own terms, and is not so revised;

(2) If a revision has been submitted for approval, a determination is issued on the revised program or portion thereof, that is inconsistent with the prior approval.

(3) A term or condition of the program, or portion thereof, or its approval is violated by the responsible government body.

(4) A flight procedure or other FAA action upon which the approved program or portion thereof is dependent is subsequently disapproved, significantly altered, or rescinded by the FAA.

(5) The airport operator requests rescission of the approval.

(6) Impacts on flight procedures, air traffic management, or air commerce occur which could not be foreseen at the time of approval.

A determination may be sooner rescinded or modified for cause with at least 30 days written notice to the airport operator of the FAA's intention to rescind or modify the determination for the reasons stated in the notice. The airport operator may, during the 30-day period, submit to the Regional Airports Division Manager for consideration any reasons and circumstances why the determination should not be rescinded or modified on the basis stated in the notice of intent. Thereafter, the FAA either rescinds or modifies the determination consistent with the notice or withdraws the notice of intent and terminates the action.

(e) Determinations may contain conditions which must be satisfied prior to implementation of any portion of the program relating to flight procedures affecting airport or aircraft operations.

(f) Noise exposure maps for current and forecast year map conditions that are submitted and approved with noise compatibility programs are considered to be the new FAA accepted noise exposure maps for purposes of part 150.

[Doc. No. 18691, 49 FR 49269, Dec. 18, 1984, as amended by Amdt. 150–2, 54 FR 39295, Sept. 25, 1989; Amdt. 150–4, 69 FR 57626, Sept. 24, 2004]

APPENDIX A TO PART 150—NOISE EXPOSURE MAPS

PART A—GENERAL

Sec. A150.1 Purpose.
Sec. A150.3 Noise descriptors.
Sec. A150.5 Noise measurement procedures and equipment.

PART B—NOISE EXPOSURE MAP DEVELOPMENT

Sec. A150.101 Noise contours and land usages.
Sec. A150.103 Use of computer prediction model.
Sec. A150.105 Identification of public agencies and planning agencies.

PART C—MATHEMATICAL DESCRIPTIONS

Sec. A150.201 General.
Sec. A150.203 Symbols.
Sec. A150.205 Mathematical computations.

PART A—GENERAL

Sec. A150.1 Purpose.

(a) This appendix establishes a uniform methodology for the development and preparation of airport noise exposure maps. That methodology includes a single system of measuring noise at airports for which there is a highly reliable relationship between projected noise exposure and surveyed reactions of people to noise along with a separate single system for determining the exposure of individuals to noise. It also identifies land uses which, for the purpose of this part are considered to be compatible with various exposures of individuals to noise around airports.

(b) This appendix provides for the use of the FAA's Integrated Noise Model (INM) or an FAA approved equivalent, for developing standardized noise exposure maps and predicting noise impacts. Noise monitoring may be utilized by airport operators for data acquisition and data refinement, but is not required by this part for the development of noise exposure maps or airport noise compatibility programs. Whenever noise monitoring is used, under this part, it should be accomplished in accordance with Sec. A150.5 of this appendix.

Sec. A150.3 Noise descriptors.

(a) *Airport Noise Measurement.* The A-Weighted Sound Level, measured, filtered and recorded in accordance with Sec. A150.5 of this appendix, must be employed as the unit for the measurement of single event noise at airports and in the areas surrounding the airports.

(b) *Airport Noise Exposure.* The yearly day-night average sound level (YDNL) must be employed for the analysis and characterization of multiple aircraft noise events and for determining the cumulative exposure of individuals to noise around airports.

Sec. A150.5 Noise measurement procedures and equipment.

(a) Sound levels must be measured or analyzed with equipment having the "A" frequency weighting, filter characteristics and the "slow response" characteristics as defined in International Electrotechnical Commission (IEC) Publication No. 179, entitled "Precision Sound Level Meters" as incorporated by reference in part 150 under §150.11. For purposes of this part, the tolerances allowed for general purpose, type 2 sound level meters in IEU 179, are acceptable.

(b) Noise measurements and documentation must be in accordance with accepted acoustical measurement methodology, such as those described in American National Standards Institute publication ANSI S1.13, dated 1971 as revised 1979, entitled "ANS—

Methods for the Measurement of Sound Pressure Levels"; ARP No. 796, dated 1969, entitled "Measurement of Aircraft Exterior Noise in the Field"; "Handbook of Noise Measurement," Ninth Ed. 1980, by Arnold P.G. Peterson; or "Acoustic Noise Measurement," dated Jan., 1979, by J.R. Hassell and K. Zaveri. For purposes of this part, measurements intended for comparison to a State or local standard or with another transportation noise source (including other aircraft) must be reported in maximum A-weighted sound levels (L_{AM}); for computation or validation of the yearly day-night average level (L_{dn}), measurements must be reported in sound exposure level (L_{AE}), as defined in Sec. A150.205 of this appendix.

PART B—NOISE EXPOSURE MAP DEVELOPMENT

Sec. A150.101 Noise contours and land usages.

(a) To determine the extent of the noise impact around an airport, airport proprietors developing noise exposure maps in accordance with this part must develop L_{dn} contours. Continuous contours must be developed for YDNL levels of 65, 70, and 75 (additional contours may be developed and depicted when appropriate). In those areas where YDNL values are 65 YDNL or greater, the airport operator shall identify land uses and determine land use compatibility in accordance with the standards and procedures of this appendix.

(b) Table 1 of this appendix describes compatible land use information for several land uses as a function of YDNL values. The ranges of YDNL values in Table 1 reflect the statistical variability for the responses of large groups of people to noise. Any particular level might not, therefore, accurately assess an individual's perception of an actual noise environment. Compatible or non-compatible land use is determined by comparing the predicted or measured YDNL values at a site with the values given. Adjustments or modifications of the descriptions of the land-use categories may be desirable after consideration of specific local conditions.

(c) Compatibility designations in Table 1 generally refer to the major use of the site. If other uses with greater sensitivity to noise are permitted by local government at a site, a determination of compatibility must be based on that use which is most adversely affected by noise. When appropriate, noise level reduction through incorporation of sound attenuation into the design and construction of a structure may be necessary to achieve compatibility.

(d) For the purpose of compliance with this part, all land uses are considered to be compatible with noise levels less than L_{dn} 65 dB. Local needs or values may dictate further delineation based on local requirements or determinations.

(e) Except as provided in (f) below, the noise exposure maps must also contain and indentify:

(1) Runway locations.

(2) Flight tracks.

(3) Noise contours of L_{dn} 65, 70, and 75 dB resulting from aircraft operations.

(4) Outline of the airport boundaries.

(5) Noncompatible land uses within the noise contours, including those within the L_{dn} 65 dB contours. (No land use has to be identified as noncompatible if the self-generated noise from that use and/or the ambient noise from other nonaircraft and nonairport uses is equal to or greater than the noise from aircraft and airport sources.)

(6) Location of noise sensitive public buildings (such as schools, hospitals, and health care facilities), and properties on or eligible for inclusion in the National Register of Historic Places.

(7) Locations of any aircraft noise monitoring sites utilized for data acquisition and refinement procedures.

(8) Estimates of the number of people residing within the L_{dn} 65, 70, and 75 dB contours.

(9) Depiction of the required noise contours over a land use map of a sufficient scale and quality to discern streets and other identifiable geographic features.

(f) Notwithstanding any other provision of this part, noise exposure maps prepared in connection with studies which were either Federally funded or Federally approved and which commenced before October 1, 1981, are not required to be modified to contain the following items:

(1) Flight tracks depicted on the map.

(2) Use of ambient noise to determine land use compatibility.

(3) The L_{dn} 70 dB noise contour and data related to L_{dn} 70 dB contour. When determinations on land use compatibility using Table 1 differ between L_{dn} 65–70 dB and the L_{dn} 70–75 dB, determinations should either use the more conservative L_{dn} 70–75 dB column or reflect determinations based on local needs and values.

(4) Estimates of the number of people residing within the L_{dn} 65, 70, and 75 dB contours.

TABLE 1—LAND USE COMPATIBILITY* WITH YEARLY DAY-NIGHT AVERAGE SOUND LEVELS

Land use	Yearly day-night average sound level (L_{dn}) in decibels					
	Below 65	65–70	70–75	75–80	80–85	Over 85
RESIDENTIAL						
Residential, other than mobile homes and transient lodgings ...	Y	N(1)	N(1)	N	N	N
Mobile home parks	Y	N	N	N	N	N
Transient lodgings	Y	N(1)	N(1)	N(1)	N	N
PUBLIC USE						
Schools	Y	N(1)	N(1)	N	N	N
Hospitals and nursing homes	Y	25	30	N	N	N
Churches, auditoriums, and concert halls	Y	25	30	N	N	N
Governmental services	Y	Y	25	30	N	N
Transportation	Y	Y	Y(2)	Y(3)	Y(4)	Y(4)
Parking	Y	Y	Y(2)	Y(3)	Y(4)	N
COMMERCIAL USE						
Offices, business and professional	Y	Y	25	30	N	N
Wholesale and retail—building materials, hardware and farm equipment.	Y	Y	Y(2)	Y(3)	Y(4)	N
Retail trade—general	Y	Y	25	30	N	N
Utilities	Y	Y	Y(2)	Y(3)	Y(4)	N
Communication	Y	Y	25	30	N	N
MANUFACTURING AND PRODUCTION						
Manufacturing, general	Y	Y	Y(2)	Y(3)	Y(4)	N
Photographic and optical	Y	Y	25	30	N	N
Agriculture (except livestock) and forestry	Y	Y(6)	Y(7)	Y(8)	Y(8)	Y(8)
Livestock farming and breeding	Y	Y(6)	Y(7)	N	N	N
Mining and fishing, resource production and extraction	Y	Y	Y	Y	Y	Y
RECREATIONAL						
Outdoor sports arenas and spectator sports	Y	Y(5)	Y(5)	N	N	N
Outdoor music shells, amphitheaters	Y	N	N	N	N	N
Nature exhibits and zoos	Y	Y	N	N	N	N
Amusements, parks, resorts and camps	Y	Y	Y	N	N	N
Golf courses, riding stables and water recreation	Y	Y	25	30	N	N

Numbers in parentheses refer to notes.

*The designations contained in this table do not constitute a Federal determination that any use of land covered by the program is acceptable or unacceptable under Federal, State, or local law. The responsibility for determining the acceptable and permissible land uses and the relationship between specific properties and specific noise contours rests with the local authorities. FAA determinations under part 150 are not intended to substitute federally determined land uses for those determined to be appropriate by local authorities in response to locally determined needs and values in achieving noise compatible land uses.

KEY TO TABLE 1

SLUCM = Standard Land Use Coding Manual.
Y (Yes) = Land Use and related structures compatible without restrictions.
N (No) = Land Use and related structures are not compatible and should be prohibited.
NLR = Noise Level Reduction (outdoor to indoor) to be achieved through incorporation of noise attenuation into the design and construction of the structure.
25, 30, or 35 = Land use and related structures generally compatible; measures to achieve NLR of 25, 30, or 35 dB must be incorporated into design and construction of structure

NOTES FOR TABLE 1

(1) Where the community determines that residential or school uses must be allowed, measures to achieve outdoor to indoor Noise Level Reduction (NLR) of at least 25 dB and 30 dB should be incorporated into building codes and be considered in individual approvals. Normal residential construction can be expected to provide a NLR of 20 dB, thus, the reduction requirements are often stated as 5, 10 or 15 dB over standard construction and normally assume mechanical ventilation and closed windows year round. However, the use of NLR criteria will not eliminate outdoor noise problems.
(2) Measures to achieve NLR 25 dB must be incorporated into the design and construction of portions of these buildings where the public is received, office areas, noise sensitive areas or where the normal noise level is low.
(3) Measures to achieve NLR of 30 dB must be incorporated into the design and construction of portions of these buildings where the public is received, office areas, noise sensitive areas or where the normal noise level is low.
(4) Measures to achieve NLR 35 dB must be incorporated into the design and construction of portions of these buildings where the public is received, office areas, noise sensitive areas or where the normal level is low.
(5) Land use compatible provided special sound reinforcement systems are installed.
(6) Residential buildings require an NLR of 25.
(7) Residential buildings require an NLR of 30.
(8) Residential buildings not permitted.

Sec. A150.103 Use of computer prediction model.

(a) The airport operator shall acquire the aviation operations data necessary to develop noise exposure contours using an FAA approved methodology or computer program, such as the Integrated Noise Model (INM) for airports or the Heliport Noise Model (HNM) for heliports. In considering approval of a methodology or computer program, key factors include the demonstrated capability to produce the required output and the public availability of the program or methodology to provide interested parties the opportunity to substantiate the results.

(b) Except as provided in paragraph (c) of this section, the following information must be obtained for input to the calculation of noise exposure contours:

(1) A map of the airport and its environs at an adequately detailed scale (not less than 1 inch to 2,000 feet) indicating runway length, alignments, landing thresholds, takeoff start-of-roll points, airport boundary, and flight tracks out to at least 30,000 feet from the end of each runway.

(2) Airport activity levels and operational data which will indicate, on an annual average-daily-basis, the number of aircraft, by type of aircraft, which utilize each flight track, in both the standard daytime (0700–2200 hours local) and nighttime (2200–0700 hours local) periods for both landings and takeoffs.

(3) For landings—glide slopes, glide slope intercept altitudes, and other pertinent information needed to establish approach profiles along with the engine power levels needed to fly that approach profile.

(4) For takeoffs—the flight profile which is the relationship of altitude to distance from

start-of-roll along with the engine power levels needed to fly that takeoff profile; these data must reflect the use of noise abatement departure procedures and, if applicable, the takeoff weight of the aircraft or some proxy for weight such as stage length.

(5) Existing topographical or airspace restrictions which preclude the utilization of alternative flight tracks.

(6) The government furnished data depicting aircraft noise characteristics (if not already a part of the computer program's stored data bank).

(7) Airport elevation and average temperature.

(c) For heliports, the map scale required by paragraph (b)(1) of this section shall not be less than 1 inch to 2,000 feet and shall indicate heliport boundaries, takeoff and landing pads, and typical flight tracks out to at least 4,000 feet horizontally from the landing pad. Where these flight tracks cannot be determined, obstructions or other limitations on flight tracks in and out of the heliport shall be identified within the map areas out to at least 4,000 feet horizontally from the landing pad. For static operation (hover), the helicopter type, the number of daily operations based on an annual average, and the duration in minutes of the hover operation shall be identified. The other information required in paragraph (b) shall be furnished in a form suitable for input to the HNM or other FAA approved methodology or computer program.

Sec. A150.105 Identification of public agencies and planning agencies.

(a) The airport proprietor shall identify each public agency and planning agency whose jurisdiction or responsibility is either wholly or partially within the L_{dn} 65 dB boundary.

(b) For those agencies identified in (a) that have land use planning and control authority, the supporting documentation shall identify their geographic areas of jurisdiction.

PART C—MATHEMATICAL DESCRIPTIONS

Sec. A150.201 General.

The following mathematical descriptions provide the most precise definition of the yearly day-night average sound level (L_{dn}), the data necessary for its calculation, and the methods for computing it.

Sec. A150.203 Symbols.

The following symbols are used in the computation of L_{dn};

Measure (in dB)	Symbol
Average Sound Level, During Time T	L_T
Day-Night Average Sound Level (individual day)	L_{dni}
Yearly Day-Night Average Sound Level	L_{dn}
Sound Exposure Level	L_{AE}

Sec. A150.205 Mathematical computations.

(a) Average sound level must be computed in accordance with the following formula:

$$L_T = 10 \log_{10} \left[\frac{1}{T} \int_O^T 10^{L_A(t)/10} \, dt \right] \quad (1)$$

where T is the length of the time period, in seconds, during which the average is taken; $L_A(t)$ is the instantaneous time varying A-weighted sound level during the time period T.

NOTE: When a noise environment is caused by a number of identifiable noise events, such as aircraft flyovers, average sound level may be conveniently calculated from the sound exposure levels of the individual events occurring within a time period T:

$$L_T = 10 \log_{10} \left[\frac{1}{T} \sum_{i=1}^n 10^{L_{AEi}/10} \right] \quad (2)$$

where L_{AEi} is the sound exposure level of the i-th event, in a series of n events in time period T, in seconds.

NOTE: When T is one hour, L_T is referred to as one-hour average sound level.

(b) Day-night average sound level (individual day) must be computed in accordance with the following formula:

$$L_{dn} = 10 \log_{10} \left[\frac{1}{86400} \left(\int_{0000}^{0700} 10^{[L_A(t)+10]/10} dt + \int_{0700}^{2200} 10^{L_A(t)/10} dt + \int_{2200}^{2400} 10^{[L_A(t)+10]/10} dt \right) \right] \quad (3)$$

Time is in seconds, so the limits shown in hours and minutes are actually interpreted in seconds. It is often convenient to compute day-night average sound level from the one-hour average sound levels obtained during successive hours.

(c) Yearly day-night average sound level must be computed in accordance with the following formula:

$$L_{dn} = 10 \log_{10} \frac{1}{365} \sum_{i=1}^{365} 10^{L_{dni}/10} \quad (4)$$

where L_{dni} is the day-night average sound level for the i-th day out of one year.

(d) Sound exposure level must be computed in accordance with the following formula:

$$L_{AE} = 10 \log_{10} \left(\frac{1}{t_o} \int_{t_1}^{t_2} 10^{L_A(t)/10} dt \right) \quad (5)$$

where t_o is one second and $L_A(t)$ is the time-varying A-weighted sound level in the time interval t_1 to t_2.

The time interval should be sufficiently large that it encompasses all the significant sound of a designated event.

The requisite integral may be approximated with sufficient accuracy by integrating $L_A(t)$ over the time interval during which $L_A(t)$ lies within 10 decibels of its maximum value, before and after the maximum occurs.

[Doc. No. 18691, 49 FR 49269, Dec. 18, 1984; 50 FR 5064, Feb. 6, 1985, as amended by Amdt. 150–1, 53 FR 8724, Mar. 16, 1988; Amdt. 150–4, 69 FR 57626, Sept. 24, 2004]

APPENDIX B TO PART 150—NOISE COMPATIBILITY PROGRAMS

Sec. B150.7 Analysis of program alternatives.
Sec. B150.9 Equivalent programs.

Sec. B150.1 Scope and purpose.

(a) This appendix prescribes the content and the methods for developing noise compatibility programs authorized under this part. Each program must set forth the measures which the airport operator (or other person or agency responsible) has taken, or proposes to take, for the reduction of existing noncompatible land uses and the prevention of the introduction of additional noncompatible land uses within the area covered by the noise exposure map submitted by the operator.

(b) The purpose of a noise compatibility program is:

(1) To promote a planning process through which the airport operator can examine and analyze the noise impact created by the operation of an airport, as well as the costs and benefits associated with various alternative noise reduction techniques, and the responsible impacted land use control jurisdictions can examine existing and forecast areas of noncompatibility and consider actions to reduce noncompatible uses.

(2) To bring together through public participation, agency coordination, and overall cooperation, all interested parties with their respective authorities and obligations, thereby facilitating the creation of an agreed upon noise abatement plan especially suited to the individual airport location while at the same time not unduly affecting the national air transportation system.

(3) To develop comprehensive and implementable noise reduction techniques and land use controls which, to the maximum extent feasible, will confine severe aircraft YDNL values of L_{dn} 75 dB or greater to areas included within the airport boundary and will establish and maintain compatible land uses in the areas affected by noise between the L_{dn} 65 and 75 dB contours.

Sec. B150.3 Requirement for noise map.

(a) It is required that a current and complete noise exposure map and its supporting documentation as found in compliance with the applicable requirements by the FAA, per § 150.21(c) be included in each noise compatibility program:

(1) To identify existing and future noncompatible land uses, based on airport operation and off-airport land uses, which have generated the need to develop a program.

(2) To identify changes in noncompatible uses to be derived from proposed program measures.

(b) If the proposed noise compatibility program would yield maps differing from those previously submitted to FAA, the program shall be accompanied by appropriately revised maps. Such revisions must be prepared in accordance with the requirements of Sec. A150.101(e) of appendix A and will be accepted by FAA in accordance with § 150.35(f).

Sec. B150.5 Program standards.

Based upon the airport noise exposure and noncompatible land uses identified in the map, the airport operator shall evaluate the several alternative noise control actions and develop a noise compatibility program which—

(a) Reduces existing noncompatible uses and prevents or reduces the probability of the establishment of additional noncompatible uses;

(b) Does not impose undue burden on interstate and foreign commerce;

(c) Provides for revision in accordance with § 150.23 of this part.

(d) Is not unjustly discriminatory.

(e) Does not derogate safety or adversely affect the safe and efficient use of airspace.

(f) To the extent practicable, meets both local needs and needs of the national air transportation system, considering tradeoffs between economic benefits derived from the airport and the noise impact.

(g) Can be implemented in a manner consistent with all of the powers and duties of the Administrator of FAA.

Sec. B150.7 Analysis of program alternatives.

(a) Noise control alternatives must be considered and presented according to the following categories:

(1) Noise abatement alternatives for which the airport operator has adequate implementation authority.

(2) Noise abatement alternatives for which the requisite implementation authority is vested in a local agency or political subdivision governing body, or a state agency or political subdivision governing body.

(3) Noise abatement options for which requisite authority is vested in the FAA or other Federal agency.

(b) At a minimum, the operator shall analyze and report on the following alternatives, subject to the constraints that the strategies are appropriate to the specific airport (for example, an evaluation of night curfews is not appropriate if there are no night flights and none are forecast):

(1) Acquisition of land and interests therein, including, but not limited to air rights, easements, and development rights, to ensure the use of property for purposes which are compatible with airport operations.

(2) The construction of barriers and acoustical shielding, including the soundproofing of public buildings.

(3) The implementation of a preferential runway system.

(4) The use of flight procedures (including the modifications of flight tracks) to control

673

the operation of aircraft to reduce exposure of individuals (or specific noise sensitive areas) to noise in the area around the airport.

(5) The implementation of any restriction on the use of airport by any type or class of aircraft based on the noise characteristics of those aircraft. Such restrictions may include, but are not limited to—

(i) Denial of use of the airport to aircraft types or classes which do not meet Federal noise standards;

(ii) Capacity limitations based on the relative noisiness of different types of aircraft;

(iii) Requirement that aircraft using the airport must use noise abatement takeoff or approach procedures previously approved as safe by the FAA;

(iv) Landing fees based on FAA certificated or estimated noise emission levels or on time of arrival; and

(v) Partial or complete curfews.

(6) Other actions or combinations of actions which would have a beneficial noise control or abatement impact on the public.

(7) Other actions recommended for analysis by the FAA for the specific airport.

(c) For those alternatives selected for implementation, the program must identify the agency or agencies responsible for such implementation, whether those agencies have agreed to the implementation, and the approximate schedule agreed upon.

Sec. B150.9 Equivalent programs.

(a) Notwithstanding any other provision of this part, noise compatibility programs prepared in connection with studies which were either Federally funded or Federally approved and commenced before October 1, 1981, are not required to be modified to contain the following items:

(1) Flight tracks.

(2) A noise contour of L_{dn} 70 dB resulting from aircraft operations and data related to the L_{dn} 70 dB contour. When determinations on land use compatibility using Table 1 of appendix A differ between L_{dn} 65–70 dB and L_{dn} 70–75 dB, the determinations should either use the more conservative L_{dn} 70–75 dB column or reflect determinations based on local needs and values.

(3) The categorization of alternatives pursuant to Sec. B150.7(a), although the persons responsible for implementation of each measure in the program must still be identified in accordance with § 150.23(e)(8).

(4) Use of ambient noise to determine land use compatibility.

(b) Previously prepared noise compatibility program documentation may be supplemented to include these and other program requirements which have not been excepted.

PART 151—FEDERAL AID TO AIRPORTS

Subpart A—General Requirements

Subpart B—Rules and Procedures for Airport Development Projects

Subpart A—General Requirements

AUTHORITY: 49 U.S.C. 106(g), 40113, 47151, 47153.

§ 151.1 Applicability.

This part prescribes the policies and procedures for administering the Federal-aid Airport Program under the Federal Airport Act, as amended (49 U.S.C. 1101 *et seq.*).

[Doc. No. 1329, 27 FR 12349, Dec. 13, 1962]

§ 151.3 National Airport Plan.

(a) Under the Federal Airport Act, the FAA prepares each year a "National Airport Plan" for developing public airports in the United States, Puerto Rico, the Virgin Islands, and Guam. In terms of general location and type of development, the National Airport Plan specifies the maximum limits of airport development that is necessary to provide a system of public airports adequate to anticipate and meet the needs of civil aeronautics.

(b) If, within the forecast period, an airport will have a substantial aeronautical necessity, it may be included in the National Airport Plan. Only work on an airport included in the current Plan is eligible for inclusion in the Federal-aid Airport Program to be undertaken within currently available appropriations and authorizations. However, the inclusion of an airport in the National Airport Plan does not commit the United States to include it in the Federal-aid Airport Program. In addition, the local community concerned is not required to proceed with planning or development of an airport included in the National Airport Plan.

[Amdt. 151-8, 30 FR 8039, June 23, 1965]

§ 151.5 General policies.

(a) *Airport layout plan.* As used in this part, "airport layout plan" means the basic plan for the layout of an eligible airport that shows, as a minimum—

(1) The present boundaries of the airport and of the offsite areas that the sponsor owns or controls for airport purposes, and of their proposed additions;

(2) The location and nature of existing and proposed airport facilities (such as runways, taxiways, aprons, terminal buildings, hangars, and roads) and of their proposed modifications and extensions; and

(3) The location of existing and proposed non-aviation areas, and of their existing improvements.

All airport development under the Federal-aid Airport Program must be done in accordance with an approved airport layout plan. Each airport layout plan, and any change in it, is subject to FAA approval. The Administrator's signature on the face of an original airport layout plan, or of any change in it, indicates FAA approval. The FAA approves an airport layout plan only if the airport development is sound and meets applicable requirements.

(b) *Safe, useful, and usable unit.* Except as provided in paragraph (d) of this section, each advance planning and engineering proposal or airport development project must provide for the planning or development of—

(1) An airport or unit of an airport that is safe, useful, and usable; or

(2) An additional facility that increases the safety, usefulness, or usability of an airport.

(c) *National defense needs.* The needs of national defense are fully considered in administering the Federal-aid Airport Program. However, approval of an advance planning and engineering proposal or a project application is limited to planning or airport development necessary for civil aviation.

(d) *Stage development.* In any case in which airport development can be accomplished more economically under stage construction, federal funds may be programmed in advance for the development over two or more years under two or more grant agreements. In such a case, the FAA makes a tentative allocation of funds for both the current and future fiscal years, rather than allocating the entire federal share in one fiscal year. A grant agreement is made only during the fiscal year in which funds are authorized to be obligated. Advance planning and engineering grants are not made under this paragraph.

[Amdt. 151–8, 30 FR 8039, June 23, 1965]

§ 151.7 Grants of funds: General policies.

(a) *Compliance with sponsorship requirements.* The FAA authorizes the expenditure of funds under the Federal-aid Airport Program for airport planning and engineering or for airport development only if the Administrator is satisfied that the sponsor has met or will meet the requirements established by existing and proposed agreements with the United States with respect to

any airport that the sponsor owns or controls.

(1) Agreements with the United States to which this requirement of compliance applies include—

(i) Any grant agreement made under the Federal-aid Airport Program;

(ii) Any covenant in a conveyance under section 16 of the Federal Airport Act;

(iii) Any covenant in a conveyance of surplus airport property either under section 13(g) of the Surplus Property Act (50 U.S.C. App. 1622(g)) or under Regulation 16 of the War Assets Administration; and

(iv) Any AP–4 agreement made under the terminated Development Landing Areas National Defense Program and the Development Civil Landing Areas Program.

This requirement does not apply to assurances required under section 602 of the Civil Rights Act of 1964 (42 U.S.C. 2000d–1) and § 15.7 of the Federal Aviation Regulations (14 CFR 15.7).

(2) If it appears that a sponsor has failed to comply with a requirement of an agreement with the United States with respect to an airport, the FAA notifies him of this fact and affords him an opportunity to submit materials to refute the allegation of noncompliance or to achieve compliance.

(3) If a project is otherwise eligible under the Federal-aid Airport Program, a grant may be made to a sponsor who has not complied with an agreement if the sponsor shows—

(i) That the noncompliance is caused by factors beyond his control; or

(ii) That the following circumstances exist:

(*a*) The noncompliance consisted of a failure, through mistake or ignorance, to perform minor conditions in old agreements with the Federal Government; and

(*b*) The sponsor is taking reasonable action promptly to correct the deficiency or the deficiency relates to an obligation that is no longer required for the safe and efficient use of the airport under existing law and policy.

(b) *Small proposals and projects.* Unless there is otherwise a special need for U.S. participation, the FAA includes an advance planning and engineering proposal or an airport development project in the Federal-aid Airport Program only if—

(1) The advance planning and engineering proposal involves more than $1,000 in United States funds; and

(2) The project application involves more than $5,000 in U.S. funds.

Whenever possible, the sponsor must consolidate small projects on a single airport in one grant agreement even though the airport development is to be accomplished over a period of years.

(c) *Previously obligated work.* Unless the Administrator specifically authorizes it, no advance planning and engineering proposal or project application may include any planning, engineering, or construction work included in a prior agreement with the United States obligating the sponsor or any other non-U.S. public agency to do the work, and entitling the sponsor or any other non-United States public agency to payment of U.S. funds for all or part of the work.

(Secs. 1–15, 17–21, 60 Stat. 170, 49 U.S.C. 1120)

[Amdt. 151–8, 30 FR 8039, June 23, 1965, as amended by Amdt. 151–17, 31 FR 16524, Dec. 28, 1966; Amdt. 151–19, 32 FR 9220, June 29, 1967]

§151.9 Runway clear zones: General.

(a) Whenever funds are allocated for developing new runways or landing strips, or to improve or repair existing runways, the sponsor must own, acquire, or agree to acquire, runway clear zones. Exceptions are considered (on the basis of a full statement of facts by the sponsor) upon a showing of uneconomical acquisition costs, or lack of necessity for the acquisition.

(b) For the purpose of this part, a runway clear zone is an area at ground level which begins at the end of each primary surface defined in §77.27(a) and extends with the width of each approach surface defined in §77.27 (b) and (c), to terminate directly below each approach surface slope at the point, or points, where the slope reaches a height of 50 feet above the elevation of the runway or 50 feet above the terrain at the outer extremity of the clear zone, whichever distance is shorter.

(c) For the purposes of this section, an airport operator or owner is considered to have an adequate property interest if it has an easement (or a covenant running with the land) giving it enough control to rid the clear zone of all obstructions (objects so far as they project above the approach surfaces established by §77.27 (b) and (c) of part 77 of this chapter), and to prevent the creation of future obstructions; together with the right of entrance and exit for those purposes, to ensure the safe and unrestricted passage of aircraft in and over the area.

[Doc. No. 1329, 27 FR 12349, Dec. 13, 1962, as amended by Amdt. 151–7, 30 FR 7484, June 8, 1965; Amdt. 151–21, 33 FR 258, Jan. 9, 1968]

§151.11 Runway clear zones; requirements.

(a) In projects involving grants-in-aid under the Federal-aid Airport Program, a sponsor must own, acquire, or agree to acquire an adequate property interest in runway clear zone areas as prescribed in paragraph (b), (c), (d), or (e) of this section, as applicable. Property interests that a sponsor acquires to meet the requirements of this section are eligible for inclusion in the Program.

(b) On new airports, the sponsor must own, acquire, or agree to acquire adequate property interests in runway clear zone areas (in connection with initial land acquisition) for all eligible runways or landing strips, without substantial deviation from standard configuration and length.

(c) On existing airports where new runways or landing strips are developed, the sponsor must own, acquire, or agree to acquire adequate property interests in runway clear zone areas for each runway and landing strip to be developed or extended, to the extent that the Administrator determines practical and feasible considering all facts presented by the airport owner or operator, preferably without substantial deviation from standard configuration and length.

(d) On existing airports where improvements are made to runways or landing strips, the sponsor must own, acquire, or agree to acquire adequate property interests in runway clear zone areas for each runway or landing strip that is to be improved to the extent that the Administrator determines is practical and feasible with regard to

677

standard configuration, length, and property interests, considering all facts presented by the airport owner or operator. Any development that improves a specific runway or landing strip is considered to be a runway improvement, including runway lighting and the developing or lighting of taxiways serving a runway.

(e) On existing airports where substantial improvements are made that do not benefit a specific runway or landing strip, such as overall grading or drainage, terminal area or building developments, the sponsor must own, acquire, or agree to acquire adequate property interests in runway clear zone areas for the dominant runway or landing strip to the extent that the Administrator determines is practical and feasible, with regard to standard configuration, length, and property interests, considering all facts presented by the airport owner or operator.

(f) If a sponsor or other public agency shows that it is legally able to prevent the future erection or creation of obstructions in the runway clear zone area, and adopts protective measures to prohibit their future erection or creation, that showing is acceptable for the purposes of paragraphs (d) and (e) of this section in place of an adequate property interest (except for rights required for removing existing obstructions). In such a case, there must be an agreement between the FAA and the sponsor for removing or marking or lighting (to be determined in each case) any existing obstruction to air navigation In each case, the sponsor must furnish information as to the specific height limitations established and as to the current and foreseeable future use of the property to which they apply. The information must include an acceptable legal opinion of the validity of the measures adopted, including a conclusion that the height limitations are not unreasonable in view of current and foreseeable future use of the property, and are a reasonable exercise of the police power, together with the reasons or basis supporting the opinion.

(g) The authority exercised by the Administrator under paragraphs (b), (c), (d), and (e) of this section to allow a deviation from, or the extent of con-

formity to, standard configuration or length of runway clear zones, or to determine the adequacy of property interests therein, is also exercised by Regional Directors.

[Doc. No. 1329, 27 FR 12350, Dec. 13, 1962, as amended by Amdt. 151–22, 33 FR 8267, June 4, 1968; Amdt. 151–25, 33 FR 14535, Sept. 27, 1968]

§ 151.13 Federal-aid Airport Program: Policy affecting landing aid requirements.

(a) *Landing aid requirements.* No project for developing or improving an airport may be approved for the Program unless it provides for acquiring or installing such of the following landing aids as the Administrator determines are needed for the safe and efficient use of the airport by aircraft, considering the category of the airport and the type and volume of traffic using it:

(1) Land needed for installing approach lighting systems (ALS).

(2) In-runway lighting.

(3) High intensity runway lighting.

(4) Runway distance markers.

For the purposes of this section "approach lighting system (ALS)" is a standard configuration of aeronautical ground lights in the approach area to a runway or channel to assist a pilot in making an approach to the runway or channel.

(b) *Specific landing aid requirements.* The landing aids set forth in paragraphs (a) (1) through (4) of this section are required for the safe and efficient use of airports by aircraft in the following cases:

(1) Lands for installing approach lighting systems are required as part of a project if the installing of the components of the system on the airport is in an approved FAA budget, unless the sponsor has already acquired the land necessary for the system or is otherwise undertaking to acquire that land. If the sponsor is otherwise undertaking to acquire the land, the grant agreement for the project must obligate the sponsor to complete the acquisition within a time limit prescribed by the Administrator. The Administrator immediately notifies a sponsor when a budget is approved providing for installing an approach lighting system at the airport concerned.

(2) In-runway lighting is required as part of a project:

(i) If the project includes:

(a) Construction of a new runway designated by the FAA as an instrument landing runway for which the installation of an IFR precision approach system including ALS and ILS, has been programmed by the FAA with funds then available therefor;

(b) An extension of 3,000 feet or more (usable for landing purposes) of the approach end of a designated instrument landing runway equipped, or programed by the FAA, with funds then available therefor, to be equipped, with an IFR precision approach system including ALS and ILS;

(c) Reconstruction of a designated instrument landing runway equipped, or programed by the FAA, with funds then available therefor, to be equipped with an IFR precision approach system including ALS and ILS, if the reconstruction requires the closing of the runway; or

(d) Any other airport development on an airport whose designated instrument landing runway is equipped, or programed by the FAA, with funds then available therefor, to be equipped with an IFR precision approach system including ALS and ILS; and

(ii) Only if a study of the airport shows that in-runway lighting is required for the safe and efficient use of the airport by aircraft, after the Administrator considers the following:

(a) The type and volume of flight activity;

(b) Other existing or planned navigational aids;

(c) Airport environmental factors such as local weather conditions and adjacent geographic profiles;

(d) Approach and departure paths;

(e) Effect on landing and takeoff minima; and

(f) In the case of projects under paragraph (b)(2)(i)(d) of this section, whether installing in-runway lighting requires closing the runway for so long a time that the adverse effect on safety of its closing would outweigh the contribution to safety that would be gained by the in-runway lights or whether it would unduly interfere with the efficiency of aircraft operations.

(3) High intensity runway edge lighting on the designated instrument landing runway is required as a part of a project whenever that runway is equipped or programmed for the installation of an ILS and high intensity runway edge lights are not then installed on the runway or included in another project. A project for extending a runway that has high intensity runway edge lights on the existing runway requires, as a part of the project, the extension of the high intensity runway edge lights.

(4) Runway distance markers whose design standards have been approved and published by the FAA are required as a part of a project on a case-by-case basis if, after reviewing the pertinent facts and circumstances of the case, the Administrator determines that they are needed for the safe and efficient use of the airport by aircraft.

[Doc. No. 1329, 27 FR 12350, Dec. 13, 1962, as amended by Amdt. 151–3, 28 FR 12613, Nov. 27, 1963; Amdt. 151–33, 34 FR 9708, June 21, 1969]

§ 151.15 Federal-aid Airport Program: Policy affecting runway or taxiway remarking.

No project for developing or improving an airport may be approved for the Program unless it provides for runway or taxiway remarking if the present marking is obliterated by construction, alteration or repair work included in a FAAP project or by the required routing of construction equipment used therein.

[Amdt. 151–17, 31 FR 16524, Dec. 28, 1966]

Subpart B—Rules and Procedures for Airport Development Projects

AUTHORITY: 49 U.S.C. 106(g), 40113, 47151, 47153.

SOURCE: Docket No. 1329, 27 FR 12351, Dec. 13, 1962, unless otherwise noted.

§ 151.21 Procedures: Application; general information.

(a) An eligible sponsor that desires to obtain Federal aid for eligible airport development must submit to the Area Manager of the area in which the sponsor is located (hereinafter in this part referred to as the "Area Manager"), a request on FAA Form 5100–3, accompanied by—

(1) The sponsor's written statement as to whether the proposed project involves the displacement and relocation of persons residing on land physically acquired or to be acquired for the project development; and

(2) The sponsor's written assurance, if the project involves displacement and relocation of such persons, that adequate replacement housing will be available or provided for (built, if necessary), without regard to their race, color, religion, sex, or national origin, before the execution of a grant agreement for the project.

(b) A proposed project is selected for inclusion in a program only if the sponsor has submitted a written assurance when required by paragraph (a)(2) of this section, or if the Administrator has determined that the project does not involve the displacement and relocation of persons residing on land to be physically acquired or to be acquired for the project development. If the Administrator selects a proposed project for inclusion in a program, a tentative allocation of funds is made for it and the sponsor is notified of the allocation. The tentative allocation may be withdrawn if the sponsor fails to submit an acceptable project application as provided in paragraph (c) of this section or fails to proceed diligently with the project, or if adequate replacement housing is not available or provided for in accordance with a written assurance when required by paragraph (a)(2) of this section.

(c) As soon as practicable after receiving notice of the tentative allocation, the sponsor must submit a project application on FAA Form 1624 to the Area Manager, without changing the language of the form, unless the change is approved in advance by the Administrator. In the case of a joint project, each sponsor executes only those provisions of the project application that apply to it. A sponsor who has executed a grant agreement for a project for the development of an airport under the Program, may, in the Administrator's discretion, submit additional project applications on FAA Form 1624 for further development of that airport.

(49 U.S.C. 1120, 1655(c); sec. 6(c), Dept. of Transportation Act; sec. 1.4(b)(1) of the regulations of the Office of the Secretary of Transportation; Federal Airport Act, as amended)

[Doc. No. 1329, 27 FR 12351, Dec. 13, 1962, as amended by Amdt. 151–11, 31 FR 6686, May 5, 1966; Amdt. 151–32, 34 FR 9617, June 19, 1969; Amdt. 151–39, 35 FR 5536, Apr. 3, 1970]

§ 151.23　Procedures: Application; funding information.

Each sponsor must state in its application that it has on hand, or show that it can obtain as needed, funds to pay all estimated costs of the proposed project that are not borne by the United States or by another sponsor. If any of the funds are to be furnished to a sponsor, or used to pay project costs on behalf of a sponsor, by a State agency or any other public agency that is not a sponsor of the project, that agency may, instead of the sponsor, submit evidence that the funds will be provided if the project is approved.

[Doc. No. 1329, 27 FR 12351, Dec. 13, 1962, as amended by Amdt. 151–34, 34 FR 12883, Aug. 8, 1969]

§ 151.24　Procedures: Application; information on estimated project costs.

(a) If any part of the estimated project costs consists of the value of donated land, labor, materials, or equipment, or of the value of a property interest in land acquired at a cost that (as represented by the sponsor) is not the actual cost or the amount of an award in eminent domain proceedings, the sponsor must so state in the application, indicating the nature of the donation or other transaction and the value it places on it.

(b) If, after the grant agreement is executed and before the final payment of the allowable project costs is made under § 151.63, it appears that the sponsor inadvertently or unknowingly failed to comply with paragraph (a) of this section as to any item, the Administrator—

(1) Makes or obtains an appraisal of the item, and if the appraised value is less than the value placed on the item in the project application, notifies the sponsor that it may, within a stated

time, ask in writing for reconsideration of the appraisal and submit statements of pertinent facts and opinion; and

(2) Adjusts the U.S. share of the project costs to reflect any decrease in value of the item below that stated in the project application.

[Amdt. 151–34, 34 FR 12883, Aug. 8, 1969]

§ 151.25 Procedures: Application; information as to property interests.

(a) Each sponsor must state in its application all of the property interests that he holds in the lands to be developed or used as part of, or in connection with, the airport as it will be when the project is completed. Each project application contains a covenant on the part of the sponsor to acquire, before starting construction work, or within a reasonable time if not needed for the construction, property interests satisfactory to the Administrator in all the lands in which it does not hold those property interests at the time it submits the application. In the case of a joint project, any one or more of the sponsors may hold or acquire the necessary property interests. In such a case, each sponsor may show on its application only those property interests that it holds or is to acquire.

(b) Each sponsor of a project must send with its application a property map (designated as Exhibit A) or incorporate such a map by reference to one in a previous application that was approved. The sponsor must clearly identify on the map all property interests required in paragraph (a) of this section, showing prior and proposed acquisitions for which United States aid is requested under the project.

(c) For the purposes of paragraphs (a) and (b) of this section, the property interest that the sponsor must have or agree to obtain, is—

(1) Title free and clear of any reversionary interest, lien, easement, lease, or other encumbrance that, in the opinion of the Administrator, would create an undue risk that it might deprive the sponsor of possession or control, interfere with its use for public airport purposes, or make it impossible for the sponsor to carry out the agreements and covenants in the application;

(2) A lease of not less than 20 years granted to the sponsor by another public agency that has title as described in paragraph (c)(1) of this section, on terms that the Administrator considers satisfactory; or

(3) In the case of an offsite area an agreement, easement, leasehold, or other right or property interest that, in the Administrator's opinion, provides reasonable assurance that the sponsor will not be deprived of its right to use the land for the intended purpose during the period necessary to meet the requirements of the grant agreement.

(d) For the purposes of this section, the word "land" includes landing areas, building areas, runway clear zones, clearways and approach zones, and areas required for offsite construction, entrance roads, drainage, protection of approaches, installation of air navigation facilities, or other airport purposes.

§ 151.26 Procedures: Applications; compatible land use information; consideration of local community interest; relocation of displaced persons.

(a) Each sponsor must state in its application the action that it has taken to restrict the use of land adjacent to or in the immediate vicinity of the airport to activities and purposes compatible with normal airport operations including landing and take-off of aircraft. The sponsor's statement must include information on—

(1) Any property interests (such as airspace easements or title to airspace) acquired by the sponsor to assure compatible land use, or to protect or control aerial approaches;

(2) Any zoning laws enacted or in force restricting the use of land adjacent to or in the vicinity of the airport, or assuring protection or control of aerial approaches, whether or not enacted by the sponsor; and

(3) Any action taken by the sponsor to induce the appropriate government authority to enact zoning laws restricting the use of land adjacent to or in the vicinity of the airport, or assuring protection or control of aerial approaches, when the sponsor lacks the power to zone the land.

(b) Each sponsor must submit with his application—

(1) A written statement—

(i) Specifying what consideration has been given to the interest of all communities in or near which the project is located; and

(ii) Containing the substance of any objection to, or approval of, the proposed project made known to the sponsor by any local individual, group or community; and

(2) A written statement showing that adequate replacement housing that is open to all persons, regardless of race, color, religion, sex, or national origin, is available and has been offered on the same nondiscriminatory basis to persons who have resided on land physically acquired or to be acquired for the project development and who will be displaced thereby.

[Amdt. 151–8, 30 FR 8039, June 23, 1965, as amended by Amdt. 151–17, 31 FR 16524, Dec. 28, 1966; Amdt. 151–39, 35 FR 5537, Apr. 3, 1970]

§ 151.27 Procedures: Application, plans, specifications, and appraisals.

(a) Except as provided in paragraph (b) of this section, each sponsor shall incorporate by reference in its project application the final plans and specifications, describing the items of airport development for which it requests United States aid. It must submit the plans and specifications with the application unless they were previously submitted or are submitted with that of another sponsor of the project.

(b) In special cases, the Administrator authorizes the postponement of the submission of final plans and specifications until a later date to be specified in the grant agreement, if the sponsor has submitted—

(1) An airport layout plan approved by the Administrator; and

(2) Preliminary plans and specifications in enough detail to identify all items of development included in the project, and prepared so as to provide for accomplishing the project in accordance with the master plan layout, the rules in subparts B and C and applicable local laws and regulations.

(c) If the project involves acquiring a property interest in land by donation, or at a cost that (as represented by the sponsor) is not the actual cost or the amount of an award in eminent domain proceedings, the Administrator, before passing on the eligibility of the project makes or obtains an appraisal of the interest. If the appraised value is less than the value placed on the interest by the sponsor (§ 151.23), the Administrator notifies the sponsor that he may within a stated time, ask in writing for reconsideration of the appraisal and submit statements of pertinent facts and opinion.

[Doc. No. 1329, 27 FR 12351, Dec. 13, 1962, as amended by Amdt. 151–8, 30 FR 8039, June 23, 1965; Amdt. 151–17, 31 FR 16524, Dec. 28, 1966]

§ 151.29 Procedures: Offer, amendment, and acceptance.

(a) Upon approving a project, the Administrator makes an offer to the sponsor to pay the United States share of the allowable project costs. The offer states a definite amount as the maximum obligation of the United States, and is subject to change or withdrawal by the Administrator, in his discretion, at any time before it is accepted.

(b) If, before the sponsor accepts the offer, it is determined that the maximum obligation of the United States stated in the offer is not enough to pay the United States share of the allowable project costs, the sponsor may request an increase in the amount in the offer, through the Area Manager.

(c) An official of the sponsor must accept the offer for the sponsor within the time prescribed in the offer, and in the required number of counterparts, by signing it in the space provided. The signing official must have been authorized to sign the acceptance by a resolution or ordinance adopted by the sponsor's governing body. The resolution or ordinance must, as appropriate under the local law—

(1) Set forth the terms of the offer at length; or

(2) Have a copy of the offer attached to the resolution or ordinance and incorporated into it by reference.

The sponsor must attach a certified copy of the resolution to each executed copy of an accepted offer or grant agreement that it is required to send to the Area Manager.

§151.31 Procedures: Grant agreement.

(a) An offer by the Administrator, and acceptance by the sponsor, as set forth in §151.29, constitute a grant agreement between the sponsor and the United States. Except as provided in §151.41(c)(3), the United States does not pay, and is not obligated to pay, any part of the project costs that have been or may be incurred, before the grant agreement is executed.

(b) The Administrator and the sponsor may agree to a change in a grant agreement if—

(1) The change does not increase the maximum obligation of the United States under the grant agreement by more than 10 percent;

(2) The change provides only for airport development that meets the requirements of subparts B and C; and

(3) The change does not prejudice the interests of the United States.

(c) When a change is agreed to, the Administrator issues a supplemental agreement incorporating the change. The sponsor must accept the supplemental agreement in the manner provided in §151.29(c).

[Doc. No. 1329, 27 FR 12351, Dec. 13, 1962, as amended by Amdt. 151–8, 30 FR 8040, June 23, 1965]

§151.33 Cosponsorship and agency.

(a) Any two or more public agencies that desire to participate either in accomplishing development under a project or in maintaining or operating the airport, may cosponsor it if they meet the requirements of subparts B and C, including—

(1) The eligibility requirements of §151.37; and

(2) The submission of a single project application, executed by each sponsor, clearly stating the certifications, representations, warranties, and obligations made or assumed by each, or a separate application by each that does not meet all the requirements of subparts B and C if in the Administrator's opinion, the applications collectively meet the requirements of subparts B and C as applied to a project with a single sponsor.

(b) A public agency that desires to participate in a project only by contributing funds to a sponsor need not become a sponsor or an agent of the sponsor, as provided in this section. However, any funds that it contributes are considered as funds of the sponsor for the purposes of the Federal Airport Act and this part.

(c) If the sponsors of a joint project are not each willing to assume, jointly and severally, the obligations that subparts B and C requires a sponsor to assume, they must send a true copy of an agreement between them, satisfactory to the Administrator, to be incorporated into the grant agreement. Each agreement must state—

(1) The responsibilities of each sponsor to the others with respect to accomplishing the proposed development and operating and maintaining the airport;

(2) The obligations that each will assume to the United States; and

(3) The name of the sponsor or sponsors who will accept, receipt for, and disburse grant payments.

If an offer is made to the sponsors of a joint project, as provided in §151.29, it contains a specific condition that it is made in accordance with the agreement between the sponsors (and the agreement is incorporated therein by reference) and that, by accepting the offer, each sponsor assumes only its respective obligations as set forth in the agreement.

(d) A public agency may, if it is authorized by local law, act as agent of the public agency that is to own and operate the airport, with or without participating financially and without becoming a sponsor. The terms and conditions of the agency and the agent's authority to act for the sponsor must be set forth in an agency agreement that is satisfactory to the Administrator. The sponsor must submit a true copy of the agreement with the project application. Such an agent may accept, on behalf of the sponsor, an offer made under §151.29, only if that acceptance has been specifically and legally authorized by the sponsor's governing body and the authority is specifically set forth in the agency agreement.

(e) When the cosponsors of an airport are not located in the same area, they must submit a joint request to the

Area Manager of the area in which the airport development will be located.

[Doc. No. 1329, 27 FR 12351, Dec. 13, 1962, as amended by Amdt. 151–8, 30 FR 8040, June 23, 1965; Amdt. 151–11, 31 FR 6686, May 5, 1966]

§ 151.35 Airport development and facilities to which subparts B and C apply.

(a) Subparts B and C applies to the following kinds of airport development:

(1) Any work involved in constructing, improving, or repairing a public airport or part thereof, including the constructing, altering, or repairing of only those buildings or parts thereof that are intended to house facilities or activities directly related to the safety of persons at the airport.

(2) Removing, lowering, relocating, marking, and lighting of airport hazards as defined in § 151.39(b).

(3) Acquiring land or an interest therein, or any easement through or other interest in air space, that is necessary to allow any work covered by paragraph (a)(1) or (2) of this section, or to remove or mitigate, or prevent or limit the establishment of, airport hazards as defined in § 151.39(b).

It does not apply to the constructing, altering, or repair of airport hangars or public parking facilities for passenger automobiles.

(b) The airport facilities to which subparts B and C applies are those structures, runways, or other items, on or at an airport, that are—

(1) Used or intended to be used, in connection with the landing, takeoff, or maneuvering of aircraft, or for or in connection with operating and maintaining the airport itself; or

(2) Required to be located at the airport for use by the users of its aeronautical facilities or by airport operators, concessionaires, and other users of the airport in connection with providing services or commodities to the users of those aeronautical facilities.

(c) For the purposes of subparts B and C, "public airport" means an airport used for public purposes, under the control of a public agency named in § 151.37(a), with a publicly owned landing area.

[Doc. No. 1329, 27 FR 12351, Dec. 13, 1962, as amended by Amdt. 151–8, 30 FR 8040, June 23, 1965]

§ 151.37 Sponsor eligibility.

To be eligible to apply for an individual or joint project for development with respect to a particular airport a sponsor must—

(a) Be a public agency, which includes for the purposes of this part only, a State, the District of Columbia, Puerto Rico, the Virgin Islands, Guam or an agency of any of them; a municipality or other political subdivision; a tax-supported organization; or the United States or an agency thereof;

(b) Be legally, financially, and otherwise able to—

(1) Make the certifications, representations, and warranties in the application form prescribed in § 151.67(a);

(2) Make, keep, and perform the assurances, agreements, and covenants in that form; and

(3) Meet the other applicable requirements of the Federal Airport Act and subparts B and C;

(c) Have, or be able to obtain, enough funds to meet the requirements of § 151.23; and

(d) Have, or be able to obtain, property interests that meet the requirements of § 151.25(a).

For the purpose of paragraph (a) of this section, the United States, or an agency thereof, is not eligible for a project under subparts B and C, unless the project—

(1) Is located in Puerto Rico, the Virgin Islands, or Guam;

(2) Is in or is in close proximity to a national park, a national recreation area, or a national monument; or

(3) Is in a national forest or a special reservation for United States purposes.

[Doc. No. 1329, 27 FR 12351, Dec. 13, 1962, as amended by Amdt. 151–8, 30 FR 8040, June 23, 1965]

§ 151.39 Project eligibility.

(a) A project for construction or land acquisition may not be approved under subparts B and C unless—

(1) It is an item of airport development described in § 151.35(a);

(2) The airport development is within the scope of the current National Airport Plan;

(3) The airport development is, in the opinion of the Administrator, reasonably necessary to provide a needed civil airport facility;

(4) The Administrator is satisfied that the project is reasonably consistent with existing plans of public agencies for the development of the area in which the airport is located and will contribute to the accomplishment of the purposes of the Federal-aid Airport Program;

(5) The Administrator is satisfied, after considering the pertinent information including the sponsor's statements required by §151.26(b), that—

(i) Fair consideration has been given to the interest of all communities in or near which the project is located; and

(ii) Adequate replacement housing that is open to all persons, regardless of race, color, religion, sex, or national origin, is available and has been offered on the same nondiscriminatory basis to persons who have resided on land physically acquired or to be acquired for the project development and have been or will be displaced thereby;

(6) The project provides for installing such of the landing aids specified in section 10(d) of the Federal Airport Act (49 U.S.C. 1109(d)) as the Administrator considers are needed for the safe and efficient use of the airport by aircraft, based on the category of the airport and the type and volume of its traffic.

(b) Only the following kinds of airport development described in §151.35(a) are eligible to be included in a project under subparts B and C:

(1) Preparing all or part of an airport site, including clearing, grubbing filling and grading.

(2) Dredging of seaplane anchorages and channels.

(3) Drainage work, on or off the airport or airport site.

(4) Constructing, altering, or repairing airport buildings or parts thereof to the extent that it is covered by §151.35(a).

(5) Constructing, altering, or repairing runways, taxiways, and aprons, including—

(i) Bituminous resurfacing of pavements with a minimum of 100 pounds of plant-mixed material for each square yard;

(ii) Applying bituminous surface treatment on a pavement (in accordance with FAA Specification P–609), the existing surface of which consists of that kind of surface treatment; and

(iii) Resealing a runway that has been substantially extended or partially reconstructed, if that resealing is necessary for the uniform color and appearance of the runway.

(6) Fencing, erosion control, seeding and sodding of an airport or airport site.

(7) Installing, altering, or repairing airport markers and runway, taxiway and apron lighting facilities and equipment.

(8) Constructing, altering, or repairing entrance roads and airport service roads.

(9) Constructing, installing, or connecting utilities, either on or off the airport or airport site.

(10) Removing, lowering, relocating marking, or lighting any airport hazard.

(11) Clearing, grading, and filling to allow the installing of landing aids.

(12) Relocating structures, roads, and utilities necessary to allow eligible airport development.

(13) Acquiring land or an interest therein, or any easement through or other interest in airspace, when necessary to—

(i) Allow other airport development to be made, whether or not a part of the Federal-aid Airport Program;

(ii) Prevent or limit the establishment of airport hazards;

(iii) Allow the removal, lowering, relocation, marking, and lighting of existing airport hazards;

(iv) Allow the installing of landing aids; or

(v) Allow the proper use, operation, maintenance, and management of the airport as a public facility.

(14) Any other airport development described in §151.35(a) that is specifically approved by the Administrator.

For the purposes of paragraph (b)(10) of this section, an airport hazard is any structure or object of natural growth located on or in the vicinity of a public airport, or any use of land in the vicinity of the airport, that obstructs the airspace needed for the landing or takeoff of aircraft or is otherwise hazardous to the landing or takeoff of aircraft. For the purposes of paragraph (b)(13) of this section, land acquisition includes the acquiring of land that is already developed as a private airport and the structures, fixtures, and improvements that are a part of realty (other than hangars, other ineligible structures and parts thereof, fixtures, and improvements).

(c) A project for acquiring land that has been or will be donated to the sponsor is not eligible for inclusion in the Federal-aid Airport Program, unless the project also includes other items of airport development that would require a sponsor's contribution equal to or more than the United States share of the value of the donated land as appraised by the Administrator.

[Doc. No. 1329, 27 FR 12351, Dec. 13, 1962, as amended by Amdt. 151-8, 30 FR 8040, June 23, 1965; Amdt. 151-17, 31 FR 16524, Dec. 28, 1966; Amdt. 151-37, 35 FR 5112, Mar. 26, 1970; Amdt. 151-39, 35 FR 5537, Apr. 3, 1970]

§ 151.41   Project costs.

(a) For the purposes of subparts B and C, project costs consist of any costs involved in accomplishing a project, including those of—

(1) Making field surveys;

(2) Preparing plans and specifications;

(3) Accomplishing or procuring the accomplishing of the work;

(4) Supervising and inspecting construction work;

(5) Acquiring land, or an interest therein, or any easement through or other interest in airspace; and

(6) Administrative and other incidental costs incurred specifically in connection with accomplishing a project, and that would not have otherwise been incurred.

(b) The costs described in paragraph (a) of this section, including the value of land, labor, materials, and equipment donated or loaned to the sponsor and appropriated to the project by the sponsor, are eligible for consideration as to their allowability, except for—

(1) That part of the cost of rehabilitation or repair for which funds have been appropriated under section 17 of the Federal Airport Act (49 U.S.C. 1116);

(2) That part of the cost of acquiring an existing private airport that represents the cost of acquiring passenger automobile parking facilities, buildings to be used as hangars, living quarters, or for nonairport purposes, at the airport, and those buildings or parts of buildings the construction of which is not airport development within the meaning of § 151.35(a);

(3) The cost of materials and supplies owned by the sponsor or furnished from a source of supply owned by the sponsor if—

(i) Those materials and supplies were used for airport development before the grant agreement was executed; or

(ii) The cost is not supported by proper evidence of quantity and value;

(4) The cost of nonexpendable machinery, tools, or equipment owned by the sponsor and used under a project by the sponsors force account, except to the extent of the fair rental value of that machinery, tools, or equipment for the period it is used on the project;

(5) The costs of general area, urban, or statewide planning of airports, as distinguished from planning a specific project;

(6) The value of any land, including improvements, donated to the sponsor by another public agency; and

(7) Any costs incurred in connection with raising funds by the sponsor, including interest and premium charges and administrative expenses involved in conducting bond elections and in the sale of bonds.

(c) To be an allowable project cost, for the purposes of computing the amount of a grant, an item that is paid or incurred must, in the opinion of the Administrator—

(1) Have been necessary to accomplish airport development in conformity with the approved plans and specifications for an approved project and with the terms of the grant agreement for the project;

(2) Be reasonable in amount (or be subject to partial disallowance under section 13(a)(3) of the Federal Airport Act (49 U.S.C. 1112(a)(3));

(3) Have been incurred after the date the grant agreement was executed, except that costs of land acquisition, field surveys, planning, preparing plans and specifications, and administrative

and incidental costs, may be allowed even though they were incurred before that date, if they were incurred after May 13, 1946; and

(4) Be supported by satisfactory evidence.

[Doc. No. 1329, 27 FR 12351, Dec. 13, 1962, as amended by Amdt. 151–8, 30 FR 8040, June 23, 1965; Amdt. 151–14, 31 FR 11747, Sept. 8, 1966]

§151.43 United States share of project costs.

(a) The United States share of the allowable costs of a project is stated in the grant agreement for the project, to be paid from appropriations made under the Federal Airport Act.

(b) Except as provided in paragraphs (c) and (d) of this section and in subpart C of this part, the United States share of the costs of an approved project for airport development (regardless of its size or location) is 50 percent of the allowable costs of the project.

(c) The U.S. share of the costs of an approved project for airport development in a State in which the unappropriated and unreserved public lands and nontaxable Indian lands (individual and tribal) is more than 5 percent of its total land, is the percentage set forth in the following table:

State	Percent
Alaska	62.50
Arizona	60.80
California	53.72
Colorado	52.98
Idaho	55.80
Montana	52.99
Nevada	62.50
New Mexico	56.14
Oregon	55.64
South Dakota	52.53
Utah	60.65
Washington	51.53
Wyoming	56.33

(d) The United States share of the costs of an approved project, representing the costs of any of the following, is 75 percent:

(1) The costs of installing high intensity runway edge lighting on a designated instrument landing runway or other runway with an approved straight-in approach procedure.

(2) The costs of installing in-runway lighting (touchdown zone lighting system, and centerline lighting system).

(3) The costs of installing runway distance markers.

(4) The costs of acquiring land, or a suitable property interest in land or in or over water, needed for installing operating, and maintaining an ALS (as described in §151.13).

(5) The costs of any project in the Virgin Islands.

[Doc. No. 1329, 27 FR 12351, Dec. 13, 1962, as amended by Amdt. 151–17, 31 FR 16524, Dec. 28, 1966; Amdt. 151–20, 32 FR 17471; Dec. 6, 1967; Amdt. 151–35, 34 FR 13699, Aug. 27, 1969; Amdt. 151–36, 34 FR 19501 Dec. 10, 1969]

§151.45 Performance of construction work: General requirements.

(a) All construction work under a project must be performed under contract, except in a case where the Administrator determines that the project, or a part of it, can be more effectively and economically accomplished on a force account basis by the sponsor or by another public agency acting for or as agent of the sponsor.

(b) Each contract under a project must meet the requirements of local law.

(c) No sponsor may issue any change order under any of its construction contracts or enter into a supplemental agreement unless three copies of that order or agreement have been sent to and approved by the Area Manager. §§151.47 and 151.49 apply to supplemental agreements as well as to original contracts.

(d) This section and §§151.47 through 151.49 do not apply to contracts with the owners of airport hazards, (as described in §151.39(b)), buildings, pipe lines, power lines, or other structures or facilities, for installing, extending, changing, removing, or relocating that structure or facility. However, the sponsor must obtain the approval of the Area Manager before entering into such a contract.

(e) No sponsor may allow a contractor or subcontractor to begin work under a project until—

(1) The sponsor has furnished three conformed copies of the contract to the Area Manager; and

(2) The Area Manager agrees to the issuance of a notice to proceed with the work to the contractor. However, the Area Manager does not agree to the

issuance of such a notice unless he is satisfied that adequate replacement housing is available and has been offered to affected persons, as required for project eligibility by § 151.39(a)(5).

(f) Except when the Area Manager determines that the sponsor has previously demonstrated satisfactory engineering and construction supervision and inspection, no sponsor may allow a contractor or subcontractor to begin work, nor may the sponsor begin force account work, until the sponsor has notified the Area Manager in writing that engineering and construction supervision and inspection have been arranged to insure that construction will conform to FAA approved plans and specifications, and that the sponsor has caused a review to be made of the qualifications of personnel who will be performing such supervision and inspection and is satisfied that they are qualified to do so.

[Doc. No. 1329, 27 FR 12351, Dec. 13, 1962, as amended by Amdt. 151–31, 34 FR 4885, Mar. 6, 1969; Amdt. 151–39, 35 FR 5537, Apr. 3, 1970]

§ 151.47 Performance of construction work: Letting of contracts.

(a) *Advertising required; exceptions.* Unless the Administrator approves another method for use on a particular airport development project, each contract for construction work on a project in the amount of more than $2,000 must be awarded on the basis of public advertising and open competitive bidding under the local law applicable to the letting of public contracts. Any oral or written agreement or understanding between a sponsor and another public agency that is not a sponsor of the project, under which that public agency undertakes construction work for or as agent of the sponsor, is not considered to be a construction contract for the purposes of this section, or §§ 151.45, 151.49, and 151.51.

(b) *Advertisement; conditions and contents.* There may be no advertisement for bids on, or negotiation of, a construction contract until the Administrator has approved the plans and specifications. The advertisement shall inform the bidders of the contract and reporting provisions required by § 151.54. Unless the estimated contract price or construction cost is $2,000 or less, there

may be no advertisement for bids or negotiation until the Administrator has given the sponsor a copy of a decision of the Secretary of Labor establishing the minimum wage rates for skilled and unskilled labor under the proposed contract. In each case, a copy of the wage determination decision must be set forth in the initial invitation for bids or proposed contract or incorporated therein by reference to a copy set forth in the advertised or negotiated specifications.

(c) *Procedure for the Secretary of Labor's wage determinations.* At least 60 days before the intended date of advertising or negotiating under paragraph (b) of this section, the sponsor shall send to the Area Manager, completed Department of Labor Form DB–11, with only the classifications needed in the performance of the work checked. General entries (such as "entire schedule" or "all applicable classifications") may not be used. Additional necessary classifications not on the form may be typed in the blank spaces or on an attached separate list. A classification that can be fitted into classifications on the form, or a classification that is not generally recognized in the area or in the industry, may not be used. Except in areas where the wage patterns are clearly established, the Form must be accompanied by any available pertinent wage payment or locally prevailing fringe benefit information.

(d) *Use and effectiveness of the Secretary of Labor's wage determinations.* (1) Wage determinations are effective only for 120 days from the date of the determinations. If it appears that a determination may expire between bid opening and award, the sponsor shall so advise the FAA as soon as possible. If he wishes a new request for wage determination to be made and if any pertinent circumstances have changed, he shall submit a new Form DB–11 and accompanying information. If he claims that the determination expires before award and after bid opening due to unavoidable circumstances, he shall submit proof of the facts which he claims support a finding to that effect.

(2) The Secretary of Labor may modify any wage determination before the award of the contract or contracts for which it was sought. If the proposed

contract is awarded on the basis of public advertisement and open competitive bidding, any modification that the FAA receives less than 10 days before the opening of bids is not effective, unless the Administrator finds that there is reasonable time to notify bidders. A modification may not continue in effect beyond the effective period of the wage determination to which it relates. The Administrator sends any modification to the sponsor as soon as possible. If the modification is effective, it must be incorporated in the invitation for bids, by issuing an addendum to the specifications or otherwise.

(e) *Requirements for awarding construction contracts.* A sponsor may not award a construction contract without the written concurrence of the Administrator (through the Area Manager) that the contract prices are reasonable and that the contract conforms to the sponsor's grant agreement with the United States. A sponsor that awards contracts on the basis of public advertising and open competitive bidding, shall, after the bids are opened, send a tabulation of the bids and its recommendations for award to the Area Manager. The allowable project costs of the work, on which the Federal participation is computed, may not be more than the bid of the lowest responsible bidder. The sponsor may not accept a bid by a contractor whose name appears on the current list of ineligible contractors published by the Comptroller General of the United States under §5.6(b) of Title 29 of the regulations of the Secretary of Labor (29 CFR part 5), or a bid by any firm, corporation, partnership, or association in which that contractor has a substantial interest.

(f) *Secretary of Labor's interpretations apply.* Where applicable by their terms, the regulations of the Secretary of Labor (29 CFR 5.20–5.32) interpreting the fringe benefit provisions of the Davis-Bacon Act apply to this section.

[Amdt. 151–6, 29 FR 18001, Dec. 18, 1964]

§151.49 Performance of construction work: Contract requirements.

(a) *Contract provisions.* In addition to any other provisions necessary to ensure completion of the work in accordance with the grant agreement, each sponsor entering into a construction contract for an airport development project shall insert in the contract the provisions required by the Secretary of Labor, as set forth in appendix H of this part. The Director, Airports Service, may amend any provision in appendix H from time to time to accord with rule-making action of the Secretary of Labor. The provisions in the following paragraphs also must be inserted in the contract:

(1) *Federal Aid to Airport Program Project.* The work in this contract is included in Federal-aid Airport Project No. __, which is being undertaken and accomplished by the [insert sponsor's name] in accordance with the terms and conditions of a grant agreement between the [insert sponsor's name] and the United States, under the Federal Airport Act (49 U.S.C. 1101) and part 151 of the Federal Aviation Regulations (14 CFR part 151), pursuant to which the United States has agreed to pay a certain percentage of the costs of the project that are determined to be allowable project costs under that Act. The United States is not a party to this contract and no reference in this contract to the FAA or any representative thereof, or to any rights granted to the FAA or any representative thereof, or the United States, by the contract, makes the United States a party to this contract.

(2) *Consent to assignment.* The contractor shall obtain the prior written consent of the [insert sponsor's name] to any proposed assignment of any interest in or part of this contract.

(3) *Convict labor.* No convict labor may be employed under this contract.

(4) *Veterans' preference.* In the employment of labor (except in executive, administrative, and supervisory positions), preference shall be given to qualified individuals who have served in the military service of the United States (as defined in section 101(1) of the Soldiers' and Sailors' Civil Relief Act of 1940) and have been honorably discharged from that service, except that preference may be given only where that labor is available locally and is qualified to perform the work to which the employment relates.

(5) *Withholding: Sponsor from contractor.* Whether or not payments or advances to the [insert sponsor's name] are withheld or suspended by the FAA, the [insert sponsor's name] may withhold or cause to be withheld from the contractor so much of the accrued payments or advances as may be considered necessary to pay laborers and mechanics employed by the contractor or any subcontractor on the work the full amount of wages required by this contract.

(6) *Nonpayment of wages.* If the contractor or subcontractor fails to pay any laborer or mechanic employed or working on the site of the work any of the wages required by this contract the [insert sponsor's name] may, after written notice to the contractor, take such action as may be necessary to cause the suspension of any further payment or advance of funds until the violations cease.

(7) *FAA inspection and review.* The contractor shall allow any authorized representative of the FAA to inspect and review any work or materials used in the performance of this contract.

(8) *Subcontracts.* The contractor shall insert in each of his subcontracts the provisions contained in paragraphs [insert designations of 6 paragraphs of contract corresponding to paragraphs (1), (3), (4), (5), (6) and (7) of this paragraph], and also a clause requiring the subcontractors to include these provisions in any lower tier subcontracts which they may enter into, together with a clause requiring this insertion in any further subcontracts that may in turn be made.

(9) *Contract termination.* A breach of paragraphs [insert designation of 3 paragraphs corresponding to paragraphs (6), (7) and (8) of this paragraph] may be grounds for termination of the contract.

(b) *Exemption of certain contracts.* Appendix H to this part and paragraph (a)(5) of this section do not apply to prime contracts of $2,000 or less.

(c) *Adjustment in liquidated damages.* A contractor or subcontractor who has become liable for liquidated damages under paragraph G of appendix H and who claims that the amount administratively determined as liquidated damages under section 104(a) of the Contract Work Hours Standards Act is incorrect or that he violated inadvertently the Contract Work Hours Standards Act notwithstanding the exercise of due care, may—

(1) If the amount determined is more than $100, apply to the Administrator for a recommendation to the Secretary of Labor that an appropriate adjustment be made or that he be relieved of liability for such liquidated damages; or

(2) If the amount determined is $100 or less, apply to the Administrator for an appropriate adjustment in liquidated damages or for release from liability for the liquidated damages.

(d) *Corrected wage determinations.* The Secretary of Labor corrects any wage determination included in any contract under this section whenever the wage determination contains clerical errors. A correction may be made at the Administrator's request or on the initiative of the Secretary of Labor.

(e) *Secretary of Labor's interpretations apply.* Where applicable by their terms, the regulations of the Secretary of Labor (29 CFR 5.20–5.32) interpreting the "fringe benefit provisions" of the Davis-Bacon Act apply to the contract provisions in appendix H, and to this section.

[Amdt. 151–6, 29 FR 18001, Dec. 18, 1964, as amended by Amdt. 151–7, 30 FR 7484, June 6, 1965]

§ 151.51   Performance of construction work: Sponsor force account.

(a) Before undertaking any force account construction work, the sponsor (or any public agency acting as agent for the sponsor) must obtain the written consent of the Administrator through the Area Manager. In requesting that consent, the sponsor must submit—

(1) Adequate plans and specifications showing the nature and extent of the construction work to be performed under that force account;

(2) A schedule of the proposed construction and of the construction equipment that will be available for the project;

(3) Assurance that adequate labor, material, equipment, engineering personnel, as well as supervisory and inspection personnel as required by §151.45(f), will be provided and

(4) A detailed estimate of the cost of the work, broken down for each class of costs involved, such as labor, materials, rental of equipment, and other pertinent items of cost.

(b) [Reserved]

[Doc. No. 1329, 27 FR 12351, Dec. 13, 1962, as amended by Amdt. 151–17, 31 FR 16525, Dec. 28, 1966; Amdt. 151–31, 34 FR 4885, Mar. 6 1969]

§151.53 Performance of construction work: Labor requirements.

A sponsor who is required to include in a construction contract the labor provisions required by §151.49 shall require the contractor to comply with those provisions and shall cooperate with the FAA in effecting that compliance. For this purpose the sponsor shall—

(a) Keep, and preserve, for a three-year period beginning on the date the contract is completed, each affidavit and payroll copy furnished by the contractor, and make those affidavits and copies available to the FAA, upon request, during that period;

(b) Have each of those affidavits and payrolls examined by its resident engineer (or any other of its employees or agents who are qualified to make the necessary determinations), as soon as possible after receiving it, to the extent necessary to determine whether the contractor is complying with the labor provisions required by §151.49 and particularly with respect to whether the contractor's employees are correctly classified;

(c) Have investigations made during the performance of work under the contract, to the extent necessary to determine whether the contractor is complying with those labor provisions, particularly with respect to whether the contractor's employees are correctly classified, including in the investigations, interviews with employees and examinations of payroll information at the work site by the sponsor's resident engineer (or any other of its employees or agents who are qualified to make the necessary determinations); and

(d) Keep the Area Manager fully advised of all examinations and investigations made under this section, all determinations made on the basis of those examinations and investigations, and all efforts made to obtain compliance with the labor provisions of the contract.

For the purposes of paragraph (c) of this section, the sponsor shall give priority to complaints of alleged violations, and shall treat as confidential any written or oral statements made by any employee. The sponsor may not disclose an employee's statement to a contractor without the employee's consent.

§151.54 Equal employment opportunity requirements: Before July 1, 1968.

In conformity with Executive Order 11246 of September 24, 1965 (30 FR 12319, 3 CFR, 1965 Supp., p. 167) the regulations of the former President's Committee on Equal Employment Opportunity, 41 CFR part 60–1 (28 FR 9812, 11305), as adopted "to the extent not inconsistent with Executive Order 11246" by the Secretary of Labor ("Transfer of Functions," Oct. 19, 1965, 30 FR 13441), are incorporated by reference into subparts B and C of this part as set forth below. They are referred to in this section by section numbers of part 60–1 of title 41.

(a) *Equal employment opportunity requirements.* There are hereby incorporated by reference into subparts B and C, as requirements, the provisions of §60–1.3(b)(1). The FAA is primarily responsible for the sponsor's compliance.

(b) *Equal employment opportunity requirements in construction contracts.* The sponsor shall cause the "equal opportunity clause" in §60–1.3(b)(1) to be incorporated into all prime contracts and subcontracts as required by §60–1.3(c).

(c) *Reporting requirements for contractors and subcontractors.* The sponsor shall cause the filing of compliance reports by contractors and subcontractors as provided in §60–1.6(a) and the furnishing of such other information as may be required under that provision.

(d) *Bidders' reports.* (1) The sponsor shall include in his invitations for bids or negotiations for contracts, and shall require his contractors to include in their invitations for bids or negotiations for subcontracts, the following provisions based on § 60–1.6(b)(1):

Each bidder, prospective contractor or proposed subcontractor shall state as an initial part of the bid or negotiations of the contract whether he has participated in any previous contract or subcontract subject to the equal opportunity clause and, if so, whether he has filed with the Office of Federal Contract Compliance in the United States Department of Labor or the contracting or administering agency all compliance reports due under applicable instructions. In any case in which a bidder or prospective contractor or proposed subcontractor who has participated in a previous contract or subcontract subject to the equal opportunity clause has not filed a compliance report due under applicable instructions, such bidder, prospective contractor or proposed subcontractors shall submit a compliance report prior to the award of the proposed contract or subcontract. When a determination has been made to award a contract to a specific contractor, such contractor shall, prior to award, furnish such other pertinent information regarding his own employment policies and practices as well as those of his proposed subcontractors as the FAA, the sponsor, or the Director of the Office of Federal Contract compliance may require.

(2) The sponsor or his contractors shall give express notice of the requirements of this paragraph (d) in all invitations for bids or negotiations for contracts.

(e) *Enforcement.* The FAA conducts compliance reviews, handles complaints and, where appropriate, conducts hearings and imposes, or recommends to the Office of Federal Contract Compliance, sanctions, as provided in subpart B—General Enforcement; Complaint Procedure of part 60–1.

(f) *Exempted contracts.* Except for subcontracts for the performance of construction work at the site of construction, the requirements of this section do not apply to subcontracts below the second tier (§ 60–1.3(c)). The requirements of this section do not apply to contracts and subcontracts exempted by § 60–1.4.

(g) *Meaning of terms.* The term *"applicant"* in the provisions of part 60–1 incorporated by reference in this section means the sponsor, except where part 60–1 refers to an applicant for employment, and the term "administering agency" therein means the FAA.

(h) *Applicability to existing agreements and contracts.* This section applies to grant agreements made after December 20, 1964, and before July 1, 1968. Except as provided in § 151.54A(b), it applies to contracts and subcontracts as defined in § 60–1.2 (i) and (k) of Title 41 made in accordance with a grant agreement to which this section applies.

(E.O. 11246, 30 FR 13441, 31 FR 6921; sec. 307, 72 Stat. 752, 49 U.S.C. 1348)

[Amdt. 151–5, 29 FR 15569, Nov. 20, 1964, as amended by Amdt. 151–8, 30 FR 8040, June 23, 1965; Amdt. 151–12, 31 FR 10261, July 29, 1966; Amdt. 151–23, 33 FR 9543, June 29, 1968]

§ 151.54a Equal employment opportunity requirements: After June 30, 1968.

(a) *Incorporation by reference.* There are hereby incorporated by reference into this part the regulations issued by the Secretary of Labor on May 21, 1968, and published in the FEDERAL REGISTER on May 28, 1968 (41 CFR part 60–1, 33 FR 7804), except for the following provisions:

(1) Paragraph (a), "Government contracts", of § 60–1.4, "Equal opportunity clause".

(2) Section 60–1.6, "Duties of agencies".

(b) *Applicability and effectiveness.* The regulations incorporated by reference in paragraph (a) of this section apply to grant agreements made after June 30, 1968. They also apply to contracts, as defined in § 60–1.3(f) of Title 41, entered into under any grant agreement made before or after that date, as provided in § 60–1.47 of Title 41.

(Sec. 307, 72 Stat. 752, 49 U.S.C. 1348)

[Amdt. 151–23, 33 FR 9543, June 29, 1968]

§ 151.55 Accounting and audit.

(a) Each sponsor shall establish and maintain, for each individual project, an adequate accounting record to allow appropriate personnel of the FAA to determine all funds received (including funds of the sponsor and funds received from the United States or other sources), and to determine the allowability of all incurred costs of the project. The sponsor shall segregate and group project costs so that it can furnish, on due notice, cost information in the following cost classifications:

(1) Purchase price or value of land.

(2) Incidental costs of land acquisition.

(3) Costs of contract construction.

(4) Costs of force account construction.

(5) Engineering costs of plans and designs.

(6) Engineering costs of supervision and inspection.

(7) Other administrative costs.

(b) The sponsor shall obtain and retain in its files for a period of three years after the date of the final grant payment, documentary evidence such as invoices, cost estimates, and payrolls supporting each item of project costs.

(c) The sponsor shall retain, for a period of three years after the date of the final grant payment, evidence of all payments for items of project costs including vouchers, cancelled checks or warrants, and receipts for cash payments.

(d) The sponsor shall allow the Administrator and the Comptroller General of the United States, or an authorized representative of either of them, access to any of its books, documents, papers, and records that are pertinent to grants received under the Federal-aid Airport Program for the purposes of accounting and audit. Appropriate FAA personnel may make progress audits at any time during the project, upon notice to the sponsor. If work is suspended on the project for an appreciable period of time, an audit will be made before any semi-final payment is made. In each case an audit is made before the final payment.

[Doc. No. 1329, 27 FR 12351, Dec. 13, 1962, as amended by Amdt. 151-8, 30 FR 8040, June 23, 1965]

§ 151.57 Grant payments: General.

(a) An application for a grant payment is made on FAA Form 5100-6, accompanied by—

(1) A summary of project costs on Form FAA-1630;

(2) A periodic cost estimate on Form FAA-1629 for each contract representing costs for which payment is requested; and

(3) Any supporting information, including appraisals of property interests, that the FAA needs to determine the allowability of any costs for which payment is requested.

(b) *Contractor's certifications.* Each application that involves work performed by a contractor must contain, in the contractor's certification in the periodic cost estimate, a statement that "there has been full compliance with all labor provisions included in the contract identified above and in all subcontracts made under that contract", and, in the case of a substantial dispute as to the nature of the contractor's or a subcontractor's obligation under the labor provisions of the contract or a subcontract, and additional phrase "except insofar as a substantial dispute exists with respect to these provisions".

(c) If a contractor or subcontractor fails or refuses to comply with the labor provisions of the contract with the sponsor, further grant payments to the sponsor are suspended until the violations stop, until the Administrator determines the allowability of the project costs to which the violations related, or, to the extent that the violations consist of underpayments to labor, until the sponsor furnishes satisfactory assurances to the FAA that restitution has been or will be made to the affected employees.

(d) If, upon final determination of the allowability of all project costs of a project, it is found that the total of grant payments to the sponsor was more than the total United States share of the allowable costs of the project, the sponsor shall promptly return the excess to the FAA.

[Doc. No. 1329, 27 FR 12351, Dec. 13, 1962, as amended by Amdt. 151-4, 29 FR 11336, Aug. 6, 1964; Amdt. 151-8, 30 FR 8040, June 23, 1965; Amdt. 151-17, 31 FR 16525, Dec. 28, 1966; Amdt. 151-32, 34 FR 9617, June 19, 1969]

§ 151.59 Grant payments: Land acquisition.

If an approved project includes land acquisition as an item of airport development, the sponsor may, at any time after executing the grant agreement and after title evidence has been approved by the Administrator for the property interest for which payment is requested, apply to the FAA, through the Area Manager, for payment of the United States share of the allowable project costs of the acquisition, including any acquisition that is completed before executing the grant agreement and is part of the airport development included in the project.

§ 151.61   Grant payments: Partial.

(a) Subject to the final determination of allowable project costs as provided in § 151.63 partial grant payments for project costs may be made to a sponsor upon application. Unless previously agreed otherwise, a sponsor may apply for partial payments on a monthly basis. The payments may be paid, upon application, on the basis of the costs of airport development that is accomplished or on the basis of the estimated cost of airport development expected to be accomplished.

(b) Except as otherwise provided, partial grant payments are made in amounts large enough to bring the aggregate amount of all partial payments to the estimated United States share of the project costs of the airport development accomplished under the project as of the date of the sponsor's latest application for payment. In addition, if the sponsor applies, a partial grant payment is made as an advance payment in an amount large enough to bring the aggregate amount of all partial payments to the estimated United States share of the estimated project costs of the airport development expected to be accomplished within 30 days after the date of the sponsor's application for advance payment. However, no partial payment may be made in an amount that would bring the aggregate amount of all partial payments for the project to more than 90 percent of the estimated United States share of the total estimated cost of all airport development included in the project, but not including contingency items, or 90 percent of the maximum obligation of the United States as stated in the grant agreement, whichever amount is the lower. In determining the amount of a partial grant payment, those project costs that the Administrator considers to be of questionable allowability are deducted both from the amount of proj- ect costs incurred

and from the amount of the estimated total project cost.

§ 151.63   Grant   payments: Semifinal and final.

(a) Whenever airport development on a project is delayed or suspended for an appreciable period of time for reasons beyond the sponsor's control and the allowability of the project costs of all airport development completed has been determined on the basis of an audit and review of all costs, a semifinal grant payment may be made in an amount large enough to bring the aggregate amount of all partial grant payments for the project to the United States share of all allowable project costs incurred, even if the amount is more than the 90 percent limitation prescribed in § 151.61(b). However, it may not be more than the maximum obligation of the United States as stated in the grant agreement.

(b) Whenever the project is completed in accordance with the grant agreement, the sponsor may apply for final payment. The final payment is made to the sponsor if—

(1) A final inspection of all work at the airport site has been made jointly by the Area Manager and representatives of the sponsor and the contractor, unless the Area Manager agrees to a different procedure for final inspection.

(2) A final audit of the project account has been completed by appropriate personnel of the FAA; and

(3) The sponsor has furnished final "as constructed" plans, unless otherwise agreed to by the Administrator.

(c) Based upon the final inspection, the final audit, the plans, and the documents and supporting information required by § 151.57(a), the Administrator determines the total amount of the allowable project costs and pays the sponsor the United States' share, less the total amount of all prior payments.

§ 151.65   Memoranda and hearings.

(a) At any time before the FAA issues a grant offer for a project, any public agency or person having a substantial interest in the disposition of the project application may file a memorandum supporting or opposing it with the Area Manager of the area in which the project is located. In addition, that public agency or person may request a public hearing on the location of the airport to be developed. If, in the Administrator's opinion, that public agency or person has a substantial interest in the matter, a public hearing is held.

(b) The Administrator sets the time and place of each hearing under this section, to avoid undue delay in disposing of the application, to afford reasonable time for all parties concerned to prepare for it, and to hold it at a place convenient to the sponsor. Notice of the time and place is mailed to the public agency or person filing the memorandum, the sponsor, and any other necessary persons.

(c) The purpose of the hearing is to help the Administrator discover facts relating to the location of the airport that is proposed to be developed under an application pending before him. There are no adverse parties or interests and no defendant or respondent. They are not hearings for the purposes of 5 U.S.C. 554, 556, and 557, and do not terminate in an adjudication as defined in that Act.

(d) Each hearing under this section is conducted by a hearing officer designated by the Administrator. The hearing officer decides the length of the hearing, the kind of testimony to be heard, and all other matters respecting the conduct of the hearing. The hearing is recorded in a manner determined by the hearing officer and the record becomes a part of the record of the project application. The Administrator's decision is not made solely on the basis of the hearing, but on all relevant facts.

[Doc. No. 1329, 27 FR 12351, Dec. 13, 1962, as amended by Amdt. 151–11, 31 FR 6686, May 5, 1966; Amdt. 151–35, 34 FR 13699, Aug. 27, 1969]

§151.67   Forms.

(a) The various forms used for the purposes of subparts B and C are as follows:

(1) Requests for Federal-aid, FAA Form 5100–3: Contains a statement requesting Federal-aid in carrying out a project under the Federal Airport Act, with appropriate spaces for inserting information needed for considering the request, including the location of the airport, the amount of funds available to the sponsor, a description of the proposed work, and its estimated cost.

(2) Project application, Form FAA–1624: A formal application for Federal-aid to carry out a project under this part. It contains four parts:

(i) Part I—For pertinent information regarding the airport and proposed work included in the project.

(ii) Part II—For incorporating the representations of the sponsor relating to its legal authority to undertake the project, the availability of funds for its share of the project costs, approvals of other non-United States agencies, the existence of any default on the compliance requirements of §151.77(a), possible disabilities, and the ownership of lands and interests in lands to be used in carrying out the project and operating the airport.

(iii) Part III—For incorporating the sponsor's assurances regarding the operation and maintenance of the airport, further development of the airport, and the acquisition of any additional interests in lands that may be needed to carry out the project or for operating the airport.

(iv) Part IV—For a statement of the sponsor's acceptance, to be executed by the sponsor and certificated by its attorney.

(3) [Reserved]

(4) Grant agreement, Form FAA–1632:

(i) Part I—Offer by the United States to pay a specified percentage of the allowable costs of the project, as described therein, on specified terms relating to the undertaking and carrying out of the project, determination of allowability of costs, payment of the United States share, and operation and maintenance of the airport in accordance with assurances in the project application.

(ii) Part II—Acceptance of the offer by the sponsor, execution of the acceptance by the sponsor, and certification by its attorney.

(5) Periodic cost estimate, Form FAA–1629: a certification to be executed by the contractor, with space for information regarding the progress of construction work as of a specific date, and the value of the completed work.

(6) Application for grant payment, FAA Form 5100–6: Application for payment under a grant agreement for work completed as of a specific date or to be completed by a specific date, with space for an appropriate breakdown of project costs among the categories shown therein, and certification provisions to be executed by the sponsor and the Area Manager.

(7) Summary of project costs, Form FAA–1630: For inserting the latest revised estimate of total project costs, the total costs incurred as of a specific date, an estimate of the aggregate of those total costs incurred to date and those to be incurred before a specific date in the future.

(b) Copies of the forms named in this section, and assistance in completing and executing them, are available from the Area Manager.

[Doc. No. 1329, 27 FR 12351, Dec. 13, 1962, as amended by Amdt. 151–8, 30 FR 8040, June 23, 1965; Amdt. 151–11, 31 FR 6686, May 5, 1966; Amdt. 151–17, 31 FR 16525, Dec. 28, 1966; Amdt. 151–25, 33 FR 14535, Sept. 27, 1968; Amdt. 151–34, 34 FR 12883, Aug. 8, 1969]

Subpart C—Project Programming Standards

AUTHORITY: 49 U.S.C. 106(g), 40113, 47151, 47153.

SOURCE: Docket No. 1329, 27 FR 12357 Dec. 13, 1962, unless otherwise noted.

§ 151.71   Applicability.

(a) This subpart prescribes programming and design and construction standards for projects under the Federal-Aid Airport Program to assure the most efficient use of Program funds and to assure that the most important elements of a national system of airports are provided.

(b) Except for the standards made mandatory by § 151.72(a), the standards prescribed in this subpart that apply to any particular project are those in effect on the date the sponsor accepts the Administrator's offer under § 151.29(c). The standards of § 151.72(a) applicable to a project are those in effect on the date written on the notification of tentative allocation of funds (§ 151.21(b)). Standards that become effective after that date may be applied

to the project by agreement between the sponsor and the Administrator.

(Secs. 1–15, 17–21, 60 Stat. 170, 49 U.S.C. 1120)

[Amdt. 151–19, 32 FR 9220, June 29, 1967]

§ 151.72   Incorporation by reference of technical guidelines in Advisory Circulars.

(a) *Provisions incorporated; mandatory standards.* The technical guidelines in the Advisory Circulars, or parts of Circulars, listed in appendix I of this part, are incorporated into this subpart by reference. Guidelines so incorporated are mandatory standards and apply in addition to the other standards in this subpart. No provision so incorporated and made mandatory supersedes any provision of this part 151 (other than of App. I) or of any other part of the Federal Aviation Regulations. Each Circular is incorporated with all amendments outstanding at any time unless the entry in appendix I of this part states otherwise.

(b) *Amendments of Appendix I.* The Director, Airports Service, may add to, or delete from, appendix I of this part any Advisory Circular or part thereof.

(c) *Availability of Advisory Circulars.* The Advisory Circulars listed in appendix I of this part may be inspected and copied at any FAA Regional Office, Area Office, or Airports District Office. Copies of the Circulars that are available free of charge may be obtained from any of the offices or from the Federal Aviation Administration, Printing Branch, HQ–438, Washington, D.C. 20553. Copies of the Circulars that are for sale may be bought from the Superintendent of Documents, U.S. Government Printing Office, Washington, D.C. 20402 for the price listed.

[Amdt. 151–13, 31 FR 11605, Sept. 2, 1966, as amended by Doc. No. 8084, 32 FR 5769, Apr. 11, 1967]

§ 151.73   Land acquisition.

(a) The acquisition of land or any interest therein, or of any easement or other interest in airspace, is eligible for inclusion in a project if it was made after May 13, 1946, and is necessary—

(1) To allow the initial development of the airport;

(2) For improvement indicated in the current National Airport Plan;

(3) For ultimate development of the airport, as indicated in the current approved airport layout plan to the extent consistent with the National Airport Plan;

(4) For approach protection meeting the standards of §77.23 as applied to §§77.25 and 77.27 of this chapter;

(5) To allow installing an ALS (as described in §151.13), in which case the costs of acquiring land needed for it are eligible for 75 percent United States participation if the need is shown in the National Airport Plan, based on the best information available to the FAA for the forecast period;

(6) To allow proper use operation, or maintenance of the airport as a public facility, including offsite lands needed for locating necessary parts of the utility systems serving the airport;

(7) To allow installing navigational aids by the FAA, if the land is within the airport boundaries; or

(8) To allow relocation of navigational aids.

(b) Appendix A of this part sets forth typical eligible and ineligible items of land acquisition as covered by this section.

[Doc. No. 1329, 27 FR 12357, Dec. 13, 1962, as amended by Amdt. 151-7, 30 FR 7484, June 8, 1965; Amdt. 151-8, 30 FR 8040 June 23, 1965]

§151.75 Preparation of site.

(a) Grading, drainage, and associated items of site preparation are eligible for inclusion in a project, but only with respect to one landing strip at any airport, unless the airport qualifies for more than one runway, based on traffic volume or wind conditions (as outlined in §151.77) and the overall site preparation required for development in accordance with the airport layout plan. The complete clearance of runway clear zone areas is desirable, but, as a minimum, all obstructions as determined by §77.23 as applied to §77.27 (b) and (c) of this chapter must be removed. Grading in runway clear zones is eligible only to remove terrain that is an obstruction. The clear zone is not a graded overrun area. Specific site preparation for an airport terminal building is eligible on the same basis as the building itself. The site preparation cost is prorated based on eligible and ineligible building space. Appendix B of this part sets forth typical eligible and ineligible items of site preparation as covered by this section.

(b) For the purposes of this section, eligible drainage work off the airport site includes drainage outfalls, drainage disposal, and interception ditches. If there is damage to adjacent property, its correction is an eligible item for inclusion in the project.

[Doc. No. 1329, 27 FR 12357, Dec. 13, 1962, as amended by Amdt. 151-7, 30 FR 7484, June 8, 1965; Amdt. 151-8, 30 FR 8040, June 23, 1965]

§151.77 Runway paving: General rules.

(a) On any airport, paving of the designated instrument landing runway (or dominant runway if there is no designated instrument runway) is eligible for inclusion in a project, within the limits of the current National Airport Plan. Program participation in constructing, reconstructing or resurfacing is limited to a single runway at each airport, unless more than one runway is eligible under a standard in §151.79 or §151.80.

(b) The kinds of runway paving that are eligible for inclusion in a project include pavement construction and reconstruction, and include runway grooving to improve skid resistance, and resurfacing to increase the load bearing capacity of the runway or to provide a leveling course to correct major irregularities in the pavement. Runway resealing or refilling joints as an ordinary maintenance matter are not eligible items, except for bituminous resurfacing consisting of at least 100 pounds of plant-mixed material for each square yard, and except for the application of a bituminous surface treatment (two applications of material and cover aggregate as prescribed in FAA Specification P-609) on a pavement the current surface of which consists of that kind of a bituminous surface treatment.

(c) On new pavement construction, the applying of a bituminous seal coat on plant hot-mix bituminous surfaces only, is an eligible item only if initial engineering analysis and design indicate the need for a seal coat. However, any delay in applying it that is caused other than by construction difficulties, makes the application a maintenance item that is not eligible.

(d) In any case in which the need for a seal coat is necessary for a new runway extension or partial reconstruction of a runway, the entire runway may be sealed.

(e) Appendix C to this part sets forth typical eligible and ineligible items of runway paving.

(49 U.S.C. 1120)

[Doc. No. 1329, 27 FR 12357, Dec. 13, 1962, as amended by Amdt. 151–17, 31 FR 16525, Dec. 28, 1966; Amdt. 151–29, 34 FR 1634, Feb. 4, 1969]

§ 151.79 Runway paving: Second runway; wind conditions.

(a) *All airports.* Paving a second runway on the basis of wind conditions is eligible for inclusion in a project only if the sponsor shows that—

(1) The airport meets the applicable standards of paragraph (b), (c), or (d) of this section;

(2) The operational experience, and the economic factors of air traffic at the location, justify an additional runway for the airport; and

(3) The second runway is oriented with the existing paved runway to achieve the maximum wind coverage, with due consideration to the airport noise factor, topography, soil conditions, and other pertinent factors affecting the economy and efficiency of the runway development.

(b) *Airports serving large and small aircraft.* The airport serves both large and small aircraft and the existing paved runway is subject to a crosswind component of more than 15 miles per hour (13 knots) more than 5 percent of the time.

(c) *Airports serving small aircraft only.* The airport serves small aircraft exclusively, and—

(1) The airport has 10,000, or more, aircraft operations each year; and

(2) The existing paved runway is subject to a crosswind component of more than 12 miles per hour (10.5 knots) more than 5 percent of the time.

(d) *Airports serving aircraft of less than 8,000 pounds only.* The airport serves small aircraft of less than 8,000 pounds maximum certificated takeoff weight exclusively and—

(1) The airport has 5,000, or more, aircraft operations each year; and

(2) The existing paved runway is subject to a crosswind component of more than 12 miles per hour (10.5 knots) more than 5 percent of the time.

[Amdt. 151–17, 31 FR 16525, Dec. 28, 1966, as amended by Amdt. 151–28, 34 FR 551, Jan. 15, 1969]

§ 151.80 Runway paving: Additional runway; other conditions.

Paving an additional runway on an airport that does not qualify for a second runway under § 151.79 is eligible if the Administrator, upon consideration on a case-to-case basis, is satisfied that—

(a) The volume of traffic justifies an additional paved runway and the layout and orientation of the additional runway will expedite traffic; or

(b) A combination of traffic volume and aircraft noise problems justifies an additional paved runway for that airport.

[Amdt. 151–17, 31 FR 16525, Dec. 28, 1966]

§ 151.81 Taxiway paving.

(a) The construction, alteration, and repair of taxiways needed to expedite the flow of ground traffic between runways and aircraft parking areas available for general public use are eligible items under the program. Taxiways to serve an area or facility that is primarily for the exclusive or near exclusive use of a tenant or operator that does not furnish aircraft servicing to the public are not eligible. In addition, the policies on resealing or refilling joints, as set forth in § 151.77, apply also to taxiway paving.

(b) Appendix D of this part sets forth typical eligible and ineligible items of taxiway paving.

§ 151.83 Aprons.

(a) The construction, alteration, and repair of aprons are eligible program items upon being shown that they are needed as public use facilities. An apron to serve an area that is primarily for the exclusive or near exclusive use of a tenant or operator who does not furnish aircraft servicing to the public is not eligible. In addition, the policies on resealing or refilling joints, as set forth in § 151.77 apply also to apron paving.

(b) In determining public use for the purposes of this section, the current use being made of a hangar governs, unless there is definite information regarding its future use. In the case of an apron area being built for future hangars, it should be shown that early hangar development is assured and that the hangars will be public facilities.

(c) Appendix E of this part sets forth typical eligible and ineligible items of apron paving.

§151.85 Special treatment areas.

The following special treatment for areas adjacent to pavement is eligible for inclusion in a project in cases where, due to the operation of turbojet powered aircraft, it may be necessary to treat those areas adjacent to runway ends, holding aprons, and taxiways to prevent erosion from the blast effects of the turbojet:

(a) Runway ends—a stabilized area the width of the runway and extending 100 to 150 feet from the end of the runway.

(b) Holding aprons—a stabilized area up to 50 feet from the edge of the pavement.

(c) Taxiway intersections—a stabilized area 25 feet on each side of the taxiway and extending 300 feet from the intersection.

(d) Taxiway (continuous movement of aircraft)—dense turf 25 feet on each side of the taxiway, or in a geographic area where dense turf cannot be established, stabilization.

§151.86 Lighting and electrical work: General.

(a) The installing of lighting facilities and related electrical work, as provided in §151.87, is eligible for inclusion in a project only if the Administrator determines, for the particular airport involved, that they are needed to ensure—

(1) Its safe and efficient use by aircraft under §151.13; or

(2) Its continued operation and adequate maintenance, and it has a large enough volume (actual or potential) of night operations.

(b) Before the Administrator makes a grant offer to the sponsor of a project that includes installing lighting facilities and related electrical work under

paragraph (a) of this section, the sponsor must—

(1) Provide in the project for removing, relocating, or adequately marking and lighting, each obstruction in the approach and turning zones, as provided in §151.91(a);

(2) Acknowledge its awareness of the cost of operating and maintaining airport lighting; and

(3) Agree to operate the airport lighting installed—

(i) Throughout each night of the year; or

(ii) According to a satisfactory plan of operation, submitted under paragraph (c) of this section.

(c) The sponsor of a project that includes installing airport lighting and related electrical work, under paragraph (a) of this section, may—

(1) Submit to the Administrator a proposed plan of operation of the airport lighting installed for periods less than throughout each night of the year;

(2) Specify, in the proposed plan, the times when the airport lighting installed will be operated; and

(3) Satisfy the Administrator that the proposed plan provides for safety in air commerce, and justifies the investment of Program funds.

(d) Paragraph (b)(3) of this section also applies to each sponsor of a project that includes installing airport lighting and related electrical work if that sponsor has not entered into a grant agreement for the project before September 5, 1968.

(e) If it agrees to comply with paragraph (b)(3) of this section, the sponsor of a project that includes installing airport lighting facilities and related electrical work that has entered into a grant agreement for that project before September 5, 1968, may—

(1) Surrender its air navigation certificate authorizing operation of a "true light" issued before that date; or

(2) Terminate its application for authority to operate a "true light" made before that date.

(Secs. 307, 606, 72 Stat. 749, 779; 49 U.S.C. 1120, 1348, 1426)

[Amdt. 151–24, 33 FR 12545, Sept. 5, 1968]

§ 151.87 Lighting and electrical work: Standards.

(a)–(b) [Reserved]

(c) The number of runways that are eligible for lighting is the same as the number eligible for paving under § 151.77, § 151.79, or § 151.80.

(d) The installing of high intensity runway edge lighting is eligible on a designated instrument landing runway and any other runway with approved straight-in approach procedures. A runway that is eligible for lighting, but does not meet the requirements for 75 percent U.S. participation under § 151.43(d), is eligible for 50 percent U.S. participation in the costs of high intensity runway edge lighting (or the allowable percentage in § 151.43(c) for public land States), if the airport is served by a navigational aid that will allow using instrument approach procedures. If a runway is not eligible for 75 or 50 percent Federal participation in high intensity runway edge lighting but is otherwise eligible for runway lighting, the U.S. share of the cost of runway edge lighting is 50 percent of the cost of the lighting installed but not more than 50 percent of the cost of medium intensity lighting.

(e) In-runway lighting (touchdown zone lighting system, and centerline lighting system) is eligible on the designated instrument landing runway.

(f) Taxiways to eligible runways on airports served by transport aircraft are eligible for lighting. On airports serving only general aviation, the lighting of connecting taxiways is eligible if the runway served is lighted or is programed to be lighted. The lighting of a parallel taxiway is eligible if the taxiway is eligible for paving. Lighting of other taxiways is eligible or not, depending on the complexity of the taxiway system.

(g) Floodlighting of aprons is eligible if there is a proven need for it, including a showing of night operations where the runway is lighted.

(h) Any airport that is eligible to participate in the costs of runway lighting is eligible for the installing of an airport beacon, lighted wind indicator, obstruction lights, lighting control equipment, and other components of basic airport lighting, including separate transformer vaults and connec-tion to the nearest available power source.

(i) The interconnection of two or more power sources on an airport property, the providing of second sources of power, and the installing of standby engine generators of reasonable capacity, are eligible under the program.

(j) Economy approach lighting aids are eligible for inclusion in a project at an airport that will not qualify within the next three years for approach lighting aids installed by FAA under the Facilities and Equipment Program if the economy approach lighting aids—

(1) Will correct a visual deficiency on one of the lighted runways of the airport; or

(2) Will permit operations at an airport at lower minimums.

"Economy approach lighting aids" includes a medium intensity approach lighting system (MALS) that may include a sequence flasher (SF); a runway end identifier lights system (REILS): and an abbreviated visual approach slope indicator (AVASI).

(k) Appendix F of this part sets forth typical eligible and ineligible items of airport lighting covered by § 151.86 and this section.

(Secs. 307, 606, 72 Stat. 749, 799; 49 U.S.C. 1120, 1348, 1426)

[Doc. No. 1329, 27 FR 12357, Dec. 13, 1962, as amended by Amdt. 151–8, 30 FR 8040, June 23, 1965; Amdt. 151–17, 31 FR 16525, Dec. 28, 1966; Amdt. 151–22, 33 FR 8267, June 4, 1968; Amdt. 151–24, 33 FR 12545, Sept. 5, 1968; Amdt. 151–35, 34 FR 13699, Aug. 27, 1969]

§ 151.89 Roads.

(a) Federal-aid Airport Program funds may not be used to resolve highway problems. Only those airport entrance roads that are definitely needed and are intended only as a way in and out of the airport are eligible.

(b) The construction, alteration, and repair of airport roads and streets that are entirely within the airport boundaries are eligible under the program, if needed for operating and maintaining the airport. In the case of an entrance road, a strip right-of-way joining the main body of the airport to the nearest public road may be considered a part of the normal boundary of the airport if—

(1) Adequate title is obtained;

(2) It was acquired to provide an airport entrance road and was not, before the existence of the airport, a public thoroughfare;

(3) The entrance road is intended only as a way in and out of the airport; and

(4) The entrance road extends only to the nearest public highway, road, or street.

(c) An entrance road may be joined to an existing highway or street with a normal fillet connection. However, acceleration-deceleration strips or grade separations are not eligible.

(d) Offsite road or street relocation needed to allow airport development or to remove an obstruction, and is not for entrance road purposes, is eligible.

(e) Appendix G sets forth typical eligible and ineligible items of road construction covered by this section.

§ 151.91 Removal of obstructions.

(a) The removal or relocation, or both, of obstructions, as defined in Technical Standard Order N18 is eligible under the Program in cases where definite arrangements are made to prevent the obstruction from being recreated. In a case where removal is not feasible, the cost of marking or lighting it is eligible. The removal and relocation of structures necessary for essential airport development is eligible. The removal of structures that are not obstructions under § 77.23 of this chapter as applied to § 77.27 of this chapter are eligible when they are located within a runway clear zone.

(b) The removal and relocation of an airport hangar that is an airport hazard (as described in § 151.39(b)) is eligible, if the reerected hangar will be substantially identical to the disassembled one.

(c) Whenever a hangar must be relocated (either for clearance of the site for other airport development or to remove a hazard) and the existing structure is to be relocated with or without disassembling, the cost of the relocation is an eligible item of project costs, including costs incidental to the relocation such as necessary footings and floors. However, if the existing structure is to be demolished and a new hangar is to be built, only the cost of

demolishing the existing hangar is an eligible item.

[Doc. No. 1329, 27 FR 12357, Dec. 13, 1962, as amended by Amdt. 151-22, 33 FR 8267, June 4, 1968]

§ 151.93 Buildings; utilities; sidewalks; parking areas; and landscaping.

(a) Only buildings or parts of buildings intended to house facilities or activities directly related to the safety of persons at the airport, including fire and rescue equipment buildings, are eligible items under the Federal-aid Airport Program. To the extent they are necessary to house snow removal and abrasive spreading equipment, and to provide minimum protection for abrasive materials, field maintenance equipment buildings are eligible items in any airport development project for an airport in a location having a mean daily minimum temperature of zero degrees Fahrenheit, or less, for at least 20 days each year for the 5 years preceding the year when Federal aid is requested under § 151.21(a), based on the statistics of the U.S. Department of Commerce Weather Bureau if available, or other evidence satisfactory to the Administrator.

(b) Airport utility construction, installation, and connection are eligible under the Federal-aid Airport Program as follows:

(1) An airport utility serving only eligible areas and facilities is eligible; and

(2) An airport utility serving both eligible and ineligible airport areas and facilities is eligible only to the extent of the additional cost of providing the capacity needed for eligible areas and facilities over and above the capacity necessary for the ineligible areas and facilities.

However, a water system is eligible only to the extent necessary to provide fire protection for aircraft operations, and to provide water for a fire and rescue equipment building.

(c) No part of the constructing, altering, or repairing (including grading, drainage, and other site preparation work) of a facility or area that is to be used as a public parking facility for passenger automobiles is eligible for inclusion in a project.

(d) Landscaping is not eligible for inclusion in a project. However, the establishment of turf on graded areas and special treatment to prevent slope erosion is eligible to the extent of the eligibility of the facilities or areas served, preserved, or protected by the turf or treatment. In the case of turfing or treatment for an area or facility that is partly eligible and partly ineligible, the eligibility of the turfing or treatment is established on a pro rata basis.

(e) The construction of sidewalks is not eligible for inclusion in a project.

[Doc. No. 1329, 27 FR 12357, Dec. 13, 1962, as amended by Amdt. 151-17, 31 FR 16525, Dec. 28, 1966; Amdt. 151-26, 33 FR 18434, Dec. 12, 1968]

§ 151.95 Fences; distance markers; navigational and landing aids; and offsite work.

(a) Boundary or perimeter fences for security purposes are eligible for inclusion in a project.

(b) A blast fence is eligible for inclusion in a project whenever—

(1) It is necessary for safety at a runway end or a holding area near the end of a runway and its installation would be more economical than the acquiring of additional property interests; or

(2) Its installation for safety at a turbojet-passenger gate will result in less separation being needed for gate positions, thereby reducing the need for apron expansion, and it is more economical to build the fence than to expand the apron.

(c) The eligibility of runway distance markers for inclusion in a project is decided on a case-by-case basis.

(d) The relocation of navigational aids is eligible for inclusion in a project whenever necessitated by development on the airport under a Program project and the sponsor is responsible under FAA Order OA 6030.1 (Agency Order 53).

(e) The installation of any of the following landing aids is eligible for inclusion in a project:

(1) Segmented circle.

(2) Wind and landing direction indicators.

(3) Boundary markers.

(f) The initial marking of runway and taxiway systems is eligible for inclusion in a project. The remarking of existing runways or taxiways is eligible if—

(1) Present marking is obsolete under current FAA standards; or

(2) Present marking is obliterated by construction, alteration or repair work included in a FAAP project or by the required routing of construction equipment used therein.

However, apron marking that is not allied with runway and taxiway marking systems, is not eligible.

(g) The following offsite work performed outside of the boundaries of an airport or airport site is eligible for inclusion in a project:

(1) Removal of obstruction as provided in § 151.91.

(2) Outfall drainage ditches, and the correction of any damage resulting from their construction.

(3) Relocating of roads and utilities that are airport hazards as defined in § 151.39(b).

(4) Clearing, grading, and grubbing to allow installing of navigational aids.

(5) Constructing and installing utilities.

(6) Lighting of obstructions.

[Doc. No. 1329, 27 FR 12359, Dec. 13, 1962, as amended by Amdt. 151-8, 30 FR 8040, June 23, 1965; Amdt. 151-17, 31 FR 16525, Dec. 28, 1966]

§ 151.97 Maintenance and repair.

(a) Maintenance work is not airport development as defined in the Federal Airport Act and is not eligible for inclusion in the Program. Therefore, it is necessary in many cases that a determination be made whether particular proposed development is maintenance or repair. For the purpose of these determinations, maintenance includes any regular or recurring work necessary to preserve existing airport facilities in good condition, any work involved in cleaning or caring for existing airport facilities, and any incidental or minor repair work on existing airport facilities, such as—

(1) Mowing and fertilizing of turfed areas;

(2) Trimming and replacing of landscaping material;

(3) Cleaning of drainage systems including ditches, pipes, catch basins, and replacing and restoring eroded

areas, except when caused by act of God or improper design;

(4) Painting of buildings (inside and outside) and replacement of damaged items normally anticipated;

(5) Repairing and replacing burned out or broken fixtures and cables, unless major reconstruction is needed;

(6) Paving repairs in localized areas, except where the size of the work is such that it constitutes a major repair item or is part of a reconstruction project; and

(7) Refilling joints and resealing surface of pavements.

(b) Repair includes any work not included in paragraph (a) of this section that is necessary to restore existing airport facilities to good condition or preserve them in good condition.

§ 151.99 Modifications of programming standards.

The Director, Airports, Service, or the Regional Director concerned may, on individual projects, when necessary for adaptation to meet local conditions, modify any standard set forth in or incorporated into this subpart, if he determines that the modification will provide an acceptable level of safety, economy, durability, or workmanship.

[Amdt. 151-13, 31 FR 11605, Sept. 2, 1966]

Subpart D—Rules and Procedures for Advance Planning and Engineering Proposals

AUTHORITY: 49 U.S.C. 106(g), 40113, 47151, 47153.

SOURCE: Docket No. 6227, 30 FR 8040, June 23, 1965, unless otherwise noted.

§ 151.111 Advance planning proposals: General.

(a) Each advance planning and engineering proposal must relate to an airport layout plan or plans and specifications for the development of a new airport, or the further development of an existing airport. Each proposal must relate to a specific airport, either existing or planned, and may not be for general area planning.

(b) Each proposal for the development or further development of an airport must have as its objective either the development of an airport layout

plan, under § 151.5(a), or the development of plans designed to lead to a project application, under §§ 151.21(c) and 151.27, or both.

(c) Each proposal must relate to planning and engineering for an airport that—

(1) Is in a location shown on the National Airport Plan; and

(2) Is not served by scheduled air carrier service and located in a large or medium hub, as identified in the current edition of "Airport Activity Statistics of Certificated Route Air Carriers" (published jointly by FAA and the Civil Aeronautics Board), that is available for inspection at any FAA Area or Regional Office, or for sale by the Superintendent of Documents, Government Printing Office, Washington, D.C. 20402.

(d) Each proposal must relate to future airport development projects eligible under subparts B and C.

(49 U.S.C. 1115; sec. 308, 72 Stat. 750, 49 U.S.C. 1349)

[Doc. No. 6227, 30 FR 8040, June 23, 1965, as amended by Amdt. 151-24, 33 FR 12545, Sept. 5, 1968]

§ 151.113 Advance planning proposals: Sponsor eligibility.

The sponsor of an advance planning and engineering proposal must be a public agency, as defined in § 151.37(a), and must be legally, financially, and otherwise able to—

(a) Make the certifications, representations, and warranties required in the advance planning proposal, FAA Form 3731;

(b) Enter into and perform the advance planning agreement;

(c) Provide enough funds to pay all estimated proposal costs not borne by the United States; and

(d) Meet any other applicable requirements of the Federal Airport Act and this subpart.

§ 151.115 Advance planning proposals: Cosponsorship and agency.

Any two or more public agencies desiring to jointly participate in an advance planning proposal may cosponsor it. The cosponsorship and agency requirements and procedures set forth in § 151.33, except § 151.33(a)(1), also apply to advance planning proposals. In addition, the sponsor eligibility requirements set forth in § 151.113 must be met by each participating public agency.

§ 151.117 Advance planning proposals: Procedures; application.

(a) Each eligible sponsor desiring to obtain Federal aid for the purpose of advance planning and engineering must submit a completed FAA Form 3731, "Advance Planning Proposal", to the Area Manager.

(b) The airport layout plan, if in existence, must accompany the advance planning proposal. If the advance planning proposal includes preparation of plans and specifications, enough details to identify the items of development to be covered by the plans and specifications must be shown. The proposal must be accompanied by evidentiary material establishing the basis for the estimated costs under the proposal, such as an offer from an engineering firm containing a schedule of services and charges therefor.

[Doc. No. 6227, 30 FR 8040, June 23, 1965, as amended by Amdt. 151–11, 31 FR 6686, May 5, 1966]

§ 151.119 Advance planning proposals: Procedures; funding.

The funding information required by § 151.23, except the last sentence, also is required in connection with an advance planning proposal. The sponsor's share of estimated proposal costs may not consist of or include the value of donated labor, materials, or equipment.

§ 151.121 Procedures: Offer; sponsor assurances.

Each sponsor must adopt the following covenant implementing the exclusive rights provisions of section 308(a) of the Federal Aviation Act of 1958, that is incorporated by reference into Part I of the Advance Planning Agreement:

The sponsor—
(a) Will not grant or permit any exclusive right forbidden by section 308(a) of the Federal Aviation Act of 1958 (49 U.S.C. 1349(a)) at the airport, or at any other airport now or hereafter owned or controlled by it;

(b) Agrees that, in furtherance of the policy of the FAA under this covenant, unless authorized by the Administrator, it will not, either directly or indirectly, grant or permit any person, firm or corporation the exclusive right at the airport, or at any other airport now or hereafter owned or controlled by it, to conduct any aeronautical activities, including, but not limited to, charter flights, pilot training, aircraft rental and sightseeing, aerial photography, crop dusting, aerial advertising and surveying, air carrier operations, aircraft sales and services, sale of aviation petroleum products whether or not conducted in conjunction with other aeronautical activity, repair and maintenance of aircraft, sale of aircraft parts, and any other activities which because of their direct relationship to the operation of aircraft can be regarded as an aeronautical activity;

(c) Agrees that it will terminate any existing exclusive right to engage in the sale of gasoline or oil, or both, granted before July 17, 1962, at such an airport, at the earliest renewal, cancellation, or expiration date applicable to the agreement that established the exclusive right; and

(d) Agrees that it will terminate any other exclusive right to conduct any aeronautical activity now existing at such an airport before the grant of any assistance under the Federal Airport Act.

[Amdt. 151–30, 34 FR 3656, Mar. 1, 1969, as amended by Amdt. 151–32, 34 FR 9617, June 19, 1969]

§ 151.123 Procedures: Offer; amendment; acceptance; advance planning agreement.

(a) The procedures and requirements of § 151.29 also apply to approved advance planning proposals. FAA's offer and the sponsor's acceptance constitute an advance planning grant agreement between the sponsor and the United States. The United States does not pay any of the advance planning costs incurred before the advance planning grant agreement is executed.

(b) No grant is made unless the sponsor intends to begin airport development within three years after the date of sponsor's written acceptance of a grant offer. The sponsor's intention must be evidenced by an appropriate written statement in the proposal.

§ 151.125 Allowable advance planning costs.

(a) The United States' share of the allowable costs of an advance planning proposal is stated in the advance planning grant agreement, but is not more than 50 percent of the total cost of the necessary and reasonable planning and engineering services.

(b) The allowable advance planning costs consist of planning and engineering expenses necessarily incurred in effecting the advance planning proposal. Allowable cost items include—

(1) Location surveys, such as preliminary topographic and soil exploration;

(2) Site evaluation;

(3) Preliminary engineering, such as stage construction outlines, cost estimates, and cost/benefit evaluation reports;

(4) Contract drawings and specifications;

(5) Testing; and

(6) Incidental costs incurred to accomplish the proposal, that would not have been incurred otherwise.

(c) To qualify as allowable, the advance planning costs paid or incurred by the sponsor must be—

(1) Reasonably necessary and directly related to the planning or engineering included in the proposal as approved by FAA;

(2) Reasonable in amount; and

(3) Verified by sufficient evidence.

§151.127 Accounting and audit.

The requirements of §151.55 relating to accounting and audit of project costs are also applicable to advance planning proposal costs. However, the requirement of segregating and grouping costs applies only to §151.55(a) (5) and (7) classifications.

§151.129 Payments.

(a) The United States' share of advance planning costs is paid in two installments unless the advance planning grant agreement provides otherwise. Upon request by sponsor, the first payment may be made in an amount not more than 50 percent of the maximum obligation of the United States stipulated in the advance planning grant agreement upon certification by sponsor that 50 percent or more of the proposed work has been completed. The final payment is made upon the sponsor's request after—

(1) The conditions of the advance planning grant agreement have been met;

(2) Evidence of cost of each item has been submitted; and

(3) Audit of submitted evidence or audit of sponsor's records, if considered desirable by FAA, has been made.

(b) When the advance planning proposal relates to the selection of an airport site, the advance planning grant agreement provides that Federal funds are paid to the sponsor only after the site is selected and the Administrator is satisfied that the site selected for the airport is reasonably consistent with existing plans of public agencies for development of the area in which the site is located, and will contribute to the accomplishment of the purposes of the Federal-aid Airport Program.

§151.131 Forms.

The forms used for the purpose of obtaining an advance planning and engineering grant are as follows:

(a) *Advance planning proposal, FAA Form 3731*—(1) *Part I.* This part of the form contains a request for the grant of Federal funds under the Federal Airport Act for the purpose of aiding in financing a proposal for the development of an airport layout plan or plans, or both, designed to lead to a project application, with spaces provided for inserting information needed for considering the request, including the location of the airport, a description of the plan or plans to be developed, and the estimate of planning and engineering costs.

(2) *Part II.* This part of the form includes the sponsor's representation that it will comply with the provisions of part 15 of the Federal Aviation Regulations (14 CFR part 15), and representations concerning its legal authority to undertake the proposal, the availability of funds for its share of the proposal costs, its intention to initiate construction of a safe, useful and usable airport facility shown on an airport layout plan developed under the proposal, or initiate the construction of the item or items of airport development shown on the plans developed under the proposal and designed to lead to a project application, or both, within three years after the date of acceptance of the offer. It also includes the sponsor's representation as to the method of financing the intended construction, approval of other agencies, defaults, possible disabilities, and a

statement concerning accept- ance to be executed by the sponsor and certified by its attorney.

(b) *Advance planning agreement, FAA Form 3732*—(1) *Part I.* This part of the form contains an offer by the United States to pay a specified percentage not to exceed 50% of the allowable proposal costs, as described therein, on specific terms relating to the carrying out of the proposal, allowability of costs, payment of the United States' share and sponsor's agreement to comply with the exclusive rights provision of section 308(a) of the Federal Aviation Act of 1958.

(2) *Part II.* This part of the form contains the acceptance of the offer by the sponsor, execution of the acceptance by the sponsor, and the certification by the sponsor's attorney.

APPENDIX A TO PART 151

There is set forth below an itemization of typical eligible and ineligible items of land acquisition as covered by § 151.73:

Typical Eligible Items

1. Land for:
(a) Initial acquisition for entire airport developments, including building areas as delineated on the approved airport layout plan.
(b) Expansion of airport facilities.
(c) Clear zones at ends of eligible runways.
(d) Approach lights (land for ALS eligible for 75 percent participation will be limited to an area 3200′ × 400′ for a Standard ALS and to an area 1700′ × 400′ for a short ALS located symmetrically about the runway centerline extended, beginning at the end of the runway).
(e) Approach protection.
(f) Airport utilities.
2. Easements for:
(a) Use of air space by aircraft.
(b) Storm-water run-off.
(c) Powerlines to serve offsite obstruction lights.
(d) Airport utilities.
3. Extinguishment of easements which interfere with airport development.

Typical Ineligible Items

1. Land required only for:
(a) Industrial and other non-airport purposes.

[Doc. No. 1329, 27 FR 12359, Dec. 13, 1962, as amended by Amdt. 151-8, 30 FR 8040, June 23, 1965; Amdt. 151-17, 31 FR 16525, Dec. 28, 1966]

APPENDIX B TO PART 151

There is set forth below an itemization of typical eligible and ineligible items of site preparation as covered by § 151.75 of this chapter:

Typical Eligible Items

1. General site preparation:
(a) Clearing of site.
(b) Grubbing of site.
(c) Grading of site.
(d) Storm drainage of site.
2. Erosion control.
3. Grading to remove obstructions.
4. Grading for installing navigation aids on airport property.
5. Dredging of seaplane anchorages and channels.

Typical Ineligible Items

1. Specific site preparation (not a part of an over-all site preparation project) for:
(a) Hangars and other buildings ineligible under the Act.
(b) Public parking facilities for passenger automobiles.
(c) Industrial and other non-airport purposes.

[Doc. No. 1329, 27 FR 12359, Dec. 13, 1962]

APPENDIX C TO PART 151

There is set forth below an itemization of typical eligible and ineligible items of runway paving as covered by § 151.77 of this chapter:

Typical Eligible Items

1. New runways for specified loadings.
2. Runway widening of extensions for specified loadings.
3. Reconstruction of existing runways for specified loadings.
4. Resurfacing runways for specified strength or for smoothness.
5. Runway grooving to improve skid resistance.

Typical Ineligible Items

1. Maintenance-type work, including:
(a) Seal coats.
(b) Crack filling.
(c) Resealing joints.
(d) Runway patching.
(e) Isolated repair.

[Doc. No. 1329, 27 FR 12360, Dec. 13, 1962, as amended by Amdt. 151-29, 34 FR 1634, Feb. 4, 1969]

APPENDIX D TO PART 151

There is set forth below an itemization of typical eligible and ineligible items of taxiway paving as covered by § 151.81 of this chapter:

Typical Eligible Items

1. Basic types of pavement listed as eligible under § 151.77.
2. Taxiway providing access to ends and intermediate points of eligible runways.
3. Bleed-off taxiways.
4. Bypass taxiways.
5. Run-up pads.
6. Primary taxiway systems providing access to hangar areas and other building areas delineated on approved airport layout plan.
7. Secondary taxiways providing access to groups of individual storage hangars and/or multiple-unit tee hangars.

Typical Ineligible Items

1. Basic types of pavement listed as ineligible under § 151.77.
2. Taxiways providing access to an area not offering aircraft storage and/or service to the public.
3. Lead-ins to individual storage hangars.

[Doc. No. 1329, 27 FR 12360, Dec. 13, 1962, as amended by Amdt. 151–8, 30 FR 8040, June 23, 1965]

APPENDIX E TO PART 151

There is set forth below an itemization of typical eligible and ineligible items of apron paving as covered by § 151.83 of this chapter:

Typical Eligible Items

1. Basic types of pavement listed as eligible under § 151.77.
2. Loading ramps.
3. Aprons available for public parking, storage, and service or a combination of any of the three.
4. Aprons serving hangars used for public storage of aircraft or service to the public, or both.
5. Aprons for cargo buildings used for public storage or service to the public, or both.

Typical Ineligible Items

1. Basic types of pavement listed as ineligible under § 151.77.
2. Aprons serving installations for non-public use.
3. Paving inside a hangar or on the proposed site of a hangar.
4. Aprons for cargo buildings not under Item 5 of the "Typical Eligible Items".
5. Apron services (pits or pipes for chemicals) will not be eligible.

[Doc. No. 1329, 27 FR 12360, Dec. 13, 1962, as amended by Amdt. 151–17, 31 FR 16525, Dec. 28, 1966]

APPENDIX F TO PART 151

There is set forth below an itemization of typical eligible and ineligible items of air-

port lighting covered by §§ 151.86 and 151.87 of this chapter:

Typical Eligible Items

1. Runway edge lights (high intensity, medium intensity, and low intensity).
2. In-runway lighting (touchdown zone lighting system, centerline lighting system, and exit taxiway lighting system).
3. Taxiway lights.
4. Taxiway guidance signs.
5. Obstruction lights.
6. Apron floodlights.
7. Beacons.
8. Wind and landing direction indicators.
9. Electrical ducts and manholes.
10. Transformer or generator vaults.
11. Control panels for field lighting.
12. Control equipment for field lighting.
13. Auxiliary power.
14. Lighting offsite obstructions.
15. Electrical vaults for field lighting.

Typical Ineligible Items

1. Electronic navigation aids.
2. Approach lights.
3. Horizon lights.
4. Isolated repair and reconstruction of airport lighting.
5. Lighting of public parking area for passenger automobiles.
6. Street or road lighting.

[Doc. No. 1329, 27 FR 12360, Dec. 13, 1962, as amended by Amdt. 151–24, 33 FR 12545, Sept. 5, 1968; Amdt. 151–35, 34 FR 13699, Aug. 27, 1969]

APPENDIX G TO PART 151

There is set forth below an itemization of typical eligible and ineligible items of road construction covered by § 151.89 of this chapter:

Typical Eligible Items

1. Entrance roads.
2. Service roads for access to public areas.
3. Service roads for airport maintenance (including perimeter airport service road within airport boundary and not for general public access).
4. Relocation of roads to permit airport development or expansion or to remove obstructions.

Typical Ineligible Items

1. Offsite roads.
2. Roads to areas of exclusive use.

[Doc. No. 1329, 27 FR 12360, Dec. 13, 1962]

APPENDIX H TO PART 151

There is set forth below the contract provision required by the regulations of the Secretary of Labor in part 5 of title 29 of the

707

Code of Federal Regulations. Section 151.49(a) requires sponsors to insert this provision in full in each construction contract.

PROVISION REQUIRED BY THE REGULATIONS OF THE SECRETARY OF LABOR

A. Minimum wages. (1) All mechanics and laborers employed or working upon the site of the work will be paid unconditionally and not less often than once a week, and without subsequent deduction or rebate on any account (except such payroll deductions as are permitted by regulations issued by the Secretary of Labor under the Copeland Act [29 CFR part 3]), the full amounts due at time of payment computed at wage rates not less than those contained in the wage determination decision(s) of the Secretary of Labor which is (are) attached hereto and made a part hereof, regardless of any contractual relationship which may be alleged to exist between the contractor and such laborers and mechanics; and the wage determination decision(s) shall be posted by the contractor at the site of the work in a prominent place where it (they) can be easily seen by the workers. For the purpose of this paragraph, contributions made or costs reasonably anticipated under section 1(b)(2) of the Davis-Bacon Act on behalf of laborers or mechanics are considered wages paid to such laborers or mechanics, subject to the provisions of subparagraph (4) below. Also for the purpose of this paragraph, regular contributions made or costs incurred for more than a weekly period under plans, funds, or programs, but covering the particular weekly period, are deemed to be constructively made or incurred during such weekly period (29 CFR 5.5(a)(1)(i)).

(2) Any class of laborers or mechanics which is not listed in the wage determination(s) and which is to be employed under the contract, shall be classified or reclassified comfortably to the wage determination(s), and a report of the action taken shall be sent by the [insert sponsor's name] to the FAA for approval and transmittal to the Secretary of Labor. In the event that the interested parties cannot agree on the proper classification or reclassification of a particular class of laborers and mechanics to be used, the question accompanied by the recommendation of the FAA shall be referred to the Secretary of Labor for final determination (29 CFR 5.5(a)(1)(ii)).

(3) Whenever the minimum wage rate prescribed in the contract for a class of laborers or mechanics includes a fringe benefit which is not expressed as an hourly wage rate and the contractor is obligated to pay a cash equivalent of such a fringe benefit, an hourly cash equivalent thereof shall be established. In the event the interested parties cannot agree upon a cash equivalent of the fringe benefit, the question, accompanied by the

recommendation of the FAA shall be referred to the Secretary of Labor for determination (29 CFR 5.5(a)(1)(iii)).

(4) If the contractor does not make payments to a trustee or other third person, he may consider as part of the wages of any laborer or mechanic the amount of any costs reasonably anticipated in providing benefits under a plan or program of a type expressly listed in the wage determination decision of the Secretary of Labor which is a part of this contract: *Provided, however,* The Secretary of Labor has found, upon the written request of the contractor, that the applicable standards of the Davis-Bacon Act have been met. The Secretary of Labor may require the contractor to set aside in a separate account assets for the meeting of obligations under the plan or program.

B. Withholding: FAA from sponsor. Pursuant to the terms of the grant agreement between the United States and [insert sponsor's name], relating to Federal-aid Airport Project No. ___, and part 151 of the Federal Aviation Regulations (14 CFR part 151), the FAA may withhold or cause to be withheld from the [insert sponsor's name] so much of the accrued payments or advances as may be considered necessary to pay laborers and mechanics employed by the contractor or any subcontractor on the work the full amount of wages required by this contract. In the event of failure to pay any laborer or mechanic employed or working on the site of the work all or part of the wages required by this contract, the FAA may, after written notice to the [insert sponsor's name], take such action as may be necessary to cause the suspension of any further payment or advance of funds until such violations have ceased (29 CFR 5.5(a)(2)).

C. Payrolls and basic records. (1) Payrolls and basic records relating thereto will be maintained during the course of the work and preserved for a period of three years thereafter for all laborers and mechanics working at the site of the work. Such records will contain the name and address of each such employee, his correct classification, rates of pay (including rates of contributions or costs anticipated of the types described in section 1(b)(2) of the Davis-Bacon Act), daily and weekly number of hours worked, deductions made and actual wages paid. Whenever the Secretary of Labor has found, under 29 CFR 5.5(a)(1)(iv) (see subparagraph (4) of subparagraph (A) above), that the wages of any laborer or mechanic include the amount of any costs reasonably anticipated in providing benefits under a plan or program described in section 1(b)(2)(B) of the Davis-Bacon Act, the contractor shall maintain records which show that the commitment to provide such benefits is enforceable, that the plan or program is financially responsible, and that the plan or program has been communicated in writing to the laborers or mechanics affected, and records which show the costs anticipated or the actual cost incurred in providing such benefits (29 CFR 5.5(a)(3)(i)).

(2) The contractor will submit weekly a copy of all payrolls to the [insert sponsor's name] for transmission to the FAA, as required by § 151.53(a). The copy shall be accompanied by a statement signed by the employer or his agent indicating that the payrolls are correct and complete, that the wage rates contained therein are not less than those determined by the Secretary of Labor and that the classifications set forth for each laborer or mechanic conform with the work he performed. A submission of a "Weekly Statement of Compliance" which is required under this contract and the Copeland regulations of the Secretary of Labor (29 CFR part 3) and the filing with the initial payroll or any subsequent payroll of a copy of any findings by the Secretary of Labor, under 29 CFR 5.5(a)(1)(iv) (see subparagraph (4) of paragraph (A) above), shall satisfy this requirement. The prime contractor shall be responsible for the submission of copies of payrolls of all subcontractors. The contractor will make the records required under the labor standards clauses of the contract available for inspection by authorized representatives of the FAA and the Department of Labor, and will permit such representatives to interview employees during working hours on the job (29 CFR 5.5(a)(3)(ii))

D. Apprentices. Apprentices will be permitted to work as such only when they are registered, individually, under a bona fide apprenticeship program registered with a State apprenticeship agency which is recognized by the Bureau of Apprenticeship and Training, United States Department of Labor; or, if no such recognized agency exists in a State, under a program registered with the Bureau of Apprenticeship and Training, United States Department of Labor. The allowable ratio of apprentices to journeymen in any craft classification shall not be greater than the ratio permitted to the contractor as to his entire work force under the registered program. Any employee listed on a payroll at an apprentice wage rate, who is not registered as above, shall be paid the wage rate determined by the Secretary of Labor for the classification of work he actually performed. The contractor or subcontractor will be required to furnish to the [insert sponsor's name] written evidence of the registration of his program and apprentices as well as of the appropriate ratios and wage rates, for the area of construction prior to using any apprentices on the contract work (29 CFR 5.5(a)(4)).

E. Compliance with Copeland Regulations. The contractor shall comply with the Copeland Regulations (29 CFR part 3) of the Secretary of Labor which are herein incorporated by reference (29 CFR 5.5(a)(5)).

F. Overtime requirements. No contractor or subcontractor contracting for any part of the contract work which may require or involve the employment of laborers or mechanics shall require or permit any laborer or mechanic in any workweek in which he is employed on such work to work in excess of eight hours in any calendar day or in excess of forty hours in such workweek unless such laborer or mechanic received compensation at a rate not less than one and one-half times his basic rate of pay for all hours worked in excess of eight hours in any calendar day or in excess of forty hours in such workweek, as the case may be (29 CFR 5.5(c)(1)).

G. Violations; liability for unpaid wages; liquidated damages. In the event of any violation of paragraph F of this provision, the contractor and any subcontractor responsible therefore shall be liable to any affected employee for his unpaid wages. In addition, such contractor and subcontractor shall be liable to the United States for liquidated damages. Such liquidated damages shall be computed, with respect to each individual laborer or mechanic employed in violation of said paragraph F of this provision, in the sum of $10 for each calendar day on which such employee was required or permitted to work in excess of eight hours or in excess of the standard workweek of forty hours without payment of the overtime wages required by said paragraph F of this provision (29 CFR 5.5 (c)(2)).

H. Withholding for unpaid wages and liquidated damages, and priority of payment (1) The FAA may withhold or cause to be withheld, from any moneys payable on account of work performed by the contractor or subcontractor, such sums as may administratively be determined to be necessary to satisfy any liabilities of such contractor or subcontractor for unpaid wages and liquidated damages as provided in paragraph G of this provision (29 CFR 5.5(c)(3)).

(2) In the event of failure or refusal of the contractor or any subcontractor to comply with overtime pay requirements of the Contract Work Hours Standards Act, if the funds withheld by the FAA for the violations are not sufficient to pay fully both the unpaid wages due laborers and mechanics and the liquidated damages due the United States, the available funds shall be used first to compensate the laborers and mechanics for the wages to which they are entitled (or an equitable portion thereof when the funds are not adequate for this purpose); and the balance, if any, shall be used for the payment of liquidated damages (29 CFR 5.14 (d)(2)).

I. Subcontracts. The contractor will insert in each of his subcontracts the clauses contained in paragraphs A through H and J of this provision, and also a clause requiring the subcontractors to include these provisions in any lower tier subcontracts which they may enter into, together with a clause requiring this insertion in any further subcontracts that may in turn be made (29 CFR 5.5(a)(6), 5.5(c)(4)).

J. Contract termination; debarment. A breach of paragraphs A through I of this provision may be grounds for termination of the contract. A breach of paragraphs A through E and I may also be grounds for debarment as provided in 29 CFR 5.6 of the regulations of the Secretary of Labor (29 CFR 5.5(a)(8)).

[Doc. No. 6387, 29 FR 18002, Dec. 18, 1964, as amended by Amdt. 151–9, 30 FR 14197, Nov. 11, 1965; Amdt. 151–38, 35 FR 5112, Mar. 26, 1970]

APPENDIX I TO PART 151

[Lists of Advisory Circulars incorporated by § 151.72: (a) *Circulars available free of charge.*]

Number	Subject
AC 150/5300–3	Adaptation of TSO-N18 Criterion to Clearways and Stopways.
AC 150/5325–2A	Airport Surface Areas Gradient Standards.
AC 150/5325–4	Runway Length Requirements for Airport Design.
AC 150/5330–2	Runway/Taxiway Widths and Clearances.
AC 150/5335–1	Airway Taxiways.
AC 150/5340–1A	Marking of Serviceable Runways and Taxiways.
AC 150/5340–3	Configuration Details of In-Runway Lighting: Touchdown Zone, Runway Centerline, and Taxiway Turnoff Lighting Systems.
AC 150/5340–4A	Installation Details for Centerline and Touchdown Zone Lighting Systems.
AC 150/5340–5	Segmented Circle Airport Marker System.
AC 150/5340–7	Marking of Deceptive, Closed, and Hazardous Areas on Airports.
AC 150/5340–13 ..	High Intensity Lighting System.
AC 150/5340–14 ..	Economy Approach Lighting Aids.
AC 150/5340–15 ..	Taxiway Lighting System.
AC 150/5345–1A	Approved Airport Lighting Equipment.
AC 150/5345–2	Specification for L–810 Obstruction Light.
AC 150/5345–3	Specification for L–821 Airport Lighting Panel for Remote Control of Airport Lighting.
AC 150/5345–4	Specification for L–829 Internally Lighted Airport Taxi Guidance Sign.
AC 150/5345–5	Specification for L–847 Circuit Selector Switch, 5000 Volt 20 Ampere.
AC 150/5345–6	Specification for L–809 Airport Light Base and Transformer Housing.
AC 150/5345–7	Specification for L–824 Underground Electrical Cables for Airport Lighting Circuits.
AC 150/5345–8	Specification for L–840 Low Intensity Runway, Landing Strip and Taxiway Light.
AC 150/5345–9A	Specification for L–819 Fixed Focus Bidirectional High Intensity Runway Light.
AC 150/5345–10A	Specification for L–828 Constant Current Regulator with Stepless Brightness Control.

[Lists of Advisory Circulars incorporated by § 151.72: (a) *Circulars available free of charge.*]

Number	Subject
AC 150/5345–11 ..	Specification for L–812 Static Indoor Type Constant Current Regulator Assembly, 4 KW and 7½ KW, with Brightness Control for Remote Operation.
AC 150/5345–12 ..	Specification for L–801 Beacon for Small Airports.
AC 150/5345–13 ..	Specification for L–841 Auxiliary Relay Cabinet Assembly for Pilot Control of Airport Lighting Circuits.
AC 150/5345–14 ..	Specification for L–827 "A" Frame Hinged Support for 12–Foot Wind Cone.
AC 150/5345–15 ..	Specification for L–842 Airport Centerline Light.
AC 150/5345–16 ..	Specification for L–843 Airport In-Runway Touchdown Zone Light.
AC 150/5345–17 ..	Specification for L–845 Semiflush Inset Prismatic Airport Light.
AC 150/5345–18 ..	Specification for L–811 Static Indoor Type Constant Current Regulator Assembly, 4 KW; With Brightness Control and Runway Selection for Direct Operation.
AC 150/5345–19 ..	Specification for L–838 Semiflush Prismatic Airport Light.
AC 150/5345–20 ..	Specification for L–802 Runway and Strip Light.
AC 150/5345–21 ..	Specification for L–813 Static Indoor Type Constant Current Regulator Assembly; 4 KW and 7½ KW; for Remote Operation of Taxiway Lights.
AC 150/5345–22 ..	Specification for L–834 Individual Lamp Series-to-Series Type Insulating Transformer for 5,000 Volt Series Circuit.
AC 150/5345–23 ..	Specification for L–822 Taxiway Edge Light.
AC 150/5345–24 ..	Specification for L–849 Condenser Discharge Type Flashing Light.
AC 150/5345–25 ..	Specification for L–848 Medium Intensity Approach Light Bar Assembly.
AC 150/5345–26 ..	Specification for L–823 Plug and Receptacle, Cable Connectors.
AC 150/5345–27 ..	Specification for L–807 Eight-Foot Illuminated Wind Cone.
AC 150/5345–30 ..	Specification for L–846 Electrical Wire for Lighting Circuits To Be Installed in Airport Pavements.
AC 150/5345–31 ..	Specification for L–833 Individual Lamp Series-to-Series Type Insulating Transformer for 600 Volt or 3,000 Volt Series Circuits.
AC 150/5345–32 ..	Specification for L–837 Large-Size Light Base and Transformer Housing.
AC 150/5345–33 ..	Specification for L–844 Individual Lamp Series-to-Series Type Insulating Transformer for 5,000 Volt Series Circuit 20/6.6 Amperes 200 Watt.
AC 150/5345–34 ..	Specification for L–839 Individual Lamp Series-to-Series Type Insulating Transformer for 5,000 Volt Series Circuit 6.6/20 Amperes 300 Watt.
AC 150/5345–35 ..	Specification for L–816 Circuit Selector Cabinet Assembly for 600 Volt Series Circuits.
AC 150/5345–36 ..	Specification for L–808 Lighted Wind Tee.
AC 150/5345–37A	FAA Specification L–850, Light Assembly, Airport Runway, Centerline.

[Amdt. 151–13, 31 FR 11606, Sept. 2, 1966, as amended by Amdt. 151–15, 31 FR 13423, Oct. 18, 1966]

PART 152—AIRPORT AID PROGRAM

Subpart A—General

AUTHORITY: 49 U.S.C. 106(g), 47106, 47127.

SOURCE: Docket No. 19430, 45 FR 34784, May 22, 1980, unless otherwise noted.

Subpart A—General

§152.1 Applicability.

This part applies to airport planning and development under the Airport and

Airway Development Act of 1970, as amended (49 U.S.C. 1701 *et seq.*).

§ 152.3 Definitions.

The following are definitions of terms used throughout this part:

AADA means the Airport and Airway Development Act of 1970, as amended (49 U.S.C. 1701 *et seq.*).

Air carrier airport means—

(1) An existing public airport regularly served, or a new public airport that the Administrator determines will be regularly served, by an air carrier, other than a charter air carrier, certificated by the Civil Aeronautics Board under section 401 of the Federal Aviation Act of 1958; and

(2) A commuter service airport.

Airport means—

(1) Any area of land or water that is used, or intended for use, for the landing and takeoff of aircraft;

(2) Any appurtenant areas that are used, or intended for use, for airport buildings, other airport facilities, or rights-of-way; and

(3) All airport buildings and facilities located on the areas specified in this definition.

Airport development means—

(1) Any work involved in constructing, improving, or repairing a public airport or portion thereof, including the removal, lowering, relocation, and marking and lighting or airport hazards, and including navigation aids used by aircraft landing at, or taking off from, a public airport, and including safety equipment required by rule or regulation for certification of the airport under section 612 of the Federal Aviation Act of 1958, and security equipment required of the sponsor by the FAA by rule or regulation for the safety and security of persons or property on the airport, and including snow removal equipment, and including the purchase of noise suppressing equipment, the construction of physical barriers, and landscaping for the purpose of diminishing the effect of aircraft noise on any area adjacent to a public airport.

(2) Any acquisition of land or of any interest therein, or of any easement through or other interest in airspace, including land for future airport development, which is necessary to permit any such work or to remove or mitigate or prevent or limit the establishment of, airport hazards; and

(3) Any acquisition of land or of any interest therein necessary to insure that such land is used only for purposes which are compatible with the noise levels of the operation of a public airport.

Airport hazard means any structure or object of natural growth located on or in the vicinity of a public airport, or any use of land near a public airport, that—

(1) Obstructs the airspace required for the flight of aircraft landing or taking off at the airport; or

(2) Is otherwise hazardous to aircraft landing or taking off at the airport.

Airport layout plan means a plan for the layout of an airport, showing existing and proposed airport facilities.

Airport master planning means the development for planning purposes of information and guidance to determine the extent, type, and nature of development needed at a specific airport.

Airport system planning means the development for planning purposes of information and guidance to determine the extent, type, nature, location, and timing of airport development needed in a specific area to establish a viable and balanced system of public airports.

Audit means the examination and verification of part or all of the documentary evidence supporting an item of project cost in accordance with Attachment P of Office of Management and Budget Circular A-102 (44 FR 60958).

Commuter service airport means an air carrier airport—

(1) That is not served by an air carrier certificated under section 401 of the Federal Aviation Act of 1958;

(2) That is regularly served by one or more air carriers operating under an exemption granted by the Civil Aeronautics Board from section 401(a) of the Federal Aviation Act of 1958; and

(3) At which not less than 2,500 passengers were enplaned during the preceding calendar year by air carriers operating under an exemption from section 401(a).

Force account means—

(1) The sponsor's or planning agency's own labor force; or

(2) The labor force of another public agency acting as an agent of the sponsor or planning agency.

General aviation airport means a public airport other than an air carrier airport.

Landing area means an area used, or intended to be used, for the landing, takeoff, or surface maneuvering of aircraft.

NASP means the National Airport System Plan.

National Airport System Plan means the plan for the development of public airports in the United States formulated by the Administrator under section 12 of the AADA.

Nonrevenue producing public-use areas means areas that are directly related to the movement of passengers and baggage in air commerce within the boundaries of the airport.

Passengers enplaned means—

(1) United States domestic, territorial, and international revenue passenger enplanements in scheduled and nonscheduled service of air carriers; and

(2) Revenue passenger enplanements by foreign air carriers in intrastate and interstate commerce.

Planning agency means a planning agency designated by the Administrator that is authorized by the laws of a State, the Commonwealth of Puerto Rico, the Virgin Islands, American Samoa, the Trust Territory of the Pacific Islands, or Guam, or by the laws of a political subdivision of any of those entities, to engage in areawide planning for the areas in which assistance under this part is to be used.

Project means a project for the accomplishment of airport development, airport master planning, or airport system planning.

Project costs means any costs involved in accomplishing a project.

Project formulation costs means, with respect to projects for airport development, any necessary costs of formulating a project including—

(1) The costs of field surveys and the preparation of plans and specifications;

(2) The acquisition of land or interests in land, or easement through or other interests in airspace; and

(3) Any necessary administrative or other incidental costs incurred by the sponsor specifically in connection with the accomplishment of a project for airport development, that would not have been incurred otherwise.

Public agency means—

(1) A state, the Commonwealth of Puerto Rico, the Virgin Islands, American Samoa, the Trust Territory of the Pacific Islands, the Government of the Northern Marianas, Guam, or any agency of those entities;

(2) A municipality or other political subdivision;

(3) A tax-supported organization; or

(4) An Indian tribe or pueblo.

Public airport means any airport that—

(1) Is used, or intended to be used, for public purposes;

(2) Is under the control of a public agency; and

(3) Has a property interest satisfactory to the Administrator in the landing area.

Reliever airport means a general aviation airport designated by the Administrator as having the primary function of relieving congestion at an air carrier airport by diverting from that airport general aviation traffic.

Runway clear zone means an area at ground level underlying a portion of the approach surface specified in the standards incorporated into this part by § 152.11.

Satisfactory property interest means—

(1) Title free and clear of any reversionary interest, lien, easement, lease, or other encumbrance that, in the opinion of the Administrator would—

(i) Create an undue risk that it might deprive the sponsor of possession or control;

(ii) Interfere with the use of the airport for public airport purposes; or

(iii) Make it impossible for the sponsor to carry out the agreements and convenants in its grant application;

(2) Unless a shorter term is authorized by the Administrator, a lease of not less than 20 years granted to the sponsor by another public agency, or the United States, that has title as described in paragraph (1) of this definition, on terms that the Administrator considers satisfactory;

(3) In the case of an off-airport area, title or an agreement, easement, leasehold or other right or property interest

that, in the Administrator's opinion, provides reasonable assurance that the sponsor will not be deprived of its right to use the land for the intended purpose during the period necessary to meet the requirements of the grant agreement; or

(4) In the case of a runway clear zone, an easement or a covenant running with the land, giving the airport operator or owner enough control to rid the clear zone of all airport hazards and prevent the creation of future airport hazards.

Sponsor means any public agency that, whether individually or jointly with one or more other public agencies, submits to the Administrator, in accordance with this part, an application for financial assistance.

Stage development means airport development accomplished under stage construction over not less than two years where the sponsor assures that any development not funded under the initial grant agreement will be completed with or without Federal funds.

State means a State of the United States or the District of Columbia.

Terminal development means airport development in the nonrevenue producing public-use areas which are associated with the terminal and which are directly related to the movement of passengers and baggage in air commerce within the boundaries of the airport, including, but not limited to, vehicles for the movement of passengers between terminal facilities and aircraft.

Unified Planning Work Program means a single document prepared by a local areawide planning agency that identifies all transportation and related planning activities that will be undertaken within the metropolitan area during a one-year or two-year period.

§ 152.5 Exemptions.

(a) Except as provided in paragraph (b) of this section, any interested person may petition the Regional Director concerned for a temporary or permanent exemption from any requirement of this part.

(b) The Regional Director concerned does not issue an exemption from any rule of this part if the grant of exemption would be inconsistent with a spe-

cific provision of, or the purpose of, the AADA, or any other applicable Federal law.

(c) Each petition filed under this section must—

(1) Unless otherwise authorized by the Regional Director concerned, be submitted not less than 60 days before the proposed effective date of the exemption;

(2) Be submitted in duplicate to the FAA Regional Office or Airports District Office having jurisdiction over the area in which the airport is located;

(3) Contain the text or substance of the rule from which the exemption is sought;

(4) Explain the nature and extent of the relief sought; and

(5) Contain any information, views, or arguments in support of the exemption.

(d) The Regional Director concerned either grants or denies the exemption and notifies the petitioner of the decision. The FAA publishes a summary of the grant or denial of petition for exemption in the FEDERAL REGISTER.

The summary includes—

(1) The docket number of the petition;

(2) The name of the petitioner;

(3) A citation of each rule from which relief is requested;

(4) A brief description of the general nature of the relief requested; and

(5) The disposition of the petition.

(e) Official FAA records, including grants and denials of exemptions, relating to petitions for exemption are maintained in current docket form in the Office of the Regional Counsel for the region concerned.

(f) Any interested person may—

(1) Examine any docketed material at the Office of the Regional Counsel, at any time after the docket is established, except material that is ordered withheld from the public under section 1104 of the Federal Aviation Act of 1958 (49 U.S.C. 1504); and

(2) Obtain a photostatic or similar copy of docketed material upon paying the same fee as that prescribed in 49 CFR part 7.

§152.7 Certifications.

(a) Subject to such terms and conditions as the Administrator may prescribe, a sponsor or a planning agency may submit, with respect to any provision of this part implementing a statutory or administrative requirement imposed on the sponsor or planning agency under the AADA, a certification that the sponsor or planning agency has complied or will comply with the provision, instead of making the showing required.

(b) The Administrator exercises discretion in determining whether to accept a certification.

(c) Acceptance by the Administrator of a certification from a sponsor or planning agency may be rescinded by the Administrator at any time if, in the Administrator's opinion, it is necessary to do so.

(d) If the Administrator determines that it is necessary, the sponsor or planning agency, on request, shall show compliance with any requirement for which a certification was accepted.

§152.9 Forms.

Any form needed to comply with this part may be obtained at any FAA Regional Office or Airports District Office.

§152.11 Incorporation by reference.

(a) *Mandatory standards.* The advisory circulars listed in appendix B to this part are incorporated into this part by reference. The Director, Office of Airport Standards, determines the scope and content of the technical standards to be included in each advisory circular in appendix B, and may add to, or delete from, appendix B any advisory circular or part thereof. Except as provided in paragraph (c) of this section, these guidelines are mandatory standards.

(b) *Modification of standards.* When necessary to meet local conditions, any technical standard set forth in appendix B may be modified for individual projects, if it is determined that the modifications will provide an acceptable level of safety, economy, durability, and workmanship. The determination and modification may be made by the Director, Office of Airport Standards, or the appropriate Regional Director, in instances where the authority has not been specifically reserved by the Director, Office of Airport Standards.

(c) *State standards.* Standards established by a state for airport development at general aviation airports in the state may be the standards applicable to those airports when they have been approved by the Director, Office of Airport Standards, or the appropriate Regional Director, in instances where approval authority has not been specifically reserved by the Director, Office of Airport Standards.

(d) *Availability of advisory circulars.* The advisory circulars listed in appendix B may be inspected and copied at any FAA Regional Office or Airports District Office. Copies of the circulars that are available free of charge may be obtained from any of those offices or from the FAA Distribution Unit, M-443.1, Washington, DC 20590. Copies of the circulars that are for sale may be bought from the Superintendent of Documents, U.S. Government Printing Office, Washington, DC 20402.

Subpart B—Eligibility Requirements and Application Procedures

SOURCE: Docket No. 19430, 45 FR 34786, May 22, 1980, unless otherwise noted.

§152.101 Applicability.

This subpart contains requirements and application procedures applicable to airport development and planning projects.

§152.103 Sponsors: Airport development.

(a) To be eligible to apply for a project for airport development with respect to a particular airport the following requirements must be met:

(1) Each sponsor must be a public agency authorized by law to submit the project application.

(2) If a sponsor is the holder of an airport operating certificate issued for the airport under part 139 of this chapter, it must be in compliance with the requirements of part 139.

(3) When any of the following agreements is applicable to an airport which

715

the sponsor owns or controls, the sponsor must have complied with the agreement, or show to the satisfaction of the Administrator that it will comply or, for reasons beyond its control, cannot comply with the agreement:

(i) Each grant agreement made with it under the Federal Airport Act (49 U.S.C. 1101 *et seq.*), or the AADA.

(ii) Each convenant in a conveyance to it under section 16 of the Federal Airport Act or section 23 of the AADA.

(iii) Each convenant in a conveyance to it of surplus airport property under section 13(a) of the Surplus Property Act (50 U.S.C. App 1622(g)) or under Regulation 16 of the War Assets Administration.

(4) The sponsor, in the case of a single sponsor, or one or more of the cosponsors must have, or be able to obtain—

(i) Funds to pay all estimated costs of the project that are not to be born by the United States; and

(ii) Satisfactory property interests in the lands to be developed or used as part of, or in connection with, the airport as it will be after the project is completed.

(b) Another public agency may act as agent of the public agency that is to own and operate the airport, for the purpose of channeling grant funds in accordance with state or local law, without becoming a sponsor.

§ 152.105 Sponsors and planning agencies: Airport planning.

(a) To be eligible to apply for a project for airport planning—

(1) If the project is for airport master planning—

(i) Each sponsor must be a public agency and meet the requirements of § 152.103(a)(3); and

(ii) The sponsor, in the case of a single sponsor, or one or more cosponsors must be legally able to implement the planning, within the existing or proposed airport boundaries, that results from the project study.

(2) If the project is for airport system planning, each sponsor must be a planning agency.

(b) Another public agency or planning agency may act as agent of another public agency or planning agency, for the purpose of channeling grant funds in accordance with state or local law, without becoming a sponsor.

§ 152.107 Project eligibility: Airport development.

(a) Except in the case of approved stage development, each project for airport development must provide for—

(1) Development of an airport or unit of an airport that is safe, useful, and usable; or,

(2) An additional facility that increases the safety, usefulness, and usability of an airport.

(b) Unless otherwise authorized by the Administrator, a project for airport development must involve more than $25,000 in United States funds.

(c) The development included in a project for airport development must—

(1) In the opinion of the Administrator, be "airport development" as defined in § 152.3;

(2) Be identified as airport development in the mandatory standards incorporated into this part by § 152.11; and

(3) Be described in an approved airport layout plan.

(d) The airport involved in a project for airport development must be included in the current NASP.

(e) In complying with paragraph (a) of this section, the sponsor must—

(1) Own, acquire, or agree to acquire control over, or a property interest in, runway clear zones that the Administrator considers adequate; and

(2) Provide for approach and runway lighting systems satisfactory to the Administrator.

§ 152.109 Project eligibility: Airport planning.

(a) *Airport master planning.* A proposed project for airport master planning is not approved unless—

(1) The location of the existing or proposed airport is included in the current NASP;

(2) In the opinion of the Administrator, the proposed planning would promote the effective location of public airports and the development of an adequate NASP;

(3) The project is airport master planning as defined in § 152.3;

(4) If the project has been determined to have areawide significance by an appropriate areawide agency, it has been incorporated into a unified planning work program; and

(5) In the case of a proposed project for airport master planning in a large or medium air traffic hub, in the opinion of the Administrator—

(i) There is an appropriate system plan identifying the need for the airport;

(ii) The absence of a system plan is due to the failure of the responsible planning agency to proceed with its preparation; or

(iii) An existing system plan is not acceptable.

(b) *Airport system planning.* A proposed project for airport system planning is not approved unless—

(1) In the opinion of the Administrator, the project promotes the effective location of public airports;

(2) In the opinion of the Administrator, the project promotes the development of an adequate NASP;

(3) The project is airport system planning as defined in § 152.3; and

(4) When the project encompasses a metropolitan area that includes a large or medium hub airport, the project is incorporated in a unified planning work program.

§ 152.111 Application requirements: Airport development.

(a) An eligible sponsor that desires to obtain Federal aid for eligible airport development must apply to the FAA in accordance with this section. The sponsor must apply on a form and in a manner prescribed by the Administrator, through the FAA Airports District Office or Airports Field Office having jurisdiction over the area where the sponsor is located or, where there is no such office, the Regional Office having that jurisdiction.

(b) *Preapplication for Federal assistance.* A preapplication for Federal assistance must be submitted unless—

(1) The Federal fund request is for $100,000 or less; or,

(2) The project does not include construction, land acquisition, or land improvement.

(c) Unless otherwise authorized by the Administrator, the preapplication

required by paragraph (b) of this section must be accompanied by the following:

(1) A list of the items of airport development requested for programming, together with an itemized estimated cost of the work involved.

(2) A sketch or sketches of the airport layout indicating the location for each item of work proposed, using the same item numbers used in the list required by paragraph (c)(1) of this section.

(3) If the proposed project involves the displacement of persons or the acquisition of real property, the assurances required by §§ 25.57 and 25.59, as applicable, of the Regulations of the Office of the Secretary of Transportation (49 CFR 25.57 and 25.59), whether or not reimbursement is being requested for the costs of displacement or real property acquisition.

(4) Any comments or statements required by appendix E, Procedures Implementing Office of Management and Budget Circular A–95, to this part, with a showing that they have been considered by the sponsor.

(5) If the proposed development involves the construction of eligible airport buildings or the acquisition of eligible fixed equipment to be contained in those buildings, a statement whether the proposed development will be in an area of the community that has been identified by the Department of Housing and Urban Development as an area of special flood hazard as defined in the Flood Disaster Protection Act of 1973 (42 U.S.C. 4002 *et seq.*).

(6) If the proposed development is in an area of special flood hazard, a statement whether the community is participating in the National Flood Insurance Program (42 U.S.C. 4011 *et seq.*).

(7) The sponsor's environmental assessment prepared in conformance with appendix 6 of FAA Order 1050.1C, "Policies and Procedures for Considering Environmental Impacts" (45 FR 2244; Jan. 10, 1980), and FAA Order 5050.4, "Airport Environmental Handbook" (45 FR 56624; Aug. 24, 1980), if an assessment is required by Order 5050.4. Copies of these orders may be examined in the Rules Docket, Office of the Chief Counsel, FAA, Washington, D.C., and may be obtained on request at any

FAA regional office headquarters or any airports district office.

(8) A showing that the sponsor has complied with the public hearing requirements in § 152.117.

(9) In the case of a proposed new airport serving any area that does not include a metropolitan area, a showing that each community in which the proposed airport is to be located has approved the proposed airport site through the body having general legislative jurisdiction over it.

(10) In the case of a proposed project at an air carrier airport, a statement that the sponsor, in making the decision to undertake the project, has consulted with air carriers using the airport.

(11) In the case of a proposed project at a general aviation airport, a statement that the sponsor, in making the decision to undertake the project, has consulted with fixed-base operators using the airport.

(12) In the case of terminal development, a certification that the airport has, or will have, all safety and security equipment required for certification of the airport under part 139 and has provided, or will provide, for access to the passenger enplaning and deplaning area to passengers enplaning or deplaning from aircraft other than air carrier aircraft.

(d) *Allocation of funds.* If the proposed project for airport development is selected by the Administrator for inclusion in a program, a tentative allocation of funds is made for the project and the sponsor is notified of the allocation. The tentative allocation may be withdrawn if the sponsor does not submit a project application in accordance with paragraph (f) of this section.

(e) *Application for Federal assistance.* As soon as practicable after receiving notice of a tentative allocation or, if a preapplication is not required (as provided in paragraph (b) of this section), an application for Federal assistance must be submitted.

(f) Unless otherwise authorized by the Administrator, the application required by paragraph (e) of this section must be accompanied by the following:

(1) When a preapplication has not been previously submitted, the information required by paragraph (c) of this section.

(2) A property map of the airport showing—

(i) The property interests of each sponsor in all the lands to be developed or used as part of, or in connection with, the airport as it will be when the project is completed; and

(ii) All property interests acquired or to be acquired, for which U.S. aid is requested under the project.

(3) With respect to all lands to be developed or used as a part of, or in connection with, the airport (as it will be when the project is completed) in which a satisfactory property interest is not held by a sponsor, a covenant by the sponsor that it will obtain a satisfactory property interest before construction is begun or within a reasonable time if not needed for construction.

(4) If the proposed project involves the displacement of persons, the relocation plan required by § 25.55 of the Regulations of the Office of the Secretary of Transportation.

(5) When the project involves an airport location, a runway location, or a major runway extension, a written certification from the Governor of the state in which the project may be located (or a delegatee), providing reasonable assurance that the project will be located, designed, constructed, and operated so as to comply with applicable air and water quality standards.

(6) A statement whether any building, installation, structure, location, or site of operations to be utilized in the performance of the grant or any contract made pursuant to the grant appears on the list of violating facilities distributed by the Environmental Protection Agency under the provisions of the Clean Air Act and Federal Water Pollution Control Act (40 CFR part 15).

(7) The assurances on Civil Rights required by § 21.7 of the Regulations of the Office of the Secretary of Transportation (49 CFR 21.7) and § 152.405.

(8) Plans and specifications for the proposed development in accordance with the design and construction standards listed in appendix B to this part.

(9) The applicable assurances required by appendix D to this part.

(10) If cosponsors are not willing to assume, jointly and severally, the obligations imposed on them by this part and the grant agreement, a statement satisfactory to the Administrator indicating—

(i) The responsibilities of each sponsor with respect to the accomplishment of the proposed project and the operation and maintenance of the airport;

(ii) The obligations each will assume to the United States; and

(iii) The name of the sponsor or sponsors who will accept, receipt for, and disburse grant payments.

(g) *Additional documentation.* The Administrator may request additional documentation as needed to support specific items of development or to comply with other Federal and local requirements as they pertain to the requested development.

(Secs. 303, 307, 308, 312, and 313, Federal Aviation Act of 1958 (49 U.S.C. 1344, 1348, 1349, 1353, and 1354); sec. 6(c), Dept. of Transportation Act (49 U.S.C. 1655(c)); Airport and Airway Development Act of 1970, as amended (49 U.S.C. 1701 *et seq.*); sec. 1.47(f)(1), Regulations of the Office of the Secretary of Transportation (49 CFR 1.47(1)); OMB Circular A-95, Revised (41 FR 2052; Jan. 13, 1976))

[Doc. No. 19430, 45 FR 34784, May 22, 1980, as amended by Amdt. 152–11, 45 FR 56622, Aug. 25, 1980; 45 FR 58107, Sept. 2, 1980; Amdt. 152–13, 46 FR 30809, June 11, 1981]

§152.113 Application requirements: Airport planning.

(a) *Application for Federal assistance.* An eligible sponsor or planning agency that desires to obtain Federal aid for eligible airport master planning or airport system planning must submit an application for Federal assistance, on a form and in a manner prescribed by the Administrator, to the appropriate FAA Airports District Office or Airports Field Office having jurisdiction over the area where the sponsor or planning agency is located or, where there is no such office, the Regional Office having that jurisdiction.

(b) Unless otherwise authorized by the Administrator, the application required by paragraph (a) of this section must be accompanied by the following:

(1) Any comments or statements required by appendix E, Procedures Implementing Office of Management and Budget Circular A-95, to this part.

(2) Budget (project costs) information subdivided into the following functions, as appropriate, and the basis for computation of these costs:

(i) Third party contracts.

(ii) Sponsor force account costs.

(iii) Administrative costs.

(3) A program narrative describing the proposed planning project including—

(i) The objective;

(ii) The results and benefits expected;

(iii) A Work Statement including—

(A) A detailed description of each work element;

(B) A list of each organization, consultant, and key individual who will work on the planning project, and the nature of the contribution of each; and

(C) A proposed schedule of work accomplishment; and

(iv) The geographic location of the airport or the boundaries of the planning area.

(4) If the sponsor proposes to accomplish the project with its own forces or those of another public or planning agency—

(i) An assurance that adequate, competent personnel are available to satisfactorily accomplish the proposed planning project, and

(ii) A description of the qualifications of the key personnel.

(5) If cosponsors are not willing to assume, jointly, and severally, the obligations imposed on them by this part and the grant agreement, a statement satisfactory to the Administrator indicating—

(i) The responsibilities of each sponsor with respect to the accomplishment of the proposed project;

(ii) The obligations each will assume to the United States; and

(iii) The name of the sponsor or sponsors who will accept, receipt for, and disburse grant payments.

(6) The assurances on Civil Rights required by §21.7 of the Regulations of the Office of the Secretary of Transportation (49 CFR 21.7).

(7) The applicable assurances required by appendix D of this part.

(c) *Additional documentation.* The Administrator may request additional documentation as needed to support a master plan or system plan, or to comply with other Federal and local requirements as they pertain to the requested plan.

(Secs. 303, 307, 308, 312, and 313, Federal Aviation Act of 1958 (49 U.S.C. 1344, 1348, 1349, 1353, and 1354); sec. 6(c), Dept. of Transportation Act (49 U.S.C. 1655(c)); Airport and Airway Development Act of 1970, as amended (49 U.S.C. 1701 *et seq.*); sec. 1.47(f)(1), Regulations of the Office of the Secretary of Transportation (49 CFR 1.47(1)); OMB Circular A–95, Revised (41 FR 2052; Jan. 13, 1976))

[Doc. No. 19430, 45 FR 34784, May 22, 1980, as amended by Amdt. 152–13, 46 FR 30809, June 11, 1981]

§ 152.115 Grant agreement: Offer, acceptance, and amendment.

(a) *Offer.* Upon approving a project for airport development, airport master planning, or airport system planning, the Administrator issues a written offer that sets forth the terms, limitations, and requirements of the proposed agreement.

(b) *Acceptance.* The acceptance of an offer or an amendment to a grant agreement must be in writing. The sponsor's or planning agency's attorney must certify that the acceptance complies with all applicable law, and constitutes a legal and binding obligation of the sponsor or planning agency.

(c) *Amendment: Airport development grants.* The maximum obligation of the United States under a grant agreement for an airport development project may be increased by an amendment if—

(1) Except as otherwise provided by the Uniform Relocation Assistance and Real Property Acquisition Policies Act of 1970, the maximum obligation of the United States is not increased by more than 10 percent;

(2) Funds are available for the increase;

(3) The sponsor shows that the increase is justified; and

(4) The change does not prejudice the interest of the United States.

(d) *Reduction of U.S. Share: Airport development grants.* When project work for which costs have been incurred is deleted from a grant agreement, the Administrator reduces the maximum obligation of the United States proportionately, based on the cost or value of the deleted work as shown on the project application.

(e) *Amendment: Airport planning.* A grant agreement for airport planning may be changed if—

(1) The change does not increase the maximum obligation of the United States under the grant agreement; and

(2) The change does not prejudice the interest of the United States.

§ 152.117 Public hearings.

(a) Before submitting a preapplication for Federal assistance for an airport development project involving the location of an airport, an airport runway, or a runway extension, the sponsor must give notice of opportunity for a public hearing, in accordance with paragraph (b) of this section, for the purpose of—

(1) Considering the economic, social, and environmental effects of the location of the airport, the airport runway, or the runway extension; and

(2) Determining the consistency of the location with the goals and objectives of any urban planning that has been carried out by the community.

(b) The notice of opportunity for public hearing must—

(1) Include a concise statement of the proposed development;

(2) Be published in a newspaper of general circulation in the communities in or near which the project may be located;

(3) Provide a minimum of 30 days from the date of the notice for submission of requests for a hearing by persons having an interest in the economic, social, or environmental effects of the project; and

(4) State that a copy is available of the sponsor's environmental assessment, if one is required by appendix 6 of FAA Order 1050.1C, "Policies and Procedures for Considering Environmental Impacts" (45 FR 2244; Jan. 10, 1980), and FAA Order 5050.4, "Airport Environmental Handbook" (45 FR 56624; Aug. 25, 1980), and will remain available, at the sponsor's place of business for examination by the public for a minimum of 30 days, beginning with the date of the notice, before any hearing held under the notice.

(c) A public hearing must be provided if requested. If a public hearing is to be held, the sponsor must publish a notice of that fact, in the same newspaper in which the notice of opportunity for a hearing was published.

(d) The notice required by paragraph (c) of this section must—

(1) Be published not less than 15 days before the date set for the hearing;

(2) Specify the date, time, and place of the hearings;

(3) Contain a concise description of the proposed project; and

(4) Indicate where and at what time more detailed information may be obtained.

(e) If a public hearing is held, the sponsor must—

(1) Provide the Administrator a summary of the issues raised, the alternatives considered, the conclusion reached, and the reasons for that conclusion; and

(2) If requested by the Administrator before the hearing, prepare a verbatim transcript of the hearing for submission to the Administrator.

(f) If a hearing is not held the sponsor must submit with its preapplication a certification that notice of opportunity for a hearing has been provided in accordance with this section and that no request for a public hearing has been received.

[Doc. No. 19430, 45 FR 34784, May 22, 1980, as amended by Amdt. 152–11, 45 FR 56622, Aug. 25, 1980]

§ 152.119 Contract requirements and procurement standards.

To the extent applicable, all grant agreements, contracts, and subcontracts involving airport development projects or airport planning must be in accordance with the contract requirements in appendices A and C, as applicable, and the procurement standards in Attachment O of Office of Management and Budget Circular A–102 (42 FR 45828).

Subpart C—Funding of Approved Projects

SOURCE: Docket No. 19430, 45 FR 34789, May 22, 1980, unless otherwise noted.

§ 152.201 Applicability.

This subpart contains the requirements for funding projects for airport development, airport master planning, and airport system planning.

§ 152.203 Allowable project costs.

(a) *Airport development.* To be an allowable project cost, for the purposes of computing the amount of an airport development grant, an item that is paid or incurred must, in the opinion of the Administrator—

(1) Have been necessary to accomplish airport development in conformity with—

(i) The approved plans and specifications for an approved project; and

(ii) The terms of the grant agreement for the project;

(2) Be reasonable in amount (subject to partial disallowance to the extent the Administrator determines it is unreasonable);

(3) Have been incurred after the date the grant agreement was executed, except that project formulation costs may be allowed even though they were incurred before that date;

(4) Be supported by satisfactory evidence;

(5) Have not been included in an airport planning grant; and

(6) Be a cost determined in accordance with the cost principles for State and local governments in Federal Management Circular 74–4 (39 FR 27133; 43 FR 50977).

(b) *Airport Planning.* To be an allowable project cost, for the purposes of computing the amount of an airport planning grant, an item that is paid or incurred must, in the opinion of the Administrator—

(1) Have been necessary to accomplish airport planning in comformity with an approved project and the terms of the grant agreement for the project;

(2) Be reasonable in amount;

(3) Have been incurred after the date the grant agreement was entered into, except for substantiated and reasonable costs incurred in designing the study effort;

(4) Be supported by satisfactory evidence; and

(5) Be figured in accordance with Federal Management Circular 74–4 (39 FR 27133; 43 FR 50977).

§ 152.205 United States share of project costs.

(a) *Airport development.* Except as provided in paragraphs (b) and (c) of this section, the following is the United

States share of the allowable cost of an airport development project approved for the specified year:

(1) 90 percent in the case of grants made from funds for fiscal years 1976, 1977, and 1978, and grants from funds for fiscal year 1980 made after February 17, 1980, for—

(i) Each air carrier airport, other than a commuter service airport, which enplanes less than one quarter of one percent of the total annual passengers enplaned as determined for purposes of making the latest annual apportionment under section 15(a)(3) of the AADA;

(ii) Each commuter service airport; and

(iii) Each general aviation or reliever airport.

(2) 80 percent in the case of grants made from funds for fiscal year 1979 and grants from funds for fiscal year 1980 made before February 18, 1980, for the airports specified in paragraph (a)(1) of this section.

(3) 75 percent in the case of grants made from funds for fiscal years 1976 through 1980 for airports other than those specified in paragraph (a)(1) of this section.

(b) In a State in which the unappropriated and unreserved public lands and nontaxable Indian lands, both individual and tribal, are more than five percent of the total land in that State, the United States' share under paragraph (a) of this section—

(1) Except as provided in paragraph (b)(2) of this section, shall be increased by the smaller of—

(i) 25 percent; or

(ii) A percentage (rounded to the nearest one-tenth of a percent) equal to one-half of the percentage which the area of those lands is of the total land area of the state; and

(2) May not exceed the greater of—

(i) The percentage share determined under paragraph (a) of this section; or

(ii) The percentage share applying on June 30, 1975, as determined under paragraph (b)(1) of this section.

(c) In the case of terminal development, the United States share shall be 50 percent.

(d) *Airport planning.* The United States share of the allowable project costs of an airport planning project shall be—

(1) In the case of an airport master plan, that percent for which a project for airport development at that airport would be eligible;

(2) In the case of an airport system plan, 75 percent.

§ 152.207 Proceeds from disposition of land.

Unless otherwise authorized by the Administrator, when a release has been granted authorizing the sponsor to dispose of land acquired with assistance under part 151 of this chapter or this part, or through conveyances under the Surplus Property Act, the proceeds realized from the disposal may not be used as matching funds for any airport development project or airport planning grant, but may be used for any other airport purpose.

§ 152.209 Grant payments: General.

(a) An application for a grant payment is made on a form and in a manner prescribed by the Administrator, and must be accompanied by any supporting information, that the FAA needs to determine the allowability of any costs for which payment is requested.

(b) *Methods of payment.* Grant payments to sponsors and planning agencies will be made by—

(1) Letter of credit;

(2) Advance by Treasury check; or

(3) Reimbursement by Treasury checks.

(c) *Letter of credit funding.* Letter of credit funding may not be used unless—

(1) There is or will be a continuing relationship between a sponsor or planning agency and the FAA for at least a 12-month period and the total amount of advances to be received within that period is $120,000 or more;

(2) The sponsor or planning agency has established or demonstrated to the FAA the willingness and ability to establish procedures that will minimize the time elapsing between the transfer of funds and their disbursement by the grantee; and

(3) The sponsor's or planning agency's financial management system meets the standards for fund control

and accountability prescribed in Attachment G of Office of Management and Budget Circular A–102 (42 FR 45828).

(d) *Advance by Treasury check.* Advance of funds by Treasury check may be made subject to the following conditions—

(1) The sponsor or planning agency meets the requirements of paragraphs (c) (2) and (3) of this section;

(2) The timing and amount of cash advances are as close as administratively feasible to actual disbursements by the sponsor or planning agency; and

(3) Except as provided in paragraph (e) of this section, in the case of an airport development project, advance payments do not exceed the estimated project costs of the airport development expected to be accomplished within 30 days after the date of the sponsor's application for the advance payment.

(e) No advance payment for airport development projects may be made in an amount that would bring the aggregate amount of all partial payments to more than the lower of the following:

(i) 90 percent of the estimated United States' share of the total estimated cost of all airport development included in the project, but not including contingency items; or

(ii) 90 percent of the maximum obligation of the United States as stated in the grant agreement.

(f) *Reimbursement by Treasury check.* Reimbursement by Treasury check will be made if the sponsor or planning agency does not meet the requirements of paragraphs (c) (2) and (3) of this section.

(g) *Withholding of payments.* Payment to the sponsor or planning agency may be withheld at any time during the grant period under the following circumstances:

(1) The sponsor or planning agency has failed to comply with the program objectives, grant award conditions, or Federal reporting requirements.

(2) The sponsor or planning agency is indebted to the United States and collection of the indebtedness will not impair accomplishment of the objectives of any grant program sponsored by the United States.

(3) The sponsor or planning agency has withheld payment to a contractor to assure satisfactory completion of work. Payment will be made to the sponsor or planning agency when it has made final payment to the contractor, including the amounts withheld.

(h) *Labor violations.* If a contractor or a subcontractor fails or refuses to comply with the labor provisions of a contract under a grant agreement for an airport development project, further grant payments to the sponsor are suspended until—

(1) The violations are corrected;

(2) The Administrator determines the allowability of the project costs to which the violations relate; or

(3) If the violations consist of underpayments to labor, the sponsor furnishes satisfactory assurances to the FAA that restitution has been or will be made to the affected employees.

(i) *Excess payments.* Upon determination of the allowability of all project costs of a project, if it is found that the total of grant payments to the sponsor or planning agency was more than the total United States share of the allowable costs of the project, the sponsor or planning agency shall promptly return the excess to FAA.

§152.211 Grant payments: Land acquisition.

If an approved project for airport development includes land acquisition as an item for which payment is requested, the sponsor may apply to the FAA for payment of the United States share of the allowable project costs of the acquisition, after—

(a) The Administrator determines that the sponsor has acquired satisfactory title to the land; or

(b) In the case of a request for advance payment under §152.209(d), the Administrator is assured that a satisfactory title will be acquired.

§152.213 Grant closeout requirements.

(a) *Program income.* Sponsors or planning agencies that are units of local government shall return all interest earned on advances of grant-in-aid funds to the Federal Government in accordance with a decision of the Comptroller General (42 Comp. Gen. 289). All other program income (gross income) earned by grant-supported activities during the grant period shall be retained by the sponsor and, if required by the grant agreement—

(1) Be added to funds committed to the project by the FAA and the sponsor and used to further eligible program objectives; or

(2) Be deducted from the total project cost for the purpose of determining the net costs on which the Federal share of costs will be based.

(b) *Financial reports.* The sponsor or planning agency shall furnish, within 90 days after completion of all items in a grant, all reports, including financial performance reports, required as a condition of the grant.

(c) *Project completion.* When the project for airport development or planning is completed in accordance with the grant agreement, the sponsor or planning agency may apply for payment for all incurred costs, as follows:

(1) *Airport development.* When allowability of costs can be determined under § 152.203, payment may be made to the sponsor if—

(i) A final inspection of all work at the airport site has been made jointly by the appropriate FAA office and representatives of the sponsor and the contractor, unless that office agrees to a different procedure for final inspection; and

(ii) The sponsor has furnished final "as constructed" plans, unless otherwise agreed to by the Administrator.

(2) *Airport planning.* When the final planning report has been received and accepted by the FAA.

(d) *Property accounting reports: Airport development projects.* The sponsor of an airport development project shall account for any property acquired with grant funds or received from the United States, in accordance with the provisions of Attachment N of Office of Management and Budget Circular A–102 (42 FR 45828).

(e) *Final determination of U.S. share.* Based upon an audit or other information considered sufficient in lieu of an audit, the Administrator determines the total amount of the allowable project costs and makes settlement for any adjustments to the Federal share of costs.

Subpart D—Accounting and Reporting Requirements

SOURCE: Docket No. 19430, 45 FR 34791, May 22, 1980, unless otherwise noted.

§ 152.301 Applicability.

This subpart contains accounting and reporting requirements applicable to—

(a) Each sponsor of a project for airport development;

(b) Each sponsor of a project for airport master planning; and

(c) Each planning agency conducting a project for airport system planning.

§ 152.303 Financial management system.

Each sponsor or planning agency shall establish and maintain a financial management system that meets the standards of Attachment G of Office of Management and Budget Circular A–102 (42 FR 45828).

§ 152.305 Accounting records.

(a) *Airport development.* Each sponsor of a project for airport development shall establish and maintain, for each individual project, an accounting record satisfactory to the Administrator which segregates cost information into the cost classifications set forth in Standard Form 271 (42 FR 45841).

(b) *Airport planning.* Each sponsor of a project for airport master planning and each planning agency conducting a project for airport system planning shall establish and maintain, for each planning project, an adequate accounting record that segregates and groups direct and indirect cost information in the following classifications:

(1) Third party contract costs.

(2) Force account costs.

(3) Administrative costs.

§ 152.307 Retention of records.

Each sponsor or planning agency shall retain, for a period of 3 years after the date of submission of the final expenditure report—

(a) Documentary evidence, such as invoices, cost estimates, and payrolls, supporting each item of project costs; and

(b) Evidence of all payments for items of project costs, including vouchers, cancelled checks or warrants, and receipts for cash payments.

§ 152.309 Availability of sponsor's records.

(a) The sponsor or planning agency shall allow any authorized representative of the Administrator, the Secretary of Transportation, or the Comptroller General of the United States access to any of its books, documents, papers, and records that are pertinent to grants received under this part for the purposes of accounting and audit.

(b) The sponsor or planning agency shall allow appropriate FAA or DOT representatives to make progress audits at any time during the project, upon reasonable notice to the sponsor or planning agency.

(c) It audit findings have not been resolved, the applicable records shall be retained by the sponsor or planning agency until those findings have been resolved.

(d) Records for nonexpendable property that was acquired with Federal funds shall be retained for three years after final disposition of the property.

(e) Microfilm copies of original records may be substituted for original records with the approval of the FAA.

(f) If the FAA determines that certain records have long-term retention value, the FAA may require transfer of custody of those records to the FAA.

§ 152.311 Availability of contractor's records.

The sponsor or planning agency shall include in each contract of the cost reimbursable type a clause that allows any authorized representative of the Administrator, the Secretary of Transportation, or the Comptroller General of the United States access to the contractor's records pertinent to the contract for the purposes of accounting and audit.

§ 152.313 Property management standards.

(a) The sponsor shall establish and maintain property management standards in accordance with Attachment N of Office of Management and Budget Circular A-102 (42 FR 45828) for the utilization and disposition of property furnished by the Federal Government, or acquired in whole or in part by the sponsor with Federal funds.

(b) A sponsor may use its own property management standards and procedures as long as the standards required by paragraph (a) of this section are included.

§ 152.315 Reporting on accrual basis.

(a) Except as provided in paragraph (b) of this section each sponsor or planning agency shall submit all financial reports on an accrual basis.

(b) If records are not maintained on an accrual basis by a sponsor or planning agency, reports may be based on an analysis of records or best estimates.

§ 152.317 Report of Federal cash transactions.

When funds are advanced to a sponsor or planning agency by Treasury check, the sponsor or planning agency shall submit the report form prescribed by the Administrator within 15 working days following the end of the quarter in which check was received.

§ 152.319 Monitoring and reporting of program performance.

(a) The sponsor or planning agency shall monitor performance under the project to ensure that—

(1) Time schedules are being met;

(2) Work units projected by time periods are being accomplished; and,

(3) Other performance goals are being achieved.

(b) Reviews shall be made for—

(1) Each item of development or work element included in the project; and

(2) All other work to be performed as a condition of the grant agreement.

(c) *Airport development.* Unless otherwise requested by the Administrator, the sponsor of a project for airport development shall submit a performance report, on an annual basis, that must include—

(1) A comparison of actual accomplishments to the goals established for the period, made, if applicable, on a quantitative basis related to cost data for computation of unit costs;

(2) The reasons for slippage in each case where an established goal was not met; and

(3) Other pertinent information including, when appropriate, an analysis and explanation of each cost overrun and high unit cost.

(d) *Airport planning.* The sponsor of a project for airport master planning or a planning agency conducting a project for airport system planning shall submit a performance report, on a quarterly basis, that must include:

(1) A comparison of actual accomplishments to the goals established for the period, made, if applicable, on a quantitative basis related to costs for computation of work element costs;

(2) Reasons for slippage in each case where an established goal was not met; and

(3) Other pertinent information including, when appropriate, an analysis and explanation of each cost overrun and high work element cost.

§ 152.321 **Notice of delay or acceleration.**

(a) The sponsor or planning agency shall promptly notify the FAA of each condition or event that may delay or accelerate accomplishment of the project.

(b) In the event that delay is anticipated, the notice required by paragraph (a) of this section must include—

(1) A statement of actions taken or contemplated; and

(2) Any Federal assistance needed.

§ 152.323 **Budget revision: Airport development.**

(a) If any performance review conducted by the sponsor discloses a need for change in the budget estimates, the sponsor shall submit a request for budget revision on a form prescribed by the Administrator.

(b) A request for prior approval for budget revision shall be made promptly by the sponsor whenever—

(1) The revision results from changes in the scope or objective of the project; or

(2) The revision increases the budgeted amounts of Federal funds needed to complete the project.

(c) The sponsor shall promptly notify the FAA whenever the amount of the grant is expected to exceed the needs of the sponsor by more than $5,000, or 5 percent of the grant amount, whichever is greater.

§ 152.325 **Financial status report: Airport planning.**

Each sponsor of a project for airport master planning and each planning agency conducting a project for airport system planning shall submit a financial status report on a form prescribed by the Administrator at the completion of the project.

Subpart E—Nondiscrimination in Airport Aid Program

AUTHORITY: Sec. 30 of the Airport and Airway Development Act of 1970 (49 U.S.C. 1730); sec. 1.47(f)(1) of the Regulations of the Office of the Secretary of Transportation (49 CFR 1.47(f)(1)).

SOURCE: Docket No. 16419, 45 FR 10188, Feb. 14, 1980, unless otherwise noted.

§ 152.401 **Applicability.**

(a) This subpart is applicable to all grantees and other covered organizations under this part, and implements the requirements of section 30 of the Airport and Airway Development Act of 1970, which provides:

The Secretary shall take affirmative action to assure that no person shall, on the grounds of race, creed, color, national origin, or sex, be excluded from participating in any activity conducted with funds received from any grant made under this title. The Secretary shall promulgate such rules as he deems necessary to carry out the purposes of this section and may enforce this section, and any rules promulgated under this section, through agency and department provisions and rules which shall be similar to those established and in effect under Title VI of the Civil Rights Act of 1964. The provisions of this section shall be considered to be in addition to and not in lieu of the provisions of Title VI of the Civil Rights Act of 1964.

(b) Each grantee, covered organization, or covered suborganization under this part shall negotiate reformation of any contract, subcontract, lease, sublease, or other agreement to include any appropriate provision necessary to effect compliance with this subpart by July 17, 1980.

§ 152.403 Definitions.

As used in this subpart—

AADA means the Airport and Airway Development Act of 1970, as amended (49 U.S.C. 1701 *et seq.*).

Affirmative action plan means a set of specific and result-oriented procedures to which a sponsor, planning agency, state, or the aviation related activity on an airport commits itself to achieve equal employment opportunity.

Airport development means—(1) Any work involved in constructing, improving, or repairing a public airport or portion thereof, including the removal, lowering, relocation, and marking and lighting of airport hazards, and including navigation aids used by aircraft landing at, or taking off from, a public airport, and including safety equipment required by rule or regulation for certification of the airport under section 612 of the Federal Aviation Act of 1958, and security equipment required of the sponsor by the Secretary by rule or regulation for the safety and security of persons and property on the airport, and including snow removal equipment, and including the purchase of noise suppressing equipment, the construction of physical barriers, and landscaping for the purpose of diminishing the effect of aircraft noise on any area adjacent to a public airport;

(2) Any acquisition of land or of any interest therein, or of any easement through or other interest in airspace, including land for future airport development, which is necessary to permit any such work or to remove or mitigate or prevent or limit the establishment of, airport hazards; and

(3) Any acquisition of land or of any interest therein necessary to insure that such land is used only for purposes which are compatible with the noise levels of the operation of a public airport.

Aviation related activity means a commercial enterprise—(1) Which is operated on the airport pursuant to an agreement with the grantee or airport operator or to a derivative subagreement;

(2) Which employs persons on the airport; and

(3) Which—(i) Is related primarily to the aeronautical activities on the airport;

(ii) Provides goods or services to the public which is attracted to the airport by aeronautical activities;

(iii) Provides services or supplies to other aeronautical related or public service airport businesses or to the airport; or

(iv) Performs construction work on the airport.

Aviation workforce includes, with respect to grantees, each person employed by the grantee on an airport or, for an aviation purpose, off the airport.

Covered organization means a grantee, a subgrantee, or an aviation related activity.

Covered suborganization is a subgrantee or sub-aviation related activity, of a covered organization.

Department means the United States Department of Transportation;

Grant means Federal financial assistance in the form of funds provided to a sponsor, planning agency, or state under this part;

Grantee means the recipient of a grant.

Minority means a person who is—(1) Black and not of Hispanic origin: A person having origins in any of the black racial groups of Africa;

(2) Hispanic: A person of Mexican, Puerto Rican, Cuban, Central or South American or other Spanish culture or origin, regardless of race;

(3) Asian or Pacific Islander: A person having origins in any or the original peoples of the Far East, Southeast Asia, the Indian subcontinent, or the Pacific Islands, including, but not limited to China, Japan, Korea, and the Philippine Islands, and Samoa; or

(4) American Indian or Alaskan Native: A person having origins in any of the original peoples of North America who maintains cultural identification through tribal affiliation or community recognition.

Planning agency means any planning agency designated by the Secretary which is authorized by the laws of the State or States (including the Commonwealth of Puerto Rico, the Virgin Islands, American Samoa, the Trust Territory of the Pacific Islands, and Guam) or political subdivisions concerned to engage in areawide planning for the area in which assistance under this part is to be used;

Secretary means the Secretary of Transportation or an authorized representative of the Secretary within the Department of Transportation;

SMSA means Standard Metropolitan Statistical Area.

Sponsor means any public agency that, either individually or jointly with one or more other public agencies, submits to the Administrator, in accordance with this part, an application for financial assistance, or that conducts a project for airport development or airport master planning, funded under this part;

Underutilization means having fewer minorities or women in a particular job group than would reasonable be expected from their availability in—

(1) The SMSA; or

(2) In the absence of a defined SMSA, in the counties contiguous to the employer's location, or the location where the work is to be performed, and in the areas from which persons may reasonably be expected to commute.

§ 152.405   Assurances.

The following assurances shall be included in each application for financial assistance under this part:

(a) *Assurance.* The grantee assures that it will undertake an affirmative action program, as required by 14 CFR part 152, subpart E, to ensure that no person shall, on the grounds of race, creed, color, national origin, or sex, be excluded from participating in any employment, contracting, or leasing activities covered in 14 CFR part 152, subpart E. The grantee assures that no person shall be excluded, on these grounds, from participating in or receiving the services or benefits of any program or activity covered by this subpart. The grantee assures that it will require that its covered organizations provide assurances to the grantee that they similarly will undertake affirmative action programs and that they will require assurances from their suborganizations, as required by 14 CFR part 152, subpart E, to the same effect.

(b) *Assurance.* The grantee agrees to comply with any affirmative action plan or steps for equal employment opportunity required by 14 CFR part 152, subpart E, as part of the affirmative action program, and by any Federal, State, or local agency or court, including those resulting from a conciliation agreement, a consent decree, court order, or similar mechanism. The grantee agrees that State or local affirmative action plans will be used in lieu of any affirmative action plan or steps required by 14 CFR part 152, subpart E, only when they fully meet the standards set forth in 14 CFR 152.409. The grantee agrees to obtain a similar assurance from its covered organizations, and to cause them to require a similar assurance of their covered suborganizations, as required by 14 CFR part 152, subpart E.

§ 152.407   Affirmative action plan: General.

(a) Except as provided in paragraph (b) of this section, each of the following shall have an affirmative action plan that meets the requirements of § 152.409 and is kept on file for review by the FAA Office of Civil Rights:

(1) Each sponsor who employs 50 or more employees in its aviation workforce.

(2) Each planning Agency which employs 50 or more employees in its agency for aviation purposes.

(3) Each state political division, administering a grant under the AADA to develop standards for airport development at general aviation airports, which employs 50 or more employees in its aviation workforce.

(b) A grantee is in compliance with paragraph (a) of this section, if it is subject to, and keeps on file for review by the FAA Office of Civil Rights, one of the following:

(1) An affirmative action plan acceptable to another Federal agency.

(2) An affirmative action plan for a State or local agency that the covered organization certifies meets the standards in § 152.409.

(3) A conciliation agreement, consent decree, or court order which provides short and long-range goals for equal employment opportunity similar to those which would be established in an affirmative action plan meeting the standards in § 152.409.

(c) Each sponsor shall require each aviation related activity (other than construction contractors) which employs 50 or more employees on the airport to prepare, and keep on file for review by the FAA Office of Civil Rights, an affirmative action plan developed in accordance with the standards in § 152.409, unless the activity is subject to one of the mechanisms described in paragraphs (b) (1) through (3) of this section.

(d) Each sponsor shall require each aviation related activity described in paragraph (c) of this section to similarly require each of its covered suborganizations (other than construction contractors) which employs 50 or more employees on the airport to prepare, and to keep on file for review by the FAA Office of Civil Rights, an affirmative action plan developed in accordance with the standards in § 152.409, unless the suborganization is subject to one of the mechanisms described in paragraphs (b) (1) through (3) of this section.

§ 152.409 Affirmative action plan standards.

(a) Each affirmative action plan required by this subpart shall be developed in accordance with the following:

(1) An analysis of the employer's aviation workforce which groups employees into the following job categories:

(i) Officials and managers.

(ii) Professionals.

(iii) Technicians.

(iv) Sales workers.

(v) Office and clerical workers.

(vi) Craft workers (skilled).

(vii) Operatives (semi-skilled).

(viii) Laborers (unskilled).

(ix) Service workers.

(2) A comparison separately made of the percent of minorities and women in the employer's present aviation workforce (in each of the job categories listed in paragraph (a)(1) of this section) with the percent of minorities and women in each of those categories in the total workforce located in the SMSA, or, in the absence of an SMSA, in the counties contiguous to the employer's location or the location where the work is to be performed and in the areas from which persons may reasonably be expected to commute. This data on the total workforce of the applicable area will be supplied to grantees by the FAA. Grantees shall make this data available to the other organizations covered by this subpart. The comparison for minorities must be made only when minorities constitute at least 2 percent of the total workforce in the geographical area used for the comparison.

(3) A comparison, for the aviation workforce, of the total number of applicants and persons hired with the total number of minority and female applicants, and minorities and females hired, for the past year. Where this data is unavailable, the employer shall establish and maintain a system to provide the data, and shall make the comparison 120 days after establishing the data system.

(4) Where the percentage of minorities and women in the employer's aviation workforce, in each job category, is less than the minority and female percentage in any job category in the workforce of the geographical area used, an analysis, based on the comparison required by paragraph (a)(3) of this section, determining whether any of the following exists:

(i) Insufficient flow of minority and female applicants.

(ii) Disparate rejection of minority and female applicants. The FAA generally considers disparate rejection to exist whenever a selection rate for any race, sex, or ethnic group is less than 80 percent of the rate for the race, sex, or ethnic group with the highest selection rate.

(b) Each affirmative action plan required by this part shall be implemented through an action-oriented program with goals and timetables designed to eliminate obstacles to equal opportunity for women and minorities in recruitment and hiring, which shall include, but not be limited to:

(1) Where disparate rejection of minority and female applicants is indicated by the analysis required by paragraph (a)(4) of this section, validation of those portions of the testing or selection procedures which cause the disparity in accordance with the "Uniform Guidelines on Employee Selection" (43 FR 38290; August 25, 1978), within 120 days of the analysis.

(2) Where testing or selection procedures cannot be validated, discontinuation of their use.

(3) Where an insufficient flow of minority and female applicants (less than the percentage available) is indicated by the analysis required by paragraph (a)(4) of this section, good faith efforts to increase the flow of minority and female applicants through the following steps, as appropriate:

(i) Development or reaffirmation of an equal opportunity policy and dissemination of that policy internally and externally.

(ii) Contact with minority and women's organizations, schools with predominant minority or female enrollments, and other recruitment sources for minorities and women.

(iii) Encouragement of State and local employment agencies, unions, and other recruiting sources to ensure that minorities and women have ample information on, and opportunity to apply for, vacancies and to participate in examinations.

(iv) Participation in special employment programs such as Co-operative Education Programs with predominantly minority and women's colleges, "After School" or Work Study programs, and Summer Employment.

(v) Participation in "Job Fairs."

(vi) Participation of minority and female employees in Career Days, Youth Motivation Programs, and counseling and related activities in the community.

(vii) Encouragement of minority and female employees to refer applicants.

(viii) Motivation, training, and employment programs for minority and female hard-core unemployed.

§ 152.411 Affirmative action steps.

(a) Each grantee which is not described in § 152.407(a) and is not subject to an affirmative action plan, regulatory goals and timetables, or other mechanism providing for short and long-range goals for equal employment opportunity, shall make good faith efforts to recruit and hire minorities and women for its aviation workforce as vacancies occur, by taking the affirmative action steps in § 152.409(b)(3), as follows:

(1) If it has 15 or more employees in its aviation workforce or employed for aviation purposes, by taking the affirmative action steps in § 152.409(b)(3), as appropriate; or

(2) If it has less than 15 employees in its aviation workforce or employed for aviation purposes, by taking the affirmative action steps in § 152.409(b)(3) (i) and (ii), as appropriate.

(b) Except as provided in paragraph (c) of this section, each sponsor shall require each of its aviation related activities on its airport, that is not subject to an affirmative action plan, regulatory goals and timetables, or other mechanism which provides short and long-range goals for equal employment opportunity, to take affirmative action steps and cause them to similarly require affirmative action steps of their covered suborganizations, as follows:

(1) Each aviation related activity or covered suborganization with less than 50 but more than 14 employees, must take the affirmative action steps enumerated in § 152.409(b)(3), as appropriate.

(2) Each aviation related activity or covered suborganization with less than 15 employees, must take the affirmative action steps enumerated in § 152.409(b)(3) (i) and (ii), as appropriate.

(c) Each sponsor shall require each construction contractor, that has a contract of $10,000 or more on its airport and that is not subject to an affirmative action plan, regulatory goals or timetables, or other mechanism which provides short and long-range goals for equal employment opportunity, to take the following affirmative action steps:

(1) The contractor must establish and maintain a current list of minority and female recruitment sources; provide written notification to these recruitment sources and to community organizations when employment opportunities are available; and maintain a record of each organization's response.

(2) The contractor must maintain a current file of the names, addresses, and telephone numbers of each minority and female walk-in applicant and each referral from a union, a recruitment source, or community organization and the action taken with respect to each individual. Where an individual

is sent to the union hiring hall for referral, but not referred back to the contractor, or, if referred, not employed by the contractor, this shall be documented. The documentation shall include an explanation of, and information on, any additional actions that the contractor may have taken.

(3) The contractor must disseminate its equal employment opportunity policy internally—

(i) By providing notice of the policy to unions and training programs;

(ii) By including it in policy manuals and collective bargaining agreements;

(iii) By publicizing it in the company newspaper, report, or other publication; and

(iv) By specific review of the policy with all management personnel and with all employees at least once a year.

(4) The contractor must disseminate the contractors's equal employment opportunity policy externally—

(i) By stating it in each employment advertisement in the news media, including news media with high minority and female readership; and

(ii) By providing written notification to, or participating in discussions with, other contractors and subcontractors with whom the contractor does business.

(5) The contractor must direct its recruitment efforts to minority and female organizations, to schools with minority and female students, and to organizations which recruit and train minorities and women, in the contractor's recruitment area.

(6) The contractor must encourage present minority and female employees to recruit other minorities and women.

(7) The contractor must, where possible, provide after school, summer, and vacation employment to minority and female youth.

(d) Each sponsor shall require each of its prime construction contractors on its airport, with a contract of $10 000 or more, to require each of the contractor's subcontractors on the airport to comply with the affirmative action steps in paragraph (c) of this section, with which it does not already comply, unless the subcontractor is subject to an affirmative action plan, regulatory goals or timetables, or other mechanism which provides short and long-range goals for equal employment opportunity, or the subcontract is less than $10,000.

§ 152.413 Notice requirement.

Each grantee shall give adequate notice to employees and applicants for employment, through posters provided by the Secretary, that the FAA is committed to the requirements of section 30 of the AADA, to ensure that no person shall, on the grounds of race, creed, color, national origin, or sex, be excluded from participating in any activity conducted with funds authorized under this part.

§ 152.415 Records and reports.

(a) Each grantee shall keep on file for a period of three years or for the period during which the Federal financial assistance is made available, whichever is longer, reports (other than those transmitted to the FAA), records, and affirmative action plans, if applicable, that will enable the FAA Office of Civil Rights to ascertain if there has been and is compliance with this subpart.

(b) Each sponsor shall require its covered organizations to keep on file, for the period set forth in paragraph (a) of this section, reports (other than those submitted to the FAA), records, and affirmative action plans, if applicable, that will enable the FAA Office of Civil Rights to ascertain if there has been and is compliance with this subpart, and shall cause them to require their covered suborganizations to keep similar records as applicable.

(c) Each grantee, employing 15 or more person, shall annually submit to the FAA a compliance report on a form provided by the FAA and a statistical report on a Form EEO–1 of the Equal Employment Opportunity Commission (EEOC) or any superseding EEOC form. If a grantee already is submitting a Form EEO–1 to another agency, the grantee may submit a copy of that form to the FAA as its statistical report. The information provided shall include goals and timetables, if established in compliance with the requirements of § 152.409 or with the requirements of another Federal agency or a State or local agency.

(d) Each sponsor shall—

(1) Require each of its aviation-related activities (except construction contractors), employing 15 or more persons, to annually submit to the sponsor the reports required by paragraph (c) of this section, on the same basis as stated in paragraph (c) of this section, and shall cause each aviation-related activity to require its covered suborganizations, with 15 or more employees, to annually submit the reports required by paragraph (c) of this section through the prime organization to the sponsor, for transmittal by the sponsor to the FAA.

(2) Annually collect from its aviation related activities employing less than 15 employees, and transmit to the FAA an aggregate employment report, that includes the employment of sponsors with less than 15 employees, on an EEO–1 or any superseding EEOC form.

(e) Each sponsor shall require each of its construction contractors on its airport, with a contract of $10,000 or more, which is not subject to E.O. 11246 and the regulations of the Department of Labor (DOL), to submit to the sponsor, at the conclusion of the project, a compliance report on a form provided by the FAA and a statistical report on a DOL Form 257 or any superseding DOL form. For projects exceeding six months, the sponsor shall require a midway compliance report. The sponsor shall submit these reports to the FAA.

(f) Each sponsor shall cause each of its construction contractors on its airport to require each of the contractor's subcontractors, with a subcontract of $10,000 or more, which are not subject to E.O. 11246 and the regulations of the DOL, to submit the reports required by paragraph (e) of this section to the prime contractor for submission to the sponsor. The sponsor shall transmit these reports to the FAA.

(g) Each organization required to prepare an affirmative action plan for the FAA under this subpart shall update it annually and as changed circumstances require. Each organization that has prepared a plan in compliance with the requirements of another Federal agency or a State or local agency, shall update it in accordance with the requirements of that agency.

§ 152.417　Monitoring employment.

(a) Each grantee shall allow the FAA Office of Civil Rights to monitor its equal employment opportunity compliance with this subpart through on-site reviews and desk audits. Reviews or audits will include the records submitted under § 152.415.

(b) As it deems necessary, the FAA Office of Civil Rights will conduct on-site or desk audits of covered aviation related activities on airports.

§ 152.419　Minority business.

Each person subject to this subpart is required to comply with the Minority Business Enterprise Regulations of the Department.

§ 152.421　Public accommodations, services, and benefits.

Requirements relating to the provision of public accommodations, services, and other benefits to beneficiaries under Title VI of the Civil Rights Act of 1964 (42 U.S.C. 2000d *et seq.*) and part 21 of the regulations of the Office of the Secretary of Transportation (49 CFR part 21) implementing Title VI are made applicable, where appropriate, to nondiscrimination and affirmative action on the basis of sex or creed, and shall be complied with by each applicant for assistance and each grantee.

§ 152.423　Investigation and enforcement.

(a) *Complaints.* Any person who believes that he or she has been subjected to discrimination prohibited by this subpart may personally, or through a representative, file a complaint with the Director of the Departmental Office of Civil Rights. A complaint must be in writing and filed not later than 180 days after the date of the alleged discrimination, unless the time for filing is extended by the Director.

(b) *Investigations and informal resolutions.* The Departmental Office of Civil Rights will make a prompt investigation whenever a complaint, compliance review, report, or any other information indicates a possible failure to comply with this subpart. The procedures in 49 CFR part 21, augmented as appropriate by the investigative procedures of part 13 of this chapter, will be followed, except that—

(1) Compliance with a regulation of the Department applicable to minority business enterprise will be investigated and enforced through the procedures contained in that regulation; and

(2) Except as provided in paragraph (c) of this section, allegations of noncompliance with regulations governing equal employment opportunity of another Federal agency or a State or local agency, will be referred, for investigation and enforcement, to the Federal agency or, in the discretion of the Departmental Office of Civil Rights, to the State or local agency.

(c) When the FAA (under section 30 of the AADA) and another Federal agency, a referral agency recognized by the Equal Employment Opportunity Commission, or a court have concurrent jurisdiction over a matter—

(1) If the other agency or court makes a finding on the record that noncompliance or discrimination has occurred, the FAA will accept the finding, and determine what sanctions or remedies are appropriate under section 30 as a result of the finding, after permitting the party against whom the finding was made to be heard on the determination of the sanctions or remedies; or

(2) If it appears that delay, through referral to another agency, will result in the continued expenditure of Federal funds under this part without compliance with this subpart, the Secretary may—

(i) Investigate the matter;

(ii) Make a determination as to compliance with section 30; and

(iii) Impose appropriate sanctions and remedies.

(d) Nothing in this section shall preclude the Director of the Departmental Office of Civil Rights from initiating an investigation when it appears that the investigation of the complaint may reveal a pattern or practice of discrimination or noncompliance with the requirements of this subpart in the employment practices of a grantee or other covered organization.

§ 152.425 Effect of subpart.

Nothing contained in this subpart diminishes or supersedes the obligations imposed by Title VI of the Civil Rights Act of 1964 (42 U.S.C. 2000d), Executive Order 11246 (42 U.S.C. 2000e (note)), or any other Federal law or Executive Order relating to civil rights.

Subpart F—Suspension and Termination of Grants

Source: Docket No. 19430, 45 FR 34792, May 22, 1980, unless otherwise noted.

§ 152.501 Applicability.

This subpart contains procedures for suspending or terminating grants for airport development projects and airport planning.

§ 152.503 Suspension of grant.

(a) If the sponsor or planning agency fails to comply with the conditions of the grant, the FAA may, by written notice to the sponsor or planning agency, suspend the grant and withhold further payments pending—

(1) Corrective action by the sponsor or planning agency; or

(2) A decision to terminate the grant.

(b) Except as provided in paragraph (c), after receipt of notice of suspension, the sponsor or planning agency may not incur additional obligations of grant funds during the suspension.

(c) All necessary and proper costs that the sponsor or planning agency could not reasonably avoid during the period of suspension will be allowed, if those costs are in accordance with appendix C of this part.

§ 152.505 Termination for cause.

(a) If the sponsor or planning agency fails to comply with the conditions of the grant, the FAA may, by written notice to the sponsor or planning agency, terminate the grant in whole, or in part.

(b) The notice of termination will contain—

(1) The reasons for the termination, and

(2) The effective date of termination.

(c) After receipt of the notice of termination, the sponsor or planning agency may not incur additional obligations of grant funds.

(d) Payments to be made to the sponsor or planning agency, or recoveries of payments by the FAA, under the grant shall be in accordance with the legal rights and liabilities of the parties.

§ 152.507 Termination for convenience.

(a) When the continuation of the project would not produce beneficial results commensurate with the further expenditure of funds, the grant may be terminated in whole, or in part, upon mutual agreement of the FAA and the sponsor or planning agency.

(b) If an agreement to terminate is made, the sponsor or planning agency—

(1) May not incur new obligations for the terminated portion after the effective date; and

(2) Shall cancel as many obligations, relating to the terminated portion, as possible.

(c) The sponsor or planning agency is allowed full credit for the Federal share of the noncancellable obligations that were properly incurred by the sponsor before the termination.

§ 152.509 Request for reconsideration.

If a grant is suspended or terminated under this subpart, the sponsor or planning agency may request the Administrator to reconsider the suspension or termination.

Subpart G—Energy Conservation in Airport Aid Program

AUTHORITY: Secs. 1–27, 84 Stat. 220–223 (49 U.S.C. 1711–1727); sec. 1.47(g), Regulations of the Office of the Secretary of Transportation; 35 FR 17044; sec. 403(b), 92 Stat. 3318; E.O. 12185.

SOURCE: Docket No. 66, 45 FR 58035, Aug. 29, 1980, unless otherwise noted.

§ 152.601 Purpose.

This subpart implements section 403 of the Powerplant and Industrial Fuel Use Act of 1978 (92 Stat. 3318; Pub. L. 95–620) in order to encourage conservation of petroleum and natural gas by recipients of Federal financial assistance.

§ 152.603 Applicability.

This subpart applies to each recipient of Federal financial assistance from the Federal Aviation Administration through the Airport Development Aid Program (ADAP) unless otherwise excluded by definition.

§ 152.605 Definitions.

As used in this subpart—

Building construction means construction of any building which receives Federal assistance under the program, which will exceed $200,000 in construction cost.

Energy assessment means an analysis of total energy requirements of a building, which, within the scope of the proposed construction activity, and at a level of detail appropriate to that scope, considers the following:

(a) Overall design of the facility or modification, and alternative designs;

(b) Materials and techniques used in construction or rehabilitation;

(c) Special or innovative conservation features that may be used;

(d) Fuel requirements for heating, cooling, and operations essential to the function of the structure, projected over the life of the facility and including projected costs of this fuel; and

(e) Kind of energy to be used, including—

(1) Consideration of opportunities for using fuels other than petroleum and natural gas, and

(2) Consideration of using alternative, renewable energy sources.

Major building modification means modification of any building which receives Federal assistance under the program, which will exceed $200,000 in construction cost.

§ 152.607 Building design requirements.

Each sponsor shall perform an energy assessment for each federally-assisted building construction or major building modification project proposed at the airport. The building design, construction, and operation shall incorporate, to the extent consistent with good engineering practice, the most cost-effective energy conservation features identified in the energy assessment.

§ 152.609 Energy conservation practices.

Each sponsor shall require fuel and energy conservation practices in the operation and maintenance of the airport and shall encourage airport tenants to use these practices.

This appendix sets forth contract and labor provisions applicable to grants under the Airport and Airway Development Act of 1970.

This appendix does not apply to: (1) Any contract with the owner of airport hazards, buildings, pipelines, powerlines, or other structures or facilities, for installing, extending, changing, removing, or relocating that structure or facility, and (2) any written agreement or understanding between a sponsor and another public agency that is not a sponsor of the project, under which the public agency undertakes construction work for or as agent of the sponsor.

I. Contract Provisions Required by the Regulations of the Secretary of Labor

Each sponsor entering into a construction contract for an airport development project shall insert in the contract and any supplemental agreement:

(1) The provisions required by the Secretary of Labor, as set forth in paragraphs A through K;

(2) The provisions set forth in paragraph L, and

(3) Any other provisions necessary to ensure completion of the work in accordance with the grant agreement.

The provisions in paragraphs A through K and provision (5) in paragraph L need not be included in prime contracts of $2,000 or less.

A. Minimum wages. (1) All mechanics and laborers employed or working upon the site of the work will be paid unconditionally and not less often than once a week, and without subsequent deduction or rebate on any account (except such payroll deductions as are permitted by regulations issued by the Secretary of Labor under the Copeland Act [29 CFR part 3], the full amounts due at time of payment computed at wage rates not less than those contained in the wage determination decision(s) of the Secretary of Labor which is (are) attached hereto and made a part hereof, regardless of any contractual relationship which may be alleged to exist between the contractor and such laborers and mechanics; and the wage determination decision(s) shall be posted by the contractor at the site of the work in a prominent place where it (they) can be easily seen by the workers. For the purpose of this paragraph, contributions made or costs reasonably anticipated under section 1(b)(2) of the Davis-Bacon Act on behalf of laborers or mechanics are considered wages paid to such laborers or mechanics, subject to the provisions of paragraph (4) below. Also for the purpose of this paragraph, regular contributions made or costs incurred for more than a weekly period

under plans, funds, or programs, but covering the particular weekly period, are deemed to be constructively made or incurred during such weekly period (29 CFR 5.5(a)(1)(i)).

(2) Any class of laborers or mechanics, including apprentices and trainees, which is not listed in the wage determination(s) and which is to be employed under the contract, shall be classified or reclassified conformably to the wage determination(s), and a report of the action taken shall be sent by the [insert sponsor's name] to the FAA for approval and transmittal to the Secretary of Labor. In the event that the interested parties cannot agree on the proper classification or reclassification of a particular class of laborers and mechanics, including apprentices and trainees, to be used, the question accompanied by the recommendation of the FAA shall be referred to the Secretary of Labor for final determination (29 CFR 5.5(a)(1)(ii)).

(3) Whenever the minimum wage rate prescribed in the contract for a class of laborers or mechanics includes a fringe benefit which is not expressed as an hourly wage rate and the contractor is obligated to pay a cash equivalent of such a fringe benefit, an hourly cash equivalent thereof shall be established. In the event the interested parties cannot agree upon a cash equivalent of the fringe benefit, the question accompanied by the recommendation of the FAA shall be referred to the Secretary of Labor for determination (29 CFR 5.5(a)(1)(iii)).

(4) If the contractor does not make payments to a trustee or other third person, he may consider as part of the wages of any laborer or mechanic the amount of any costs reasonably anticipated in providing benefits under a plan or program of a type expressly listed in the wage determination decision of the Secretary of Labor which is a part of this contract: *Provided, however,* the Secretary of Labor has found, upon written request of the contractor, that the applicable standards of the Davis-Bacon Act have been met. The Secretary of Labor may require the contractor to set aside in a separate account assets for the meeting of obligations under the plan or program (29 CFR 5.5(a)(1)(iv)).

B. Withholding: FAA from sponsor. Pursuant to the terms of the grant agreement between the United States and [insert sponsor's name], relating to Airport Development Aid Project No. __, and part 152 of the Federal Aviation Regulations (14 CFR part 152), the FAA may withhold or cause to be withheld from the [insert sponsor's name] so much of the accrued payments or advances as may be considered necessary to pay laborers and mechanics, including apprentices and trainees, employed by the contractor or any subcontractor on the work the full amount of wages required by this contract. In the event of failure to pay any laborer or mechanics, including any apprentice or trainee, employed or working on the site of the work all or part of the wages required by this contract, the FAA may, after written notice to the [insert sponsor's name], take such action as may be necessary to cause the suspension of any further payment or advance of funds until such violations have ceased (29 CFR 5.5(a)(2)).

C. Payrolls and basic records. (1) Payrolls and basic records relating thereto will be maintained during the course of the work and preserved for a period of 3 years thereafter for all laborers and mechanics working at the site of the work. Such records will contain the name and address of each such employee, his correct classification, rates of pay (including rates of contributions or costs anticipated of the types described in section 1(b)(2) of the Davis-Bacon Act), daily and weekly number of hours worked, deductions made and actual wages paid. Whenever the Secretary of Labor has found, under 29 CFR 5.5(a)(1)(iv) (see paragraph (4) of paragraph A above), that the wages of any laborer or mechanic include the amount of any costs reasonably anticipated in providing benefits under a plan or program described in section 1(b)(2)(B) of the Davis-Bacon Act, the contractor shall maintain records which show that the commitment to provide such benefits is enforceable, that the plan or program is financially responsible, and that the plan or program has been communicated in writing to the laborers or mechanics affected, and records which show the costs anticipated or the actual costs incurred in providing such benefits (29 CFR 5.5(a)(3)(i)).

(2) The contractor will submit weekly a copy of all payrolls to the [insert sponsor's name] for availability to the FAA. The copy shall be accompanied by a statement signed by the employer or his agent indicating that the payrolls are correct and complete, that the wage rates contained therein are not less than those determined by the Secretary of Labor and that the classifications set forth for each laborer or mechanic conform with the work he performed. A submission of a "Weekly Statement of Compliance" which is required under this contract and the Copeland regulations of the Secretary of Labor (29 CFR part 3) and the filing with the initial payroll or any subsequent payroll of a copy of any findings by the Secretary of Labor under 29 CFR 5.5(a)(1)(iv) (see paragraph (4) of paragraph A above), shall satisfy this requirement. The prime contractor shall be responsible for submission of copies of payrolls of all subcontractors. The contractor will make the records required under the labor standards clauses of the contract available for inspection by authorized representatives of the FAA and the Department of Labor, and will permit such representatives to interview employees during working hours on the job. Contractors employing apprentices or trainees under approved programs shall include a notation on the first

weekly certified payrolls submitted to the [insert sponsor's name] for availability to the FAA, that their employment is pursuant to an approved program and shall identify the program (29 CFR 5.5(a)(3)(ii)).

D. Apprentices and trainees—(1) *Apprentices.* Apprentices will be permitted to work at less than the predetermined rate for the work they performed when they are employed and individually registered in a bona fide apprenticeship program registered with the U.S. Department of Labor, Employment and Training Administration, Bureau of Apprenticeship and Training, or with a State Apprenticeship Agency recognized by the Bureau, or if a person is employed in his first 90 days of probationary employment as an apprentice in such an apprenticeship program, who is not individually registered in the program, but who has been certified by the Bureau of Apprenticeship and Training or a State Apprenticeship Agency (where appropriate) to be eligible for probationary employment as an apprentice. The allowable ratio of apprentices to journeymen in any craft classification shall not be greater than the ratio permitted to the contractor as to his entire work force under the registered program. Any employee listed on a payroll at an apprentice wage rate, who is not a trainee as defined in paragraph (2) of this paragraph or is not registered or otherwise employed as stated above, shall be paid the wage rate determined by the Secretary of Labor for the classification of work he actually performed. The contractor or subcontractor will be required to furnish to the [insert sponsor's name] or a representative of the Wage-Hour Division of the U.S. Department of Labor written evidence of the registration of his program and apprentices as well as the appropriate ratios and wage rates (expressed in percentages of the journeyman hourly rates), for the area of construction prior to using any apprentices on the contract work. The wage rate paid apprentices shall be not less than the appropriate percentage of the journeyman's rate contained in the applicable wage determination (29 CFR 5.5(a)(4)(i)).

(2) *Trainees.* Except as provided in 29 CFR 5.15 trainees will not be permitted to work at less than the predetermined rate for the work performed unless they are employed pursuant to and individually registered in a program which has received prior approval, evidenced by formal certification by the U.S. Department of Labor, Employment and Training Administration. Bureau of Apprenticeship and Training. The ratio of trainees to journeymen shall not be greater than permitted under the plan approved by the Bureau of Apprenticeship and Training. Every trainee must be paid at not less than the rate specified in the approved program for his level of progress. Any employee listed on

the payroll at a trainee rate who is not registered and participating in a training plan approved by the Bureau of Apprenticeship and Training shall be paid not less than the wage rate determined by the Secretary of Labor for the classification of work he actually performed. The contractor or subcontractor will be required to furnish the [insert sponsor's name] or a representative of the Wage-Hour Division of the U.S. Department of Labor written evidence of the certification of his program, the registration of the trainees, and the ratios and wage rates prescribed in that program. In the event the Bureau of Apprenticeship and Training withdraws approval of a training program, the contractor will no longer be permitted to utilize trainees at less than the applicable predetermined rate for the work performed until an acceptable program is approved (29 CFR 5.5(a)(4)(ii)).

(3) *Equal employment opportunity.* The utilization of apprentices, trainees and journeymen under this paragraph shall be in conformity with the equal employment opportunity requirements of Executive Order 11246, as amended, and 29 CFR part 30 (29 CFR 5.5(a)(4)(iii)).

(4) *Application of 29 CFR 5.5(a)(4).* On contracts in excess of $2,000 the employment of all apprentices and trainees as defined in 29 CFR 5.2(c) shall be subject to the provisions of 29 CFR 5.5(a)(4) (see paragraph D(1), (2), and (3) above).

E. Compliance with Copeland Regulations. The contractor shall comply with the Copeland Regulations (29 CFR part 3) of the Secretary of Labor which are herein incorporated by reference (29 CFR 5.5(a)(5)).

F. Overtime requirements. No contractor or subcontractor contracting for any part of the contract work which may require or involve the employment of laborers or mechanics shall require or permit any laborer or mechanic in any workweek in which he is employed on such work to work in excess of 8 hours in any calendar day or in excess of 40 hours in such workweek unless such laborer or mechanic received compensation at a rate not less than 1½ times his basic rate of pay for all hours worked in excess of 8 hours in any calendar day or in excess of 40 hours in such workweek, as the case may be (29 CFR 5.5(c)(1)).

G. Violations; liability for unpaid wages; liquidated damages. In the event of any violation of paragraph F of this provision, the contractor and any subcontractor responsible therefor shall be liable to any affected employee for his unpaid wages. In addition, such contractor and subcontractor shall be liable to the United States for liquidated damages. Such liquidated damages shall be computed, with respect to each individual laborer or mechanic employed in violation of said paragraph F of this provision, in the sum of $10 for each calendar day on which

such employee was required or permitted to work in excess of 8 hours or in excess of the standard workweek of 40 hours without payment of the overtime wages required by said paragraph F of this provision (29 CFR 5.5(c)(2)).

H. Withholding for unpaid wages and liquidated damages. The FAA may withhold or cause to be withheld, from any monies payable on account of work performed by the contractor or subcontractor, such sums as may administratively be determined to be necessary to satisfy any liabilities of such contractor or subcontractor for unpaid wages and liquidated damages as provided in paragraph G of this provision (29 CFR 5.5(c)(3)).

I. Working conditions. No contractor may require any laborer or mechanic employed in the performance of any contract to work in surroundings or under working conditions that are unsanitary, hazardous, or dangerous to his health or safety as determined under construction safety and health standards (29 CFR part 1926) and other occupational and health standards (29 CFR part 1910) issued by the Department of Labor.

J. Subcontracts. The contractor will insert in each of his subcontracts the clauses contained in paragraphs A through K of this provision, and also a clause requiring the subcontractors to include these provisions in any lower tier subcontracts which they may enter into, together with a clause requiring this insertion in any further subcontracts that may in turn be made (29 CFR 5.5(a)(6), 5.5(c)(4)).

K. Contract termination debarment. A breach of clause A, B, C, D, E, or J may be grounds for termination of the contract, and for debarment as provided in §5.6 of the Regulations of the Secretary of Labor as codified in 29 CFR 5.6 (29 CFR 5.5(a)(7)).

L. Additional contract provisions—(1) *Airport Development Aid Program Project.* The work in this contract is included in Airport Development Aid Program Project No. __, which is being undertaken and accomplished by the [insert sponsor's name] in accordance with the terms and conditions of a grant agreement between the [insert sponsor's name] and the United States, under the Airport and Airway Development Act of 1970 (84 Stat. 219) and part 152 of the Federal Aviation Regulations (14 CFR part 152), pursuant to which the United States has agreed to pay a certain percentage of the costs of the project that are determined to be allowable project costs under that Act. The United States is not a party to this contract and no reference in this contract to the FAA or any representative thereof, or to any rights granted to the FAA or any representative thereof, or the United States, by the contract, makes United States a party to this contract.

(2) *Consent to assignment.* The contractor shall obtain the prior written consent of the

[insert sponsor's name] to any proposed assignment of any interest in or part of this contract.

(3) *Convict labor.* No convict labor may be employed under this contract.

(4) *Veterans preference.* In the employment of labor (except in executive, administrative, and supervisory positions), preference shall be given to qualified individuals who have served in the military service of the United States (as defined in section 101(1) of the Soldiers' and Sailors' Civil Relief Act of 1940 (50 U.S.C. App. 501) and have been honorably discharged from the service, except that preference may be given only where that labor is available locally and is qualified to perform the work to which the employment relates.

(5) *Withholding: sponsor from contractor.* Whether or not payments or advances to the [insert sponsor's name] are withheld or suspended by the FAA, the [insert sponsor's name] may withhold or cause to be withheld from the contractor so much of the accrued payments or advances as may be considered necessary to pay laborers and mechanics employed by the contractor or any subcontractor on the work the full amount of wages required by this contract.

(6) *Nonpayment of wages.* If the contractor or subcontractor fails to pay any laborer or mechanic employed or working on the site of the work any of the wages required by this contract the [insert sponsor's name] may, after written notice to the contractor, take such action as may be necessary to cause the suspension of any further payment or advance of funds until the violations cease.

(7) *FAA inspection and review.* The contractor shall allow any authorized representative of the FAA to inspect and review any work or materials used in the performance of this contract.

(8) *Subcontracts.* The contractor shall insert in each of his subcontracts the provisions contained in paragraphs [insert designation of 6 paragraphs of contract corresponding to paragraphs (1), (3), (4), (5), (6), and (7) of this paragraph], and also a clause requiring the subcontractors to include these provisions in any lower tier subcontracts which they may enter into, together with a clause requiring this insertion in any further subcontracts that may in turn be made.

(9) *Contract termination.* A breach of paragraphs [insert designation of 3 paragraphs corresponding to paragraphs (6), (7), and (8) of this paragraph] may be grounds for termination of the contract.

II. Adjustment in Liquidated Damages

A contractor or subcontractor who has become liable for liquidated damages under the provision set out in paragraph I.G of this appendix and who claims that the amount administratively determined as liquidated damages under section 104(a) of the Contract Work Hours and Safety Standards Act is in-

correct or that he violated inadvertently the Contract Work Hours and Safety Standards Act, notwithstanding the exercise of due care, may—

(1) If the amount determined is more than $100, apply to the Administrator for a recommendation to the Secretary of Labor that an appropriate adjustment be made or that he be relieved of liability for the liquidated damages; or

(2) If the amount determined is $100 or less, apply to the Administrator for an appropriate adjustment in liquidated damages or for release from liability for the liquidated damages.

III. Corrected Wage Determinations

The Secretary of Labor corrects any wage determination included in any contract under this appendix whenever the wage determination contains clerical errors. A correction may be made at the Administrator's request or on the initiative of the Secretary of Labor.

IV. Applicability of Interpretations of the Secretary of Labor

When applicable by their terms, the regulations of the Secretary of Labor (29 CFR 5.20–5.32) interpreting the "fringe benefit provisions" of the Davis-Bacon Act apply to the contract provisions in this appendix.

V. Records

A sponsor who is required to include in a construction contract the labor provisions required by this appendix shall require the contractor to comply with those provisions and shall cooperate with the FAA in effecting that compliance. For this purpose the sponsor shall—

(1) Keep, and preserve, the record described in paragraph IC for a 3-year period beginning on the date the contract is completed, each affidavit and payroll copy furnished by the contractor, and make those affidavits and copies available to the FAA, upon request, during that period;

(2) Have each of those affidavits and payrolls examined by its resident engineer (or any other of its employees or agents who is qualified to make the necessary determinations), as soon as possible after receiving it, to the extent necessary to determine whether the contractor is complying with the labor provisions required by this appendix and particularly with respect to whether the contractor's employees are correctly classified;

(3) Have investigations made during the performance of work under the contract, to the extent necessary to determine whether the contractor is complying with those labor provisions, including in the investigations, interviews with employees and examinations of payroll information at the work site by

the sponsor's resident engineer (or any other of its employees or agents who is qualified to make the necessary determinations);

(4) Keep the appropriate FAA office fully advised of all examinations and investigations made under this appendix, all determinations made on the basis of those examinations and investigations, and all efforts made to obtain compliance with the labor provisions of the contract; and

(5) Give priority to complaints of alleged violations, and treat as confidential any written or oral statements made by any employee in connection with a complaint, and not disclose an employee's statement made in connection with a complaint to a contractor without the employee's consent.

[Doc. No. 19430, 45 FR 34793, May 22, 1980]

APPENDIX B TO PART 152—LIST OF ADVISORY CIRCULARS INCORPORATED BY § 152.11

(a) *Circulars available free of charge.*

Number and Subject

150/5100–12—Electronic Navigational Aids Approved for Funding Under the Airport Development Aid Program (ADAP).

150/5190–3A—Model Airport Hazard Zoning Ordinance.

150/5210–7A—Aircraft Fire and Rescue Communications.

150/5210–10—Airport Fire and Rescue Equipment Building Guide.

150/5300–2C—Airport Design Standards—Site Requirements for Terminal Navigational Facilities.

150/5300–4B—Utility Airports—Air Access to National Transportation.

150/5300–6—Airport Design Standards—General Aviation Airports—Basic and General Transport.

150/5300–8—Planning and Design Criteria for Metropolitan STOL Ports.

150/5320–6B—Airport Pavement Design and Evaluation.

150/5320–10—Environmental Enhancement at Airports—Industrial Waste Treatment.

150/5320–12—Methods for the Design, Construction, and Maintenance of Skid Resistant Airport Pavement Surfaces.

150/5325–2C—Airport Design Standards—Airports Served by Air Carriers—Surface Gradient and Line-of-Sight.

150/5325–4—Runway Length Requirements for Airport Design.

150/5325–6A—Airport Design Standards—Effect and Treatment of Jet Blast.

150/5325–8—Compass Calibration Pad.

150/5335–1A—Airport Design Standards—Airports Served by Air Carriers—Taxiways.

150/5335–2—Airport Aprons.

150/5335–3—Airport Design Standards—Airports Served by Air Carriers—Bridges and Tunnels on Airports.

150/5335–4—Airport Design Standards—Airports Served by Air Carriers—Runway Geometrics.

150/5340–1D—Marking of Paved Areas on Airports.

150/5340–4C—Installation Details for Runway Centerline and Touchdown Zone Lighting Systems.

150/5340–5A—Segmented Circle Airport Marker System.

150/5340–8—Airport 51-foot Tubular Beacon Tower.

150/5340–14B—Economy Approach Lighting Aids.

150/5340–17A—Standby Power for Non-FAA Airport Lighting System.

150/5340–18—Taxiway Guidance Sign System.

150/5340–19—Taxiway Centerline Lighting System.

150/5340–20—Installation Details and Maintenance Standards for Reflective Markers for Airport Runway and Taxiway Centerlines.

150/5340–21—Airport Miscellaneous Lighting Visual Aids.

AC/5340–22—Maintenance Guide for Determining Degradation and Cleaning of Centerline and Touchdown Zone Lights.

150/5340–23A—Supplemental Wind Cones.

150/5340–24—Runway and Taxiway Edge Lighting System.

150/5340–25—Visual Approach Slope Indicator (VASI) Systems.

150/5345–1E—Approved Airport Lighting Equipment.

150/5345–2—Specification for L–810 Obstruction Light.

150/5345–3C—Specification for L–821 Panels for Remote Control of Airport Lighting.

150/5345–4—Specification for L–829 Internally Lighted Airport Taxi Guidance Sign.

150/5345–5—Specification for L–847 Circuit Selector Switch, 5,000 Volt 20 Ampere.

150/5345–7C—Specification for L–824 Underground Electrical Cable for Airport Lighting Circuits.

150/5345–10C—Specification for L–828 Constant Current Regulators.

150/5345–11—Specification for L–812 Static Indoor Type Constant Current Regulator Assembly; 4 KW and 7½ KW, With Brightness Control for Remote Operation.

150/5345–12A—Specification for L–801 Beacon.

150/5345–13—Specification for L–841 Auxiliary Relay Cabinet Assembly for Pilot Control of Airport Lighting Circuits.

150/5345–18—Specification for L–811 Static Indoor Type Constant Current Regulator Assembly, 4 KW; With Brightness Control and Runway Selection for Direct Operation.

150/5345–21—Specification for L–813 Static Indoor Type Constant Current Regulator Assembly; 4 KW and 7½ KW; for Remote Operation of Taxiway Lights.

150/5345–26A—Specification for L–823 Plug and Receptacle. Cable Connectors.

150/5345–27A—Specification for L–807 Eight-foot and Twelve-foot Unlighted or Externally Lighted Wind Cone Assemblies.

150/5345–28C—Specification for L–851 Visual Approach Slope Indicators and Accessories.

150/5345–36—Specification for L–808 Lighted Wind Tee.

150/5345–39A—FAA Specification for L–853, Runway and Taxiway Retroreflective Markers.

150/5345–42A—FAA Specification L–857, Airport Light Bases, Transformer Housings, and Junction Boxes.

150/5345–43B—FAA/DOD Specification L–856, High Intensity Obstruction Lighting Systems.

150/5345–44A—Specification for L–858 Retroreflective Taxiway Guidance Sign.

150/5345–45—Lightweight Approach Light Structure.

150/5345–46—Specification for Semiflush Airport Lights.

150/5345–47—Isolation Transformers for Airport Lighting Systems.

150/5345–48—Specification for Runway and Taxiway Edge Lights.

150/5360–6—Airport Terminal Building Development with Federal Participation.

150/5360–7—Planning and Design Considerations for Airport Terminal Building Development.

150/5370–7—Airport Construction Controls to Prevent Air and Water Pollution.

150/5370–9—Slip-Form Paving—Portland Cement Concrete.

150/5370–11—Use of Nondestructive Testing Devices in the Evaluation of Airport Pavements.

(b) *Circulars for sale.*

Number and Subject

150/5320–5B—Airport Drainage; $1.30.

150/5370–10—Standards for Specifying Construction of Airports; $7.25.

150/5390–1A—Heliport Design Guide; $1.50.

[Doc. No. 19430, 45 FR 34795, May 22, 1980]

APPENDIX C TO PART 152—PROCUREMENT PROCEDURES AND REQUIREMENTS

There is set forth below procurement procedures and requirements applicable to grants for airport development under the Airport and Airway Development Act of 1970.

1. *General.* Each contract under a project must meet the requirements of local law and the requirements and standards contained in this appendix. The sponsor shall establish procedures for procurement of supplies, equipment, construction, and services funded under the project which meet the requirements of Attachment O of Office of Management and Budget (OMB) Circular A–102 (44 FR 47874) and of this appendix. Subject to funding and time limitations, the FAA reviews the sponsor's procurement system to

determine whether it may be certified in accordance with Attachment O of OMB Circular A–102.

2. *Out-of-state labor.* No procedure or requirement shall be imposed by any grantee which will operate to discriminate against the employment of labor from any other State, possession, or territory of the United States in the construction of a project.

3. *Bid guarantee.* All bids for construction or facility improvement in excess of $100,000 shall be accompanied by a bid guarantee consisting of a firm commitment such as a bid bond, certified check or other negotiable instrument equivalent to five percent of the bid price as assurance that the bidder will, upon acceptance of his bid, execute such contractual documents as may be required within the time specified.

4. *Construction work.* All construction work under a project must be performed under contract, except in a case where the Administrator determines that the project, or a part of it, can be more effectively and economically accomplished on a force account basis by the sponsor or by another public agency acting for or as agent of the sponsor.

5. *Change order.* Unless otherwise authorized by the Administrator, no sponsor may issue any change order under any of its construction contracts or enter into a supplemental agreement unless three copies of that order or agreement have been sent to, and approved by, the FAA.

6. *Beginning work.* No sponsor may allow a contractor or subcontractor to begin work under a project until—

a. The sponsor has furnished three conformed copies of the contract to the appropriate FAA office;

b. The sponsor has, if applicable, submitted a statement that comparable replacement housing, as defined in § 25.15 of the Regulations of the Office of the Secretary of Transportation, will be available within a reasonable period of time before displacement.

c. The appropriate FAA office has agreed to the issuance of a notice to proceed with the work to the contractor.

7. *Supervision and inspection.* No work will be commenced until the sponsor has provided for adequate supervision and inspection of construction and advised the appropriate FAA office.

8. *Engineering and planning services.* Unless otherwise authorized by the Administrator, each proposal for engineering and planning services shall be reviewed by FAA before the commencement of the development of design plans and specifications.

9. *Advertising general.* Unless the Administrator approves another method for use on a particular airport development project, each contract and supplemental agreement for construction work on a project in the amount of more than $10,000 must be awarded on the basis of public advertising and

open competitive bidding under the local law applicable to the letting of public contracts.

10. *Advertising: conditions and contents.* There may be no advertisement for bids on, or negotiation of, a construction contract or supplemental agreement until the Administrator has either approved the plans and specifications or accepted a certification in accordance with § 152.7 that they meet all applicable standards prescribed by this part. The advertisement shall inform the bidders of the equal employment opportunity requirements of part 152. Unless the estimated contract price or construction cost is $2,000 or less, there may be no advertisement for bids or negotiations until the Administrator has given the sponsor a copy of a decision of the Secretary of Labor establishing the minimum wage rates for skilled and unskilled labor under the proposed contract. In each case, a copy of the wage determination decision, including fringe benefits, must be set forth in the initial invitation for bids or proposed contract, or incorporated therein by reference to a copy set forth in the advertised or negotiated specifications.

11. *Procedures for obtaining wage determinations.* (a) *Specific request for wage determination.* At least 60 days before the intended date of advertising or negotiating of this section, the sponsor shall send to the appropriate FAA office, completed Department of Labor Form DB–11 or DB–11(a), as appropriate, with only the classifications needed in the performance of the work checked. General entries (such as "entire schedule" or "all applicable classifications") may not be used. Additional necessary classifications not on the form may be typed in the blank spaces or on an attached separate list. A classification that can be fitted into classifications on the form, or a classification that is not generally recognized in the area or in the industry, may not be used. Except in areas where the wage patterns are clearly established, the Form must be accompanied by any available pertinent wage payment or locally prevailing fringe benefit information.

(b) *General wage determination.* Whenever the wage patterns in a particular area for a particular type of construction are well settled and whenever it may be reasonably anticipated that there will be a large volume of procurement in that area for that type of construction, the Secretary of Labor, upon the request of a Federal agency or in his discretion, may issue a general wage determination when, after consideration of the facts and circumstances involved, he finds that the applicable statutory standards and those of part 1, 29 CFR, subtitle A, will be met. This general wage determination is used for all projects located in the area and for the type of construction covered by the general wage determination.

12. *Advertising: wage determinations.* (a) Wage determinations are effective only for

120 days from the date of the determinations. If it appears that a determination may expire between bid opening and award, the sponsor shall so advise the FAA as soon as possible. If it wishes a new request for wage determination to be made and if any pertinent circumstances have changed, it shall submit the appropriate form of the Department of Labor and accompanying information. If it claims that the determination expires before award and after bid opening due to unavoidable circumstances, it shall submit proof of the facts which it claims support a finding to that effect.

(b) The Secretary of Labor may modify any wage determination before the award of the contract or contracts for which it was sought. If the proposed contract is awarded on the basis of public advertisement and open competitive bidding, any modification that the FAA receives less than 10 days before the opening of bids is not effective, unless the Administrator finds that there is reasonable time to notify bidders. A modification may not continue in effect beyond the effective period of the wage determination to which it relates. The Administrator sends any modification to the sponsor as soon as possible. If the modification is effective, it must be incorporated in the invitation for bids, by issuing an addendum to the specifications or otherwise.

13. *Awarding contracts.* (a) A sponsor may not award a construction contract without the written concurrence of the Administrator (through the appropriate FAA office) that the contract prices are reasonable. A sponsor that awards contracts on the basis of public advertising and open competitive bidding, shall, after the bids are opened, send a tabulation of the bids and its recommendations for award to the appropriate FAA office. The sponsor may not accept a bid by a contractor whose name appears on the current list of ineligible contractors published by the Comptroller General of the United States under § 5.6(b) of the regulations of the Secretary of Labor (29 CFR part 5), or a bid by any firm, corporation, partnership, or association in which an ineligible contractor has a substantial interest.

(b) A sponsor's proposed contract must have pre-award review and approval by the FAA in any of the following circumstances:

(1) The sponsor's procurement system is not in compliance with one or more significant aspects of Attachment O of OMB Circular A–102 or with the standards of this appendix.

(2) The procurement is expected to exceed $10,000 and is to be awarded without competition or only one bid or offer is received in response to solicitation.

(3) The procurement is expected to exceed $10,000 and specifies a "brand name" product.

(c) The FAA may require pre-award review and approval of a sponsor's proposed contract under any of the following circumstances:

(1) The sponsor's procurement system has not yet been reviewed by the FAA for compliance with OMB Circular A-102 and this appendix.

(2) The sponsor has requested pre-award assistance.

(3) The proposal is for automatic data processing in accordance with paragraph C1 of Attachment B to Federal Management Circular 74-4 (39 FR 27133; 43 FR 50977).

(4) The proposal is one of a series with the same firm.

(5) The proposal is to be performed outside the recipient's established procurement system or office.

(6) The proposal is for construction and is to be awarded through the negotiation procurement method or without competition.

14. *Force account work.* Before undertaking any force account construction work, the sponsor (or any public agency acting as agent for the sponsor) must obtain the written consent of the Administrator through the appropriate FAA office. In requesting that consent, the sponsor must submit—

(a) Adequate plans and specifications showing the nature and extent of the construction work to be performed under that force account;

(b) A schedule of the proposed construction and of the construction equipment that will be available for the project;

(c) Assurance that adequate labor, material, equipment, engineering personnel, as well as supervisory and inspection personnel as required by this appendix, will be provided; and

(d) A detailed estimate of the cost of the work, broken down for each class of costs involved, such as labor, materials, rental of equipment, and other pertinent items of cost.

15. *Each sponsor shall—*

(a) Include the equal opportunity clause required by 41 CFR 60-1.4(b) in each nonexempt construction contract and subcontract;

(b) Prior to the award of each nonexempt contract, require each prime contractor and subcontractor to submit the certification required by 41 CFR 60-1.8(b);

(c) Include the Notice of Requirement for Affirmative Action to Ensure Equal Employment Opportunity (Executive Order 11246) required by 41 CFR 60-4.2 in all solicitations for offers and bids on each nonexempt construction contract and subcontract;

(d) Include the Standard Federal Equal Employment Opportunity Construction Contract Specifications (Executive Order 11246) required by 41 CFR 60-4.3(a) in each nonexempt construction contract and subcontract.

16. *Exceptions.* (a) Paragraphs 1 through 5 and paragraphs 9 through 13 of this section do not apply to contracts with the owners of airport hazards, buildings, pipelines, powerlines, or other structures or facilities, for installing, extending, changing, removing, or relocating any of those structures or facilities. However, the sponsor must obtain the approval of the appropriate FAA office before entering into such a contract.

(b) Any oral or written agreement or understanding between a sponsor and another public agency that is not a sponsor of the project, under which that public agency undertakes construction work for or as agent of the sponsor, is not considered to be a construction contract for the purposes of this appendix.

[Doc. No. 19430, 45 FR 34796, May 22, 1980]

APPENDIX D TO PART 152—ASSURANCES

There is set forth below the assurances that the sponsor or planning agency must submit with its application in accordance with §§ 152.111 or 152.113, as applicable.

I. General Assurance

Each applicant for an airport development grant or an airport planning grant shall submit the following assurance:

The applicant hereby assures and certifies that it will comply with the regulations, policies, guidelines, and requirements, including Office of Management and Budget Circulars No. A-95 (41 FR 2052), A-102 (42 FR 45828), and FMC 74-4 (39 FR 27133; as amended by 43 FR 50977), as they relate to the application, acceptance, and use of Federal funds for this federally-assisted project.

II. Airport Development

A. *Assurances.* Each applicant for an airport development grant shall submit the following assurances:

1. *Authority of applicant.* It possesses legal authority to apply for the grant, and to finance and construct the proposed facilities; that a resolution, motion or similar action has been duly adopted or passed as an official act of the applicant's governing body, authorizing the filing of the application, including all understandings and assurances contained therein, and directing and authorizing the person identified as the official representative of the applicant to act in connection with the application and to provide such additional information as may be required.

2. *E.O. 11296 and E.O. 11288.* It will comply with the provisions of: Executive Order 11296, relating to evaluation of flood hazards, and Executive Order 11288, relating to the prevention, control, and abatement of water pollution.

3. *Sufficiency of funds.* It will have sufficient funds available to meet the non-Federal share of the cost for construction projects. Sufficient funds will be available when construction is completed to assure effective operation and maintenance of the facility for the purposes constructed.

4. *Construction.* It will obtain approval by the appropriate Federal agency of the final working drawings and specifications before the project is advertised or placed on the market for bidding; that it will construct the project, or cause it to be constructed, to final completion in accordance with the application and approved plans and specification; that it will submit to the appropriate Federal agency for prior approval changes that alter the costs of the project, use of space, or functional layout; that it will not enter into a construction contract(s) for the project or undertake other activities until the conditions of the construction grant program(s) have been met.

5. *Supervision, inspection, and reporting.* It will provide and maintain competent adequate architectural engineering supervision and inspection at the construction site to insure that the completed work conforms with the approved plans and specifications; that it will furnish progress reports and such other information as the Federal grantor agency may require.

6. *Operation of facility.* It will operate and maintain the facility in accordance with the minimum standards as may be required or prescribed by the applicable Federal, State and local agencies for the maintenance and operation of such facilities.

7. *Access to records.* It will give the grantor agency and the Comptroller General through any authorized representative access to and the right to examine all records, books, papers, or documents related to the grant.

8. *Access for handicapped.* It will require the facility to be designed to comply with part 27, Nondiscrimination on the Basis of Handicap in Federally Assisted Programs and Activities Receiving or Benefiting from Federal Financial Assistance, of the Regulations of the Office of the Secretary of Transportation (49 CFR part 27). The applicant will be responsible for conducting inspections to insure compliance with these specifications by the contractor.

9. *Commencement and completion.* It will cause work on the project to be commenced within a reasonable time after receipt of notification from the approving Federal agency that funds have been approved and that the project will be prosecuted to completion with reasonable diligence.

10. *Disposition of interest.* It will not dispose of or encumber its title or other interests in the site and facilities during the period of Federal interest or while the Government holds bonds, whichever is the longer.

11. *Civil Rights.* It will comply with Title VI of the Civil Rights Act of 1964 (Pub. L. 88–352) and in accordance with Title VI of that Act, no person in the United States shall, on the ground of race, color, or national origin, be excluded from participation in, be denied the benefits of, or be otherwise subjected to discrimination under any program or activity for which the applicant receives Federal financial assistance and will immediately take any measures necessary to effectuate this agreement. If any real property or structure thereon is provided or improved with the aid of Federal financial assistance extended to the Applicant, this assurance shall obligate the Applicant, or in the case of any transfer of such property, any transferee, for the period during which the real property or structure is used for a purpose for which the Federal financial assistance is extended or for another purpose involving the provision of similar services or benefits.

12. *Private gain.* It will establish safeguards to prohibit employees from using their positions for a purpose that is or gives the appearance of being motivated by a desire for private gain for themselves or others, particularly those with whom they have family, business, or other ties.

13. *Relocation assistance.* It will comply with the requirements of Title II and Title III of the Uniform Relocation Assistance and Real Property Acquisition Policies Act of 1970 (Pub. L. 91–646) which provides for fair and equitable treatment of persons displaced as a result of Federal and federally assisted programs.

14. *OMB Circular A–102.* It will comply with all requirements imposed by the Federal grantor agency concerning special requirements of law, program requirements, and other administrative requirements approved in accordance with Office of Management and Budget Circular No. A–102.

15. *Hatch Act.* It will comply with the provisions of the Hatch Act which limit the political activity of employees.

16. *Federal Fair Labor Standards Act.* It will comply with the minimum wage and maximum hours provisions of the Federal Fair Labor Standards Act, as they apply to hospital and eduational institution employees of State and local governments.

17. *Effective date and duration.* These covenants shall become effective upon acceptance by the sponsor of an offer of Federal aid for the Project or any portion thereof, made by the FAA and shall constitute a part of the Grant Agreement thus formed. These covenants shall remain in full force and effect throughout the useful life of the facilities developed under this Project, but in any event not to exceed twenty (20) years from the date of said acceptance of an offer of Federal aid for the Project. However, these limitations on the duration of the covenants

do not apply to the covenant against exclusive rights and real property acquired with Federal funds. Any breach of these covenants on the part of the sponsor may result in the suspension or termination of, or refusal to grant Federal assistance under, FAA administered programs, or such other action which may be necessary to enforce the rights of the United States under this agreement.

18. *Conditions and limitations on airport use.* The Sponsor will operate the Airport as such for the use and benefit of the public. In furtherance of this covenant (but without limiting its general applicability and effect), the Sponsor specifically agrees that it will keep the Airport open to all types, kinds, and classes of aeronautical use on fair and reasonable terms without discrimination between such types, kinds, and classes. *Provided,* that the sponsor may establish such fair, equal, and not unjustly discriminatory conditions to be met by all users of the airport as may be necessary for the safe and efficient operation of the Airport; and *Provided further,* That the Sponsor may prohibit or limit any given type, kind, or class of aeronautical use of the Airport if such action is necessary for the safe operation of the Airport or necessary to serve the civil aviation needs of the public.

19. *Exclusive right.* The Sponsor—

a. Will not grant or permit any exclusive right forbidden by Section 308(a) of the Federal Aviation Act of 1958 (49 U.S.C. 1349(a)) at the Airport, or at any other airport now owned or controlled by it;

b. Agrees that, in furtherance of the policy of the FAA under this covenant, unless authorized by the Administrator, it will not, either directly or indirectly, grant or permit any person, firm or corporation the exclusive right at the Airport, or at any other airport now owned or controlled by it, to conduct any aeronautical activities, including, but not limited to charter flights, pilot training, aircraft rental and 'sightseeing, aerial photography, crop dusting, aerial advertising and surveying, air carrier operations, aircraft sales and services, sale of aviation petroleum products whether or not conducted in conjunction with other aeronautical activity, repair and maintenance of aircraft, sale of aircraft parts, and any other activities which because of their direct relationship to the operation of aircraft can be regarded as an aeronautical activity.

c. Agrees that it will terminate any existing exclusive right to engage in the sale of gasoline or oil, or both, granted before July 17, 1962, at such an airport, at the earliest renewal, cancellation, or expiration date applicable to the agreement that established the exclusive right; and

d. Agrees that it will terminate any other exclusive right to conduct an aeronautical activity now existing at such an airport before the grant of any assistance under the Airport and Airway Development Act.

20. *Public use and benefit.* The Sponsor agrees that it will operate the Airport for the use and benefit of the public, on fair and reasonable terms, and without unjust discrimination. In furtherance of the covenant (but without limiting its general applicability and effect), the Sponsor specifically covenants and agrees:

a. That in its operation and the operation of all facilities on the Airport, neither it nor any person or organization occupying space or facilities thereon will discriminate against any person or class of persons by reason of race, color, creed, or national origin in the use of any of the facilities provided for the public on the Airport.

b. That in any agreement, contract, lease or other arrangement under which a right or privilege at the Airport is granted to any person, firm, or corporation to conduct or engage in any aeronautical activity for furnishing services to the public at the Airport, the Sponsor will insert and enforce provisions requiring the contractor—

(1) To furnish said service on a fair, equal, and not unjustly discriminatory basis to all users thereof, and

(2) To charge fair, reasonable, and not unjustly discriminatory prices for each unit or service; Provided, That the contractor may be allowed to make reasonable and non-discriminatory discounts, rebates, or other similar types of price reductions to volume purchasers.

c. That it will not exercise or grant any right or privilege which would operate to prevent any person, firm or corporation operating aircraft on the Airport from performing any services on its own aircraft with its own employees (including, but not limited to maintenance and repair) that it may choose to perform.

d. In the event the Sponsor itself exercises any of the rights and privileges referred to in subsection b, the services involved will be provided on the same conditions as would apply to the furnishing of such services by contractors or concessionaires of the Sponsor under the provisions of such subsection b.

21. *Nonaviation activities.* Nothing contained herein shall be construed to prohibit the granting or exercise of an exclusive right for the furnishing of nonaviation products and supplies or any service of a nonaeronautical nature or to obligate the Sponsor to furnish any particular nonaeronautical service at the Airport.

22. *Operation and maintenance of the airport.* The Sponsor will operate and maintain in a safe and serviceable condition the Airport and all facilities thereon and connected therewith which are necessary to serve the aeronautical users of the Airport other than facilities owned or controlled by the United

States, and will not permit any activity thereon which would interfere with its use for airport purposes; *Provided,* That nothing contained herein shall be construed to require that the Airport be operated for aeronautical uses during temporary periods when snow, flood, or other climatic conditions interfere with such operation and maintenance; and *Provided further,* That nothing herein shall be construed as requiring the maintenance, repair, restoration or replacement of any structure or facility which is substantially damaged or destroyed due to an act of God or other condition or circumstance beyond the control of the Sponsor. In furtherance of this covenant the sponsor will have in effect at all times arrangements for—

a. Operating the airport's aeronautical facilities whenever required;

b. Promptly marking and lighting hazards resulting from airport conditions, including temporary conditions; and

c. Promptly notifying airmen of any condition affecting aeronautical use of the Airport.

23. *Airport Hazards.* Insofar as it is within its power and reasonable, the Sponsor will, either by the acquisition and retention of easements or other interests in or rights for the use of land or airspace or by the adoption and enforcement of zoning regulations prevent the construction, erection, alteration, or growth of any structure, tree, or other object in the approach areas of the runways of the Airport, which would constitute an airport hazard.

In addition, the Sponsor will not erect or permit the erection of any permanent structure or facility which would interfere materially with the use, operation, or future development of the Airport, in any portion of a runway approach area in which the Sponsor has acquired, or hereafter acquires, property interests permitting it to so control the use made of the surface of the land.

24. *Use of adjacent land.* Insofar as it is within its power and reasonable, the Sponsor will, either by the acquisition and retention of easements or other interests in or rights for the use of land or airspace or by the adoption and enforcement of zoning regulations, take action to restrict the use of land adjacent to or in the immediate vicinity of the Airport to activities and purposes compatible with normal airport operations including landing and takeoff of aircraft.

25. *Airport layout plan.* The Sponsor will keep up to date at all times an airport layout plan of the Airport showing (1) boundaries of the Airport and all proposed additions thereto, together with the boundaries of all offsite areas owned or controlled by the Sponsor for airport purposes, and proposed additions thereto; (2) the location and nature of all existing and proposed airport facilities and structures (such as runways,

taxiways, aprons, terminal buildings, hangars and roads), including all proposed extensions and reductions of existing airport facilities; and (3) the location of all existing and proposed nonaviation areas and of all existing improvements thereon. Such airport layout plan and each amendment, revision, or modification thereof, shall be subject to the approval of the FAA, which approval shall be evidenced by the signature of a duly authorized representative of the FAA on the face of the airport layout plan. The Sponsor will not make or permit any changes or alterations in the airport or in any of its facilities other than in conformity with the airport layout plan as so approved by the FAA, if such changes or alterations might adversely affect the safety, utility, or efficiency of the Airport.

26. *Federal use of facilities.* All facilities of the Airport developed with Federal aid and all those usable for the landing and taking off of aircraft, will be available to the United States at all times, without charge, for use by government aircraft in common with other aircraft, except that if the use by government aircraft is substantial, a reasonable share, proportional to such use, of the cost of operating and maintaining facilities so used, may be charged. Unless otherwise determined by the FAA, or otherwise agreed to by the Sponsor and the using agency, substantial use of an airport by government aircraft will be considered to exist when operations of such aircraft are in excess of those which, in the opinion of the FAA, would unduly interfere with use of the landing area by other authorized aircraft, or during any calendar month that—

a. Five (5) or more government aircraft are regularly based at the airport or on land adjacent thereto; or

b. The total number of movements (counting each landing as a movement and each takeoff as a movement) of government aircraft is 300 or more, or the gross accumulative weight of government aircraft using the Airport (the total movements of government aircraft multiplied by gross certified weights of such aircraft) is in excess of five million pounds.

27. *Areas for FAA Use.* Whenever so requested by the FAA, the Sponsor will furnish without cost to the Federal Government, for construction, operation, and maintenance of facilities for air traffic control activities, or weather reporting activities and communication activities related to air traffic control, such areas of land or water, or estate therein, or rights in buildings of the Sponsor as the FAA may consider necessary or desirable for construction at Federal expense of space or facilities for such purposes. The approximate amounts of areas and the nature of the property interests and/or rights so required

will be set forth in the Grant Agreement relating to the project. Such areas or any portion thereof will be made available as provided herein within 4 months after receipt of written requests from the FAA.

28. *Fee and rental structure.* The airport operator or owner will maintain a fee and rental structure for the facilities and services being provided the airport users which will make the Airport as self-sustaining as possible under the circumstances existing at the Airport, taking into account such factors as the volume of traffic and economy of collection.

29. *Reports to FAA.* The Sponsor will furnish the FAA with such annual or special airport financial and operational reports as may be reasonably requested. Such reports may be submitted on forms furnished by the FAA, or may be submitted in such manner as the Sponsor elects so long as the essential data are furnished. The Airport and all airport records and documents affecting the Airport, including deeds, leases, operation and use agreements, regulations, and other instruments, will be made available of inspection and audit by the Secretary and the Comptroller General of the United States, or their duly authorized representatives, upon reasonable request. The Sponsor will furnish to the FAA or to the General Accounting Office, upon request, a true copy of any such document.

30. *System of accounting.* All project accounts and records will be kept in accordance with a standard system of accounting if so prescribed by the Secretary.

31. *Interfering right.* If at any time it is determined by the FAA that there is any outstanding right or claim of right in or to the Airport property, other than those set forth in Part II of the Application for Federal Assistance, the existence of which creates an undue risk of interference with the operation of the Airport or the performance of the covenants of this part, the sponsor will acquire, extinguish, or modify such right or claim of right in a manner acceptable to the FAA.

32. *Performance obligation.* The Sponsor will not enter into any transaction which would operate to deprive it of any of the rights and powers necessary to perform any or all of the covenants made herein, unless by such transaction the obligation to perform all such covenants is assumed by another public agency found by the FAA to be eligible under the Act and Regulations to assume such obligations and having the power, authority, and financial resources to carry out all such obligations. If an arrangement is made for management or operation of the Airport by any agency or person other than the Sponsor or an employee of the Sponsor, the Sponsor will reserve sufficient rights and authority to insure that the Airport will be operated and maintained in accordance with the Act, the Regulations, and these covenants.

33. *Meaning of terms.* Unless the context otherwise requires, all terms used in these covenants which are defined in the Act and the Regulations shall have the meanings assigned to them therein.

B. *Airport Layout Plan Approval.* A sponsor seeking FAA approval of a new or revised airport layout plan shall submit with the plan an environmental assessment prepared in conformance with Appendix 6 of FAA Order 1050.1C, "Policies and Procedures for Considering Environmental Impacts" (45 FR 2244; January 10, 1980) and FAA Order 5050.4 "Airport Environmental Handbook" (45 FR 56622; August 25, 1980), if an assessment is required by Order 5050.4.

III. Airport Planning

Each applicant for an airport planning grant shall submit the assurances numbered 1 (except for the phrase "and to finance and construct the proposed facilities"), 7, 9, 11 (except for the last sentence), and 12, 14, 15, 30, and 33 of Part II of this appendix.

(Airport and Airway Development Act of 1970, as amended (49 U.S.C. 1701 *et seq.*); sec. 1.47(f)(1) Regulations of the Office of the Secretary of Transportation (49 CFR 1.47(f) (1)))

[Doc. No. 19430, 45 FR 34797, May 22, 1980, as amended by Amdt. 152–11, 45 FR 56622, Aug. 25, 1980]

PART 153—AIRPORT OPERATIONS

Subpart A—Aviation Safety Inspector Access

Sec.
153.1   Applicability.
153.3   Definitions.
153.5   Aviation safety inspector airport access.

Subpart B [Reserved]

AUTHORITY: 49 U.S.C. 106(g), 40113, and 44701.

SOURCE: Docket No. FAA–2007–29237, 73 FR 47827, Aug. 15, 2008, unless otherwise noted.

Subpart A—Aviation Safety Inspector Access

§ 153.1   Applicability.

This subpart prescribes requirements governing Aviation Safety Inspector access to public-use airports and facilities to perform official duties.

§ 153.3   Definitions.

The following definitions apply in this subpart:

Air Operations Area (AOA) means a portion of an airport, specified in the airport security program, in which security measures specified in Title 49 of the Code of Federal Regulations are carried out. This area includes aircraft movement areas, aircraft parking areas, loading ramps, and safety areas, for use by aircraft regulated under 49 CFR parts 1542, 1544, and 1546, and any adjacent areas (such as general aviation areas) that are not separated by adequate security systems, measures, or procedures. This area does not include the secured area.

Airport means any public-use airport, including heliports, as defined in 49 U.S.C. 47102, including:

(1) A public airport; or

(2) A privately-owned airport used or intended to be used for public purposes that is—

(i) A reliever airport; or

(ii) Determined by the Secretary to have at least 2,500 passenger boardings each year and to receive scheduled passenger aircraft service.

Aviation Safety Inspector means a properly credentialed individual who bears FAA Form 110A and is authorized under the provisions of 49 U.S.C. 40113 to perform inspections and investigations.

FAA Form 110A means the credentials issued to qualified Aviation Safety Inspectors by the FAA for use in the performance of official duties.

Secured area means a portion of an airport, specified in the airport security program, in which certain security measures specified in Title 49 of the Code of Federal Regulations are carried out. This area is where aircraft operators and foreign air carriers that have a security program under 49 CFR part 1544 or part 1546 enplane and deplane passengers and sort and load baggage and any adjacent areas that are not separated by adequate security systems, measures, or procedures.

Security Identification Display Area (SIDA) means a portion of an airport, specified in the airport security program, in which security measures specified in Title 49 of the Code of Federal Regulations are carried out. This area includes the secured area and may include other areas of the airport.

§153.5 Aviation safety inspector airport access.

Airports, aircraft operators, aircraft owners, airport tenants, and air agencies must grant Aviation Safety Inspectors bearing FAA Form 110A free and uninterrupted access to public-use airports and facilities, including AOAs, SIDAs, and other secured and restricted areas. Aviation Safety Inspectors displaying FAA Form 110A do not require access media or identification media issued or approved by an airport operator or aircraft operator in order to inspect or test compliance, or perform other such duties as the FAA may direct.

Subpart B [Reserved]

PART 155—RELEASE OF AIRPORT PROPERTY FROM SURPLUS PROPERTY DISPOSAL RESTRICTIONS

Sec.
155.1 Applicability.
155.3 Applicable law.
155.5 Property and releases covered by this part.
155.7 General policies.
155.9 Release from war or national emergency restrictions.
155.11 Form and content of requests for release.
155.13 Determinations by FAA.

AUTHORITY: 49 U.S.C. 106(g), 40113, 47151–47153.

SOURCE: Docket No. 1329, 27 FR 12361, Dec. 13, 1962, unless otherwise noted.

§155.1 Applicability.

This part applies to releases from terms, conditions, reservations, or restrictions in any deed, surrender of leasehold, or other instrument of transfer or conveyance (in this part called "instrument of disposal") by which some right, title, or interest of the United States in real or personal property was conveyed to a non-Federal public agency under section 13 of the Surplus Property Act of 1944 (58 Stat. 765; 61 Stat. 678) to be used by that agency in developing, improving, operating, or maintaining a public airport or to provide a source of revenue from non-aviation business at a public airport.

§ 155.3 Applicable law.

(a) Section 4 of the Act of October 1, 1949 (63 Stat. 700) authorizes the Administrator to grant the releases described in § 155.1, if he determines that—

(1) The property to which the release relates no longer serves the purpose for which it was made subject to the terms, conditions, reservations, or restrictions concerned; or

(2) The release will not prevent accomplishing the purpose for which the property was made subject to the terms, conditions, reservations, or restrictions, and is necessary to protect or advance the interests of the United States in civil aviation.

In addition, section 4 of that Act authorizes the Administrator to grant the releases subject to terms and conditions that he considers necessary to protect or advance the interests of the United States in civil aviation.

(b) Section 2 of the Act of October 1, 1949 (63 Stat. 700) provides that the restrictions against using structures for industrial purposes in any instrument of disposal issued under section 13(g)(2)(A) of the Surplus Property Act of 1944, as amended (61 Stat. 678) are considered to be extinguished. In addition, section 2 authorizes the Administrator to issue any instruments of release or conveyance necessary to remove, of record, such a restriction, without monetary consideration to the United States.

(c) Section 68 of the Atomic Energy Act of 1954, as amended (42 U.S.C. 2098) releases, remises, and quitclaims, to persons entitled thereto, all reserved rights of the United States in radioactive minerals in instruments of disposal of public or acquired lands. In addition, section 3 of the Act of October 1, 1949 (50 U.S.C. App. 1622b) authorizes the Administrator to issue instruments that he considers necessary to correct any instrument of disposal by which surplus property was transferred to a non-Federal public agency for airport purposes or to conform the transfer to the requirements of applicable law. Based on the laws cited in this paragraph, the Administrator issues appropriate instruments of correction upon the written request of persons entitled to ownership, occupancy, or use of the lands concerned.

§ 155.5 Property and releases covered by this part.

This part applies to—

(a) Any real or personal property that is subject to the terms, conditions, reservations, or restrictions in an instrument of disposal described in § 155.1; and

(b) Any release from a term, condition, reservation, or restriction in such an instrument, including a release of—

(1) Personal property, equipment, or structures from any term, condition, reservation, or restriction so far as necessary to allow it to be disposed of for salvage purposes;

(2) Land, personal property, equipment or structures from any term, condition, reservation, or restriction requiring that it be used for airport purposes to allow its use, lease, or sale for nonairport use in place;

(3) Land, personal property, equipment, or structures from any term, condition, reservation, or restriction requiring its maintenance for airport use;

(4) Land, personal property, equipment, or structures from all terms, conditions, restrictions, or reservations to allow its use, lease, sale, or other disposal for nonairport purposes; and

(5) Land, personal property, equipment, or structures from the reservation of right of use by the United States in time of war or national emergency, to facilitate financing the operation and maintenance or further development of a public airport.

§ 155.7 General policies.

(a) Upon a request under § 155.11, the Administrator issues any instrument that is necessary to remove, of record, any restriction against the use of property for industrial purposes that is in an instrument of disposal covered by this part.

(b) The Administrator does not issue a release under this part if it would allow the sale of the property concerned to a third party, unless the public agency concerned has obligated itself to use the proceeds from the sale exclusively for developing, improving,

748

operating, or maintaining a public airport.

(c) Except for a release from a restriction against using property for industrial purposes, the Administrator does not issue a release under this part unless it is justified under §155.3(a) (1) or (2).

(d) The Administrator may issue a release from the terms, conditions, reservations, or restrictions of an instrument of disposal subject to any other terms or conditions that he considers necessary to protect or advance the interests of the United States in civil aviation. Such a term or condition, including one regarding the use of proceeds from the sale of property, is imposed as a personal covenant or obligation of the public agency concerned rather than as a term or condition to the release or as a covenant running with the land, unless the Administrator determines that the purpose of the term or condition would be better achieved as a condition or covenant running with the land.

(e) A letter or other document issued by the Administrator that merely grants consent to or approval of a lease, or to the use of the property for other than the airport use contemplated by the instrument of disposal, does not otherwise release the property from the terms, conditions, reservations, or restrictions of the instrument of disposal.

§155.9 Release from war or national emergency restrictions.

(a) The primary purpose of each transfer of surplus airport property under section 13 of the Surplus Property Act of 1944 was to make the property available for public or civil airport needs. However, it was also intended to ensure the availability of the property transferred, and of the entire airport, for use by the United States during a war or national emergency, if needed. As evidence of this purpose, most instruments of disposal of surplus airport property reserved or granted to the United States a right of exclusive possession and control of the airport during a war or emergency, substantially the same as one of the following:

(1) That during the existence of any emergency declared by the President or

the Congress, the Government shall have the right without charge except as indicated below to the full, unrestricted possession, control, and use of the landing area, building areas, and airport facilities or any part thereof, including any additions or improvements thereto made subsequent to the declaration of the airport property as surplus: *Provided, however,* That the Government shall be responsible during the period of such use for the entire cost of maintaining all such areas, facilities, and improvements, or the portions used, and shall pay a fair rental for the use of any installations or structures which have been added thereto without Federal aid.

(2) During any national emergency declared by the President or by Congress, the United States shall have the right to make exclusive or nonexclusive use and have exclusive or nonexclusive control and possession, without charge, of the airport at which the surplus property is located or used or of such portion thereof as it may desire: *Provided, however,* That the United States shall be responsible for the entire cost of maintaining such part of the airport as it may use exclusively, or over which it may have exclusive possession and control, during the period of such use, possession, or control and shall be obligated to contribute a reasonable share, commensurate with the use made by it, of the cost of maintenance of such property as it may use nonexclusively or over which it may have nonexclusive control and possession: *Provided further,* That the United States shall pay a fair rental for its use, control, or possession, exclusively or nonexclusively, of any improvements to the airport made without U.S. aid.

(b) A release from the terms, conditions, reservations, or restrictions of an instrument of disposal that might prejudice the needs or interests of the armed forces, is granted only after consultation with the Department of Defense.

§155.11 Form and content of requests for release.

(a) A request for the release of surplus airport property from a term, condition, reservation, or restriction in an instrument of disposal need not be in any special form, but must be in writing and signed by an authorized official of the public agency that owns the airport.

(b) A request for a release under this part must be submitted in triplicate to the District Airport Engineer in whose district the airport is located.

(c) Each request for a release must include the following information, if applicable and available:

(1) Identification of the instruments of disposal to which the property concerned is subject.

(2) A description of the property concerned.

(3) The condition of the property concerned.

(4) The purpose for which the property was transferred, such as for use as a part of, or in connection with, operating the airport or for producing revenues from nonaviation business.

(5) The kind of release requested.

(6) The purpose of the release.

(7) A statement of the circumstances justifying the release on the basis set forth in § 155.3(a) (1) or (2) with supporting documents.

(8) Maps, photographs, plans, or similar material of the airport and the property concerned that are appropriate to determining whether the release is justified under § 155.9.

(9) The proposed use or disposition of the property, including the terms and conditions of any proposed sale or lease and the status of negotiations therefor.

(10) If the release would allow sale of any part of the property, a certified copy of a resolution or ordinance of the governing body of the public agency that owns the airport obligating itself to use the proceeds of the sale exclusively for developing, improving, operating, or maintaining a public airport.

(11) A suggested letter or other instrument of release that would meet the requirements of State and local law for the release requested.

(12) The sponsor's environmental assessment prepared in conformance with Appendix 6 of FAA Order 1050.1C, "Policies and Procedures for Considering Environmental Impacts" (45 FR 2244; Jan. 10, 1980), and FAA Order 5050.4, "Airport Environmental Handbook" (45 FR 56624; Aug. 25, 1980), if an assessment is required by Order 5050.4. Copies of these orders may be examined in the Rules Docket, Office of the Chief Counsel, FAA, Washington, D.C., and may be obtained on request at any FAA regional office headquarters or any airports district office.

[Doc. No. 1329, 27 FR 12361, Dec. 13, 1962, as amended by Amdt. 155–1, 45 FR 56622, Aug. 25, 1980]

§ 155.13 Determinations by FAA.

(a) An FAA office that receives a request for a release under this part, and supporting documents therefore, examines it to determine whether the request meets the requirements of the Act of October 1, 1949 (63 Stat. 700) so far as it concerns the interests of the United States in civil aviation and whether it might prejudice the needs and interests of the armed forces. Upon a determination that the release might prejudice those needs and interests, the Department of Defense is consulted as provided in § 155.9(b).

(b) Upon completing the review, and receiving the advice of the Department of Defense if the case was referred to it, the FAA advises the airport owner as to whether the release or a modification of it, may be granted. If the release, or a modification of it acceptable to the owner, is granted, the FAA prepares the necessary instruments and delivers them to the airport owner.

PART 156—STATE BLOCK GRANT PILOT PROGRAM

Sec.
156.1 Applicability.
156.2 Letters of interest.
156.3 Application and grant process.
156.4 Airport and project eligibility.
156.5 Project cost allowability.
156.6 State program responsibilities.
156.7 Enforcement of State block grant agreements and other related grant assurances.

AUTHORITY: 49 U.S.C. 106(g), 47101, 47128; 49 CFR 1.47(f), (k).

SOURCE: Docket No. 35723, 53 FR 41303, Oct. 20, 1988, unless otherwise noted.

§ 156.1 Applicability.

(a) This part applies to grant applicants for the State block grant pilot program and to those States receiving block grants available under the Airport and Airway Improvement Act of 1982, as amended.

(b) This part sets forth—

(1) The procedures by which a State may apply to participate in the State block grant pilot program;

(2) The program administration requirements for a participating State;

(3) The program responsibilities for a participating State; and

(4) The enforcement responsibilities of a participating State.

§ 156.2 Letters of interest.

(a) Any state that desires to participate in the State block grant pilot program shall submit a letter of interest, by November 30, 1988, to the Associate Administrator for Airports, Federal Aviation Administration, 800 Independence Avenue SW., Room 1000E, Washington, DC 20591.

(b) A State's letter of interest shall contain the name, title, address, and telephone number of the individual who will serve as the liaison with the Administrator regarding the State block grant pilot program.

(c) The FAA will provide an application form and program guidance material to each State that submits a letter of interest to the Associate Administrator for Airports.

§ 156.3 Application and grant process.

(a) A State desiring to participate shall submit a completed application to the Associate Administrator for Airports.

(b) After review of the applications submitted by the States, the Administrator shall select three States for participation in the State block grant pilot program.

(c) The Administrator shall issue a written grant offer that sets forth the terms and conditions of the State block grant agreement to each selected State.

(d) A State's participation in the State block grant pilot program begins when a State accepts the Administrator's written grant offer in writing and within any time limit specified by the Administrator. The State shall certify, in its written acceptance that the acceptance complies with all applicable Federal and State law, that the accept-

ance constitutes a legal and binding obligation of the State, and that the State has the authority to carry out all the terms and conditions of the written grant offer.

§ 156.4 Airport and project eligibility.

(a) A participating State shall use monies distributed pursuant to a State block grant agreement for airport development and airport planning, for airport noise compatibility planning, or to carry out airport noise compatibility programs, in accordance with the Airport and Airway Improvement Act of 1982, as amended.

(b) A participating State shall administer the airport development and airport planning projects for airports within the State.

(c) A participating State shall not use any monies distributed pursuant to a State block grant agreement for integrated airport system planning, projects related to any primary airport, or any airports—

(1) Outside the State's boundaries; or

(2) Inside the State's boundaries that are not included in the National Plan of Integrated Airport Systems.

§ 156.5 Project cost allowability.

(a) A participating State shall not use State block grant funds for reimbursement of project costs that would not be eligible for reimbursement under a project grant administered by the FAA.

(b) A participating State shall not use State block grant funds for reimbursement or funding of administrative costs incurred by the State pursuant to the State block grant program.

§ 156.6 State program responsibilities.

(a) A participating State shall comply with the terms of the State block grant agreement.

(b) A participating State shall ensure that each person or entity, to which the State distributes funds received pursuant to the State block grant pilot program, complies with any terms that the State block grant agreement requires to be imposed on a recipient for airport projects funded pursuant to the State block grant pilot program.

(c) Unless otherwise agreed by a participating State and the Administrator in writing, a participating State shall not delegate or relinquish, either expressly or by implication, any State authority, rights, or power that would interfere with the State's ability to comply with the terms of a State block grant agreement.

§ 156.7 Enforcement of State block grant agreements and other related grant assurances.

The Administrator may take any action, pursuant to the authority of the Airport and Airway Improvement Act of 1982, as amended, to enforce the terms of a State block grant agreement including any terms imposed upon subsequent recipients of State block agreement funds.

PART 157—NOTICE OF CONSTRUCTION, ALTERATION, ACTIVATION, AND DEACTIVATION OF AIRPORTS

Sec.
157.1 Applicability.
157.2 Definition of terms.
157.3 Projects requiring notice.
157.5 Notice of intent.
157.7 FAA determinations.
157.9 Notice of completion.

AUTHORITY: 49 U.S.C. 106(g), 40103, 40113, 44502.

SOURCE: Docket No. 25708, 56 FR 33996, July 24, 1991, unless otherwise noted.

§ 157.1 Applicability.

This part applies to persons proposing to construct, alter, activate, or deactivate a civil or joint-use (civil/military) airport or to alter the status or use of such an airport. Requirements for persons to notify the Administrator concerning certain airport activities are prescribed in this part. This part does not apply to projects involving:

(a) An airport subject to conditions of a Federal agreement that requires an approved current airport layout plan to be on file with the Federal Aviation Administration; or

(b) An airport at which flight operations will be conducted under visual flight rules (VFR) and which is used or intended to be used for a period of less than 30 consecutive days with no more than 10 operations per day.

(c) The intermittent use of a site that is not an established airport, which is used or intended to be used for less than one year and at which flight operations will be conducted only under VFR. For the purposes of this part, *intermittent use of a site* means:

(1) The site is used or is intended to be used for no more than 3 days in any one week; and

(2) No more than 10 operations will be conducted in any one day at that site.

§ 157.2 Definition of terms.

For the purpose of this part:

Airport means any airport, heliport, helistop, vertiport, gliderport, seaplane base, ultralight flightpark, manned balloon launching facility, or other aircraft landing or takeoff area.

Heliport means any landing or takeoff area intended for use by helicopters or other rotary wing type aircraft capable of vertical takeoff and landing profiles.

Private use means available for use by the owner only or by the owner and other persons authorized by the owner.

Private use of public lands means that the landing and takeoff area of the proposed airport is publicly owned and the proponent is a non-government entity, regardless of whether that landing and takeoff area is on land or on water and whether the controlling entity be local, State, or Federal Government.

Public use means available for use by the general public without a requirement for prior approval of the owner or operator.

Traffic pattern means the traffic flow that is prescribed for aircraft landing or taking off from an airport, including departure and arrival procedures utilized within a 5-mile radius of the airport for ingress, egress, and noise abatement.

§ 157.3 Projects requiring notice.

Each person who intends to do any of the following shall notify the Administrator in the manner prescribed in § 157.5:

(a) Construct or otherwise establish a new airport or activate an airport.

(b) Construct, realign, alter, or activate any runway or other aircraft landing or takeoff area of an airport.

(c) Deactivate, discontinue using, or abandon an airport or any landing or takeoff area of an airport for a period of one year or more.

(d) Construct, realign, alter, activate, deactivate, abandon, or discontinue using a taxiway associated with a landing or takeoff area on a public-use airport.

(e) Change the status of an airport from private use to public use or from public use to another status.

(f) Change any traffic pattern or traffic pattern altitude or direction.

(g) Change status from IFR to VFR or VFR to IFR.

§157.5 Notice of intent.

(a) Notice shall be submitted on FAA Form 7480-1, copies of which may be obtained from an FAA Airport District/Field Office or Regional Office, to one of those offices and shall be submitted at least—

(1) In the cases prescribed in paragraphs (a) through (d) of §157.3, 90 days in advance of the day that work is to begin; or

(2) In the cases prescribed in paragraphs (e) through (g) of §157.3, 90 days in advance of the planned implementation date.

(b) Notwithstanding paragraph (a) of this section—

(1) In an emergency involving essential public service, public health, or public safety or when the delay arising from the 90-day advance notice requirement would result in an unreasonable hardship, a proponent may provide notice to the appropriate FAA Airport District/Field Office or Regional Office by telephone or other expeditious means as soon as practicable in lieu of submitting FAA Form 7480-1. However, the proponent shall provide full notice, through the submission of FAA Form 7480-1, when otherwise requested or required by the FAA.

(2) notice concerning the deactivation, discontinued use, or abandonment of an airport, an airport landing or takeoff area, or associated taxiway may be submitted by letter. Prior notice is not required; except that a 30-day prior notice is required when an established instrument approach procedure is involved or when the affected property is subject to any agreement with the United States requiring that it be maintained and operated as a public-use airport.

§157.7 FAA determinations.

(a) The FAA will conduct an aeronautical study of an airport proposal and, after consultations with interested persons, as appropriate, issue a determination to the proponent and advise those concerned of the FAA determination. The FAA will consider matters such as the effects the proposed action would have on existing or contemplated traffic patterns of neighboring airports; the effects the proposed action would have on the existing airspace structure and projected programs of the FAA; and the effects that existing or proposed manmade objects (on file with the FAA) and natural objects within the affected area would have on the airport proposal. While determinations consider the effects of the proposed action on the safe and efficient use of airspace by aircraft and the safety of persons and property on the ground, the determinations are only advisory. Except for an objectionable determination, each determination will contain a determination-void date to facilitate efficient planning of the use of the navigable airspace. A determination does not relieve the proponent of responsibility for compliance with any local law, ordinance or regulation, or state or other Federal regulation. Aeronautical studies and determinations will not consider environmental or land use compatibility impacts.

(b) An airport determination issued under this part will be one of the following:

(1) *No objection.*

(2) *Conditional.* A conditional determination will identify the objectionable aspects of a project or action and specify the conditions which must be met and sustained to preclude an objectionable determination.

(3) *Objectionable.* An objectionable determination will specify the FAA's reasons for issuing such a determination.

(c) *Determination void date.* All work or action for which notice is required by this sub-part must be completed by the determination void date. Unless otherwise extended, revised, or terminated, an FAA determination becomes invalid on the day specified as the determination void date. Interested persons may, at least 15 days in advance of the determination void date, petition the FAA official who issued the determination to:

(1) Revise the determination based on new facts that change the basis on which it was made; or

(2) Extend the determination void date. Determinations will be furnished to the proponent, aviation officials of the state concerned, and, when appropriate, local political bodies and other interested persons.

§ 157.9 Notice of completion.

Within 15 days after completion of any airport project covered by this part, the proponent of such project shall notify the FAA Airport District Office or Regional Office by submission of FAA Form 5010-5 or by letter. A copy of FAA Form 5010-5 will be provided with the FAA determination.

PART 158—PASSENGER FACILITY CHARGES (PFC'S)

Subpart A—General

Subpart B—Application and Approval

Subpart C—Collection, Handling, and Remittance of PFC's

Subpart D—Reporting, Recordkeeping and Audits

Subpart E—Termination

Subpart F—Reduction in Airport Improvement Program Apportionments

AUTHORITY: 49 U.S.C. 106(g), 40116–40117, 47106, 47111, 47114–47116, 47524, 47526.

SOURCE: Docket No. 26385, 56 FR 24278, May 29, 1991, unless otherwise noted.

Subpart A—General

§ 158.1 Applicability.

This part applies to passenger facility charges (PFC's) as may be approved by the Administrator of the Federal Aviation Administration (FAA) and imposed by a public agency that controls a commercial service airport. This part also describes the procedures for reducing funds to a large or medium hub airport that imposes a PFC.

[Doc. No. FAA–2000–7402, 65 FR 34540, May 30, 2000]

§ 158.3 Definitions.

The following definitions apply in this part:

Airport means any area of land or water, including any heliport, that is used or intended to be used for the landing and takeoff of aircraft, and any appurtenant areas that are used or intended to be used for airport buildings or other airport facilities or rights-of-way, together with all airport buildings and facilities located thereon.

Airport capital plan means a capital improvement program that lists airport-related planning, development or noise compatibility projects expected to be accomplished with anticipated available funds.

Airport layout plan (ALP) means a plan showing the existing and proposed airport facilities and boundaries in a form prescribed by the Administrator.

Airport revenue means revenue generated by a public airport (1) through any lease, rent, fee, PFC or other charge collected, directly or indirectly, in connection with any aeronautical activity conducted on an airport that it controls; or (2) In connection with any activity conducted on airport land acquired with Federal financial assistance, or with PFC revenue under this part, or conveyed to such public agency under the provisions of any Federal surplus property program or any provision enacted to authorize the conveyance of Federal property to a public agency for airport purposes.

Air travel ticket includes all documents, electronic records, boarding passes, and any other ticketing medium about a passenger's itinerary necessary to transport a passenger by air, including passenger manifests.

Allowable cost means the reasonable and necessary costs of carrying out an approved project including costs incurred prior to and subsequent to the approval to impose a PFC, and making payments for debt service on bonds and other indebtedness incurred to carry out such projects. Allowable costs include only those costs incurred on or after November 5, 1990. Costs of terminal development incurred after August 1, 1986, at an airport that did not have more than .25 percent of the total annual passenger boardings in the U.S. in the most recent calendar year for which data is available and at which total passenger boardings declined by at least 16 percent between calendar year 1989 and calendar year 1997 are allowable.

Approved project means a project for which the FAA has approved using PFC revenue under this part. The FAA may also approve specific projects contained in a single or multi-phased project or development described in an airport capital plan separately. This includes projects acknowledged by the FAA under § 158.30 of this part.

Bond financing costs means the costs of financing a bond and includes such costs as those associated with issuance, underwriting discount, original issue discount, capitalized interest, debt service reserve funds, initial credit enhancement costs, and initial trustee and paying agent fees.

Charge effective date means the date on which carriers are obliged to collect a PFC.

Charge expiration date means the date on which carriers are to cease to collect a PFC.

Collecting carrier means an issuing carrier or other carrier collecting a PFC, whether or not such carrier issues the air travel ticket.

Collection means the acceptance of payment of a PFC from a passenger.

Commercial service airport means a public airport that annually enplanes 2,500 or more passengers and receives scheduled passenger service of aircraft.

Covered air carrier means an air carrier that files for bankruptcy protection or has an involuntary bankruptcy proceeding started against it after December 12, 2003. An air carrier that is currently in compliance with PFC remittance requirements and has an involuntary bankruptcy proceeding commenced against it has 90 days from the date such proceeding was filed to obtain dismissal of the involuntary petition before becoming a covered air carrier. An air carrier ceases to be a covered air carrier when it emerges from bankruptcy protection.

Covered airport means a medium or large hub airport at which one or two air carriers control more than 50 percent of passenger boardings.

Debt service means payments for such items as principal and interest, sinking funds, call premiums, periodic credit enhancement fees, trustee and paying agent fees, coverage, and remarketing fees.

Exclusive long-term lease or use agreement means an exclusive lease or use agreement between a public agency and an air carrier or foreign air carrier with a term of 5 years or more.

FAA Airports office means a regional, district or field office of the Federal Aviation Administration that administers Federal airport-related matters.

Financial need means that a public agency cannot meet its operational or debt service obligations and does not have at least a 2-month capital reserve fund.

Frequent flier award coupon means a zero-fare award of air transportation that an air carrier or foreign air carrier provides to a passenger in exchange for accumulated travel mileage credits in a customer loyalty program, whether or not the term "frequent flier" is used in the definition of that program. The definition of "frequent flier award coupon" does not extend to redemption of accumulated credits for awards of additional or upgraded service on trips for which the passenger has paid a published fare, "two-for-the-price-of-one" and similar marketing programs, or to air transportation purchased for a passenger by other parties.

Ground support equipment means service and maintenance equipment used at an airport to support aeronautical operations and related activities. Baggage tugs, belt loaders, cargo loaders, forklifts, fuel trucks, lavatory trucks, and pushback tractors are among the types of vehicles that fit this definition.

Implementation of an approved project means: (1) With respect to construction, issuance to a contractor of notice to proceed or the start of physical construction; (2) with respect to non-construction projects other than property acquisition, commencement of work by a contractor or public agency to carry out the statement of work; or (3) with respect to property acquisition projects, commencement of title search, surveying, or appraisal for a significant portion of the property to be acquired.

Issuing carrier means any air carrier or foreign air carrier that issues an air travel ticket or whose imprinted ticket stock is used in issuing such ticket by an agent.

Medium or large hub airport means a commercial service airport that has more than 0.25 percent of the total number of passenger boardings at all such airports in the U.S. for the prior calendar year, as determined by the Administrator.

Non-hub airport means a commercial service airport (as defined in 49 U.S.C. 47102) that has less than 0.05 percent of the passenger boardings in the U.S. in the prior calendar year on an aircraft in service in air commerce.

Nonrevenue passenger means a passenger receiving air transportation from an air carrier or foreign air carrier for which remuneration is not received by the air carrier or foreign air carrier as defined under Department of Transportation Regulations or as otherwise determined by the Administrator. Air carrier employees or others receiving air transportation against whom token service charges are levied are considered nonrevenue passengers. Infants for whom a token fare is charged are also considered nonrevenue passengers.

Notice of intent (to impose or use PFC revenue) means a notice under § 158.30 from a public agency controlling a non-hub airport that it intends to impose a PFC and/or use PFC revenue. Except for §§ 158.25 through 30, "notice of intent" can be used interchangeably with "application."

One-way trip means any trip that is not a round trip.

Passenger enplaned means a domestic, territorial or international revenue passenger enplaned in the States in scheduled or nonscheduled service on aircraft in intrastate, interstate, or foreign commerce.

PFC means a passenger facility charge covered by this part imposed by a public agency on passengers enplaned at a commercial service airport it controls.

PFC administrative support costs means the reasonable and necessary costs of developing a PFC application or amendment, issuing and maintaining the required PFC records, and performing the required audit of the public agency's PFC account. These costs may include reasonable monthly financial account charges and transaction fees.

Project means airport planning airport land acquisition or development of a single project, a multi-phased development program, (including but not limited to development described in an airport capital plan) or a new airport for which PFC financing is sought or approved under this part.

Public agency means a State or any agency of one or more States; a municipality or other political subdivision of a State; an authority created by Federal, State or local law; a tax-supported organization; an Indian tribe or pueblo that controls a commercial service airport; or for the purposes of this part, a private sponsor of an airport approved to participate in the Pilot Program on Private Ownership of Airports.

Round trip means a trip on a complete air travel itinerary which terminates at the origin point.

Significant business interest means an air carrier or foreign air carrier that:

(1) Had no less than 1.0 percent of passenger boardings at that airport in the prior calendar year,

(2) Had at least 25,000 passenger boardings at the airport in that prior calendar year, or

(3) Provides scheduled service at that airport.

State means a State of the United States, the District of Columbia, the Commonwealth of Puerto Rico, the Virgin Islands, American Samoa, the Commonwealth of the Northern Mariana Islands, and Guam.

Unliquidated PFC revenue means revenue received by a public agency from collecting carriers but not yet used on approved projects.

[Doc. No. 26385, 56 FR 24278, May 29, 1991, as amended by Amdt. 158–2, 65 FR 34540, May 30, 2000; Amdt. 158–3, 70 FR 14934, Mar. 23, 2005; Amdt. 158–4, 72 FR 28847, May 23, 2007]

§158.5 Authority to impose PFC's.

Subject to the provisions of this part, the Administrator may grant authority to a public agency that controls a commercial service airport to impose a PFC of $1, $2, $3, $4, or $4.50 on passengers enplaned at such an airport. No public agency may impose a PFC under this part unless authorized by the Administrator. No State or political subdivision or agency thereof that is not a public agency may impose a PFC covered by this part.

[Doc. No. 26385, 56 FR 24278, May 29, 1991, as amended by Amdt. 158–2, 65 FR 34541, May 30, 2000]

§158.7 Exclusivity of authority.

(a) A State, political subdivision of a State, or authority of a State or political subdivision that is not the eligible public agency may not tax, regulate, prohibit, or otherwise attempt to control in any manner the imposition or collection of a PFC or the use of PFC revenue.

(b) No contract or agreement between an air carrier or foreign air carrier and a public agency may impair the authority of such public agency to impose a PFC or use the PFC revenue in accordance with this part.

[Doc. No. 26385, 56 FR 24278, May 29, 1991, as amended by Amdt. 158–2, 65 FR 34541, May 30, 2000]

§158.9 Limitations.

(a) No public agency may impose a PFC on any passenger—

(1) For more than 2 boardings on a one-way trip or in each direction of a round trip;

(2) On any flight to an eligible point on an air carrier that receives essential air service compensation on that route. The Administrator makes available a list of carriers and eligible routes determined by the Department of Transportation for which PFC's may not be imposed under this section;

757

(3) Who is a nonrevenue passenger or obtained the ticket for air transportation with a frequent flier award coupon;

(4) On flights, including flight segments, between 2 or more points in Hawaii;

(5) In Alaska aboard an aircraft having a certificated seating capacity of fewer than 60 passengers; or

(6) Enplaning at an airport if the passenger did not pay for the air transportation that resulted in the enplanement due to Department of Defense charter arrangements and payments.

(b) No public agency may require a foreign airline that does not serve a point or points in the U.S. to collect a PFC from a passenger.

[Doc. No. 26385, 56 FR 24278, May 29, 1991, as amended by Amdt. 158–2, 65 FR 34541, May 30, 2000; Amdt. 158–4, 72 FR 28847, May 23, 2007]

§ 158.11 Public agency request not to require collection of PFC's by a class of air carriers or foreign air carriers or for service to isolated communities.

(a) Subject to the requirements of this part, a public agency may request that collection of PFC's not be required for—

(1) Passengers enplaned by any class of air carrier or foreign air carrier if the number of passengers enplaned by the carriers in the class constitutes not more than one percent of the total number of passengers enplaned annually at the airport at which the fee is imposed; or

(2) Passengers enplaned on a flight to an airport—

(i) That has fewer than 2,500 passenger boardings each year and receives scheduled passenger service; or

(ii) In a community that has a population of less than 10,000 and is not connected by a land highway or vehicular way to the land-connected National Highway System within a State.

(b) The public agency may request this exclusion authority under paragraph (a)(1) or (a)(2) of this section or both.

[Doc. No. FAA-2000-7402, 65 FR 34541, May 30, 2000]

§ 158.13 Use of PFC revenue.

PFC revenue, including any interest earned after such revenue has been remitted to a public agency, may be used only to finance the allowable costs of approved projects at any airport the public agency controls.

(a) *Total cost.* PFC revenue may be used to pay all or part of the allowable cost of an approved project.

(b) *PFC administrative support costs.* Public agencies may use PFC revenue to pay for allowable administrative support costs. Public agencies must submit these costs as a separate project in each PFC application.

(c) *Maximum cost for certain low-emission technology projects.* If a project involves a vehicle or ground support equipment using low emission technology eligible under § 158.15(b), the FAA will determine the maximum cost that may be financed by PFC revenue. The maximum cost for a new vehicle is the incremental amount between the purchase price of a new low emission vehicle and the purchase price of a standard emission vehicle, or the cost of converting a standard emission vehicle to a low emission vehicle.

(d) *Bond-associated debt service and financing costs.* (1) Public agencies may use PFC revenue to pay debt service and financing costs incurred for a bond issued to carry out approved projects.

(2) If the public agency's bond documents require that PFC revenue be commingled in the general revenue stream of the airport and pledged for the benefit of holders of obligations, the FAA considers PFC revenue to have paid the costs covered in § 158.13(d)(1) if—

(i) An amount equal to the part of the proceeds of the bond issued to carry out approved projects is used to pay allowable costs of such projects; and

(ii) To the extent the PFC revenue collected in any year exceeds the debt service and financing costs on such bonds during that year, an amount equal to the excess is applied as required by § 158.39.

(e) *Exception providing for the use of PFC revenue to pay for debt service for non-eligible projects.* The FAA may authorize a public agency under § 158.18 to impose a PFC for payments for debt service on indebtedness incurred to carry out an airport project that is not eligible if the FAA determines that such use is necessary because of the financial need of the airport.

(f) *Combination of PFC revenue and Federal grant funds.* A public agency may combine PFC revenue and airport grant funds to carry out an approved project. These projects are subject to the record keeping and auditing requirements of this part, as well as the reporting, record keeping and auditing requirements imposed by the Airport and Airway Improvement Act of 1982 (AAIA).

(g) *Non-Federal share.* Public agencies may use PFC revenue to meet the non-Federal share of the cost of projects funded under the Federal airport grant program or the FAA "Program to Permit Cost-Sharing of Air Traffic Modernization Projects" under 49 U.S.C. 44517.

(h) *Approval of project following approval to impose a PFC.* The public agency may not use PFC revenue or interest earned thereon except on an approved project.

[Doc. No. 26385, 56 FR 24278, May 29, 1991, as amended by Amdt. 158–4, 72 FR 28847, May 23, 2007]

§158.15 Project eligibility at PFC levels of $1, $2, or $3.

(a) To be eligible, a project must—

(1) Preserve or enhance safety, security, or capacity of the national air transportation system;

(2) Reduce noise or mitigate noise impacts resulting from an airport; or

(3) Furnish opportunities for enhanced competition between or among air carriers.

(b) Eligible projects are any of the following projects—

(1) Airport development eligible under subchapter I of chapter 471 of 49 U.S.C.;

(2) Airport planning eligible under subchapter I of chapter 471 of 49 U.S.C.;

(3) Terminal development as described in 49 U.S.C. 47110(d);

(4) Airport noise compatibility planning as described in 49 U.S.C. 47505;

(5) Noise compatibility measures eligible for Federal assistance under 49 U.S.C. 47504, without regard to whether the measures are approved under 49 U.S.C. 47504;

(6) Construction of gates and related areas at which passengers are enplaned or deplaned and other areas directly related to the movement of passengers and baggage in air commerce within the boundaries of the airport. These areas do not include restaurants, car rental and automobile parking facilities, or other concessions. Projects required to enable added air service by an air carrier with less than 50 percent of the annual passenger boardings at an airport have added eligibility. Such projects may include structural foundations and floor systems, exterior building walls and load-bearing interior columns or walls, windows, door and roof systems, building utilities (including heating, air conditioning, ventilation, plumbing, and electrical service), and aircraft fueling facilities next to the gate;

(7) A project approved under the FAA's "Program to Permit Cost-Sharing of Air Traffic Modernization Projects" under 49 U.S.C. 44517; or

(8) If the airport is in an air quality nonattainment area (as defined by section 171(2) of the Clean Air Act (42 U.S.C. 7501(2)) or a maintenance area referred to in section 175A of such Act (42 U.S.C. 7505a), and the project will result in the airport receiving appropriate emission credits as described in 49 U.S.C. 47139, a project for:

(i) Converting vehicles eligible under §158.15(b)(1) and ground support equipment powered by a diesel or gasoline engine used at a commercial service airport to low-emission technology certified or verified by the Environmental Protection Agency to reduce emissions or to use cleaner burning conventional fuels; or

(ii) Acquiring for use at a commercial service airport vehicles eligible under §158.15(b)(1) and, subject to §158.13(c), ground support equipment that include low-emission technology or use cleaner burning fuels.

(c) An eligible project must be adequately justified to qualify for PFC funding.

[Doc. No. 26385, 56 FR 24278, May 29, 1991; 56 FR 37127, Aug. 2, 1991; Amdt. 158–2, 65 FR 34541, May 30, 2000; Amdt. 158–4, 72 FR 28848, May 23, 2007]

§ 158.17 Project eligibility at PFC levels of $4 or $4.50.

(a) A project for any airport is eligible for PFC funding at levels of $4 or $4.50 if—

(1) The project meets the eligibility requirements of § 158.15;

(2) The project costs requested for collection at $4 or $4.50 cannot be paid for from funds reasonably expected to be available for the programs referred to in 49 U.S.C. 48103; and

(3) In the case of a surface transportation or terminal project, the public agency has made adequate provision for financing the airside needs of the airport, including runways, taxiways, aprons, and aircraft gates.

(b) In addition, a project for a medium or large airport is only eligible for PFC funding at levels of $4 or $4.50 if the project will make a significant contribution to improving air safety and security, increasing competition among air carriers, reducing current or anticipated congestion, or reducing the impact of aviation noise on people living near the airport.

[Doc. No. FAA–2000–7402, 65 FR 34541, May 30, 2000]

§ 158.18 Use of PFC revenue to pay for debt service for non-eligible projects.

(a) The FAA may authorize a public agency to impose a PFC to make payments for debt service on indebtedness incurred to carry out at the airport a project that is not eligible if the FAA determines it is necessary because of the financial need of the airport. The FAA defines financial need in § 158.3.

(b) A public agency may request authority to impose a PFC and use PFC revenue under this section using the PFC application procedures in § 158.25. The public agency must document its financial position and explain its financial recovery plan that uses all available resources.

(c) The FAA reviews the application using the procedures in § 158.27. The FAA will issue its decision on the public agency's request under § 158.29.

[Doc. No. FAA–2006–23730, 72 FR 28848, May 23, 2007]

§ 158.19 Requirement for competition plans.

(a) Beginning in fiscal year 2001, no public agency may impose a PFC with respect to a covered airport unless the public agency has submitted a written competition plan. This requirement does not apply to PFC authority approved prior to April 5, 2000.

(b) The Administrator will review any plan submitted under paragraph (a) of this section to ensure that it meets the requirements of 49 U.S.C. 47106(f) and periodically will review its implementation to ensure that each covered airport successfully implements its plan.

[Doc. No. FAA–2000–7402, 65 FR 34541, May 30, 2000]

Subpart B—Application and Approval

§ 158.20 Submission of required documents.

(a) Letters and reports required by this part may be transmitted to the appropriate recipient (the public agency, air carrier, and/or the FAA) via e-mail, courier, facsimile, or U.S. Postal Service.

(1) Documents sent electronically to the FAA must be prepared in a format readable by the FAA. Interested parties can obtain the format at their local FAA Airports Office.

(2) Any transmission to FAA Headquarters, using regular U.S. Postal Service, is subject to inspection that may result in delay and damage due to the security process.

(b) Once the database development is completed with air carrier capability, public agencies and air carriers may use the FAA's national PFC database to post their required quarterly reports, and, in that case, do not have to distribute the reports in any other way.

[Doc. No. FAA–2006–23730, 72 FR 28848, May 23, 2007]

§ 158.21 General.

This subpart specifies the consultation and application requirements under which a public agency may obtain approval to impose a PFC and use PFC revenue on a project. This subpart also establishes the procedure for the Administrator's review and approval of applications and amendments and establishes requirements for use of excess PFC revenue.

§158.23 Consultation with air carriers and foreign air carriers.

(a) *Notice by public agency.* A public agency must provide written notice to air carriers and foreign air carriers having a significant business interest at the airport where the PFC is proposed. A public agency must provide this notice before the public agency files an application with the FAA for authority to impose a PFC under §158.25(b). In addition, public agencies must provide this notice before filing an application with the FAA for authority to use PFC revenue under §158.25(c). Public agencies must also provide this notice before filing a notice of intent to impose and/or use a PFC under §158.30. Finally, a public agency must provide this notice before filing a request to amend the FAA's decision with respect to an approved PFC as discussed in §158.37(b)(1). The notice shall include:

(1) Descriptions of projects being considered for funding by PFC's;

(2) The PFC level for each project, the proposed charge effective date, the estimated charge expiration date, and the estimated total PFC revenue;

(3) For a request by a public agency that any class or classes of carriers not be required to collect the PFC—

(i) The designation of each such class,

(ii) The names of the carriers belonging to each such class, to the extent the names are known,

(iii) The estimated number of passengers enplaned annually by each such class, and

(iv) The public agency's reasons for requesting that carriers in each such class not be required to collect the PFC; and

(4) Except as provided in §158.25(c)(2), the date and location of a meeting at which the public agency will present such projects to air carriers and foreign air carriers operating at the airport.

(b) *Meeting.* The meeting required by paragraph (a)(4) of this section shall be held no sooner than 30 days nor later than 45 days after issuance of the written notice required by paragraph (a) of this section. At or before the meeting, the public agency shall provide air carriers and foreign air carriers with—

(1) A description of projects;

(2) An explanation of the need for the projects; and

(3) A detailed financial plan for the projects, including—

(i) The estimated allowable project costs allocated to major project elements;

(ii) The anticipated total amount of PFC revenue that will be used to finance the projects; and

(iii) The source and amount of other funds, if any, needed to finance the projects.

(c) *Requirements of air carriers and foreign air carriers.* (1) Within 30 days following issuance of the notice required by paragraph (a) of this section, each carrier must provide the public agency with a written acknowledgement that it received the notice.

(2) Within 30 days following the meeting, each carrier must provide the public agency with a written certification of its agreement or disagreement with the proposed project. A certification of disagreement shall contain the reasons for such disagreement. The absence of such reasons shall void a certification of disagreement.

(3) If a carrier fails to provide the public agency with timely acknowledgement of the notice or timely certification of agreement or disagreement with the proposed project, the carrier is considered to have certified its agreement.

[Doc. No. 26385, 56 FR 24278, May 29, 1991, as amended by Amdt. 158–2, 65 FR 34541, May 30, 2000; Amdt. 158–3, 70 FR 14934, Mar. 23, 2005]

§158.24 Notice and opportunity for public comment.

(a)(1) *Notice by public agency.* A public agency must provide written notice and an opportunity for public comment before:

(i) Filing an application with the FAA for authority to impose a PFC under §158.25(b);

(ii) Filing an application with the FAA for authority to use PFC revenue under §158.25(c);

(iii) Filing a notice of intent to impose and/or use a PFC under § 158.30; and

(iv) Filing a request to amend a previously approved PFC as discussed in § 158.37(b)(1).

(2) The notice must allow the public to file comments for at least 30 days, but no more than 45 days, after the date of publication of the notice or posting on the public agency's Web site, as applicable.

(b)(1) *Notice contents.* The notice required by § 158.24(a) must include:

(i) A description of the project(s) the public agency is considering for funding by PFC's;

(ii) A brief justification for each project the public agency is considering for funding by PFC's;

(iii) The PFC level for each project;

(iv) The estimated total PFC revenue the public agency will use for each project;

(v) The proposed charge effective date for the application or notice of intent;

(vi) The estimated charge expiration date for the application or notice of intent;

(vii) The estimated total PFC revenue the public agency will collect for the application or notice of intent; and

(viii) The name of and contact information for the person within the public agency to whom comments should be sent.

(2) The public agency must make available a more detailed project justification or the justification documents to the public upon request.

(c) *Distribution of notice.* The public agency must make the notice available to the public and interested agencies through one or more of the following methods:

(1) Publication in local newspapers of general circulation;

(2) Publication in other local media;

(3) Posting the notice on the public agency's Internet Web site; or

(4) Any other method acceptable to the Administrator.

[Doc. No. FAA–2004–17999, 70 FR 14934, Mar. 23, 2005]

§ 158.25　Applications.

(a) *General.* This section specifies the information the public agency must file when applying for authority to impose a PFC and for authority to use PFC revenue on a project. A public agency may apply for such authority at any commercial service airport it controls. The public agency must use the proposed PFC to finance airport-related projects at that airport or at any existing or proposed airport that the public agency controls. A public agency may apply for authority to impose a PFC before or concurrent with an application to use PFC revenue. If a public agency chooses to apply, it must do so by using FAA Form 5500–1, PFC Application (latest edition) and all applicable Attachments. The public agency must provide the information required under paragraphs (b) or (c), or both, of this section.

(b) *Application for authority to impose a PFC.* This paragraph sets forth the information to be submitted by all public agencies seeking authority to impose a PFC. A separate application shall be submitted for each airport at which a PFC is to be imposed. The application shall be signed by an authorized official of the public agency, and, unless otherwise authorized by the Administrator, must include the following:

(1) The name and address of the public agency.

(2) The name and telephone number of the official submitting the application on behalf of the public agency.

(3) The official name of the airport at which the PFC is to be imposed.

(4) The official name of the airport at which a project is proposed.

(5) A copy of the airport capital plan or other documentation of planned improvements for each airport at which a PFC financed project is proposed.

(6) A description of each project proposed.

(7) The project justification, including the extent to which the project achieves one or more of the objectives set forth in § 158.15(a) and (if a PFC level above $3 is requested) the requirements of § 158.17. In addition—

(i) For any project for terminal development, including gates and related areas, the public agency shall discuss

any existing conditions that limit competition between and among air carriers and foreign air carriers at the airport, any initiatives it proposes to foster opportunities for enhanced competition between and among such carriers, and the expected results of such
initiatives; or

(ii) For any terminal development
project at a covered airport, the public
agency shall submit a competition plan
in accordance with §158.19.

(8) The charge to be imposed for each
project.

(9) The proposed charge effective
date.

(10) The estimated charge expiration
date.

(11) Information on the consultation
with air carriers and foreign air carriers having a significant business interest at the airport and the public
comment process, including:

(i) A list of such carriers and those
notified;

(ii) A list of carriers that acknowledged receipt of the notice provided
under §158.23(a);

(iii) Lists of carriers that certified
agreement and that certified disagreement with the project;

(iv) Information on which method
under §158.24(b) the public agency used
to meet the public notice requirement;
and

(v) A summary of substantive comments by carriers contained in any certifications of disagreement with each
project and disagreements with each
project provided by the public, and the
public agency's reasons for continuing
despite such disagreements.

(12) If the public agency is also filing
a request under §158.11—

(i) The request;

(ii) A copy of the information provided to the carriers under §158.23(a)(3);

(iii) A copy of the carriers' comments
with respect to such information;

(iv) A list of any class or classes of
carriers that would not be required to
collect a PFC if the request is approved; and

(v) The public agency's reasons for
submitting the request in the face of
opposing comments.

(13) A copy of information regarding
the financing of the project presented
to the carriers and foreign air carriers

under §158.23 of this part and as revised
during the consultation.

(14) A copy of all comments received
as a result of the carrier consultation
and public comment processes.

(15) For an application not accompanied by a concurrent application for
authority to use PFC revenue:

(i) A description of any alternative
methods being considered by the public
agency to accomplish the objectives of
the project;

(ii) A description of alternative uses
of the PFC revenue to ensure such revenue will be used only on eligible
projects in the event the proposed
project is not ultimately approved for
use of PFC revenue;

(iii) A timetable with projected dates
for completion of project formulation
activities and submission of an application to use PFC revenue; and

(iv) A projected date of project implementation and completion.

(16) A signed statement certifying
that the public agency will comply
with the assurances set forth in Appendix A to this part.

(17) Such additional information as
the Administrator may require.

(c) *Application for authority to use PFC
revenue.* A public agency may use PFC
revenue only for projects approved
under this paragraph. This paragraph
sets forth the information that a public
agency shall submit, unless otherwise
authorized by the Administrator, when
applying for the authority to use PFC
revenue to finance specific projects.

(1) An application submitted concurrently with an application for the authority to impose a PFC, must include:

(i) The information required under
paragraphs (b)(1) through (15) of this
section;

(ii) An FAA Form 5500–1, Attachment
G, Airport Layout Plan, Airspace, and
Environmental Findings (latest edition) providing the following information:

(A) For projects required to be shown
on an ALP, the ALP depicting the
project has been approved by the FAA
and the date of such approval;

(B) All environmental reviews required by the National Environmental
Policy Act (NEPA) of 1969 have been
completed and a copy of the final FAA

environmental determination with respect to the project has been approved, and the date of such approval, if such determination is required; and

(C) The final FAA airspace determination with respect to the project has been completed, and the date of such determination, if an airspace study is required.

(iii) The information required by §§ 158.25(b)(16) and 158.25(b)(17).

(2) An application where the authority to impose a PFC has been previously approved:

(i) Must not be filed until the public agency conducts further consultation with air carriers and foreign air carriers under § 158.23. However, the meeting required under § 158.23(a)(4) is optional if there are no changes to the projects after approval of the impose authority and further opportunity for public comment under § 158.24; and

(ii) Must include a summary of further air carrier consultation and the public agency's response to any disagreements submitted under the air carrier consultation and public comment processes conducted under paragraph (c)(2)(i) of this section;

(iii) Must include the following, updated and changed where appropriate:

(A) FAA Form 5500–1 without attachments except as required below;

(B) For any projects where there have been no changes since the FAA approved authority to impose a PFC for those projects, a list of projects included in this application for use authority. The FAA will consider the information on these projects, filed with the impose authority application, incorporated by reference; and

(C) For any project that has changed since receiving impose authority, the public agency must file an Attachment B for that project clearly describing the changes to the project.

(iv) An FAA Form 5500–1, Attachment G, Airport Layout Plan, Airspace, and Environmental Findings (latest edition) providing the following information:

(A) For projects required to be shown on an ALP, the ALP depicting the project has been approved by the FAA and the date of such approval;

(B) All environmental reviews required by the National Environmental

Policy Act (NEPA) of 1969 have been completed and a copy of the final FAA environmental determination with respect to the project has been approved, and the date of such approval, if such determination is required; and

(C) The final FAA airspace determination with respect to the project has been completed, and the date of such determination, if an airspace study is required; and

(v) The information required by §§ 158.25(b)(16) and 158.25(b)(17).

[Doc. No. FAA–2004–17999, 70 FR 14935, Mar. 23, 2005]

§ 158.27   Review of applications.

(a) *General.* This section describes the process for review of all applications filed under § 158.25 of this part.

(b) *Determination of completeness.* Within 30 days after receipt of an application by the FAA Airports office, the Administrator determines whether the application substantially complies with the requirements of § 158.25.

(c) *Process for substantially complete application.* If the Administrator determines the application is substantially complete, the following procedures apply:

(1) The Administrator advises the public agency by letter that its application is substantially complete.

(2) The Administrator may opt to publish a notice in the FEDERAL REGISTER advising that the Administrator intends to rule on the application and inviting public comment, as set forth in paragraph (e) of this section. If the Administrator publishes a notice, the Administrator will provide a copy of the notice to the public agency.

(3) If the Administrator publishes a notice, the public agency—

(i) Shall make available for inspection, upon request, a copy of the application, notice, and other documents germane to the application, and

(ii) May publish the notice in a newspaper of general circulation in the area where the airport covered by the application is located.

(4) After reviewing the application and any public comments received from a FEDERAL REGISTER notice, the Administrator issues a final decision approving or disapproving the application, in whole or in part, before 120

days after the FAA Airports office received the application.

(d) *Process for applications not substantially complete.* If the Administrator determines an application is not substantially complete, the following procedures apply:

(1) The Administrator notifies the public agency in writing that its application is not substantially complete. The notification will list the information required to complete the application.

(2) Within 15 days after the Administrator sends such notification, the public agency shall advise the Administrator in writing whether it intends to supplement its application.

(3) If the public agency declines to supplement the application, the Administrator follows the procedures for review of an application set forth in paragraph (c) of this section and issues a final decision approving or disapproving the application, in whole or in part, no later than 120 days after the application was received by the FAA Airports office.

(4) If the public agency supplements its application, the original application is deemed to be withdrawn for purposes of applying the statutory deadline for the Administrator's decision. Upon receipt of the supplement, the Administrator issues a final decision approving or disapproving the supplemented application, in whole or in part, no later than 120 days after the supplement was received by the FAA Airports office.

(e) *The Federal Register notice.* The FEDERAL REGISTER notice includes the following information:

(1) The name of the public agency and the airport at which the PFC is to be imposed;

(2) A brief description of the PFC project, the level of the proposed PFC, the proposed charge effective date, the proposed charge expiration date and the total estimated PFC revenue;

(3) The address and telephone number of the FAA Airports office at which the application may be inspected;

(4) The Administrator's determination on whether the application is substantially complete and any information required to complete the application; and

(5) The due dates for any public comments.

(f) *Public comments.* (1) Interested persons may file comments on the application within 30 days after publication of the Administrator's notice in the FEDERAL REGISTER.

(2) Three copies of these comments shall be submitted to the FAA Airports office identified in the FEDERAL REGISTER notice.

(3) Commenters shall also provide one copy of their comments to the public agency.

(4) Comments from air carriers and foreign air carriers may be in the same form as provided to the public agency under §158.23.

[Doc. No. 26385, 56 FR 24278, May 29, 1991; 56 FR 30867, July 8, 1991, as amended by Amdt. 158–3, 70 FR 14936, Mar. 23, 2005]

§158.29   The Administrator's decision.

(a) *Authority to impose a PFC.* (1) An application to impose a PFC will be approved in whole or in part only after a determination that—

(i) The amount and duration of the PFC will not result in revenue that exceeds amounts necessary to finance the project;

(ii) The project will achieve the objectives and criteria set forth in §158.15 except for those projects approved under §158.18.

(iii) If a PFC level above $3 is being approved, the project meets the criteria set forth in §158.17;

(iv) The collection process, including any request by the public agency not to require a class of carriers to collect PFC's, is reasonable, not arbitrary, nondiscriminatory, and otherwise in compliance with the law;

(v) The public agency has not been found to be in violation of 49 U.S.C. 47524 and 47526;

(vi) The public agency has not been found to be in violation of 49 U.S.C. 47107(b) governing the use of airport revenue;

(vii) If the public agency has not applied for authority to use PFC revenue, a finding that there are alternative uses of the PFC revenue to ensure that such revenue will be used on approved projects; and

(viii) If applicable, the public agency has submitted a competition plan in accordance with § 158.19.

(2) The Administrator notifies the public agency in writing of the decision on the application. The notification will list the projects and alternative uses that may qualify for PFC financing under § 158.15, and (if a PFC level above $3 is being approved) § 158.17, PFC level, total approved PFC revenue including the amounts approved at $3 and less, $4, and/or $4.50, duration of authority to impose and earliest permissible charge effective date.

(b) *Authority to use PFC revenue on an approved project.* (1) An application for authority to use PFC revenue will be approved in whole or in part only after a determination that—

(i) The amount and duration of the PFC will not result in revenue that exceeds amounts necessary to finance the project;

(ii) The project will achieve the objectives and criteria set forth in § 158.15 except for those projects approved under § 158.18.

(iii) If a PFC level above $3 is being approved, the project meets the criteria set forth in § 158.17; and

(iv) All applicable requirements pertaining to the ALP for the airport, airspace studies for the project, and the National Environmental Policy Act of 1969 (NEPA), have been satisfied.

(2) The Administrator notifies the public agency in writing of the decision on the application. The notification will list the approved projects, PFC level, total approved PFC revenue, total approved for collection, including the amounts approved at $3 and less, $4, and/or $4.50, and any limit on the duration of authority to impose a PFC as prescribed under § 158.33.

(3) Approval to use PFC revenue to finance a project shall be construed as approval of that project.

(c) *Disapproval of application.* (1) If an application is disapproved, the Administrator notifies the public agency in writing of the decision and the reasons for the disapproval.

(2) A public agency reapplying for approval to impose or use a PFC must comply with §§ 158.23, 158.24, and 158.25.

(d) The Administrator publishes a monthly notice of PFC approvals and disapprovals in the FEDERAL REGISTER.

[Doc. No. 26385, 56 FR 24278, May 29, 1991; 56 FR 30867, July 8, 1991, as amended by Amdt. 158-2, 65 FR 34542, May 30, 2000; Amdt. 158-3, 70 FR 14936, Mar. 23, 2005; Amdt. 158-4, 72 FR 28848, May 23, 2007]

§ 158.30 PFC Authorization at Non-Hub Airports.

(a) *General.* This section specifies the procedures a public agency controlling a non-hub airport must follow when notifying the FAA of its intent to impose a PFC and to use PFC revenue on a project under this section. In addition, this section describes the FAA's rules for reviewing and acknowledging a notice of intent filed under this section. A public agency may notify the FAA of its intent to impose a PFC before or concurrent with a notice of intent to use PFC revenue. A public agency must file a notice of intent in the manner and form prescribed by the Administrator and must include the information required under paragraphs (b), (c), or both, of this section.

(b) *Notice of intent to impose a PFC.* This paragraph sets forth the information a public agency must file to notify the FAA of its intent to impose a PFC under this section. The public agency must file a separate notice of intent for each airport at which the public agency plans on imposing a PFC. An authorized official of the public agency must sign the notice of intent and, unless authorized by the Administrator, must include:

(1) A completed FAA Form 5500-1, PFC Application (latest edition) without attachments except as required below;

(2) Project information (in the form and manner prescribed by the FAA) including the project title, PFC funds sought, PFC level sought, and, if an existing Airport Improvement Program (AIP) grant already covers this project, the grant agreement number.

(3) If an existing AIP grant does not cover this project, the notice of intent must include the information in paragraph (b)(2) of this section as well as the following:

(i) Additional information describing the proposed schedule for the project,

(ii) A description of how this project meets one of the PFC objectives in § 158.15(a), and

(iii) A description of how this project meets the adequate justification requirement in § 158.15(c).

(4) A copy of any comments received by the public agency during the air carrier consultation and public comment processes (§§ 158.23 and 158.24) and the public agency's response to any disagreements.

(5) If applicable, a request to exclude a class of carriers from the requirement to collect the PFC (§ 158.11).

(6) A signed statement certifying that the public agency will comply with the assurances set forth in Appendix A to this part.

(7) Any additional information the Administrator may require.

(c) *Notice of intent to use PFC revenue.* A public agency may use PFC revenue only for projects included in notices filed under this paragraph or approved under § 158.29. This paragraph sets forth the information that a public agency must file, unless otherwise authorized by the Administrator, in its notice of intent to use PFC revenue to finance specific projects under this section.

(1) A notice of intent to use PFC revenue filed concurrently with a notice of intent to impose a PFC must include:

(i) The information required under paragraphs (b)(1) through (7) of this section;

(ii) A completed FAA Form 5500–1, Attachment G, Airport Layout Plan, Airspace, and Environmental Findings (latest edition) for all projects not included in an existing Federal airport program grant.

(2) A notice of intent to use PFC revenue where the FAA has previously acknowledged a notice of intent to impose a PFC must:

(i) Be preceded by further consultation with air carriers and the opportunity for public comment under §§ 158.23 and 158.24 of this part. However, a meeting with the air carriers is optional if all information is the same as that provided with the impose authority notice;

(ii) Include a copy of any comments received by the public agency during the air carrier consultation and public comment processes (§§ 158.23 and 158.24)

and the public agency's response to any disagreements or negative comments; and

(iii) Include any updated and changed information:

(A) Required by paragraphs (b)(1), (2), (5), (6), and (7) of this section; and

(B) Required by paragraph (c)(1)(ii) of this section.

(d) *FAA review of notices of intent.* (1) The FAA will review the notice of intent to determine that:

(A) The amount and duration of the PFC will not result in revenue that exceeds the amount necessary to finance the project(s);

(B) Each proposed project meets the requirements of § 158.15;

(C) Each project proposed at a PFC level above $3.00 meets the requirements of § 158.17(a)(2) and (3);

(D) All applicable airport layout plan, airspace, and environmental requirements have been met for each project;

(E) Any request by the public agency to exclude a class of carriers from the requirement to collect the PFC is reasonable, not arbitrary, nondiscriminatory, and otherwise complies with the law; and

(F) The consultation and public comment processes complied with §§ 158.23 and 158.24.

(2) The FAA will also make a determination regarding the public agency's compliance with 49 U.S.C. 47524 and 47526 governing airport noise and access restrictions and 49 U.S.C. 47107(b) governing the use of airport revenue. Finally, the FAA will review all comments filed during the air carrier consultation and public comment processes.

(e) *FAA acknowledgment of notices of intent.* Within 30 days of receipt of the public agency's notice of intent about its PFC program, the FAA will issue a written acknowledgment of the public agency's notice. The FAA's acknowledgment may concur with all proposed projects, may object to some or all proposed projects, or may object to the notice of intent in its entirety. The FAA's acknowledgment will include the reason(s) for any objection(s).

(f) Public agency actions following issuance of FAA acknowledgment letter. If the FAA does not object to either a project or the notice of intent in its entirety, the public agency may implement its PFC program. The public agency's implementation must follow the information specified in its notice of intent. If the FAA objects to a project, the public agency may not collect or use PFC revenue on that project. If the FAA objects to the notice of intent in its entirety, the public agency may not implement the PFC program proposed in that notice. When implementing a PFC under this section, except for § 158.25, a public agency must comply with all sections of part 158.

(g) *Acknowledgment not an order.* An FAA acknowledgment issued under this section is not considered an order issued by the Secretary for purposes of 49 U.S.C. 46110 (Judicial Review).

(h) *Sunset provision.* This section will expire May 9, 2008.

[Doc. No. FAA-2004-17999, 70 FR 14936, Mar. 23, 2005]

§ 158.31 **Duration of authority to impose a PFC after project implementation.**

A public agency that has begun implementing an approved project may impose a PFC until—

(a) The charge expiration date is reached;

(b) The total PFC revenue collected plus interest earned thereon equals the allowable cost of the approved project;

(c) The authority to collect the PFC is terminated by the Administrator under subpart E of this part; or

(d) The public agency is determined by the Administrator to be in violation of 49 U.S.C. 47524 and 47526, and the authority to collect the PFC is terminated under that statute's implementing regulations under this title.

[Doc. No. 26385, 56 FR 24278, May 29, 1991, as amended by Amdt. 158-2, 65 FR 34542, May 30, 2000; Amdt. 158-4, 72 FR 28849, May 23, 2007]

§ 158.33 **Duration of authority to impose a PFC before project implementation.**

(a) A public agency shall not impose a PFC beyond the lesser of the following—

(1) 2 years after approval to use PFC revenue on an approved project if the project has not been implemented, or

(2) 5 years after the charge effective date; or

(3) 5 years after the FAA's decision on the application (if the charge effective date is more than 60 days after the decision date) if an approved project is not implemented.

(b) If, in the Administrator's judgment, the public agency has not made sufficient progress toward implementation of an approved project within the times specified in paragraph (a) of this section, the Administrator begins termination proceedings under subpart E of this part.

(c) The authority to impose a PFC following approval shall automatically expire without further action by the Administrator on the following dates:

(1) 3 years after the charge effective date; or 3 years after the FAA's decision on the application if the charge effective date is more than 60 days after the decision date unless—

(i) The public agency has filed an application for approval to use PFC revenue for an eligible project that is pending before the FAA;

(ii) An application to use PFC revenue has been approved; or

(iii) A request for extension (not to exceed 2 years) to submit an application for project approval, under § 158.35, has been granted; or

(2) 5 years after the charge effective date; or 5 years after the FAA's decision on the application (if the charge effective date is more than 60 days after the decision date) unless the public agency has obtained project approval.

(d) If the authority to impose a PFC expires under paragraph (c) of this section, the public agency must provide the FAA with a list of the air carriers and foreign air carriers operating at the airport and all other collecting carriers that have remitted PFC revenue to the public agency in the preceding 12 months. The FAA notifies each of the listed carriers to terminate PFC collection no later than 30 days after the date of notification by the FAA.

(e) Restriction on reauthorization to impose a PFC. Whenever the authority to impose a PFC has expired or been terminated under this section, the Administrator will not grant new approval to impose a PFC in advance of implementation of an approved project.

[Doc. No. 26385, 56 FR 24278, May 29, 1991; 56 FR 37127, Aug. 2, 1991; Amdt. 158–4, 72 FR 28849, May 23, 2007]

§158.35 Extension of time to submit application to use PFC revenue.

(a) A public agency may request an extension of time to submit an application to use PFC revenue after approval of an application to impose PFC's. At least 30 days prior to submitting such request, the public agency shall publish notice of its intention to request an extension in a local newspaper of general circulation and shall request comments. The notice shall include progress on the project, a revised schedule for obtaining project approval and reasons for the delay in submitting the application.

(b) The request shall be submitted at least 120 days prior to the charge expiration date and, unless otherwise authorized by the Administrator, shall be accompanied by the following:

(1) A description of progress on the project application to date.

(2) A revised schedule for submitting the application.

(3) An explanation of the reasons for delay in submitting the application.

(4) A summary financial report depicting the total amount of PFC revenue collected plus interest, the projected amount to be collected during the period of the requested extension, and any public agency funds used on the project for which reimbursement may be sought.

(5) A summary of any further consultation with air carriers and foreign air carriers operating at the airport.

(6) A summary of comments received in response to the local notice.

(c) The Administrator reviews the request for extension and accompanying information, to determine whether—

(1) The public agency has shown good cause for the delay in applying for project approval;

(2) The revised schedule is satisfactory; and

(3) Further collection will not result in excessive accumulation of PFC revenue.

(d) The Administrator, upon determining that the agency has shown good cause for the delay and that other elements of the request are satisfactory, grants the request for extension to the public agency. The Administrator advises the public agency in writing not more than 90 days after receipt of the request. The duration of the extension shall be as specified in §158.33 of this part.

§158.37 Amendment of approved PFC.

(a)(1) A public agency may amend the FAA's decision with respect to an approved PFC to:

(i) Increase or decrease the level of PFC the public agency wants to collect from each passenger,

(ii) Increase or decrease the total approved PFC revenue,

(iii) Change the scope of an approved project,

(iv) Delete an approved project, or

(v) Establish a new class of carriers under §158.11 or amend any such class previously approved.

(2) A public agency may not amend the FAA's decision with respect to an approved PFC to add projects, change an approved project to a different facility type, or alter an approved project to accomplish a different purpose.

(b) The public agency must file a request to the Administrator to amend the FAA's decision with respect to an approved PFC. The request must include or demonstrate:

(1)(i) Further consultation with the air carriers and foreign air carriers and seek public comment in accordance with §§158.23 and 158.24 when applying for those requests to:

(A) Amend the approved PFC amount for a project by more than 25 percent of the original approved amount if the amount was $1,000,000 or greater,

(B) Amend the approved PFC amount for a project by any percentage if the original approved amount was below $1,000,000 and the amended approved amount is $1,000,000 or greater,

(C) Change the scope of a project, or

(D) Increase the PFC level to be collected from each passenger.

(ii) No further consultation with air carriers and foreign air carriers or public comment is required by a public agency in accordance with §§158.23 and

158.24 when applying for an amendment in the following situations:

(A) To institute a decrease in the level of PFC to be collected from each passenger;

(B) To institute a decrease in the total PFC revenue;

(C) To institute an increase of 25 percent or less of the original approved amount if the amount was more than $1,000,000; or

(D) To institute an increase of any amount if the original approved amount of the project was less than $1,000,000 and if the amended approved amount of the project remains below $1,000,000; or

(E) To establish a new class of carriers under § 158.11 or amend any such class previously approved; or

(F) To delete an approved project.

(2) A copy of any comments received from the processes in paragraph (b)(1)(A) of this section for the carrier consultation and the opportunity for public comment in accordance with §§ 158.23 and 158.24;

(3) The public agency's reasons for continuing despite any objections;

(4) A description of the proposed amendment;

(5) Justification, if the amendment involves an increase in the PFC amount for a project by more than 25 percent of the original approved amount if that amount is $1,000,000 or greater, an increase in the PFC amount by any percentage if the original approved amount was less than $1,000,000 and the amended approved amount is $1,000,000 or greater, a change in the approved project scope, or any increase in the approved PFC level to be collected from each passenger.

(6) A description of how each project meets the requirements of § 158.17(b), for each project proposed for an increase of the PFC level above $3.00 at a medium or large hub airport;

(7) A signed statement certifying that the public agency has met the requiements of § 158.19, if applicable, for any amendment proposing to increase the PFC level above $3.00 at a medium or large hub airport; and

(8) Any other information the Administrator may require.

(c) The Administrator will approve, partially approve or disapprove the amendment request and notify the public agency of the decision within 30 days of receipt of the request. If a PFC level of more than $3.00 is approved, the Administrator must find the project meets the requirements of §§ 158.17 and 158.19, if applicable, before the public agency can implement the new PFC level.

(d) The public agency must notify the carriers of any change to the FAA's decision with respect to an approved PFC resulting from an amendment. The effective date of any new PFC level must be no earlier than the first day of a month which is at least 30 days from the date the public agency notifies the carriers.

[Doc. No. FAA–2004–17999, 70 FR 14937, Mar. 23, 2005, as amended by Amdt. 158–4, 72 FR 28849, May 23, 2007]

§ 158.39   Use of excess PFC revenue.

(a) If the PFC revenue remitted to the public agency, plus interest earned thereon, exceeds the allowable cost of the project, the public agency must use the excess funds for approved projects or to retire outstanding PFC-financed bonds.

(b) For bond-financed projects, any excess PFC revenue collected under debt servicing requirements shall be retained by the public agency and used for approved projects or retirement of outstanding PFC-financed bonds.

(c) When the authority to impose a PFC has expired or has been terminated, accumulated PFC revenue shall be used for approved projects or retirement of outstanding PFC-financed bonds.

(d) Within 30 days after the authority to impose a PFC has expired or been terminated, the public agency must present a plan to the appropriate FAA Airports office to begin using accumulated PFC revenue. The plan must include a timetable for submitting any necessary application under this part. If the public agency fails to submit such a plan, or if the plan is not acceptable to the Administrator, the Administrator may reduce Federal airport grant program apportioned funds.

[Doc. No. 26385, 56 FR 24278, May 29, 1991, as amended by Amdt. 158–4, 72 FR 28849, May 23, 2007]

Subpart C—Collection, Handling, and Remittance of PFC's

§158.41 General.

This subpart contains the requirements for notification, collection, handling and remittance of PFC's.

§158.43 Public agency notification to collect PFC's.

(a) Following approval of an application to impose a PFC under subpart B of this part, the public agency shall notify the air carriers and foreign air carriers required to collect PFC's at its airport of the Administrator's approval. Each notified carrier shall notify its agents, including other issuing carriers, of the collection requirement.

(b) The notification shall be in writing and contain at a minimum the following information:

(1) The level of PFC to be imposed.

(2) The total revenue to be collected.

(3) The charge effective date will always be the first day of the month; however, it must be at least 30 days after the date the public agency notified the air carriers of the FAA's approval to impose the PFC.

(4) The proposed charge expiration date.

(5) A copy of the Administrator's notice of approval.

(6) The address where remittances and reports are to be filed by carriers.

(c) The public agency must notify air carriers required to collect PFCs at its airport and the FAA of changes in the charge expiration date at least 30 days before the existing charge expiration date or new charge expiration date, whichever comes first. Each notified air carrier must notify its agents, including other issuing carriers, of such changes.

(d) The public agency shall provide a copy of the notification to the appropriate FAA Airports office.

[Doc. No. 26385, 56 FR 24278, May 29, 1991, as amended by Amdt. 158–4, 72 FR 28849, May 23, 2007]

§158.45 Collection of PFC's on tickets issued in the U.S.

(a) On and after the charge effective date, tickets issued in the U.S. shall include the required PFC except as provided in paragraphs (c) and (d) of this section.

(1) Issuing carriers shall be responsible for all funds from time of collection to remittance.

(2) The appropriate charge is the PFC in effect at the time the ticket is issued.

(3) Issuing carriers and their agents shall collect PFCs based on the itinerary at the time of issuance.

(i) Any change in itinerary initiated by a passenger that requires an adjustment to the amount paid by the passenger is subject to collection or refund of the PFC as appropriate.

(ii) Failure to travel on a nonrefundable or expired ticket is not a change in itinerary. If the ticket purchaser is not permitted any fare refund on the unused ticket, the ticket purchaser is not permitted a refund of any PFC associated with that ticket.

(b) Issuing carriers and their agents shall note as a separate item on each air travel ticket upon which a PFC is shown, the total amount of PFC's paid by the passenger and the airports for which the PFC's are collected.

(c) For each one-way trip shown on the complete itinerary of an air travel ticket, issuing air carriers and their agents shall collect a PFC from a passenger only for the first two airports where PFC's are imposed. For each round trip, a PFC shall be collected only for enplanements at the first two enplaning airports and the last two enplaning airports where PFC's are imposed.

(d) In addition to the restriction in paragraph (c) of this section, issuing carriers and their agents shall not collect PFC's from a passenger covered by any of the other limitations described in §158.9(a).

(e) Collected PFC's shall be distributed as noted on the air travel ticket.

(f) Issuing carriers and their agents shall stop collecting the PFC's on the charge expiration date stated in a notice from the public agency, or as required by the Administrator.

[Doc. No. 26385, 56 FR 24278, May 29, 1991, as amended by Amdt. 158–2, 65 FR 34542, May 30, 2000; Amdt. 158–4, 72 FR 28849, May 23, 2007]

§ 158.47 Collection of PFC's on tickets issued outside the U.S.

(a) For tickets issued outside the U.S., an air carrier or foreign air carrier may follow the requirements of either § 158.45 or this section, unless the itinerary is for travel wholly within the U.S. Air carriers and foreign air carriers must comply with § 158.45 where the itinerary is for travel wholly within the U.S. regardless of where the ticket is issued.

(b) Notwithstanding any other provisions of this part, no foreign airline is required to collect a PFC on air travel tickets issued on its own ticket stock unless it serves a point or points in the U.S.

(c) If an air carrier or foreign air carrier elects not to comply with § 158.45 for tickets issued outside the U.S.—

(1) The carrier is required to collect PFC's on such tickets only for the public agency controlling the last airport at which the passenger is enplaned prior to departure from the U.S.

(2) The carrier may collect the PFC either at the time the ticket is issued or at the time the passenger is last enplaned prior to departure from the U.S. The carrier may vary the method of collection among its flights.

(3) The carrier shall provide a written record to the passenger that a PFC has been collected. Such a record shall appear on or with the air travel ticket and shall include the same information as required by § 158.45(b), but need not be preprinted on the ticket stock.

(4) Issuing carriers and their agents shall collect PFCs based on the itinerary at the time of issuance.

(i) Any change in itinerary initiated by a passenger that requires an adjustment to the amount paid by the passenger is subject to collection or refund of the PFC as appropriate.

(ii) Failure to travel on a nonrefundable or expired ticket is not a change in itinerary. If the ticket purchaser is not permitted any fare refund on the unused ticket, the ticket purchaser is not permitted a refund of any PFC associated with that ticket.

(d) With respect to a flight on which the air carrier or foreign air carrier chooses to collect the PFC at the time the air travel ticket is issued—

(1) The carrier and its agents shall collect the required PFC on tickets issued on or after the charge effective date.

(2) The carrier is not required to collect PFC's at the time of enplanement for tickets sold by other air carriers or foreign air carriers or their agents.

(e) With respect to a flight on which the air carrier or foreign air carrier chooses to collect the PFC at the time of enplanement, the carrier shall examine the air travel ticket of each passenger enplaning at the airport on and after the charge effective date and shall collect the PFC from any passenger whose air travel ticket does not include a written record indicating that the PFC was collected at the time of issuance.

(f) Collected PFC's shall be distributed as noted on the written record provided to the passenger.

(g) Collecting carriers shall be responsible for all funds from time of collection to remittance.

(h) Collecting carriers and their agents shall stop collecting the PFC on the charge expiration date stated in a notice from the public agency, or as required by the Administrator.

[Doc. No. 26385, 56 FR 24278, May 29, 1991; 56 FR 37127, Aug. 2, 1991; Amdt. 158–4, 72 FR 28849, May 23, 2007]

§ 158.49 Handling of PFC's.

(a) Collecting carriers shall establish and maintain a financial management system to account for PFC's in accordance with the Department of Transportation's Uniform System of Accounts and Reports (14 CFR part 241). For carriers not subject to 14 CFR part 241, such carriers shall establish and maintain an accounts payable system to handle PFC revenue with subaccounts for each public agency to which such carrier remits PFC revenue.

(b) Collecting carriers must account for PFC revenue separately. PFC revenue may be commingled with the air carrier's other sources of revenue except for covered air carriers discussed in paragraph (c) of this section. PFC revenues held by an air carrier or an agent of the air carrier after collection are held in trust for the beneficial interest of the public agency imposing the PFC. Such air carrier or agent holds neither legal nor equitable interest in the PFC revenues except for any handling fee or interest collected on unremitted proceeds as authorized in §158.53.

(c)(1) A covered air carrier must segregate PFC revenue in a designated separate PFC account. Regardless of the amount of PFC revenue in the covered air carrier's account at the time the bankruptcy petition is filed, the covered air carrier must deposit into the separate PFC account an amount equal to the average monthly liability for PFCs collected under this section by such air carrier or any of its agents.

(i) The covered air carrier is required to create one PFC account to cover all PFC revenue it collects. The designated PFC account is solely for PFC transactions and the covered air carrier must make all PFC transactions from that PFC account. The covered air carrier is not required to create separate PFC accounts for each airport where a PFC is imposed.

(ii) The covered air carrier must transfer PFCs from its general accounts into the separate PFC account in an amount equal to the average monthly liability for PFCs as the "PFC reserve." The PFC reserve must equal a one-month average of the sum of the total PFCs collected by the covered air carrier, net of any credits or handling fees allowed by law, during the past 12-month period of PFC collections immediately before entering bankruptcy.

(iii) The minimum PFC reserve balance must never fall below the fixed amount defined in paragraph (c)(1)(ii) of this section.

(iv) A covered air carrier may continue to deposit the PFCs it collects into its general operating accounts combined with ticket sales revenue. However, at least once every business day, the covered air carrier must remove all PFC revenue (Daily PFC amount) from those accounts and transfer it to the new PFC account. An estimate based on 1/30 of the PFC reserve balance is permitted in substitution of the Daily PFC amount.

(A) In the event a covered air carrier ceases operations while still owing PFC remittances, the PFC reserve fund may be used to make those remittances. If there is any balance in the PFC reserve fund after all PFC remittances are made, that balance will be returned to the covered air carrier's general account.

(B) In the event a covered air carrier emerges from bankruptcy protection and ceases to be a covered air carrier, any balance remaining in the PFC reserve fund after any outstanding PFC obligations are met will be returned to the air carrier's general account.

(v) If the covered air carrier uses an estimate rather than the daily PFC amount, the covered air carrier shall reconcile the estimated amount with the actual amount of PFCs collected for the prior month (Actual Monthly PFCs). This reconciliation must take place no later than the 20th day of the month (or the next business day if the date is not a business day). In the event the Actual Monthly PFCs are greater than the aggregate estimated PFC amount, the covered air carrier will, within one business day of the reconciliation, deposit the difference into the PFC account. If the Actual Monthly PFCs are less than the aggregate estimated PFC amount, the covered air carrier will be entitled to a credit in the amount of the difference to be applied to the daily PFC amount due.

(vi) The covered air carrier is permitted to recalculate and reset the PFC reserve and daily PFC amount on each successive anniversary date of its bankruptcy petition using the methodology described above.

(2) If a covered air carrier or its agent fails to segregate PFC revenue in violation of paragraph (c)(1) of this section, the trust fund status of such revenue shall not be defeated by an inability of any party to identify and trace the precise funds in the accounts of the air carrier.

(3) A covered air carrier and its agents may not grant to any third party any security or other interest in PFC revenue.

(4) A covered air carrier that fails to comply with any requirement of paragraph (c) of this section, or causes an eligible public agency to spend funds to recover or retain payment of PFC revenue, must compensate that public agency for those cost incurred to recover the PFCs owed.

(5) The provisions of paragraph (b) of this section that allow the commingling of PFCs with other air carrier revenue do not apply to a covered air carrier.

(d) All collecting air carriers must disclose the existence and amount of PFC funds regarded as trust funds in their financial statements.

[Doc. No. 26385, 56 FR 24278, May 29, 1991, as amended by Amdt. 158–2, 65 FR 34542, May 30, 2000; Amdt. 158–4, 72 FR 28850, May 23, 2007]

§ 158.51 Remittance of PFC's.

Passenger facility charges collected by carriers shall be remitted to the public agency on a monthly basis. PFC revenue recorded in the accounting system of the carrier, as set forth in § 158.49 of this part, shall be remitted to the public agency no later than the last day of the following calendar month (or if that date falls on a weekend or holiday, the first business day thereafter).

§ 158.53 Collection compensation.

(a) As compensation for collecting, handling, and remitting the PFC revenue, the collecting air carrier is entitled to:

(1) $0.11 of each PFC collected.

(2) Any interest or other investment return earned on PFC revenue between the time of collection and remittance to the public agency.

(b) A covered air carrier that fails to designate a separate PFC account is prohibited from collecting interest on the PFC revenue. Where a covered air carrier maintains a separate PFC account in compliance with § 158.49(c), it will receive the interest on PFC accounts as described in paragraph (a)(2) of this section.

(c)(1) Collecting air carriers may provide collection cost data periodically to the FAA after the agency issues a notice in the FEDERAL REGISTER that specifies the information and deadline for filing the information. Submission of the information is voluntary. The requested information must include data on interest earned by the air carriers on PFC revenue and air carrier collection, handling, and remittance costs in the following categories:

(i) Credit card fees;

(ii) Audit fees;

(iii) PFC disclosure fees;

(iv) Reservations costs;

(v) Passenger service costs;

(vi) Revenue accounting, data entry, accounts payable, tax, and legal fees;

(vii) Corporate property department costs;

(viii) Training for reservations agents, ticket agents, and other departments;

(ix) Ongoing carrier information systems costs;

(x) Ongoing computer reservations systems costs; and

(xi) Airline Reporting Corporation fees.

(2) The FAA may determine a new compensation level based on an analysis of the data provided under paragraph (c)(1) of this section, if the data is submitted by carriers representing at least 75 percent of PFCs collected nationwide.

(3) Any new compensation level determined by the FAA under paragraph (c)(2) of this section will replace the level identified in paragraph (a)(1) of this section.

[Doc. No. FAA–2006–23730, 72 FR 28850, May 23, 2007; Amdt. 158–4, 72 FR 31714, June 8, 2007]

Subpart D—Reporting, Recordkeeping and Audits

§ 158.61 General.

This subpart contains the requirements for reporting, recordkeeping and auditing of accounts maintained by collecting carriers and by public agencies.

§ 158.63 Reporting requirements: Public agency.

(a) The public agency must provide quarterly reports to air carriers collecting PFCs for the public agency with a copy to the appropriate FAA Airports Office. The quarterly report must include:

(1) Actual PFC revenue received from collecting air carriers, interest earned, and project expenditures for the quarter;

(2) Cumulative actual PFC revenue received, interest earned, project expenditures, and the amount committed for use on currently approved projects, including the quarter;

(3) The PFC level for each project; and

(4) Each project's current schedule.

(b) The report shall be provided on or before the last day of the calendar month following the calendar quarter or other period agreed by the public agency and collecting carrier.

(c) For medium and large hub airports, the public agency must provide to the FAA, by July 1 of each year, an estimate of PFC revenue to be collected for each airport in the following fiscal year.

[Doc. No. 26385, 56 FR 24278, May 29, 1991, as amended by Amdt. 158-2, 65 FR 34542, May 30, 2000; Amdt. 158-4, 72 FR 28851, May 23, 2007]

§ 158.65 Reporting requirements: Collecting air carriers.

(a) Each air carrier collecting PFCs for a public agency must provide quarterly reports to the public agency unless otherwise agreed by the collecting air carrier and public agency, providing an accounting of funds collected and funds remitted.

(1) Unless otherwise agreed by the collecting air carrier and public agency, reports must state:

(i) The collecting air carrier and airport involved,

(ii) The total PFC revenue collected,

(iii) The total PFC revenue refunded to passengers,

(iv) The collected revenue withheld for reimbursement of expenses under § 158.53, and

(v) The dates and amounts of each remittance for the quarter.

(2) The report must be filed by the last day of the month following the calendar quarter or other period agreed by the collecting carrier and public agency for which funds were collected.

(b) A covered air carrier must provide the FAA with:

(1) A copy of its quarterly report by the established schedule under paragraph (a) of this section; and

(2) A monthly PFC account statement delivered not later than the fifth day of the following month. This monthly statement must include:

(i) The balance in the account on the first day of the month,

(ii) The total funds deposited during the month,

(iii) The total funds disbursed during the month, and

(iv) The closing balance in the account.

[Doc. No. FAA-2006-23730, 72 FR 28851, May 23, 2007]

§ 158.67 Recordkeeping and auditing: Public agency.

(a) Each public agency shall keep any unliquidated PFC revenue remitted to it by collecting carriers on deposit in an interest bearing account or in other interest bearing instruments used by the public agency's airport capital fund. Interest earned on such PFC revenue shall be used, in addition to the principal, to pay the allowable costs of PFC-funded projects. PFC revenue may only be commingled with other public agency airport capital funds in deposits or interest bearing instruments.

(b) Each public agency shall establish and maintain for each approved application a separate accounting record. The accounting record shall identify the PFC revenue received from the collecting carriers, interest earned on such revenue, the amounts used on each project, and the amount reserved for currently approved projects.

(c) At least annually during the period the PFC is collected, held or used, each public agency shall provide for an audit of its PFC account. The audit shall be performed by an accredited independent public accountant and may be of limited scope. The accountant shall express an opinion of the fairness and reasonableness of the public agency's procedures for receiving, holding, and using PFC revenue. The accountant shall also express an opinion on whether the quarterly report required under § 158.63 fairly represents the net transactions within the PFC account. The audit may be—

(1) Performed specifically for the PFC account; or

(2) Conducted as part of an audit under Office of Management and Budget Circular A-133 (the Single Audit Act of 1984, Pub. L. 98-502, and the Single Audit Act Amendments of 1996, Pub. L. 104-156) provided the auditor specifically addresses the PFC.

(3) Upon request, a copy of the audit shall be provided to each collecting carrier that remitted PFC revenue to

the public agency in the period covered by the audit and to the Administrator.

[Doc. No. 26385, 56 FR 24278, May 29, 1991, as amended by Amdt. 158–4, 72 FR 28851, May 23, 2007]

§ 158.69 Recordkeeping and auditing: Collecting carriers.

(a) Collecting carriers shall establish and maintain for each public agency for which they collect a PFC an accounting record of PFC revenue collected, remitted, refunded and compensation retained under § 158.53(a) of this part. The accounting record shall identify the airport at which the passengers were enplaned.

(b) Each collecting carrier that collects more than 50,000 PFC's annually shall provide for an audit at least annually of its PFC account.

(1) The audit shall be performed by an accredited independent public accountant and may be of limited scope. The accountant shall express an opinion on the fairness and reasonableness of the carrier's procedures for collecting, holding, and dispersing PFC revenue. The opinion shall also address whether the quarterly reports required under § 158.65 fairly represent the net transactions in the PFC account.

(2) For the purposes of an audit under this section, collection is defined as the point when agents or other intermediaries remit PFC revenue to the carrier.

(3) Upon request, a copy of the audit shall be provided to each public agency for which a PFC is collected.

§ 158.71 Federal oversight.

(a) The Administrator may periodically audit and/or review the use of PFC revenue by a public agency. The purpose of the audit or review is to ensure that the public agency is in compliance with the requirements of this part and 49 U.S.C. 40117.

(b) The Administrator may periodically audit and/or review the collection and remittance by the collecting carriers of PFC revenue. The purpose of the audit or review is to ensure collecting carriers are in compliance with the requirements of this part and 49 U.S.C. 40117.

(c) Public agencies and carriers shall allow any authorized representative of the Administrator, the Secretary of Transportation, or the Comptroller General of the U.S., access to any of its books, documents, papers, and records pertinent to PFC's

[Doc. No. 26385, 56 FR 24278, May 29, 1991, as amended by Amdt. 158–2, 65 FR 34543, May 30, 2000]

Subpart E—Termination

§ 158.81 General.

This subpart contains the procedures for termination of PFCs or loss of Federal airport grant funds for violations of this part or 49 U.S.C. 40117. This subpart does not address the circumstances under which the authority to collect PFCs may be terminated for violations of 49 U.S.C. 47523 through 47528.

[Doc. No. FAA–2006–23730, 72 FR 28851, May 23, 2007]

§ 158.83 Informal resolution.

The Administrator shall undertake informal resolution with the public agency or any other affected party if, after review under § 158.71, the Administrator cannot determine that PFC revenue is being used for the approved projects in accordance with the terms of the Administrator's approval to impose a PFC for those projects or with 49 U.S.C. 40117.

[Doc. No. 26385, 56 FR 24278, May 29, 1991, as amended by Amdt. 158–2, 65 FR 34543, May 30, 2000]

§ 158.85 Termination of authority to impose PFC's.

(a) The FAA begins proceedings to terminate the public agency's authority to impose a PFC only if the Administrator determines that informal resolution is not successful.

(b) The Administrator publishes a notice of proposed termination in the FEDERAL REGISTER and supplies a copy to the public agency. This notice will state the scope of the proposed termination, the basis for the proposed action and the date for filing written comments or objections by all interested parties. This notice will also identify any corrective actions the public agency can take to avoid further proceedings. The due date for comments and corrective action shall be no less than 60 days after publication of the notice.

(c) If corrective action has not been taken as prescribed by the Administrator, the FAA holds a public hearing, and notice is given to the public agency and published in the FEDERAL REGISTER at least 30 days prior to the hearing. The hearing will be in a form determined by the Administrator to be appropriate to the circumstances and to the matters in dispute.

(d) The Administrator publishes the final decision in the FEDERAL REGISTER. Where appropriate, the Administrator may prescribe corrective action, including any corrective action the public agency may yet take. A copy of the notice is also provided to the public agency.

(e) Within 10 days of the date of publication of the notice of the Administrator's decision, the public agency shall—

(1) Advise the FAA in writing that it will complete any corrective action prescribed in the decision within 30 days; or

(2) Provide the FAA with a listing of the air carriers and foreign air carriers operating at the airport and all other issuing carriers that have remitted PFC revenue to the public agency in the preceding 12 months.

(f) When the Administrator's decision does not provide for corrective action or the public agency fails to complete such action, the FAA provides a copy of the FEDERAL REGISTER notice to each air carrier and foreign air carrier identified in paragraph (e) of this section. Such carriers are responsible for terminating or modifying PFC collection no later than 30 days after the date of notification by the FAA.

§ 158.87 Loss of Federal airport grant funds.

(a) If the Administrator determines that revenue derived from a PFC is excessive or is not being used as approved, the Administrator may reduce the amount of funds otherwise payable to the public agency under 49 U.S.C. 47114. Such a reduction may be made as a corrective action under § 158.83 or § 158.85 of this part.

(b) The amount of the reduction under paragraph (a) of this section shall equal the excess collected, or the amount not used in accordance with this part.

(c) A reduction under paragraph (a) of this section shall not constitute a withholding of approval of a grant application or the payment of funds under an approved grant within the meaning of 49 U.S.C. 47111(d).

[Doc. No. 26385, 56 FR 24278, May 29, 1991, as amended by Amdt. 158–2, 65 FR 34543, May 30, 2000]

Subpart F—Reduction in Airport Improvement Program Apportionment

§ 158.91 General.

This subpart describes the required reduction in funds apportioned to a large or medium hub airport that imposes a PFC.

§ 158.93 Public agencies subject to reduction.

The funds apportioned under 49 U.S.C. 47114 to a public agency for a specific primary commercial service airport that it controls are reduced if—

(a) Such airport enplanes 0.25 percent or more of the total annual enplanements in the U.S., and

(b) The public agency imposes a PFC at such airport.

[Doc. No. 26385, 56 FR 24278, May 29, 1991, as amended by Amdt. 158–2, 65 FR 34543, May 30, 2000]

§ 158.95 Implementation of reduction.

(a) A reduction in apportioned funds will not take effect until the first fiscal year following the year in which the collection of the PFC is begun and will be applied in each succeeding fiscal year in which the public agency imposes the PFC.

(b) The reduction in apportioned funds is calculated at the beginning of each fiscal year and shall be an amount equal to—

(1) In the case of a fee of $3 or less, 50 percent of the projected revenues from the fee in the fiscal year but not by more than 50 percent of the amount that otherwise would be apportioned under this section; and

(2) In the case of a fee of more than $3, 75 percent of the projected revenues from the fee in the fiscal year but not by more than 75 percent of the amount that otherwise would be apportioned under this section.

(c) If the projection of PFC revenue in a fiscal year is inaccurate, the reduction in apportioned funds may be increased or decreased in the following fiscal year, except that any further reduction shall not cause the total reduction to exceed 50 percent of such apportioned amount as would otherwise be apportioned in any fiscal year.

[Doc. No. 26385, 56 FR 24278, May 29, 1991, as amended by Amdt. 158–2, 65 FR 34543, May 30, 2000]

APPENDIX A TO PART 158—ASSURANCES

A. *General.*

1. These assurances shall be complied with in the conduct of a project funded with passenger facility charge (PFC) revenue.

2. These assurances are required to be submitted as part of the application for approval of authority to impose a PFC under the provisions of 49 U.S.C. 40117.

3. Upon approval by the Administrator of an application, the public agency is responsible for compliance with these assurances.

B. *Public agency certification.* The public agency hereby assures and certifies, with respect to this project that:

1. Responsibility and authority of the public agency. It has legal authority to impose a PFC and to finance and carry out the proposed project; that a resolution, motion or similar action has been duly adopted or passed as an official act of the public agency's governing body authorizing the filing of the application, including all understandings and assurances contained therein, and directing and authorizing the person identified as the official representative of the public agency to act in connection with the application.

2. Compliance with regulation. It will comply with all provisions of 14 CFR part 158.

3. Compliance with state and local laws and regulations. It has complied, or will comply, with all applicable State and local laws and regulations.

4. Environmental, airspace and airport layout plan requirements. It will not use PFC revenue on a project until the FAA has notified the public agency that—

(a) Any actions required under the National Environmental Policy Act of 1969 have been completed;

(b) The appropriate airspace finding has been made; and

(c) The FAA Airport Layout Plan with respect to the project has been approved.

5. Nonexclusivity of contractual agreements. It will not enter into an exclusive long-term lease or use agreement with an air carrier or foreign air carrier for projects funded by PFC revenue. Such leases or use agreements will not preclude the public agency from funding, developing, or assigning new capacity at the airport with PFC revenue.

6. Carryover provisions. It will not enter into any lease or use agreement with any air carrier or foreign air carrier for any facility financed in whole or in part with revenue derived from a passenger facility charge if such agreement for such facility contains a carryover provision regarding a renewal option which, upon expiration of the original lease, would operate to automatically extend the term of such agreement with such carrier in preference to any potentially competing air carrier or foreign air carrier seeking to negotiate a lease or use agreement for such facilities.

7. Competitive access. It agrees that any lease or use agreements between the public agency and any air carrier or foreign air carrier for any facility financed in whole or in part with revenue derived from a passenger facility charge will contain a provision that permits the public agency to terminate the lease or use agreement if—

(a) The air carrier or foreign air carrier has an exclusive lease or use agreement for existing facilities at such airport; and

(b) Any portion of its existing exclusive use facilities is not fully utilized and is not made available for use by potentially competing air carriers or foreign air carriers.

8. Rates, fees and charges.

(a) It will not treat PFC revenue as airport revenue for the purpose of establishing a rate, fee or charge pursuant to a contract with an air carrier or foreign air carrier.

(b) It will not include in its rate base by means of depreciation, amortization, or any other method, that portion of the capital costs of a project paid for by PFC revenue for the purpose of establishing a rate, fee or charge pursuant to a contract with an air carrier or foreign air carrier.

(c) Notwithstanding the limitation provided in subparagraph (b), with respect to a project for terminal development, gates and related areas, or a facility occupied or used by one or more air carriers or foreign air carriers on an exclusive or preferential basis, the rates, fees, and charges payable by such carriers that use such facilities will be no less than the rates, fees, and charges paid by such carriers using similar facilities at the airport that were not financed by PFC revenue.

9. Standards and specifications. It will carry out the project in accordance with FAA airport design, construction and equipment standards and specifications contained in advisory circulars current on the date of project approval.

10. Recordkeeping and Audit. It will maintain an accounting record for audit purposes for 3 years after physical and financial completion of the project. All records must satisfy the requirements of 14 CFR part 158 and contain documentary evidence for all items of project costs.

11. Reports. It will submit reports in accordance with the requirements of 14 CFR part 158, subpart D, and as the Administrator may reasonably request.

12. Compliance with 49 U.S.C. 47523 through 47528. It understands 49 U.S.C. 47524 and 47526 require that the authority to impose a PFC be terminated if the Administrator determines the public agency has failed to comply with those sections of the United States Code or with the implementing regulations published under the Code.

[Doc. No. 26385, 56 FR 24278, May 29, 1991, as amended by Amdt. 158–2, 65 FR 34543, May 30, 2000; Amdt. 158–4, 72 FR 28851, May 23, 2007]

PART 161—NOTICE AND APPROVAL OF AIRPORT NOISE AND ACCESS RESTRICTIONS

Subpart A—General Provisions

AUTHORITY: 49 U.S.C. 106(g), 47523–47527, 47533.

SOURCE: Docket No. 26432, 56 FR 48698, Sept. 25, 1991, unless otherwise noted.

Subpart A—General Provisions

§161.1 Purpose.

This part implements the Airport Noise and Capacity Act of 1990 (49

779

U.S.C. App. 2153, 2154, 2155, and 2156). It prescribes:

(a) Notice requirements and procedures for airport operators implementing Stage 3 aircraft noise and access restrictions pursuant to agreements between airport operators and aircraft operators;

(b) Analysis and notice requirements for airport operators proposing Stage 2 aircraft noise and access restrictions;

(c) Notice, review, and approval requirements for airport operators proposing Stage 3 aircraft noise and access restrictions; and

(d) Procedures for Federal Aviation Administration reevaluation of agreements containing restrictions on Stage 3 aircraft operations and of aircraft noise and access restrictions affecting Stage 3 aircraft operations imposed by airport operators.

§ 161.3 Applicability.

(a) This part applies to airports imposing restrictions on Stage 2 aircraft operations proposed after October 1, 1990, and to airports imposing restrictions on Stage 3 aircraft operations that became effective after October 1, 1990.

(b) This part also applies to airports enacting amendments to airport noise and access restrictions in effect on October 1, 1990, but amended after that date, where the amendment reduces or limits aircraft operations or affects aircraft safety.

(c) The notice, review, and approval requirements set forth in this part apply to all airports imposing noise or access restrictions as defined in § 161.5 of this part.

§ 161.5 Definitions.

For the purposes of this part, the following definitions apply:

Agreement means a document in writing signed by the airport operator; those aircraft operators currently operating at the airport that would be affected by the noise or access restriction; and all affected new entrants planning to provide new air service within 180 days of the effective date of the restriction that have submitted to the airport operator a plan of operations and notice of agreement to the restriction.

Aircraft operator, for purposes of this part, means any owner of an aircraft that operates the aircraft, i.e., uses, causes to use, or authorizes the use of the aircraft; or in the case of a leased aircraft, any lessee that operates the aircraft pursuant to a lease. As used in this part, aircraft operator also means any representative of the aircraft owner, or in the case of a leased aircraft, any representative of the lessee empowered to enter into agreements with the airport operator regarding use of the airport by an aircraft.

Airport means any area of land or water, including any heliport, that is used or intended to be used for the landing and takeoff of aircraft, and any appurtenant areas that are used or intended to be used for airport buildings or other airport facilities or rights-of-way, together with all airport buildings and facilities located thereon.

Airport noise study area means that area surrounding the airport within the noise contour selected by the applicant for study and must include the noise contours required to be developed for noise exposure maps specified in 14 CFR part 150.

Airport operator means the airport proprietor.

Aviation user class means the following categories of aircraft operators: air carriers operating under parts 121 or 129 of this chapter; commuters and other carriers operating under part 135 of this chapter; general aviation, military, or government operations.

Day-night average sound level (DNL) means the 24-hour average sound level, in decibels, for the period from midnight to midnight, obtained after the addition of ten decibels to sound levels for the periods between midnight and 7 a.m., and between 10 p.m. and midnight, local time, as defined in 14 CFR part 150. (The scientific notation for DNL is L_{dn}).

Noise or access restrictions means restrictions (including but not limited to provisions of ordinances and leases) affecting access or noise that affect the operations of Stage 2 or Stage 3 aircraft, such as limits on the noise generated on either a single-event or cumulative basis; a limit, direct or indirect, on the total number of Stage 2 or Stage 3 aircraft operations; a noise budget or noise allocation program that includes Stage 2 or Stage 3 aircraft; a restriction imposing limits on hours of operations; a program of airport-use charges that has the direct or indirect effect of controlling airport noise; and any other limit on Stage 2 or Stage 3 aircraft that has the effect of controlling airport noise. This definition does not include peak-period pricing programs where the objective is to align the number of aircraft operations with airport capacity.

Stage 2 aircraft means an aircraft that has been shown to comply with the Stage 2 requirements under 14 CFR part 36.

Stage 3 aircraft means an aircraft that has been shown to comply with the Stage 3 requirements under 14 CFR part 36.

[Doc. No. 26432, 56 FR 48698, Sept. 25, 1991, as amended by Amdt. 161–2, 66 FR 21067, Apr. 27, 2001]

§161.7 Limitations.

(a) Aircraft operational procedures that must be submitted for adoption by the FAA, such as preferential runway use, noise abatement approach and departure procedures and profiles and flight tracks, are not subject to this part. Other noise abatement procedures, such as taxiing and engine runups, are not subject to this part unless the procedures imposed limit the total number of Stage 2 or Stage 3 aircraft operations, or limit the hours of Stage 2 or Stage 3 aircraft operations, at the airport.

(b) The notice, review, and approval requirements set forth in this part do not apply to airports with restrictions as specified in 49 U.S.C. App. 2153(a)(2)(C):

(1) A local action to enforce a negotiated or executed airport aircraft noise or access agreement between the airport operator and the aircraft operator in effect on November 5, 1990.

(2) A local action to enforce a negotiated or executed airport aircraft noise or access restriction the airport operator and the aircraft operators agreed to before November 5, 1990.

(3) An intergovernmental agreement including airport aircraft noise or access restriction in effect on November 5, 1990.

(4) A subsequent amendment to an airport aircraft noise or access agreement or restriction in effect on November 5, 1990, where the amendment does not reduce or limit aircraft operations or affect aircraft safety.

(5) A restriction that was adopted by an airport operator on or before October 1, 1990, and that was stayed as of October 1, 1990, by a court order or as a result of litigation, if such restriction, or a part thereof, is subsequently allowed by a court to take effect.

(6) In any case in which a restriction described in paragraph (b)(5) of this section is either partially or totally disallowed by a court, any new restriction imposed by an airport operator to replace such disallowed restriction, if such new restriction would not prohibit aircraft operations in effect on November 5, 1990.

(7) A local action that represents the adoption of the final portion of a program of a staged airport aircraft noise or access restriction, where the initial portion of such program was adopted during calendar year 1988 and was in effect on November 5, 1990.

(c) The notice, review, and approval requirements of subpart D of this part with regard to Stage 3 aircraft restrictions do not apply if the FAA has, prior to November 5, 1990, formed a working group (outside of the process established by 14 CFR part 150) with a local airport operator to examine the noise impact of air traffic control procedure changes. In any case in which an agreement relating to noise reductions at such airport is then entered into between the airport proprietor and an air carrier or air carrier constituting a majority of the air carrier users of such airport, the requirements of subparts B and D of this part with respect to restrictions on Stage 3 aircraft operations do apply to local actions to enforce such agreements.

(d) Except to the extent required by the application of the provisions of the Act, nothing in this part eliminates, invalidates, or supersedes the following:

(1) Existing law with respect to airport noise or access restrictions by local authorities;

(2) Any proposed airport noise or access regulation at a general aviation

airport where the airport proprietor has formally initiated a regulatory or legislative process on or before October 1, 1990; and

(3) The authority of the Secretary of Transportation to seek and obtain such legal remedies as the Secretary considers appropriate, including injunctive relief.

§ 161.9 Designation of noise description methods.

For purposes of this part, the following requirements apply:

(a) The sound level at an airport and surrounding areas, and the exposure of individuals to noise resulting from operations at an airport, must be established in accordance with the specifications and methods prescribed under appendix A of 14 CFR part 150; and

(b) Use of computer models to create noise contours must be in accordance with the criteria prescribed under appendix A of 14 CFR part 150.

§ 161.11 Identification of land uses in airport noise study area.

For the purposes of this part, uses of land that are normally compatible or noncompatible with various noise-exposure levels to individuals around airports must be identified in accordance with the criteria prescribed under appendix A of 14 CFR part 150. Determination of land use must be based on professional planning, zoning, and building and site design information and expertise.

Subpart B—Agreements

§ 161.101 Scope.

(a) This subpart applies to an airport operator's noise or access restriction on the operation of Stage 3 aircraft that is implemented pursuant to an agreement between an airport operator and all aircraft operators affected by the proposed restriction that are serving or will be serving such airport within 180 days of the date of the proposed restriction.

(b) For purposes of this subpart, an agreement shall be in writing and signed by:

(1) The airport operator;

(2) Those aircraft operators currently operating at the airport who would be affected by the noise or access restriction; and

(3) All new entrants that have submitted the information required under § 161.105(a) of this part.

(c) This subpart does not apply to restrictions exempted in § 161.7 of this part.

(d) This subpart does not limit the right of an airport operator to enter into an agreement with one or more aircraft operators that restricts the operation of Stage 2 or Stage 3 aircraft as long as the restriction is not enforced against aircraft operators that are not party to the agreement. Such an agreement is not covered by this subpart except that an aircraft operator may apply for sanctions pursuant to subpart F of this part for restrictions the airport operator seeks to impose other than those in the agreement.

§ 161.103 Notice of the proposed restriction.

(a) An airport operator may not implement a Stage 3 restriction pursuant to an agreement with all affected aircraft operators unless there has been public notice and an opportunity for comment as prescribed in this subpart.

(b) In order to establish a restriction in accordance with this subpart, the airport operator shall, at least 45 days before implementing the restriction, publish a notice of the proposed restriction in an areawide newspaper or newspapers that either singly or together has general circulation throughout the airport vicinity or airport noise study area, if one has been delineated; post a notice in the airport in a prominent location accessible to airport users and the public; and directly notify in writing the following parties:

(1) Aircraft operators providing scheduled passenger or cargo service at the airport; affected operators of aircraft based at the airport; potential new entrants that are known to be interested in serving the airport; and aircraft operators known to be routinely providing non-scheduled service;

(2) The Federal Aviation Administration;

(3) Each Federal, state, and local agency with land use control jurisdiction within the vicinity of the airport,

or the airport noise study area, if one has been delineated;

(4) Fixed-base operators and other airport tenants whose operations may be affected by the proposed restriction; and

(5) Community groups and business organizations that are known to be interested in the proposed restriction.

(c) Each direct notice provided in accordance with paragraph (b) of this section shall include:

(1) The name of the airport and associated cities and states;

(2) A clear, concise description of the proposed restriction, including sanctions for noncompliance and a statement that it will be implemented pursuant to a signed agreement;

(3) A brief discussion of the specific need for and goal of the proposed restriction;

(4) Identification of the operators and the types of aircraft expected to be affected;

(5) The proposed effective date of the restriction and any proposed enforcement mechanism;

(6) An invitation to comment on the proposed restriction, with a minimum 45-day comment period;

(7) Information on how to request copies of the restriction portion of the agreement, including any sanctions for noncompliance;

(8) A notice to potential new entrant aircraft operators that are known to be interested in serving the airport of the requirements set forth in §161.105 of this part; and

(9) Information on how to submit a new entrant application, comments, and the address for submitting applications and comments to the airport operator, including identification of a contact person at the airport.

(d) The Federal Aviation Administration will publish an announcement of the proposed restriction in the FEDERAL REGISTER.

[Doc. No. 26432, 56 FR 48698, Sept. 25, 1991; 56 FR 51258, Oct. 10, 1991]

§161.105 Requirements for new entrants.

(a) Within 45 days of the publication of the notice of a proposed restriction by the airport operator under §161.103(b) of this part, any person in-

tending to provide new air service to the airport within 180 days of the proposed date of implementation of the restriction (as evidenced by submission of a plan of operations to the airport operator) must notify the airport operator if it would be affected by the restriction contained in the proposed agreement, and either that it—

(1) Agrees to the restriction; or

(2) Objects to the restriction.

(b) Failure of any person described in §161.105(a) of this part to notify the airport operator that it objects to the proposed restriction will constitute waiver of the right to claim that it did not consent to the agreement and render that person ineligible to use lack of signature as ground to apply for sanctions under subpart F of this part for two years following the effective date of the restriction. The signature of such a person need not be obtained by the airport operator in order to comply with §161.107(a) of this part.

(c) All other new entrants are also ineligible to use lack of signature as ground to apply for sanctions under subpart F of this part for two years.

§161.107 Implementation of the restriction.

(a) To be eligible to implement a Stage 3 noise or access restriction under this subpart, an airport operator shall have the restriction contained in an agreement as defined in §161.101(b) of this part.

(b) An airport operator may not implement a restriction pursuant to an agreement until the notice and comment requirements of §161.103 of this part have been met.

(c) Each airport operator must notify the Federal Aviation Administration the implementation of a restriction pursuant to an agreement and must include in the notice evidence of compliance with §161.103 and a copy of the signed agreement.

§161.109 Notice of termination of restriction pursuant to an agreement.

An airport operator must notify the FAA within 10 days of the date of termination of a restriction pursuant to an agreement under this subpart.

§ 161.111 Availability of data and comments on a restriction implemented pursuant to an agreement.

The airport operator shall retain all relevant supporting data and all comments relating to a restriction implemented pursuant to an agreement for as long as the restriction is in effect. The airport operator shall make these materials available for inspection upon request by the FAA. The information shall be made available for inspection by any person during the pendency of any petition for reevaluation found justified by the FAA.

§ 161.113 Effect of agreements; limitation on reevaluation.

(a) Except as otherwise provided in this subpart, a restriction implemented by an airport operator pursuant to this subpart shall have the same force and effect as if it had been a restriction implemented in accordance with subpart D of this part.

(b) A restriction implemented by an airport operator pursuant to this subpart may be subject to reevaluation by the FAA under subpart E of this part.

Subpart C—Notice Requirements for Stage 2 Restrictions

§ 161.201 Scope.

(a) This subpart applies to:

(1) An airport imposing a noise or access restriction on the operation of Stage 2 aircraft, but not Stage 3 aircraft, proposed after October 1, 1990.

(2) An airport imposing an amendment to a Stage 2 restriction, if the amendment is proposed after October 1, 1990, and reduces or limits Stage 2 aircraft operations (compared to the restriction that it amends) or affects aircraft safety.

(b) This subpart does not apply to an airport imposing a Stage 2 restriction specifically exempted in § 161.7 or a Stage 2 restriction contained in an agreement as long as the restriction is not enforced against aircraft operators that are not parties to the agreement.

§ 161.203 Notice of proposed restriction.

(a) An airport operator may not implement a Stage 2 restriction within the scope of § 161.201 unless the airport operator provides an analysis of the proposed restriction, prepared in accordance with § 161.205, and a public notice and opportunity for comment as prescribed in this subpart. The notice and analysis required by this subpart shall be completed at least 180 days prior to the effective date of the restriction.

(b) Except as provided in § 161.211, an airport operator must publish a notice of the proposed restriction in an areawide newspaper or newspapers that either singly or together has general circulation throughout the airport noise study area; post a notice in the airport in a prominent location accessible to airport users and the public; and directly notify in writing the following parties:

(1) Aircraft operators providing scheduled passenger or cargo service at the airport; operators of aircraft based at the airport; potential new entrants that are known to be interested in serving the airport; and aircraft operators known to be routinely providing nonscheduled service that may be affected by the proposed restriction;

(2) The Federal Aviation Administration;

(3) Each Federal, state, and local agency with land-use control jurisdiction within the airport noise study area;

(4) Fixed-base operators and other airport tenants whose operations may be affected by the proposed restriction; and

(5) Community groups and business organizations that are known to be interested in the proposed restriction.

(c) Each notice provided in accordance with paragraph (b) of this section shall include:

(1) The name of the airport and associated cities and states;

(2) A clear, concise description of the proposed restriction, including a statement that it will be a mandatory Stage 2 restriction, and where the complete text of the restriction, and any sanctions for noncompliance, are available for public inspection;

(3) A brief discussion of the specific need for, and goal of, the restriction;

(4) Identification of the operators and the types of aircraft expected to be affected;

(5) The proposed effective date of the restriction, the proposed method of implementation (e.g., city ordinance, airport rule, lease), and any proposed enforcement mechanism;

(6) An analysis of the proposed restriction, as required by §161.205 of this subpart, or an announcement of where the analysis is available for public inspection;

(7) An invitation to comment on the proposed restriction and analysis, with a minimum 45-day comment period;

(8) Information on how to request copies of the complete text of the proposed restriction, including any sanctions for noncompliance, and the analysis (if not included with the notice); and

(9) The address for submitting comments to the airport operator, including identification of a contact person at the airport.

(d) At the time of notice, the airport operator shall provide the FAA with a full text of the proposed restriction, including any sanctions for noncompliance.

(e) The Federal Aviation Administration will publish an announcement of the proposed Stage 2 restriction in the FEDERAL REGISTER.

§161.205 Required analysis of proposed restriction and alternatives.

(a) Each airport operator proposing a noise or access restriction on Stage 2 aircraft operations shall prepare the following and make it available for public comment:

(1) An analysis of the anticipated or actual costs and benefits of the proposed noise or access restriction;

(2) A description of alternative restrictions; and

(3) A description of the alternative measures considered that do not involve aircraft restrictions, and a comparison of the costs and benefits of such alternative measures to costs and benefits of the proposed noise or access restriction.

(b) In preparing the analyses required by this section, the airport operator shall use the noise measurement systems and identify the airport noise study area as specified in §§161.9 and 161.11, respectively; shall use currently accepted economic methodology; and

shall provide separate detail on the costs and benefits of the proposed restriction with respect to the operations of Stage 2 aircraft weighing less than 75,000 pounds if the restriction applies to this class. The airport operator shall specify the methods used to analyze the costs and benefits of the proposed restriction and the alternatives.

(c) The kinds of information set forth in §161.305 are useful elements of an adequate analysis of a noise or access restriction on Stage 2 aircraft operations.

§161.207 Comment by interested parties.

Each airport operator shall establish a public docket or similar method for receiving and considering comments, and shall make comments available for inspection by interested parties upon request. Comments must be retained as long as the restriction is in effect.

§161.209 Requirements for proposal changes.

(a) Each airport operator shall promptly advise interested parties of any changes to a proposed restriction, including changes that affect noncompatible land uses, and make available any changes to the proposed restriction and its analysis. Interested parties include those that received direct notice under §161.203(b), or those that were required to be consulted in accordance with the procedures in §161.211 of this part, and those that have commented on the proposed restriction.

(b) If there are substantial changes to the proposed restriction or the analysis during the 180-day notice period, the airport operator shall initiate new notice following the procedures in §161.203 or, alternatively, the procedures in §161.211. A substantial change includes, but is not limited to, a proposal that would increase the burden on any aviation user class.

(c) In addition to the information in §161.203(c), new notice must indicate that the airport operator is revising a previous notice, provide the reason for making the revision, and provide a new effective date (if any) for the restriction. The effective date of the restriction must be at least 180 days after the date the new notice and revised analysis are made available for public comment.

§ 161.211 Optional use of 14 CFR part 150 procedures.

(a) An airport operator may use the procedures in part 150 of this chapter, instead of the procedures described in §§ 161.203(b) and 161.209(b), as a means of providing an adequate public notice and comment opportunity on a proposed Stage 2 restriction.

(b) If the airport operator elects to use 14 CFR part 150 procedures to comply with this subpart, the operator shall:

(1) Ensure that all parties identified for direct notice under § 161.203(b) are notified that the airport's 14 CFR part 150 program will include a proposed Stage 2 restriction under part 161, and that these parties are offered the opportunity to participate as consulted parties during the development of the 14 CFR part 150 program;

(2) Provide the FAA with a full text of the proposed restriction, including any sanctions for noncompliance, at the time of the notice;

(3) Include the information in § 161.203 (c)(2) through (c)(5) and 161.205 in the analysis of the proposed restriction for the part 14 CFR part 150 program;

(4) Wait 180 days following the availability of the above analysis for review by the consulted parties and compliance with the above notice requirements before implementing the Stage 2 restriction; and

(5) Include in its 14 CFR part 150 submission to the FAA evidence of compliance with paragraphs (b)(1) and (b)(4) of this section, and the analysis in paragraph (b)(3) of this section, together with a clear identification that the 14 CFR part 150 program includes a proposed Stage 2 restriction under part 161.

(c) The FAA determination on the 14 CFR part 150 submission does not constitute approval or disapproval of the proposed Stage 2 restriction under part 161.

(d) An amendment of a restriction may also be processed under 14 CFR part 150 procedures in accordance with this section.

§ 161.213 Notification of a decision not to implement a restriction.

If a proposed restriction has been through the procedures prescribed in this subpart and the restriction is not subsequently implemented, the airport operator shall so advise the interested parties. Interested parties are described in § 161.209(a).

Subpart D—Notice, Review, and Approval Requirements for Stage 3 Restrictions

§ 161.301 Scope.

(a) This subpart applies to:

(1) An airport imposing a noise or access restriction on the operation of Stage 3 aircraft that first became effective after October 1, 1990.

(2) An airport imposing an amendment to a Stage 3 restriction, if the amendment becomes effective after October 1, 1990, and reduces or limits Stage 3 aircraft operations (compared to the restriction that it amends) or affects aircraft safety.

(b) This subpart does not apply to an airport imposing a Stage 3 restriction specifically exempted in § 161.7, or an agreement complying with subpart B of this part.

(c) A Stage 3 restriction within the scope of this subpart may not become effective unless it has been submitted to and approved by the FAA. The FAA will review only those Stage 3 restrictions that are proposed by, or on behalf of, an entity empowered to implement the restriction.

§ 161.303 Notice of proposed restrictions.

(a) Each airport operator or aircraft operator (hereinafter referred to as applicant) proposing a Stage 3 restriction shall provide public notice and an opportunity for public comment, as prescribed in this subpart, before submitting the restriction to the FAA for review and approval.

(b) Except as provided in § 161.321, an applicant shall publish a notice of the proposed restriction in an areawide newspaper or newspapers that either singly or together has general circulation throughout the airport noise study area; post a notice in the airport in a prominent location accessible to airport users and the public; and directly notify in writing the following parties:

(1) Aircraft operators providing scheduled passenger or cargo service at the airport; operators of aircraft based at the airport; potential new entrants that are known to be interested in serving the airport; and aircraft operators known to be routinely providing nonscheduled service that may be affected by the proposed restriction;

(2) The Federal Aviation Administration;

(3) Each Federal, state, and local agency with land-use control jurisdiction within the airport noise study area;

(4) Fixed-base operators and other airport tenants whose operations may be affected by the proposed restriction; and

(5) Community groups and business organizations that are known to be interested in the proposed restriction.

(c) Each notice provided in accordance with paragraph (b) of this section shall include:

(1) The name of the airport and associated cities and states;

(2) A clear, concise description of the proposed restriction (and any alternatives, in order of preference), including a statement that it will be a mandatory Stage 3 restriction; and where the complete text of the restriction, and any sanctions for noncompliance, are available for public inspection;

(3) A brief discussion of the specific need for, and goal of, the restriction;

(4) Identification of the operators and types of aircraft expected to be affected;

(5) The proposed effective date of the restriction, the proposed method of implementation (e.g., city ordinance, airport rule, lease, or other document), and any proposed enforcement mechanism;

(6) An analysis of the proposed restriction, in accordance with §161.305 of this part, or an announcement regarding where the analysis is available for public inspection;

(7) An invitation to comment on the proposed restriction and the analysis, with a minimum 45-day comment period;

(8) Information on how to request a copy of the complete text of the restriction, including any sanctions for noncompliance, and the analysis (if not included with the notice); and

(9) The address for submitting comments to the airport operator or aircraft operator proposing the restriction, including identification of a contact person.

(d) Applicants may propose alternative restrictions, including partial implementation of any proposal, and indicate an order of preference. If alternative restriction proposals are submitted, the requirements listed in paragraphs (c)(2) through (c)(6) of this section should address the alternative proposals where appropriate.

§161.305 Required analysis and conditions for approval of proposed restrictions.

Each applicant proposing a noise or access restriction on Stage 3 operations shall prepare and make available for public comment an analysis that supports, by substantial evidence, that the six statutory conditions for approval have been met for each restriction and any alternatives submitted. The statutory conditions are set forth in 49 U.S.C. App. 2153(d)(2) and paragraph (e) of this section. Any proposed restriction (including alternatives) on Stage 3 aircraft operations that also affects the operation of Stage 2 aircraft must include analysis of the proposals in a manner that permits the proposal to be understood in its entirety. (Nothing in this section is intended to add a requirement for the issuance of restrictions on Stage 2 aircraft to those of subpart C of this part.) The applicant shall provide:

(a) The complete text of the proposed restriction and any submitted alternatives, including the proposed wording in a city ordinance, airport rule, lease, or other document, and any sanctions for noncompliance;

(b) Maps denoting the airport geographic boundary, and the geographic boundaries and names of each jurisdiction that controls land use within the airport noise study area;

(c) An adequate environmental assessment of the proposed restriction or adequate information supporting a categorical exclusion in accordance with FAA orders and procedures regarding compliance with the National Environmental Policy Act of 1969 (42 U.S.C. 4321);

(d) A summary of the evidence in the submission supporting the six statutory conditions for approval; and

(e) An analysis of the restriction, demonstrating by substantial evidence that the statutory conditions are met. The analysis must:

(1) Be sufficiently detailed to allow the FAA to evaluate the merits of the proposed restriction; and

(2) Contain the following essential elements needed to provide substantial evidence supporting each condition for approval:

(i) *Condition 1: The restriction is reasonable, nonarbitrary, and nondiscriminatory.* (A) Essential information needed to demonstrate this condition includes the following:

(*1*) Evidence that a current or projected noise or access problem exists, and that the proposed action(s) could relieve the problem, including:

(*i*) A detailed description of the problem precipitating the proposed restriction with relevant background information on factors contributing to the proposal and any court-ordered action or estimated liability concerns; a description of any noise agreements or noise or access restrictions currently in effect at the airport; and measures taken to achieve land-use compatibility, such as controls or restrictions on land use in the vicinity of the airport and measures carried out in response to 14 CFR part 150; and actions taken to comply with grant assurances requiring that:

(*A*) Airport development projects be reasonably consistent with plans of public agencies that are authorized to plan for the development of the area around the airport; and

(*B*) The sponsor give fair consideration to the interests of communities in or near where the project may be located; take appropriate action, including the adoption of zoning laws, to the extent reasonable, to restrict the use of land near the airport to activities and purposes compatible with normal airport operations; and not cause or permit any change in land use, within its jurisdiction, that will reduce the compatibility (with respect to the airport) of any noise compatibility program measures upon which federal funds have been expended.

(*ii*) An analysis of the estimated noise impact of aircraft operations with and without the proposed restriction for the year the restriction is expected to be implemented, for a forecast timeframe after implementation, and for any other years critical to understanding the noise impact of the proposed restriction. The analysis of noise impact with and without the proposed restriction including:

(*A*) Maps of the airport noise study area overlaid with noise contours as specified in §§ 161.9 and 161.11 of this part;

(*B*) The number of people and the noncompatible land uses within the airport noise study area with and without the proposed restriction for each year the noise restriction is analyzed;

(*C*) Technical data supporting the noise impact analysis, including the classes of aircraft, fleet mix, runway use percentage, and day/night breakout of operations; and

(*D*) Data on current and projected airport activity that would exist in the absence of the proposed restriction.

(*2*) Evidence that other available remedies are infeasible or would be less cost-effective, including descriptions of any alternative aircraft restrictions that have been considered and rejected, and the reasons for the rejection; and of any land use or other nonaircraft controls or restrictions that have been considered and rejected, including those proposed under 14 CFR part 150 and not implemented, and the reasons for the rejection or failure to implement.

(*3*) Evidence that the noise or access standards are the same for all aviation user classes or that the differences are justified, such as:

(*i*) A description of the relationship of the effect of the proposed restriction on airport users (by aviation user class); and

(*ii*) The noise attributable to these users in the absence of the proposed restriction.

(B) At the applicant's discretion, information may also be submitted as follows:

(*1*) Evidence not submitted under paragraph (e)(2)(ii)(A) of this section (Condition 2) that there is a reasonable chance that expected benefits will equal or exceed expected cost; for example, comparative economic analyses of the costs and benefits of the proposed restriction and aircraft and nonaircraft alternative measures. For detailed elements of analysis, see paragraph (e)(2)(ii)(A) of this section.

(*2*) Evidence not submitted under paragraph (e)(2)(ii)(A) of this section that the level of any noise-based fees that may be imposed reflects the cost of mitigating noise impacts produced by the aircraft, or that the fees are reasonably related to the intended level of noise impact mitigation.

(ii) *Condition 2: The restriction does not create an undue burden on interstate or foreign commerce.* (A) Essential information needed to demonstrate this statutory condition includes:

(*1*) Evidence, based on a cost-benefit analysis, that the estimated potential benefits of the restriction have a reasonable chance to exceed the estimated potential cost of the adverse effects on interstate and foreign commerce. In preparing the economic analysis required by this section, the applicant shall use currently accepted economic methodology, specify the methods used and assumptions underlying the analysis, and consider:

(*i*) The effect of the proposed restriction on operations of aircraft by aviation user class (and for air carriers the number of operations of aircraft by carrier), and on the volume of passengers and cargo for the year the restriction is expected to be implemented and for the forecast timeframe.

(*ii*) The estimated costs of the proposed restriction and alternative nonaircraft restrictions including the following, as appropriate:

(*A*) Any additional cost of continuing aircraft operations under the restriction, including reasonably available information concerning any net capital costs of acquiring or retrofitting aircraft (net of salvage value and operating efficiencies) by aviation user

class; and any incremental recurring costs;

(*B*) Costs associated with altered or discontinued aircraft operations, such as reasonably available information concerning loss to carriers of operating profits; decreases in passenger and shipper consumer surplus by aviation user class; loss in profits associated with other airport services or other entities; and/or any significant economic effect on parties other than aviation users.

(*C*) Costs associated with implementing nonaircraft restrictions or nonaircraft components of restrictions, such as reasonably available information concerning estimates of capital costs for real property, including redevelopment, soundproofing, noise easements, and purchase of property interests; and estimates of associated incremental recurring costs; or an explanation of the legal or other impediments to implementing such restrictions.

(*D*) Estimated benefits of the proposed restriction and alternative restrictions that consider, as appropriate, anticipated increase in real estate values and future construction cost (such as sound insulation) savings; anticipated increase in airport revenues; quantification of the noise benefits, such as number of people removed from noise contours and improved work force and/or educational productivity, if any; valuation of positive safety effects, if any; and/or other qualitative benefits, including improvements in quality of life.

(B) At the applicant's discretion, information may also be submitted as follows:

(*1*) Evidence that the affected carriers have a reasonable chance to continue service at the airport or at other points in the national airport system.

(*2*) Evidence that other air carriers are able to provide adequate service to the airport and other points in the system without diminishing competition.

(*3*) Evidence that comparable services or facilities are available at another airport controlled by the airport operator in the market area, including services available at other airports.

(*4*) Evidence that alternative transportation service can be attained through other means of transportation.

(*5*) Information on the absence of adverse evidence or adverse comments with respect to undue burden in the notice process required in § 161.303, or alternatively in § 161.321, of this part as evidence that there is no undue burden.

(iii) *Condition 3: The proposed restriction maintains safe and efficient use of the navigable airspace.* Essential information needed to demonstrate this statutory condition includes evidence that the proposed restriction maintains safe and efficient use of the navigable airspace based upon:

(A) Identification of airspace and obstacles to navigation in the vicinity of the airport; and

(B) An analysis of the effects of the proposed restriction with respect to use of airspace in the vicinity of the airport, substantiating that the restriction maintains or enhances safe and efficient use of the navigable airspace. The analysis shall include a description of the methods and data used.

(iv) *Condition 4: The proposed restriction does not conflict with any existing Federal statute or regulation.* Essential information needed to demonstrate this condition includes evidence demonstrating that no conflict is presented between the proposed restriction and any existing Federal statute or regulation, including those governing:

(A) Exclusive rights;

(B) Control of aircraft operations; and

(C) Existing Federal grant agreements.

(v) *Condition 5: The applicant has provided adequate opportunity for public comment on the proposed restriction.* Essential information needed to demonstrate this condition includes evidence that there has been adequate opportunity for public comment on the restriction as specified in § 161.303 or § 161.321 of this part.

(vi) *Condition 6: The proposed restriction does not create an undue burden on the national aviation system.* Essential information needed to demonstrate this condition includes evidence that the proposed restriction does not create an undue burden on the national aviation system such as:

(A) An analysis demonstrating that the proposed restriction does not have a substantial adverse effect on existing or planned airport system capacity, on observed or forecast airport system congestion and aircraft delay, and on airspace system capacity or workload;

(B) An analysis demonstrating that nonaircraft alternative measures to achieve the same goals as the proposed subject restrictions are inappropriate;

(C) The absence of comments with respect to imposition of an undue burden on the national aviation system in response to the notice required in § 161.303 or § 161.321.

§ 161.307 Comment by interested parties.

(a) Each applicant proposing a restriction shall establish a public docket or similar method for receiving and considering comments, and shall make comments available for inspection by interested parties upon request. Comments must be retained as long as the restriction is in effect.

(b) Each applicant shall submit to the FAA a summary of any comments received. Upon request by the FAA, the applicant shall submit copies of the comments.

§ 161.309 Requirements for proposal changes.

(a) Each applicant shall promptly advise interested parties of any changes to a proposed restriction or alternative restriction that are not encompassed in the proposals submitted, including changes that affect noncompatible land uses or that take place before the effective date of the restriction, and make available these changes to the proposed restriction and its analysis. For the purpose of this paragraph, interested parties include those who received direct notice under § 161.303(b) of this part, or those who were required to be consulted in accordance with the procedures in § 161.321 of this part, and those who commented on the proposed restriction.

(b) If there are substantial changes to a proposed restriction or the analysis made available prior to the effective date of the restriction, the applicant proposing the restriction shall initiate new notice in accordance with the procedures in §161.303 or, alternatively, the procedures in §161.321. These requirements apply to substantial changes that are not encompassed in submitted alternative restriction proposals and their analyses. A substantial change to a restriction includes, but is not limited to, any proposal that would increase the burden on any aviation user class.

(c) In addition to the information in §161.303(c), a new notice must indicate that the applicant is revising a previous notice, provide the reason for making the revision, and provide a new effective date (if any) for the restriction.

(d) If substantial changes requiring a new notice are made during the FAA's 180-day review of the proposed restriction, the applicant submitting the proposed restriction shall notify the FAA in writing that it is withdrawing its proposal from the review process until it has completed additional analysis, public review, and documentation of the public review. Resubmission to the FAA will restart the 180-day review.

§161.311 Application procedure for approval of proposed restriction.

Each applicant proposing a Stage 3 restriction shall submit to the FAA the following information for each restriction and alternative restriction submitted, with a request that the FAA review and approve the proposed Stage 3 noise or access restriction:

(a) A summary of evidence of the fulfillment of conditions for approval, as specified in §161.305;

(b) An analysis as specified in §161.305, as appropriate to the proposed restriction;

(c) A statement that the entity submitting the proposal is the party empowered to implement the restriction, or is submitting the proposal on behalf of such party; and

(d) A statement as to whether the airport requests, in the event of disapproval of the proposed restriction or any alternatives, that the FAA approve any portion of the restriction or any alternative that meets the statutory requirements for approval. An applicant requesting partial approval of any proposal should indicate its priorities

as to portions of the proposal to be approved.

§161.313 Review of application.

(a) *Determination of completeness.* The FAA, within 30 days of receipt of an application, will determine whether the application is complete in accordance with §161.311. Determinations of completeness will be made on all proposed restrictions and alternatives. This completeness determination is not an approval or disapproval of the proposed restriction.

(b) *Process for complete application.* When the FAA determines that a complete application has been submitted, the following procedures apply:

(1) The FAA notifies the applicant that it intends to act on the proposed restriction and publishes notice of the proposed restriction in the FEDERAL REGISTER in accordance with §161.315. The 180-day period for approving or disapproving the proposed restriction will start on the date of original FAA receipt of the application.

(2) Following review of the application, public comments, and any other information obtained under §161.317(b), the FAA will issue a decision approving or disapproving the proposed restriction. This decision is a final decision of the Administrator for purpose of judicial review.

(c) *Process for incomplete application.* If the FAA determines that an application is not complete with respect to any submitted restriction or alternative restriction, the following procedures apply:

(1) The FAA shall notify the applicant in writing, returning the application and setting forth the type of information and analysis needed to complete the application in accordance with §161.311.

(2) Within 30 days after the receipt of this notice, the applicant shall advise the FAA in writing whether or not it intends to resubmit and supplement its application.

(3) If the applicant does not respond in 30 days, or advises the FAA that it does not intend to resubmit and/or supplement the application, the application will be denied. This closes the

matter without prejudice to later application and does not constitute disapproval of the proposed restriction.

(4) If the applicant chooses to resubmit and supplement the application, the following procedures apply:

(i) Upon receipt of the resubmitted application, the FAA determines whether the application, as supplemented, is complete as set forth in paragraph (a) of this section.

(ii) If the application is complete, the procedures set forth in § 161.315 shall be followed. The 180-day review period starts on the date of receipt of the last supplement to the application.

(iii) If the application is still not complete with respect to the proposed restriction or at least one submitted alternative, the FAA so advises the applicant as set forth in paragraph (c)(1) of this section and provides the applicant with an additional opportunity to supplement the application as set forth in paragraph (c)(2) of this section.

(iv) If the environmental documentation (either an environmental assessment or information supporting a categorical exclusion) is incomplete, the FAA will so notify the applicant in writing, returning the application and setting forth the types of information and analysis needed to complete the documentation. The FAA will continue to return an application until adequate environmental documentation is provided. When the application is determined to be complete, including the environmental documentation, the 180-day period for approval or disapproval will begin upon receipt of the last supplement to the application.

(v) Following review of the application and its supplements, public comments, and any other information obtained under § 161.317(b), the FAA will issue a decision approving or disapproving the application. This decision is a final decision of the Administrator for the purpose of judicial review.

(5) The FAA will deny the application and return it to the applicant if:

(i) None of the proposals submitted are found to be complete;

(ii) The application has been returned twice to the applicant for reasons other than completion of the environmental documentation; and

(iii) The applicant declines to complete the application. This closes the matter without prejudice to later application, and does not constitute disapproval of the proposed restriction.

§ 161.315   Receipt of complete application.

(a) When a complete application has been received, the FAA will notify the applicant by letter that the FAA intends to act on the application.

(b) The FAA will publish notice of the proposed restriction in the FEDERAL REGISTER, inviting interested parties to file comments on the application within 30 days after publication of the FEDERAL REGISTER notice.

§ 161.317   Approval or disapproval of proposed restriction.

(a) Upon determination that an application is complete with respect to at least one of the proposals submitted by the applicant, the FAA will act upon the complete proposals in the application. The FAA will not act on any proposal for which the applicant has declined to submit additional necessary information.

(b) The FAA will review the applicant's proposals in the preference order specified by the applicant. The FAA may request additional information from aircraft operators, or any other party, and may convene an informal meeting to gather facts relevant to its determination.

(c) The FAA will evaluate the proposal and issue an order approving or disapproving the proposed restriction and any submitted alternatives, in whole or in part, in the order of preference indicated by the applicant. Once the FAA approves a proposed restriction, the FAA will not consider any proposals of lower applicant-stated preference. Approval or disapproval will be given by the FAA within 180 days after receipt of the application or last supplement thereto under § 161.313. The FAA will publish its decision in the FEDERAL REGISTER and notify the applicant in writing.

(d) The applicant's failure to provide substantial evidence supporting the statutory conditions for approval of a particular proposal is grounds for disapproval of that proposed restriction.

(e) The FAA will approve or disapprove only the Stage 3 aspects of a restriction if the restriction applies to both Stage 2 and Stage 3 aircraft operations.

(f) An order approving a restriction may be subject to requirements that the applicant:

(1) Comply with factual representations and commitments in support of the restriction; and

(2) Ensure that any environmental mitigation actions or commitments by any party that are set forth in the environmental documentation provided in support of the restriction are implemented.

§161.319 Withdrawal or revision of restriction.

(a) The applicant may withdraw or revise a proposed restriction at any time prior to FAA approval or disapproval, and must do so if substantial changes are made as described in §161.309. The applicant shall notify the FAA in writing of a decision to withdraw the proposed restriction for any reason. The FAA will publish a notice in the FEDERAL REGISTER that it has terminated its review without prejudice to resubmission. A resubmission will be considered a new application.

(b) A subsequent amendment to a Stage 3 restriction that was in effect after October 1, 1990, or an amendment to a Stage 3 restriction previously approved by the FAA, is subject to the procedures in this subpart if the amendment will further reduce or limit aircraft operations or affect aircraft safety. The applicant may, at its option, revise or amend a restriction previously disapproved by the FAA and resubmit it for approval. Amendments are subject to the same requirements and procedures as initial submissions.

§161.321 Optional use of 14 CFR part 150 procedures.

(a) An airport operator may use the procedures in part 150 of this chapter, instead of the procedures described in §§161.303(b) and 161.309(b) of this part, as a means of providing an adequate public notice and opportunity to comment on proposed Stage 3 restrictions, including submitted alternatives.

(b) If the airport operator elects to use 14 CFR part 150 procedures to comply with this subpart, the operator shall:

(1) Ensure that all parties identified for direct notice under §161.303(b) are notified that the airport's 14 CFR part 150 program submission will include a proposed Stage 3 restriction under part 161, and that these parties are offered the opportunity to participate as consulted parties during the development of the 14 CFR part 150 program;

(2) Include the information required in §161.303(c)(2) through (5) and §161.305 in the analysis of the proposed restriction in the 14 CFR part 150 program submission; and

(3) Include in its 14 CFR part 150 submission to the FAA evidence of compliance with the notice requirements in paragraph (b)(1) of this section and include the information required for a part 161 application in §161.311, together with a clear identification that the 14 CFR part 150 submission includes a proposed Stage 3 restriction for FAA review and approval under §§161.313, 161.315, and 161.317.

(c) The FAA will evaluate the proposed part 161 restriction on Stage 3 aircraft operations included in the 14 CFR part 150 submission in accordance with the procedures and standards of this part, and will review the total 14 CFR part 150 submission in accordance with the procedures and standards of 14 CFR part 150.

(d) An amendment of a restriction, as specified in §161.319(b) of this part, may also be processed under 14 CFR part 150 procedures.

§161.323 Notification of a decision not to implement a restriction.

If a Stage 3 restriction has been approved by the FAA and the restriction is not subsequently implemented, the applicant shall so advise the interested parties specified in §161.309(a) of this part.

§161.325 Availability of data and comments on an implemented restriction.

The applicant shall retain all relevant supporting data and all comments relating to an approved restriction for as long as the restriction is in effect and shall make these materials available for inspection upon request by the FAA. This information shall be made available for inspection by any person during the pendency of any petition for reevaluation found justified by the FAA.

Subpart E—Reevaluation of Stage 3 Restrictions

§ 161.401 Scope.

This subpart applies to an airport imposing a noise or access restriction on the operation of Stage 3 aircraft that first became effective after October 1, 1990, and had either been agreed to in compliance with the procedures in subpart B of this part or approved by the FAA in accordance with the procedures in subpart D of this part. This subpart does not apply to Stage 2 restrictions imposed by airports. This subpart does not apply to Stage 3 restrictions specifically exempted in § 161.7.

§ 161.403 Criteria for reevaluation.

(a) A request for reevaluation must be submitted by an aircraft operator.

(b) An aircraft operator must demonstrate to the satisfaction of the FAA that there has been a change in the noise environment of the affected airport and that a review and reevaluation pursuant to the criteria in § 161.305 is therefore justified.

(1) A change in the noise environment sufficient to justify reevaluation is either a DNL change of 1.5 dB or greater (from the restriction's anticipated target noise level result) over noncompatible land uses, or a change of 17 percent or greater in the noncompatible land uses, within an airport noise study area. For approved restrictions, calculation of change shall be based on the divergence of actual noise impact of the restriction from the estimated noise impact of the restriction predicted in the analysis required in § 161.305(e)(2)(i)(A)(I)(ii). The change in the noise environment or in the noncompatible land uses may be either an increase or decrease in noise or in noncompatible land uses. An aircraft operator may submit to the FAA reasons why a change that does not fall within either of these parameters justifies reevaluation, and the FAA will consider

such arguments on a case-by-case basis.

(2) A change in the noise environment justifies reevaluation if the change is likely to result in the restriction not meeting one or more of the conditions for approval set forth in § 161.305 of this part for approval. The aircraft operator must demonstrate that such a result is likely to occur.

(c) A reevaluation may not occur less than 2 years after the date of the FAA approval. The FAA will normally apply the same 2-year requirement to agreements under subpart B of this part that affect Stage 3 aircraft operations. An aircraft operator may submit to the FAA reasons why an agreement under subpart B of this part should be reevaluated in less than 2 years, and the FAA will consider such arguments on a case-by-case basis.

(d) An aircraft operator must demonstrate that it has made a good faith attempt to resolve locally any dispute over a restriction with the affected parties, including the airport operator, before requesting reevaluation by the FAA. Such demonstration and certification shall document all attempts of local dispute resolution.

[Doc. No. 26432, 56 FR 48698, Sept. 25, 1991; 56 FR 51258, Oct. 10, 1991]

§ 161.405 Request for reevaluation.

(a) A request for reevaluation submitted to the FAA by an aircraft operator must include the following information:

(1) The name of the airport and associated cities and states;

(2) A clear, concise description of the restriction and any sanctions for noncompliance, whether the restriction was approved by the FAA or agreed to by the airport operator and aircraft operators, the date of the approval or agreement, and a copy of the restriction as incorporated in a local ordinance, airport rule, lease, or other document;

(3) The quantified change in the noise environment using methodology specified in this part;

(4) Evidence of the relationship between this change and the likelihood that the restriction does not meet one or more of the conditions in § 161.305;

(5) The aircraft operator's status under the restriction (e.g., currently affected operator, potential new entrant) and an explanation of the aircraft operator's specific objection; and

(6) A description and evidence of the aircraft operator's attempt to resolve the dispute locally with the affected parties, including the airport operator.

(b) The FAA will evaluate the aircraft operator's submission and determine whether or not a reevaluation is justified. The FAA may request additional information from the airport operator or any other party and may convene an informal meeting to gather facts relevant to its determination.

(c) The FAA will notify the aircraft operator in writing, with a copy to the affected airport operator, of its determination.

(1) If the FAA determines that a reevaluation is not justified, it will indicate the reasons for this decision.

(2) If the FAA determines that a reevaluation is justified, the aircraft operator will be notified to complete its analysis and to begin the public notice procedure, as set forth in this subpart.

§161.407   Notice of reevaluation.

(a) After receiving an FAA determination that a reevaluation is justified, an aircraft operator desiring continuation of the reevaluation process shall publish a notice of request for reevaluation in an areawide newspaper or newspapers that either singly or together has general circulation throughout the airport noise study area (or the airport vicinity for agreements where an airport noise study area has not been delineated); post a notice in the airport in a prominent location accessible to airport users and the public; and directly notify in writing the following parties:

(1) The airport operator, other aircraft operators providing scheduled passenger or cargo service at the airport, operators of aircraft based at the airport, potential new entrants that are known to be interested in serving the airport, and aircraft operators known to be routinely providing nonscheduled service;

(2) The Federal Aviation Administration;

(3) Each Federal, State, and local agency with land-use control jurisdiction within the airport noise study area (or the airport vicinity for agreements where an airport noise study area has not been delineated);

(4) Fixed-base operators and other airport tenants whose operations may be affected by the agreement or the restriction;

(5) Community groups and business organizations that are known to be interested in the restriction; and

(6) Any other party that commented on the original restriction.

(b) Each notice provided in accordance with paragraph (a) of this section shall include:

(1) The name of the airport and associated cities and states;

(2) A clear, concise description of the restriction, including whether the restriction was approved by the FAA or agreed to by the airport operator and aircraft operators, and the date of the approval or agreement;

(3) The name of the aircraft operator requesting a reevaluation, and a statement that a reevaluation has been requested and that the FAA has determined that a reevaluation is justified;

(4) A brief discussion of the reasons why a reevaluation is justified;

(5) An analysis prepared in accordance with §161.409 of this part supporting the aircraft operator's reevaluation request, or an announcement of where the analysis is available for public inspection;

(6) An invitation to comment on the analysis supporting the proposed reevaluation, with a minimum 45-day comment period;

(7) Information on how to request a copy of the analysis (if not in the notice); and

(8) The address for submitting comments to the aircraft operator, including identification of a contact person.

§161.409   Required analysis by reevaluation petitioner.

(a) An aircraft operator that has petitioned the FAA to reevaluate a restriction shall assume the burden of analysis for the reevaluation.

(b) The aircraft operator's analysis shall be made available for public review under the procedures in § 161.407 and shall include the following:

(1) A copy of the restriction or the language of the agreement as incorporated in a local ordinance, airport rule, lease, or other document;

(2) The aircraft operator's status under the restriction (e.g., currently affected operator, potential new entrant) and an explanation of the aircraft operator's specific objection to the restriction;

(3) The quantified change in the noise environment using methodology specified in this part;

(4) Evidence of the relationship between this change and the likelihood that the restriction does not meet one or more of the conditions in § 161.305; and

(5) Sufficient data and analysis selected from § 161.305, as applicable to the restriction at issue, to support the contention made in paragraph (b)(4) of this section. This is to include either an adequate environmental assessment of the impacts of discontinuing all or part of a restriction in accordance with the aircraft operator's petition, or adequate information supporting a categorical exclusion under FAA orders implementing the National Environmental Policy Act of 1969 (42 U.S.C. 4321).

(c) The amount of analysis may vary with the complexity of the restriction, the number and nature of the conditions in § 161.305 that are alleged to be unsupported, and the amount of previous analysis developed in support of the restriction. The aircraft operator may incorporate analysis previously developed in support of the restriction, including previous environmental documentation to the extent applicable. The applicant is responsible for providing substantial evidence, as described in § 161.305, that one or more of the conditions are not supported.

§ 161.411 Comment by interested parties.

(a) Each aircraft operator requesting a reevaluation shall establish a docket or similar method for receiving and considering comments and shall make comments available for inspection to

interested parties specified in paragraph (b) of this section upon request. Comments must be retained for two years.

(b) Each aircraft operator shall promptly notify interested parties if it makes a substantial change in its analysis that affects either the costs or benefits analyzed, or the criteria in § 161.305, differently from the analysis made available for comment in accordance with § 161.407. Interested parties include those who received direct notice under paragraph (a) of § 161.407 and those who have commented on the reevaluation. If an aircraft operator revises its analysis, it shall make the revised analysis available to an interested party upon request and shall extend the comment period at least 45 days from the date the revised analysis is made available.

§ 161.413 Reevaluation procedure.

(a) Each aircraft operator requesting a reevaluation shall submit to the FAA:

(1) The analysis described in § 161.409;

(2) Evidence that the public review process was carried out in accordance with §§ 161.407 and 161.411, including the aircraft operator's summary of the comments received; and

(3) A request that the FAA complete a reevaluation of the restriction and issue findings.

(b) Following confirmation by the FAA that the aircraft operator's documentation is complete according to the requirements of this subpart, the FAA will publish a notice of reevaluation in the FEDERAL REGISTER and provide for a 45-day comment period during which interested parties may submit comments to the FAA. The FAA will specifically solicit comments from the affected airport operator and affected local governments. A submission that is not complete will be returned to the aircraft operator with a letter indicating the deficiency, and no notice will be published. No further action will be taken by the FAA until a complete submission is received.

(c) The FAA will review all submitted documentation and comments pursuant to the conditions of § 161.305. To the extent necessary, the FAA may request additional information from the aircraft operator, airport operator, and others known to have information material to the reevaluation, and may convene an informal meeting to gather facts relevant to a reevaluation finding.

§161.415 Reevaluation action.

(a) Upon completing the reevaluation, the FAA will issue appropriate orders regarding whether or not there is substantial evidence that the restriction meets the criteria in §161.305 of this part.

(b) If the FAA's reevaluation confirms that the restriction meets the criteria, the restriction may remain as previously agreed to or approved. If the FAA's reevaluation concludes that the restriction does not meet the criteria, the FAA will withdraw a previous approval of the restriction issued under subpart D of this part to the extent necessary to bring the restriction into compliance with this part or, with respect to a restriction agreed to under subpart B of this part, the FAA will specify which criteria are not met.

(c) The FAA will publish a notice of its reevaluation findings in the FEDERAL REGISTER and notify in writing the aircraft operator that petitioned the FAA for reevaluation and the affected airport operator.

§161.417 Notification of status of restrictions and agreements not meeting conditions-of-approval criteria.

If the FAA has withdrawn all or part of a previous approval made under subpart D of this part, the relevant portion of the Stage 3 restriction must be rescinded. The operator of the affected airport shall notify the FAA of the operator's action with regard to a restriction affecting Stage 3 aircraft operations that has been found not to meet the criteria of §161.305. Restrictions in agreements determined by the FAA not to meet conditions for approval may not be enforced with respect to Stage 3 aircraft operations.

Subpart F—Failure To Comply With This Part

§161.501 Scope.

(a) This subpart describes the procedures to terminate eligibility for air-port grant funds and authority to impose or collect passenger facility charges for an airport operator's failure to comply with the Airport Noise and Capacity Act of 1990 (49 U.S.C. App. 2151 *et seq.*) or this part. These procedures may be used with or in addition to any judicial proceedings initiated by the FAA to protect the national aviation system and related Federal interests.

(b) Under no conditions shall any airport operator receive revenues under the provisions of the Airport and Airway Improvement Act of 1982 or impose or collect a passenger facility charge under section 1113(e) of the Federal Aviation Act of 1958 if the FAA determines that the airport is imposing any noise or access restriction not in compliance with the Airport Noise and Capacity Act of 1990 or this part. Recision of, or a commitment in writing signed by an authorized official of the airport operator to rescind or permanently not enforce, a noncomplying restriction will be treated by the FAA as action restoring compliance with the Airport Noise and Capacity Act of 1990 or this part with respect to that restriction.

§161.503 Informal resolution; notice of apparent violation.

Prior to the initiation of formal action to terminate eligibility for airport grant funds or authority to impose or collect passenger facility charges under this subpart, the FAA shall undertake informal resolution with the airport operator to assure compliance with the Airport Noise and Capacity Act of 1990 or this part upon receipt of a complaint or other evidence that an airport operator has taken action to impose a noise or access restriction that appears to be in violation. This shall not preclude a FAA application for expedited judicial action for other than termination of airport grants and passenger facility charges to protect the national aviation system and violated federal interests. If informal resolution is not successful, the FAA will notify the airport operator in writing of the apparent violation. The airport operator shall respond to the notice in writing not later than 20 days after receipt of the notice, and also state whether the airport operator will agree to defer implementation or enforcement of its noise or access restriction until completion of the process under this subpart to determine compliance.

§ 161.505 Notice of proposed termination of airport grant funds and passenger facility charges.

(a) The FAA begins proceedings under this section to terminate an airport operator's eligibility for airport grant funds and authority to impose or collect passenger facility charges only if the FAA determines that informal resolution is not successful.

(b) The following procedures shall apply if an airport operator agrees in writing, within 20 days of receipt of the FAA's notice of apparent violation under § 161.503, to defer implementation or enforcement of a noise or access restriction until completion of the process under this subpart to determine compliance.

(1) The FAA will issue a notice of proposed termination to the airport operator and publish notice of the proposed action in the FEDERAL REGISTER. This notice will state the scope of the proposed termination, the basis for the proposed action, and the date for filing written comments or objections by all interested parties. This notice will also identify any corrective action the airport operator can take to avoid further proceedings. The due date for comments and corrective action by the airport operator shall be specified in the notice of proposed termination and shall not be less than 60 days after publication of the notice.

(2) The FAA will review the comments, statements, and data supplied by the airport operator, and any other available information, to determine if the airport operator has provided satisfactory evidence of compliance or has taken satisfactory corrective action. The FAA will consult with the airport operator to attempt resolution and may request additional information from other parties to determine compliance. The review and consultation process shall take not less than 30 days. If the FAA finds satisfactory evidence of compliance, the FAA will notify the airport operator in writing and publish notice of compliance in the FEDERAL REGISTER.

(3) If the FAA determines that the airport operator has taken action to impose a noise or access restriction in violation of the Airport Noise and Capacity Act of 1990 or this part, the FAA will notify the airport operator in writing of such determination. Where appropriate, the FAA may prescribe corrective action, including corrective action the airport operator may still need to take. Within 10 days of receipt of the FAA's determination, the airport operator shall—

(i) Advise the FAA in writing that it will complete any corrective action prescribed by the FAA within 30 days; or

(ii) Provide the FAA with a list of the domestic air carriers and foreign air carriers operating at the airport and all other issuing carriers, as defined in § 158.3 of this chapter, that have remitted passenger facility charge revenue to the airport in the preceding 12 months.

(4) If the FAA finds that the airport operator has taken satisfactory corrective action, the FAA will notify the airport operator in writing and publish notice of compliance in the FEDERAL REGISTER. If the FAA has determined that the airport operator has imposed a noise or access restriction in violation of the Airport Noise and Capacity Act of 1990 or this part and satisfactory corrective action has not been taken, the FAA will issue an order that—

(i) Terminates eligibility for new airport grant agreements and discontinues payments of airport grant funds, including payments of costs incurred prior to the notice; and

(ii) Terminates authority to impose or collect a passenger facility charge or, if the airport operator has not received approval to impose a passenger facility charge, advises the airport operator that future applications for such approval will be denied in accordance with § 158.29(a)(1)(v) of this chapter.

(5) The FAA will publish notice of the order in the FEDERAL REGISTER and notify air carriers of the FAA's order and actions to be taken to terminate or modify collection of passenger facility charges in accordance with § 158.85(f) of this chapter.

(c) The following procedures shall apply if an airport operator does not agree in writing, within 20 days of receipt of the FAA's notice of apparent violation under §161.503, to defer implementation or enforcement of its noise or access restriction until completion of the process under this subpart to determine compliance.

(1) The FAA will issue a notice of proposed termination to the airport operator and publish notice of the proposed action in the FEDERAL REGISTER. This notice will state the scope of the proposed termination, the basis for the proposed action, and the date for filing written comments or objections by all interested parties. This notice will also identify any corrective action the airport operator can take to avoid further proceedings. The due date for comments and corrective action by the airport operator shall be specified in the notice of proposed termination and shall not be less than 30 days after publication of the notice.

(2) The FAA will review the comments, statements, and data supplied by the airport operator, and any other available information, to determine if the airport operator has provided satisfactory evidence of compliance or has taken satisfactory corrective action. If the FAA finds satisfactory evidence of compliance, the FAA will notify the airport operator in writing and publish notice of compliance in the FEDERAL REGISTER.

(3) If the FAA determines that the airport operator has taken action to impose a noise or access restriction in violation of the Airport Noise and Capacity Act of 1990 or this part, the procedures in paragraphs (b)(3) through (b)(5) of this section will be followed.

PART 169—EXPENDITURE OF FEDERAL FUNDS FOR NONMILITARY AIRPORTS OR AIR NAVIGATION FACILITIES THEREON

Sec.
169.1 Applicability.
169.3 Application for recommendation and certification.
169.5 FAA determination.

AUTHORITY: 49 U.S.C. 106(g), 40101–40107, 40113–40114, 44501–44502, 46104, 47122, 47151–47153, 47302–47306.

§ 169.1 Applicability.

(a) This part prescribes the requirements for issuing a written recommendation and certification that a proposed project is reasonably necessary for use in air commerce or in the interests of national defense. The first two sentences of section 308(a) of the Federal Aviation Act of 1958 (49 U.S.C. 1349(a)): (1) Require such a recommendation and certification where Federal funds are to be expended for nonmilitary purposes for airports or air navigation facilities thereon; and (2) provide that any interested person may apply to the Administrator, under regulations prescribed by him, for a recommendation and certification.

(b) This part does not apply to projects for the expenditure of Federal funds for military purposes or for airports, or air navigation facilities thereon, operated by the Federal Aviation Administration.

[Doc. No. 9256, 34 FR 5718, Mar. 27, 1969]

§ 169.3 Application for recommendation and certification.

(a) Any interested person may apply to the Administrator for a recommendation and certification with respect to a proposed project for the acquisition, establishment, construction, alteration, repair, maintenance, or operation of an airport or an air navigation facility thereon by or in his interests, on which Federal funds are proposed to be expended for nonmilitary purposes. The application shall be filed with the Regional Airports Division or Airports District Office, whichever is appropriate, in whose geographical area the airport is located. The application must state—

(1) The name and address of the applicant, the owner of the airport, and the individual responsible for its operation and maintenance, and the interest of the applicant in the matter;

(2) The location of the airport, and of any air navigation facilities thereon;

(3) A technical description of the project;

(4) The information contained in the notice required by §157.3 of this chapter; and

(5) All available pertinent data relating to the necessity of the airport or

air navigation facility for use in air commerce including where applicable—

(i) The number and type of aircraft that use or would use the airport or facility;

(ii) The present and expected level of activity;

(iii) Any special use of the airport or facility such as its providing access to places of recreation as national forests or parks or to isolated communities where access by other means is not available or is curtailed by climatic condition; and

(iv) In the case of an airport or air navigation facility owned, operated, or maintained by a Federal agency other than the FAA, the relationship of the airport or facility to the performance of that agency's functions.

(b) Each of the following has the effect of a recommendation and certification, and a separate application under this part with respect thereto is not required:

(1) Approval of a project under section 16 of the Airport and Airway Development Act of 1970 (49 U.S.C. 1701).

(2) Inclusion of an airport in the National Airport System Plan, if—

(i) Notice of construction or alteration required by § 157.3 of this chapter has been given; and

(ii) The Administrator has determined that there is no objection to the proposed construction or alteration.

[Doc. No. 9256, 34 FR 5718, Mar. 27, 1969, as amended by Amdt. 169–1, 37 FR 21322, Oct. 7, 1972; Amdt. 169–2, 54 FR 39295, Sept. 25, 1989]

§ 169.5 FAA determination.

(a) The Administrator issues a recommendation and certification if he finds that the airport or facility is reasonably necessary for use in air commerce or in the interests of national defense; that it conforms to all applicable plans and policies for, and allocations of, airspace; and that it otherwise complies with requirements of Federal law properly considered by the Administrator. The Administrator may grant the recommendation and certification subject to conditions that ensure conformity of the airport or facility with these standards.

(b) A recommendation and certification under this part, express or implied, does not extend to a modified version of an airport or facility to which it applies, or to an additional area or facility at the same airport.

(c) If the application is denied the Administrator notifies the applicant of the grounds for the denial. The Administrator may revoke a recommendation and certification for proper cause.

(d) The authority of the Administrator under this part is exercised by Regional Airports Division Managers as to airports or facilities within their respective regions.

[Doc. No. 9256, 34 FR 5718, Mar. 27, 1969, as amended by Amdt. 169–1, 37 FR 21322, Oct. 7, 1972; Amdt. 169–2, 54 FR 39295, Sept. 25, 1989]

SUBCHAPTER J—NAVIGATIONAL FACILITIES

PART 170—ESTABLISHMENT AND DISCONTINUANCE CRITERIA FOR AIR TRAFFIC CONTROL SERVICES AND NAVIGATIONAL FACILITIES

AUTHORITY: 49 U.S.C. 106(g), 40103–40107, 40113, 44502, 44701–44702, 44708–44709, 44719, 44721–44722, 46308.

SOURCE: 56 FR 341, Jan. 3, 1991, unless otherwise noted.

Subpart A—General

§ 170.1 Scope.

This subpart sets forth establishment and discontinuance criteria for navigation aids operated and maintained by the United States.

§ 170.3 Definitions.

For purposes of this subpart—

Air navigation facility (NAVAID) means any facility used, available for use, or designated for use in the aid of air navigation. Included are landing areas; lights; signaling, radio direction-finding, or radio or other electronic communication; and any other structure or mechanism having a similar purpose of guiding or controlling flight or the landing or takeoff of aircraft.

Air traffic clearance means an authorization by air traffic control for an aircraft to proceed under specified traffic conditions within controlled airspace for the purpose of preventing collision between known aircraft.

Air traffic control (ATC) means a service that promotes the safe, orderly, and expeditious flow of air traffic, including airport, approach, departure, and en route air traffic control.

Air traffic controller means a person authorized to provide air traffic service, specifically en route and terminal control personnel.

Aircraft operations means the airborne movement of aircraft in controlled or noncontrolled airport terminal areas, and counts at en route fixes or other points where counts can be made. There are two types of operations: local and itinerant.

(1) *Local operations* mean operations performed by aircraft which:

(i) Operate in the local traffic pattern or within sight of the airport;

(ii) Are known to be departing for, or arriving from flight in local practice areas located within a 20-mile radius of the airport; or

(iii) Execute simulated instrument approaches or low passes at the airport.

(2) *Itinerant operations* mean all aircraft operations other than local operations.

Airport traffic control tower means a terminal facility, which through the use of air/ground communications, visual signaling, and other devices, provides ATC services to airborne aircraft operating in the vicinity of an airport and to aircraft operating on the airport area.

Alternate airport means an airport, specified on a flight plan, to which a flight may proceed when a landing at the point of first intended landing becomes inadvisable.

Approach means the flight path established by the FAA to be used by aircraft landing on a runway.

Approach control facility means a terminal air traffic control facility providing approach control service.

Arrival means any aircraft arriving at an airport.

Benefit-cost ratio means the quotient of the discounted life cycle benefits of an air traffic control service or navigation aid facility (i.e., ATCT) divided by the discounted life cycle costs.

Ceiling means the vertical distance between the ground or water and the lowest layer of clouds or obscuring phenomena that is reported as "broken," "overcast," or "obstruction."

Control Tower—See Airport Traffic Control Tower.

Criteria means the standards used by the FAA for the determination of establishment or discontinuance of a service or facility at an airport.

Departure means any aircraft taking off from an airport.

Discontinuance means the withdrawal of a service and/or facility from an airport.

Establishment means the provision of a service or facility at a candidate airport.

Instrument approach means a series of predetermined maneuvers for the orderly transfer of an aircraft under instrument flight conditions from the beginning of the initial approach to a landing, or to a point from which a landing may be made visually. It is prescribed and approved for a specific airport by competent authority.

Instrument flight rules (IFR) means rules governing the procedures for conducting flight under instrument meteorological conditions (IMC) instrument flight.

Instrument landing system (ILS) means an instrument landing system whereby the pilot guides his approach to a runway solely by reference to instruments in the cockpit. In some instances, the signals received from the ground can be fed into the automatic pilot for automatically controlled approaches.

Instrument meteorological conditions (IMC) means weather conditions below the minimums prescribed for flight under Visual Flight Rules (VFR).

Instrument operation means an aircraft operation in accordance with an IFT flight plan or an operation where IFR separation between aircraft is provided by a terminal control facility or air route traffic control center (ARTCC).

Life cycle benefits means the value of services provided to aviation users over the life span of a facility or service.

Life cycle costs means the value of research and development costs, investment costs, operation costs, maintenance costs, and termination costs over the life span of a facility or service.

Maintenance costs means the costs incurred in servicing and maintaining a facility after establishment.

Mean sea level (MSL) means the base commonly used in measuring altitudes.

Microwave landing system (MLS) means a landing system which enables equipped aircraft to make curved and closely spaced approaches to properly instrumented airports.

Noncommercial traffic means all aircraft operations that are conducted free of compensation.

Nonprecision approach procedure means an FAA standard for approaching an IFR runway where no electronic glide slope is available.

Nonscheduled commercial service means the carriage by aircraft in air commerce of persons or property for compensation or hire that are not operated in regularly scheduled service such as charter flights.

Present value (PV) means the value of a stream of future benefits or costs that are discounted to the present.

PVB or *BPV* means the discounted value of life cycle benefits.

PVC or *CPV* means the discounted value of life cycle benefits.

PVCM or *CMPV* means the discounted value of operations and maintenance costs less termination costs over a facility's remaining life cycle.

Runway means a defined rectangular area on a land airport prepared for the landing and takeoff of aircraft along its length.

Runway visual range means an instrumentally derived value based on standard calibrations that represent the horizontal distance a pilot will see down the runway from the approach end.

Scheduled commercial service means the carriage by aircraft in air commerce under parts 121 and 135 of persons or property for compensation or hire based on published flight schedules.

Separation means the spacing of aircraft in flight and while landing and taking off to achieve their safe and orderly movement.

Takeoff clearance means authorization by an airport traffic control tower for an aircraft to take off.

Tower cab means an ATC facility located at an airport. Controllers at these facilities direct ground traffic, takeoffs, and landings.

Traffic advisories means advisories issued to alert pilots to other known or observed air traffic which may be in such proximity to the position or intended route of flight of their aircraft to warrant attention.

Traffic pattern means the flow of aircraft operating on and in the vicinity of an airport during specified wind conditions as established by appropriate authority.

VFR traffic means aircraft operated solely in accordance with Visual Flight Rules.

Visual flight rules (VFR) means rules that govern the procedures for conducting flight under visual conditions. The term "VFR" is also used in the United States to indicate weather conditions that are equal to or greater than minimum VFR requirements. In addition, "VFR" is used by pilots and controllers to indicate the type of flight plan.

Visual meteorological conditions (VMC) means meteorological conditions expressed in terms of visibility, distance from clouds, and ceiling equal to or better than specified minima.

[56 FR 341, Jan. 3, 1991, as amended by Amdt. 170–3, 66 FR 21067, Apr. 27, 2001; Docket FAA–2017–0733, Amdt. 170–4, 82 FR 34400, July 25, 2017]

Subpart B—Airport Traffic Control Towers

§ 170.11   Scope.

This subpart sets forth establishment and discontinuance criteria for Airport Traffic Control Towers.

§ 170.13   Airport Traffic Control Tower (ATCT) establishment criteria.

(a) The following criteria along with general facility establishment standards must be met before an airport can qualify for an ATCT:

(1) The airport, whether publicly or privately owned, must be open to and available for use by the public as defined in the Airport and Airway Improvement Act of 1982;

(2) The airport must be recognized by and contained within the National Plan of Integrated Airport Systems;

(3) The airport owners/authorities must have entered into appropriate assurances and covenants to guarantee that the airport will continue in operation for a long enough period to per-

mit the amortization of the ATCT investment;

(4) The FAA must be furnished appropriate land without cost for construction of the ATCT; and

(5) The airport must meet the benefit-cost ratio criteria specified herein utilizing three consecutive FAA annual counts and projections of future traffic during the expected life of the tower facility. (An FAA annual count is a fiscal year or a calendar year activity summary. Where actual traffic counts are unavailable or not recorded, adequately documented FAA estimates of the scheduled and nonscheduled activity may be used.)

(b) An airport meets the establishment criteria when it satisfies paragraphs (a)(1) through (a)(5) of this section and its benefit-cost ratio equals or exceeds one. As defined in § 170.3 of this part, the benefit-cost ratio is the ratio of the present value of the ATCT life cycle benefits (BPV) to the present value of ATCT life cycle costs (CPV).

BPV/CPV≥1.0

(c) The satisfaction of all the criteria listed in this section does not guarantee that the airport will receive an ATCT.

§ 170.15   ATCT discontinuance criteria.

An ATCT will be subject to discontinuance when the continued operation and maintenance costs less termination costs (CMPV) of the ATCT exceed the present value of its remaining life-cycle benefits (BPV):

BPV/CMPV<1.0

Subpart C [Reserved]

PART 171—NON-FEDERAL NAVIGATION FACILITIES

Subpart A—VOR Facilities

AUTHORITY: 49 U.S.C. 106(g), 40103–40107, 40109, 40113, 44502, 44701–44702, 44708–44709, 44711, 44719–44721, 45303, 46308.

SOURCE: Docket No. 5034, 29 FR 11337, Aug. 6, 1964, unless otherwise noted.

Subpart A—VOR Facilities

§ 171.1 Scope.

This subpart sets forth minimum requirements for the approval and operation on non-Federal VOR facilities that are to be involved in the approval of instrument flight rules and air traffic control procedures related to those facilities.

[Doc. No. 5034, 29 FR 11337, Aug. 6, 1964, as amended by Amdt. 171–2, 31 FR 5408, Apr. 6, 1966; Amdt. 171–7, 35 FR 12711, Aug. 11, 1970]

§171.3 Requests for IFR procedure.

(a) Each person who requests an IFR procedure based on a VOR facility that he owns must submit the following information with that request:

(1) A description of the facility and evidence that the equipment meets the performance requirements of §171.7 and is installed in accordance with §171.9.

(2) A proposed procedure for operating the facility.

(3) A proposed maintenance organization and maintenance manual that meets the requirements of §171.11.

(4) A statement of intention to meet the requirements of this subpart.

(5) A showing that the facility has an acceptable level of operational reliability and an acceptable standard of performance. Previous equivalent operational experience with a facility with identical design and operational characteristics will be considered in showing compliance with this paragraph.

(b) After the FAA inspects and evaluates the facility, it advises the owner of the results and of any required changes in the facility or the maintenance manual or maintenance organization. The owner must then correct the deficiencies, if any, and operate the facility for an in-service evaluation by the FAA.

[Doc. No. 5034, 29 FR 11337, Aug. 6, 1964, as amended by Amdt. 171–7, 35 FR 12711, Aug. 11, 1970]

§171.5 Minimum requirements for approval.

(a) The following are the minimum requirements that must be met before the FAA will approve an IFR procedure for a non-Federal VOR:

(1) The facility's performance, as determined by air and ground inspection, must meet the requirements of §171.7.

(2) The installation of the equipment must meet the requirements of §171.9.

(3) The owner must agree to operate and maintain the facility in accordance with §171.11.

(4) The owner must agree to furnish periodic reports, as set forth in §171.13, and must agree to allow the FAA to inspect the facility and its operation whenever necessary.

(5) The owner must assure the FAA that he will not withdraw the facility from service without the permission of the FAA.

(6) The owner must bear all costs of meeting the requirements of this section and of any flight or ground inspections made before the facility is commissioned, except that the Federal Aviation Administration may bear certain of these costs subject to budgetary limitations and policy established by the Administrator.

(b) If the applicant for approval meets the requirements of paragraph (a) of this section, the FAA commissions the facility as a prerequisite to its approval for use in an IFR procedure. The approval is withdrawn at any time the facility does not continue to meet those requirements.

[Doc. No. 5034, 29 FR 11337, Aug. 6, 1964, as amended by Amdt. 171–6, 35 FR 10288, June 24, 1970]

§171.7 Performance requirements.

(a) The VOR must perform in accordance with the "International Standards and Recommended Practices, Aeronautical Telecommunications," Part I, paragraph 3.3 (Annex 10 to the Convention on International Civil Aviation), except that part of paragraph 3.3.2.1 specifying a radio frequency tolerance of 0.005 percent, and that part of paragraph 3.3.7 requiring removal of only the bearing information. In place thereof, the frequency tolerance of the radio frequency carrier must not exceed plus or minus 0.002 percent, and all radiation must be removed during the specified deviations from established conditions and during periods of monitor failure.

(b) Ground inspection consists of an examination of the design features of the equipment to determine that there will not be conditions that will allow unsafe operations because of component failure or deterioration.

(c) The monitor is checked periodically, during the in-service test evaluation period, for calibration and stability The tests are made with a standard "Reference and variable phase signal generator" and associated test equipment, including an oscilloscope and portable field detector. In general, the ground check is conducted in accord- ance with section 8.4 of FAA Handbook AF P 6790.9 "Maintenance Instruction for VHF Omniranges", adapted for the facility concerned.

(d) Flight tests to determine the facility's adequacy for operational requirements and compliance with applicable "Standards and Recommended Practices" are conducted in accordance with the "U.S. Standard Flight Inspection Manual", particularly section 201.

(e) After January 1, 1975, the owner of the VOR shall modify the facility to perform in accordance with paragraph 3.3.5.7 of Annex 10 to the Convention on International Civil Aviation within 180 days after receipt of notice from the Administrator that 50 kHz channel spacing is to be implemented in the area and that a requirement exists for suppression of 9960 Hz subcarrier harmonics.

[Doc. No. 5034, 29 FR 11337, Aug. 6, 1964, as amended by Amdt. 171-7, 35 FR 12711, Aug. 11, 1970; Amdt. 171-9, 38 FR 28557, Oct. 15, 1973]

§ 171.9 Installation requirements.

(a) The facility must be installed according to accepted good engineering practices, applicable electric and safety codes, and the installation must meet at least the Federal Communication Commission's licensing requirements.

(b) The facility must have a reliable source of suitable primary power, either from a power distribution system or locally generated, with a supplemental standby system, if needed.

(c) Dual transmitting equipment with automatic changeover is preferred and may be required to support certain IFR procedures.

(d) There must be a means for determining, from the ground, the performance of the equipment, including the antenna, initially and periodically.

(e) A facility intended for use as an instrument approach aid for an airport must have or be supplemented by (depending on circumstances) the following ground-air or landline communications services:

(1) At facilities outside of and not immediately adjacent to controlled airspace, there must be ground-air communications from the airport served by the facility. Separate communications channels are acceptable.

(2) At facilities within or immediately adjacent to controlled airspace, there must be the ground-air communications required by paragraph (e)(1) of this section and reliable communications (at least a landline telephone) from the airport to the nearest FAA air traffic control or communication facility.

Paragraphs (e) (1) and (2) of this section are not mandatory at airports where an adjacent FAA facility can communicate with aircraft on the ground at the airport and during the entire proposed instrument approach procedure. In addition, at low traffic density airports within or immediately adjacent to controlled airspace and where extensive delays are not a factor, the requirements of paragraphs (e) (1) and (2) of this section may be reduced to reliable communications (at least a landline telephone) from the airport to the nearest FAA air traffic control or communication facility, if an adjacent FAA facility can communicate with aircraft during the proposed instrument approach procedure, at least down to the minimum en route altitude for the controlled airspace area.

[Doc. No. 5034, 29 FR 11337, Aug. 6, 1964, as amended by Amdt. 171-7, 35 FR 12711, Aug. 11, 1970; Amdt. 171-16, 56 FR 65664, Dec. 17, 1991]

§ 171.11 Maintenance and operations requirements.

(a) The owner of the facility must establish an adequate maintenance system and provide qualified maintenance personnel to maintain the facility at the level attained at the time it was commissioned. Each person who maintains a facility must meet at least the Federal Communications Commission's licensing requirements and show that he has the special knowledge and skills

needed to maintain the facility including proficiency in maintenance procedures and the use of specialized test
equipment.

(b) The owner must prepare, and obtain FAA approval of, an operations
and maintenance manual that sets
forth mandatory procedures for operations, preventive maintenance, and
emergency maintenance, including instructions on each of the following:

(1) Physical security of the facility.

(2) Maintenance and operations by
authorized persons only.

(3) FCC licensing requirements for
operating and maintenance personnel.

(4) Posting of licenses and signs.

(5) Relations between the facility and
FAA air traffic control facilities, with
a description of the boundaries of controlled airspace over or near the facility, instructions for relaying air traffic
control instructions and information
(if applicable), and instructions for the
operation of an air traffic advisory
service if the VOR is located outside of
controlled airspace.

(6) Notice to the Administrator of
any suspension of service.

(7) Detailed and specific maintenance
procedures and servicing guides stating
the frequency of servicing.

(8) Air-ground communications, if
provided, expressly written or incorporating appropriate sections of FAA
manuals by reference.

(9) Keeping of station logs and other
technical reports, and the submission
of reports required by §171.13.

(10) Monitoring of the facility.

(11) Inspections by United States personnel.

(12) Names, addresses, and telephone
numbers of persons to be notified in an
emergency.

(13) Shutdowns for routine maintenance and issue of "Notices to Airmen"
for routine or emergency shutdowns
(private use facilities may omit the
"Notices to Airmen").

(14) An explanation of the kinds of
activity (such as construction or grading) in the vicinity of the facility that
may require shutdown or recertification of the facility by FAA flight
check.

(15) Procedures for conducting a
ground check of course accuracy.

(16) Commissioning of the facility.

(17) An acceptable procedure for
amending or revising the manual.

(18) The following information concerning the facility:

(i) Location by latitude and longitude to the nearest second, and its
position with respect to airport layouts.

(ii) The type, make, and model of the
basic radio equipment that will provide
the service.

(iii) The station power emission and
frequency.

(iv) The hours of operation.

(v) Station identification call letters
and method of station identification,
whether by Morse code or recorded
voice announcement, and the time
spacing of the identification.

(vi) A description of the critical parts
that may not be changed, adjusted, or
repaired without an FAA flight check
to confirm published operations.

(c) The owner shall make a ground
check of course accuracy each month
in accordance with procedures approved by the FAA at the time of commissioning, and shall report the results
of the checks as provided in §171.13.

(d) If the owner desires to modify the
facility, he must submit the proposal
to the FAA and may not allow any
modifications to be made without specific approval.

(e) The owner's maintenance personnel must participate in initial inspections made by the FAA. In the case
of subsequent inspections, the owner or
his representative shall participate.

(f) Whenever it is required by the
FAA, the owner shall incorporate improvements in VOR maintenance
brought about by progress in the state
of the art. In addition, he shall provide
a stock of spare parts, including vacuum tubes, of such a quantity to make
possible the prompt replacement of
components that fail or deteriorate in
service.

(g) The owner shall provide all approved test instruments needed for
maintenance of the facility.

(h) The owner shall close the facility
upon receiving two successive pilot reports of its malfunctioning.

[Doc. No. 5034, 29 FR 11337, Aug. 6, 1964, as
amended by Amdt. 171–2, 31 FR 5408, Apr. 6,
1966]

§ 171.13 Reports.

The owner of each facility to which this subpart applies shall make the following reports on forms furnished by the FAA, at the times indicated, to the FAA Regional office for the area in which the facility is located:

(a) *Record of meter readings and adjustments (Form FAA–198).* To be filled out by the owner with the equipment adjustments and meter readings as of the time of commissioning, with one copy to be kept in the permanent records of the facility and two copies to the appropriate Regional office of the FAA. The owner shall revise the form after any major repair, modernization, or returning, to reflect an accurate record of facility operation and adjustment.

(b) *Facility maintenance log (FAA Form 6003–1).* This form is a permanent record of all equipment malfunctioning met in maintaining the facility, including information on the kind of work and adjustments made, equipment failures, causes (if determined), and corrective action taken. The owner shall keep the original of each report at the facility and send a copy to the appropriate Regional office of the FAA at the end of the month in which it is prepared.

(c) *Radio equipment operation record (Form FAA–418).* To contain a complete record of meter readings, recorded on each scheduled visit to the facility. The owner shall keep the original of each month's record at the facility and send a copy of it to the appropriate Regional office of the FAA.

(d) [Reserved]

(e) *VOR ground check error data (Forms FAA–2396 and 2397).* To contain results of the monthly course accuracy ground check in accordance with FAA Handbook AF P 6790.9 "Maintenance Instructions for VHF Omniranges". The owner shall keep the originals in the facility and send a copy of each form to the appropriate Regional office of the FAA on a monthly basis.

(49 U.S.C. 1348)

[Doc. No. 5034, 29 FR 11337, Aug. 6, 1964, as amended by Amdt. 171–5, 34 FR 15245, Sept. 30, 1969; Amdt. 171–10, 40 FR 36110, Aug. 19, 1975]

Subpart B—Nondirectional Radio Beacon Facilities

§ 171.21 Scope.

(a) This subpart sets forth minimum requirements for the approval and operation of non-Federal, nondirectional radio beacon facilities that are to be involved in the approval of instrument flight rules and air traffic control procedures related to those facilities.

(b) A nondirectional radio beacon ("H" facilities domestically—NDB facilities internationally) radiates a continuous carrier of approximately equal intensity at all azimuths. The carrier is modulated at 1020 cycles per second for station identification purposes.

[Doc. No. 5034, 29 FR 11337, Aug. 6, 1964, as amended by Amdt. 171–2, 31 FR 5408, Apr. 6, 1966; Amdt. 171–7, 35 FR 12711, Aug. 11, 1970]

§ 171.23 Requests for IFR procedure.

(a) Each person who requests an IFR procedure based on a nondirectional radio beacon facility that he owns must submit the following information with that request:

(1) A description of the facility and evidence that the equipment meets the performance requirements of § 171.27 and is installed in accordance with § 171.29.

(2) A proposed procedure for operating the facility.

(3) A proposed maintenance arrangement and a maintenance manual that meets the requirements of § 171.31.

(4) A statement of intention to meet the requirements of this subpart.

(5) A showing that the facility has an acceptable level of operational reliability and an acceptable standard of performance. Previous equivalent operational experience with a facility with identical design and operational characteristics will be considered in showing compliance with this subparagraph.

(b) After the FAA inspects and evaluates the facility, it advises the owner of the results and of any required changes in the facility or the maintenance manual or maintenance organization. The owner must then correct the deficiencies, if any, and operate the facility for an in-service evaluation by the FAA.

[Doc. No. 5034, 29 FR 11337, Aug. 6, 1964, as amended by Amdt. 171-7, 35 FR 12711, Aug. 11, 1970]

§171.25 Minimum requirements for approval.

(a) The following are the minimum requirements that must be met before the FAA will approve an IFR procedure for a non-Federal, nondirectional radio beacon facility under this subpart:

(1) The facility's performances, as determined by air and ground inspection, must meet the requirements of §171.27.

(2) The installation of the equipment must meet the requirements of §171.29.

(3) The owner must agree to operate and maintain the facility in accordance with §171.31.

(4) The owner must agree to furnish periodic reports, as set forth in §171.33, and agree to allow the FAA to inspect the facility and its operation whenever necessary.

(5) The owner must assure the FAA that he will not withdraw the facility from service without the permission of the FAA.

(6) The owner must bear all costs of meeting the requirements of this section and of any flight or ground inspections made before the facility is commissioned, except that the Federal Aviation Administration may bear certain of these costs subject to budgetary limitations and policy established by the Administrator.

(b) If the applicant for approval meets the requirements of paragraph (a) of this section, the FAA commissions the facility as a prerequisite to its approval for use in an IFR procedure. The approval is withdrawn at any time the facility does not continue to meet those requirements. In addition, the facility may be de-commissioned whenever the frequency channel is needed for higher priority common system service.

[Doc. No. 5034, 29 FR 11337, Aug. 6, 1964, as amended by Amdt. 171-6, 35 FR 10233, June 24, 1970]

§171.27 Performance requirements.

(a) The facility must meet the performance requirements set forth in the "International Standards and Rec-

ommended Practices, Aeronautical Telecommunications, Part I, paragraph 3.4" (Annex 10 to the Convention on International Civil Aviation), except that identification by on-off keying of a second carrier frequency, separated from the main carrier by 1020 Hz plus or minus 50 Hz, is also acceptable.

(b) The facility must perform in accordance with recognized and accepted good electronic engineering practices for the desired service.

(c) Ground inspection consists of an examination of the design features of the equipment to determine (based on recognized and accepted good engineering practices) that there will not be conditions that will allow unsafe operations because of component failure or deterioration.

(d) Flight tests to determine the facility's adequacy for operational requirements and compliance with applicable "Standards and Recommended Practices" are conducted in accordance with the "U.S. Standard Flight Inspection Manual", particularly section 207. The original test is made by the FAA and later tests shall be made under arrangements, satisfactory to the FAA, that are made by the owner.

[Doc. No. 5034, 29 FR 11337, Aug. 6, 1964, as amended by Amdt. 171-7, 35 FR 12711, Aug. 11, 1970]

§171.29 Installation requirements.

(a) The facility must be installed according to accepted good engineering practices, applicable electric and safety codes, and FCC licensing requirements.

(b) The facility must have a reliable source of suitable primary power.

(c) Dual transmitting equipment may be required to support some IFR procedures.

(d) A facility intended for use as an instrument approach aid for an airport must have or be supplemented by (depending on the circumstances) the following ground-air or landline communications services:

(1) At facilities outside of and not immediately adjacent to controlled airspace, there must be ground-air communications from the airport served by the facility. Voice on the aid controlled from the airport is acceptable.

(2) At facilities within or immediately adjacent to controlled airspace, there must be the ground-air communications required by paragraph (d)(1) of this section and reliable communications (at least a landline telephone) from the airport to the nearest FAA air traffic control or communication facility.

Paragraphs (d) (1) and (2) of this section are not mandatory at airports where an adjacent FAA facility can communicate with aircraft on the ground at the airport and during the entire proposed instrument approach procedure. In addition, at low traffic density airports within or immediately adjacent to controlled airspace, and where extensive delays are not a factor, the requirements of paragraphs (d) (1) and (2) of this section may be reduced to reliable communications (at least a landline telephone) from the airport to the nearest FAA air traffic control or communications facility, if an adjacent FAA facility can communicate with aircraft during the proposed instrument approach procedure, at least down to the minimum en route altitude for the controlled airspace area.

[Doc. No. 5034, 29 FR 11337, Aug. 6, 1964, as amended by Amdt. 171-16, 56 FR 65664, Dec. 17, 1991]

§ 171.31 Maintenance and operations requirements.

(a) The owner of the facility must establish an adequate maintenance system and provide qualified maintenance personnel to maintain the facility at the level attained at the time it was commissioned. Each person who maintains a facility must meet at least the Federal Communications Commission's licensing requirements and show that he has the special knowledge and skills needed to maintain the facility including proficiency in maintenance procedures and the use of specialized test equipment.

(b) The owner must prepare, and obtain approval of, an operations and maintenance manual that sets forth mandatory procedures for operations, preventive maintenance, and emergency maintenance, including instructions on each of the following:

(1) Physical security of the facility.

(2) Maintenance and operations by authorized persons only.

(3) FCC licensing requirements for operating and maintenance personnel.

(4) Posting of licenses and signs.

(5) Relations between the facility and FAA air traffic control facilities, with a description of the boundaries of controlled airspace over or near the facility, instructions for relaying air traffic control instructions and information (if applicable), and instructions for the operation of an air traffic advisory service if the facility is located outside of controlled airspace.

(6) Notice to the Administrator of any suspension of service.

(7) Detailed arrangements for maintenance flight inspection and servicing stating the frequency of servicing.

(8) Air-ground communications, if provided, expressly written or incorporating appropriate sections of FAA manuals by reference.

(9) Keeping of station logs and other technical reports, and the submission of reports required by § 171.33.

(10) Monitoring of the facility, at least once each half hour, to assure continuous operation.

(11) Inspections by United States personnel.

(12) Names, addresses, and telephone numbers of persons to be notified in an emergency.

(13) Shutdowns for routine maintenance and issue of "Notices to Airmen" for routine or emergency shutdowns (private use facilities may omit the "Notices to Airmen").

(14) Commissioning of the facility.

(15) An acceptable procedure for amending or revising the manual.

(16) The following information concerning the facility:

(i) Location by latitude and longitude to the nearest second, and its position with respect to airport layouts.

(ii) The type, make, and model of the basic radio equipment that will provide the service.

(iii) The station power emission and frequency.

(iv) The hours of operation.

(v) Station identification call letters and method of station identification, whether by Morse code or recorded voice announcement, and the time spacing of the identification.

(c) If the owner desires to modify the facility, he must submit the proposal to the FAA and meet applicable requirements of the FCC.

(d) The owner's maintenance personnel must participate in initial inspections made by the FAA. In the case of subsequent inspections, the owner or his representative shall participate.

(e) The owner shall provide a stock of spare parts, including vacuum tubes, of such a quantity to make possible the prompt replacement of components that fail or deteriorate in service.

(f) The owner shall close the facility upon receiving two successive pilot reports of its malfunctioning.

[Doc. No. 5034, 29 FR 11337, Aug. 6, 1964, as amended by Amdt. 171–2, 31 FR 5408, Apr. 6, 1966]

§171.33 Reports.

The owner of each facility to which this subpart applies shall make the following reports, at the times indicated, to the FAA Regional office for the area in which the facility is located:

(a) *Record of meter readings and adjustments (Form FAA–198).* To be filled out by the owner or his maintenance representative with the equipment adjustments and meter readings as of the time of commissioning, with one copy to be kept in the permanent records of the facility and two copies to the appropriate Regional Office of the FAA. The owner shall revise the form after any major repair, modernization, or returning, to reflect an accurate record of facility operation and adjustment.

(b) *Facility maintenance log (FAA Form 6030–1).* This form is a permanent record of all equipment malfunctioning met in maintaining the facility, including information on the kind of work and adjustments made, equipment failures, causes (if determined), and corrective action taken. The owner shall keep the original of each report at the facility and send a copy to the appropriate Regional Office of the FAA at the end of the month in which it is prepared.

(c) *Radio equipment operation record (Form FAA–418).* To contain a complete record of meter readings, recorded on each scheduled visit to the facility.

The owner shall keep the original of each month's record at the facility and send a copy of it to the appropriate Regional Office of the FAA.

[Doc. No. 5034, 29 FR 11337, Aug. 6, 1964, as amended by Amdt. 171–10, 40 FR 36110, Aug. 19, 1975]

Subpart C—Instrument Landing System (ILS) Facilities

§171.41 Scope.

This subpart sets forth minimum requirements for the approval and operation of non-Federal Instrument Landing System (ILS) Facilities that are to be involved in the approval of instrument flight rules and air traffic control procedures related to those facilities.

[Doc. No. 5034, 29 FR 11337, Aug. 6, 1964, as amended by Amdt. 171–2, 31 FR 5408, Apr. 6, 1966; Amdt. 171–7, 35 FR 12711, Aug. 11, 1970]

§171.43 Requests for IFR procedure.

(a) Each person who requests an IFR procedure based on an ILS facility that he owns must submit the following information with that request:

(1) A description of the facility and evidence that the equipment meets the performance requirements of §171.47 and is installed in accordance with §171.49.

(2) A proposed procedure for operating the facility.

(3) A proposed maintenance organization and a maintenance manual that meets the requirements of §171.51.

(4) A statement of intent to meet the requirements of this subpart.

(5) A showing that the facility has an acceptable level of operational reliability and an acceptable standard of performance. Previous equivalent operational experience with a facility with identical design and operational characteristics will be considered in showing compliance with this subparagraph.

(b) After the FAA inspects and evaluates the facility, it advises the owner of the results and of any required changes in the facility or the maintenance manual or maintenance organization. The owner must then correct the deficiencies, if any, and operate the facility for an in-service evaluation by the FAA.

[Doc. No. 5034, 29 FR 11337, Aug. 6, 1964, as amended by Amdt. 171–7, 35 FR 12711, Aug. 11, 1970]

§ 171.45   Minimum requirements for approval.

(a) The following are the minimum requirements that must be met before the FAA will approve an IFR procedure for a non-Federal Instrument Landing System:

(1) The facility's performance, as determined by air and ground inspection, must meet the requirements of § 171.47.

(2) The installation of the equipment must meet the requirements of § 171.49.

(3) The owner must agree to operate and maintain the facility in accordance with § 171.51.

(4) The owner must agree to furnish periodic reports, as set forth in § 171.53 and agree to allow the FAA to inspect the facility and its operation whenever necessary.

(5) The owner must assure the FAA that he will not withdraw the facility from service without the permission of the FAA.

(6) The owner must bear all costs of meeting the requirements of this section and of any flight or ground inspections made before the facility is commissioned, except that the Federal Aviation Administration may bear certain of these costs subject to budgetary limitations and policy established by the Administrator.

(b) If the applicant for approval meets the requirements of paragraph (a) of this section, the FAA commissions the facility as a prerequisite to its approval for use in an IFR procedure. The approval is withdrawn at any time the facility does not continue to meet those requirements. In addition, the facility may be de-commissioned whenever the frequency channel is needed for higher priority common system service.

[Doc. No. 5034, 29 FR 11337, Aug. 6, 1964, as amended by Amdt. 171–6, 35 FR 10288, June 24, 1970]

§ 171.47   Performance requirements.

(a) The Instrument Landing System must perform in accordance with the "International Standards and Rec-

ommended Practices, Aeronautical Telecommunications, Part I, Paragraph 3.1" (Annex 10 to the Convention on International Civil Aviation) except as follows:

(1) The first part of paragraph 3.1.3, relating to suppression of radiation wholly or in part in any or all directions outside the 20-degree sector centered on the course line to reduce localizer does not apply.

(2) Radiation patterns must conform to limits specified in 3.1.3.3 and 3.1.3.4, but this does not mean that suppression of radiation to the rear of the antenna array to satisfy difficult siting positions (as per 3.1.3.1.4) is not allowed. For example, if a reflector screen for the antenna array is required to overcome a siting problem, the area to the rear of the localizer may be made unusable and should be so advertised.

(3) A third marker beacon (inner marker) is not required.

(4) The frequency tolerance of the radio frequency carrier must not exceed plus or minus 0.002 percent.

(b) Ground inspection consists of an examination of the design features of the equipment to determine that there will not be conditions that will allow unsafe operations because of component failure or deterioration.

(c) The monitor is checked periodically, during the in-service test evaluation period, for calibration and stability. These tests, and ground checks of glide slope and localizer radiation characteristics, are conducted in accordance with FAA Handbooks AF P 6750.1 and AF P 6750.2 "Maintenance Instructions for ILS Localizer Equipment" and "Maintenance Instructions for ILS Glide Slope Equipment".

(d) Flight tests to determine the facility's adequacy for operational requirements and compliance with applicable "Standards and Recommended Practices" are conducted in accordance with the "U.S. Standard Flight Inspection Manual", particularly section 217.

[Doc. No. 5034, 29 FR 11337, Aug. 6, 1974, as amended by Amdt. 171–9, 38 FR 28557, Oct. 15, 1973]

§ 171.49 Installation requirements.

(a) The facility must be of a permanent nature, located, constructed, and installed according to ICAO Standards (Annex 10), accepted good engineering practices, applicable electric and safety codes, and FCC licensing requirements.

(b) The facility must have a reliable source of suitable primary power, either from a power distribution system or locally generated. A determination by the Administrator as to whether a facility will be required to have standby power for the localizer, glide slope and monitor accessories to supplement the primary power, will be made for each airport based upon operational minimums and density of air traffic.

(c) A determination by the Administrator as to whether a facility will be required to have dual transmitting equipment with automatic changeover for localizer and glide slope components, will be made for each airport based upon operational minimums and density of air traffic.

(d) There must be a means for determining, from the ground, the performance of the equipment (including antennae), initially and periodically

(e) The facility must have, or be supplemented by (depending on the circumstances) the following ground-air or landline communications services:

(1) At facilities outside of and not immediately adjacent to controlled airspace, there must be ground-air communications from the airport served by the facility. The utilization of voice on the ILS frequency should be determined by the facility operator on an individual basis.

(2) At facilities within or immediately adjacent to controlled airspace, there must be the ground-air communications required by paragraph (e)(1) of this section and reliable communications (at least a landline telephone) from the airport to the nearest FAA air traffic control or communications facility.

Paragraphs (e)(1) and (e)(2) of this section are not mandatory at airports where an adjacent FAA facility can communicate with aircraft on the ground at the airport and during the entire proposed instrument approach procedure. In addition, at low traffic density airports within or immediately adjacent to controlled airspace, and where extensive delays are not a factor, the requirements of paragraphs (e)(1) and (e)(2) of this section may be reduced to reliable communications (at least a landline telephone) from the airport to the nearest FAA air traffic control or communications facility, if an adjacent FAA facility can communicate with aircraft during the proposed instrument approach procedure down to the airport surface or at least to the minimum approach altitude.

[Doc. No. 5034, 29 FR 11337, Aug. 6, 1964, as amended by Amdt. 171–6, 35 FR 10288, June 24, 1970; Amdt. 171–16, 56 FR 65664, Dec. 17, 1991]

§ 171.51 Maintenance and operations requirements.

(a) The owner of the facility must establish an adequate maintenance system and provide qualified maintenance personnel to maintain the facility at the level attained at the time it was commissioned. Each person who maintains a facility must meet at least the Federal Communications Commission's licensing requirements and show that he has the special knowledge and skills needed to maintain the facility including proficiency in maintenance procedures and the use of specialized test equipment.

(b) The owner must prepare, and obtain approval of, an operations and maintenance manual that sets forth mandatory procedures for operations, preventive maintenance, and emergency maintenance, including instructions on each of the following:

(1) Physical security of the facility.

(2) Maintenance and operations by authorized persons only.

(3) FCC licensing requirements for operating and maintenance personnel.

(4) Posting of licenses and signs.

(5) Relation between the facility and FAA air traffic control facilities, with a description of the boundaries of controlled airspace over or near the facility, instructions for relaying air traffic control instructions and information (if applicable), and instructions for the operations of an air traffic advisory service if the facility is located outside of controlled airspace.

(6) Notice to the Administrator of any suspension of service.

(7) Detailed and specific maintenance procedures and servicing guides stating the frequency of servicing.

(8) Air-ground communications, if provided, expressly written or incorporating appropriate sections of FAA manuals by reference.

(9) Keeping of station logs and other technical reports, and the submission of reports required by § 171.53.

(10) Monitoring of the facility.

(11) Inspections by United States personnel.

(12) Names, addresses, and telephone numbers of persons to be notified in an emergency.

(13) Shutdowns for routine maintenance and issue of "Notices to Airmen" for routine or emergency shutdowns (private use facilities may omit the "Notices to Airmen").

(14) Commissioning of the facility.

(15) An acceptable procedure for amending or revising the manual.

(16) An explanation of the kinds of activities (such as construction or grading) in the vicinity of the facility that may require shutdown or recertification of the facility by FAA flight check.

(17) Procedures for conducting a ground check or localizer course alignment width, and clearance, and glide slope elevation angle and width.

(18) The following information concerning the facility:

(i) Facility component locations with respect to airport layout, instrument runway, and similar areas.

(ii) The type, make, and model of the basic radio equipment that will provide the service.

(iii) The station power emission and frequencies of the localizer, glide slope, markers, and associated compass locators, if any.

(iv) The hours of operation.

(v) Station identification call letters and method of station identification and the time spacing of the identification.

(vi) A description of the critical parts that may not be changed, adjusted, or repaired without an FAA flight check to confirm published operations.

(c) The owner shall make a ground check of the facility each month in accordance with procedures approved by the FAA at the time of commissioning, and shall report the results of the checks as provided in § 171.53.

(d) If the owner desires to modify the facility, he must submit the proposal to the FAA and may not allow any modifications to be made without specific approval.

(e) "The owner's maintenance personnel must participate in initial inspections made by the FAA. In the case of subsequent inspections, the owner or his representative shall participate."

(f) Whenever it is required by the FAA, the owner shall incorporate improvements in ILS maintenance brought about by progress in the state of the art. In addition, he shall provide a stock of spare parts, including vacuum tubes, of such a quantity to make possible the prompt replacement of components that fail or deteriorate in service.

(g) The owner shall provide FAA approved test instruments needed for maintenance of the facility.

(h) The owner shall close the facility upon receiving two successive pilot reports of its malfunctioning.

[Doc. No. 5034, 29 FR 11337, Aug. 6, 1964, as amended by Amdt. 171–2, 31 FR 5408, Apr. 6, 1966]

§ 171.53 Reports.

The owner of each facility to which this subpart applies shall make the following reports, at the times indicated, to the FAA Regional Office for the area in which the facility is located:

(a) *Record of meter readings and adjustments (Form FAA–198).* To be filled out by the owner or his maintenance representative with the equipment adjustments and meter readings as of the time of commissioning, with one copy to be kept in the permanent records of the facility and two copies to the appropriate Regional Office of the FAA. The owner shall revise the form after any major repair, modernization, or retuning, to reflect an accurate record of facility operation and adjustment.

(b) *Facility maintenance log (FormFAA 6030–1).* This form is a permanent record of all equipment malfunctioning met in maintaining the facility, including information on the kind of work and adjustments made, equipment failures, causes (if determined), and corrective action taken. The owner shall keep the original of each report at the facility and send a copy to the appropriate Regional Office of the FAA at the end of each month in which it is prepared.

(c) *Radio equipment operation record (Form FAA-418)*. To contain a complete record of meter readings, recorded on each scheduled visit to the facility. The owner shall keep the original of each month's record at the facility and send a copy of it to the appropriate Regional Office of the FAA.

[Doc. No. 5034, 29 FR 11337, Aug. 6, 1964, as amended by Amdt. 171-5, 34 FR 15245, Sept. 30, 1969; Amdt. 171-10, 40 FR 36110, Aug. 19, 1975]

Subpart D—True Lights

§171.61 Air navigation certificate: Revocation and termination.

(a) Except as provided in paragraph (b) of this section, each air navigation certificate of "Lawful Authority to Operate a True Light" is hereby revoked, and each application therefor is hereby terminated.

(b) Paragraph (a) of this section does not apply to—

(1) A certificate issued to a Federal-Aid Airport Program sponsor who was required to apply for that certificate under regulations then in effect, and who has not surrendered that certificate under §151.86(e) of this chapter; or

(2) An application made by a Federal-Aid Airport Program sponsor who was required to make that application under regulations then in effect, and who has not terminated that application under §151.86(e) of this chapter.

(49 U.S.C. 1101–1120; sec. 307, 72 Stat. 749, 49 U.S.C. 1348)

[Amdt. 171-4, 33 FR 12545, Sept. 5, 1968]

Subpart E—General

§171.71 Materials incorporated by reference.

Copies of standards, recommended practices and documents incorporated by reference in this part are available for the use of interested persons at any FAA Regional Office and FAA Head-quarters. An historical file of these materials is maintained at Headquarters, Federal Aviation Administration, 800 Independence Avenue SW., Washington, DC 20590.

[Amdt. 171-8, 36 FR 5584, Mar. 25, 1971]

§171.73 Alternative forms of reports.

On a case-by-case basis, a Regional Administrator may accept any report in a format other than the FAA form required by this part if he is satisfied that the report contains all the information required on the FAA form and can be processed by FAA as conveniently as the FAA form.

(49 U.S.C. 1348)

[Amdt. 171-5, 34 FR 15245, Sept. 30, 1969, as amended by Amdt. 171-15, 54 FR 39296, Sept. 25, 1989]

§171.75 Submission of requests.

(a) Requests for approval of facilities not having design and operational characteristics identical to those of facilities currently approved under this part, including requests for deviations from this part for such facilities, must be submitted to the Director, Advanced Systems Design Service.

(b) The following requests must be submitted to the Regional Administrator of the region in which the facility is located:

(1) Requests for approval of facilities that have design and operational characteristics identical to those of facilities currently approved under this part, including requests for deviations from this part for such facilities.

(2) Requests for deviations from this part for facilities currently approved under this part.

(3) Requests for modification of facilities currently approved under this part.

[Amdt. 171-7, 35 FR 12711, Aug. 11, 1970, as amended by Amdt. 171-15, 54 FR 39296, Sept. 25, 1989]

Subpart F—Simplified Directional Facility (SDF)

SOURCE: Docket No. 10116, 35 FR 12711, Aug. 11, 1970, unless otherwise noted.

§ 171.101 Scope.

This subpart sets forth minimum requirements for the approval and operation of non-Federal Simplified Directional Facilities (SDF) that are to be involved in the approval of instrument flight rules and air traffic control procedures related to those facilities.

§ 171.103 Requests for IFR procedure.

(a) Each person who requests an IFR procedure based on an SDF that he owns must submit the following information with that request:

(1) A description of the facility and evidence that the equipment meets the performance requirements of § 171.109 and the standards and tolerances of § 171.111, and is installed in accordance with § 171.113.

(2) A proposed procedure for operating the facility.

(3) A proposed maintenance organization and a maintenance manual that meets the requirements of § 171.115.

(4) A statement of intent to meet the requirements of this subpart.

(5) A showing that the facility has an acceptable level of operational reliability as prescribed in § 171.111(k), and an acceptable standard of performance. Previous equivalent operational experience with a facility with identical design and operational characteristics will be considered in showing compliance with this paragraph.

(b) After the Federal Aviation Administration inspects and evaluates the facility, it advises the owner of the results and of any required changes in the facility or the maintenance manual or maintenance organization. The owner must then correct the deficiencies, if any, and operate the facility for an in-service evaluation by the Federal Aviation Administration.

§ 171.105 Minimum requirements for approval.

(a) The following are the minimum requirements that must be met before the Federal Aviation Administration will approve an IFR procedure for a non-Federal Simplified Directional Facility:

(1) A suitable frequency channel must be available.

(2) The facility's performance, as determined by air and ground inspection, must meet the requirements of §§ 171.109 and 171.111.

(3) The installation of the equipment must meet the requirements of § 171.113.

(4) The owner must agree to operate and maintain the facility in accordance with § 171.115.

(5) The owner must agree to furnish periodic reports as set forth in § 171.117, and agree to allow the FAA to inspect the facility and its operation whenever necessary.

(6) The owner must assure the FAA that he will not withdraw the facility from service without the permission of the FAA.

(7) The owner must bear all costs of meeting the requirements of this section and of any flight or ground inspections made before the facility is commissioned, except that the FAA may bear certain of these costs subject to budgetary limitations and policy established by the Administrator.

(b) If the applicant for approval meets the requirements of paragraph (a) of this section, the FAA commissions the facility as a prerequisite to its approval for use in an IFR procedure. The approval is withdrawn at any time the facility does not continue to meet those requirements. In addition, the facility is licensed by the Federal Communications Commission. The Federal Aviation Administration recommends cancellation or nonrenewal of the Federal Communications Commission license whenever the frequency channel is needed for higher priority common system service.

§ 171.107 Definition.

As used in this subpart:

SDF (simplified directional facility) means a directional aid facility providing only lateral guidance (front or back course) for approach from a final approach fix.

DDM (difference in depth of modulation) means the percentage modulation depth of the larger signal minus the percentage modulation depth of the smaller signal, divided by 100.

Angular displacement sensitivity means the ratio of measured DDM to the corresponding angular displacement from the appropriate reference line.

Back course sector means the course sector on the opposite end of the runway from the front course sector.

Course line means the locus of points along the final approach course at which the DDM is zero.

Course sector means a sector in a horizontal plane containing the course line and limited by the loci of points nearest to the course line at which the DDM is 0.155.

Displacement sensitivity means the ratio of measured DDM to the corresponding lateral displacement from the appropriate reference line.

Front course sector means the course sector centered on the course line in the direction from the runway in which a normal final approach is made.

Half course sector means the sector in a horizontal plane containing the course line and limited by the loci of points nearest to the course line, at which the DDM is 0.0775.

Point A means a point on the front course in the approach direction a distance of 4 nautical miles from the threshold.

Point A1 means a point on the front course in the approach direction a distance of 1 statute mile from the threshold.

Point A2 means a point on the front course at the threshold.

Reference datum means a point at a specified height located vertically above the intersection of the course and the threshold.

Missed approach point means the point on the final approach course, not farther from the final approach fix than Point "A2", at which the approach must be abandoned, if the approach and subsequent landing cannot be safely completed by visual reference, whether or not the aircraft has descended to the minimum descent altitude.

§ 171.109 Performance requirements.

(a) The Simplified Directional Facility must perform in accordance with the following standards and practices:

(1) The radiation from the SDF antenna system must produce a composite field pattern which is amplitude modulated by a 90 Hz and a 150 Hz tone. The radiation field pattern must produce a course sector with the 90 Hz tone predominating on one side of the course and with the 150 Hz tone predominating on the opposite side.

(2) When an observer faces the SDF from the approach end of runway, the depth of modulation of the radio frequency carrier due to the 150 Hz tone must predominate on his right hand and that due to the 90 Hz tone must predominate on his left hand.

(3) All horizontal angles employed in specifying the SDF field patterns must originate from the center of the antenna system which provides the signals used in the front course sector.

(4) The SDF must operate on odd tenths or odd tenths plus a twentieth MHz within the frequency band 108.1 MHz to 111.95 MHz. The frequency tolerance of the radio frequency carrier must not exceed plus or minus 0.002 percent.

(5) The radiated emission from the SDF must be horizontally polarized. The vertically polarized component of the radiation on the course line must not exceed that which corresponds to an error one-twentieth of the course sector width when an aircraft is positioned on the course line and is in a roll attitude of 20° from the horizontal.

(6) The SDF must provide signals sufficient to allow satisfactory operation of a typical aircraft installation within the sector which extends from the center of the SDF antenna system to distances of 18 nautical miles within a plus or minus 10° sector and 10 nautical miles within the remainder of the coverage when alternative navigational facilities provide satisfactory coverage within the intermediate approach area. SDF signals must be receivable at the distances specified at and above a height of 1,000 feet above the elevation of the threshold, or the lowest altitude authorized for transition, whichever is higher. Such signals must be receivable, to the distances specified, up to a surface extending outward from the SDF antenna and inclined at 7° above the horizontal.

(7) The modulation tones must be phase-locked so that within the half course sector, the demodulated 90 Hz and 150 Hz wave forms pass through zero in the same direction within 20° of phase relative to the 150 Hz component, every half cycle of the combined 90 Hz

and 150 Hz wave form. However, the phase need not be measured within the half course sector.

(8) The angle of convergence of the final approach course and the extended runway centerline must not exceed 30°. The final approach course must be aligned to intersect the extended runway centerline between points A1 and the runway threshold. When an operational advantage can be achieved, a final approach course that does not intersect the runway or that intersects it at a distance greater than point A1 from the threshold, may be established, if that course lies within 500 feet laterally of the extended runway centerline at a point 3,000 feet outward from the runway threshold. The mean course line must be maintained within ±10 percent of the course sector width.

(9) The nominal displacement sensitivity within the half course sector must be 50 microamperes/degree. The nominal course sector width must be 6°. When an operational advantage can be achieved, a nominal displacement sensitivity of 25 microamperes/degree may be established, with a nominal course sector width of 12° with proportional displacement sensitivity. The lateral displacement sensitivity must be adjusted and maintained within the limits of plus or minus 17 percent of the nominal value.

(10) The off-course (clearance) signal must increase at a substantially linear rate with respect to the angular displacement from the course line up to an angle on either side of the course line where 175 microamperes of deflection is obtained. From that angle to ±10°, the off-course deflection must not be less than 175 microamperes. From ±10° to ±35° the off-course deflection must not be less than 150 microamperes. With the course adjusted to cause any of several monitor alarm conditions, the aforementioned values of 175 microamperes in the sector 10° each side of course and 150 microamperes in the sector ±10° to ±35° may be reduced to 160 microamperes and 135 microamperes, respectively. These conditions must be met at a distance of 18 nautical miles from the SDF antenna within the sector 10° each side of course line and 10 nautical miles from the SDF antenna within the sector ±10° to ±35° each side of course line.

(11) The SDF may provide a ground-to-air radiotelephone communication channel to be operated simultaneously with the navigation and identification signals, if that operation does not interfere with the basic function. If a channel is provided, it must conform with the following standards:

(i) The channel must be on the same radio frequency carrier or carriers as used for the SDF function, and the radiation must be horizontally polarized. Where two carriers are modulated with speech, the relative phases of the modulations on the two carriers must avoid the occurrence of nulls within the coverage of the SDF.

(ii) On centerline, the peak modulation depth of the carrier or carriers due to the radiotelephone communications must not exceed 50 percent but must be adjusted so that the ratio of peak modulation depth due to the radiotelephone communications to that due to the identification signal is approximately 9:1.

(iii) The audio frequency characteristics of the radiotelephone channel must be flat to within 3 db relative to the level at 1,000 Hz over the range from 300 Hz to 3,000 Hz.

(12)(i) The SDF must provide for the simultaneous transmission of an identification signal, specific to the runway and approach direction, on the same radio frequency carrier or carriers as used for the SDF function. The transmission of the identification signal must not interfere in any way with the basic SDF function.

(ii) The identification signal must be produced by Class A2 modulation of the radio frequency carrier or carriers using a modulation tone of 1020 Hz within ±50 Hz. The depth of modulation must be between the limits of 5 and 15 percent except that, where a radiotelephone communication channel is provided, the depth of modulation must be adjusted so that the ratio of peak modulation depth due to radiotelephone communications to that due to the identification signal modulation is approximately 9:1. The emissions carrying the identification signal must be horizontally polarized.

(iii) The identification signal must employ the International Morse Code and consist of three letters.

(iv) The identification signal must be transmitted at a speed corresponding to approximately seven words per minute, and must be repeated at approximately equal intervals, not less than six times per minute. When SDF transmission is not available for operational use, including periods of removal of navigational components or during maintenance or test transmissions, the identification signal must be suppressed.

(b) It must be shown during ground inspection of the design features of the equipment that there will not be conditions that will allow unsafe operations because of component failure or deterioration.

(c) The monitor must be checked periodically during the in-service test evaluation period for calibration and stability. These tests, and ground checks of SDF radiation characteristics must be conducted in accordance with the maintenance manual required by § 171.115(c) and must meet the standards and tolerances contained in § 171.111(j).

(d) The monitor system must provide a warning to the designated control point(s) when any of the conditions of § 171.111(j) occur, within the time periods specified in that paragraph.

(e) Flight inspection to determine the adequacy of the facility's operational performance and compliance with applicable performance requirements must be conducted in accordance with the "U.S. Standard Flight Inspection Manual." Tolerances contained in the U.S. Standard Flight Inspection Manual, section 217, must be complied with except as stated in paragraph (f) of this section.

(f) Flight inspection tolerances specified in section 217 of the "U.S. Standard Flight Inspection Manual" must be complied with except as follows:

(1) *Course sector width.* The nominal course sector width must be 6°. When an operational advantage can be achieved, a nominal course sector width of 12° may be established. Course sector width must be adjusted and maintained within the limits of ±17 percent of the nominal value.

(2) *Course alignment.* The mean course line must be adjusted and maintained within the limits of ±10 percent of the nominal course sector width.

(3) *Course structure.* Course deviations due to roughness, scalloping, or bends must be within the following limitations:

(i) *Front course.* (*a*) Course structure from 18 miles from runway threshold to Point A must not exceed ±40 microamperes;

(*b*) Point A to Point A–1—linear decrease from not more than ±40 microamperes at Point A to not more than ±20 microamperes at Point A–1;

(*c*) Point A–1 to Missed Approach Point—not more than ±20 microamperes;

(*d*) Monitor tolerances: width ±17 percent of nominal; alignment—±10 percent of nominal course sector width.

(ii) *Back course.* (*a*) Course structure 18 miles from runway threshold to 4 miles from runway threshold must not exceed ±40 microamperes. Four miles to 1 mile from R/W must not exceed ±40 microamperes decreasing to not more than ±20 microamperes, at a linear rate.

(*b*) Monitor tolerances: width—±17 percent of nominal; alignment—±10 percent of nominal course sector width.

[Doc. No. 10116, 35 FR 12711, Aug. 11, 1970, as amended by Amdt. 171–9, 38 FR 28557, Oct. 15, 1973]

§ 171.111   Ground standards and tolerances.

Compliance with this section must be shown as a condition to approval and must be maintained during operation of the SDF.

(a) *Frequency.* (1) The SDF must operate on odd tenths or odd tenths plus a twentieth MHz within the frequency band 108.1 MHz to 111.95 MHz. The frequency tolerance of the radio frequency carrier must not exceed plus or minus 0.002 percent.

(2) The modulating tones must be 90 Hz and 150 Hz within ±2.5 percent.

(3) The identification signal must be 1020 Hz within ±50 Hz.

(4) The total harmonic content of the 90 Hz tone must not exceed 10 percent.

(5) The total harmonic content of the 150 Hz tone must not exceed 10 percent.

(b) *Power output.* The normal carrier power output must be of a value which will provide coverage requirements of §171.109(a)(6) when reduced by 3 dB to the monitor RF power reduction alarm point specified in §171.111(j)(3).

(c) *VSWR.* (1) The VSWR of carrier and sideband feedlines must be a nominal value of 1/1 and must not exceed 1.2/1.

(2) The sponsor will also provide additional manufacturer's ground standards and tolerances for all VSWR parameters peculiar to the equipment which can effect performance of the facility in meeting the requirements specified in §§ 171.109 and 171.111.

(d) *Insulation resistance.* The insulation resistance of all coaxial feedlines must be greater than 20 megohms.

(e) *Depth of modulation.* (1) The depth of modulation of the radio frequency carrier due to each of the 90 Hz and 150 Hz tones must be 20 percent ±2 percent along the course line.

(2) The depth of modulation of the radio frequency carrier due to the 1020 Hz identification signal must be within 5 percent to 15 percent.

(f) *Course sector width.* The standard course sector width must be 6° or 12°. The course sector must be maintained with ±17 percent of the standard.

(g) *Course alignment.* Course alignment must be as specified in §171.109(a)(8).

(h) *Back course alignment and width.* If a back course is provided, standards and tolerances for back course sector width and alignment must be the same as course sector width and course alignment specified in paragraphs (f) and (g) of this section.

(i) *Clearance.* Clearance must be as specified in §171.109(a)(10).

(j) *Monitor standards and tolerances.* (1) The monitor system must provide a warning to the designated control point(s) when any of the conditions described in this paragraph occur, within the time periods specified in paragraph (j)(6) of this section.

(2) Course shift alarm: The monitor must alarm and cause radiation to cease, or identification and navigation signals must be removed, if the course alignment deviates from standard alignment by 10 percent or more of the standard course sector width.

(3) RF power reduction alarm: The monitor must alarm and cause radiation to cease, or identification and navigation signals must be removed, if the output power is reduced by 3 db or more from normal.

(4) Modulation level alarm: The monitor must alarm and cause radiation to cease, or identification and navigation signals must be removed, if the 90 Hz and 150 Hz modulation levels decrease by 17 percent or more.

(5) Course sector width alarm: The monitor must alarm and cause radiation to cease, or identification and navigation signals must be removed, for a change in course sector width to a value differing by ±17 percent or more from the standard.

(6) Monitor delay before shutdown: Radiation must cease, or identification and navigation signals must be removed, within 10 seconds after a fault is detected by the monitor, and no attempt must be made to resume radiation for a period of at least 20 seconds. If an automatic recycle device is used, not more than three successive recycles may be permitted before a complete SDF shutdown occurs.

(k) *Mean time between failures.* The mean time between failures must not be less than 800 hours. This measure is applied only to equipment failures (monitor or transmitting equipment, including out of tolerance conditions) which result in facility shutdown. It does not relate to the responsiveness of the maintenance organization.

(l) *Course alignment stability.* Drift of the course alignment must not exceed one-half the monitor limit in a 1-week period.

[Doc. No. 10116, 35 FR 12711, Aug. 11, 1970, as amended by Amdt. 171-9, 38 FR 28558, Oct. 15, 1973]

§ 171.113   Installation requirements.

(a) The facility must be installed according to accepted good engineering practices, applicable electric and safety codes, and FCC requirements.

(b) The SDF facility must have the following basic components:

(1) VHF SDF equipment and associated monitor system;

(2) Remote control, and indicator equipment (remote monitor) when required by the FAA;

9

(3) A final approach fix; and

(4) Compass locator (COMLO) or marker if suitable fixes and initial approach routes are not available from existing facilities.

(c) The facility must have a reliable source of suitable primary power, either from a power distribution system or locally generated. Also, adequate power capacity must be provided for operation of test and working equipment at the SDF. A determination by the Federal Aviation Administration as to whether a facility will be required to have standby power for the SDF and monitor accessories to supplement the primary power will be made for each airport based upon operational minimums and density of air traffic.

(d) A determination by the Federal Aviation Administration as to whether a facility will be required to have dual transmitting equipment with automatic changeover for the SDF will be made for each airport based upon operational minimums and density of air traffic.

(e) There must be a means for determining, from the ground, the performance of the equipment (including antennae), initially and periodically.

(f) The facility must have the following ground-air or landline communication services:

(1) At facilities outside of and not immediately adjacent to controlled airspace, there must be ground-air communications from the airport served by the facility. The utilization of voice on the SDF should be determined by the facility operator on an individual basis.

(2) At facilities within or immediately adjacent to controlled airspace, there must be ground/air communications required by paragraph (b)(1) of this section and reliable communications (at least a landline telephone) from the airport to the nearest Federal Aviation Administration air traffic control or communications facility.

Compliance with paragraphs (f) (1) and (2) of this section need not be shown at airports where an adjacent Federal Aviation Administration facility can communicate with aircraft on the ground at the airport and during the entire proposed instrument approach procedure. In addition, at low traffic density airports within or immediately

adjacent to controlled airspace, and where extensive delays are not a factor, the requirements of paragraphs (f) (1) and (2) of this section may be reduced to reliable communications (at least a landline telephone) from the airport to the nearest Federal Aviation Administration air traffic control or communications facility, if an adjacent Federal Aviation Administration facility can communicate with aircraft during the proposed instrument approach procedure down to the airport surface or at least down to the minimum approach altitude.

(g) At those locations where two separate SDF facilities serve opposite ends of a single runway, an interlock must insure that only the facility serving the approach direction in use can radiate, except where no operationally harmful interference results.

(h) At those locations where, in order to alleviate frequency congestion, the SDF facilities serving opposite ends of one runway employ identical frequencies, an interlock must insure that the facility not in operational use cannot radiate.

(i) Provisions for maintenance and operations by authorized persons only.

(j) Where an operational advantage exists, the installation may omit a back course.

[Doc. No. 10116, 35 FR 12711, Aug. 11, 1970, as amended by Amdt. 171–16, 56 FR 65664, Dec. 17, 1991]

§171.115 Maintenance and operations requirements.

(a) The owner of the facility shall establish an adequate maintenance system and provide qualified maintenance personnel to maintain the facility at the level attained at the time it was commissioned. Each person who maintains a facility shall meet at a minimum the Federal Communications Commission's licensing requirements and show that he has the special knowledge and skills needed to maintain the facility, including proficiency in maintenance procedures and the use of specialized test equipment.

(b) The SDF must be designed and maintained so that the probability of operation within the performance requirements specified is high enough to insure an adequate level of safety. In the event out-of-tolerance conditions develop, the facility shall be removed from operation, and the designated control point notified.

(c) The owner must prepare, and obtain approval of, and each person operating or maintaining the facility shall comply with, an operations and maintenance manual that sets forth procedures for operations, preventive maintenance, and emergency maintenance, including instructions on each of the following:

(1) Physical security of the facility. This includes provisions for designating critical areas relative to the facility and preventing or controlling movements within the facility that may adversely affect SDF operations.

(2) Maintenance and operations by authorized persons only.

(3) Federal Communications Commission requirements for operating personnel and maintenance personnel.

(4) Posting of licenses and signs.

(5) Relation between the facility and Federal Aviation Administration air traffic control facilities, with a description of the boundaries of controlled airspace over or near the facility, instructions for relaying air traffic control instructions and information (if applicable), and instructions for the operation of an air traffic advisory service if the facility is located outside of controlled airspace.

(6) Notice to the Administrator of any suspension of service.

(7) Detailed and specific maintenance procedures and servicing guides stating the frequency of servicing.

(8) Air-ground communications, if provided, expressly written or incorporating appropriate sections of Federal Aviation Administration manuals by reference.

(9) Keeping of station logs and other technical reports, and the submission of reports required by § 171.117.

(10) Monitoring of the facility.

(11) Names, addresses, and telephone numbers of persons to be notified in an emergency.

(12) Inspection by U.S. personnel.

(13) Shutdowns for routine maintenance and issue of "Notices to Airmen" for routine or emergency shutdowns, except that private use facilities may omit "Notices to Airmen."

(14) Commissioning of the facility.

(15) An acceptable procedure for amending or revising the manual.

(16) An explanation of the kinds of activities (such as construction or grading) in the vicinity of the facility that may require shutdown or certification of the facility by Federal Aviation Administration flight check.

(17) Procedure for conducting a ground check of SDF course alignment, width and clearance.

(18) The following information concerning the facility:

(i) Facility component locations with respect to airport layout, instrument runway, and similar areas;

(ii) The type, make, and model of the basic radio equipment that will provide the service;

(iii) The station power emission and frequencies of the SDF, markers and associated COMLOs, if any;

(iv) The hours of operation;

(v) Station identification call letters and method of station identification and the time spacing of the identification;

(vi) A description of the critical parts that may not be changed, adjusted, or repaired without a Federal Aviation Administration flight check to confirm published operations.

(d) The owner shall make a ground check of the facility each month in accordance with procedures approved by the Federal Aviation Administration at the time of commissioning, and shall report the results of the checks as provided in § 171.117.

(e) If the owner desires to modify the facility, he shall submit the proposal to the Federal Aviation Administration and may not allow any modifications to be made without specific approval.

(f) The owner's maintenance personnel shall participate in initial inspections made by the Federal Aviation Administration. In the case of subsequent inspections, the owner or his representatives shall participate.

(g) Whenever it is required by the Federal Aviation Administration, the owner shall incorporate improvements in SDF maintenance. In addition, he shall provide a stock of spare parts, of such a quantity, to make possible the prompt replacement of components that fail or deteriorate in service.

(h) The owner shall provide Federal Aviation Administration approved test instruments needed for maintenance of the facility.

(i) The owner shall close the facility by ceasing radiation and shall issue a "Notice to Airmen" that the facility is out of service (except that private use facilities may omit "Notices to Airmen"), upon receiving two successive pilot reports of its malfunctioning.

§ 171.117 Reports.

The owner of each facility to which this subpart applies shall make the following reports, at the time indicated, to the Federal Aviation Administration Regional Office for the area in which the facility is located:

(a) Record of meter readings and adjustments (Form FAA–198). To be filled out by the owner or his maintenance representative with the equipment adjustments and meter readings as of the time of commissioning, with one copy to be kept in the permanent records of the facility and two copies to the appropriate Regional Office of the Federal Aviation Administration. The owner shall revise the form after any major repair, modification, or retuning, to reflect an accurate record of facility operation and adjustment.

(b) Facility maintenance log (FAA Form 6030–1) This form is a permanent record of all equipment malfunctioning met in maintaining the facility, including information on the kind of work and adjustments made, equipment failures, causes (if determined), and corrective action taken. The owner shall keep the original of each report at the facility and send a copy to the appropriate Regional Office of the Federal Aviation Administration at the end of each month in which it is prepared.

(c) Radio equipment operation record (Form FAA–418), containing a complete record of meter readings, recorded on each scheduled visit to the facility. The owner shall keep the original of each month's record at the facility and send a copy of it to the appropriate Re-

gional Office of the Federal Aviation Administration.

[Doc. No. 10116, 35 FR 12711, Aug. 11, 1970, as amended by Amdt. 171–10, 40 FR 36110, Aug. 19, 1975]

Subpart G—Distance Measuring Equipment (DME)

Source: Docket No. 10116, 35 FR 12715, Aug. 11, 1970, unless otherwise noted.

§ 171.151 Scope.

This subpart sets forth minimum requirements for the approval and operation of non-Federal DME facilities that are to be involved in the approval of instrument flight rules and air traffic control procedures related to those facilities.

§ 171.153 Requests for IFR procedure.

(a) Each person who requests an IFR procedure based on a DME facility that he owns must submit the following information with that request:

(1) A description of the facility and evidence that the equipment meets the performance requirements of § 171.157 and is installed in accordance with § 171.159.

(2) A proposed procedure for operating the facility.

(3) A proposed maintenance organization and maintenance manual that meets the requirement of § 171.161.

(4) A statement of intention to meet the requirements of this subpart.

(5) A showing that the facility has an acceptable level of operational reliability and an acceptable standard of performance. Previous equivalent operational experience with a facility with identical design and operational characteristics will be considered in showing compliance with this paragraph.

(b) After the Federal Aviation Administration inspects and evaluates the facility, it advises the owner of the results and of any required changes in the facility or the maintenance manual or maintenance organization. The owner must then correct the deficiencies, if any, and operate the facility for an in-service evaluation by the Federal Aviation Administration.

§ 171.155 Minimum requirements for approval.

(a) The following are the minimum requirements that must be met before the Federal Aviation Administration will approve an IFR procedure for a non-Federal DME:

(1) A suitable frequency channel must be available.

(2) The facility's performance, as determined by air and ground inspection, must meet the requirements of § 171.157.

(3) The installation of the equipment must meet the requirements of § 171.159.

(4) The owner must agree to operate and maintain the facility in accordance with § 171.161.

(5) The owner must agree to furnish periodic reports, as set forth in § 171.163, and must agree to allow the Federal Aviation Administration to inspect the facility and its operation whenever necessary.

(6) The owner must assure the Federal Aviation Administration that he will not withdraw the facility from service without the permission of the Federal Aviation Administration.

(7) The owner must bear all costs of meeting the requirements of this section and of any flight or ground inspections made before the facility is commissioned, except that the Federal Aviation Administration may bear certain of these costs subject to budgetary limitations and policy established by the Administrator.

(b) If the applicant for approval meets the requirements of paragraph (a) of this section, the Federal Aviation Administration commissions the facility as a prerequisite to its approval for use in an IFR procedure. The approval is withdrawn at any time the facility does not continue to meet those requirements.

§ 171.157 Performance requirements.

(a) The DME must meet the performance requirements set forth in the "International Standards and Recommended Practices. Aeronautical Telecommunications, Part I, Paragraph 3.5" (Annex 10 to the Convention of International Civil Aviation).

(b) It must be shown during ground inspection of the design features of the equipment that there will not be conditions that will allow unsafe operations because of component failure or deterioration.

(c) The monitor must be checked periodically, during the in-service test evaluation period, for calibration and stability. These tests and ground tests of the functional and performance characteristics of the DME transponder must be conducted in accordance with the maintenance manual required by § 171.161(b).

(d) Flight inspection to determine the adequacy of the facility's operational performance and compliance with applicable "Standards and Recommended Practices" must be accomplished in accordance with the "U.S. Standard Flight Inspection Manual."

[Doc. No. 10116, 35 FR 12715, Aug. 11, 1970, as amended by Amdt. 171-13, 50 FR 4875, Nov. 27, 1985]

§ 171.159 Installation requirements.

(a) The facility must be installed according to accepted good engineering practices, applicable electric and safety codes, and Federal Communications Commission requirements.

(b) The facility must have a reliable source of suitable primary power, either from a power distribution system or locally generated, with a supplemental standby system, if needed.

(c) Dual transmitting equipment with automatic changeover is preferred and may be required to support certain IFR procedures.

(d) There must be a means for determining from the ground, the performance of the equipment, initially and periodically.

(e) A facility intended for use as an instrument approach aid for an airport must have or be supplemented by the following ground air or landline communications services:

(1) At facilities outside of and not immediately adjacent to controlled airspace, there must be ground-air communications from the airport served by the facility. Separate communications channels are acceptable.

(2) At facilities within or immediately adjacent to controlled airspace, there must be the ground-air communications required by paragraph (e)(1)

of this section and reliable communications (at least a landline telephone) from the airport to the nearest Federal Aviation Administration air traffic control or communications facility. Separate communications channels are acceptable.

Compliance with paragraphs (e) (1) and (2) of this section need not be shown at airports where an adjacent Federal Aviation Administration facility can communicate with aircraft on the ground at the airport and during the entire proposed instrument approach procedure. In addition, at low traffic density airports within or immediately adjacent to controlled airspace, and where extensive delays are not a factor, the requirements of paragraphs (e) (1) and (2) of this section may be reduced to reliable communications (at least a landline telephone) from the airport to the nearest Federal Aviation Administration air traffic control or communications facility, if an adjacent Federal Aviation Administration facility can communicate with aircraft during the proposed instrument approach procedure, at least down to the minimum en route altitude for the controlled airspace area.

[Doc. No. 10116, 35 FR 12715, Aug. 11, 1970, as amended by Amdt. 171–16, 56 FR 65665, Dec. 17, 1991]

§ 171.161 Maintenance and operations requirements.

(a) The owner of the facility shall establish an adequate maintenance system and provide qualified maintenance personnel to maintain the facility at the level attained at the time it was commissioned. Each person who maintains a facility shall meet at a minimum the Federal Communications Commission's licensing requirements and show that he has the special knowledge and skills needed to maintain the facility, including proficiency in maintenance procedures and the use of specialized test equipment.

(b) The owner must prepare and obtain Federal Aviation Administration approval of, and each person operating or maintaining the facility shall comply with, an operations and maintenance manual that sets forth procedures for operations, preventive maintenance, and emergency maintenance, including instructions on each of the following:

(1) Physical security of the facility.

(2) Maintenance and operations by authorized persons only.

(3) Federal Communications Commission's requirements and maintenance personnel.

(4) Posting of licenses and signs.

(5) Relations between the facility and Federal Aviation Administration air traffic control facilities, with a description of the boundaries of controlled airspace over or near the facility, instructions for relaying air traffic control instructions and information (if applicable), and instructions for the operation of an air traffic advisory service if the DME is located outside of controlled airspace.

(6) Notice to the Administrator of any suspension of service.

(7) Detailed and specific maintenance procedures and servicing guides stating the frequency of servicing.

(8) Air-ground communications, if provided, expressly written or incorporating appropriate sections of Federal Aviation Administration manuals by reference.

(9) Keeping of station logs and other technical reports, and the submission of reports required by § 171.163.

(10) Monitoring of the facility.

(11) Inspections by U.S. personnel.

(12) Names, addresses, and telephone numbers of persons to be notified in an emergency.

(13) Shutdowns for routine maintenance and issue of "Notices to Airmen" for routine or emergency shutdowns, except that private use facilities may omit the "Notices to Airmen."

(14) An explanation of the kinds of activity (such as construction or grading) in the vicinity of the facility that may require shutdown or reapproval of the facility by Federal Aviation Administration flight check.

(15) Commissioning of the facility.

(16) An acceptable procedure for amending or revising the manual.

(17) The following information concerning the facility:

(i) Location by latitude and longitude to the nearest second, and its position with respect to airport layouts.

(ii) The type, make, and model of the basic radio equipment that will provide the service.

(iii) The station power emission and frequency.

(iv) The hours of operation.

(v) Station identification call letters and methods of station identification, whether by Morse code or recorded voice announcement, and the time spacing of the identification.

(vi) A description of the critical parts that may not be changed, adjusted, or repaired without an FAA flight check to confirm published operations.

(c) The owner shall make a monthly ground operational check in accordance with procedures approved by the FAA at the time of commissioning, and shall report the results of the checks as provided in § 171.163.

(d) If the owner desires to modify the facility, he shall submit the proposal to the FAA and may not allow any modifications to be made without specific approval.

(e) The owner's maintenance personnel shall participate in initial inspections made by the FAA. In the case of subsequent inspections, the owner or his representative shall participate.

(f) Whenever it is required by the FAA, the owner shall incorporate improvements in DME maintenance.

(g) The owner shall provide a stock of spare parts of such a quantity to make possible the prompt replacement of components that fail or deteriorate in service.

(h) The owner shall provide FAA-approved test instruments needed for maintenance of the facility.

(i) The owner shall shut down the facility (i.e., cease radiation and issue a NOTAM that the facility is out-of-service) upon receiving two successive pilot reports of its malfunctioning.

§ 171.163   Reports.

The owner of each facility to which this subpart applies shall make the following reports on forms furnished by the FAA, at the time indicated, to the FAA Regional office for the area in which the facility is located:

(a) Record of meter readings and adjustments (Form FAA-198). To be filled out by the owner with the equipment adjustments and meter readings as of the time of commissioning, with one copy to be kept in the permanent records of the facility and two copies to the appropriate Regional office of the FAA. The owner shall revise the form after any major repair, modification, or returning, to reflect an accurate record of facility operation and adjustment.

(b) Facility maintenance log (FAA Form 6030-1). This form is a permanent record of all equipment malfunctioning met in maintaining the facility, including information on the kind of work and adjustments made, equipment failures, causes (if determined), and corrective action taken. The owner shall keep the original of each report at the facility and send a copy to the appropriate Regional Office of the Federal Aviation Administration at the end of the month in which it is prepared.

(c) Radio equipment operation record (Form FAA-418), containing a complete record of meter readings, recorded on each scheduled visit to the facility. The owner shall keep the original of each month's record at the facility and send a copy of it to the appropriate Regional Office of the Federal Aviation Administration.

[Doc. No. 10116, 35 FR 12715, Aug. 11, 1970, as amended by Amdt. 171-10, 40 FR 36110, Aug. 19, 1975]

Subpart H—VHF Marker Beacons

SOURCE: Docket No. 10116, 35 FR 12716, Aug. 11, 1970, unless otherwise noted.

§ 171.201   Scope.

(a) This subpart sets forth minimum requirements for the approval and operation of non-Federal VHF marker beacon facilities that are to be involved in the approval of instrument flight rules and air traffic control procedures related to those facilities.

(b) [Reserved]

§ 171.203   Requests for IFR procedure.

(a) Each person who requests an IFR procedure which will incorporate the use of a VHF marker beacon facility that he owns must submit the following information with that request:

(1) A description of the facility and evidence that the equipment meets the performance requirements of §171.207 and is installed in accordance with §171.209.

(2) A proposed procedure for operating the facility.

(3) A proposed maintenance organization and a maintenance manual that meets the requirements of §171.211.

(4) A statement of intent to meet the requirement of this subpart.

(5) A showing that the facility has an acceptable level of operational reliability, and an acceptable standard of performance. Previous equivalent operational experience may be shown to comply with this subparagraph.

(b) After the Federal Aviation Administration inspects and evaluates the facility, it advises the owner of the results and of any required changes in the facility or the maintenance manual or maintenance organization. The owner shall then correct the deficiencies, if any, and operate the facility for an in-service evaluation by the Federal Aviation Administration.

§171.205 Minimum requirements for approval.

(a) The following are the minimum requirements that must be met before the Federal Aviation Administration will approve an IFR procedure which incorporates the use of a non-Federal VHF marker beacon facility under this subpart:

(1) The facility's performances, as determined by air and ground inspection, must meet the requirements of §171.207.

(2) The installation of the equipment must meet the requirements of §171.209.

(3) The owner must agree to operate and maintain the facility in accordance with §171.211.

(4) The owner must agree to furnish periodic reports, as set forth in §171.213, and agree to allow the Federal Aviation Administration to inspect the facility and its operation whenever necessary.

(5) The owner must assure the Federal Aviation Administration that he will not withdraw the facility from service without the permission of the Federal Aviation Administration.

(6) The owner must bear all costs of meeting the requirements of this section and of any flight or ground inspections made before the facility is commissioned, except that the Federal Aviation Administration may bear certain of these costs subject to budgetary limitations and policy established by the Administrator.

(b) If the applicant for approval meets the requirements of paragraph (a) of this section, the Federal Aviation Administration commissions the facility as a prerequisite to its approval for use in an IFR procedure. The approval is withdrawn at any time the facility does not continue to meet those requirements.

§171.207 Performance requirements.

(a) VHF Marker Beacons must meet the performance requirements set forth in the "International Standards and Recommended Practices, Aeronautical Telecommunications, Part I, paragraphs 3.1.6 and 3.6." (Annex 10 to the Convention on International Civil Aviation) except those portions that pertain to identification. Identification of a marker beacon (75 MHz) must be in accordance with "U.S. Standard Flight Inspection Manual," §219.

(b) The facility must perform in accordance with recognized and accepted good electronic engineering practices for the desired service. The facility must be checked periodically during the in-service test evaluation period for calibration and stability. These tests and ground tests of the marker radiation characteristics must be conducted in accordance with the maintenance manual required by §171.211(b).

(c) It must be shown during ground inspection of the design features of the equipment that there will not be conditions that will allow unsafe operations because of component failure or deterioration.

(d) Flight inspection to determine the adequacy of the facility's operational performance and compliance with applicable "Standards and Recommended Practices" are conducted in accordance with the "U.S. Standard Flight Inspection Manual." The original test is made by the Federal Aviation Administration and later tests must be made under arrangements, satisfactory to the Federal Aviation Administration, that are made by the owner.

§ 171.209 **Installation requirements.**

(a) The facility must be installed according to accepted good engineering practices, applicable electric and safety codes, and Federal Communications Commission requirements.

(b) The facility must have a reliable source of suitable primary power.

(c) Dual transmitting equipment may be required, if applicable, to support certain IFR procedures.

(d) At facilities within or immediately adjacent to controlled airspace and that are intended for use as instrument approach aids for an airport, there must be ground-air communications or reliable communications (at least a landline telephone) from the airport to the nearest Federal Aviation Administration air traffic control or communication facility. Compliance with this paragraph need not be shown at airports where an adjacent Federal Aviation Administration facility can communicate with aircraft on the ground at the airport and during the entire proposed instrument approach procedure. In addition, at low traffic density airports within or immediately adjacent to controlled airspace, and where extensive delays are not a factor, the requirements of this paragraph may be reduced to reliable communications (at least a landline telephone) from the airport to the nearest Federal Aviation Administration air traffic control or communications facility, if an adjacent Federal Aviation Administration facility can communicate with aircraft during the proposed instrument approach procedure, at least down to the minimum en route altitude for the controlled airspace area.

[Doc. No. 10116, 35 FR 12716, Aug. 11, 1970, as amended by Amdt. 171–16, 56 FR 65665, Dec. 17, 1991]

§ 171.211 **Maintenance and operations requirements.**

(a) The owner of the facility shall establish an adequate maintenance system and provide qualified maintenance personnel to maintain the facility at the level attained at the time it was commissioned. Each person who maintains a facility shall meet at a minimum the Federal Communications Commission's licensing requirements and show that he has the special knowledge and skills needed to maintain the facility, including proficiency in maintenance procedures and the use of specialized test equipment.

(b) The owner must prepare, and obtain approval of, and each person who operates or maintains the facility shall comply with, an operations and maintenance manual that sets forth procedures for operations, preventive maintenance, and emergency maintenance, including instructions on each of the following:

(1) Physical security of the facility.

(2) Maintenance and operations by authorized persons only.

(3) Federal Communications Commission's requirements for operating and maintenance personnel.

(4) Posting of licenses and signs.

(5) Relations between the facility and Federal Aviation Administration air traffic control facilities, with a description of the boundaries of controlled airspace over or near the facility, instructions for relaying air traffic control instructions and information (if applicable).

(6) Notice to the Administrator of any suspension of service.

(7) Detailed arrangements for maintenance, flight inspection, and servicing, stating the frequency of servicing.

(8) Keeping of station logs and other technical reports, and the submission of reports required by § 171.213.

(9) Monitoring of the facility, at least once each half hour, to assure continuous operation.

(10) Inspections by U.S. personnel.

(11) Names, addresses, and telephone numbers of persons to be notified in an emergency.

(12) Shutdowns for routine maintenance and issue of "Notices to Airmen" for routine or emergency shutdowns (private use facilities may omit the "Notice to Airmen").

(13) Commissioning of the facility.

(14) An acceptable procedure for amending or revising the manual.

(15) The following information concerning the facility:

(i) Location by latitude and longitude to the nearest second, and its position with respect to airport layouts.

(ii) The type, make, and model of the basic radio equipment that will provide the service.

(iii) The station power emission and frequency.

(iv) The hours of operation.

(v) Station identification call letters and methods of station identification, whether by Morse Code or recorded voice announcement, and the time spacing of the identification.

(c) If the owner desires to modify the facility, he shall submit the proposal to the Federal Aviation Administration and meet applicable requirements of the Federal Communications Commission, and must not allow any modification to be made without specific approval by the Federal Aviation Administration.

(d) The owner's maintenance personnel shall participate in initial inspections made by the Federal Aviation Administration. In the case of subsequent inspections, the owner or his representative shall participate.

(e) The owner shall provide a stock of spare parts, of such a quantity to make possible the prompt replacement of components that fail or deteriorate in service.

(f) The owner shall shut down the facility by ceasing radiation, and shall issue a "Notice to Airmen" that the facility is out of service (except that private use facilities may omit "Notices to Airmen") upon receiving two successive pilot reports of its malfunctioning.

§171.213 Reports.

The owner of each facility to which this subpart applies shall make the following reports, at the times indicated, to the Federal Aviation Administration Regional Office for the area in which the facility is located:

(a) Record of meter readings and adjustments (Form FAA-198). To be filled out by the owner or his maintenance representative with the equipment adjustments and meter readings as of the time of commissioning, with one copy to be kept in the permanent records of the facility and two copies to the appropriate Regional Office of the Federal Aviation Administration. The owner must revise the form after any major repair, modification, or retuning, to reflect an accurate record of facility operation and adjustment.

(b) Facility maintenance log (FAA Form 6030-1). This form is a permanent record of all equipment malfunctioning met in maintaining the facility, including information on the kind of work and adjustments made, equipment failures, causes (if determined), and corrective action taken. The owner shall keep the original of each report at the facility and send a copy to the appropriate Regional Office of the Federal Aviation Administration at the end of the month in which it is prepared.

(c) Radio equipment operation record (Form FAA-418), containing a complete record of meter readings, recorded on each scheduled visit to the facility. The owner shall keep the original of each month's record at the facility and send a copy of it to the appropriate Regional Office of the Federal Aviation Administration.

[Doc. No. 10116, 35 FR 12716, Aug. 11, 1970, as amended by Amdt. 171-10, 40 FR 36110, Aug. 19, 1975]

Subpart I—Interim Standard Microwave Landing System (ISMLS)

SOURCE: Docket No. 14120, 40 FR 36110, Aug. 19, 1975, unless otherwise noted.

§171.251 Scope.

This subpart sets forth minimum requirements for the approval and operation of non-Federal Interim Standard Microwave Landing System (ISMLS) facilities that are to be involved in the approval of instrument flight rules and air traffic control procedures related to those facilities.

§171.253 Definitions.

As used in this subpart:

Angular displacement sensitivity (Glide Slope) means the ratio of measured DDM to the corresponding angular displacement from the appropriate reference line.

Collocated ground station means the type of ground station which transmits two or more guidance signals simultaneously from a common location.

Course line means the locus of points nearest to the runway centerline in any horizontal plane at which the DDM is zero.

Course sector (full) means a sector in a horizontal plane containing the course line and limited by the loci of points nearest to the course line at which the DDM is 0.155.

Course sector (half) means the sector in a horizontal plane containing the course line and limited by the loci of points nearest to the course line at which DDM is 0.0775.

DDM means difference in depth of modulation. The percentage modulation depth of the larger signal minus the percentage modulation depth of the smaller signal, divided by 100.

Displacement sensitivity (Localizer) means the ratio of measured DDM to the corresponding lateral displacement from the appropriate reference line.

Facility Performance Category I—ISMLS means an ISMLS which provides guidance information from the coverage limit of the ISMLS to the point at which the localizer course line intersects the ISMLS glide path at a height of 200 feet or less above the horizontal plane containing the threshold.

Glide path means that locus of points in the vertical plane containing the runway center line at which the DDM is zero, which, of all such loci, is the closest to the horizontal plane.

Glide path angle (θ) means the angle between a straight line which represents the mean of the ISMLS glide path and the horizontal.

Glide path sector (full) means the sector in the vertical plane containing the ISMLS glide path and limited by the loci of points nearest to the glide path at which the DDM is 0.175. The ISMLS glide path sector is located in the vertical plane containing the runway centerline, and is divided by the radiated glide path in two parts called upper sector and lower sector, referring respectively to the sectors above and below the glide path.

Glide path sector (half) means the sector in the vertical plane containing the ISMLS glide path and limited by the loci of points nearest to the glide path at which the DDM is 0.0875.

ISMLS Point 'A' means an imaginary point on the glide path/localizer course measured along the runway centerline extended, in the approach direction, four nautical miles from the runway threshold.

ISMLS Point 'B' means an imaginary point on the glide path/localizer course measured along the runway centerline extended, in the approach direction, 3500 feet from the runway threshold.

ISMLS Point 'C' means a point through which the downward extended straight portion of the glide path (at the commissioned angle) passes at a height of 100 feet above the horizontal plane containing the runway threshold.

Interim standard microwave landing system (ISMLS) means a ground station which transmits azimuth and elevation angle information which, when decoded and processed by the airborne unit, provides signal performance capable of supporting approach minima for V/STOL and CTOL operations and operates with the signal format and tolerances specified in §§ 171.259, 171.261, 171.263, 171.265, and 171.267.

Integrity means that quality which relates to the trust which can be placed in the correctness of the information supplied by the facility.

Mean corrective time means the average time required to correct an equipment failure over a given period, after a service man reaches the facility.

Mean time between failures means the average time between equipment failure over a given period.

Reference datum means a point at a specified height located vertically above the intersection of the runway centerline and the threshold and through which the downward extended straight portion of the ISMLS glide path passes.

Split type ground station means the type of ground station in which the electronic components for the azimuth and elevation guidance are contained in separate housings or shelters at different locations, with the azimuth portion of the ground station located at the stop end of the runway, and elevation guidance near the approach end of the runway.

§171.255 Requests for IFR procedures.

(a) Each person who requests an IFR procedure based on an ISMLS facility that he owns must submit the following information with that request:

(1) A description of the facility and evidence that the equipment meets the performance requirements of §§171.259, 171.261, 171.263, 171.265, 171.267, and 171.269, and is installed in accordance with §171.271.

(2) A proposed procedure for operating the facility.

(3) A proposed maintenance organization and a maintenance manual that meets the requirements of §171.273.

(4) A statement of intent to meet the requirements of this subpart.

(5) A showing that the ISMLS facility has an acceptable level of operational reliability, maintainability and acceptable standard of performance. Previous equivalent operational experience with a facility with identical design and operational characteristics will be considered in showing compliance with this paragraph.

(b) After the FAA inspects and evaluates the ISMLS facility, it advises the owner of the results and of any required changes in the ISMLS facility or in the maintenance manual or maintenance organization. The owner must then correct the deficiencies, if any, and operate the ISMLS facility for an inservice evaluation by the FAA.

§171.257 Minimum requirements for approval.

(a) The following are the minimum requirements that must be met before the FAA approves an IFR procedure for a non-Federal ISMLS facility:

(1) The performance of the ISMLS facility, as determined by flight and ground inspection conducted by the FAA, must meet the requirements of §§171.259, 171.261, 171.263, 171.265, 171.267, and 171.269.

(2) The installation of the equipment must meet the requirements of §171.271.

(3) The owner must agree to operate and maintain the ISMLS facility in accordance with §171.273.

(4) The owner must agree to furnish periodic reports as set forth in §171.275 and agree to allow the FAA to inspect the facility and its operation whenever necessary.

(5) The owner must assure the FAA that he will not withdraw the ISMLS facility from service without the permission of the FAA.

(6) The owner must bear all costs of meeting the requirements of this section and of any flight or ground inspection made before the ISMLS facility is commissioned, except that the FAA may bear certain costs subject to budgetary limitations and policy established by the Administrator.

(b) If the applicant for approval meets the requirements of paragraph (a) of this section, the FAA approves the ISMLS facility for use in an IFR procedure. The approval is withdrawn at any time that the ISMLS facility does not continue to meet those requirements. In addition, the ISMLS facility may be de-commissioned whenever the frequency channel is needed for higher priority common system service.

§171.259 Performance requirements: General.

(a) The ISMLS consists of the following basic components:

(1) C-Band (5000 MHz–5030 MHz) localizer equipment, associated monitor system, and remote indicator equipment;

(2) C-Band (5220 MHz–5250 MHz) glide path equipment, associated monitor system, and remote indicator equipment;

(3) VHF marker beacons (75 MHz), associated monitor systems, and remote indicator equipment.

(4) An ISMLS airborne receiver or a VHF/UHF ILS receiver modified to be capable of receiving the ISMLS signals. This modification requires the addition of a C-Band antenna, a converter unit, a microwave/ILS mode control, and a VHF/UHF receiver modification kit.

(b) The electronic ground equipments in paragraph (a)(1), (2), and (3) of this section, must be designed to operate on a nominal 120/240 volt, 60 Hz, 3-wire single phase AC power source.

(c) ISMLS ground equipment must meet the following service conditions:

(1) AC line parameters, DC voltage, elevation, and duty:

120 V nominal value, 102 V to 138 V (±1 V).*

208 V nominal value, 177 V to 239 V (±2 V).*
240 V nominal value, 204 V to 276 V (±0.2 V).*

AC line frequency (60 Hz), 57 Hz to 63 Hz (±0.2 Hz).*

DC voltage (48 V), 44 V to 52 V (±0.5 V).*

*NOTE: Where discrete values of the above frequency or voltages are specified for testing purposes, the tolerances given in parentheses indicated by an asterisk apply to the test instruments used to measure these parameters.

Elevation, 0 to 10,000 ft. above sea level.
Duty, continuous, unattended.

(2) Ambient conditions for localizer and glide path equipment:

Temperature, −10 °C to + 50 °C.
Relative humidity, 5% to 90%.

(3) Ambient conditions for marker beacon facilities and all other equipment installed outdoors (for example, antennae, field detectors, and shelters):

Temperature, −50 °C. to + 70 °C.
Relative humidity, 5% to 100%.

(4) All equipment installed outdoors must operate satisfactorily under the following conditions:

Wind velocity, 0–100 MPH (not including gusts).
Hail stones, ½″ diameter.
Rain, provide coverage through a distance of 5 nautical miles with rain falling at a rate of 50 millimeters per hour, and with rain falling at the rate of 25 millimeters per hour for the additional design performance range of the system.
Ice loading, encased in ½″ radial thickness of clear ice.

(d) The ISMLS must perform in accordance with the following standards and practices for Facility Performance Category I operation:

(1) The ISMLS must be constructed and adjusted so that, at a specified distance from the threshold, similar instrumental indications in the aircraft represent similar displacements from the course line or ISMLS glide path, as appropriate, regardless of the particular ground installation in use.

(2) The localizer and glide path components listed in paragraphs (a)(1) and (a)(2) of this section which form part of an ISMLS, must comply at least with the standard performance requirements specified herein. The marker beacon components listed in paragraph (a)(3) of this section which form part of an ISMLS, must comply at least with the

standard performance requirements specified in subpart H of this part.

(3) The ISMLS must be so designed and maintained that the probability of operation is within the performance requirements specified in § 171.273(k).

(e) The signal format and pairing of the runway localizer and glide path transmitter frequencies of an ISMLS must be in accordance with the frequency plan approved by the FAA, and must meet the following signal format requirements:

(1) The localizer and glide slope stations must transmit angular guidance information on a C-band microwave carrier on narrow, scanned antenna beams that are encoded to produce a modulation in space which, after averaging over several beam scans, is equivalent to the modulation used for conventional ILS as specified in subpart C of this part, except that the frequency tolerance may not exceed ±0.0001 percent.

(2) Guidance modulation must be impressed on the microwave carrier of the radiated signal in the form of a summation of 90 Hz and 150 Hz sinusoidal modulation corresponding to the pointing direction of the particular beam which radiates the signal.

(3) Each of the effective beam positions must be illuminated in a particular sequence for a short time interval. The modulation impressed on each beam must be a sample of the combined 90 Hz and 150 Hz waveform appropriate for that particular beam direction and time slot, and must be accomplished by appropriately varying the length of time the carrier is radiated during each beam illumination interval.

(4) For those cases where the scanning beam fills the coverage space in steps, the incremental step must not exceed 0.6 times the beam width where the beam is in the proportional guidance sector. In the clearance region, the step may not exceed 0.8 times the beam width.

(5) At least one pulse duration modulation (pdm) sample pulse per beam width of scan must be provided.

(6) The minimum pulse duration must be 40 microseconds.

(7) The minimum beam scan cycle must be 600 Hz.

(8) The minimum duty ratio detectable by a receiver located anywhere in the coverage areas defined by this specification may not be less than 0.1. Detected duty ratio means the ratio of the average energy per scan detected at a point in space to the average energy per scan transmitted in all directions through the transmitting antenna.

(9) The localizer must produce a C-band unmodulated reference frequency signal of sufficient strength to allow satisfactory operation of an aircraft receiver within the specified localizer and glide path coverage sectors. Pairing of this reference frequency with the localizer and glide slope frequencies must be in accordance with a frequency plan approved by the FAA.

§ 171.261 Localizer performance requirements.

This section prescribes the performance requirements for localizer equipment components of the ISMLS.

(a) The localizer antenna system must:

(1) Be located on the extension of the centerline of the runway at the stop end;

(2) Be adjusted so that the course line be on a vertical plane containing the centerline of the runway served;

(3) Have the minimum height necessary to comply with the coverage requirements prescribed in paragraph (j) of this section;

(4) Be located at a distance from the stop end of the runway that is consistent with safe obstruction clearance practices;

(5) Not obscure any light of the approach landing system; and

(6) Be installed on frangible mounts or beyond the 1000′ light bar.

(b) On runways where limited terrain prevents the localizer antennae from being positioned on the runway centerline extended, and the cost of the land fill or a tall tower antenna support is prohibitive, the localizer antenna array may be offset, including a collocated ground station, so that the course intercepts the centerline at a point determined by the amount of the angular offset and the glide path angle. If other than a runway centerline localizer is used, the criteria in subpart C of part 97 of this chapter is applicable.

(c) At locations where two separate ISMLS facilities serve opposite ends of of a single runway, an interlock must ensure that only the facility serving the approach direction being used will radiate.

(d) The radiation from the localizer antenna system must produce a composite field pattern which is pulse duration modulated, the time average equivalent to amplitude modulation by a 90 Hz and 150 Hz tone. The localizer station must transmit angular guidance information over a C-band microwave carrier on narrow, scanned antenna beams that are encoded to produce a modulation in space which, after averaging over several beam scans, is equivalent to the modulation used for conventional ILS as specified in subpart C of this part. The radiation field pattern must produce a course sector with one tone predominating on one side of the course and with the other tone predominating on the opposite side. When an observer faces the localizer from the approach end of the runway, the depth of modulation of the radio frequency carrier due to the 150 Hz tone must predominate on his right hand and that due to the 90 Hz tone must predominate on his left hand.

(e) All horizontal angles employed in specifying the localizer field patterns must originate from the center of the localizer antenna system which provides the signals used in the front course sector.

(f) The ISMLS course sector angle must be adjustable between 3 degrees and 9 degrees. The applicable course sector angle will be established and approved on an individual basis.

(g) The ISMLS localizer must operate in the band 5000 MHz to 5030 MHz. The frequency tolerance may not exceed ±0.0001 percent.

(h) The emission from the localizer must be vertically polarized. The horizontally polarized component of the radiation of the course line may not exceed that which corresponds to a DDM error of 0.016 when an aircraft is positioned on the course line and is in a roll attitude of 20 degrees from the horizontal.

(i) The localizer must provide signals sufficient to allow satisfactory operation of a typical aircraft installation within the localizer and glide path coverage sectors. The localizer coverage sector must extend from the center of the localizer antenna system to distances of 18 nautical miles minimum within ±10 degrees from the front course line, and 10 nautical miles minimum between ±10 degrees and ±35 degrees from the front course line. The ISMLS localizer signals must be receivable at the distances specified up from a surface extending outward from the localizer antenna and within a sector in the elevation plane from 0.300 to 1.750 of the established glide path angle (θ).

(j) Except as provided in paragraph (k) of this section, in all parts of the coverage volume specified in paragraph (i) of this section, the peak field strength may not be less than -87 dBW/m^2, and must permit satisfactory operational usage of ISMLS localizer facilities.

(k) The minimum peak field strength on the ISMLS glide path and within the localizer course sector from a distance of 10 nautical miles to a height of 100 feet (30 meters) above the horizontal plane containing the threshold, may not be less than $+ 87$ dBW/m^2.

(l) Above 16 degrees, the ISMLS localizer signals must be reduced to as low a value as practicable.

(m) Bends in the course line may not have amplitudes which exceed the following:

Zone	Amplitude (DDM) (95 pct. probability)
Outer limit of coverage to:	
ISMLS point "A"	0.031.
ISMLS point "A" to ISMLS point "B".	0.031 at ISMLS point "A" decreasing at linear rate to 0.015 at ISMLS point "B".
ISMLS point "B" to ISMLS point "C".	0.015.

(n) The amplitudes referred to in paragraph (m) of this section are the DDMs due to bends as realized on the mean course line, when correctly adjusted.

(o) The radio frequency carrier must meet the following requirements:

(1) The nominal depth of modulation of the radio frequency carrier due to each of the 90 Hz and 150 Hz tones must be 20 percent along the course line.

(2) The depth of modulation of the radio frequency carrier due to each of the 90 Hz and 150 Hz tones must be between 18 and 22 percent.

(3) The frequency tolerance of the 90 Hz and 150 Hz modulated tones must be within ±25 percent.

(4) Total harmonic content of the 90 Hz tone may not exceed 10 percent.

(5) Total harmonic content of the 150 Hz tone may not exceed 10 percent. However, a 300 Hz tone may be transmitted for identification purposes.

(6) At every half cycle of the combined 90 Hz and 150 Hz wave form, the modulation tones must be phase-locked so that within the half course sector, the demodulated 90 Hz and 150 Hz wave forms pass through zero in the same direction within 20 degrees with phase relative to the 150 Hz component. However, the phase need not be measured within the half course sector.

(p) The mean course line must be adjusted and maintained within ±.015DDM from the runway centerline at the ISMLS reference datum.

(q) The nominal displacement sensitivity within the half course sector at the ISMLS reference datum, must be 0.00145 DDM/meter (0.00044DDM/foot). However, where the specified nominal displacement sensitivity cannot be met, the displacement sensitivity must be adjusted as near as possible to that value.

(r) The lateral displacement sensitivity must be adjusted and maintained within 17 percent of the nominal value. Nominal sector width at the ISMLS reference datum is 210 meters (700 feet).

(s) The increase of DDM must be substantially linear with respect to angular displacement from the front course line where DDM is zero, up to angle on either side of the front course line where the DDM is 0.180. From that angle to ±10 degrees, the DDM may not be less than 0.180. From ±10 degrees to ±35 degrees, the DDM may not be less than 0.155.

(t) The localizer must provide for the simultaneous transmission of an identification signal which meets the following:

(1) It must be specific to the runway and approach direction, on the same radio frequency carrier, as used for the localizer function.

(2) Transmission of the identification signal may not interfere in any way with the basic localizer function.

(3) The signal must be produced by pulse duration modulation of the radio frequency carrier resulting in a detected audio tone in the airborne VHF receiver of 1020 Hz ±50Hz.

(4) The depth of modulation must be between the limits of 10 and 12 percent.

(5) The emissions carrying the identification signal must be vertically polarized.

(6) The identification signal must employ the International Morse Code and consist of three letters. It must be preceded by the International Morse Code signal of the letter "M" followed by a short pause where it is necessary to distinguish the ISMLS facility from other navigational facilities in the immediate area. At airports where both an ISMLS and an ILS are in operation, each facility must have a different identification call sign.

(7) The signal must be transmitted at a speed corresponding to approximately seven words per minute, and must be repeated at approximately equal intervals, not less than six times per minute, during which time the localizer is available for operational use. When the localizer is not available for transmission, the identification signal must be suppressed.

§171.263 Localizer automatic monitor system.

(a) The ISMLS localizer equipment must provide an automatic monitor system that transmits a warning to designated local and remote control points when any of the following occurs:

(1) A shift of the mean course line of the localizer from the runway centerline equivalent to more than 0.015 DDM at the ISMLS reference datum.

(2) For localizers in which the basic functions are provided by the use of a single-frequency system, a reduction of power output to less than 50 percent of normal or a loss of ground station identification transmissions.

(3) Changes of displacement sensitivity to a value differing by more than 17 percent from nominal value for the localizer.

(4) Failure of any part of the monitor itself. Such failure must automatically produce the same results as the malfunctioning of the element being monitored.

(b) Within 10 seconds of the occurrence of any of the conditions prescribed in paragraph (a) of this section, including periods of zero radiation, localizer signal radiation must cease or the navigation and identification components must be removed.

§171.265 Glide path performance requirements.

This section prescribes the performance requirements for glide path equipment components of the ISMLS. These requirements are based on the assumption that the aircraft is heading directly toward the facility.

(a) The glide slope antenna system must be located near the approach end of the runway, and the equipment must be adjusted so that the vertical path line will be in a sloping horizontal plane containing the centerline of the runway being served, and satisfy the coverage requirements prescribed in paragraph (g) of this section. For the purpose of obstacle clearance, location of the glide slope antenna system must be in accordance with the criteria specified in subpart C of part 97 of this chapter.

(b) The radiation from the glide path antenna system must produce a composite field pattern which is pulse duration modulated by a 90 Hz and a 150 Hz tone, which is the time average equivalent to amplitude modulation. The pattern must be arranged to provide a straight line descent path in the vertical plane containing the centerline of the runway, with the 150 Hz tone predominating below the path and the 90 Hz tone predominating above the path to at least an angle equal to 1.75θ. As used in this section theta (θ), denotes the nominal glide path angle. The glide path angle must be adjusted and maintained within 0.075θ.

(c) The glide path equipment must be capable of producing a radiated glide path from 3 to 9 degrees with respect to the horizontal. However, ISMLS glide path angles in excess of 3 degrees may be used to satisfy instrument approach procedures or to overcome an obstruction clearance problem, only in accordance with the criteria specified in subpart C of part 97 of this chapter.

(d) The downward extended straight portion of the ISMLS glide path must pass through the ISMLS reference datum at a height ensuring safe guidance over obstructions and safe and efficient use of the runway served. The height of the ISMLS reference datum must be in accordance with subpart C of part 97 of this chapter.

(e) The glide path equipment must operate in the band 5220 MHz to 5250 MHz. The frequency tolerance may not exceed ±0.0001 percent.

(f) The emission from the glide path equipment must be vertically polarized.

(g) The glide path equipment must provide signals sufficient to allow satisfactory operation of a typical aircraft installation insectors of 8 degrees on each side of the centerline of the ISMLS glide path, to a distance of at least 10 nautical miles up to 1.75θ and down to 0.45θ above the horizontal or to such lower angle at which 0.22 DDM is realized.

(h) To provide the coverage for glide path performance specified in paragraph (g) of this section, the minimum peak field strength within this coverage sector must be −82 dBW/m². The peak field strength must be provided on the glide path down to a height of 30 meters (100 feet) above the horizontal plane containing the threshold.

(i) Bends in the glide path may not have amplitudes which exceed the following:

Zone	Amplitude (DDM) (95 pct. probability)
Outer limit of coverage to ISMLS point "C."	0.035.

The amplitude referred to is the DDM due to bends as realized on the mean ISMLS glide path correctly adjusted. In regions of the approach where ISMLS glide path curvature is significant, bend amplitude is calculated from the mean curved path, and not the downward extended straight line.

(j) Guidance modulation must be impressed on the microwave carrier of the radiated glide slope signal in the form of a unique summation of 90 Hz and 150 Hz sinusoidal modulation corresponding to the point direction of the particular beam which radiates the signal. Each of the effective beam positions must be illuminated in sequence for a short time interval. The scan rate must be synchronous with the 90 and 150 Hz tone base. The modulation impressed on each beam must be a sample of the combined 90 Hz and 150 Hz waveform appropriate for that particular beam direction and time slot. The actual modulation must be accomplished by appropriately varying the length of time the carrier is radiated during each beam illumination interval.

(k) The nominal depth of modulation of the radio frequency carrier due to each of the 90 Hz and 150 Hz tones must be 40 percent along the ISMLS glide path. The depth of modulation may not deviate outside the limits of 37.5 percent to 42.5 percent.

(l) The following tolerances apply to the frequencies of the modulating tones:

(1) The modulating tones must be 90 Hz and 150 Hz within 2.5 percent.

(2) The total harmonic content of the 90 Hz tone may not exceed 10 percent.

(3) The total harmonic content of the 150 Hz tone may not exceed 10 percent.

(m) At every half cycle of the combined 90 Hz and 150 Hz wave form, the modulation must be phase-locked so that, within the ISMLS half glide path sector, the demodulated 90 Hz and 150 Hz wave forms pass through zero in the same direction within 20 degrees of phase relative to the 150 Hz component. However, the phase need not be measured within the ISMLS half glide path sector.

(n) The nominal angular displacement sensitivity must correspond to a DDM of 0.0875 at an angular displacement above and below the glide path of 0.12θ. The glide path angular displacement sensitivity must be adjusted and maintained within ±25 percent of the nominal value selected. The upper and lower sectors must be as symmetrical as practicable within the limits prescribed in this paragraph.

(o) The DDM below the ISMLS glide path must increase smoothly for decreasing angle until a value of 0.22 DDM is reached. This value must be achieved at an angle not less than 0.30θ above the horizontal. However, if it is achieved at an angle above 0.45θ, the DDM value may not be less than 0.22 at least down to an angle of 0.45θ.

[Doc. No. 14120, 40 FR 36110, Aug. 19, 1975; 40 FR 41093, Sept. 5, 1975; 40 FR 43719, Sept. 23, 1975]

§ 171.267 Glide path automatic monitor system.

(a) The ISMLS glide path equipment must provide an automatic monitor system that transmits a warning to designated local and remote control points when any of the following occurs:

(1) A shift of the mean ISMLS glide path angle equivalent to more than 0.075θ.

(2) For glide paths in which the basic functions are provided by the use of a single frequency system, a reduction of power output to less than 50 percent.

(3) A change of the angle between the glide path and the line below the glide path (150 Hz predominating), at which a DDM of 0.0875 is realized by more than ±0.0375θ.

(4) Lowering of the line beneath the ISMLS glide path at which a DDM of 0.0875 is realized to less than 0.75θ from the horizontal.

(5) Failure of any part of the monitor itself. Such failure must automatically produce the same results as the malfunctioning of the element being monitored.

(b) At glide path facilities where the selected nominal angular displacement sensitivity corresponds to an angle below the ISMLS glide path, which is close to or at the maximum limits specified, an adjustment to the monitor operating limits may be made to protect against sector deviations below 0.75θ from the horizontal.

(c) Within 10 seconds of the occurrence of any of the conditions prescribed in paragraph (a) of this section, including periods of zero radiation, glide path signal radiation must cease.

§ 171.269 Marker beacon performance requirements.

ISMLS marker beacon equipment must meet the performance requirements prescribed in subpart H of this part.

§ 171.271 Installation requirements.

(a) The ISMLS facility must be permanent in nature, located, constructed, and installed according to accepted good engineering practices, applicable electric and safety codes, FCC licensing requirements, and paragraphs (a) and (c) of § 171.261.

(b) The ISMLS facility must have a reliable source of suitable primary power, either from a power distribution system or locally generated. Adequate power capacity must be provided for the operation of test and working equipment of the ISMLS.

(c) The ISMLS facility must have a continuously engaged or floating battery power source for the ground station for continued normal operation if the primary power fails. A trickle charge must be supplied to recharge the batteries during the period of available primary power. Upon loss and subsequent restoration of power, the batteries must be restored to full charge within 24 hours. When primary power is applied, the state of the battery charge may not affect the operation of the ISMLS ground station. The battery must permit continuation of normal operation for at least two hours under the normal operating conditions. The equipment must meet all specification requirements with or without batteries installed.

(d) There must be a means for determining, from the ground, the performance of the equipment including antennae, both initially and periodically.

(e) The facility must have, or be supplemented by, ground-air or landline communications services. At facilities within or immediately adjacent to controlled airspace and that are intended for use as instrument approach aids for an airport, there must be ground-air communications or reliable communications (at least a landline telephone) from the airport to the nearest Federal Aviation Administration air traffic control or communication facility. Compliance with this paragraph need not be shown at airports where an adjacent Federal Aviation Administration facility can communicate with aircraft on the ground at the airport and during the entire proposed instrument approach procedure. In addition, at low traffic density airports within or immediately adjacent to controlled airspace, and where extensive delays are not a factor, the requirements of this paragraph may be reduced to reliable communications (at least a landline telephone) from the airport to the nearest Federal Aviation Administration air traffic control or communications facility, if an adjacent Federal Aviation Administration facility can communicate with aircraft during the proposed instrument approach procedure, at least down to the minimum en route altitude for the controlled area.

(f) Except where no operationally harmful interference will result, at locations where two separate ISMLS facilities serve opposite ends of a single runway, an interlock must ensure that only the facility serving the approach direction in use can radiate.

[Doc. No. 14120, 40 FR 36110, Aug. 19, 1975, as amended by Amdt. 171–16, 56 FR 65665, Dec. 17, 1991]

§ 171.273 Maintenance and operations requirements.

(a) The owner of the facility must establish an adequate maintenance system and provide qualified maintenance personnel to maintain the facility at the level attained at the time it was commissioned. Each person who maintains a facility must meet at least the Federal Communications Commission's licensing requirements and show that he has the special knowledge and skills needed to maintain the facility, including proficiency in maintenance procedures and the use of specialized test equipment.

(b) In the event of out-of-tolerance conditions or malfunctions, as evidenced by receiving two successive pilot reports, the owner must close the facility be ceasing radiation, and issue a "Notice to Airman" (NOTAM) that the facility is out of service.

(c) The owner must prepare, and obtain approval of, an operations and maintenance manual that sets forth mandatory procedures for operations, periodic maintenance, and emergency maintenance, including instructions on each of the following:

(1) Physical security of the facility.

(2) Maintenance and operations by authorized persons.

(3) FCC licensing requirements for operations and maintenance personnel.

(4) Posting of licenses and signs.

(5) Relation between the facility and FAA air traffic control facilities, with a description of the boundaries of controlled airspace over or near the facility, instructions for relaying air traffic control instructions and information, if applicable, and instructions for the operation of an air traffic advisory service if the facility is located outside of controlled airspace.

(6) Notice to the Administrator of any suspension of service.

(7) Detailed and specific maintenance procedures and servicing guides stating the frequency of servicing.

(8) Air-ground communications, if provided, expressly written or incorporating appropriate sections of FAA manuals by reference.

(9) Keeping of station logs and other technical reports, and the submission of reports required by § 171.275.

(10) Monitoring of the ISMLS facility.

(11) Inspections by United States personnel.

(12) Names, addresses, and telephone numbers of persons to be notified in an emergency.

(13) Shutdowns for periodic maintenance and issue of "Notices to Airmen" for routine or emergency shutdowns.

(14) Commissioning of the ISMLS facility.

(15) An acceptable procedure for amending or revising the manual.

(16) An explanation of the kinds of activities (such as construction or grading) in the vicinity of the ISMLS facility that may require shutdown or recertification of the ISMLS facility by FAA flight check.

(17) Procedures for conducting a ground check of the localizer course alignment, width, and clearance, glide path elevation angle and course width, and marker beacon power, and modulation.

(18) The following information concerning the ISMLS facility:

(i) Facility component locations with respect to airport layout, instrument runways, and similar areas.

(ii) The type, make, and model of the basic radio equipment that provides the service.

(iii) The station power emission and frequencies of the ISMLS localizer, glide path, beacon markers, and associated compass locators, if any.

(iv) The hours of operation.

(v) Station identification call letters and method of station identification and the time spacing of the identification.

(vi) A description of the critical parts that may not be changed, adjusted, or repaired without an FAA flight check to confirm published operations.

(d) The owner or his maintenance representative must make a ground check of the ISMLS facility periodically in accordance with procedures approved by the FAA at the time of commissioning, and must report the results of the checks as provided in §171.275.

(e) Modifications to an ISMLS facility may be made only after approval by the FAA of the proposed modification submitted by the owner.

(f) The owner or the owner's maintenance representative must participate in inspections made by the FAA.

(g) Whenever it is required by the FAA, the owner must incorporate improvements in ISMLS maintenance.

(h) The owner or his maintenance representative must provide a sufficient stock of spare parts, including solid state components, or modules to make possible the prompt replacement of components or modules that fail or deteriorate in service.

(i) FAA approved test instruments must be used for maintenance of the ISMLS facility.

(j) The mean corrective maintenance time of the ISMLS equipment may not exceed 0.5 hours, with a maximum corrective maintenance time of not greater than 1.5 hours. This measure applies to failures of the monitor, transmitter and associated antenna assemblies, limited to unscheduled outage and out-of-tolerance conditions.

(k) The mean time between failures of the ISMLS equipment may not be less than 1,500 hours. This measure applies to unscheduled outages, out-of-tolerance conditions, and failures of the monitor, transmitter, and associated antenna assemblies.

(l) Inspection consists of an examination of the ISMLS equipment to ensure that unsafe operating conditions do not exist.

(m) Monitoring of the ISMLS radiated signal must ensure a high degree of integrity and minimize the requirements for ground and flight inspection. The monitor must be checked periodically during the in-service test evaluation period for calibration and stability. These tests and ground checks of glide slope, localizer, and marker beacon radiation characteristics must be conducted in accordance with the maintenance requirements of this section.

§ 171.275 Reports.

The owner of the ISMLS facility or his maintenance representative must make the following reports at the indicated time to the appropriate FAA Regional Office where the facility is located.

(a) *Facility Equipment Performance and Adjustment Data (FAA Form 198).* The FAA Form 198 shall be filled out by the owner or his maintenance representative with the equipment adjustments and meter readings as of the time of facility commissioning. One copy must be kept in the permanent records of the facility and two copies must be sent to the appropriate FAA Regional Office. The owner or his maintenance representative must revise the FAA Form 198 data after any major repair, modernization, or retuning to reflect an accurate record of facility operation and adjustment. In the event the data are revised, the owner or his maintenance representative shall notify the appropriate FAA Regional Office of such revisions, and forward copies of the revisions to the appropriate FAA Regional Office.

(b) *Facility Maintenance Log (FAA Form 6030–1).* FAA Form 6030–1 is a permanent record of all the activities required to maintain the ISMLS facility. The entries must include all malfunctions met in maintaining the facility including information on the kind of work and adjustments made, equipment failures, causes (if determined) and corrective action taken. In addition, the entries must include completion of periodic maintenance required to maintain the facility. The owner or his maintenance representative must keep the original of each form at the facility and send a copy to the appropriate FAA Regional Office at the end of each month in which it is prepared. However, where an FAA approved remote monitoring system is installed which precludes the need for periodic maintenance visits to the facility, monthly reports from the remote monitoring system control point must be forwarded to the appropriate FAA Regional Office, and a hard copy retained at the control point.

(c) *Technical Performance Record (FAA Form 418)*. FAA Form 418 contains a record of system parameters, recorded on each scheduled visit to the facility. The owner or his maintenance representative shall keep the original of each month's record at the facility and send a copy of the form to the appropriate FAA Regional Office.

Subpart J—Microwave Landing System (MLS)

SOURCE: Docket No. 20669, 51 FR 33177, Sept. 18, 1986, unless otherwise noted.

§ 171.301 Scope.

This subpart sets forth minimum requirements for the approval, installation, operation and maintenance of non-Federal Microwave Landing System (MLS) facilities that provide the basis for instrument flight rules (IFR) and air traffic control procedures.

§ 171.303 Definitions.

As used in this subpart:

Auxiliary data means data transmitted in addition to basic data that provide ground equipment siting information for use in refining airborne position calculations and other supplementary information.

Basic data means data transmitted by the ground equipment that are associated directly with the operation of the landing guidance system.

Beam center means the midpoint between the −3 dB points on the leading and trailing edges of the scanning beam main lobe.

Beamwidth means the width of the scanning beam main lobe measured at the −3 dB points and defined in angular units on the boresight, in the horizontal plane for the azimuth function

and in the vertical plane for the elevation function.

Clearance guidance sector means the volume of airspace, inside the coverage sector, within which the azimuth guidance information provided is not proportional to the angular displacement of the aircraft, but is a constant fly-left or fly-right indication of the direction relative to the approach course the aircraft should proceed in order to enter the proportional guidance sector.

Control Motion Noise (CMN) means those fluctuations in the guidance which affect aircraft attitude, control surface motion, column motion, and wheel motion. Control motion noise is evaluated by filtering the flight error record with a band-pass filter which has corner frequencies at 0.3 radian/sec and 10 radians/sec for azimuth data and 0.5 radian/sec and 10 radians/sec for elevation data.

Data rate means the average number of times per second that transmissions occur for a given function.

Differential Phase Shift Keying (DPSK) means differential phase modulation of the radio frequency carrier with relative phase states of 0 degree or 180 degrees.

Failure means the inability of an item to perform within previously specified limits.

Guard time means an unused period of time provided in the transmitted signal format to allow for equipment tolerances.

Integrity means that quality which relates to the trust which can be placed in the correctness of the information supplied by the facility.

Mean corrective time means the average time required to correct an equipment failure over a given period, after a service technician reaches the facility.

Mean course error means the mean value of the azimuth error along a specified radial of the azimuth function.

Mean glide path error means the mean value of the elevation error along a specified glidepath of the elevation function.

Mean-time-between-failures (MTBF) means the average time between equipment failures over a given period.

Microwave Landing System (MLS) means the MLS selected by ICAO for international standardization.

Minimum glidepath means the lowest angle of descent along the zero degree azimuth that is consistent with published approach procedures and obstacle clearance criteria.

MLS Approach Reference Datum is a point at a specified height located vertically above the intersection of the runway centerline and the threshold.

MLS back azimuth reference datum means a point 15 meters (50 feet) above the runway centerline at the runway midpoint.

MLS datum point means a point defined by the intersection of the runway centerline with a vertical plane perpendicular to the centerline and passing through the elevation antenna phase center.

Out of coverage indication (OCI) means a signal radiated into areas outside the intended coverage sector, where required, to specifically prevent invalid removal of an airborne warning indication in the presence of misleading guidance information.

Path Following Error (PFE) means the guidance perturbations which could cause aircraft displacement from the desired course or glidepath. It is composed of the path following noise and the mean course error in the case of azimuth functions, or the mean glidepath error in the case of elevation functions. Path following errors are evaluated by filtering the flight error record with a second order low pass filter which has a corner frequency at 0.5 radian/sec for azimuth data or 1.5 radians/sec for elevation data.

Path following noise (PFN) means that portion of the guidance signal error which could cause displacement from the actual mean course line or mean glidepath as appropriate.

Split-site ground station means the type of ground station in which the azimuth portion of the ground station is located near the stop end of the runway, and the elevation portion is located near the approach end.

Time division multiplex (TDM) means that each function is transmitted on the same frequency in time sequence, with a distinct preamble preceding each function transmission.

§ 171.305   **Requests for IFR procedure.**

(a) Each person who requests an IFR procedure based on an MLS facility which that person owns must submit the following information with that request:

(1) A description of the facility and evidence that the equipment meets the performance requirements of §§ 171.309, 171.311, 171.313, 171.315, 171.317, 171.319, and 171.321 and is fabricated and installed in accordance with § 171.323.

(2) A proposed procedure for operating the facility.

(3) A proposed maintenance organization and a maintenance manual that meets the requirements of § 171.325.

(4) A statement of intent to meet the requirements of this subpart.

(5) A showing that the facility has an acceptable level of operational reliability and an acceptable standard of performance. Previous equivalent operational experience with a facility with identical design and operational characteristics will be considered in showing compliance with this subparagraph.

(b) FAA inspects and evaluates the MLS facility; it advises the owner of the results, and of any required changes in the MLS facility or in the maintenance manual or maintenance organization. The owner must then correct the deficiencies, if any, and operate the MLS facility for an in-service evaluation by the FAA.

§ 171.307   **Minimum requirements for approval.**

(a) The following are the minimum requirements that must be met before the FAA approves an IFR procedure for a non-Federal MLS facility:

(1) The performance of the MLS facility, as determined by flight and ground inspection conducted by the FAA, must meet the requirements of §§ 171.309, 171.311, 171.313, 171.315, 171.317, 171.319, and 171.321.

(2) The fabrication and installation of the equipment must meet the requirements of § 171.323.

(3) The owner must agree to operate and maintain the MLS facility in accordance with § 171.325.

(4) The owner must agree to furnish operational records as set forth in § 171.327 and agree to allow the FAA to

inspect the facility and its operation whenever necessary.

(5) The owner must assure the FAA that he will not withdraw the MLS facility from service without the permission of the FAA.

(6) The owner must bear all costs of meeting the requirements of this section and of any flight or ground inspection made before the MLS facility is commissioned.

(b) [Reserved]

§ 171.309 General requirements.

The MLS is a precision approach and landing guidance system which provides position information and various ground-to-air data. The position information is provided in a wide coverage sector and is determined by an azimuth angle measurement, an elevation angle measurement and a range (distance) measurement.

(a) An MLS constructed to meet the requirements of this subpart must include:

(1) Approach azimuth equipment, associated monitor, remote control and indicator equipment.

(2) Approach elevation equipment, associated monitor, remote control and indicator equipment.

(3) A means for the encoding and transmission of essential data words, associated monitor, remote control and indicator equipment. Essential data are basic data words 1, 2, 3, 4, and 6 and auxiliary data words A1, A2 and A3.

(4) Distance measuring equipment (DME), associated monitor, remote control and indicator equipment.

(5) Remote controls for paragraphs (a) (1), (2), (3), and (4) of this section must include as a minimum on/off and reset capabilities and may be integrated in the same equipment.

(6) At locations where a VHF marker beacon (75 MHz) is already installed, it may be used in lieu of the DME equipment.

(b) In addition to the equipment required in paragraph (a) of this section the MLS may include:

(1) Back azimuth equipment, associated monitor, remote control and indicator equipment. When Back Azimuth is provided, a means for transmission of Basic Data Word 5 and Auxiliary Data Word A4 shall also be provided.

(2) A wider proportional guidance sector which exceeds the minimum specified in §§ 171.313 and 171.317.

(3) Precision DME, associated monitor, remote control and indicator equipment.

(4) VHF marker beacon (75 MHz), associated monitor, remote control and indicator equipment.

(5) The MLS signal format will accommodate additional functions (e.g., flare elevation) which may be included as desired. Remote controls for paragraphs (b) (1), (3) and (4) of this section must include as a minimum on/off and reset capabilities, and may be integrated in the same equipment.

(6) Provisions for the encoding and transmission of additional auxiliary data words, associated monitor, remote control and indicator equipment.

(c) MLS ground equipment must be designed to operate on a nominal 120/240 volt, 60 Hz, 3-wire single phase AC power source and must meet the following service conditions:

(1) AC line parameters, DC voltage, elevation and duty:

120 VAC nominal value—102 V to 138 V (±1 V)*

240 VAC nominal value—204 V to 276 V (±2 V)*

60 Hz AC line frequency—57 Hz to 63 Hz (±0.2 Hz)*

*NOTE: Where discrete values of the above frequency or voltages are specified for testing purposes, the tolerances given in parentheses indicated by an asterisk apply to the test instruments used to measure these parameters.

Elevation—0 to 3000 meters (10,000 feet) above sea level
Duty—Continuous, unattended

(2) Ambient conditions within the shelter for electronic equipment installed in shelters are:

Temperature, −10 °C to + 50 °C
Relative humidity, 5% to 90%

(3) Ambient conditions for electronic equipment and all other equipment installed outdoors (for example, antenna, field detectors, and shelters):

Temperature, −50 °C to + 70 °C
Relative humidity, 5% to 100%

(4) All equipment installed outdoors must operate satisfactorily under the following conditions:

Wind Velocity: The ground equipment shall remain within monitor limits with wind velocities of up to 70 knots from such directions that the velocity component perpendicular to runway centerline does not exceed 35 knots. The ground equipment shall withstand winds up to 100 knots from any direction without damage.

Hail Stones: 1.25 centimeters (½ inch) diameter.

Rain: Provide required coverage with rain falling at a rate of 50 millimeters (2 inches) per hour, through a distance of 9 kilometers (5 nautical miles) and with rain falling at the rate of 25 millimeters (1 inch) per hour for the additional 28 kilometers (15 nautical miles).

Ice Loading: Encased in 1.25 centimeters (½ inch) radial thickness of clear ice.

Antenna Radome De-Icing: Down to −6 °C (20 °F) and wind up to 35 knots.

(d) The transmitter frequencies of an MLS must be in accordance with the frequency plan approved by the FAA.

(e) The DME component listed in paragraph (a)(4) of this section must comply with the minimum standard performance requirements specified in subpart G of this part.

(f) The marker beacon components listed in paragraph (b)(4) of this section must comply with the minimum standard performance requirements specified in subpart H of this part.

§171.311 Signal format requirements.

The signals radiated by the MLS must conform to the signal format in which angle guidance functions and data functions are transmitted sequentially on the same C-band frequency. Each function is identified by a unique digital code which initializes the airborne receiver for proper processing.

The signal format must meet the following minimum requirements:

(a) *Frequency assignment.* The ground components (except DME/Marker Beacon) must operate on a single frequency assignment or channel, using time division multiplexing. These components must be capable of operating on any one of the 200 channels spaced 300 KHz apart with center frequencies from 5031.0 MHz to 5090.7 MHz and with channel numbering as shown in Table 1a. The operating radio frequencies of all ground components must not vary by more than ±10 KHz from the assigned frequency. Any one transmitter frequency must not vary more than ±50 Hz in any one second period. The MLS angle/data and DME equipment must operate on one of the paired channels as shown in Table 1b.

TABLE 1a—FREQUENCY CHANNEL PLAN

Channel No.	Frequency (MHz)
500	5031.0
501	5031.3
502	5031.6
503	5031.9
504	5032.2
505	5032.5
506	5032.8
507	5033.1
508	5033.4
509	5033.7
510	5034.0
511	5034.3
* * * * *	
598	5060.4
599	5060.7
600	5061.0
601	5061.3
* * * * *	
698	5090.4
699	5090.7

TABLE 1b—CHANNELS

DME No.	Channel pairing			DME parameters					
	VHF freq. MHz	MLS angle freq. MHz	MLS Ch. No.	Interrogation				Reply	
				Freq. MHz	Pulse codes			Freq. MHz	Pulse codes µs
					DME/N µs	DME/P Mode			
						IA µs	FA µs		
* 1X				1025	12			962	12
** 1Y				1025	36			1088	30
* 2X				1026	12			963	12
** 2Y				1026	36			1089	30
* 3X				1027	12			964	12
** 3Y				1027	36			1090	30
* 4X				1028	12			965	12
** 4Y				1028	36			1091	30
* 5X				1029	12			966	12

TABLE 1b—CHANNELS—Continued

	Channel pairing			DME parameters					
				Interrogation				Reply	
						Pulse codes			
DME No.	VHF freq. MHz	MLS angle freq. MHz	MLS Ch. No.	Freq. MHz	DME/N µs	DME/P Mode		Freq. MHz	Pulse codes µs
						IA µs	FA µs		
**5Y				1029	36			1092	30
*6X				1030	12			967	12
**6Y				1030	36			1093	30
*7X				1031	12			968	12
**7Y				1031	36			1094	30
*8X				1032	12			969	12
**8Y				1032	36			1095	30
*9X				1033	12			970	12
**9Y				1033	36			1096	30
*10X				1034	12			971	12
**10Y				1034	36			1097	30
*11X				1035	12			972	12
**11Y				1035	36			1098	30
*12X				1036	12			973	12
**12Y				1036	36			1099	30
*13X				1037	12			974	12
**13Y				1037	36			1100	30
*14X				1038	12			975	12
**14Y				1038	36			1101	30
*15X				1039	12			976	12
**15Y				1039	36			1102	30
*16X				1040	12			977	12
**16Y				1040	36			1103	30
▽17X	108.00			1041	12			978	12
17Y	108.05	5043.0	540	1041	36	36	42	1104	30
17Z		5043.3	541	1041		21	27	1104	15
18X	108.10	5031.0	500	1042	12	12	18	979	12
18W		5031.3	501	1042		24	30	979	24
18Y	108.15	5043.6	542	1042	36	36	42	1105	30
18Z		5043.9	543	1042		21	27	1105	15
19X	108.20			1043	12			980	12
19Y	108.25	5044.2	544	1043	36	36	42	1106	30
19Z		5044.5	545	1043		21	27	1106	15
20X	108.30	5031.6	502	1044	12	12	18	981	12
20W		5031.9	503	1044		24	30	981	24
20Y	108.35	5044.8	546	1044	36	36	42	1107	30
20Z		5045.1	547	1044		21	27	1107	15
21X	108.40			1045	12			982	12
21Y	108.45	5045.4	548	1045	36	36	42	1108	30
21Z		5045.7	549	1045		21	27	1108	15
22X	108.50	5032.2	504	1046	12	12	18	983	12
22W		5032.5	505	1046		24	30	983	24
22Y	108.55	5046.0	550	1046	36	36	42	1109	30
22Z		5046.3	551	1046		21	27	1109	15
23X	108.60			1047	12			984	12
23Y	108.65	5046.6	552	1047	36	36	42	1110	30
23Z		5046.9	553	1047		21	27	1110	15
24X	108.70	5032.8	506	1048	12	12	18	985	12
24W		5033.1	507	1048		24	30	985	24
24Y	108.75	5047.2	554	1048	36	36	42	1111	30
24Z		5047.5	555	1048		21	27	1111	15
25X	108.80			1049	12			986	12
25Y	108.85	5047.8	556	1049	36	36	42	1112	30
25Z		5048.1	557	1049		21	27	1112	15
26X	108.90	5033.4	508	1050	12	12	18	987	12
26W		5033.7	509	1050		24	30	987	24
26Y	108.95	5048.4	558	1050	36	36	42	1113	30
26Z		5048.7	559	1050		21	27	1113	15
27X	109.00			1051	12			988	12
27Y	109.05	5049.0	560	1051	36	36	42	1114	30
27Z		5049.3	561	1051		21	27	1114	15
28X	109.10	5034.0	510	1052	12	12	18	989	12
28W		5034.3	511	1052		24	30	989	24
28Y	109.15	5049.6	562	1052	36	36	42	1115	30
28Z		5049.9	563	1052		21	27	1115	15

TABLE 1b—CHANNELS—Continued

Channel pairing				DME parameters					
				Interrogation				Reply	
					Pulse codes				
DME No.	VHF freq. MHz	MLS angle freq. MHz	MLS Ch. No.	Freq. MHz	DME/N μs	DME/P Mode		Freq. MHz	Pulse codes μs
						IA μs	FA μs		
29X	109.20			1053	12			990	12
29Y	109.25	5050.2	564	1053	36	36	42	1116	30
29Z		5050.5	565	1043		21	27	1116	15
30X	109.30	5034.6	512	1054	12	12	18	991	12
30W		5034.9	513	1054		24	30	991	24
30Y	109.35	5050.8	566	1054	36	36	42	1117	30
30Z		5051.1	567	1054		21	27	1117	15
31X	109.40			1055	12			992	12
31Y	109.45	5051.4	568	1055	36	36	42	1118	30
31Z		5051.7	569	1055		21	27	1118	15
32X	109.50	5035.2	514	1056	12	12	18	993	12
32W		5035.5	515	1056		24	30	993	24
32Y	109.55	5052.0	570	1056	36	36	42	1119	30
32Z		5052.3	571	1056		21	27	1119	15
33X	109.60			1057	12			994	12
33Y	109.65	5052.6	572	1057	36	36	42	1120	30
33Z		5052.9	573	1057		21	27	1120	15
34X	109.70	5035.8	516	1058	12	12	18	995	12
34W		5036.1	517	1058		24	30	995	24
34Y	109.75	5053.2	574	1058	36	36	42	1121	30
34Z		5053.5	575	1058		21	27	1121	15
35X	109.80			1059	12			996	12
35Y	109.85	5053.8	576	1059	36	36	42	1122	30
35Z		5054.1	577	1059		21	27	1122	15
36X	109.90	5036.4	518	1060	12	12	18	997	12
36W		5036.7	519	1060		24	30	997	24
36Y	109.95	5054.4	578	1060	36	36	42	1123	30
36Z		5054.7	579	1060		21	27	1123	15
37X	110.00			1061	12			998	12
37Y	110.05	5055.0	580	1061	36	36	42	1124	30
37Z		5055.3	581	1061		21	27	1124	15
38X	110.10	5037.0	520	1062	12	12	18	999	12
38W		5037.3	521	1062		24	30	999	24
38Y	110.15	5055.6	582	1062	36	36	42	1125	30
38Z		5055.9	583	1062		21	27	1125	15
39X	110.20			1063	12			1000	12
39Y	110.25	5056.2	584	1063	36	36	42	1126	30
39Z		5056.5	585	1063		21	27	1126	15
40X	110.30	5037.6	522	1064	12	12	18	1001	12
40W		5037.9	523	1064		24	30	1001	24
40Y	110.35	5056.8	586	1064	36	36	42	1127	30
40Z		5057.1	587	1064		21	27	1127	15
41X	110.40			1065	12			1002	12
41Y	110.45	5057.4	588	1065	36	36	42	1128	30
41Z		5057.7	589	1065		21	27	1128	15
42X	110.50	5038.2	524	1066	12	12	18	1003	12
42W		5038.5	525	1066		24	30	1003	24
42Y	110.55	5058.0	590	1066	36	36	42	1129	30
42Z		5058.3	591	1066		21	27	1129	15
43X	110.60			1067	12			1004	12
43Y	110.65	5058.6	592	1067	36	36	42	1130	30
43Z		5058.9	593	1067		21	27	1130	15
44X	110.70	5038.8	526	1068	12	12	18	1005	12
44W		5039.1	527	1068		24	30	1005	24
44Y	110.75	5059.2	594	1068	36	36	42	1131	30
44Z		5059.5	595	1068		21	27	1131	15
45X	110.80			1069	12			1006	12
45Y	110.85	5059.8	596	1069	36	36	42	1132	30
45Z		5060.1	597	1069		21	27	1132	15
46X	110.90	5039.4	528	1070	12	12	18	1007	12
46W		5039.7	529	1070		24	30	1007	24
46Y	110.95	5060.4	598	1070	36	36	42	1133	30
46Z		5060.7	599	1070		21	27	1133	15
47X	111.00			1071	12			1008	12
47Y	111.05	5061.0	600	1071	36	36	42	1134	30

TABLE 1b—CHANNELS—Continued

DME No.	VHF freq. MHz	MLS angle freq. MHz	MLS Ch. No.	Interrogation Freq. MHz	DME/N µs	DME/P Mode IA µs	DME/P Mode FA µs	Reply Freq. MHz	Reply Pulse codes µs
47Z		5061.3	601	1071	....	21	27	1134	15
48X	111.10	5040.0	530	1072	12	12	18	1009	12
48W		5040.3	531	1072	....	24	30	1009	24
48Y	111.15	5061.6	602	1072	36	36	42	1135	30
48Z		5061.9	603	1072	....	21	27	1135	15
49X	111.20			1073	12	....	....	1010	12
49Y	111.25	5062.2	604	1073	36	36	42	1136	30
49Z		5062.5	605	1073	....	21	27	1136	15
50X	111.30	5040.6	532	1074	12	12	18	1011	12
50W		5040.9	533	1074	....	24	30	1011	24
50Y	111.35	5062.8	606	1074	36	36	42	1137	30
50Z		5063.1	607	1074	....	21	27	1137	15
51X	111.40			1075	12	....	....	1012	12
51Y	111.45	5063.4	608	1075	36	36	42	1138	30
51Z		5063.7	609	1075	....	21	27	1138	15
52X	111.50	5041.2	534	1076	12	12	18	1013	12
52W		5041.5	535	1076	....	24	30	1013	24
52Y	111.55	5064.0	610	1076	36	36	42	1139	30
52Z		5064.3	611	1076	....	21	27	1139	15
53X	111.60			1077	12	....	....	1014	12
53Y	111.65	5064.6	612	1077	36	36	42	1140	30
53Z		5064.9	613	1077	....	21	27	1140	15
54X	111.70	5041.8	536	1078	12	12	18	1015	12
54W		5042.1	537	1078	....	24	30	1015	24
54Y	111.75	5065.2	614	1078	36	36	42	1141	30
54Z		5065.5	615	1078	....	21	27	1141	15
55X	111.80			1079	12	....	....	1016	12
55Y	111.85	5065.8	616	1079	36	36	42	1142	30
55Z		5066.1	617	1079	....	21	27	1142	15
56X	111.90	5042.4	538	1080	12	12	18	1017	12
56W		5042.7	539	1080	....	24	30	1017	24
56Y	111.95	5066.4	618	1080	36	36	42	1143	30
56Z		5066.7	619	1080	....	21	27	1143	15
57X	112.00			1081	12	....	....	1018	12
57Y	112.05			1081	36	....	....	1144	30
58X	112.10			1082	12	....	....	1019	12
58Y	112.15			1082	36	....	....	1145	30
59X	112.20			1083	12	....	....	1020	12
59Y	122.25			1083	36	....	....	1146	30
** 60X				1084	12	....	....	1021	12
** 60Y				1084	36	....	....	1147	30
** 61X				1085	12	....	....	1022	12
** 61Y				1085	36	....	....	1148	30
** 62X				1086	12	....	....	1023	12
** 62Y				1086	36	....	....	1149	30
** 63X				1037	12	....	....	1024	12
** 63Y				1087	36	....	....	1150	30
** 64X				1088	12	....	....	1151	12
** 64Y				1088	36	....	....	1025	30
** 65X				1089	12	....	....	1152	12
** 65Y				1089	36	....	....	1026	30
** 66X				1090	12	....	....	1153	12
** 66Y				1090	36	....	....	1027	30
** 67X				1091	12	....	....	1154	12
** 67Y				1091	36	....	....	1028	30
** 68X				1092	12	....	....	1155	12
** 68Y				1092	36	....	....	1029	30
** 69X				1093	12	....	....	1156	12
** 69Y				1093	36	....	....	1030	30
70X	112.30			1094	12	....	....	1157	12
** 70Y	112.35			1094	36	....	....	1031	30
71X	112.40			1095	12	....	....	1158	12
** 71Y	112.45			1095	36	....	....	1032	30
72X	112.50			1096	12	....	....	1159	12
** 72Y	112.55			1096	36	....	....	1033	30

TABLE 1b—CHANNELS—Continued

	Channel pairing			DME parameters					
				Interrogation				Reply	
						Pulse codes			
DME No.	VHF freq. MHz	MLS angle freq. MHz	MLS Ch. No.	Freq. MHz	DME/N μs	DME/P Mode		Freq. MHz	Pulse codes μs
						IA μs	FA μs		
73X	112.60			1097	12			1160	12
**73Y	112.65			1097	36			1034	30
74X	112.70			1098	12			1161	12
**74Y	112.75			1098	36			1035	30
75X	112.80			1099	12			1162	12
**75Y	112.85			1099	36			1036	30
76X	112.90			1100	12			1163	12
**76Y	112.95			1100	36			1037	30
77X	113.00			1101	12			1164	12
**77Y	113.05			1101	36			1038	30
78X	113.10			1102	12			1165	12
**78Y	113.15			1102	36			1039	30
79X	113.20			1103	12			1166	12
**79Y	113.25			1103	36			1040	30
80X	113.30			1104	12			1167	12
80Y	113.35	5067.0	620	1104	36	36	42	1041	30
80Z		5067.3	621	1104		21	27	1041	15
81X	113.40			1105	12			1168	12
81Y	113.45	5067.6	622	1105	36	36	42	1042	30
81Z		5067.9	623	1005		21	27	1042	15
82X	113.50			1106	12			1169	12
82Y	113.55	5068.2	624	1106	36	36	42	1043	30
82Z		5068.5	625	1106		21	27	1043	15
83X	113.60			1107	12			1170	12
83Y	113.65	5068.8	626	1107	36	36	42	1044	30
83Z		5069.1	627	1107		21	27	1044	15
84X	113.70			1108	12			1171	12
84Y	113.75	5069.4	628	1108	36	36	42	1045	30
84Z		6069.7	629	1108		21	27	1045	15
85X	113.80			1109	12			1172	12
85Y	113.85	5070.0	630	1109	36	36	42	1046	30
85Z		5070.3	631	1109		21	27	1046	15
86X	113.90			1110	12			1173	12
86Y	113.95	5070.6	632	1110	36	36	42	1047	30
86Z		5070.9	633	1110		21	27	1047	15
87X	114.00			1111	12			1174	12
87Y	114.05	5071.2	634	1111	36	36	42	1048	30
87Z		5071.5	635	1111		21	27	1048	15
88X	114.10			1112	12			1175	12
88Y	114.15	5071.8	636	1112	36	36	42	1049	30
88Z		5072.1	637	1112		21	27	1049	15
89X	114.20			1113	12			1176	12
89Y	114.25	5072.4	638	1113	36	36	42	1050	30
89Z		5072.7	639	1113		21	27	1050	15
90X	114.30			1114	12			1177	12
90Y	114.35	5073.0	640	1114	36	36	42	1051	30
90Z		5073.3	641	1114		21	27	1051	15
91X	114.40			1115	12			1178	12
91Y	114.45	5073.6	642	1115	36	36	42	1052	30
91Z		5073.9	643	1115		21	27	1052	15
92X	114.50			1116	12			1179	12
92Y	114.55	5074.2	644	1116	36	36	42	1053	30
92Z		5074.5	645	1116		21	27	1053	15
93X	114.60			1117	12			1180	12
93Y	114.65	5074.8	646	1117	36	36	42	1054	30
93Z		5075.1	647	1117		21	27	1054	15
94X	114.70			1118	12			1181	12
94Y	114.75	5075.4	648	1118	36	36	42	1055	30
94Z		5075.7	649	1118		21	27	1055	15
95X	114.80			1119	12			1182	12
95Y	114.85	5076.0	650	1119	36	36	42	1056	30
95Z		5076.3	651	1119		21	27	1056	15
96X	114.90			1120	12			1183	12
96Y	114.95	5076.6	652	1120	36	36	42	1057	30
96Z		5076.9	653	1120		21	27	1057	15

TABLE 1b—CHANNELS—Continued

DME No.	VHF freq. MHz	MLS angle freq. MHz	MLS Ch. No.	Freq. MHz	DME/N µs	DME/P Mode IA µs	DME/P Mode FA µs	Reply Freq. MHz	Reply Pulse codes µs
97X	115.00			1121	12			1184	12
97Y	115.05	5077.2	654	1121	36	36	42	1058	30
97Z		5077.5	655	1121		21	27	1058	15
98X	115.10			1122	12			1185	12
98Y	115.15	5077.8	656	1122	36	36	42	1059	30
98Z		5078.1	657	1122		21	27	1059	15
99X	115.20			1123	12			1186	12
99Y	115.25	5078.4	658	1123	36	36	42	1060	30
99Z		5078.7	659	1123		21	27	1060	15
100X	115.30			1124	12			1187	12
100Y	115.35	5079.0	660	1124	36	36	42	1061	30
100Z		5079.3	661	1124		21	27	1061	15
101X	115.40			1125	12			1188	12
101Y	115.45	5079.6	662	1125	36	36	42	1062	30
101Z		5079.9	663	1125		21	27	1062	15
102X	115.50			1126	12			1189	12
102Y	115.55	5080.2	664	1126	36	36	42	1063	30
102Z		5080.5	665	1126		21	27	1063	15
103X	115.60			1127	12			1190	12
103Y	115.65	5080.B	666	1127	36	36	42	1064	30
103Z		5081.1	667	1127		21	27	1064	19
104X	115.70			1128	12			1191	12
104Y	115.75	5081.4	668	1128	36	36	42	1065	30
104Z		5081.7	669	1128		21	27	1065	19
105X	115.80			1129	12			1192	12
105Y	115.85	5082.0	670	1129	36	36	42	1066	30
105Z		5082.3	671	1129		21	27	1066	15
106X	115.90			1130	12			1193	12
106Y	115.95	5082.6	672	1130	36	36	42	1067	30
106Z		5082.9	673	1130		21	27	1067	15
107X	116.00			1131	12			1194	12
107Y	116.05	5083.2	674	1131	36	36	42	1068	30
107Z		5083.5	675	1131		21	27	1068	15
108X	116.10	508		1132	12			1195	12
108Y	116.15	5083.8	676	1132	36	36	42	1069	30
108Z		5084.1	677	1132		21	27	1069	15
109X	116.20			1133	12			1196	12
109Y	116.25	5084.4	678	1133	36	36	42	1070	30
109Z		5084.7	679	1133		21	27	1070	15
110X	116.30			1134	12			1197	12
110Y	116.35	5085.0	680	1134	36	36	42	1071	30
110Z		5085.3	681	1134		21	27	1071	15
111X	116.40			1135	12			1198	12
111Y	116.45	5086.6	682	1135	36	36	42	1072	30
111Z		5085.9	683	1135		21	27	1072	15
112X	116.50			1136	12			1199	12
112Y	116.55	5086.2	684	1136	36	36	42	1073	30
112Z		5086.5	685	1136		21	27	1073	15
113X	116.60			1137	12			1200	12
113Y	116.65	5086.8	686	1137	36	36	42	1074	30
113Z		5087.1	687	1137		21	27	1074	15
114X	116.70			1138	12			1201	12
114Y	116.75	5087.4	688	1138	36	36	42	1075	30
114Z		5087.7	689	1138		21	27	1075	15
115X	116.80			1139	12			1202	12
115Y	116.85	5088.0	690	1139	36	36	42	1076	30
115Z		5088.3	691	1139		21	27	1076	15
116X	116.90			1140	12			1203	12
116Y	116.95	5088.6	692	1140	36	36	42	1077	30
116Z		5088.9	693	1140		21	27	1077	15
117X	117.00			1141	12			1204	12
117Y	117.05	5089.2	694	1141	36	36	42	1078	30
117Z		5089.5	695	1141		21	27	1078	15
118X	117.10			1142	12			12.5	12
118Y	117.15	5089.8	696	1142	36	36	42	1079	30

TABLE 1b—CHANNELS—Continued

DME No.	Channel pairing			DME parameters					
	VHF freq. MHz	MLS angle freq. MHz	MLS Ch. No.	Interrogation				Reply	
				Freq. MHz	Pulse codes				
					DME/N µs	DME/P Mode		Freq. MHz	Pulse codes µs
						IA µs	FA µs		
118Z		5090.1	697	1142		21	27	1079	12
119X	117.20			1143	12			1206	12
119Y	117.25	5090.4	698	1143	36	36	42	1080	30
119Z		5090.7	699	1143		21	27	1080	15
120X	117.30			1144	12			1207	12
120Y	117.35			1144	36			1081	30
121X	117.40			1145	12			1208	12
121Y	117.45			1145	36			1082	30
122X	117.50			1146	12			1209	12
122Y	117.55			1146	36			1083	30
123X	117.60			1147	12			1210	12
123Y	117.65			1147	36			1084	30
124X	117.70			1148	12			1211	12
** 124Y	117.75			1148	36			1085	30
125X	117.80			1149	12			1212	12
** 125Y	117.85			1149	36			1086	30
126X	117.90			1150	12			1213	12
** 126Y	117.95			1150	36			1087	30

Notes:
* These channels are reserved exclusively for national allotments.
** These channels may be used for national allotment on a secondary basis. The primary reason for reserving these channels is to provide protection for the secondary Surveillance Radar (SSR) system.
∇ 108.0 MHz is not scheduled for assignment to ILS service. The associated DME operating channel No. 17X may be assigned to the emergency service.

(b) *Polarization.* (1) The radio frequency emissions from all ground equipment must be nominally vertically polarized. Any horizontally polarized radio frequency emission component from the ground equipment must not have incorrectly coded angle information such that the limits specified in paragraphs (b) (2) and (3) of this section are exceeded.

(2) Rotation of the receiving antenna thirty degrees from the vertically polarized position must not cause the path following error to exceed the allowed error at that location.

(c) *Modulation requirements.* Each function transmitter must be capable

of DPSK and continuous wave (CW) modulations of the RF carrier which have the following characteristics.

(1) DPSK. The DPSK signal must have the following characteristics:

bit rate	15.625 KHz
bit length	64 microseconds
logic "0"	no phase transition
logic "1"	phase transition
phase transition	less than 10 microseconds
phase tolerance	±10 degrees

The phase shall advance (or retard) monotonically throughout the transition region. Amplitude modulation during the phase transition period shall not be used.

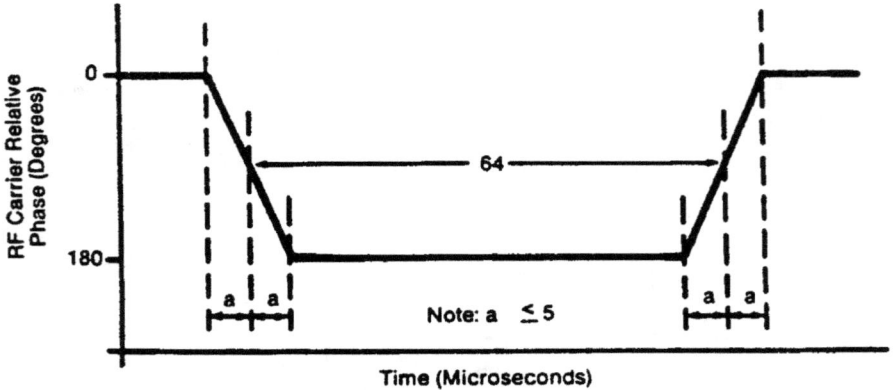

Figure 1.—DPSK Phase Characteristic

(2) CW. The CW pulse transmissions and the CW angle transmissions as may be required in the signal format of any function must have characteristics such that the requirements of paragraph (d) of this section are met.

(d) *Radio frequency signal spectrum.* The transmitted signal must be such that during the transmission time, the mean power density above a height of 600 meters (2000 feet) does not exceed -100.5 dBW/m^2 for angle guidance and -95.5 dBW/m^2 for data, as measured in a 150 KHz bandwidth centered at a frequency of 840 KHz or more from the assigned frequency.

(e) *Synchronization.* Synchronization between the azimuth and elevation components is required and, in split-site configurations, would normally be accomplished by landline interconnections. Synchronization monitoring must be provided to preclude function overlap.

(f) *Transmission rates.* Angle guidance and data signals must be transmitted at the following average repetition rates:

Function	Average data rate (Hertz)
Approach Azimuth	13 ±0.5
High Rate Approach Azimuth	[1] 39 ±1.5
Approach Elevation	39 ±1.5
Back Azimuth	6.5 ±0.25
Basic Data	[2]
Auxiliary Data	[3]

[1] The higher rate is recommended for azimuth scanning antennas with beamwidths greater than two degrees. It should be noted that the time available in the signal format for additional functions is limited when the higher rate is used.

[2] Refer to Table 8a.

[3] Refer to Table 8c.

(g) *Transmission sequences.* Sequences of angle transmissions which will generate the required repetition rates are shown in Figures 2 and 3.

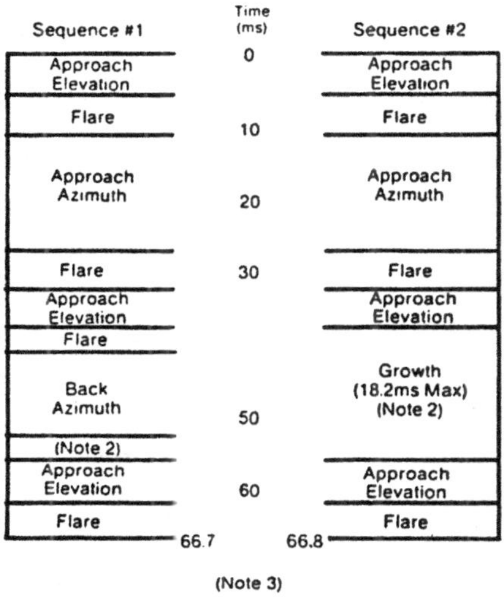

Notes:

1. When Back Azimuth is Provided, Basic Data Word #2 Must Be Transmitted Only In This Position.

2. Data Words May Be Transmitted In Any Open Time Periods.

3. The Total Time Duration of Sequence #1 Plus Sequence #2 Must Not exceed 134 ms.

Figure 2.   Transmission sequence pair which provides for all

MLS angle guidance functions.

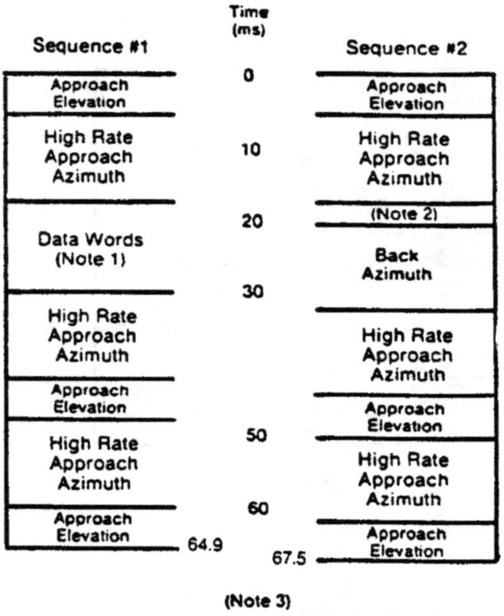

Figure 3. Transmission sequence pair which provides for the MLS high rate approach azimuth angle guidance function.

(h) *TDM cycle.* The time periods between angle transmission sequences must be varied so that exact repetitions do not occur within periods of less than 0.5 second in order to protect against synchronous interference. One such combination of sequences is shown in Figure 4 which forms a full multiplex cycle. Data may be transmitted during suitable open times within or between the sequences.

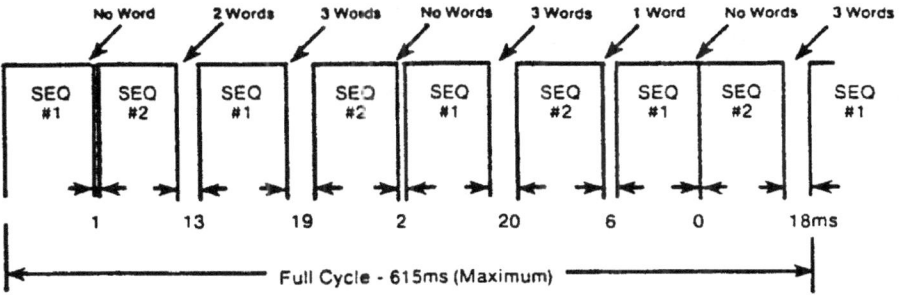

Note: Angle Sequence Are Those From Figure 2 Or 3. Do Not Mix Sequences.

Figure 4.   A complete function multiplex cycle.

(i) *Function Formats (General)*. Each angle function must contain the following elements: a preamble; sector signals; and a TO and FRO angle scan organized as shown in Figure 5a. Each data function must contain a preamble and a data transmission period organized as shown in Figure 5b.

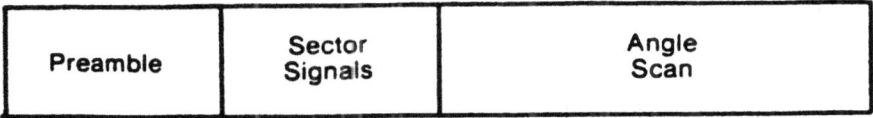

(a) Angle Function

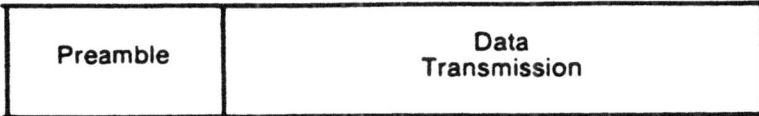

(b) Data Function

Figure 5 — Function format.

(1) *Preamble format*. The transmitted angle and date functions must use the preamble format shown in Figure 6. This format consists of a carrier acquisition period of unmodulated CW transmission followed by a receiver synchronization code and a function identification code. The preamble timing must be in accordance with Table 2.

Clock Pulse 0	Carrier Acquisition	Synchronization Code	Function Identification Code
	13	18	25

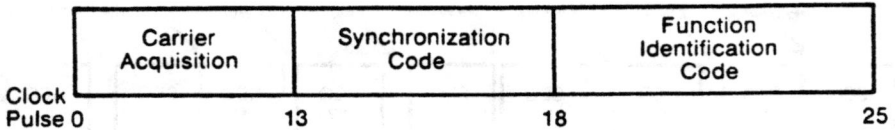

Figure 6 - Preamble organization.

(i) *Digital codes.* The coding used in the preamble for receiver synchronization is a Barker code logic 11101. The time of the last phase transition midpoint in the code shall be the receiver reference time (see Table 2). The function identification codes must be as shown in Table 3. The last two bits (I_{11} and I_{12}) of the code are parity bits obeying the equations:

$$I_6 + I_7 + I_8 + I_9 + I_{10} + I_{11} = \text{Even}$$
$$I_6 + I_8 + I_{10} + I_{12} = \text{Even}$$

(ii) *Data modulation.* The digital code portions of the preamble must be DPSK modulated in accordance with § 171.311(c)(1) and must be transmitted throughout the function coverage volume.

(2) *Angle function formats.* The timing of the angle transmissions must be in accordance with Tables 4a, 4b, and 5. The actual timing of the TO and FRO scans must be as required to meet the accuracy requirements of §§ 171.313 and 171.317.

(i) Preamble. Must be in accordance with requirements of § 171.311(i)(1).

TABLE 2—PREAMBLE TIMING [1]

Event	Event time slot begins at—	
	15.625 kHz clock pulse (number)	Time (milli-seconds)
Carrier acquisition:		
(CW transmission)	0	0
Receiver reference time code:		
$I_1 = 1$	13	0.832
$I_2 = 1$	14	0.896
$I_3 = 1$	15	0.960
$I_4 = 0$	16	1.024
$I_5 = 1$	17	[2] 1.088
Function identification:		
I_6	18	1.152
I_7	19	1.216
I_8	20	1.280
I_9	21	1.344
I_{10} (see table 1)	22	1.408
I_{11}	23	1.472
I_{12}	24	1.536

TABLE 2—PREAMBLE TIMING [1]—Continued

Event	Event time slot begins at—	
	15.625 kHz clock pulse (number)	Time (milli-seconds)
END PREAMBLE	25	1.600

[1] Applies to all functions transmitted.
[2] Reference time for receiver synchronization for all function timing.

TABLE 3—FUNCTION IDENTIFICATION CODES

Function	Code						
	I_6	I_7	I_8	I_9	I_{10}	I_{11}	I_{12}
Approach azimuth	0	0	1	1	0	0	1
High rate approach azimuth	0	0	1	0	1	0	0
Approach elevation	1	1	0	0	0	0	1
Back azimuth	1	0	0	1	0	0	1
Basic data 1	0	1	0	1	0	0	0
Basic data 2	0	1	1	1	1	0	0
Basic data 3	1	0	1	0	0	0	0
Basic data 4	1	0	0	0	1	0	0
Basic data 5	1	1	0	1	1	0	0
Dasic data 6	0	0	0	1	1	0	1
Auxiliary data A	1	1	1	0	0	1	0
Auxiliary data B	1	0	1	0	1	1	1
Auxiliary data C	1	1	1	1	0	0	0

(ii) *Sector signals.* In all azimuth formats, sector signals must be transmitted to provide Morse Code identification, airborne antenna selection, and system test signals. These signals are not required in the elevation formats. In addition, if the signal from an installed ground component results in a valid indication in an area where no valid guidance should exist, OCI signals must be radiated as provided for in the signal format (see Tables 4a, 4b, and 5). The sector signals are defined as follows:

(A) *Morse Code.* DPSK transmissions that will permit Morse Code facility identification in the aircraft by a four letter code starting with the letter "M" must be included in all azimuth functions. They must be transmitted and repeated at approximately equal intervals, not less than six times per minute, during which time the ground subsystem is available for operational use. When the transmissions of the ground subsystem are not available, the identification signal must be suppressed. The audible tone in the aircraft is started by setting the Morse Code bit to logic "1" and stopped by a logic "0" (see Tables 4a and 4b). The identification code characteristics must conform to the following: the dot must be between 0.13 and 0.16 second in duration, and the dash between 0.39 and 0.48 second. The duration between dots and/or dashes must be one dot plus or minus 10%. The duration between characters (letters) must not be less than three dots. When back azimuth is provided, the code shall be transmitted by the approach azimuth and back azimuth within plus or minus 0.08 seconds.

(B) *Airborne antenna selection.* A signal for airborne antenna selection shall be transmitted as a "zero" DPSK signal lasting for a six-bit period (see Tables 4a and 4b).

TABLE 4a—APPROACH AZIMUTH FUNCTION TIMING

| Event | Event time slot begins at— | |
	15.625 kHz clock pulse (number)	Time (milli-sec-onds)
Preamble	0	0
Morse code	25	1.600
Antenna select	26	1.664
Rear OCI	32	2.048
Left OCI	34	2.176
Right OCI	36	2.304
To test	38	2.432
To scan [1]	40	2.560
Pause	....	8.760
Midscan point	....	9.060
FRO scan [1]	....	9.360
FRO test	....	15.560
End Function (Airborne)	....	15.688
End guard time; end function (ground)	....	15.900

AA[1] The actual commencement and completion of the TO and the FRO scan transmissions are dependent on the amount of proportional guidance provided. The time slots provided shall accommodate a maximum scan of plus or minus 62.0 degrees. Scan timing shall be compatible with accuracy requirements.

TABLE 4b—HIGH RATE APPROACH AZIMUTH AND BACK AZIMUTH FUNCTION TIMING

| Event | Event time slot begins at— | |
	15.625 kHz clock pulse (number)	Time (milli-sec-onds)
Preamble	0	0
Morse Code	25	1.600
Antenna select	26	1.664
Rear OCI	32	2.048
Left OCI	34	2.176
Right OCI	36	2.304
To test	38	2.432
To scan [1]	40	2.560
Pause	....	6.760
Midscan point	....	7.060
FRO scan [1]	....	7.360
FRO test pulse	....	11.560
End function (airborne)	....	11.688
End guard time; end function (ground)	....	11.900

[1] The actual commencement and completion of the TO and the FRO scan transmissions are dependent on the amount of proportional guidance provided. The time slots provided will accommodate a maximum scan of plus or minus 42.0 degrees. Scan timing shall be compatible with accuracy requirements.

(C) *OCI.* Where OCI pulses are used, they must be: (1) greater than any guidance signal in the OCI sector; (2) at least 5 dB less than the level of the scanning beam within the proportional guidance sector; and (3) for azimuth functions with clearance signals, at least 5 dB less than the level of the left (right) clearance pulses within the left (right) clearance sector.

TABLE 5—APPROACH ELEVATION FUNCTION TIMING

| Event | Event time slot begins at: | |
	15.625 kHz clock pluse (number)	Time (milli-sec-onds)
Preamble	0	0
Processor pause	25	1.600
OCI	27	1.728
To scan [1]	29	1.856
Pause	....	3.406
Midscan point	....	3.606
FRO scan [1]	....	3.806
End function (airborne)	....	5.356
End guard time; end function (ground)	....	5.600

[1] The actual commencement and completion of the TO and FRO scan transmissions are dependent upon the amount of proportional guidance provided. The time slots provided will accommodate a maximum scan of −1.5 degrees to + 29.5 degrees. Scan timing shall be compatible with accuracy requirements.

The duration of each pulse measured at the half amplitude point shall be at least 100 microseconds, and the rise and fall times shall be less then 10 microseconds. It shall be permissible to sequentially transmit two pulses in each out-of-coverage indication time slot. Where pulse pairs are used, the duration of each pulse shall be at least 50 microseconds, and the rise and fall times shall be less then 10 microseconds. The transmission of out-of-coverage indication pulses radiated from antennas with overlapping coverage patterns shall be separated by at least 10 microseconds.

NOTE: If desired, two pulses may be sequentially transmitted in each OCI time slot. Where pulse pairs are used, the duration of each pulse must be 45 (±5) microseconds and the rise and fall times must be less than 10 microseconds.

(D) *System test.* Time slots are provided in Tables 4a and 4b to allow radiation of TO and FRO test pulses. However, radiation of these pulses is not required since the characteristics of these pulses have not yet been standardized.

(iii) *Angle encoding.* The encoding must be as follows:

(A) *General.* Azimuth and elevation angles are encoded by scanning a narrow beam between the limits of the proportional coverage sector first in one direction (the TO scan) and then in the opposite direction (the FRO scan). Angular information must be encoded by the amount of time separation between the beam centers of the TO and FRO scanning beam pulses. The TO and FRO transmissions must be symmetrically disposed about the midscan point listed in Tables 4a, 4b, 5, and 7. The midscan point and the center of the time interval between the TO and FRO scan transmissions must coincide with a tolerance of ±10 microseconds. Angular coding must be linear with angle and properly decoded using the formula:

$$\theta = \frac{V}{2}\left(T_0 - t\right)$$

where:

θ = Receiver angle in degrees.
V = Scan velocity in degrees per microsecond.
T_0 = Time separation in microseconds between TO and FRO beam centers corresponding to zero degrees.
t = Time separation in microseconds between TO and FRO beam centers.

The timing requirements are listed in Table 6 and illustrated in Figure 7.

Signal Format
Time Slots

▦ Preamble

▤ Sector Signals

▨ "To" Angle Scan

▨ "Fro" Angle Scan

▨ Pause Time

▢ Guard Time

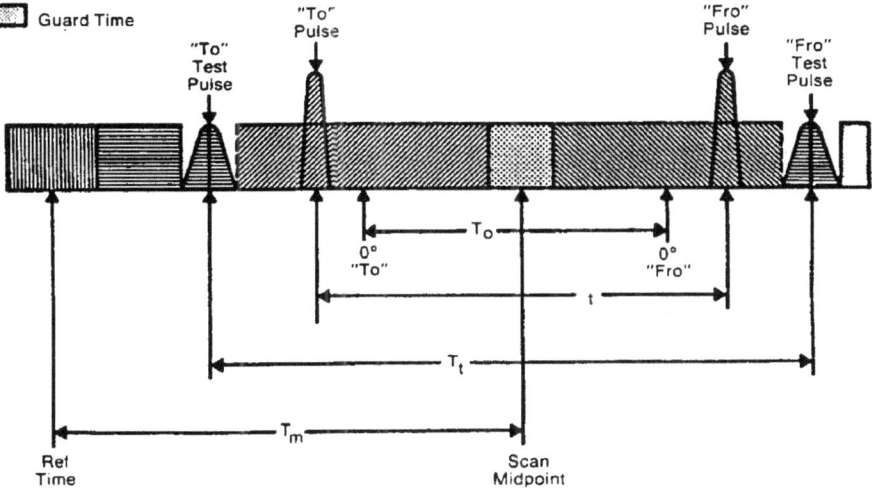

Figure 7.   Azimuth Angle Scan Timing (Not to Scale)

(B) *Azimuth angle encoding.* Each guidance angle transmitted must consist of a clockwise TO scan followed by a counterclockwise FRO scan as viewed from above the antenna. For approach azimuth functions, increasing angle values must be in the direction of the TO scan; for the back azimuth function, increasing angle values must be in the direction of the FRO scan. The antenna has a narrow beam in the plane of the scan direction and a broad beam in the orthogonal plane which fills the vertical coverage.

(C) *Elevation angle encoding.* The radiation from elevation equipment must produce a beam which scans from the horizon up to the highest elevation angle and then scans back down to the horizon. The antenna has a narrow beam in the plane of the scan direction and a broad beam in the orthogonal plane which fills the horizontal cov-erage. Elevation angles are defined from the horizontal plane containing the antenna phase center; positive angles are above the horizontal and zero angle is along the horizontal.

(iv) *Clearance guidance.* The timing of the clearance pulses must be in accordance with Figure 8. For azimuth elements with proportional coverage of less than ±40 degrees (±20 degrees for back azimuth), clearance guidance information must be provided by transmitting pulses in a TO and FRO format adjacent to the stop/start times of the scanning beam signal. The fly-right clearance pulses must represent positive angles and the fly-left clearance pulses must represent negative angles. The duration of each clearance pulse must be 50 microseconds with a tolerance of ±5 microseconds. The transmitter switching time between the clearance pulses and the scanning

857

beam transmissions must not exceed 10 microseconds. The rise time at the edge of each clearance pulse must be less than 10 microseconds. Within the fly-right clearance guidance section, the fly-right clearance guidance signal shall exceed scanning beam antenna sidelobes and other guidance and OCI signals by at least 5 dB; within the fly-left clearance guidance sector, the fly left clearance guidance signal shall exceed scanning beam antenna sidelobes and all other guidance and OCI signals by at least 5 dB; within the proportional guidance sector, the clearance guidance signals shall be at least 5dB below the proportional guidance signal. Optionally, clearance guidance may be provided by scanning throughout the approach guidance sector. For angles outside the approach azimuth proportional coverage limits as set in Basic Data Word One (Basic Data Word 5 for back azimuth), proper decode and display of clearance guidance must occur to the limits of the guidance region.

Where used, clearance pulses shall be transmitted adjacent to the scanning beam signals at the edges of proportional coverage as shown in Figure 8. The proportional coverage boundary shall be established at one beamwidth inside the scan start/stop angles, such that the transition between scanning beam and clearance signals occurs outside the proportional coverage sector. When clearance pulses are provided in conjunction with a narrow beamwidth (e.g., one degree) scanning antenna, the scanning beam antenna shall radiate for 15 microseconds while stationary at the scan start/stop angles.

(3) *Data function format.* Basic data words provide equipment characteristics and certain siting information. Basic data words must be transmitted from an antenna located at the approach azimuth or back azimuth site which provides coverage throughout the appropriate sector. Data function timing must be in accordance with Table 7a.

TABLE 6—ANGLE SCAN TIMING CONSTANTS

Function	Max value of $_t$(usec)	T_o(usec)	V(deg/ usec)	T_m (usec)	Pause time (usec)	T_t (usec)
Approach azimuth	13,000	6,800	0.02	7,972	600	13,128
High rate approach azimuth	9,000	4,800	0.02	5,972	600	9,128
Approach elevation	3,500	3,350	0.02	2,518	400	N/A
Back azimuth	9,000	4,800	−0.02	5,972	600	9,128

TABLE 7a—BASIC DATA FUNCTION TIMING

Event	Event time slot begins at:[1]	
	15.625 kHz clock pulse (number)	Time (milli- sec- onds)
Preamble	0	0
Data transmission (bits I_{13}–I_{30})	25	1.600
Parity transmission (bits I_{31}–I_{32})	43	2.752
End function (airborne)	45	2.880
End guard time: end function (ground)		3.100

[1] The previous event time slot ends at this time.

TABLE 7b—AUXILIARY DATA FUNCTION TIMING— (DIGITAL)

Event	Event time slot begins at:	
	15.625 kHz clock pulse (number)	Time (milli- sec- onds)
Preamble	0	0
Address transmission (bits I_{13}–I_{20})	25	1.600
Data transmission: (bits I_{21}–I_{69})	33	2.112

TABLE 7b—AUXILIARY DATA FUNCTION TIMING— (DIGITAL)—Continued

Event	Event time slot begins at:	
	15.625 kHz clock pulse (number)	Time (milli- sec- onds)
Parity transmission (bits I_{70}–I_{76})	82	5.248
End function (airborne)	89	5.696
End guard time; end function (ground)		5.900

TABLE 7c—AUXILIARY DATA FUNCTION TIMING— (ALPHANUMERIC)

Event	Event time slot begins at:	
	15.615 kHz clock pulse (number)	Time (milli- sec- onds)
Preamble	0	0
Address transmission (bits I_{13}–I_{20})	25	1.600
Data transmission: (bits I_{21}–I_{76})	33	2.112
End function (airborne)	89	5.696

TABLE 7c—AUXILIARY DATA FUNCTION TIMING—
(ALPHANUMERIC)—Continued

| Event | Event time slot begins at: | |
	15.615 kHz clock pulse (number)	Time (milli-sec-onds)
End guard time; (end function ground)	....	5.900

(i) *Preamble.* Must be in accordance with requirements of § 171.311(i)(1)

(ii) *Data transmissions.* Basic data must be transmitted using DPSK modulation. The content and repetition rate of each basic data word must be in accordance with Table 8a. For data containing digital information, binary number 1 must represent the lower range limit with increments in binary steps to the upper range limit shown in Table 8a. Data containing digital information shall be transmitted with the least significant bit first

(j) *Basic Data word requirements.* Basic Data shall consist of the items specified in Table 8a. Basic Data word contents shall be defined as follows:

(1) *Approach azimuth to threshold distance* shall represent the minimum distance between the Approach Azimuth antenna phase center and the vertical plane perpendicular to the centerline which contains the landing threshold.

(2) *Approach azimuth proportional coverage limit* shall represent the limit of the sector in which proportional approach azimuth guidance is transmitted.

(3) *Clearance signal type* shall represent the type of clearance when used. Pulse clearance is that which is in accordance with § 171.311 (i) (2) (iv). Scanning Beam (SB) clearance indicates that the proportional guidance sector is limited by the proportional coverage limits set in basic data.

859

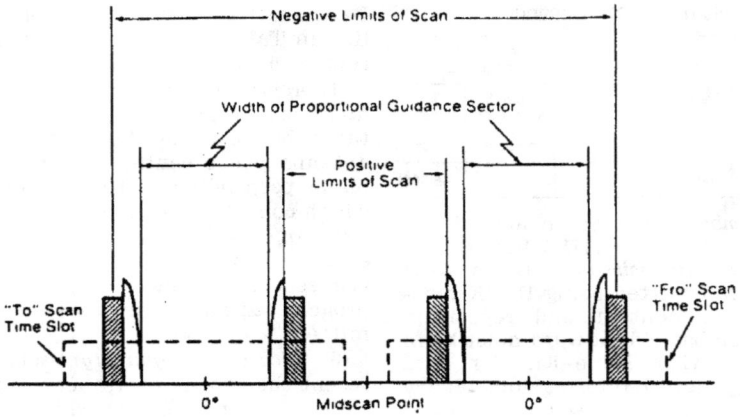

(a) APPROACH AZIMUTH

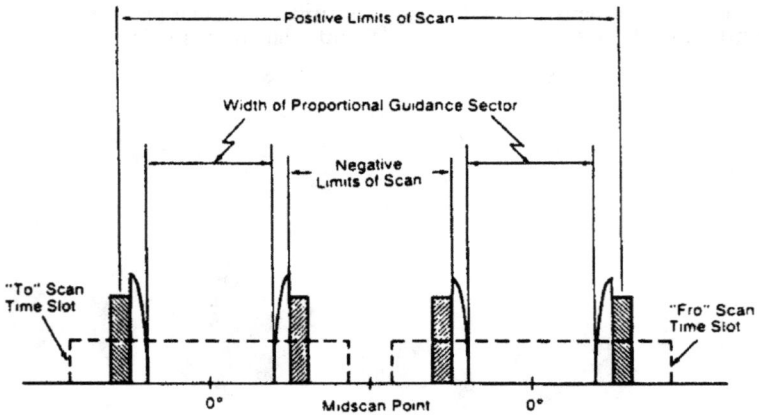

(b) BACK AZIMUTH

Legend

Clearance Pulses

▨ Fly-Left

▨ Fly-Right

Scanning Beam Pulses

⋀ Start Scan

⋂ Stop Scan

Figure 8. Clearance Pulse Timing for Azimuth Functions

TABLE 8a—BASIC DATA WORDS

Data bit #	Data item definition	LSB value	Data bit value
	Basic Data Word No. 1		
1	Preamble	N/A	1
2	....	....	1
3	....	....	1
4	....	....	0
5	....	....	1
6	....	....	0
7	....	....	1
8	....	....	0
9	....	....	1
10	....	....	0
11	....	....	0
12	....	....	0
13	Approach azimuth to threshold distance (Om − 630m).	100m	100m
14	....	....	200m
15	....	....	400m
16	....	....	800m
17	....	....	1600m
18	....	....	3200m
19	Approach azimuth proportional coverage limit (negative limit) (0° to −62°).	2°	−2°
20	....	....	−4°
21	....	....	−8°
22	....	....	−13°
23	....	....	−32°
24	Approach azimuth proportional coverage limit (positive limit) (0° to + 62°).	2°	2°
25	....	....	4°
26	....	....	8°
27	....	....	16°
28	....	....	32°
29	Clearance signal type	N/A	0 = pulse; 1 = SB
30	Spare	....	Transmit zero
31	Parity: (13 + 14 + 15. . . + 30 + 31 = odd).	N/A	N/A
32	Parity: (14 + 16 + 18. . . + 30 + 32 = odd).	N/A	N/A

Note 1: Transmit throughout the Approach Azimuth guidance sector at intervals of 1.0 seconds or less.
Note 2: The all zero state of the data field represents the lower limit of the absolute value of the coded parameter unless otherwise noted.

Data bit #	Data item definition	LSB value	Data bit value
	Basic Data Word No. 2		
1	Preamble	N/A	1
2	....	....	1
3	....	....	1
4	....	....	0
5	....	....	1
6	....	....	0
7	....	....	1
8	....	....	0
9	....	....	1
10	....	....	1
11	....	....	0
12	....	....	0
13	Minimum glide path (2.0° to 14.7°).	0.1°	0.1°
14	....	....	0.2°
15	....	....	0.4°
16	....	....	0.8°

TABLE 8a—BASIC DATA WORDS—Continued

Data bit #	Data item definition	LSB value	Data bit value
17	....	....	1.6°
18	....	....	3.2°
19	....	....	6.4°
20	Back azimuth status	....	see note 4
21	DME status	....	see note 6
22	....	....	
23	Approach azimuth status ...	....	see note 4
24	Approach azimuth status	....	see note 4
25	Spare	....	Transmit zero
26	......do	....	Do.
27	......do	....	Do.
28	......do	....	Do.
29	......do	....	Do.
30	......do	....	Do.
31	Parity: (13 + 14 + 15. . . + 30 + 31) = odd).	N/A	N/A
32	Parity: (14 + 16 + 18. . . + 30 + 32 = odd).	N/A	N/A

Note 1: Transmit throughout the Approach Azimuth guidance sector at intervals of 0.16 seconds or less.
Note 2: The all zero state of the data field represents the lower limit of the absolute range of the coded parameter unless otherwise noted.

Data bit #	Data item definition	LSB value	Data bit value
	Basic Data Word No. 3		
1	Preamble	N/A	1
2	....	....	1
3	....	....	1
4	....	....	0
5	....	....	1
6	....	....	1
7	....	....	0
8	....	....	1
9	....	....	0
10	....	....	0
11	....	....	0
12	....	....	0
13	Approach azimuth beamwidth (0.5° − 4.0°) See note 7.	0.5°	0.5°
14	....	....	1.0°
15	....	....	2.0°
16	Approach elevation beamwidth (0.5° to 2.5°) See note 7.	0.5°	0.5°
17	....	....	1.0°
18	Note: values greater than 2.5° are invalid.	....	2.0°
19	DME distance (Om to 6387.5m.	12.5m	12.5m
20	....	....	25.0m
21	....	....	50.0m
22	....	....	100.0m
23	....	....	200.0m
24	....	....	400.0m
25	....	....	800.0m
26	....	....	1600.0m
27	....	....	3200.0m
28	Spare	....	Transmit zero
29	......do	....	Do.
30	......do	....	Do.
31	Parity: (13 + 14 + 15. . . + 30 + 31 = odd).	....	
32	Parity: (14 + 16 + 18. . . + 30 + 32 = odd).	N/A	N/A

861

TABLE 8a—BASIC DATA WORDS—Continued

Data bit #	Data item definition	LSB value	Data bit value

Note 1: Transmit throughout the Approach Azimuth guidance sector at intervals of 1.0 seconds or less.

Note 2: The all zero state of the data field represents the lower limit of the absolute range of the coded parameter unless otherwise noted.

Basic Data Word No. 4

Data bit #	Data item definition	LSB value	Data bit value
1	Preamble	N/A	1
2			1
3			1
4			0
5			1
6			1
7			0
8			0
9			0
10			1
11			0
12			0
13	Approach azimuth magnetic orientation (0° to 359°).	1°	1°
14			2°
15			4°
16			8°
17			16°
18			32°
19			64°
20			128°
21			256°
22	Back azimuth magnetic orientation (0° to 359°).	1°	1°
23			2°
24			4°
25			8°
26			16°
27			32°
28			64°
29			128°
30			256°
31	Parity: (13 + 14 + 15. . . + 30 + 31 = odd).	N/A	N/A
32	Parity: (14 + 16 + 18. . . + 30 + 32 = odd).	N/A	N/A

Note 1: Transmit at intervals of 1.0 second or less throughout the Approach Azimuth guidance sector, except when Back Azimuth guidance is provided. See Note 8.

Note 2: The all zero state of the data field represents the lower limit of the absolute range of the coded parameter unless otherwise noted.

Basic Data Word No. 5

Data bit #	Data item definition	LSB value	Data bit value
1	Preamble	N/A	1
2			1
3			1
4			0
5			1
6			1
7			1
8			0
9			1
10			1
11			0
12			0
13	Back azimuth proportional coverage negative limit (0° to −42°).	2°	−2°
14			−4°
15			−8°

TABLE 8a—BASIC DATA WORDS—Continued

Data bit #	Data item definition	LSB value	Data bit value
16			−16°
17			−32°
18	Back azimuth proportional coverage positive limit (0° to +42°).	2°	2°
19			4°
20			8°
21			16°
22			32°
23	Back azimuth beamwidth (0.5° to 4.0°) See note 7.	0.5°	0.5°
24			1.0°
25			2.0°
26	Back azimuth status		See Note 10
27	..do		Do.
28	..do		Do.
29	..do		Do.
30	..do		Do.
31	Parity: (13 + 14 + 15. . . + 30 + 31 = odd).	N/A	N/A
32	Parity: (14 + 16 + 18. . . + 30 + 32 = odd).	N/A	N/A

Note 1: Transmit only when Back Azimuth guidance is provided. See note 9.

Note 2: The all zero state of the data filed represents the lower limit of the absolute range of the coded parameter unless otherwise noted.

Basic Data Word No. 6

Data bit #	Data item definition	LSB value	Data bit value
1	Preamble	N/A	1
2			1
3			1
4			0
5			1
6			0
7			0
8			0
9			1
10			1
11			0
12			1
(13–30)	MLS ground equipment identification (Note 3).		
13	Character 2	N/A	B1
14			B2
15			B3
16			B4
17			B5
18			B6
19	Character 3	N/A	B1
20			B2
21			B3
22			B4
23			B5
24			B6
25	Character 4	N/A	B1
26			B2
27			B3
28			B4
29			B5
30			B6
31	Parity: (13 + 14 + 15. . . + 30 + 31 = odd).	N/A	N/A
32	Parity: (14 + 16 + 18. . . + 30 + 32 = odd).	N/A	N/A

Note 1: Transmit at intervals of 1.0 second or less throughout the Approach Azimuth guidance sector, except when Back Azimuth guidance is provided. See note 8.

Note 3: Characters are encoded using the International Alphabet Number 5, (IA–5):
Note 4: Coding for status bit:
0 = Function not radiated, or radiated in test mode (not reliable for navigation).
1 = Function radiated in normal mode (for Back Azimuth, this also indicates that a Back Azimuth transmission follows).
Note 5: Date items which are not applicable to a particular ground equipment shall be transmitted as all zeros.
Note 6: Coding for status bits:

I_{21}	I_{22}	
0	0	DME transponder inoperative or not available.
1	0	Only IA mode or DME/N available.
0	0	FA mode, Standard 1, available.
1	1	FA mode, Standard 2, available.

Note 7: The value coded shall be the actual beamwidth (as defined in § 171.311 (j)(9) rounded to the nearest 0.5 degree.
Note 8: When back Azimuth guidance is provided, Data Words 4 and 6 shall be transmitted at intervals of 1.33 seconds or less throughout the Approach Azimuth coverage and 4 seconds or less throughout the Back Azimuth coverage.
Note 9: When Back Azimuth guidance is provided, Data Word 5 shall be transmitted at an interval of 1.33 seconds or less throughout the Back Azimuth coverage sector and 4 seconds or less throughout the Approach Azimuth coverage sector.
Note 10: Coding for status bit:
0 = Function not radiated, or radiated in test mode (not reliable for navigation).
1 = Function radiated in normal mode.

(4) *Minimum glidepath* the lowest angle of descent along the zero degree azimuth that is consistent with published approach procedures and obstacle clearance criteria.

(5) *Back azimuth status* shall represent the operational status of the Back Azimuth equipment.

(6) *DME status* shall represent the operational status of the DME equipment.

(7) *Approach azimuth status* shall represent the operational status of the approach azimuth equipment.

(8) *Approach elevation status* shall represent the operational status of the approach elevation equipment.

(9) *Beamwidth* the width of the scanning beam main lobe measured at the −3 dB points and defined in angular units on the antenna boresight, in the horizontal plane for the azimuth function and in the vertical plane for the elevation function.

(10) *DME distance* shall represent the minimum distance between the DME antenna phase center and the vertical plane perpendicular to the runway centerline which contains the MLS datum point.

(11) *Approach azimuth magnetic orientation* shall represent the angle measured in the horizontal plane clockwise from Magnetic North to the zero-degree angle guidance radial originating from the approach azimuth antenna phase center. The vertex of the meas-

ured angle shall be at the approach azimuth antenna phase center.

NOTE: For example, this data item would be encoded 090 for an approach azimuth antenna serving runway 27 (assuming the magnetic heading is 270 degrees) when sited such that the zero degree radial is parallel to centerline.

(12) *Back azimuth magnetic orientation* shall represent the angle measured in the horizontal plane clockwise from Magnetic North to the zero-degree angle guidance radial originating from the Back Azimuth antenna. The vertex of the measured angle shall be at the Back Azimuth antenna phase center.

NOTE: For example, this data item would be encoded 270 for a Back Azimuth Antenna serving runway 27 (assuming the magnetic heading is 270 degrees) when sited such that the zero degree radial is parallel to centerline.

(13) *Back azimuth proportional coverage limit* shall represent the limit of the sector in which proportional back azimuth guidance is transmitted.

(14) *MLS ground equipment identification* shall represent the last three characters of the system identification specified in §171.311(i)(2). The characters shall be encoded in accordance with International Alphabet No. 5 (IA–5) using bits b_1 through b_6.

NOTE: Bit b_7 of this code may be reconstructed in the airborne receiver by taking the complement of bit b_6.

(k) *Residual radiation.* The residual radiation of a transmitter associated with an MLS function during time intervals when it should not be transmitting shall not adversely affect the reception of any other function. The residual radiation of an MLS function at times when another function is radiating shall be at least 70 dB below the level provided when transmitting.

(1) *Symmetrical scanning.* The TO and FRO scan transmissions shall be symmetrically disposed about the mid-scan point listed in Tables 4a, 4b and 5. The mid-scan point and the center of the time interval between the TO and FRO scan shall coincide with a tolerance of plus or minus 10 microseconds.

(m) *Auxiliary data*—(1) *Addresses.* Three function identification codes are reserved to indicate transmission of Auxiliary Data A, Auxiliary Data B, and Auxiliary Data C. Auxiliary Data A contents are specified below, Auxiliary Data B contents are reserved for future use, and Auxiliary Data C contents are reserved for national use. The address codes of the auxiliary data words shall be as shown in Table 8b.

(2) *Organization and timing.* The organization and timing of digital auxiliary data must be as specified in Table 7b. Data containing digital information must be transmitted with the least significant bit first. Alphanumeric data characters must be encoded in accordance with the 7-unit code character set as defined by the American National Standard Code for Information Interchange (ASCII). An even parity bit is added to each character. Alphanumeric data must be transmitted in the order in which they are to be read. The serial transmission of a character must be with the lower order bit transmitted first and the parity bit transmitted last. The timing for alphanumeric auxiliary data must be as shown in Table 7c.

(3) *Auxiliary Data A content:* The data items specified in Table 8c are defined as follows:

(i) *Approach azimuth antenna offset* shall represent the minimum distance between the Approach Azimuth antenna phase center and the vertical plane containing the runway centerline.

(ii) *Approach azimuth to MLS datum point distance* shall represent the minimum distance between the Approach Azimuth antenna phase center and the vertical plane perpendicular to the centerline which contains the MLS datum point.

(iii) *Approach azimuth alignment with runway centerline* shall represent the minimum angle between the approach azimuth antenna zero-degree guidance plane and the runway certerline.

(iv) *Approach azimuth antenna coordinate system* shall represent the coordinate system (planar or conical) of the angle data transmitted by the approach azimuth antenna.

(v) *Approach elevation antenna offset* shall represent the minimum distance between the elevation antenna phase center and the vertical plane containing the runway centerline.

(vi) *MLS datum point to threshold distance* shall represent the distance measured along the runway centerline from the MLS datum point to the runway threshold.

(vii) *Approach elevation antenna height* shall represent the height of the elevation antenna phase center relative to the height of the MLS datum point.

(viii) *DME offset* shall represent the minimum distance between the DME antenna phase center and the vertical plane containing the runway centerline.

(ix) *DME to MLS datum point distance* shall represent the minimum distance between the DME antenna phase center and the vertical plane perpendicular to the centerline which contains the MLS datum point.

(x) *Back azimuth antenna offset* shall represent the minimum distance between the back azimuth antenna phase center and the vertical plane containing the runway centerline.

(xi) *Back azimuth to MLS datum point distance* shall represent the minimum distance between the Back Azimuth antenna and the vertical plane perpendicular to the centerline which contains the MLS datum point.

(xii) *Back azimuth antenna alignment with runway centerline* shall represent the minimum angle between the back azimuth antenna zero-degree guidance plane and the runway centerline.

§ 171.313 Azimuth performance requirements.

This section prescribes the performance requirements for the azimuth equipment of the MLS as follows:

(a) *Approach azimuth coverage requirements.* The approach azimuth equipment must provide guidance information in at least the following volume of space (see Figure 9):

TABLE 8b—AUXILIARY DATA WORD ADDRESS CODES

No.	I_{13}	I_{14}	I_{15}	I_{16}	I_{17}	I_{18}	I_{19}	I_{20}
1.	0	0	0	0	0	1	1	1
2.	0	0	0	0	1	0	1	0
3.	0	0	0	0	1	1	0	1
4.	0	0	0	1	0	0	1	1
5.	0	0	0	1	0	1	0	0
6.	0	0	0	1	1	0	0	1
7.	0	0	0	1	1	1	1	0
8.	0	0	1	0	0	0	1	0

TABLE 8b—AUXILIARY DATA WORD ADDRESS CODES—Continued

No.	I_{13}	I_{14}	I_{15}	I_{16}	I_{17}	I_{18}	I_{19}	I_{20}
9.	0	0	1	0	0	1	0	1
10.	0	0	1	0	1	0	0	0
11.	0	0	1	0	1	0	1	1
12.	0	0	1	1	0	0	0	1
13.	0	0	1	1	0	1	1	0
14.	0	0	1	1	1	0	1	1
15.	0	0	1	1	1	1	0	0
16.	0	1	0	0	0	0	1	1
17.	0	1	0	0	0	1	0	0
18.	0	1	0	0	1	0	0	1
19.	0	1	0	0	1	1	1	0
20.	0	1	0	1	0	0	0	0
21.	0	1	0	1	0	1	1	1
22.	0	1	0	1	1	0	1	0
23.	0	1	0	1	1	1	0	1
24.	0	1	1	0	0	0	0	1
25.	0	1	1	0	0	1	1	0
26.	0	1	1	0	1	0	1	1
27.	0	1	1	0	1	1	0	0
28.	0	1	1	1	0	0	1	0
29.	0	1	1	1	0	1	0	1
30.	0	1	1	1	1	0	0	0
31.	0	1	1	1	1	1	1	1
32.	1	0	0	0	0	0	1	0
33.	1	0	0	0	0	1	0	1
34.	1	0	0	0	1	0	0	0
35.	1	0	0	0	1	1	1	1
36.	1	0	0	1	0	0	0	1
37.	1	0	0	1	0	1	1	0
38.	1	0	0	1	1	0	1	1
39.	1	0	0	1	1	1	0	0
40.	1	0	1	0	0	0	0	0

TABLE 8b—AUXILIARY DATA WORD ADDRESS CODES—Continued

No.	I_{13}	I_{14}	I_{15}	I_{16}	I_{17}	I_{18}	I_{19}	I_{20}
41.	1	0	1	0	0	1	1	1
42.	1	0	1	0	1	0	1	0
43.	1	0	1	0	1	1	0	1
44.	1	0	1	1	0	0	1	1
45.	1	0	1	1	0	1	0	0
46.	1	0	1	1	1	0	0	1
47.	1	0	1	1	1	1	1	0
48.	1	1	0	0	0	0	0	1
49.	1	1	0	0	0	1	1	0
50.	1	1	0	0	1	0	1	1
51.	1	1	0	0	1	1	0	0
52.	1	1	0	1	0	0	1	0
53.	1	1	0	1	0	1	0	1
54.	1	1	0	1	1	0	0	0
55.	1	1	0	1	1	1	1	1
56.	1	1	1	0	0	0	1	1
57.	1	1	1	0	0	1	0	0
58.	1	1	1	0	1	0	0	1
59.	1	1	1	0	1	1	1	0
60.	1	1	1	1	0	0	0	0
61.	1	1	1	1	0	1	1	1
62.	1	1	1	1	1	0	1	0
63.	1	1	1	1	1	1	0	1
64.	0	0	0	0	0	0	0	0

NOTE 1: Parity bits I_{19} and I_{20} are chosen to satisfy the equations:

$$I_{13} + I_{14} + I_{15} + I_{16} + I_{17} + I_{18} + I_{19} = \text{EVEN}$$
$$I_{14} + I_{16} + I_{18} + I_{20} = \text{EVEN}$$

TABLE 8C—AUXILIARY DATA

Word (See note 6)	Data content	Type of data	Maximum time between trans-missions (Seconds)	Bits used	Range of values	Least significant bit
A1	Preamble	Digital	1.0	12		
	Address			8		
	Approach azimuth antenna offset			10	−511 m to + 511 m (See note 3)	1 m
	Approach azimuth to MLS datum point distance.			13	0 m to 8 191 m	1 m
	Approach azimuth antenna alignment with runway centerline.			12	−20.47° to 20.47° (See note 3) ..	0.01°
	Approach azimuth antenna coordinate system.			1	(See note 2)	
	Spare			13		
	Parity			7	(See note 1)	
A2	Preamble	Digital	1.0	12		
	Address			8		
	Approach elevation antenna offset			10	−511 m to + 511 m (See note 3)	1 m
	MLS datum point to threshold distance			10	0 m to 1 023 m	1 m
	Approach elevation antenna height			7	−6.3 m to + 6.3 m (See note 3)	0.1 m
	Spare			22		
	Parity			7	(See note 1)	
A3	Preamble	Digital	(See note 4)	12		
	Address			8		
	DME offset			10	−511 m to + 511 m	1 m
	DME to MLS datum point distance			14	−8 191 m to + 8 191 m (See note 3).	1 m
	Spare			25		
	Parity			7	(See note 1)	
A4	Preamble	Digital	(See note 5)	12		
	Address			8		
	Back azimuth antenna			10	−511 m to + 511 m (See note 3)	1 m
	Back azimuth to MLS datum point distance			11	0 m to 2 047 m	1 m

TABLE 8C—AUXILIARY DATA—Continued

Word (See note 6)	Data content	Type of data	Maximun time between trans- missions (Seconds)	Bits used	Range of values	Least sig- nifi- cant bit
	Back azimuth antenna alignment with run- way centerline.	....	....	12	− 20.47° to 20.47° (See note 3) ..	0.01°
	Spare	....	....	16	....	....
	Parity	....	....	7	(See note 1)	....

NOTE 1: Parity bits I_{70} to I_{76} are chosen to satisfy the equations which follow:

For BIT I_{70}:
Even = $(I_{13} + ... + I_{18}) + I_{20} + I_{22} + I_{24} + I_{25} + I_{28} + I_{29} + I_{31} + I_{32} + I_{33} + I_{35} + I_{36} + I_{38} + L_{41} + L_{44} + L_{45} + L_{46} + I_{50} + (I_{52} + ... + I_{55}) + I_{58} + I_{60} + I_{64} + I_{65} + I_{70}$

For BIT I_{71}:
Even = $(I_{14} + ... + I_{19}) + I_{21} + I_{23} + I_{25} + I_{26} + I_{29} + I_{30} + I_{32} + I_{33} + I_{34} + I_{36} + I_{37} + I_{39} + I_{42} + L_{45} + L_{46} + L_{47} + I_{51} + (I_{53} + ... + I_{56}) + I_{59} + I_{61} + I_{65} + I_{66} + I_{71}$

For BIT I_{72}:
Even = $(I_{15} + ... + I_{20}) + I_{22} + I_{24} + I_{26} + I_{27} + I_{30} + I_{31} + I_{33} + I_{34} + I_{35} + I_{37} + I_{38} + L_{40} + L_{43} + L_{46} + L_{47} + L_{48} + I_{52} + (I_{54} + ... + I_{57}) + I_{60} + I_{62} + I_{66} + I_{67} + I_{72}$

For BIT I_{73}:
Even = $(I_{16} + ... + I_{21}) + I_{23} + I_{25} + I_{27} + I_{28} + I_{31} + I_{32} + I_{34} + I_{35} + I_{36} + I_{38} + I_{39} + L_{41} + L_{44} + L_{47} + L_{48} + L_{49} + I_{53} + (I_{55} + ... + I_{58}) + I_{61} + I_{63} + I_{67} + I_{68} + I_{73}$

For BIT I_{74}:
Even = $(I_{17} + ... + I_{22}) + I_{24} + I_{26} + I_{28} + I_{29} + I_{32} + I_{33} + I_{35} + I_{36} + I_{37} + I_{39} + L_{40} + L_{42} + L_{45} + L_{48} + L_{49} + I_{50} + I_{54} + (I_{56} + ... + I_{59}) + I_{62} + I_{64} + I_{68} + I_{69} + I_{74}$

For BIT I_{75}:
Even = $(I_{13} + ... + I_{17}) + I_{19} + I_{21} + I_{23} + I_{24} + I_{27} + I_{28} + I_{30} + I_{31} + I_{32} + I_{34} + I_{35} + I_{37} + L_{40} + L_{43} + L_{44} + L_{45} + L_{49} + (I_{51} + ... + I_{54}) + I_{57} + I_{59} + I_{63} + I_{64} + I_{69} + I_{75}$

For BIT I_{76}:
Even = $I_{13} + I_{14} + ... + I_{75} + I_{76}$

NOTE 2: Code for I_{56} is: 0 = conical; 1 = planar.

NOTE 3: The convention for the coding of negative numbers is as follows: − MSB is the sign bit; 0 = + ; 1 = −.

—Other bits represent the absolute value.

The convention for the antenna location is as follows: As viewed from the MLS approach reference datum looking toward the datum point, a positive number shall represent a lo- cation to the right of the runway centerline (lateral offset) or above the runway (vertical offset), or towards the stop end of the run- way (longitudinal distance).

The convention for the antenna alignment is as follows: As viewed from above, a posi- tive number shall represent clockwise rota- tion from the runway centerline to the re- spective zero-degree guidance plane.

NOTE 4: Data Word A3 is transmitted at in- tervals of 1.0 seconds or less throughout the approach Azimuth coverage sector, except when back Azimuth guidance is provided. Where back Azimuth is provided transmit at intervals of 1.33 seconds or less throughout the approach Azimuth sector and 4.0 seconds or less throughout the back Azimuth cov- erage sector.

NOTE 5: When back Azimuth guidance is provided, transmit at intervals of 1.33 sec- onds or less throughout the back Azimuth coverage sector and 4.0 seconds or less throughout the approach Azimuth coverage sector.

NOTE 6: The designation "A1" represents the function identification code for "Auxil- iary Data A" and address code number 1.

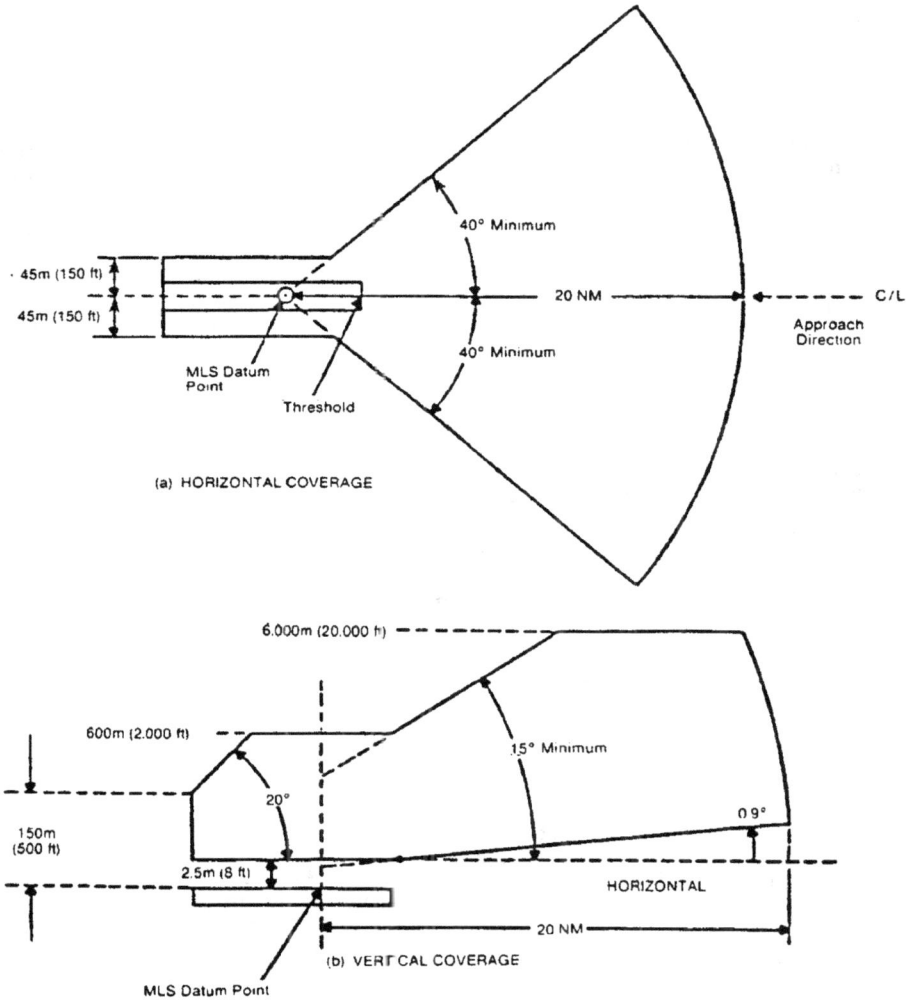

Figure 9. Approach Azimuth/Data Coverage

(1) Horizontally within a sector plus or minus 40 degrees about the runway centerline originating at the datum point and extending in the direction of the approach to 20 nautical miles from the runway threshold. The minimum proportional guidance sector must be plus or minus 10 degrees about the runway centerline. Clearance signals must be used to provide the balance of the required coverage, where the proportional sector is less than plus or minus 40 degrees. When intervening obstacles prevent full coverage, the ±40° guidance sector can be reduced as required. For systems providing ±60° lateral guidance

867

the coverage requirement is reduced to 14 nm beyond ±40°.

(2) Vertically between:

(i) A conical surface originating 2.5 meters (8 feet) above the runway centerline at threshold inclined at 0.9 degree above the horizontal.

(ii) A conical surface originating at the azimuth ground equipment antenna inclined at 15 degrees above the horizontal to a height of 6,000 meters (20,000 feet).

(iii) Where intervening obstacles penetrate the lower surface, coverage need be provided only to the minimum line of sight.

(3) Runway region:

(i) Proportional guidance horizontally within a sector 45 meters (150 feet) each side of the runway centerline beginning at the stop end and extending parallel with the runway centerline in the direction of the approach to join the approach region. This requirement does not apply to offset azimuth installations.

(ii) Vertically between a horizontal surface which is 2.5 meters (8 feet) above the farthest point of runway centerline which is in line of sight of the azimuth antenna, and in a conical surface originating at the azimuth ground equipment antenna inclined at 20 degrees above the horizontal up to a height to 600 meters (2,000 feet). This requirement does not apply to offset azimuth installations.

(4) Within the approach azimuth coverage sector defined in paragraphs (a) (1), and (2) and (3) of this section, the power densities must not be less than those shown in Table 9 but the equipment design must also allow for:

(i) Transmitter power degradation from normal by −1.5 dB;

TABLE 9—MINIMUM POWER DENSITY WITHIN COVERAGE BOUNDARIES(DBW/M²)

Function	Data signals	Angle signals for various antenna beamwidths				Clearance signals
		1°	1.5°	2°	3°	
Approach azimuth	−89.5	−88	....	−85.5	−82	−88
High rate approach azimuth	−89.5	−88	....	−88	−86.5	−88
Back azimuth	−89.5	−88	....	−85.5	−82	−88
Approach elevation	−89.5	−88	−88	−88	....	....

(ii) Rain loss of −2.2 dB at the longitudinal coverage extremes.

(b) *Siting requirements.* The approach azimuth antenna system must, except as allowed in paragraph (c) of this section:

(1) Be located on the extension of the centerline of the runway beyond the stop end;

(2) Be adjusted so that the zero degree azimuth plane will be a vertical plane which contains the centerline of the runway served;

(3) Have the minimum height necessary to comply with the coverage requirements prescribed in paragraph (a) of this section;

(4) Be located at a distance from the stop end of the runway that is consistent with safe obstruction clearance practices;

(5) Not obscure any light of an approach lighting system; and

(6) Be installed on frangible mounts or beyond the 300 meter (1,000 feet) light bar.

(c) On runways where limited terrain prevents the azimuth antenna from being positioned on the runway centerline extended, and the cost of the land fill or a tall tower antenna support is prohibitive, the azimuth antenna may be offset.

(d) *Antenna coordinates.* The scanning beams transmitted by the approach azimuth equipment within ±40° of the centerline may be either conical or planar.

(e) *Approach azimuth accuracy.* (1) The system and subsystem errors shall not exceed those listed in Table 10 at the approach reference datum.

At the approach reference datum, temporal sinusoidal noise components shall not exceed 0.025 degree peak in the frequency band 0.01 Hz to 1.6 Hz, and the CMN shall not exceed 0.10 degree. From the approach reference datum to the coverage limit, the PFE, PFN and CMN limits, expressed in angular terms, shall be allowed to linearly increase as follows:

(i) With distance along the runway centerline extended, by a factor of 1.2 for the PFE and PFN limits and to ±0.10 degree for the CMN limits.

(ii) With azimuth angle, by a factor of 1.5 at the ±40 degree and a factor of 2.0 at the ±60 degree azimuth angles for the PFE, PFN and CMN limits.

(iii) With elevation angle from + 9 degrees to + 15 degrees, by a factor of 1.5 for the PFE and PFN limits.

(iv) Maximum angular limits. The PFE limits shall not exceed ±0.25 degree in any coverage region below an elevation angle of + 9 degrees nor exceed ±0.50 degree in any coverage region above that elevation angle. The CMN limits shall not exceed ±0.10 degree in any coverage region within ±10 degrees of runway centerline extended nor exceed ±0.20 degree in any other region within coverage.

NOTE: It is desirable that the CMN not exceed ±0.10 degree throughout the coverage.

(f) Approach azimuth antenna characteristics are as follows:

(1) *Drift.* Any azimuth angle as encoded by the scanning beam at any point within the proportional coverage must not vary more than ±0.07 degree over the range of service conditions specified in § 171.309(d) without the use of internal environmental controls. Multipath effects are excluded from this requirement.

(2) *Beam pointing errors.* The azimuth angle as encoded by the scanning beam at any point within ±0.5 degree of the zero degree azimuth must not deviate from the true azimuth angle at that point by more than ±.05 degree. Multipath and drift effects are excluded from this requirement.

TABLE 10—APPROACH AZIMUTH ACCURACIES AT THE APPROACH REFERENCE DATUM

Error type	System	Angular error (degrees)	
		Ground subsystem	Airborne subsystem
PFE	±20 ft. (6.1m) [1][2]	±0.118° [3] ..	±0.017°
CMN	±10.5 ft. (3.2m) [1][2][4]	±0.030°	±0.050°

Notes:
[1] Includes errors due to ground and airborne equipment and propagation effects.

[2] The system PFN component must not exceed ±3.5 meters (11.5 feet).
[3] The mean (bias) error component contributed by the ground equipment should not exceed ±10 feet.
[4] The system control motion noise must not exceed 0.1 degree.
[5] The airborne subsystem angular errors are provided for information only.

(3) *Antenna alignment.* The antenna must be equipped with suitable optical, electrical or mechanical means or any combination of the three, to bring the zero degree azimuth radial into coincidence with the approach reference datum (for centerline siting) with a maximum error of 0.02 degree. Additionally, the azimuth antenna bias adjustment must be electronically steerable at least to the monitor limits in steps not greater than 0.005 degree.

(4) *Antenna far field patterns in the plane of scan.* On boresight, the azimuth antenna mainlobe pattern must conform to Figure 10, and the beamwidth must be such that, in the installed environment, no significant lateral reflections of the mainlobe exist along the approach course. In any case the beamwidth must not exceed three degrees. Anywhere within coverage the −3 dB width of the antenna mainlobe, while scanning normally, must not be less than 25 microseconds (0.5 degree) or greater than 250 microseconds (5 degrees). The antenna mainlobe may be allowed to broaden from the value at boresight by a factor of 1/cosθ, where θ is the angle off boresight. The sidelobe levels must be as follows:

(i) *Dynamic sidelobe levels.* With the antenna scanning normally, the dynamic sidelobe level that is detected by a receiver at any point within the proportional coverage sector must be down at least 10 dB from the peak of the main beam. Outside the coverage sector, the radiation from the scanning beam antenna must be of such a nature that receiver warning will not be removed or suitable OCI signals must be provided.

(ii) *Effective sidelobe levels.* With the antenna scanning normally, the sidelobe levels in the plane of scan must be such that, in the installed environment, the CMN contributed by sidelobe reflections will not exceed the angular equivalent of 9 feet at approach reference datum over the required range of aircraft approach speeds.

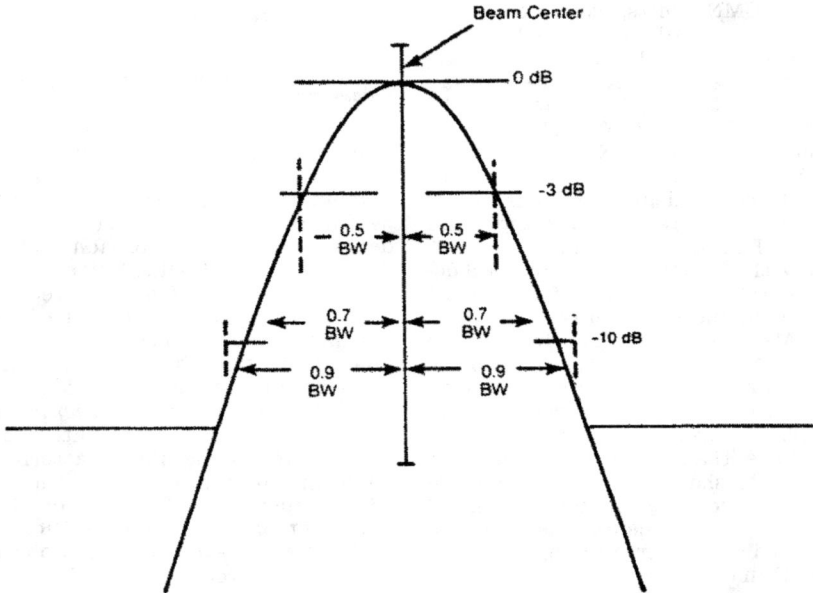

NOTES: 1. The beam envelope is smoothed by a 26 kHz video filter
          before measurement.
       2. BW = Beamwidth.

Figure 10. Far Field Dynamic Signal in Space

(5) *Antenna far field pattern in the vertical plane.* The azimuth antenna free space radiation pattern below the horizon must have a slope of at least −8 dB/degree at the horizon and all sidelobes below the horizon must be at least 13 dB below the pattern peak. The antenna radiation pattern above the horizon must satisfy both the system coverage requirements and the spurious radiation requirement.

(6) *Data antenna.* The data antenna must have horizontal and vertical patterns as required for its function.

(g) *Back azimuth coverage requirements.* The back azimuth equipment where used must provide guidance information in at least the following volume of space (see Figure 11):

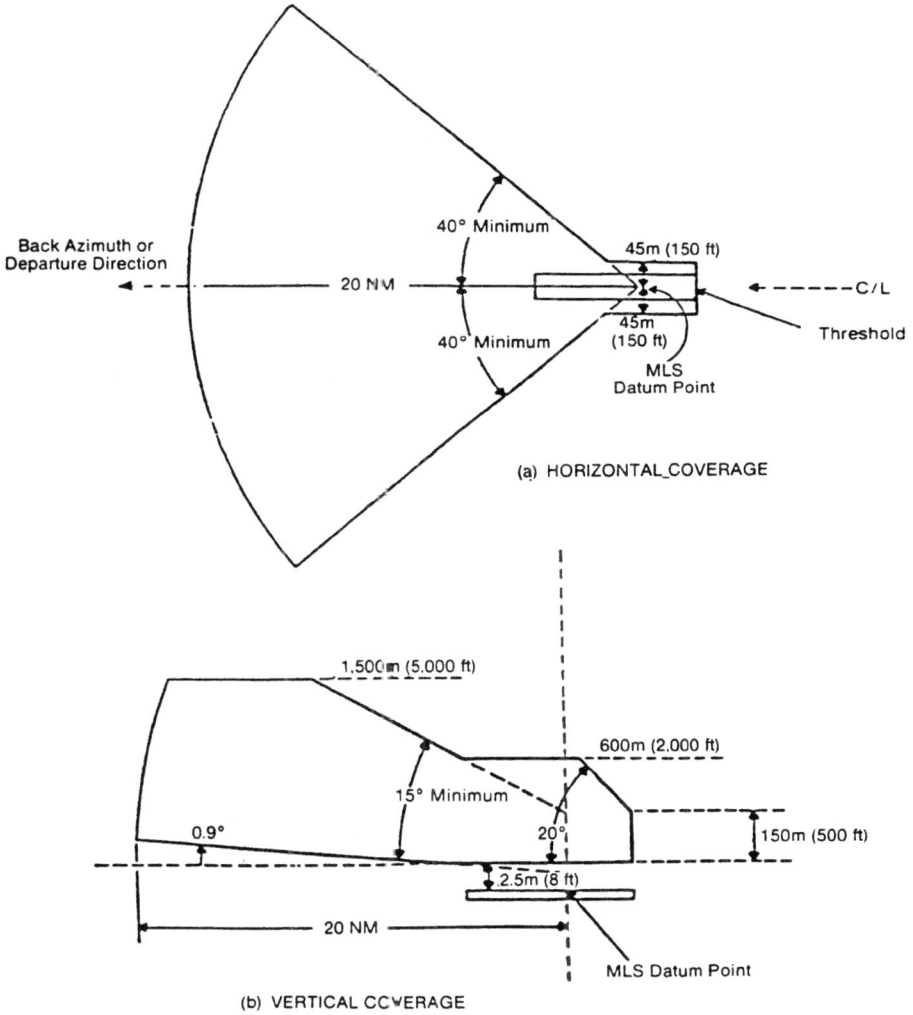

(a) HORIZONTAL COVERAGE

(b) VERTICAL COVERAGE

Figure 11.   Back Azimuth/Data Coverage

(1) Horizontally within a sector ±40 degrees about the runway centerline originating at the back azimuth ground equipment antenna and extending in the direction of the missed approach at least to 20 nautical miles from the runway stop end. The minimum proportional guidance sector must be ±10 degrees about the runway centerline. Clearance signals must be

871

used to provide the balance of the required coverage where the proportional sector is less than ±40 degrees.

(2) Vertically in the runway region between:

(i) A horizontal surface 2.5 meters (8 feet) above the farthest point of runway centerline which is in line of sight of the azimuth antenna, and,

(ii) A conical surface originating at the azimuth ground equipment antenna inclined at 20 degrees above the horizontal up to a height of 600 meters (2000 feet).

(3) Vertically in the back azimuth region between:

(i) A conical surface originating 2.5 meters (8 feet) above the runway stop end, included at 0.9 degree above the horizontal, and,

(ii) A conical surface orginating at the missed approach azimuth ground equipment antenna, inclined at 15 degrees above the horizontal up to a height of 1500 meters (5000 feet).

(iii) Where obstacles penetrate the lower coverage limits, coverage need be provided only to minimum line of sight.

(4) Within the back azimuth coverage sector defined in paragraph (q) (1), (2), and (3) of this section the power densities must not be less than those shown in Table 9, but the equipment design must also allow for:

(i) Transmitter power degradation from normal −1.5 dB.

(ii) Rain loss of −2.2 dB at the longitudinal coverage extremes.

(h) *Back azimuth siting.* The back azimuth equipment antenna must:

(1) Normally be located on the extension of the runway centerline at the threshold end;

(2) Be adjusted so that the vertical plane containing the zero degree course line contains the back azimuth reference datum;

(3) Have minimum height necessary to comply with the course requirements prescribed in paragraph (g) of this section;

(4) Be located at a distance from the threshold end that is consistent with safe obstruction clearance practices;

(5) Not obscure any light of an approach lighting system; and

(6) Be installed on frangible mounts or beyond the 300 meter (1000 feet) light bar.

(i) *Back azimuth antenna coordinates.* The scanning beams transmitted by the back azimuth equipment may be either conical or planar.

(j) *Back azimuth accuracy.* The requirements specified in § 171.313(e) apply except that the reference point is the back azimuth reference datum.

(k) *Back azimuth antenna characteristics.* The requirements specified in § 171.313(f) apply.

(1) *Scanning conventions.* Figure 12 shows the approach azimuth and back azimuth scanning conventions.

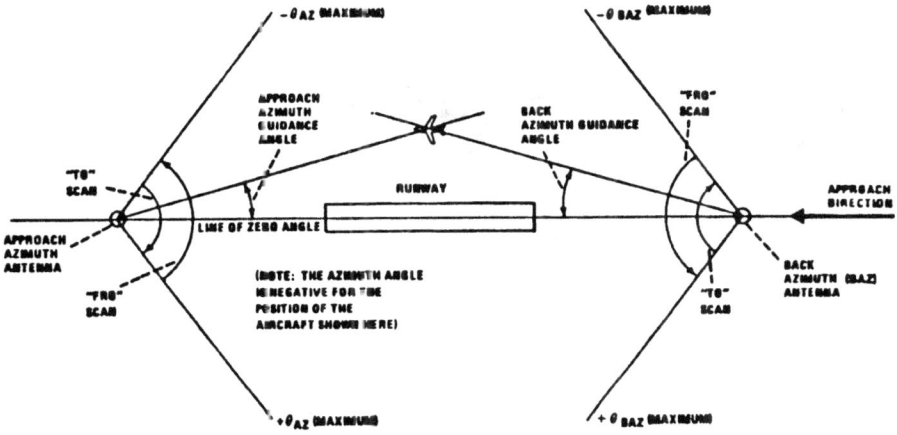

Figure 12. Azimuth Guidance Functions Scanning Conventions

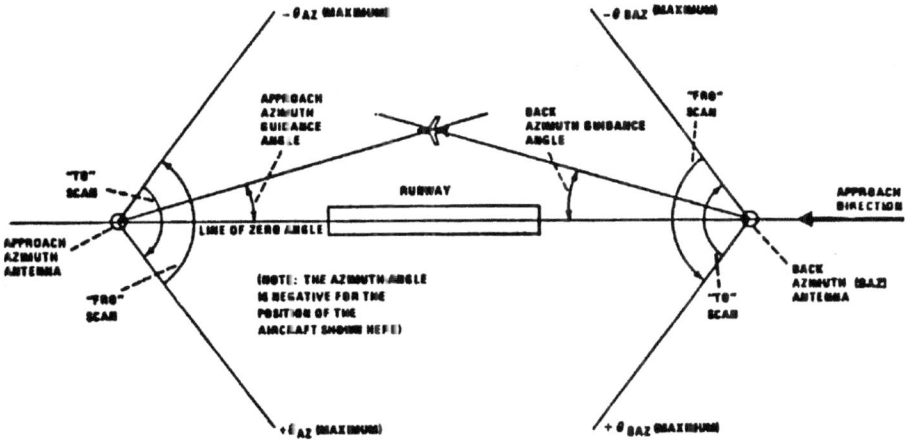

Figure 12. Azimuth Guidance Functions Scanning Conventions

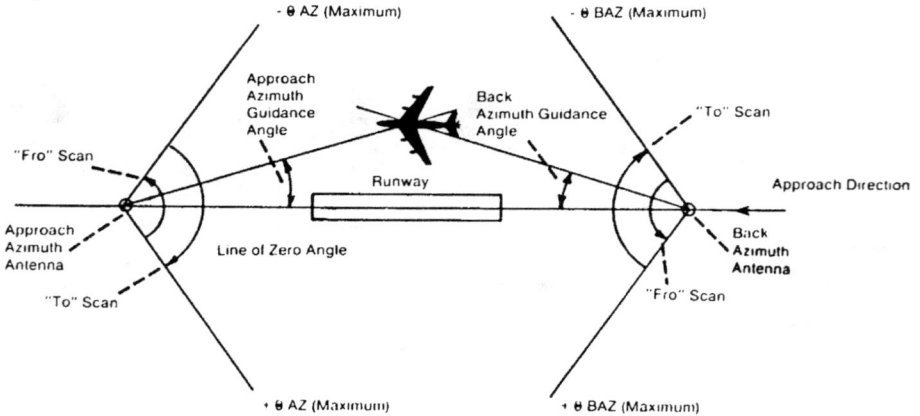

Figure 12.   Azimuth Guidance Functions Scanning Conventions

(m) *False guidance.* False courses which can be acquired and tracked by an aircraft shall not exist anywhere either inside or outside of the MLS coverage sector. False courses which exist outside of the minimum coverage sector may be suppressed by the use of OCI.

NOTE: False courses may be due to (but not limited to) MLS airborne receiver acquisition of the following types of false guidance: reflections of the scanning beam, scanning beam antenna sidelobes and grating lobes, and incorrect clearance.

§ 171.315 Azimuth monitor system requirements.

(a) The approach azimuth or back azimuth monitor system must cause the radiation to cease and a warning must be provided at the designated control point if any of the following conditions persist for longer than the periods specified:

(1) There is a change in the ground equipment contribution to the mean course error component such that the path following error at the reference datum or in the direction of any azimuth radial, exceeds the limits specified in §§ 171.313(e)(1) or 171.313(j) for a period of more than one second.

NOTE: The above requirement and the requirement to limit the ground equipment mean error to ±10 ft. can be satisfied by the following procedure. The integral monitor alarm limit should be set to the angular equivalent of ±10 ft. at the approach reference datum. This will limit the electrical component of the mean course error to ±10 ft. The field monitor alarm limit should be set such that with the mean course error at the alarm limit the total allowed PFE is not exceeded on any commissioned approach course from the limit of coverage to an altitude of 100 feet.

(2) There are errors in two consecutive transmissions of Basic Data Words 1, 2, 4 or 5.

(3) There is a reduction in the radiated power to a level not less than that specified in §§ 171.313(a)(4) or 171.313(g)(4) for a period of more than one second.

(4) There is an error in the preamble DPSK transmissions which occurs more than once in any one second period.

(5) There is an error in the time division multiplex synchronization of a particular azimuth function that the requirement specified in § 171.311(e) is not satisfied and if this condition persists for more than one second.

(6) A failure of the monitor is detected.

(b) Radiation of the following fuctions must cease and a warning provided at the designated control point if there are errors in 2 consecutive transmissions:

(1) Morse Code Identification,

(2) Basic Data Words 3 and 6,

(3) Auxiliary Data Words.

(c) The period during which erroneous guidance information is radiated must not exceed the periods specified in §171.315(a). If the fault is not cleared within the time allowed, the ground equipment must be shut down. After shutdown, no attempt must be made to restore service until a period of 20 seconds has elapsed.

§171.317 Approach elevation performance requirements.

This section prescribes the performance requirements for the elevation equipment components of the MLS as follows:

(a) *Elevation coverage requirements.* The approach elevation facility must provide proportional guidance information in at least the following volume of space (see Figure 13):

(1) Laterally within a sector originating at the datum point which is at least equal to the proportional guidance sector provided by the approach azimuth ground equipment.

(2) Longitudinally from 75 meters (250 feet) from the datum point to 20 nautical miles from threshold in the direction of the approach.

(3) Vertically within the sector bounded by:

(i) A surface which is the locus of points 2.5 meters (8 feet) above the runway surface;

(ii) A conical surface originating at the datum point and inclined 0.9 degree above the horizontal and,

(iii) A conical surface originating at the datum point and inclined at 15.0 degrees above the horizontal up to a height of 6000 meters (20,000 feet).

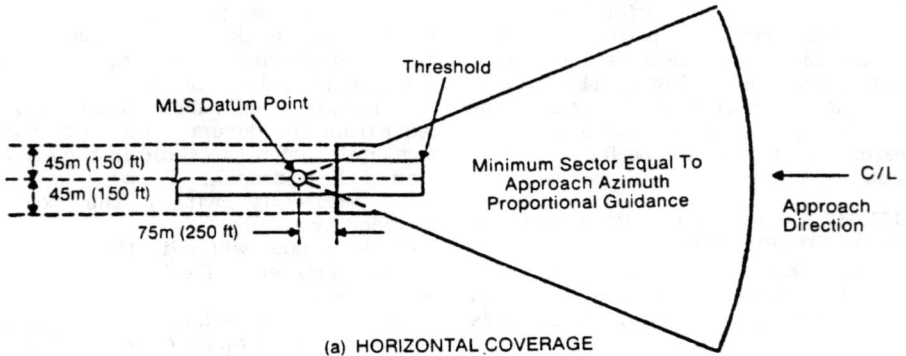

(a) HORIZONTAL COVERAGE

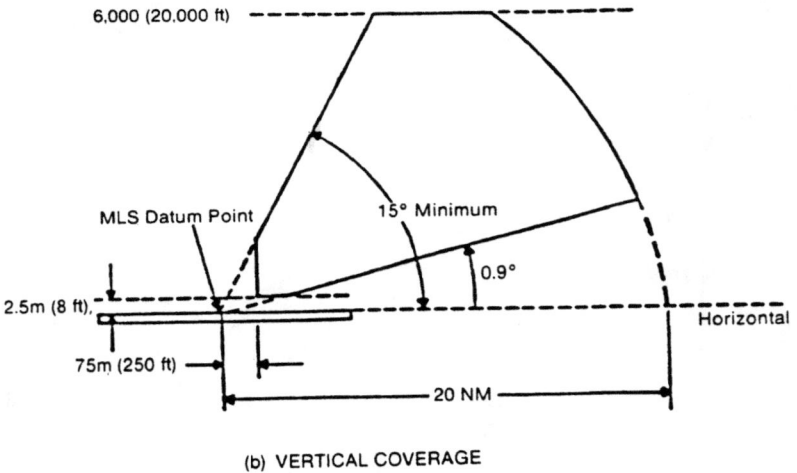

(b) VERTICAL COVERAGE

Figure 13. Approach Elevation Coverage

Where the physical characteristics of the approach region prevent theachievement of the standards under paragraphs (a) (1), (2), and (3) of this section, guidance need not be provided below a conical surface originating at the elevation antenna and inclined 0.9 degree above the line of sight.

(4) Within the elevation coverage sector defined in paragraphs (a) (1), (2) and (3) of this section, the power densities must not be less than those shown in Table 9, but the equipment design must also allow for:

(i) Transmitter power degradation from normal by −1.5 dB.

(ii) Rain loss of −2.2 dB at the coverage extremes.

(b) *Elevation siting requirements.* The Elevation Antenna System must:

(1) Be located as close to runway centerline as possible (without violating obstacle clearance criteria).

(2) Be located near runway threshold such that the asymptote of the minimum glidepath crosses the threshold of the runway at the Approach Reference Datum height. Normally, the minimum glidepath should be 3 degrees and the Approach Reference Datum height should be 50 feet. However, there are circumstances where other glideslopes and reference datum heights are appropriate. Some of these instances are discussed in FAA Order 8260.34 (Glide Slope Threshold Crossing Height Requirements) and Order 8260.3 (IFR Approval of MLS.)

(3) Be located such that the MLS Approach Reference Datum and ILS Reference Datum heights are coincident within a tolerance of 3 feet when MLS is installed on a runway already served by an ILS. This requirement applies only if the ILS glide slope is sited such that the height of the reference datum meets the requirements of FAA Order 8260.34.

(c) *Antenna coordinates.* The scanning beams transmitted by the elevation subsystem must be conical.

(d) *Elevation accuracy.* (1) The accuracies shown in Table 13 are required at the approach reference datum. From the approach reference datum to the coverage limit, the PFE, PFN and CMN limits shall be allowed to linearly increase as follows:

(i) With distance along the runway centerline extended at the minimum glide path angle, by a factor of 1.2 for the PFE and PFN limits and to ±0.10 degree for the CMN limits;

(ii) With azimuth angle, from runway centerline extended to the coverage extreme, by a factor of 1.2 for the PFE

and PFN limits and by a factor of 2.0 for the CMN limits;

(iii) With increasing elevation angles from + 3 degrees to + 15 degrees, by a factor of 2.0 for the PFE and PFN limits;

TABLE 13—ELEVATION ACCURACIES AT THE APPROACH REFERENCE DATUM

| Error type | System | Angular error (degrees) | |
		Ground subsystem	Airborne subsystem [4]
PFE	[1] [2] ±0.133	([3])	±0.017
CMN	[1]±0.050	±0.020	±0.010

Notes:

[1] Includes errors due to ground and airborne equipment and propagation effects.

[2] The system PFN component must not exceed ±0.087 degree.

[3] The mean (bias) error component contributed by the ground equipment should not exceed ±0.067 degree.

[4] The airborne subsystem angular errors are provided for information only.

(iv) With decreasing elevation angle from + 3 degrees (or 60% of the minimum glide path angle, whichever is less) to the coverage extreme, by a factor of 3 for the PFE, PFN and CMN limits; and

(v) Maximum angular limits. the CMN limits shall not exceed ±0.10 degree in any coverage region within ±10 degrees laterally of runway centerline extended which is above the elevation angle specified in (iv) above.

NOTE: It is desirable that the CMN not exceed ±0.10 degree throughout the coverage region above the elevation angle specified in paragraph (d)(1)(iv) of this section.

(2) The system and ground subsystem accuracies shown in Table 13 are to be demonstrated at commissioning as maximum error limits. Subsequent to commissioning, the accuracies are to be considered at 95% probability limits.

(e) Elevation antenna characteristics are as follows:

(1) *Drift.* Any elevation angle as encoded by the scanning beam at any point within the coverage sector must not vary more than 0.04 degree over the range of service conditions specified in § 171.309(d) without the use of internal environmental controls. Multipath effects are excluded from this requirement.

(2) *Beam pointing errors.* The elevation angle as encoded by the scanning beam at any point within the coverage sector

must not deviate from the true elevation angle at that point by more than ±0.04 degree for elevation angles from 2.5° to 3.5°. Above 3.5° these errors may linearly increase to ±0.1 degree at 7.5°. Multipath and drift effects are excluded from this requirement.

(3) *Antenna alignment*. The antenna must be equipped with suitable optical, electrical, or mechanical means or any combination of the three, to align the lowest operationally required glidepath to the true glidepath angle with a maximum error of 0.01 degree. Additionally, the elevation antenna bias adjustment must be electronically steerable at least to the monitor limits in steps not greater than 0.005 degrees.

(4) *Antenna far field patterns in the plane of scan*. On the lowest operationally required glidepath, the antenna mainlobe pattern must conform to Figure 10, and the beamwidth must be such that in the installed environment, no significant ground reflections of the mainlobe exist. In any case, the beamwidth must not exceed 2 degrees. The antenna mainlobe may be allowed to broaden from the value at boresight by a factor of 1/cosθ, where θ is the angle of boresight. Anywhere within coverage, the −3 dB width of the antenna mainlobe, while scanning normally, must not be less than 25 microseconds (0.5 degrees) or greater than 250 microseconds (5 degrees). The sidelobe levels must be as follows:

(i) *Dynamic sidelobe levels*. With the antenna scanning normally, the dynamic sidelobe level that is detected by a receiver at any point within the proportional coverage sector must be down at least 10 dB from the peak of the mainlobe. Outside the proportional coverage sector, the radiation from the scanning beam antenna must be of such a nature that receiver warnings will not be removed or a suitable OCI signal must be provided.

(ii) *Effective sidelobe levels*. With the antenna scanning normally, the sidelobe levels in the plane of scan must be such that, when reflected from the ground, the resultant PFE along any glidepath does not exceed 0.083 degrees.

(5) *Antenna far field pattern in the horizontal plane*. The horizontal pattern of the antenna must gradually de-empha-

size the signal away from antenna boresight. Typically, the horizontal pattern should be reduced by at least 3 dB at 20 degrees off boresight and by at least 6 dB at 40 degrees off boresight. Depending on the actual multipath conditions, the horizontal radiation patterns may require more or less de-emphasis.

(6) *Data antenna*. The data antenna must have horizontal and vertical patterns as required for its function.

(f) *False guidance*. False courses which can be acquired and tracked by an aircraft shall not exist anywhere either inside or outside of the MLS coverage sector. False courses which exist outside of the minimum coverage sector may be suppressed by the use of OCI.

NOTE: False courses may be due to (but not limited to) MLS airborne receiver acquisition of the following types of false guidance: reflections of the scanning beam and scanning beam antenna sidelobes and grating lobes.

§ 171.319 Approach elevation monitor system requirements.

(a) The monitor system must act to ensure that any of the following conditions do not persist for longer than the periods specified when:

(1) There is a change in the ground component contribution to the mean glidepath error component such that the path following error on any glidepath exceeds the limits specified in § 171.317(d) for a period of more than one second.

NOTE: The above requirement and the requirement to limit the ground equipment mean error to ±0.067 degree can be satisfied by the following procedure. The integral monitor alarm limit should be set to ±0.067 degree. This will limit the electrical component of mean glidepath error to ±0.067 degree. The field monitor alarm limit should be set such that with the mean glidepath error at the alarm limit the total allowed PFE is not exceeded on any commissioned glidepath from the limit of coverage to an altitude of 100 feet.

(2) There is a reduction in the radiated power to a level not less than that specified in § 171.317(a)(4) for a period of more than one second.

(3) There is an error in the preamble DPSK transmission which occurs more than once in any one second period.

(4) There is an error in the time division multiplex synchronization of a particular elevation function such that the requirement specified in § 171 311(e) is not satisfied and this condition persists for more than one second.

(5) A failure of the monitor is detected.

(b) The period during which erroneous guidance information is radiated must not exceed the periods specified in § 171.319(a). If the fault is not cleared within the time allowed, radiation shall cease. After shutdown, no attempt must be made to restore service until a period of 20 seconds has elapsed.

§ 171.321 DME and marker beacon performance requirements.

(a) The DME equipment must meet the performance requirements prescribed in subpart G of the part. This subpart imposes requirements that performance features must comply with International Standards and Recommended Practices, Aeronautical Telecommunications, Vol. I of Annex 10 to ICAO. It is available from ICAO, Aviation Building, 1080 University Street, Montreal 101, Quebec, Canada, Attention: Distribution Officer and also available for inspection at the National Archives and Records Administration (NARA). For information on the availability of this material at NARA, call 202–741–6030, or go to: *http://www.archives.gov/federal_register/code_of_federal_regulations/ibr_locations.html.*

(b) MLS marker beacon equipment must meet the performance requirements prescribed in subpart H of this part. This subpart imposes requirements that performance features must comply with International Standards and Recommended Practices, Aeronautical Telecommuncations, Vol. I of Annex 10 to ICAO.

[Doc. No. 5034, 29 FR 11337, Aug. 6, 1964, as amended at 69 FR 18803, Apr. 9, 2004]

§ 171.323 Fabrication and installation requirements.

(a) The MLS facility must be permanent and must be located, constructed, and installed in accordance with best commercial engineering practices, using applicable electric and safety codes and Federal Communications Commission (FCC) licensing requirements and siting requirements of §§ 171.313(b) and 171.317(b).

(b) The MLS facility components must utilize solid state technology except that traveling wave tube amplifiers (TWTA) may be used. A maximum level of common modularity must be provided along with diagnostics to facilitate maintenance and trouble-shooting.

(c) An approved monitoring capability must be provided which indicates the status of the equipment at the site and at a remotely located maintenance area, with monitor capability that provides pre-alarm of impending system failures. This monitoring feature must be capable of transmitting the status and pre-alarm over standard phone lines to a remote section. In the event the sponsor requests the FAA to assume ownership of the facility, the monitoring feature must also be capable of interfacing with FAA remote monitoring requirements. This requirement may be complied with by the addition of optional software and/or hardware in space provided in the original equipment.

(d) The mean corrective maintenance time of the MLS equipment must be equal to or less than 0.5 hours with a maximum corrective maintenance time not to exceed 1.5 hours. This measure applies to correction of unscheduled failures of the monitor, transmitter and associated antenna assemblies, limited to unscheduled outage and out of tolerance conditions.

(e) The mean-time-between-failures of the MLS angle system must not be less than 1,500 hours. This measure applies to unscheduled outage, out-of-tolerance conditions, and failures of the monitor, transmitter, and associated antenna assemblies.

(f) The MLS facility must have a reliable source of suitable primary power, either from a power distribution system or locally generated. Adequate power capacity must be provided for the operation of the MLS as well as the test and working equipment of the MLS.

(g) The MLS facility must have a continuously engaged or floating battery power source for the continued normal operation of the ground station operation if the primary power fails. A trickle charge must be supplied to recharge the batteries during the period of available primary power. Upon loss and subsequent restoration of power, the battery must be restored to full charge within 24 hours. When primary power is applied, the state of the battery charge must not affect the operation of the MLS ground station. The battery must allow continuation of normal operation of the MLS facility for at least 2 hours without the use of additional sources of power. When the system is operating from the battery supply without prime power, the radome deicers and the environmental system need not operate. The equipment must meet all specification requirements with or without batteries installed.

(h) There must be a means for determining, from the ground, the performance of the system including antenna, both initially and periodically.

(i) The facility must have, or be supplemented by, ground, air, or landline communications services. At facilities within or immediately adjacent to controlled airspace, that are intended for use as instrument approach aids for an airport, there must be ground air communications or reliable communications (at least a landline telephone) from the airport to the nearest FAA air traffic control or communication facility. Compliance with this paragraph need not be shown at airports where an adjacent FAA facility can communicate with aircraft on the ground at the airport and during the entire proposed instrument approach procedure. In addition, at low traffic density airports within or immediately adjacent to controlled airspace, and where extensive delays are not a factor, the requirements of this paragraph may be reduced to reliable communications from the airport to the nearest FAA air traffic control or communications facility. If the adjacent FAA facility can communicate with aircraft during the proposed instrument approach procedure down to the airport surface or at least down to the minimum en route altitude, this would require at least a landline telephone.

(j) The location of the phase center for all antennas must be clearly marked on the antenna enclosures.

(k) The latitude, longitude and mean sea level elevation of all MLS antennas, runway threshold and runway stop end must be determined by survey with an accuracy of ±3 meters (±10 feet) laterally and ±0.3 meter (±1.0 foot) vertically. The relative lateral and vertical offsets of all antenna phase centers, and both runway ends must be determined with an accuracy of ±0.3 meter (±1.0 foot) laterally and ±0.03 meter (±0.1 foot) vertically. The owner must bear all costs of the survey. The results of this survey must be included in the "operations and maintenance" manual required by section 171.325 of this subpart and will be noted on FAA Form 198 required by § 171.327.

[Doc. No. 20669, 51 FR 33177, Sept. 18, 1986, as amended by Amdt. 171–16, 56 FR 65665, Dec. 17, 1991]

§ 171.325 Maintenance and operations requirements.

(a) The owner of the facility must establish an adequate maintenance system and provide MLS qualified maintenance personnel to maintain the facility at the level attained at the time it was commissioned. Each person who maintains a facility must meet the FCC licensing requirements and demonstrate that he has the special knowledge and skills needed to maintain an MLS facility, including proficiency in maintenance procedures and the use of specialized test equipment.

(b) In the event of out-of-tolerance conditions or malfunctions, as evidenced by receiving two successive pilot reports, the owner must close the facility by encasing radiation, and issue a "Notice to Airmen" (NOTAM) that the facility is out of service.

(c) The owner must prepare, and obtain approval of, an operations and maintenance manual that sets forth mandatory procedures for operations, periodic maintenance, and emergency maintenance, including instructions on each of the following:

(1) Physical security of the facility.

(2) Maintenance and operations by authorized persons.

(3) FCC licensing requirements for operations and maintenance personnel.

(4) Posting of licenses and signs.

(5) Relations between the facility and FAA air traffic control facilities, with a description of the boundaries of controlled airspace over or near the facility, instructions for relaying air traffic control instructions and information, if applicable, and instructions for the operation of an air traffic advisory service if the facility is located outside of controlled airspace.

(6) Notice to the Administrator of any suspension of service.

(7) Detailed and specific maintenance procedures and servicing guides stating the frequency of servicing.

(8) Air-ground communications, if provided, expressly written or incorporating appropriate sections of FAA manuals by reference.

(9) Keeping the station logs and other technical reports, and the submission of reports required by §171.327.

(10) Monitoring of the MLS facility.

(11) Inspections by United States personnel.

(12) Names, addresses, and telephone numbers of persons to be notified in an emergency.

(13) Shutdowns for periodic maintenance and issuing of NOTAM for routine or emergency shutdowns.

(14) Commissioning of the MLS facility.

(15) An acceptable procedure for amending or revising the manual.

(16) An explanation of the kinds of activities (such as construction or grading) in the vicinity of the MLS facility that may require shutdown or recertification of the MLS facility by FAA flight check.

(17) Procedures for conducting a ground check of the azimuth and elevation alignment.

(18) The following information concerning the MLS facility:

(i) Facility component locations with respect to airport layout, instrument runways, and similar areas.

(ii) The type, make and model of the basic radio equipment that provides the service including required test equipment.

(iii) The station power emission, channel, and frequency of the azimuth, elevation, DME, marker beacon, and associated compass locators, if any.

(iv) The hours of operation.

(v) Station identification call letters and method of station identification and the time spacing of the identification.

(vi) A description of the critical parts that may not be changed, adjusted, or repaired without an FAA flight check to confirm published operations.

(d) The owner or his maintenance representative must make a ground check of the MLS facility periodically in accordance with procedures approved by the FAA at the time of commissioning, and must report the results of the checks as provided in §171.327.

(e) The only modifications permitted are those that are submitted to FAA for approval by the MLS equipment manufacturer. The owner or sponsor of the facility must incorporate these modifications in the MLS equipment. Associated changes must also be made to the operations and maintenance manual required in paragraph (c) of this section. This and all other corrections and additions to this operations and maintenance manual must also be submitted to FAA for approval.

(f) The owner or the owner's maintenance representative must participate in inspections made by the FAA.

(g) The owner must ensure the availability of a sufficient stock of spare parts, including solid state components, or modules to make possible the prompt replacement of components or modules that fail or deteriorate in service.

(h) FAA approved test instruments must be used for maintenance of the MLS facility.

(i) Inspection consists of an examination of the MLS equipment to ensure that unsafe operating conditions do not exist.

(j) Monitoring of the MLS radiated signal must ensure a high degree of integrity and minimize the requirements for ground and flight inspection. The monitor must be checked daily during the in-service test evaluation period (96 hour burn in) for calibration and stability. These tests and ground checks or azimuth, elevation, DME, and marker beacon radiation characteristics must be conducted in accordance with the maintenance requirements of this section.

§ 171.327 Operational records.

The owner of the MLS facility or his maintenance representative must submit the following operational records at the indicated time to the appropriate FAA regional office where the facility is located.

(a) *Facility Equipment Performance & Adjustment Data (FAA Form 198).* The FAA Form 198 shall be filled out by the owner or his maintenance representative with the equipment adjustments and meter readings as of the time of facility commissioning. One copy must be kept in the permanent records of the facility and two copies must be sent to the appropriate FAA regional office. The owner or his maintenance representative must revise the FAA Form 198 data after any major repair, modernization, or retuning to reflect an accurate record of facility operation and adjustment.

(b) *Facility Maintenance Log (FAA Form 6030-1).* FAA Form 6030-1 is permanent record of all the activities required to maintain the MLS facility. The entries must include all malfunctions met in maintaining the facility including information on the kind of work and adjustments made, equipment failures, causes (if determined) and corrective action taken. In addition, the entries must include completion of periodic maintenance required to maintain the facility. The owner or his maintenance representative must keep the original of each form at the facility and send a copy to the appropriate FAA regional office at the end of each month in which it is prepared. However, where an FAA approved remote monitoring system is installed which precludes the need for periodic maintenance visits to the facility, monthly reports from the remote monitoring system control point must be forwarded to the appropriate FAA regional office, and a hard copy retained at the control point.

(c) *Technical Performance Record (FAA Form 6830 (formerly FAA Form 418)).* This form contains a record of system parameters as specified in the manufacturer's equipment manual. This data will be recorded on each scheduled visit to the facility. The owner or his maintenance representative shall keep the original of each record at the facility and send a copy of the form to the appropriate FAA regional office.

SUBCHAPTER K—ADMINISTRATIVE REGULATIONS

PART 183—REPRESENTATIVES OF THE ADMINISTRATOR

Subpart A—General

Sec.
183.1 Scope.

Subpart B—Certification of Representatives

183.11 Selection.
183.13 Certification.
183.15 Duration of certificates.
183.17 Reports.

Subpart C—Kinds of Designations: Privileges

183.21 Aviation Medical Examiners.
183.23 Pilot examiners.
183.25 Technical personnel examiners.
183.27 Designated aircraft maintenance inspectors.
183.29 Designated engineering representatives.
183.31 Designated manufacturing inspection representatives.
183.33 Designated Airworthiness Representative.

Subpart D—Organization Designation Authorization

183.41 Applicability and definitions.
183.43 Application.
183.45 Issuance of Organization Designation Authorizations.
183.47 Qualifications.
183.49 Authorized functions.
183.51 ODA Unit personnel.
183.53 Procedures manual.
183.55 Limitations.
183.57 Responsibilities of an ODA Holder.
183.59 Inspection.
183.61 Records and reports.
183.63 Continuing requirements: Products, parts or appliances.
183.65 Continuing requirements: Operational approvals.
183.67 Transferability and duration.

AUTHORITY: 31 U.S.C. 9701; 49 U.S.C. 106(f), 106(g), 40113, 44702, 45303.

SOURCE: Docket No. 1151, 27 FR 4951, May 26, 1962, unless otherwise noted.

EDITORIAL NOTE: For miscellaneous amendments to cross references in this part 183 see Amdt. 183–1, 31 FR 9211, July 6, 1966.

Subpart A—General

§ 183.1 Scope.

This part describes the requirements for designating private persons to act as representatives of the Administrator in examining, inspecting, and testing persons and aircraft for the purpose of issuing airman, operating, and aircraft certificates. In addition, this part states the privileges of those representatives and prescribes rules for the exercising of those privileges, as follows:

(a) An individual may be designated as a representative of the Administrator under subparts B or C of this part.

(b) An organization may be designated as a representative of the Administrator by obtaining an Organization Designation Authorization under subpart D of this part.

[Doc. No. FAA–2003–16685, 70 FR 59946, Oct. 13, 2005]

Subpart B—Certification of Representatives

§ 183.11 Selection.

(a) The Federal Air Surgeon, or his or her authorized representatives within the FAA, may select Aviation Medical Examiners from qualified physicians who apply. In addition, the Federal Air Surgeon may designate qualified forensic pathologists to assist in the medical investigation of aircraft accidents.

(b) Any local Flight Standards Inspector may select a pilot examiner, technical personnel examiner, or a designated aircraft maintenance inspector whenever he determines there is a need for one.

(c)(1) The Aircraft Certification Service may select Designated Engineering Representatives from qualified persons who apply by a letter accompanied by a "Statement of Qualifications of Designated Engineering Representative."

(2) The Aircraft Certification Service may select Designated Manufacturing

Inspection Representatives from qualified persons who apply by a letter accompanied by a "Statement of Qualifications of Designated Manufacturing Inspection Representative."

(d) The Associate Administrator for Air Traffic, may select Air Traffic Control Tower Operator Examiners.

(e) The Aircraft Certification Service may select Designated Airworthiness Representatives from qualified persons who apply by a letter accompanied by a "Statement of Qualifications of Designated Airworthiness Representative."

(Approved by the Office of Management and Budget under control number 2120-0035)

(Secs. 313(a), 314, 601, 603, 605, and 1102, Federal Aviation Act of 1958, as amended (49 U.S.C. 1354(a), 1355, 1421, 1423, 1425, and 1502); sec. 6(c) Department of Transportation Act (49 U.S.C. 1655(c)))

[Doc. No. 1151, 27 FR 4951, May 26, 1962, as amended by Amdt. 183-7, 45 FR 32669, May 19, 1980; Amdt. 183-8, 48 FR 16179, Apr. 14, 1983; Amdt. 183-9, 54 FR 39296, Sept. 25, 1989; Amdt. 183-13, 73 FR 43066, July 24, 2008; Docket FAA-2018-0119, Amdt. 183-17, 83 FR 9176, Mar. 5, 2018]

§ 183.13 Certification.

(a) A "Certificate of Designation" and an appropriate Identification Card is issued to each Aviation Medical Examiner and to each forensic pathologist designated under § 183.11(a).

(b) A "Certificate of Authority" specifying the kinds of designation for which the person concerned is qualified and stating an expiration date is issued to each Flight Standards Designated Representative, along with a "Certificate of Designation" for display purposes, designating the holder as a Flight Standards Representative and specifying the kind of designation for which he is qualified.

(c) A "Certificate of Authority," stating the specific functions which the person concerned is authorized to perform and stating an expiration date, is issued to each Designated Airworthiness Representative, along with a "Certificate of Designation" for display purposes.

(Secs. 601 and 602, 72 Stat. 752, 49 U.S.C. 1421-1422; secs. 313(a), 314, 601, 603, 605, and 1102, Federal Aviation Act of 1958, as amended (49 U.S.C. 1354(a), 1355, 1421, 1423, 1425, and 1502); sec. 6(c) Department of Transportation Act (49 U.S.C. 1655(c)))

[Doc. No. 1151, 27 FR 4951, May 26, 1962, as amended by Amdt. 183-2, 32 FR 46, Jan. 5, 1967; Amdt. 183-8, 48 FR 16179, Apr. 14, 1983]

§ 183.15 Duration of certificates.

(a) Unless sooner terminated under paragraph (b) of this section, a designation as an Aviation Medical Examiner or as a Flight Standards or Aircraft Certification Service Designated Representative as described in §§ 183.21, 183.23, 183.25, 183.27, 183.29, 183.31, or 183.33 is effective until the expiration date shown on the document granting the authorization.

(b) A designation made under this subpart terminates:

(1) Upon the written request of the representative;

(2) Upon the written request of the employer in any case in which the recommendation of the employer is required for the designation;

(3) Upon the representative being separated from the employment of the employer who recommended him or her for certification;

(4) Upon a finding by the Administrator that the representative has not properly performed his or her duties under the designation;

(5) Upon the assistance of the representative being no longer needed by the Administrator; or

(6) For any reason the Administrator considers appropriate.

[Doc. No. FAA-2007-27812, 73 FR 43066, July 24, 2008]

§ 183.17 Reports.

Each representative designated under this part shall make such reports as are prescribed by the Administrator.

Subpart C—Kinds of Designations: Privileges

§ 183.21 Aviation Medical Examiners.

An Aviation Medical Examiner may—

(a) Accept applications for physical examinations necessary for issuing medical certificates under part 67 of this chapter;

(b) Under the general supervision of the Federal Air Surgeon or the appropriate senior regional flight surgeon, conduct those physical examinations;

(c) Issue or deny medical certificates in accordance with part 67 of this chapter, subject to reconsideration by the Federal Air Surgeon or his or her authorized representatives within the FAA; and

(d) [Reserved]

(e) As requested, participate in investigating aircraft accidents.

(Secs. 601 and 602, 72 Stat. 752, 49 U.S.C 1421–1422)

[Doc. No. 1151, 27 FR 4951, May 26, 1962, as amended by Amdt. 183–2, 32 FR 46, Jan. 5, 1967; Amdt. 183–5, 38 FR 12203, May 10, 1973; Docket FAA–2010–1127, Amdt. 183–15, 81 FR 1307, Jan. 12, 2016]

§183.23 Pilot examiners.

Any pilot examiner, instrument rating examiner, or airline transport pilot examiner may—

(a) As authorized in his designation, accept applications for flight tests necessary for issuing pilot certificates and ratings under this chapter;

(b) Under the general supervision of the appropriate local Flight Standards Inspector, conduct those tests;

(c) In the discretion of the appropriate local Flight Standards Inspector, issue temporary pilot certificates and ratings to qualified applicants; and

(d) Accept an application for a remote pilot certificate with a small UAS rating and verify the identity of the applicant in a form and manner acceptable to the Administrator.

[Docket 1151, 27 FR 4951, May 26, 1962, as amended by Docket FAA–2015–0150, Amdt. 183–16, 81 FR 42214, June 28, 2016]

§183.25 Technical personnel examiners.

(a) A designated mechanic examiner (DME) (airframe and power plant) may—

(1) Accept applications for, and conduct, mechanic, oral and practical tests necessary for issuing mechanic certificates under part 65 of this chapter; and

(2) In the discretion of the appropriate local Flight Standards Inspector, issue temporary mechanic certificates to qualified applicants.

(b) A designated parachute rigger examiner (DPRE) may—

(1) Accept applications for, and conduct, oral and practical tests necessary for issuing parachute rigger certificates under part 65 of this chapter; and

(2) In the discretion of the appropriate local Flight Standards Inspector, issue temporary parachute rigger certificates to qualified applicants.

(c) An air traffic control tower operator examiner may—

(1) Accept applications for, and conduct, written and practical tests necessary for issuing control tower operator certificates under part 65 of this chapter; and

(2) In the discretion of the Associate Administrator for Air Traffic issue temporary control tower operator certificates to qualified applicants.

(d) A designated flight engineer examiner (DFEE) may—

(1) Accept applications for, and conduct, oral and practical tests necessary for issuing flight engineer certificates under part 63 of this chapter; and

(2) In the discretion of the appropriate local Flight Standards Inspector, issue temporary flight engineer certificates to qualified applicants.

(e) A designated flight navigator examiner (DFNE) may—

(1) Accept applications for, and conduct, oral and practical tests necessary for issuing flight navigator certificates under part 63 of this chapter; and

(2) In the discretion of the appropriate local Flight Standards Inspector, issue temporary flight navigator certificates to qualified applicants.

(f) A designated aircraft dispatcher examiner (DADE) may—

(1) Accept applications for, and conduct, written and practical tests necessary for issuing aircraft dispatcher certificates under part 65 of this chapter; and

(2) In the discretion of the appropriate local Flight Standards Inspector, issue temporary aircraft dispatcher certificates to qualified applicants.

[Doc. No. 1151, 27 FR 4951, May 26, 1962, as amended by Amdt. 183-9, 54 FR 39296, Sept. 25, 1989]

§ 183.27　Designated aircraft maintenance inspectors.

A designated aircraft maintenance inspector (DAMI) may approve maintenance on civil aircraft used by United States military flying clubs in foreign countries.

§ 183.29　Designated engineering representatives.

(a) A structural engineering representative may approve structural engineering information and other structural considerations within limits prescribed by and under the general supervision of the Administrator, whenever the representative determines that information and other structural considerations comply with the applicable regulations of this chapter.

(b) A power plant engineering representative may approve information relating to power plant installations within limitations prescribed by and under the general supervision of the Administrator whenever the representative determines that information complies with the applicable regulations of this chapter.

(c) A systems and equipment engineering representative may approve engineering information relating to equipment and systems, other than those of a structural, powerplant, or radio nature, within limits prescribed by and under the general supervision of the Administrator, whenever the representative determines that information complies with the applicable regulations of this chapter.

(d) A radio engineering representative may approve engineering information relating to the design and operating characteristics of radio equipment, within limits prescribed by and under the general supervision of the Administrator whenever the representative determines that information complies with the applicable regulations of this chapter.

(e) An engine engineering representative may approve engineering information relating to engine design, operation and service, within limits prescribed by and under the general supervision of the Administrator, whenever the representative determines that information complies with the applicable regulations of this chapter.

(f) A propeller engineering representative may approve engineering information relating to propeller design, operation, and maintenance, within limits prescribed by and under the general supervision of the Administrator whenever the representative determines that information complies with the applicable regulations of this chapter.

(g) A flight analyst representative may approve flight test information, within limits prescribed by and under the general supervision of the Administrator, whenever the representative determines that information complies with the applicable regulations of this chapter.

(h) A flight test pilot representative may make flight tests, and prepare and approve flight test information relating to compliance with the regulations of this chapter, within limits prescribed by and under the general supervision of the Administrator.

(i) An acoustical engineering representative may witness and approve aircraft noise certification tests and approve measured noise data and evaluated noise data analyses, within the limits prescribed by, and under the general supervision of, the Administrator, whenever the representative determines that the noise test, test data, and associated analyses are in conformity with the applicable regulations of this chapter. Those regulations include, where appropriate, the methodologies and any equivalencies previously approved by the Director of Environment and Energy, for that noise test series. No designated acoustical engineering representative may determine that a type design change is not an acoustical change, or approve equivalencies to prescribed noise procedures or standards.

[Doc. No. 1151, 27 FR 4951, May 26, 1962, as amended by Amdt. 183-7, 45 FR 32669, May 19, 1980; Amdt. 183-9, 54 FR 39296, Sept. 25, 1989]

§183.31 Designated manufacturing inspection representatives.

A designated manufacturing inspection representative (DMIR) may, within limits prescribed by, and under the general supervision of, the Administrator, do the following:

(a) Issue—

(1) Original airworthiness certificates for aircraft and airworthiness approvals for engines, propellers, and product parts that conform to the approved design requirements and are in a condition for safe operation;

(2) Export certificates of airworthiness and airworthiness approval tags in accordance with subpart L of part 21 of this chapter;

(3) Experimental certificates for aircraft for which the manufacturer holds the type certificate and which have undergone changes to the type design requiring a flight test; and

(4) Special flight permits to export aircraft.

(b) Conduct any inspections that may be necessary to determine that—

(1) Prototype products and related parts conform to design specifications; and

(2) Production products and related parts conform to the approved type design and are in condition for safe operation.

(c) Perform functions authorized by this section for the manufacturer, or the manufacturer's supplier, at any location authorized by the FAA.

[Doc. No. 16622, 45 FR 1416, Jan. 7, 1980]

§183.33 Designated Airworthiness Representative.

A Designated Airworthiness Representative (DAR) may, within limits prescribed by and under the general supervision of the Administrator, do the following:

(a) Perform examination, inspection, and testing services necessary to issue, and to determine the continuing effectiveness of, certificates, including issuing certificates, as authorized by the Executive Director, Flight Standards Service in the area of maintenance or as authorized by the Executive Director, Aircraft Certification Service in the areas of manufacturing and engineering.

(b) Charge a fee for his or her services.

(c) Perform authorized functions at any authorized location.

(Secs. 313(a), 314, 601, 603, 605, and 1102, Federal Aviation Act of 1958, as amended (49 U.S.C. 1354(a), 1355, 1421, 1423, 1425, and 1502); sec.6(c) Department of Transportation Act (49 U.S.C. 1655(c)))

[Doc. No. 23140, 48 FR 16179, Apr. 14, 1983, as amended by Amdt. 183–9, 54 FR 39296, Sept. 25, 1989; Amdt. 183–11, 67 FR 72766, Dec. 6, 2002; Docket FAA–2018–0119, Amdt. 183–17, 83 FR 9176, Mar. 5, 2018]

Subpart D—Organization Designation Authorization

SOURCE: Docket No. FAA–2003–16685, 70 FR 59947, Oct. 13, 2005, unless otherwise noted.

§183.41 Applicability and definitions.

(a) This subpart contains the procedures required to obtain an Organization Designation Authorization, which allows an organization to perform specified functions on behalf of the Administrator related to engineering, manufacturing, operations, airworthiness, or maintenance.

(b) *Definitions.* For the purposes of this subpart:

Organization Designation Authorization (ODA) means the authorization to perform approved functions on behalf of the Administrator.

ODA Holder means the organization that obtains the authorization from the Administrator, as identified in a Letter of Designation.

ODA Unit means an identifiable group of two or more individuals within the ODA Holder's organization that performs the authorized functions.

§183.43 Application.

An application for an ODA may be submitted after November 14, 2006. An application for an ODA must be submitted in a form and manner prescribed by the Administrator and must include the following:

(a) A description of the functions for which authorization is requested.

(b) A description of how the applicant satisfies the requirements of §183.47 of this part;

(c) A description of the applicant's organizational structure, including a description of the proposed ODA Unit as it relates to the applicant's organizational structure; and

(d) A proposed procedures manual as described in § 183.53 of this part.

§ 183.45   Issuance of Organization Designation Authorizations.

(a) The Administrator may issue an ODA Letter of Designation if:

(1) The applicant meets the applicable requirements of this subpart; and

(2) A need exists for a delegation of the function.

(b) An ODA Holder must apply to and obtain approval from the Administrator for any proposed changes to the functions or limitations described in the ODA Holder's authorization.

§ 183.47   Qualifications.

To qualify for consideration as an ODA, the applicant must—

(a) Have sufficient facilities, resources, and personnel, to perform the functions for which authorization is requested;

(b) Have sufficient experience with FAA requirements, processes, and procedures to perform the functions for which authorization is requested; and

(c) Have sufficient, relevant experience to perform the functions for which authorization is requested.

§ 183.49   Authorized functions.

(a) Consistent with an ODA Holder's qualifications, the Administrator may delegate any function determined appropriate under 49 U.S.C. 44702(d).

(b) Under the general supervision of the Administrator, an ODA Unit may perform only those functions, and is subject to the limitations, listed in the ODA Holder's procedures manual.

§ 183.51   ODA Unit personnel.

Each ODA Holder must have within its ODA Unit—

(a) At least one qualified ODA administrator; and either

(b) A staff consisting of the engineering, flight test, inspection, or maintenance personnel needed to perform the functions authorized. Staff members must have the experience and expertise to find compliance, determine conformity, determine airworthiness, issue certificates or issue approvals; or

(c) A staff consisting of operations personnel who have the experience and expertise to find compliance with the regulations governing the issuance of pilot, crew member, or operating certificates, authorizations, or endorsements as needed to perform the functions authorized.

§ 183.53   Procedures manual.

No ODA Letter of Designation may be issued before the Administrator approves an applicant's procedures manual. The approved manual must:

(a) Be available to each member of the ODA Unit;

(b) Include a description of those changes to the manual or procedures that may be made by the ODA Holder. All other changes to the manual or procedures must be approved by the Administrator before they are implemented.

(c) Contain the following:

(1) The authorized functions and limitations, including the products, certificates, and ratings;

(2) The procedures for performing the authorized functions;

(3) Description of the ODA Holder's and the ODA Unit's organizational structure and responsibilities;

(4) A description of the facilities at which the authorized functions are performed;

(5) A process and a procedure for periodic audit by the ODA Holder of the ODA Unit and its procedures;

(6) The procedures outlining actions required based on audit results, including documentation of all corrective actions;

(7) The procedures for communicating with the appropriate FAA offices regarding administration of the delegation authorization;

(8) The procedures for acquiring and maintaining regulatory guidance material associated with each authorized function;

(9) The training requirements for ODA Unit personnel;

(10) For authorized functions, the procedures and requirements related to maintaining and submitting records;

(11) A description of each ODA Unit position, and the knowledge and experience required for each position;

(12) The procedures for appointing ODA Unit members and the means of documenting Unit membership, as required under §183.61(a)(4) of this part;

(13) The procedures for performing the activities required by §183 63 or §183.65 of this part;

(14) The procedures for revising the manual, pursuant to the limitations of paragraph (b) of this section; and

(15) Any other information required by the Administrator necessary to supervise the ODA Holder in the performance of its authorized functions.

§183.55 Limitations.

(a) If any change occurs that may affect an ODA Unit's qualifications or ability to perform a function (such as a change in the location of facilities, resources, personnel or the organizational structure), no Unit member may perform that function until the Administrator is notified of the change, and the change is approved and appropriately documented as required by the procedures manual.

(b) No ODA Unit member may issue a certificate, authorization or other approval until any findings reserved for the Administrator have been made.

(c) An ODA Holder is subject to any other limitations as specified by the Administrator.

§183.57 Responsibilities of an ODA Holder.

The ODA Holder must—

(a) Comply with the procedures contained in its approved procedures manual;

(b) Give ODA Unit members sufficient authority to perform the authorized functions;

(c) Ensure that no conflicting non-ODA Unit duties or other interference affects the performance of authorized functions by ODA Unit members.

(d) Cooperate with the Administrator in his performance of oversight of the ODA Holder and the ODA Unit.

(e) Notify the Administrator of any change that could affect the ODA Holder's ability to continue to meet the requirements of this part within 48 hours of the change occurring.

§183.59 Inspection.

The Administrator, at any time and for any reason, may inspect an ODA Holder's or applicant's facilities, products, components, parts, appliances, procedures, operations, and records associated with the authorized or requested functions.

§183.61 Records and reports.

(a) Each ODA Holder must ensure that the following records are maintained for the duration of the authorization:

(1) [Reserved]

(2) For any approval or certificate issued by an ODA Unit member (except those airworthiness certificates and approvals not issued in support of type design approval projects):

(i) The application and data required to be submitted under this chapter to obtain the certificate or approval; and

(ii) The data and records documenting the ODA Unit member's approval or determination of compliance.

(3) A list of the products, components, parts, or appliances for which ODA Unit members have issued a certificate or approval.

(4) The names, responsibilities, qualifications and example signature of each member of the ODA Unit who performs an authorized function.

(5) A copy of each manual approved or accepted by the ODA Unit, including all historical changes.

(6) Training records for ODA Unit members and ODA administrators.

(7) Any other records specified in the ODA Holder's procedures manual.

(8) The procedures manual required under §183.53 of this part, including all changes.

(b) Each ODA Holder must ensure that the following are maintained for five years:

(1) A record of each periodic audit and any corrective actions resulting from them; and

(2) A record of any reported service difficulties associated with approvals or certificates issued by an ODA Unit member.

(c) For airworthiness certificates and approvals not issued in support of a type design approval project, each ODA Holder must ensure the following are maintained for two years;

(1) The application and data required to be submitted under this chapter to obtain the certificate or approval; and

(2) The data and records documenting the ODA Unit member's approval or determination of compliance.

(d) For all records required by this section to be maintained, each ODA Holder must:

(1) Ensure that the records and data are available to the Administrator for inspection at any time;

(2) Submit all records and data to the Administrator upon surrender or termination of the authorization.

(e) Each ODA Holder must compile and submit any report required by the Administrator to exercise his supervision of the ODA Holder.

[Doc. No. FAA–2003–16685, 70 FR 59947, Oct. 13, 2005, as amended by Amdt. 183–14, 76 FR 8893, Feb. 16, 2011]

§ 183.63 Continuing requirements: Products, parts or appliances.

For any approval or certificate for a product, part or appliance issued under the authority of this subpart, an ODA Holder must:

(a) Monitor reported service problems related to certificates or approvals it holds;

(b) Notify the Administrator of:

(1) A condition in a product, part or appliance that could result in a finding of unsafe condition by the Administrator; or

(2) A product, part or appliance not meeting the applicable airworthiness requirements for which the ODA Holder has obtained or issued a certificate or approval.

(c) Investigate any suspected unsafe condition or finding of noncompliance with the airworthiness requirements for any product, part or appliance, as required by the Administrator, and report to the Administrator the results of the investigation and any action taken or proposed.

(d) Submit to the Administrator the information necessary to implement corrective action needed for safe operation of the product, part or appliance.

[Doc. No. FAA–2003–16685, 70 FR 59947, Oct. 13, 2005, as amended by Amdt. 183–14, 76 FR 8893, Feb. 16, 2011]

§ 183.65 Continuing requirements: Operational approvals.

For any operational authorization, airman certificate, air carrier certificate, air operator certificate, or air agency certificate issued under the authority of this subpart, an ODA Holder must:

(a) Notify the Administrator of any error that the ODA Holder finds it made in issuing an authorization or certificate;

(b) Notify the Administrator of any authorization or certificate that the ODA Holder finds it issued to an applicant not meeting the applicable requirements;

(c) When required by the Administrator, investigate any problem concerning the issuance of an authorization or certificate; and

(d) When notified by the Administrator, suspend issuance of similar authorizations or certificates until the ODA Holder implements all corrective action required by the Administrator.

§ 183.67 Transferability and duration.

(a) An ODA is effective until the date shown on the Letter of Designation, unless sooner terminated by the Administrator.

(b) No ODA may be transferred at any time.

(c) The Administrator may terminate or temporarily suspend an ODA for any reason, including that the ODA Holder:

(1) Has requested in writing that the authorization be suspended or terminated;

(2) Has not properly performed its duties;

(3) Is no longer needed; or

(4) No longer meets the qualifications required to perform authorized functions.

PART 185—TESTIMONY BY EMPLOYEES AND PRODUCTION OF RECORDS IN LEGAL PROCEEDINGS, AND SERVICE OF LEGAL PROCESS AND PLEADINGS

185.5 Testimony by employees and production of records in legal proceedings.

AUTHORITY: 49 U.S.C. 106(g), 40113–40114, 46104; 49 CFR part 9.

SOURCE: Docket No. 9900, 34 FR 16622, Oct. 17, 1969, unless otherwise noted.

§185.1 Purpose.

(a) The purpose of this part is to name the FAA officials who, pursuant to part 9 of the regulations of the Office of the Secretary of Transportation (49 CFR part 9) as amended (34 FR 11972, July 16, 1969), are those:

(1) Upon whom legal process or pleadings may be served in any legal proceeding concerning the FAA, and who have authority to acknowledge the service and take further action thereon; and

(2) Who otherwise perform the functions prescribed by part 9 in legal proceedings concerning the FAA with respect to testimony by FAA employees and production of FAA records in legal proceedings.

(b) For purposes of this part, "legal proceedings" includes any proceeding before a court of law, administrative board or commission, hearing officer, or other body conducting a legal or administrative proceeding.

§185.3 Acceptance of service on behalf of the Secretary of Transportation or the Administrator.

Legal process or pleadings in any legal proceeding concerning the FAA may be served, at the option of the server, on the Chief Counsel, Deputy Chief Counsel, Assistant Chief Counsel, Litigation Division, of the FAA, or any other FAA official designated by the Chief Counsel, with the same effect as if served upon the Secretary of Transportation or the Administrator. The official accepting the service under this section acknowledges the service and takes further action as appropriate.

§185.5 Testimony by employees and production of records in legal proceedings.

The Chief Counsel, and each Assistant Chief Counsel, each Regional Counsel, the Aeronautical Center Counsel, and the Technical Center Counsel, with respect to matters arising within their respective jurisdictions, and any other

FAA official designated by the Chief Counsel, perform the functions in legal proceedings (other than one described in §185.3 of this part) as prescribed by part 9 of the regulations of the Office of the Secretary of Transportation, with respect to testimony by FAA employees and production of FAA records in legal proceedings.

[Doc. No. 9900, 34 FR 16622, Oct. 17, 1969, as amended by Amdt. 185–1, 54 FR 39296, Sept. 25, 1989; Amdt. 185–3, 62 FR 46866, Sept. 4, 1997]

PART 187—FEES

Sec.
187.1 Scope.
187.3 Definitions.
187.5 Duplicates of licenses.
187.7 Copies; seal.
187.15 Payment of fees.
187.17 Failure of applicant to pay prescribed fees.
187.51 Applicability of overflight fees.
187.53 Calculation of overflight fees.
187.55 Overflight fees billing and payment procedures.

APPENDIX A TO PART 187—METHODOLOGY FOR COMPUTATION OF FEES FOR CERTIFICATION SERVICES PERFORMED OUTSIDE THE UNITED STATES

APPENDIX B TO PART 187 [RESERVED]

APPENDIX C TO PART 187—FEES FOR PRODUCTION CERTIFICATION-RELATED SERVICES PERFORMED OUTSIDE THE UNITED STATES

AUTHORITY: 31 U.S.C. 9701; 49 U.S.C. 106(f), 106(g), 106(l)(6), 40104–40105, 40109, 40113–40114, 44702, 45301.

SOURCE: Docket No. 8347, 32 FR 12051, Aug. 22, 1967, unless otherwise noted.

§187.1 Scope.

This part prescribes fees only for FAA services for which fees are not prescribed in other parts of this chapter or in 49 CFR part 7. The fees for services furnished in connection with making information available to the public are prescribed exclusively in 49 CFR part 7. Appendix A to this part prescribes the methodology for computation of fees for certification services performed outside the United

States. Appendix C to this part prescribes the methodology for computation of fees for production certification-related services performed outside the United States.

[Docket FAA–2015–3597, Amdt. 187–36, 81 FR 85853, Nov. 29, 2016]

§ 187.3 Definitions.

For the purpose of this part:

Great circle distance means the shortest distance between two points on the surface of the Earth.

Overflight means a flight through U.S.-controlled airspace that does not include a landing in or takeoff from the United States.

Overflight through Enroute airspace means an overflight through U.S.-controlled airspace where primarily radar-based air traffic services are provided.

Overflight through Oceanic airspace means an overflight through U.S.-controlled airspace where primarily procedural air traffic services are provided.

U.S.-controlled airspace means all airspace over the territory of the United States, extending 12 nautical miles from the coastline of U.S. territory; any airspace delegated to the United States for U.S. control by other countries or under a regional air navigation agreement; or any international airspace, or airspace of undetermined sovereignty, for which the United States has accepted responsibility for providing air traffic control services.

[Docket FAA–2015–3597, Amdt. 187–36, 81 FR 85853, Nov. 29, 2016]

§ 187.5 Duplicates of licenses.

The fee for furnishing to a person entitled thereto a replacement, duplicate, or facsimile of a certificate or other document evidencing a license, for which a fee is not specifically provided elsewhere in this chapter, is $2.

§ 187.7 Copies; seal.

The fees for furnishing photostatic or similar copies of documents and for affixation of the seal for a certification or validation are the same as those provided in subpart H of 49 CFR part 7.

§ 187.15 Payment of fees.

(a) The fees of this part are payable to the Federal Aviation Administration by check, money order, wire transfers, draft, payable in U.S. currency and drawn on a U.S. bank, or by credit card payable in U.S. currency, prior to the provision of any service under this part.

(b) Applicants for the FAA services provided under this part shall pay any bank processing charges on fees collected under this part, when such charges are assessed on U.S. Government.

(c) Applicants for the FAA services described in Appendix A of this part shall pay bank processing charges, when such charges are assessed by banks on U.S. Government deposits.

(d) The fees described in appendix B of this part are payable to the Federal Aviation Administration in U.S. currency. Remittance of fees of $1,000 or more are to be paid by electronic funds transfer. Remittance of amounts less than $1,000 may be paid by electronic funds transfer, check, money order, credit card, or draft.

[Doc. No. 27809, 60 FR 19631, Apr. 19, 1995, as amended by Amdt. 187–7, 62 FR 13503, Mar. 20, 1997; Amdt. 187–7, 62 FR 23295, Apr. 29, 1997; Amdt. 187–10, 62 FR 55703, Oct. 27, 1997; Amdt. 187–7, 63 FR 40000, July 24, 1998; Amdt. 187–11, 65 FR 36008, June 6, 2000; Amdt. 187–12, 66 FR 43718, Aug. 20, 2001; Amdt. 187–4, 72 FR 18559, Apr. 12, 2007]

§ 187.17 Failure by applicant to pay prescribed fees.

If an applicant fails to pay fees agreed to under appendix C of this part, the FAA may suspend or deny any application for service and may suspend or revoke any production certification-related approval granted.

[Doc. No. 28967, 62 FR 55703, Oct. 27, 1997]

§ 187.51 Applicability of overflight fees.

(a) Except as provided in paragraphs (c) or (d) of this section, any person who conducts an overflight through either Enroute or Oceanic airspace must pay a fee as calculated in § 187.53.

(b) *Services.* Persons covered by paragraph (a) of this section must pay a fee for the FAA's rendering or providing of certain services, including but not limited to the following:

(1) Air traffic management.

(2) Communications.

(3) Navigation.

(4) Radar surveillance, including separation services.

(5) Flight information services

(6) Procedural control.

(7) Emergency services and training.

(c) The FAA does not assess a fee for any military or civilian overflight operated by the United States Government or by any foreign government.

(d) Fees for overflights through U.S.-controlled airspace covered by a written FAA agreement or other binding arrangement are charged according to the terms of that agreement or arrangement unless the terms are silent on fees.

[Docket FAA–2015–3597, Amdt. 187–36, 81 FR 85853, Nov. 29, 2016]

§ 187.53 Calculation of overflight fees.

(a) The FAA assesses a total fee that is the sum of the Enroute and Oceanic calculated fees.

(1) *Enroute fee.* The Enroute fee is calculated by multiplying the Enroute rate in paragraph (c) of this section by the total number of nautical miles flown through each segment of Enroute airspace divided by 100 (because the Enroute rate is expressed per 100 nautical miles).

(2) *Oceanic fee.* The Oceanic fee is calculated by multiplying the Oceanic rate in paragraph (c) of this section by the total number of nautical miles flown through each segment of Oceanic airspace divided by 100 (because the Oceanic rate is expressed per 100 nautical miles).

(b) Distance flown through each segment of Enroute or Oceanic airspace is based on the great circle distance (GCD) from the point of entry into U.S.-controlled airspace to the point of exit from U.S.-controlled airspace based on FAA flight data. Where actual entry and exit points are not available, the FAA will use the best available flight data to calculate the entry and exit points.

(c) The rate for each 100 nautical miles flown through Enroute or Oceanic airspace is:

Time period	Enroute rate	Oceanic rate
January 1, 2017 to January 1, 2018	58.45	23.15

Time period	Enroute rate	Oceanic rate
January 1, 2018 to January 1, 2019	60.07	24.77
January 1, 2019 and Beyond	61.75	26.51

(d) The formula for the total overflight fee is:

$$Rij = E*DEij/100 + O*DOij/100$$

Where:

Rij = the total fee charged to aircraft flying between entry point i and exit point j.

$DEij$ = total distance flown through each segment of Enroute airspace between entry point i and exit point j.

$DOij$ = total distance flown through each segment of Oceanic airspace between entry point i and exit point j.

E and O = the Enroute and Oceanic rates, respectively, set forth in paragraph (c) of this section.

(e) The FAA will review the rates described in this section at least once every 2 years and will adjust them to reflect the current costs and volume of the services provided.

[Docket FAA–2015–3597, Amdt. 187–36, 81 FR 85853, Nov. 29, 2016]

§ 187.55 Overflight fees billing and payment procedures.

(a) The FAA will send an invoice to each user when fees are owed to the FAA. If the FAA cannot identify the user, then an invoice will be sent to the registered owner. Users will be billed at the address of record in the country where the aircraft is registered, unless a billing address is otherwise provided.

(b) The FAA will send an invoice if the monthly (based on Universal Coordinated Time) fees equal or exceed $400.

(c) Payment must be made by one of the methods described in § 187.15(d).

[Docket FAA–2015–3597, Amdt. 187–36, 81 FR 85853, Nov. 29, 2016]

APPENDIX A TO PART 187—METHODOLOGY FOR COMPUTATION OF FEES FOR CERTIFICATION SERVICES PERFORMED OUTSIDE THE UNITED STATES

(a) Fixed fees and hourly rates have been derived using the methodology described below to ensure full cost recovery for certification actions or approvals provided by the FAA for persons outside the United States.

(b) These rates are based on aviation safety inspector time rather than calculating a separate rate for managerial or clerical time because the inspector is the individual performing the actual service. Charging for inspector time, while building in all costs into the rate base, provides for efficient cost recovery and time management.

(c) The hourly billing rate has been determined by using the annual operations budget of the Flight Standards Service. The budget is comprised of the following:

(1) Personnel compensation and benefits, budget code series 1100 (excluding codes 1151 and 1152—overtime, Sunday and holiday pay), 1200, and 1300.

(2) Travel and transportation of persons, budget code series 2100 (excluding code 2100—site visit travel).

(3) Transportation of things, budget code series 2200.

(4) Rental, communications, utilities, budget code series 2300.

(5) Printing and reproduction, budget code series 2400.

(6) Contractual services, budget code series 2500.

(7) Supplies and materials, budget code series 2600.

(8) Equipment, budget code series 3100.

(9) Lands and structures, budget code series 3200.

(10) Insurance claims and indemnities, budget code series 4200.

(d) In order to recover overhead costs attributable to the budget, all costs other than direct inspector transportation and subsistence, overtime, and Sunday/holiday costs,
are assigned to the number of inspector positions. An hourly cost per inspector is developed by dividing the annual Flight Standards Operations Budget, excluding the items enumerated above, by the number of aviation safety inspections (OMB position series 1825) on board at the beginning of the fiscal year, to determine the annual cost of an aviation safety inspector. This annual cost of an aviation safety inspector is divided by 2,087 hours, which is the annual paid hours of a U.S. Federal Government employee. This result in the hourly government paid cost of an aviation safety inspector.

(e) To ensure that the hourly inspector cost represents a billing rate that ensures full recovery of costs, the hourly cost per inspector must be multiplied by an indirect work factor to determine the hourly inspector billing rate. This is necessary for the following reasons:

(1) Inspectors spend a significant amount of time in indirect work to support their inspection activities, much of which cannot be allocated to any one client.

(2) Not all 2,087 annual paid hours are available as work hours because training, providing technical assistance, leave, and other indirect work activities reduce the work time that may be directly billed. Consequently, the hourly cost per inspector must be adjusted upwards by an indirect work factor. The calculation of an indirect work factor is discussed in paragraph (f) of this appendix.

(f)(1) The indirect work factor is determined using the following formula:

$$\left(1+\sum_{1}^{k} a_i\right)(1+b) = \text{indirect work factor}$$

where:

a = indirect work rate, and

b = leave usage (total leave hours divided by total hours available for work.

(2) The components of the formula are derived as follows:

(i) *a = indirect work rate.* Indirect work rate is take from the Flight Standards Staffing Standard Order and is used to project the amount of time an aviation safety inspector spends in indirect activities, as opposed to certification and surveillance work. The indirect work activities are:

(A) Development of master minimum equipment lists on Flight Operations Evaluation Board.

(B) Development of aircraft training documents on Flight Standardization Board.

(C) Development of Maintenance program documents on Maintenance Review Board.

(D) Providing technical assistance.

(E) Assisting legal counsel.

(F) Evaluation of technical documents.

(G) Leave (all types).

(H) Training.

(I) Administrative time.

(J) Travel for indirect work.

(ii) *b = leave usage (total leave hours divided by total hours available for work).* This is computed by using OMB guidelines of 280 average annual leave hours and 1,800 average annual hours available for work for computer manpower requirements.

(g) The hourly inspector cost, when multiplied by the indirect work factor, yields the hourly inspector billing rate and ensures full cost recovery by incorporating the total amount of FAA paid hours needed to produce one hour of direct billable inspector time.

(h) Certifications and approvals for which there are fixed times, such as airman tests, are determined by multiplying the time used in the Flight Standards Staffing Standard or airman test guidelines by the inspector hourly billing rate.

(i) Certifications and approvals for which there are no fixed work rates, such as airman and repair station facilities (air agencies), are billed at the hourly inspector billing rate.

(j) Actual transportation and subsistence expenses incurred in certification or approval actions will be billed in addition to the hourly inspector billing rate, where such expenses are incurred.

(k) In no event will the fees exceed the actual costs of providing certification or approval services.

(l) The methodology for computing user fees is published in this Appendix. The User fee schedule is published in an FAA Advisory Circular entitled "Flight Standards Service Schedule of Charges Outside the United States." A copy of this publication may be obtained from: New Orders, Superintendent of Documents, P.O. Box 371954, Pittsburgh, PA 15250–7954.

(m) Fees will be reviewed every year, at the beginning of the fiscal year, and adjusted either upward or downward in order to reflect the current costs of performing tests, authorizations, certifications, permits, or ratings.

(n) Notice of each change to a fee for a service described in the user fee schedule will be published in the "Notices" section of the FEDERAL REGISTER.

[Amdt. 187–5, 60 FR 19631, Apr. 19, 1995]

APPENDIX B TO PART 187 [RESERVED]

APPENDIX C TO PART 187—FEES FOR PRODUCTION CERTIFICATION-RE-LATED SERVICES PERFORMED OUT-SIDE THE UNITED STATES

(a) *Purpose.* This appendix describes the methodology for the calculation of fees for production certification-related services outside the United States that are performed by the FAA.

(b) *Applicability.* This appendix applies to production approval holders who elect to use manufacturing facilities or supplier facilities located outside the United States to manufacture or assemble aeronautical products after September 30, 1997.

(c) *Definitions.* For the purpose of this appendix, the following definitions apply:

Manufacturing facility means a place where production of a complete aircraft, aircraft engine, propeller, part, component, or appliance is performed.

Production certification-related service means a service associated with initial production approval holder qualification; ongoing production approval holder and supplier surveillance; designee management; initial production approval holder qualification and ongoing surveillance for production certificate extensions outside the United States; conformity inspections; and witnessing of tests.

Supplier facility means a place where production of a part, component, or subassembly is performed for a production approval holder.

Production approval holder means a person who holds an FAA approval for production under type certificate only, an FAA approval for production under an approved production inspection system, a production certificate, a technical standard order authorization, or a parts manufacturer approval.

(d) *Procedural requirements.* (1) Applicants may apply for FAA production certification-related services provided outside the United States by a letter of application to the FAA detailing when and where the particular services are required.

(2) The FAA will notify the applicant in writing of the estimated cost and schedule to provide the services.

(3) The applicant will review the estimated costs and schedule of services. If the applicant agrees with the estimated costs and schedule of services, the applicant will propose to the FAA that the services be provided. If the FAA agrees and can provide the services requested, a written agreement will be executed between the applicant and the FAA.

(4) The applicant must provide advance payment for each 12-month period of agreed FAA service unless a shorter period is agreed to between the Production Approval Holder and FAA.

(e) *Fee determination.* (1) Fees for FAA production certification-related services will consist of: personnel compensation and benefit (PC&B) for each participating FAA employee, actual travel and transportation expenses incurred in providing the service, other agency costs and an overhead percentage.

(2) Fees will be determined on a case-by-case basis according to the following general formula:

$$W_1H_1 + W_2H_2 \text{ etc.,} + T + O$$

Where:

W_1H_1 = hourly PC&B rate for employee 1, times estimated hours

W_2H_2 = hourly PC&B rate for employee 2, etc., times estimated hours

T = estimated travel and transportation expenses

O = other agency costs related to each activity including overhead.

(3) In no event will the applicant be charged more than the actual FAA costs of providing production certification-related services.

(4) If the actual FAA costs vary from the estimated fees by more than 10 percent, written notice by the FAA will be given to the applicant as soon as possible.

(5) If FAA costs exceed the estimated fees, the applicant will be required to pay the difference prior to receiving further services. If the estimated fees exceed the FAA costs, the applicant may elect to apply the balance to future agreements or to receive a refund.

(f) Fees will be reviewed by the FAA periodically and adjusted either upward or downward in order to reflect the current costs of performing production certification-related services outside the United States.

(1) Notice of any change to the elements of the fee formula in this Appendix will be published in the FEDERAL REGISTER.

(2) Notice of any change to the methodology in this Appendix and other changes for the fees will be published in the FEDERAL REGISTER.

[Doc. No. 28967, 62 FR 55703, Oct. 27, 1997]

PART 189—USE OF FEDERAL AVIATION ADMINISTRATION COMMUNICATIONS SYSTEM

Sec.
189.1 Scope.
189.3 Kinds of messages accepted or relayed.
189.5 Limitation of liability.

AUTHORITY: 31 U.S.C. 9701; 49 U.S.C. 106(g), 40104, 40113, 44502, 45303.

SOURCE: Docket No. 27778, 60 FR 39615, Aug. 2, 1995, unless otherwise noted.

§ 189.1 Scope.

This part describes the kinds of messages that may be transmitted or relayed by FAA Flight Service Stations.

§ 189.3 Kinds of messages accepted or relayed.

(a) Flight Service Stations may accept for transmission over FAA communication systems any messages concerning international or overseas aircraft operations described in paragraphs (a) (1) through (6) of this section. In addition, Flight Service Stations may relay any message described in this section that was originally accepted for transmission at an FAA Flight Service Station outside the 48 contiguous States, or was received from a foreign station of the Aeronautical Fixed Telecommunications Network that, in normal routing, would require transit of the United States to reach an overseas address:

(1) Distress messages and distress traffic.

(2) Messages concerning the safety of human life.

(3) Flight safety messages concerning—

(i) Air traffic control, including—

(A) Messages concerning aircraft in flight or about to depart;

(B) Departure messages;

(C) Flight plan departure messages;

(D) Arrival messages;

(E) Flight plan messages;

(F) Flight notification messages;

(G) Messages concerning flight cancellation; and

(H) Messages concerning delayed departure;

(ii) Position reports from aircraft;

(iii) Messages originated by an aircraft operating agency of immediate concern to an aircraft in flight or about to depart; and

(iv) Meteorological advice of immediate concern to an aircraft in flight or about to depart.

(4) Meteorological messages concerning—

(i) Meteorological forecasts;

(ii) Meteorological observations exclusively; or

(iii) Other meteorological information exchanged between meteorological offices.

(5) Aeronautical administrative messages—

(i) Concerning the operation or maintenance of facilities essential to the safety or regulatory of aircraft operation;

(ii) Essential to efficient functioning of aeronautical telecommunications; or

(iii) Between civil aviation authorities concerning aircraft operation.

(6) Notices to airmen.

(b) The following messages may only be relayed through the FAA communications systems:

(1) Flight regularity messages—

(i) Addressed to the point of intended landing and to not more than two other addressees in the general area of the route segment of the flight to which the message refers, containing information required for weight and balance computation and remarks essential to the rapid unloading of the aircraft;

(ii) Concerning changes, taking effect within 72 hours, in aircraft operating schedules;

(iii) Concerning the servicing of aircraft en route or scheduled to depart within 48 hours;

(iv) Concerning changes in the collective requirements for passengers, crew, or cargo of aircraft en route or about to depart, if the changes are caused by unavoidable deviations from normal operating schedules and are necessary for flight regularity;

(v) Concerning non-routine landings to be made by aircraft en route or about to depart;

(vi) Concerning parts or materials urgently needed to operate aircraft en route or scheduled to depart within 48 hours; or

(vii) Concerning pre-flight arrangement of air navigation services and, in the case of non-scheduled or irregular operations, operational servicing of aircraft scheduled to depart within 48 hours.

(2) Messages originated by and addressed to aircraft operating agencies or their representatives that directly bear on the efficient and economic conduct or day to day operations, if adequate non-United States communications facilities are not available and the messages concern—

(i) Matter described in paragraph (b)(1) of this section, but not meeting the time limitations described in paragraph (b)(1) of this section;

(ii) Aircraft parts, equipment, or supplies, air navigation or communications, or essential ground facilities;

(iii) Train or hotel reservations for passengers or employees;

(iv) Lost baggage or personal effects;

(v) Tickets or cargo shipments and payment therefore;

(vi) Location of passengers and cargo;

(vii) New or revised passenger or cargo rates;

(viii) Crew assignments and similar operations personnel matters taking effect within 7 days;

(ix) Post flight reports for record purposes;

(x) Publicity and special handling regarding dignitaries; or

(xi) Reservations, when originated by aircraft operating agencies to secure space required in transport aircraft.

§189.5   Limitation of liability.

The United States is not liable for any omission, error, or delay in transmitting or relaying, or for any failure to transmit or relay, any message accepted for transmission or relayed under this part, even if the omission, error, delay, or failure to transmit or relay is caused by the negligence of an employee of the United States.

PART 193—PROTECTION OF VOLUNTARILY SUBMITTED INFORMATION

AUTHORITY: 49 U.S.C. 106(g), 40113, 40123.

SOURCE: 66 FR 33805, June 25, 2001, unless otherwise noted.

§193.1   What does this part cover?

This part describes when and how the FAA protects from disclosure safety and security information that you submit voluntarily to the FAA. This part carries out 49 U.S.C. 40123, protection of voluntarily submitted information.

§193.3   Definitions.

Agency means each authority of the Government of the United States, whether or not the agency is within or subject to review by another agency, but does not include—

(1) The Congress;

(2) The courts of the United States;

(3) The governments of the territories or possessions of the United States;

(4) The government of the District of Columbia;

(5) Court martial and military commissions.

De-identified means that the identity of the source of the information, and the names of persons have been removed from the information.

Disclose means to release information to a person other than another agency. Examples are disclosures under the Freedom of Information Act (5 U.S.C. 552), in rulemaking proceedings, in a press release, or to a party to a legal action.

Information includes data, reports, source, and other information. "Information" may be used to describe the whole or a portion of a submission of information.

Summarized means that individual incidents are not specifically described, but are presented in statistical or other general form.

Voluntary means that the information was not required to be submitted as part of a mandatory program, and was not submitted as a condition of doing business with the government. "Voluntarily-provided information" does not include information submitted as part of complying with statutory, regulatory, or contractual requirements, except that information submitted as part of complying with a voluntary program under this part is considered to be voluntarily provided.

§ 193.5 How may I submit safety or security information and have it protected from disclosure?

(a) You may do so under a program under this part. The program may be developed based on your proposal, a proposal from another person, or a proposal developed by the FAA.

(b) You may be any person, including an individual, a company, or an organization.

(c) You may propose to develop a program under this part using either the notice procedure in § 193.11 or the no-notice procedure in § 193.13.

(d) If the FAA decides to protect the information that you propose to submit it issues an order designating the

information as protected under this part.

(e) The FAA only issues an order designating information as protected if the FAA makes the findings in § 193.7.

(f) The designation may be for a program in which all similar persons may participate, or for a program in which only you submit information.

(g) Even if you receive protection from disclosure under this part, this part does not establish the extent to which the FAA may or may not use the information to take enforcement action. Limits on enforcement action applicable to a program under this part will be in another policy or rule.

§ 193.7 What does it mean for the FAA to designate information as protected?

(a) *General.* When the FAA issues an order designating information as protected under this part, the FAA does not disclose the information except as provided in this part.

(b) *What findings does the FAA make before designating information as protected?* The FAA designates information as protected under this part when the FAA finds that—

(1) The information is provided voluntarily;

(2) The information is safety or security related;

(3) The disclosure of the information would inhibit the voluntary provision of that type of information;

(4) The receipt of that type of information aids in fulfilling the FAA's safety and security responsibilities; and

(5) Withholding such information from disclosure, under the circumstances provided in this part, will be consistent with the FAA's safety and security responsibilities.

(c) *How will the FAA handle requests for information under the Freedom of Information Act (FOIA)?* The FAA does not disclose information that is designated as protected under this part in response to a FOIA request.

(d) *What if the FAA obtains from another source the same information I submit?* Only information received under a program under this part is protected from disclosure under this part. Information obtained by the FAA through another means is not protected under this part.

(e) *Sharing information with other agencies.* The FAA may provide information that you have submitted under this part to other agencies with safety or security responsibilities. The agencies are subject to the requirements of 49 U.S.C. 40123 regarding nondisclosure of information. The FAA will give the information to another agency only if, for each such request, the other agency provides the FAA with adequate assurance, in writing, that—

(1) The agency has a safety or security need for the information, including the general nature of the need.

(2) The agency will protect the information from disclosure as required in 49 U.S.C. 40123, this part, and the designation. This includes a commitment that the agency will mark the information as provided in the designation.

(3) The agency will limit access to those with a need to know to carry out safety or security responsibilities

(f) *What if the FAA receives a subpoena for the information I submit?* When the FAA receives a subpoena for information you have submitted under this part, the FAA contacts you to determine whether you object to disclosure of the information or you wish to participate in responding to the subpoena. If both you and the FAA determine that release of the information is appropriate, the information is released. Otherwise, the FAA will not release information designated as protected under this part unless ordered to do so by a court of competent jurisdiction.

§ 193.9 **Will the FAA ever disclose information that is designated as protected under this part?**

The FAA discloses information that is designated as protected under this part when withholding it would not be consistent with the FAA's safety and security responsibilities, as follows:

(a) *Disclosure in all programs.* (1) The FAA may disclose de-identified, summarized information submitted under this part to explain the need for changes in policies and regulations. An example is the FAA publishing a notice of proposed rulemaking based on your information, and including a de-identified, summarized version of your infor-

mation (and the information from other persons, if applicable) to explain the need for the notice of proposed rulemaking.

(2) The FAA may disclose information provided under this part to correct a condition that compromises safety or security, if that condition continues uncorrected.

(3) The FAA may disclose information provided under this part to carry out a criminal investigation or prosecution.

(4) The FAA may disclose information provided under this part to comply with 49 U.S.C. 44905, regarding information about threats to civil aviation.

(b) *Additional disclosures.* For each program, the FAA may find that there are additional circumstances under which withholding information provided under this part would not be consistent with the FAA's safety and security responsibilities. Those circumstances are described in the designation for that program.

§ 193.11 **What is the notice procedure?**

This section states the notice procedure for the FAA to designate information as protected under this part. This procedure is used when there is not an immediate safety or security need for the information. This procedure generally is used to specify a type of information that you and others like you will provide on an on-going basis.

(a) *Application.* You may apply to have information designated as protected under this part by submitting an application addressed to the U.S. Department of Transportation, Docket Operations, West Building Ground Floor, Room W12–140, 1200 New Jersey Avenue, SE., Washington, DC 20590 for paper submissions, and the Federal Docket Management System (FDMS) Web page at *http://www.regulations.gov* for electronic submissions. Your application must include the designation described in paragraph (c) of this section that you want the FAA to issue. You should not include in your application any information that you do not want available to the public. The FAA may issue a proposed designation based on the application or may deny your application.

(b) *Proposed designation.* Before issuing a designation under this section, based either on your application or the FAA's own initiative, the FAA publishes a proposed designation in the FEDERAL REGISTER and requests comment.

(c) *Designation.* The FAA designates information as protected under this part if, after review of the comments, the FAA makes the findings in § 193.7. The FAA publishes in the FEDERAL REGISTER an order designating the information provided under the program as protected under this part. The designation includes the following:

(1) A summary of why the FAA finds that you and others, if applicable, will provide the information voluntarily.

(2) A description of the type of information that you and others, if applicable, may voluntarily provide under the program and a summary of why the FAA finds that the information is safety or security related.

(3) A summary of why the FAA finds that the disclosure of the information would inhibit you and others, if applicable, from voluntarily providing of that type of information.

(4) A summary of why the receipt of that type of information aids in fulfilling the FAA's safety and security responsibilities.

(5) A summary of why withholding such information from disclosure would be consistent with the FAA's safety and security responsibilities, including a statement as to the circumstances under which, and a summary of why, withholding such information from disclosure would not be consistent with the FAA's safety and security responsibilities, as described in § 193.9.

(6) A summary of how the FAA will distinguish information protected under this part from information the FAA receives from other sources.

(7) A summary of the significant comments received and the FAA's responses.

(d) *Amendment of designation.* The FAA may amend a designation using the procedures in paragraphs (a), (b), and (c) of this section.

(e) *Withdrawal of designation.* The FAA may withdraw a designation under this section at any time the FAA finds that continuation of the designation does not meet the elements of § 193.7, or if the requirements of the designation are not met. The FAA withdraws the designation by publishing a notice in the FEDERAL REGISTER. The withdrawal is effective on the date of publication or such later date as the notice may state. Information provided during the time the program was designated remains protected under this part and the program. Information provided after the withdrawal of the designation is effective is not protected under this part or the program.

[66 FR 33805, June 25, 2001, as amended at 72 FR 68475, Dec. 5, 2007]

§ 193.13 **What is the no-notice procedure?**

This section states the no-notice procedure for the FAA to designate information as protected under this part. This procedure is used when there is an immediate safety or security need for the information. This procedure generally is used for specific information that you will provide on a short-term basis.

(a) *Application.* You may request that the FAA designate information you are offering as protected under this part. You must state your name, at least the general nature of information, and whether you will provide the information without the protection of this part. Your request may be verbal or writing.

(b) *Designation.* The FAA issues a written order designating information provided under this section as protected under this part. The FAA designates the information as protected under this part if the FAA—

(1) Makes the findings as § 193.7; and

(2) Finds that there is an immediate safety or security need to obtain the information without carrying out the procedures in § 193.11 of this part.

(c) *Time limit.* Except as provided in paragraphs (c)(1) and (c)(2) of this section, no designation under this section continues in effect for more than 60 days after the date of designation. Information provided during the time the designation was in effect remains protected under this part. Information provided that the designation ceases to be in effect is not protected under this part. The designation remains in effect for more than 60 days if—

(1) The procedures to designate such information under § 193.11(a) have been initiated, or

(2) There is an ongoing enforcement or criminal investigation, in which case the designation may continue until the investigation is completed.

(d) *Amendment of designation.* The FAA may amend a designation under this section using the procedures in paragraphs (a) and (b) of this section.

(e) *Withdrawal of designation.* The FAA may withdraw a designation under this section at any time the FAA finds that continuation does not meet the elements of § 193.7, or if the requirements of the designation are not met. The FAA withdraws the designation by notifying the person in writing that the designation is withdrawn. The withdrawal is effective on the date of receipt of the notice or such later date as the notice may state. Information provided during the time the designation was in effect remains protected under this part. Information provided after the withdrawal is effective is not protected under this part.

§ 193.15 What FAA officials exercise the authority of the Administrator under this part?

(a) The authority to issue proposed and final designations, to issue pro-posed and final amendments of designations, and to withdraw designations under this part, and to disclose information that has been designated as protected under this part, is delegated by the Administrator to Associate Administrators and Assistant Administrators and to the Chief Counsel, their Deputies, and any individual formally designated as Acting Associate or Assistant Administrator, Acting Chief Counsel, or Acting Deputy of such offices.

(b) The officials identified in paragraph (a) of this section may further delegate the authority to issue proposed designations and proposed amendments to designations.

§ 193.17 How must design and production approval holders handle information they receive from the FAA under this part?

(a) If the FAA discloses information under § 193.9(a)(2) to the holders of design approvals of production approvals issued by the FAA, the approval holder must disclose that information only to persons who need to know the information to address the safety or security condition.

(b) Unless an emergency exists, before disclosing information to approval holders the FAA will contact the submitter of the information.

SUBCHAPTERS L–M [RESERVED]

SUBCHAPTER N—WAR RISK INSURANCE

PART 198—AVIATION INSURANCE

AUTHORITY: 49 U.S.C. 106(g), 40113, 44301–44310; 49 CFR 1.47(b).

SOURCE: Docket No. 28893, 63 FR 13739, Mar. 20, 1998, unless otherwise noted.

§ 198.1 Eligibility of aircraft operation for insurance.

An aircraft operation is eligible for insurance if—

(a) The President of the United States has determined that the continuation of that aircraft operation is necessary to carry out the foreign policy of the United States;

(b) The aircraft operation is—

(1) In foreign air commerce or between two or more places all of which are outside the United States if insurance with premium is sought; or

(2) In domestic or foreign air commerce, or between two or more places all of which are outside the United States if insurance without premium is sought; and

(c) The Administrator finds that commercial insurance against loss or damage arising out of any risk from the aircraft operation cannot be obtained on reasonable terms from an insurance carrier.

§ 198.3 Basis of insurance.

(a) Premium insurance may be issued by the FAA is the requirements of §198.1 (a), (b)(1) and (c) are met.

(b) Subject to §198.9(c), standby insurance without premium may be issued by the FAA if all of the following conditions have been met:

(1) A department, agency, or instrumentality of the U.S. Government seeks performance of air services operations, pursuant to a contract of the department, agency, or instrumentality; or transportation of military forces or materiel on behalf of the United States, pursuant to an agreement between the United States and a foreign government.

(2) Such department, agency, or instrumentality of the U.S. Government has agreed in writing to indemnify the Secretary of Transportation against all losses covered by such insurance. Such an agreement, when countersigned by the President, constitutes a determination that the continuation of that aircraft operation is necessary to carry out the foreign policy of the United States.

(3) A current copy of the aircraft operator's applicable commercial insurance policy or policies is on file with the FAA, including every endorsement making a material change to the policy. Updated copies of these policies must be provided upon each renewal of the commercial policy. Every subsequent material change by endorsement must be promptly provided to the FAA.

(c) Insurance is activated, placing the insurance in full force, as specified by the FAA's written notification to the operator and remains in force until such time as either of the following occurs:

(1) The requirements in §198.1 are no longer met; or

(2) In the case of non-premium insurance, an aircraft operation is no longer performed under contract to a department, agency, or instrumentality of the U.S. Government; or pursuant to an agreement between the United States and a foreign government; or the Administrator finds that commercial insurance can now be obtained on reasonable terms.

(d) Insurance policies revert to standby status upon written notification by the FAA to the aircraft operator. A policy will remain in standby status until either—

(1) The insurance is activated by written notice; or

(2) The policy is canceled.

§198.5 Types of insurance coverage available.

Application may be made for insurance against loss or damage to the following persons, property, or interests:

(a) Aircraft, or insurable items of an aircraft, engaged in eligible operations under §198.1.

(b) Any individual employed or transported on the aircraft referred to in paragraph (a) of this section.

(c) The baggage of persons referred to in paragraph (b) of this section.

(d) Property transported, or to be transported, on the aircraft referred to in paragraph (a) of this section.

(e) Statutory or contractual obligations, or any other liability, of the aircraft referred to in paragraph (a) of this section or of its owner or operator, of the nature customarily covered by insurance.

§198.7 Amount of insurance coverage available.

(a) For each aircraft or insurable item, the amount insured may not exceed the amount for which the applicant has otherwise insured or self-insured the aircraft or insurable item against damage or liability arising from any risk. In the case of hull insurance, the amount insured may not exceed the reasonable value of the aircraft as determined by the FAA or its designated agent.

(b) Policies issued without premium may be revised from time to time by the FAA with notice to the insured, to add aircraft or insurable items or to amend amounts of coverage if the insured has changed the amount by which it has otherwise insured or self-insured the aircraft or itself.

§198.9 Applicant for insurance.

(a) Application for premium or non-premium insurance must be made in accordance with the applicable form supplied by the FAA.

(b) Each applicant for insurance with the premium under this part must submit to the FAA with its application a letter describing in detail the operations in which the aircraft is or will be engaged and stating the type of insurance coverage being sought and the reason it is being sought. The applicant must also submit any other information deemed pertinent by the FAA.

(c) Each applicant for premium or non-premium insurance must, upon request by the FAA, submit to the FAA evidence that commercial insurance is not available on reasonable terms for each flight or ground operation for which insurance is sought. Each aircraft operator who has a standby non-premium insurance policy must, upon request by the FAA, submit evidence to the FAA that commercial insurance is not available on reasonable terms before the FAA activates that policy. The adequacy of the evidence submitted is determined solely by the FAA.

(d) The standby non-premium policy issued to the aircraft operator does not provide actual coverage until formally activated by the FAA.

§198.11 Change in status of aircraft.

In the event of sale, lease, confiscation, requisition, total loss, or other change in the status of an aircraft or insurable items covered by insurance under this part, the insured party must notify the office administering the Aviation Insurance Program before, or as soon as practicable after, the change in status.

§198.13 Premium insurance—payment of premiums.

The insured must pay the premium for insurance issued under this part within the stated period after receipt of notice that premium payment is due and in accordance with the provisions of the applicable FAA insurance policy. Premiums must be sent to the FAA, and made payable to the FAA.

§198.15 Non-premium insurance—payment of registration binders.

(a) The binder for initial registration is $575 for each aircraft or insurable item. This binder is adjusted not more frequently than annually based on changes in the Consumer Price Index of All Urban Consumers published by the Secretary of Labor.

(b) An application for non-premium insurance must be accompanied by the proper binder, payable to the FAA. A binder is not returnable unless the application is rejected.

(c) Requests made after issuance of a non-premium policy for the addition of an aircraft or insurable item must be accompanied by the binder for each aircraft and insurable item.

(d) When an operator acquires an aircraft or insurable item that was previously covered under an active or standby policy, the new operator must register that aircraft or item on its policy and pay the binder for each aircraft and insurable item.

§ 198.17 Ground support and other coverage.

An aircraft operator may apply for insurance to cover any risks arising from the provision of goods or services directly supporting the operation of an aircraft that meets the requirements of § 198.3(b).

PART 199 [RESERVED]

FINDING AIDS

A list of CFR titles, subtitles, chapters, subchapters and parts and an alphabetical list of agencies publishing in the CFR are included in the CFR Index and Finding Aids volume to the Code of Federal Regulations which is published separately and revised annually.

Table of CFR Titles and Chapters
(Revised as of January 1, 2019)

Title 1—General Provisions

Title 2—Grants and Agreements

Title 2—Grants and Agreements—Continued

Title 3—The President

Title 4—Accounts

Title 5—Administrative Personnel

909

Title 5—Administrative Personnel—Continued

Title 12—Banks and Banking—Continued

Title 13—Business Credit and Assistance

Title 14—Aeronautics and Space

Title 15—Commerce and Foreign Trade

Title 15—Commerce and Foreign Trade—Continued

Title 16—Commercial Practices

Title 17—Commodity and Securities Exchanges

Title 18—Conservation of Power and Water Resources

Title 19—Customs Duties

Title 20—Employees' Benefits

Title 20—Employees' Benefits—Continued

Title 21—Food and Drugs

Title 22—Foreign Relations

Title 23—Highways

Title 25—Indians

Title 26—Internal Revenue

Title 27—Alcohol, Tobacco Products and Firearms

Title 28—Judicial Administration

Title 29—Labor

Title 29—Labor—Continued

Title 30—Mineral Resources

Title 31—Money and Finance: Treasury

Title 41—Public Contracts and Property Management—Continued
Chap.

Title 42—Public Health

Title 43—Public Lands: Interior

Title 44—Emergency Management and Assistance

Title 45—Public Welfare

Title 45—Public Welfare—Continued

Title 46—Shipping

Title 47—Telecommunication

Title 48—Federal Acquisition Regulations System

Alphabetical List of Agencies Appearing in the CFR

(Revised as of January 1, 2019)

Agency	CFR Title, Subtitle or Chapter
Administrative Conference of the United States	1, III
Advisory Council on Historic Preservation	36, VIII
Advocacy and Outreach, Office of	7, XXV
Afghanistan Reconstruction, Special Inspector General for	5, LXXXIII
African Development Foundation	22, XV
Federal Acquisition Regulation	48, 57
Agency for International Development	2, VII; 22, II
Federal Acquisition Regulation	48, 7
Agricultural Marketing Service	7, I, IX, X, XI
Agricultural Research Service	7, V
Agriculture, Department of	2, IV; 5, LXXIII
Advocacy and Outreach, Office of	7, XXV
Agricultural Marketing Service	7, I, IX, X, XI
Agricultural Research Service	7, V
Animal and Plant Health Inspection Service	7, III; 9, I
Chief Financial Officer, Office of	7, XXX
Commodity Credit Corporation	7, XIV
Economic Research Service	7, XXXVII
Energy Policy and New Uses, Office of	2, IX; 7, XXIX
Environmental Quality, Office of	7, XXXI
Farm Service Agency	7, VII, XVIII
Federal Acquisition Regulation	48, 4
Federal Crop Insurance Corporation	7, IV
Food and Nutrition Service	7, II
Food Safety and Inspection Service	9, III
Foreign Agricultural Service	7, XV
Forest Service	36, II
Grain Inspection, Packers and Stockyards Administration	7, VIII; 9, II
Information Resources Management, Office of	7, XXVII
Inspector General, Office of	7, XXVI
National Agricultural Library	7, XLI
National Agricultural Statistics Service	7, XXXVI
National Institute of Food and Agriculture	7, XXXIV
Natural Resources Conservation Service	7, VI
Operations, Office of	7, XXVIII
Procurement and Property Management, Office of	7, XXXII
Rural Business-Cooperative Service	7, XVIII, XLII
Rural Development Administration	7, XLII
Rural Housing Service	7, XVIII, XXXV
Rural Telephone Bank	7, XVI
Rural Utilities Service	7, XVII, XVIII, XLII
Secretary of Agriculture, Office of	7, Subtitle A
Transportation, Office of	7, XXXIII
World Agricultural Outlook Board	7, XXXVIII
Air Force, Department of	32, VII
Federal Acquisition Regulation Supplement	48, 53
Air Transportation Stabilization Board	14, VI
Alcohol and Tobacco Tax and Trade Bureau	27, I
Alcohol, Tobacco, Firearms, and Explosives, Bureau of	27, II
AMTRAK	49, VII
American Battle Monuments Commission	36, IV
American Indians, Office of the Special Trustee	25, VII
Animal and Plant Health Inspection Service	7, III; 9, I

932

List of CFR Sections Affected

All changes in this volume of the Code of Federal Regulations (CFR) that were made by documents published in the FEDERAL REGISTER since January 1, 2014 are enumerated in the following list. Entries indicate the nature of the changes effected. Page numbers refer to FEDERAL REGISTER pages. The user should consult the entries for chapters, parts and subparts as well as sections for revisions.

For changes to this volume of the CFR prior to this listing, consult the annual edition of the monthly List of CFR Sections Affected (LSA). The LSA is available at *www.govinfo.gov*. For changes to this volume of the CFR prior to 2001, see the "List of CFR Sections Affected, 1949–1963, 1964–1972, 1973–1985, and 1986–2000" published in 11 separate volumes. The "List of CFR Sections Affected 1986–2000" is available at *www.govinfo.gov*.

List of CFR Sections Affected

○

941